Stanley Gibbons
STAMP CATALOGUE

PART 8

Italy and Switzerland

Sixth Edition, 2003

Stanley Gibbons Ltd
London and Ringwood

By Appointment to Her Majesty The Queen
Stanley Gibbons Ltd., London
Philatelists

Published by **Stanley Gibbons Ltd.**
Publications Editorial, Sales Offices and
Distribution Centre:
7 Parkside, Christchurch, Ringwood,
Hants, BH24 3SH

**1st Edition in this form - July 1980
2nd Edition - August 1983
3rd Edition -November 1986
4th Edition - June 1993
5th Edition - June 1997
6th Edition - December 2003**

© Stanley Gibbons Ltd. 2003

ISBN: 0-85259-554-9

Copyright Notice
The contents of this catalogue, including the numbering system and illustrations, are fully protected by copyright. No part of this publication may be reproduced, stored in a retrieval system, or transmitted in any form or by any means, electronic, mechanical, photocopying, recording or otherwise, without the prior permission of Stanley Gibbons Limited. Requests for such permission should be addressed to the Catalogue Editor at Ringwood.
    This catalogue is sold on condition that it is not, by way of trade or otherwise, lent, re-sold, hired out, circulated or otherwise disposed of other than in its complete original and unaltered form and without a similar condition including this condition being imposed on the subsequent purchaser.

Item No. 2837 (03)

Printed in Great Britain by Unwin Brothers Ltd., Old Woking, Surrey

Stanley Gibbons Foreign Catalogue Parts 2–22

Edward Stanley Gibbons published his first catalogue of postage stamps from Plymouth in November 1865. Its unillustrated twenty pages listed stamps and postal stationery from Antigua to Wurttemburg with price columns provided for unused or used, either as singles or by the dozen.

Since 1865 the catalogue range has grown to over forty current titles, all profusely illustrated and reflecting current research and price information.

The foreign listings, of which this volume forms a part, were published as Part II of the Stanley Gibbons catalogue from 1897 to 1945. Circumstances were difficult in the austerity period following the Second World War so the foreign listings were split into seven smaller catalogues. From 1951 to 1970 these were consolidated into Part II Europe and Colonies and Part III America, Asia and Africa.

Collecting patterns do change, however, so in 1970–71 an experimental series of Sectional catalogues appeared which were, in turn, replaced by a series of three alphabetical volumes covering Europe and four covering Overseas.

The present system of twenty-one catalogues, covering individual countries or collecting groups, was initiated in 1979. Full details of each volume and its contents are provided on the back cover. The scheme has the advantage of allowing flexibility in response to changing collecting habits with the listings being continually improved, currently by notes covering certain postal history aspects and by the addition of stamp booklet listings.

About this edition

This edition contains a number of new features.
- It is the first of our specialised Foreign catalogues to be produced electronically
- It is the first to be produced in colour
- A design index has been added for Switzerland

A certain amount of re-laying out and re-numbering has been undertaken, converting the old four column price listings to two column.

Prices have been reviewed throughout and considerable increases recorded, particularly in Italian Colonies. We are grateful to the following for supplying copies of their price lists: The Amateur Collector, London; J. Barefoot, York; Leo Baresch Ltd, West Sussex; D.J.M. Kerr, Earlston; Pitteri S.A., Chiasso, Switzerland; Robstine Stamps, Hampshire.

Addresses of specialist societies for this area can be found on page IV.

New Issues
The first supplement to this catalogue appeared in *Gibbons Stamp Monthly* for October 2003

Stamps added
Italy 1132a
Italian Social Republic 11a
Switzerland D92a
283b
1175a

Number Changes
Old	New
Arbe	
5B	5
6B	6
Veglia	
5B	5
6B	6
Libya Cyrenaica	
40a	deleted
58a	deleted

Hugh Jefferies
Geoff Wilson

Stanley Gibbons Holdings Plc.

HEAD OFFICE, 399 STRAND, LONDON WC2R 0LX
Telephone 020 7836 8444 and Fax 020 7836 7342
Website: www.stanleygibbons.com for all departments.

Stanley Gibbons Ltd, Stanley Gibbons Auctions.
Auction Room and Specialist Stamp Departments: Open Monday-Friday,
9.30 a.m. to 5 p.m.
Shop: Open Monday-Friday 9 a.m. to 5.30 p.m. and Saturday 9.30 a.m. to 5.30 p.m.
E-mail: enquiries@stanleygibbons.co.uk

Fraser's. Autographs, photographs, letters, documents. Open Monday-Friday 9 a.m. to 5.30 p.m.
and
Saturday 10 a.m. to 4 p.m.
Website: www.frasersautographs.com **E-mail:** info@frasersautographs.co.uk

RINGWOOD OFFICE, PARKSIDE, CHRISTCHURCH ROAD, RINGWOOD, HANTS BH24 3SH
Telephone 01425 472363 (24 hour answer phone service), **Fax** 01425 470247.
Website: www.stanleygibbons.com **E-mail:** info@stanleygibbons.co.uk

Stanley Gibbons Publications.
Publications Mail Order: FREEPHONE 0800 611 622 Monday-Friday 8.30 a.m. to 5 p.m.

Stanley Gibbons Publications has overseas licensees and distributors for Australia, Belgium, Canada, Denmark, Finland, France, Hong Kong, Israel, Italy, Japan, Luxembourg, Netherlands, New Zealand, Norway, Singapore, Sweden and Switzerland. Please contact the Ringwood address for details.

Specialist Societies

Italy and Colonies Study Circle
Hon. Secretary: R. Harlow
7 Duncombe House,
8 Manor Road
Teddington,
TW11 8BG

Helvetia Philatelic Society
Hon. Secretary: Peter Vonwiller
Telephone: 01494 782472

American Helvetia Philatelic Society
Secretary: Richard T. Hall
Post Office 15053
Asheville
North Carolina
28813-0053
U.S.A.

General Philatelic Information
and Guidelines to the Scope of the Foreign Catalogue

The notes which follow seek to reflect current practice in compiling the Foreign Catalogue.

It scarcely needs emphasising that the Stanley Gibbons Stamp Catalogue has a very long history and that the vast quantity of information it contains has been carefully built up by successive generations through the work of countless individuals. Philately itself is never static and the Catalogue has evolved and developed during this long time-span. Thus, while these notes are important for today's criteria, they may be less precise the farther back in the listings one travels. They are not intended to inaugurate some unwanted series of piecemeal alterations in a widely respected work, but it does seem to us useful that Catalogue users know as exactly as possible the policies currently in operation.

THE CATALOGUE IN GENERAL

Contents. The Catalogue is confined to adhesive postage stamps, including miniature sheets. For particular categories the rules are

(*a*) Revenue (fiscal) stamps or telegraph stamps are listed only where they have been expressly authorised for postal duty.

(*b*) Stamps issued only precancelled are included, but normally issued stamps available additionally with precancel have no separate precancel listing unless the face value is changed.

(*c*) Stamps prepared for use but not issued, hitherto accorded full listing, are nowadays footnoted with a price (where possible).

(*d*) Bisects (trisects, etc.) are only listed where such usage was officially authorised.

(*e*) Stamps issued only on first day covers and not available separately are not listed but priced (on the cover) in a footnote.

(*f*) New printings, as such, are not listed, though stamps from them may qualify under another category, e.g. when a prominent new shade results.

(*g*) Official and unofficial reprints are dealt with by footnote.

(*h*) Stamps from imperforate printings of modern issues which also occur perforated are covered by footnotes or general notes, but are listed where widely available for postal use.

Exclusions. The following are excluded: (a) non-postal revenue or fiscal stamps; (b) postage stamps used fiscally; (c) local carriage labels and private local issues; (d) telegraph stamps; (e) bogus or phantom stamps; (f) railway or airline letter fee stamps, bus or road transport company labels; (g) cut-outs; (h) all types of non-postal labels; (i) documentary labels for the postal service, e.g. registration, recorded delivery, airmail etiquettes, etc.; (j) privately applied embellishments to official issues and privately commissioned items generally; (k) stamps for training postal officers; (l) specimen stamps.

Full listing. "Full listing" confers our recognition and implies allotting a catalogue number and (wherever possible) a price quotation.

In judging status for inclusion in the catalogue broad considerations are applied to stamps. They must be issued by a legitimate postal authority, recognised by the government concerned, and must be adhesives valid for proper postal use in the class of service for which they are inscribed. Stamps, with the exception of such categories as postage dues and officials, must be available to the general public, at face value, in reasonable quantities without any artificial restrictions being imposed on their distribution.

We record as abbreviated, Appendix entries, without catalogue numbers or prices, stamps from countries which either persist in having far more issues than can be justified by postal need or have failed to maintain control over their distribution so that they have not been available to the public in reasonable quantities at face value. Miniature sheets and imperforate stamps are not mentioned in these entries.

The publishers of this catalogue have observed, with concern, the proliferation of "artificial" stamp-issuing territories. On several occasions this has resulted in separately inscribed issues for various component parts of otherwise united states or territories.

Stanley Gibbons Publications have decided that where such circumstances occur, they will not, in the future, list these items in the SG catalogue without first satisfying themselves that the stamps represent a genuine political, historical or postal division within the country concerned. Any such issues which do not fulfil this stipulation will be recorded in the Catalogue Appendix only.

For errors and varieties the criterion is legitimate (albeit inadvertent) sale over a post office counter in the normal course of business. Details of provenance are always important; printers' waste and fraudulently manufactured material is excluded.

Certificates. In assessing unlisted items due weight is given to Certificates from recognised Expert Committees and, where appropriate, we will usually ask to see them.

New Issues. New issues are listed regularly in the Catalogue Supplement published in *Gibbons Stamp Monthly*, whence they are consolidated into the next available edition of the Catalogue.

Date of Issue. Where local issue dates differ from dates of release by agencies, "date of issue" is the local date. Fortuitous stray usage before the officially intended date is disregarded in listing.

Catalogue numbers. Stamps of each country are catalogued chronologically by date of issue. Subsidiary classes (e.g. postage due stamps) are integrated into one list with postage and commemorative stamps and distinguished by a letter prefix to the catalogue number.

The catalogue number appears in the extreme left column. The boldface Type numbers in the next column are merely cross-references to illustrations. Catalogue numbers in the *Gibbons Stamp Monthly* Supplement are provisional only and may need to be altered when the lists are consolidated. Miniature sheets only purchasable intact at a post office have a single **MS** number; sheetlets – individual stamps available – number each stamp separately. The catalogue no longer gives full listing to designs, originally issued in normal sheets, which subsequently appear in sheetlets showing changes of colour, perforation, printing process or face value. Such stamps will be covered by footnotes.

Information (contd.)

Once published in the Catalogue, numbers are changed as little as possible; really serious renumbering is reserved for the occasions when a complete country or an entire issue is being rewritten. The edition first affected includes cross-reference tables of old and new numbers.

Our catalogue numbers are universally recognised in specifying stamps and as a hallmark of status.

Illustrations. Stamps are illustrated at three-quarters linear size. Stamps not illustrated are the same size and format as the value shown unless otherwise indicated. Stamps issued only as miniature sheets usually have the stamp alone illustrated but sheet size is also quoted. Overprints, surcharges, watermarks and postmarks are normally actual size. Illustrations of varieties are often enlarged to show the detail.

CONTACTING THE CATALOGUE EDITOR

The editor is always interested in hearing from people who have new information which will improve or correct the Catalogue. As a general rule he must see and examine the actual stamps before they can be considered for listing; photographs or photocopies are insufficient evidence. Neither he nor his staff give opinions as to the genuineness of stamps.

Submissions should be made in writing to the Catalogue Editor, Stanley Gibbons Publications, 7 Parkside, Christchurch Road, Ringwood, Hants BH24 3SH. The cost of return postage for items submitted is appreciated, and this should include the registration fee if required.

Where information is solicited purely for the benefit of the enquirer, the editor cannot undertake to reply if the answer is already contained in these published notes or if return postage is omitted. Written communications are greatly preferred to enquiries by telephone and the editor regrets that he or his staff cannot see personal callers without a prior appointment being made.

The editor welcomes close contact with study circles and is interested, too, in finding reliable local correspondents who will verify and supplement official information in overseas countries where this is deficient.

We regret we do not give opinions as the genuineness of stamps, nor do we identify stamps or number them by our Catalogue.

TECHNICAL MATTERS

The meanings of the technical terms used in the Catalogue will be found in Stanley Gibbons *Philatelic Terms Illustrated* by James Mackay (price £14·95 plus postage).

1. Printing

Printing errors. Errors in printing are of major interest to the Catalogue. Authenticated items meriting consideration would include background, centre or frame inverted or omitted; centre or subject transposed; error of colour; error or omission of value; double prints and impressions; printed both sides; and so on. Designs *tête-bêche*, whether intentionally or by accident, are listable. *Se-tenant* arrangements of stamps are recognised in the listings or footnotes. Gutter pairs (a pair of stamps separated by blank margin) are excluded unless they have some philatelic importance. Colours only partially omitted are not listed, neither are stamps printed on the gummed side.

Printing Varieties. Listing is accorded to major changes in the printing base which lead to completely new types. In recess-printing this could be a design re-engraved, in photogravure or photolithography a screen altered in whole or in part. It can also encompass flat-bed and rotary printing if the results are readily distinguishable.

To be considered at all, varieties must be constant. Early stamps, produced by primitive methods, were prone to numerous imperfections; the lists reflect this, recognising re-entries, retouches, broken frames, misshapen letters, and so on. Printing technology has, however, radically improved over the years, during which time photogravure and lithography have become predominant. Varieties nowadays are more in the nature of flaws and these, being too specialised for a general catalogue, are almost always outside the scope. We therefore do not list such items as dry prints, kiss prints, doctor-blade flaws, blanket set-offs, doubling through blanket stretch, plate cracks and scratches, registration flaws (leading to colour shifts), lithographic ring flaws, and so on. Neither do we recognise fortuitous happenings like paper creases or confetti flaws.

Overprints (and surcharges). Overprints of different types qualify for separate listing. These include overprints in different colours; overprints from different printing processes such as litho and typo; overprints in totally different typefaces, etc.

Overprint errors and varieties. Major errors in machine-printed overprints are important and listable. They include overprint inverted or omitted; overprint double (treble, etc); overprint diagonal; overprint double, one inverted; pairs with one overprint omitted, e.g. from a radical shift to an adjoining stamp; error of colour; error of type fount; letters inverted or omitted, etc. If the overprint is handstamped, few of these would qualify and a distinction is drawn.

Varieties occurring in overprints will often take the form of broken letters, slight differences in spacing, rising spacers, etc. Only the most important would be considered for footnote mention.

Sheet positions. If space permits we quote sheet positions of listed varieties, and authenticated data is solicited for this purpose.

2. Paper

All stamps listed are deemed to be on "ordinary" paper of the wove type and white in colour; only departures from this are mentioned.

Types. Where classification so requires we distinguish such other types of paper as, for example, vertically and horizontally laid; wove and laid bâtonné; card(board); carton; cartridge; enamelled; glazed; GC (Grande Consommation); granite; native; pelure; porous; quadrillé; ribbed; rice; and silk thread.

Our chalky (chalk-surfaced) paper is specifically one which shows a black mark when touched with a silver wire. This and other coatings are easily lost or damaged through immersion in water.

The various makeshifts for normal paper are listed as appropriate. They include printing on: unfinished banknotes, war maps, ruled paper, Post Office forms, and the unprinted side of glossy magazines.

Descriptive terms. The fact that a paper is handmade (and thus probably of uneven thickness) is mentioned where necessary. Such descriptive terms as "hard" and "soft"; "smooth" and "rough"; "thick", "medium" and "thin" are applied where there is philatelic merit in classifying papers.

Coloured, very white and toned papers. A coloured paper is one that is coloured right through (front and back of the stamp). In the Catalogue the colour of the paper is given in *italics*, thus

black/*rose* = black design on rose paper.

Papers have been made specially white in recent years by, for example, a very heavy coating of chalk. We do not classify shades of whiteness of paper as distinct varieties. There does exist, however, a type of paper from early days called toned. This is off-white, often brownish or buffish, but it cannot be assigned any definite colour. A toning effect brought on by climate, incorrect storage or gum staining is disregarded here, as this was not the state of the paper when issued.

Safety devices. The Catalogue takes account of such safety devices as varnish lines, grills, burelage or imprinted patterns on the front or moire on the back of stamps.

Modern Developments. Two modern developments also affect the listings, printing on self-adhesive paper and the tendency, philatelic in origin, for conventional paper to be reinforced or replaced by different materials. Some examples are the use of foils in gold, silver, aluminium, palladium and steel; application of an imitation wood veneer; printing on plastic moulded in relief; and use of a plastic laminate to give a three-dimensional effect. Examples also occur of stamps impregnated with scent; printed on silk; and incorporating miniature gramophone records.

3. Perforation and Rouletting

Perforation gauge. The gauge of a perforation is the number of holes in a length of 2 cm. For correct classification the size of the holes (large or small) may need to be distinguished; in a few cases the actual number of holes on each edge of the stamp needs to be quoted.

Measurement. The Gibbons *Instanta* gauge is the standard for measuring perforations. The stamp is viewed against a dark background with the transparent gauge put on top of it. Though the gauge measures to decimal accuracy, perforations read from it are generally quoted in the Catalogue to the nearest half. For example:

Just over perf. $12^{3}/_{4}$ to just under perf. $13^{1}/_{4}$ = perf. 13
Perf. $13^{1}/_{4}$ exactly, rounded up = perf. $13^{1}/_{2}$
Just over perf. $13^{1}/_{4}$ to just under perf. $3^{3}/_{4}$ = perf. $13^{1}/_{2}$
Perf. $13^{3}/_{4}$ exactly, rounded up = perf. 14

However, where classification depends on it, actual quarter-perforations are quoted.

Notation. Where no perforation is quoted for an issue it is imperforate. Perforations are usually abbreviated (and spoken) as follows, though sometimes they may be spelled out for clarity. This notation for rectangular stamps (the majority) applies to diamond shapes if "top" is read as the edge to the top right.

P 14: perforated alike on all sides (read: "perf.14").

P 14×15: the first figure refers to top and bottom, the second to left and right sides (read: "perf. 14 by 15"). This is a compound perforation. For an upright triangular stamp the first figure refers to the two sloping sides and the second to the base. In inverted triangulars the base is first and the second figure refers to the sloping sides.

P 14–15: perforation measuring anything between 14 and 15: the holes are irregularly spaced, thus the gauge may vary along a single line or even along a single edge of the stamp (read: "perf. 14 to 15").

P 14 *irregular*: perforated 14 from a worn perforator, giving badly aligned holes irregularly spaced (read: "irregular perf. 14").

P comp(ound) 14×15: two gauges in use but not necessarily on opposite sides of the stamp. It could be one side in one gauge and three in the other, or two adjacent sides with the same gauge (Read: "perf. compound of 14 and 15"). For three gauges or more, abbreviated as "*P* 14, $14^{1}/_{2}$, 15 or *compound*" for example.

P 14, $14^{1}/_{2}$: perforated approximately $14^{1}/_{2}$ (read: "perf. 14 or $14^{1}/_{2}$). It does *not* mean two stamps, one perf. 14 and the other perf. $14^{1}/_{2}$. This obsolescent notation is gradually being replaced in the Catalogue.

Imperf: imperforate (not perforated).

Imperf×*P* 14: imperforate at top and bottom and perf 14 at sides.

P 14×*imperf*: perf 14 at top and bottom and imperforate at sides.

Such headings as "*P* 13×14 (*vert*) and *P* 14×13 (*horiz*)" indicate which perforations apply to which stamp format – vertical or horizontal.

Some stamps are additionally perforated so that a label or tab is detachable; others have been perforated suitably for use as two halves. Listings are normally for whole stamps, unless stated otherwise.

Other terms. Perforation almost always gives circular holes; where other shapes have been used they are specified, e.g. square holes; lozenge perf. Interrupted perfs are brought about by the omission of pins at regular intervals. Perforations have occasionally been simulated by being printed as part of the design. With few exceptions, privately applied perforations are not listed.

Perforation errors and varieties. Authenticated errors, where a stamp normally perforated is accidentally issued imperforate, are listed provided no traces of perforation (blind holes or indentations) remain. They must be provided as pairs, both stamps wholly imperforate, and are only priced in that form.

Stamps merely imperforate between stamp and margin (fantails) are not listed.

Imperforate-between varieties are recognised, where one row of perfs has been missed. They are listed and priced in pairs:

Imperf between (horiz pair): a horizontal pair of stamps with perfs all around the edges but none between the stamps.

Imperf between (vert pair): a vertical pair of stamps with perfs all around the edges but none between the stamps.

Where several of the rows have escaped perforation the resulting varieties are listable. Thus:

Imperf vert (horiz pair): a horizontal pair of stamps perforated top and bottom; all three vertical directions are imperf – the two outer edges and between the stamps.

Imperf horiz (vert pair): a vertical pair perforated at left and right edges; all three horizontal directions are imperf – the top, bottom and between the stamps.

Straight edges. Large sheets cut up before issue to post offices can cause stamps with straight edges, i.e. imperf on one side or on two sides at right angles. They are not usually listable in this condition and are worth less than corresponding stamps properly perforated all round.

This does not, however, apply to certain stamps, mainly from coils and booklets, where straight edges on various sides are the manufacturing norm affecting every stamp. The listings and notes make clear which sides are correctly imperf.

Information (contd.)

Malfunction. Varieties of double, misplaced or partial perforation caused by error or machine malfunction are not listable, neither are freaks, such as perforations placed diagonally from paper folds. Likewise disregarded are missing holes caused by broken pins, and perforations "fading out" down a sheet, the machinery progressively disengaging to leave blind perfs and indentations to the paper.

Centring. Well-centred stamps have designs surrounded by equal opposite margins. Catalogue prices are for stamps with fine centring; poorly centred stamps should usually be available at a lower price.

Types of perforating. Where necessary for classification, perforation types are distinguished. These include:

Line perforation from one line of pins punching single rows of holes at a time.

Comb perforation from pins disposed across the sheet in comb formation, punching out holes at three sides of the stamp a row at a time.

Harrow perforation applied to a whole pane or sheet at one stroke.

Rotary perforation from the toothed wheels operating across a sheet, then crosswise.

Sewing-machine perforation. The resultant condition, clean-cut or rough, is distinguished where required.

Pin-perforation is the commonly applied term for pin-roulette in which, instead of being punched out, round holes are pricked by sharp-pointed pins and no paper is removed.

Punctured stamps. Perforation holes can be punched into the face of the stamp. Patterns of small holes, often in the shape of initial letters, are privately applied devices against pilferage. These "perfins" are outside the scope. Identification devices, when officially inspired, are listed or noted; they can be shapes, or letters or words formed from holes, sometimes converting one class of stamp into another.

Rouletting. In rouletting the paper is cut, for ease of separation, but none is removed. The gauge is measured, when needed, as for perforations. Traditional French terms descriptive of the type of cut are often used and types include:

Arc roulette (percé en arc). Cuts are minute, spaced arcs, each roughly a semicircle.

Cross roulette (percé en croix). Cuts are tiny diagonal crosses.

Line roulette (percé en ligne or *en ligne droite).* Short straight cuts parallel to the frame of the stamp. The commonest basic roulette. Where not further described, "roulette" means this type.

Rouletted in colour or *coloured roulette (percé en lignes colorées* or *en lignes de couleur).* Cuts with coloured edges, arising from notched rule inked simultaneously with the printing plate.

Saw-tooth roulette (percé en scie). Cuts applied zigzag fashion to resemble the teeth of a saw.

Serpentine roulette (percé en serpentin). Cuts as sharply wavy lines.

Zigzag roulettes (percé en zigzags). Short straight cuts at angles in alternate directions, producing sharp points on separation. U.S. usage favours "serrate(d) roulette" for this type.

Pin-roulette (originally *percé en points* and now *perforés trous d'epingle*) is commonly called pin-perforation in English.

4. Gum

All stamps listed are assumed to have gum of some kind; if they were issued without gum this is stated. Original gum (o.g.) means that which was present on the stamp as issued to the public. Deleterious climates and the presence of certain chemicals can cause gum to crack and, with early stamps, even make the paper deteriorate. Unscrupulous fakers are adept in removing it and regumming the stamp to meet the unreasoning demand often made for "full o.g." in cases where such a thing is virtually impossible.

Until recent times the gum used for stamps has been gum arabic, but various synthetic adhesives – tinted or invisible-looking – have been in use since the 1960s. Stamps existing with more than one type of gum are not normally listed separately, though the fact is noted where it is of philatelic significance, e.g. in distinguishing reprints or new printings.

The distinct variety of grilled gum is, however, recognised. In this the paper is passed through a gum breaker prior to printing to prevent subsequent curling. As the patterned rollers were sufficient to impress a grill into the paper beneath the gum we can quote prices for both unused and used examples.

Self-adhesive stamps are issued on backing paper from which they are peeled before affixing to mail. Unused examples are prices as for backing paper intact. Used examples are best kept on cover or on piece.

5. Watermarks

Stamps are on unwatermarked paper except where the heading to the set says otherwise.

Detection. Watermarks are detected for Catalogue description by one of four methods: (1) holding stamps to the light; (2) laying stamps face down on a dark background; (3) adding a few drops of petroleum ether 40/60 to the stamp laid face down in a watermark tray; or (4) by use of the Morley-Bright Detector, or other equipment, which works by revealing the thinning of the paper at the watermark. (Note that petroleum ether is highly inflammable in use and can damage photogravure stamps.)

Listable types. Stamps occurring on both watermarked and unwatermarked papers are different types and both receive full listing.

Single watermarks (devices occurring once on every stamp) can be modified in size and shape as between different issues; the types are noted but not usually separately listed. Fortuitous absence of watermark from a single stamp or its gross displacement would not be listable.

To overcome registration difficulties the device may be repeated at close intervals (a *multiple watermark*), single stamps thus showing parts of several devices. Similarly a large sheet watermark (or *all-over watermark*) covering numerous stamps can be used. We give informative notes and illustrations for them. The designs may be such that numbers of stamps in the sheet automatically lack watermark; this is not a listable variety. Multiple and all-over watermarks sometimes undergo modifications, but if the various types are difficult to distinguish from single stamps, notes are given but not separate listings.

Papermakers' watermarks are noted where known but not listed separately, since most stamps in the sheet will lack them. Sheet watermarks which are nothing more than officially adopted papermakers' watermarks are, however, given normal listing.

Marginal watermarks, falling outside the pane of stamps, are ignored except where misplacement causes the adjoining row to be affected, in which case they may be footnoted.

Watermark errors and varieties. Watermark errors are recognised as of major importance. They comprise stamps intended to be on unwatermarked paper but issued watermarked by mistake, or stamps printed on paper with the wrong watermark. Watermark varieties, on the other hand, such as broken or deformed bits on the dandy roll, are not listable.

Watermark positions. Paper has a side intended for printing and watermarks are usually impressed so that they read normally when looked through from that printed side.

Illustrations in the Catalogue are of watermarks in normal positions (from the front of the stamps) and are actual size where possible.

Differences in watermark position are collectable as distinct varieties. In this Catalogue, however, only normal and sideways watermarks are listed (and "sideways inverted" is treated as "sideways"). Inverted and reversed watermarks have always been outside its scope: in the early days of flat-bed printing, sheets of watermarked paper were fed indiscriminately through the press and the resulting watermark positions had no particular philatelic significance. Similarly, the special make-up of sheets for booklets can in some cases give equal quantities of normal and inverted watermarks.

6. Colours

Stamps in two or three colours have these named in order of apearance, from the centre moving outwards. Four colours or more are usually listed as multicoloured.

In compound colour names the second is the predominant one, thus:

orange-red = a red tending towards orange;
red-orange = an orange containing more red than usual.

Standard colours used. The 200 colours most used for stamp identification are given in the Stanley Gibbons Colour Key. The Catalogue has used the Key as a standard for describing new issues for some years. The names are also introduced as lists are rewritten, though exceptions are made for those early issues where traditional names have become universally established.

Determining colours. When comparing actual stamps with colour samples in the Key, view in a good north daylight (or its best substitute: fluorescent "colour-matching" light). Sunshine is not recommended. Choose a solid portion of the stamp design; if available, marginal markings such as solid bars of colour or colour check dots are helpful. Shading lines in the design can be misleading as they appear lighter than solid colour. Postmarked portions of a stamp appear darker than normal. If more than one colour is present, mask off the extraneous ones as the eye tends to mix them.

Errors of colour. Major colour errors in stamps or overprints which qualify for listing are: wrong colours; one colour inverted in relation to the rest; albinos (colourless impressions), where these have Expert Committee certificates; colours completely omitted, but only on unused stamps (if found on used stamps the information is footnoted).

Colours only partially omitted are not recognised. Colour shifts, however spectacular, are not listed.

Shades. Shades in philately refer to variations in the intensity of a colour or the presence of differing amounts of other colours. They are particularly significant when they can be linked to specific printings. In general, shades need to be quite marked to fall within the scope of this Catalogue; it does not favour nowadays listing the often numerous shades of a stamp, but chooses a single applicable colour name which will indicate particular groups of outstanding shades. Furthermore, the listings refer to colours as issued: they may deteriorate into something different through the passage of time.

Modern colour printing by lithography is prone to marked differences of shade, even within a single run, and variations can occur within the same sheet. Such shades are not listed.

Aniline colours. An aniline colour meant originally one derived from coal-tar; it now refers more widely to colour of a particular brightness suffused on the surface of a stamp and showing clearly on the back.

Colours of overprints and surcharges. All overprints and surcharges are in black unless stated otherwise in the heading or after the description of the stamp.

7. Luminescence

Machines which sort mail electronically have been introduced in recent years. In consequence some countries have issued stamps on fluorescent or phosphorescent papers, while others have marked their stamps with phosphor bands.

The various papers can only be distinguised by ultra-violet lamps emitting particular wavelengths. They are separately listed only when the stamps have some other means of distinguishing them, visible without the use of these lamps. Where this is not so, the papers are recorded in footnotes or headings. (Collectors using the lamps, nevertheless, should exercise great care in their use as exposure to their light is extremely dangerous to the eyes.)

Phosphor bands are listable, since they are visible to the naked eye (by holding stamps at an angle to the light and looking along them, the bands appear dark). Stamps existing with and without phosphor bands or with differing numbers of bands are given separate listings. Varieties such as double bands, misplaced or omitted bands, bands printed on the wrong side, are not listed.

8. Coil Stamps

Stamps issued only in coil form are given full listing. If stamps are issued in both sheets and coils the coil stamps are listed separately only where there is some feature (e.g. perforation) by which singles can be distinguished. Coil strips containing different stamps *se-tenant* are also listed.

Coil join pairs are too random and too easily faked to permit of listing; similarly ignored are coil stamps which have accidentally suffered an extra row of perforations from the claw mechanism in a malfunctioning vending machine.

9. Booklet Stamps

Single stamps from booklets are listed if they are distinguishable in some way (such as watermark or perforation) from similar sheet stamps. Booklet panes, provided they are distinguishable from blocks of sheet stamps, are listed for most countries; booklet panes containing more than one value *se-tenant* are listed under the lowest of the values concerned.

Lists of stamp booklets are given for certain countries and it is intended to extend this generally.

Information (contd.)

10. Forgeries and Fakes

Forgeries. Where space permits, notes are considered if they can give a concise description that will permit unequivocal detection of a forgery. Generalised warnings, lacking detail, are not nowadays inserted since their value to the collector is problematic.

Fakes. Unwitting fakes are numerous, particularly "new shades" which are colour changelings brought about by exposure to sunlight, soaking in water contaminated with dyes from adherent paper, contact with oil and dirt from a pocketbook, and so on. Fraudulent operators, in addition, can offer to arrange: removal of hinge marks; repairs of thins on white or coloured papers; replacement of missing margins or perforations; reperforating in true or false gauges; removal of fiscal cancellations; rejoining of severed pairs, strips and blocks; and (a major hazard) regumming. Collectors can only be urged to purchase from reputable sources and to insist upon Expert Committee certification where there is any kind of doubt.

The Catalogue can consider footnotes about fakes where these are specific enough to assist in detection.

PRICES

Prices quoted in this Catalogue are the selling prices of Stanley Gibbons Ltd at the time when the book went to press. They are for stamps in fine condition; in issues where condition varies they may ask more for the superb and less for the sub-standard.

All prices are subject to change without prior notice and Stanley Gibbons Ltd may from time to time offer stamps at other than catalogue prices in consequence of special purchases or particular promotions.

No guarantee is given to supply all stamps priced, since it is not possible to keep every catalogued item in stock. Commemorative issues may, at times, only be available in complete sets and not as individual values.

Quotations of prices. The prices in the left-hand column are for unused stamps and those in the right-hand column are for used.

Prices are expressed in pounds and pence sterling. One pound comprises 100 pence (£1 = 100p).

The method of notation is as follows: pence in numerals (e.g. 10 denotes ten pence); pounds and pence up to £100, in numerals (e.g. 4·25 denotes four pounds and twenty-five pence); prices above £100 expressed in whole pounds with the "£" sign shown.

Unused stamps. Prices for stamps issued up to the end of the Second World War (1945) are for lightly hinged examples and more may be asked if they are in unmounted mint condition. Prices for all later unused stamps are for unmounted mint. Where not available in this condition, lightly hinged stamps supplied are often at a lower price.

Used stamps. The used prices are normally for stamps postally used but may be for stamps cancelled-to-order where this practice exists.

A pen-cancellation on early issues can sometimes correctly denote postal use. Instances are individually noted in the Catalogue in explanation of the used price given.

Prices quoted for bisects on cover or on large piece are for those dated during the period officially authorised.

Stamps not sold unused to the public but affixed by postal officials before use (e.g. some parcel post stamps) are priced used only.

Minimum price. The minimum catalogue price quoted is 10p. For individual stamps prices between 10p and 95p are provided as a guide for catalogue users. The lowest price *charged* for individual stamps purchased from Stanley Gibbons Ltd. is £1.

Set Prices. Set prices are generally for one of each value, excluding shades and varieties, but including major colour changes. Where there are alternative shades, etc, the cheapest is usually included. The number of stamps in the set is always stated for clarity.

Where prices are given for *se-tenant* blocks or strips, any mint set price quoted for such an issue is for the complete *se-tenant* strip plus any other stamps included in the set. Used set prices are always for a set of single stamps.

Repricing. Collectors will be aware that the market factors of supply and demand influence the prices quoted in this Catalogue. Whatever the scarcity of a particular stamp, if there is no one in the market who wishes to buy it, it cannot be expected to achieve a high price. Conversely, the same item actively sought by numerous potential buyers may cause the price to rise.

All the prices in this Catalogue are examined during the preparation of each new edition by expert staff of Stanley Gibbons and repriced as necessary. They take many factors into account, including supply and demand, and are in close touch with the international stamp market and the auction world.

GUARANTEE

All stamps are guaranteed genuine originals in the following terms:

If not as described, and returned by the purchaser, we undertake to refund the price paid to us in the original transaction. If any stamp is certified as genuine by the Expert Committee of the Royal Philatelic Society, London, or by B.P.A. Expertising Ltd, the purchaser shall not be entitled to make claim against us for any error, omission or mistake in such certificate. Consumers' statutory rights are not affected by this guarantee.

The established Expert Committees in this country are those of the Royal Philatelic Society, 41 Devonshire Place, London W1G 6JY, and B.P.A. Expertising Ltd, P.O. Box 137, Leatherhead, Surrey, KT22 0RG. They do not undertake valuations under any circumstances and fees are payable for their services.

International Philatelic Glossary

English	French	German	Spanish	Italian
Agate	Agate	Achat	Agata	Agata
Air stamp	Timbre de la poste aérienne	Flugpostmarke	Sello de correo aéreo	Francobollo per posta aerea
Apple Green	Vert-pomme	Apfelgrün	Verde manzana	Verde mela
Barred	Annulé par barres	Balkenentwertung	Anulado con barras	Sbarrato
Bisected	Timbre coupé	Halbiert	Partido en dos	Frazionato
Bistre	Bistre	Bister	Bistre	Bistro
Bistre-brown	Brun-bistre	Bisterbraun	Castaño bistre	Bruno-bistro
Black	Noir	Schwarz	Negro	Nero
Blackish Brown	Brun-noir	Schwärzlichbraun	Castaño negruzco	Bruno nerastro
Blackish Green	Vert foncé	Schwärzlichgrün	Verde negruzco	Verde nerastro
Blackish Olive	Olive foncé	Schwärzlicholiv	Oliva negruzco	Oliva nerastro
Block of four	Bloc de quatre	Viererblock	Bloque de cuatro	Bloco di quattro
Blue	Bleu	Blau	Azul	Azzurro
Blue-green	Vert-bleu	Blaugrün	Verde azul	Verde azzurro
Bluish Violet	Violet bleuâtre	Bläulichviolett	Violeta azulado	Violtto azzurrastro
Booklet	Carnet	Heft	Cuadernillo	Libretto
Bright Blue	Bleu vif	Lebhaftblau	Azul vivo	Azzurro vivo
Bright Green	Vert vif	Lebhaftgrün	Verde vivo	Verde vivo
Bright Purple	Mauve vif	Lebhaftpurpur	Púrpura vivo	Porpora vivo
Bronze Green	Vert-bronze	Bronzegrün	Verde bronce	Verde bronzo
Brown	Brun	Braun	Castaño	Bruno
Brown-lake	Carmin-brun	Braunlack	Laca castaño	Lacca bruno
Brown-purple	Pourpre-brun	Braunpurpur	Púrpura castaño	Porpora bruno
Brown-red	Rouge-brun	Braunrot	Rojo castaño	Rosso bruno
Buff	Chamois	Sämisch	Anteado	Camoscio
Cancellation	Oblitération	Entwertung	Cancelación	Annullamento
Cancelled	Annulé	Gestempelt	Cancelado	Annullato
Carmine	Carmin	Karmin	Carmín	Carminio
Carmine-red	Rouge-carmin	Karminrot	Rojo carmín	Rosso carminio
Centred	Centré	Zentriert	Centrado	Centrato
Cerise	Rouge-cerise	Kirschrot	Color de ceresa	Color Ciliegia
Chalk-surfaced paper	Papier couché	Kreidepapier	Papel estucado	Carta gessata
Chalky Blue	Bleu terne	Kreideblau	Azul turbio	Azzurro smorto
Charity stamp	Timbre de bienfaisance	Wohltätigkeitsmarke	Sello de beneficenza	Francobollo di beneficenza
Chestnut	Marron	Kastanienbraun	Castaño rojo	Marrone
Chocolate	Chocolat	Schokolade	Chocolate	Cioccolato
Cinnamon	Cannelle	Zimtbraun	Canela	Cannella
Claret	Grenat	Weinrot	Rojo vinoso	Vinaccia
Cobalt	Cobalt	Kobalt	Cobalto	Cobalto
Colour	Couleur	Farbe	Color	Colore
Comb-perforation	Dentelure en peigne	Kammzähnung, Reihenzähnung	Dentado de peine	Dentellatura e pettine
Commemorative stamp	Timbre commémoratif	Gedenkmarke	Sello conmemorativo	Francobollo commemorativo
Crimson	Cramoisi	Karmesin	Carmesí	Cremisi
Deep Blue	Blue foncé	Dunkelblau	Azul oscuro	Azzurro scuro
Deep bluish Green	Vert-bleu foncé	Dunkelbläulichgrün	Verde azulado oscuro	Verde azzurro scuro
Design	Dessin	Markenbild	Diseño	Disegno
Die	Matrice	Urstempel. Type, Platte	Cuño	Conio, Matrice

xi

English	French	German	Spanish	Italian
Double	Double	Doppelt	Doble	Doppio
Drab	Olive terne	Trüboliv	Oliva turbio	Oliva smorto
Dull Green	Vert terne	Trübgrün	Verde turbio	Verde smorto
Dull purple	Mauve terne	Trübpurpur	Púrpura turbio	Porpora smorto
Embossing	Impression en relief	Prägedruck	Impresión en relieve	Impressione a relievo
Emerald	Vert-émeraude	Smaragdgrün	Esmeralda	Smeraldo
Engraved	Gravé	Graviert	Grabado	Inciso
Error	Erreur	Fehler, Fehldruck	Error	Errore
Essay	Essai	Probedruck	Ensayo	Saggio
Express letter stamp	Timbre pour lettres par exprès	Eilmarke	Sello de urgencia	Francobollo per espresso
Fiscal stamp	Timbre fiscal	Stempelmarke	Sello fiscal	Francobollo fiscale
Flesh	Chair	Fleischfarben	Carne	Carnicino
Forgery	Faux, Falsification	Fälschung	Falsificación	Falso, Falsificazione
Frame	Cadre	Rahmen	Marco	Cornice
Granite paper	Papier avec fragments de fils de soie	Faserpapier	Papel con filamentos	Carto con fili di seta
Green	Vert	Grün	Verde	Verde
Greenish Blue	Bleu verdâtre	Grünlichblau	Azul verdoso	Azzurro verdastro
Greenish Yellow	Jaune-vert	Grünlichgelb	Amarillo verdoso	Giallo verdastro
Grey	Gris	Grau	Gris	Grigio
Grey-blue	Bleu-gris	Graublau	Azul gris	Azzurro grigio
Grey-green	Vert gris	Graugrün	Verde gris	Verde grigio
Gum	Gomme	Gummi	Goma	Gomma
Gutter	Interpanneau	Zwischensteg	Espacio blanco entre dos grupos	Ponte
Imperforate	Non-dentelé	Geschnitten	Sin dentar	Non dentellato
Indigo	Indigo	Indigo	Azul indigo	Indaco
Inscription	Inscription	Inschrift	Inscripción	Dicitura
Inverted	Renversé	Kopfstehend	Invertido	Capovolto
Issue	Émission	Ausgabe	Emisión	Emissione
Laid	Vergé	Gestreift	Listado	Vergato
Lake	Lie de vin	Lackfarbe	Laca	Lacca
Lake-brown	Brun-carmin	Lackbraun	Castaño laca	Bruno lacca
Lavender	Bleu-lavande	Lavendel	Color de alhucema	Lavanda
Lemon	Jaune-citron	Zitrongelb	Limón	Limone
Light Blue	Bleu clair	Hellblau	Azul claro	Azzurro chiaro
Lilac	Lilas	Lila	Lila	Lilla
Line perforation	Dentelure en lignes	Linienzähnung	Dentado en linea	Dentellatura lineare
Lithography	Lithographie	Steindruck	Litografía	Litografia
Local	Timbre de poste locale	Lokalpostmarke	Emisión local	Emissione locale
Lozenge roulette	Percé en losanges	Rautenförmiger Durchstich	Picadura en rombos	Perforazione a losanghe
Magenta	Magenta	Magentarot	Magenta	Magenta
Margin	Marge	Rand	Borde	Margine
Maroon	Marron pourpré	Dunkelrotpurpur	Púrpura rojo oscuro	Marrone rossastro
Mauve	Mauve	Malvenfarbe	Malva	Malva
Multicoloured	Polychrome	Mehrfarbig	Multicolores	Policromo
Myrtle Green	Vert myrte	Myrtengrün	Verde mirto	Verde mirto
New Blue	Bleu ciel vif	Neublau	Azul nuevo	Azzurro nuovo
Newspaper stamp	Timbre pour journaux	Zeitungsmarke	Sello para periódicos	Francobollo per giornali

English	French	German	Spanish	Italian
Obliteration	Oblitération	Abstempelung	Matasello	Annullamento
Obsolete	Hors (de) cours	Ausser Kurs	Fuera de curso	Fuori corso
Ochre	Ocre	Ocker	Ocre	Ocra
Official stamp	Timbre de service	Dienstmarke	Sello de servicio	Francobollo di servizio
Olive-brown	Brun-olive	Olivbraun	Castaño oliva	Bruno oliva
Olive-green	Vert-olive	Olivgrün	Verde oliva	Verde oliva
Olive-grey	Gris-olive	Olivgrau	Gris oliva	Grigio oliva
Olive-yellow	Jaune-olive	Olivgelb	Amarillo oliva	Giallo oliva
Orange	Orange	Orange	Naranja	Arancio
Orange-brown	Brun-orange	Orangebraun	Castaño naranja	Bruno arancio
Orange-red	Rouge-orange	Orangerot	Rojo naranja	Rosso arancio
Orange-yellow	Jaune-orange	Orangegelb	Amarillo naranja	Giallo arancio
Overprint	Surcharge	Aufdruck	Sobrecarga	Soprastampa
Pair	Paire	Paar	Pareja	Coppia
Pale	Pâle	Blass	Pálido	Pallido
Pane	Panneau	Gruppe	Grupo	Gruppo
Paper	Papier	Papier	Papel	Carta
Parcel post stamp	Timbre pour colis postaux	Paketmarke	Sello para paquete postal	Francobollo per pacchi postali
Pen-cancelled	Oblitéré à plume	Federzugentwertung	Cancelado a pluma	Annullato a penna
Percé en arc	Percé en arc	Bogenförmiger Durchstich	Picadura en forma de arco	Perforazione ad arco
Percé en scie	Percé en scie	Bogenförmiger Durchstich	Picado en sierra	Foratura a sega
Perforated	Dentelé	Gezähnt	Dentado	Dentellato
Perforation	Dentelure	Zähnung	Dentar	Dentellatura
Photogravure	Photogravure, Heliogravure	Rastertiefdruck	Fotograbado	Rotocalco
Pin perforation	Percé en points	In Punkten durchstochen	Horadado con alfileres	Perforato a punti
Plate	Planche	Platte	Plancha	Lastra, Tavola
Plum	Prune	Pflaumenfarbe	Color de ciruela	Prugna
Postage Due stamp	Timbre-taxe	Portomarke	Sello de tasa	Segnatasse
Postage stamp	Timbre-poste	Briefmarke, Freimarke, Postmarke	Sello de correos	Francobollo postale
Postal fiscal stamp	Timbre fiscal-postal	Stempelmarke als Postmarke verwendet	Sello fiscal-postal	Fiscale postale
Postmark	Oblitération postale	Poststempel	Matasello	Bollo
Printing	Impression, Tirage	Druck	Impresión	Stampa, Tiratura
Proof	Épreuve	Druckprobe	Prueba de impresión	Prova
Provisionals	Timbres provisoires	Provisorische Marken. Provisorien	Provisionales	Provvisori
Prussian Blue	Bleu de Prusse	Preussischblau	Azul de Prusia	Azzurro di Prussia
Purple	Pourpre	Purpur	Púrpura	Porpora
Purple-brown	Brun-pourpre	Purpurbraun	Castaño púrpura	Bruno porpora
Recess-printing	Impression en taille douce	Tiefdruck	Grabado	Incisione
Red	Rouge	Rot	Rojo	Rosso
Red-brown	Brun-rouge	Rotbraun	Castaño rojizo	Bruno rosso
Reddish Lilac	Lilas rougeâtre	Rötlichlila	Lila rojizo	Lilla rossastro
Reddish Purple	Poupre-rouge	Rötlichpurpur	Púrpura rojizo	Porpora rossastro
Reddish Violet	Violet rougeâtre	Rötlichviolett	Violeta rojizo	Violetto rossastro
Red-orange	Orange rougeâtre	Rotorange	Naranja rojizo	Arancio rosso
Registration stamp	Timbre pour lettre chargée (recommandée)	Einschreibemarke	Sello de certificado	Francobollo per raccomandate

English	French	German	Spanish	Italian
Reprint	Réimpression	Neudruck	Reimpresión	Ristampa
Reversed	Retourné	Umgekehrt	Invertido	Rovesciato
Rose	Rose	Rosa	Rosa	Rosa
Rose-red	Rouge rosé	Rosarot	Rojo rosado	Rosso rosa
Rosine	Rose vif	Lebhaftrosa	Rosa vivo	Rosa vivo
Roulette	Perçage	Durchstich	Picadura	Foratura
Rouletted	Percé	Durchstochen	Picado	Forato
Royal Blue	Bleu-roi	Königblau	Azul real	Azzurro reale
Sage green	Vert-sauge	Salbeigrün	Verde salvia	Verde salvia
Salmon	Saumon	Lachs	Salmón	Salmone
Scarlet	Écarlate	Scharlach	Escarlata	Scarlatto
Sepia	Sépia	Sepia	Sepia	Seppia
Serpentine roulette	Percé en serpentin	Schlangenliniger Durchstich	Picado a serpentina	Perforazione a serpentina
Shade	Nuance	Tönung	Tono	Gradazione de colore
Sheet	Feuille	Bogen	Hoja	Foglio
Slate	Ardoise	Schiefer	Pizarra	Ardesia
Slate-blue	Bleu-ardoise	Schieferblau	Azul pizarra	Azzurro ardesia
Slate-green	Vert-ardoise	Schiefergrün	Verde pizarra	Verde ardesia
Slate-lilac	Lilas-gris	Schierferlila	Lila pizarra	Lilla ardesia
Slate-purple	Mauve-gris	Schieferpurpur	Púrpura pizarra	Porpora ardesia
Slate-violet	Violet-gris	Schieferviolett	Violeta pizarra	Violetto ardesia
Special delivery stamp	Timbre pour exprès	Eilmarke	Sello de urgencia	Francobollo per espressi
Specimen	Spécimen	Muster	Muestra	Saggio
Steel Blue	Bleu acier	Stahlblau	Azul acero	Azzurro acciaio
Strip	Bande	Streifen	Tira	Striscia
Surcharge	Surcharge	Aufdruck	Sobrecarga	Soprastampa
Tête-bêche	Tête-bêche	Kehrdruck	Tête-bêche	Tête-bêche
Tinted paper	Papier teinté	Getöntes Papier	Papel coloreado	Carta tinta
Too-late stamp	Timbre pour lettres en retard	Verspätungsmarke	Sello para cartas retardadas	Francobollo per le lettere in ritardo
Turquoise-blue	Bleu-turquoise	Türkisblau	Azul turquesa	Azzurro turchese
Turquoise-green	Vert-turquoise	Türkisgrün	Verde turquesa	Verde turchese
Typography	Typographie	Buchdruck	Tipografia	Tipografia
Ultramarine	Outremer	Ultramarin	Ultramar	Oltremare
Unused	Neuf	Ungebraucht	Nuevo	Nuovo
Used	Oblitéré, Usé	Gebraucht	Usado	Usato
Venetian Red	Rouge-brun terne	Venezianischrot	Rojo veneciano	Rosso veneziano
Vermilion	Vermillon	Zinnober	Cinabrio	Vermiglione
Violet	Violet	Violett	Violeta	Violetto
Violet-blue	Bleu-violet	Violettblau	Azul violeta	Azzurro violetto
Watermark	Filigrane	Wasserzeichen	Filigrana	Filigrana
Watermark sideways	Filigrane couché liegend	Wasserzeichen	Filigrana acostado	Filigrana coricata
Wove paper	Papier ordinaire, Papier uni	Einfaches Papier	Papel avitelado	Carta unita
Yellow	Jaune	Gelb	Amarillo	Giallo
Yellow-brown	Brun-jaune	Gelbbraun	Castaño amarillo	Bruno giallo
Yellow-green	Vert-jaune	Gelbgrün	Verde amarillo	Verde giallo
Yellow-olive	Olive-jaunâtre	Gelboliv	Oliva amarillo	Oliva giallastro
Yellow-orange	Orange jaunâtre	Gelborange	Naranja amarillo	Arancio giallastro
Zig-zag roulette	Percé en zigzag	Sägezahnartiger	Picado en zigzag	Perforazione a zigzag

Visit the world's most famous stamp shop - 399 Strand, London

- Browse through our stockbooks of over 4 million stamps - everything from Abu Dhabi to Zanzibar

- Everything from Penny Blacks to the latest New Issues and FDC's - all backed by the SG guarantee.

- Choose from the widest range of catalogues, albums and accessories - with expert help to find exactly what you need.

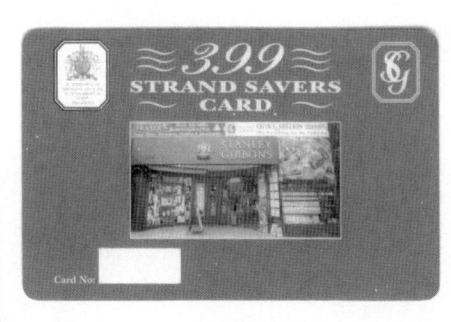

Strand Savers Card

- Only £20 to join
- 10% discount on all purchases at 399 Strand (excludes stamps over £100)
- Up to 20% Off on regular Double Discount days

- Win up to £250 SG vouchers in Free monthly prize draws
- Late night shopping and special events
- Rejoin for only £15

Opening times:
9.00am - 5.30pm Monday to Friday
9.30am - 5.30pm Saturday

Don't miss the Manager's Weekly Specials, plus many more fantastic offers

Stanley Gibbons Limited
399 Strand, London WC2R 0LX
Tel: +44 (0)20 7836 8444
Fax: +44 (0)20 7836 7342
Email: shop@stanleygibbons.co.uk

www.stanleygibbons.com

Quote ref.: PART804

www.allworldstamps.com

Now featuring data from our 2004 catalogues

STANLEY GIBBONS ONLINE CATALOGUE

We have just re-launched allworldstamps.com.

- Commonwealth and British Empire (1840-1952), 2004 edition data now online

- Create your own Virtual Collection online.

- Value your Virtual Collection.

- Stamps of the World data available to search for non-commonwealth countries

Features

Value Collection
Online Wants List
Stamp Exchange
Multi Currency

Advanced Search
Auction Search
Keep Previous Searches

Online Shop
Auto Shopping List

Colour Images
Helpful Notes
Custom Print Options

Choose between two subscription packages

▶ **STANDARD SUBSCRIPTION**
only £14.95 per year

▶ **SUBSCRIPTION PLUS**
Includes Virtual Collection
only £22.95 per year

Visit www.allworldstamps.com and join today.

Selling Through Auction
Has Never Been Easier

Bulk Accumulations

Single items

Free appraisals*

Specialised collections

Material Required for next sale

One Country Albums

View and bid online at www.stanleygibbons.com

For details on submitting similar material for auction, contact Colin Avery or Ryan Epps
* For material accepted for auction

STANLEY GIBBONS Auctions

Stanley Gibbons Auctions Dept.
399 Strand, London WC2R 0LX UK
Tel: +44 (0)20 7836 8444   Fax: +44 (0)20 7836 7342
email: auctions@stanleygibbons.co.uk
Internet: www.stanleygibbons.com

ITALIAN STATES Modena 1852

Italian States

MODENA

100 Centesimi = 1 Lira

Duke Francis V, 21 Jan 1846–11 June 1859

1 Arms of Este   **2**

(Dies engraved and electrotypes made by Rocca, Rinaldi and Algeri, Modena. Typo State Stamp Office, Modena)

1852 (1 June)–57. *Black impression on coloured paper.* W **2** (1l.), no wmk (others). Imperf.

(i) First Setting. Without full point after figures of value.

1	**1**	5c. on *green* (2.9.1852)		£1500	£110
3		10c. on *rose* (2.6.1852)		£325	65·00
		a. No full point after "CENT" (I/19, II/7)		£1400	£650
		b. Inverted figure "1" (II/30)		£6500	£2750
		c. "EENT. 10" (III/38)		£6500	£2750
4		15c. on *yellow*		40·00	25·00
		a. No full point after "CENT" (IV/2)		£160	£400
		b. "CETN 15." (IV/51)		—	£1700
5		25c. on *buff*		42·00	29·00
		a. No full point after "CENT" (I/19)		£190	£500
		b. Raised point after "CENT" (II/8)		£2500	
		c. "C" ("ENT. 25" omitted (III/3))		£1000	
6		40c. on *pale blue* (2.6.1852)		£10000	£900
		a. On *deep blue* (17.10.1852)		£160	90·00
		b. No full point after "CENT" (I/19)		£900	£1300
		c. Space between figures "4" and "0" (III/10)			

(ii) Second Setting. With full point after figures of value.

9	**1**	5c. on *green* (17.7.1852)		25·00	44·00
		a. No full point after "CENT"; "5" closer to "T" (II/36)		£15000	£6500
		b. "C" of "CENT" omitted (III/19)		—	£6000
		c. "CENT .5" (III/28)		£2000	£1500
		d. "CNET. 5." (IV/18)		£13000	£4500
		e. "E" of "CENT" sideways (IV/46)		—	£7000
		f. No inscription of value		—	£3000
10		5c. on *olive-green* (8.10.1855)		£225	90·00
		a. Raised point after "5" (I/8, 9; III/15, 25, 33, 60)		£850	£1200
		b. No full point after "5" (II/10, 54; III/31, 50, 53; IV/7 15, 28, 33)		£700	£600
		c. "CENT .5" (III/28)		£1700	£1900
		d. "CNET. 5." (IV/18)		£4000	£2500
		e. Figure "1" for "T" in "CENT" (IV/50)		£4000	£2500
		f. "5" omitted			
11		10c. on *rose* (22.4.1857)		£275	£160
		a. "CNET. 10" (no point after "10") (II/1)		£1100	£1700
		b. Raised full point after "10" (II/52)		£1100	£850
		c. "CE6T. 10." (III/22)		£1500	£1400
		d. "CENE. 10." (III/54)		£2000	£1600
		e. "CNET 10." (full point after "10") (IV/15, 55)		£850	£1200
		f. "N" of "CENT" sideways (IV/33)		£13000	£4500
12		40c. on *deep blue* (2.12.1855)		40·00	£120
		a. "CENT. 49." (I/19, 38)		£275	£700
		b. "CNET. 40" (with or without full point after "40") (II/1, IV/15, 55)		£350	£1000
		c. "CEN .T40." (II/12)			
		d. "CENT .40." (III/19; IV/45)		£250	£700
		e. "CE6T. 40." (III/22)		£700	£1800
		f. "CENE. 40." (III/54)		£700	£1800
		g. "CENT. 4C." (IV/39)		£750	£1900
13		1l. on *white* ("LIRA 1.") (7.5.1853)		55·00	£2250
		a. No full point after figure "1" (I/41)		£150	£3500
		b. "LIRA. 1" (II/12)		£375	£4500

Dates are those of earliest known use.

Nos. 1/13 were printed in sheets of 240, divided into four panes of 60 (10 × 6). Positions (in brackets) of errors and varieties are quoted by the pane: I, top left; II, top right; III, bottom left, IV, bottom right.

The watermark "A" on the 1 lira is the initial of the papermaker's name: Agostino Amici.

The 5c. on *yellow* or *blue* and 25c. on *green* are proofs.

N 3   **N 4**

A   B

1853 (1 Apr). *NEWSPAPER TAX. Large inscription as* A. Typo. Imperf.

N14	**N 3**	9c. black on dull mauve		£12000	£3250

Nos. N14/16 were made from the same die as those of Type **1**, the values of which were inserted in movable type. The letters "B.G." stand for "BOLLO GAZZETTE" = Stamp for Journals. Prior to the issue of No. N14, in February and March 1853, the tax was indicated by a double-circle handstamp, inscribed "STATI ESTENSI CENT. 9." in the outer circle and "GAZZETTE ESTERE" in the centre, applied directly to the newspaper (*Price on piece* £160).

All known unused examples of No. N14 are without gum.

1853 (21 May). *NEWSPAPER TAX. Small inscription as* B. Typo. Imperf.

N15	**N 3**	9c. black on *dull mauve*		£600	75·00
		a. No stop after 9		£800	£200

Printed in sheets of 240 divided into panes as for Nos. 1/13. No. N15a occurs on I/4, 25; II/6, 18, 34; and IV/32.

1857 (1 Nov). *NEWSPAPER TAX. Without full point after figure of value.* Typo. Imperf.

N16	**1**	10c. black on *grey-lilac*		55·00	£275
		a. Error. "CEN1" for "CENT" (I/53, III/14)		£300	£2000

A 9c. on *violet* as No. N16 was prepared in 1855 but not issued (*Price* £2.40 *un*).

(Eng F. Riccò, Modena. Typo State Stamp Office)

1859 (17 Feb). *NEWSPAPER TAX.* Imperf.

N17	**N 4**	10c. black		£1000	£2000

On 11 June 1859 the Duke left Modena and a Provisional Government was set up to prepare for union with Sardinia.

ITALIAN STATES Modena, Naples — 1859

PROVISIONAL GOVERNMENT,
11 June 1859–18 March 1860

5 Cross of Savoy

(Dies engraved and electrotypes made by Carlo Setti. Typo Carlo Vincenzi, Modena)

1859 (15 Oct–Nov). *White paper.* Imperf.

18	5	5c. pale green		£1300	£600
		a. *Deep green*		£700	£525
19		15c. brown		£2500	£3500
		a. *Greyish brown*		£2750	£3500
		b. Raised point before "CENT." (I/17)		£3000	
		c. No full point after "15" (III/8, 27; IV/4, 27)		£2500	
20		15c. grey (Nov)		£300	
		a. Raised point before "CENT." (I/17)		£500	
		b. No full point after "15" (III/8, 27, IV/4, 27)		£325	
21		20c. violet-black		£1800	£150
		a. No full point after "20" (I/6)		£1500	£140
		b. "C" of "CENT" omitted (IV/26)			
22		20c. lilac (8 Nov)		60·00	£1000
		a. *Pale lilac*		60·00	£1000
		b. "ECNT" (III/3)		£225	£2250
		c. "N" of "CENT" inverted (III/30)		£170	£1200
		d. No full point after "20" (III/8, 12, 27; IV/4, 5, 14)		£120	£900
23		40c. pale rose		£180	£1200
		a. *Rose-red*		£350	£1200
		b. Raised point before "CENT" (I/17)		£350	£2750
		c. Inverted 5 before "CENT" (I/19)			
		d. No full point after "40" (II/8)		£275	£2750
24		80c. buff		£180	£19000
		a. *Orange-brown*		£180	£19000
		b. Figure "0" omitted (I/6)		£350	
		c. Figure "8" omitted (I/21)		£350	
		d. "N" of "CENT" inverted (I/22)		£350	
		e. No full point after "80" (I/25)		£350	

Nos. 18/24 were printed in sheets of 120 stamps divided into four panes of 30 (5 × 6). Positions of errors are quoted as for Nos. 1/13.

At the Milan Exibition, held in 1906, the original steel die that was engraved for the above stamps was shown by Captain A. E. Fiecchi, the Secretary to the Committee. He later had some reprints made by means of this die, which intentionally differ from the stamps of 1859. They were produced in sheets of 24 on very thin paper and there is no point after the figures of value.

On 18 March 1860, after a plebiscite, Modena became part of the Kingdom of Sardinia; the stamps of Sardinia replaced those for Modena.

NAPLES

(KINGDOM OF THE TWO SICILIES)

200 Tornesi = 100 Grano = 1 Ducato

In 1816 the Kingdoms of Naples and Sicily were united under the tiltle of the Kingdom of the Two Sicilies.

King Ferdinand II, 8 Nov 1830–22 May 1859

1    **2**

The above design bears the Arms of the Two Sicilies, composed of the horse for Naples, the three legs with head of Medusa for Sicily, and the three *fleurs-de-lis* for Bourbon.

(Eng G. Masini. Recess G. de Maja)

1858 (1 Jan). *T* **1** *(various shapes and frames).* W **2**, *40 times in sheet of 200 stamps.* Imperf.

1	½ grano lake	£2250	£475
1A	½ grano rose	£1800	£325
2	1 grano lake	£450	40·00
2A	1 grano rose	£900	44·00
3	2 grana lake	£275	12·00
3A	2 grana rose	£275	12·00
4	5 grana lake	£4500	£900
4A	5 grana rose	£2250	50·00
5	10 grana lake	£5000	£250
5A	10 grana rose	£4750	£170
6	20 grana lake	£6500	£1300
6A	20 grana rose	£4250	£600
7	50 grana lake	£10000	£3000
7A	50 grana rose	£10000	£3000

Varieties. Printed on both sides.

2A	1 grano rose	—	£1400
3A	2 grana rose (1 grano on back)	—	£3000
4A	5 grana rose	—	£9500
5A	10 grana rose	—	£32000

The designer introduced a different letter of his name, "G. MASINI", in the outer border of each value as a secret mark.

There are three plates of the 2gr. and two of each of the other values except the 50gr., of which there is only one.

No. 1A is known used bisected in 1861 from Chieti and Campobasso.

There are numerous forgeries of the 2, 10 and 20gr. of this issue that were made to deceive the postal authorities. These are normally found with genuine postal obliterations, unused rare.

All the values except the 2gr. were reprinted in 1898 on thick white wove unwatermarked paper. The impression of the reprints is very clear; the colour varies from pale to bright pink.

King Francis II, 22 May 1859–7 Sept 1860

Garibaldi and his redshirts landed in Sicily on 11 May 1860 and entered Naples, from which the King had fled, on 7 September 1860.

GARIBALDI RÉGIME, 7 Sept–7 Nov 1860

On 21 October 1860 Naples and Sicily voted by plebiscite to join the Kingdom of Sardinia as a further step towards a united Italy. On 26 October Garibaldi hailed Victor Emmanuel II of Sardinia as king, and the latter entered Naples on 7 November. No. 9, though issued under Sardinian authority, is the last stamp inscribed "Posta Napoletana".

3 Arms under Bourbon Dynasty    **4** Cross of Savoy

1860 (6 Nov). W **2**. Recess. Imperf.

8	3	½t. blue	£150000	£10000

Printed from the ½ grano, Plate II, the letter "G." on each stamp having been altered to a "T". This was done by Gennariello de Maja. There are 100 varieties of the stamp caused by this alteration, as each stamp on the plate was altered by hand.

ITALIAN STATES Naples, Neapolitan Provinces, Papal States 1860

1860 (6 Dec). W **2**. Recess. Imperf.
9	**4**	¼t. pale blue	£38000	£3750
		a. Deep blue	£38000	£3750

Like the ½ tornese, No. 8, this stamp was printed from the old plate of the ½ grano, after the centre of each stamp had been more or less removed, and re-engraved. Consequently there are likewise 100 varieties of this stamp.

NEAPOLITAN PROVINCES

Currency as Naples

These stamps were issues of the Kingdom of Sardinia for the newly-acquired provinces of Naples and Sicily; they are similar to the contemporary stamps of Sardinia, but, pending the introduction of a unified currency, the values were in Neapolitan money.

King Victor Emmanuel II

1

(Head embossed in colourless relief. Frame litho F. Matraire, Turin)

1861 (15 Feb–Mar). Imperf.
1	**1**	½t. blue-green	£450	£180
2		½t. green	9·25	£140
		a. Head inverted	£130	£9000
		b. Printed both sides	—	£18000
3		½t. apple-green	9·25	£140
4		½t. olive-green	£6000	£400
		a. Head inverted	—	£12000
5		½g. brown	£130	£150
		a. Head inverted	£1500	
6		½g. yellow-brown	£220	£160
7		½g. grey-brown	£3750	£190
8		1g. black	£450	16·00
9		1g. grey-black	£325	19·00
		a. Head inverted	—	£1400
10		2g. blue	80·00	9·50
11		2g. pale blue	90·00	7·50
		a. Head inverted	£180	£525
12		2g. indigo	£5500	£200
13		5g. lilac-rose	£225	£180
14		5g. rose	£225	£130
15		5g. red	£140	90·00
		a. Head inverted	£700	£4500
16		5g. vermilion	£200	95·00
		a. Printed both sides	—	£12000
17		10g. dull orange	£130	£140
		a. Head double	£180	£275
18		10g. orange	£100	£170
19		20g. yellow	£425	£1600
		a. Head inverted	—	£16000
20		20g. yellow-ochre	£1200	£3750
21		50g. bluish grey	16·00	£11000
22		50g. slate-blue	10·00	£11000
23		50g. pale grey	23·00	£7000

Errors of colour.
24	**1**	¼t. black	£30000	£31000
25		2g. black	—	£36000

These errors were issued at Roccagloriosa and Cosenza respectively.

Forgeries of some of the values, made to deceive the Post Office, may be met with duly cancelled.

Stamps similar to T **1** of Sardinia, but with inscription in larger, clearer lettering, were prepared in 1862 for use at Naples. Values 5c. green, 10c. grey-brown, 20c. blue, 40c. carmine-red, 80c. bright orange. These were not officially issued but a few are known postally used.

The above were superseded by the stamps of Italy in 1862.

PAPAL STATES

1852. 100 Bajocchi = 1 Scudo
1866. 100 Centesimi = 1 Lira

The temporal sovereignty of the Popes began in 754, with the gift to the Pope of territory won from the Lombards by Pepin the Short, King of the Franks.

In 1850, in addition to Rome and the surrounding district, the Papal States included the provinces of Romagna, the Marches and Umbria.

Pope Pius IX
15 June 1846–7 February 1878

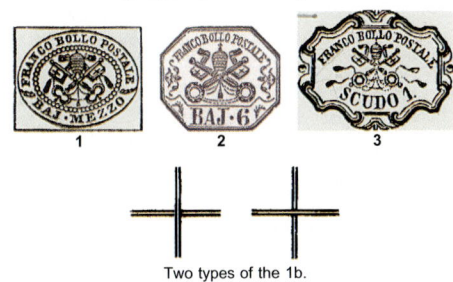

1 2 3

Two types of the 1b.

The illustration shows two types of intersection of the outer framelines in a block of four Single stamps of Type I show an extension of the vertical framelines and stamps of Type II have an extension of the horizontal framelines Type II only occurred in the last printing in bluish green.

(Dies eng Doublet and Decoppet. Stereos made by F. Coppet & Co. Typo Rev. Camera Apostolica, Rome)

1852 (1 Jan)–64. As T **1** to **3** *(various shapes and frames). Black impression, except for 50b. and 1s. Imperf.*
1		½b. drab	£450	75·00
2		½b. bluish grey	£425	42·00
		a. Tête-bêche (pair)	—	£24000
3		½b. greenish grey	£700	£150
4		½b. lilac-grey	£350	£225
		a. Printed on both sides	—	£20000
5		½b. dull lilac	35·00	£120
6		½b. dull purple	£225	£275
7		1b. greyish green (I)	£180	6·25
		a. Printed on both sides	—	£20000
8		1b. light green (I)	£150	7·25
9		1b. bluish green (I)	£425	41·00
10		1b. bluish green (II)	46·00	55·00
11		2b. olive-green	£130	11·00
		a. No stop after "BAJ" (No. 14)	£325	22·00
12		2b. deep green	85·00	6·00
13		2b. greenish white	70·00	11·50
14		2b. white	8·50	50·00
		a. No stop after "BAJ" (No. 14)	9·75	£120
15		3b. brown	60·00	26·00
		a. Printed on both sides	—	£20000
16		3b. yellow-buff (1858)	23·00	£160
		a. Printed on both sides	—	£20000
17		4b. buff	£4500	65·00
18		4b. lemon	£160	65·00
		a. Printed on both sides	—	£20000
19		4b. yellow	£120	34·00
20		5b. rose	£150	7·50
		a. Printed on both sides	—	£20000
21		5b. pale rose	£160	11·50
22		5b. lavender	£850	£190
23		6b. greenish grey	£550	48·00
24		6b. greyish	£500	£120
25		7b. blue	£850	60·00
26		8b. white (1.10.52)	£400	32·00
27		50b. dull blue (12.7.52)	£12000	£1500
28		50b. deep blue (*worn impression*) (20.5.64)	£16000	£2500
29		1sc. dull rose (12.7.52)	£3000	£3000

Nearly all values of this issue are known cut into fractions and used for a corresponding proportion of their original value.

3

ITALIAN STATES Papal States, Parma — 1852

The first printing of the ½b. had position 62 inverted. thus giving No. 2a. The error was corrected in later printings.
Stamps can be found with part of the papermakers' watermarks: "PIETRO MILIANI FABRIANO" (3b.), "CANSON FRERES" (50b., 1s.). "BATH" (2, 6b.) or with a stitch watermark.
Examples with all outer double framelines complete are worth a premium.
A 20b. on *yellow* (similar to Type **2**) was prepared but not issued.

(Dies altered by M. Montarsolo. Stereos made by Giuseppe Coccapieller. Typo Rev. Camera Apostolica, Rome)

1867 (21 Sept). As T **1** and **2** *(various shapes and frames)* but value in cent *(esimi)*. Black on coloured glazed paper. Imperf.

30	2c. *green*	£110	£200
	a. No stop after "Cent"	£120	£300
31	3c. *drab*	£500	£4750
32	3c. *rosy drab*	£1800	£2250
33	5c. *greenish blue*	£130	£170
	a. No stop after figures	£400	£950
34	10c. *vermilion*	£850	55·00
35	20c. *Indian red*	£120	75·00
	a. No stop after "Cent"	£475	£300
36	40c. *lemon*	£140	£170
	a. No stop after figures	£160	£190
37	80c. *rose*	£140	£450

Prepared for use, but never issued. Unglazed paper. Ungummed.
Imperf.

37a	3c. *green*		£80000
38	5c. *greenish blue*		55·00
39	10c. *vermilion*		90
40	20c. *bronze green/solferino*		1·80
41	20c. *bronze green/magenta*		1·80

No. 37a was prepared in 1867 The other values date from 1870, and may represent imperforate examples of the 1868 issue.
The variety with no stop after figures is to be found on Nos. 38 and 40/41.

1868 (Mar)–**70**. As last. P 13.

42	2c. *green*	8·00	60·00
	a. No stop after "Cent"	10·00	£180
43	3c. *drab*	35·00	£3000
44	3c. *rosy drab*	£3750	£12000
45	5c. *greenish blue*	9·75	38·00
	a. No stop after "Cent"	55·00	£275
	b. No stop after figures	10·50	70·00
46	10c. *orange-vermilion*	2·75	11·00
47	10c. *vermilion*	£130	14·00
48	20c. *Indian red*	£700	23·00
	a. No stop after figures	£1400	75·00
49	20c. *magenta*	3·75	30·00
	a. No stop after "Cent"	10·00	£120
	b. No stop after figures	10·00	£120
50	20c. *solferino*	2·20	13·00
	a. No stop after figures	10·00	£120
51	20c. *deep crimson*	5·50	85·00
52	40c. *lemon*	5·50	85·00
	a. No stop after figures	6·00	£110
53	40c. *chrome-yellow*	5·50	85·00
	a. No stop after figures	6·00	£110
54	40c. *orange-yellow*	75·00	£800
	a. No stop after figures	£100	£1000
55	80c. *rose*	25·00	£325
56	80c. *pale rose*	28·00	£450
57	80c. *carmine* (1870)	£2500	£16000

All the values of both the imperf and the perforated series have been privately reprinted many times. The reprints are imperf or perf 11½, 12 or 13.

After the withdrawal of a French garrison from Rome during the Franco-Prussian war, Italian troops took the city on 20 September 1870. A plebiscite in the Papal States on 2 October led to their incorporation in the Kingdom of Italy.

PARMA

100 Centesimi = 1 Lira

The Duchy of Parma and Piacenza was created in 1545.

Duke Charles III, 25 Aug 1849–26 March 1854

1 Bourbon *fleur-de-lis*

(Die eng D. Bentelli. Typo Rossi-Ubaldi, Parma)

1852 (1 June). Imperf.

1	**1**	5c. grey-black/*yellow*	70·00	95·00
2		5c. black/*yellow*	42·00	85·00
3		10c. grey-black/*white*	70·00	95·00
4		10c. black/*white*	70·00	95·00
5		15c. grey-black/*dull rose*	£1900	42·00
		a. Tête-bêche (pair)		
6		15c. black/*rose*	£2000	40·00
7		25c. black/*purple*	£9500	£140
8		40c. black/*pale blue*	£2000	£225
9		40c. black/*blue*	£1700	£225

Position 9 of the lower left-hand pane of 20 was inverted, giving No. 5a; the error was corrected during the first printing. Five used horizontal pairs (three on cover) are known, together with one vertical pair on cover and one almost complete unused sheet.
The 5c. and 10c. *tête-bêche* are forgeries. Varieties are also known of genuine stamps printed on the back with the same or other value, but these are bogus. No genuine variety printed on both sides is known.
No. 8 unused is only known without gum

1853–57. NEWSPAPER. Type of 1859 issue. Black impression. Imperf.

N1	**3**	6c. on *rose* (1.11.57)	£1100	£250
N2		6c. on *pale rose*	70·00	
N3		9c. on *pale blue* (4.53)	£600	£17000
N4		9c. on *blue*	44·00	

1853–55. Coloured impression. Imperf.

10	**1**	5c. *pale yellow* (4.1.54)	£5500	£700
11		5c. *orange-yellow*	£5000	£600
12		15c. *pale red* (30.12.53)	£6000	£120
13		15c. *red*	£6000	£130
14		25c. *red brown* (28.5.55)	£8500	£275
15		25c. *deep brown*	£8500	£275

In both the preceding issues the impressions vary from sharply-printed, with all the lines distinct, to blurred impressions, with very little visible.
The 25c. unused is only known without gum.

Duchess Marie Louise, Regent
26 March 1854–9 June 1859

2

(Die eng D. Bentelli. Typo Rossi-Ubaldi, Parma)

1857–59. Imperf.

16	**2**	15c. *pale red* (4.3.59)	£200	£325
17		15c. *red*	£200	£325
18		25c. *brown-lilac* (3.7.57)	£475	£180
19		25c. *brown-purple*	£375	£150
20		40c. *pale blue* (30.6.57)	46·00	£400
		a. Narrow "0" in "40"	£160	£1200
21		40c. *blue*	46·00	£400
		a. Narrow "0" in "40"	£160	£1200

ITALIAN STATES Parma, Romagna, Sardinia   1857

The narrow "0" occurs 20 times in the sheet of 72 stamps.

On 9 June 1859 the Regent handed over her authority to a Provisional Government, to prepare for union with Sardinia.

PROVISIONAL GOVERNMENT
9 June 1859–18 March 1860

3 (Typo at Parma)

1859 (27 Aug). *Coloured impression.* Imperf.

27	3	5c. yellow-green	£950	£13000
28		5c. blue-green	£1900	£3250
29		10c. brown	£700	£350
	a.	Figure "1" inverted	£1100	£3000
30		10c. deep brown	£850	£400
31		20c. blue	£1000	£700
32		20c. deep blue	£1000	£160
33		40c. red	£475	£7000
34		40c. brown-red	£16000	£8500
35		80c. bistre-yellow	£6000	
36		80c. bistre-orange	£7000	

No 29a occurs on position 36 in the sheet of 60, in the second printing only.

All values exist with "A" in "STATI" shorter than usual, and with "CFN" for "CEN", in "CENTESIMI", etc. The 10, 20, 40 and 80c. exist with thick "0" in value, and the 10 and 20c. with small "o".

Parma and Piacenza, after a plebiscite, became part of the Kingdom of Sardinia on 18 March 1860, the stamps of Sardinia replaced those of Parma.

ROMAGNA
100 Bajocchi = 1 Scudo

Romagna was, in theory, one of the Papal States from 756. Papal authority was fully exercised there from 1503, it ended on 12 June 1859 with the formation of a Provisional Government to prepare for union with Sardinia.

PROVISIONAL GOVERNMENT
12 June 1859–25 March 1860

1

(Electrotypes made by Amoretti Bros. Typo Volpe and del Sassi, Bologna)

1859 (1 Sept). *Black impression.* Imperf.

1	½b. on *buff*		18·00	£225
2	½b. on *yellow*		18·00	£225
3	1b. on *drab*		18·00	£110
4	2b. on *orange-buff*		32·00	£120
5	3b. on *deep green*		37·00	£250
6	4b. on *pale brown*		£500	£120
7	5b. on *grey-lilac*		46·00	£300
8	6b. on *yellow-green*		£250	£6000
9	8b. on *rose*		£180	£1400
10	20b. on *grey-green*		£180	£2000

These stamps are frequently found with forged obliterations. They have been twice privately reprinted—in 1892 and 1897. The blocks used for the reprints were more or less damaged, so that the impression is thick and blurred. The small "Y"-shaped ornament between the pearls in the corners is indistinct, and in some cases has entirely disappeared, and the four dots outside the pearls are either altogether absent, or are joined to the pearls.

The ½, 2 and 4 to 8b. values are known bisected or otherwise divided and used for a corresponding fraction of their original value.

Proofs or colour trials of some of the values are known printed on other papers than those assigned to them in the above list.

After a plebiscite Romagna became part of the Kingdom of Sardinia on 25 March 1860, and the stamps of Sardinia came into use.

SARDINIA
100 Centesimi = 1 Lira

The Kingdom of Sardinia, to give its official title, comprised Savoy (till 1860), Piedmont, Liguria and Sardinia; it is often called Piedmont, for the capital was Turin.

King Victor Emmanuel II

1  **2**  **N 3**

(T **1** and **2** des and ptd F. Matraire, Turin)

1851 (1 Jan). *Lithographed.* Imperf.

1	1	5c. grey-black	£6000	£1700
2		5c. black	£6000	£1700
3		20c. blue	£6000	£130
4		20c. deep blue	£6000	£350
5		40c. lilac-rose	£11000	£21000
6		40c. pink	£8500	£4250
7		40c. rose	£8000	£3500
8		40c. deep rose	£8500	£4250

1853 (1 Oct). *Embossed on coloured paper.* Imperf.

9	1	5c. blue-green	£9500	£1000
10		20c. blue	£11000	£120
11		40c. pale rose	£7500	£800

Numerous private reprints of the stamps of this issue exist. These reprints have been made in several colours, and are frequently found with forged postmarks, sometimes on pieces of paper. The original stamps are only known in one shade of colour (for each value).

1854 (18 Apr). *Embossed on white paper, the head in colourless relief, the frame in relief on colour, lithographed before embossing.* Imperf.

12	1	5c. green	—	£500
13		5c. yellow-green	£29000	£500
14		5c. bright green	—	£500
15		20c. pale blue	£12000	£100
16		20c. blue	—	£110
17		20c. deep blue	—	£110
18		40c. dull rose	£86000	£2500
19		40c. deep rose	—	£2750
20		40c. deep brown-red	—	£2750

All three values have been privately reprinted many times in the colours of the issue and in other colours also.

See note at the end of Neapolitan Provinces regarding stamps as T **1** of Sardinia which were prepared for use in Naples in 1862.

ITALIAN STATES Sardinia, Sicily — 1855

1855 (July)–**63**. *Frame typographed in colour, head embossed in colourless relief.* Imperf.

21	**2**	5c. pea-green (1855)	£2000	£1100
22		5c. emerald-green (1855)	£1400	£160
		a. Head inverted	—	£6000
23		5c. myrtle (1857)	£2250	£225
24		5c. bright yellow-green (1857)	£550	85·00
		a. Head inverted	—	£3500
25		5c. olive-green (1859)	£190	£100
26		5c. deep olive-green (1861)	£225	£110
		a. Head inverted	—	£2250
27		5c. deep green (1862)	5·50	12·50
		a. Head inverted	—	£2500
28		5c. yellowish green (1862)	5·50	12·50
29		5c. pale green (1863)	5·50	12·50
30		10c. dark brown (1858)	£375	£190
		a. Head inverted		
31		10c. violet-brown (1859)	£300	£190
32		10c. grey-brown (1859)	28·00	90·00
		a. Head inverted	—	£7000
33		10c. olive-brown (1860)	85·00	70·00
34		10c. pale brown (1861)	38·00	26·00
35		10c. olive-grey (1861)	28·00	90·00
36		10c. chocolate-brown (1861)	£130	40·00
37		10c. bistre-olive (1862)	19·00	19·00
		a. Head inverted	—	£3000
38		10c. ochre-yellow (1862)	80·00	17·00
39		10c. orange-brown (1862)	85·00	70·00
		a. Head inverted	—	£2750
40		10c. bistre (1863)	5·50	12·00
41		10c. pale bistre (1863)	5·50	12·00
42		10c. deep bistre (1863)	5·50	12·00
43		20c. cobalt-blue (1855)	£1400	75·00
44		20c. milky blue (1855)	£2250	60·00
45		20c. dark blue (1859)	£200	30·00
		a. Head inverted	—	£850
46		20c. blue (1860)	£200	19·00
		a. Head inverted	—	£900
47		20c. grey-blue (1861)	90·00	10·00
		a. Head inverted	—	£900
48		20c. indigo (1862)	95·00	18·00
49		40c. vermilion (1855)	£1900	£180
50		40c. scarlet (1857)	£1200	65·00
		a. Head inverted	—	£5000
51		40c. brick-red (1859)	£170	£160
52		40c. carmine (1860)	£160	£130
53		40c. red-carmine (1861)	40·00	35·00
		a. Head inverted	—	£3500
54		40c. rose-carmine (1862)	40·00	35·00
55		40c. pale red (1863)	20·00	30·00
56		80c. orange-bistre (1858)	95·00	£250
57		80c. buff (1858)	90·00	£250
58		80c. pale ochre-yellow (1859)	£450	£325
		a. Head inverted	—	£11000
59		80c. bright orange (1861)	17·00	£225
60		80c. orange-yellow (1862)	24·00	£325
		a. Head inverted	—	£12000
61		3l. bronze (1861)	£350	£2500

All values except the 1c. (Newspaper), 5c. and 3 lire, are known divided and used for a half or other fraction of their original value.

The 5c., 20c. and 40c. have been privately reprinted. The impression is not so clear as that of the originals, the ornaments in the spandrels being very thick and smudgy. These reprints are found perf 11½.

For stamps of similar design but with larger, clearer inscriptions, see Neapolitan Provinces.

(Des and ptd F. Matraire, Turin)

1861 (1 Jan). NEWSPAPER. *Frame typographed in black, numeral embossed in colourless relief.* Imperf.

N62	**N 3**	1c. black	5·75	10·00
		a. Figure in centre inverted	£1000	
		b. Figure "2" for "1"	£425	£1300
N63		2c. black	£130	90·00
		a. Figure in centre inverted	£1000	
		b. Figure "1" for "2"	£3750	£18000

On 17 March 1861 King Victor Emmanuel of Sardinia was declared to be King of Italy.

From 1859 to 1862 the issues of the Kingdom of Sardinia were provisionally used in those States and parts of Italy which from time to time during that period were united with the Kingdom of Sardinia, until they were superseded by stamps for the Kingdom of Italy in 1862.

SICILY

(KINGDOM OF THE TWO SICILIES)

100 Grano = 1 Ducato

In 1816 the Kingdoms of Naples and Sicily were united under the title of the Kingdom of the Two Sicilies.

King Ferdinand 11, 8 Nov 1830–22 May 1859

King Francis 11, 22 May 1859–7 Sept 1860

1

(Eng T. Aloisio Juvara, Messina. Recess F. Lao, Palermo)

1859 (1 Jan). Imperf.

1	**1**	½g. orange-yellow (Pl. I, II)	from	£350	£1200
		a. Olive-yellow (Pl. I)		—	£23000
		b. Orange (Pl. I, II)	from	£800	£650
		c. Retouch (Pl. I, II)	from	£400	£1200
		d. Error. Cobalt (Pl. II)			
2		1g. russet-brown (Pl. I)		£12000	£550
		a. Olive-brown (Pl. I)	from	£600	95·00
		ab. Printed double (Pl. II)		£4500	£5000
		b. Olive-green (Pl. II, III)	from	£375	£130
		c. Deep olive-green (Pl. III)		£110	£150
		d. Head and background entirely redrawn (Pl. I)		—	£6500
		e. Retouch (Pl. I, II)	from	£200	£170
		f. Double impression (constant) (Pl. II)	from	£450	£250
3		2g. dull blue (Pl. I, II, III)		95·00	75·00
		b. Pale blue (Pl. I, II, III)		95·00	75·00
		c. Ultramarine (Pl. I, II, III)		£6500	£450
		d. Deep cobalt (Pl. I, II, III)		£3250	£200
		e. Deep blue (Pl. III)		£2250	£225
		f. Retouch (Pl. I, II)	from	£120	£100
4		5g. carmine (Pl. I, 1st ptg)		£450	£300
		b. Rose-red (Pl. I, 1st ptg)		£425	£325
		c. Brick-red (Pl. I, 1st ptg)		£2000	£1000
		d. Red-brown (Pl. I, 1st ptg)		£5000	£2500
		e. Dull rose (Pl. I, 2nd ptg)		£3000	£2250
		f. Vermilion (Pl. I, (2nd ptg), II)		£140	£1000
		h. Orange-red (Pl. II)		£130	£1200
		i. Retouch (Pl. I)	from	£275	£550
5		10g. indigo		£550	£250
		a. Retouch (8 on sheet)		£650	£350
6		20g. slate-grey		£550	£450
		b. Purple-slate		£2250	£850
		c. Bluish slate		£425	£350
		d. Retouch (pos. 72)		£850	£900
7		50g. brown-lake		£550	£3500
		b. Chocolate		£450	£3250
		c. Retouch (pos. 93)		£700	£5500
		d. Double impression (pos. 62)		£700	£5500

Printed in sheets of 100 on soft or hard paper. There was one plate only for Nos. 5/7, plates for the other values are detailed below. Although some examples can easily be distinguished as coming from a particular plate, others can only be assigned by reference to a plating study (e.g. the handbook by Emilio Diena). For this reason they are no longer listed individually.

½g. Plate I. 2–2½ mm between rows. The 50 positions from the left-hand side have the right upper corner incomplete. 23 positions from the right-hand side have a white dot touching "A" of "POSTA". Retouches on positions 19, 31, 68, 69, 79 and 99. Colour trials in shades of blue, milky blue and dull blue were made from part of this plate and should not be confused with No. 1d.

Plate II. 1½ mm between rows. Most positions have a white dot inside the bottom right corner of the white frame. No retouches.

Used stamps from this plate are worth about three times quoted

ITALIAN STATES Sicily, Tuscany — 1859

prices of Nos. 1 and 1b. Only two examples of the colour error (No. 1d.) are known, both used (one on piece).

1g. Plate I. 2–2½ mm between rows. About 80 positions have the "S" and "T" of "POSTA" joined by a white flaw. Stamps in olive-brown from this plate are worth about four times unused and ten times used prices quoted for No. 2a. There were two states of this plate, the second state showing further retouches. Three stamps in the sheet show the head almost entirely redrawn (No. 2d.) There are about 20 less prominent retouches which are worth about five times quoted price of No. 2e.

Plate II. 1–1½ mm between rows. Most positions have a short white dash under beard. *Unused* examples in olive-green are worth twice quoted price. Positions 30, 32 and 35 show a re-entry, causing a doubling of the impression (particularly noticeable as thicker inscriptions) (No. 2f) on all shades. It should not be confused with No. 2ab which results from the whole sheet being printed double; this occurs only on the olive-brown shade and the two impressions are offset by about 3 mm. There are six slight retouches.

Plate III. 1½ mm between rows. Numerous very minor retouches.

2g. Plates I, II and III. Stamps with a white dot under the nose come from Plates I or II but is not present on all examples. Plate I has 16 retouches and Plate II has 5, none very prominent.

5g. Plate I. Stamps either have the right upper corner incomplete together with a white dot on the nose or there is a white dot next to "A" of "DELLA". Seven slight retouches. There were two printings from this plate, the second printing is blurred and indistinct.

Plate II. No distinguishing features. 1 retouch (position 90).

In November 1860 Sicily, with Naples, became part of the Kingdom of Sardinia. See note after Naples.

TUSCANY

1851. 60 Quattrini = 20 Soldi = 12 Crazie = 1 Tuscan Lira
1859. (1 Nov). 1 Tuscan Lira = 1 Italian Lira

Tuscany became a Grand Duchy in 1569

Grand Duke Leopold 11, 8 June 1824–27 April 1859

1 Arms of Tuscany
2

T **2** and **4** are reduced illustrations of the complete watermarks of the whole sheet.

(Engraved and electrotypes made by M. Alessandri, Florence. Typo Grand Ducal Printing Office, Florence)

1851 (1 Apr)–**52**. *Blue to greyish blue paper.* Wmk Crowns. T **2**, in sheet. Imperf.

1	1	1q. black/azure (1.9.52)	£5000	£950
2		1q. black/grey	£4750	£900
3		1s. lemon/azure	£8000	£1000
4		1s. orange/azure	£8000	£1000
5		1s. orange/grey	£6000	£950
6		2s. brick-red/azure	£20000	£3000
7		1c. deep carmine/azure (1.7.52)	£3750	£110
8		1c. claret/grey	£3750	48·00
9		1c. carmine/grey	£3750	48·00
10		2c. bright blue/azure	£3750	£110
11		2c. blue/grey	£1800	55·00
12		2c. dull blue/grey	£1800	55·00
13		4c. myrtle-green/azure	£4000	£140
14		4c. deep green/grey	£3000	60·00
15		4c. yellow-green/grey	£3000	60·00
16		6c. deep blue/azure	£4000	£110
17		6c. violet-blue/grey	£5000	80·00
18		6c. indigo/grey	£5000	80·00
19		6c. slate-blue/grey	£5000	80·00
20		9c. plum/azure (1.7.52)	£8000	£190
21		9c. dull purple/azure	£9000	£190
22		9c. dull purple/grey	£8000	90·00
23		60c. brick-red/azure (11.52)	£36000	£18000

Stamps printed on white, porous, unwatermarked paper are proofs. Some values are known used for postage.

N 3
4

1854 (1 Oct). NEWSPAPER TAX. *Framed with faint pink ruled lines. Yellowish white pelure paper.*
N1 N **3** 2s. black 32·00
         a. Tête-bêche (pair) £650

The tax on newspapers was suppressed on 18 November 1859. This stamp was reprinted in 1864 on thick white paper.

1857–59. W **4** *("Il E R R POSTE TOSCANE" double lined) in sheet.* Imperf.

24	1	1q. black (24.7.57)	£800	£550
25		1s. yellow-buff (6.7.57)	£18000	£2750
26		1c. carmine (5.12.57)	£4500	£250
27		1c. pale carmine	£4500	£250
28		2c. blue (6.10.57)	£1000	50·00
29		2c. greenish blue	£1000	50·00
30		4c. deep green (24.7.57)	£4250	85·00
		a. Bottom label inverted		
31		6c. deep blue (14.3.57)	£5000	95·00
32		6c. dull blue	£5000	£130
33		9c. purple-brown (8.7.59)	£16000	£2750

Only one example is known of No. 30a, in used condition.

The 9c. is listed here for convenience of reference, though it was issued after the setting-up of the Provisional Government.

Grand Duke Leopold was expelled from Tuscany on 27 April 1859 and a Provisional Government was set up to prepare for union with Sardinia.

PROVISIONAL GOVERNMENT
27 April 1859–22 March 1860

5 Arms of Savoy

1860 (1 Jan). W **4** in sheet. Imperf.

36	5	1c. deep purple	£1100	£400
37		1c. plum	£1100	£400
38		1c. dull purple	£1100	£400
39		5c. olive-green	£6500	£150
40		5c. deep green	£5000	£150
41		5c. pale green	£5000	£150
42		10c. deep brown	£1100	18·00
43		10c. red-brown	£1100	18·00
44		10c. purple-brown	£1100	18·00

ITALIAN STATES Tuscany 1860

45	20c. deep blue	£4250	80·00
46	20c. blue	£4250	80·00
47	20c. grey-blue	£4750	95·00
48	40c. rose-carmine	£6000	£120
49	40c. rose	£6000	£120
50	80c. pale red-brown	£14000	£600
51	3 lire, yellow-buff	£100000	£40000

The 40c. is known bisected and used as 20c.

There are many so-called *unused* Tuscany stamps offered for sale, especially from the Continent, which are only *used* stamps *cleaned*. Our prices are for undoubtedly *unused* specimens in good condition.

After a plebiscite Tuscany became part of the Kingdom of Sardinia on 22 March 1860; the stamps of Sardinia replaced those of Tuscany.

ITALY 1862

Italy

100 Centesimi = 1 Lira

KINGDOM
King Victor Emmanuel II
17 March 1861–9 January 1878

1   **N 2**

(Printed by F. Matraire, Turin)

1862. Frame typographed in colour, head embossed in colourless relief. P 11½ × 12.

1	1	10c. bistre (24.2.62)	£4500	£100
		a. Deep bistre	£8000	£225
		b. Bistre-brown	£9000	£225
		c. Olive-bistre	£12000	£275
		d. Yellow-bistre	£11000	£225
2		20c. blue (1.3.62)	£600	£550
		a. Indigo	16·00	14·00
		b. Violet-blue	18·00	32·00
3		40c. rose (10.4.62)	£200	60·00
		a. Rose-red	£275	£160
		b. Deep red	£275	£160
4		80c. yellow (3.10.62)	55·00	£1200
		a. Orange-yellow	50·00	£1200

These stamps which are similar, except as regards perforation, to the 1855–61 issue of Sardinia, *imperf.*, are also known perf. 9½, 10, 11, 12½, 13, 13½ and 14, but these are fraudulent. The same remark applies to all perforated specimens of the 5c. *green* and 3l. *bronze* as these two values were never issued perforated.

1862 (1 May). NEWSPAPER. Frame typographed in colour, numeral embossed in colourless relief. Imperf.

N5	N 2	2c. yellow	40·00	85·00
		a. Orange-buff	41·00	85·00

1863 (1 Jan). Lithographed, and head embossed. Imperf.

5	1	15c. pale blue	50·00	22·00
		a. Deep blue	70·00	41·00
		b. Pair, one with head omitted	£1000	
		c. Head inverted	—	£53000

Only six examples of No. 5c. are known, all used (one is on cover and one on piece).
This stamp is found with several varieties of perforation, all of which are fraudulent.

D 3   **3**

(Litho F. Matraire, Turin)

1863 (1 Jan). POSTAGE DUE. Imperf. *A. Unused with gum; B. Unused without gum; C. Used.*

			A.	B.	C.
D6	D 3	10c. yellow	£1700	35·00	80·00
		a. Orange	£1700	£120	£160
		b. Brown-orange	£1700	£120	£160

(Litho F. Matraire, Turin)

1863. Imperf. *Two types.*
(a) First "C" in bottom inscr half closed (11 Feb).

6	3	15c. blue	£350	21·00
		a. Deep blue	£350	21·00
		b. "C" completely closed (= "O")	£1500	£110

(b) "C" open and line broken below "Q" (16 Apr).

7	3	15c. blue	3·50	1·90
		a. Deep blue	5·50	9·25
		b. Line below "Q" unbroken	8·25	12·50

No. 6 unused but without gum is worth £40.
This issue is also known with fraudulent perforation.
There are three types of postal forgeries of No. 7. The first, used in Naples, is litho and in ultramarine-blue; the second, also used in Naples is recess printed and in greenish blue; the third, used in Aquila, is also recess printed but in slate-grey. All are rare.

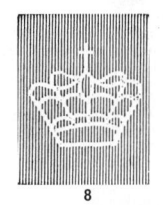

4   **5**   **6**

7   **8**

1863 (1 Dec)–**65**. *Corners vary for each value in T* **6**. W **8**. *Typo.* P 14.

8	4	1c. olive-green	3·50	50
		a. Pale bronze-green	3·50	70
		b. Deep bronze-green	3·50	70
9	5	2c. pale brown (1.3.65)	7·50	35
		a. Brown	7·50	35
		b. Deep brown	7·50	35
		c. Imperf (pair)	£150	£225
10	6	5c. greenish grey	£1600	60
		a. Pale grey	£1600	1·10
		b. Slate-grey	£1600	1·10
11		10c. buff	£2000	65
		a. Brown-buff	£2000	1·00
		b. Orange-buff	£2000	1·00
12		15c. blue	£2000	85
		a. Pale blue	£2000	1·30
13		30c. brown	10·00	1·40
		a. Chocolate	10·00	2·00
14		40c. rose	£4000	1·30
		a. Carmine	£4000	1·30
15		60c. pale mauve	10·00	6·25
		a. Mauve	10·00	6·50
16	7	2l. pale scarlet	16·00	30·00
		a. Deep scarlet	16·00	30·00

The original printings were made by De La Rue & Co. until the end of 1865 when the plates were sent to the Government Printing Works at Turin. The 15c. was only printed by De La Rue.
There is some doubt as to who designed and engraved this issue. Leonard Wyon has been credited on the basis of De La Rue correspondence from April 1863. However it appears that by then trial engravings had already been made by J. F Joubert de la Ferté. It is uncertain who prepared the final dies.
The 2c. imperforate comes from the Turin printing. The 1, 15 and 30c. from the De La Rue printing are also known imperf; these are rare.

9

ITALY 1865

```
   C    20

    20    C
      (9)
```

I II III

The new plates (I) and (II) differ from the original (III) by the addition of white dots and in the position of the head within the oval. Pl. I has dot in ornament above "O" and another before "P". Pl. II has dot before "P" only.

1865. T **6**, *printed from the original and two new plates surch. with* T **9** *in brown.* W **8**. P 14.

17	20c.on 15c. dull blue (I) (1 Jan)	£600	75
	a. Surch omitted	£19000	
	b. Surch inverted	—	£45000
	c. Imperf		
18	20c.on 15c. dull blue (II) (Feb)	£6000	16·00
19	20c.on 15c. dull blue (III) (Mar)	£1400	6·25

One unused and three used (one on cover) examples are known of No. 17b.

PRINTERS. From 1866 all stamps were printed at the Government Printing Works at Turin (Officina Governativa Carte Valori) until 1928 and from 1929 at Rome (Istituto Poligrafico dello Stato), *unless otherwise stated*.

10   D 11   D 12

1867 (April). *New value*. Typo. W **8**. P 14.
20	**10**	20c. pale blue	£1300	3·00
		a. *Bright blue*	£650	50

No. 20 was printed by De La Rue and No. 20a from the same plates at Turin.

(Eng L. Bigola. Typo)

1869 (1 Mar). *POSTAGE DUE*. W **8**. P 14.
| D21 | D **11** | 10c. orange-brown | £4000 | 12·50 |

1870 (1 Jan)–**1925**. *POSTAGE DUE. As Type D* **12**. *Typo*. W **8**. P 14.

D22	1c. magenta and orange	4·25	2·20
	a. Numeral inverted	£3250	£2250
D23	2c. magenta and orange	9·00	7·25
	a. Numeral inverted	£8500	£3000
D24	5c. magenta and orange	35	10
	a. Numeral inverted	4·00	4·00
D25	10c. magenta and orange (8.71)	35	10
	a. Numerals inverted	5·50	7·00
	b. Numerals double	48·00	55·00
D26	20c. magenta and orange (10.94)	1·50	10
	a. Numerals inverted	28·00	28·00
	b. Numerals double	90·00	£110
	c. Imperf (pair)	£150	£170
D27	30c. magenta and orange	3·50	30
	a. Numerals inverted	8·25	14·00
	b. Imperf (pair)	£3500	
D28	40c. magenta and orange	3·00	40
	a. Numerals inverted	£350	£450
D29	50c. magenta and orange	3·50	20
	a. Numerals inverted	50·00	55·00
D30	60c. magenta and orange	£750	95
	a. Numerals inverted	£275	£275
D31	60c. brown and orange (7.25)	20·00	3·00
D32	1l. brown and pale blue	£5500	4·50
	a. Numeral inverted		
D33	1l. magenta and blue ('92)	6·50	20
	a. Numeral double	£700	£700
	b. Numeral inverted	£2750	£2000
	c. Imperf (pair)	£140	£250
D34	2l. brown and pale blue	£5500	7·50
	a. Numeral inverted	—	£2250
D35	2l. magenta and blue ('03)	55·00	55
	a. Numeral inverted	£2000	£2250
D36	5l. brown and blue (1.1.74)	£375	10·00
	a. Numeral inverted	—	£1100
	b. Numeral double	—	£1600
D37	5l. magenta and blue ('03)	85·00	3·50
	a. Numeral inverted		
D38	10l. brown and blue (1.1.74)	£8000	9·25
	a. Numerals inverted	—	£275
D39	10l. magenta and blue (1893)	90·00	15·00

The earlier printings of the 1c. to 60c. were in pale orange and later printings in deeper browner orange. The former are usually scarcer than the latter.

The pale orange shades of the 5c., 10c., 30c., 40c., 50c. and 60c. with inverted numerals are much rarer than the later shades.

Stamps as Type D **12**, but with an orange numeral in a green frame are fiscals.

Stamps printed by lithography, with no watermark and perf 12½, are forgeries.

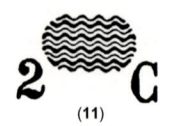

O 11   (11)

1875 (1 Jan). *OFFICIAL*. *Typo*. W **8**. P 14.
O21	O **11**	2c. claret	75	65
O22		5c. claret	75	65
O23		20c. claret	15	15
O24		30c. claret	25	20
O25		1l. claret	1·60	3·00
O26		2l. claret	10·50	8·00
O27		5l. claret	55·00	60·00
O28		10l. claret	60·00	28·00

1877 (1 Aug). *Colours changed*. *Typo*. W **8**. P 14.
21	**6**	10c. claret	£4500	1·00
		a. *Deep blue*	£5500	4·50
22	**10**	20c. orange-buff	£3500	80
		a. *Orange*	£3750	2·75

The 20c. is from a new die engraved by Professor L. Bigola.

1878 (1 Jan). *Official stamps surch with* T **11**, *In blue for use as postage stamps*.

23	O **11**	2c.on 2c. claret	£160	4·25
		a. Surch inverted	—	£1200
24		2c.on 5c. claret	£160	5·75
		a. Surch inverted	—	£900
25		2c.on 20c. claret	£300	1·60
		a. Surch inverted	£29000	£650
26		2c.on 30c. claret	£200	2·30
		a. Surch inverted	—	£650
27		2c.on 1l. claret	£250	1·70
		a. Surch inverted	£36000	£800
28		2c.on 2l. claret	£250	2·75
		a. Surch inverted	£36000	£950
29		2c.on 5l. claret	£300	3·75
		a. Surch inverted	—	£950
30		2c.on 10l. claret	£200	4·50
		a. Surch inverted	—	£800

ITALY 1879

King Umberto I, 9 Jan 1878–29 July 1900

1879 (15 Aug)–**82**. *Corners vary for each value.* Typo. W **8**. P 14.
31	12	5c. green	7·50	30
		a. *Pale green*	8·25	1·40
32		10c. pale rose-red	£350	35
		a. *Deep rose-red*	£450	1·60
33		20c. orange	£350	30
		a. *Deep orange*	£400	1·80
		b. Perf 11½		
34		25c. deep blue	£500	65
		a. *Blue*	£700	4·50
35		30c. brown	£110	£800
36		50c. mauve	10·00	3·25
37		2l. vermilion (1882)	45·00	£120

One used example only of No. 33b. is known.
Beware of forged and non-contemporary postmarks on Nos. 35 and 37.

1884 (1 Jan). POSTAGE DUE. Typo. W **8**. P 14.
D40	D 13	50l. green	90·00	15·00
D41		100l. carmine-red	95·00	4·75

The background and frame of the 100l. differ from those of the 50l.
For new colours, see Nos. D73/4.

1884 (1 July)–**86**. PARCEL POST. Type P **13** *(various frames, etc)*. Typo. W **8**. P 14.
P38	10c. olive-grey (1.5.86)	70·00	16·00
P39	20c. blue (1.5.86)	£110	26·00
P40	50c. rose	11·50	3·75
P41	75c. green	10·50	3·75
P42	1l.25, orange	15·00	9·75
P43	1l.75, brown	20·00	29·00

1889 (1 Aug–Oct). Typo. W **8**. P 14.
38	13	5c. green (10.89)	£550	80
		a. *Blue-green*	£350	2·10
39	14	40c. brown	8·25	2·00
40	14a	45c. dull green (shades)	£2000	1·70
41	15	60c. mauve	14·50	6·75
42	16	1l. brown and orange	10·00	1·90
		a. *Brown and buff*	14·00	10·50
43	17	5l. red and green	16·00	£250

1890 (1 June)–**91**. *Stamps of 1879 surch with T* **18** *or* **19**.
44	12	2c.on 5c. green (20.4.91)	30·00	24·00
		a. "2" with thin foot (pos. 15)	£100	£250
45		20c.on 30c. brown	£300	2·30
46		20c.on 50c. mauve	£300	11·50

1890 (1 Oct)–**91**. POSTAGE DUE. Type D **12** *surch as Type D* **20**.
D47	10on 2c. magenta & orange (1.3.91)	60·00	14·00
D48	20on 1c. magenta and orange	£250	7·50
	a. Surch inverted	—	£6500
D49	30on 2c. magenta and orange (1.3.91)	£950	3·50
	a. Surch inverted	—	£1800

1890 (1 Dec). *Parcel Post stamps, Nos. P38/43, surch with T* **20**, *for use as postage stamps.*
47	2c.on 10c. olive-grey	5·25	2·50
	a. Surch inverted	£325	£2250
48	2c.on 20c. blue	5·75	2·20
49	2c.on 50c. rose	43·00	16·00
	a. Surch inverted	—	£26000
50	2c.on 75c. green	9·00	2·50
51	2c.on 1l.25, orange	30·00	10·00
	a. Surch inverted	£47000	£24000
52	2c.on 1l.75, brown	22·00	25·00

1891–97. Typo. W **8**. P 14.
53	21	1c. pale brown (7.96)	4·25	95
		a. *Deep brown*	5·50	95
54	22	2c. red-brown (7.96)	7·25	50
		a. Imperf (pair)		
55	23	5c. green (11.91)	£400	55

ITALY 1891

56	24	5c. green (2.97)	26·00	45
57	25	10c. lake (7.96)	7·25	35
58	26	20c. orange-yellow (6.95)	7·25	35
		a. Orange	5·50	1·80
59	27	25c. pale blue (3.93)	5·25	60
		a. Blue	5·50	4·50
60	28	45c. reseda-green (3.95)	7·25	90
		a. Pale green	5·50	4·50
61	29	5l. carmine and blue (1.5.91)	50·00	65·00

King Victor Emmanuel III, 29 July 1900–5 June, 1944

(Des G. Cellini. Typo.)

1901 (1 July–1 Oct). *Laureated design (which varies for each value) in second colour.* W **8**. P 14.

62	30	1c. brown	25	10
		a. Imperf (pair)	£550	£850
63	31	2c. orange-brown	25	10
		a. Double impression	85·00	£160
		b. Imperf (pair)	£170	£250
64	32	5c. deep bluish green	47·00	15
65	33	10c. lake	60·00	25
		a. Imperf (pair)	—	£11000
66		20c. orange	9·00	25
67		25c. blue	90·00	35
		a. Deep blue	90·00	35
68		40c. brown (1 Oct)	£400	1·90
69		45c. olive-green (1 Oct)	7·75	10
		a. Imperf (pair)	£250	£350
70		50c. mauve (1 Oct)	£500	3·25
		a. Violet	£500	3·25
71	34	1l. brown and green (1 Oct)	3·00	10
		a. Imperf (pair)	£110	£180
		b. Double impression of brown	55·00	85·00
72		5l. blue and rose (1 Oct)	17·00	50

See also Nos. 85, 111, 181 and 185/7.

1903 (1 June). *EXPRESS LETTER. Inland. Typo.* W **8**, twice. P 14.

E73	E **35**	25c. rose	26·00	25
		a. Imperf (pair)	£400	£450

See also Nos. E113, E129 and E178/9.

Examples without watermark and perforated 11½ are postal forgeries.

1903 (1 July). *POSTAGE DUE. Colours changed. Typo.* W **8**. P 14.

D73	D **13**	50l. yellow	45·00	10·00
D74		100l. blue	60·00	4·50

1905 (1 Sept). *No. 66 surch with T* **35**.

73	33	15c. on 20c. orange	60·00	 40

(Des F. P. Michetti Eng M. Savage. Recess L'Officina Calcografica Italiana, Rome)

1906 (20 Mar). *No wmk.* P 12.

74	**36**	15c. slate	55·00	90
		a. Imperf between (pair)	£275	£300

Exists on thin and on thick paper.
See also Nos. 80 and 90.

(T **37**/8 des N. Leoni. T **39**/40 des F. P. Michetti. Typo at Turin and by Petiti, Rome)

1906 (Oct)–**08**. W **8**. P 14.

75	37	5c. green	45	30
		a. Blue-green	45	30
		b. Yellow-green	45	30
		c. Imperf (pair)	70·00	70·00
		d. Double impression	55·00	55·00
76	38	10c. rose-red	45	10
		a. Imperf (pair)	70·00	70·00
		b. Double impression	55·00	55·00
77	39	25c. blue (1.08)	2·00	10
		a. Imperf (pair)	£130	£130
		b. Double impression, one on back	£275	
78	40	40c. brown (1.08)	2·50	10
		a. Imperf (pair)	£170	£170
79		50c. violet (1.08)	2·50	10
		a. Imperf (pair)	£150	£150

Examples perforated 10½, 11½ or 13½, all without watermark, are postal forgeries.
See also Nos. 104, 106/10, 178/80 and 182/4.

ITALY 1908

1908 (1 Sept). *EXPRESS LETTER. Foreign. Typo.* W **8**. P 14.
E80   E **41**   30c. blue and rose . . . . . 1·00   85
See also Nos. E180/1.

(Eng A. Repettati)

1909 (1 June). T **41** *(as T **36**, but typo, and redrawn slightly smaller). Crown as type **36b**.* No wmk. P 13½.
80   **41**   15c. slate-black . . . . . £225   1·80
See also Nos. 101 and 105.

42 Garibaldi   **43**   **44**

(Des L. Morandi. Typo)

1910 (15 Apr). *50th Anniv of Plebiscite in Naples and Sicily.* No wmk. P 14 × 13½.
81   **42**   5c.(+5c.) deep green . . . . . 25·00   11·00
82   15c.(+5c.) rose-red . . . . . 50·00   34·00

(Des L. Morandi. Typo)

1910 (1 Nov). *National Plebiscite of Southern States, 1860.* No wmk. P 14 × 13½.
83   **43**   5c.(+5c.) rose . . . . . £120   43·00
84   15c.(+5c.) green . . . . . £200   60·00
The use of Nos. 81/4 was restricted to the interior of the Kingdom of Italy.

(Des G. Cellini. Typo)

1910 (1 Nov). W **8**. P 14.
85   **44**   10l. sage-green and pale rose . . . 60·00   3·00

45   **46**   **47**   **48**

(Des A. Sezanne (**45**), E. Morelli (**46**) and V. Grassi (**47/8**).
(Eng A. Repettati. Recess)

1911 (1 May). *Jubilee of the Kingdom of Italy.* No wmk. P 14 × 13½.
86   **45**   2c.(+3c.) brown . . . . . 8·50   1·30
87   **46**   5c.(+5c.) deep green . . . . . 11·00   8·00
88   **47**   10c.(+5c.) scarlet . . . . . 14·00   14·00
89   **48**   15c.(+5c.) slate . . . . . 14·00   14·00
86/89 *Set of 4* . . . . . 43·00   34·00

49   **50**

(Eng A. Repettati. Recess)

1911 (Oct). T **49** (as T **36**, *but redrawn*). No wmk. P 13½.
90   **49**   15c. slate . . . . . 27·00   35
              a. Printed both sides . . £225   £325
              b. Imperf (pair) £140   £180
This can be distinguished from T 36 by the thicker "C" in "Cent" and by the star on the far side of the collar, which is absent from T 36, crown as type **36c**; the perforation also identifies it. No. 74 is perf 12, No. 94 perf 13¼ × 13¾, No. 104 perf 13½ × 14.

(Des A. Sezanne. Recess)

1912 (25 Apr). *Re-erection of the Campanile of St. Mark, Venice.* P 14 × 13½.
91   **50**   5c. black . . . . . 6·50   3·25
92   15c. brown . . . . . 17·00   13·00

2   **2**   **2**   **2**
(51) (spaced 13½ mm)   (52) (spaced 12 mm)

1913 (1 Mar). Nos. 87/9 surch.
93   **51**   2 on 5c. deep green . . . . . 1·10   1·30
              a. Spaced wider, 15½ mm . . 14·50   21·00
94   2 on 10c. scarlet . . . . . 1·60   1·20
              a. Spaced wider, 15½ mm . . 7·25   10·50
95   **52**   2 on 15c. slate (V.) . . . . . 1·20   1·20
              a. Spaced wider, 13½ mm . . 29·00   43·00
No. 95a occurs on positions 55 and 65 in the sheet of 100; Nos. 93a and 94a occur on all stamps in the fifth vertical row.

PNEUMATIC POST. This service carried letters by underground pneumatic tubes between post offices and functions in Rome, Milan, Naples, Turin and Genoa.

PE **53**

1913 (Apr)–**23**. *PNEUMATIC POST. Typo.* W **8**. P 14.
PE96   PE **53**   10c. brown . . . . . 1·60   5·50
PE97   15c. lilac (9.21) . . . . . 1·70   8·75
PE98   30c. blue (6.23) . . . . . 4·75   42·00
See also Nos. PE191/5.

PRICES FOR PARCEL POST STAMPS. The left-hand portion is affixed to the packet-card, the right-hand portion to the receipt. Prices in the first column are for unused complete pairs, in the second column for used pairs (usually cancelled-to-order) and in the third column for the left half used.

P **53**

1914 (16 July)–**22**. *PARCEL POST. Typo.* W **8**. P 13½.
                                            Un   Used   Used
                                            pair pair   half
P 96   P **53**   5c. brown 40   60   10

13

ITALY 1914

P 97	10c. deep blue	40	60	10
P 98	20c. black (7.17)	60	60	10
	a. Imperf (pair)	£225		
P 99	25c. red	70	60	10
	a. Imperf (pair)	£225		
P100	50c. orange	95	70	10
	a. Imperf (pair)	£225		
P101	1l. violet	1·20	80	10
P102	2l. green	1·60	60	10
	a. Imperf (pair)	£225		
P103	3l. yellow	3·25	70	10
	a. Imperf (pair)	£225		
P104	4l. slate	4·75	70	10
	a. Imperf (pair)	£225		
P105	10l. pale purple (2.21)	27·00	3·50	1·75
	a. Imperf (pair)	£225		
P106	12l. red-brown (10.22)	£100	£140	19·00
P107	15l. olive-green (12.21)	£100	£140	19·00
P108	20l. deep purple (10.22)	£100	£140	19·00
P96/108 Set of 13		£300	£400	55·00

53 Banner of United Italy
54 Italian Eagle and Arms of Savoy 
(55)

1915 (20 Nov)–**16**. *Red Cross Society. No. 98 is surch with T* **55**. *Typo.* W **8**. P 14.

96	53	10c.+5c. carmine	2·50	2·50
97	54	15c.+5c. slate	5·00	3·50
98		20c.on 15c.+5c. slate (2.16)	7·00	10·50
		a. Surch inverted	£450	£700
99		20c.+5c. orange (3.16)	7·25	9·25

ESPERIMENTO POSTA AEREA
MAGGIO 1917
CENT. 20 TORINO·ROMA · ROMA·TORINO
(56) (57)

1916 (Jan). *No. 90 surch with T* **56**.
100	49	20c.on 15c. slate	14·00	35
		a. Surch inverted	£300	£300

1916 (8 Dec). *No wmk.* P 13½.
101	41	20c. orange	35·00	4·00

1917 (20 May). *AIR. Optd with T* **57**.
102	E **35**	25c. rose	11·00	8·50

This was the first air stamp to be issued by any country.

IDROVOLANTE

NAPOLI · PALERMO NAPOLI
25 CENT 25
(58)

1917 (27 June). *AIR. Surch with T* **58**.
103	E **59**	25c. on 40c. violet	11·50	9·00

1917–**23**. *Typo.* W **8**. P 14.
104	37	15c. slate (9.19)	2·75	15
		a. Imperf (pair)	£300	£450
105	41	20c. brown (10.17)	7·50	15
		a. Imperf (pair)	30·00	38·00
106	39	30c. orange-brown (9.22)	2·30	20
107		55c. dull purple (12.20)	11·00	2·75

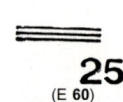

108		60c. carmine-red (1.18)	2·40	15
109		60c. blue (17.12.23)	5·50	11·00
110		85c. red-brown (12.20)	6·75	70
111	**34**	2l. myrtle and orange (11.23)	15·00	1·00
104/111 Set of 8			48·00	14·50

(E 59) (E 60)

1917 (Nov). *EXPRESS LETTER. Inland. Surch with Type E* **60**. *Typo.* W **8**. P 14.
E112	E **59**	25c. on 40c. violet	20·00	17·00

No. E112 was never issued without the surcharge.

1920 (May). *EXPRESS LETTER. Inland. Typo.* W **8**. P 14.
E113	E **35**	50c. red	1·70	45

PUBLICITY ENVELOPES.—These stamps were sold at a discount of 5 per cent to a Society and were affixed to envelopes or letter-cards bearing advertisements, the scheme being in aid of disabled soldiers. Unused prices are for stamps with gum.

B.L.P.
(B 59)

("B.L.P." = "Buste Lettere Postali")

1921 (Jan–July). *PUBLICITY ENVELOPE STAMPS. Postage stamps with litho opt. Type B* **59**.
B112	**38**	10c. rose-red (B.)	£650	£650
B113	**41**	20c. orange (B.) (July)	£900	£250
B114	**39**	25c. blue (R.)	£150	85·00
B115	**40**	40c. brown (B)	60·00	11·00

See also Nos. B129/33.

59 Ancient Seal of Republic of Trieste
60 
61 

(Des G. Petronio. Typo Petiti, Rome)

1921 (5 June). *Union of Venezia Giulia with Italy.* W **8**. P 14.
112	**59**	15c. rose and black	3·00	12·50
113		25c. rose and blue	3·00	12·50
114		40c. rose and brown	3·00	12·50

(Des G. Cellini. Typo Petiti, Rome)

1921 (28 Sept). *600th Anniv of Dante's Death. T* **60/1** *and similar vert design.* W **8**. P 14.
115		15c. purple-lake	3·75	6·25
116		25c. green	3·75	6·25
117		40c. brown (Dante)	3·75	6·25

Nos. 115/17 exist overprinted with Type B **59** but were not issued (*Price for set of 3: £2250 un*).

LIRE 1,20
(E 62)

ITALY 1921

1921 (3 Oct). EXPRESS LETTER. Foreign. Surch with Type E **62**.
E118 E **41** L.1.20on 30c. blue and rose .. 2·50 10
            a. Comma omitted (pos.
                13) .. .. 9·00 35·00

62 "Victory" (E **63**) IX CONGRESSO FILATELICO ITALIANO TRIESTE 1922 (**63**)

(Des and eng A. Repetati. Recess)

1921 (1 Nov). Victory Issue, 1918. W **8**. P 14 × 13½.
118 **62** 5c. green 50 70
119   10c. carmine 75 85
120   15c. slate .. .. 1·80 3·25
121   25c. ultramarine .. .. 90 1·90
118/121 Set of 4 .. .. 3·50 6·00
Nos. 118/21 exist overprinted with Type B **59** but were not issued (Price for set of 4: £400 un).

1922 (9 Jan). EXPRESS LETTER. Inland. Surch with Type E **63**.
E122 E **35** 60c.on 50c. red .. 34·00 25·00
            a. Imperf (pair) .. £350 £425

1922 (4 June). Ninth Italian Philatelic Congress, Trieste. Optd with T **63**.
122 **38** 10c. rose-red £250 £130
123 **37** 15c. slate £180 £130
124 **39** 25c. blue £180 £130
125 **40** 40c. brown £275 £130
122/125 Set of 4 .. .. £800 £450

64   65 Mazzini   B.L.P. (B **66**)

(Des V. Grassi. Eng A. Blasi. Typo Petiti, Rome)

1922 (20 Sept). 50th Anniv of Mazzini's Death. T **64/5** and similar horiz design. W **8**. P 14.
126 25c. maroon .. .. 5·00 10·00
127 40c. purple .. .. 7·00 10·50
128 80c. blue (Tomb of Mazzini) .. 5·00 13·00
Nos. 126/8 exist overprinted with Type B **59** but were not issued (Price for set of 3: £700 un).

1922 (Sept)–**23**. PUBLICITY ENVELOPE STAMPS. Postage stamps optd with Type B **66**.

(a) Litho opt (Sept 1922–23).
B129 **38** 10c. rose-red .. .. 75·00 55·00
B130 **37** 15c. slate (B.) .. £550 £475
B131 **41** 20c. orange (B.) .. £500 £225
B132 **39** 25c. blue £100 £225
B133 **40** 40c. brown (B.) .. £130 65·00
            a. Black opt .. .. £130 65·00
B134   50c. violet £550 £375
B135 **39** 60c. carmine-lake .. £1600 £1400
B136 **34** 1l. brown and green .. £2750 £1500

(b) Typo opt (1923).
B137 **37** 15c. slate (R.) .. £250 £250
B138 **41** 20c. orange £250 £250
B139 **39** 25c. blue (R.) .. £250 £250
B140   30c. orange-brown .. £170 £100

B141   85c. red-brown £250 £250
The 10c. also exists with typo overprint in black but is difficult to distinguish. Prices apply to either state.
See note above No. B112.

1922 (Oct). EXPRESS LETTER. New values. W **8**. P 14.

(a) Inland.
E129 E **35** 60c. rose-red .. .. 3·25 40

(b) Foreign.
E130 E **41** 1l.20, blue and rose .. £140
No. E130 was prepared but not issued.

66

(Des G. B. Conti. Eng A. Blasi. Typo Petiti, Rome)

1923 (11 June). Tercentenary of the Congregation "DE PROPAGANDA FIDE". Centre in orange. W **8**. P 14.
129 **66** 20c. bronze-green .. 1·80 23·00
130   30c. carmine .. .. 1·80 23·00
131 **66** 50c. violet .. .. .. 1·80 23·00
132   1l. blue .. .. 2·50 23·00
129/132 Set of 4 .. .. 7·00 85·00
The portrait and arms in the corners at right vary for each value.

Cent. 7½ (67)   Cent. 7½ (68) Smaller "½"   10 CENTESIMI (69)
DIECI (70)   Cent. 25 (71)   Lire 1,75 (72)

1923 (July)–**27**. Surch.
133 **39** 7½c.on 85c. (T **67**) (1.1.24) .. 10 80
134   7½c.on 85c. (T **68**) (17.10.27) .. 9·00 32·00
135 **30** 10c.on 1c. (T **69**) (18.9.23) .. 35 15
            a. Surch inverted .. 21·00 32·00
136 **31** 10c.on 2c. (T **69**) (23.7.23) .. 35 15
            a. Surch inverted .. 55·00 80·00
137 **37** 10c.on 15c. (T **70**) (5.25) .. 10 15
138 **39** 20c.on 25c. (As T **71**) (4.25) .. 10 25
139 **33** 25c.on 45c. (T **71**) (8.24) .. 10 6·50
140 **39** 25c.on 60c. (T **67**) (1.24) .. 70 40
141 **40** 30c.on 50c. (As T **67**) (4.25) .. 10 15
142 **39** 30c.on 55c. (As T **67**) (8.25) .. 10 25
143 **40** 50c.on 40c. (As T **67**) (4.8.23) .. 75 15
            a. Surch inverted .. £180 £250
144 **39** 50c.on 55c. (As T **67**) (10.10.23) .. 27·00 2·50
            a. Surch inverted .. £750 £1300
145 **44** 1l.75on 10l. (T **72**) (28.2.25) .. 10·00 8·25
A second setting of No. 140 has shorter, thinner bars.

30 (P **73**)   CENT. 30

1923 (Oct)–**25**. PARCEL POST. Surch as Type P **73**.
                                   Un   Used Used
                                   pair pair half
P146 P **53** 30c.on 5c. brown .. 1·20 38·00 75
P147   60c.on 5c. brown .. 2·10 38·00 75

ITALY 1923

P148	1l.50 on 5c. brown	6·75	£100	5·25
P149	3l.on 10l. pale pur (9.25)	4·25	£100	3·25
P146/149 Set of 4		12·00	£250	9·00

159	1l. blue		25·00	95·00
160	5l. dull purple		£350	£650
155/160 Set of 6			£350	£750

Designs:—10c. to 50c. Scenes from *I Promessi Sposi*; 1l. Manzoni's home. Milan.

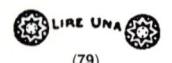

(79)

1924. Surch with T **79**.

161	62	1l.on 5c. green (17.2)	19·00	38·00
162		1l.on 10c. carmine (2.1)	12·00	38·00
163		1l.on 15c. slate (18.2)	19·00	38·00
164		1l.on 25c. ultramarine (18.2)	12·00	38·00
161/164 Set of 4			55·00	£140

Cent. 15 CROCIERA ITALIANA 1924

(PE 80) (80)

1924 (Jan)–27. PNEUMATIC POST. Surch as Type PE **80**.

PE165	PE **53**	15c. on 10c. brown	4·50	10·50
PE166		15c. on 20c. dull pur (22.6.27)	6·25	12·00
PE167		20c. on 10c. brown (18.3.25)	3·50	12·00
PE168		20c. on 15c. dull pur (18.3.25)	5·75	8·75
PE169		35c. on 40c. rose-red (22.6.27)	10·50	60·00
PE170		40c. on 30c. blue (18.3.25)	4·00	55·00

1924 (16 Feb). Trade Propaganda. Optd with T **80**.

165	**38**	10c. rose-red	2·30	5·50
166	**39**	30c. orange-brown	2·30	5·50
167	**40**	50c. violet	2·30	5·50
168	**39**	60c. blue (R.)	12·00	23·00
169		85c. red-brown (R.)	8·25	23·00
170	**34**	1l. brown and green	35·00	95·00
171		2l. myrtle and orange	55·00	95·00
165/171 Set of 7			£100	£225

These stamps were used for the despatch of correspondence posted on an Italian warship which conveyed a trade delegation and display on a South American propaganda tour.

1924–25. EXPRESS LETTER.

(a) Inland. Surch as Type E **63**.

E172	E **35**	70c.on 60c. rose-red (11.4.25)	30	25
		a. Surch inverted	£250	£300

(b) Foreign. Surch as Type E **62**.

E173	E **41**	L.1.60 on 1l.20 blue and rose (5.24)	70	11·00

1924 (Nov)–25. Stamps of 1901–22 with attached vert advertising labels (imperf between stamp and label). Labels in colours given. W **8**. P 14.

171a	15c. (104)+Columbia (ultramarine)	29·00	24·00
171b	15c. (104)+Bitter Campari (blue) (1.25)	2·40	9·00
171c	15c. (104)+Cordial Campari (blk) (1.25)	2·40	9·00
171d	25c. (77)+Coen (green)	£180	24·00
171e	25c. (77)+Piperno (brown)	£1200	£375
171f	25c. (77)+Tagliacozzo (brown)	£600	£375
171g	25c. (77)+Abrador (blue) (1.25)	75·00	60·00
171h	25c. (77)+Reinach (green) (1.25)	75·00	45·00
171i	30c. (106)+Columbia (green)	24·00	23·00
171j	50c. (79)+Coen (ultramarine)	£1200	45·00
171k	50c. (79)+Columbia (red)	16·00	2·50
171l	50c. (79)+De Montel (blue)	2·75	8·00
171m	50c. (79)+Piperno (green)	£1300	£140
171n	50c. (79)+Reinach (blue)	£180	13·00
171o	50c. (79)+Singer (red)	2·75	95
171p	50c. (79)+Tagliacozzo (green)	£1800	£275
171q	50c. (79)+Siero Casali (ultramarine) (12.24)	16·00	9·75

---

73 74

75

(Des D. Cambellotti, recess (**73**) and G. Balla, typo (**74/5**))

1923 (24 Oct). *1st Anniv of Fascist March on Rome.* No wmk. (10c. to 50c.), W **8** (others). P 14.

146	**73**	10c. deep green	3·25	1·60
147		30c. violet	3·50	1·60
148		50c. carmine-red	4·50	2·50
149	**74**	1l. light blue	4·25	1·70
150		2l. brown	4·25	4·00
151	**75**	5l. black and blue	6·50	14·00
146/151 Set of 6			24·00	23·00

76 77

78 Manzoni

(Des E. Federici. Typo Petiti, Rome)

1923 (29 Oct). *Fascist "Black Shirt" Fund.* W **8**. P 14.

152	**76**	30c.+30c. brown	23·00	33·00
153		50c.+50c. bright mauve	27·00	33·00
154		1l.+1l. grey	23·00	33·00

(Des E. Federici. Typo Petiti, Rome)

1923 (29 Dec). *50th Death Anniv of A. Manzoni (writer)*. T **77** and similar types, and **78**. Centres in black or grey-black. W **8**. P 14.

155		10c. claret	2·40	24·00
156		15c. green	2·40	24·00
157		30c. black	2·40	24·00
158		50c. chestnut	2·40	24·00

ITALY 1924

171r	50c. (79)+Tantal (red) (1.25)	£225	65·00
171s	1l. (71)+Columbia (blue) (12.24)	£550	£450

Prices are for average badly centred copies. Well centred copies and used on cover worth much more.

Nos. 178+Columbia (green) and E129+Perugina (blue) were prepared but not issued.

81 Church of St. John Lateran   **82**

(Des E. Federici (20c. to 60c.), A. Blasi (1l., 5l.). Typo Staderini, Rome).

1924 (24 Dec). *Holy Year (1925)*. T **81** *and similar horiz designs*. W **8**. P 12.

172	20c.+10c. brown and myrtle green	2·50	3·25
173	30c.+15c. brown and chocolate	2·50	3·25
174	50c.+25c. brown and violet	2·50	3·25
175	60c.+30c. brown and carmine	2·50	10·00
176	1l.+50c. purple and blue	2·50	9·75
177	5l.+2.50l. purple and orange-red	2·50	22·00
172/177	Set of 6	14·00	46·00

Designs:—20c. Church of St. Maria Maggiore; 50c. Church of St. Paul; 60c. St. Peter's; 1l. Pope opening Holy Door; 5l. Pope shutting Holy Door.

1925–26. EXPRESS LETTER. New values. W **8**. P 14.

(a) Inland.

E178	E **35**	70c. rose-red (6.25)	25	15
E179		1l.25, blue (20.9.26)	15	10

(b) Foreign.

E180	E **41**	2l. blue and rose (2.25)	2·30	15
E181		2l.50, blue and rose (7.26)	65	1·30

1925–27. *New values and colours*. W **8**. P 14.

178	**39**	20c. orange (20.3.25)	75	80
179		20c. green (6.25)	35	10
180		20c. purple (7.26)	2·30	15
181	**34**	25c. green and yellow green (6.26)	1·70	10
182	**39**	25c. green (21.8.27)	7·75	3·50
183		30c. slate (8.25)	1·90	10
184		60c. orange (7.26)	7·00	15
185	**34**	75c. lake-red and carmine (3.26)	1·50	10
186		1l.25, blue and ultramarine (3.26)	5·50	10
187		2l.50, myrtle and orange (11.26)	40·00	1·30
178/187	Set of 10		60·00	7·75

(Des C. Parmeggiani. Recess)

1925–26. *Royal Jubilee*. No wmk.

A. P 13½.

188A	**82**	60c. lake-red	4·00	1·60
		d. Watermarked letters	21·00	5·75
		e. Watermarked crown	95·00	24·00
189A		1l. blue	6·75	2·10
		d. Watermarked letters	18·00	3·50
		e. Watermarked crown	70·00	17·50
190A		1l.25, blue	4·25	50

B. P 11.

188B	**82**	60c. lake-red	25	25
		c. Compound perf	£550	£275
		d. Watermarked letters	4·75	4·75
		e. Watermarked crown	19·00	19·00
189B		1l. blue	55	20
		c. Compound perf	£350	£180
		d. Watermarked letters	3·50	3·50
		e. Watermarked crown	14·00	14·00
190B		1l.25, blue	70·00	38·00
		c. Compound perf	£550	£275

Dates of issue: 188/9A, 6.6.25; 190A, 12.1.26; 188/9B, 10.6.25; 190B, 5.26.

The edge of the sheet was watermarked "MINISTERIO DEL TESORO" flanked by sloping crowns 60c. and 1l. values from the margin row are found with part of this watermark.

1925 (Oct)–**28**. PNEUMATIC POST. *New values and colours*. W **8**. P 14.

PE191	PE **53**	15c. rose (8.2.28)	5·00	5·50
PE192		15c. claret (1.12.28)	1·70	8·00
PE193		20c. dull purple	11·50	14·00
PE194		35c. rose-red (14.10.27)	9·50	55·00
PE195		40c. rose-red	18·00	60·00

83 Vision of St. Francis   **86** Death of St. Francis from fresco in Church of The Holy Cross, Florence

(Des D. Cambellotti (20c.), G. Guerrini (30c., 5l.), A. Blasi (40c.), E. del Neri (60c.), A. Rizzini (5l.). Litho from woodcuts by Blasi (20, 40, 60c.) Eng A. Repettati; recess (30c., 1l.25, 5l.))

1926 (30 Jan–Oct). *700th Death Anniv of St. Francis of Assisi*.

(a) W **8**. P 14.

191	20c. dull green	35	25
192	40c. violet	35	25
193	60c. dull lake	35	25

(b) No wmk.

A. P 13½.

194A	30c. blue-black	14·00	8·25
195A	1l.25, blue	£325	20·00
	c. Watermarked letters	£700	
196A	5l.+2l.50, sepia	3·00	34·00

B. P 11.

194B	30c. blue-black	35	25
195B	1l.25, blue	35	25
	c. Watermarked letters	18·00	9·50

Designs: *Vert*—30c., 5l. St. Francis (after Luca della Robbia); *Horiz*—40c. St. Damian's Church and Monastery, Assisi; 60c. St. Francis's Monastery, Assisi.

Dates of issue: 194A, 10.26; 194B, 4.10.26; others, 30.1.26. The watermark consists of letters from "MINISTERIO FINANZE".

88   **89** Castle of St. Angelo

1926 (15 Mar)–**28**. AIR. *Typo*. W **8**. P 14.

197	**88**	50c. rose (24.3.28)	5·25	2·00
198		60c. grey	2·50	1·90
199		80c. red-brown and purple (11.6.28)	29·00	17·00
200		1l. blue	1·70	3·00
201		1l.20, pale brown (2.27)	10·50	28·00
202		1l.50, orange	9·50	7·50
203		5l. green	23·00	21·00
197/203	Set of 7		75·00	75·00

(Des E. Cavalletti. Eng A. Repettati. Recess)

1926 (26 Oct). *First National Defence issue*. T **89** (*and similar types*). *No wmk*. P 11.

204	40c.+20c. black and brown	2·00	3·25
205	60c.+30c. brown and lake	2·00	3·25

17

ITALY 1926

```
206      1l.25+60c. black and blue-green       2·00    8·75
207      5l.+2l.50 black and blue              3·25   32·00
204/207  Set of 4                              8·25   42·00
```
Designs:—60c. Aqueduct of Claudius; 1l.25, Capitol; 5l. Porta del Popolo.
See also Nos. 219/22 and 278/81.

90 Volta

91

(Des Prof Giulio Cisari. Litho)

1927 (5 Mar). *Centenary of Volta's Death.* W **8**. P. 14.
```
208   90   20c. crimson                              55      30
209        50c. blackish green                     1·50      15
210        60c. brown-purple                       2·75      85
211        1l.25, bright ultramarine               3·25    1·20
208/211  Set of 4                                  7·25    2·25
```
For 20c., T **90**, in violet, see Libya (Cyrenaica) No. 40a.

(Des C. Parmeggiani)

1927 (9 Apr)–**29**.
(a) *Recess.* No wmk. P 11. *Size* 19 × 23½ *mm.*
```
212   91   1l.75, brown (13.9.27)                  3·75       15
           a. Perf 14 (1.29)                    £21000    £1600
           b. Perf 11 × 14 (1929)                    —    £1200
213        1l.85, black                              80       30
214        2l.55, carmine (16.9.27)                5·25     3·00
215        2l.65, purple                           5·25    23·00
212/215  Set of 4                                 13·50    24·00
```
The side panels and value tables of Nos. 212/3 differ slightly from those of Nos. 214/5.

(b) *Litho.* W **8**. P 14. *Size* 17½ × 21½ *mm.*
```
216   91   50c. slate and brown (16.8.27)         2·50      10
```

P **92**   **92**

1927–39. *PARCEL POST. As Type* P **92**. *Typo.* W **8**. P 13½.
```
                                                Un    Used   Used
                                               pair   pair   half
P217  P 92  5c. brown (19.12.38)                 25     30     10
P218        10c. deep blue
              (5.9.39)                           25     30     10
P219        25c. carmine (16.6.32)               25     30     10
P220        30c. ultramarine
              (14.10.27)                         25     40     10
P221        50c. orange (30.5.32)                25     30     10
P222      — 60c. rose-scarlet
              (14.10.27)                         25     40     10
P223  P 92  1l. violet (9.31)                    25     30     10
P224        2l. green (16.5.32)                  25     40     10
P225        3l. yellow-bistre
              (4.27)                             25     80     10
P226        4l. grey-black
              (9.5.27)                           25     80     10
P227        10l. purple (4.7.34)               1·10  13·50     45
P228        20l. dull purple
              (2.1.33)                         1·60  22·00     55
P217/228  Set of 12                            4·75  36·00   1·80
```
The value in the right-hand portion of the 60c. is in figures.

1927 (16 Sept). *AIR. Surch as Type PE* **80**.
```
217   88   50c.on 60c. grey                      6·25   11·00
218        80c.on 1l. blue                      19·00   60·00
```

1928 (1 Mar). *Second National Defence issue. As Nos 204/7 but values and colours changed.*
```
219        30c.+10c. black and violet              5·25   6·25
220        50c.+20c. black and olive-green         5·25   6·00
221        1l.25+50c. black and blue              10·50  17·00
222        5l.+2l. black and carmine              20·00  50·00
219/222  Set of 4                                 37·00  75·00
```

1928–29. *Typo.* W **8**. P. 14.
```
223   92   7½c. brown (21.6.28)                    3·50   2·00
224        15c. orange (4.2.29)                    3·00     15
225        35c. slate (4.2.29)                     7·00   1·00
226        50c. bright mauve (7.28)               11·00     10
223/226  Set of 4                                 22·00   3·00
```

CONCESSIONAL LETTER POST. These stamps are for the use of private organizations and agencies, which the Italian Post Office allows to undertake the delivery of mail on payment of a fee for each letter. They are normally found cancelled with private handstamps.

CL **93** Arms of Savoy and Fasces

1928 (1 July). *CONCESSIONAL LETTER POST. Typo.* W **8**. P 14.
```
CL227  CL 93  10c. blue                            3·00    15
              a. Perf 11                          17·00  2·10
              b. Perf 11 × 14                      £750  £500
```

93 Emmanuele Filiberto

94 Soldier of First World War and Statue

95 Statue, Turin (Maroghetti)

(Des G. da Milano (T **93**), F. Serracchiani (others). Typo)

1928. *400th Birth Anniv of Emmanuele Filiberto, Duke of Savoy and Tenth Anniv of Victory in World War.* W **8**. P 13½ (Nos. 227/9), 11 (No. 234) or 14 (others).
```
227  93   20c. blue and lake-brown (4.8)        £100   75·00
          a. Perf 11                              60      55
228       25c. deep bluish green & scarlet
            (4.8)                              35·00   21·00
          a. Perf 11                              60      55
229       30c. lake-brown & dp bluish grn
            (4.8)                              14·00   14·00
          a. Perf 11                              85      75
          ab. Centre inverted                £31000   £4500
230  94   50c. Indian red and light blue
            (17.9)                                50      20
231       75c. carmine-red and rose (17.9)        65      30
232  95   1l.25, black and blue (27.7)            90      40
233  94   1l.75, myrtle green & lt blue
            (18.9)                              1·90    2·00
234  93   5l. dp bluish green & dp mauve
            (7.8)                               8·75   25·00
235  94   10l. black and rose (21.9)           22·00   60·00
236  96   20l. blackish green & brt mauve
            (4.8)                              35·00    £325
227/236  Set of 10 (cheapest)                  65·00    £375
```

ITALY 1929

96 King Victor Emmanuel II

(Des G. Cisari. Photo)

1929 (4 Jan). *50th Death Anniv of King Victor Emmanuel II. Veterans Fund.* W **8**. P 14.
237 **96** 50c.+10c. deep olive-green . . . . . 2·75 2·20

97 Fascist Arms of Italy 
98 Romulus, Remus and Wolf 
99 Julius Caesar

100 Augustus the Great
101 Italia 
102 King Victor Emmanuel III 
103 King Victor Emmanuel III 

(Des P. Paschetto (T **98**, **101**, **103**), G. Cisari (T **99**, **100**, **102**). Photo)

1929 (21 Apr)–**42**. *Imperial Series.* W **8**. P 14.
238	**97**	2c. orange (16.12.30)	10	20
239	**98**	5c. brown	20	10
240	**99**	7½c. deep violet	20	10
241	**100**	10c. sepia	20	10
242	**101**	15c. blue-green	20	10
243	**99**	20c. carmine	20	10
244	**102**	25c. green	20	10
245	**103**	30c. brown	20	10
246	**101**	35c. blue	20	10
247	**103**	50c. bright violet	20	10
248	**102**	75c. carmine	20	10
249	**99**	1l. violet (14.7.42)	10	15
250	**102**	1l.25, blue	20	10
251	**100**	1l.75, orange-vermilion	20	10
252	**101**	2l. brown-lake	20	10
253	**98**	2l.55, grey-green	20	15
254		3l.70, bright violet (30.9.30)	10	10
255		5l. carmine	25	10
256	**101**	10l. violet	1·60	35
257	**99**	20l. yellow-green	3·75	2·75
258	**100**	25l. blue-black	8·00	11·00
259	**102**	50l. deep violet	10·00	20·00
238/259	*Set of 22*		27·00	35·00

Nos. 253/5 differ slightly from T **98** in having the value and shields, at the foot, transposed, while No. 257 varies from T **99** in that the value tablets are enclosed as in T **97**.

For Nos. 244/5 and 247 with *se-tenant* war propaganda labels, see Nos. 563/74.

For stamps without watermark see Nos. 630/2 and stamps without Fascist emblems see Nos. 620/6 and 633/46.

104 Bramante Courtyard 
106 Monks building the Abbey

108 St. Benedict

1929 (1 Aug–27 Sept). *14th Centenary of Abbey of Montecassino.* P 14.

(a) W **8**. *Photo.*
260	**104**	20c. red-orange	80	25
261	–	25c. deep green	80	25
262	**106**	50c.+10c. sepia	3·25	4·00
263	–	75c.+15c. bright scarlet	4·25	6·00
264	**104**	1l.25+25c. blue	4·50	7·00
265	–	5l.+1l. deep purple	4·75	24·00

(b) No wmk. *Recess.*
266	**108**	10l.+2l. slate-green (27.9)	7·75	48·00
260/266	*Set of 7*		23·00	80·00

Designs: As T **104**—25c. "Death of St Benedict" (fresco). As T **106**—75c., 5l. Abbey of Montecassino.

CL 109 Arms and Fasces
109 

1930 (7 Jan). CONCESSIONAL LETTER POST. *Photo.* P 14.
CL267 CL **109** 10c. brown 10 15

(Des A. della Torre. Photo)

1930 (8 Jan). *Marriage of Prince Umberto and Princess Marie Jose.* W **8**. P 14.
267	**109**	20c. orange-vermilion	50	15
268		50c.+10c. sepia	1·20	1·10
269		1l.25+25c. deep blue	1·90	4·50

For 20c. green see Libya (Cyrenaica) No. 58a.

110 Pegasus 
111 Wings 
112 Angel

113

(Des E. del Neri (**110**/1). G. Marussig (**112**), N. Brunetti (**113**). Photo)

1930 (12 Mar)–**32**. *AIR.* W **8**. P 14.
270	**111**	25c. grey-green (19.4.32)	10	10
271	**110**	50c. sepia	10	10
272	**112**	75c. chestnut (19.4.32)	10	10
273	**111**	80c. orange-vermilion	10	20
274	**112**	1l. bright violet	10	10
275	**113**	2l. blue	10	15

ITALY   1930

276	110	5l. green	10	25
277		10l. carmine-red (9.12.30)	15	80
270/277		Set of 8	70	1·60

1930 (1 July). *Third National Defence issue. As Nos. 204/7 but values and colours changed.* P. 14.

278		30c.+10c. violet and deep green	1·10	4·50
279		50c.+10c. greenish blue & deep green	1·60	3·00
280		1l.25+30c. green and deep blue	4·50	8·75
281		5l.+1l.50, chocolate and brown	7·50	31·00
278/281		Set of 4	13·00	48·00

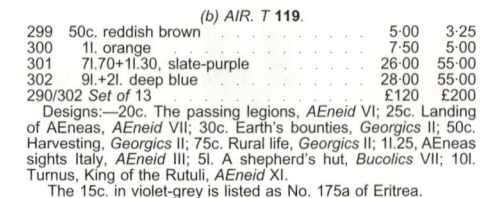

114 Ferrucci on Horseback 
115 Ferrucci assassinated by Maramaldo

116 Francesco Ferrucci
117 Francesco Ferrucci 

(Des D. Tofani (**114/5**, **117**), I. Marchesi (**116**). Photo)

1930 (10 July). *4th Centenary of Francesco Ferrucci's Death.* W **8**. P. 14.

(a) POSTAGE.

282	114	20c. carmine-red	35	30
283	115	25c. green	45	30
284		50c. bright violet	30	15
285		1l.25, blue	2·00	90
286	116	5l.+2l. orange-vermilion	6·00	39·00

(b) AIR.

287	117	50c. bright violet	85	3·50
288		1l. chestnut	85	4·00
289		5l.+2l. purple	2·10	31·00
282/289		Set of 8	11·50	70·00

118 Helenus and Anchises, *AEneid* III
119 Jupiter sending forth Eagle 

(Des C. Mezzana. Photo (290/6, 299/300), recess (others))

1930 (21 Oct). *Birth Bimillenary of Virgil.* No wmk (Nos. 297/8, 301/2) or W **8** (others). P. 14.

(a) POSTAGE. T **118** *and similar designs.*

290		15c. brown	70	35
291		20c. orange	70	20
292		25c. green	85	20
293		30c. purple	1·00	40
294		50c. bright violet	70	15
295		75c. carmine-red	1·40	70
296		1l.25, blue	1·40	65
297		5l.+1.50 lake-brown	28·00	48·00
298		10l.+2l.50, grey-green	28·00	60·00

(b) AIR. T **119**.

299		50c. reddish brown	5·00	3·25
300		1l. orange	7·50	5·00
301		7l.70+1l.30, slate-purple	26·00	55·00
302		9l.+2l. deep blue	28·00	55·00
290/302		Set of 13	£120	£200

Designs:—20c. The passing legions, *AEneid* VI; 25c. Landing of AEneas, *AEneid* VII; 30c. Earth's bounties, *Georgics* II; 50c. Harvesting, *Georgics* II; 75c. Rural life, *Georgics* II; 1l.25, AEneas sights Italy, *AEneid* III; 5l. A shepherd's hut, *Bucolics* VII; 10l. Turnus, King of the Rutuli, *AEneid* XI.

The 15c. in violet-grey is listed as No. 175a of Eritrea.

120 Savoia Marchetti S-55A Flying Boats 
121 St. Antony's Installation as a Franciscan

122 The Vision of St. Antony
123 Tower of the Marzocco 

1930 (Dec). *AIR. Transatlantic Mass Formation Flight.* Photo. W **8**. P. 14.

303	120	7l.70, light blue and drab	£300	£850
		a. Seven stars instead of six	£800	

Issued privately in December 1930 for use on the flight. Issued to the public on 27 June 1931.

Issued in sheets of 200, divided into panes of 50. No. 303a occurs on row 5/2 of the first pane.

(Des C. Vincenti. 75c. and 5l. eng A. Repettati, recess, others photo)

1931 (9 Mar). *700th Death Anniv of St. Antony of Padua.* T **121**/**2** *and similar designs.* No wmk (75c., 5l.). W **8** (others). P. 14.

304		20c. purple	70	25
305		25c. green	80	20
306		30c. brown	1·40	30
307		50c. bright violet	70	15
308		75c. lake	8·00	1·20
		a. Perf 12	70·00	£140
309		1l.25, blue	6·25	95
310		5l.+2l.50, bronze-green	36·00	46·00
304/310		Set of 7	48·00	44·00

Designs: *Horiz*—25c. Sermon to the Fishes; 30c. Hermitage of Olivares; 50c. Basilica of the Saint at Padua; 75c. Death of St. Antony; 1l.25, St. Antony liberating prisoners.

(Des A. Pittalis. Photo)

1931 (29 Nov). *50th Anniv of Naval Academy, Leghorn.* T **123** *and similar horiz designs.* W **8**. P. 14.

311		20c. carmine-red	2·50	25
312		50c. bright violet	2·50	15
313		1l.25, blue	8·00	55

Designs:—50c. Cadet ship *Amerigo Vespucci*; 1l.25, Cruiser *Trento*.

ITALY 1932

124 Dante, 1265–1321
125 Leonardo Da Vinci's Drawing "Flying Man" 
126 Leonardo da Vinci 
127 Leonardo da Vinci 

(Postage des F. Chiapelli. Air des C. Mezzana. 100l. recess, others photo)

1932 (14 Mar–6 Aug). *Dante Alighieri Society*. No wmk (100l.) or W **8** (others). P 14.

*(a) POSTAGE. T **124** and similar designs.*

314	10c. sepia	65	25
315	15c. blue-green	70	20
316	20c. carmine-red	70	20
317	25c. green	70	20
318	30c. sepia	1·30	25
319	50c. bright violet	55	15
320	75c. carmine-red	2·00	95
321	1l.25, blue	1·40	65
322	1l.75, orange	1·50	95
323	2l.75, slate-green	11·50	6·75
324	5l.+2l. carmine-red	18·00	48·00
325	10l.+2l.50, olive-green	18·00	60·00

(b) AIR.

326	**125**	50c. sepia	1·40	1·50
327	**126**	1l. bright violet	2·10	1·80
328		3l. brown-lake	3·75	5·25
329		5l. green	4·25	7·50
330	**125**	7l.70+2l. blue	8·00	27·00
331	**126**	10l.+2l.50, violet-grey	9·25	36·00
332	**127**	100l. olive-green and blue (6 Aug)	33·00	£130
314/332 Set of 19			£110	£300

Designs:—10c. Giovanni Boccaccio (writer); 15c. Niccolò Machiavelli (statesman); 20c. Fra Paolo Sarpi (philosopher); 25c. Vittorio Alfieri (poet); 30c. Ugo Foscolo (writer); 50c. Giacomo Leopardi (poet); 75c. Giosué Carducci (poet); 1l.25, Carlo Botta (historian); 1l.75, Torquato Tasso (poet); 2l.75, Francesco Petrarch (poet); 5l. Ludovico Ariosto (poet).

128 Garibaldi and Victor Emmanuel
129 Garibaldi 
130 Caprera 
E **131** "Garibaldi" (statue). Savoia Marchetti S-55A Flying Boat and "Anita Garibaldi" (statue) 

(Des C. Mezzana (**131**), F. Chiapelli (others). Photo)

1932 (6 Apr–2 June). *50th Anniv of Garibaldi's Death*. W **8**. P 14.

*(a) POSTAGE. T **128/9** and similar types.*

333	10c. slate-blue	85	35
334	20c. sepia	95	20
335	25c. grey-green	1·30	30
336	30c. orange-vermilion	1·50	35
337	50c. bright violet	85	20
338	75c. carmine-red	3·00	1·10
339	1l.25, blue	2·30	70
340	1l.75+25c. deep blue	12·00	30·00
341	2l.55+50c. lake-brown	20·00	40·00
342	5l.+1l. lake	20·00	45·00

Designs: *Horiz*—10c. Garibaldi's birthplace, Nice; 20c., 30c. T **128**; 25c., 50c. "Here we make Italy or die"; 75c. Death of Anita (Garibaldi's wife); 1l.25, Garibaldi's tomb; 1l.75, Quarto Rock. *Vert*—2l.55, Garibaldi's statue, Rome.

*(b) AIR. T **130** and similar types.*

343	50c. lake	1·50	1·60
344	80c. green	2·75	3·00
345	1l.+25c. lake-brown	5·50	8·00
346	2l.+50c. blue	7·25	13·00
347	5l.+1l. green	9·00	15·00

Designs: *Vert*—50c., 1l. T **130**; 80c. The Ravenna hut; 2l. Anita; 5l. Garibaldi.

(c) AIR EXPRESS (2 June).

E348	E **131**	2l.25+1l. violet and carmine	6·00	15·00
E349		4l.50+1l.50, brown and green	6·25	15·00
333/E349 Set of 17			90·00	£170

E **132** King Victor Emmanuel III
132 

1932 (2 Sept)–33. *EXPRESS LETTER*. Photo. W **8**. P 14.

E350	E **132**	1l.25, green	25	10
E351		2l.50, red-orange (14.3.33)	25	95

(Des C. Mezzana. Photo)

1932 (27 Oct). *10th Anniv of Fascist March on Rome*. W **8**. P 14. T **132** and similar types inscr "X ANNUALE".

(a) POSTAGE. Inscr "POSTE ITALIANE".

350	5c. sepia	60	15
351	10c. sepia	60	15
352	15c. blue-green	85	30
353	20c. carmine-red	75	15
354	25c. green	85	15
355	30c. sepia	90	45
356	35c. blue	3·00	1·90
357	50c. bright violet	60	15
358	60c. chestnut	3·00	1·20
359	75c. carmine-red	1·40	50
360	1l. violet-slate	3·00	75
361	1l.25, blue	1·40	40
362	1l.75, orange-vermilion	2·10	40

ITALY   1932

363	2l.55, slate-green	18·00	11·50
364	2l.75, deep green	18·00	11·50
365	5l.+2l.50, carmine-red	30·00	85·00

Symbolic designs:—5c. Agriculture; 10c. Fascist soldier; 15c. Fascist coastguard; 20c. Italian youth; 25c. Tools forming a shadow of the Fasces; 30c. Religion; 35c. Imperial highways; 50c. Equestrian statue of Mussolini; 60c. Land reclamation; 75c. Colonial expansion; 1l. Marine development; 1l.25, Italians abroad; 1l.75, Sport; 2l.55, Child welfare; 2l.75, "O.N.D." recreation; 5l. Caesar's statue.

(b) AIR. Inscr "POSTA AEREA".

366	50c. brown	3·50	3·00
367	75c. chestnut	9·25	7·25

Designs:—50c. Eagle (front of Air Ministry Building, Rome); 75c. Aerial view of Italian Cathedrals.

(c) EXPRESS LETTER.
(i) Inland. Inscr "ESPRESSO".

E368	1l.25, green	75	70

(ii) Foreign. Inscr "EXPRES".

E369	2l.50, orange-vermilion	2·75	55·00
350/E369	Set of 20	90·00	£160

Designs:—1l.25, Roman road; 2l.50, Flags and head of Mussolini.

135 Italian flag   **King Victor Emmanuel III**   **"Flight"**

136 Italian flag   **King Victor Emmanuel III**   **Rome-Chicago**

(½-size illustrations)

E 133 Savoia Marchetti S-55A Flying Boat

PE 134 Galileo

(Des A. Ortona. Photo)

1933 (20 Jan)—**34**. AIR EXPRESS. W **8**. P 14.

E370	E **133**	2l. blue-black (4.7.34)	10	80
E371		2l.25, blue-black	3·25	55·00

1933 (29 Mar). PNEUMATIC POST. Type PE **134** and another portrait. W **8**. P 14.

PE372	15c. purple (Dante)	20	50
PE373	35c. carmine-red	20	85

See also Nos. PE679/80.

(Des C. Mezzana. Photo)

1933 (20 May). AIR. Balbo Transatlantic Mass Formation Flight by Savoia Marchetti S-55X Flying Boats. Centres in ultramarine. W **8**. P 14.

378	**135**	5l.25+19l.75, scarlet and green/green/scarlet	85·00	£1300
379	**136**	5l.25+44l.75, green and scarlet/scarlet/green	85·00	£1300

The colours of the frame and flag are given in the order of the stamps, reading from left to right.

The first illustration in each group is of the Registered Air Express label and has an abbreviation of one of the pilots' names overprinted on it; the second is of the stamp for Ordinary Postage and the third is the actual Air Mail stamp. Each value was issued in twenty strips of three, differing only in the name of the pilots.

No. 379 exists overprinted "VOLO DI RITORNO" but was not issued (Price £17000 un).

1933 (20 May). OFFICIAL AIR. As No. 379 optd "SERVIZIO DI STATO" on stamp at left. Centres in reddish violet.

O379	**136**	5l.25+44l.75, green and scarlet/scarlet/green	£1800	£8000

134 Airship *Graf Zeppelin*

137 Athlete   **138** Dome of St. Peter's

(Des C. Mezzana. Photo)

1933 (24 Apr). AIR. "Graf Zeppelin" issue. T **134** (views with airship above). W **8**. P 14.

372	3l. green and black	6·50	14·00
373	5l. brown and green	9·75	14·00
374	10l. grey-blue and scarlet	9·75	35·00
375	12l. orange-vermilion and blue	13·50	55·00
376	15l. black and brown	13·50	65·00
377	20l. ultramarine and red-brown	20l.	70·00
372/377	Set of 6	65·00	£225

Designs:—3l. S. Paolo Gate and tomb of Consul Caius Cestius; 5l. Old Appian Way and tomb of Cecilia Metella; 10l. Portion of Forum Mussolini; 12l. S. Angelo Castle; 15l. Forum Romanum; 20l. Empire Way, Colosseum and Baths of Domitian.

139 St. Peter's and Church of the Holy Sepulchre

PRIMO VOLO DIRETTO
ROMA = BUENOS-AYRES
TRIMOTORE · LOMBARDI-MAZZOTTI

2
(140)

22

ITALY 1933

(Des A. Pesci. Photo)

1933 (16 Aug). *International University Games, Turin.* W **8**. P 14.
380	**137**	10c. brown	20	20
381		20c. carmine-red	20	25
382		50c. bright violet	35	15
383		1l.25, blue	1·70	1·40
380/383	Set of 4		2·20	1·80

(Des C. Mezzana. Photo)

1933 (23 Oct). *"Holy Year".* W **8**. P 14.

(a) POSTAGE. T **138** and similar types inscr "ANNO SANTO".
384	20c. carmine-red	1·60	15
385	25c. green	2·30	25
386	50c. bright violet	1·90	10
387	1l.25, blue	2·40	55
388	2l.55+2l.50, black	6·75	32·00

(b) AIR.
389	**139**	50c.+25c. red-brown	85	6·75
390		75c.+50c. purple	1·60	8·75
384/390	Set of 7		16·00	44·00

Designs:—25c., 50c. Angel with Cross; 1l.25, T **138**; 2l.55, Cross with Doves of Peace.

1934 (15 Jan). AIR. *Rome–Buenos Aires Flight.* T **113** *(new colours)* surch. as T **140**.
391	**113**	2l. on 2l. yellow	3·25	32·00
392		3l. on 2l. sage-green	3·25	38·00
393		5l. on 2l. rose-carmine	3·25	50·00
394		10l. on 2l. dull violet	3·25	60·00
391/394	Set of 4		12·00	£160

D **141**
D **142**

1934 (3 Feb). POSTAGE DUE. Photo. W **8**. P 14.
D395	D **141**	5c. brown	25	15
D396		10c. deep blue	25	15
D397		20c. bright scarlet	40	15
D398		25c. green	40	15
D399		30c. orange-red	40	15
D400		40c. agate	40	45
D401		50c. violet	25	10
D402		60c. indigo	35	1·90
D403	D **142**	1l. reddish orange	40	15
D404		2l. green	40	20
D405		5l. violet	95	35
D406		10l. blue	3·00	70
D407		20l. carmine-red	7·50	3·75
D395/407	Set of 13		13·50	7·50

141 Anchor of the Emmanuele Filiberto
142 Antonio Pacinotti

(Des C. Mezzana. Photo)

1934 (12 Mar–July). *10th Anniv of the Annexation of Fiume.* T **141** and similar types inscr "DECENNALE DI FIVME". W **8**. P 14.

(a) POSTAGE. Inscr "POSTE ITALIANE".
395	10c. sepia	3·50	30
396	20c. carmine-red	40	20
397	50c. bright violet	40	15
398	1l.25, blue	45	1·10
399	1l.75+1l. slate-blue	70	15·00
400	2l.55+2l. purple	90	20·00
401	2l.75+2l.50, olive-green	90	20·00

Designs:—10, 20c. Type **141**, 50c. Gabriele d'Annunzio; 1l.25. St. Vito's tower barricaded; 1l.75, Hands supporting crown of historical monuments; 2l.55, Victor Emmanuel III's arrival in the *Brindisi*; 2l.75, Galley, gondola and battleship.

(b) AIR. Inscr "POSTA AEREA".
402	25c. green	55	80
403	50c. brown	55	50
404	75c. red brown	55	1·90
405	1l.+50c. purple	55	5·25
406	2l.+1l.50, deep blue	55	7·50
407	3l.+2l. brownish black	55	7·50

Designs: Marina Fiat MF.5 flying boat over—25, 75c. Fiume Harbour; 50c., 1l. War memorial; 2l. Three Venetian lions; 3l. Roman wall.

(c) AIR EXPRESS. Inscr "POSTA AEREA ESPRESSO".
E408	2l.+1l.25, blue (July)	1·40	10·00
E409	2l.25+1l.25, olive-green	55	9·50
E410	4l.50+2l. carmine	55	9·50
395/E410	Set of 16	12·00	£100

Design:—2l., 2l.25, 4l.50, Foundation of Fiume.

(Des R. Pierbattista and Sartori. Photo)

1934 (23 May). *75th Anniv of the Invention of Pacinotti's Dynamo.* W **8**. P 14.
| 411 | **142** | 50c. violet | 70 | 15 |
| 412 | | 1l.25, blue | 1·00 | 85 |

143
144 Savoia Marchetti S-55X Flying Boat over Footballer
145 Luigi Galvani

(Des A. Ortona (5l.). L. Ferri (others). Photo)

1934 (24 May). *World Cup Football Championship, Italy.* W **8**. P 14.

(a) POSTAGE. As T **143**.
413	20c. orange-red	9·50	1·90
414	25c. green	8·00	80
415	50c. violet	9·50	30
416	1l.25, blue	21·00	3·75
417	5l.+2l.50, brown	55·00	£120

Designs: *Horiz*—25c., 50c., 1l.25, Two footballers. *Vert*—5l. Heading the ball.

(b) AIR. As T **144**.
418	50c. carmine	6·00	5·25
419	75c. slate-blue	6·25	6·25
420	5l.+2l.50, blackish olive	26·00	65·00
421	10l.+5l. agate	31·00	75·00
413/421	Set of 9	£160	£250

Designs (Marina Fiat MF.5 flying boat over): *Horiz*—50c. Mussolini Stadium, Turin; 5l. Stadium, Rome. *Vert*—10l. Littoral Stadium, Bologna.

(Des R. Garrasi. Photo)

1934 (16 Aug). *First International Congress of Electro-Radio-Biology.* W **8**. P 14.
| 422 | **145** | 30c. brown/*buff* | 85 | 25 |
| 423 | | 75c. carmine/*pink* | 1·20 | 1·40 |

23

ITALY 1934

146 Military Symbol

147 Italian "P" Type Airship under Fire

(Des G. Rondini. Photo)

1934 (6 Sept). *Military Medal Centenary. Various military types all inscr "1 CENTENARIO DELLE MEDAGLIE AL VALORE MILITARE".* W **8**. P 14.

(a) POSTAGE. Inscr "POSTE ITALIANE" as T **146**.

424	10c. brown	1·00	40
425	15c. deep green	1·10	80
426	20c. carmine-red	1·00	30
427	25c. green	1·30	30
428	30c. brown	1·80	90
429	50c. bright violet	1·40	20
430	75c. carmine	5·50	1·60
431	1l.25, blue	4·25	1·00
432	1l.75+1l. orange-vermilion	10·00	20·00
433	2l.55+2l. claret	16·00	19·00
434	2l.75+2l. deep violet	18·00	22·00

Designs:—Vert—25c. Mountaineers; 1l.75, Cavalry. Horiz—15c., 50c. Barbed-wire cutter; 20c. Throwing hand-grenade; 30c. Cripple wielding crutch; 75c. Artillery; 1l.25, Soldiers cheering; 2l.55, Sapper; 2l.75, First aid.

(b) AIR. Inscr "POSTA AEREA" as T **147**.

435	25c. green	1·30	1·40
436	50c. grey	1·30	1·60
437	75c. brown	1·30	2·30
438	80c. grey-blue	2·40	2·75
439	1l.+50c. red-brown	4·25	9·00
440	2l.+1l. blue	5·50	15·00
441	3l.+2l. brown-black	8·75	15·00

Designs:—Horiz—50c., 75c. Naval launch; 80c. Type **147**; 1l. Caproni Ca 101 airplane and troops in desert; 2l. Pomilio PC type biplane and troops. Vert—3l. Unknown soldier's tomb.

(c) AIR EXPRESS. Inscr "POSTA AEREA ESPRESSO" as T **147**.

E442	2l.+1l.25, brown	5·25	14·00
E443	4l.50+2l. lake	7·25	14·00
424/E443 Set of 20		90·00	£130

Design: Horiz—2l., 4l.50, Caproni Ca 101 airplane over triumphal arch.

148 King Victor Emmanuel III

149 Man with Fasces

(Des G. Rondini. Photo)

1934 (5 Nov). AIR. *Rome–Mogadiscio flight and King of Italy's visit to Italian Somaliland.* W **8**. P 14.

444	**148**	1l. bright violet	1·40	6·75
445		2l. blue	1·40	8·50
446		4l. red-brown	2·50	35·00
447		5l. green	2·50	56·00
448		8l. carmine-red	11·50	65·00
449		10l. brown	12·50	70·00
444/449 Set of 6			29·00	£225

1934 (5 Nov). *OFFICIAL AIR. As No. 449 (colour changed) optd "SERVIZIO DI STATO", in gold.*

| O450 | **148** | 10l. slate | 6·50 | £7500 |

(Des Garelli. Photo)

1935 (23 Apr). *University Contests.* T **149** *and allegorical types inscr "LITTORIALI".* W **8**. P 14.

450	20c. carmine-red	30	15
451	30c. brown	2·20	1·20
452	50c. bright violet	30	15

Designs:—30c. Eagle and soldier; 50c. Standard-bearer and bayonet attack.

150

151 Emblematical of Italian Air Force

(Des C. Mezzana. Photo)

1935 (1 July). *National Militia.* W **8**. P 14.

(a) T **150** and similar types inscr "PRO OPERA PREVID. MILIZIA".

453	20c.+10c. carmine-red	5·75	3·75
454	25c.+15c. green	5·75	5·00
455	50c.+30c. bright violet	5·75	6·00
456	1l.25+75c. blue	5·75	9·50

Designs:—25c. Roman standards (labara); 50c. Soldier and cross; 1l.25, Solders marching through arch.

(b) AIR. T **151**.

457	50c.+50c. brown	9·25	11·00
453/457 Set of 5		29·00	32·00

152 Symbolical of Flight

153 Leonardo da Vinci

(Des Garelli. Photo)

1935 (1 Oct). *International Aeronautical Exhibition, Milan.* W **8**. P 14.

458	**152**	20c. carmine-red	5·75	45
459		30c. brown	15·00	1·30
460	**153**	50c. bright violet	22·00	25
461		1l.25, blue	20·00	90
458/461 Set of 4			55·00	2·50

154 Vincenzo Bellini

155 "Music"

24

ITALY 1935

(Des G. Rondini. Photo)

1935 (15 Oct). *Death Centenary of Vincenzo Bellini (composer).* W **8**. P 14.

(a) POSTAGE. T **154** *and similar designs.*

462	20c. carmine-red	3·50	40
463	30c. brown	5·75	60
464	50c. bright violet	5·25	25
465	1l.25, blue	7·25	1·60
466	1l.75+1l. orange-vermilion	25·00	32·00
467	2l.75+2l. olive-green	41·00	40·00

Designs: *Vert*—20c. to 1l.25. T **154**; 2l.75, Bellini's villa. *Horiz*—1l.75, Hands at the piano.

(b) AIR. T **155** *and similar designs.*

468	25c. ochre	1·70	1·20
469	50c. brown	1·70	1·20
470	60c. carmine	4·25	1·60
471	1l.+1l. bright violet	9·75	28·00
472	5l.+2l. green	14·50	40·00
462/472 Set of 11		£110	£130

Designs:—50c., 60c. T **155**; 1l. Angelic musicians; 5l. Mountain landscape.

156 "Commerce" and Industrial Map of Italy

(Des M. Parrini. Photo)

1936 (23 Mar). *17th Milan Fair. T* **156** *and similar horiz design.* W **8**. P 14.

473	**156**	20c. vermilion	45	25
474	–	30c. dp brn (Cogwheel and plough)	45	40
475	–	50c. violet (As 30c.)	55	20
476	**156**	1l.25, blue	80	65
473/476 Set of 4			2·00	1·40

157 "Fertility"

158 Savoia Marchetti S-55A Flying Boat

(Des G. Rondini. Photo)

1936 (1 July). *2000th Anniv of Birth of Horace, Symbolic types inscr "BIMILLENARIO ORAZIANO".* W **8**. P 14.

(a) POSTAGE. T **157** *and similar designs.*

477	10c. green	2·10	25
478	20c. scarlet	1·60	25
479	30c. sepia	4·25	65
480	50c. bright violet	4·25	15
481	75c. scarlet	7·25	80
482	1l.25+1l. blue	17·00	30·00
483	1l.75+1l. carmine	24·00	42·00
484	2l.55+1l. slate-blue	27·00	46·00

Designs: *Horiz*—20c. and 1l.25, Landscape; 75c. The Capitol; 2l.55, Dying gladiator. *Vert*—30c. Ajax defying the lightning; 50c. Medallion portrait of Horace; 1l.75, Pan.

(b) AIR. T **158** *and similar designs.*

485	25c. green	1·80	1·40
486	50c. sepia	2·50	1·40
487	60c. vermilion	3·00	2·30
488	1l.+1l. violet	9·00	30·00
489	5l.+2l. grey-green	12·00	55·00
477/489 Set of 13		£100	£190

Designs: *Horiz*—50c., 1l. Caproni Ca 101 airplane over lake; 60c. Eagle and oak tree; 5l. Rome.

159

160

161  **162**

(Des R. Maffei (30c., 1l.75), R. Garrasi (others). Photo)

1937 (28 June). *Child Welfare. Allegorical types inscr "MOSTRA COLONIE ESTIVE E ASSISTENZA ALL'INFANZIE".* W **8**. P 14.

(a) POSTAGE. T **159/60** *and similar designs.*

490	10c. red-brown	1·70	50
491	20c. carmine	1·70	40
492	25c. green	1·70	50
493	30c. sepia	1·90	1·20
494	50c. bright violet	1·80	20
495	75c. scarlet	5·25	1·60
496	1l.25, blue	6·25	1·70
497	1l.75+75c. orange	29·00	42·00
498	2l.75+1l.25 pale blue-green	23·00	45·00
499	5l.+3l. slate-blue	25·00	50·00

Designs:—25c. T **159**; 30c., 1l.75, Boy between Fasces (21 × 37 mm.); 50c., 1l.25, 5l. T **160**; 75c., 2l.75, "Bambino" after della Robbia.

(b) AIR.

500	**161**	25c. blue-green	5·00	2·00
501	**162**	50c. olive-brown	5·25	1·40
502	**161**	1l. bright violet	5·00	3·00
503	**162**	2l.+1l. blue	7·50	30·00
504	**161**	3l.+2l. orange	10·50	34·00
505	**162**	5l.+3l. lake	16·00	38·00
490/505 Set of 16			£130	£225

163 Naval Memorial

164 Augustus the Great

(Des C. Mezzana. Photo)

1937 (23 Sept). *2000th Anniv of Birth of Augustus the Great. Symbolic types inscr "BIMILLENARIO AUGUSTEO".* W **8**. P 14.

(a) POSTAGE. T **163** *and similar designs.*

506	10c. deep blue-green	80	20
507	15c. olive-brown	80	25
508	20c. scarlet	80	25
509	25c. green	80	25

25

ITALY 1937

510	30c. bronze-green	1·00	25
511	50c. bright violet	90	10
512	75c. scarlet	1·10	70
513	1l.25, deep blue	1·80	75
514	1l.75+1l. purple	29·00	30·00
515	2l.55+2l. slate-black	32·00	35·00

Designs:—15c. Military trophies; 20c. Reconstructing temples of Rome; 25c. Census (with reference to birth of Jesus Christ); 30c. Statue of Julius Caesar; 50c. Election of Augustus as Emperor; 75c. Conquest of Ethiopia; 1l.25, Constructing a new fleet; 1l.75, Building the Altar of Peace; 2l.55, The Capitol.

(b) AIR. T 164 and similar designs.

516	25c. purple	3·50	2·20
517	50c. olive-brown	3·50	2·40
518	80c. chestnut	6·25	3·75
519	1l.+1l. blue	24·00	25·00
520	5l.+1l. slate-violet	30·00	40·00
506/520 Set of 15		£120	£130

Designs:—25c. "Agriculture"; 50c. Prosperity of the Romans; 80c. Horses of the Sun Chariot; 1l. Staff and Map of Roman Empire.

165 Gasparo Spontini (composer)

166 Marconi

(Des R. Pierbattista. Photo)

1937 (25 Oct). *Famous Italians. As T 165 (inscribed portraits).* W **8**. P 14.

521	10c. sepia	35	35
522	20c. carmine	35	35
523	25c. green	35	30
524	30c. olive-brown	35	40
525	50c. bright violet	35	15
526	75c. scarlet	95	1·00
527	1l.25, blue	1·20	1·00
528	1l.75, orange	1·20	1·00
529	2l.55+2l. grey-green	11·00	35·00
530	2l.75+2l. brown	11·00	38·00
521/530 Set of 10		24·00	70·00

Portraits:—20c., 2l.55, Antonio Stradivarius (violin maker); 25c. Giacomo Leopardi (poet); 30, 75c. Giovanni Battista Pergolesi (composer); 1l.25, 2l.75, Giotto di Bordone (painter and architect); 1l.75, Type **165**.

1938 (24 Jan). *Guglielmo Marconi (telegraph pioneer) Commemoration. Photo.* W **8**. P 14.

531	**166** 20c. carmine-red	1·60	20
532	50c. bright violet	45	15
533	1l.25, blue	60	1·50

167 Founding of Rome

168 Victor Emmanuel III

169 Steam Locomotive *Bayard*, 1839, and 1939 Railcar

(Des C. Mezzana. Photo)

1938 (28 Oct). *2nd Anniv of Proclamation of Italian Empire.* W **8**. P 14.

(a) POSTAGE. T 167 and similar types.

534	10c. sepia	70	15
535	20c. carmine	1·00	15
536	25c. green	1·00	15
537	30c. olive-brown	85	15
538	50c. bright violet	1·50	15
539	75c. scarlet	2·30	30
540	1l.25, blue	3·00	25
541	1l.75, slate-violet	3·50	55
542	2l.75, grey-green	12·50	8·75
543	5l. brown-red	23·00	11·00

Designs:—20c. Emperor Augustus; 25c. Dante; 30c. Columbus; 50c. Leonardo da Vinci; 75c. Garibaldi and Victor Emmanuel II; 1l.25, Italian Unknown Warrior's Tomb; 1l.75, "March on Rome"; 2l.75, Wedding Ring on Map of Ethiopia; 5l. Victor Emmanuel III.

(b) AIR. T 168 and similar types.

544	25c. blue-green	85	1·00
545	50c. olive-brown	1·40	1·00
546	1l. bright violet	1·70	3·25
547	2l. grey-blue	2·30	6·00
548	3l. brown-lake	4·50	10·00
549	5l. green	4·75	15·00
534/549 Set of 16		60·00	70·00

Designs:—50c. and 1l. Dante; 2l. and 5l. Leonardo da Vinci; 3l. Victor Emmanuel III.

(Des G. Cametti. Photo)

1939 (15 Dec). *Centenary of Italian Railways.*

550	**169** 20c. scarlet	50	20
551	50c. bright violet	65	20
552	1l.25, blue	1·10	1·50

170 Hitler and Mussolini

171 Hitler and Mussolini

(Des C. Mezzana (**170**), A. Pesci (**171**). Photo)

1941 (30 Jan–2 Apr). *Italo-German Friendship.* W **8**. P 14.

553	**170** 10c. brown (2.4)	1·40	45
554	20c. orange-red (2.4)	1·40	35
555	25c. blue-green (2.4)	1·40	40
556	**171** 50c. violet	1·90	35
557	75c. carmine	2·30	80
558	1l.25, blue	2·30	1·20
553/558 Set of 6		9·75	3·25

172 Roman Cavalry

173 Galileo Teaching at Padua

174 Rossini

(Des C. Mezzana. Photo)

1941 (13 Dec). *2000th Birth Anniv of Livy (Latin historian).* T **172** and similar design. W **8**. P 14.

559	20c.+10c. carmine	35	55
560	30c.+15c. brown	35	70
561	50c.+25c. violet	40	75
562	1l.25+1l. blue	40	90
559/562 Set of 4		1·40	2·75

Designs:—20c., 30c. T **172**; 50c., 1l.25, Roman legionary.

ITALY 1942

1942 (14 Aug). *War Propaganda. Nos. 244/5 and 247 with attached labels (imperf between stamp and label) to encourage war effort.* W **8**. P 14.

563	102	25c. green (Navy)		20	40
564		25c. green (Army)		20	40
565		25c. green (Air Force)		20	40
566		25c. green (Militia)		20	40
567	103	30c. brown (Navy)		20	1·20
568		30c. brown (Army)		20	1·20
569		30c. brown (Air Force)		20	1·20
570		30c. brown (Militia)		20	1·20
571		50c. bright violet (Navy)		20	40
572		50c. bright violet (Army)		20	40
573		50c. bright violet (Air Force)		20	40
574		50c. bright violet (Militia)		20	40
563/574 Set of 12				2·20	7·25

Nos. 271, 274 and 275 were also produced with similar propaganda labels, but were not issued as events overtook the promise of victory inscribed on them.

(Des C. Mezzana. Photo)

1942 (28 Sept). *Death Tercentenary of Galileo. As T* **173** *(various designs).* W **8**. P 14.

575	10c. lake and orange		35	25
576	25c. blue-green and grey-olive		35	25
577	50c. violet and purple		35	25
578	1l.25, ultramarine and grey-blue		50	1·30
575/578 Set of 4			1·40	2·00

Designs:—25c. Galileo at Venice; 50c. Portrait of Galileo; 1l.25, Galileo at Arcetri, near Florence.

1942 (23 Nov). *150th Birth Anniv of Rossini (composer). As T* **174** *inscr "CL/ANNIVERSARIO ROSSINIANO 1792–1942". Photo.* W **8**. P 14.

579	25c. green		20	25
580	30c. brown		20	25
581	50c. violet		20	25
582	1l. blue		20	40
579/582 Set of 4			70	1·00

Designs:—25c., 30c. Rossini Monument. Pescaro: 50c., 1l. Type **174**.

P.M.
(M **175**)

1943 (June). *MILITARY POST. Optd photo with Type M* **175**.

(a) Postage stamps of 1929–42 (Nos. 239/56).

M583	5c. brown	25	35
M584	10c. sepia	25	70
M585	15c. blue-green	25	70
M586	20c. carmine	25	70
M587	25c. green	25	70
M588	30c. brown	25	70
M589	50c. bright violet	25	70
M590	1l. violet	1·40	11·00
M591	1l.25, blue	25	85
M592	1l.75, orange-vermilion	25	70
M593	2l. brown-lake	25	85
M594	5l. carmine	25	2·40
M595	10l. violet	25	17·00

(b) Air stamps of 1930 (Nos. 271/7).

M596	50c. sepia	20	70
M597	1l. bright violet	20	70
M598	2l. blue	30	8·50
M599	5l. green	1·40	15·00
M600	10l. carmine-red	1·40	21·00

(c) Air Express stamp of 1934 (No. E370).

M601	2l. blue-black	1·40	17·00

(d) Express Letter stamp of 1932 (No. E350).

M602	1l.25, green	20	1·40
M583/602 Set of 20		18·00	95·00

ITALIAN SOCIAL REPUBLIC. The issues made by Mussolini's government in Northern Italy during 1943–45 are listed at the end of Italy.

ALLIED MILITARY GOVERNMENT

British and American troops landed in Sicily on 10 July 1943 and in Italy on 3 September.

175   **GOVERNO MILITARE ALLEATO** (**176**)

(Litho Bureau of Engraving and Printing. Washington)

1943 (17 Sept). *For use in Sicily.* P 11.

(a) Optd "ITALY CENTESIMI" in black.

583	175	15c. orange	35	50
584		25c. olive-bistre	35	50
585		30c. grey	35	50
586		50c. violet	35	50
587		60c. yellow	35	65

(b) Optd "ITALY LIRA" or "LIRE" in black.

588	175	1l. emerald-green	35	50
589		2l. carmine	35	65
590		5l. greenish blue	35	1·20
591		10l. brown	35	1·50
583/591 Set of 9			2·75	6·00

1943 (10 Dec). *For use in Naples. Stamps of 1929–42 optd with T* **176**.

592	99	20c. carmine (B.)	45	1·20
593	101	35c. blue (R.)	5·00	7·25
594	103	50c. bright violet (R.)	30	1·10

ROYAL GOVERNMENT 10 Sept 1943–13 June 1946

On 10 Sept 1943 King Victor Emmanuel III and Marshal Badoglio set up a government at Brindisi; on 11 Feb 1944 they moved to Salerno and administration of the southern provinces was transferred to them by the Allies.

Mussolini set up a rival government as the Italian Social Republic in Northern Italy on 23 September 1943 and exercised control in those areas occupied by the German army until April 1945.

The King handed over his powers to Crown Prince Umberto on 5 June 1944 and abdicated on 9 May 1946.

187 Romulus, Remus and Wolf (after Pollaiuolo)

(Des De Simone. Litho Richter, Naples)

1943–44. *Pinkish grey burelé background. No gum.*

(a) Wmk Honeycomb. P 11 × 11½.

618	187	50c. reddish purple (30.12.43)	1·40	2·40

(b) No wmk. P 11.

619	187	50c. reddish purple (16.5.44)	10	65

Crown Prince Umberto, Regent
5 June 1944–9 May 1946

A   B

C   D

ITALY 1943

10c. In Type B "POSTE ITALIANE" is more to the right and the "I" further from the stop after "CENT".
1l. In Type D the "L" in "LIRE" extends only as far as the "I" whereas in Type C it extends as far as the "E". The letters of "POSTE ITALIANE" are larger in Type C.

1944–45. Printed at Rome. As postage stamps of 1929–42 but without Fascist emblems. P 14.

(a) W 8.

620	103	30c. brown (11.44)	20	25
621		50c. violet (12.44)	20	1·80
622		60c. green (2.45)	20	90
623		1l. violet (D) (2.45)	20	20

(b) No wmk (April 1945).

624	100	10c. sepia (A)	2·25	3·25
625	103	60c. green	20	70
626	99	1l. violet (D)	20	20
620/626	Set of 7		4·25	6·50

See Nos. 630/46.

(188) (189) (190)

1945. Nos. 108/9 of Italian Social Republic and No. 251 of Italy surch with T **188/90**.

627	1l.20 on 20c. carmine (2.5)		10	10
628	2l. on 25c. green (2.5)		10	15
629	2l.50 on 1l.75, orange-vermilion (3.3)		10	25
	a. Six bars at left (No. 91 in sheet)		3·50	3·50

D 191    D 192

1945 (April). POSTAGE DUE. Fascist emblems removed. No wmk. P 14.

D630	D **191**	5c. brown	45	70
D631		10c. blue	10	10
D632		20c. carmine	45	45
D633		25c. green	10	10
D634		30c. orange	10	10
D635		40c. black	10	10
D636		50c. violet	10	10
D637		60c. indigo	10	30
D638	D **192**	1l. orange	30	70
D639		2l. green	10	10
D640		5l. violet	10	10
D641		10l. blue	10	10
D642		20l. carmine	10	1·20
D630/642	Set of 13		2·00	3·75

See Nos. D679/89.

1945 (May). Printed at Novara. As stamps of 1929–42 but without wmk. P 14.

630	101	15c. blue-green	10	10
631		35c. blue	10	35
632	99	1l. violet (C)	25	10

1945–46. Printed at Novara. As stamps of 1929–42 but without Fascist emblems. No wmk. P 14.

633	100	10c. sepia (B) (8.45)	10	40
634	99	20c. carmine (7.45)	10	70
635	101	50c. violet (6.45)	10	20
636		60c. orange-vermilion (8.45)	10	25
637	99	1l. violet (C) (5.45)	10	15
638	101	2l. brown-lake (8.45)	10	30
639		10l. violet (3.46)	2·40	5·00
633/639	Set of 7		2·75	6·25

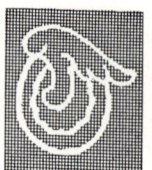

191 Winged Wheel    E **192** Italia    (P **192**)

There are three different types of this watermark.

1945. Printed at Rome. As stamps of 1929–42 but without Fascist emblems with wmk. T **191**. P 14.

640	99	20c. carmine (7.45)	10	30
641	103	60c. green (7.45)	10	35
642	99	1l. violet (D) (5.45)	10	10
643	101	1l.20, chocolate (8.45)	10	30
644		2l. brown-lake (7.45)	55	90
645	98	5l. carmine (7.45)	10	30
646	101	10l. violet (11.45)	2·10	5·00
640/646	Set of 7		2·75	6·50

1945 (May). CONCESSIONAL LETTER POST. No. CL267 surch with Royal Arms (obliterating fasces) and new value.

CL647	CL **109**	40c. on 10c. brown	10	1·30

1945 (Aug)–**46.** CONCESSIONAL LETTER POST. As Type CL **109**, but Arms redrawn without fasces. Photo. W **191**. P 14.

CL648	40c. brown	10	1·00
CL649	1l. brown (5.46)	2·10	2·10

(Des P. Paschetto. Photo)

1945 (Aug). EXPRESS LETTER. W **191**. P 14.

E647	E **192**	5l. carmine	10	1·00

1945 (Aug). PARCEL POST. Nos. P217/28 optd with Type P **192** obliterating Fascist emblems between stamps.

		Un pair	Used pair	Used half
P647	5c. brown	55	1·25	10
P648	10c. deep blue	55	1·25	10
P649	25c. carmine	55	1·25	10
P650	30c. ultramarine	10·50	13·00	2·20
P651	50c. orange	55	80	10
P652	60c. rose-scarlet	55	80	10
P653	1l. violet	55	80	10
P654	2l. green	55	80	10
P655	5l. yellow-bistre	55	80	10
P656	4l. grey-black	55	80	10
P657	10l. purple	12·50	27·00	1·50
P658	20l. dull purple	18·00	60·00	3·75
P647/658	Set of 12	42·00	£100	7·50

192 "Freedom"    **193** "Work, Justice and Family"    **194** "Enlightenment"

ITALY 1945

195 Planting a Sapling
196 "Peace"
197 "Work, Justice and Family" 

(Des A. Lalia (T **192**), R Garrasi (T **193**, T **196**), P. Paschetto (T **194**, 60c., 2l.), M. Melis and A. Mazzotta (T **195**). Photo. T **197** eng M. Colombati. Recess)

1945 (1 Oct)–**48**. T **192/7** and similar design. W **191**. P 14.
647	**192**	10c. red-brown	15	10
648	**193**	20c. sepia	15	10
649	**194**	25c. greenish blue (10.10.46)	15	10
650	**195**	40c. grey	15	10
651	**192**	50c. violet (3.7.46)	15	10
652	–	60c. deep green	15	15
653	**192**	80c. carmine	15	10
654	**195**	1l. green	15	10
655	**194**	1l.20, brown	15	25
656	–	2l. purple-brown	15	10
657	**194**	3l. scarlet	15	10
658		4l. vermilion (10.5.46)	20	10
659	**193**	5l. dull blue	45	10
660	**195**	6l. bluish violet (5.5.47)	6·75	10
661	**192**	8l. blue-green (19.1.48)	3·25	10
662		10l. grey	1·50	10
663	**193**	10l. vermilion (20.10.47)	32·00	10
664	**195**	15l. pale blue (3.7.46)	7·00	10
665	**194**	20l. purple	3·25	10
666	**196**	25l. deep green	19·00	10
667	**194**	30l. bright blue (16.12.47)	£275	25
668	**196**	50l. brown-purple	7·75	10
669	**197**	100l. carmine (shades) (29.7.46)	£275	95
647/669 Set of 23			£575	3·00

Design: (17 × 21 mm)—60c., 2l. Gardener tying sapling to stake.
The 10l. grey and 100l. carmine printed by typography or lithography on unwatermarked paper are forgeries; the 10l. is line perforated 14½ or imperf, the 100l. is perf 11½.

E **200** Winged Foot of Mercury
E **201** Horse and Torchbearer 

(Des P. Paschetto (E **200**), M. Melis and A. Mazzotta (E **201**). Photo)

1945 (1 Oct)–**51**. EXPRESS LETTER. W **191**. P 14.
E679	E **200**	5l. brown-red	10	10
E680	E **201**	10l. blue	10	30
E681		15l. lake (28.7.47)	1·90	15
E682	E **200**	25l. red-orange (15.11.47)	27·00	10
E683		30l. violet (3.7.46)	2·75	75
E684		50l. bright purple (19.12.51)	26·00	10
E685	E **201**	60l. carmine (10.12.47)	40·00	15
E679/685 Set of 7			65·00	1·50

See also No. E915.

1945 (22 Oct). PNEUMATIC POST. Portraits as Type PE **134**, but inscr "ITALIA". Photo. W **191**. P 14.
PE679	60c. brown (Dante)	25	1·10
PE680	1l.40, blue (Galileo)	25	1·10

1945 (8 Dec). POSTAGE DUE. As Nos. D631, 633/42 but W **191**. P 14.
D679	D **191**	10c. blue	10	2·40
D680		25c. green	1·10	3·00
D681		30c. orange	1·10	3·00
D682		40c. black	10	10
D683		50c. violet	5·00	2·75
D684		60c. indigo	6·00	10·00
D685	D **192**	1l. orange	10	10
D686		2l. green	10	10
D687		5l. violet	5·50	3·50
D688		10l. blue	15·00	5·50
D689		20l. carmine	24·00	10·00
D679/689 Set of 11			50·00	36·00

King Umberto II, 9 May 1946–13 June 1946

1946 (10 May–3 July). PARCEL POST. As Type P **92**, but without fasces between stamps. W **8** (sideways). P 13.
		Un pair	Used pair	Used half
P679	1l. mauve (3.7)	1·20	45	15
P680	2l. grey-green	85	45	15
P681	3l. yellow-orange (3.7)	1·50	45	15
P682	4l. grey-black	2·10	45	15
P683	10l. claret	36·00	34·00	2·30
P684	20l. dull purple	48·00	65·00	6·50
P679/684 Set of 6		80·00	90·00	8·50

REPUBLIC, 10 June 1946

198 Clasped Hands and Caproni Campini N-1 Jet
199 Barn Swallows

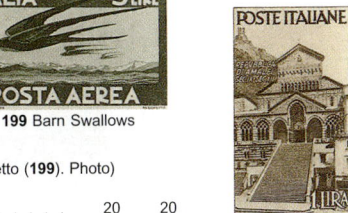

(Des A. Lalia (**198**), P. Paschetto (**199**). Photo)

1945 (1 Oct)–**47**. AIR. W **191**. P 14.
670	**198**	1l. greenish slate	20	20
671	**199**	2l. dull ultramarine	20	20
672	**198**	3l.20, orange-red	20	20
673	**199**	5l. deep green	20	20
674	**198**	10l. carmine-red	20	10
675	**199**	25l. blue (13.7.46)	10·00	5·25
676		25l. yellow-brown (21.4.47)	15	10
677	**198**	50l. deep green (13.7.46)	18·00	9·25
678		50l. reddish violet (21.4.47)	15	10
670/678 Set of 9			26·00	14·00

See also Nos. 952/3.

200 Amalfi
P **201** 

(Des C. Mezzana. Photo)

1946 (31 Oct). Mediaeval Italian Republics. T **200** and similar designs. W **191**. P 14.
679	1l. sepia	15	10
680	2l. blue	15	10
681	3l. green	15	10
682	4l. orange	15	10

ITALY 1946

683	5l. violet	10	10
684	10l. carmine	20	10
685	15l. ultramarine	65	60
686	20l. red-brown	25	10
679/686 Set of 8		1·70	1·30

Designs: *Vert*—2l. Lucca; 3l. Siena; 4l. Florence. *Horiz*—5l. Pisa; 10l. Genoa; 15l. Venice; 20l. "Il Giuramento di Pontida" (*trans* "The Oath of Pontida").

1946 (7 Dec)–**57**. PARCEL POST. Type P **201**. Photo. W **191** (sideways). P 13.

		Un pair	Used pair	Used half
P687	25c. ultramarine (20.10.47)	15	10	10
	a. P 12½ × 13½. Wmk upright (7.55)	10	10	10
P688	50c. bistre-brown (12.5.47)	35	15	10
P689	1l. yellow-brown (12.5.47)	35	15	10
P690	2l. turquoise-blue (5.5.47)	80	30	10
P691	3l. red-orange (24.3.47)	40	15	10
P692	4l. grey (21.4.47)	7·00	7·25	75
P693	5l. bright purple (20.10.47)	45	10	10
	a. P 12½ × 13½. Wmk upright (23.2.57)	30	10	10
P694	10l. violet (6.2.47)	6·75	10	10
P695	20l. brown-purple	1·60	65	15
	a. P 12½ × 13½. Wmk upright (3.54)	4·50	75	50
P696	30l. reddish purple (19.1.52)	3·25	65	15
	a. P 12½ × 13½. Wmk upright (12.55)	5·25	3·50	50
P697	50l. vermilion	15·00	30	10
	a. P 12½ × 13½. Wmk upright (11.54)	17·00	1·20	30
P698	100l. blue	40·00	10·00	20
	a. P 12½ × 13½. Wmk upright (11.54)	60·00	35·00	95
P699	200l. deep green (2.1.48)	50·00	15·00	70
	a. P 12½ × 13½. Wmk upright (11.54)	95·00	70·00	4·50
P700	300l. deep claret (2.1.48)	£1500	£500	4·00
P701	500l. deep brown (2.1.48)	£120	£100	4·00
	a. P 12½ × 13½. Wmk upright (11.56)	£225	£160	18·00
P687/701 Set of 15 (cheapest)		£1600	£550	10·00

See also Nos. P908/29 and P1347/8.

CL 201 Italia

D 201

(Des R. Garrasi. Photo)

1947 (1 June–15 Nov). CONCESSIONAL LETTER POST. W **191**. P 14.

CL687	CL **201**	1l. blue-green	60	30
CL688		8l. rose-red (15.11)	18·00	15

(Des E. Pizzi. Recess (500l.), photo (others))

1947–54. POSTAGE DUE. W **191** (sideways). P 13½ × 14 (500l.) or 14 (others).

D690	D **201**	1l. red-orange (11.6.47)	30	10
D691		2l. dull blue-green (11.6.47)	30	10
D692		3l. carmine (1.7.47)	60	85
D693		4l. sepia (1.7.47)	65	50
D694		5l. bluish violet (11.6.47)	95	10
D695		6l. ultramarine (1.7.47)	2·20	80
D696		8l. bright mauve (1.7.47)	7·25	1·10
D697		10l. blue (1.7.47)	1·50	10
D698		12l. bistre-brown (1.7.47)	3·00	1·00
D699		20l. bright purple (1.7.47)	50·00	10
D700		25l. brown-red (1.2.54)	65·00	25
D701		50l. turquoise-green (1.7.47)	39·00	10
D702		100l. dull orange (1.2.52)	10·00	10

D703		500l. lake and deep blue (31.5.52)	10·00	10
		a. Perf 11½ × 13½	21·00	50
		b. Perf 13½	21·00	50
D690/703 Set of 14 (cheapest)			£170	4·75

See also Nos. D924/35.

LIRE 6–

(**201**)

1947 (1 July). AIR. No. 672 surch with T **201**.

687	**198**	6l.on 3l.20, red-orange	15	10
		a. Pair, one without surch	£1600	

202 Wireless Mast   **203** Ship's Aerial   PE **204** Minerva

(Des R. Garrasi. Photo)

1947 (1 Sept). AIR. 50th Anniv of Radio. As T **202**/3. W **191** (sideways). P 14.

688	**202**	6l. bluish violet	20	15
689	**203**	10l. deep carmine-red	20	15
690		20l. reddish orange	85	55
691	**202**	25l. turquoise-blue	90	65
692	**203**	35l. deep dull blue	1·30	75
693		50l. bright purple	2·50	1·40
688/693 Set of 6			5·50	3·25

Designs:—20l., 50l. Heinkel He 70 Blitz wireless-equipped airplane.

(Des R. Garrasi. Photo)

1947 (15 Nov). PNEUMATIC POST. W **191** (sideways). P 14.

PE694	PE **204**	3l. bright purple	4·00	5·50
PE695		5l. greenish blue	10	15

See also Nos. PE961 /2.

204 Douglas DC-2 Airplane over Rome

205 St. Catherine Giving her Cloak to a Beggar

206 St. Catherine Carrying the Cross

ITALY 1948

(Des R. Garrasi. Eng T. Méle (697). Photo (694/6), recess (697))

1948 (16 Feb–10 Sept). *AIR.* W **191**. P 14.
694	**204**	100l. deep bluish green	3·50	20
695		300l. magenta	55	55
696		500l. dull ultramarine	1·60	1·10
697		1000l. purple-brown (10.9)	3·00	2·10
694/697	*Set of* 4		8·00	3·50

See also Nos. 911/14 and 1297.

(Des C. Mezzana. Photo)

1948 (1 Mar). *600th Anniv of Birth of St. Catherine of Siena.* P 14.

(a) POSTAGE. As T **205**. W **191** (sideways).
698		3l. slate-blue and yellow-green	15	30
699		5l. blue and violet	15	40
700		10l. violet and purple-brown	3·25	2·75
701		30l. olive-grey and bistre	20·00	10·00

Designs show St. Catherine:—5l. Carrying the Cross; 10l. Extending her arms to Italy; 30l. Dictating a Dialogue to a Disciple.

(b) AIR. As T **206**. W **191**.
702		100l. violet and red-brown	55·00	32·00
703		200l. blue and bistre	30·00	13·00
698/703	*Set of* 6		£100	55·00

Design:—200l. St Catherine extending her arms to Italy.

207 "Proclamation of New Constitution"
208 Rising at Palermo 

(Des R. Garrasi. Photo)

1948 (12 Apr). *Proclamation of New Constitution.* W **191**. P 14.
704	**207**	10l. reddish violet	95	70
705		30l. blue	2·40	1·50

(Des C. Mezzana. Photo)

1948 (3 May). *Centenary of 1848 Revolution. As T* **208** *(inscr "PRIMO CENTENARIO DEL RISORGIMENTO ITALIANO").* W **191**. P 14.
706		3l. sepia	35	35
707		4l. bright purple	35	35
708		5l. blue	85	50
709		6l. green	55	60
710		8l. chocolate	55	45
711		10l. rose-red	1·20	25
712		12l. grey-green	3·00	1·70
713		15l. black	7·25	85
714		20l. carmine	21·00	5·25
715		30l. blue	6·25	50
716		50l. violet	75·00	2·75
717		100l. slate-blue	£140	11·50
706/717	*Set of* 12		£400	23·00

Designs: 4l. Rising at Padua; 5l. Concession of Statute, Turin; 6l. Storming Porta Tosa, Milan, 8l. Proclamation of Venetian Republic; 10l. Defence of Vicenza; 12l. Hero of Curtatone; 15l. Hero of Goito; 20l. Austrian retreat from Bologna; 30l. Fighting at Brescia; 50l. Garibaldi; 100l. Goffredo Mameli (poet and patriot) on death bed, July 1849.

E **209** Rising at Naples

(Des C. Mezzana. Photo)

1948 (18 Sept). *EXPRESS LETTER. Centenary of 1848 Revolution.* W **191**. P 14.
E718	E **209**	35l. violet	85·00	11·00

209 Alpinist and Bassano Bridge
210 Gaetano Donizetti 

(Des E. Pizzi. Photo)

1948 (1 Oct). *Rebuilding of Bassano Bridge.* W **191**. P 14.
718	**209**	15l. deep blue-green	1·10	1·10

(Des E. Pizzi. Photo)

1948 (23 Oct). *Death Centenary of Gaetano Donizetti (composer).* W **191**. P 14.
719	**210**	15l. sepia	80	2·10

211 Exhibition Grounds
212 

(Des P. Caccia Dominioni. Photo)

1949 (12 Apr). *27th Milan Fair.* W **191**. P 14.
720	**211**	20l. sepia	7·00	2·50

(Des G. Cisari. Photo)

1949 (12 Apr). *Twenty-fifth Biennial Art Exhibition, Venice. T* **212** *and similar designs.* W **191** (sideways). P 14.
721		5l. brown-red and flesh	65	20
722		15l. green and cream	3·50	95
723		20l. red-brown and buff	9·00	1·40
724		50l. blue and lemon	40·00	1·20
721/724	*Set of* 4		48·00	3·50

Designs:—15l. Clock bell-ringers, St. Mark's Column and Campanile; 20l. Emblem of Venice and *Bucentaur* (state galley); 50l. Winged lion on St. Mark's Column.

213 Globes and Forms of Transport
214 Vascello Castle 

(Des E. Pizzi. Photo)

1949 (2 May). *75th Anniv of Universal Postal Union.* W **191**. P 14.
725	**213**	50l. ultramarine	50·00	4·25

(Des C. Mezzana. Photo)

1949 (18 May). *Centenary of Roman Republic.* W **191**. P 14.
726	**214**	100l. brown	£160	60·00

ITALY 1949

215 Worker and Ship
216 Statue of Mazzini 

(Des L. Lazzarini and Scaramucci. Photo)
1949 (30 May). *European Recovery Plan.* W **191** (sideways). P 14.
727 **215** 5l. blue-green . . . . 7·00 2·50
728 15l. violet . . . . 19·00 10·00
729 20l. brown . . . . 55·00 11·00

(Des E. Pizzi. Photo)
1949 (1 June). *Honouring Giuseppe Mazzini (founder of "Young Italy").* W **191**. P 14.
730 **216** 20l. grey-black . . . . 7·00 1·50

217 V. Alfieri
218 San Giusto Cathedral 

(Des E. Pizzi. Photo)
1949 (4 June). *Birth Bicentenary of Vittorio Alfieri (poet).* W **191**. P 14.
731 **217** 20l. sepia . . . . 6·00 1·50

1949 (8 June). *First Trieste Free Election.* W **191**. Photo. P 14.
732 **218** 20l. lake . . . . 10·50 10·00

219 Staff of Aesculapius and Globe
CL 220 Italia 
220 A. Palladio and Vicenza Basilica 

(Des V. Retrosi. Photo)
1949 (13 June). *Second World Health Congress, Rome.* W **191**. P 14.
733 **219** 20l. violet . . . . 30·00 6·25

(Des R. Garrasi. Photo)
1949 (2 July)–**52**. CONCESSIONAL LETTER POST. W **191**. P 14.
CL734 **CL 220** 15l. violet . . . . 50·00 15
CL735 20l. reddish violet (1.2.52) . . 1·50 10
See also Nos. CL916/22.

(Des E. Pizzi. Photo)
1949 (4 Aug). *400th Anniv of Completion of Palladio's Basilica at Vicenza.* W **191**. P 14.
734 **220** 20l. violet . . . . 9·00 4·50

221 Lorenzo de Medici
222 Galleon and Exhibition Buildings 

(Des E. Pizzi. Photo)
1949 (4 Aug). *500th Anniv of Birth of Lorenzo de Medici "The Magnificent".* W **191**. P 14.
735 **221** 20l. violet-blue . . . . 6·75 1·50

(Des L. Lazzarini. Photo)
1949 (16 Aug). *13th Levant Fair. Bari.* W **191**. P 14.
736 **222** 20l. scarlet . . . . 3·50 1·70

223 Voltaic Pile
224 Count Alessandro Volta 

(Des F. Frigerio. Eng O. Mele (20l.) and M. Canfarini (50l.). Recess)
1949 (14 Sept). *150th Anniv of Volta's Discovery of the Electric Cell.* W **191**. P 14.
737 **223** 20l. carmine-red . . . . 6·50 1·50
738 **224** 50l. blue . . . . 75·00 23·00

225 Holy Trinity Bridge, Florence
226 Caius Valerius Catullus 
227 Domenico Cimarosa 

(Des E. Pizzi. Photo)
1949 (19 Sept). *Rebuilding of Holy Trinity Bridge, Florence.* W **191**. P 14.
739 **225** 20l. green . . . . 10·00 1·30

(Des C. Tomiolo. Photo)
1949 (19 Sept). *Bimillenary of Death of Catullus (poet).* W **191**. P 14.
740 **226** 20l. blue . . . . 10·00 1·30

(Des E. Pizzi. Photo)
1949 (28 Dec). *Bicentenary of Birth of Domenico Cimarosa (composer).* W **191**. P 14.
741 **227** 20l. slate-violet . . . . 8·50 1·00

ITALY 1950

228 Entrance to Exhibition
229 Car and Flags 

(Des L. Lazzarini. Photo)
1950 (12 Apr). *28th Milan Fair.* W **191**. P 14.
742 228 20l. brown . . . . 3·00   1·00

(Des L. Lazzarini. Photo)
1950 (29 Apr). *32nd International Automobile Exhibition, Turin.* W **191**. P 14.
743 229 20l. grey-violet . . . . 9·00   1·00

230 Statue of Perseus
231 St. Peter's Basilica 
232 Gaudenzio Ferrari 

(Des R. Pierbattista and R. De Sanctis. Photo)
1950 (22 May). *Fifth General Conference of United Nations Educational, Scientific and Cultural Organization, Florence.* T **230** and similar horiz design. W **191**. P 14.
744   20l. grey-green . . . . 7·00   1·20
745   55l. blue . . . . 45·00   4·75
Design:—20l. Pitti Palace, Florence.

(Des C. Mezzana. Photo)
1950 (29 May). *Holy Year.* W **191**. P 14.
746 231 20l. violet . . . . 6·00   45
747   55l. blue . . . . 45·00   1·70

(Des E. Contini. Photo)
1950 (1 July). *Honouring Gaudenzio Ferrari (painter).* W **191**. P 14.
748 232 20l. grey-green . . . . 10·00   1·50

233 Town Hall, Florence, Statue of Columbus and Wireless Mast
234 L. Muratori 
235 Guido D'Arezzo 

(Des L. Giani. Photo)
1950 (15 July). *International Radio Conference.* W **191**. P 14.
749 233 20l. violet . . . . 10·50   5·50
750   55l. blue . . . . £160   95·00

(Des E. Pizzi. Photo)
1950 (22 July). *Death Bicentenary of Ludovico Muratori (historian).* W **191**. P 14.
751 234 20l. brown . . . . 4·75   1·20

(Des R. Pierbattista and R. De Sanctis. Photo)
1950 (29 July). *900th Death Anniv of Guido D'Arezzo (musician).* W **191**. P 14.
752 235 20l. green . . . . 15·00   2·10

236
237 Marzotto and Rossi 

(Des R. De Sanctis. Photo)
1950 (21 Aug). *14th Levant Fair, Bari.* W **191**. P 14.
753 236 20l. red-brown . . . . 6·75   1·10

(Des L. Lazzarini. Photo)
1950 (11 Sept). *Wool Industry Pioneers.* W **191**. P 14.
754 237 20l. deep blue . . . . 1·80   65

238 Tobacco Plant and Factory
239 Seal of Academy 
240 A. Righi 

(Des C. Mezzana. Photo)
1950 (11 Sept). *European Tobacco Conference, Rome.* T **238** and similar types inscr "CONFERENZA EUROPEA DEL TOBACCO 'ROMA' MCML". W **191**. P 14.
755   5l. green and magenta . . . . . 3·00   1·20
756   20l. green and brown . . . . . . 5·00   50
757   55l. brown and bright blue . . . 46·00   12·50
Designs:—20l. Plant; 55l. Girl and plant.

1950 (16 Sept). *Bicentenary of Academy of Fine Arts. Venice Photo.* W **191**. P 14.
758 239 20l. red-brown and brown . . . 2·20   1·10

(Des R. Pierbattista and D. Mancini. Photo)
1950 (16 Sept). *Birth Centenary of Augusto Righi (physicist).* W **191**. P 14.
759 240 20l. black and buff . . . . . . 2·30   1·10

33

ITALY 1950

241 Blacksmith
242 First Tuscan Stamp 
245 Westland W.81 Helicopter over Fair
246 Fair Buildings
247 Allegory

(Des C. Mezzana. Recess (100l., 200l.), photo (others).)

1950 (20 Oct). *Designs as T 241 showing provincial occupations.* W **191** (sideways). P 14½ (100, 200l.) or 14 (others).

760	50c. violet-blue	20	30
761	1l. blackish violet	20	10
762	2l. black-brown	20	15
763	5l. black	40	15
764	6l. purple-brown	20	15
765	10l. green	3·25	15
766	12l. turquoise-green	20	15
767	15l. slate-blue	1·40	15
768	20l. bright violet	10·50	15
769	25l. orange-brown	3·50	15
770	30l. bright purple	1·30	15
771	35l. carmine	8·50	30
772	40l. brown	75	15
773	50l. violet	10·00	15
774	55l. blue	50	30
775	60l. scarlet	4·00	30
776	65l. blue-green	1·10	30
777	100l. chestnut	65·00	30
778	200l. yellow-brown	13·00	30
760/778	Set of 19	£120	4·25

Designs:—1l. Motor mechanic; 2l. Stonemason; 5l. Potter; 6l. Girls embroidering and water-carrying; 10l. Weaver; 12l. Fisherman at tiller; 15l. Boat builder; 20l. Fisherman trawling; 25l. Girl packing oranges; 30l. Girl carrying grapes; 35l. Gathering olives; 40l. Carter and wagon; 50l. Shepherd; 55l. Ploughman; 60l. Ox-cart; 65l. Girl harvester; 100l. Women handling maize; 200l. Woodcutter.

See also Nos. 880/6.

(Des R. Rossi. Photo)

1951 (27 Mar). *Centenary of First Tuscan Stamp.* W **191**. P 14.

779	**242**	20l. scarlet and bright purple	1·40	85
780		55l. blue and ultramarine	27·00	25·00

243 Car and Flags
244 Peace Hall, Rome 

(Des L. Lazzarini. Photo)

1951 (2 Apr). *33rd International Automobile Exhibition, Turin.* W **191**. P 14.

781	**243**	20l. blue-green	9·00	1·40

(Des R. Pierbattista. Photo)

1951 (11 Apr). *Consecration of Hall of Peace, Rome.* W **191**. P 14.

782	**244**	20l. bright violet	6·25	1·60

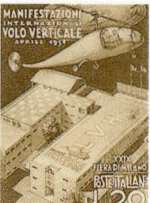

(Des C. Mezzana (20l.), E. Pizzi and R. Mura (55l.). Photo)

1951 (12 Apr). *29th Milan Fair.* W **191**. P 14.

783	**245**	20l. yellow-brown	7·50	1·00
784	**246**	55l. blue	60·00	31·00

(Des L. Lazzarini. Photo)

1951 (25 Apr). *Tenth International Textile Art and Fashion Exhibition, Turin.* W **191**. P 14.

785	**247**	20l. violet	20·00	2·10

248 Columbus Disembarking
249 Gymnastic Symbols 

(Des R. Pierbattista and R. De Sanctis. Photo)

1951 (5 May). *Fifth Birth Centenary of Columbus.* W **191**. P 14.

786	**248**	20l. turquoise-green	15·00	1·80

(Des E. Pizzi and R. Pierbattista. Photo)

1951 (18 May). *International Gymnastic Festival, Florence.* W **191**. P 14.

787	**249**	5l. scarlet and sepia	33·00	£120
788		10l. scarlet and turquoise-green	33·00	£120
789		15l. scarlet and ultramarine	33·00	£120

250 Montecassino Abbey Restored
251 Perugino 

(Des R. Mura and D. Mancini. Photo)

1951 (18 June). *Restoration of Montecassino Abbey. T* **250** *and similar horiz type inscr* "MONTECASSINO". W **191**. P 14.

790		20l. violet	4·50	1·40
791		55l. blue	55·00	28·00

Design:—55l. Abbey in ruins, 1944.

(Des E. Pizzi. Photo)

1951 (23 July). *500th Birth Anniv of Perugino (painter).* W **191**. P 14.

792	**251**	20l. red-brown and sepia	2·50	1·70

ITALY 1951

252 Modern Art
253 Cyclist and Globe 
257 "Industry and Commerce"
258 Census in Ancient Rome

(Des E. Bonini (20l.), B. Buffoni (55l.). Photo)

1951 (23 July). *Triennial Art Exhibition, Milan.* T **252** *and similar horiz design.* W **191**. P 14.
793   20l. black and grey-green . . . . 7·75   1·30
794   55l. pink and blue . . . . 35·00   26·00
Design:—55l. Jug and symbols.

(Des G. Savini and D. Mancini. Photo)

1951 (31 Oct). *Third Industrial and Commercial Census.* W **191**. P 14.
801   **257**   10l. green . . . . 1·00   80

(Des R. Pierbattista and D. Mancini. Photo)

1951 (31 Oct). *Ninth National Census.* W **191**. P 14.
802   **258**   25l. violet-black . . . . 2·50   2·10

(Des R. Pierbattista. Photo)

1951 (23 Aug). *World Cycling Championship.* W **191**. P 14.
795   **253**   25l. grey-black . . . . 6·00   2·10

254 Galleon and Hemispheres
255 "Jorio's Daughter" 
259 G. Verdi and Roncole Church
260 Mountain Forest

(Des R. De Sanctis. Photo)

1951 (8 Sept). *Fifteenth Levant Fair, Bari.* W **191**. P 14.
796   **254**   25l. bright blue . . . . 5·50   1·40

(Des E. Pizzi. Recess)

1951 (19 Nov). *50th Death Anniv of Verdi (composer).* T **259** *and similar designs inscr* "1901 1951". W **191**. P 14.
803   10l. blue-green and purple . . . . . . 1·40   2·10
804   25l. sepia and reddish brown . . . . . 6·00   2·00
805   60l. deep blue and blue-green . . . . 25·00   8·00
Designs: *Horiz*—10l. Verdi, Theatre Royal and Cathedral, Parma; 60l. Verdi, La Scala Opera House and Cathedral, Milan.

(Des R. Pierbattista and R. De Sanctis. Photo)

1951 (15 Sept). *Birth Centenary of Francesco Paolo Michetti (painter).* W **191**. P 14.
797   **255**   25l. deep brown . . . . 6·00   2·10

(10l. des F. M. Caruso and D. Mancini. 25l. des G. Savini, D. Mancini and Confalonieri. Photo)

1951 (21 Nov). *Forestry Festival.* T **260** *and similar design inscr* "FESTA DEGLI ALBERI". W **191**. P 14.
806   10l. deep green and olive-green . . . . 1·50   2·10
807   25l. deep green . . . . 3·75   1·30
Design: *Horiz*—25l. Tree and wooded hills.

256 Type **1** of Sardinia and Arms of Cagliari

(Des G. Savini. Photo)

1951 (9 Oct). *Sardinian Postage Stamp Centenary.* T **256** *and similar horiz designs showing stamps and different coats of arms.* W **191**. P 14.
798   10l. black and sepia . . . . 1·40   1·60
799   25l. blue-green and carmine . . . . . 2·00   1·30
800   60l. orange-red and blue . . . . . . 10·00   10·50
Designs:—25l., 20c. stamp and arms of Genoa; 60l., 40c. stamp and arms of Turin.

261 V. Bellini
262 Royal Palace, Caserta 

(Des E. Pizzi. Photo)

1952 (28 Jan). *150th Birth Anniv of Bellini (composer).* W **191**. P 14.
808   **261**   25l. grey-black . . . . 2·50   60

35

ITALY 1952

(Des R. De Sanctis. Photo)
1952 (1 Feb). *200th Anniv of Construction of Caserta Palace by Vanvitelli.* W **191**. P 14.
809 **262** 25l. bistre and deep green .... 2·75   80

263
264 Motor-boat Pavilion

(Des R. De Sanctis. Photo)
1952 (22 Mar). *First International Sports Stamps Exhibition, Rome.* W **191**. P 14.
810 **263** 25l. brown and grey-black 85   60

(Des C. Mezzana. Recess)
1952 (12 Apr). *30th Milan Fair.* W **191**. P 14.
811 **264** 60l. bright blue .... 25·00   7·00

265 Leonardo da Vinci
266 "The Virgin of the Rocks"

(Des E. Pizzi. Photo (25l.) Recess (others))
1952. *Fifth Birth Centenary of Leonardo da Vinci.*
    (a) W **191**. P 14.
812 **265** 25l. orange (15 Apr) 40   20
    (b) No wmk (60l.). W **191** (80l.). P 13.
813 **266** 60l. ultramarine (31 Dec) .... 3·75 3·75
814 **265** 80l. brown-red (31 Dec) .... 18·00   30

267 Campaniles and First Stamps
268 Hand, Torch and Globe

(Des C. Mezzana. Photo)
1952 (29 May). *Centenary of First Stamps of Modena and Parma.* W **191**. P 14.
815 **267** 25l. black and red-brown ..... 1·00   65
816   60l. indigo and blue ..... 6·50 6·50

(Des A. Ortona. Photo)
1952 (7 June). *Overseas Fair, Naples.* W **191**. P 14.
817 **268** 25l. dull ultramarine ..... 1·30   65

269 Lion of St. Mark
270 Emblem of Fair
271 San Giusto Cathedral and Flag

(Des B. Buffoni. Photo)
1952 (14 June). *Twenty-sixth Biennial Art Exhibition, Venice.* W **191**. P 14.
818 **269** 25l. black and cream ..... 1·40   60

(Des R. Pierbattista and R. De Sanctis. Photo)
1952 (19 June). *Thirtieth Padua Fair.* W **191**. P 14.
819 **270** 25l. red and slate-blue ..... 2·00   65

(Des C. Mezzana. Photo)
1952 (28 June). *Fourth Trieste Fair.* W **191**. P 14.
820 **271** 25l. green, red and brown ..... 1·50   65

272 Caravel and Bari Fair
273 Girolamo Savonarola

(Des R. De Sanctis. Photo)
1952 (6 Sept). *Sixteenth Levant Fair, Bari.* W **191**. P 14.
821 **272** 25l. deep green ..... 1·20   65

(Des E. Pizzi. Photo)
1952 (20 Sept). *Fifth Birth Centenary of Savonarola (reformer).* W **191**. P 14.
822 **273** 25l. bluish violet ..... 2·75   65

274 Savoia Marchetti S.M.95C Airliner over Colosseum
275 Alpine Climbing Equipment

(Des C. Mezzana. Photo)
1952 (29 Sept). *First Civil Aeronautics Law Conference, Rome.* W **191**. P 14.
823 **274** 60l. blue and ultramarine ..... 12·00 11·50

ITALY 1952

(Des R. Damiani. Photo)
1952 (4 Oct). *Alpine Troops National Exhibition.* W **191** (sideways). P 14.
824 **275** 25l. grey-black 45   40

276 Army, Navy and Air Force Symbols
277 Sailor, Soldier and Airman 

(Des O. Grassetti (10l., 25l.), R. Glaudus (60l.). Photo)
1952 (3 Nov). *Armed Forces Day.* T **276/7** and similar horiz design inscr "GIORNATA DELLE FORZE ARMATE". W **191** (sideways on 25l. and 60l.). P 14.
825 10l. myrtle-green 25   10
826 25l. black-brown and grey-brown . . . 60   10
827 60l. black and pale blue . . . 5·00 1·80
Design: As T **277**—60l. Airplane, motor torpedo boat and tank.

278 Cardinal Massaia and Map
279 V. Gemito 

(Des C. Mezzana. Eng M. Colombati. Recess)
1952 (21 Nov). *Centenary of Mission to Ethiopia.* W **191**. P 14.
828 **278** 25l. brown and orange-brown . . . 85 1·20

(Des E. Pizzi. Photo)
1952 (6 Dec). *Birth Centenary of Gemito (sculptor).* W **191**. P 14.
829 **279** 25l. red-brown 40   50

280 A. Mancini
281 

(Des E. Pizzi. Photo)
1952 (6 Dec). *Birth Centenary of Mancini (painter).* W **191**. P 14.
830 **280** 25l. blackish green 40   45

(Des R. De Sanctis. Photo)
1952 (31 Dec). *Centenary of Martyrdom of Belfiore.* W **191**. P 14.
831 **281** 25l. deep blue and black . . . . 1·40 45

282 Antonello da Messina
283 Cars Racing 

(T **282/3** des V. Grassi. Photo)
1953 (21 Feb). *Antonello Exhibition, Messina.* W **191** (sideways). P 14.
832 **282** 25l. brown-red . . . . 1·20 70

1953 (24 Apr). *Twentieth "Mille Miglia" Car Race.* W **191**. P 14.
833 **283** 25l. bright violet 45   60

284 Bee and Medals
285 Arcangelo Corelli 
286 Coin of Syracuse 

(T **284/5** des V. Grassi. Photo)
1953 (30 Apr). *Creation of Orders of Meritorious Labour.* W **191** (sideways). P 14.
834 **284** 25l. bright violet 45   45

1953 (30 May). *Birth Tercentenary of Corelli (composer).* W **191** (sideways). P 14.
835 **285** 25l. brown 50   85

(Des V. Grassi. Eng M. Colombati (Nos. 845/6)
1953 (6 June)–**54**. W **191**.
    (a) Size 17 × 21 mm. Photo. P 14.
836 **286** 5l. slate 10   10
837   10l. orange-red 30   10
838   12l. deep bluish green . . . 10   10
839   13l. bright reddish purple (1.2.54) 10   10
840   20l. sepia . . . . 3·00 10
841   25l. reddish violet . . . . 2·25 10
842   35l. carmine-red 70   55
843   60l. blue . . . . 15·00 3·50
844   80l. orange-brown . . . . 65·00 55
    (b) Size 22½ × 28 mm. Recess. P 13½.
845 **286** 100l. brown (28.12.54) . . . £140   30
         a. Perf 13½ × 12 . . . . £15000 £2500
846   200l. deep blue (28.12.54) . . 4·75   60
836/846 Set of 11 . . . . £200 5·50
200l. printed by typography on unwatermarked paper, perf 11½, is a forgery.
See also Nos. 887/906, 1008/9 and 1202/19b.

37

ITALY 1953

287 St. Clare of Assisi
CP 288 

(Des E. Pizzi. Photo)
1953 (27 June). *Seventh Death Centenary of St. Clare.* W **191** (sideways). P 14.
847 **287** 25l. brown-red and deep brown 40 55

CONCESSIONAL PARCEL POST. These are for the payment of a special tax for the authorised delivery of parcels privately instead of through the post office. Prices in the first column are for unused complete pairs, in the second column for the left half used and in the third column for the right half used.

1953 (1 July). CONCESSIONAL PARCEL POST. *Photo.* W **191**. P 13½.

			Un pair	Used left	Used right
CP848	CP **288**	40l. brown-orange	4·75	30	2·75
CP849		50l. blue	£130	4·50	80·00
CP850		75l. sepia	£120	2·10	12·00
CP851		110l. lilac-rose	75·00	2·40	12·00

See Nos. CP918/34.

288 Mountains and Reservoirs
289 "Agriculture" 

(Des N. Barbi. Photo)
1953 (11 July). *Mountains Festival.* W **191** (sideways). P 14.
848 **288** 25l. blue-green 1·00 40

(Des V. Retrosi. Photo)
1953 (26 July). *International Agricultural Exhibition, Rome.* W **191**. P 14.
849 **289** 25l. sepia 70 30
850 60l. blue 2·75 1·30

290 Rainbow over Atlantic
291 L. Signorelli 

(Des V. Grassi. Photo)
1953 (6 Aug). *Fourth Anniv of Atlantic Pact.* W **191**. P 14.
851 **290** 25l. dp turquoise & yellow-orange 3·50 20
852 60l. violet-blue and mauve 7·00 2·00

(Des V. Grassi. Photo)
1953 (13 Aug). *Fifth Birth Centenary of Signorelli (painter).* W **191** (sideways). P 14.
853 **291** 25l. grey-green and sepia 45 20

292 A. Bassi
293 Capri 

(Des E. Pizzi. Photo)
1953 (5 Sept). *Sixth International Microbiological Congress, Rome.* W **191**. P 14.
854 **292** 25l. sepia and greenish black 40 20

1953 (31 Dec). *Tourist Series. Views as T* **293**. *Photo.* W **191** (sideways on vert designs). P 14.
855 10l. red-brown and sepia 35 10
856 12l. black and greenish blue 35 10
857 20l. reddish brown and brown-orange 75 10
858 deep blue-green and pale blue 75 10
859 35l. brown and buff 1·20 20
860 60l. deep blue and turquoise-green 1·60 40
855/860 Set of 6 5·00 1·10
Designs:—*Vert*—10l. Siena; 25l. Cortina d'Ampezzo. *Horiz*—12l. Rapallo; 20l. Gardone; 35l. Taormina.

294 Lateran Palace
295 Television Aerial and Screen 

(Des E. Pizzi. Photo)
1954 (11 Feb). *25th Anniv of Lateran Treaty.* W **191** (sideways). P 14.
861 **294** 25l. sepia and bistre-brown 45 20
862 60l. blue and bright blue 1·80 1·40

(Des L. Lazzarini. Photo)
1954 (25 Feb). *Introduction of Television in Italy.* W **191** (sideways). P 14.
863 **295** 25l. bluish violet 1·30 20
864 60l. deep turquoise-green 3·75 1·80

296 "Everyone Must Contribute to the Public Expense"

ITALY 1954

(Des V. Grassi. Photo)
1954 (20 Mar). *"Encouragement to Tax-payers".* W **191**. P. 14.
865 **296** 25l. reddish violet   1·00   10

297 Vertical Flight Trophy
298 Golden Eagle and Campanile

(Des A. Mistruzzi. Photo)
1954 (24 Apr). *First Experimental Helicopter Mail Flight, Milan-Turin.* W **191** (sideways). P. 14.
866 **297** 25l. blackish green   30   35

(Des V. Grassi. Photo)
1954 (1 June). *Tenth Anniv of Resistance Movement.* W **191** (sideways). P. 14.
867 **298** 25l. grey-black and orange-brown   25   20

P 298
299 A. Catalani

1954 (14 June). PARCEL POST. Recess. W **191**. P 13½.
                      Un   Used   Used
                     pair   pair   half
P868 P **298** 1000l. ultramarine   £2500 £2000 6·00
See also Nos. P928/9.

(Des G. Savini. Photo)
1954 (19 June). *Birth Centenary of Catalani (composer).* W **191**. P 14.
868 **299** 25l. deep grey-green   25   30

300 Marco Polo, Lion of St. Mark, Venice, and Dragon Pillar, Peking
301 Cyclist, Car and Landscape

(Des V. Grassi and L. Gasbarra after R. de Catarini. Eng M. Colombati. Recess.)
1954 (8 July). *Seventh Birth Centenary of Marco Polo.* W **191**.
869 **300**   25l. brown P 14 × 13½   30   20
870   60l. slate-green P 13   2·75   2·50
           a. Perf 13 × 12   11·00   5·50

(Des R. Franzoni. Photo)
1954 (6 Sept). *60th Anniv of Italian Touring Club.* W **191**. P. 14.
871 **301** 25l. deep green and scarlet   30   30

302 "St. Michael the Archangel" (after Guido Reni)
303 "Pinocchio"
304 Amerigo Vespucci

(Des R. De Sanctis. Photo)
1954 (9 Oct). *International Police Congress, Rome.* W **191** (sideways). P 14.
872 **302** 25l. carmine-red   15   20
873   60l. bright blue   80   1·20

(Des G. Savini after K. Mussino. Photo)
1954 (26 Oct). *64th Death Anniv of Carlo Lorenzini (Collodi) (writer).* W **191** (sideways). P. 14.
874 **303** 25l. scarlet   35   30

(Des F. M. Caruso. Eng M. Colombati. Recess)
1954 (31 Dec). *Fifth Birth Centenary of Amerigo Vespucci (explorer).* W **191** (sideways). P 13½.
875 **304** 25l. deep reddish purple   25   25
876   60l. indigo   1·20   1·50

305 "Madonna" (Perugino)
306 Silvio Pellico

(Des R. Pierbattista and D. Mancini. Photo)
1954 (31 Dec). *Termination of Marian Year.* T **305** *and similar vert design.* W **191** (sideways). P. 14.
877   25l. brown and buff   20   20
878   60l. black and cream   85   1·30
Design:—60l. Madonna's head (Michelangelo).

(Des F. M. Caruso. Photo)
1955 (24 Jan). *Death Centenary of Pellico (dramatist).* W **191** (sideways). P. 14.
879 **306** 25l. bright blue and violet   25   20

ITALY 1955

307 Mult. Stars

308 "The Nation Expects a Faithful Declaration of Your Income"

There are two types of this watermark. In the first the stars are in horizontal (shown) or vertical alignment, in the second they align diagonally.

1955 (1 Mar)–**66**. W **307**.

(a) As Nos. 760/76 (provincial occupations). P 14.

880	50c. violet-blue (12.55)		10	10
881	1l. blackish violet		10	10
882	2l. black-brown		10	10
883	15l. slate-blue		50	10
884	30l. bright purple (7.7.55)		60·00	10
885	50l. violet (23.5.55)		19·00	10
886	65l. blue-green (4.4.57)		32·00	35·00
880/886	Set of 7		£100	32·00

(b) As Nos. 836/46 and new values. Size 17 × 21 mm. Recess (100, 200l.), photo (others). P 13½ (100, 200l.) or 14 (others).

887	286	1l. black (27.1.58)	10	20
888		5l. slate	10	10
889		6l. yellow-brown (27.5.57)	10	10
890		10l. orange-red	10	10
891		12l. deep bluish green (20.6.55)	10	10
892		13l. bright reddish purple (7.7.55)	10	10
893		15l. violet-grey (3.5.56)	10	10
894		20l. sepia	10	10
895		25l. reddish violet	30	10
896		30l. yellow-brown (1.7.60)	15	10
897		35l. carmine-red (11.55)	10	10
898		40l. magenta (1.7.60)	60	10
899		50l. yellow-olive (27.1.58)	50	10
900		60l. blue (7.7.55)	10	10
901		70l. deep bluish green (1.7.60)	20	10
902		80l. orange-brown (14.4.55)	10	10
903		90l. red-brown (27.1.58)	20	10
904		100l. brown (22½ × 28 mm) (1.56)	15·00	10
		a. Perf 13½ × 12 (10.55)	15·00	10
905		130l. brown-red and greenish grey (17 × 21 mm) (15.3.66)	10	20
906		200l. deep blue (22½ × 28 mm) (15.6.57)	8·25	10
887/906	Set of 20		25·00	2·20

See also Nos. 1008/9 and 1202/19b.

(Des F. M. Caruso. Photo)

1955 (15 Mar). *"Encouragement to Taxpayers".* W **307**. P 14.

907	308	25l. reddish violet	1·10	10

1955–**79**. PARCEL POST. Recess (1000, 2000l.), photo (others). W **307**.

(a) Type P **201**. P 12½ × 13.

		Un pair	Used pair	Used half
P908	25c. ultramarine (10.55)	10	10	10
P909	50c. sepia (1.56)	2·40	2·40	20
P910	5l. bright purple (8.59)	10	15	10
P911	10l. violet (14.4.55)	10	15	10
P912	20l. brown-purple (3.55)	15	15	10
P913	30l. reddish purple (2.56)	10	10	10
P914	40l. slate-violet (1.8.57)	10	15	10
P915	50l. scarlet (11.55)	10	15	10
P916	60l. brt reddish violet (28.3.60)	10	15	10
P917	100l. blue (10.55)	10	15	10
P918	140l. brown-red (28.3.60)	10	15	10
P919	150l. orange-brown (1.8.57)	10	15	10
P920	200l. myrtle green (11.55)	10	15	10
P921	280l. orange-yellow (28.3.60)	10	15	10
P922	300l. claret (10.57)	10	15	10
P923	400l. olive-black (1.8.57)	20	20	10
P924	500l. deep brown (11.56)	35	30	10
P925	600l. olive-brown (28.3.60)	30	30	10
P926	700l. new blue (15.3.66)	70	55	15
P927	800l. orange (15.3.66)	1·20	85	15

(b) Type P **298**. P 13½.

P928	1000l. dull ultramarine (worn impression) (2.57)		1·90	70	15
	a. Blue (fine impression) (1979)		85	70	10
P929	2000l. carmine-red & brn (4.57)		3·00	2·50	20
P908/929	Set of 22		9·50	9·50	2·30

No. P928a appears to come from a new plate.
For 20l. and 30l. values with "I.P.S." at foot, see Nos. P1347/8.

309

310 A. Rosmini

(Des R. Ferrini. Photo)

1955 (6 June). *Fourth World Petroleum Congress.* T **309** and similar vert design inscr "IV CONGRESSO MONDIALE DEL PETROLIO". W **307**. P 14.

908		25l. deep grey-green	20	20
909		60l. brown-red	60	1·10

Design:—60l. Oil derricks and globe.

(Des R. Pierbattista and R. De Sanctis. Photo)

1955 (1 July). *Death Centenary of Rosmini (theologian).* W **307**. P 14.

910	310	25l. sepia	50	20

1955 (7 July)–**59**. AIR. W **307**. P 14.

911	204	100l. blue-green	3·00	10
912		300l. magenta (11.55)	40	30
913		500l. blue (11.55)	90	55
914		1000l. brown-purple (12.59)	1·60	1·30
911/914	Set of 4		5·25	2·00

For 100l. in smaller size, 20 × 36 mm, see No. 1297.

1955 (7 July). EXPRESS LETTER. W **307**. P 14.

E915	E **200**	50l. bright purple	23·00	15

311 Girolamo Fracastoro (physician) and Roman Arena, Verona

312 Basilica of St. Francis

(Des L. Gasbarra. Photo)

1955 (1 Sept). *International Medical Conference, Verona.* W **307**. P 14.

915	311	25l. brown and black	35	20

ITALY 1955

1955 (Sept)–**90**. *CONCESSIONAL LETTER POST.* As Nos. CL734/5 but W **307**. *Photo.* P 14.

CL916	CL **220**	20l. reddish violet	10	15
CL917		30l. blue-green (9.65)	10	15
CL918		35l. orange-brown (15.5.74)	10	15
CL919		110l. blue (20.6.77)	10	15
CL920		270l. deep magenta (21.7.84)	50	40
CL921		300l. grn & carm-rose (13.4.87)	35	55
CL922		370l. agate and pale orange (24.9.90)	35	55

(Des G. Lerario. Photo)

1955 (4 Oct). *200th Anniv of Elevation of Basilica of St. Francis of Assisi to Papal Chapel.* W **307**. P 14.

916	**312**	25l. black and cream	20	20

313 Scholar and Drawing-board

314 "The Harvester"

(Des G. Savini. Photo)

1955 (15 Oct). *Centenary of "Montani" Institute, Fermo.* W **307**. P 14.

917	**313**	25l. deep bluish green	20	30

1955 (Oct)–**81**. *CONCESSIONAL PARCEL POST.* Type CP **288**. W **307**. Recess (500, 600, 900l.), photo (others). P 13½ (500, 600, 900l.) or 12½ × 13½ (others).

			Un pair	Used left	Used right
CP918		40l. brown-orange (5.56)	45	10	40
CP919		50l. blue (11.55)	50	10	40
CP920		60l. violet (13.1.58)	4·25	2·10	6·00
CP921		70l. green (15.3.66)	16·00	2·80	12·00
CP922		75l. sepia (10.55)	£250	7·50	55·00
CP923		80l. dp purple-brown (28.3.60)	10	10	10
CP924		90l. lilac (13.1.58)	20	10	10
CP925		110l. lilac-rose (10.55)	£250	4·25	33·00
CP926		110l. golden yellow (28.3.60)	10	10	10
CP927		120l. blue-green (13.1.58)	10	10	10
CP928		140l. slate-black (28.3.60)	15	10	10
CP929		150l. bright rose (16.12.68)	10	10	10
CP930		180l. vermilion (15.3.66)	25	10	10
CP931		240l. slate (15.3.66)	30	10	10
CP932		500l. orange-brown (26.7.76)	70	10	15
CP933		600l. blue-green (1979)	70	10	15
CP934		900l. ultramarine (16.11.81)	65	10	15
CP918/934	*Set of 17*		£475	16·00	95·00

(Des L. Gasbarra. Photo)

1955 (3 Nov). *50th Anniv of International Agricultural Institute.* W **307**. P 14.

918	**314**	25l. brown and rose-red	15	20

315 F.A.O. Building, Rome

(Des R. Pierbattista. Photo)

1955 (3 Nov). *Tenth Anniv of Food and Agriculture Organization.* W **307**. P 14.

919	**315**	60l. reddish violet and black	60	60

316 G. Matteotti

317 B. Grassi

318 "St. Stephen giving Alms to the Poor"

(Des R. Pierbattista and R. De Sanctis. Photo)

1955 (10 Nov). *70th Birth Anniv of Giacomo Matteotti (politician).* W **307**. P 14.

920	**316**	25l. brown-red	55	20

(Des R. Mura. Photo)

1955 (19 Nov). *Thirtieth Death Anniv of Grassi (biologist).* W **307**. P 14.

921	**317**	25l. bronze-green	20	20

(Des R. de Sanctis (after Fra Angelico). Photo)

1955 (26 Nov). *Fifth Death Centenary of Fra Angelico (painter).* T **318** and similar design inscr "BEATO ANGELICO". W **307**. P 14.

922		10l. black and cream	10	30
923		25l. blue and cream	15	30

Design: *Horiz*—25l. "St Lawrence giving goods of the Church to the poor".

1955–**92**. *POSTAGE DUE.* W **307**. Recess (500, 1500l.), photo (others).

*(a) With imprint "*IST. POL. STATO-OFF. CARTE VALORI*".* P 14.

D924	D **201**	5l. bluish violet (12.55)	10	10
D925		8l. bright mauve (5.56)	£150	£160
D926		10l. blue (2.57)	10	10
D927		20l. bright purple (1.56)	10	10
D928		25l. brown-red (3.56)	10	10
D929		30l. slate-purple (27.4.61)	20	10
D930		40l. sepia (15.3.66)	10	10
D931		50l. turquoise-green (2.57)	25	10
D932		100l. dull orange (4.57)	15	10

*(b) With imprint "*I.P.Z.S. - OFF. CARTE VALORI*".* P 14.

D933	D **201**	50l. turquoise-green (1992)	10	10
D934		100l. dull orange (1992)	10	10

(c) No imprint. P 14 × 13½.

D935	D **201**	500l. carmine-lake & dp blue (12.61)	2·30	10

*(d) With imprint "*I.P.Z.S. ROMA*".* P 14.

D936	D **201**	500l. reddish purple & dp bl (1992)	45	10
D937		900l. bright magenta, black & dp turquoise-green (6.7.84)	55	40
D938		1500l. reddish orange and deep brown (20.2.91)	1·30	45

ITALY 1955

319 G. Pascoli  **320** G. Mazzini

(Des G. Savini. Photo)
1955 (31 Dec). *Birth Centenary of Pascoli (poet)*. W **307**. P 14.
924 **319** 25l. black 15 20

(Des F. M. Caruso. Photo)
1955 (31 Dec). AIR. *150th Anniv of Birth of Mazzini (founder of "Young Italy")*. W **307**. P 14.
925 **320** 100l. deep bluish green . . . . . 1·40 85

321 "Italia" Ski-jump

(Des C. Mancioli. Photo)
1956 (26 Jan). *Seventh Winter Olympic Games, Cortina d Ampezzo*. T **321** and similar horiz designs inscr "CORTINA 1956". W **307**. P 14.
926   10l. deep turquoise-green and orange . . 10 20
927   12l. black and yellow 10 20
928   25l. slate-purple and red-orange 10 20
929   60l. blue and yellow-orange . . . . . 95 1·50
926/929 *Set of 4* . . . . 1·10 1·90
Designs:—12l. Snow Stadium; 25l. Ice Stadium; 60l. Skating Arena, Misurina.

1956

(322)

1956 (24 Feb). AIR. *Visit of Italian President to U.S.A. and Canada*. As No. 678 but colour changed. W **307**. Surch with T **322**, in blue.
930 **198** 120l. on 50l. deep magenta . . . . 65 1·60

323 Coach and Train  **324**

(Des A. Frailich. Photo)
1956 (19 May). *50th Anniv of Simplon Tunnel*. W **307**. P 14.
931 **323** 25l. deep bluish green . . . . . . 3·50 55

(Des L. Gasbarra. Photo)
1956 (2 June). *Tenth Anniv of Republic*. W **307**. P 14.
932 **324** 10l. grey and blue-grey 15 20
933   25l. carmine and rose-red 20 20

934   60l. light blue and blue . . . . . . 2·10 1·80
935   80l. orange and brown . . . . . . 3·25 20
932/935 *Set of 4* . . . . 5·25 2·20

325 Count Avogadro  **326**

(Des G. Savini. Photo)
1956 (8 Sept). *Death Centenary of Avogadro (physicist)*. W **307**. P 14.
936 **325** 25l. violet-black 15 20

(Des D. Gonzague. Photo)
1956 (15 Sept). *Europa*. W **307**. P 14.
937 **326** 25l. deep green and green 65 10
938   60l. deep blue and grey-blue . . . 6·00 35

327  **328** The Globe

(Des C. Mancioli. Photo)
1956 (22 Sept). *International Astronautical Congress, Rome*. W **307**. P 14.
939 **327** 25l. deep greenish blue 15 20

(Des C. Donati. Litho)
1956 (29 Dec). *First Anniv of Admission of Italy to United Nations Organization*. No wmk. P 14.
940 **328** 25l. scarlet & turq-green/*pale pink* . . 15 20
941   60l. turq-green & scarlet/*pale green* . 20 20
In the above design an image of the globe is superimposed on a similar image slightly out of alignment, to provide a three-dimensional effect when viewed through the appropriately coloured spectacles.

329 Savings Bank, Books and Certificates  **330** Ovid

42

ITALY 1956

(Des R. Pierbattista. Photo)
1956 (31 Dec). *80th Anniv of Post Office Savings Bank.* W **307**. P 14.
942　**329**　25l. grey-blue and slate-blue　　10　　20

(Des B. Bramanti. Photo)
1957 (10 June). *Bimillenary of Birth of Ovid (poet).* W **307**. P 14.
943　**330**　25l. black and olive　　10　　20

331 St. George (after Donatello)
332 Antonio Canova
333 Traffic Lights at Crossroads

(Des E. Pizzi. Eng M. Colombati. Recess)
1957 (24 June)—**67**. W **307**. P 13.
944　**331**　500l. deep green　　1·60　　10
　　　　　　a. Perf 14 × 13½ (1967)　1·50　　10
945　　　　1000l. carmine　　5·00　　55
　　　　　　a. Perf 14 × 13½ (1967)　1·90　　15
Printings of No. 944 from 14.3.69, of No. 944a from 1970 and of No 945a from 9.11.74 were on fluorescent paper.

(Des and eng M. Colombati (25l.), M. Canfarini (60l.) and V. Nicastro (80l.). Recess)
1957 (15 July). *Birth Bicentenary of Antonio Canova (sculptor).* T **332** *and similar designs.* W **307**. P 14.
946　　25l. brown　　　　　　　10　　20
947　　60l. deep slate　　　　　10　　40
948　　80l. deep blue　　　　　10　　20
Designs: *Vert*—60l. Hercules and Lica. *Horiz*—80l. Pauline Borghese (bust).

(Des R. Mura. Photo)
1957 (7 Aug). *Road Safety Campaign.* W **307**. P 14.
949　**333**　25l. red, black and deep bluish green　　15　　10

334 "Europa" Flags
335 Giosué Carducci
336 Filippino Lippi (after self-portrait)

(Des C. Mancioli. Litho)
1957 (16 Sept). *Europa. Flags in national colours; background (25l.) or frame (60l.) colours given below.* W **307**. P 14 (25l.) or 13½ × 13 (60l.).
950　**334**　25l. blue　　　　20　　10
951　　　　60l. bright blue　　1·70　　35

1957 (Sept)—**62**. *AIR.* W **307**. P 14.
952　**199**　5l. deep green (5.62)　　10　　10
953　**198**　50l. violet　　　　　　　10　　10

(Des and eng M. Colombati. Recess)
1957 (14 Oct). *50th Death Anniv of Carducci (poet).* W **307**. P 14.
954　**335**　25l. sepia　　15　　20

(Des and eng V. Nicastro. Recess)
1957 (25 Nov). *500th Birth Anniv of Filippino Lippi (painter).* W **307**. P 14.
955　**336**　25l. brown　　10　　20

337 Cicero (bust)
338 Garibaldi (after M. Lorusso)

(Des R. Pierbattista. Photo)
1957 (30 Nov). *Death Bimillenary of Cicero (statesman).* W **307**. P 14.
956　**337**　25l. brown-red　　10　　20

(Des and eng M. Canfarini (15l.). Des C. Mancioli. Eng M. Colombati (110l.). Recess)
1957 (14 Dec). *150th Birth Anniv of Garibaldi.* T **338** *and similar designs.* W **307**. P 14 × 13½ (15l.) or 13½ × 14 (110l.).
957　　15l. deep grey-green　　10　　20
958　　110l. deep lilac　　　　15　　20
Design: *Horiz*—110l. Statue of Garibaldi on horseback (after Romanelli).

339 St. Domenico Savio and Youths
340 St. Francis of Paola

(Des G. Savini. Photo)
1957 (14 Dec). *Death Centenary of St. Domenico Savio.* W **307**. P 14.
959　**339**　15l. black and bright reddish violet　　10　　20

(Des C. Mancioli. Eng V. Nicastro. Recess)
1957 (21 Dec). *450th Death Anniv of St. Francis of Paola.* W **307**. P 14.
960　**340**　25l. black　　10　　20

E **341** Etruscan Horses
341 Dams, Peasant and Map of Sardinia

43

ITALY 1958

(Des L. Gasbarra. Photo)
1958 (13 Jan)–**66**. *EXPRESS LETTER*. W **307**. *Size 37 × 21 mm.* P 14.
| E961 | E **341** | 75l. reddish purple | 10 | 10 |
| E962 | | 150l. deep bluish green (15.3.66) | 20 | 10 |

See Nos. E1220/2.

1958 (31 Jan)–**66**. *PNEUMATIC POST*. W **307**. P 14.
| PE961 | PE **204** | 10l. scarlet | 10 | 30 |
| PE962 | | 20l. blue (15.3.66) | 10 | 30 |

(Des C. Mancioli and A. Santini. Eng M. Colombati. Recess)
1958 (1 Feb). *Inauguration of Flumendosa-Mulargia Irrigation Scheme, Sardinia*. W **307**. P 14.
| 961 | **341** | 25l. deep turquoise-green | 10 | 20 |

342 Statue of the Holy Virgin and Lourdes Basilica

343 "The Constitution"

(Des R. Mura. Eng V. Nicastro. Recess)
1958 (16 Apr). *Centenary of the Apparition of the Virgin Mary at Lourdes*. W **307**. P 14.
| 962 | **342** | 15l. claret | 10 | 15 |
| 963 | | 60l. deep blue | 10 | 20 |

(Des T. Marangoni. Photo)
1958 (9 May). *Tenth Anniv of Constitution*. T **343** *and similar designs*. W **307**. P $13\frac{1}{2}$ × 14.
964		25l. blue-green and yellow-brown	10	10
965		60l. sepia and cobalt	10	10
966		110l. sepia and olive-brown	10	10

Designs: *Vert*—60l. Oak tree with new growth. *Horiz*—110l. Montecitorio Palace, Rome.

344 Exhibition Emblem and Ancient Roman Road

345 Rodolfo's Attic (*La Bohme*)

(Des C. Mancioli. Photo)
1958 (12 June). *Brussels International Exhibition*. W **307**. P 14.
| 967 | **344** | 60l. yellow and pale blue | 10 | 20 |

(Des C. Parravicini. Eng M. Canfarini. Recess)
1958 (10 July). *Birth Centenary of Puccini (operatic composer)*. P 14.
| 968 | **345** | 25l. deep blue | 10 | 20 |

346 The Prologue (*Pagliacci*)

347 "Ave Maria" (after Segantini)

348 "Fattori in his studio" (self-portrait)

(Des T. Marangoni. Photo)
1958 (10 July). *Birth Centenary of Leoncavallo (operatic composer)*. W **307**. P 14.
| 969 | **346** | 25l. rose-red and indigo | 10 | 20 |

(Des and eng. E. V. de Cresci. Recess; background photo)
1958 (7 Aug). *Birth Centenary of Giovanni Segantini (painter)*. W **307**. P 14.
| 970 | **347** | 110l. deep grey-green/cream | 20 | 20 |

(Des and eng V. Nicastro. Recess)
1958 (7 Aug). *50th Death Anniv of Giovanni Fattori (painter)*. W **307**. P 13 × 14.
| 971 | **348** | 110l. brown | 20 | 20 |

349 Federal Palace, Brasilia, and Arch of Titus, Rome

(Des C. Mancioli. Photo)
1958 (23 Aug). *Visit of President Gronchi to Brazil*. W **307**. P 14.
| 972 | **349** | 175l. deep bluish green | 40 | 70 |

349a "Europa"

350 Naples $\frac{1}{2}$ grano stamp of 1858

351 "Winged Horse" (sculpture in Sorrento Cathedral)

(Des A. van der Vossen. Photo)
1958 (13 Sept). *Europa*. W **307**. P 14.
| 973 | **349a** | 25l. cobalt and orange-red | 10 | 10 |
| 974 | | 60l. orange-red and cobalt | 20 | 20 |

(Eng V. Nicastro (25l.), M. Colombati (60l.). Recess)
1958 (4 Oct). *Centenary of First Naples Postage Stamps*. T **350** *and similar vert design*. W **307**. P 14 × $13\frac{1}{2}$.
| 975 | | 25l. deep Venetian red | 10 | 10 |
| 976 | | 60l. red-brown and sepia | 10 | 20 |

Design:—60l. Naples 1 grano stamp of 1858.

44

ITALY 1958

1958 (9 Oct). *Visit of Shah of Iran. Photo.* W **307**. P 14.
977 **351** 25l. sepia and pale lavender . . . 10 20
978 60l. deep violet-blue and pale blue . . . 25 50
This issue had been prepared for release on 9 Oct but the visit was postponed owing to the death of the Pope. They went generally on sale on 27 Nov but certain offices had released them in error on 9 Oct.

352 E. Torricelli
353 "Triumphs of Julius Caesar" (after fresco by Mantegna) 
354 Eleonora Duse 

(Des G. Savini. Eng V. Nicastro. Recess)

1958 (20 Oct). *350th Birth Anniv of Evangelista Torricelli (physicist).* W **307**. P 14.
979 **352** 25l. claret . . . 35 45

(Des and eng A. Quieti (15l.); des G. Savini, eng F. Pagani (25l.), M. Colombati (60l.). Recess)

1958 (3 Nov). *40th Anniv of Victory in World War I.* T **353** and similar designs. W **307**. P 14.
980 15l. green . . . 10 10
981 25l. slate . . . 10 10
982 60l. claret . . . 10 25
Designs: *Horiz*—25l. Arms of Trieste, Rome and Trento. *Vert*—60l. Memorial bell of Rovereto.

(Eng M. Colombati, after photograph. Recess)

1958 (11 Dec). *Birth Centenary of Eleonora Duse (actress).* P 14.
983 **354** 25l. deep bright blue . . . 10 20

355 "Drama"
356 Sicily 5 gr stamp of 1859 

(Des E. Carboni. Photo)

1958 (29 Dec). *Tenth Anniv of "Premio Italia" (international contest for radio and television plays).* T **355** and similar vert design inscr "X ANNUALE PREMIO ITALIA". W **307**. P 14.
984 25l. black, blue and scarlet . . . 10 20
985 60l. black and blue . . . 10 20
Design:—60l. "Music" (radio mast and grand piano).

(Eng V. Nicastro. Recess)

1959 (2 Jan). *Centenary of First Sicilian Postage Stamps.* T **356** and similar vert design. P 14 × 13½.
986 25l. deep turquoise-blue . . . 10 10
987 60l. red-orange . . . 10 20
Design:—25l. Sicily 2gr. stamp of 1859.

357 Capitol, Quirinal Square Obelisk and Dome of St. Peter's
358 N.A.T.O. Emblem and Map 

1959 (11 Feb). *30th Anniv of Lateran Treaty. Photo.* W **307**. P 14.
988 **357** 25l. blue . . . 10 10

(Des L. Gasbarra. Photo)

1959 (4 Apr). *Tenth Anniv of North Atlantic Treaty Organization.* W **307**. P 14.
989 **358** 25l. blue and yellow . . . 10 20
990 60l. blue and green . . . 10 20

359 Arms of Paris and Rome
360 Olive branch growing from shattered tree 

(Des R. Mura. Photo)

1959 (9 Apr). *Rome-Paris Friendship.* W **307**. P 14.
991 **359** 15l. red, brown-red and blue . . . 10 10
992 25l. red, brown-red and blue . . . 10 10
On the 25l. stamp the whole of the background is blue.

(Des L. Gasbarra. Eng S. Vana. Recess)

1959 (13 Apr). *International War Veterans Association Convention, Rome.* P 14.
993 **360** 25l. bronze-green . . . 10 10

361 Lord Byron Monument
362 C. Prampolini 
363 Quirinal Square Obelisk, Rome 

(Eng M. Colombati and V. Nicastro. Recess)

1959 (21 Apr). *Unveiling of Lord Byron Monument, Rome.* P 14.
994 **361** 15l. deep grey-green . . . 10 20

(Des and eng V. Nicastro. Recess)

1959 (27 Apr). *Birth Centenary of Camillo Prampolini (politician).* P 14.
995 **362** 15l. carmine . . . 1·60 2·25

45

ITALY 1959

(Des C. Mancioli (15l., 25l.) or photographs (others). Photo)

1959 (23 June). *Olympic Games Propaganda. Roman Monuments and Ruins.* T **363** *and designs inscr* "ROMA MCMLX". W **307**. P 14.

996	15l. sepia and bright orange	10	10
997	25l. sepia and chalky blue	10	10
998	35l. sepia and buff	10	20
999	60l. sepia and mauve	10	20
1000	110l. sepia and yellow	15	10
996/1000	Set of 5	50	65

Designs: *Vert*—25l. Tower of City Hall, Quirinal Hill. *Horiz*—35l. Baths of Caracalla; 60l. Arch of Constantine (Colosseum); 110l. Basilica of Maxentius.

364 Victor Emmanuel II, Garibaldi, Cavour and Mazzini

365 Workers' Monument and I.L.O. Building, Geneva

(15l. des L. Gasbarra. Eng M. Colombati (15l., 25l.), E. Donnini (35l.), S. Vana (60l.), A. Quieti (110l.). Recess; red cross, photo (25l.))

1959 (27 June). *Centenary of Second War of Independence.* T **364** *and designs inscr* "GUERRA DELL'INDIPENDENZA 1859". P 14.

1001	15l. black	10	10
1002	25l. red and brown	10	10
1003	35l. deep violet	10	10
1004	60l. ultramarine	10	20
1005	110l. carmine-lake	10	20
1001/1005	Set of 5	45	65

Designs: *Vert*—25l. Italian camp after the Battle of Magenta (after painting by Fattori); 110l. Battle of Magenta (after painting by Induno). *Horiz*—35l. Battle of San Fermo (after painting by Trezzini); 60l. Battle of Palestro.

No. 1002 is also a Red Cross commemorative.

(Des and eng E. Vangelli. Recess)

1959 (20 July). *40th Anniv of the International Labour Organization.* P 14 × 13.

1006	**365**	25l. violet	10	10
1007		60l. brown	10	20

1959 (8 Aug). *As Nos. 904 and 906, but redrawn. Size 17 × 21 mm and coin and inscriptions on plain background.* Recess. W **307**. P 14.

1008	**286**	100l. brown	55	10
1009		200l. deep blue	55	10

366 Romagna 8b. stamp of 1859

366a "Europa"

367

(Des D. Mancini. Photo)

1959 (1 Sept). *Centenary of Romagna Postage Stamps.* T **366** *and a similar vert design.* W **307**. P 14.

1010	25l. brown and black	10	10
1011	60l. dull green and black	10	10

Design:—60l. Romagna 20b. stamp of 1859.

1959 (19 Sept). *Europa.* Photo. Wove or laid paper. W **307**. P 14.

1012	**366a**	25l. olive-green	25	10
1013		60l. grey-blue	25	10

(Des R. Mura. Photo)

1959 (20 Dec). *Stamp Day.* W **307**. P 14.

1014	**367**	15l. carmine-red, black and grey	10	10

368 "The Fire of Borgo" (after Raphael)

369 Garibaldi's Message to Sicilians

(Des and eng V. Nicastro. Recess)

1960 (7 Apr). *World Refugee Year.* W **307**. P 14.

1015	**368**	25l. claret	10	10
1016		60l. deep slate-purple	10	20

(Des G. Savini. Photo (15l.). Des and eng E. Vangelli (25l.), E. Donnini (60l.). Recess)

1960 (5 May). *Centenary of Garibaldi's Expedition to Sicily.* T **369** *and similar designs inscr* "1860 SPEDIZIONE DEI MILLE 1960". W **307** (15l.); no wmk (others). P 14 (15l.), 13 × 14 (25l.) or 14 × 13 (60l.).

1017	15l. sepia	10	10
1018	25l. claret	10	10
1019	60l. ultramarine	10	25

Designs: *Vert*—25l. Garibaldi meeting King Victor Emmanuel II near Naples (after Matania). *Horiz*—60l. Embarkation of volunteers at Quarto, near Genoa (after T. van Elven).

370 "The Discus-Thrower" (after Miron)

371 V. Bottego (after E. Ximenes)

(Des T. Marangoni (10l., 25l., 60l., 150l.). Photo (incl 5l.). Eng A. Quieti (15l.), M. Canfarini (25l.), M. Colombati (110l.), T. Mele (200l.). Recess)

1960 (25 June). *Olympic Games.* T **370** *and designs inscr* "GIOCHI XVII OLIMPIADE". W **307** (5l., 10l., 25l., 60l., 150l.) or no wmk (others). P 14.

1020	5l. yellow-brown	10	10
1021	10l. grey-blue and red-orange	10	10
1022	15l. ultramarine	10	10
1023	25l. sepia and lilac	10	10
1024	35l. claret	10	10

46

ITALY 1960

1025	60l. sepia and bluish green		10	20
1026	110l. reddish purple		10	10
1027	150l. brown and blue		65	1·00
1028	200l. green		35	20
1020/1028	Set of 9		1·50	1·80

Designs:—*Vert*—5l. Games emblem; 15l. "Starting the Race" (statue); 110l. "Pugilist at rest" (after Apollonius); 200l. "The Apoxiomenos" (after Lisippos). *Horiz*—10l. Olympic Stadium, Rome; 25l. Cycling Stadium, Rome; 60l. Sports Palace, Rome; 150l. Little Sports Palace.

(Eng V. Nicastro. Recess)

1960 (23 July). *Birth Centenary of Bottego (explorer)*. P 14.
1029	371	30l. brown		10	20

371a Conference Emblem
372 Caravaggio

(Des P. Rahikainen. Photo)

1960 (19 Sept). *Europa*. W **307**. P 14.
1030	371a	30l. yellow-brown & myrtle-green		20	10
1031		70l. salmon and blue		20	10

(Des after O. Lioni. Eng M. Colombati. Recess)

1960 (25 Nov). *350th Death Anniv of Caravaggio (painter)*. P 13 × 14.
1032	372	25l. orange-brown		10	10

373 Coach and Posthorn
374 Michelangelo

(Des L. Gasbarra. Photo)

1960 (18 Dec). *Stamp Day*. W **307**. P 14.
1033	373	15l. black-brown and brown-red		10	10

(Nos. 1049/52 eng respectively E. Donnini, A. Quieti, M. Colombati, V. Nicastro. Recess. Others photo)

1961 (6 Mar). *Works of Michelangelo*. T **374** *and similar designs*. W **307**. P 13½ (500l. and 1000l.) or 14 (others).

(a) Size 17 × 20½ mm.
1034	1l. greenish black		10	20
1035	5l. brown-orange		10	10
1036	10l. orange-red		10	10
1037	15l. bright reddish purple		10	10
1038	20l. deep bluish green		10	10
1039	25l. sepia		20	10
1040	30l. plum		10	10
1041	40l. rose-red		10	10
1042	50l. olive		15	10
1043	55l. red-brown		10	10
1044	70l. blue		15	10
1045	85l. deep grey-green		15	20
1046	90l. magenta		20	20
1047	100l. slate-violet		30	10
1048	115l. ultramarine		15	20
1049	150l. brown		65	20
1050	200l. deep blue		1·10	20

(b) Size 22 × 26½ mm.
1051	500l. blue-green		3·50	25
1052	1000l. brown-red		2·40	4·00
1034/1052	Set of 19		8·75	6·00

Designs: (Frescoes on ceiling of Sistine Chapel)—1l., 5l., 10l., 115l., 150l. Ignudo (diff versions); 15l. Joel; 20l. Libyan Sibyl; 25l. Isaiah; 30l. Erythraean Sibyl; 40l. Daniel; 50l. Delphic Sibyl; 55l. Cumaean Sibyl; 70l. Zachariah; 85l. Jonah; 90l. Jeremiah; 100l. Ezekiel; 500l. Adam; 1000l. Eve.

375 Douglas DC-8 Jetliner crossing Atlantic Ocean
376 Pliny the Younger

(Des R. Mura. Photo)

1961 (6 Apr). *Visit of President Gronchi to South America*. T **375** *and similar designs*. W **307**. P 14.
1053	170l. blue		2·30	4·25
1054	185l. deep green		2·30	5·25
1055	205l. slate-violet		8·50	13·00

Designs:—As T **375** but with Argentina (170l.) and Uruguay (185l.) marked in deep colours instead of Peru (205l.) on map.

Nos. 1053/4 were placed on sale on 3 April with the 205l. value in *rose*, but were not valid for postal use until 6 April. The 205l. showed an error in the map of Peru and was withdrawn from sale on the 4th, being replaced with No. 1055. A few examples of the rose are known cancelled on cover but in most cases the Postal Administration covered the stamp with an example of No. 1055. (*Price for 205l. rose:* £1300 *un.*). Forgeries on genuine watermarked paper exist.

(Des L. Maraja. Photo)

1961 (27 May). *19th Birth Centenary of Pliny the Younger*. W **307**. P 14.
1056	376	30l. bistre-brown and buff		10	20

377 Ippolito Nievo
378 St. Paul in ship (from 15th century Bible of Borso d'Este)

(Des R. Mura. Photo)

1961 (8 June). *Death Centenary of Nievo (poet)*. W **307**. P 14.
1057	377	30l. greenish blue and red		10	20

1961 (28 June). *19th Centenary of St. Paul's Arrival in Rome*. Photo. W **307**. P 14.
1058	378	30l. multicoloured		10	30
1059		70l. multicoloured		15	55

47

ITALY 1961

379 Cannon and Gaeta Fortress
380 Doves 

(Des T. Marangoni. Photo)

1961 (12 Aug). *Centenary of Italian Unification and Independence.* T **379** and similar horiz designs inscr "1861 CENTENARIO UNITA' D'ITALIA 1961". W **307**. P 14.
1060	15l. chocolate and blue	10	20
1061	30l. red-brown and grey-blue	10	10
1062	40l. brown and light blue	15	20
1063	70l. mauve and bistre-brown	20	20
1064	115l. grey-blue and chestnut	85	20
1065	300l. scarlet, brown and green	4·25	8·00
1060/1065	Set of 6	5·00	8·00

Designs:—30l. Carignano Palace, Turin; 40l. Montecitorio Palace, Rome; 70l. Vecchio Palace, Florence; 115l. Madama Palace, Rome; 300l. Capitals, "Palace of Work", International Exhibition of Work, Turin.

(Des T. Kurpershoek. Photo)

1961 (18 Sept). *Europa.* W **307**. P 14.
1066	**380**	30l. rose	15	10
1067		70l. green	15	20

381 G. Romagnosi
382 Imprint of 50c. Provisional Postal Franked Paper of Sardinia, 1819 

(Eng M. Colombati. Recess)

1961 (28 Nov). *Birth Bicentenary of Romagnosi (philosopher).* P 13½.
1068	**381**	30l. green	10	30

(Des L. Gasbarra. Photo)

1961 (3 Dec). *Stamp Day.* W **307**. P 14.
1069	**382**	15l. magenta and black	10	10

383 "The Sweet-burning Lamp" from Pascoli's *La Poesia* (after wood-eng by P. Morbiducci)
384 Pacinotti's Dynamo (diagram) 

1962 (6 Apr). *50th Death Anniv of G. Pascoli (poet).* Photo. W **307**. P 14.
1070	**383**	30l. red	10	10
1071		70l. blue	10	30

(Des C. Mancioli. Photo)

1962 (12 June). *50th Death Anniv of Antonio Pacinotti (physicist).* W **307**. P 14.
1072	**384**	30l. black and carmine	10	10
1073		70l. black and blue	10	30

385 St. Catherine (after 15th-century woodcut)
386 Camera Lens 

(Photo (30l.). Eng M. Colombati. Recess and photo (70l.))

1962 (26 June). *Fifth Centenary of Canonization of St. Catherine of Siena.* T **385** and similar vert design. W **307** (30l.), no wmk (70l.). P 14.
1074	30l. deep slate-violet	10	10
1075	70l. black and carmine	10	45

Design:—30l. St. Catherine (after A. Vanni).

(Des E. Carboni. Photo)

1962 (25 Aug). *30th Anniv of International Cinematograph Art Fair, Venice.* T **386** and similar vert design. W **307**. P 14.
1076	30l. black and blue	10	20
1077	70l. black and orange-red	10	30

Design:—70l. Lion of St. Mark.

387 Cyclist being paced
388 Europa "Tree" 

(Des C. Mancioli. Photo)

1962 (30 Aug). *World Cycling Championships.* T **387** and similar horiz designs inscr "CAMPIONATI MONDIALI DI CICLISMO 1962". W **307**. P 14.
1078	30l. black and green	10	10
1079	70l. blue and black	10	10
1080	300l. black and orange-red	1·90	6·25

Designs:—70l. Cyclists road-racing; 300l. Cyclist on track.

(Des Lex Weyer. Photo)

1962 (17 Sept). *Europa.* W **307**. P 14.
1081	**388**	30l. carmine-red and carmine	30	10
1082		70l. ultramarine and blue	30	25

389 Balzan Medal
390 Campaign Emblem 

1962 (25 Oct). *International Balzan Foundation.* Photo. W **307**. P 14.
1083	**389**	70l. red and green	25	30

1962 (31 Oct). *Malaria Eradication.* Photo. W **307**. P 14.
1084	**390**	30l. reddish violet	10	30
1085		70l. blue	10	40

ITALY 1962

391 10c. stamp of 1862 and 30l. stamp of 1961
392 "The Pentecost" (from *Codex Syriacus*) 

1962 (2 Dec). *Stamp Day.* Photo. W **307**. P 14.
1086 **391** 15l. plum, bistre, dp violet & lt yell 10 10

1962 (8 Dec). *Ecumenical Council, Vatican City.* Photo. W **307**. P 14.
1087 **392** 30l. orange and blue/*cream* . . . 10 10
1088 70l. blue and orange/*cream* . . . 10 10

393 Statue of Cavour (statesman)
394 Pico della Mirandola 
395 D'Annunzio 

(Eng V. Nicastro. Recess)

1962 (10 Dec). *Centenary of Court of Accounts.* P 14.
1089 **393** 30l. deep bluish green 10 30

1963 (25 Feb). *500th Anniv of Birth of G. Pico della Mirandola (scholar).* Photo. W **307**. P 14.
1090 **394** 30l. slate-violet 10 10

(Des G. Barbieri, Eng A. Quieti. Recess)

1963 (12 Mar). *Centenary of Birth of Gabriele D'Annunzio (author and soldier).* P 14.
1091 **395** 30l. deep green 10 30

396 "Sowing" (bas-relief after G. and N. Pisano)
397 Monviso, Italian Alps, Ice-axe and Rope 

1963 (21 Mar). *Freedom from Hunger.* T **396** and similar vert design. Photo. W **307**. P 14.
1092 30l. sepia and rose-carmine 10 30
1093 70l. sepia and blue 15 40
Design:—70l. "Harvesting" (bas-relief after G. and N. Pisano).

1963 (30 Mar). *Italian Alpine Club Centenary.* Photo. W **307**. P 14.
1094 **397** 115l. sepia and light blue 10 30

398 "I.N.A." Lighthouse
399 Posthorn and Globe 

(Des C. Mancioli. Photo)

1963 (4 Apr). *50th Anniv of Italian National Insurance Corporation.* W **307**. P 14.
1095 **398** 30l. black and green 10 30

(Des L. Gasbarra. Photo)

1963 (7 May). *Paris Postal Conference Centenary.* W **307**. P 14.
1096 **399** 70l. blue and green 10 30

400 Three-dimensional Emblem
401 "World Tourism" 

(Des C. Mancioli. Photo)

1963 (8 June). *Centenary of Red Cross.* W **307**. P 14.
1097 **400** 30l. red and slate-purple 10 30
1098 70l. red and blue 10 40

(Des L. Gasbarra. Photo)

1963 (21 Aug). *U.N. Tourism Conference, Rome.* W **307**. P 14.
1099 **401** 15l. blue and olive 10 30
1100 70l. brown and blue 10 30

402 "Co-operation"
403 "Naples" 

(Des A. Holm. Photo)

1963 (16 Sept). *Europa.* W **307**. P 14.
1101 **402** 30l. brown and rose-red 15 10
1102 70l. green and brown 15 10

(Des C. Mancioli. Photo)

1963 (21 Sept). *Fourth Mediterranean Games. Naples.* T **403** and similar vert design. W **307**. P 14.
1103 15l. blue and yellow-brown 10 10
1104 70l. orange and deep bluish green . . . 10 30
Design:—70l. Greek "Olympic" vase.

49

ITALY 1963

404 Mascagni and Costanzi Theatre
405 G. Belli 
406 Stamp "Flower" 

1963. *150th Birth Anniv of Verdi and Birth Centenary of Mascagni (composers).* T **404** *and similar design. Photo.* W **307**. P 14.
1105   30l. brown and olive (10 Oct) 10   30
1106   30l. olive and brown (7 Dec) 10   30
Design:—No. 1105, Verdi and La Scala Opera House.

1963 (14 Nov). *Death Centenary of Giuseppe Belli (poet). Photo.* W **307**. P 14.
1107   **405**   30l. light brown 10   30

(Des L. Gasbarra. Photo)
1963 (1 Dec). *Stamp Day.* W **307**. P 14.
1108   **406**   15l. red and blue 10   10

407 Galileo Galilei
408 Nicodemus (from Michelangelo's "Pietà") 
409 Michelangelo's "Madonna of Bruges"

1964 (15 Feb). *400th Anniv of Birth of Galileo Galilei. Photo.* W **307**. P 14.
1109   **407**   30l. chestnut 15   30
1110   70l. black 15   30

1964 (18 Feb). *400th Death Anniv of Michelangelo. Photo.* W **307**. P 14.
(a) POSTAGE.
1111   **408**   30l. sepia 10   30
(b) AIR.
1112   **409**   185l. black 10   55

410 Carabinieri on Parade

1964 (5 June). *150th Anniv of the Carabinieri.* T **410** *and similar horiz design. Photo.* W **307**. P 14.
1113   30l. red and blue 10   10
1114   70l. sepia 10   30
Design:—70l. "The Charge at Pastrengo (1848)", after De Albertis.

411 G. Bodoni
412 Europa "Flower" 
413 European Buildings 

(Eng E. Vangelli, after portrait by Appiani and Rosaspina. Recess)
1964 (30 July). *150th Death Anniv (1963) of Giambattista Bodoni (type-designer and printer).* P 14 × 13½.
1115   **411**   30l. carmine 10   30

(Des G. Bétemps. Photo)
1964 (14 Sept). *Europa.* W **307**. P 14.
1116   **412**   30l. bright purple 15   10
1117   70l. turquoise-blue 15   10

(Des I. Bergomas. Photo (30l., 70l.). Eng G. Denza. Recess (500l.))
1964 (15 Oct). *Seventh European Municipalities Assembly.* W **307** (30l., 70l.), or no wmk (500l.). P 14.
1118   **413**   30l. chocolate and green 10   10
1119   70l. chocolate and blue 10   10
1120   500l. red 40   1·70

414 Victor Emmanuel Monument, Rome
415 G. da Verrazzano and Verrazano Bridge 

(Des L. Gasbarra. Photo)
1964 (14 Nov). *War Veterans' Pilgrimage to Rome.* W **307**. P 14.
1121   **414**   30l. brown 10   10
1122   70l. blue 10   10

(Des R. Mura. Photo)
1964 (21 Nov). *Opening of Verrazano Narrows Bridge, New York.* W **307**. P 14.
(a) POSTAGE.
1123   **415**   30l. black and brown 10   10
(b) AIR. Inscr "POSTA AEREA".
1124   **415**   130l. black and green 10   30
This American bridge is designated "Verrazano" with one "z".

ITALY 1964

416 Italian Stamps

417 Prisoners of War

420 Mont Blanc and Tunnel

421 A. Tassoni and Episode from his "Secchia Rapita"

1964 (6 Dec). *Stamp Day.* Photo. W **307**. P 14.
1125 **416** 15l. brown and yellow-brown 10 10

(Des G. Verdi (10l., 115l.), G. Savini (15l.), R. Ferrini (30l., 130l.), P. Renzulli (70l.). Photo)

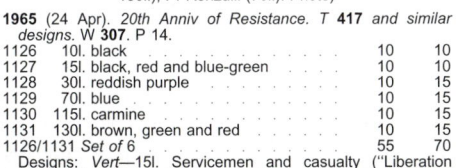

1965 (24 Apr). *20th Anniv of Resistance.* T **417** *and similar designs.* W **307**. P 14.
1126 10l. black 10 10
1127 15l. black, red and blue-green 10 10
1128 30l. reddish purple 10 15
1129 70l. blue 10 15
1130 115l. carmine 10 15
1131 130l. brown, green and red 10 15
1126/1131 *Set of 6* 55 70

Designs: *Vert*—15l. Servicemen and casualty ("Liberation Army"); 70l. Alpine soldiers ("Resistance in the Mountains"). *Horiz*—30l. Gaunt hands and arms on swastika ("Political and Racial Persecution"); 115l. Patriots with banners ("Resistance in the Towns"); 130l. Ruined building and torn flags ("Martyred Cities").

418 I.T.U. Emblem, Meucci and Marconi

419 Yachts of "Flying Dutchman" Class

(Des L. Gasbarra. Photo)

1965 (17 May). *Centenary of International Telecommunications Union.* W **307**. P 14.
1132 **418** 70l. red and deep bluish green 10 30
 a. red (inscription) omitted . . . .

(Des C. Mancioli. Photo)

1965 (31 May). *World Sailing Championships, Alassio and Naples.* T **419** *and similar designs.* W **307**. P 14.
1133 30l. black and crimson 10 10
1134 70l. black and blue 10 30
1135 500l. black and grey-blue 20 70

Designs: *Vert*—70l. "5.5 S.1" class yachts. *Horiz*—500l. "Lightning" class yachts.

(Des R. Mura. Photo)

1965 (16 July). *Opening of Mont Blanc Road Tunnel.* W **307**. P 14.
1136 **420** 30l. black 10 30

1965 (20 Sept). *400th Birth Anniv of Alessandro Tassoni (poet).* Photo. W **307**. P 14.
1137 **421** 40l. multicoloured 10 10

422 Europa "Sprig"

423 "Hell" (Codex, Vatican Library)

(Des H. Karlsson. Photo)

1965 (27 Sept). *Europa.* W **307**. P 14.
1138 **422** 40l. olive-green and yellow-orange 15 10
1139 90l. olive-green and blue 10 10

1965 (21 Oct). *700th Anniv of Dante's Birth.* T **423** *and similar designs.* Photo. W **307** (500l.) or no wmk (others). P 14 × 13 (130l.) or 13 × 14 (others).
1140 40l. multicoloured 10 10
1141 90l. multicoloured 10 10
1142 130l. multicoloured 10 20
1143 500l. bronze-green 20 70
1140/1143 *Set of 4* . . . . 45 1·00

Designs: *Vert*—90l. "Purgatory" (codex, Marciana Library, Venice); 500l. Head of Dante, bronze, Naples Museum. *Horiz*—130l. "Paradise" (codex, British Museum).

424 House and Savings-bank

425 Douglas DC-6B Airliner passing Control Tower

(Des T. Granati. Photo)

1965 (30 Oct). *Savings Day.* W **307**. P 14.
1144 **424** 40l. multicoloured 10 10

51

ITALY 1965

(Des L. Gasbarra (40l.), S. Destefani (90l.). Photo)

1965 (3 Nov). *Night Airmail Service.* T **425** *and similar horiz design.* W **307** (40l.) or no wmk (90l.). P 14.
| 1145 | 40l. red and deep Prussian blue | 10 | 10 |
| 1146 | 90l. blue, cream, red and green | 10 | 30 |

Design:—90l. Sud Aviation SE 210 Caravelle jetliner within airmail envelope "border".

426 Map of "Highway to the Sun"

427 Two-man Bobsleigh

(Des N. Vitullo. Photo)

1965 (5 Dec). *Stamp Day.* W **307**. P 13 × 14.
| 1147 | **426** | 20l. multicoloured | 10 | 10 |

(Des F. Cuzzani (40l.), C. Fontani (90l.). Photo)

1966 (24 Jan). *World Bobsleigh Championships, Cortina d'Ampezzo.* T **427** *and similar vert design.* W **307**. P 14.
| 1148 | 40l. red, greenish blue and grey | 10 | 10 |
| 1149 | 90l. reddish violet and light blue | 10 | 30 |

Design:—90l. Four-man bobsleigh.

428 Skier carrying Torch

429 B. Croce

(Des E. de Stefani (40l.), L. Gasbarra (90l.) E. Consolazione (500l.). Photo)

1966 (5 Feb). *University Winter Games, Turin.* T **428** *and similar designs.* W **307**. P 14.
1150	40l. black and red	10	10
1151	90l. violet and red	10	10
1152	500l. brown and red	20	45

Designs: Vert—90l. Ice skating; 500l. Ice hockey.

1966 (22 Feb). *Birth Centenary of Benedetto Croce (philosopher).* Photo. W **307**. P 14.
| 1153 | **429** | 40l. sepia | 10 | 15 |

430 Arms of Cities of Venezia

431 Pine, Palatine Hill, Rome

(Des L. Gasbarra. Photo)

1966 (22 Mar). *Centenary of Union of Venezia and Italy.* P 14.
| 1154 | **430** | 40l. multicoloured | 10 | 15 |

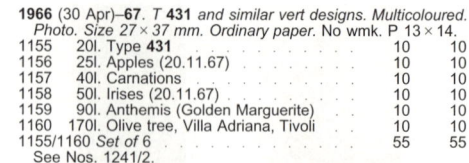

1966 (30 Apr)–**67**. T **431** *and similar vert designs. Multicoloured. Photo. Size 27 × 37 mm. Ordinary paper. No wmk.* P 13 × 14.
1155	20l. Type 431	10	10
1156	25l. Apples (20.11.67)	10	10
1157	40l. Carnations	10	10
1158	50l. Irises (20.11.67)	10	10
1159	90l. Anthemis (Golden Marguerite)	10	10
1160	170l. Olive tree, Villa Adriana, Tivoli	10	10
1155/1160	Set of 6	55	55

See Nos. 1241/2.

432 "Visit Italy"

433 Capital "I"

(Des P. Cuzzano. Photo)

1966 (28 May). *Tourist Propaganda.* W **307**. P 14.
| 1161 | **432** | 20l. multicoloured | 10 | 15 |

(Des R. Ferrini. Photo)

1966 (1 June). *20th Anniv of Republic.* P 13 × 14.
| 1162 | **433** | 40l. multicoloured | 10 | 15 |
| 1163 | | 90l. multicoloured | 10 | 20 |

434 Battle Scene

435 "Singing Angels" (from copper panel on altar of St. Antony's Basilica, Padua)

(Des F. Zanaro. Photo)

1966 (21 July). *Centenary of Battle of Bezzecca.* W **307**. P 14.
| 1164 | **434** | 90l. olive | 10 | 15 |

1966 (24 Sept). *Fifth Death Centenary of Donatello.* Photo. P 13 × 14.
| 1165 | **435** | 40l. multicoloured | 10 | 15 |

436 Europa "Ship"

437 "Madonna in Maesta" (after Giotto)

52

ITALY   1966

(Des G. & J. Bender. Photo)
1966 (26 Sept). *Europa.* W **307**. P 14.
1166   **436**   40l. reddish violet   15   15
1167   90l. new blue   15   15

1966 (20 Oct). *Giotto's 700th Birth Anniv* Photo. P 14.
1168   **437**   40l. multicoloured   10   10

438 Filzi, Battisti, Chiesa and Sauro
439 Postal Emblem

1966 (3 Nov). *50th Death Anniversaries of World War I Heroes.* Photo. W **307**. P 14.
1169   **438**   40l. deep bluish green and slate   10   10

(Des E. Consolazione. Photo)
1966 (4 Dec). *Stamp Day.* P 14 × 13½.
1170   **439**   20l. carmine, olive-green, blk & yell   10   10

440 Compass and Globe
441 Toscanini

(Des L. Gasbarra. Photo)
1967 (20 Mar). *Centenary of Italian Geographical Society.* W **307**. P 14.
1171   **440**   40l. grey-blue and black   10   10

(Des R. Ferrini. Photo)
1967 (25 Mar). *Birth Centenary of Arturo Toscanini (orchestral conductor).* W **307**. P 14.
1172   **441**   40l. buff and deep violet-blue . . .   10   10

442 Campidoglio, Rome
443 Cogwheels

1967 (25 Mar). *Tenth Anniv of the Rome Treaties.* Photo. W **307**. P 14.
1173   **442**   40l. bistre-brown and black   10   15
1174   90l. reddish purple and black . . .   10   20

(Des O. Bonnevalle. Photo)
1967 (10 Apr). *Europa.* W **307**. P 14.
1175   **443**   40l. purple and pale pink   10   10
1176   90l. ultramarine and pale cream . .   10   20

444 Brown Bear (Abruzzo Park)
445 Monteverdi

(Des C. Mancioli. Photo)
1967 (22 Apr). *Italian National Parks.* T **444** and similar designs. Multicoloured. P 13 × 14 (vert) or 14 × 13 (horiz).
1177   20l. Ibex (Gran Paradiso Park) (vert)   10   10
1178   40l. Type **444**   10   10
1179   90l. Red deer stag (Stelvio Park) .   10   10
1180   170l. Tree (Circeo Park) (*vert*) . . .   10   20
1177/1180 *Set of* 4   35   45

(Des G. Savini. Photo)
1967 (15 May). *400th Birth Anniv of Claudio Monteverdi (composer).* W **307**. P 14.
1181   **445**   40l. brown and yellow-brown . . .   10   10

446 Racing Cyclists
447 Pirandello and Stage

(Des E. Consolazione, P. Cuzzani and A. de Stefani. Photo)
1967 (20 May). *50th Tour of Italy Cycle Race.* T **446** and similar horiz designs showing cyclists. P 14 × 13.
1182   40l. multicoloured   10   10
1183   90l. multicoloured   10   10
1184   500l. multicoloured   45   80

(Des P. Cuzzani and E. Consolazione. Photo)
1967 (28 June). *Birth Centenary of Luigi Pirandello (dramatist).* P 14 × 13.
1185   **447**   40l. multicoloured   10   10

448 Stylised Mask
449 Coded Addresses

(Des S. Avenali. Photo)
1967 (30 June). *Two Worlds Festival, Spoleto.* W **307**. P 14.
1186   **448**   20l. black and green   10   10
1187   40l. black and carmine   10   10

(Des H. Ferrini. Photo)
1967–68. *Introduction of Postal Codes.* P 14.
(*a*) No wmk (1.7.67).
1188   **449**   20l. black, new blue and yellow .   10   10
1189   40l. black, carmine and yellow . .   10   10
(*b*) Fluorescent paper. W **307** (25.1.68).
1190   **449**   25l. black, light purple and yellow   10   10
1191   50l. black, green and yellow . . .   10   10

53

ITALY 1967

450 Pomilio PE Type Biplane and Postmark
451 St. Ivo's Church, Rome  
456 Sentry
457 E. Fermi (scientist) and Reactor

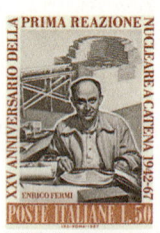

1967 (18 July). *50th Anniv of First Airmail Stamp. Photo.* W **307**. P 14.
1192   **450**   40l. black and light blue   10   10

1967 (2 Aug). *300th Death Anniv of Francesco Borromini (architect). Photo.* P 14.
1193   **451**   90l. multicoloured   10   10

(Des C. Mancioli. Photo)

1967 (9 Nov). *50th Anniv of Stand on the Piave.* P 14.
1199   **456**   50l. multicoloured   10   10

1967 (2 Dec). *25th Anniv of First Nuclear Chain Reaction. Photo.* W **307**. P 14.
1200   **457**   50l. black and chestnut   10   10

452 Giordano and Music from *Andrea Chénier*
453 "The Oath of Pontida" (from painting by Adolfo Cao)
458 Stamp and Dove
459 Scouts around Campfire 

1967 (28 Aug). *Birth Centenary of Umberto Giordano (composer). Photo.* W **307**. P 14.
1194   **452**   20l. chestnut and black   10   10

1967 (2 Sept). *800th Anniv of Oath of Pontida. Photo.* W **307**. P 14.
1195   **453**   20l. brown   10   10

(Des G. Belli. Photo)

1967 (3 Dec). *Stamp Day.* P 13 × 14.
1201   **458**   25l. multicoloured   10   10

1968–77. As Nos. 887 etc. and 1008/9 but smaller (16 × 20 mm). Fluorescent paper. Recess (100, 150, 200, 300, 400l.), recess and litho (170, 350l.), photo (others). W **307**. P 14.

1202	**286**	1l. black (6.5.68)	10	30
1203		5l. slate (20.2.68)	10	10
1204		6l. yellow-brown (6.5.68)	10	30
1205		10l. orange-red (20.2.68)	10	10
1206		15l. slate-violet (20.2.68)	10	10
1207		20l. sepia (20.2.68)	10	10
1208		25l. reddish violet (20.2.68)	10	10
1209		30l. yellow-brown (20.2.68)	10	10
1210		40l. bright purple (6.5.68)	10	10
1211		50l. yellow-olive (20.2.68)	10	10
1212		55l. bluish violet (24.5.69)	10	10
1213		60l. blue (6.5.68)	10	10
1214		70l. bluish green (6.5.68)	10	10
1215		80l. orange-brown (6.5.68)	10	10
1215a		90l. red-brown (20.2.68)	10	10
1216		100l. brown (11.3.68)	10	10
1216a		120l. dp bl & light grn (22.11.77)	10	10
1216b		125l. reddish purple and orange-brown (1.3.74)	10	20
1217		130l. brn-red & dp grey (11.3.68)	10	10
1217a		150l. deep violet (15.3.76)	10	10
1217b		170l. dp dull green & brown-ochre (22.11.77)	15	10
1218		180l. dull purple and greenish grey (15.11.71)	10	10
1218a		200l. slate-blue (6.5.68)	10	10
1219		300l. blue-green (18.7.72)	10	10
1219a		350l. orange-vermilion, crimson and orange-yellow (22.11.77)	20	20

454 I.T.Y. Emblem
455 Lions Emblem

1967 (23 Oct). *International Tourist Year Photo.* P 13½ × 14.
1196   **454**   20l. black, new blue & olive-yellow   10   10
1197   50l. black, new blue and orange   10   10

1967 (30 Oct). *50th Anniv of Lions International. Photo.* P 14 × 13½.
1198   **455**   50l. multicoloured   10   10

ITALY   1968

1219b	400l. scarlet (15.3.76)	15	10
	ba. Imperf (pair)	75·00	
1202/1219b Set of 26		2·50	2·75

40, 150, 200, 300 and 400l. on non-fluorescent paper without watermark or with printed "watermark" are forgeries. Most were printed by lithography or typography.

1968 (11 Mar)–**76**. EXPRESS LETTER. As Nos. E961/2 but slightly smaller (36 × 20½ mm). Fluorescent paper. W **307**. P 14.

E1220	E **341**	150l. deep bluish green	10	10
E1221		250l. blue & pale blue (12.8.74)	15	15
E1222		300l. deep brown & pale brown (15.4.76)	20	15

(Des C. Pontani. Photo)

1968 (23 Apr). Italian Boy Scouts. P 14.
| 1220 | **459** | 50l. multicoloured | 15 | 10 |

464 Giambattista Vico (300th Birth Anniv)

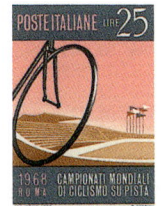

465 Cycle Wheel and Stadium

(Des and eng M. Colombati (No. 1226), V. Nicastro (No. 1227). Recess)

1968. Italian Philosophers' Birth Anniversaries. T **464** and similar horiz portrait. W **307**. P 14 × 13½ (No. 1226) or 13½ (No. 1227).
| 1226 | **464** | 50l. ultramarine (24 June) | 10 | 10 |
| 1227 | | 50l. black (5 Sept) | 10 | 20 |

Design:—No. 1227, Tommaso Campanella (400th birth anniv).

(Des R. Ferrini. Photo)

1968 (26 Aug). World Road Cycling Championships. T **465** and similar vert design. P 13 × 14.
| 1228 | | 25l. indigo, pink and brown | 15 | 10 |
| 1229 | | 90l. indigo, red and greenish blue | 15 | 20 |

Design:—90l. Cyclist and Imola Castle.

460 Europa "Key"

461 "Tending the Sick"

(Des H. Schwarzenbach. Photo)

1968 (29 Apr). Europa. W **307**. P 14.
| 1221 | **460** | 50l. grey-green and pink | 15 | 10 |
| 1222 | | 90l. yellow-brown & greenish blue | 15 | 20 |

FLUORESCENT PAPER. From No. 1223 all issues were printed on fluorescent paper unless otherwise stated. Originally paper reacted yellow under U.V. light, but from March 1973 some values come on a range of white fluorescent papers.

1968 (28 May). 400th Birth Anniv of Luigi Gonzaga (St. Aloysius). Photo. W **307**. P 13 × 14.
| 1223 | **461** | 25l. slate-violet and chestnut | 10 | 30 |

466 "St. Mark's Square, Venice" (Canaletto)

467 Rossini

1968 (30 Sept). Death Bicentenary of Canaletto (painter). Photo. P 14.
| 1230 | **466** | 50l. multicoloured | 10 | 20 |

(Des and eng E. Donnini. Recess)

1968 (25 Oct). Death Centenary of Gioacchino Rossini (composer). Photo. W **307**. P 14 × 13½.
| 1231 | **467** | 50l. carmine-red | 10 | 20 |

462 Boito and "Mephistopheles"

463 F. Baracca and "Aerial Combat" (abstract by G. Balla)

468 Mobilization

469 "Conti Correnti Postali"

(Des C. Pontani. Photo)

1968 (10 June). 50th Death Anniv of Arrigo Boito (composer and librettist). P 14.
| 1224 | **462** | 50l. multicoloured | 10 | 10 |

1968 (19 June). 50th Death Anniv of Francesco Baracca (airman of World War I). Photo. P 14.
| 1225 | **463** | 25l. multicoloured | 10 | 10 |

(Des T. Marangoni. Photo)

1968 (2 Nov). 50th Anniv of Victory in World War 1. T **468** and similar horiz designs. Multicoloured. P 14 × 13.
1232		20l. Type **468**	10	10
1233		25l. Trench warfare	10	10
1234		40l. Naval forces	10	10
1235		50l. Air Force	10	10
1236		90l. Battle of Vittorio Veneto	10	10
1237		180l. Tomb of Unknown Soldier	10	15
1232/1237 Set of 6			55	65

55

ITALY 1968

(Des G. Belli. Photo)
1968 (20 Nov). *50th Anniv of Postal Cheque Service.* P 14 × 13½.
1238   **469**   50l. red, green, black and light blue 10   10

470 Tracking Equipment and Buildings

471 "Postal Development"

1968 (25 Nov). *Space Telecommunications Centre, Fucino.* Photo. P 14.
1239   **470**   50l. multicoloured 10   10

(Des P. Renzulli. Photo)
1968 (1 Dec). *Stamp Day.* W **307**. P 14.
1240   **471**   25l. carmine-red and yellow 10   10

1968 (20 Dec). *New values as T* **431** *but smaller (26 × 35½ mm.) and on fluorescent paper. Multicoloured.* Photo. P 13 × 14.
1241   55l. Cypresses 10   10
1242   180l. Broom 10   10

472 Commemorative Medal

473 Colonnade

(Des G. Monassi. Photo)
1969 (22 Apr). *Centenary of State Audit Department.* P 14.
1243   **472**   50l. black and light pink 10   10

(Des L. Gasbarra, G. Belli and A. Ponsiglione. Photo)
1969 (28 Apr). *Europa.* P 14 × 13.
1244   **473**   50l. multicoloured 15   10
1245   90l. multicoloured 15   20

474 Machiavelli

475 I.L.O. Emblem

1969 (3 May). *500th Birth Anniv of Niccolo Machiavelli (statesman).* Photo. P 14 × 13½.
1246   **474**   50l. multicoloured 10   10

1969 (7 June). *50th Anniv of International Labour Organization.* Photo. W **307**. P 14.
1247   **475**   50l. black and emerald 10   10
1248   90l. black and red 10   10

476 Postal Emblem

477 Sondrio-Tirano Mailcoach of 1903

(Des F. Filanci. Photo)
1969 (26 June). *50th Anniv of Italian Philatelic Federation.* P 14.
1249   **476**   50l. multicoloured 10   30

(Eng T. Mele. Recess)
1969 (7 Dec). *Stamp Day.* W **307**. P 14.
1250   **477**   25l. ultramarine 10   10

478 Skiing

479 "Galatea" (detail of fresco by Raphael)

(Des R. Prünster. Photo)
1970 (6 Feb). *World Skiing Championships, Val Gardena. T* **478** *and similar vert design. Multicoloured.* W **307**. P 13 × 14.
1251   50l. Type **478** 10   20
1252   90l. Dolomites 10   10

1970 (6 Apr). *450th Death Anniv of Raphael. T* **479** *and similar horiz design. Multicoloured.* Photo. P 14 × 13.
1253   20l. Type **479** 10   10
1254   50l. "Madonna of the Goldfinch" (Raphael) 10   10

480 Symbols of Flight

481 "Flaming Sun"

(Des S. Salaroli and F. Piludi. Photo)
1970 (2 May). *50th Anniv of Rome—Tokyo Flight by A. Ferrarin.* P 14 × 13.
1255   **480**   50l. new bl, scar, brt emer & blk 10   10
1256   90l. royal bl, scar, brt emer & blk 10   10

(Des L. le Brocquy. Photo)
1970 (4 May). *Europa.* W **307**. P 14.
1257   **481**   50l. yellow and vermilion 15   10
1258   90l. orange-yellow & bluish green 15   20

56

ITALY 1970

482 Erasmo da Narni (from statue by Donatello)
483 Running 
487 "Garibaldi at Dijon" (engraving)
488 U.N. Emblem within Tree

(Des and eng V. Nicastro. Recess)

1970 (30 May). *600th Birth Anniv of Erasmo da Narni, "Il Gattamelata" (condottiere).* W **307**. P 14 × 13½.
1259　482　50l. slate-green　　　　　　10　10

1970 (15 Oct). *Centenary of Garibaldi's Participation in Franco-Prussian War.* Photo. W **307**. P 14.
1265　487　20l. grey and deep blue　　　10　10
1266　　　50l. bright purple and blue　　10　20

(Des S. Dabovich. Photo)

1970 (26 Aug). *World University Games, Turin.* T **483** and similar horiz design. Multicoloured. P 14.
1260　　20l. Type **483**　　　　　　　10　10
1261　　180l. Swimming　　　　　　　10　20

1970 (24 Oct). *25th Anniversary of United Nations.* Photo. P 13 × 14.
1267　488　25l. yellow-green, black and sepia　　　　　　　　　　　10　20
1268　　　90l. olive-yellow, black & light blue　　　　　　　　　　　10　20

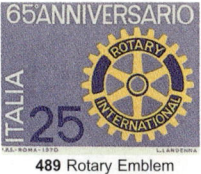

484 Dr. Montessori and Children
486 Loggia of Campanile, St. Mark's Square, Venice
489 Rotary Emblem
490 Telephone Dial and "Network" 

(Des L. Landenna. Photo)

1970 (12 Nov). *65th Anniversary of Rotary International.* W **307**. P 14.
1269　489　25l. ultramarine, yellow & violet-blue　　　　　　　　　10　10
1270　　　90l. ultramarine, yellow & violet-blue　　　　　　　　　10　20

485 Map and Cavour's Declaration

1970 (31 Aug). *Birth Centenary of Dr. Maria Montessori (educationalist).* Photo. P 14 × 13.
1262　484　50l. multicoloured　　　　　10　10

(Des S. Teglia. Photo)

1970 (24 Nov). *Completion of Telephone Trunk-dialling System.* W **307**. P 14.
1271　490　25l. bright green and scarlet　10　10
1272　　　90l. dull ultramarine and scarlet　10　10

491 Urban Complex and Tree
492 Electric Train 

1970 (19 Sept). *Centenary of Union of Rome and Papal States with Italy.* Photo. P 14.
1263　485　50l. brown, red, green and black　　　　　　　　　　　10　10

(Des E. Vangelli. Photo)

1970 (28 Nov). *Nature Conservation Year.* W **307**. P 14.
1273　491　20l. brown-red and green　　10　10
1274　　　25l. slate and bright green　　10　10

(Eng V. Nicastro. Recess)

1970 (26 Sept). *400th Death Anniv of Jacopo Tatti, "Il Sansovino" (architect).* W **307**. P 14 × 13.
1264　486　50l. chestnut　　　　　　　10　10

(Eng E. Donnini. Recess)

1970 (6 Dec). *Stamp Day.* W **307**. P 14.
1275　492　25l. black　　　　　　　　　10　20

57

ITALY 1970

493 "The Adoration" (F. Lippi)
494 S. Mercadante 

1970 (12 Dec). *Christmas.* T **493** and similar multicoloured design. Photo. P 14.

(a) POSTAGE.
1276   25l. Type **493** 10   10

(b) AIR.
1277   150l. "The Adoration of the Magi" (G. da Fabriano) (horiz—44 × 35 *mm*.) . . 10   30

(Des E. and S. Consolazione. Photo)

1970 (17 Dec). *Death Centenary of Saverio Mercadante* (composer). W **307**. P 14.
1278 **494** 25l. violet and grey 10   10

495 "Mercury" (detail of "Perseus with the Head of Medusa" by Cellini)
496 Bramante's "Little Temple", St. Peter's in Montorio, Rome 

1971 (20 Mar). *400th Death Anniv of Benvenuto Cellini (goldsmith and sculptor). Photo.* W **307**. P 14.
1279 **495** 50l. turquoise-blue 10   10

(Des and eng T. Mele. Recess and photo)
1971 (8 Apr). W **307**. P 13 × 14.
1280 **496** 50l. black and orange-brown . . . 10   10

497 Adenauer, Schuman and De Gasperi
498 Europa Chain 

(Des E. Donnini. Photo)
1971 (28 Apr). *20th Anniversary of European Coal and Steel Community.* W **307**. P 14 × 13.
1281 **497** 50l. sepia, black & turquoise-green 10   20
1282   90l. sepia, black and claret 10   10

(Des H. Haflidason. Photo)
1971 (3 May). *Europa.* W **307**. P 14.
1283 **498** 50l. red 15   10
1284   90l. bright purple 15   10

499 Mazzini
500 Canoeist in Slalom 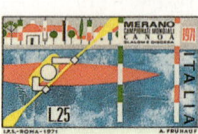

(Des A. Quieti. Photo)
1971 (12 June). *25th Anniversary of the Republic.* P 13½.
1285 **499** 50l. multicoloured 10   30
1286   90l. multicoloured 10   10

(Des A. Frühauf. Photo)
1971 (16 June). *World Canoeing Slalom and Free Descent Championships, Merano.* T **500** and similar horiz design. Multicoloured. P 14.
1287   25l. Type **500** 10   10
1288   90l. Canoeist making free descent . . 10   10

501 Three Sports
502 Alitalia Emblem 

(Des A. Perone. Photo)
1971 (26 June). *Youth Games.* T **501** and similar vert design. P 13 × 14.
1289   20l. black, bright green and ochre . . 10   10
1290   50l. black, lavender and orange . . 10   10
Design:—50l. Four other sports

(Des E. Ciocca (50l.), T. Mele (90l.), L. Landenna (150l.). Photo)
1971 (16 Sept). *25th Anniv of Alitalia State Airline.* T **502** and similar horiz designs. Multicoloured. P 14 × 13.
1291   50l. Type **502** 10   10
1292   90l. Emblem and Globe 10   10
1293   150l. Tailplane of Boeing "747" . . . 10   20

503 Grazia Deledda
504 Boy in "Savings" Barrel

ITALY　　　　　　　　　　　　　　　　　　　　　　　　　　　　　　　　　1971

(Des and eng V. Nicastro. Recess and photo)
1971 (28 Sept). *Birth Centenary of Grazia Deledda (writer).* W **307**. P 13 × 14.
1294　**503**　50l. black and light orange-brown　　　10　10

(Des HG. Pubblicita & Marketing. Photo)
1971 (27 Oct). *Postal Savings Bank Campaign.* P 13 × 14.
1295　**504**　25l. multicoloured　　　10　20
1296　　　50l. multicoloured　　　10　10

1971 (15 Nov). *AIR. As No. 911, but smaller, 20 × 36 mm, and on fluorescent paper.* W **307**. P 14.
1297　**204**　100l. blue-green　　　15　25

505 U.N.I.C.E.F. Emblem and Paper Dolls　　　**506** Liner *Tirrenia*

(Des E. Tomei (25l.), R. Ferrini (90l.) Photo)
1971 (26 Nov). *25th Anniv of United Nation's Children's Fund. T* **505** *and similar horiz design.* Multicoloured. P 14 × 13.
1301　25l. Type **505**　　　10　10
1302　90l. Children acclaiming U.N.I.C.E.F. emblem　　　10　20

(Des and eng T. Mele. Recess)
1971 (5 Dec). *Stamp Day.* W **307**. P 14.
1303　**506**　25l. slate-green　　　10　20

507 "The Nativity"　　　**508** G. Verga and Sicilian Cart

1971 (10 Dec). *Christmas. T* **507** *and similar horiz design, showing miniatures from "Matilda's Evangelarium", Nonantola Abbey, Modena.* Multicoloured. Photo. P 14 × 13.
1304　25l. Type **507**　　　10　20
1305　90l. "The Adoration of the Magi"　　　10　10

(Des P. Bellanca, A. de Stefani and T. Mele. Photo)
1972 (27 Jan). *50th Death Anniv of Giovanni Verga writer.* P 14 × 13.
1306　**508**　25l. multicoloured　　　15　10
1307　　　50l. multicoloured　　　15　10

509 G. Mazzini　　　**510** Stylized Flags

(Des and eng E. Donnini. Recess and photo)
1972 (10 Mar). *Death Centenary of Giuseppe Mazzini (statesman).* W **307**. P 13½.
1308　**509**　25l. deep bluish green and black　　　10　20
1309　　　90l. grey-black and black　　　10　10
1310　　　150l. red and black　　　10　10

(Des E. Carboni. Photo)
1972 (14 Apr). *50th International Fair, Milan. T* **510** *and similar horiz designs.* P 14 × 13.
1311　25l. green and black　　　10　20
1312　50l. orange-red and black　　　10　10
1313　90l. new blue and black　　　10　10
Designs:—50l. "Windows, stands and pavilions" (abstract); 90l. Abstract general view of Fair.

511 "Communications"　　　**512** Alpine Soldier

(Des P. Huovinen. Photo)
1972 (2 May). *Europa.* P 13 × 14.
1314　**511**　50l. multicoloured　　　15　30
1315　　　90l. multicoloured　　　15　30

(Des E. Tomei. Photo)
1972 (10 May). *Centenary of Alpine Corps. T* **512** *and similar horiz designs.* Multicoloured. P 14 × 13.
1316　25l. Type **512**　　　10　10
1317　50l. Soldier's hat　　　10　30
1318　90l. Soldier and mountains　　　10　10

513 Brenta Mountains　　　**514** Diagram of Conference Hall

(Des M. P. Gelmi (25l.), A. Quieti (50l.), D. Zuffi (180l.). Photo)
1972 (2 Sept). *Centenary of Tridentine Alpinists Society. T* **513** *and similar horiz designs.* Multicoloured. P 14 × 13.
1319　25l. Type **513**　　　10　30
1320　50l. Alpinist　　　10　10
1321　180l. Mt. Crozzon　　　10　30

(Des A. de Stefani. Photo)
1972 (21 Sept). *60th Interparliamentary Union Conference, Rome.* P 14 × 13.
1322　**514**　50l. multicoloured　　　10　10
1323　　　90l. multicoloured　　　10　10

59

ITALY 1972

515 "St. Peter Damiani"
(miniature, after G. di Paolo)

516 "The Three Graces" (Canova)

521 L. Perosi

522 Don Orione

523 Oceanic Survey

(Des E. Donnini. Photo)

1972 (30 Sept). *900th Death Anniv of St. Peter Damiani. Photo.* P 14 × 13.
1324 **515** 50l. multicoloured 10 10

(Des and eng V. Nicastro. Recess)

1972 (13 Oct). *150th Death Anniv of Antonio Canova (sculptor).* W **307**. P 13 × 14.
1325 **516** 50l. blue-green 10 10

1972 (20 Dec). *Birth Centenary of Lorenzo Perosi (composer and priest).* P 14.
1334 **521** 50l. purple-brown and yellow . . . 10 10
1335 90l. black and bright yellow-green 10 10

1972 (30 Dec). *Birth Centenary of Don Orione (child-welfare pioneer). Photo.* P 14.
1336 **522** 50l. blue and pale turquoise-blue 10 10
1337 90l. deep dull green and yellow . . 10 10

(Des E. Vangelli. Photo)

1973 (15 Feb). *Centenary of Military Marine Institute of Hydrography.* P 13 × 14.
1338 **523** 50l. multicoloured 10 10

517 Initial and First Verse (Foligno edition)

518 "Angel"

1972 (23 Nov). *500th Anniv of "The Divine Comedy". T* **517** *and similar multicoloured designs. Photo.* P 13 × 14 (90l.) or 14 × 13 (others).
1326 50l. Type **517** 10 10
1327 90l. Initial and first verse (Mantua edition) (*vert*) 10 10
1328 180l. Initial and first verse ("Jesino" edition) 10 20

1972 (6 Dec). *Christmas. T* **518** *and similar multicoloured designs. Photo.* P 14 × 13 (25l.) or 13 × 14 (others).
1329 20l. Type **518** 10 10
1330 25l. "Holy Child in Crib" (*horiz*) . . . 10 10
1331 150l. "Angel" (looking to left) . . . 10 30

524 Grand Staircase, Royal Palace, Caserta

526 Fair Theme

525 Schiavoni Shore

(Des and eng R. di Giuseppe. Recess)

1973 (1 Mar). *200th Death Anniv of Luigi Vanvitelli (architect).* P 14 × 13.
1339 **524** 25l. bronze-green 10 30

1973 (5 Mar–10 Apr). *"Save Venice" Campaign. T* **525** *and similar multicoloured designs. Photo.* P 14.
1340 20l. Type **525** 10 10
1341 25l. "The Tetrarchs" (sculpture) (*vert*) (10.4.) 10 10
1342 50l. "The Triumph of Venice" (V. Carpaccio) (10.4.) . . . 10 10
1343 90l. Bronze horses, St. Mark's Basilica (*vert*) (10.4.) 10 15
1344 300l. Piazzetta S. Marco (10.4.) . . 20 45
1340/1344 Set of 5 . . . . 55 75

519 Postal Coach

520 L. B. Alberti (from bronze by M. de Pasti)

(Des and eng E. Donnini. Recess)

1972 (10 Dec). *Stamp Day.* W **307**. P 14.
1332 **519** 25l. crimson 10 30

(Des E. Vangelli. Photo)

1972 (16 Dec). *500th Death Anniv of Leon B. Alberti (writer and savant).* P 14.
1333 **520** 50l. blue and orange-yellow . . . 10 30

ITALY 1973

Nos. 1341 and 1343 are smaller, size 20 × 37 mm.

(Des E. Vangelli. Photo)
1973 (10 Mar). *75th International Agricultural Fair, Verona.*
P 13 × 14.
1345 **526** 50l. multicoloured   10   10

527 Title-page of "Diverse Figure"
528 Formation of Fiat G-91 PAN Acrobatic Jet Aircraft 

(Des G. M. Stanzani. Photo)
1973 (15 Mar). *300th Death Anniv of Salvator Rosa (painter and poet).* P 14.
1346 **527** 25l. black and orange   10   10

1973 (Mar). PARCEL POST. As Nos. P912/13 but inscr "I.P.S.-OFF. CARTE VALORI-ROMA" at foot. Ordinary paper. Photo. W **307**. P 12½ × 13½.

			Un pair	Used pair	Used half
P1347	P **201**	20l. brown-purple	15	10	10
P1348		30l. reddish purple	15	10	10

(Des A. de Stefani (20l.), T. Mele (150l.), E. Tomei (others). Photo)
1973 (28 Mar). *50th Anniv of Italian Military Aviation.* T **528** and similar horiz designs. Multicoloured. P 14 × 13.

(a) POSTAGE.
1349 20l. Type **528**   10   10
1350 25l. Formation of Savoia Marchetti S-55X flying boats   10   10
1351 50l. Fiat G-91Y jet fighters on patrol   10   10
1352 90l. Fiat CR-32 biplanes performing aerobatics   10   30
1353 180l. Caproni Campini N-1 jet airplane   10   30

(b) AIR. Inscr "POSTA AEREA".
1354 150l. Lockheed F-104S Starfighter over Aeronautical Academy, Pozzuoli   10   30
1349/1354 Set of 6   55   1·10

529 Football and Pitch
530 A. Manzoni (after F. Hayez) 

(Des C. Tomei (25l.) and G. Vero (90l.). Photo)
1973 (19 May). *75th Anniv of Italian Football Association.* T **529** and similar horiz design. Multicoloured. P 14 × 13.
1355 25l. Type **529**   10   30
1356 90l. Players in goalmouth   40   40

(Des and eng E. Donnini. Recess and litho)
1973 (22 May). *Death Centenary of Alessandro Manzoni (writer and politician).* P 14 × 13.
1357 **530** 25l. brown and black   10   30

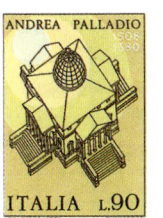

531 Palladio's "Rotunda", Vicenza
532 Spring and Cogwheels 

(Des E. Vangelli. Photo)
1973 (30 May). *Andrea Palladio Commemoration.* P 13 × 14.
1358 **531** 90l. multicoloured   10   10

(Des E. Vangelli. Photo)
1973 (20 June). *50th Anniv of Italian State Supplies Office.* P 14 × 13.
1359 **532** 50l. multicoloured   10   10

533 Europa "Posthorn"
534 "Catcher" and Baseball Field 

(Des L. F. Anisdahl. Litho)
1973 (30 June). *Europa.* P 14.
1360 **533** 50l. gold, reddish lilac and lemon   15   15
1361 90l. gold, turquoise-green & lemon   15   15

(Des T. Mele. Photo)
1973 (31 July). *1st Inter-continental Baseball Cup.* T **534** and similar horiz design. Multicoloured. P 14 × 13.
1362 25l. Type **534**   10   30
1363 90l. "Striker" and baseball field   10   10

535 Carnival Setting
536 "Argenta Episode" 

(Des E. Vangelli. Photo)
1973 (10 Aug). *Viareggio Carnival.* P 13 × 14.
1364 **535** 25l. multicoloured   10   10

1973 (25 Aug). *50th Death Anniv of Don Giovanni Minzoni (military chaplain).* Photo. P 14 × 13.
1365 **536** 50l. multicoloured   10   10

61

ITALY 1973

537 G. Salvemini
538 Farnese Palace, Caprarola 

(Des E. Vangelli. Photo)
1973 (18 Sept). *Birth Centenary of Gaetano Salvemini (political historian)*. P 14 × 13½.
1366 537 50l. multicoloured 10 10

(Des and eng R. di Giuseppe. Recess and litho)
1973 (21 Sept). *400th Death Anniv of "Vignola" (Jacopo Barozzi–architect)*. P 14 × 13.
1367 538 90l. dull purple and light yellow . . 10 10

539 "St. John the Baptist"
540 Leaning Tower of Pisa 

(Des and eng V. Nicastro. Recess and litho)
1973 (28 Sept). *400th Birth Anniv of Caravaggio*. P 14.
1368 539 25l. black and yellow 10 10

1973 (8 Oct). *Tourism. Photo*. P 14.
1369 540 50l. multicoloured 10 10

541 Botticelli
542 Immacolatella Fountain, Naples 

1973 (5 Nov). *Italian Painters (1st series)*. T **541** and similar vert designs. Photo. P 14 × 13½.
1370 50l. sepia and orange-red 10 10
1371 50l. indigo and yellow-brown 10 10
1372 50l. blackish green and emerald . . . 10 10
1373 50l. black and carmine 10 10
1374 50l. blackish brown and greenish blue . 10 10
1370/1374 Set of 5 . . . . 45 45
Painters:—No. 1371, Piranesi; 1372, Veronese; 1373, Verrocchio; 1374, Tiepolo.
See also Nos. 1392/6 and 1495/9.

(Des and eng E. Donnini. Recess and litho)
1973 (10 Nov). *Italian Fountains (1st series)*. T **542** and similar vert designs. Multicoloured. P 13 × 14.
1375 25l. Type **542** 10 20
1376 25l. Trevi Fountain, Rome 10 20
1377 25l. Pretoria Fountain, Palermo . . . 10 20
See also Nos. 1418/20, 1453/5, 1503/5, 1529/31, 1570/2 and 1618/20.

543 "Angels"
544 Map and Emblems 

(Des and eng R. di Giuseppe. Recess and litho)
1973 (27 Nov). *Christmas. Sculptures by A. di Duccio*. T **543** and similar vert designs. P 13 × 14.
1378 20l. black and yellow-green 10 10
1379 25l. black and light blue 10 10
1380 150l. black and yellow 10 30
Designs:—25l. "Virgin and Child"; 150l. "Angels" (different).

(Des S. Teglia and D. Zuffi. Photo)
1973 (29 Nov). *50th Anniv of Italian Rotary*. P 13 × 14.
1381 544 50l. deep blue, emerald and red . 10 10

545 Sud Aviation Super Caravelle 12
546 Military Medal for Valour 

(Des and eng A. Gigli. Recess)
1973 (2 Dec). *Stamp Day*. W **89**. P 14.
1382 545 25l. greenish blue 10 30

(Des R. Severi. Photo)
1973 (10 Dec). *150th Anniv of Holders of the Gold Medal for Military Valour Organisation*. P 13 × 14.
1383 546 50l. multicoloured 10 10

547 Caruso as Duke of Mantua in Verdi's *Rigoletto*
548 "Christ crowning King Roger" (Martorana Church, Palermo)

ITALY   1973

(Des and eng V. Nicastro. Recess)
1973 (15 Dec). *Birth Centenary of Enrico Caruso (operatic tenor).* P 13 × 14.
| 1384 | **547** | 50l. claret | 10 | 20 |

(Des and eng A. Quieti. Recess and litho)
1974 (14 Mar). *Norman Art in Sicily. Mosaics.* T **548** and similar vert design. P 13 × 14.
| 1385 | | 20l. deep blue and pale yellow | 10 | 20 |
| 1386 | | 50l. red and pale green | 10 | 10 |

Design:—50l. "King William offering Church to the Virgin Mary" (Monreale Cathedral).

549 Pres. L. Einaudi

550 G. Marconi in Headphones

(Des and eng V. Nicastro Recess)
1974 (23 Mar). *Birth Centenary of Luigi Einaudi (President 1948–55).* P 14 × 13.
| 1387 | **549** | 50l. green | 10 | 10 |

(Des A. de Stefani (50l.), E. Emanuele (90l.). Photo)
1974 (24 Apr). *Birth Centenary of Guglielmo Marconi (radio pioneer).* T **550** and similar horiz design. P 14 × 13.
| 1388 | | 50l. pale drab and deep bluish green | 10 | 10 |
| 1389 | | 90l. multicoloured | 10 | 30 |

Design:—90l. Marconi on world map.

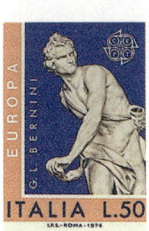

551 "David" (Bernini)

552 Guards from Lombardy-Venetia (1848), Sardinian Marines (1848) and Tebro Battalion (1849)

1974 (29 Apr). *Europa. Sculptures.* T **551** and similar vert design. Multicoloured. Photo. P 13 × 14.
| 1390 | | 50l. Type **551** | 15 | 10 |
| 1391 | | 90l. "Spirit of Victory" (Michelangelo) | 15 | 20 |

1974 (25 May). *Italian Painters (2nd series). Vert portraits as* T **541**. Photo. P 14 × 13½.
1392		50l. indigo and yellow-olive	10	15
1393		50l. sepia and light blue	10	15
1394		50l. black and rose-red	10	15
1395		50l. brown and olive-yellow	10	15
1396		50l. slate-blue and red-brown	10	15
1392/1396		Set of 5	45	70

Portraits:—No. 1392, Borromini; 1393, Carriera; 1394, Giambellino (Giovanni Bellini); 1395, Mantegna; 1396, Raphael.

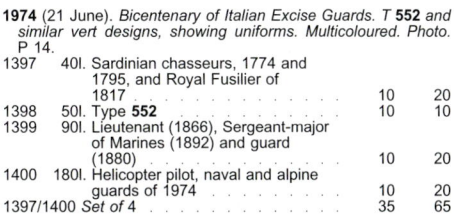

1974 (21 June). *Bicentenary of Italian Excise Guards.* T **552** and similar vert designs, showing uniforms. Multicoloured. Photo. P 14.
1397		40l. Sardinian chasseurs, 1774 and 1795, and Royal Fusilier of 1817	10	20
1398		50l. Type **552**	10	10
1399		90l. Lieutenant (1866), Sergeant-major of Marines (1892) and guard (1880)	10	20
1400		180l. Helicopter pilot, naval and alpine guards of 1974	10	20
1397/1400		Set of 4	35	65

553 Feather Headdress

(Des E. Tomei (40l.), C. Tomei (50l.). Photo)
1974 (27 June). *50th Anniv of National Bersaglieri Association.* T **553** and similar horiz design. Multicoloured. P 14 × 13½.
| 1401 | | 40l. Type **553** | 10 | 10 |
| 1402 | | 50l. Organisation emblem | 10 | 10 |

554 Running

555 Francesco Petrarch

(Des E. Consolazione and P. Guzzani. Photo)
1974 (28 June). *European Athletics Championships, Rome.* T **554** and similar design. Multicoloured. P 14 × 13½.
| 1403 | | 40l. Type **554** | 10 | 10 |
| 1404 | | 50l. Pole vaulting | 10 | 10 |

(Des and eng A. Quieti. Recess and photo)
1974 (19 July). *600th Death Anniv of Francesco Petrarch (poet and scholar).* T **555** and similar vert design. P 13½ × 14.
| 1405 | | 40l. multicoloured | 10 | 20 |
| 1406 | | 50l. dp ultram, greenish yell & brn-ochre | 10 | 20 |

Design:—50l. Petrarch at work in his study.

556 Portofino

557 Tommaseo's Statue, Sebenico

63

ITALY 1974

(Des E. Vangelli. Photo)
1974 (23 July). *Tourist Publicity (1st series).* T **556** *and similar horiz design. Multicoloured.* P 14.
1407 40l. Type **556** 10   20
1408 40l. Gradara 10   20
For similar designs see Design Index under "Tourist Publicity" and under town names on each stamp.

(Des and eng G. Verdelocco. Recess and litho)
1974 (30 July). *Death Centenary of Niccolo Tommaseo (writer).* P 13½ × 14.
1409 **557** 50l. deep green and pale pink .. 10   10

558 Giacomo Puccini
559 Cover Engraving of Ariosto's "Orlando Furioso" 

(Des A. Saporetti. Photo)
1974 (8 Aug). *50th Death Anniv of Giacomo Puccini (composer).* P 13½ × 14.
1410 **558** 40l. multicoloured 10   10

(Des and eng G Bertossi. Recess and photo)
1974 (7 Sept). *500th Birth Anniv of Ludovico Ariosto (poet).* P 14 × 13.
1411 **559** 50l. deep ultramarine and carmine 10   10

560 Commemorative Tablet (Quotation from Varrone's "Menippean Satire")
561 "The Month of October" (detail from 15th-century mural) 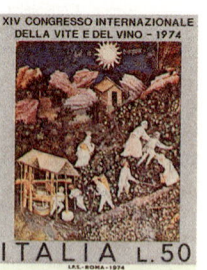

(Des and eng F. Tulli. Recess and photo)
1974 (21 Sept). *2000th Death Anniv of Marco Varrone (Varrone Reatino) (author).* P 14 × 13½.
1412 **560** 50l. lake, brownish red & pale yell 10   10

1974 (28 Sept). *14th International Wine Congress, Italy.* Photo. P 14.
1413 **561** 50l. multicoloured 10   10

562 "U.P.U." and Emblem
563 Detail from "Triumph of St. Thomas Aquinas" (F. Traini) 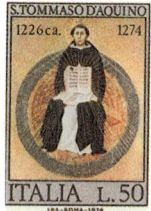

(Des A. de Stefani. Photo)
1974 (19 Oct). *Centenary of Universal Postal Union.* T **562** *and similar horiz design. Multicoloured.* P 14.
1414 50l. Type **562** 10   10
1415 90l. "U.P.U.", emblem and letters 10   10

(Des A. de Stefani. Photo)
1974 (25 Oct). *700th Death Anniv of St. Thomas Aquinas.* Photo. P 13½ × 14.
1416 **563** 50l. multicoloured 10   10

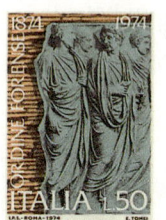

564 Detail of Bas-relief Ara Pacis
565 "The Adoration" (P. di Greccio) 

(Des E. Tomei. Photo)
1974 (26 Oct). *Centenary of Italian Order of Advocates.* P 13½ × 14.
1417 **564** 50l. black, dull blue-green & yell brn 10   10

(Des and eng E. Donnini. Recess and photo)
1974 (9 Nov). *Italian Fountains (2nd series). Vert designs similar to* T **542**. *Multicoloured.* P 13½ × 14.
1418 40l. Oceanus Fountain, Florence 10   20
1419 40l. Neptune Fountain, Bologna 10   20
1420 40l. Maggiore Fountain, Perugia 10   20

(Des and eng T. Mele. Recess and photo)
1974 (26 Nov). *Christmas.* P 14 × 13½.
1421 **565** 40l. multicoloured 10   10

ITALY 1974

566 Pulcinella

567 "God admonishing Adam" (Jacopo Della Quercia (sculptor) (1374–1438))

(Des L. Bocchini (40l.), G. Faccincani (50l.), A. Burdino (90l.) Photo)

1974 (1 Dec). *Children's Comic Characters. T* **566** *and similar vert designs. Multicoloured.* P $13\frac{1}{2} \times 14$.
1422	40l. Type **566**	10	10
1423	50l. Clowns	10	10
1424	90l. Pantaloon from Bisognosi	10	10

(Des and eng R. di Giuseppe, recess (1425). Des and eng T. Mele; recess and litho (1426))

1974 (21 Dec). *Anniversaries of Italian Artists (1st series). T* **567** *and similar vert design.* P 14.
1425	90l. deep grey-violet	10	20
1426	90l. multicoloured	10	20

Design:—No. 1426, Uffizi Gallery, Florence (Giorgio Vasari (architect and painter) (1511–1574)).

See also Nos. 1445/6, 1480/2, 1523/4, 1564/5, 1593/4, 1699/1700, 1731/2, 1774/5, 1824/5, 1885/6, 1949/50 and 1987.

568 Angel with Tablet

569 "Pitti Madonna"

1975 (25 Mar). *Holy Year. T* **568** *and similar multicoloured designs. Photo.* P 14.
1427	40l. Type **568**	10	10
1428	50l. Angel with column	10	10
1429	90l. Bridge of the Holy Angels, Rome (49 × 40 mm)	10	20
1430	150l. Angel with crown of thorns	10	10
1431	180l. Angel with cross	10	20
1427/1431	Set of 5	45	65

(Des and eng R. di Giuseppe (40l.), G. Verdelocco (50l.), A. Quieti (90l.). Recess)

1975 (18 Apr). *500th Birth Anniv of Michelangelo. T* **569** *and similar vert designs.* P $13\frac{1}{2} \times 14$.
1432	40l. deep blue-green	10	10
1433	50l. sepia	10	10
1434	90l. brown-red	10	20

Designs:—50l. Sculptured niche, Vatican Palace; 90l. Detail from fresco "Flood of the Universe" (Sistine Chapel).

570 "The Four Days of Naples" (M. Mazzacurati)

571 "The Flagellation of Christ" (Caravaggio)

(Des S. Mura. Photo)

1975 (23 Apr). *30th Anniv of Italian Resistance Movement. Monuments. T* **570** *and similar vert designs. Multicoloured.* P $13\frac{1}{2} \times 14$.
1435	70l. Type **570**	10	20
1436	100l. "Martyrs of the Ardeatine Caves" (F. Coccia)	10	10
1437	150l. "The Resistance Fighters of Cuneo" (U. Mastroianni)	10	20

1975 (29 Apr). *Europe. Paintings. T* **571** *and similar vert design. Multicoloured. Photo.* P $13\frac{1}{2} \times 14$.
1438	100l. Type **571**	20	10
1439	150l. "Appearance of the Angel to Agar and Ishmael in the Desert" (Tiepolo)	20	10

572 Globe and Emblems

573 "San Marco III" (satellite) and "Santa Rita" (marine launching pad)

(Des E. Vangelli. Photo)

1975 (15 May). *International Women's Year.* P $14 \times 13\frac{1}{2}$.
1440	**572** 70l. multicoloured	10	10

1975 (28 May). *Italian Space Project. Photo.* P 13×14.
1441	**573** 70l. multicoloured	10	10

(Des E. Vangelli. Photo)

1975 (15 June). *Tourist Publicity (2nd series). Horiz designs similar to T* **556**. *Multicoloured.* P 14.
1442	150l. Cefalu	10	20
1443	150l. Isola Bella	10	20
1444	150l. Montecatini Terme	10	20

(Eng T. Mele. Recess and photo)

1975 (18 June). *Anniversaries of Italian Artists (2nd series). Vert designs similar to T* **567**. *Multicoloured.* P 14.
1445	90l. "Flora" (Guido Reni) (1575–1642)	10	20
1446	90l. "Artist and Model" (Armando Spadini (1883–1925))	10	20

65

ITALY 1975

574 Cover Engraving from Palestrina's *Primo Libro delle Messe*

575 Boat in Harbour

(Des and eng G. Verdelocco. Recess and litho)
1975 (27 June). *450th Birth Anniv of Giovanni Pierluigi da Palestrina (composer).* P 13½ × 14.
1447 574 100l. dull claret and pale drab   10   20

(Des Rita Cavacece. Photo)
1975 (30 June). *Italian Emigration.* P 14 × 13½.
1448 575 70l. multicoloured   10   20

576 Notoriat Emblem

577 Railway Steam Locomotive Driving-wheels

(Des and eng G. Toffoletti. Recess and photo)
1975 (25 July). *Centenary of Unification of Italian Law.* P 14 × 13½.
1449 576 100l. bright magenta, yell-ochre & bl   10   10

(Des E. Vangelli. Photo)
1975 (15 Sept). *21st International Railway Congress. Bologna.* P 14 × 13½.
1450 577 70l. multicoloured   10   10

578 "D'Acquisto's Sacrifice" (Vittorio Pisani)

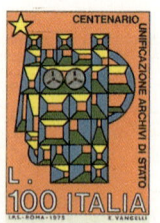

579 Symbolised Head representing Files

(Des S. Campeggi. Photo)
1975 (22 Sept). *32nd Death Anniv of Salvo d'Acquisto (carabiniere who sacrificed himself to save 22 hostages).* P 14 × 13½.
1451 578 100l. multicoloured   10   10

(Des E. Vangelli. Photo)
1975 (26 Sept). *Centenary of State Archives' Unification.* P 13½ × 14.
1452 579 100l. multicoloured   10   10

(Des and eng E. Donnini. Recess and litho)
1975 (30 Oct). *Italian Fountains (3rd series). Vert designs similar to T 542. Multicoloured.* P 13½ × 14.
1453 70l. Rosello Fountain, Sassari   10   20
1454 70l. 99 Channel Fountain, L'Aquila   10   20
1455 70l. Piazza Fountain, Milan   10   20

580 Ferruccio Busoni

581 "Annunciation to the Shepherds"

1975 (14 Nov). *Italian Composers. T 580 and similar vert designs. Photo.* P 14 × 13½.
1456 100l. chalky blue, brown-rose and lake   10   10
1457 100l. deep ultram, dull grn & deep grn   10   10
1458 100l. slate-grn, orge-brn & deep brn   10   10
1459 100l. olive-brown, red and brown lake   10   10
1460 100l. maroon, bl-grey & deep grey-grn   10   10
1461 100l. grey-black, greenish yell & yell   10   10
1456/1461 Set of 6   55   55
Designs:—Nos. 1457, Alessandro Scarlatti; 1458, Francesco Cilea; 1459, Antonio Vivaldi; 1460, Franco Alfano; 1461, Gaspare Spontini.

(Des and eng T. Mele. Recess and litho)
1975 (25 Nov). *Christmas. Alatri Cathedral carvings. T 581 and similar vert designs. Multicoloured.* P 13½ × 14.
1462 70l. Type **581**   10   20
1463 100l. "The Nativity"   10   10
1464 150l. "Annunciation to the Kings"   10   20

582 "Children on Horseback"

583 "Boccaccio" (from fresco, A. del Castagno)

(Des C. Chiocchetti (70l.), E. Tommaselli (100l.), M. Fabro (150l.). Photo)
1975 (7 Dec). *Stamp Day. Children's Stories. T 582 and similar multicoloured designs.* P 14 × 13½ (horiz) or 13½ × 14 (vert).
1465 70l. Type **582**   10   10
1466 100l. "The Magic Orchard" (vert)   10   10
1467 150l. "Church procession"   10   20

(Des and eng M. Ramassotto (100l.), G. Bertossi (150l.) Recess and litho)
1975 (22 Dec). *600th Death Anniv of Giovanni Boccaccio (writer). T 583 and similar vert design. Multicoloured.* P 13½ × 14.
1468 100l. Type **583**   10   10
1469 150l. Cover engraving from Boccaccio's "Fiammetta"   10   20

ITALY 1976

584 Entrance of State Advocate's Office

585 "Italia 1976" Emblem

1976 (30 Jan). *Centenary of State Advocate's Office.* Photo. P 13½ × 14.
1470 **584** 150l. multicoloured 10 10

(Des L. M. Boschini. Photo)

1976 (27 Mar). *"Italia 1976" International Stamp Exhibition, Milan (1st issue).* T **585** and similar vert design. P 13½ × 14.
1471 150l. bright scarlet, emerald and black 10 20
1472 180l. multicoloured 10 20
Design:—180l.. Exhibition Hall, Milan.
See also Nos. 1487/91.

(Des E. Vangelli. Photo)

1976 (21 May). *Tourist Publicity (3rd series).* Horiz designs similar to T **556**. Multicoloured. P 14.
1473 150l. Fenis Castle, Aosta 10 20
1474 150l. Forio, Ischia 10 20
1475 150l. Itria valley 10 20

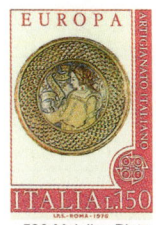

586 Majolica Plate

587 Republican Flags

1976 (22 May). *Europa, Italian Crafts.* T **586** and similar vert design. Multicoloured. Photo. P 13½ × 14.
1476 150l. Type **586** 20 10
1477 180l. Vase 20 20

(Des E. Vangelli (100l.), A. Ferrari (150l.). Photo)

1976 (1 June). *30th Anniv of Republic.* T **587** and similar vert design. Multicoloured. P 13½ × 14.
1478 100l. Type **587** 10 10
1479 150l. Statesmen 10 10

588 "Fortitude" (Giacomo Serpotta (1656–1732))

589 "The Dragon"

(Des and eng R. di Giuseppe (1480), T. Mele (1481, 1482). Recess (1480) or recess and litho)

1976 (26 July). *Anniversaries of Italian Artists (3rd series).* T **588** and similar vert designs. P 14.
1480 150l. deep violet-blue 10 10
    a. Imperf (pair) £170
1481 150l. multicoloured 10 20
1482 150l. black and rosine 10 10
Designs: No. 1481, "Woman at Table" (Umberto Boccioni (1882–1916)), 1482, "Gunner's Letter from the Front" (Filippo Tommaso Marinetti (1876–1944)).

(Des and eng R. di Giuseppe. Recess)

1976 (30 July). *450th Death Anniv of Vittore Carpaccio (painter).* T **589** and similar horiz design. P 14 × 13½.
1483 150l. brown-lake 15 20
    a. Horiz pair. Nos. 1483/4 . . . . . . 30 40
1484 150l. brown-lake 15 20
Design:—No. 1484, "St. George".
Nos. 1483/4 were issued together in horizontal *se-tenant* pairs within sheets of 40 stamps and 20 half stamp-size labels, the latter occupying the centre two vertical rows. The left and right halves of the sheet are *tête-bêche*. Each pair forms a composite design.

590 "Flora" (Titian)

591 "St. Francis" (13th-century fresco)

(Des and eng F. Tulli. Recess)

1976 (15 Sept). *400th Death Anniv of Titian.* P 14.
1485 **590** 150l. rose-carmine 10 20

(Des and eng Maria Tuccelli. Recess)

1976 (2 Oct). *750th Death Anniv of St. Francis of Assisi.* P 14.
1486 **591** 150l. sepia and light brown 10 10

592 "Cursus Publicus" Post Cart

593 Girl with "Protective Umbrella" and Animals

(Des T. Mele. Photo)

1976 (14 Oct). *"Italia 1976" International Stamp Exhibition, Milan (2nd issue). Development of Italian Postal Service.* T **592** and similar horiz designs. P 14 × 13½.
1487 70l. black, greenish grey & steel-blue 10 20
1488 100l. black, greenish grey & bistre-yell 10 10
1489 150l. black, grey and yellow brown 10 20

67

ITALY 1976

1490	200l. multicoloured	10	10
1491	400l. multicoloured	15	40
1487/1491	Set of 5	50	90

Designs:—100l. Emblem of Royal Sardinian Posts; 150l. 19th-century "Lions head" letter-box; 200l. Early cancelling machine; 400l. Modern letter-coding machine.

(Des M. Palazzo (40l.), A. Grasselli (100l.), G. Sanguineti (150l.). Photo)

1976 (17 Oct). *Stamp Day. Nature Protection.* T **593** and similar vert designs. Multicoloured. P 13½ × 14.

1492	40l. Type **593**	10	10
1493	100l. "Protective scarf"	10	10
1494	150l. Doctor with bandaged tree	10	10

1976 (22 Nov). *Italian Painters (3rd series). Vert portraits as* T **541**. *Photo.* P 13½.

1495	170l. myrtle-green, orange-yellow & red	10	10
1496	170l. black, turquoise-grn & blkish grn	10	10
1497	170l. black, bright purple & deep mag	10	10
1498	170l. bistre-brown, lavender & bluish vio	10	10
1499	170l. black and light olive-brown	10	10
1495/1499	Set of 5	45	45

Portraits:—No. 1495, Carlo Dolci; 1496, Lorenzo Ghiberti (sculptor); 1497, Domenico Ghirlandaio; 1498, Giovanni Piazzetta; 1499, "Sassoferrato" (Giovanni Salvi).

594 "The Visit" (S. Lega)
595 "Adoration of the Magi" (Bartolo di Fredi) 

1976 (7 Dec). *150th Birth Anniv of Silvestro Lega (painter).* P 14 × 13½.

1500	**594**	170l. multicoloured	10	10

1976 (11 Dec). *Christmas.* T **595** *and similar vert design. Multicoloured. Photo.* P 13½ × 14.

1501	70l. Type **595**	10	20
1502	120l. "The Nativity" (Taddeo Gaddi)	10	20

(Des and eng E. Donnini. Recess and litho)

1976 (21 Dec). *Italian Fountains (4th series). Vert designs as* T **542**. *Multicoloured.* P 13½ × 14.

1503	170l. Gallipoli Fountain	10	20
1504	170l. Madonna Fountain, Verona	10	20
1505	170l. Palazzo Doria Fountain, Genoa	10	20

596 Net of Serpents
597 Igniting Explosives 

(Des T. Mele (120l.), Rita Cavacece (170l.). Photo)

1977 (28 Feb). *Campaign against Drug Abuse.* T **596** *and similar horiz design. Multicoloured.* P 14 × 13½.

1506	120l. Type **596**	10	10
1507	170l. "Addict" and poppy	10	10

(Des G. Ascari. Photo)

1977 (5 Mar). *300th Birth Anniv of Pietro Micca (national hero).* P 14 × 13½.

1508	**597**	170l. multicoloured	10	10

598 "Globe" and Cross
599 Article 53 of Italian Constitution 

(Des A. Locca and S. Consolazione. Photo)

1977 (29 Mar). *Salesian Missionaries.* T **598** *and similar vert design. Multicoloured.* P 13½ × 14.

1509	70l. Type **598**	10	20
1510	120l. St. John Bosco and "United people"	10	20

(Des Central Philatelic Institute, Rome. Photo)

1977 (14 Apr). *"Encouragement to Taxpayers".* P 14.

1511	**599**	120l. black, bistre-brown and stone	10	10
1512		170l. blk, deep olive & dull apple-grn	10	10

(Des E. Vangelli. Photo)

1977 (2 May). *Europa. Horiz designs as* T **556** *but with CEPT emblem. Multicoloured.* P 14.

1513	170l. Mount Etna	25	20
1514	200l. Castel del Monte	25	20

(Des E. Vangelli. Photo)

1977 (30 May). *Tourist Publicity (4th series). Horiz designs as* T **556**. *Multicoloured.* P 14.

1515	170l. Canossa Castle	10	20
1516	170l. Castellana Grotto	10	20
1517	170l. Fermo	10	20

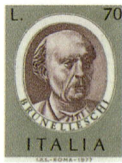

600 Filippo Brunelleschi (architect)
601 Paddle-steamer *Ferdinando Primo* 

1977 (27 June). *Famous Italians.* T **600** *and similar vert designs. Photo.* P 13.

1518	70l. sepia, dull grn & blackish green	10	20
1519	70l. slate-blk, turq-bl & greenish black	10	20
1520	70l. purple-brn, greenish yell & light brn	10	20
1521	70l. greenish-bl, salmon pk & bright scar	10	20
1522	70l. blk, red-brown & deep brown	10	20
1518/1522	Set of 5	45	90

Portraits:—No. 1519, Pietro Aretino (satirist); 1520, Carlo Goldoni (dramatist); 1521, Luigi Cherubini (composer); 1522, Edoardo Bassini (surgeon).

ITALY 1977

(Des and eng A. Quieti (1523), T. Mele (1524). Recess and litho)

1977 (5 Sept). *Anniversaries of Italian Artists (4th series). Vert designs as T* **567**. *Multicoloured.* P 14.
1523 170l. "Winter" (G. Arcimboldi (c. 1527–1593))   10   10
1524 170l. "Justice" (A. Delitio (15th cent.))   10   20

(Des F. Gay. Eng G. Toffoletti. Recess and litho)

1977 (23 Sept). *Italian Ship-building (1st series). T* **601** *and similar horiz designs. Multicoloured.* P 14 × 13.
1525 170l. Type **601**   15   30
    a. Block. Nos. 1525/8 plus 2 labels   55
1526 170l. Sail corvette *Caracciolo*   15   30
1527 170l. Liner *Saturnia*   15   30
1528 170l. Hydrofoil missile boat *Sparviero*   15   30
1525/1528 Set of 4   55   1·10

Nos. 1525/8 were issued *se-tenant* in blocks of four stamps and two half stamp-size labels depicting the arms of the Italian Navy and of the merchant navy, each sheet containing ten blocks.
See also Nos. 1552/5, 1621/4 and 1691/4.

(Des and eng E. Donnini. Recess and litho)

1977 (18 Oct). *Italian Fountains (5th series). Vert designs as T* **542**. *Multicoloured.* P 13 × 14.
1529 120l. Pacassi Fountain, Gorizia   10   20
1530 120l. Fraterna Fountain, Isernia   10   20
1531 120l. Palma Fountain, Palmi   10   20

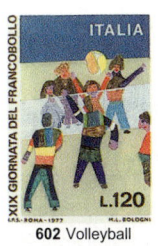

602 Volleyball 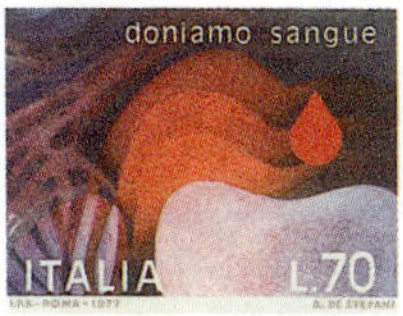   **603** "Pulse"

(Des M. L. Bologni (1532), M. L. Uderzo (1533), A. Pomponi (1534). Photo)

1977 (23 Oct). *Stamp Day. "Leisure Time". T* **602** *and similar vert designs. Multicoloured.* P 13½ × 14.
1532 120l. Type **602**   10   10
    a. Block. Nos. 1532/4 plus label   30
1533 120l. Catching butterflies   10   10
1534 120l. Kites   10   10

Nos. 1532/4 were issued together in *se-tenant* blocks of three stamps and one label within the sheet.

(Des A. de Stefani. Photo)

1977 (26 Oct). *"Give Blood". T* **603** *and similar horiz design. Multicoloured.* P 14 × 13.
1535 70l. Type **603**   10   20
1536 120l. "Transfusion"   10   10

604 Quintino Sella and 1863 1l. Stamps    **605** Dina Galli

(Des E. Brotzu and S. Vespaziani. Photo)

1977 (28 Oct). *150th Birth Anniv of Quintino Sella (statesman).* P 13½.
1537 **604** 170l. yellow-olive & blackish brn   10   10

(Des E. Vangelli. Photo)

1977 (2 Dec). *Birth Centenary of Dina Galli (actress).* P 13½ × 14.
1538 **605** 170l. multicoloured   10   10

606 "Adoration of the Shepherds" (P. Testa)    **607** La Scala Opera House

(Des and eng E. Donnini. Recess and litho)

1977 (13 Dec). *Christmas. T* **606** *and similar horiz design.* P 14.
1539 70l. black and pale brown-olive   10   20
1540 120l. black and turquoise green   10   20

Design:—120l. "The Adoration of the Shepherds" (J. Caraglio).

(Eng F. Tulli. Recess and litho)

1978 (15 Mar). *Bicentenary of La Scala Opera House. T* **607** *and similar vert design. Multicoloured.* P 13½ × 14.
1541 170l. Type **607**   15   20
1542 200l. La Scala interior   20   20

(Des E. Vangelli. Photo)

1978 (30 Mar). *Tourist Publicity (5th series). Horiz designs as T* **556**. *Multicoloured.* P 14.
1543 70l. Gubbio   10   30
1544 200l. Udine   10   20
1545 600l. Paestum   35   40

608 Grouper

(Des B. Pecciarini. Photo)

1978 (3 Apr). *Environmental Protection. Mediterranean Fauna. T* **608** *and similar horiz designs. Multicoloured.* P 14 × 13½.
1546 170l. Type **608**   25   20
    a. Strip. Nos. 1546/9 plus label   90
1547 170l. Leathery turtle   25   20
1548 170l. Mediterranean monk seal   25   20
1549 170l. Audouin's gull   25   20
1546/1549 Set of 4   90   70

Nos. 1546/9 were issued together in *se-tenant* strips of four stamps and one label depicting a stylized sea-horse.

ITALY 1978

609 Maschio Angioino Castle, Naples
610 Matilde Serao (writer) 

(Des and eng E. Donnini. Recess and litho.)

1978 (29 Apr). *Europa. T* **609** *and similar horiz design. Multicoloured.* P 14 × 13.
1550   170l. Type **609**   20   20
1551   200l. Pantheon, Rome   30   30

(Des F. Gay. Eng G. Toffoletti. Recess and litho.)

1978 (8 May). *Italian Ship-building (2nd series). Horiz designs as T* **601**. *Multicoloured.* P 14 × 13.
1552   170l. Ligurian brigantine *Fortuna* . . .   30   30
   a. Block. Nos. 1552/5 plus 2
    labels . . . .   1·10
1553   170l. Cruiser *Benedetto Brin*   30   30
1554   170l. Frigate *Lupo*   30   30
1555   170l. Container ship *Africa*   30   30
1552/1555 Set of 4 . . . .   1·10   1·10
   Nos. 1552/5 were issued together in *se-tenant* blocks of four stamps and two half stamp-size labels depicting nautical instruments.

(Des and eng T. Mele. Recess)

1978 (10 May). *Famous Italians. T* **610** *and similar vert designs.* P 14 × 13.
1556   170l. black and carmine   15   20
   a. Block of 6. Nos. 1556/61   80
1557   170l. blackish brown and grey-blue . .   15   20
1558   170l. indigo and grey-blue   15   20
1559   170l. black and dull yellowish green . .   15   20
1560   170l. reddish brown & dull yellowish
    grn   15   20
1561   170l. indigo and carmine   15   20
1556/1561 Set of 6   80   1·10
   Designs:—No. 1557, Vittorino da Feltre (scientist); 1558, Victor Emmanuel II; 1559, Pope Pius IX; 1560, Marcello Malpighi (biologist); 1561, Antonio Meucci (telephone pioneer).
   Nos. 1556/61 were issued *se-tenant* in blocks of six within the sheet.
   See also Nos. 1600/4.

611 First and Last Paragraphs of Constitution
612 Telephone Wires and Lens 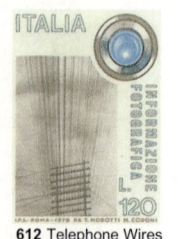

(Des and eng F. Borrelli. Recess and litho.)

1978 (2 June). *30th Anniv of Constitution.* P 13 × 14.
1562   611   170l. multicoloured   15   20

(Des Maria Codoni. Photo)

1978 (30 June). *Photographic Information.* P 13 × 14.
1563   612   120l. brownish grey, new blue and
    blue-green   10   20

(Des and eng T. Mele. Recess and litho)

1978 (12 July). *Anniversaries of Italian Artists (5th series). Vert designs, as T* **567**. *Multicoloured.* P 14.
1564   170l. "The Ivy" (Tranquillo Cremona
    (1837–1878))   25   20
1565   520l. "The Cook" (Bernardo Strozzi
    (1581–1644))   70   90

613 Holy Shroud of Turin
614 Volleyball Players 

(Des T. Mele. Photo)

1978 (8 Sept). *400th Anniv of Translation of Holy Shroud from Savoy to Turin.* P 13½.
1566   613   220l. stone, grey-black and
    carmine   20   20

(Des and eng A. Ciaburro. Photo)

1978 (20 Sept). *World Volleyball Championships. T* **614** *and similar vert design.* P 14.
1567   80l. black, red and new blue   15   20
1568   120l. black, new blue and orange . . .   15   20
   Design:—120l. Players with ball.

615 Detail from "St. Peter distributing Ananias's Silver"
616 "Madonna and Child" (Giorgione) 

(Des and eng A. Quieti. Recess)

1978 (18 Oct). *550th Death Anniv of Tommaso Guidi (Masaccio).* P 13 × 14.
1569   615   170l. blackish blue   10   10

(Des and eng E. Donnini. Recess and litho)

1978 (25 Oct). *Italian Fountains (6th series). Vert designs similar to T* **542**. *Multicoloured.* P 13 × 14.
1570   120l. Neptune Fountain, Trento   10   20
1571   120l. Fountain of Fortune, Fano   10   20
1572   120l. Cavallina Fountain, Genzano di
    Lucania   10   20

(Eng F. Tulli (80l.). Recess and litho (80l.), photo (120l.).)

1978 (8 Nov). *Christmas. T* **616** *and similar horiz design.* P 13 × 14 (80l.) or 13½ (120l.).
1573   80l. carmine and drab   10   20
1574   120l. multicoloured   10   20

ITALY 1978

Design: 48 × 27 mm—120l. "The Adoration of the Magi" (Giorgione).

617 "Flowers"
618

(Des S. Colazilli (1575), G Gazzarri (1576), P. Porceddu (1577). Photo)

1978 (26 Nov). *Stamp Day. United Europe.* T **617** and similar vert designs. Multicoloured. P 13 × 14.
1575	120l. Type **617**	10	20
1576	120l. Flags and ribbon	10	20
1577	120l. Figures raising globe inscribed "E"	10	20

(Des E. Vangelli. Eng V. Puliti. Recess)

1978 (4 Dec)–**87**. P 14 × 13½.
(a) No watermark.
1578	**618**	1500l. multicoloured (14.5.79)	35	10
1579		2000l. multicoloured (12.4.79)	45	10
1580		3000l. multicoloured (12.3.79)	1·20	10
1581		4000l. multicoloured (12.2.79)	1·50	20
1582		5000l. multicoloured	2·10	25
1583		10000l. multicoloured (27.6.83)	3·50	1·20

(b) Wmk **307**.
| 1584 | **618** | 20000l. multicoloured (5.1.87) | 7·50 | 6·00 |
| 1578/1584 | Set of 7 | | 15·00 | 7·25 |

Nos. 1585/7 are vacant.

619 State Polygraphic Institute
620 "St. Francis washing the Feet of a Leper" (Maestro di Francesco Bardi)

1979 (6 Jan). *50th Anniv of State Polygraphic Institute.* T **619** and similar horiz design. Multicoloured. Photo. P 14 × 13.
| 1588 | 170l. Type **619** | 10 | 15 |
| 1589 | 220l. Printing press | 10 | 15 |

1979 (22 Jan). *Leprosy Relief.* Photo. P 14 × 13.
| 1590 | **620** | 80l. multicoloured | 10 | 15 |

621 Cyclist carrying Bicycle
622 Albert Einstein

(Des G. Pirrotta. Photo)

1979 (27 Jan). *World Cyclo-cross Championships.* P 13 × 14.
| 1591 | **621** | 170l. multicoloured | 10 | 15 |
| 1592 | | 220l. multicoloured | 15 | 15 |

(Des and eng T. Mele. Recess and litho)

1979 (15 Feb). *Anniversaries of Italian Artists (6th series).* Vert designs as T **567**. Multicoloured. P 14.
| 1593 | 170l. "The Annunciation" (Antonella da Messina (c. 1430–1479)) | 20 | 15 |
| 1594 | 520l. "Field with Haystack" (Ardengo Soffici (1879–1964)) | 75 | 1·10 |

(Eng F. Tulli. Recess and litho)

1979 (14 Mar). *Birth Centenary of Albert Einstein (physicist).* P 13 × 14.
| 1595 | **622** | 120l. dp dull pur, greenish grey & bl | 10 | 15 |

(Des E. Vangelli. Photo)

1979 (30 Mar). *Tourist Publicity (6th series).* Horiz designs as T **556**. Multicoloured. P 14.
1596	70l. Asiago	10	20
1597	90l. Castelsardo, Sardinia	10	15
1598	170l. Orvieto	15	15
1599	220l. Scilla	20	15
1596/1599	Set of 4	40	60

(Des and eng T. Mele. Recess)

1979 (23 Apr). *Famous Italians.* Vert designs as T **610**. P 14 × 13.
1600	170l. red brown, light blue and black	10	15
1601	170l. deep green, yellow and violet	10	15
1602	170l. deep blue and carmine-rose	10	15
1603	170l. deep brown and brown-ochre	10	15
1604	170l. violet, brown and deep green	10	15
1600/1604	Set of 5	45	70

Designs:—No. 1600, Carlo Maderno (architect); 1601, Lazzaro Spallanzani (biologist); 1602, Ugo Foscolo (writer); 1603, Massimo Bontempelli (writer); 1604, Francesco Severi (mathematician).

623 Morse Telegraph Apparatus
624 Flags of Member States forming "E"

(Eng G. Toffoletti. Photo)

1979 (30 Apr). *Europa.* T **623** and similar horiz design. Multicoloured. P 14.
| 1605 | 170l. Type **623** | 30 | 15 |
| 1606 | 220l. Carrier pigeon with message tube | 45 | 15 |

(Des A. and M. Iocca. Photo)

1979 (5 May). *First Direct Elections to European Parliament.* P 14 × 13.
| 1607 | **624** | 170l. multicoloured | 15 | 15 |
| 1608 | | 220l. multicoloured | 20 | 15 |

ITALY 1979

625 Head of Aeneas (bas-relief, Ara Pacis)
626 Ball in Basket (poster) 

1979 (9 June). *70th World Rotary Congress, Rome.* Photo. P 13 × 14.
1609   625   220l. multicoloured 15   15

(Des Studio GIOB, Turin (80l.), A. Ciaburro (120l.). Photo)

1979 (13 June). *21st European Basketball Championships.* T **626** and similar vert design. P 14.
1610   80l. multicoloured 10   15
1611   120l. crimson, black and orange-yellow 15   15
Design:—120l. Two players.

627 "Doctor Examining Patient with Stomach Ailment" (woodcut from Giovanni da Cuba's *Hortus Sanitatis*)
628 Emblem, Ribbon "3" and Milan Cathedral

(Eng M. Ramassotto. Recess and litho)

1979 (16 June). *Prevention of Digestive Illnesses.* P 14.
1612   627   120l. multicoloured 10   15

1979 (22 June). *Third World Machine Tool Exhibition, Milan.* Photo. P 14 × 13.
1613   628   170l. multicoloured 15   15
1614   220l. multicoloured 20   15

629 Ottorino Respighi and Appian Way, Rome
630 Woman with Telephone and Morse Key 

(Eng A. Morena. Recess and litho)

1979 (9 July). *Birth Centenary of Ottorino Respighi (musician).* P 13 × 14.
1615   629   120l. multicoloured 10   15

(Des E. Greco. Photo)

1979 (20 Sept). *Third World Telecommunications Exhibition, Geneva.* T **630** and similar vert design. P 14.
1616   170l. grey-black and red 10   15
1617   220l. greenish slate and emerald . . . 15   15
Design:—220l. Woman with early telephone and communications satellite.

(Des and eng E. Donnini. Recess and litho)

1979 (22 Sept). *Italian Fountains (7th series).* Vert designs similar to T **542**. Multicoloured. P 13 × 14.
1618   120l. Melograno Fountain, Issogne . . . 15   15
1619   120l. Bollente Fountain, Acqui Terme . . 15   15
1620   120l. Fontana Grande, Viterbo 15   15

(Des F. Gay. Eng G. Toffoletti. Recess and litho)

1979 (12 Oct). *Italian Ship-building (3rd series).* Horiz designs as T **601**. Multicoloured. P 14 × 13.
1621   170l. Full-rigged sailing ship *Cosmos* . . 25   15
          a. Block. Nos 1621/4 plus 2 labels . . 90
1622   170l. Cruiser *Dandolo* 25   15
1623   170l. Ferry *Deledda* 25   15
1624   170l. Submarine *Carlo Fecia di Cossato* . . 25   15
1621/1624 *Set of* 4 90   55
Nos. 1621/4 were issued together in *se-tenant* blocks of four stamps and two half stamp-size labels depicting nautical instruments.

631 Sir Rowland Hill and "Penny Black"
632 Christmas Landscape 

(Des A. and M. Iocca. Photo)

1979 (25 Oct). *Death Centenary of Sir Rowland Hill.* P 14 × 13.
1625   631   220l. multicoloured 20   15

(Des A. Raimondi. Photo)

1979 (7 Nov). *Christmas.* P 14 × 13½.
1626   632   120l. multicoloured 10   15

633 Children under Umbrella (Group IIB, Varapodio School)
634 Solar Energy (alternative sources)

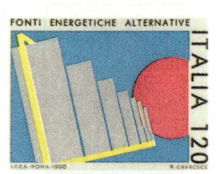

ITALY   1979

1979 (25 Nov). *Stamp Day. International Year of the Child.* T **633** and similar horiz designs, showing drawings by schoolchildren. Multicoloured. Photo. P 14 × 13½ (horiz) or 13½ × 14 (vert).
1627	70l. Children of different races holding hands (L. Carra)	10	15
1628	120l. Type **633**	10	15
1629	150l. Children with balloons (V. Fedon)	10	15

(Des Rita Cavacece. Photo)

1980 (25 Feb). *Conservation of Energy.* T **634** and similar horiz design. Multicoloured. P 14 × 13½.
1630	120l. Type **634**	15	15
1631	170l. Oil well (reduction of consumption)	15	15

635 "St. Benedict" (detail, fresco by Sodoma in Monastery of Monteoliveto Maggiore)

636 Royal Palace, Naples

(Des V. Puliti. Recess)

1980 (21 Mar). *1500th Birth Anniv of St. Benedict of Nursia (founder of Benedictine Order).* P 13½ × 14.
1632	**635**	220l. indigo	15	15

(Des S. Consolazione. Eng F. Borrelli. Recess and litho)

1980 (26 Apr). *"Europa 80" International Stamp Exhibition, Naples.* P 13½ × 14.
1633	**636**	220l. multicoloured	15	15

637 Antonio Pigafetta (navigator) and *Vitoria*

638 St. Catherine (reliquary bust)

(Des L. Vangelli. Litho)

1980 (28 Apr). *Europa.* T **637** and similar horiz design. Multicoloured. P 14 × 13½.
1634	170l. Type **637**	35	15
1635	220l. Antonio lo Surdo (geophysicist)	50	15

1980 (29 Apr). *600th Death Anniv of St. Catherine of Siena.* Photo. P 13½ × 14.
1636	**638**	170l. multicoloured	15	15

639 Red Cross Flags

(Des Rita Cavacece. Photo)

1980 (15 May). *First International Exhibition of Red Cross Stamps.* P 14 × 13½.
1637	**639**	70l. multicoloured	15	15
1638		80l. multicoloured	15	15

640 Philae Temples

(Des A. Ciaburro. Photo)

1980 (20 May). *Italian Work for the World (1st series). Preservation of Philae Temples, Egypt.* T **640** and similar horiz design. Multicoloured. P 14 × 13½.
1639	**640**	220l. Type **640**	15	15
		a. Horiz pair. Nos. 1639/40	30	30
1640		220l. Philae Temples (*different*)	15	15

Nos. 1639/40 were issued together in horizontal *se-tenant* pairs within sheets of 40 stamps and 20 half stamp-size labels depicting capitals, the stamps forming a composite design.
See also Nos. 1720/1, 1758/9, 1780/1, 1830/1, 1865/6 and 1937/40.

641 Footballer

642 "Cosimo I with his Artists" (Vasari)

(Des A. Sassu. Photo)

1980 (11 June). *European Football Championship, Italy.* P 14 × 13½.
1641	**641**	80l. multicoloured	1·10	95

(Des E. Vangelli. Photo)

1980 (28 June). *Tourist Publicity (7th series).* Horiz designs as T **556**. Multicoloured. P 14.
1642	80l. Erice	10	30
1643	150l. Ravello	15	15
1644	200l. Roseto degli Abruzzi	20	30
1645	670l. Salsomaggiore Terme	45	90
1642/1645	Set of 4	80	1·50

1980 (2 July). *Exhibition "Florence and Tuscany of the Medicis in 16th-century Europe".* T **642** and similar vert design. Multicoloured. Photo. P 13½ × 14.
1646	170l. Type **642** (ceiling medallion, Palazzo Vecchio, Florence)	15	15
	a. Horiz strip. Nos. 1646/7 plus label	30	

73

ITALY 1980

1647	170l. Armillary sphere		15	15

Nos. 1646/7 were issued together with intervening stamp-size label depicting the Medici arms in *se-tenant* strips within the sheet.

643 Fonte Avellana Monastery

644 Castel Sant'Angelo, Rome

(Des E. Donnini. Eng F. Tulli. Recess)

1980 (3 Sept). *Millenary of Fonte Avellana Monastery*. P 14 × 13½.

1648	**643**	200l. bronze-green, yellowish green and deep brown	20	15

(Des T. Mele (5 to 40, 60, 120, 150l.), E. Vangelli (50, 90, 100, 550l.), A. Ciaburro (70, 80l.), G. Toffoletti (380l.), P. Gabriele (650l.), A. Cosentino (850l.). Des and eng E. Donnini (200, 250l.). Eng P. Arghittu (170, 180, 600l., coil 600l.), F. Bonnelli (300l.), Maria Tuccelli (450l., coil 300, 500l.), F. Tulli (700l.), A. Ciaburro (750l.), G. Verdelocco (350, 400, 500, 800, 900, 1000l., coils 30 to 200l., 400, 450, 650 to 800l.), Rita Morena (1400l.). Photo (1649/61, 1664*a*, 1665*a*, 1666*a*, 1667*a*, 1669*a*, 1675), recess and litho (1662/4, 1665, 1666, 1669, 1671, 1672), recess (1667, 1668, 1670, 1673, 1674, 1676/8 and coils))

1980 (22 Sept)–**94**. *Castles*. T **644** *and similar vert designs.* W **307**.

(a) Size 22 × 27 mm. P 14 × 13½.

1649		5l. new blue and red	20	10
1650		10l. olive-brown and brown-ochre	20	10
1651		20l. orange-brown & deep ultramarine	20	10
1652		30l. pale orange & dull ultram (20.8.81)	20	10
1653		40l. red-brown and turquoise-blue	20	10
1654		50l. multicoloured (no imprint date)	20	10
		a. With imprint date "1980" at foot (1991)	20	10
1655		60l. yellow-olive and magenta	20	15
1656		70l. multicoloured (20.8.81)	10	10
1657		80l. multicoloured (20.8.81)	10	10
1658		90l. multicoloured	20	15
1659		100l. multicoloured	20	10
1660		120l. grey-blue and salmon-pink	20	10
1661		150l. dull violet and brown-ochre	20	10
1662		170l. black and greenish yellow	20	15
1663		180l. ultramarine and rose	55	80
1664		200l. multicoloured (*recess and litho*)	20	10
1664*a*		200l. multicoloured (*photo*) (21.2.94)	20	10
1665		250l. multicoloured (*recess and litho*)	25	10
1665*a*		250l. multicoloured (*photo*) (21.2.94)	25	10
1666		300l. multicoloured (*recess and litho*)	30	10
1666*a*		300l. multicoloured (*photo*) (21.2.94)	25	10
1667		350l. orange-brown, grey-blue & green	30	10
1667*a*		380l. multicoloured (5.2.87)	30	10
1668		400l. grey-blue, green and deep brown	35	10
1669		450l. multicoloured (*recess and litho*)	40	10
1669*a*		450l. multicoloured (*photo*) (21.2.94)	40	10
1670		500l. grey-blue, deep brown and green	45	10
1670*a*		550l. multicoloured (14.2.84)	40	10
1671		600l. black and turquoise-green	55	10
1671*a*		650l. multicoloured (15.3.86)	45	10
1672		700l. multicoloured	65	10
1673		750l. reddish brown, emerald and deep turquoise-blue (20.9.90)	65	10
1674		800l. dp brown, myrtle green & mag	75	15
1675		850l. multicoloured (7.3.92)	80	15
1676		900l. multicoloured	80	15
1677		1000l. multicoloured	85	15
1678		1400l. orange-brn, ultram & vio (9.7.83)	1·10	15

(b) Coil stamps. Size 16 × 21 mm. Imperf × p 14.

1679		30l. magenta	20	15
		a. Coil pair. Nos. 1679 and 1681	60	60
		b. Coil pair. Nos. 1679 and 1682	75	55
1680		50l. slate-blue (*creamy paper*) (5.7.85)	25	15
		a. Coil pair. Nos. 1680 and 1686	65	95
		b. Steel blue (*white paper*) (1.3.88)	20	15
1680*c*		100l. brown (1.3.88)	15	15
1681		120l. deep brown	25	15
1682		170l. violet	40	40
1683		200l. bluish violet & ultram (30.9.81)	3·00	5·50
1684		300l. yellowish green & bl-grn (30.9.81)	55	65
1685		400l. reddish brown and dull yellow-green (25.6.83)	85	1·10
1686		450l. yellowish green (*creamy paper*) (25.7.85)	25	80
		a. Dull yellowish green (*white paper*) (1.3.88)	25	80
1687		500l. deep turquoise-blue (1.3.88)	45	1·10
1687*a*		600l. emerald (23.3.91)	60	80
1688		650l. deep magenta (1.3.88)	50	80
1689		750l. bright violet (1.3.88)	60	95
1690		800l. bright scarlet (23.3.91)	85	95
1649/1690 Set of 47 (one of each value/size)			19·00	16·00

Designs:—10l. Sforzesco Castle, Milan; 20l. Castel del Monte, Andria; 30l. (1652), L'Aquila Castle; 30l. (1679), 100l. (1680*c*), Santa Severa Castle; 40l. Ursino Castle, Catania; 50l. (1654), Rocca di Calascio, L'Aquila; 50l. (1680), Scilla; 60l. Norman Tower, San Mauro; 70l. Aragonese Castle, Reggio Calabria; 80l. Sabbionara, Avio; 90l. Isola Capo Rizzuto; 100l. (1659), Aragonese Castle, Ischia; 120l. (1660), Estense Castle, Ferrara; 120l. (1681), Lombardia Enna; 150l. Miramare, Trieste; 170l. (1662), Ostia; 170l. (1682), 650l. (1688), Serralunga d'Alba; 180l. Castel Gavone, Finale Ligure; 200l. (1664/*a*), Cerro al Volturno; 200l. (1683), Svevo Angioina Fortress, Lucera; 250l. Rocca di Mondavio, Pesaro; 300l. (1666/*a*), Norman Castle, Svevo, Bari; 300l. (1684), 500l. (1687), Norman Castle, Melfi; 350l. Mussomeli; 380l. Rocca di Vignola, Modena; 400l. (1668), Emperor's Castle, Prato; 400l. (1685), 750l. (1689), Venafro; 450l. (1669/*a*), Bosa; 450l. (1686), Piobbico Castle, Pesaro; 500l. (1670), Rovereto; 550l. Rocca Sinibalda; 600l. Scaligero Castle, Sirmione; 650l. (1671*a*), Montecchio; 700l. Ivrea; 750l. (1673), Rocca di Urbisaglia; 800l. Rocca Maggiore, Assisi; 850l. Castello di Arechi, Salerno; 900l. Castello di Saint-Pierre, Aosta; 1000l. Montagnana, Padua; 1400l. Caldoresco Castle, Vasto.

The coils have every fifth stamp numbered on the back. Nos. 1680 and 1686 were issued together in the same coil, Nos. 1680*b* and 1686*a* in separate coils.

Apart from the process, Nos. 1664*a*, 1665*a*, 1666*a* and 1669*a* can be distinguished from the recess and litho printings by the addition of a dash between "I.P.Z.S." and "ROMA" at the foot.

A booklet containing 4 × 300l., 4 × 250l. and 3 × 200l., the cover with imprint "I.P.Z.S. Roma 3–1982", was not issued by the postal authority.

(Des F Gay. Eng G. Toffoletti. Recess and litho)

1980 (11 Oct). *Italian Ship-building* (4th series). Horiz designs as T **601**. Multicoloured. P 14 × 13.

1691		200l. Corvette *Gabbiano*	65	50
		a. Block. Nos. 1691/4 plus 2 labels	2·30	
1692		200l. Destroyer *Audace*	65	50
1693		200l. Barque *Italia*	65	50
1694		200l. Pipe-layer *Castoro Sei*	65	50
1691/1694 Set of 4			2·30	1·80

Nos. 1691/4 were issued together in *se-tenant* blocks of four stamps and two half stamp-size labels depicting ships' fittings.

ITALY 1980

645 Filippo Mazzei

646 Villa Foscari Malcontenta, Venice

(Des L. Vangelli. Photo)

1980 (18 Oct). *250th Birth Anniv of Filippo Mazzei (writer and American revolutionary)*. P 13 × 14.
1695 645 320l. multicoloured 25 15

(Des and eng E. Donnini. Recess and litho)

1980 (31 Oct). *Villas (1st series). T 646 and similar horiz designs. Multicoloured.* P 14 × 13½.
1696 80l. Type **646** 20 30
1697 150l. Villa Barbaro Maser, Treviso . . . 25 15
1698 170l. Villa Godi Valmarana, Vicenza . . 35 45
See also Nos. 1737/9, 1770/2, 1811/14, 1853/6, 1893/6 and 1943/7.

(Des and eng T. Mele. Recess and litho)

1980 (20 Nov). *Anniversaries of Italian Artists (7th series). Vert designs as T 567. Multicoloured.* P 14.
1699 520l. "Saint Barbara" (Jacopo Palma, the Elder (1480–1528)) 40 55
1700 520l. "Apollo and Daphne" (Gian Lorenzo Bernini (1598–1680)) . . 40 55

647 "Nativity" (Federico Brandani)

(Eng E. Donnini. Recess)

1980 (22 Nov). *Christmas*. P 14.
1701 647 120l. slate-green & chestnut . . . 10 15

648 "My Town" (Treviso)

649 Daniele Comboni and African Village

(Des G. Botter (70l.), E. Casolari (120l.), G. Cesile (170l.). Photo)

1980 (30 Nov). *Stamp Day. T 648 and similar horiz designs showing paintings by schoolchildren entitled "My Town". Multicoloured.* P 14 × 13½.
1702 70l. Type **648** 10 15
1703 120l. Sansepolcro 15 15
1704 170l. Sansepolcro (*different*) 15 15

(Eng N. Arghittu. Recess)

1981 (14 Mar). *150th Birth Anniv and Death Centenary of Daniele Comboni (missionary)*. P 14 × 13½.
1705 649 80l. chestnut, indigo & dull ultram 10 15

650 Alcide de Gasperi

651 Landscape outlined by Person in Wheelchair

(Eng V. Puliti. Recess)

1981 (3 Apr). *Birth Centenary of Alcide de Gasperi (statesman)*. P 13½ × 14.
1706 650 200l. blackish olive 15 15

(Des A. Ciaburro. Photo)

1981 (11 Apr). *International Year of Disabled Persons*. P 13½ × 14.
1707 651 300l. multicoloured 25 15

652 Anemones

653 Human Chess Game, Marostica

(Des A. Raimondi. Photo)

1981 (27 Apr). *Flowers (1st series). T 652 and similar vert designs. Multicoloured.* P 13½ × 14.
1708 200l. Type **652** 15 15
1709 200l. Oleander 15 15
1710 200l. Roses 15 15
See also Nos. 1753/5 and 1797/9.

(Des A. Ciaburro. Photo)

1981 (May). *Europa. T 653 and similar vert design. Multicoloured.* P 13 × 14.
1711 300l. Type **653** 65 15
1712 300l. Horse race, Siena 65 15

654 St. Rita of Cascia

655 Ciro Menotti

75

ITALY 1981

(Des G. Toffoletti. Photo)
1981 (22 May). *600th Birth Anniv of St. Rita of Cascia.* P 13½ × 14.
1713 **654** 600l. multicoloured 40 40

(Des and eng F. Tulli. Recess)
1981 (26 May). *150th Death Anniv of Ciro Menotti (patriot).*
P 14 × 13½.
1714 **655** 80l. black and reddish brown . . . 10 10

656 Agusta A.109 Helicopter
657 Fertile and Barren Soil 
658 Naval Academy and Badge
659 Spada Palace, Rome, and Decorative Motif from Grand Hall

(Des F. Gay. Photo)
1981 (24 July). *Centenary of Naval Academy, Livorno.* T **658** and similar horiz designs. Multicoloured. P 14 × 13.
1726 80l. Type **658** 10 15
1727 150l. Aerial view of Academy . . . 10 30
1728 200l. Cadet ship *Amerigo Vespucci* and sailor using sextant 15 15

(Eng N. Arghittu. Recess)
1981 (31 Aug). *150th Anniv of Council of State.* P 14 × 13½.
1729 **659** 200l. brown, green and indigo . . 10 15

(Des G. Toffoletti. Litho)
1981 (1 June). *Italian Aircraft (1st series).* T **656** and similar horiz designs. Multicoloured. P 14 × 13.
1715 200l. Type **656** 15 15
      a. Block. Nos. 1715/18 plus 2 labels 55
1716 200l. Partenavia P.68B Victor airplane 15 15
1717 200l. Aeritalia G.222 transport . . 15 15
1718 200l. Aermacchi MB 339 jet trainer . 15 15
1715/1718 *Set of 4* 55 55
Nos. 1715/18 were issued together in *se-tenant* blocks of four stamps and two half stamp-size labels depicting airplane engines, the order of the stamps differing in alternate blocks.
See also Nos. 1748/51 and 1792/5.

(Des G. Belli and A. Sanna. Photo)
1981 (8 June). *Water Conservation.* P 13½ × 14.
1719 **657** 80l. multicoloured 10 15

(Eng G. Verdelocco. Recess)
1981 (26 June). *Italian Work for the World (2nd series). Dam Construction.* Horiz designs as T **640**. P 14 × 13½.
1720 300l. indigo 25 15
      a. Horiz strip. Nos. 1720/21 plus label 50 30
1721 300l. bright crimson 25 15
Designs:—No 1720, São Simão, Brazil; 1721, High Island, Hong Kong.
Nos. 1720/1 were issued together with intervening half stamp-size inscribed label in horizontal *se-tenant* strips within the sheet.

(Des E. Vangelli. Photo)
1981 (4 July). *Tourist Publicity (8th series).* Horiz designs as T **556**. P 14.
1722 80l. Matera 15 15
1723 150l. Riva del Garda 20 80
1724 300l. Santa Teresa di Gallura . . . 40 30
1725 900l. Tarquinia . . . . . 1·30 55
1722/1725 *Set of 4* . . . . . 1·80 1·60

660 Running
661 Riace Bronze 

(Des A. Ciaburro. Photo)
1981 (4 Sept). *World Cup Light Athletics Championships, Rome.* P 13½ × 14.
1730 **660** 300l. multicoloured 25 30

(Eng T. Mele. Recess and litho)
1981 (7 Sept). *Anniversaries of Italian Artists (8th series).* Horiz designs as T **567**. Multicoloured. P 14.
1731 200l. "Harbour" (Carlo Cerra (1881–1966)) 10 15
1732 200l. "Nightfall" Giuseppe Ugonia (1881–1944)) 10 15

1981 (9 Sept). *Riace Bronzes (ancient Greek statues).* T **661** and similar vert design. Multicoloured. P 13½ × 14.
1733 200l. Type **661** 20 15
      a. Pair. Nos. 1733/4 . . . . . 40 30
1734 200l. Riace bronze (*different*) . . . 20 15
Nos. 1733/4 were issued together in *se-tenant* pairs within the sheet.

ITALY 1981

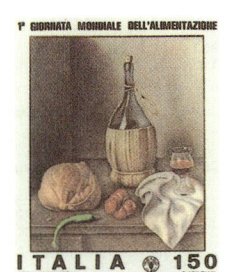

662 Virgil (Treviri mosaic)

663 "Still-life" (Gregorio Sciltian)

1981 (19 Sept). *Death Bimillenary of Virgil (poet)*. Photo. P 14.
1735   662   600l. multicoloured   40   45

1981 (16 Oct). *World Food Day*. Litho. P 14.
1736   663   150l. multicoloured   25   20

(Des and eng E. Donnini. Recess and litho)

1981 (17 Oct). *Villas (2nd series)*. Horiz designs as *T* 646. Multicoloured. P 14 × 13½.
1737   100l. Villa Campolieto, Ercolano   10   25
1738   200l. Villa Cimbrone, Ravello   20   25
1739   300l. Villa Pignatelli, Naples   30   30

664 "Adoration of the Magi" (Giovanni da Campione d'Italia)

665 Pope John XXIII

(Des and eng E. Donnini. Recess)

1981 (21 Nov). *Christmas*. P 14.
1740   664   200l. indigo, orange-brn & ultram   15   15

1981 (25 Nov). *Birth Centenary of Pope John XXIII*. Photo. P 13½ × 14.
1741   665   200l. multicoloured   20   15

666 Envelopes forming Railway Track

667 "St. Francis receiving the Stigmata" (Pietro Cavaro)

(Des P. Magri-Tilli (120l.), F. Borrelli (300l.); photo. Des and eng L. Vangelli (200l.); recess and litho)

1981 (29 Nov). *Stamp Day*. T 666 *and similar designs*. P 13½ × 14 (200l.) or 14 × 13½ (others).
1742   120l. green, rose-red and black   10   15
1743   200l. multicoloured   20   30
1744   300l. multicoloured   30   15
   Designs: *Vert*—200l. Caduceus, chest, envelopes and cherub blowing posthorn. *Horiz*—300l. Letter seal.

(Eng Maria M. Tuccelli. Recess)

1982 (6 Jan). *800th Birth Anniv of St. Francis of Assisi*. P 13½ × 14.
1745   667   300l. brown and deep blue   20   30

668 Paganini (after Ingres)

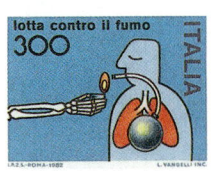

669 Skeletal Hand lighting Cigarette "Bomb"

1982 (19 Feb). *Birth Bicentenary of Niccolo Paganini (composer and violinist)*. Photo. P 13½ × 14.
1746   668   900l. multicoloured   70   1·90

(Des L. Vangelli. Photo)

1982 (2 Mar). *Anti-smoking Campaign*. P 14 × 13½.
1747   669   300l. multicoloured   25   15

(Des G. Toffoletti. Litho)

1982 (27 Mar). *Italian Aircraft (2nd series)*. Horiz designs as *T* 656. Multicoloured. P 14 × 13.
1748   300l. Panavia (inscr "Aeritalia") MRCA Tornado jet fighter   45   65
   a. Block. Nos. 1748/51 plus 2 labels . . . .   1·60
1749   300l. Savoia SIAI 260 Turbo trainer . .   45   65
1750   300l. Piaggio P-166 DL-3 Turbo . . .   45   65
1751   300l. Nardi NH 500 helicopter   45   65
1748/1751 *Set of 4* . . . . . .   1·60   2·30
   Nos. 1748/51 were issued together in *se-tenant* blocks of four stamps and two half stamp-size labels depicting "ATCR 33" radar and Alfa Romeo "AR 318" engine, the order of the stamps differing in alternate blocks.

670 Church of Santo Spirito o del Vespro, Palermo

671 Coronation of Charlemagne, 799

(Eng F. Borrelli. Recess)

1982 (31 Mar). *700th Anniv of Sicilian Vespers (uprising)*. P 13½ × 14.
1752   670   120l. carmine, deep turquoise-blue and deep reddish purple . .   10   30

77

ITALY 1982

(Des A. Raimondi. Photo)

1982 (10 Apr). *Flowers (2nd series). Vert designs as T **652**. Multicoloured.* P 13 × 14.
1753	300l. Camellias	30	80
1754	300l. Carnations	30	80
1755	300l. Cyclamen	30	80

(Eng Maria M. Tuccelli (2001.), F. Borrelli (4501.). Recess and litho)

1982 (3 May). *Europa. T **671** and similar vert design.* P 13 × 14.
1756	200l. grey-brown, black & steel blue	40	80
1757	450l. multicoloured	75	50

Design:—450l. Stars and signatures to Treaty of Rome, 1957.

(Des Maria Codoni. Photo)

1982 (29 May). *Italian Work for the World (3rd series). Horiz designs as T **640**. Multicoloured.* P 14 × 13½.
1758	450l. Radio communication across Red Sea	35	15
	a. Horiz strip. Nos. 1758/9 plus label	70	30
1759	450l. Automatic letter sorting	35	15

Nos. 1758/9 were issued together with intervening half stamp-size inscribed label in horizontal *se-tenant* strips within the sheet.

672 Garibaldi

673 Bridge Game, Pisa

1982 (2 June). *Death Centenary of Giuseppe Garibaldi. Photo.* P 13½ × 14.
1760	**672** 200l. multicoloured	35	65

(Des A. Ciaburro. Photo)

1982 (5 June). *Folk Customs (1st series).* P 13½ × 14.
1761	**673** 200l. multicoloured	20	65

See also Nos. 1804, 1850, 1875/6, 1914, 1972, 2004, 2028 and 2092.

(Des E. Vangelli. Photo)

1982 (28 June). *Tourist Publicity (9th series). Horiz designs as T **556**. Multicoloured.* P 14.
1762	200l. Frasassi Grotto	25	95
1763	200l. Fai della Paganella	25	95
1764	450l. Rodi Garganico	40	50
1765	450l. Temple of Agrigento	40	50
1762/1765	Set of 4	1·20	2·50

674 Coxless Four

675 Ducal Palace, Urbino, Montefeltro and Palazzo dei Consoli, Gubbio

(Des C. Venturi. Photo)

1982 (4 Aug). *World Junior Rowing Championships.* P 14.
1766	**674** 200l. multicoloured	20	50

(Des and eng E. Donnini. Recess and litho)

1982 (10 Sept). *500th Death Anniv of Federico da Montefeltro, Duke of Urbino.* P 14 × 13½.
1767	**675** 200l. multicoloured	15	15

676 Footballer holding aloft World Cup

677 Seating plan

(Des R. Guttuso. Photo)

1982 (12 Sept). *Italy's Victory in World Cup Football Championship.* P 14.
1768	**676** 1000l. multicoloured	1·40	3·00

(Des P. Gabriele. Photo)

1982 (14 Sept). *69th Interparliamentary Conference.* P 14 × 13½.
1769	**677** 450l. multicoloured	35	15

(Des and eng E. Donnini. Recess and litho)

1982 (1 Oct). *Villas (3rd series). Horiz designs as T **646**. Multicoloured.* P 14 × 13½.
1770	150l. Temple of Aesculapius, Villa Borghese, Rome	20	50
1771	250l. Villa d'Este, Tivoli	35	15
1772	350l. Villa Lante, Bagnaia, Viterbo	95	1·40

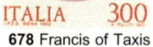

678 Francis of Taxis

679 Tree, Chair and Bed (Maria dl Pastena)

(Eng V. Puliti. Recess)

1982 (23 Oct). *Commemoration of Establishment of First Public Postal System in Europe.* P 13½ × 14.
1773	**678** 300l. crimson, dp ultram & verm	25	15

(Eng V. Puliti. Recess and litho)

1982 (3 Nov). *Anniversaries of Italian Artists (9th series). Vert designs as T **567**. Multicoloured.* P 14.
1774	300l. "Portrait of Antonietta Negroni Prati Morosini" (Francesco Hayez (1791–1882))	30	50
1775	300l. "The Fortune-teller" (Giovanni Battista Piazzetta (1682–1754))	30	50

78

ITALY 1982

1982 (28 Nov). *Stamp Day. Timber in Human Life.* T **679** and similar horiz designs showing drawings by schoolchildren. *Multicoloured. Photo.* P 14 × 13½.
1776	150l. Type **679**	15	15
1777	250l. Tree with timber products in branches (Lucia Andreoli)	20	50
1778	350l. Forest (Marco Gallea)	80	65

680 Microscope
681 Academy Emblem

1983 (14 Jan). *Cancer Control. Photo.* P 13½ × 14.
1779	**680** 400l. multicoloured	35	50

1983 (20 Jan). *Italian Work for the World (4th series). Automobile Industry.* Horiz designs as T **640**. *Multicoloured. Photo.* P 13½.
1780	400l. Factories on globe	35	50
	a. Pair. Nos. 1780/1	70	1·00
1781	400l. Assembly line	35	50

Nos. 1780/1 were issued together in *se-tenant* pairs within the sheet.

(Eng A. Ciaburro. Recess)

1983 (25 Jan). *400th Anniv of Accademia della Crusca (Florentine Academy of Letters).* P 14 × 13½.
1782	**681** 400l. crimson, sepia and deep blue	35	50

682 Shooting
683 Rossetti

(Des C. Venturi. Photo)

1983 (5 Feb). *World Biathlon Championships, Antholz.* P 14.
1783	**682** 200l. multicoloured	20	65

(Eng Rita Morena. Recess)

1983 (28 Feb). *Birth Bicentenary of Gabriele Rossetti (poet).* P 14 × 13½.
1784	**683** 300l. deep blue and deep brown	25	50

684 Guicciardini (after G. Bugiardini)
685 Saba and Trieste

(Des and eng G. Verdelocco. Recess)

1983 (5 Mar). *500th Birth Anniv of Francesco Guicciardini (lawyer and diplomat).* P 13½ × 14.
1785	**684** 450l. agate	35	15

(Des E. Vangelli. Photo)

1983 (9 Mar). *Birth Centenary of Umberto Saba (poet).* P 14 × 13½.
1786	**685** 600l. multicoloured	45	50

686 Pius XII
687 Pope and St. Paul's Basilica
688 Launch of Ship

(Eng A. Ciaburro. Recess)

1983 (21 Mar). *25th Death Anniv of Pope Pius XII.* P 13½ × 14.
1787	**686** 1400l. indigo	1·00	80

1983 (25 Mar). *Holy Year.* T **687** and similar vert designs. *Multicoloured. Photo.* P 14.
1788	250l. Type **687**	45	30
1789	300l. Pope John Paul II and Basilica of Santa Maria Maggiore	25	15
1790	400l. Pope and St. John's Basilica	30	15
1791	500l. Pope and St. Peter's Cathedral	90	15
1788/1791	Set of 4	1·70	70

(Des G. Toffoletti. Litho)

1983 (28 Mar). *Italian Aircraft (3rd series).* Horiz designs as T **656**. *Multicoloured.* P 14 × 13½.
1792	400l. Savoia SIAI 211	40	65
	a. Block. Nos. 1792/5 plus 2 labels	1·40	
1793	400l. Agusta A.129 Mangusta helicopter	40	65
1794	400l. Caproni C22J glider	40	65
1795	400l. Aeritalia/Aermacchi AM-X jet fighter	40	65
1792/1795	Set of 4	1·40	2·30

Nos. 1792/5 were issued together in *se-tenant* blocks of four stamps and two half stamp-size labels depicting "San Marco II" or "L-SAT" satellite, the order of the stamps differing in alternate blocks.

(Eng. L. Vangelli. Recess)

1983 (29 Apr). *Labour Day.* P 14 × 13½.
1796	**688** 1200l. ultramarine	1·20	95

(Des A. Raimondi. Photo)

1983 (30 Apr). *Flowers (3rd series).* Vert designs as T **652**. *Multicoloured.* P 13½ × 14.
1797	200l. Gladioli	60	1·30
1798	200l. Mimosa	60	1·30
1799	200l. Rhododendron	60	1·30

79

ITALY 1983

689 Galileo (after O. Leoni) and Telescope
690 Moneta and Doves 

(Des and eng E. Donnini. Recess and litho)

1983 (2 May). *Europa. T* **689** *and similar horiz design. Multicoloured.* P 14 × 13½.
1800   400l. Type **689** . . . . 4·50   1·10
1801   500l. Archimedes (marble bust) and screw . . . . 4·50   80

(Eng P. Arghittu. Recess)

1983 (5 May). *150th Birth Anniv of Ernesto Teodoro Moneta (Nobel Peace Prize winner).* P 13½ × 13½.
1802   **690**   500l. multicoloured 35   30

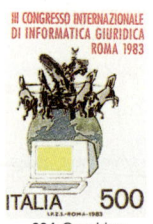

691 Quadriga, Globe and V.D.U.
692 Elevation of Host 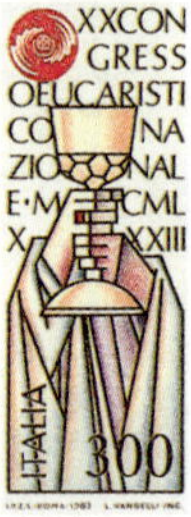
693 Frescobaldi 

1983 (9 May). *Third International Juridical Information Congress, Rome. Photo.* P 13½ × 14.
1803   **691**   500l. multicoloured 35   30

(Des A. Ciaburro. Photo)

1983 (13 May). *Folk Customs (2nd series). Vert design as T* **673**. *Multicoloured.* P 13½.
1804   300l. Ceri procession, Gubbio 35   50

(Des L. Vangelli. Photo)

1983 (14 May). *20th National Eucharistic Congress, Milan.* P 14.
1805   **692**   300l. multicoloured 25   15

1983 (30 July). *Tourist Publicity (10th series). Horiz designs as T* **556**. *Multicoloured. Photo.* P 14.
1806   250l. Alghero 40   1·60
1807   300l. Bardonecchia 50   80
1808   400l. Riccione 75   65
1809   500l. Taranto . . . . 1·50   15
1806/1809 Set of 4 . . . . 2·75   2·75

(Eng F. Borrelli. Recess)

1983 (15 Sept). *400th Birth Anniv of Girolamo Frescobaldi (composer).* P 13½ × 14.
1810   **693**   400l. myrtle green, indigo and brown 35   50

(Des and eng E. Donnini. Recess and litho)

1983 (10 Oct). *Villas (4th series). Horiz designs as T* **646**. *Multicoloured.* P 14 × 13½.
1811   250l. Villa Fidelia, Spello 50   1·20
1812   300l. Villa Imperiale, Pesaro 40   65

1813   400l. Michetti Convent, Francavilla al Mare 65   65
1814   500l. Villa di Riccia 80   15
1811/1814 Set of 4 . . . . 2·10   2·40

694 Francesco de Sanctis
695 "Madonna of the Chair" 

(Des V. Puliti. Photo)

1983 (28 Oct). *Death Centenary of Francesco de Sanctis (writer).* P 14 × 13½.
1815   **694**   300l. multicoloured 25   15

1983 (10 Nov). *Christmas. 500th Birth Anniv of Raphael (artist). T* **695** *and similar vert designs. Multicoloured. Photo.* P 13½ × 14.
1816   250l. Type **695** 20   15
1817   400l. "Sistine Madonna" 25   15
1818   500l. "Madonna of the Candles" . . . 60   15

696 Chain of Letters (Roberta Rizzi)
697 Battered Road Sign 

1983 (27 Nov). *Stamp Day. T* **696** *and similar multicoloured designs showing drawings by schoolchildren. Multicoloured.* P 13½ × 14 (300l.) or 14 × 13 (others).
1819   200l. Type **696** 15   50
1820   300l. Space postman delivering letter (Maria Grazia Federico) (*vert*) . . 35   20
1821   400l. Train leaving envelope and globe (Paolo Bucciarelli) 50   20

(Des R. Ferrini (300l.), C. Venturi (400l.). Photo)

1984 (20 Jan). *Road Safety. T* **697** *and similar horiz design. Multicoloured.* P 13½ × 14 (300l.) or 14 × 13½ (400l.).
1822   300l. Type **697** 20   50
1823   400l. Crashed car and policeman . . . 30   50

(Eng V. Puliti. Recess and litho)

1984 (25 Jan). *Anniversaries of Italian Artists (10th series). Vert designs as T* **567**. *Multicoloured.* P 14.
1824   300l. "Races at Bois de Boulogne" (Giuseppe de Nittis (1846–1884)) 35   15
1825   400l. "Paul Guillaume" (Amedeo Modigliani (1884–1920)) 45   50

80

ITALY   1984

698 Maserati "Biturbo"

(Des G. Toffoletti. Photo)

1984 (10 Mar). *Italian Motor Industry (1st series).* T **698** *and similar horiz designs. Multicoloured.* P 14 × 13½.
1826	450l. Type **698**	75	65
	a. Block. Nos. 1826/9 plus 2 labels	2·75	
1827	450l. Iveco "190.38 Special" lorry	75	65
1828	450l. Same Trattori "Galaxy" tractor	75	65
1829	450l. Alfa "33"	75	65
1826/1829	*Set of* 4	2·75	2·30

Nos. 1826/9 were issued together in *se-tenant* blocks of four stamps and two half stamp-size labels depicting Isotta Fraschini or Italia manufacturers' emblems.
See also Nos. 1867/70 and 1933/6.

699 Glassblower, Glasses and Jug

(Des P. Arghittu. Photo)

1984 (10 Apr). *Italian Work for the World (5th series). Ceramic and Glass Industries.* T **699** *and similar horiz design. Multicoloured.* P 14 × 13½.
1830	300l. Ceramic plaque and furnace	25	15
	a. Horiz strip. Nos. 1830/1 plus label	50	30
1831	300l. Type **699**	25	15

Nos. 1830/1 were issued together with intervening half stamp-size label inscr "LAVORO ITALIANO PER IL MONDO" in horizontal *se-tenant* strips within the sheet.

700 European Parliament Building, Strasbourg

(Des P. Gabriele. Photo)

1984 (16 Apr). *Second European Parliament Direct Elections.* P 14 × 13½.
| 1832 | **700** | 400l. multicoloured | 35 | 65 |

701 State Forest Corps Helicopter

702 Ministry of Posts and Telecommunications, Rome

(Des G. Ascari. Photo)

1984 (24 Apr). *Nature Protection. Forests.* T **701** *and similar horiz designs. Multicoloured.* P 14 × 13½.
1833	450l. Type **701**	1·20	65
	a. Block of 4. Nos. 1833/6	4·25	
1834	450l. Forest animals and burning cigarette	1·20	65
1835	450l. River and litter	1·20	65
1836	450l. Wildlife and building construction	1·20	65
1833/1836	*Set of* 4	4·25	2·30

Nos. 1833/6 were issued together in *se-tenant* blocks of four within the sheet.

(Des M. Codoni. Photo)

1984 (26 Apr). *"Italia '85" International Stamp Exhibition, Rome (1st issue).* T **702** *and similar horiz design. Multicoloured.* P 14.
1837	450l. Type **702**	45	25
1838	550l. Appian Way	55	30

See also Nos. 1857/9, 1862/4, 1871/3 and 1898/**MS**1912.

703 G. di Vittorio, B. Buozzi and A. Grandi

704 Bridge

(Des Maria M. Tuccelli. Photo)

1984 (30 Apr). *40th Anniv of Rome Pact (foundation of Italian Trade Unions).* P 14 × 13½.
| 1839 | **703** | 450l. multicoloured | 70 | 50 |

(Des J. Larriviere. Photo)

1984 (4 May). *Europa. 25th Anniv of European Post and Telecommunications Conference.* P 14 × 13½.
| 1840 | **704** | 450l. multicoloured | 2·00 | 1·10 |
| 1841 | | 550l. multicoloured | 3·75 | 4·75 |

705 Symposium Emblem

706 Horse-race

1984 (7 May). *International Telecommunications Symposium, Florence. Photo.* P 14.
| 1842 | **705** | 550l. multicoloured | 50 | 65 |

(Eng A. Ciaburro. Recess and litho)

1984 (12 May). *Centenary of Italian Derby.* T **706** *and similar horiz design. Multicoloured.* P 14 × 13½.
1843	250l. Type **706**	70	3·25
1844	400l. Horse-race (*different*)	1·10	1·10

1984 (19 May). *Tourist Publicity (11th series). Horiz designs as* T **556**. *Multicoloured. Photo.* P 14.
1845	350l. Campione d'Italia	80	3·00
1846	450l. Chianciano Terme	60	1·10
1847	450l. Padula	85	95
1848	550l. Syracuse	85	1·40
1845/1848	*Set of* 4	2·75	5·75

81

ITALY　　　　　　　　　　　　　　　　　　　　　　　　　　　　　　　1984

CP 707

708 Harvester, Thresher and Medieval Fields Map

1984 (27 July). *CONCESSIONAL PARCEL POST.* W **307**. *Photo.*
P 14 × 13½.
CP1849　CP **707**　3000l. blue and bright
　　　　　　　　　carmine　．．．．．．．．　3·25　2·10

(Des A. Ciaburro. Photo)

1984 (3 Sept). *Folk Customs (3rd issue). Vert design as T* **673**.
Multicoloured. P 13½ × 14.
1850　400l. Procession of Shrine of Santa
　　　　Rosa, Viterbo．．．．．．．．．．．　40　50

(Des Laura Bedetti. Photo)

1984 (1 Oct). *Peasant Farming. T* **708** *and similar horiz design.*
Multicoloured. P 14 × 13½.
1851　250l. Type **708**．．．．．．．．．．．．．　25　1·40
1852　350l. Hand oil press, cart and medieval
　　　　fields map．．．．．．．．．．．．．．．　30　50

(Des E. Donnini. Recess and litho)

1984 (6 Oct). *Villas (5th series). Horiz designs as T* **646**.
Multicoloured. P 14 × 13½.
1853　250l. Villa Caristo, Stignano．．．．．．．　60　2·10
1854　350l. Villa Doria Pamphili, Genoa．．．．　60　1·90
1855　400l. Villa Reale, Stupinigi．．．．．．．　80　65
1856　450l. Villa Mellone, Lecce．．．．．．．．　80　50
1853/1856 Set of 4．．．．．．．．．．．．．．．．．　2·50　3·75

709 Etruscan Bronze of Warrior

710 Dish Aerial, Globe and Punched Tape

(Des A. Ciaburro. Recess and litho (1857, 1859). litho (1858))

1984 (9 Nov). *"Italia '85" International Stamp Exhibition, Rome*
(2nd issue). T **709** *and similar vert designs. Multicoloured.*
P 13½ × 14.
1857　550l. Type **709**．．．．．．．．．．．．．　60　50
　　　　a. Strip of 3. Nos. 1857/9．．．．．．．．　1·80
1858　550l. Exhibition emblem．．．．．．．．．　60　50
1859　550l. Etruscan silver-backed mirror．．．　60　50
Nos. 1857/9 were issued together in *se-tenant* strips of three within the sheet.

(Des E. Donnini. Photo)

1985 (15 Jan). *Information Technology.* P 13½ × 14.
1860　**710**　350l. multicoloured．．．．．．．．．　25　50

711 Man helping Old Woman

712 "Venus in her Chariot" (fresco, Raphael)

(Des G. Hajnal. Photo)

1985 (23 Jan). *Problems of Elderly People.* P 13½ × 14.
1861　**711**　250l. multicoloured．．．．．．．．．　25　65

(Eng G. Verdelocco (1862), L. Vangeli (1864). Recess and litho (1862, 1864), litho (1863))

1985 (13 Feb). *"Italia '85" International Stamp Exhibition, Rome*
(3rd issue). T **712** *and similar vert designs. Multicoloured.*
P 13½ × 14.
1862　600l. Type **712**．．．．．．．．．．．．．　60　15
　　　　a. Strip of 3. Nos. 1862/4．．．．．．．．　1·80
1863　600l. Exhibition emblem．．．．．．．．．　60　15
1864　600l. Warriors (detail of fresco,
　　　　Baldassare Peruzzi)．．．．．．．．　60　15
Nos. 1862/4 were issued together in *se-tenant* strips of three within the sheet.

713 Plate, Vase and Pot

714 St. Mary of Peace Church, Rome

(Des E. Donnini. Photo)

1985 (2 Mar). *Italian Work for the World (6th series).*
Ceramics. T **713** *and similar horiz design. Multicoloured.*
P 14 × 13½.
1865　600l. Type **713**．．．．．．．．．．．．．　60　15
　　　　a. Horiz strip. Nos. 1865/6 plus
　　　　label．．．．．．．．．．．．．．．．．．．　1·20　30
1866　600l. Decorated plate．．．．．．．．．．．　60　15
Nos. 1865/6 were issued together with intervening half stamp-size label inscr "LAVORO ITALIANO PER IL MONDO" in horizontal *se-tenant* strips within the sheet.

(Des G. Toffoletti. Photo)

1985 (21 Mar). *Italian Motor Industry (2nd series). Horiz designs*
as T **698**. P 14 × 13½.
1867　450l. Fiat "Uno"．．．．．．．．．．．．．　1·20　50
　　　　a. Block. Nos. 1867/70 plus 2
　　　　labels．．．．．．．．．．．．．．．．．．．　4·25
1868　450l. Lamborghini "Countach LP500"．．　1·20　50
1869　450l. Lancia "Thema"．．．．．．．．．．．　1·20　50
1870　450l. Fiat Abarth "100 Bialbero"．．．．．　1·20　50
1867/1870 *Set of* 4．．．．．．．．．．．．．．．．．　4·25　1·80
Nos. 1867/70 were issued together in *se-tenant* blocks of four stamps and two half stamp-size labels depicting De Vecchi and Cisitalia manufacturers' emblems.

82

ITALY 1985

(Eng F. Tulli. Recess and litho (1871, 1873), litho (1872))

1985 (30 Mar). *"Italia '85" International Stamp Exhibition, Rome (4th issue). Baroque Art.* T **714** *and similar vert designs. Multicoloured.* P $13\frac{1}{2} \times 14$.
1871	250l. Type **714**		25	50
	a. Strip of 3. Nos. 1871/3		75	
1872	250l. Exhibition emblem		25	50
1873	250l. Fountain, obelisk and Saint Agnes's Church, Rome		25	50

Nos. 1871/3 were issued together in *se-tenant* strips of three within the sheet.

715 Pope Sixtus V
716 European Otter 

(Eng Rita Morena. Recess and litho)

1985 (24 Apr). *400th Anniv of Election of Pope Sixtus V.* P $13\frac{1}{2} \times 14$.
1874	**715**	1500l. multicoloured	1·60	95

(Des A. Ciaburro. Photo)

1985 (29 May). *Folk Customs (4th series). Vert designs as* T **673**. *Multicoloured.* P $13\frac{1}{2} \times 14$.
1875	250l. March of the Turks, Potenza		45	65
1876	350l. Republican regatta, Amalfi		65	65

(Des G. Ascari. Photo)

1985 (1 June). *Tourist Publicity (12th series). Horiz designs as* T **556**. *Multicoloured. Photo.* P 14.
1877	350l. Bormio		35	1·90
1878	400l. Castellammare di Stabia		50	65
1879	450l. Stromboli		60	65
1880	600l. Termoli		1·60	25
1877/1880	Set of 4		2·75	3·00

(Des G. Ascari. Photo)

1985 (5 June). *Nature Protection.* T **716** *and similar vert designs. Multicoloured.* P $13\frac{1}{2} \times 14$.
1881	500l. Type **716**		55	50
	a. Block of 4. Nos. 1881/4		2·00	
1882	500l. Primulas		55	50
1883	500l. Fir tree		55	50
1884	500l. Black-winged stilts		55	50
1881/1884	Set of 4		2·00	1·80

Nos. 1881/4 were issued together in *se-tenant* blocks of four within the sheet.

(Des and eng Rita Morena (350l.), R. Tulli (400l.). Recess and litho)

1985 (15 June). *Anniversaries of Italian Artists (11th series). Vert designs as* T **567**. *Multicoloured.* P 14.
1885	350l. "Madonna" (Giambattista Salvi (1609–85))		55	95
1886	400l. "The Pride of Work" (Mario Sironi (1885–1961))		70	95

717 Aureliano Pertile and Giovanni Martinelli (singers)
718 San Salvatore Abbey 

(Des D. C. Vangelli. Photo)

1985 (20 June). *Europa.* T **717** *and similar vert design. Multicoloured.* P $13\frac{1}{2} \times 14$.
1887	500l. Type **717**		2·75	95
1888	600l. Vincenzo Bellini and Johann Sebastian Bach (composers)		4·75	1·30

(Eng Laura Bedetti. Recess and litho)

1985 (1 Aug). *950th Anniv of San Salvatore Abbey, Mt. Amiata.* P $14 \times 13\frac{1}{2}$.
1889	**718**	450l. multicoloured	40	15

719 Cyclists
720 U.N. and Congress Emblems and Globe 

(Des F. Borrelli. Photo)

1985 (21 Aug). *World Cycling Championships, Bassano del Grappa.* P $14 \times 13\frac{1}{2}$.
1890	**719**	400l. multicoloured	70	50

(Des M. Codoni. Photo)

1985 (26 Aug). *Seventh United Nations Crime Prevention Congress, Milan.* P $14 \times 13\frac{1}{2}$.
1891	**720**	600l. multicoloured	55	15

721 Profile and Emblem
722 State Emblems of Italy and Vatican City and Medallion (Mario Soccorsi) 

(Des R. Ferrini. Photo)

1985 (3 Sept). *International Youth Year.* P $14 \times 13\frac{1}{2}$.
1892	**721**	600l. multicoloured	60	15

(Des and eng E. Donnini. Recess and litho)

1985 (1 Oct). *Villas (6th series). Horiz designs as* T **646**. *Multicoloured.* P $14 \times 13\frac{1}{2}$.
1893	300l. Villa Nitti, Maratea		65	50
1894	400l. Villa Aldrovandi Mazzacorati, Bologna		85	15

ITALY 1985

1895	500l. Villa Santa Maria, Pula	1·10	10
1896	600l. Villa de Mersi, Villazzano	1·40	15
1893/1896	Set of 4	3·50	85

(Des Luciana de Simoni. Photo)

1985 (15 Oct). *Ratification of the Modification of 1929 Lateran Concordat.* P 14 × 13½.

1897	722	400l. multicoloured	70	50

723 Parma Town Hall and 1857 25c. Stamp

724 Basel 1845 2½r. Stamp

(Des G. Toffoletti (1898/1906). Eng V. Puliti (**MS**1912). Recess and litho (1908, 1910, **MS**1912), litho (others))

1985 (25 Oct). *"Italia '85" International Stamp Exhibition, Rome (5th issue).* Multicoloured.

(a) T **723** and similar horiz designs. P 14.

1898	300l. Type **723**	25	65
	a. Sheetlet. Nos. 1898/1906	2·00	
1899	300l. Naples New Castle and 1858 2g. stamp	25	65
1900	300l. Palermo Cathedral and Sicily 1859 ½g. stamp	25	65
1901	300l. Modena Cathedral and 1852 15c. stamp	25	65
1902	300l. Piazzo Navona, Rome, and Papal States 1852 7b. stamp	25	65
1903	300l. Palazzo Vecchio, Florence, and Tuscany 1851 2c. stamp	25	65
1904	300l. Turin and Sardinia 1861 3l. stamp	25	65
1905	300l. Bologna and Romagna 1859 6b. stamp	25	65
1906	300l. Palazzo Litta, Milan, and Lombardy and Venetia 1850 15c. stamp	25	65

Nos. 1898/1906 were printed together in *se-tenant* sheetlets.

(b) T **724** and similar horiz designs. P 14 × 13½.

1907	500l. Type **724**	50	80
	a. Sheetlet. Nos. 1907/11 plus label	2·25	
1908	500l. Japan 1871 48m. stamp	50	80
1909	500l. United States 1847 10c. stamp	50	80
1910	500l. Western Australia 1854 1d. stamp	50	80
1911	500l. Mauritius 1848 2d. stamp	50	80
1898/1911	Set of 14	4·25	8·75

Nos. 1907/11 were printed together in *se-tenant* sheetlets.

(c) Sheet 86 × 56 mm. Imperf.
MS1912 4000l. Sardinia 1851 5c. stamp and Great Britain "Penny Black" ... 3·00 5·00
No. **MS**1912 was on sale at the exhibition or by subscription.

725 Skiers

726 Amilcare Ponchielli and Scene from *La Gioconda*

(Des A. de Stefani. Photo)

1986 (25 Jan). *Cross-country Skiing.* P 14 × 13½.

1913	**725**	450l. multicoloured	35	50

(Des A. Ciaburro. Photo)

1986 (3 Feb). *Folk Customs (5th series).* Vert design as T **673**. Multicoloured. P 13½ × 14.

1914	450l. Le Candelore, Catania	40	50

(Des P. Fazzini (1916). Eng Rita Morena (1915). Recess and litho (1915), photo (1916))

1986 (8–15 Mar). *Composers.* T **726** and similar vert design. Multicoloured. P 14 × 13½ (1915) or 13½ × 14 (1916).

1915	2000l. Type **726** (death centenary)	2·10	65
1916	2000l. Giovan Battista Pergolesi (250th death anniv) (15.3)	2·30	80

727 Acitrezza

(Des E. Vangelli. Photo)

1986 (24 Mar). *Tourist Publicity (13th series).* T **727** and similar horiz designs. Multicoloured. P 14.

1917	350l. Type **727**	45	50
1918	450l. Capri	55	80
1919	550l. Merano	70	50
1920	650l. San Benedetto del Tronto	85	15
1917/1920	Set of 4	2·30	1·70

728 Heart-shaped Tree (life)

729 "Eyes"

(Des E. Consolazione. Photo)

1986 (28 Apr). *Europa.* T **728** and similar vert designs. Multicoloured. P 13½ × 14.

1921	650l. Type **728**	1·80	50
	a. Block of 4. Nos. 1921/4	6·50	
1922	650l. Star-shaped tree (poetry)	1·80	50
1923	650l. Butterfly-shaped tree (colour)	1·80	50
1924	650l. Sun-shaped tree (energy)	1·80	50
1921/1924	Set of 4	6·50	1·80

Nos. 1921/4 were issued together in *se-tenant* blocks of four within the sheet.

(Des E. Greco. Photo)

1986 (3 May). *25th International Ophthalmology Congress, Rome.* P 14.

1925	**729**	550l. multicoloured	45	15

ITALY 1986

730 Italian Police

(Des G. Toffoletti. Photo)
1986 (10 May). *European Police Meeting, Chianciano Terme.* P 14.
1926	**730**	550l. multicoloured	95	50
1927		650l. multicoloured	1·20	95

Nos. 1926/7 were each issued with *se-tenant* half stamp-size label depicting a policeman or policewoman respectively.

731 Battle Scene    **732** Figure with Flag

1986 (31 May). *120th Anniv of Battle of Bezzecca.* Photo. P 14 × 13½.
1928	**731**	550l. multicoloured	50	50

(Des E. Vangelli. Photo)
1986 (31 May). *National Independence Martyrs' Day.* P 14.
1929	**732**	2000l. multicoloured	2·40	65

733 Bersagliere and Helmets 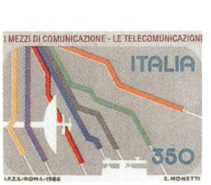   **734** Dish Aerial, Transmitter and "Messages"

(Des Anna Maresca. Photo)
1986 (7 June). *150th Anniv of Turin Bersaglieri Corps (alpine troops).* P 13½ × 14.
1930	**733**	450l. multicoloured	85	50

(Des E. Monetti. Photo)
1986 (16 June). *Telecommunications.* P 14 × 13½.
1931	**734**	350l. multicoloured	50	15

735 Varallo

(Des and eng F. Tulli. Recess)
1986 (28 June). *Holy Mountain of Varallo.* P 14.
1932	**735**	2000l. bronze green & turquoise-blue	1·90	65

(Des G. Toffoletti. Photo)
1986 (4 July). *Italian Motor Industry (3rd series).* Horiz designs as T **698**. Multicoloured. P 14 × 13½.
1933	450l. Alfa Romeo "AR 8 Turbo"	90	50
	a. Block. Nos. 1933/6 plus 2 labels	3·25	
1934	450l. Innocenti "650 SE"	90	50
1935	450l. Ferrari "Testarossa"	90	50
1936	450l. Fiatallis "FR 10B"	90	50
1933/1936	Set of 4	3·25	1·80

Nos. 1933/6 were issued together in *se-tenant* blocks of four stamps and two half stamp-size labels bearing Scat and Simit manufacturers' emblems.

736 Clothes and Woman (fashion)

(Des Luciana de Simoni (450l.). Photo)
1986 (14 July). *Italian Work for the World (7th series).* T **736** and similar horiz designs. Multicoloured. P 14 × 13½.
1937	450l. Type **736**	75	15
	a. Horiz strip. Nos. 1937/8 plus label	5·00	
1938	450l. Man and clothes (fashion)	75	15
1939	650l. Olivetti personal computer, keyboard and screen	2·10	50
1940	650l. Breda steam turbine	2·10	50
1937/1940	Set of 4	5·00	1·20

Nos. 1937/8 were issued together with intervening half stamp-size label showing fashion accessories in horizontal *se-tenant* strips within the sheet.

737 Airplane flying through "40"    **738** "Madonna and Child" (bronze sculpture, Donatello)

85

ITALY 1986

(Des F. Losso and M. Sciarrini (550l.), G. Toffoletti (650l.). Photo)
1986 (16 Sept). *40th Anniv of Alitalia (national airline). T* **737** *and similar horiz design. Multicoloured.* P 14 × 13½.
1941	550l. Type **737**		55	15
1942	650l. Airplane and landing lights		70	15

(Des and eng E. Donnini. Recess and litho)
1986 (1 Oct). *Villas (7th series). Horiz designs as T* **646**. *Multicoloured.* P 14 × 13½.
1943	350l. Villa Necker, Trieste		40	50
1944	350l. Villa Borromeo, Cassano d'Adda		40	50
1945	450l. Villa Palagonia, Bagheria		60	15
1946	550l. Villa Medicea, Poggio a Caiano		60	15
1947	650l. Issogne Castle		80	15
1943/1947	Set of 5		2·50	1·30

(Eng P. Arghittu. Recess)
1986 (10 Oct). *Christmas.* P 14.
1948	**738** 450l. bistre		45	15

(Des and eng F. Tulli. Recess and litho)
1986 (11 Oct). *Anniversaries of Italian Artists (12th series). Vert designs as T* **567**. P 14.
1949	450l. black and pale orange		1·00	15
1950	550l. multicoloured		1·20	15

Designs:—450l. Drawing of woman (Andrea del Sarto 1486–1531)); 550l. "Daphne at Pavarola" (Felice Casorati (1883–1963)).

739 Lockheed Hercules Transport dropping Squares in National Colours onto Globe

740 Engraving 1862 Stamp

(Des U. Monaco (550l.), A. Rampelli (650l.) Photo)
1986 (11 Nov). *International Peace Year. T* **739** *and similar vert design. Multicoloured.* P 13½ × 14.
1951	550l. Type **739**		50	15
1952	650l. Airplane, Cross and people (commemoration of Italian airmen killed on mission to Kindu, Congo)		60	15

(Des G. Verdelocco. Photo)
1986 (29 Nov). *Stamp Day. Francesco Maria Matraire (engraver).* P 14 × 13½.
1953	**740** 550l. multicoloured		85	15

741 Woven Threads (Marzotto Textile Industry)

(Des V. Barison (1954), Procom (1955). Photo)
1987 (27 Feb). *Italian Industry. T* **741** *and similar horiz design.* P 14 × 13½.
1954	700l. multicoloured		65	15
1955	700l. new blue and deep turquoise-blue		65	15

Design:—No. 1955, Clouds and flame (Italgas Gas Corporation).

742 River Volturno

743 Gramsci

(Des Laura Mezzana. Photo)
1987 (6 Mar). *Nature Protection. Rivers and Lakes. T* **742** *and similar horiz designs. Multicoloured.* P 14 × 13½.
1956	500l. Type **742**		75	15
	a. Block of 4. Nos. 1956/9		2·75	
1957	500l. Lake Garda		75	15
1958	500l. Lake Trasimeno		75	15
1959	500l. River Tirso		75	15
1956/1959	Set of 4		2·75	55

Nos. 1956/9 were issued together in *se-tenant* blocks of four within the sheet.

(Des G. Manzu. Photo)
1987 (27 Apr). *50th Death Anniv of Antonio Gramsci (politician).* P 14 × 13½.
1960	**743** 600l. brownish grey, black and scarlet		70	50

744 Church of the Motorway of the Sun, Florence (Giovanni Michelucci)

745 View of Naples on Football

(Des E. Vangelli. Photo)
1987 (4 May). *Europa. Architecture. T* **744** *and similar horiz design. Multicoloured. Photo.* P 14 × 13½.
1961	600l. Type **744**		1·20	65
1962	700l. Termini station, Rome (Nervi)		1·50	65

(Des E. Vangelli. Photo)
1987 (9 May). *Tourist Publicity (14th series). Horiz designs as T* **556**. *Multicoloured.* P 14.
1963	380l. Verbania Pallanza		50	1·40
1964	400l. Palmi		55	80
1965	500l. Vasto		70	50
1966	600l. Villacidro		80	80
1963/1966	Set of 4		2·30	3·00

(Des V. Cozzella. Litho)
1987 (18 May). *S.S.C. Naples, National Football Champion, 1986–87.* P 13½ × 14.
1967	**745** 500l. multicoloured		1·10	1·10

ITALY 1987

746 "The Absinthe Drinker" (Edgar Degas)
747 Liguori and Gulf of Naples 

1987 (29 May). Anti-alcoholism Campaign. Photo. P $13\frac{1}{2} \times 14$.
1968   746   380l. multicoloured 55   50

(Des and eng A. Ciaburro. Recess and litho)

1987 (1 Aug). Death Bicentenary of St. Alfonso Maria de Liguori (co-founder of Redemptorists). P $14 \times 13\frac{1}{2}$.
1969   747   400l. multicoloured 35   50

748 Emblem and Olympic Stadium, Rome
749 Piazza del Popolo, Ascoli Piceno 

(Des A. Rinnaudo. Photo)

1987 (29 Aug). World Light Athletics Championships, Rome (1970) and "Olymphilex '87" Stamp Exhibition, Rome (1971). T **748** and similar horiz design. Multicoloured. P 14.
1970   700l. Type **748** 55   15
1971   700l. International Olympic Committee building, Foro Italico, Rome 55   15

(Des A. Ciaburro. Photo)

1987 (12 Sept). Folk Customs (6th series). Vert design as T **673**. Multicoloured. P $13\frac{1}{2} \times 14$.
1972   380l. Joust, Foligno 45   50

(Des and eng F. Tulli. Recess and litho)

1987 (10 Oct). Piazzas (1st series). T **749** and similar horiz designs. Multicoloured. P $14 \times 13\frac{1}{2}$.
1973   380l. Type **749** 45   50
1974   500l. Piazza Giuseppe Verdi, Palermo 60   15
1975   600l. Piazza San Carlo, Turin . . . 75   15
1976   700l. Piazza dei Signori, Verona . . . 85   65
1973/1976 Set of 4 . . . . 2·40   1·30
See also Nos. 2002/3 and 2023/4.

750 "The Adoration in the Manger" (St. Francis's Basilica, Assisi)
751 Battle Scene 

1987 (15 Oct). Christmas. Frescoes by Giotto. T **750** and similar vert design. Multicoloured. Photo. P $13\frac{1}{2} \times 14$.
1977   500l. Type **750** 65   15
1978   600l. "Epiphany" (Scrovegni Chapel, Padua) 75   15

(Des and eng E. Donnini. Recess and litho)

1987 (3 Nov). 120th Anniv of Battle of Mentana. P $14 \times 13\frac{1}{2}$.
1979   751   380l. multicoloured 50   50

752 "Christ Pantocrator" (mosaic, Monreale Cathedral)

(Des and eng P. Arghittu. Recess and litho)

1987 (4 Nov). Artistic Heritage. T **752** and similar horiz design. Multicoloured. P 14.
1980   500l. Type **752** 85   50
1981   500l. San Carlo Theatre, Naples (18th-century engraving) 85   50

753 College and 1787 and 1987 Uniforms
754 Marco de Marchi (philatelist) and Milan Cathedral 

(Des G. Toffoletti. Recess and litho)

1987 (14 Nov). Bicentenary of Nunziatella Military Academy, Naples. P $14 \times 13\frac{1}{2}$.
1982   753   600l. multicoloured 60   50

(Des P. Arghittu. Photo)

1987 (20 Nov). Stamp Day. P $13\frac{1}{2} \times 14$.
1983   754   500l. multicoloured 90   50

755 Man chipping Flints
756 Lyceum 

(Des U. Taccola. Eng E. Donnini. Recess and litho)

1988 (6 Feb). Homo aeserniensis. P $13\frac{1}{2} \times 14$.
1984   755   500l. multicoloured 40   65

ITALY   1988

(Eng E. Donnini. Recess and litho)

1988 (1 Mar). *E. Q. Visconti Lyceum, Rome.* P 14 × 13½.
1985 **756** 500l. multicoloured 45 30
See also Nos. 2019, 2109 and 2127.

757 Statue, Bosco and Boy

758 15th-Century Soncino Bible

(Des C. Mezzana. Photo)

1988 (2 Apr). *Death Centenary of St. John Bosco (founder of Salesian Brothers).* P 13½ × 14.
1986 **757** 500l. multicoloured 40 50

(Des and eng P. Arghittu. Recess and litho)

1988 (7 Apr). *Anniversaries of Italian Artists (13th series).* Vert design as T **567**. Multicoloured. P 14.
1987 650l. "Archaeologists" (Giorgio de Chirico (1888–1978)) . . . . . 1·00 65

(Des E. Vangelli. Photo)

1988 (22 Apr). *500th Anniv of First Printing of Bible in Hebrew.* P 14 × 13½.
1988 **758** 550l. multicoloured 60 30

759 St. Valentine, Epileptics and Wave Patterns

760 "ETR 450" Electric Train in Station

(Des G. Toffoletti. Photo)

1988 (23 Apr). *Anti-epilepsy Campaign.* P 14 × 13½.
1989 **759** 500l. multicoloured 60 65

(Des M. Codoni (650l.), G. Micheletto (750l.) Photo)

1988 (2 May). *Europa. Transport and Communications.* T **760** and similar horiz designs. Multicoloured. P 14 × 13½.
1990 650l. Type **760** . . . . . 1·20 95
1991 750l. Map and keyboard operator (electronic postal systems) . . . 1·40 1·40

(Des E. Vangelli. Photo)

1988 (7 May). *Tourist Publicity (15th series).* Horiz designs as T **556**. Multicoloured. P 14.
1992 400l. Castiglione della Pescaia 35 65
1993 500l. Lignano Sabbiadoro 50 50
1994 650l. St. Domenico's Church, Noto . . . 60 50
1995 750l. Vieste 70 80
1992/1995 Set of 4 . . . . . 1·90 2·20

761 Golfer on Ball

762 Stadium and Mascot

(Des A. Testa. Photo)

1988 (16 May). *Golf.* P 14.
1996 **761** 500l. multicoloured 45 65

1988 (16 May). *World Cup Football Championship, Italy (1990) (1st issue).* Photo. P 14 × 13½.
1997 **762** 3150l. multicoloured . . . . . 2·30 4·75
See also Nos. 2049 and 2052/87.

763 Milan Cathedral on Football

764 Horse's Head

(Des V. Cozzella. Photo)

1988 (23 May). *A.C Milan, National Football Champion, 1987–88.* P 13½ × 14.
1998 **763** 650l. multicoloured . . . . . 55 1·10

(Eng Rita Morena. Recess and litho)

1988 (4 June). *Artistic Heritage. Pergola Bronzes.* T **764** and similar horiz design. Multicoloured. P 14.
1999 500l. Type **764** 40 95
2000 650l. Bust of woman 55 95

765 Student (bas-relief)

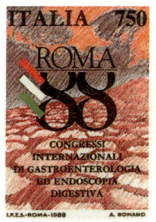

766 Emblem and Appian Way

(Eng L. Vangelli. Recess)

1988 (10 June). *900th Anniv of Bologna University.* P 13½ × 14.
2001 **765** 500l. dull violet 40 65

ITALY 1988

(Des and eng F. Tulli. Recess and litho)

1988 (2 July). *Piazzas (2nd series). Horiz designs as T* **749**. *Multicoloured.* P 14 × 13½.
| 2002 | 400l. Piazza del Duomo, Pistoia | 50 | 50 |
| 2003 | 550l. Piazza del Unita d'Italia, Trieste | 65 | 50 |

(Des A. Ciaburro. Photo)

1988 (13 Aug). *Folk Customs (7th series). Vert design as T* **673**. *Multicoloured.* P 13½ × 14.
| 2004 | 550l. Candle procession, Sassari | 90 | 50 |

(Des A. Romano. Photo)

1988 (5 Sept). *"Roma 88" International Gastroenterology and Digestive Endoscopy Congress.* P 13½ × 14.
| 2005 | 766 | 750l. multicoloured | 80 | 50 |

767 *Ossessione* (Luchino Visconti, 1942)

(Des F. Filanci T.P.A. Photo)

1988 (13 Oct). *Italian Films. T* **767** *and similar horiz designs showing scene from and advertising poster of named film. Multicoloured.* P 14 × 13½.
2006	500l. Type 767	90	1·10
2007	650l. *Ladri di Biciclette* (Vittorio de Sica, 1948)	90	95
2008	2400l. *Roma Citta Aperta* (Roberto Rossellini, 1945)	3·25	1·30
2009	3050l. *Riso Amaro* (Giuseppe de Santis, 1949)	3·50	2·20
2006/2009	Set of 4	7·50	5·00

768 Bird (aluminium)

769 "Holy Family" (Pasquale Celommi)

(Des G. Micheletto (2011). Eng F. Borrelli (2012). Recess and photo (2012), photo (others))

1988 (19 Oct). *Italian Industry. T* **768** *and similar horiz designs. Multicoloured.* P 14 × 13½.
2010	750l. Type 768	50	15
2011	750l. Oscilloscope display (electronics)	50	50
2012	750l. Banknote engraving, 1986 tourism stamp and medals (60th anniv of State Polygraphic Institute)	50	50

1988 (29 Oct). *Christmas (1st issue). Photo.* P 13½ × 14.
| 2013 | 769 | 650l. multicoloured | 85 | 30 |

See also No. 2015.

770 Borromeo and Plague Victims

771 "Nativity" (bas-relief)

(Des and eng A. Ciaburro. Recess and litho)

1988 (4 Nov). *450th Birth Anniv of St. Carlo Borromeo, Archbishop of Milan.* P 14 × 13½.
| 2014 | 770 | 2400l. multicoloured | 1·90 | 1·30 |

(Des and eng P. Arghittu. Recess and litho)

1988 (12 Nov). *Christmas (2nd issue).* P 14 × 13½.
| 2015 | 771 | 500l. deep bluish green & lake-brown | 90 | 50 |

772 Edoardo Chiossone (stamp designer) and Japanese 1879 2s. "Koban" Stamp

773 AIDS Virus

(Des N. Suezawa. Photo)

1988 (9 Dec). *Stamp Day.* P 13½ × 14.
| 2016 | 772 | 500l. multicoloured | 50 | 15 |

1989 (13 Jan). *Anti-AIDS Campaign. Photo.* P 13½ × 14.
| 2017 | 773 | 650l. multicoloured | 55 | 15 |

774 1907 Itala Car and Route Map

(Des G. Toffoletti. Photo)

1989 (21 Jan). *Re-enactment of 1907 Peking–Paris Car Rally.* P 14 × 13½.
| 2018 | 774 | 3150l. multicoloured | 2·75 | 6·50 |

(Des and eng E. Donnini. Recess and litho)

1989 (31 Mar). *Giuseppe Parini Lyceum, Milan. Horiz design as T* **756**. P 14 × 13½.
| 2019 | 650l. multicoloured | 50 | 15 |

ITALY   1989

776 Fresco, Ragione Palace, Padua

(Des and eng P. Arghittu. Recess and litho (500l.), recess (650l.))

1989 (8 Apr). *Artistic Heritage.* T **776** and similar vert design. P 14.
2020	500l. multicoloured	50	80
2021	650l. slate-blue	65	50

Design:—650l. Crypt, Basilica of St. Nicolas, Bari.

777 Stylized Yachts
778 Leap-frog (Luca Rizzello)

(Des A. Rinnaudo. Photo)

1989 (8 Apr). *World Sailing Championships, Alassio, Naples and Porto Cervo.* P 14.
2022	777	3050l. multicoloured	2·50	2·10

(Des and eng F. Tulli. Recess and litho)

1989 (10 Apr). *Piazzas (3rd series).* Horiz designs as T **749**. Multicoloured. P 14 × 13½.
2023	400l. Piazza di Spagna, Rome	45	65
2024	400l. Piazza del Duomo, Catanzaro	45	65

1989 (8 May). *Europa. Children's Games.* T **778** and similar multicoloured designs. Photo. P 13½ × 14 (650l.) or 14 × 13½ (others).
2025	500l. Type 778	80	65
2026	650l. Girl dressing up (Serena Forcuti) (vert)	1·20	50
2027	750l. Sack race (Adelise Lahner)	1·50	50

(Des A. Ciaburro. Photo)

1989 (27 May). *Folk Customs (8th series).* Vert design as T **673**. Multicoloured. P 13½ × 14.
2028	400l. Spello flower paintings	35	65

779 Cloisters
780 Parliamentary Emblem as Tree on Map

(Des L. Vangelli. Recess)

1989 (29 May). *Pisa University.* P 14 × 13½.
2029	779	500l. dull violet	40	50

(Des Class 3C, G. Carducci Elementary School, Legnano. Photo)

1989 (3 June). *Third Direct Elections to European Parliament.* P 13½ × 14.
2030	780	500l. multicoloured	60	50

No. 2030 is also inscribed with the European Currency Unit rate of 0.31 ECU.

(Des E. Vangelli. Photo)

1989 (10 June). *Tourist Publicity (16th series).* Horiz designs as T **556**. Multicoloured. P 14.
2031	500l. Grottammare	55	80
2032	500l. Spotorno	55	80
2033	500l. Pompeii	55	80
2034	500l. Giardini Naxos	55	80
2031/2034	Set of 4	2·00	2·75

781 1889 5c. Savoy Arms Stamp
782 Ball and Club Emblem

1989 (24 June). *Centenary of Ministry of Posts and Telecommunications.* T **781** and similar horiz design. Photo. P 14 × 13½.
2035	500l. Type 781	50	1·60
2036	2400l. Globe within posthorn	1·80	1·60

(Des V. Cozzella. Photo)

1989 (26 June). *Inter Milan, National Football Champion, 1988–89.* P 14 × 13½.
2037	782	650l. multicoloured	50	65

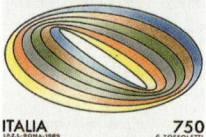

783 Stylized Chamber

(Des G. Toffoletti. Photo)

1989 (28 June). *Centenary of Interparliamentary Union.* P 14 × 13½.
2038	783	750l. multicoloured	55	50

ITALY 1989

784 Phrygian Cap

(Des F. M. Ricci. Photo)

1989 (7 July). *Bicentenary of French Revolution.* P 14.
2039 784   3150l. multicoloured   2·75   6·50

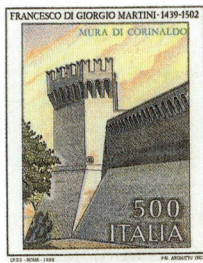

785 Corinaldo Wall   **786** Chaplin in Film Scenes

(Des and eng P. Arghittu. Recess and litho)

1989 (2 Sept). *Artistic Heritage. 550th Birth Anniv of Francesco di Giorgio Martini (architect).* P 14.
2040 785   500l. multicoloured   55   50

(Des and eng Rita Morena. Recess)

1989 (23 Sept). *Birth Centenary of Charlie Chaplin (film actor and director).* P 14 × 13½.
2041 786   750l. black and blackish brown   70   50

787 "Inauguration of Naples–Portici Line" (S. Fergola) (left-hand detail)

(Eng A. Ciaburro. Recess and litho)

1989 (3 Oct). *150th Anniv of Naples–Portici Railway.* T **787** and similar horiz design. Multicoloured. P 14 × 13½.
2042 550l. Type **787**   45   50
   a. Horiz pair. Nos. 2042/3   90   1·00
2043 550l. Right-hand detail   45   50
Nos. 2042/3 were issued together in horizontal *se-tenant* pairs within the sheet, each pair forming a composite design.

788 Castelfidardo, Accordion and Stradella

(Des A. Ciaburro. Photo)

1989 (14 Oct). *Italian Industry.* T **788** and similar horiz design. Multicoloured. P 14 × 13½.
2044 450l. Type **788**   40   50
2045 450l. Books (Arnoldo Mondadori Publishing House)   40   50

789 Madonna and Child   **790** Emilio Diena (stamp dealer)

1989 (21 Oct). *Christmas.* T **789** and similar vert design showing details of "Adoration of the Magi" by Correggio. Multicoloured. Photo. P 13½ × 14.
2046 500l. Type **789**   55   50
   a. Horiz pair. Nos. 2046/7   1·10   1·00
2047 500l. Magi   55   50
Nos. 2046/7 were issued together in *se-tenant* pairs, each pair forming a composite design.

(Des S. Consolazione. Photo)

1989 (24 Nov). *Stamp Day.* P 13½ × 14.
2048 790   500l. black, chestnut and new blue   60   50

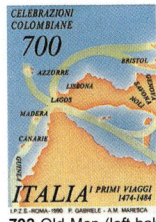

791 Monument (Mario Ceroli) and Football Pitch   **792** Old Map (left half) with Route superimposed

(Eng Maria M. Tuccelli. Recess and litho)

1989 (9 Dec). *World Cup Football Championship, Italy (1990) (2nd issue).* P 13½ × 14.
2049 791   450l. multicoloured   40   65

(Des P. Gabriele and Anna Maresca. Photo)

1990 (24 Feb). *Columbus's First Voyages, 1474–84.* T **792** and similar vert design. Multicoloured. P 13½ × 14.
2050 700l. Type **792**   60   50
   a. Horiz pair. Nos. 2050/1   1·10   1·00
2051 700l. Right half of map   60   50
Nos. 2050/1 were issued together in *se-tenant* pairs within the sheet, each pair forming a composite design.

793 Italy   **794** National Colours

91

ITALY 1990

(Des G. Toffoletti and M. Codoni. Photo)
1990 (24 Mar). *World Cup Football Championship, Italy (3rd issue).* T **793** and similar horiz designs showing finalists' emblems or playing venues. Multicoloured. P 14 × 13½.

2052	450l. Type **793**	30	65
	a. Sheetlet. Nos. 2052/7	1·60	
2053	450l. U.S.A.	30	65
2054	450l. Olympic Stadium, Rome	30	65
2055	450l. Comunale Stadium, Florence	30	65
2056	450l. Austria	30	65
2057	450l. Czechoslovakia	30	65
2058	600l. Argentina	40	65
	a. Sheetlet. Nos. 2058/63	2·10	
2059	600l. U.S.S.R.	40	65
2060	600l. San Paolo Stadium, Naples	40	65
2061	600l. New Stadium, Bari	40	65
2062	600l. Cameroun	40	65
2063	600l. Rumania	40	65
2064	650l. Brazil	50	65
	a. Sheetlet. Nos. 2064/9	2·75	
2065	650l. Costa Rica	50	65
2066	650l. Delle Alpi Stadium, Turin	50	65
2067	650l. Ferraris Stadium, Genoa	50	65
2068	650l. Sweden	50	65
2069	650l. Scotland	50	65
2070	700l. United Arab Emirates	50	65
	a. Sheetlet. Nos. 2070/5	2·75	
2071	700l. West Germany	50	65
2072	700l. Dall'Ara Stadium, Bologna	50	65
2073	700l. Meazza Stadium, Milan	50	65
2074	700l. Colombia	50	65
2075	700l. Yugoslavia	50	65
2076	800l. Belgium	60	1·30
	a. Sheetlet. Nos. 2076/81	3·25	
2077	800l. Uruguay	60	1·30
2078	800l. Bentegodi Stadium, Verona	60	1·30
2079	800l. Friuli Stadium, Udine	60	1·30
2080	800l. South Korea	60	1·30
2081	800l. Spain	60	1·30
2082	1200l. England	85	1·30
	a. Sheetlet. Nos. 2082/7	4·50	
2083	1200l. Netherlands	85	1·60
2084	1200l. Sant'Elia Stadium, Cagliari	85	1·60
2085	1200l. La Favorita Stadium, Palermo	85	1·60
2086	1200l. Ireland	85	1·60
2087	1200l. Egypt	85	1·60
2052/2087	Set of 36	17·00	30·00

Designs of the same value were issued together in *se-tenant* sheetlets of six stamps, each sheetlet covering one of the round-robin groups.

Overprints on No. 2070a of the Cup (on No. 2071), "GERMANIA CAMPIONE DEL MONDO" (on No. 2073), the FIFA emblem, a copyright note and a number (in the margin) were privately applied.

See also No. 2104.

(Des E. Vangelli (2088/90). Photo)
1990 (30 Mar). *Tourist Publicity (17th series).* Horiz designs as T **558**. Multicoloured. P 14.

2088	600l. San Felice Circeo	55	50
2089	600l. Castellammare del Golfo	55	50
2090	600l. Montepulciano	55	50
2091	600l. Sabbioneta	55	50
2088/2091	Set of 4	2·00	1·80

(Des A. Ciaburro and Maria Perrini. Photo)
1990 (9 Apr). *Folk Customs (9th series).* Vert design as T **673**. Multicoloured. P 13½ × 14.

2092	600l. Avelignesi horse-race, Merano	45	50

(Des M. Spera. Photo)
1990 (10 Apr). *Death Centenary of Aurelio Saffi.* P 14.

2093	794 700l. multicoloured	50	40

795 Giovanni Giorgi (inventor)

796 Flags, Globe and Workers (after "The Four States" (Pellizza da Volpedo))

(Des Maria Tuccelli. Photo)
1990 (23 Apr). *55th Anniv of Invention of Giorgi/MKSA System of Electrotechnical Units.* P 14 × 13½.

2094	795 600l. multicoloured	40	50

(Des E. Donnini. Photo)
1990 (28 Apr). *Centenary of Labour Day.* P 13½ × 14.

2095	796 600l. multicoloured	40	50

797 Ball on Map

798 Piazza San Silvestro Post Office, Rome

(Des V. Cozzella. Photo)
1990 (30 Apr). *S.S.C. Naples, National Football Champion, 1989–90.* P 13½ × 14.

2096	797 700l. multicoloured	50	50

(Des P. Gabriele and A. Maresca. Photo)
1990 (7 May). *Europa. Post Office Buildings.* T **798** and similar horiz designs. Multicoloured. P 14 × 13½.

2097	700l. Type **798**	1·00	50
2098	800l. Fondaco Tedeschi post office, Venice	1·50	65

799 Paisiello

800 Globe, Open Book and Bust of Dante

(Des P. Gabriele. Photo)
1990 (9 May). *250th Birth Anniv of Giovanni Paisiello (composer).* P 13½ × 14.

2099	799 450l. multicoloured	30	50

(Des M. Codoni. Photo)
1990 (12 May). *Centenary of Dante Alighieri Society.* P 14 × 13½.

2100	800 700l. multicoloured	45	80

ITALY 1990

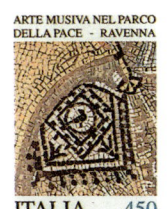

801 Byzantine Mosaic, Ravenna
802 Malatestiana Temple, Rimini

(Des Academy of Fine Arts, Ravenna; photo (450l.). Des and eng L. Vangelli, recess and litho (700l.))

1990 (19 May). *Artistic Heritage.* T **801** and similar vert design. Multicoloured. P 13½ × 14.
2101   450l. Type **801** 30   50
2102   700l. "Christ and Angels" (detail of Rachis altar, Friuli) (Lombard art) 50   40

(Des M. Dolcini. Photo)

1990 (15 June). *40th Anniv of Maletestiana Religious Music Festival.* P 14.
2103   **802**   600l. multicoloured 45   50

(Des G. Toffoletti and M. Codoni. Photo)

1990 (9 July). *West Germany. Winner of World Cup Football Championship.* As No. 2071 but value changed and additionally inscr "CAMPIONE DEL MONDO". P 14 × 13½.
2104   600l. multicoloured . . . . 2·00   1·90

803 "Still Life"
804 Ancient and Modern Wrestlers

(Eng P. Arghittu. Recess)

1990 (20 July). *Birth Centenary of Giorgio Morandi (painter).* P 14.
2105   **803**   750l. black 60   50

(Des A. Rinnaudo. Photo)

1990 (11 Oct). *World Greco-Roman Wrestling Championships, Rome.* P 14 × 13½.
2106   **804**   3200l. multicoloured . . . . . . 2·75   2·40

805 "New Life" (Emidio Vangelli)

1990 (26 Oct). *Christmas.* T **805** and similar horiz design. Multicoloured. Photo. P 14.
2107   600l. Type **805** 45   50
2108   750l. "Adoration of the Shepherds" (fresco by Pellegrino in St. Daniel's Church, Friuli) 60   50

806 Catania University
807 Corrado Mezzana (stamp designer, self-portrait)

(Des and eng E. Donnini and F. Barbarossa (600l.); recess and litho. Des and eng F. Tulli; recess (750l.))

1990 (5 Nov). T **806** and another horiz design. P 14 × 13½.
2109   600l. multicoloured 45   50
2110   750l. indigo and ultramarine 60   50
Design: As T **756**—600l. Bernardino Telesio High School, Cosenza.

1990 (16 Nov). *Stamp Day.* Photo. P 13½ × 14.
2111   **807**   600l. multicoloured 55   50

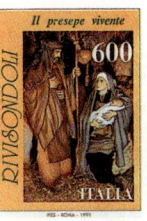

808 Holy Family
809 Fair Emblem
810 Emblem

1991 (5 Jan). *"The Living Tableau", Rivisondoli.* Photo. P 13½ × 14.
2112   **808**   600l. multicoloured 55   50

(Des E. Tenti. Photo)

1991 (10 Jan). *"EuroFlora '91" Fair, Genoa.* P 14.
2113   **809**   750l. multicoloured 60   50

(Des L. Vangelli. Photo)

1991 (15 Jan). *750th Anniv of Siena University.* P 13½ × 14.
2114   **810**   750l. gold, black and turquoise-blue 60   50

(Des E. Vangelli. Photo)

1991 (23 Feb). *Tourist Publicity (18th series).* Horiz designs as T **556**. Multicoloured. P 14.
2115   600l. Cagli 50   50
2116   600l. La Maddalena 50   50
2117   600l. Roccaraso 50   50
2118   600l. Sanremo 50   50
2115/2118 Set of 4 . . . . 1·80   1·80

93

ITALY 1991

811 European Community Flag
812 City and Columbus's Fleet 

(Des Complan. Photo)
1991 (12 Mar). *Europa Youth Meeting, Venice.* P 14 × 13½.
2119   811   750l. multicoloured 65   15
No. 2119 is also valued in ECUs (European Currency Unit).

(Des F. Filanci and M. Antomelli. Photo)
1991 (22 Mar). *500th Anniv (1992) of Discovery of America by Christopher Columbus (1st issue).* T **812** and similar horiz design. Multicoloured. P 14 × 13½.
2120   750l. Type **812** 60   50
         a. Horiz pair. Nos. 2120/1 . . . . . 1·20   1·00
2121   750l. Map, Columbus, seal and King and Queen of Spain 60   50
Nos. 2120/1 were issued together in horizontal *se-tenant* pairs within the sheet, each pair forming a composite design.
See also Nos. 2151/4 and **MS**2158.

813 Belli and View of Rome

(Des A. Riso. Photo)
1991 (15 Apr). *Birth Bicentenary of Giuseppe Gioachino Belli (poet).* P 14 × 13½.
2122   813   600l. blackish brown and blue 45   50

814 St. Gregory's Church, Rome

(Des E. Vangelin. Photo)
1991 (20 Apr). *Artistic Heritage.* P 14 × 13½.
2123   814   3200l. multicoloured . . . . 2·30   1·30

815 "DRS" Satellite
816 Sta. Maria Maggiore Church, Lanciano 

1991 (29 Apr). *Europa. Europe in Space.* T **815** and similar horiz design. Multicoloured. Photo. P 14 × 13½.
2124   750l. Type **815** . . . . 1·30   50
2125   800l. "Hermes" spaceship and "Columbus" space station . . . . 1·30   50

(Eng P. Arghittu. Recess)
1991 (2 May). *Artistic Heritage.* P 13½ × 14.
2126   816   600l. reddish brown 50   50

(Des and eng E. Donnini. Recess and litho)
1991 (3 May). *D. A. Azuni Lyceum, Sassari.* Horiz design as T **756**. P 14 × 13½.
2127   600l. multicoloured 50   50

817 Football and Genoa Lantern
818 Hands and Ball 

(Des V. Cozzella. Photo)
1991 (27 May). *Sampdoria, National Football Champion, 1990–91.* P 13½ × 14.
2128   817   3000l. multicoloured . . . . . . 2·30   4·00

(Des A. Rinnaudo. Photo)
1991 (5 June). *Centenary of Basketball.* P 13½ × 14.
2129   818   500l. multicoloured 40   50

819 Children and Butterflies
820 "Youth and Gulls" (sculpture, Pericle Fazzini) 

(Des Grazia Musmeci (600l.), G. Polino (750l.). Photo)
1991 (14 June). *United Nations Conference on Rights of the Child.* T **819** and similar vert design. Multicoloured. P 13½ × 14.
2130   600l. Type **819** 50   50
2131   750l. Child with balloon on man's shoulders 65   50

(Eng P. Arghittu (600l.), G.Toffoletti (3200l.). Recess and litho)
1991 (21 June). *Artistic Heritage.* T **820** and similar vert design. P 14.
2132   600l. chrome-yellow, greenish bl & blk 45   65
2133   3200l. multicoloured . . . . 2·50   2·40
Design:—3200l. Palazzo Esposizioni, Turin (Pier Luigi Nervi (birth centenary).

ITALY 1991

821 Winged Sphinx

822 Luigi Galvani (physiologist) and Experimental Equipment

(Des Anna Maresca. Photo)
1991 (31 Aug). *Egyptian Museum, Turin.* P 13½ × 14.
2134   821   750l. gold, emerald and yellow . .   65   50

(Des A. Ciaburro. Photo)
1991 (24 Sept). *One Hundred Years of Radio (1st issue).* P 14 × 13½.
2135   822   750l. multicoloured   65   50
Galvani carried out experiments in electricity.
See also Nos. 2148, 2203, 2241 and 2321/2.

823 Mozart at Spinet

824 Bear

(Des G. Toffoletti and Rita Fantini. Photo)
1991 (7 Oct). *Death Bicentenary of Wolfgang Amadeus Mozart (composer).* P 13½ × 14.
2136   823   800l. multicoloured   70   65

(Des Anna Maresca (3137/8), Anna Maresca and Cristina Bruscaglia (others). Photo)
1991 (10 Oct). *Nature Protection.* T **824** *and similar horiz designs. Multicoloured.* P 14 × 13½.
2137   500l. Type **824**   50   65
2138   500l. Peregrine falcon (Uccellina Park)   50   65
2139   500l. Deer   50   65
2140   500l. Marine life   50   65
2137/2140 Set of 4 . . . .   1·80   2·20

825 "The Angel of Life" (Giovanni Segantini)

826 Giulio and Alberto Bolaffi (stamp catalogue publishers)

(Des Anna Maresca. Photo)
1991 (18 Oct). *Christmas.* P 13½ × 14.
2141   825   600l. multicoloured   50   60

(Des E. Vangelli and Anna Maresca. Photo)
1991 (25 Oct). *Stamp Day.* P 14.
2142   826   750l. multicoloured   50   50

827 Signature and National Flag

(Des E. Vitali. Photo)
1991 (30 Oct). *Birth Centenary of Pietro Nenni (politician).* P 14.
2143   827   750l. multicoloured   60   65

828 Runners

829 Neptune Fountain, Florence

(Des A. Rinnaudo. Photo)
1992 (30 Jan). *22nd European Indoor Light Athletics Championships, Genoa.* P 13½ × 13½.
2144   828   600l. multicoloured   55   50

1992 (6 Feb). *400th Death Anniv of Bartolomeo Ammannati (architect and sculptor). Photo.* P 13½ × 14.
2145   829   750l. multicoloured   60   50

830 Statue of Marchese Alberto V of Este (founder) and University

831 Pediment

(Des L. Vangelli. Photo)
1992 (4 Mar). *600th Anniv (1991) of Ferrara University.* P 13½ × 14.
2146   830   750l. multicoloured   60   50

(Des A. Ciaburro. Photo)
1992 (9 Mar). *Naples University.* P 14 × 13½.
2147   831   750l. multicoloured   60   50

95

ITALY 1992

(Des A. Ciaburro. Photo)

1992 (26 Mar). *One Hundred Years of Radio (2nd issue).* Horiz design as T **822**. Multicoloured. P 14 × 13½.
2148 750l. Alessandro Volta (physicist) and Voltaic pile 75 60

Volta formulated the theory of current electricity and invented an electric battery.

832 Emblem and Venue
833 Medal of Lorenzo (Renato Berardi) 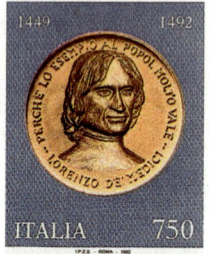

(Des G. Toffoletti. Photo)

1992 (27 Mar). *"Genova '92" International Thematic Stamp Exhibition (1st issue).* P 13½ × 14.
2149 **832** 750l. multicoloured 60 15

See also Nos. 2170/5.

1992 (8 Apr). *500th Death Anniv of Lorenzo de Medici, "The Magnificent"* Photo. P 14.
2150 **833** 750l. multicoloured 60 50

834 Columbus before Queen Isabella
835 Scenes from Life of St. Maria Filippini (altar, Montefiascone Cathedral) 

(Des R. Schlecht. Photo)

1992 (24 Apr). *500th Anniv of Discovery of America by Columbus (2nd issue).* T **834** and similar horiz designs. Multicoloured. P 14 × 13½.
2151 500l. Type **834** 50 80
    a. Block of 4. Nos. 2151/4 . . . . 1·80
2152 500l. Columbus's fleet 50 80
2153 500l. Sighting land 50 80
2154 500l. Landing in the New World . . 50 80
2151/2154 Set of 4 . . . . 1·80 2·75

Nos. 2151/4 were issued together in *se-tenant* blocks of four within the sheet.

(Des Maria Perrini. Photo)

1992 (2 May). *300th Anniv of Maestre Pie Filippini Institute.* P 13½ × 14.
2155 **835** 750l. multicoloured 60 50

836 Columbus Monument, Genoa (G. Giannetti)
837 Columbus presenting Natives 

1992 (2 May). *Europa. 500th Anniv of Discovery of America by Columbus.* T **836** and similar vert design. Multicoloured. Photo. P 13½ × 14.
2156 750l. Type **836** . . . . . . 1·10 50
2157 850l. Emblem of "Colombo '92" exhibition, Genoa . . . . 1·40 50

(Des A. Major and D. Sheaff. Eng F. Sarandrea (**MS**2518a, **MS**2518f), P. Leoni (**MS**2518c), M. Robiati (others). Recess)

1992 (22 May). *500th Anniv of Discovery of America by Columbus (3rd issue).* Six sheets, each 113 × 93 mm, containing horiz designs as T **837** reproducing scenes from United States 1893 Columbian Exposition issue. P 10½.
MS2158 Six sheets. (a) 50l. blackish olive (Type **837**); 300l. turq-bl (Columbus announcing discovery); 4000l. deep magenta (Columbus in chains). (b) 100l. blackish lilac (Columbus welcomed at Barcelona); 800l. bright crimson (Columbus restored to favour); 3000l. emerald (Columbus describing third voyage). (c) 200l. indigo (Columbus sighting land); 900l. violet-blue (Columbus's feet); 1500l. orange-red (Queen Isabella pledging jewels). (d) 400l. brown (Columbus soliciting aid of Queen Isabella); 700l. bright scarlet (Columbus at La Rabida); 1000l. deep blue (Recall of Columbus). (e) 500l. choc (Landing of Columbus); 600l. bottle green (*Santa Maria*); 2000l. brt carm (Portraits of Queen Isabella and Columbus). (f) 5000l. slate-green ("America", Columbus and "Liberty") *Set of 6 sheets* . . . . 22·00 27·00

Some examples of the 600l. show a deformed final "O" (resembling "G") in "COLOMBO".

838 Seascape and Cyclists
839 Ball, Team Badge and Stylization of Milan Cathedral 

(Des F. la Cava. Photo)

1992 (23 May). *75th "Tour of Italy" Cycle Race.* T **838** and similar horiz design. Multicoloured. P 14 × 13½.
2159 750l. Type **838** 75 65
    a. Horiz pair. Nos. 2159/60 . . . 1·50 1·30
2160 750l. Mountains and cyclists . . . 75 65

Nos. 2159/60 were issued together in horizontal *se-tenant* pairs within the sheet, each pair forming a composite design.

(Des V. Cozzella. Photo)

1992 (25 May). *A.C. Milan, National Football Champion, 1991–92.* P 13½ × 14.
2161 **839** 750l. light green, scarlet and black 75 50

ITALY   1992

840 Viareggio    **841** Nuvolari

(Des L. Vangelli. Photo)
1992 (30 May–13 June). *Seaside Resorts.* T **840** *and similar horiz design. Multicoloured.* P 14 × 13½.
| 2162 | 750l. Type **840** | 60 | 50 |
| 2163 | 750l. Rimini (June) | 60 | 50 |

(Des Cristina Bruscaglia. Photo)
1992 (5 June). *Birth Centenary of Tazio Nuvolari (racing driver).* P 14 × 13½.
| 2164 | **841** | 3200l. multicoloured | 2·75 | 2·10 |

(Des E. Vangelli (2165), E. Vangelli and Maria Perrini (2167), E. Vangelli and Anna Maresca (others). Photo)
1992 (30 June). *Tourist Publicity (19th series). Horiz designs as* T **556.** *Multicoloured.* P 14.
2165	600l. Arcevia	50	65
2166	600l. Braies	50	65
2167	600l. Maratea	50	65
2168	600l. Pantelleria	50	65
2165/2168	Set of 4	1·80	2·10

842 "Adoration of the Shepherds" (detail)    **843** Columbus's House, Genoa

(Des and eng P. Arghittu. Recess and litho)
1992 (5 Sept). *400th Death Anniv of Jacopo da Ponte (painter).* P 14.
| 2169 | **842** | 750l. multicoloured | 60 | 50 |

(Des E. Donnini. Photo)
1992 (18 Sept). *"Genova '92" International Thematic Stamp Exhibition (2nd issue).* T **843** *and similar vert designs. Multicoloured.* P 13½ × 14.
2170	500l. Type **843**	40	50
2171	600l. Departure of Columbus's fleet from Palos, 1492	50	50
2172	750l. Route map of Columbus's first voyage	60	50
2173	850l. Columbus sighting land	65	50
2174	1200l. Columbus landing on San Salvador	1·00	1·40
2175	3200l. Columbus, "Man" (Leonardo da Vinci), "Fury" (Michelangelo) and Raphael's portrait of Michelangelo	2·50	1·40
2170/2175	Set of 6	5·00	4·25

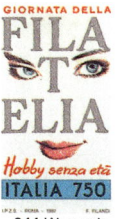

844 Woman's Eyes and Mouth    **845** Map of Europe and Lions Emblem

(Des F. Filanci. Photo)
1992 (22 Sept). *Stamp Day.*
(a) Sheet stamps. P 14.
| 2176 | **844** | 750l. multicoloured | 75 | 50 |
(b) Booklet stamps. Self adhesive. P 13½.
2177	**844**	750l. multicoloured	3·00	2·00
	a. Booklet pane. No. 2177 × 5	15·00	
	b. Perf 14	50·00	50·00

1992 (24 Sept). *75th Anniv of Lions International and 38th Europa Forum, Genoa. Photo.* P 14 × 13½.
| 2178 | **845** | 3000l. multicoloured | 2·30 | 50 |

846 European Community Emblem and Members' Flags    **847** Woman with Food Bowl

(Des G. Toffoletti. Photo)
1992 (5 Oct). *European Single Market (1st issue).* P 14 × 13½.
| 2179 | **846** | 600l. multicoloured | 50 | 1·60 |

See also Nos. 2182/93.

(Des L. Vangelli. Photo)
1992 (16 Sept). *International Nutrition Conference, Rome.*
| 2180 | **847** | 500l. multicoloured | 45 | 50 |

848 Caltagirone Crib    **849** Buildings on Flag of Italy

(Des E. Donnini. Photo)
1992 (31 Oct). *Christmas.* P 14 × 13½.
| 2181 | **848** | 600l. multicoloured | 55 | 50 |

(Des S. Isola and E. Donnini. Photo)
1993 (20 Jan). *European Single Market (2nd Issue).* T **849** *and similar vert designs differing in flag of country and language of inscription. Multicoloured.* P 13½ × 14.
| 2182 | 750l. Type **849** | 55 | 50 |
| | a. Sheetlet of 12. Nos. 2182/93 | 6·00 | |

97

ITALY 1993

2183	750l. Belgium	55	50
2184	750l. Denmark	55	50
2185	750l. France	55	50
2186	750l. Germany	55	50
2187	750l. Greece	55	50
2188	750l. Ireland	55	50
2189	750l. Luxembourg	55	50
2190	750l. Netherlands	55	50
2191	750l. Portugal	55	50
2192	750l. United Kingdom	55	50
2193	750l. Spain	55	50
2182/2193	*Set of* 12	6·00	5·50

Nos. 2182/93 were issued together in *se-tenant* sheetlets of 12 stamps.

854 Tabby    855 "The Piazza"

1993 (6 Mar). *Domestic Cats. T* **854** *and similar multicoloured designs. Photo.* P 14 × 13½ (horiz) or 13½ × 14 (vert).
2199	600l. Type **854**	45	50
2200	600l. White Persian	45	50
2201	600l. Devon rex (*vert*)	45	50
2202	600l. Maine coon (*vert*)	45	50
2199/2202	*Set of* 4	1·60	1·80

850 Russian and Italian Alpine Veterans   851 Mezzettino, Colombina and Arlecchino

(Des G. Prati. Photo)

1993 (23 Jan). *50th Anniversary Meeting of Veterans of Battle of Nikolayevka.* P 14 × 13½.
2194 **850** 600l. multicoloured   50   50

(Des A. Ciaburro. Photo)

1993 (26 Mar). *One Hundred Years of Radio (3rd issue). Horiz design as T* **822**. *Multicoloured.* P 14 × 13½.
2203 750l. Temistocle Calzecchi Onesti (physicist) and apparatus for detecting electromagnetic waves   65   50

(Des M. Donizetti. Photo)

1993 (6 Feb). *Death Bicentenary of Carlo Goldoni (dramatist). T* **851** *and similar vert design. Multicoloured.* P 13½ × 14.
2195 500l. Type **851**   45   50
2196 500l. Arlecchino and portrait of Goldoni   45   65

(Des and eng P. Arghittu. Recess and litho)

1993 (6 Apr). *Death Bicentenary of Francesco Guardi (artist).* P 14.
2204 **855** 3200l. multicoloured   2·50   2·75

852 "Africa" (mosaic, Roman villa, Piazza Armerina)   853 Wedge stopping Heart-shaped Cog

(Des and eng P. Arghittu. Recess and litho)

1993 (20 Feb). *Artistic Heritage.* P 14.
2197 **852** 750l. multicoloured   65   50

856 Horace    857 Cottolengo and Small House of the Divine Providence, Turin

(Des D. Vangelli. Photo)

1993 (19 Apr). *2000th Death Anniv of Horace (Quintus Horatius Flaccus) (poet).* P 13½ × 14.
2205 **856** 600l. multicoloured   50   50

(Des L. Vangelli. Photo)

1993 (5 Mar). *National Health Day. Campaign against Heart Disease.* P 14 × 13½.
2198 **853** 750l. multicoloured   65   50

(Des F. Tulli. Photo)

1993 (30 Apr). *St. Giuseppe Benedetto Cottolengo Commemoration.* P 13½ × 14.
2206 **857** 750l. multicoloured   65   50

ITALY 1993

858 "Carousel Horses" (Lino Bianchi Barriviera)
859 Medal (Giuseppe Romagnoli) 

1993 (3 May). *Europa. Contemporary Art.* T **858** *and similar vert design. Multicoloured.* P 13½ × 14.
2207　750l. Type **858** . . . . 70　50
2208　850l. "Dynamism of Coloured Shapes" (Gino Severini) . . . . . 80　50

(Des G. Toffoletti. Photo)

1993 (31 May). *400th Anniv of San Luca National Academy.* P 13½ × 14.
2209　**859**　750l. multicoloured . . . . . . 65　50

860 Emblem
861 Player and Club Badge 

(Des V. Sedini. Photo)

1993 (5 June). *"Family Fest '93" International Conference, Rome.* P 14 × 13½.
2210　**860**　750l. multicoloured . . . . . . 65　50

(Des M. Pajè. Photo)

1993 (7 June). *Milan, National Football Champion, 1992–93.* P 13½ × 14.
2211　**861**　750l. multicoloured . . . . . . 65　50

862 Carloforte
863 Canoeing 

(Des E. Vangelli. Photo)

1993 (26 June). *Tourist Publicity (20th series).* T **862** *and similar horiz designs. Multicoloured.* P 14 × 13½.
2212　600l. Type **862** . . . . 50　50
2213　600l. Palmanova . . . . 50　50
2214　600l. Senigallia . . . . 50　50
2215　600l. Sorrento . . . . 50　50
2212/2215 *Set of* 4 . . . . 1·80　1·80

1993 (1 July). *World Canoeing Championships, Trentino. Photo.* P 13½ × 14.
2216　**863**　750l. multicoloured . . . . . . 65　50

864 Observatory
865 Staircase, St. Salome's Cathedral, Veroli 

(Des Anna Maresca. Photo)

1993 (4 Sept). *Centenary of Regina Margherita Observatory.* P 14 × 13½.
2217　**864**　500l. multicoloured . . . . . . 45　50

(Des Maria Perrini. Litho)

1993 (25 Sept). *Artistic Heritage.* P 13½ × 14.
2218　**865**　750l. multicoloured . . . . . . 65　50

866 Soldier, Boy with Rifle and German Helmet
867 Carriage 

(Des G. Toffoletti (2219), Eva Fischer (2220), E. Treccani (2221). Photo)

1993 (25 Sept). *Second World War 50th Anniversaries (1st series).* T **866** *and similar vert designs. Multicoloured.* P 13½ × 14.
2219　750l. Type **866** (the Four Days of Naples) . . . . 75　50
2220　750l. Menorah, people in railway truck and Star of David (deportation of Roman Jews) . . . . 75　50
2221　750l. Seven Cervi brothers (execution) . . . . 75　50
See also Nos. 2259/61.

(Des Accademia Tassiana. Photo)

1993 (2 Oct). *The Taxis Family in Postal History.* T **867** *and similar horiz designs. Multicoloured.* P 14 × 13½.
2222　750l. Type **867** . . . . 60　50
　　　　a. P 14 × imperf. Booklets . . . 60　50
　　　　ab. Booklet pane. Nos. 2222a, 2223a, 2224a, 2225a and 2226a . . . 3·00
2223　750l. Taxis arms . . . . 60　50
　　　　a. P 14 × imperf. Booklets . . . 60　50
2224　750l. Gig . . . . 60　50
　　　　a. P 14 × imperf. Booklets . . . 60　50
2225　750l. 17th-century postal messenger . . 60　50
　　　　a. P 14 × imperf. Booklets . . . 60　50
2226　750l. 18th-century postal messenger . . 60　50
　　　　a. P 14 × imperf. Booklets . . . 60　50
2222/2226 *Set of* 5 . . . . 2·75　2·30

ITALY 1993

868 Head Office, Rome
869 Colonies Express Letter Stamp Design 

1993 (14 Oct). *Centenary of Bank of Italy.* T **868** *and similar horiz design. Multicoloured. Photo.* P 14 × 13½.
| 2227 | 750l. Type **868** | 1·10 | 50 |
| 2228 | 1000l. 1000 lire banknote (first note issued by Bank) | 1·50 | 80 |

Nos. 2227/8 were each issued in sheets of 40 stamps and 20 half stamp-size labels showing the Bank emblem.

1993 (12 Nov). *Stamp Day. Centenary of First Italian Colonies Stamps. Photo.* P 14.
| 2229 | **869** | 600l. scarlet and deep grey-blue | 50 | 50 |

870 Tableau Vivant, Corchiano
871 17th-century Map of Foggia 

(Des Maria Perrini (600l.). Photo)

1993 (13 Nov). *Christmas.* T **870** *and similar vert design. Multicoloured.* P 13½ × 14.
| 2230 | 600l. Type **870** | 50 | 50 |
| 2231 | 750l. "The Annunciation" (Piero della Francesca) | 60 | 50 |

1993 (27 Nov). *Treasures from State Archives and Museums (1st series).* T **871** *and similar multicoloured designs. Photo.* P 13½ × 14 (750l.) or 14 × 13½ (others).
2232	600l. Type **871** (Foggia Archives)	50	50
2233	600l. "Concert" (Bartolomeo Manfredi) (Uffizi Gallery, Florence)	50	50
2234	750l. View of Siena from 15th-century illuminated manuscript (Siena Archives) (*vert*)	50	50
2235	850l. "The Death of Adonis" (Sebastiano del Piombo) (Uffizi Gallery)	65	50
2232/2235	Set of 4	2·00	1·80

See also Nos. 2266/9, 2306/9 and 2346/9.

872 Ringmaster and Bareback Riders
873 Mother and Child inside House 

(Des D. Vangelli. Photo)

1994 (8 Jan). *The Circus.* T **872** *and similar vert design. Multicoloured.* P 13½ × 14.
| 2236 | 600l. Type **872** | 45 | 50 |
| 2237 | 750l. Clowns | 55 | 50 |

(Des W. Werth and U. Zellir. Photo)

1994 (14 Feb). *"The Housewife, a Presence that Counts".* P 14.
| 2238 | **873** | 750l. multicoloured | 60 | 50 |

874 "Bread" (Dario Piazza)
875 Boxer 

1994 (5 Mar). *Paintings of Italian Food.* T **874** *and similar vert design. Multicoloured. Photo.* P 13½ × 14.
| 2239 | 500l. Type **874** | 45 | 50 |
| 2240 | 600l. "Italian Pasta in the World" (Erminia Scaglione) | 60 | 50 |

(Des A. Ciaburro. Photo)

1994 (11 Mar). *One Hundred Years of Radio (4th issue). Horiz design as* T **822**. *Multicoloured.* P 14 × 13½.
| 2241 | 750l. Augusto Righi (physicist) and his Hertzian oscillator | 65 | 50 |

1994 (12 Mar). *Dogs.* T **875** *and similar horiz designs. Multicoloured. Photo.* P 14 × 13½.
2242	600l. Type **875**	45	50
2243	600l. Dalmatian	45	50
2244	600l. Maremma sheepdog	45	50
2245	600l. German shepherd	45	50
2242/2245	Set of 4	1·60	1·80

876 "The Risen Christ" (statue)
877 Pacioli in Study 

(Des G. Toffoletti. Photo)

1994 (2 Apr). *Procession of "The Risen Christ", Tarquinia.* P 13½ × 14.
| 2246 | **876** | 750l. multicoloured | 60 | 50 |

1994 (13 Apr). *500th Anniv of Publication of Summary of Arithmetic, Geometry, Proportion and Proportionality by Fra' Luca Pacioli. Photo.* P 14 × 13½.
| 2247 | **877** | 750l. multicoloured | 60 | 50 |

ITALY 1994

(Des E. Vangelli. Photo)

1994 (23 Apr). *Tourist Publicity (21st series). Horiz designs as T* **862**. *Multicoloured.* P 14 × 13½.
2248	600l. Odescalchi Castle, Santa Marinella		45	50
2249	600l. St. Michael's Abbey, Monticchio		45	50
2250	600l. Orta San Giulio		45	50
2251	600l. Cathedral, Messina		45	50
2248/2251	*Set of* 4		1·60	1·80

878 Kossuth
879 Women's High-diving

(Des D. Vangelli. Photo)

1994 (30 Apr). *Death Centenary of Lajos Kossuth (Hungarian statesman).* P 13½ × 14.
2252	**878**	3750l. multicoloured	2·75	1·60

(Des Nani Tedeschi. Photo)

1994 (2 May). *World Water Sports Championships. T* **879** *and similar vert designs. Multicoloured.* P 13½ × 14.
2253	600l. Type **879**		50	50
2254	750l. Water polo		60	50

880 Club Badge, Football and Colours
881 Camillo Golgi (cytologist) and Golgi Cells

(Des M. de Rosa. Photo)

1994 (2 May). *Milan, National Football Champion, 1993–94.* P 14 × 13½.
2255	**880**	750l. multicoloured	70	50

(Des Laura Mezzana. Photo)

1994 (2 May). *Europa. Discoveries. T* **881** *and similar vert designs showing Italian Nobel Prize winners. Multicoloured.* P 13½ × 14.
2256	750l. Type **881** (medicine, 1906)		65	50
2257	850l. Giulio Natta (chemist) and diagram of polymer structure (chemistry, 1963)		75	50

882 "Goddess of Caldevigo" (bronze statuette, 5th century B.C.)
883 Destruction of Montecassino

1994 (6 May). *"Ancient Peoples of Italy" Archaeological Exhibition, Rimini. Photo.* P 13½ × 14.
2258	**882**	750l. multicoloured	60	50

(Des Eva Fischer. Photo)

1994 (18 May). *Second World War 50th Anniversaries (2nd series). T* **883** *and similar vert designs. Multicoloured.* P 13½ × 14.
2259	750l. Type **883**		45	50
2260	750l. Bound prisoners (Ardeatine Caves Massacre)		45	50
2261	750l. Family (Marzabotto Massacre)		45	50

884 Washing of Feet
885 "Ariadne, Venus and Bacchus"

1994 (28 May). *22nd National Eucharistic Congress, Siena. Photo.* P 13½ × 14.
2262	**884**	600l. multicoloured	45	50

1994 (31 May). *Artistic Heritage. 400th Death Anniv of Tintoretto (artist). Photo.* P 14.
2263	**885**	750l. multicoloured	60	50

886 "Piazza del Duomo during the Plague, 1630" (attr. Cigoli)
887 "E", European Union Emblem and Parliament

1994 (4 June). *750th Anniv of Arciconfraternita della Misericordia, Florence. Photo.* P 14 × 13½.
2264	**886**	750l. multicoloured	50	50

(Des Cristina Bruscaglia. Photo)

1994 (11 June). *European Parliament Elections.* P 13½ × 14.
2265	**887**	600l. multicoloured	50	50

ITALY 1994

(Des Maria Perrini (2266, 2269). Photo)

1994 (16 June). *Treasures from State Archives and Museums (2nd series). Vert designs as T* **871**. *Multicoloured.* P $13\frac{1}{2} \times 14$.

2266	600l. Frontispiece of notary's register, 1623–24 (Catania Archives)	45	50
2267	600l. "Death of Patroclus" (Attic vase, 5th century B.C.) (Agrigento Archaeological Museum)	50	50
2268	750l. "Galata and his Wife" (statue) (National Roman Museum)	50	50
2269	850l. Civic seal, 1745 (Campobasso Archives)	60	50
2266/2269 Set of 4		1·80	1·80

888 Olympic Rings and Pierre de Coubertin (founder)

889 Vesuvius and "G 7"

(Des Nani Tedeschi. Photo)

1994 (23 June). *Centenary of International Olympic Committee.* P $13\frac{1}{2} \times 14$.
2270 **888** 850l. multicoloured 70 50

1994 (8 July). *Group of Seven (industrialized countries) Summit, Naples. Photo.* P $13\frac{1}{2} \times 14$.
2271 **889** 600l. new blue, dull ultram & emer 50 50
Examples with 750l. value are known imperf, but these were not issued.

890 Church of the Holy House and "Madonna and Child"

891 Pietro Miliani (papermaker) (after Francesco Rosaspina)

892 Frederick II (sculpture, Bitonto Cathedral)

(Des Maria Perrini. Photo)

1994 (8 Sept). *700th Anniv of Shrine of the Nativity of the Virgin, Loreto.* P 14.
2272 **890** 500l. multicoloured 50 50

(Des Anna Maresca. Photo)

1994 (16 Sept). *Stamp Day. T* **891** *and similar vert design. Multicoloured.* P $13\frac{1}{2} \times 14$.
2273 600l. Type **891** 45 50
2274 750l. Paper and Watermark Museum (former St. Dominic's Monastery), Fabriano 60 50

(Des Maria Perrini. Photo)

1994 (19 Sept). *800th Birth Anniv of Frederick II, Holy Roman Emperor.* P 14.
2275 **892** 750l. multicoloured 65 50

893 St. Mark's Basilica

894 "The Annunciation" (Melozzo da Forli)

(Des F. Ramberti. Litho)

1994 (8 Oct). *900th Anniv of Dedication of St Mark's Basilica, Venice.* P $14 \times 13\frac{1}{2}$.
2276 **893** 750l. multicoloured 70 70
         a. Tête-bêche (vert pair) . . . . 1·40 1·30
MS2277 80×115 mm. No. 2276 together with No. 1491 of San Marino . . . . 1·30 2·75
No. 2276 was issued in vertical *tête-bêche* pairs within sheets of twenty, each stamp *se-tenant* with a half stamp-size inscribed label.
No. **MS**2277 was issued simultaneously in Italy and San Marino. Each stamp bears an inscription on the back, over the gum, limiting its validity to the appropriate country.

1994 (5 Nov). *Christmas. T* **894** *and similar vert design. Multicoloured. Photo.* P $13\frac{1}{2} \times 14$.
2278 600l. Type **894** 50 50
2279 750l. "Sacred Conversation" (detail, Lattanzio da Rimini) 65 50

895 Club Emblem on Globe

896 Headquarters, Rome

(Des R. Sambonet. Photo)

1994 (8 Nov). *Centenary of Italian Touring Club.* P $13\frac{1}{2} \times 14$.
2280 **895** 600l. multicoloured 45 50

1994 (11 Nov). *75th Anniv of Credit for Businesses and Public Works. Photo.* P $13\frac{1}{2} \times 14$.
2281 **896** 750l. multicoloured 70 50
No. 2281 was issued in sheets of 40 stamps and 20 half stamp-size inscribed labels.

897 New Emblem

898 Gentile

ITALY 1994

(Des M. Checchi (600l.), F. Ricci (others). Photo)
1994 (18 Nov). *Incorporation of Italian Post.* T **897** *and similar design.* Size 34 × 26 mm. P 13½ × 14 (600l.) or 14 × 13½ (others).

2282	—	600l. bright rose-red and silver	60	50
2283	897	750l. black, emerald and rosine	85	50
		a. Pair. Nos. 2283/4	1·70	1·00
2284		750l. carmine-vermilion	85	50

Design: *Vert*—600l. Palazzo Querini Dubois, Venice (restored with Post Office help).
Nos. 2283/4 were issued together in *se-tenant* pairs within the sheet.
For 750 and 850l. values, size 26 × 17 mm, see Nos. 2343/4.

(Des D. Vangelli. Photo)
1994 (21 Nov). *50th Death Anniv of Giovanni Gentile (philosopher).* P 13½ × 14.

2285	898	750l. multicoloured	65	50

899 Rainbow, Dove, Olive Tree and Flood
900 Skater

(Des L. Vangelli. Photo)
1995 (2 Jan). *For Flood Victims.* P 13½ × 14.

2286	899	750l.+2250l. multicoloured	3·25	5·50

(Des P. Arghittu. Photo)
1995 (6 Feb). *World Speed Skating Championships, Baselga di Pine.* P 14 × 13½.

2287	900	750l. multicoloured	65	50

901 First Issue of La Domenica del Corriere
902 Rice

1995 (18 Feb). *50th Death Anniv of Achille Beltrame (painter).* Photo. P 13½ × 14.

2288	901	500l. multicoloured	55	50

(Des Maria Tuccelli. Photo)
1995 (4 Mar). *Italian Food.* T **902** *and similar vert design. Multicoloured.* P 13½ × 14.

2289	500l. Type **902**	50	50
2290	750l. Olives and olive oil	65	50

903 Grey Herons
904 Anniversary Emblem

(Des Anna Maresca. Photo)
1995 (11 Mar). *Birds.* T **903** *and similar horiz designs. Multicoloured.* P 14 × 13½.

2291	600l. Type **903**	45	50
2292	600l. Griffon vultures ("Grifone")	45	50
2293	600l. Golden eagles ("Aquila Reale")	45	50
2294	600l. Snow finches ("Fringuello Alpino")	45	50
2291/2294 Set of 4		1·60	1·80

(Des L. Vangelli. Photo)
1995 (24 Mar). *50th Anniv of United Nations Organization.* P 14 × 13½.

2295	904	850l. black, new blue and gold	65	50

905 Detail of Monument (Giuseppe Grande)
906 Princess Mafalda of Savoy and Concentration Camp

1995 (25 Mar). *Centenary of Monument to the Fallen of the Five Days of Milan (1848 uprising).* P 14 × 13½.

2296	905	750l. multicoloured	60	50

(Des Anna Maresca (2297/9), Maria Tuccelli (2300), Maria Tuccelli and Cristina Bruscaglia (2301), Cristina Bruscaglia (2302), A. Ciaburm (2303, 2305), P. Arghittu (2304). Photo)
1995 (31 Mar). *50th Anniv of End of Second World War.* T **906** *and similar horiz designs. Multicoloured.* P 13½ × 14.

2297	750l. Type **906**	55	65
	a. Sheetlet of 9. Nos. 2297/2305	4·50	
2298	750l. DUKW at Anzio	55	65
2299	750l. Teresa Gullace and scene of her death	55	65
2300	750l. Florence Town Hall and Military Medal	55	65
2301	750l. Vittorio Veneto Town Hall and Military Medal	55	65
2302	750l. Cagliari Town Hall and Military Medal	55	65
2303	750l. Battle of Mount Lungo	55	65
2304	750l. Parachuting supplies in the Balkans	55	65
2305	750l. Light cruisers of the Eighth Division in Atlantic	55	65
2297/2305 Set of 9	4·50	5·25

Nos. 2297/2305 were issued together in *se-tenant* sheetlets of nine stamps.

1995 (28 Apr). *Treasures from State Archives and Museums (3rd series). Multicoloured designs as* T **871**. Photo. P 13½ × 14 (vert) or 14 × 13½ (horiz).

2306	500l. Illuminated letter "P" from statute of Pope Innocent III (Rome Archives) (*vert*)	35	50
2307	500l. "Port of Naples" (detail, Bernardo Strozzi) (St. Martin National Museum, Naples)	45	50

103

ITALY 1995

2308 750l. Illuminated letter "I" showing the Risen Christ from 1481 document (Mantua Archives) (vert) 50 50
2309 850l. "Sacred Love and Profane Love" (Titian) (Borghese Museum and Gallery, Rome) 60 50
2306/2309 Set of 4 . . . . 1·70 1·80

907 Emblem
908 Santa Croce Basilica, Florence 

(Des E. Camplani and G. Pescolderung. Photo)
1995 (29 Apr). *Centenary of Venice Biennale.* P $13\frac{1}{2} \times 14$.
2310 **907** 750l. blue, gold and lemon 60 50

(Des F. Tulli. Recess)
1995 (3 May). *Artistic Heritage.* P $13\frac{1}{2} \times 14$.
2311 **908** 750l. agate 60 50

909 Soldiers and Civilians celebrating
910 Players 

(Des L. Vangelli. Photo)
1995 (5 May). *Europa. Peace and Freedom.* T **909** and similar vert design. Multicoloured. P $13\frac{1}{2} \times 14$.
2312 750l. Type **909** (50th anniv of end of Second World War in Europe) 65 50
2313 850l. Mostar Bridge (Bosnia) and Council of Europe emblem 75 50

(Des Cristina Bruscaglia. Litho)
1995 (8 May). *Centenary of Volleyball.* P $13\frac{1}{2} \times 14$.
2314 **910** 750l. dp new blue, red-orge & turq-grn 60 50

(Des P. Arghittu. Photo)
1995 (12 May). *Tourist Publicity (22nd series).* Horiz designs as T **862**. Multicoloured. P $14 \times 13\frac{1}{2}$.
2315 750l. Alatri 55 50
2316 750l. Nuoro 55 50
2317 750l. Susa 55 50
2318 750l. Venosa 55 50
2315/2318 Set of 4 . . . . 2·00 1·80

911 Experiment demonstrating X-rays
912 Player and Club Badge 

(Des Anna Maresca. Photo)
1995 (2 June). *Centenary of Discovery of X-rays by Wilhelm Röntgen.* P $14 \times 13\frac{1}{2}$.
2319 **911** 750l. multicoloured 60 50

(Des U. Nespolo. Photo)
1995 (5 June). *Juventus, National Football Champion, 1994–95.* P $13\frac{1}{2} \times 14$.
2320 **912** 750l. multicoloured 60 50

913 Villa Griffone (site of Marconi's early experiments)
914 St. Antony, Holy Basilica (Padua) and Page of Gospel 

(Des E. Junger (850l.). Photo)
1995 (8 June). *One Hundred Years of Radio (5th issue). Centenary of First Radio Transmission.* T **913** and similar horiz design. Multicoloured. P $14 \times 13\frac{1}{2}$ (750l.) or 14 (850l.).
2321 750l. Type **913** 60 50
2322 850l. Guglielmo Marconi and transmitter (36×21 mm) 70 50

(Des Nicola Russo. Photo)
1995 (13 June). *800th Birth Anniv of St. Antony of Padua.* T **914** and similar multicoloured design. P $13\frac{1}{2} \times 14$ (750l.) or $14 \times 13\frac{1}{2}$ (850l.).
2323 750l. Type **914** 60 50
2324 850l. St. Antony holding Child Jesus (painting, Vieira Lusitano) (horiz) 70 50

915 Durazzo Pallavicini, Pegli
916 Milan Cathedral and Eye (congress emblem) 

104

ITALY 1995

(Des and eng Rita Morena (2325/6), Maria Tuccelli (2327/8). Recess and litho)

1995 (24 June). *Public Gardens (1st series).* T **915** and similar horiz designs. Multicoloured. P 14 × 13½.
2325	750l. Type **915**	60	50
2326	750l. Boboli, Florence	60	50
2327	750l. Ninfa, Cisterna di Latina	60	50
2328	750l. Parco della Reggia, Caserta	60	50
2325/2328	Set of 4	2·20	1·80

See also Nos. 2439/42.

(Des P. Buttafava. Litho)

1995 (24 June). *Tenth European Ophthalmological Society Congress, Milan.* P 13½ × 14.
2329 **916** 750l. multicoloured 60 50

917 "Sailors' Wives"

1995 (4 July). *Birth Centenary of Massimo Campigli (painter).* Photo. P 14.
2330 **917** 750l. multicoloured 75 50

918 Dome of Santa Maria del Fiore (Florence), Galileo and Albert Einstein

919 Rudolph Valentino in *The Son of the Sheik*

(Des Cristina Bruscaglia. Litho)

1995 (7 Aug). *14th World Relative Physics Conference, Florence.* P 14 × 13½.
2331 **918** 750l. royal blue, orange-brown & black 60 50

(Des and eng Rita Morena. Recess and litho)

1995 (29 Aug). *Centenary of Motion Pictures.* T **919** and similar vert designs. P 13½ × 14.
2332	750l. black, indigo and vermilion	55	50
2333	750l. multicoloured	55	50
2334	750l. multicoloured	55	50
2335	750l. multicoloured	55	50
2332/2335	Set of 4	2·00	1·80

Designs:—No. 2333, Totò in *The Gold of Naples*; 2334, Frederico Fellini's *Cabiria Nights*; 2335, Poster (by Massimo Geleng) for "Cinecittà 95" film festival.

920 Wheatfield and Anniversary Emblem

921 St. Albert's Stone Coffin (detail) and Basilica

(Des Cristina Bruscaglia. Photo)

1995 (1 Sept). *50th Anniv of Food and Agriculture Organization.* P 14 × 13½.
2336 **920** 850l. multicoloured 70 65

(Des and eng A. Ciaburro. Recess)

1995 (2 Sept). *900th Anniversaries of Pontida Basilica and Death of St. Albert of Prezzate.* P 14 × 13½.
2337 **921** 1000l. reddish brown & dp turq-bl 80 80

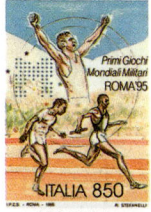

922 Athletes

923 Globe and Means of Communication

(Des R. Stefanelli. Photo)

1995 (6 Sept). *First World Military Games, Rome.* P 13½ × 14.
2338 **922** 850l. multicoloured 75 65

(Des U. d'Arro and M. Sala. Photo)

1995 (27 Oct). *50th Anniv of Ansa News Agency.* P 14 × 13½.
2339 **923** 750l. multicoloured 60 50

924 Crib (Stefano da Putignano), Polignano Cathedral

925 Renato Mondolfo (philatelist) and Trieste 1949 20l. Stamp

(Des Maria Perrini (750l.), E. Donnini (850l.). Photo)

1995 (18 Nov). *Christmas.* T **924** and similar horiz design. Multicoloured. P 14 × 13½.
2340	750l. Type **924**	85	50
2341	850l. "Adoration of the Wise Men" (detail, Fra Angelico)	1·00	65

(Des A. Marcon and EM Studio. Photo)

1995 (9 Dec). *Stamp Day.* P 14 × 13½.
2342 **925** 750l. multicoloured 55 50

ITALY 1995

(Des F. Ricci. Litho)

1995 (9 Dec). *First Anniv of Incorporation of Italian Post. Size 26 × 17 mm.* P 13½ × 14.

2343	897	750l. scarlet-vermilion	55	50
		a. Perf 3 sides. Booklets	55	50
		ab. Booklet pane. Nos. 2343a × 8	4·50	
2344		850l. black, emerald & carmine-verm	70	65
		a. Perf 3 sides. Booklets	70	65
		ab. Booklet pane. Nos. 2344a × 8	5·50	

926 Collage representing Marinetti's Works

927 "Sarah and the Angel" (fresco, Archbishops Palace, Udine)

1996 (19 Jan). *120th Birth Anniv of Filippo Marinetti (writer and founder of Futurist movement). Photo.* P 14.

2345	926	750l. multicoloured	55	50

(Des Cristina Bruscaglia. Photo)

1996 (26 Feb). *Treasures from State Archives and Museums (4th series). Multicoloured designs as T 871.* P 13½ × 14 (2347) or 14 × 13½ (others).

2346		750l. Arms (Georgofili Academy, Florence)	55	50
2347		750l. Illuminated letter showing St. Luke and his ox from Constitution of 1372 (Lucca Archives) (*vert*)	55	50
2348		850l. Inkwells, pen and manuscript of Gabriele d'Annunzio (writer) (Il Vittoriale, Gardone Riviera)	60	50
2349		850l. "Life of King Modus and Queen Racio" from 1486 miniature (Turin Archives)	60	50
2346/2349		Set of 4	2·10	1·80

1996 (5 Mar). *300th Birth Anniv of Giambattista Tiepolo (painter).* P 14.

2350	927	1000l. multicoloured	90	80

928 White Wine

929 Marco Polo and Palace in the Forbidden City

(Des Maria Tuccelli. Photo)

1996 (20 Mar). *Italian Wine Production. T 928 and similar vert design. Multicoloured.* P 13½ × 14.

2351		500l. Type 928	30	50
2352		750l. Red wine	45	50

(Des Cristina Bruscaglia. Photo)

1996 (22 Mar). *700th Anniv (1995) of Marco Polo's Return from Asia and "China '96" International Stamp Exhibition, Peking.* P 14 × 13½.

2353	929	1250l. multicoloured	1·10	1·10

930 Milan Cathedral (left detail)

931 Quill Pen and Satellite (50th anniv of National Federation of Italian Press)

(Des A. Marcon. Litho)

1996 (23 Mar). *"Italia 98" International Stamp Exhibition, Milan (1st issue). T 930 and similar vert design. Multicoloured.* P 13½ × 14.

2354		750l. Type 930	1·90	50
		a. Horiz pair. Nos. 2354/5	4·00	1·00
		b. Booklet pane. No. 2354a × 4	16·00	
2355		750l. Cathedral (right detail)	1·90	50

Nos. 2354/5 were issued together in horizontal *se-tenant* pairs within the sheet, each pair forming a composite design of the Cathedral.

The booklet pane has a perforated margin around the block.

(Des L. Vangelli, litho (2356). Des F. Cocchi, photo (2357))

1996 (3 Apr). *Anniversaries. T 931 and similar design.* P 13½ × 14 (2356) or 14 × 13½ (2357).

2356		750l. multicoloured	65	50
2357		750l. dull ultramarine, bright rose & black	65	50

Design: *Horiz*—No. 2357, Globe (centenary of *La Gazetta dello Sport* (newspaper)).

932 Postman and Emblem

933 Uniforms of Different Periods

(Des Rita Fantini. Photo)

1996 (13 Apr). *International Museum of Postal Images, Belvedere Ostrense.* P 13½ × 14.

2358	932	500l. multicoloured	50	50

(Des P. Arghittu. Photo)

1996 (13 Apr). *Centenary of Academy of Excise Guards.* P 13½ × 14.

2359	933	750l. multicoloured	70	50

ITALY 1996

934 Truck and Route Map
935 Carina Negrone (pilot) 

(Des G. Tenti. Photo)
1996 (13 Apr). *Trans-continental Drive, Rome–New York.* P 13½ × 14.
2360 934   4650l. multicoloured . . . .   4·25   3·25

(Des Tiziana Trinca (750l.), Giustina Milite (850l.). Photo)
1996 (29 Apr). *Europa. Famous Women. T* **935** *and similar vert design. Multicoloured.* P 13½ × 14.
2361 750l. Type **935**   60   50
2362 850l. Adelaide Ristori (actress)   75   50

936 Fishes, Sea and Coastline from St. Raphael to Genoa
937 Celestino V and Town of Fumone 

(Des C. Andreotto. Eng Maria Tuccelli. Recess and litho)
1996 (14 May). *20th Anniv of Ramoge Agreement on Environmental Protection of the Mediterranean.* P 13½ × 14.
2363 936   750l. multicoloured   65   50

(Des and eng P. Arghittu. Recess and Litho)
1996 (18 May). *700th Death Anniv of Pope Celestino V.* P 14 × 13½.
2364 937   750l. multicoloured   70   50

938 St. Anthony's Church, Diano Marina
939 Abbey and Relief from 12th-century Ivory Reliquary 

(Des Maria Tuccelli (2365), A. Paolucci (2366), P. Arghittu (2367), Tiziana Trinca (2368). Photo)
1996 (18 May). *Tourist Publicity (23rd series). T* **938** *and similar horiz designs. Multicoloured.* P 14 × 13½.
2365 750l. Type **938**   60   50
2366 750l. Pienza Cathedral   60   50
2367 750l. Belltower of St. Michael the Archangel's Church, Monte Sant' Angelo   60   50
2368 750l. Prehistoric stone dwelling, Lampedusa   60   50
2365/2368 *Set of* 4 . . . .   2·20   1·80

(Des Rita Fantini. Photo)
1996 (18 May). *500th Anniv of Reconsecration of Farfa Abbey.* P 13½ × 14.
2369 939   1000l. black, lemon and dull orange   90   80

940 Fair Entrance and Mt. Pellegrino
941 State Arms 

(Des Maria Perrini. Photo)
1996 (25 May). *Mediterranean Fair, Palermo.* P 14 × 13½.
2370 940   750l. multicoloured   65   50

(Des L. Vangelli. Photo)
1996 (1 June). *50th Anniv of Italian Republic.* P 13½ × 14.
2371 941   750l. multicoloured   60   50

942 Rider and Emblem
943 Views of Messina and Venice 

1996 (20 June). *50th Anniv of Production of Vespa Motor Scooters. Photo.* P 13½ × 14.
2372 942   750l. multicoloured   60   50

(Des Cristina Bruscaglia. Photo)
1996 (21 June). *40th Anniv of Founding Meetings of European Economic Community, Messina and Venice.* P 14.
2373 943   750l. multicoloured   60   50

944 Athlete on Starting Block and 1896 Athletes
945 *Acanthobrahmaea europaea* 

107

ITALY 1996

(Des A. Rinnaudo. Photo)

1996 (1 July). *Centenary of Modern Olympic Games and Olympic Games, Atlanta. T 944 and similar multicoloured designs.* P 14 × 13½.
2374	500l. Type **944**	45	50
2375	750l. Putting the shot and view of Atlanta (*vert*)	65	50
2376	850l. Gymnast, stadium and basketball player	75	50
2377	1250l. 1896 stadium, Athens, and 1996 stadium, Atlanta (*vert*)	1·00	1·10
2374/2377	Set of 4	2·50	2·30

(Des Maria Tuccelli. Photo)

1996 (26 Aug). *Butterflies. T 945 and similar horiz designs.* Multicoloured. P 14 × 13½.
2378	750l. Type **945**	55	50
2379	750l. *Melanargia arge*	55	50
2380	750l. *Papilio hospiton*	55	50
2381	750l. *Zygaena rubicundus*	55	50
2378/2381	Set of 4	2·00	1·80

946 *Prima Comunione*  **947** Santa Maria del Fiore

(Des and eng Rita Morena. Recess and litho)

1996 (30 Aug). *Italian Films. T 946 and similar vert designs.* P 13½ × 14.
2382	750l. black, bright scarlet and indigo	60	50
2383	750l. multicoloured	60	50
2384	750l. multicoloured	60	50

Designs:—No. 2383, Poster for *Cabiria*; 2384, *Scusate il Ritardo*.

(Eng F. Tulli. Recess)

1996 (7 Sept). *700th Anniv of Cathedral of Santa Maria del Fiore, Florence.* P 14 × 13½.
2385	**947** 750l. deep blue	70	50

948 Player, Shield and Club Badge  **949** Choppy (congress mascot)

(Des Anna Maresca. Photo)

1996 (7 Sept). *Milan, National Football Champion, 1995–96.* P 13½ × 14.
2386	**948** 750l. multicoloured	85	50

(Des U. Betotti. Photo)

1996 (9 Sept). *13th International Prehistoric and Protohistoric Sciences Congress.* P 13½ × 14.
2387	**949** 850l. multicoloured	75	50

950 Games Emblem and Pictograms  **951** Fair Entrance

(Des Maria Perrini. Photo)

1996 (13 Sept). *Mediterranean Games, Bari (1997).* P 13½ × 14.
2388	**950** 750l. multicoloured	70	50

(Des Maria Perrini. Photo)

1996 (13 Sept). *Levant Fair, Bari.* P 14 × 13½.
2389	**951** 750l. multicoloured	70	50

952 Rejoicing Crowd and Club Badge 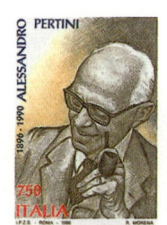 **953** Pertini

(Des Puzzle Ltd. Photo)

1996 (14 Sept). *Juventus, European Football Champion, 1995–96.* P 13½ × 14.
2390	**952** 750l. multicoloured	70	50

(Des Rita Morena. Photo)

1996 (25 Sept). *Birth Centenary of Alessandro Pertini (President, 1978–85).* P 13½ × 14.
2391	**953** 750l. multicoloured	65	50

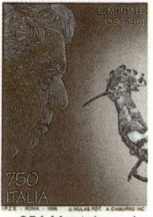

954 Montale and Hoopoe  **955** "The Annunciation"

(Eng A. Ciaburro. Recess and litho)

1996 (12 Oct). *Birth Centenary of Eugenio Montale (poet).* P 13½ × 14.
2392	**954** 750l. blackish brown and deep blue	65	50

1996 (31 Oct). *400th Birth Anniv of Pietro Berrettini da Cortona (artist).* Photo. P 13½ × 14.
2393	**955** 500l. multicoloured	55	50

ITALY 1996

956 *Tex Willer* (Galep)

957 Vortex and "Stamps"

(Eng Rita Morena. Recess and litho)

1996 (31 Oct). *Stamp Collecting. Strip Cartoons.* T **956** *and similar horiz design. Multicoloured.* P 14 × 13½.
2394	750l. Type **956**	65	50
2395	850l. *Corto Maltese* (Hugo Pratt)	75	50

(Des Tiziana Trinca. Photo)

1996 (8 Nov). *Stamp Day.* P 13½ × 14.
2396	**957** 750l. multicoloured	60	50

958 Bell Tower and Former Benedictine Abbey (seat of faculty)

959 Emblem

(Des and eng F. Tulli. Recess)

1996 (9 Nov). *Universities.* T **958** *and similar designs.* P 14 × 13½ (2399) or 13½ × 14 (others).
2397	750l. brown	60	50
2398	750l. deep blue	60	50
2399	750l. deep olive	60	50

Designs: *Vert*—No. 2397, Type **958** (centenary of Faculty of Agriculture, Perugia University); 2398, Former St. Matthew's Cathedral (seat of Medical School), Salerno University. *Horiz*—No. 2399, Athenaeum, Sassari University.

(Des G. de Pol. Photo)

1996 (13 Nov). *World Food Summit, Rome.* P 14 × 13½.
2400	**959** 850l. myrtle green and black	65	50

960 "Madonna of the Quail" (Antonio Pisanello)

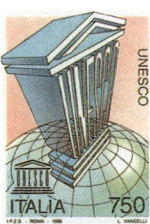

961 "UNESCO" and Globe

(Des Maria Tuccelli (850l.). Photo)

1996 (15 Nov). *Christmas.* T **960** *and similar multicoloured design.* P 13½ × 14 (750l.) or 14 × 13½ (850l.).
2401	750l. Type **960**	60	50
2402	850l. Father Christmas and toys (*horiz*)	75	50

(Des L. Vangelli. Photo)

1996 (20 Nov). *50th Anniversaries of United Nations Educational, Scientific and Cultural Organization (750l.)* T **961** *and similar vert design. Multicoloured.* P 13½ × 14.
2403	750l. Type **961**	55	50
2404	850l. U.N.I.C.E.F. emblem on kite, baby and globe	70	50

962 Headquarters, Rome

963 Bookcase

(Des M. Bonsignori. Photo)

1996 (26 Nov). *70th Anniv of National Statistics Institute.* P 13½ × 14.
2405	**962** 750l. multicoloured	60	50

(Des L. Vangelli. Photo)

1996 (29 Nov). *50th Anniv of Strega Prize.* P 13½ × 14.
2406	**963** 3400l. multicoloured	2·30	2·40

964 Hall of the Tricolour, Reggio Emilia

965 Tower Blocks and Skier

(Des Rita Fantini. Photo)

1997 (7 Jan). *Bicentenary of First Tricolour (now national flag), Cisalpine Republic.* P 13½ × 14.
2407	**964** 750l. multicoloured	60	50

(Des A. Testa. Photo)

1997 (1 Feb). *World Alpine Skiing Championships, Sestriere.* T **965** *and similar vert design. Multicoloured.* P 13½ × 14.
2408	750l. Type **965**	60	50
2409	850l. Olympic colours forming ski run and ski	60	50

ITALY 1997

966 Ferraris, Early Motor and Ferraris National Electrotechnology Institute, Turin

967 Loi

(Des T. Aime. Photo)
1997 (7 Feb). *Death Centenary of Galileo Ferraris (physicist).* P 14 × 13½.
2410   966   750l. multicoloured   60   50

(Des L. Vangelli. Photo)
1997 (8 Mar). *Fifth Death Anniv of Emanuela Loi (bodyguard killed in Mafia car bombing).* P 14 × 13½.
2411   967   750l. multicoloured   60   50

968 1819 Letter and Handstamps of Italian States

(Des M. Picardi. Litho)
1997 (21 Mar). *"Italia 98" International Stamp Exhibition, Milan (2nd issue). Sheet 150 × 80 mm containing T* **968** *and similar vert designs. Multicoloured.* P 13½ × 14.
MS2412 750l. Bologna 1910 cancellation, aerogramme from Balboa 1933 Transatlantic Mass Formation flight and postcard with 1917 25c. airmail stamp (Aerophilately); 750l. Cancellations used for the signing of the Rome Treaty (forming European Economic Community), Rome Olympic Games and Holy Year, 1952 Leonardo da Vinci 80l. stamp and 1931 inauguration of Milan railway station postcard (Thematic Philately); 750l. Type **968** (Postal History); 750l. *Democratica,* Italian stamp catalogue and L'Italia Filatelica (stamp review) (Philatelic Literature) . . . . . 5·25 4·00

969 Statue of Marcus Aurelius

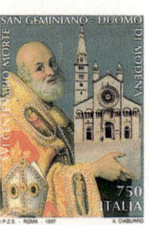

970 St. Germiniano (after Bartolomeo Schedoni) holding Modena Cathedral

(Des Cristina Bruscaglia. Photo)
1997 (25 Mar). *40th Anniv of Treaty of Rome (foundation of European Economic Community).* P 13½ × 14.
2413   969   750l. multicoloured   60   50

(Des A. Ciaburro. Photo)
1997 (4 Apr). *1600th Death Anniv of St. Germiniano (patron saint of Modena).* P 13½ × 14.
2414   970   750l. multicoloured   60   50

971 "Baptism of St. Ambrose" and "Hand of God recalling him to City"

972 Statue of Minerva, Central Square

(Des Maria Tuccelli. Litho)
1997 (4 Apr). *1600th Death Anniv of St. Ambrose, Bishop of Milan.* P 14.
2415   971   1000l. multicoloured   75   50
The illustrations are taken from reliefs by Volvinio on the Golden Altar in St. Ambrose's Cathedral, Milan.

(Des and eng F. Tulli. Recess)
1997 (14 Apr). *Universities.* T **972** *and similar horiz design.* P 14 × 13½.
2416   750l. bright crimson   60   50
2417   750l. indigo   60   50
Designs:—No. 2416, Type **972** (Rome University); 2417, Palace of Bo, Padua University.

973 St. Peter's Cathedral and Colosseum within "Wolf suckling Romulus and Remus"

974 Pre-Roman Walls, Gela

(Des Cristina Bruscaglia. Photo)
1997 (21 Apr). *2750th Anniv of Foundation of Rome.* P 14 × 13½.
2418   973   850l. multicoloured   70   50

(Des Maria Perrini. Photo)
1997 (24 Apr). P 14 × 13½.
2419   974   750l. multicoloured   60   50

975 First Page of Prison Notebook and Signature

976 Terracotta Relief and Cloisters

110

ITALY　　　　　　　　　　　　　　　　　　　　　　　　　　　　　　1997

(Des A. Olivetti. Photo)
1997 (26 Apr). *60th Death Anniv of Antonio Gramsci (politician).*
P 14.
2420　**975**　850l. multicoloured　　　　　60　　50

(Des Rita Fantini. Photo)
1997 (3 May). *500th Anniv of Consecration of Pavia Church.*
P 13½ × 14.
2421　**976**　1000l. multicoloured　　　　85　　50

977 Shoemaker's Workshop
978 Detail of 1901 Poster for Tosca and Theatre

1997 (5 May). *Europa. Tales and Legends.* T **977** and similar multicoloured design. Photo. P 14 × 13½ (800l.) or 13½ × 14 (900l.).
2422　　800l. Type **977** ("He who becomes the Property of Others works for his Soup")　　　　　　　　55　　50
2423　　900l. Street singer (19th-century copper etching)　　　　　　　　　65　　50

(Des Rita Morena. Photo)
1997 (16 May). *Centenary of Teatro Massimo, Palermo.*
P 13½ × 14.
2424　**978**　800l. multicoloured　　　　65　　50

979 St. Sebastian's Church, Acireale
980 Books and Marble Floor

(Des P. Arghittu. Litho)
1997 (17 May). *Tourist Publicity (24th series).* T **979** and similar horiz designs. Multicoloured. P 14 × 13½.
2425　　800l. Type **979**　　　　　　　65　　50
2426　　800l. Cicero and his tomb, Formia　65　　50
2427　　800l. St. Mary of the Assumption, Positano　　　　　　　　　65　　50
2428　　800l. St. Vitale's Basilica, Ravenna　　65　　50
2425/2428 *Set of 4*　　　　　　2·30　1·80

(Des Tiziana Trinca. Photo)
1997 (22 May). *Tenth Book Salon, Turin.* P 13½ × 14.
2429　**980**　800l. multicoloured　　　　70　　50

981 Queen Paola and Castel Sant'Angelo, Rome
982 Palazzo della Civiltà del Lavoro and Fair Pavilions

(Des Myriam Voz and T. Martin. Photo)
1997 (23 May). *60th Birth Anniv of Queen Paola of Belgium.*
P 14 × 13½.
2430　**981**　750l. multicoloured　　　　70　　50

(Des Maria Perrini. Photo)
1997 (24 May). *Rome Fair.* P 14 × 13½.
2431　**982**　800l. multicoloured　　　　70　　50

983 Orvieto Cathedral
984 Morosini in Via Tasso Prison, 1944

(Des F. Tulli. Recess)
1997 (31 May). P 13½ × 14.
2432　**983**　450l. bluish violet　　　　　40　　50

(Des Giustina Milite. Photo)
1997 (4 June). *53rd Death Anniv of Father Giuseppe Morosini.*
P 13½ × 14.
2433　**984**　800l. multicoloured　　　　65　　50

985 Player, Club Emblem and Football
986 Chamois (*Rupicapra ornata*) and Iris marsica

(Des A. Ciaburro. Photo)
1997 (7 June). *Juventus, National Football Champion, 1996–1997.*
P 13½ × 14.
2434　**985**　800l. multicoloured　　　　65　　50

(Des Maria Tuccelli. Photo)
1997 (7 June). *75th Anniv of Abruzzo National Park.* P 13½ × 14.
2435　**986**　800l. multicoloured　　　　55　　50

111

ITALY 1997

987 Towers and Fair Complex

988 Pennant and Ships' Bows

(Des G. Lanzi. Photo)
1997 (7 June). *Bologna Fair*. P 14 × 13½.
2436 987 800l. multicoloured 65 50

(Des Giustina Milite. Photo)
1997 (10 June). *Centenary of Italian Naval League*. P 13½ × 14.
2437 988 800l. multicoloured 70 50

989 Runner, High Jumper and Gymnast

990 Cogwheel and Robot Arm (industry)

(Des L. Vangelli. Photo)
1997 (13 June). *13th Mediterranean Games, Bari*. P 14 × 13½.
2438 989 900l. multicoloured 75 50

(Des and eng Maria Tuccelli (2439, 2441), Rita Morena (others). Recess and litho)
1997 (14 June). *Public Gardens (2nd series). Horiz designs as T* **915**. *Multicoloured*. P 14 × 13½.
2439   800l. Orto Botanico, Palermo 60 50
2440   800l. Villa Sciarra, Rome 60 50
2441   800l. Cavour, Sántena 60 50
2442   800l. Miramare, Trieste 60 50
2439/2442 Set of 4 . . . . 2·20 1·80

(Des P. Arghittu (800 l.), L. Vangelli (900 l.). Photo)
1997 (20 June). *Italian Work. T* **990** *and similar multicoloured design*. P 13½ × 14 (800l.) or 14 × 13½ (900l.).
2443   800l. Type **990** 55 50
2444   900l. Cereals, fruit trees, grapes and sun (agriculture) (*horiz*) 60 50

991 Globe and the *Matthew*

992 Verri

(Des Susan Warr. Litho)
1997 (24 June). *500th Anniv of John Cabot's Discovery of North America*. P 14.
2445 991 1300l. multicoloured . . . . . . 1·10 80

(Des Anna Maresca. Photo)
1997 (28 June). *Death Bicentenary of Pietro Verri (illuminist)*. P 13½ × 14.
2446 992 3600l. multicoloured . . . . . . 3·75 2·40

993 "Madonna of the Rosary" (Pomarancio il Vecchio)

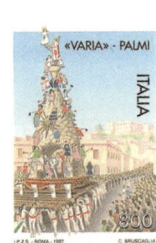

994 Procession

1997 (19 July). *Painters' Anniversaries. T* **993** *and similar vert design. Multicoloured. Photo*. P 14 (450l.) or 13½ × 14 (650l.).
2447   450l. Type **993** (400th death anniv) . . . 55 50
2448   650l. "The Miracle of Ostia" ((detail, Paolo Uccello) (600th birth anniv) (26 × 37 mm) 45 50

(Des Cristina Bruscaglia. Photo)
1997 (2 Aug). *Varia Festival, Palmi*. P 13½ × 14.
2449 994 800l. multicoloured 70 50

995 Basketball

996 Rosmini

(Des Anna Maresca. Photo)
1997 (19 Aug). *University Games, Sicily. T* **995** *and similar horiz designs. Multicoloured*. P 14 × 13½.
2450   450l. Type **995** 35 50
2451   800l. High jumping 65 50

(Des Tiziana Trinca. Photo)
1997 (26 Aug). *Birth Bicentenary of Antonio Rosmini (philosopher)*. P 14 × 13½.
2452 996 800l. multicoloured 70 50

(Des Rita Morena. Recess and litho)
1997 (27 Aug). *Italian Films (2nd series). Vert designs as T* **946**. P 13½ × 14.
2453   800l. multicoloured 55 50
2454   800l. black, blue and carmine-red . . . 55 50
2455   800l. multicoloured 55 50
Designs:—No. 2453, Pietro Germi in *Il Ferroviere*; 2454, Anna Magnani in *Mamma Roma*; 2455, Ugo Tognazzi in *Amici Miei*.

ITALY 1997

997 Open Book and Beach, Viareggio
998 Venue and Bell Tower 

(Des Rita Fantini. Photo)
1997 (30 Aug). *Viareggio–Repaci Prize.* P 14 × 13½.
2456 997   400l. multicoloured . . . . 3·25   2·40

(Des Maria Perrini. Photo)
1997 (1 Sept). *International Trade Fair, Bolzano.* P 14 × 13½.
2457 998   800l. multicoloured 70   50

999 Bronze Head (500 B.C.)
1000 Pope Paul VI and Door of Death, St. Peter's Cathedral, Rome 

(Des E. Donnini (800l.). Photo)
1997 (13 Sept). *Museum Exhibits. T* **999** *and similar vert designs. Multicoloured.* P 13½ × 14.
2458   450l. Type **999** (National Museum, Reggio Calabria) 40   50
2459   650l. "Madonna and Child with Two Vases of Roses" (Ercole de Roberti) (National Picture Gallery, Ferrara) 45   50
2460   800l. Miniature of poet Sordello da Goito (Arco Palace Museum, Mantua) . . . 50   50
2461   900l. "St. George and the Dragon" (Vitale di Bologna) (National Picture Gallery, Bologna) 55   50
2458/2461   Set of 4 . . . . 1·70   1·80

(Des and eng A. Ciaburro. Recess.)
1997 (26 Sept). *Birth Centenary of Pope Paul VI.* P 13½ × 14.
2462 1000 4000l. indigo . . . . 3·25   2·10

1001 Portello Pavilion (venue) and Milan Cathedral
1002 War-ravaged and Reconstructed Cities 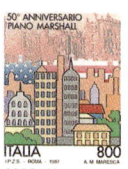

(Des Maria Perrini. Photo)
1997 (30 Sept). *Milan Fair.* P 14 × 13½.
2463 1001 800l. multicoloured 65   50

(Des Anna Maresca. Photo)
1997 (17 Oct). *50th Anniv of European Recovery Programme ("Marshall Plan").* P 14 × 13½.
2464 1002 800l. multicoloured 65   50

1003 Nativity (crib, St. Francis's Church, Leonessa)
1004 Production Plant and Merloni 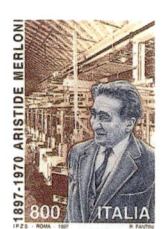

(Des E. Donnini (800l.). Photo)
1997 (18 Oct). *Christmas. T* **1003** *and similar horiz design. Multicoloured.* P 14 × 13½.
2465   800l. Type **1003** 65   50
2466   900l. "Nativity" (painting, Sta. Maria Maggiore, Spelo) 85   50

(Des Rita Fantini. Photo)
1997 (24 Oct). *Birth Centenary of Aristide Merloni (entrepreneur).* P 13½ × 14.
2467 1004 800l. multicoloured 65   50

1005 Cavalcaselle and Drawings
1006 Magnifying Glass and Fleur-de-lis 

(Des and eng A. Ciaburro. Recess and litho)
1997 (31 Oct). *Death Centenary of Giovanni Battista Cavalcaselle (art historian).* P 13½ × 14.
2468 1005 800l. multicoloured 70   50

(Des Giustina Milite. Photo)
1997 (5 Dec). *Stamp Day.* P 13½ × 14.
2469 1006 800l. multicoloured 70   50

1007 Refugees aboard *Toscana* (steamer)
1008 Arms of State Police and Badge of Traffic Police 

(Des A. Ciaburro. Photo)
1997 (6 Dec). *50th Anniv of Exodus of Italian Inhabitants from Istria, Fiume and Dalmatia.* P 14 × 13½.
2470 1007 800l. multicoloured 70   50

ITALY 1997

(Des Maria Tuccelli. Photo)
1997 (12 Dec). *50th Anniv of Traffic Police.* P 14 × 13½.
2471 **1008** 800l. multicoloured 70 50

1009 Map of Italy in Column and Flag
1010 "Hercules and the Hydra"

(Des Cristina Bruscaglia. Photo)
1998 (2 Jan). *50th Anniv of Constitution.* P 13½ × 14.
2472 **1009** 800l. black, rosine and emerald 65 50

1998 (3 Jan). *500th Death Anniv of Antonio del Pollaiolo (painter). Photo.* P 14.
2473 **1010** 800l. multicoloured 65 50

1011 Bertolt Brecht
1012 Fair Complex

1998 (2 Feb). *Writers' Birth Centenaries.* T **1011** *and similar designs.* P 13½ × 14 (900l.) or 14 × 13½ (others).
2474 450l. multicoloured 40 50
2475 650l. multicoloured 55 60
2476 800l. multicoloured 65 65
2477 900l. blue, blue-green and black . . . 75 50
2474/2477 *Set of* 4 . . . . 2·10 1·90
Designs: *Horiz*—650l. Federico García Lorca (poet); 800l. Curzio Malaparte. *Vert*—900l. Leonida Repaci.

(Des Cristina Bruscaglia. Photo)
1998 (11 Feb). *Verona Fair.* P 14 × 13½.
2478 **1012** 800l. multicoloured 65 50

1013 Memorial Tablet in Casale Montferrato Synagogue
1014 Trombonist

(Des G. Bourbon. Photo)
1998 (28 Mar). *150th Anniv of Granting of Full Citizen Rights to Italian Jews.* P 14.
2479 **1013** 800l. multicoloured 55 50

(Des Giustina Milite. Litho)
1998 (3 Apr). *Europa. National Festivals.* T **1014** *and similar vert design. Multicoloured.* P 13½ × 14.
2480 800l. Type **1014** (Umbria Jazz Festival) 60 50
2481 900l. Boy holding animal (Giffoni Film Festival) 65 50

1015 "The Last Supper"
1016 Costumes designed by Bernardo Buontalenti for First Opera in Florence

1998 (4 Apr). *500th Anniv of Completion of "The Last Supper" (mural) by Leonardo da Vinci.* P 14 × 13½.
2482 **1015** 800l. red-brown 65 50

(Des L. Vangelli. Photo)
1998 (8 Apr). *Italian Theatre.* T **1016** *and similar multicoloured design.* P 13½ × 14 (2483) or 14 × 13½ (2484).
2483 800l. Type **1016** (400th anniv of opera) 55 50
2484 800l. Gaetano Donizetti (composer, 150th death anniv) (*horiz*) 55 50

1017 Turin Cathedral and Holy Shroud
1018 Otranto Castle

(Des Rita Fantini. Photo)
1998 (19 Apr). *500th Anniv of Turin Cathedral. Display of the Holy Shroud.* P 13½ × 14.
2485 **1017** 800l. multicoloured 65 50

(Des P. Arghittu. Litho)
1998 (18 Apr). *Tourism Publicity (25th series).* T **1018** *and similar horiz designs. Multicoloured.* P 14 × 13½.
2486 800l. Type **1018** 65 50
2487 800l. Mori Fountain and Orsini Tower, Marino 65 50
2488 800l. Valfederia Chapel, Livigno . . . 65 50
2489 800l. Marciana Marina, Elba 65 50
2486/2489 *Set of* 4 . . . . 2·30 1·80

ITALY 1998

1019 Cagliari Cathedral, Drummer and Fair Building

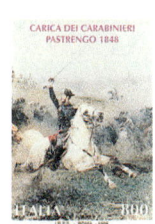

1020 "Charge of the Carabinieri at Pastrengo" (Sebastiano de Albertis)

1025 Santa Maria de Pesio Carthusian Monastery

1026 Ammonites and Pergola

(Des Rita Fantini. Photo)
1998 (30 May). *Artistic Heritage.* P 14 × 13½.
2496   **1025**   800l. multicoloured   60   50

(Des Giustina Milite. Photo)
1998 (23 Apr). *International Sardinia Fair, Cagliari.* P 14 × 13½.
2490   **1019**   800l. multicoloured   65   50

(Des G. Lancia. Photo)
1998 (30 May). *Fourth International "Fossils, Evolution, Ambience" Congress, Pergola.* P 14 × 13½.
2497   **1026**   800l. multicoloured   60   50

1998 (30 Apr). *150th Anniv of Battle of Pastrengo. Photo.* P 13½ × 14.
2491   **1020**   800l. multicoloured   65   50

1027 Flag at Half-mast

1028 Endoscope and Globe

(Des A. Cappuccio. Photo)
1998 (2 June). *"The Forces of Order, the Fallen".* P 13½ × 14.
2498   **1027**   800l. multicoloured   60   50

1021 Flags

1022 Player and Club Badge

(Des N. Russo. Photo)
1998 (11 May). *Padua Fair.* P 13½ × 14.
2492   **1021**   800l. multicoloured   60   50

(Des Tiziana Trinca. Photo)
1998 (3 June). *Sixth World General Endoscopic Surgery Congress, Rome.* P 13½ × 14.
2499   **1028**   900l. multicoloured   85   50

(Des Tiziana Trinca. Photo)
1998 (18 May). *Juventus, National Football Champion, 1997–98.* P 13½ × 14.
2493   **1022**   800l. multicoloured   65   50

1029 First Parliamentary Chamber

1030 Fair Complex and Basilica

(Des Cristina Bruscaglia. Photo)
1998 (6 June). *National Museums.* T **1029** and similar multicoloured designs. P 13½ × 14 (2501) or 14 × 13½ (others).
2500   800l. Type **1029** (Italian Risorgimento Museum, Turin)   60   50
2501   800l. Statue of an ephebus (Athenian youth), Temple of Concord and column of Temple of Vulcan (Regional Archaeology Museum, Agrigento) (*vert*)   60   50
2502   800l. Sculpture by Umberto Boccioni and Palazzo Venier dei Leoni (venue) (Peggy Guggenheim Collection, Venice)   60   50

1023 Turin Polytechnic

1024 Emblem

(Des F. Tulli. Recess)
1998 (18 May). *Universities.* P 14 × 13½.
2494   **1023**   800l. steel-blue   60   50

1998 (22 May). *World Food Programme. Photo.* P 14 × 13½.
2495   **1024**   900l. multicoloured   85   50

ITALY 1998

(Des Michele Novello and C. Bellani. Photo)
1998 (13 June). *Vicenza Trade Fair.* P 13½ × 14.
2503 **1030** 800l. multicoloured 65 50

1031 Leopardi (after Luigi Lolli) and Palazzo Leopardi Recanati

1032 Young Etruscan Girl (detail of tomb painting)

1998 (29 June). *Birth Bicentenary of Giacomo Leopardi, (poet). Photo.* P 14 × 13½.
2504 **1031** 800l. brown and black 55 50

(Des G. Toffoletti (100l.), Maria Tuccelli (450l.), L. Vangelli (650l.). Des and eng F. Tulli (800l.), A. Ciaburro (1000l.). Photo (100 to 650l.) or recess (others))
1998 (8 July). *Women in Art.* T **1032** *and similar vert designs.* W **1032** (800, 1000l.). P 14 × 13½.
2505 100l. black, blue-green and silver 15 15
2506 450l. multicoloured 40 15
2507 650l. multicoloured 60 15
2508 800l. lake-brown and black 70 15
2509 1000l. deep turquoise-blue, chestnut and black 90 65
2505/2509 *Set of* 5 . . . . 2·50 1·10
Designs:—450l. Detail of "Herod's Banquet and the Dance of Salome" (fresco by Filippo Lippi in Prato Cathedral); 650l. "Profile of a Woman" (Antonio del Pollaiuolo; 800l. "Lady with a Unicorn" (detail, Raphael); 1000l. "Constanza Buonarelli" (bust by Gian Lorenzo Bernini).

1033 Pitch, Pitcher and Batter

1034 Columbus and Vespucci

(Des A. Rinnaudo. Photo)
1998 (21 July). *33rd World Cup Baseball Championship, Florence.* P 14 × 13½.
2510 **1033** 900l. multicoloured 75 50

(Des J. de Faria. Photo)
1998 (12 Aug). *500th Anniversaries of Landing of Christopher Columbus in Venezuela and of Amerigo Vespucci's Explorations.* P 14 × 13½.
2511 **1034** 1300l. multicoloured . . . . . . 1·00 80

1035 Emblem

1036 Mother Teresa and Child

(Des R. Russo. Photo)
1998 (28 Aug). *50th International Stamp Fair, Riccione.* P 13½ × 14.
2512 **1035** 800l. multicoloured 65 50

(Des Rita Moreno (800l.), M. Temo (900l.). Photo)
1998 (5 Sept). *First Death Anniv of Mother Teresa (founder of Missionaries of Charity).* T **1036** *and similar multicoloured design.* P 14 × 13½ (800l.) or 13½ × 14 (900l.).
2513 800l. Type **1036** 65 50
2514 900l. Mother Teresa (*vert*) 75 50

1037 Father Pio and Monastery Church, San Giovanni Rotondo

1038 Titus Arch, Rome, and Sicilian Mosaic of Rider

(Des and eng A. Ciaburro. Recess)
1998 (23 Sept). *30th Death Anniv of Father Pio da Pietrelcina (Capuchin friar who bore the stigmata).* P 14 × 13½.
2515 **1037** 800l. deep blue 65 50

(Des Maria Perrini. Photo)
1998 (2 Oct). *World Equestrian Championships, Rome.* P 14 × 13½.
2516 **1038** 4000l. multicoloured . . . . . 3·25 1·90

1039 Telecommunications College, Rome

(Des and eng F. Tulli. Recess)
1998 (9 Oct). *Universities.* P 14 × 13½.
2517 **1039** 800l. deep blue 65 50

1040 Pope John Paul II and his Message

(Des I. Fantini. Photo)
1998 (23 Oct). *"Italia 98" International Stamp Exhibition, Milan (3rd issue). Stamp Day.* P 14.
2518 **1040** 800l. multicoloured 65 50

ITALY 1998

1041 *Giuseppe Garibaldi* (aircraft carrier)
1042 "Dionysus" (bronze statue) 
1045 Cogwheels and "Proportions of Man" (Leonardo da Vinci)
1046 Satellite Dish, Type, Book and "Internet"

(Des Anna Maresca (2519/20), A. Cappuccio (2521), A. Squadrone (2522). Photo)

1998 (24 Oct). *Armed Forces Day.* T **1041** and similar multicoloured designs. P 14 × 13½ (horiz) or 13½ × 14 (vert).
2519	800l.	Type **1041** (Navy)	65	50
2520	800l.	Eurofighter 2000 (75th anniv of Air Force)	65	50
2521	800l.	Carabiniere (*vert*)	65	50
2522	800l.	Battle of El-Alamein at night (Army) (*vert*)	65	50
2519/2522		*Set of 4*	2·30	1·80

Nos. 2519/22 were each issued with *se-tenant* label showing "Italia 98" International Stamp Exhibition emblem.

1998 (25 Oct). *"Italia 98" International Stamp Exhibition, Milan (4th issue). Art Day.* Photo. P 13½ × 14.
2523	**1042**	800l. multicoloured	65	50

1043 Ferrari competing in Race, 1931

(Des Anna Maresca. Litho)

1998 (26 Oct). *"Italia 98" International Stamp Exhibition, Milan (5th issue). Birth Centenary of Enzo Ferrari (car designer).* Sheet 160 × 110 mm containing T **1043** and similar horiz designs. Multicoloured. P 13½.
MS2524 800l. Type **1043**; 800l. Formula 1 Ferrari, 1952; 800l. Ferrari GTO, 1963; 800l. Formula 1 Ferrari, 1998 . . . . 3·50 4·00

1044 Hand releasing Birds

(Des J.-M. Folon. Photo)

1998 (27 Oct). *50th Anniv of Universal Declaration of Human Rights.* P 14 × 13½.
2525 **1044** 1400l. multicoloured . . . . 1·10 80

No. 2525 was issued with *se-tenant* half stamp-size label showing "Italia 98" International Stamp Exhibition emblem.

(Des Tiziana Trinca)

1998 (28 Oct). *Europa Day.*
 (a) Ordinary gum. Photo. P 13½ × 14.
2526 **1045** 800l. multicoloured 65 50
 (b) Booklet stamps. Self-adhesive. Litho. Die-cut perf 11.
2527 **1045** 800l. multicoloured 65 50
 a. Booklet pane. Nos. 2527 × 6 . . . . 4·00

(Des Rita Morena. Recess and litho)

1998 (29 Oct). *"Italia 98" International Stamp Exhibition, Milan (6th issue). Cinema Day.* Vert designs as T **946**. Multicoloured. P 13½ × 14.
2528	450l.	*Ti Conosco Mascherino* (dir. Eduardo de Filippo)	40	50
2529	800l.	*Fantasmia a Roma* (Antonio Pietrangeli)	65	50
2530	900l.	*Il Signor Max* (Mario Camerini)	75	50

Nos. 2528/30 were each issued with *se-tenant* label showing the exhibition emblem.

(Des Anna Maresca. Photo)

1998 (31 Oct). *"Italia 98" International Stamp Exhibition, Milan (7th issue). Communications Day.* P 13½ × 14.
2531 **1046** 800l. multicoloured 55 50

1047 Arrows circling Letter
1048 "Epiphany" (sculpture, St. Mark's Church, Seminara) 

(Des L. Vangelli. Litho)

1998 (1 Nov). *"Italia 98" International Stamp Exhibition, Milan (8th issue). Post Day.* Sheet 130 × 90 mm. P 13½ × 14.
MS2532 **1047** 4000l. multicoloured . . . . 3·00 5·50

(Des Maria Tuccelli (800l.), Rita Morena (900l.). Recess)

1998 (28 Nov). *Christmas.* T **1048** and similar design. P 13½ × 14.
2533 800l. indigo 60 50
2534 900l. red-brown 65 50

Design: Horiz—900l. "Adoration of the Shepherds" (drawing, Giulio Romano).

ITALY 1998

1049 "Ecstasy of St. Teresa"
1050 Royal Decree and Waldensian Emblem 

1998 (1 Dec). *400th Birth Anniv of Gian Lorenzo Bernini (sculptor). Photo.* P $13\frac{1}{2} \times 14$.
2535 **1049** 900l. multicoloured 65 50

(Des S. Calorio. Photo)

1998 (4 Dec). *150th Anniv of Toleration of the Waldenses (religious sect).* P 14.
2536 **1050** 800l. multicoloured 55 50

DENOMINATION. From No. 2537 Italian stamps were denominated both in lira and in euros. The catalogue listings use the former until the introduction of euro notes and coins on 1 January 2002.

1999 (28 Jan). *As Nos. 2505/9 but with face value in euros added.*
2537 100l. brown, blue-green and gold 10 15
2538 450l. multicoloured 35 15
2539 650l. multicoloured 50 15
2540 800l. lake-brown and black 65 50
2541 1000l. deep turquoise-blue, chestnut and black 75 65
2537/2541 Set of 5 . . . . 2·10 1·40

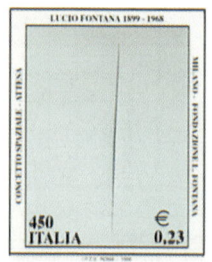

1051 "Space Concept–Wait"
1052 La Sila National Park, Calabria 

1999 (19 Feb). *Birth Centenary of Lucio Fontana (artist). Photo.* P 14.
2542 **1051** 450l. grey-blue and black 35 50

(Des Anna Maresca (800l.) and Rita Fantini (900l.). Photo)

1999 (12 Mar). *Europa. Parks and Gardens.* T **1052** *and similar multicoloured design.* P $13\frac{1}{2} \times 14$ (800l.) or $14 \times 13\frac{1}{2}$ (900l.).
2543 800l. Type **1052** 60 50
2544 900l. Tuscan Archipelago National Park (horiz) 70 50

1053 Holy Door, St. Peter's Cathedral
1054 St. Egidius's Church, Cellere 

(Des A. Ciaburro. Photo)

1999 (13 Mar). *Holy Year 2000.* P $13\frac{1}{2} \times 14$.
2545 **1053** 1400l. multicoloured . . . . 1·00 95

(Des and eng Maria Tuccelli. Recess)

1999 (10 Apr). *Artistic Heritage.* P $14 \times 13\frac{1}{2}$.
2546 **1054** 800l. lake-brown 55 50

1055 Holy Year 2000 and 11th-century Bells
1056 Earth Pyramids, Segonzano 

(Des Anna Maresca. Photo)

1999 (17 Apr). *Museums.* T **1055** *and similar multicoloured designs.* P $13\frac{1}{2} \times 14$ (2549) or $14 \times 13\frac{1}{2}$ (others).
2547 800l. Type **1055** (History of Campanology Museum, Agnone) 55 50
2548 800l. "Lake with Swan" (stained glass) (Casina delle Civette Museum, Rome) 55 50
2549 800l. Renaissance majolica dish (International Ceramics Museum, Faenza) (vert) 55 50

(Des P. Arghittu. Photo)

1999 (17 Apr). *Tourist Publicity (26th series).* T **1056** *and similar horiz designs. Multicoloured.* P $14 \times 13\frac{1}{2}$.
2550 800l. Type **1056** 55 50
2551 800l. Marmore Waterfall, Terni 55 50
2552 800l. Cathedral, Lecce 55 50
2553 800l. Lipari 55 50
2550/2553 Set of 4 . . . . 2·00 1·80

1057 Audience Chamber
1058 Fire Engine at Fire 

(Des Anna Maresca. Photo)

1999 (23 Apr). *Constitutional Court.* P $14 \times 13\frac{1}{2}$.
2554 **1057** 800l. multicoloured 55 50

(Des S. Silvestrini. Photo)

1999 (29 Apr). *Fire Brigade.* P $14 \times 13\frac{1}{2}$.
2555 **1058** 800l. multicoloured 55 50

ITALY 1999

1059 Cadet and Academy
1060 Players and Airplane
1065 "P"
1066 First Fiat Car (advertising poster)

(Des Cristina Bruscaglia. Photo)

1999 (3 May). *Modena Military Academy.* P $13\frac{1}{2} \times 14$.
2556 **1059** 800l. multicoloured 55 50

(Des Batesitalia. Typo)

1999 (14 June). *Priority Mail stamp. Self-adhesive.* Die-cut perf 11.
2563 **1065** 1200l. black and gold . . . . . 85 1·40
  a. Booklet pane. No. 2563 × 8
    (without labels) . . . . . . 7·00
No. 2563 was issued in sheets and booklets of four, each stamp with attached label inscribed "POSTA PRIORITARIA Priority Mail". It was also issued in booklets of eight without attached label.

(Des Tiziana Trinca (800l.), L. Vangelli (900l.). Photo)

1999 (4 May). *50th Anniv of Death in Aircrash of Grand Turin Football Team.* T **1060** *and similar horiz design.* Multicoloured. P $14 \times 13\frac{1}{2}$.
2557   800l. Type **1060** 65 50
2558   900l. Superga Basilica, club arms and
       names of victims 75 50

1999 (10 July). *Centenary of Fiat (motor manufacturer).* Photo. P $13\frac{1}{2} \times 14$.
2564 **1066** 4800l. multicoloured . . . . . 3·25 1·60

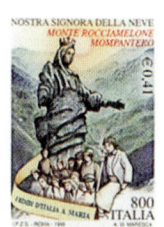

1061 Council Seat, Strasbourg
1062 Players and Club Emblem
1067 "Our Lady of the Snow"
1068 Pimentel and St. Elmo Castle, Naples 

(Des Maria Perrini. Photo)

1999 (5 May). *50th Anniv of Council of Europe.* P $14 \times 13\frac{1}{2}$.
2559 **1061** 800l. multicoloured 55 50

(Des Anna Maresca. Photo)

1999 (19 July). *Centenary of Erection of Statue of "Our Lady of the Snow" on Mt. Rocciamelone.* P $13\frac{1}{2} \times 14$.
2565 **1067** 800l. multicoloured 55 50

(Des L. Vangelli. Photo)

1999 (7 June). *Milan, National Football Champion, 1998–99.* P $13\frac{1}{2} \times 14$.
2560 **1062** 800l. multicoloured 70 50

(Des Giustina Milite. Photo)

1999 (20 Aug). *Death Bicentenary of Eleonora de Fonseca Pimentel (writer and revolutionary).* P $14 \times 13\frac{1}{2}$.
2566 **1068** 800l. multicoloured 55 50

1063 Ballot Box and Parliament Chamber, Strasbourg
1064 Coppi
1069 Canoes

(Des L. Vangelli. Photo)

1999 (10 June). *20th Anniv of First Direct Elections to European Parliament.* P $14 \times 13\frac{1}{2}$.
2561 **1063** 800l. multicoloured 55 50

(Des Cristina Bruscaglia. Photo)

1999 (12 June). *80th Birth Anniv of Fausto Coppi (racing cyclist).* P $14 \times 13\frac{1}{2}$.
2562 **1064** 800l. multicoloured 55 50

1999 (26 Aug). *30th World Speed Canoeing Championships.* P $14 \times 13\frac{1}{2}$.
2567 **1069** 900l. multicoloured 60 50

ITALY　　　　　　　　　　　　　　　　　　　　　　　　　　　　　　1999

1070 "Goethe in the Rome Countryside" (Johann Tischbein)

1071 Cyclist and Stopwatch

1999 (28 Aug). *250th Birth Anniv of Johann Wolfgang Goethe (poet and playwright). Photo.* P 14 × 13½.
2568　**1070**　400l. multicoloured　.　.　.　.　.　.　2·75　1·80

(Des Rita Fantini. Photo)
1999 (15 Sept). *World Cycling Championships, Treviso and Verona.* P 13½ × 14.
2569　**1071**　1400l. multicoloured　.　.　.　.　.　1·00　80

1072 Child with Rucksack

(Des Anna Maresca. Photo)
1999 (25 Sept). *Stamp Day.* P 13½ × 14.
2570　**1072**　800l. multicoloured　.　.　.　.　.　55　50

1073 Architectural Drawing of Basilica

(Des Rita Morena. Recess)
1999 (25 Sept). *Re-opening of Upper Basilica of St. Francis of Assisi.* P 14 × 13½.
2571　**1073**　800l. multicoloured　.　.　.　.　.　55　50

1074 Parini (after Francesco Rosaspina)

1075 Volta (bust by Giovan Comolli) and Voltaic Pile

(Des A. Ciaburro. Recess)
1999 (2 Oct). *Death Bicentenary of Giuseppe Parini (poet).* P 13½ × 14.
2572　**1074**　800l. steel blue　.　.　.　.　.　55　50

(Des Rita Morena. Photo)
1999 (11 Oct). *Bicentenary of Invention of Electrochemical Battery by Alessandro Volta.* P 13½ × 14.
2573　**1075**　3000l. multicoloured　.　.　.　.　2·10　1·60

1076 Forms and U.P.U. Emblem

(Des Tiziana Trinca. Photo)
1999 (18 Oct). *125th Anniv of Universal Postal Union.* P 14 × 13½.
2574　**1076**　900l. multicoloured　.　.　.　.　.　65　50

1077 Mameli and 1948 and 1949 100l. Stamps

(Des Tiziana Trinca. Photo)
1999 (22 Oct). *150th Death Anniv of Goffredo Mameli (poet and patriot) and 150th Anniv of Roman Republic.* P 14.
2575　**1077**　1500l. multicoloured　.　.　.　.　1·10　1·30

1078 Man and Town

1079 First World War Soldiers (after postcard)

(Des Valentina Mincolelli (450l.), Laura Gori (650l.), Franca Palombi (800l.), Frederica Trani (1000l.). Photo)
1999 (23 Oct). *"The Stamp Our Friend". T* **1078** *and similar vert designs. Multicoloured.* P 13½ × 14.
2576　　450l. Type **1078**　.　.　.　.　.　.　35　80
　　　　a. Sheetlet of 4. Nos. 2576/9　.　.　1·90
2577　　650l. Campaign emblem　.　.　.　.　50　95
2578　　800l. Schoolchildren　.　.　.　.　.　60　1·10
2579　　1000l. Windmill (toy)　.　.　.　.　.　70　1·10
2576/2579 Set of 4　.　.　.　.　.　.　.　.　1·90　3·50

Nos. 2576/9 were issued together in *se-tenant* sheetlets of four stamps.

120

ITALY   1999

(Des Tiziana Trinca. Photo)
1999 (4 Nov). *Centenary of Generation of '99.* P 13½ × 14.
2580   **1079**   900l. multicoloured   65   50

1080 Santa Claus

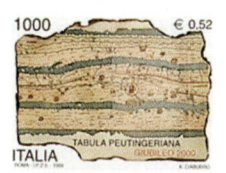

1081 Peutinger Tablet (medieval map showing pilgrim route by C. Celtes and Conrad Peutinger)

(Des Pirkko Vahtero (800l.). Photo)
1999 (5 Nov). *Christmas.* T **1080** *and similar vert design. Multicoloured.* P 13½ × 14.
2581   800l. Type **1080**   60   50
2582   1000l. "Nativity" (Dosso Dossi)   75   50

(Des A. Ciaburro. Photo)
1999 (24 Nov). *Holy Year 2000.* T **1081** *and similar horiz designs. Multicoloured.* P 14 × 13½.
2583   1000l. Type **1081**   70   50
2584   1000l. 18th-century pilgrim's stamp   70   50
2585   1000l. 13th-century bas-relief of pilgrims (facade of Fidenza Cathedral)   70   50

1082 Urbino State Art Institute

(Des and eng P. Arghittu. Recess)
1999 (27 Nov). *Schools and Universities.* T **1082** *and similar horiz design.* P 14 × 13½.
2586   450l. black   35   50
2587   650l. red-brown   45   50
Design:—650l. Pisa High School.

1083 "Leopard bitten by Tarantula"

1999 (27 Nov). *Birth Centenary of Antonio Ligabue (artist). Photo.* P 14.
2588   **1083**   1000l. multicoloured   70   50

1084 Robot's Hand meeting Man's Hand (after Michelangelo)

(Des E. Manera. Photo)
1999 (27 Nov). *Year 2000.* P 14 × 13½.
2589   **1084**   4800l. multicoloured   3·25   2·40

1085 Child looking at Aspects of Earth

(Des Tiziana Trinca. Litho)
2000 (1 Jan). *New Millennium. "The Past and the Future". Sheet* 110 × 80 *mm containing T* **1085** *and similar horiz design. Multicoloured.* P 14 × 13½.
MS2590   2000l. Type **1085**; 2000l. Astronaut looking at Moon   3·00   4·75

(Des Batisitalia. Typo)
2000 (10 Jan). *Priority Mail Stamp.* As T **1065** *but different colour. Self-adhesive.* Die-cut perf 11.
2591   1200l. black, greenish-yellow and gold   85   65
No. 2591 was issued with attached label inscribed "POSTA PRIORITARIA Priority Mail".

1086 Tosca and Scenery

1087 St. Paul (statue) and Holy Door, St. Peter's Basilica, Rome

(Des Rita Morena. Recess and litho)
2000 (14 Jan). *Centenary of the First Performance of Tosca (opera).* P 14 × 13½.
2592   **1086**   800l. multicoloured   55   50

(Des Anna Maria Maresca. Photo)
2000 (18 Jan). *Holy Year 2000.* P 13½ × 14.
2593   **1087**   1000l. multicoloured   70   50

121

# ITALY													2000

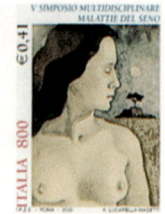

1088 Players

1089 Painting (Antonella Lucarella Masetti)

(Des P. Volpi. Photo)
2000 (5 Feb). *Six Nations Rugby Championship.* P 14 × 13½.
2594 **1088** 800l. multicoloured 55   50

2000 (12 Feb). *Fifth Conference on Breast Diseases.* T **1089** and similar vert design. Multicoloured. Photo. P 13½ × 14.
2595 800l. Type **1089** 55   50
2596 1000l. Painting (Cristina Bruscaglia) . . 70   50

1090 "Enigma of an Autumn Afternoon"

1091 Skier and Trophy

2000 (4 Mar). *New Millennium (1st issue). Art and Science.* Sheet 111 × 80 mm containing T **1090** and similar horiz design, showing paintings by Giorgio de Chirico. Litho. P 14 × 13½.
MS2597 800l. Type **1090** (art); 800l. "The Inevitable Temple" (science) . . . . . . 2·00   2·40

(Des Giustina Milite. Photo)
2000 (7 Mar). *World Cup Skiing Championships.* P 13½ × 14.
2598 **1091** 4800l. multicoloured . . . . . 3·25   2·40

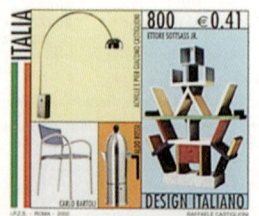

1092 Lamp (Achille and Pier Giacomo Castiglioni), Chair (Carlo Bartoli), Coffee Pot (Aldo Rossi) and Bookcase (Ettore Sottsass Jr.)

(Des R. Castiglioni. Litho)
2000 (9 Mar). *Italian Design.* Sheet 154 × 138 mm containing T **1092** and similar horiz designs. Multicoloured. P 13½.
MS2599 800l. Type **1092**; 800l. Armchair (Mario Bellini), corkscrew (Alessandro Mendini), table lamp (Vico Magistretti) and suspended lamp (Alberto Meda and Paolo Rizzatto); 800l. Chair (Gio Ponti), bean bag (Gatti Paolini Teodoro), pasta set (Massimo Morozzi) and standard uplighter (Tobia Scarpa); 800l. White standard uplighter (Pietro Chiesa), hostess trolley (Joe Colombo), chair (Cini Boeri and Tomu Katayanagi) and sideboard (Lodovico Acerbis and Giotto Stoppino); 800l. Easy chairs (Gaetano Pesce), chair (Enzo Mari), clothes horse (De Pas d'Urbino Lomazzi) and mobile filing cabinet (Antonio Citterio and Oliver Loew); 800l. Chair (Marco Zanuso), anglepoise lamp (Michele de Lucchi and Giancarlo Fassina), ice bucket (Bruno Munari) and stool (Anna Castelli Ferrieri) . . . 3·50   6·50

1093 "Adoration of the Magi" (Domenico Ghirlandaio)

1094 Library and Emblem

2000 (10 Mar). *Holy Year 2000.* T **1093** and similar multicoloured designs. Photo. P 14 × 13½.
2600 450l. Type **1093** 40   50
2601 650l. "Baptism of Christ" (Paolo Caliari Veronese) (*vert*) 55   50
2602 800l. "The Last Supper" (Ghirlandaio) (*vert*) 70   50
2603 1000l. "Regret of Christ's Death" (Giotto di Bondone) 85   50
2604 1200l. "The Resurrection" (Piero della Francesca) (*vert*) . . . . . 1·00   80
2600/2604 Set of 5 . . . . . . 3·25   2·50

(Des Anna Maria Maresca. Photo)
2000 (6 Apr). *150th Anniv of La Civilta Cattolica Foundation (collection of Church publications).* P 14 × 13½.
2605 **1094** 800l. multicoloured 55   50

1095 Courtyard

(Des Rita Fantini. Photo)
2000 (8 Apr). *150th Anniv of St. Joseph's College, Rome.* P 14 × 13½.
2606 **1095** 800l. multicoloured 55   50

ITALY 2000

1096 Terre di Franciacorta, Erbrusco

2000 (14 Apr). *Tourist Publicity (27th series)*. T **1096** and similar horiz designs. Multicoloured. P 14 × 13½.
2607	800l. Type **1096**	55	50
2608	800l. Dunarobba fossil forest, Avigliano Umbro	55	50
2609	800l. View of Ercolano	55	50
2610	800l. Beauty Island, Taormina	55	50
2607/2610	Set of 4	2·00	1·80

1097 Cyclist **1098** Christ carrying Cross

(Des A. Rinnaudo. Photo)

2000 (14 Apr). *Centenary of International Cycling Union.* P 13½ × 14.
| 2611 | **1097** | 1500l. multicoloured | 1·10 | 80 |

(Des A. Ciaburro. Photo)

2000 (19 Apr). *Papier-mâché Figurines, Caltanisetta.* P 14 × 13½.
| 2612 | **1098** | 800l. multicoloured | 55 | 50 |

1099 Landscape (Giorgione) **1100** Piccinni

(Des Tiziana Trinca. Litho)

2000 (4 May). *New Millennium (2nd issue). Countryside and City.* Sheet 110 × 80 mm containing T **1099** and similar horiz design. Multicoloured. P 14 × 13½.
MS2613 800l. Type **1099**; 800l. "Perspective of an Ideal Town" (Piero della Francesca) ... 2·30 1·20

(Des Rita Morena. Photo)

2000 (6 May). *Death Bicentenary of Niccolò Piccinni (composer).* P 13½ × 14.
| 2614 | **1100** | 4000l. multicoloured | 2·75 | 2·40 |

1101 "Building Europe" **1102** Sardinia 1851 5, 20 and 40c. Stamps

(Des. J.-P. Cousin. Photo)

2000 (9 May). *Europa.* P 13½ × 14.
| 2615 | **1101** | 800l. multicoloured | 55 | 50 |

(Des Cristina Bruscaglia. Photo)

2000 (9 May). *Museum of Posts and Telecommunications.* T **1102** and similar horiz design. Multicoloured. P 14 × 13½.
| 2616 | 800l. Type **1102** | 60 | 50 |
| 2617 | 800l. Reconstruction of radio and telegraph cabin aboard *Elettra* (Marconi's steam yacht) | 60 | 50 |

1103 Footballer and Pitch **1104** Cathedral Facade

(Des L. Vangelli. Photo)

2000 (20 May). *Lazio, National Football Champion, 1999–2000.* P 13½ × 14.
| 2618 | **1103** | 800l. multicoloured | 55 | 50 |

(Des Maria Carmela Perrini. Photo)

2000 (31 May). *700th Anniv of Monza Cathedral.* P 13½ × 14.
| 2619 | **1104** | 800l. multicoloured | 55 | 50 |

1105 Globe and Ears of Corn **1106** Statue

(Des Cristina Bruscaglia. Photo)

2000 (17 June). *United Nations World Food Programme.* P 13½ × 14.
| 2620 | **1105** | 1000l. multicoloured | 70 | 50 |

(Des Anna Maria Maresca. Photo)

2000 (24 June). *Centenary of the Jesus the Redeemer Monument, Nuoro.* P 13½ × 14.
| 2621 | **1106** | 800l. multicoloured | 55 | 50 |

ITALY 2000

1107 Bridge, Parana River, Argentina

1108 Profiles

(Des Anna Maria Maresca. Photo)

2000 (28 June). *120th Anniv of Italian Water Board.* P 14 × 13½.
2622 **1107** 800l. multicoloured 55 50

(Des Tiziana Trinca. Litho)

2000 (4 July). *New Millennium (3rd issue). Technology and Space. Sheet 110 × 80 mm containing T* **1108** *and similar horiz design. Multicoloured.* P 14 × 13½.
MS2623 800l. Type **1108**; 800l. Symbolic man . . . . 2·30 1·20

1113 "Madonna and Child" (Crivelli)

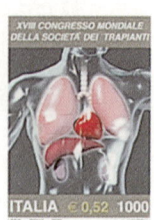

1114 Internal Organs

(Des Rita Morena. Recess and photo)

2000 (8 Aug). *570th Birth Anniv of Carlo Crivelli (artist).* P 14.
2628 **1113** 800l. multicoloured 55 50

(Des L. Vangelli. Photo)

2000 (26 Aug). *18th International Transplantation Society Congress, Rome.* P 13½ × 14.
2629 **1114** 1000l. multicoloured 70 80

1109 Child with Ladder to Moon (Giacomo Chiesa)

1110 Archer

2000 (7 July). *"Stampin the Future". Winning Entry in Children's International Painting Competition. Photo.* P 13½ × 14.
2624 **1109** 1000l. multicoloured 70 50

(Des A. Rinnaudo. Photo)

2000 (8 July). *World Archery Championship, Campagna.* P 13½ × 14.
2625 **1110** 1500l. multicoloured . . . . 1·10 80

1115 Athlete and Stadium

1116 "War"

(Des Maria Carmela Perrini and Rita Fantini (800l.), Maria Carmela Perrini (1000l.). Photo)

2000 (1 Sept). *Olympic Games, Sydney. T* **1115** *and similar vert design. Multicoloured.* P 13½ × 14.
2630 800l. Type **1115** 55 50
2631 1000l. "Discus Thrower" (statue) and Sydney Harbour 70 80

2000 (4 Sept). *New Millennium (4th issue). War and Peace. Frescoes by Taddeo Zuccari. Sheet 110 × 80 mm containing T* **1116** *and similar vert design. Multicoloured. Litho.* P 13½ × 14.
MS2632 800l. Type **1116**; 800l. "Peace" . . . . 2·30 1·20

1111 Cyclist and Globe

1112 Fair Attractions

(Des Rita Morena. Photo)

2000 (31 July). *World Junior Cycling Championships.* P 13½ × 14.
2626 **1111** 800l. multicoloured 55 50

(Des Anna Maria Maresca. Photo)

2000 (8 Aug). *Millenary Fair of St. Orso.* P 14 × 13½.
2627 **1112** 1000l. multicoloured 70 50

1117 Battle Scene (Jacques Maries Gaston Oufray Debreville)

1118 Figures in Evening Dress and City Skyline

2000 (8 Sept). *Bicentenary of Marengo Battle. Photo.* P 13½ × 14.
2633 **1117** 800l. multicoloured 55 50

ITALY 2000

(Des A. Cremonese. Photo)
2000 (20 Sept). *New Year.* P 13½ × 14.
2634 **1118** 800l. multicoloured 55 50

1119 Child holding Magnifying Glass
1120 Monti and Sick Child
1125 Quill, Text and Bust of Bruno (Pietro Masulli)
1126 "Madonna of the Rose Garden"

(Des L. Vangelli. Photo)
2000 (23 Sept). *Stamp Day.* P 14 × 13½.
2635 **1119** 800l. multicoloured 55 50

(Des Anna Maresca. Photo)
2000 (30 Sept). *Death Centenary of Father Luigi Maria Monti.* P 14 × 13½.
2636 **1120** 800l. multicoloured 55 50

(Des Cristina Bruscaglia. Photo)
2000 (20 Oct). *400th Death Anniv of Giordano Bruno (writer and philosopher).* P 14 × 13½.
2641 **1125** 800l. multicoloured 55 50

(Des Rita Morena. Recess and litho)
2000 (25 Oct). *600th Birth Anniv of Luca della Robbia (artist).* P 14.
2642 **1126** 800l. multicoloured 55 50

1121 Salieri
1122 Disabled Athletes
1127 Arms of Academy
1128 Martino and Map of Europe

(Des Rita Morena. Photo)
2000 (30 Sept). *250th Birth Anniv of Antonio Salieri (composer).* P 13½ × 14.
2637 **1121** 4800l. multicoloured . . . . . 3·25 2·40

(Des Rita Fantini. Photo)
2000 (26 Oct). *250th Anniv of Roveretana degli Agiati Academy.* P 13½ × 14.
2643 **1127** 800l. multicoloured 55 50

(Des A. Rinnaudo. Photo)
2000 (2 Oct). *Paralympic Games, Sydney.* P 13½ × 14.
2638 **1122** 1500l. multicoloured . . . . . 1·10 1·30

(Des Cristina Bruscaglia. Photo)
2000 (3 Nov). *Birth Centenary of Gaetano Martino (politician).* P 14.
2644 **1128** 800l. multicoloured 55 50

1123 Emblem, Chaos Model and Globe in Container
1124 Couple and Globe
1129 "Perseus with the Head of Medusa" (bronze statue)

(Des Giustina Milite. Photo)
2000 (14 Oct). *World Mathematics Year.* P 14 × 13½.
2639 **1123** 800l. multicoloured 55 50

(Des Cristina Bruscaglia. Photo)
2000 (18 Oct). *Volunteers.* P 13½ × 14.
2640 **1124** 800l. multicoloured 55 50

(Des A. Ciaburro. Recess and litho)
2000 (3 Nov). *500th Birth Anniv of Benvenuto Cellini (goldsmith and sculptor).* P 14.
2645 **1129** 1200l. multicoloured 85 95

125

ITALY 2000

1130 Young Woman
1131 Camerino University 

(Des A. Ciaburro. Litho)

2001 (27 Jan). *Composers' Anniversaries*. Sheet 87 × 180 mm containing T **1135** and similar vert designs. Multicoloured. P $13\frac{1}{2}$ × 14.
MS2653 800l. Type **1135**; 800l. Domenico Cimarosa (death bicentenary); 800l. Gasparo Luigi Pacifico Spontini (150th death anniv); 800l. Giuseppe Verdi (death centenary) ... 2·40   4·00

(Des Tiziana Trinca. Litho)

2000 (4 Nov). *New Millennium (5th series). Meditation and Expression*. Sheet 110 × 80 mm containing T **1130** and similar horiz design. Multicoloured. P 14 × $13\frac{1}{2}$.
MS2646 800l. Type **1130**; 800l. Dancing figures ... 2·30   1·20

1136 St. Rose and Angels (Francesco Podesti of Ancona)
1137 Racing Car 

(Des A. Ciaburro. Recess)

2000 (6 Nov). *Universities*. T **1131** and similar horiz design. Each indigo. P 14 × $13\frac{1}{2}$.
2647 800l. Type **1131** ... 55   50
2648 1000l. Calabria University ... 70   65

2001 (6 Mar). *750th Death Anniv of St. Rose of Viterbo*. Photo. P $13\frac{1}{2}$ × 14.
2654 **1136** 800l. multicoloured ... 55   50

(Des Tiziana Trinca. Litho)

2001 (9 Mar). *Ferrari, Formula One Constructor's Championship Winner (2000)*. Sheet 110 × 81 mm. P 14 × $13\frac{1}{2}$.
MS2655 1137 5000l. multicoloured ... 3·50   6·50

1132 Snowflakes and Globe
1133 Snowboarding

1138 Abbey of Santa Maria in Sylvis, Sesto al Reghena
1139 Lombardy and Venetia 1850 5c. Stamp (151st anniv) 

(Des Maria Tuccelli (800l.), Maria Perrini (1000l.). Photo)

2000 (6 Nov). *Christmas*. T **1132** and similar multicoloured design. P $13\frac{1}{2}$ × 14 (800l.) or 14 × $13\frac{1}{2}$ (1000l.).
2649 800l. Type **1132** ... 55   50
2650 1000l. Crib, Matera Cathedral ... 70   80

(Des and eng A. Ciaburro. Recess)

2001 (10 Mar). P 14.
2656 **1138** 800l. Prussian blue ... 55   50

(Des Anna Maresca. Photo)

2001 (15 Jan). *World Snowboarding Championships, Madonna di Campiglio*. P $13\frac{1}{2}$ × 14.
2651 **1133** 1000l. multicoloured ... 70   50

2001 (31 Mar). *Stamp Anniversaries*. T **1139** and similar vert designs. Multicoloured. Photo. P $13\frac{1}{2}$ × 14.
2657 800l. Type **1139** ... 55   50
2658 800l. Sardinia 1851 5c. stamp (150th anniv) ... 55   50
2659 800l. Tuscany 1851 1q. stamp (150th anniv) ... 55   50

1134 "The Annunciation" (detail, Botticelli)
1135 Vincenzo Bellini (composer, birth bicentenary)

(Des Batestitalia. Typo)

2001 (10 Apr). *Priority Mail Stamp*. As T **1065** but central "P" larger, 12 × 12 mm. Self-adhesive. Die-cut perf 11.
2660 1200l. black, greenish yellow and gold ... 85   50
No. 2660 was issued in sheets and booklets of four stamps with attached label inscribed "POSTA PRIORITARIA Priority Mail".

(Des Cristina Bruscaglia. Photo)

2001 (18 Jan). *"Italy in Japan 2001" (cultural and scientific event)*. P 14.
2652 **1134** 1000l. multicoloured ... 70   50

126

ITALY 2001

1140 Bridge, Comacchio **1141** Campanula

(Des Guistina Milite. Photo)

2001 (14 Apr). *Tourist Publicity (28th series).* T **1140** *and similar horiz designs. Multicoloured.* P 14 × 13½.
2661	800l. Type **1140**	55	50
2662	800l. Diamante	55	50
2663	800l. Pioraco	55	50
2664	800l. Stintino	55	50
2661/2664	Set of 4	2·00	1·80

(Des Anna Maresca (Nos. 2665, 2668), Cristina Bruscaglia (Nos. 2666/7). Photo)

2001 (21 Apr). *World Day to Combat Desertification and Drought.* T **1141** *and similar vert designs. Multicoloured.* P 13½ × 14.
2665	450l. Type **1141**	30	15
2666	650l. Marmosets	45	50
2667	800l. European storks	50	50
2668	1000l. Desert and emblem	65	65
2665/2668	Set of 4	1·70	1·60

1142 Map of Italy and Tractors **1143** Castle and Emblem

(Des Rita Fantini. Photo)

2001 (24 Apr). *Confederation General of Italian Agriculture.* P 13½ × 14.
| 2669 | **1142** | 800l. multicoloured | 55 | 50 |

(Des Tiziana Trinca. Photo)

2001 (28 Apr). *Millenary of Gorzia City.* P 14 × 13½.
| 2670 | **1143** | 800l. multicoloured | 55 | 50 |

1144 Water pouring from Vase **1145** Profiles

(Des Anna Maresca. Photo)

2001 (4 May). *Europa. Water Resources.* P 14 × 13½.
| 2671 | **1144** | 800l. multicoloured | 65 | 50 |

(Des Tiziana Tinca. Photo)

2001 (9 May). *European Union.* P 14 × 13½.
| 2672 | **1145** | 800l. multicoloured | 55 | 50 |

1146 Medals **1147** Rose and Workers' Silhouettes

(Des Cristina Bruscaglia. Photo)

2001 (9 May). *Centenary of Order of Merit for Labour.* P 13½ × 14.
| 2673 | **1146** | 800l. multicoloured | 55 | 50 |

(Des P. Longo. Photo)

2001 (19 May). *National Day for Victims of Industrial Accidents.* P 13½ × 14.
| 2674 | **1147** | 800l. multicoloured | 55 | 50 |

1148 Child with Stamp and Magnifying Glass (Rita Vergari) **1149** "St. Peter healing with his Shadow"

2001 (26 May). *Day for Art and Student Creativity.* T **1148** *and similar multicoloured designs. Photo.* P 13½ × 14 (No. 2675) or 14 × 13½ (others).
2675	800l. Type **1148**	55	50
2676	800l. People standing on rainbow (Lucia Catena)	55	50
2677	800l. Painting with eye (Luigi di Cristo)	55	50
2678	800l. Colours and profile (Barbara Grilli)	55	50
2675/2678	Set of 4	2·00	1·80

2001 (1 June). *600th Birth Anniv of Tommaso de Giovanni di Simone Guidi "Masaccio" (painter). Photo.* P 13½ × 14.
| 2679 | **1149** | 800l. multicoloured | 55 | 50 |

1150 "Madonna and Child" (Piero della Francesca) **1151** Emblem

ITALY 2001

(Des Rita Morena. Recess and litho)

2001 (9 June). *500th Death Anniv of Giovanni della Rovere.* P 14.
2680　**1150**　800l. multicoloured . . . . . . 55　50

(Des E. Camplani and G. Pescolderung. Photo)

2001 (12 June). *50th Anniv of Panathlon International (sports organization).* P 13½ × 14.
2681　**1151**　800l. multicoloured . . . . . . 55　50

1152 Guaita Tower, Mt. Titano

1153 Footballer and Net

(Des Anna Maresca. Photo)

2001 (23 June). *1700th Anniv of San Marino.* P 13½ × 14.
2682　**1152**　800l. multicoloured . . . . . . 55　50

(Des L. Vangelli. Photo)

2001 (23 June). *A S Roma, National Football Champion, 2000–01.* P 13½ × 14.
2683　**1153**　800l. multicoloured . . . . . . 55　50

1154 Motorboat and Helicopter

1155 Quasimodo

(Des Tiziana Trinca. Photo)

2001 (20 July). *Harbour Master's Office.* P 14 × 13½.
2684　**1154**　800l. multicoloured . . . . . . 55　50

(Des Anna Maresca. Photo)

2001 (20 Aug). *Birth Centenary of Salvatore Quasimodo (writer).* P 13½ × 14.
2685　**1155**　1500l. multicoloured . . . . . . 1·10　1·30

1156 Octagonal Hall, Domus Aurea, Rome

(Des and eng Rita Morena. Recess)

2001 (31 Aug). P 14.
2686　**1156**　1000l. red-brown . . . . . . 70　50

1157 Bookcase (Piero Lissoni and Patricia Urquiola) and Chair (Anna Bartolli)

(Des R. Castiglioni and Adriana Rigamonti. Litho)

2001 (1 Sept). *Italian Design.* Sheet 155 × 137 mm containing T **1157** and similar horiz designs. Multicoloured. P 13½.
MS2687　800l. Type **1157**; 800l. Chair (Monica Graffeo) and table lamp (Rodolfo Dordoni); 800l. Lamp (Ferruccio Laviani) and sofa (Massimo Iosa Ghini); 800l. Armchair (Anna Gili) and side table (Miki Astori); 800l. Vertical storage unit (Marco Ferreri) and double seat (M. Cananzi and R. Semprini); 800l. Stool (Stefano Giovannoni) and flexible-necked lamp (Massimiliano Datti) . . . . . . 3·00　3·00

1158 "The Fourth State" (detail, Guiseppe Pellizza da Volpedo)

(Des and eng Rita Moreno. Recess)

2001 (15 Sept). P 14 × 13½.
2688　**1158**　1000l. lake-brown . . . . . . 70　50

1159 Stone Age Man and Pick

1160 Schoolchildren

(Des G. Gut. Photo)

2001 (19 Sept). *Archaeological Museum, Alto Adige.* P 13½ × 14.
2689　**1159**　800l. multicoloured . . . . . . 55　50

(Des Maria Perrini. Photo)

2001 (22 Sept). *Youth Philately.* P 14 × 13½.
2690　**1160**　800l. multicoloured . . . . . . 55　50

ITALY 2001

1161 Fermi
1162 Pavia University

(Des Cristina Bruscaglia. Photo)

2001 (29 Sept). *Birth Centenary of Enrico Fermi (physicist)*. P 13½ × 14.
| 2691 | **1161** | 800l. multicoloured | 55 | 50 |

(Des L. Vangelli (2694), A. Ciaburro (others). Recess)

2001 (29 Sept). *Universities*. T **1162** *and similar designs*. P 13½ × 14 (2693) or 14 × 13½ (others).
2692		800l. indigo	55	50
2693		800l. lake-brown (*vert*)	55	50
2694		800l. deep turquoise-blue	55	50

Designs:—No. 2693, Bari University; 2694, School of Science, Rome.

1163 Latinas and Messanger
1164 Exhibits

(Des J. Vertiz Hoyos. Photo)

2001 (12 Oct). *Unione Latina (Romance language speaking countries)*. P 14 × 13½.
| 2695 | **1163** | 800l. black, yellow and deep ultramarine | 55 | 50 |

(Des Maria Perrini. Photo)

2001 (12 Oct). *National Archaeological Museum, Taranto*. P 14 × 13½.
| 2696 | **1164** | 1000l. multicoloured | 70 | 50 |

1165 International Fund for Agricultural Development Emblem
1166 "Enthroned Christ with Angels" (painting on wood)

2001 (16 Oct). *World Food Day*. T **1165** *and similar multicoloured designs, each stamp featuring "The Seed" (sculpture) by Roberto Joppolo. Photo*. P 14 × 13½.
2697		800l. Type **1165**	50	25
		a. Horiz strip of 3. Nos. 2697/9	1·50	
2698		800l. Plants and woman hoeing (50th anniv of Food and Agriculture Organization Summit Conference, Rome) (50 × 29)	50	25
2699		800l. World Food Programme emblem	50	25

Nos. 2698/9 were issued together in *se-tenant* strips of three stamps.

(Des and eng Rita Morena. Recess and litho)

2001 (19 Oct). P 14.
| 2700 | **1166** | 800l. multicoloured | 50 | 25 |

1167 "Madonna and Child" (painting from triptych)
1168 "Dawn of Peace" (collage, San Vito dei Normani Primary School)

(Des and eng A. Ciaburro. Recess and litho)

2001 (20 Oct). *500th Anniv of "Madonna and Child, Angels, St. Francis, St. Thomas Aquinas and two Donors" (triptych, Macrino d'Alba)*. P 14.
| 2701 | **1167** | 800l. multicoloured | 50 | 25 |

2001 (30 Oct). *Christmas*. T **1168** *and similar horiz design. Multicoloured. Photo*. P 14 × 13½.
| 2702 | | 800l. Type **1168** | 50 | 25 |
| 2703 | | 1000l. "Nativity" (painting, St. Mary Major Basilica) | 65 | 30 |

1169 Fabric

(Des Marchi. Litho)

2001 (29 Nov). *Italian Silk Industry. Sheet 140 × 92 mm. Self-adhesive gum. Imperf*.
MS2704 **1169** 5000l. multicoloured . . . . . . 3·25 3·25

No. **MS**2704 was printed on fabric mounted on silk jacquard. A peel-off plastic backing featured instructions for use. If required, the address could be written in the blank area at the bottom right of the sheet.

129

ITALY 2001

(Des A. Ciaburro (1c.), Christina Bruscaglia (2c. and 3c.), G. Toffoletti (5c.), L. Vangelli (10c. and 20c.), Maria Tucelli (23c.), F. Tulli (41c.) and Rita Morena (50c. and 77c.). Photo (Nos. 2705/11) and recess (Nos. 2715/17))

2002. *Women in Art. Designs as T* **1032** *but with values expressed in euros.* P $14 \times 13\frac{1}{2}$.

(a) No Watermark.

2705	1c. multicoloured (1.3.02)	10	10
2706	2c. multicoloured (2.2.02)	10	10
2707	3c. multicoloured (1.3.02)	10	10
2708	5c. multicoloured (2.2.02)	10	10
2709	10c. multicoloured (2.2.02)	15	10
2710	20c. multicoloured (1.3.02)	30	15
2711	23c. multicoloured (2.2.02)	30	15

(b) W **307**.

2715	41c. lake-brown, greenish slate and black (2.2.02)	60	30
2716	50c. deep turquoise, Indian red and black (2.2.02)	70	35
2717	77c. orange-brown, deep olive and black (2.2.02)	1·10	55

Designs: 1c. "Ebe" (painting detail, Antonia Canova); 2c. Profile (5th-century B.C. coin, Syracuse); 3c. Woman's head (detail from murel, Pierro della Francesca); 5c. As No. 2505; 10c. Head (3rd-century B.C. sculpture, "G. Fiorello" civic museum, Lucera); 20c. Portrait of a lady (Correggio); 23c. As No. 2506; 41c. As No. 2508; 50c. "Portrait of a young girl" (detail, painting, Francesco Mazzola); 77c. "Spring" (detail, painting, Botticelli).

Numbers have been left for additions to this series.

1170 "Ducato" (Venetian coin), 1285

1171 Woman's Head and State Arms

(Des R. di Luzzo (No. 2727) Photo)

2002 (2 Jan). *European Coins.* T **1170** *and similar horiz designs. Multicoloured. Fluorescent paper. Photo.* P $14 \times 13\frac{1}{2}$.

2725	41c. Type **1170**	60	30
	a. Horiz pair. Nos. 2725/6	1·20	60
2726	41c. "Genovino" (Genoa) and "Fiorino" (Florence), 1252	60	30
2727	41c. Flags of EU forming Euro symbol	60	30
	a. Horiz pair. Nos. 2727/8	1·20	60
2728	41c. 1946 lira coin transforming into euro coin	60	30
2725/2728	Set of 4	2·20	1·10

Nos. 2725/6 and 2727/8 respectively were issued in horizontal se-tenant pairs within the sheet.

(Des Batesitalia Typo)

2002 (2 Jan). *Priority Mail Stamps. Designs as No. 2660 but with face values in euros only. Multicoloured, background colour given. Self-adhesive gum. Die-cut perf 11.*

2729	62c. greenish yellow	90	45
2730	77c. pale turquoise	1·10	55
2731	€1 lavender	1·40	70
2732	€1.24 bright yellow green	1·80	90
2733	€1.86 bright rose	2·75	1·30
2734	€4.13 reddish lilac	6·00	3·00
2729/2734	Set of 6	12·50	6·25

Nos. 2729/34 were each issued with an attached label inscribed "postaprioritaria Priority Mail".

(Des L. Vangelli. Eng V. Puliti. Recess and litho)

2002 (2 Jan). *Fluorescent paper.* P $14 \times 13\frac{1}{2}$.

2735	**1171** €1 multicoloured	1·40	70
2736	€1.24 multicoloured (2.1.02)	1·40	70
2737	€1.55 multicoloured (2.1.02)	1·80	90
2738	€2.17 multicoloured (2.1.02)	2·20	1·10
2739	€2.58 multicoloured (2.1.02)	3·10	1·50

2740	€3.62 multicoloured (2.1.02)	3·75	1·80
2741	€6.20 multicoloured (1.3.02)	9·00	4·75

Numbers have been left for additions to this series.

1172 Escrivá

(Des Anna Maresca. Photo)

2002 (9 Jan). *Birth Centenary of Josemaría Escrivá de Balaguer (founder of Opus Dei (religious organization)).* P $14 \times 13\frac{1}{2}$.

2745	**1172**	41c. multicoloured	60	30

1173 Luigi Bocconi and University Building

1174 1852 5c. Stamp

(Des Cristina Bruscaglia. Photo)

2002 (24 Jan). *Centenary of Bocconi University.* P $14 \times 13\frac{1}{2}$.

2746	**1173**	41c. purple-brown and stone	60	30

The University was established with an endowment from Ferinando Bocconi in memory of his son Luigi.

2002 (26 Jan). *150th Anniv of First Stamp of Parma.* P $13\frac{1}{2} \times 14$.

2747	**1174**	41c. multicoloured	60	30

1175 Mountain Peak

1176 Emblem and Olympic Rings

(Des Cristina Bruscaglia. Photo)

2002 (1 Feb). *International Year of Mountains.* P $13\frac{1}{2} \times 14$.

2748	**1175**	41c. multicoloured	55	30

2002 (23 Feb). *Winter Olympic Games, Turin (2006). Photo.* P $13\frac{1}{2} \times 14$.

2749	**1176**	41c. multicoloured	60	30

ITALY 2002

1177 Queen Elena  **1178** Sculpture (Arnolfo di Cambio)

2002 (2 Mar). *50th Death Anniv of Queen Elena of Savoy. Photo.*
P 13½ × 14.
2750　**1177**　41c. + 21c. multicoloured　　90　45

(Des Rita Moreno. Recess)
2002 (8 Mar). *700th Death Anniv of Arnolfo di Cambio (sculptor).*
P 14.
2751　**1178**　41c. deep magenta　　60　30

1179 Venaria Reale

(Des Giustina Milite. Photo)
2002 (23 Mar). *Tourist Publicity (29th series). T* **1179** *and similar horiz designs. Multicoloured.* P 14 × 13½.
2752　41c. Type **1179**　　　60　30
2753　41c. Capo d'Orlando　　60　30
2754　41c. San Gimignano　　60　30
2755　41c. Sannicandro di Bari　60　30
2752/2755　Set of 4　　　　2·00　1·10

1180 Santa Maria delle Grazie Sanctuary

(Des A. Ciaburro. Recess)
2002 (3 Apr). P 14.
2756　**1180**　41c. red-brown　　60　30

1181 Police Officers, Computer Screen and Patrol Car

(Des Anna Maresca and Rita Fantini. Photo)
2002 (12 Apr). *150th Anniv of State Police Force.* P 14 × 13½.
2757　**1181**　41c. multicoloured　　60　30

1182 Ricci and World Map

(Des Giustina Milite. Photo)
2002 (20 Apr). *450th Birth Anniv of Matteo Rici (missionary).*
P 14 × 13½.
2758　**1182**　41c. multicoloured　　60　30

1183 Circus Performers

(Des Tiziana Trinca. Photo)
2002 (4 May). *Europa. Circus.* P 14 × 13½.
2759　**1183**　41c. multicoloured　　60　30

1184 Sailing Ship and Student  **1185** Vittorio de Sica (film director, birth centenary)

(Des Maria Perrini. Photo)
2002 (4 May). *Francesco Morosini Naval Military School, Venice.*
P 14 × 13½.
2760　**1184**　41c. multicoloured　　60　30

(Des Rita Morena. Recess and litho)
2002 (10 May). *Cinema Anniversaries. T* **1185** *and similar vert designs. Multicoloured.* P 13½ × 14.
2761　41c. Type **1185**　　　60　30
2762　41c. Text and clouds (birth centenary (1901) of Cesare Zavattini (screen writer))　　　　60　30

1186 Football Player and Emblem  **1187** Falcone and Boresellino

131

ITALY 2002

(Des L. Vangelli. Photo)
2002 (18 May). *Juventus, National Football Champion, 2001–02.* P 13½ × 14.
2763 **1186** 41c. multicoloured 60 30

(Des Tiziana Trinca. Photo)
2002 (23 May). *Tenth Death Anniv of Giovanni Falcone and Paolo Borsellino (judges).* P 14 × 13½.
2764 **1187** 62c. multicoloured 90 45

1188 Emblems and Member Flags
1189 Kayaking 

2002 (28 May). *Russia's Membership of North Atlantic Treaty Organization (N.A.T.O.).* Photo. P 14 × 13½.
2765 **1188** 41c. multicoloured 60 30

(Des A. Saliola. Photo)
2002 (30 May). *World Kayaking Championships, Valsesia.* P 13½ × 14.
2766 **1189** 52c. multicoloured 75 35

1190 Modena 1853 1 lira Arms of Este Stamp
1191 Arms 

2002 (1 June). *150th Anniv of Modena (Italian State) Stamps.* Photo. P 13½ × 14.
2767 **1190** 41c. multicoloured 60 30

2002 (1 June). *Italian Military Involvement in Peace Missions.* Photo. P 13½ × 14.
2768 **1191** 41c. multicoloured 60 30

1192 Binda
1193 Padre Pio 

(Des Maria Perrini. Photo)
2002 (14 June). *Birth Centenary of Alfredo Binda (cyclist).* P 13½ × 14.
2769 **1192** 41c. multicoloured 60 30

(Des S. Rovai. Photo)
2002 (16 June). *Canonization of Padre Pio Santo.* P 14.
2770 **1193** 41c. multicoloured 60 30

1194 Divisione Acqui (monument, Mario Salazzari)
1195 Crucifixion (Arezzo Basilica) 

(Des Maria Perrini. Photo)
2002 (21 June). *"Divisione Acqui" (World War II resistance group on Cephalonia).* P 13½ × 14.
2771 **1194** 41c. multicoloured 60 30

(Des A. Ciaburro. Recess and photo)
2002 (22 June). P 14.
2772 **1195** €2.58 multicoloured . . . . . 3·75 1·90

1196 Building Faade
1197 Maria Goretti 

(Des G. Leluzzo. Photo)
2002 (24 June). *Bicentenary of Ministry of Interior.* P 14 × 13½.
2773 **1196** 41c. multicoloured 60 30

(Des Giustina Milite. Photo)
2002 (6 July). *Death Centenary of Saint Maria Goretti.* P 13½ × 14.
2774 **1197** 41c. multicoloured 60 30

1198 Mazarin
1199 National Colours encircling Globe 

(Des G. Ieluzzo. Photo)
2002 (13 July). *400th Birth Anniv of Cardinal Jules Mazarin (minister to Louis XIV of France).* P 14 × 13½.
2775 **1198** 41c. multicoloured 60 30

132

ITALY   2002

2002 (8 Aug). *"Italians in the World"*. Photo. P 13½ × 14.
2776 **1199** 52c. multicoloured 75   35

1200 Monument
(Vincenzo Gasperetti)

1201 Jacket (Krizia)

(Des Maria Perrini. Photo)

2002 (17 Aug). *Monument to the Victims of Massacre at Sant' Anna di Stazzema*. P 13½ × 14.
2777 **1200** 41c. multicoloured 60   30

2002 (30 Aug). *Italian Design*. Sheet 157 × 137 mm containing T **1201** and similar vert designs. Multicoloured. Litho. P 14.
MS2778 41c. Type **1201**; 41c. Brassiere (Dolce & Gabbana); 41c. Drawing of dress (Gianfranco Ferre); 41c. Drawing of suit (Giorgio Armani); 41c. Dress (Laura Biagiotti); 41c. Shoes (Prada) . . . . 8·75   8·75

1202 Cathedral and Tower, Pisa

2002 (30 Aug). *UNESCO World Heritage Sites*. T **1202** and similar horiz design. Multicoloured. Photo. P 14.
2779 41c. Type **1202** 60   30
2780 52c. Aeolian Islands 75   35
Nos. 2779/80 were each issued with a half stamp-sized label bearing the "Riccione 2002" stamp exhibition emblem.
Stamps of a similar design were issued by the United Nations.

1203 Dalla Chiesa

1204 Teatro della Concordia, Monte Castello di Vibio, Perugia

(Des Tiziana Trinca. Photo)

2002 (3 Sept). *20th Anniv of Assassination of Carlo Alberto Dalla Chiesa (police chief and prefect of Palermo)*. P 13½ × 14.
2781 **1203** 41c. multicoloured 60   30

(Des and eng Rita Morena. Recess and litho)
2002 (7 Sept). P 14.
2782 **1204** 41c. multicoloured 60   30

1205 Yacht

1206 Papal States 1852 5b. Stamp

(Des A. Novaro. Photo)

2002 (11 Sept). *12th Prada Classic Yacht Challenge, Imperia*. P 14 × 13½.
2783 **1205** 41c. multicoloured 60   30

2002 (4 Oct). *150th Anniv of First Papal States Stamp*. P 13½ × 14.
2784 **1206** 41c. multicoloured 60   30

1207 Cross, City Museum, Santa Giulia, Brescia

1208 Orchid

(Des G. Ieluzzo (2785), Cristina Bruscaglia (2786). Photo)

2002 (4 Oct). *Museum Exhibitss*. T **1207** and similar multicoloured design. P 13½ × 14 (2785) or 14 × 13½ (horiz).
2785 41c. Type **1207** 60   30
2786 41c. Busts, Museo Nazionale, Palazzo Altemps, Rome (*horiz*) 60   30

(Des Cristina Bruscaglia (52c.), Anna Maria Maresca (others). Photo)

2002 (11 Oct). *Flora and Fauna*. T **1208** and similar vert designs. Multicoloured. P 13½ × 14.
2787 23c. Type **1208** 30   15
2788 52c. European lynx 75   35
2789 77c. Stag beetle . . . . 1·10 55

1209 Emblem

1210 Corps Member and Emblem

(Des S. Fermariello. Photo)

2002 (16 Oct). *World Food Day*. P 13½ × 14.
2790 **1209** 41c. multicoloured 60   30

133

ITALY 2002

(Des G. Ieluzzo. Photo)
2002 (22 Oct). *State Forestry Corps.* P 13½ × 14.
2791 **1210** 41c. multicoloured ... 60 30

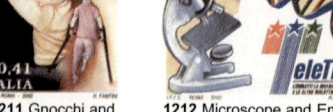

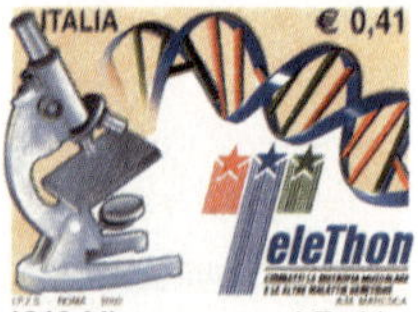

1211 Gnocchi and Children
1212 Microscope and Emblem

(Des Rita Fantini. Photo)
2002 (25 Oct). *Birth Centenary of Carlo Gnocchi (founder of rehabilitation centres for disabled children).* P 13½ × 14.
2792 **1211** 41c. multicoloured ... 60 30

(Des Anna Maresca. Photo)
2002 (31 Oct). *"Telethon 2002" (campaign to combat muscular dystrophy and genetic disease).* P 14 × 13½.
2793 **1212** 41c. multicoloured ... 60 30

1213 The Holy Family
1214 "Nike di Samotracia" (statue) and Athlete 

(Des A. Saliola (41c.) and Rita Fantini (62c.). Photo)
2002 (31 Oct). *Christmas.* T **1213** and similar multicoloured design. Ordinary paper. P 14 × 13½ (41c.) or 13½ × 14 (62c.).
2794 41c. Type **1213** ... 60 30
2795 62c. Child and Christmas tree ... 90 45

(Des A. Saliola. Photo)
2002 (20 Nov). *Women in Sport.* P 13½ × 14.
2796 **1214** 41c. multicoloured ... 60 30

1215 Flags of Championship Winners and Football
1216 Magnifying Glass, Stamps and Children 

(Des Andrea Acker. Litho)
2002 (29 Nov). *20th-century World Cup Football Champions.* T **1215** and similar multicoloured design. P 13½ × 14.
2797 52c. Type **1215** ... 75 35
    a. Horiz pair. Nos. 3109/10 ... 1·50 75
2798 52c. Italian footballer ... 75 35

Nos. 2797/8 were issued together in horizontal *se-tenant* pairs within the sheet. No. 2797 is perforated in a circle contained within an outer perforated square.

(Des Silvia Isola. Photo)
2002 (29 Nov). *Stamp Day. Philately in Schools.* P 14 × 13½.
2799 **1216** 62c. multicoloured ... 90 45

1217 Vittorio Orlando
1218 Event Emblem 

2002 (4 Dec). *50th Death Anniv of Vittorio Emanuele Orlando (politician).* Photo. P 13½ × 14.
2800 **1217** 41c. multicoloured ... 60 30

(Des D. Biasizzo. Photo)
2003 (16 Jan). *"Tarvisio 2003" (winter sports competition).* P 13½ × 14.
2801 **1218** 52c. multicoloured ... 75 35

1219 Family and Scales
1220 Cyclist carrying Cycle 

2003 (16 Jan). *The Italian Republic on Stamps.* Photo. P 14.
2802 **1219** 62c. multicoloured ... 90 45
    a. Booklet pane. No. 2802 × 5 plus 5 labels ... 4·50

No. 2802 was issued in sheets and booklets of five stamps with attached label inscribed "POSTA PRIORITARIA Priority Mail".

(Des A. Saliola. Photo)
2003 (1 Feb). *World Cyclo-cross Championship, Monopoli.* P 13½ × 14.
2803 **1220** 41c. multicoloured ... 60 30

1221 Building and Tandem

(Des G. Ieluzzo. Photo)
2003 (1 Feb). *150th Anniv (2002) of Fratelli Alinari (photographic company).* P 14 × 13½.
2804 **1221** 77c. multicoloured ... 1·10 55

134

ITALY STAMP BOOKLETS 2003

1222 Jigsaw Puzzle

(Des Cristina Bruscaglia. Photo)
2003 (14 Feb). *European Year of the Disabled.* P 14 × 13½.
2805 **1222** 41c. multicoloured 60 30

1223 Skiers

(Des Nicoletta Sasudelli. Photo)
2003 (18 Feb). *World Nordic Skiing Championships, Val di Fiemme.* P 14 × 13½.
2806 **1223** 41c. multicoloured 60 30

1224 Couple, Flower and Emblem

(Des G. Ieluzzo. Photo)
2003 (25 Feb). *National Civil Service.* P 14 × 13½.
2807 **1224** 62c. multicoloured 90 45

SB6S	1970	(a) Cover inscr "POSTE ITALIANE"	£1400
		(b) Milan Fair issue. Cover inscr "Vend System"	£1200
		Coin of Syracuse (T **286**) 1 pane, No. 1208 × 4 (100l.) Serif or sans-serif cover inscriptions (Rome and Naples printings). Sold at Ischia	£140
SB7	24.6.89	*Centenary of Ministry of Posts* (T **781**) 1 pane, No. 2035 × 6 (3000l.). Sold at Postal Museum, Rome	18·00
SB8	22.9.92	*Stamp Day* (T **844**) 1 pane, No. 2177a (3750l.)	14·00
SB9	2.10.93	*The Taxis Family in Postal History* 1 pane, No. 2222ab (3750l.)	3·00
SB10	9.12.95	*Postal Emblem* (T **897**) 1 pane, No. 2343ab (6000l.)	4·00
SB11	9.12.95	*Postal Emblem* (T **897**) 1 pane, No. 2344ab (6800l.)	5·50
SB12	23.3.96	*"Italia 98"* 1 pane, No. 2354b (6000l.)	16·00
SB13	28.10.98	*Europa Day* (T **1045**) 1 pane, No. 2527a (4800l.)	4·00
SB14	14.6.99	*Priority Mail* (T **1065**) One pane, No. 2563 × 4 (with attached labels) (4800l.)	3·50
SB15	14.6.99	*Priority Mail* (T **1065**) One pane, No. 2563a (booklet included separate loose sheet of labels) (9600l.)	8·00
SB16	10.4.01	*Priority Mail* One pane, No. 2660 × 4 (with attached labels) (4800l.)	3·50

STAMP BOOKLETS

The following checklist covers, in simplified form, booklets issued by Italy. It is intended that it should be used in conjunction with the main listings and details of stamps and panes listed there are not repeated.

Booklets prepared for automatic machines have the suffix S.

Booklets containing two panes of No. 64 × 6 or one pane of No. 65 × 6 or two panes of No. 73 × 6 or all five panes were prepared in Genoa and submitted to the Post Office for approval. They were not issued and are very rare.

A booklet containing "castle" stamps, Nos. 1664/6, was not an official issue.

Prices are for complete booklets

Booklet No.	Date	Contents and Face Value	Price
SB1	4.06	*Victor Emmanuel III* (T **36**) 4 panes, No. 74 × 6. Green cover	
		(a) Cover price 3l.65	£7000
		(b) Cover price 3l.60	—
SB2	1911	*Victor Emmanuel III* (T **49**) 4 panes, No. 90 × 6, blue cover (3l.60)	£2750
SB3	1916	*Victor Emmanuel III* (T **49**) *surch* 4 panes, No. 100 × 6 (4l.80)	£1400
SB4S	1957	*Coin of Syracuse* (T **286**) 1 pane, No. 890 × 10 (100l.)	
		(a) Cover inscr "POSTE ITALIANE"	£1400
		(b) Milan Fair issue. Cover inscr "Vend System"	£1200
SB5S	1957	*Coin of Syracuse* (T **286**) 1 pane, No. 895 × 4 (100l.)	

135

ITALY   Design Index

INDEX TO STAMP DESIGNS

This index provides in a condensed form a key to designs and subjects of Italian stamps. In all sections, where the same design, or subject, appears more than once in a set only the first number is given.
In section A stamps are listed under the inscription. In sections B and C, scenes and buildings are listed under the town or geographical area in which they are situated. Portraits are listed under surnames only; those without surnames (e.g. rulers and some saints) are under forenames. Works of art and inventions are indexed under the artist's, or inventor's, name, where this appears on the stamp. Other issues appear under the main subject or part of the inscription. In the latter case words such as anniversary, conference, fair, museum, society etc are ignored, as are also initial definite and indefinite articles.

A. SUBSIDIARY GROUPS
B.L.P. (opt) B112, B129
Espresso E73, E113, E122, E129, E172, E178, E350, E368, E370, E647, E679, E718, E915, E961, E1220
Espresso Urgente E112
Expres. . E80, E118, E130, E173, E180, E369
Francobollo di Stato O21
Giornati Stampi N5
P.M. (opt) M583
Pacchi Postali P38
Pacchi sul Bolletino P96, P146, P217, P647, P679, P687, P868, P908, P1347
Posta Pneumatica PE36, PE165, PE191, PE372, PE679, PE694, PE961
Postali sulla Ricevuta. P96, P146, P217, P647, P679, P687, P868, P908, P1347
Racapito Autorizzato . . . CL227, CL267, CL647, CL648, CL687, CL734, CL916
Raccomandata per Espresso 378
Segna Tassa D6, D21, D47
Segnatasse D22, D40, D73, D395, D630, D679, D690, D924
Servizio di Stato (opt) O379, O450
Trasporto Pacchi in Concessione CP848, CP918, CP1849

B. AIR STAMPS
Augusto 516
Bellini 468
Belltower 694, 911, 1297
Birds 687, 952
Calcio . . . . see Football
Caterina, St. 702
Clasped hands 670, 930, 953
Crociera Aerea Transatlantica 303
Crociera Nord Atlantica 378
Dante 326
Esperimento Posta Aerea (opt) 102
Espresso E348, E370, E408, E442
Ferucci 287
Fiume 402
Football 418
Garibaldi 343
Idrovolante (opt) 391
Mazzini 925
Medaglie al Valore Militaire 435
Orazione 485
Pegasus 270
Primo Volo Diretto (opt) 391
Pro Opera Previo Milizia 457
Rischiare la Vita 366
Roma Mogadiscio 444
Victor Emmanuel III 197
Volare Necesse Est 367
Zeppelin 372, 435

C. POSTAGE STAMPS
A87 1970
Abbazia di Santa Maria 2656
Accademia dell Crusca 1782
Accademia di Belle Arti 758
Accademia Navale 311
Accademia Roveretana 2643
Accordo Ramoge 2363
Acireale 2425
Acitrezza 1917
Acqui Terme 1619
Acquisto 1451
Adenauer 1281
Aeronautica Militare 1349, 2520
Agenzia Ansa 2339
Agnone 2547
Agricoltura 849, 1345, 2444
Agrigento 1765, 2501
AIDS Difenditil 2017
Aircraft 783, 823, 827, 1053, 1145, 1192, 1349, 1382, 1715, 1748, 1792, 1951, 2303
Alatri 1462, 2315
Alberi 806
Alberti 1333
Alberto da Prezzate, St. 2337
Alfano 1460
Alfieri 731
Alghero 1806
Alghieri . . . . see Dante
Alitalia 1291, 1941
Allied Military Postage 583
Amalfi 679, 1875
Anchor 396
Anemone 1708
Angel 1329
Angelico 922, 2341
Animals 1177, 1881, 2137
Anniversario 2525
Anno del Rifugiato 1015
Anno Felliniano 2634
Anno Int. del Turismo 1196
Anno Int. della Donna 1440
Anno Int. della Gioventu 1892
Anno Int. delle Persone Handicappate 1707
Anno Mariano 877
Anno Mondiale della Pace 1951
Anno Santo 172, 384, 746, 1427, 1788
Annunzio 1011
Antiche Genti d'Italia 2258
Antonello 832
Antoniano 304
Antonio, St., of Padua 2323
Anziani e loro Problemi 1861
Anzio e Nettuno 2298
Aosta 1473
Apples 1156
Aquila, L' 1454, 1652
Aquino 1416
Ara Pacis 782
Arance 769
Arcevia 2165
Archimedes 1801

Arciconfraternita della misericordia 2264
Arcimboldi 1523
Ardeatine Caves 2260
Aretino 1519
Arezzo 752, 2772
Ariosto 1411
Arma dei Carabinieri 1113, 2521
Arms . . 38, 53, 62, 238, 798, 991, 1154, 2223, 2269, 2346
Arte Barocca 1871
Arte del Vetro 1830
Arte Etrusca 1857
Arte Normanna in Sicilia 1385
Arte Rinascimental 1862
Arte Tessile e della Moda 785
Artigianato Italiano 1476
Ascoli Piceno 1973
Asiago 1596
Assemblea Mondiale della Sanita 733
Assisi 916, 2571
Astronautico Internazionale 939
Athens, Greece 2377
Atlanta, U.S.A. 2377
Attic vase 2267
Augusteo the Great 238, 506, 624
Aurora di Pace 2702
Automobiles . . . . see Cars
Avigliano Umbro 2608
Avio 1657
Avogadro 936
Avvento Anno Duemila MS2590, MS2597, MS2613, MS2623, MS2632, MS2646
Avvocatura dello Stato 1470

Bach and Bellini 1888
Bagheria 1945
Balloon 2335
Balzan 1083
Banca d'Italia 2227
Baracca 1225
Bardonecchia 1807
Bari . . . 736, 753, 796, 821, 1666, 2021, 2389, 2438
"Bari '97" 2388
Barriviera 2207
Baseball 1362, 2510
Basilica San Paolo 2593
Basketball 1289, 1610, 2129, 2376
Bassano 718
Bassi 854
Bassini 1522
Bee 834
Beetle 2789
Belfiore 831
Belli 1107, 2122
Bellini 462, 808, 1888, MS2653
Bells 2547
Beltrame 2288
Belvedere Ostrense 2358
Benedetto, St. 1632
Benvenuta Europa 2182
Bernini 1390, 1700, 2535
Berrettini 2393

136

ITALY Design Index

Bersaglieri . . . 1401, 1930
Bezzecca, Battle of . . . 1164, 1928
Biathlon . . . 1783
Bibbia . . . 1988
Biella . . . 824
Binda . . . 2769
Birds . . . 675, 867, 1549, 1884, 2138, 2291
Bobsleighing . . . 1148
Boccaccio . . . 1468
Boccioni . . . 1481
Bocconi . . . 2746
Bodoni . . . 1115
Boito . . . 1224
Bolaffi . . . 2142
Bologna . . . 714, 1419, 1894, 1905, 2436, 2461, 2693
Bologna University . . . 2001
Bolzano . . . 2457, 2689
Bondone . . . 2603
Bontempelli . . . 1603
Bordone . . . 527
Bormio . . . 1877
Borromeo . . . 2014
Borromini . . . 1193, 1392
Bosco . . . 1986
Bossorilievo . . . 2585
Bottego . . . 1029
Botticelli . . . 1370, 2652
Boy in barrel . . . 1295
Boy scouts . . . *see* Scouts
Braies . . . 2166
Bramante . . . 1280
Brazil . . . 972
Brecht . . . 2474
Brescia . . . 715, 2607
Brunelleschi . . . 1518
Bruno . . . 2641
Brussels . . . 967
Bruxelles . . . *see* Brussels
Buozzi . . . 1839
Busoni . . . 1456
Butterflies . . . 1533, 2378
Byron . . . 994

Cabot's Voyage . . . 2445
Caesar . . . 623, 634, 640
Cagli . . . 2115
Cagliari . . . 2303, 2490
Calabria . . . 765, 2648
Calcio . . . *see* Football
Caltanisetta . . . 2612
Cambio . . . 2751
Camerino . . . 2647
Campagna . . . 2625
Campagna...la Fame . . . 1092
Campanella . . . 1227
Campania . . . 768
Campanula . . . 2665
Campigli . . . 2330
Campione d'Italia, G. . . . 1740
Campione d'Italia (town) . . . 1845
Campobasso . . . 2269
Canaletto . . . 1230
Canoeing . . . 1287, 2216, 2567, 2776
Canossa . . . 1515
Canova . . . 946, 1325
Cantiere . . . 762, 882
Capo d'Orlando . . . 2753
Capri . . . 860, 1918
Carabinieri . . . 1113, 2521
Caraglio . . . 1540
Caravaggio . . . 1032, 1368, 1438
Carducci . . . 954
Carlo Magno . . . 1756
Carloforte . . . 2212
Carpaccio . . . 1483
Carrà . . . 1731
Carriages . . . 2222
Carriera . . . 1393
Cars . . 743, 781, 833, 871, 1826, 1867, 1933, 2018
Caruso . . . 1384
Casalinga . . . 2238
Caserta . . . 809, 2328
Casorati . . . 1950
Cassa Previd . . . 152
Cassano d'Adda . . . 1944
Castel de Monte . . . 1514, 1651
Castellammare del Golfo . . . 2089
Castellammare di Stabia . . . 1878
Castellana . . . 1516
Castellated head . . . *see* Italia
Castelsardo . . . 1597
Castiglione della Pescaia . . . 1992
Catalani . . . 868
Catania . . . 1654, 1914, 2110, 2266
Catanzaro . . . 2024
Caterina, St., of Siena 698, 1074, 1636
Cats . . . 2199
Catullus . . . 740
Cavalcaselle . . . 2468
Cavour . . . 1089
Cefalu . . . 1442
Celestino V . . . 2364
Cellere . . . 2546
Cellini . . . 1279, 2645
Censimento Generale . . . 802
Censimento Industriale . . . 801
Ceramics . . . 1865
Chaplin . . . 2041
Cherubini . . . 1521
Chianciano Terme . . . 1846
Chiara, St., of Assisi . . . 847
Chiesa . . . 2781
Child . . . 1295
Chirico . . . 1987
Christ . . . 2246
Christo . . . 2700
Church and musicians . . . 1626
Ciaburro . . . 2509, 2541
Cibi Italiani . . . 2239, 2289
Cicerone . . . 956
Cicogna . . . 2667
Cilea . . . 1458
Cimarosa . . . 741
Cinema 2006, 2332, 2382, 2453, 2528, 2761
Cinematografica . . . 1076
Cinque Giornate di Milano . . . 2296
Circus . . . 2236
Cisterna di Latina . . . 2327
Civil service . . . 2807
Civilta Contadine . . . 1851
Club Alpino Italiano . . . 1094
Coach (motor) . . . 1332
Coach and horses . . . 931, 1033, 1250
Codice Avviamento Postale . . . 1188
Cogwheels . . . 1175, 1359
Coins 836, 865, 887, 907, 1008, 1083, 1105, 1202, 1243
Colombiano . . . *see* Columbus
"Colombo '92" . . . 2157
Columbus . . . 786, 2511
Comacchio . . . 2661
Comboni . . . 1705
Comuni e Poteri Locali . . . 1118
Concilio Ecumenico Vaticano . . . 1087
Cone Vedie Futuro . . . 2624
Consiglio D'Europa . . . 2559
Consiglio di Stato . . . 1729
Conti Correnti Postali . . . 1238
Coppi . . . 2562
Corchiano . . . 2230
Corelli . . . 835
Corpi di Polizia . . . 1926
Corpo degli Alpini . . . 1316
Correggio . . . 2046
Corte Costituzione . . . 2554
Corte dei Conti . . . 1089
Corte Maltese . . . 2395
Cortina d'Ampezzo . . . 858, 926
Cosenza . . . 2109
Costituzione . . . 964, 1562, 2472
Cottolengo . . . 2206
Coubertin . . . 2270
Crediop . . . 2281
Cremona . . . 1564
Crib . . . 1320, 2015
Crivelli . . . 2628
Croce . . . 1153
Croce Rossa . . . *see* Red Cross
Crociera Italiana (opt) . . . 165
Cross . . . 2785
Cursus publicus . . . 1487
Curtatone . . . 712
Cycling . . . 795, 871, 1078, 1182, 1228, 1290, 1591, 1890, 2159, 2569, 2611, 2626, 2803

Damiani . . . 1324
Dams . . . 1720
Dante . . . 115, 314, 1140, 2100
De Sica . . . 2761
Dea Roma . . . 89
Deledda . . . 1294
Delitio . . . 1524
Deportazione Ebrei Romani . . . 2220
Design Italiano . . . **MS**2599, **MS**2687, **MS**2778
Diamante . . . 2662
Diano Marina . . . 2365
Diena . . . 2048
Diritto Aeronautico Privato . . . 823
Dish aerials . . . 1239
Dissesto idrogeologico . . . 1719
Divina Commedia . . . 1326
Diving . . . 2253
Divisione Acqui . . . 2771
Dogs . . . 2242
Dolci . . . 1495
Domenica del Corriere (paper) . . . 2288
Donatello . . . 944, 1165, 1948
Doniamo sangue . . . 1535
Donizetto . . . 719, 2484
Dritti dell'Infanzia . . . 2130
Droga Uccide . . . 1506
Duccio . . . 1378
Duse . . . 983

Earth . . . 939
Eccidio dei Fratelli Cervi . . . 2221
Eccidio di Marzabotto . . . 2261
Eccidio Fosse Ardeatine . . . 2260
Einaudi . . . 1387, 1479
Einstein . . . 1595
El-Alamein . . . 2522
Elba . . . 2486
Emancipazione Israelita . . . 2479
Emigrazione Italiana del Mondo . . 1448
Endoscopia . . . 2499
Eolie Islands . . . 2780
Epilessia si può Guarire . . . 1989
Ercolano . . . 1737, 2609
Erice . . . 1642
Escriva . . . 2745
Esperimento Trasporto...Elicottero 866
Etna, Mt. . . . 1513
Etruscan art . . . 1857
Eucharistic Congress . . . 1805, 2262
"Euroflora '91" . . . 2113
Europa . . . 937, 950, 973, 1012, 1030, 1066, 1081, 1101, 1116, 1138, 1166, 1175, 1221, 1244, 1257, 1283, 1314, 1360, 1390, 1438, 1476, 1513, 1550, 1605, 1634, 1711, 1756, 1800, 1840, 1887, 1921, 1961, 1990, 2025, 2097, 2124, 2156, 2207, 2256, 2312, 2361, 2422, 2480, 2543, 2615, 2671, 2759
"Europa 80" . . . 1633
Europa Unita . . . 2182
European Parliament 1607, 1832, 2030, 2265
Evangelario di Matilde . . . 1304
EVII . . . 1118
Ex Combattenti . . . 993

Fabiano . . . 1277
Fabriano . . . 2274
Fabric . . . **MS**2704
Fabrizi . . . 2382
Faenza . . . 2549
Fai della Paganella . . . 1763
Falcone . . . 2764
Family . . . 648
"Family Fest '93" . . . 2210
Fano . . . 1571
F.A.O. . . . 919, 2336, 2620

ITALY Design Index

Farfa . . . 2369
Fattori . . . 971
Fauna da Salvare . . . 1881
Fazzini . . . 2132
Federazione società filateliche . . . 1249
Federico II . . . 2275
Fellini . . . 2334
Feltre . . . 1557
Fermi . . . 1200, 2691
Fermo . . . 917, 1517
Ferrara . . . 1660, 2459
Ferrara University . . . 2146
Ferrais . . . 2410
Ferrari . . . 748, **MS**2524, **MS**2655
Ferrovie . . . 550
Ferrucci . . . 282
Festa degli Alberi . . . 806
Festa del Lavoro . . . 1796
Festa della montagna . . . 848
Festival dei Due Mondi . . . 1186
Fiat . . . 2564
Fiera di Roma . . . 2431
Fiera Milano . . . 2463
Filatelico Italiano (opt) . . . 122
Filiberto . . . 227
Filzi etc. . . . 1169
Fire engine . . . 2555
Firenze . . . *see* Florence
Fish . . . 1546, 2140
Fiume . . . 395
Flacco . . . 2205
Flags . . . 1478, 1607, 2182
Florence . . . 682, 739, 787, 1418, 1646, 1842, 1903, 1961, 2145, 2264, 2300, 2311, 2326, 2346, 2385
Flowers 1157, 1708, 1753, 1797, 1882
Flumendosa Mulargia . . . 961
Foggia . . . 2232
Foligno . . . 1972
Fondazione de Roma . . . 2418
Fontana . . . 2542
Fonte Avellana . . . 1648
Fonti Enegetiche Alternative . . . 1630
Football 1355, 1641, 1768, 1967, 1997, 1998, 2037, 2049, 2052, 2096, 2128, 2161, 2211, 2255, 2320, 2386, 2390, 2434, 2493, 2557, 2560, 2618, 2683, 2797
Forestry Corps . . . 2791
Forio . . . 1474
Forli . . . 2278
Formia . . . 2426
Forze Armate . . . 825, 2303
Forze dell ordine . . . 2498
Foscolo . . . 1602
Fracastoro . . . 915
Francavilla al Mare . . . 1813
Francesca . . . 2231, 2604, 2680
Francescano . . . 191
Francesco di Paola, St. . . . 960
Francis, St., of Assisi . . . 1486, 1745
Francobollo Coloniale . . . 2229
Francobollo Sportivo . . . 810
Frasassi . . . 1762
Fratelli Alinari . . . 2804
Fredi . . . 1501
Frescobaldi . . . 1810
Friuli . . . 777
Fucina . . . 760, 880
Fucino . . . 1239

Gaddi . . . 1502
"Galata Suicida" (statue) . . . 2268
Galilei . . . 575, 1109, 1800
Galli . . . 1538
Gallipoli . . . 1503
Galvani . . . 422, 2135
Garda, Lake . . . 1957
Gardone . . . 857
Gardone Riviera . . . 2348
Garibaldi . . . 81, 333, 957, 1017, 1265, 1760
Gasperi . . . 1706
Gasperi, Adenauer etc. . . . 1281
Gazzetta dello Sport . . . 2357
Gela . . . 2419
Gemito . . . 829
Genoa . . . 684, 1505, 1854, 2156
Genova . . . *see* Genoa
"Genova '92" . . . 2170
Gentile . . . 2285
Genzano di Luciana . . . 1572
George, St. . . . 944
Ghiberti . . . 1496
Ghirlandaio . . . 1497, 2602
Giambellino . . . 1394
Giardini Naxos . . . 2034
Ginnastici . . . 787
Giochi del Mediterraneo . . . 1103
Giochi della gioventù . . . 1289
Giochi Olimpici . . . *see* Olympic Games
Giordano . . . 1194
Giorgi . . . 2094
Giorgione . . . 1573
Giornata dei Martiri . . . 1929
Giornata del francobollo *see* Stamp Day
Giornata del Risparmio . . . 1144
Giornata della filatelia . . *see* Stamp Day
Giornata delle forze armate . . . 825
Giornata mondiale dell'Alimentazione . . . 1736
Giotto . . . 527, 1168, 1977
Giovani Incontrano l'Europa . . . 2119
Giovanni XXIII . . . *see* John XXIII
Giro d'Italia . . . 2159
Giuochi Universitari . . . 380
Giuramento di Pontida . . . 686, 1195
Glassblowing . . . 1831
Globe and posthorn . . . 2036
Globe and stamp . . . 1096
Gloria in Excelsis . . . 1329
Gnocchi . . . 2792
Goethe . . . 2568
Goito . . . 713
Goldoni . . . 1520, 2195
Golf . . . 1996
Golgi . . . 2256
Gonzaga . . . 1223
Goretti . . . 2773
Gorizia . . . 1529
Gorzia City . . . 2670
Governo Militaire Alleato (opt) . . . 592
Gradara . . . 1408
Gramsci . . . 1960, 2420
Grandi etc. . . . 1839
Grassi . . . 921
Greccio . . . 1421
Gronchi . . . 1479
Grottammare . . . 2031
Guardi . . . 2204
Guardia di Finanza . . . 1397, 2359
Gubbio . . . 1543, 1804
Guerra dell'Indipendenza . . . 1001
Guicciardini . . . 1785
Gullace . . . 2299
Gymnastics . . . 1290, 2376

Hammer . . . 647
Hayez . . . 1774
Head of statue . . . 944
Helicopter . . . 783, 1833
Hill . . . 1625
Homo aeserniensis . . . 1984
Horace . . . 477, 2205
Horse racing . . . 1843

ICAO . . . 823
Ice hockey . . . 1152
I.F.A.D. . . . 2697
Il Francobollo . . . 2576
Illuminated letter . . . 2306, 2347
Immagine Postale . . . 2358
Industria Italia . . . 2443
Informatica Giuridica . . . 1805
Informazione Fotografica . . . 1563
Informazione Giornalistica . . . 1860
Infortunistica Stradale . . . 1822
Insects . . . 834, 1533, 2378
International Year of Mountains . . 2748
Interparliamentary Union . . . 1322, 2038
Interpol . . . 872
Invito alla Filatelia . . . 2394
Ischia . . . 1474, 1659
Isernia . . . 1530
Isola Bella . . . 1443
Issogne . . . 1618, 1947
Istituto Idrografico . . . 1338
Istituto Internazionale di Agricoltura 918
Istituto Maestre Pie Filippini . . . 2155
Istituto Nazionale Assicurazioni . . . 1095
Istituto Poligrafico . . . 1588
Istituzione Avvocatura . . . 1470
Istruzione Professionale . . . 917
Italia . . . 241, 635, 643
"Italia 76" . . . 1471, 1487
"Italia 85" 1837, 1857, 1862, 1871, 1898
"Italia 90" . . . 1997, 2049, 2052, 2104
"Italia 98" . . 2354, **MS**2412, 2518, 2523, 2525, 2528, 2531, **MS**2532
Italian design . . . **MS**2778
Itria Valley . . . 1475

Jigsaw . . . 2805
John XXIII, Pope . . . 1741
Juventus Football Club . . . 2320, 2390, 2434, 2493, 2763

Key . . . 1221
Kites . . . 1534
Kossuth . . . 2252

La Civilta Cattolica . . . 2605
La Porta Santa . . . 2545
Lampedusa . . . 2368
Lanciano . . . 2126
Lauretane . . . 2272
Lavoro Italiano 1639, 1720, 1758, 1780, 1937, 1954, 2010, 2044
Lazio . . . 772
Lecce . . . 1856, 2552
Lega . . . 1500
Lega Navale . . . 2437
Leoncavallo . . . 969
Leone . . . 1479
Leopardi . . . 523, 2504
Levant Fair . . 736, 753, 796, 821, 2389
Liberté, égalité, fraternité . . . 2039
Liberty (statue) . . . 668
Ligabue . . . 2588
Lignano Sabbiadoro . . . 1993
Liguna . . . 767, 883
Liguori . . . 1969
Lions International . . . 1198, 2178
Lipari . . . 2553
Lippi . . . 955, 1276
Littorali . . . 450
Livigno . . . 2488
Livio . . . *see* Livy
Livorno . . . 1726
Livy . . . 559
Locomotives . . . *see* Railways
Loi . . . 2411
Lombardia . . . 763, 882
Longobardi . . . 2102
Lorca . . . 2475
Lorenzini . . . 874
Lorenzo il Magnifico . . . 735
Lorry . . . 1827
Lotta contro il fumo . . . 1747
Lotta contro l'alcolismo . . . 1968
Lotta contro l'infarto . . . 2198
Lourdes . . . 962
Lucca . . . 680
Lucca Archives . . . 2347
Lucera . . . 1683
Lusitano . . . 2324
Lynx . . . 2788

Macchine Utensili . . . 1613
Machiavelli . . . 1246
Maciste . . . 2383
Maddalena, La . . . 2116
Maderno . . . 1600
Madonna and child . . . 2701
Madre Teresa . . . 2513
Mafalda, Princess, of Savoy . . . 2297
Maggio, 1 . . . 2095
Malaparte . . . 2476

ITALY Design Index

Malaria . . . 1084
Malattie Digestive . . . 1612
Malpighi . . . 1560
Mameli Goffredo . . . 2575
Mameli Morente . . . 717
Mancini . . . 830
Manfredi . . . 2233
Mantana . . . 2460
Mantegna . . . 1395
Mantova . . . *see* Mantua
Mantua Archives . . . 2308
Manzoni . . . 155, 1357
Maps . . . 961, 1053, 1147, 1263, 1381, 1991, 2050, 2096, 2172, 2232, 2360
Maratea . . . 1893, 2167
Marche . . . 775
Marchi . . . 1983
Marconi . . . 1388, 2321
Marconi and Meucci . . . 1132
Marengo . . . 2633
Marina Militare . . . 2519
Marinetti . . . 1482, 2345
Marino . . . 2487
Marmotta . . . 2666
Marostica . . . 1711
Martinelli and Pertile . . . 1887
Martini . . . 2040
Martino . . . 2644
Marzabotto . . . 2261
Marzotto and Rossi . . . 754
Masaccio . . . 1569, 2679
Mascagni . . . 1106
Masettie . . . 2595
Massaia . . . 828
Matematica . . . 2639
Matera . . . 1722
Matteotti . . . 920
Mazaria . . . 2775
Mazzei . . . 1695
Mazzini . . . 126, 730, 925, 1308
Medaglie al Valore Militaire . . . 424
Medal . . . 1383, 2150, 2300, 2673
Medici . . . 2150
Medici nell'Europa . . . 1646
Mediterranean Fair . . . 237
Mediterranean Games . . . 2388
Melfi . . . 1684
Menotti . . . 1714
Mentana, Battle of . . . 1979
Merano . . . 1919, 2092
Mercadente . . . 1278
Mercato Comune Europeo . . . 2179
Merloni . . . 2467
Messina, A. da . . . 1593
Messina (town) . . . 2251, 2373
Meucci . . . 1561
Meucci and Marconi . . . 1132
Micca . . . 1508
Michelangelo . . 1034, 1111, 1391, 1432
Michetti . . . 797
Milan . . . 709, 1455, 1650, 1906, 2019, 2354, 2523, 2560
Milan Fair . . . 473, 720, 742, 783, 811, 1311
Milan Football Club . . 2161, 2211, 2255, 2386
Milan Triennale . . . 793
Miliani . . . 2273
Ministry of Interior . . . 2773
Minzoni . . . 1365
Mirandula . . . 1090
Missionari Salesiani . . . 1509
Modena . . . 1667*a*, 1901, 2556
Modena e Palma . . . 815
Modificazione del Concordato . . . 1897
Modigliani . . . 1825
Mondolfo . . . 2342
Moneta . . . 1802, 2725
Monreale . . . 1980
Montale . . . 2392
Monte Amiata . . . 1889
Monte Bianco . . . 1136
Monte Lungo, Battle of . . . 2303
Monte Rocciamelone . . . 2565
Monte Sant'Angelo . . . 2367
Montecassino . . . 260, 790, 2259
Montecatini Terme . . . 1444
Montefeltro . . . 1767
Montepulciano . . . 2090
Montessori . . . 1262
Monteverdi . . . 1181
Monti . . . 2636
Monti Castello . . . 2782
Monticchio . . . 2249
Monza . . . 2619
Morandi . . . 2105
Morosini . . . 2433
Mosaic . . . 2101, 2197
Mostra d'Oltremare . . . 817
Mozart . . . 2136
Muratori . . . 751
Museo Storico Delle Postee . . . 2617
Musicians and church . . . 1626

Naples . . 817, 1375, 1435, 1550, 1739, 1899, 1967, 1981
Naples Summit . . . 2271
Naples University . . . 2147
Napoli . . . *see* Naples
Narni . . . 1259
Natale . . . 2581, 2649, 2703, 2794
National Museum of Rome . . . 2786
Nativity 1539, 1701, 2230, 2340, 2465, 2582, 2600, 2650
NATO . . . 989, 2675
Natta . . . 2257
Natura e Vita . . . 1921
Naval Military school . . . 2760
Nazioni Unite . . . *see* United Nations
Negrone . . . 2361
Nenni . . . 2143
Nervi . . . 2133
Nicola etc. . . . 1479
Nievo . . . 1057
Nikolajewka, Battle of . . . 2194
Nittis . . . 1824
Noto . . . 1994
Nudes . . . 2595
Numeral . . . 8
Nunziatella . . . 2316
Nuoro . . . 2316, 2621
Nutrizione . . . 2180
Nuvolari . . . 2164

Officina . . . 761, 881
Oftalmologia . . . 1925, 2329
Olive . . . 771
Olives . . . 2290
"Olymphilex '87" . . . 1971
Olympic Games 926, 996, 1020, 2374, 2630, 2638, 2749
Olympic rings . . . 810, 2270
Onesti . . . 2203
ONU . . . *see* United Nations
Orazio . . . *see* Horace
Orazione . . . *see* Horace
Orchid . . . 2787
Ordine Forense . . . 1417
Ordini al Merito del Lavoro . . . 834
Organizzazione Int del Lavoro . . . 1006, 1247
Orione . . . 1336
Orlando . . . 2800
Orta San Giulio . . . 2250
Orvieto . . . 1598, 2432
Otranto . . . 2486
Ovidio . . . 943

Pace e Libertà . . . 2312
Pacelli . . . 1787
Pacinotti . . . 420, 1072
Pacioli . . . 2247
Padova . . . *see* Padua
Padua . . . 707, 2020, 2417, 2492
Padua Fair . . . 819
Padula . . . 1847
Paestum . . . 1545
Paganini . . . 1746
Paisiello . . . 2099
Palermo . . 706, 1377, 1900, 1974, 2439
Palestrina . . . 1447
Palladio . . . 734, 1358
Palma . . . 1699
Palmanova . . . 2213
Palmi . . . 1531, 1964, 2449
Panathlon . . . 2681
Pantelleria . . . 2168
Paola . . . 2430
Paolo VI, Pope . . . 2462
Parachutists . . . 2304
Paraco Nazionale . . . 2435, 2543
Parigi . . . *see* Paris
Parini . . . 2572
Paris . . . 1096
Parlamento Europeo 1607, 1832, 2561
Parma . . . 1898
Pascoli . . . 924, 1070,
Pastrengo . . . 2491
Patti Laternensi . . . 861, 988
Patto Atlantico . . . 851
Patto di Roma . . . 1839
Pavia . . . 2692
Peace Mission . . . 2768
Pegli . . . 2325
Pellegrinaggio degli Ex Combattenti . . . 1121
Pellegrino . . . 2108
Pellico . . . 879
Pen and ink set . . . 2348
Pergola . . . 2497
Pergola bronze . . . 1999
Pergolesi . . . 524, 1916
Perosi . . . 1334
Pertile and Martinelli . . . 1887
Pertini . . . 2391
Perugia . . . 1420
Perugia University . . . 2397
Perugino . . . 792
Pesaro . . . 1686, 1812
Petrarch . . . 1405
Petrolio . . . 908
Philately . . . 2799
Piano Marshall . . . 2464
Piave . . . 1199
Piazza Armerina . . . 2197
Piazzetta . . . 1498, 1775
Picciani . . . 2614
Pienza . . . 2366
Pigafetta . . . 1634
Pimentel . . . 2566
Pio IX, Pope . . . 1559
Pio XII, Pope . . . 1787
Piombo . . . 2235
Pioraco . . . 2663
Pirandello . . . 1185
Piranesi . . . 1371
Pisa . . . 683, 1369, 1761, 2587, 2779
Pisa University . . . 2029
Pistoia . . . 2002
Plants . . . 650, 1242, 2140
Plebiscito Meridionale . . . 83
Plinio il Giovane . . . 1056
Pliny . . . 1056
Poggio a Caiano . . . 1946
Pole vaulting . . . 1404
Polignano a Mare . . . 2340
Polizia . . . 1926, 2471
Pollaiolo . . . 2473
Polo . . . 869, 2353
Pompeii . . . 2033
Ponchielli . . . 1915
Ponte . . . 2169, 2622
Pontida, Oath of . . . 686, 1195
Pontida Basilica . . . 2337
Portofino . . . 1407
Positano . . . 2427
Post codes . . . 1188
Post emblem . . . 2283, 2343
Post riders . . . 1069, 1170, 2225
Posta Napoletana . . . 975, 1633
Posta Prioritaria . . . 2563, 2591, 2660, 2729
Postale Internazionale . . . 1096
Posthorn . . . 2035
Potenza . . . 1875
Prampolini . . . 995
Prato . . . 1668
Premio Italia . . . 984

ITALY

Design Index

Prevenzione del Crimine 1891
Pro Alluvionati 2286
Pro Hanseniani 1590
Pro Opera Previd Milizia 453
Progetto San Marco........... 1441
Propaganda Fide............... 129
Provveditorato Generale 1359
Prudenza sulla Strada.......... 949
Puccini................. 968, 1410
Puglia.................. 770, 884
Pula 1895

Quasimodo 2685
Quattro Giornate di Napoli 2219
Queen Elena 2750
Quercia 1425

Radio 688
Radiodiffusione 749
Raffaello .... see Raphael
Ragazzi Del '99 2580
Railways 550, 931, 1275, 1450, 1990, 2042
Rainbow and map 851
Rapallo...................... 856
Raphael............ 1253, 1396, 1816
Rapporto Spaak............... 2372
Ratificato Accordo............ 1897
Ravello................. 1643, 1738
Ravenna 2101, 2428
Reatino...................... 1412
Red Cross 96, 1097, 1637
Reggio Calabria.............. 2458
Regina Margherita Observatory... 2217
Regno d'Italia, Roma e Torina..... 86
Relativity Conference.......... 2331
Relay 2338
Reni 1445
Repaci...................... 2477
Repubblica 932, 1162, 1478
Repubblica Italiana 2371
Repubblica Roma 726
Resistenza 867, 1126, 1435
Resistenza sul Piave 1199
Respighi 1615
Rete Aerea Postale Notturna..... 1145
Rete Telefonica Teleselettiva ... 1271
Riace bronze 1733
Riccia 1814
Riccione 1808
Rice 2289
Rici 2758
Righi 759, 2241
Rimini.......... 2103, 2163, 2258
Rimini, L. da................. 2279
Risorgimento Italiano........... 706
Risparmio Postale 942
Ristori....................... 2362
Rita da Cascia, St. 1713
Riva del Garda................ 1723
Rivisondoli 2112
Roadsign 1822
Robbia 2642
Roccaraso 2117
Rodi Garganico 1764
"Roma '88" 2005
Roma Gemellaggio Parigi 991
Roma New York via terra........ 2360
Romagne 1010
Romagnosi................... 1068
Romano 2534
Rome 716, 823, 996, 1376, 1551, 1649,
  1770, 1902, 1962, 1985, 2023, 2097,
  2123, 2431, 2440, 2516, 2548, 2606,
                          2686, 2694
Rome Archives................ 2306
Roncalli 1741
Rosa........................ 1346
Rose........................ 2674
Roseto degli Abruzzi 1644
Rosmini 910, 2452
Rossetti 1784
Rossi e Marzotto 754
Rossini................. 574, 1231
Rotary 1269, 1381, 1609
Rowing 1766

Rugby....................... 2594
Running 1260, 1403, 1730, 2144, 2374

Saba........................ 1786
Sabbioneta 2091
Saffi 2093
Sailing 1133
Salerno..................... 1675
Salerno University 2398
Salieri 2637
Salone Aeronautico Int......... 458
Salsomaggiore Terme 1645
Salvaguardia della Natura 1273
Salvaguardiamo i boschi 1833
Salvemini 1366
Salvi 1885
Salviamo Venezia 1340
Sampdoria 2128
San Benedetto del Tronto 1920
San Felice Circeo 2088
San Gimignano 2754
San Luca Academy 2209
"San Marco" (satellite)........ 1441
San Marino 2682
Sanctis 1815
Sanita...................... 733
Sannicandro di Bari 2755
Sanremo 2118
Sant Germiniano 2414
Sant Orso 2627
Santa Ambrose 2414
Santa Maria De Pesio 2756
Santa Marinella 2248
Santa Teresa di Gallura 1724
Santenna 2441
Santo 2770
Sanzio .... see Raphael
Saragat 1479
Sardegna .... see Sardinia
Sardinia 773, 798, 885, 961
Sardo .... see Sardinia
Sarto....................... 1949
Sassari............... 1453, 2127
Sassari University 2399
Sassoferrato................. 1499
Satellite .... see Space
Savio 959
Savonarola 822
Scales and family............. 648
Scarlatti 1457
Schuman, Adenauer etc........ 1281
Scienze Preistoriche e
  Protostoriche 2387
Scilla 1599
Scouts 1220
Seal (animal) 1548
Seal 2114, 2269
Segantini 970
Segni 1479
Segonzano 2550
Sella 1537
Seminara 2533
Sempione 931
Senigallia 2214
Serao 1556
Serpotta 1480
Sestrieres '97 2408
Severi...................... 1604
Severini 2208
Ships........ 727, 796, 1303, 1338, 1525,
  1552, 1621, 1634, 1691, 1728, 1796,
                    2120, 2171, 2305
Shooting 1783
Shot, Putting the 2375
Sicily 769, 986, 1385
Siena 681, 855, 1712, 2234
Signorelli 853
Sindone a Turino 1566
Siracusa .... see Syracuse
Sirmione 1671
Sironi 1886
Sisto V, Pope 1874
Skiing .. 1150, 1251, 1289, 1913, 2598, 2806
Snowboarding 2651
Società Alpinisti Tridentini 1319

Società Geografica Italiana 1171
Società Nazionale Dante Alighieri 314
Soffici....................... 1594
Sorrento 2215
Sower...................... 1092
Space 1441, 2124
Spadini...................... 1446
Spallanzani 1601
Spedizione dei Mille........... 1017
Speed skating 2287
Spello 1811, 2028
Spoleto..................... 1186
Spontini 521, 1461
Spotorno 2032
Stadiums 1970, 2377
Stamp Day . . . 1014, 1033, 1069, 1086,
  1108, 1125, 1147, 1170, 1201, 1240,
  1250, 1275, 1303, 1332, 1382, 1422,
  1465, 1492, 1532, 1575, 1627, 1702,
  1742, 1776, 1819, 1953, 1983, 2016,
  2048, 2111, 2142, 2176, 2229, 2273,
  2342, 2396, 2469, 2570, 2635, 2690
Stampa Del Secolo 2584
Stampa Italiana 2356
Stamps 779, 798, 815, 975, 986, 1010,
  1014, 1086, 1201, 1537, 1588, 1625,
  1898, 2035, 2149, 2229, 2616, 2657,
                    2747, 2767, 2784
Stati Gen. dei Comuni 1118
Stignano.................... 1853
Stintino..................... 2664
Stradivarius 529
Stromboli 1879
Strozzi 1565, 2307
Stupinigi 1855
Surdo 1635
Susa........................ 2317
Swimming 1261, 1290
Sword........................ 86
Syracuse 1848

Tabacco 755
Tabula Peutingeriana 2583
Taormina 859, 2610
Taranto 1809, 2696
Tarquinia 1725, 2246
Tarvisso 2801
Tasso 1773, 2222
Tassoni..................... 1137
Tatti 1264
Teatro alla Scala 1541
Teatro Massino 2424
Telaio 765
Telecomunicazione 1616, 1842, 1931
Telephone 1271
Television 863
Termi....................... 2551
Termoli 1880
Testa....................... 1539
Tex 2394
Tiepolo 1374, 1439, 2350
Timone 766
Tintoretto 2263
Tirso, River.................. 1959
Titian 1485, 2309
Tivoli....................... 1771
Tiziano .... see Titian
Tobacco 755
Toffoletti 2505, 2537
Tommaseo 1409
Torch 649
Torino .... see Turin
Tornio 763
Torricelli 979
Tosca....................... 2592
Toscana .... see Tuscany
Toscanini 1172
Totò 2333
Touring Club Italiano 871, 2280
Tourist Publicity...... 1407, 1442, 1473,
  1513, 1515, 1543, 1596, 1642, 1722,
  1762, 1806, 1845, 1877, 1917, 1963,
  1992, 2031, 2088, 2115, 2165, 2212,
  2248, 2315, 2365, 2425, 2486, 2550,
                    2607, 2661, 2752
Tractor 1828

140

ITALY
Design Index

Traffic lights 949
Traforco del Monte Bianco 1136
Trains . . . . see Railways
Trasimeno, Lake 1958
Tratti di Roma 1173, 1757, 2413
Trees 1155, 1241, 1883
Trentino 778
Trento 1570
Treviso 1697
Trieste . . . 732, 1661, 1943, 2003, 2442
Trieste Fair 820
Trinca 2525
Troisi 2384
Truck 2360
Truppe Alpine 824
Tuccelli 2506, 2538
Tulli 2508, 2540
Tumbolo 764
Turin 708, 1904, 1975, 2134, 2429,
2485, 2494, 2500, 2557
Turin Archives 2349
Turin Shroud 1566, 2485
Turismo 1099
Turtle 1547
Tuscany 779, 1646
Tutti Sono Tenutia 865, 1511

Uccello 2448
Udine 1544
Ugonia 1732
Umberto I 31, 39, 57
Umbria 774
UNESCO 744
UNICEF 1301
Unificazione Archivi di Stato 1452
Unificazione Ordinamenti Notarili   1449
Unione all'Italia 1154
Unione di Roma all'Italia 1263
Unione Europea 2672
Unione Interparlamentare 1769
Unione Latina 2695
Unione Postale Universale . . 725, 1414
Unità d'Italia 1060
United Nations 940, 1267, 2295
Universiade Sicilia 2450

Universiade torino '70 1260
Universita Padua 2417
Universita Rome 2416
Universitatis Senarum 2114
UPU 725, 1414, 2574
Urbino 1701, 2586
Uruguay 1054

Valdesi 2536
Valentino 2332
Van 1933
Vangelli 2107, 2507, 2539
Vanvitelli 1339
Varallo 1932
Vasari 1426
Vase 2267
Vasto 1678, 1965
Vecellio . . . . see Titian
Vecchio 2447
Venaria Reale 2752
Vendemmia 770, 884
Venezia . . . . see Venice
Venezia Giulia 112
Venice 91, 685, 710, 1340, 1696,
2098, 2276, 2282, 2373, 2502
Venice Academy of Fine Arts 758
Venice Biennale 721, 818, 2310
Venosa 2318
Verbania Pallanza 1963
Verdi 803, 1105
Verga 1306
Vergilius . . . . see Virgil
Veroli 2218
Verona 915, 1504, 1976, 2478
Veronese 1372, 2601
Verrazzano 1123
Verri 2446
Verrocchio 1373
Verso il Duemila 2589
Vespa 2372
Vespri Siciliani 1752
Vespucci 875
Viareggio 2162
Viareggio Carnival 1364
Viareggio repaci 2456

Vicenza 711, 1698, 2503
Vico 1226
Victor Emmanuel II . . . 1, 6, 10, 20, 237
Victor Emmanuel III   65, 74, 75, 80, 85,
90, 104, 178, 188, 212, 223, 244, 620,
1558
Vieste 1995
Vignola 1367
Villacidro 1966
Villas . . . 1696, 1737, 1770, 1811, 1853,
1893, 1943, 2321
Villazzano 1896
Vinci 460, 812, 2482, 2586
Virgil 290, 1735
Visita del Presidente...Peru 1053
Visita del Presidente...U.S.A.
(surch) 930
Visita di...Sciahinsciah dell'Iran 977
Visitate l'Italia 1161
Vite e del Vino 1413
Viterbo 1620, 1772, 1850, 2654
Vittoria 980, 1232
Vittorio, Buozzi etc 1839
Vittorio Veneto 118, 2301
Vivaldi 1459
Volleyball 1289, 1532, 1567, 2314
Volo Roma–Tokio 1255
Volontariato 2640
Volpedo 2688
Volta 208, 737, 2148, 2573
Volturno, River 1956

Water polo 2254
Welcome Europe 2182
Wheelchair 1707
Wine 2351
Wolf 618
Wrestling 2106

X-rays 2319

Yachts 1133, 2022

Zavattini 2762

ITALY Italian Social Republic 1944

ITALIAN SOCIAL REPUBLIC
23 September 1943–25 April 1945

Following the surrender of Italy on 3 September 1943, and his rescue from imprisonment on 12 September, Mussolini proclaimed the Italian Social Republic at Salò on 23 September 1943. From this town on Lake Garda the republican government administered those parts of Italy, north of the Gustav Line, which were under German occupation.

Initially the postal authorities utilized stamps of the current "Imperial" series, first issued in 1929.

During December 1943, at the instigation of National Republican Guard members, the current stamps were overprinted "G.N.R." by Bontacchio at Brescia. Three different type faces were used for these overprints which were issued on 20 December, only to be withdrawn three days later.

Early in the following year, in an attempt to prevent speculation in these Brescia overprints, the postal authorities ordered a similar issue to be prepared at Verona and put the Brescia issue back on sale. These Verona overprints, produced by Chiamenti, utilized zincos made in the first two type faces used at Brescia and in consequence there are problems of identification.

Our listing is confined to the Verona overprints, although the same values exist from the Brescia issue. To aid identification the third type face (Type 3) only used at Brescia is also shown.

G. N. R. (1)   **G.N.R.** (2)   **G. N. R.** (3)

Types 1 and 2 were used at both Brescia and Verona; Type 3 at Brescia only.

Stamps of Italy overprinted

1944 (Feb). *Verona overprint.*

(a) POSTAGE.
(i) Nos. 239 and 241/59 optd with T 1.

1	98	5c. brown	2·20	5·50
2	100	10c. sepia	2·20	5·50
3	101	15c. blue-green (R.)	2·20	5·50
4	99	20c. carmine	2·20	5·50
5	102	25c. green (R.)	2·20	5·50
6	103	30c. brown	2·20	5·50
7	101	35c. blue (R.)	75·00	£140
8	103	50c. bright violet	2·20	5·50
9	102	75c. carmine	3·50	5·50
10	99	1l. violet	2·20	5·50
11	102	1l.25 blue (R.)	3·50	5·50
12	100	1l.75 orange-vermilion	5·25	30·00
13	101	2l. brown-lake	13·00	30·00
14	98	2l.55 grey-green (R.)	£190	£180
15		3l.70 bright violet	£100	£140
16		5l. carmine	26·00	50·00
17	101	10l. violet	65·00	£140
18	99	20l. yellow-green (R.)	£225	£450
19	100	25l. blue-black (R.)	£650	£1400
20	102	50l. deep violet	£500	£1400
1/20		Set of 20	£1700	£3750

(ii) War Propaganda issue. Nos. 563/74 optd with T 2 across stamp and label.

21	102	25c. green (Navy) (R.)	5·00	16·00
22		25c. green (Army) (R.)	5·00	16·00
23		25c. green (Air Force) (R.)	5·00	16·00
24		25c. green (Militia) (R.)	5·00	16·00
25	103	30c. brown (Navy)	6·50	21·00
26		30c. brown (Army)	6·50	21·00
27		30c. brown (Air Force)	6·50	21·00
28		30c. brown (Militia)	6·50	21·00
29		50c. bright violet (Navy)	4·50	16·00
30		50c. bright violet (Army)	4·50	16·00
31		50c. bright violet (Air Force)	4·50	16·00
32		50c. bright violet (Militia)	4·50	16·00
21/32		Set of 12	60·00	£190

(b) AIR. Nos. 270/7 optd with T 2 (2l.) or T 1 (others).

33	111	25c. grey-green (R.)	25·00	45·00
34	110	50c. sepia	3·50	9·00
35	112	75c. chestnut	33·00	45·00
36	111	80c. orange-vermilion	95·00	£140
37	112	1l. bright violet	3·50	9·00
38	113	2l. blue (R.)	£275	£160

39	110	5l. green (R.)	£130	£225
40		10l. carmine-red	£1100	£1800
33/40		Set of 8	£1500	£2250

The 10l. does not exist with the Brescia overprint.

(c) EXPRESS. Nos. E350/1 optd with T 2.

E41	E 132	1l.25 green (R.)	31·00	45·00
E42		2l.50 red-orange	£190	£400

(d) AIR EXPRESS. No. E370 optd with T 2.

E43	E 133	2l. blue-black (R.)	£700	£1100

(e) POSTAGE DUE. Nos. D395/407 optd with T 1.

D44	D 141	5c. chocolate	16·00	42·00
D45		10c. blue (R.)	12·50	42·00
D46		20c. bright carmine	16·00	24·00
D47		25c. green (R.)	9·75	24·00
D48		30c. orange-vermilion	16·00	42·00
D49		40c. sepia (R.)	25·00	24·00
D50		50c. bright violet	50·00	£200
D51		60c. slate-blue (R.)	£250	£800
D52	D 142	1l. orange	12·50	32·00
D53		2l. green (R.)	80·00	85·00
D54		5l. bright violet	£190	£325
D55		10l. blue (R.)	65·00	£225
D56		20l. carmine	65·00	£225
D44/56		Set of 13	£750	£1900

Nos. D50/1 with Brescia overprints are worth approximately 75% (mint) and 60% (used) of the prices quoted.

The 10l. and 20l. do not exist with the Brescia overprint.

(Optd at Florence, Genoa, Rome or Verona from stereos prepared at Brescia)

1944 (22 Jan). *Nos. 244/5, 247/8 and 250 optd.*

57	4	25c. green	30	1·80
		a. Error. Opt in red	55·00	£190
58	5	30c. brown (R.)	35	1·80
59	6	50c. bright violet (R.)	30	1·80
60	4	75c. carmine	75	1·80
		a. Error. Optd on 20c. (No. 243)	£250	£950
61	5	1l.25 blue (R.)	35	1·80

No. 60a resulted from the inclusion of sheets of No. 243 in the stacks of 75c. stamps intended for overprinting.

1944 (24 Jan). EXPRESS LETTER. *Nos. E350/1 optd with Type E 7.*

E62	E 132	1l.25 green (R.)	25	1·90
E63		2l.50 red-orange	25	12·50

1944 (Feb). *War Propaganda stamps, Nos. 563/74 optd.*
A. Once, on stamp only.

64A	4	25c. green (Navy)	30	2·10
65A		25c. green (Army)	30	2·10
66A		25c. green (Air Force)	30	2·10
67A		25c. green (Militia)	30	2·10
68A	5	30c. brown (Navy) (R.)	60	6·50
69A		30c. brown (Army) (R.)	60	6·50
70A		30c. brown (Air Force) (R.)	60	6·50
71A		30c. brown (Militia) (R.)	60	6·50
72A	6	50c. bright violet (Navy) (R.)	35	4·00
73A		50c. bright violet (Army) (R.)	35	4·00

ITALY Italian Social Republic 1944

74A	50c. bright violet (Air Force) (R.)	35	4·00
75A	50c. bright violet (Militia) (R.)	35	4·00
64A/75A	Set of 12	4·50	45·00

B. Twice, on both stamp and label.

64B	4	25c. green (Navy)	24·00	80·00
65B		25c. green (Army)	24·00	80·00
66B		25c. green (Air Force)	24·00	80·00
67B		25c. green (Militia)	24·00	80·00
68B	5	30c. brown (Navy) (R.)	24·00	80·00
69B		30c. brown (Army) (R.)	24·00	80·00
70B		30c. brown (Air Force) (R.)	24·00	80·00
71B		30c. brown (Militia) (R.)	24·00	80·00
72B	6	50c. bright violet (Navy) (R.)	24·00	80·00
73B		50c. bright violet (Army) (R.)	24·00	80·00
74B		50c. bright violet (Air Force) (R.)	24·00	80·00
75B		50c. bright violet (Militia) (R.)	24·00	80·00
64B/75B	Set of 12		£275	£900

The colour of the red overprints varies from red to lilac-carmine.

1944 (Mar). *CONCESSIONAL LETTER POST. No. CL267 optd with Type CL* **8**.

CL76	CL **109**	10c. brown	15	1·00

No. CL267 overprinted with Type **4** was not issued.

1944 (April). *No. 259 optd with T* **5** *at Verona.*

77	**102**	50l. deep violet (R.)	£200	£1800

REP. SOC. ITALIANA
(P **9**)

1944 (April). *PARCEL POST. Nos. P217/28 optd with Type P* **9**.

P77	5c. brown	9·00	10·50
P78	10c. deep blue	9·00	10·50
P79	25c. carmine	9·00	10·50
P80	30c. ultramarine	9·00	10·50
P81	50c. orange	9·00	10·50
P82	60c. rose-scarlet	9·00	10·50
P83	1l. violet	9·00	10·50
P84	2l. green	£350	£550
P85	3l. yellow-bistre	15·00	35·00
P86	4l. grey-black	28·00	55·00
P87	10l. purple	£180	
P88	20l. dull-purple	£425	
P77/88	Set of 12	£950	

The used prices for Nos. P77/88 are for unsevered stamps. Unoverprinted parcel post stamps of Italy (P217/28) were used unsevered in the Republic for normal postage.

1944 (Apr). *POSTAGE DUE. Nos. D395/407 optd with Type[f]CL* **8**.

D 89	D **141**	5c. chocolate	1·70	4·50
D 90		10c. blue	1·70	3·75
D 91		20c. bright carmine	1·70	3·75
D 92		25c. green	1·70	3·75
D 93		30c. orange-vermilion	1·70	5·25
D 94		40c. sepia	1·70	8·75
D 95		50c. bright violet	1·70	3·00
D 96		50c. slate-blue	3·75	18·00
D 97	D **142**	1l. orange	1·70	3·00
D 98		2l. green	5·50	12·50
D 99		5l. bright violet	55·00	£110
D100		10l. blue	95·00	£170
D101		20l. carmine	95·00	£170
D89/101	Set of 13		£250	£475

10 Loggia dei Mercanti, Bologna 
11 
12 Basilica de St. Lorenzo, Rome

13 Basilica de St. Lorenzo, Rome 
14 Drummer 
15 Fascist Allegory

11a

(Photo State Polygraphic Institute, Novara)

1944–45. *T* **10/15** *and similar vert designs.* P 14.

(a) W **8** of Italy (5 June).

102	**10**	20c. carmine	20	55
103	**12**	25c. green	20	55
104	**14**	30c. brown	10	55
105		75c. carmine	10	90

(b) Without wmk (1944–45).

106	–	5c. brown	10	50
107	–	10c. brown	10	20
108	**11**	20c. carmine	10	20
11a		a. SOCIAIE instead of SOCIALE	40·00	55·00
109	**13**	25c. green	20	55
110	**14**	30c. brown	10	20
111	**15**	50c. violet	10	20
112	**14**	75c. red	10	5·00
113	–	1l. violet	10	20
114	–	1l.25 blue	45	9·00
115	–	3l. green	60	33·00
102/115	Set of 14		2·20	47·00

Designs:—5c. St. Ciriaco's Church, Ancona; 10c., 1l. Montecassino Abbey; 1l.25, 3l. St. Mary of Grace, Milan.

E **16** Palermo Cathedral
17 Bandiera Brothers 

1944. *EXPRESS LETTER. Photo.* W **8** of Italy. P 14.

E116	E **16**	1l.25 green	10	90

(Des Maioli. Photo State Polygraphic Institute, Novara)

1944 (6 Dec). *Death Centenary of Attilio and Emilio Bandiera (revolutionaries)*. No wmk. P 14.

117	**17**	25c. green	15	50
118		1l. violet	15	50
119		2l.50 carmine	15	4·50

CAMPIONE

In 1944 the Italian town of Campione, on Lake Lugano, which is an enclave surrounded by Swiss territory, issued the stamps listed below. When King Victor Emmanuel and Marshal Badoglio broke with the Axis Powers in 1943, Campione supported the king. As stamps could not be obtained from southern Italy, stamps bearing the Cross of Savoy were printed for use in Campione and on mail to Switzerland only.

100 Centesimi = 1 Swiss Franc

1 Arms of Campione

2 Campione and Lake Lugano

(Typo Orell Fussli, Zurich)

1944.

A. P 11½ (large holes) (20 May).

1A	1	0.05f. green	33·00	27·00
2A		0.10f. red-brown	4·00	15·00
3A		0.20f. red	4·00	15·00
4A		0.30f. blue	£200	£300
5A		1f. pale violet	£200	£300
1A/5A	Set of 5		£400	£600

B. P 11 (small holes) (23 June).

1B	1	0.05f. green	3·25	4·50
2B		0.10f. red-brown	3·25	4·50
3B		0.20f. red	3·25	4·50
4B		0.30f. blue	3·25	4·50
5B		1f. pale violet	41·00	55·00
1B/5B	Set of 5		50·00	65·00

(Photo Courvoisier)

1944 (7 Sept). T **2** and similar designs. Granite paper. P 11½.

6	0.05f. deep green	1·80	3·75
7	0.10f. deep purple-brown	1·80	3·75
8	0.20f. carmine	1·80	3·75
9	0.30f. deep blue	1·80	3·75
10	0.40f. deep violet	2·75	5·75
11	0.60f. deep reddish purple	3·50	7·25
12	1f. slate-blue	5·00	10·00
6/12	Set of 7	17·00	35·00

Designs:—0.10f. Church of the Madonna, Ghirli; 0.20f. Church of the Holy Zenone; 0.30f. View of Campione; 0.40f. Modena Cathedral; 0.60f. Gravestone to the Grand Masters of Scala, Verona; 1f. Basilica of Santa Maria Maggiore of Bergamo.

The stamps of Campione were withdrawn on 1 June 1952. Since then Swiss stamps (obtainable from Lugano) are used for mail to Switzerland and Italian stamps on mail to Italy but both are valid for international mail.

AUSTRIAN TERRITORIES ACQUIRED BY ITALY 1918

Austrian Territories Acquired by Italy

1918. 100 Heller = 1 Krone

1918. 100 Centesimi = 1 Lira

1919. 100 Centesimi = 1 Corona

I. TRENTINO

After the Battle of Vittorio Veneto and the Armistice of 3 November 1918, Italian troops occupied the Trentino (South Tyrol) up to the Brenner Pass. The area was awarded to Italy by the Treaty of St. Germain, 10 September 1919.

Regno d'Italia

(1) Trentino 3 nov 1918

(2) Venezia Tridentina

(3) Venezia Tridentina 10 Heller

1918 (11 Nov). Stamps of Austria, 1916-18, optd by Signor Seiser, Trento, with T **1**.

1	49	3h. purple (Austrian crown)	2·00	2·50
		a. Opt double	45·00	50·00
		b. Opt inverted	35·00	35·00
2		5h. pale green	1·50	1·60
		a. "8 nov. 1918"	£1400	
		b. Opt inverted	40·00	40·00
3		6h. orange	32·00	30·00
4		10h. lake	1·25	1·60
		a. "8 nov. 1918"	70·00	80·00
5		12h. blue-green	£100	£100
6	60	15h. red-brown (Charles I)	2·50	2·75
7		20h. deep blue-green	1·00	1·10
		a. Opt inverted	12·00	14·00
		b. Opt double	45·00	45·00
		c. "8 nov. 1918"	70·00	70·00
		d. yellow-green		
8		25h. blue	21·00	24·00
9		30h. dull violet	7·00	8·00
10	51	40h. olive (Arms)	32·00	30·00
11		50h. green	14·00	18·00
		a. Opt inverted	60·00	65·00
12		60h. deep blue	28·00	26·00
		a. Opt double	60·00	65·00
13		80h. chestnut	32·00	35·00
14		90h. lake	£600	£550
15		1k. vermilion/*yellow*	32·00	35·00
16	52	2k. blue (Arms)	£160	£180
		a. Granite paper	£225	£275
17		4k. green	£900	£950
18		10k. violet	£16000	

The normal overprint is with stop after "nov." but stamps exist without stop.

The "8 nov 1918" error occurs on position 94 of the first printing.

No. 18 was prepared for presentation purposes only. The first printing of 11, of which only 5 or 6 were distributed, was overprinted in black and is worth about four times the quoted price The second printing of 20 has the overprint in greyish black; the only two used examples known are on cover.

1918 (20 Dec). Stamps of Italy, 1901-17, optd by Signor Seiser, Trento, with T **2**.

19	30	1c. brown	80	1·40
		a. Opt inverted	30·00	30·00
20	31	2c. red-brown	80	1·40
		a. Opt inverted	30·00	30·00
21	37	5c. green	80	1·40
		a. Opt inverted	30·00	30·00
		b. Opt double	32·00	32·00
22	38	10c. rose	80	1·40
		a. Opt inverted	35·00	35·00
		b. Opt double	32·00	32·00
23	41	20c. orange (No. 105)	80	1·40
		a. Opt inverted	35·00	35·00
24	40	40c. brown	18·00	18·00
25	33	45c. olive-green	11·00	18·00
		a. Opt double	£100	£100
26	40	50c. bright mauve	12·00	22·00
27	34	1l. brown and green	12·00	22·00
		a. Opt double	£100	£100

1919 (Jan). Stamps of Italy, 1906-17, surch in Rome as T **3**.

28	37	5h. on 5c. green	40	85
		a. "5" omitted (pos. 69)	15·00	15·00
		b. "V" omitted	30·00	30·00
		c. "er" of "Heller" omitted (pos. 24)	22·00	22·00
29	38	10h. on 10c. rose	40	85
		a. "Trldentina" (pos. 17)	30·00	30·00
		b. Surch inverted	40·00	40·00
30	41	20h. on 20c. orange (No 105)	40	85
		a. "r" of "Heller" omitted (pos. 29)	22·00	22·00
		b. "0" for "20"	30·00	30·00
		c. " 2" inserted by hand	80·00	80·00
		d. Surch double	40·00	40·00

The errors occur on only part of the printing.

These stamps are known handstamped with a large "T". They were used at Bolzano as Postage Due stamps. but were not officially authorised.

II. VENEZIA GIULIA

Trieste, Gorizia and the adjoining areas, with the Istrian peninsula, were also occupied in 1918 and awarded to Italy in 1919.

Regno d'Italia Venezia Giulia 3. XI. 18.
(4)

Venezia Giulia
(5)

1918 (14 Nov). Stamps of Austria. 1916-18, optd by the Printers' Association. Trieste, as T **4**.

31	49	3h. purple (21.11) (Austrian crown)	50	70
32		5h. pale green	50	70
33		6h. orange (21.11)	75	1·10
34		10h. lake (15.11)	2·75	85
35		12h. blue-green (21.11)	1·40	1·90
36	60	15h. red-brown (Charles I)	50	70
37		20h. dark green (15.11)	50	70
38		25h. blue	3·50	4·25
39		30h. purple (21.11)	1·60	1·90
40	51	40h. olive (Arms)	26·00	32·00
41		50h. green	3·50	4·00
42		60h. deep blue	5·50	7·00
43		80h. chestnut	5·50	7·00
44		1k. vermilion/*yellow*	5·50	7·00
45	52	2k. blue (4.12) (Arms)	70·00	80·00
		a. On granite paper	£400	£400
46		3k. carmine/*granite* (4.12)	£120	£140
47		4k. green (4.12)	£160	£180
48		10k. deep violet	£12000	£14000

The overprint on the 10 k. was struck by hand and differs from that on the other values. The 37 examples produced were distributed to senior officials.

145

AUSTRIAN TERRITORIES ACQUIRED BY ITALY 1918

Errors and Varieties

The overprint on this issue was set very loosely, resulting in a number of varieties caused by a letter or a stop falling out; there were also errors consisting of wrong founts.
No stop after "XI".
No stop after "18".
No stop on first "i" in "Giulia".
Tall "X" with serifs, and short defective "I" in "XI".
"d'talia", first "I" missing.
"d'Ita is", "I" missing.
"d'Ita Ira" word spaced in middle.
"Regnod'Italia", close up; no space between the words.
"G ulia", first "i" omitted.
Date " .18." for "3.X.1.1 B."
Inverted and double overprints also exist.

1918 (6 Dec)–**19**. *Stamps o1 Italy 1901-17, optd at Trieste with T 5.*

49	**30**	1c. brown (1.19)	75	1·25
		a. Opt inverted	14·00	18·00
50	**31**	2c. red-brown (1.19)	75	1·25
		a. Opt inverted	10·00	12·00
51	**37**	5c. green	20	40
		a. Opt inverted	20·00	24·00
52	**38**	10c. rose-red	15	40
		a. Opt inverted	24·00	30·00
53	**41**	20c. orange (No. 105)	25	50
		a. Opt inverted	40·00	45·00
54	**39**	25c. blue	35	70
		a. Opt inverted	45·00	45·00
55	**40**	40c. brown (16.12.18)	4·00	6·00
56	**33**	45c. olive-green (12.12.18)	1·25	2·00
		a. Opt inverted	50·00	60·00
57	**40**	50c. violet (11.12.18)	1·60	2·75
58	**39**	60c. carmine-red (21.12.18)	18·00	30·00
59	**34**	1l. brown and green (21.12.18)	8·00	12·00
49/59	Set of 11		32·00	50·00

1918 (Dec). *POSTAGE DUE. Postage Due stamps of Italy. 1870–94, optd with T 5.*

D60	D **12**	5c. magenta and orange	15	40
D61		10c. magenta and orange	25	50
D62		20c. magenta and orange	60	1·10
D63		30c. magenta and orange	2·00	3·25
D64		40c. magenta and orange	12·00	20·00
D65		50c. magenta and orange	24·00	35·00
D66		1l. magenta and blue	85·00	£100
D60/66	Set of 7		£110	£140

Venezia Giulia
(E **6**)

1919 (3 Jan). *EXPRESS LETTER. Express Letter stamp of Italy. 1903, optd with Type E **6**.*

E60	E **35**	25c. rose-red	10·00	18·00

1919 (20 Feb). *Stamps of Italy, 1906–17, surch as T **6**.*

60	**37**	5h. on 5c. green	35	75
61	**41**	20h. on 20c. orange (105)	35	75

These two stamps surcharged with Austrian currency were issued for two days only during a temporary shortage of Italian currency stamps.

For the stamps issued in this area under Yugoslav occupation and under Allied Military Government, 1945–47, see under Trieste and under Venezia Giulia.

III. GENERAL ISSUE

This was for use throughout the areas of Trentmo, Venezia Giulia and Dalmatia.

1
centesimo
di corona
(7)

25 centesimi
di corona
(E 8)

1919 (Jan). *Stamps of Italy, 1901–18, surch as T **7** in Rome.*

62	30	1c. di c. on 1c. brown (Feb)	30	45
63	31	2c. di c. on 2 c. dark red-brown	30	45
		a. "Contesimi"	27·00	27·00
		b. "2" omitted	90·00	90·00
		c. "2" handstamped	£150	£150
64		2c. di c. on 2 c. pale chestnut-brown	30	35
65	37	5c. di c. on 5 c. deep green	30	35
66		5c. di c. on 5 c. pale green	30	35
		a. "entesimi"	75·00	75·00
		b. "d" of "di" omitted	30·00	30·00
		c. "centesim"	32·00	32·00
67	38	10c. di c. on 10 c. rose-red	30	35
		a. "corena"	70·00	70·00
		b. "centcsimi"	32·00	32·00
		c. "centesim"	32·00	32·00
68	41	20c. di c. on 20 c. orge (No. 105) (Feb)	30	35
69		20c. di c. on 20 c. dark orange	30	35
		a. "entesima"	30·00	30·00
70	39	25c. di c. on 25 c. blue (Feb)	30	45
71	40	40c. di c. on 40 c. brown (Mar)	30	70
		a. "ccrona"	70·00	70·00
72	33	45c. di c. on 45 c. olive-green (Mar)	30	70
73	40	50c. di c. on 50 c. violet (Apr)	30	70
74	39	60c. di c. on 60 c. carmine-red (Feb)	30	85
		a. "00" for "60"	70·00	70·00
75	34	1cor. on 1l. brown and green (Mar)	30	85
		a. "coron"	85·00	85·00
62/75	Set of 14		3·75	6·50

The 5 l. and 10 l. of this series were never issued officially.
The 2, 5, 10 and 20 c. are known overprinted "T" at Bolzano for use as Postage Due stamps. These were made for collectors and were not officially authorised.

1919 (Jan). *POSTAGE DUE Postage Due stamps of Italy, 1870–1903, surch as T **7** (Nos. D76/81) or as Type E **8** (Nos. D82/4).*

D76	D **12**	5c. di c. on 5 c. magenta & orange	20	75
D77		10c. di c. on 10 c. magenta & orge	20	75
		a. Figs of value and surch inverted	65·00	65·00
D78		20c. di c. on 20 c. magenta & orge	30	75
D79		30c. di c. on 30 c. magenta & orge	40	75
D80		40c. di c. on 40 c. magenta & orge	40	75
D81		50c. di c. on 50 c. magenta & orge	40	75
D82		una corona on 1l. magenta & blue	40	75
D83		due corone on 2l. magenta & blue	19·00	38·00
D84		cinque corone on 5l. magenta & blue	19·00	38·00
D75/84	Set of 9		35·00	75·00

No. D82 also exists with the surcharge in the smaller typeface, as Type **7** (*Price* £900 *un*).

AUSTRIAN TERRITORIES ACQUIRED BY ITALY 1919

1919. EXPRESS LETTER, Express Letter stamps of Italy, 1903–08, surch as Type E **8**.
E76	E **35**	25c. di c. on 25 c. rose (Feb)	30	55
		a. Surch double	30·00	30·00
		b. "2" omitted	85·00	85·00
		c. "25" omitted	85·00	85·00
E77	E **41**	30c. di c. on 30 c. blue and rose (Mar)	50	1·10
		a. "centesimi"	85·00	85·00

IV. DALMATIA

Italian troops occuped Dalmatia in 1918 until, by the Treaty of Rapallo, 12 November 1920, Italy gave up all except Zara.

Stamps of Italy surcharged.

1919 (May). As Type E **8**
76	**34**	una corona on 1 l. brown and green	1·00	3·75
		a. "c" of "corona" omitted	55·00	£120

5 centesimi di corona (8)

1921 (Feb)–**22**. Surch as T **8** (corona values in one line).
77	**37**	5c. di c. on 5 c. green	20	50
78	**38**	10c. di c. on 10 c. Carmine	20	50
		a. Pair, one with surch omitted	30·00	
79	**39**	25c. di c. on 25 c. blue (7.10.22)	80	1·40
80	**40**	50c. di c. on 50 c. mauve (7.10.22)	1·00	2·00
		a. Pair, one with surch omitted	60·00	
81	**34**	1 cor. on 1 l. brown and green (7.10.22)	1·40	3·25
82		5 cor. on 5 l. blue and rose (7.10.22)	12·00	30·00
83	**44**	10 cor. on 10l. sage-grn & rose (7.10.22)	12·00	30·00
77/83	Set of 7		25·00	60·00

1921 (Feb). EXPRESS LETTER. No. E73 surch as T **8**.
E84		25c. di c. on 25 c. rose	70	1·75
		a. Surch double	70·00	£180

The 1l.20, No. E130, was surcharged "LIRE 1, 20 DI CORONA" in two lines but was not issued (Price £30 un).

1922 (Oct). POSTAGE DUE. Postage Due stamps, surch as T **8**.
D85	D **12**	50c. dic. on 50c. magenta & orange	75	2·50
D86		1 cor. on 1 l. magenta and blue	2·50	7·00
D87		2 cor. on 2 l. magenta and blue	8·00	17·00
D88		5 cor. on 5 l. magenta and blue	8·00	17·00
D85/88	Set of 4		17·00	40·00

Nos. 79/83 and D85/8 were used only in Zara (Zadar).

CASTELROSSO 1922

Castelrosso

ITALIAN OCCUPATION
100 Centesimi = 1 Lira

This island off the coast of Asia Minor, formerly part of the Turkish Empire, was occupied by the French Navy in 1915. Stamps issued during this occupation are listed in Part 3 (*Balkans*) of this catalogue.

In accordance with the Treaty of Svres on 10 August 1920 Castelrosso was awarded to Italy and on 21 August the French forces withdrew. After a temporary transference to Italian naval administration on 1 March 1921, it later came under the rule of the Governor of the Dodecanese and Castelrosso.

CASTELROSSO
(1)

(2)

1922 (11 July). *Contemporary stamps of Italy (various portraits of Victor Emmanuel III) optd with T* **1**.

1	37	5c. green	3·00	11·00
2	38	10c. rose-red	95	11·00
3	37	15c. slate	2·25	11·00
4	41	20c. orange (No. 105)	95	11·00
5	39	25c. blue	95	11·00
6	40	40c. brown	32·00	15·00
7		50c. violet	32·00	15·00
8	39	60c. carmine-red	32·00	20·00
9		85c. red-brown	2·25	38·00
1/9	Set of 9		95·00	£130

1923 (Jan). *Typo. Wmk Crown. P* 14.

10	2	5c. green	1·90	11·00
11		10c. carmine	1·90	11·00
12		25c. blue	1·90	11·00
13		50c. dull purple	1·90	11·00
14		1l. brown	1·90	11·00
10/14	Set of 5		8·50	50·00

CASTELROSSO
(3)

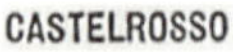

CASTELROSSO
(4)

1924 (Mar). *Contemporary stamps of Italy optd with T* **3**.

15	37	5c. green	90	15·00
16	38	10c. rose-red	90	15·00
17	37	15c. slate	90	18·00
18	41	20c. orange (No. 105)	90	18·00
19	39	25c. blue	90	15·00
20	40	40c. brown	90	15·00
21		50c. violet	90	17·00
22	39	60c. carmine-red	90	21·00
23		85c. red-brown	90	26·00
24	34	1l. brown and green	90	26·00
15/24	Set of 10		9·00	£150

1930 (20 Oct). *Ferrucci issue of Italy (colours changed) optd with T* **4**.

25	114	20c. bright violet (R.)	4·25	3·25
26	115	25c. deep green (R.)	4·25	6·00
27		50c. black (R.)	4·25	3·25
28		1l.25 blue (R.)	4·25	8·00
29	116	5l.+2l. carmine-red (B.)	15·00	35·00
25/29	Set of 5		29·00	50·00

1932 (28 Aug). *T* **128/9** *and similar types (Garibaldi) of Italy, with colours changed, optd with T* **4**.

30	10c. sepia (R.)	15·00	25·00
31	20c. lake-brown (B.)	15·00	25·00
32	25c. green (R.)	15·00	25·00
33	30c. slate-blue (R.)	15·00	25·00
34	50c. purple (B.)	15·00	25·00
35	75c. lake (B.)	15·00	25·00
36	1l.25c. deep blue (R.)	15·00	25·00
37	1l.75+25c. sepia (R.)	15·00	25·00
38	2l.55+50c. orange-vermilion (B.)	15·00	25·00
39	5l.+1l. violet (R.)	15·00	25·00
30/39	Set of 10	£140	£225

Castelrosso was transferred to Greece with the Dodecanese Islands by the Treaty of Paris, which came into force on 15 September 1947. It is now called Kastellorizon.

DODECANESE ISLANDS 1912

Dodecanese Islands

100 Centesimi = 1 Lira

ITALIAN OCCUPATION

These islands (literally, in Greek, the "Twelve Islands") consist of twelve small islands in the south-east Aegean Sea, with the larger island of Rhodes. In 1912 they declared their independence from Turkey but they were occupied by Italy in May of that year, during the Turco-Italian War; her possession of them was not recognised until the Greco-Italian Agreement of 10 August 1920. Castelrosso was placed under the same administration in 1921.

1912 (22 Sept). Nos. 77 and 79 of Italy optd "EGEO".

1	39	25c. blue	14·50	30·00
		a. Opt inverted	£170	£170
2	40	50c. violet	14·50	30·00
		a. Opt inverted	£170	£170

1912 (1 Dec)–21. Stamps of Italy (Arms (T **31**) or various portraits of Victor Emmanuel III (others)) optd for the individual islands (in capitals on Nos. 6 and 10, in upper and lower case on others).

A. Calimno

3A	31	2c. orange-brown	4·50	4·25
4A	37	5c. green	1·40	4·25
5A	38	10c. rose-red	40	4·25
6A	49	15c. slate (90, no wmk) (V)	19·00	8·25
7A	37	15c. slate (104, wmkd) (10.21)	2·75	25·00
8A	49	20c.on 15c. slate (100) (1.1.16)	10·00	17·00
9A	41	20c. orange (101, no wmk) (6.17)	55·00	85·00
10A		20c. orange (105, wmkd) (9.21)	2·75	25·00
11A	39	25c. blue	4·00	4·25
12A	40	40c. brown	40	4·25
13A		50c. violet	40	4·25
3A/13A Set of 11			90·00	£170

B. Caso

3B	31	2c. orange-brown	4·75	4·25
4B	37	5c. green	1·60	4·25
5B	38	10c. rose- red	40	4·25
6B	49	15c. slate (90, no wmk) (V)	22·00	8·25
7B	37	15c. slate (104, wmkd) (10.21)	2·75	25·00
8B	49	20c.on 15c. slate (100) (1.1.16)	65	12·00
9B	41	20c. orange (101, no wmk) (6.17)	75·00	85·00
10B		20c. orange (105,wmkd) (9.21)	2·10	20·00
11B	39	25c. blue	40	4·25
12B	40	40c. brown	40	4·25
13B		50c. violet	40	7·50
3B/13B Set of 11			£100	£160

C. Cos

3C	31	2c. orange-brown	4·75	4·25
4C	37	5c. green	45·00	4·25
5C	38	10c. rose-red	2·25	4·25
6C	49	15c. slate (90, no wmk) (V)	22·00	8·25
7C	37	15c. slate (104, wmkd) (10.21)	2·75	35·00
8C	49	20c. on 15c.slate(100) (1.1.16)	10·00	21·00
9C	41	20c. orange (101 wmkd) (6.17)	27·00	85·00
10C		20c. orange (105, wmkd) (9.21)	2·10	21·00
11C	39	25c. blue	19·00	4·25
12C	40	40c. brown	40	4·25
13C		50c. violet	40	7·50
3C/13C Set of 11			£120	£180

D. Karki

3D	31	2c. orange-brown	4·75	4·25
4D	37	5c. green	1·60	4·25
5D	38	10c. rose- red	1·60	4·25
6D	49	15c. slate (90 no wmk) (V)	22·00	8·25
7D	37	15c. slate(104, wmkd) (10.21)	2·75	26·00
8D	49	20c.on 15c. slate (100) (1.1.16)	1·25	15·00
9D	41	20c. orange (101, no wmk) (6.17)	75·00	85·00
10D		20c. orange (105, wmkd) (9.21)	2·75	24·00
11D	39	25c. blue	40	4·25
12D	40	40c. brown	40	4·25
13D		50c. violet	40	7·50
3D/13D Set of 11			£100	£170

E. Leros

3E	31	2c. orange-brown	4·75	4·25
4E	37	5c. green	3·50	4·25
5E	38	10c. rose-red	70	4·25
6E	49	15c. slate (90, no wmk) (V)	35·00	8·25
7E	37	15c. slate (104, wmkd) (10.21)	2·75	22·00
8E	49	20c.on 15c. slate (100) (1.1.16)	10·00	16·50
9E	41	20c. orange (101 no wmk) (6.17)	27·00	85·00
10E		20c. orange (105, wmkd) (9.21)	95·00	55·00
11E	39	25c. blue	21·00	4·25
12E	40	40c. brown	2·75	4·25
13E		50c. violet	40	7·50
3E/13E Set of 11			£180	£190

F. Lipso

3F	31	2c. orange-brown	4·75	4·25
4F	37	5c. green	1·90	4·25
5F	38	10c. rose-red	85	4·25
6F	49	15c. slate (90,no wmk) (V)	21·00	8·25
7F	37	15c. Slate (104 wmkd) (10.21)	2·75	22·00
8F	49	20c.on 15c. slate (100) (1.1.16)	80	15·00
9F	41	20c. orange (101 no wmk) (6.17)	45·00	55·00
10F		20c. orange (105 wmkd) (9.21)	2·75	25·00
11F	39	25c. blue	40	4·25
12F	40	40c. brown	1·25	4·25
13F		50c. violet	40	7·50
3F/13F Set of 11			75·00	£170

G. Nisiros

3G	31	2c. orange-brown	4·75	4·25
4G	37	3c. green	1·60	4·25
5G	38	10c. rose-red	40	4·25
6G	49	15c. slate (90, no wmk) (V)	19·00	8·25
7G	37	15c. slate (104, wmkd) (10.21)	13·50	23·00
8G	49	20c.on 15c. slate (100) (1.1.16)	80	15·00
9G	41	20c. orange (101, no wmk) (6.17)	75·00	85·00
10G		20c. orange (105, wmkd.) (9.21)	55·00	65·00
11G	39	25c. blue	1·40	4·25
12G	40	40c. brown	40	4·25
13G		50c. violet	2·75	7·50
3G/13G Set of 11			£160	£200

H. Patmos

3H	31	2c. orange-brown	4·75	4·25
4H	37	3c. green	1·60	4·25
5H	38	10c. rose-red	1·40	4·25
6H	49	15c. slate (90, no wmk) (V)	19·00	8·25
7H	37	15c. slate (104, wmkd) (10.21)	2·75	25·00
8H	49	20c.on 15c. slate (100) (1.1.16)	10·00	20·00
9H	41	20c. orange (101, no wmkd) (6.17)	45·00	85·00
10H		20c. orange (105, wmkd.) (9.21)	90·00	85·00
11H	39	25c. blue	55	4·25
12H	40	40c. brown	2·50	4·25
13H		50c. violet	40	7·50
3H/13H Set of 11			£120	£225

I. Piscopi

3I	31	2c. orange-brown	4·75	4·25
4I	37	3c. green	1·50	4·25
5I	38	10c. rose-red	40	4·25
6I	49	15c. slate (90, no wmk) (V)	22·00	8·25
7I	37	15c. slate (104, wmkd) (10.21)	10·00	25·00
8I	49	20c. on 15c. slate (100) (1.1.16)	80	15·00
9I	41	20c. orange (101, no wmk) (6.17)	45·00	85·00
10I		20c. orange (105, wmkd.) (9.21)	27·00	38·00
11I	39	25c. blue	40	4·25
12I	40	40c. brown	40	4·25
13I		50c. violet	40	7·50
3I/13I Set of 11			£100	£180

J. Rodi

3J	31	2c. orange-brown	40	4·25
4J	37	3c. green	1·40	4·25
5J	38	10c. rose-red	40	4·25
6J	49	15c. slate (90, no wmk) (V)	23·00	8·25
7J	37	15c. slate (104, wmkd) (10.21)	85·00	38·00
8J	49	20c.on 15c. slate (100) (1.1.16)	75·00	80·00
9J	41	20c. orange (101, no wmk) (6.17)	£100	85·00
10J		20c. orange (105, wmkd) (9.21)	4·25	10·00
11J	39	25c. blue	1·40	4·25
12J	40	40c. brown	2·25	4·25
13J		50c. violet	40	7·50
3J/13J Set of 11			£275	£225

DODECANESE ISLANDS 1912

*Dates of issue of Nos. 7, 9 and 10 with the "Rodi" overprint were 4.22, 5.17 and 8.19 respectively.

K. Scarpanto

3K	31	2c. orange-brown	4·75	4·25
4K	37	3c. green	1·40	4·25
5K	38	10c. rose-red	40	4·25
6K	49	15c. slate (90, no wmk) (V)	17·00	8·25
7K	37	15c. slate (104, wmkd) (10.21)	10·00	19·00
8K	49	20c.on 15c. slate (100) (1.1.16)	80	17·00
9K	41	20c. orange (101, no wmk) (6.17)	75·00	85·00
10K		20c. orange (105, wmkd.) (9.21)	27·00	27·00
11K	39	25c. blue	4·50	4·25
12K	40	40c. brown	40	4·25
13K		50c. violet	1·40	7·50
3K/13K Set of 11			£130	£170

L. Simi

3L	31	2c. orange-brown	4·75	4·25
4L	37	3c. green	14·50	4·25
5L	38	10c. rose-red	40	4·25
6L	49	15c. slate (90, no wmk) (V)	28·00	28·00
7L	37	15c. slate (104, wmkd) (10.21)	75·00	75·00
8L	49	20c.on 15c. slate (100) (1.1.16)	5·75	5·75
9L	41	20c. orange (101, no wmk) (6.17)	40·00	60·00
10L		20c. orange (105, wmkd.) (9.21)	38·00	38·00
11L	39	25c. blue	1·90	4·25
12L	40	40c. brown	40	4·25
13L		50c. violet	40	7·50
3L/13L Set of 11			£190	£200

M. Stampalia

3M	31	2c. orange-brown	4·75	4·25
4M	37	3c. green	40	4·25
5M	38	10c. rose-red	40	4·25
6M	49	15c. slate (90, no wmk) (V)	21·00	8·25
7M	37	15c. slate (104, wmkd) (10.21)	6·75	19·00
8M	49	20c.on 15c. slate (100) (1.1.16)	65	12·00
9M	41	20c. orange (101, no wmk) (6.17)	50·00	60·00
10M		20c. orange (105, wmkd.) (9.21)	25·00	27·00
11M	39	25c. blue	55	4·25
12M	40	40c. brown	2·25	4·25
13M		50c. violet	40	7·50
3M/13M Set of 11			£100	£130

1916–24. Nos. 66, 110 and 71 of Italy optd "Rodi".

14	33	20c. orange (1.16)	2·00	4·25
15	39	85c. red-brown (9.22)	40·00	60·00
16	34	1l. brown and green ('24)	2·00	

1 Rhodian Windmill
2 Knight kneeling before the Holy City

(Des F. Di Fausto. Litho (A) by Bestelli & Tuminelli, Milan, (B) by Govt Ptg Wks, Rome)

1929 (19 May)–**32**. King of Italy's Visit to the Aegean Islands T **1**/**2** (and similar types).

A. Without printers' imprint. No wmk. P 11.

17A		5c. claret	3·50	1·10
18A		10c. sepia	3·50	80
19A		20c. scarlet	3·50	30
20A		25c. green	3·50	30
21A		30c. deep blue	3·50	40
22A		50c. chocolate	3·50	40
23A		1l.25, deep blue	3·50	20
24A		5l. claret	3·50	1·10
25A		10l. olive-green	38·00	55·00
17A/25A Set of 9			55·00	55·00

B. With imprint (8.32). Wmk Crown. P 14.

17B		5c. claret	15	85
18B		10c. sepia	15	85
19B		20c. scarlet	15	85
20B		25c. green	15	85
21B		30c. deep blue	15	85
22B		50c. chocolate	15	85
23B		1l.25, deep blue	15	85
24B		5l. claret	15	85
25B		10l. olive-green	1·60	1·75
17B/25B Set of 9			3·00	8·50

Designs: *Vert*—10c. Galley of Knights of St. John, 20, 25c. Knight defending Christianity; 50c., 1l.25, A Knight's tomb. As Type **2**: 30c., 5l.

Although these stamps are inscribed "RODI" they were issued for general use in all the Dodecanese Islands.

Nos. 17B/25B and 124/7 were also used in eastern Crete during its Italian occupation, 1941–43.

XXI Congresso Idrologico (3) ISOLE ITALIANE DELL'EGEO (4)

1930 (25 Sept). Twenty-first Hydrological Congress. Nos 17A/25A optd with T **3**.

26		5c. claret	13·50	11·50
27		10c. sepia	15·00	11·50
28		20c. scarlet	23·00	10·00
29		25c. green	30·00	10·00
30		30c. deep blue	15·00	12·00
31		50c. chocolate	£375	30·00
32		1l.25, deep blue	£300	50·00
33		5l. claret	£160	£250
34		10l. olive-green	£160	£275
26/34 Set of 9			£1000	£600

1930 (20 Oct). Ferrucci issue of Italy (colours changed), optd in capital letters for the individual Islands.

A. CALINO F. LISSO J. RODI
B. CASO G. NISIRO K. SCARPANTO
C. COO H. PATMO L. SIMI
D. CALCHI I. PISCOPI M. STAMPALIA
E. LERO

Same prices for each island

35	114	20c. bright violet (R.)	1·90	3·00
36	115	25c. deep green (R.)	1·90	3·00
37		50c. black (R.)	1·90	5·75
38		1l.25, blue (R.)	1·90	5·75
39	116	5l.+2l. carmine-red (B.)	2·75	10·00
35/39 Set of 5			9·25	25·00

See also Castelrosso Nos 25/9.

1930 (20 Oct). AIR. Ferrucci air stamps of Italy (colours changed) optd with T **4**.

40	117	50c. purple (B)	5·75	11·50
41		1l. deep blue (R)	5·75	11·50
42		5l.+2l. carmine-red (B)	12·00	32·00

1931 CONGRESSO EUCARISTICO ITALIANO
ISOLE ITALIANE DELL'EGEO (5) (6)

1930 (1 Dec). Virgil. Nos. 290/302 of Italy optd as T **5**. Colours changed.

*(a) POSTAGE. As T **118**.*

43		15c. slate-violet (R.)	1·00	5·75
44		20c. chestnut (B.)	1·00	5·75
45		25c. blue-green (R.)	1·00	2·50
46		30c. brown (B.)	1·00	2·50
47		50c. purple (R.)	1·00	2·50
48		75c. carmine-red (B.)	1·00	5·75
49		1l.25, greenish blue (R.)	1·00	8·25
50		5l.+1l.50 purple (R.)	2·40	17·00
51		10l.+2l.50 brown (B.)	2·40	17·00

*(b) AIR. T **119**.*

52		50c. blue-green (B.)	1·40	12·00
53		1l. carmine-red (B.)	1·40	12·00
54		7l.70+1l.30 brown (R.)	3·00	24·00
55		9l.+2l. slate-blue (R.)	3·00	25·00
43/55 Set of 13			19·00	£130

DODECANESE ISLANDS 1931

1931 (16 Sept). *Italian Eucharistic Congress. Nos.* 17A/23A *optd with T* **6**.
56	5c. claret (B.)	4·00	5·75
57	10c. sepia (R.)	4·00	5·75
58	20c. scarlet (B.)	4·00	10·00
	a. Opt inverted	£275	
59	25c. green (R.)	4·00	10·00
60	30c. deep blue (R.)	4·00	10·00
61	50c. chocolate (R.)	30·00	24·00
62	1l.25, deep blue (R.)	23·00	42·00
56/62 *Set of 7*		65·00	95·00

1932 (21 Feb). *T* **121/2** *and similar types of Italy (St Anthony) optd as T* **4**. *Colours changed.*
63	20c. slate-purple (B.)	15·00	9·00
64	25c. green (R.)	15·00	9·00
65	30c. red-brown (B.)	15·00	11·00
66	50c. purple (B.)	15·00	7·50
67	75c. carmine-rose (B.)	15·00	12·50
68	1l.25, light blue (R.)	15·00	14·50
69	5l.+2l.50 orange (B.)	15·00	55·00
63/69 *Set of 7*		95·00	£110

```
  ISOLE        ITALIANE
  DELL'        EGEO
```
(7)

1932 (May–Nov). *Dante. Nos.* 314/32 *of Italy optd as T* **7**. *Colours changed.*

(a) POSTAGE. As T **124**.
70	10c. olive-green	95	2·40
71	15c. violet-slate	95	2·40
72	20c. chestnut	95	2·40
73	25c. green	95	2·40
74	30c. orange-vermilion	95	2·40
75	50c. purple	95	1·00
76	75c. carmine-red	95	3·00
77	1l.25, blue	95	2·40
78	1l.75, sepia	1·10	3·00
79	2l.75, carmine	1·10	3·00
80	5l.+2l. bright violet	1·40	9·25
81	10l.+2l.50 chocolate	1·40	13·50
70/81 *Set of 12*		11·00	42·00

(b) AIR.
82	**125**	50c. carmine	1·00	2·40
83	**126**	1l. green	1·00	2·40
84		3l. purple	1·00	2·75
85		5l. orange-vermilion	1·00	2·75
86	**125**	7l.70+2l. sepia	1·40	6·75
87	**126**	10l.+2l.50 deep blue	1·40	12·00

Inscr "ISOLE ITALIANE DELL'EGEO".
88	**127**	100 l. olive-green and blue (Nov)	15·00	70·00
82/88 *Set of 7*			20·00	90·00

1932 (28 Aug). *Garibaldi issue (T* **128/9** *and similar types) of Italy, optd in capital letters for the individual Islands. Colours changed.*
A.	CALINO	F.	LISSO
B.	CASO	G.	NISIRO
C.	COO	H.	PATMO
D.	CALCHI	I.	PISCOPI
E.	LERO		
		J.	RODI
		K.	SCARPANTO
		L.	SIMI
		M.	STAMPALIA

Same prices for each island
89	10c. sepia (R.)	8·00	12·00
90	20c. lake-brown (B.)	8·00	12·00
91	25c. green (R.)	8·00	12·00
92	30c. slate-blue (B.)	8·00	12·00
93	50c. purple (B.)	8·00	12·00
94	75c. lake (B.)	8·00	12·00
95	1l.25c. deep blue (R.)	8·00	12·00
96	1l.75+25c. sepia (R.)	8·00	12·00
97	2l.55+50c. orange-vermilion (B.)	8·00	12·00
98	5l.+1l. deep violet (R.)	8·00	12·00
89/98 *Set of 10*		70·00	£110

See also Castelrosso Nos. 30/9.

1932 (28 Aug). *AIR. Garibaldi air stamps as T* **130** *optd as T* **4**. *Colours changed.*
99	50c. olive-green (R.)	30·00	55·00
100	80c. lake (B.)	30·00	55·00
101	1l.+25c. deep blue (R.)	30·00	55·00
102	2l.+50c. lake-brown (B.)	30·00	55·00
103	5l.+1l. slate (R.)	30·00	55·00
99/103 *Set of 5*		£140	£250

1932 (28 Aug). *AIR EXPRESS. Garibaldi Air Express stamps as T* **131** *optd as T* **4**. *Colours changed*
E104	2l.25+1l. carmine and blue (B)	38·00	70·00
E105	4l.50+1l.50 grey and yellow (V.)	38·00	70·00

 8 9

(Litho Bestelli & Tuminelli, Milan)

1932 (Oct). *20th Anniv of Italian Occupation of Dodecanese Islands. Wmk Crown. P* 11.
106	**8**	5c. scarlet, black and emerald	5·00	8·25
107		10c. scarlet, black and blue	5·00	5·00
108		20c. scarlet, black and yellow	5·00	5·00
109		25c. scarlet, black and violet	5·00	5·00
110		30c. scarlet, black and rose	5·00	5·00
111	**9**	50c. scarlet, black and pale blue	5·00	5·00
112		1l.25, scarlet, maroon and pale blue	5·00	12·00
113		5l. scarlet, blue and pale blue	15·00	35·00
114		10l. scarlet, green and pale blue	42·00	55·00
115		25l. scarlet, chocolate and pale blue	£275	£600
106/115 *Set of 10*			£325	£650

 10 Airship Graf Zeppelin   11 Wing from the Arms of Francesco Sans

(Des G. Rondini. Photo)

1933 (12 May). *AIR. Wmk Crown. P* 14.
116	**10**	3l. brown	32·00	90·00
117		5l. purple	32·00	£110
118		10l. blue-green	32·00	£180
119		12l. blue	32·00	£225
120		15l. carmine	32·00	£225
121		20l. black	32·00	£225
116/121 *Set of 6*			£170	£950

1933 (20 May). *AIR. Balbo Transatlantic Mass Formation Flight. As T* **135/6** *of Italy, without the pilot's name, optd T* **5** *(smaller) on both left and right sides. Centres in slate-blue.*
122	5l.25+19l.75 scarlet & grn/grn/scar	27·00	75·00
123	5l.25+44l.75 green & scar/scar/grn	27·00	75·00

(Des B. Bramanti. Typo)

1934 (Jan). *AIR. Wmk Crown. P* 14.
124	**11**	50c. black and yellow	20	20
125		80c. black and carmine	3·00	2·75

151

DODECANESE ISLANDS 1934

126	1l. black and turquoise-green		1·75	20
127	5l. black and magenta		5·25	7·25
124/127 Set of 4			9·00	9·50

See note below No 25.

1934 (15 June). *World Cup Football Championship. As Nos. 413/21 of Italy optd "ISOLE ITALIANE DELL'EGEO" as T 5, but smaller. Colours changed.*

(a) POSTAGE.

128	20c. lake-red	40·00	40·00
129	25c. green (R.)	40·00	40·00
130	50c. bright violet (R.)	£140	20·00
131	1l.25, deep blue (R.)	40·00	70·00
132	5l.+2l.50 bright blue (R.)	40·00	£170

(b) AIR.

133	50c. brown (R.)	4·25	25·00
134	75c. carmine-red	4·25	25·00
135	5l.+2l.50 orange-vermilion	12·50	50·00
136	10l.+5l. green (R.)	12·50	70·00
128/136 Set of 9		£300	£450

P **12** Galley and Rose

P **13** Stag and St. Paul's Gate, Rhodes

(Des B. Bramanti. Photo)

1934 (1 July). PARCEL POST. Wmk Crown. P 13½.

		Un pair	Used pair	Used half
P137	P **12** 5c. orange	1·75	1·75	85
P138	10c. scarlet	1·75	1·75	85
P139	20c. green	1·75	1·75	85
P140	25c. bright violet	1·75	1·75	85
P141	50c. deep blue	1·75	1·75	85
P142	60c. black	1·75	1·75	85
P143	P **13** 1l. orange	1·75	1·75	85
P144	2l. scarlet	1·75	1·75	85
P145	3l. green	1·75	1·75	85
P146	4l. bright violet	1·75	1·75	85
P147	10l. deep blue	1·75	1·75	85
P137/147 Set of 11		17·00	17·00	8·50

See note on Parcel Post Stamps below No. PE98 of Italy.

D **14** Badge of the Knights of St. John

D **15** Immortelle

(Des B. Bramanti. Photo)

1934 (1 July). POSTAGE DUE. Wmk Crown. P 14.

D148	D **14**	5c. orange	1·10	1·40
D149		10c. scarlet	1·10	1·40
D150		20c. green	1·10	70
D151		30c. bright violet	1·10	1·00
D152		40c. deep blue	1·10	2·40
D153	D **15**	50c. orange	1·10	70
D154		60c. scarlet	1·10	3·75
D155		1l. green	1·10	3·75
D156		2l. bright violet	1·10	2·40
D148/156 Set of 9			9·00	16·00

1934 (Dec). *Military Medal Centenary As Nos. 424/41 of Italy, optd "ISOLE ITALIANE DELL'EGEO" as T 5, but smaller. Colours changed.*

(a) POSTAGE.

157	10c. slate (R.)	30·00	40·00
158	15c. brown	30·00	40·00
159	20c. orange-vermilion	30·00	40·00
160	25c. green (R.)	30·00	40·00
161	30c. claret	30·00	40·00
162	50c. olive-green	30·00	40·00
163	75c. carmine-red	30·00	40·00
164	1l.25, blue (R.)	30·00	40·00
165	1l.75+1l. bright violet (R.)	19·00	40·00
166	2l.55+2l. lake	19·00	40·00
167	2l.75+2l. chestnut	19·00	40·00
157/167 Set of 11		£275	£400

(b) AIR.

168	25 c. green	38·00	50·00
169	50 c. brown-black (R.)	38·00	50·00
170	75 c. rose-carmine	38·00	50·00
171	80 c. brown	38·00	50·00
172	1l.+50c. olive-green	29·00	50·00
173	2l.+1l. blue (R.)	29·00	50·00
174	3l.+2l. bright violet (R.)	29·00	50·00

(c) AIR EXPRESS.

E175	2l.+1l.25, blue	30·00	48·00
E176	4l.50+2l. green	30·00	48·00
168/E176 Set of 9		£275	£400

16   E **17**   (18)

ISOLE ITALIANE DELL'ECEO

(Des B. Bramanti. Photo)

1935 (Apr). *Holy Year. Wmk Crown. P 14*

177	**16** 5c. orange	8·25	11·50
178	10c. brown	8·25	11·50
179	20c. carmine	8·25	13·50
180	25c. green	8·25	13·50
181	30c. purple	8·25	15·00
182	50c. chestnut	8·25	15·00
183	1l.25 blue	8·25	38·00
177/183 Set of 7		50·00	£110

A 5l. value was prepared but not issued (*Price* £100 *un*).

1935 (6 Dec). *EXPRESS LETTER. Wmk Crown. P 14*

E184	E **17** 1l.25 green	1·75	1·40
E185	2l.50 orange	2·50	3·00

1938 (10 May). *Augustus Bimillenary. As Nos. 506/20 of Italy, optd with T **18**. Colours changed.*

(a) POSTAGE.

186	10c. olive-brown (B.)	2·25	4·50
187	15c. bright violet (R.)	2·25	4·50
188	20c. red-brown (B.)	2·25	4·50
189	25c. grey-green (R.)	2·25	4·50
190	30c. purple (B.)	2·25	4·50
191	50c. deep blue-green (R)	2·25	4·50
192	75c. carmine (B.)	2·25	4·50
193	1l.25, deep blue (R.)	2·25	4·50
194	1l.75+1l. orange (B.)	3·00	10·00
195	2l.55+2l. sepia (R.)	3·00	10·00
186/195 Set of 10		22·00	50·00

(b) AIR.

196	25c. slate-violet (R)	1·75	2·75
197	50c. green (R.)	1·75	2·75
198	80c. blue (R.)	1·75	8·00
199	1l.+1l. purple (B.)	3·00	12·00
200	5l.+1l. scarlet (8.)	4·00	25·00
196/200 Set of 5		11·00	50·00

152

DODECANESE ISLANDS 1938

1938 (20 Aug). *1600th Death Anniv of Giotto (painter)* Nos. 527 and 530 *of Italy optd with T* **18**.
201	1l.25 blue (R.)	95	1·75
202	2l.75+2l. brown (R.)	1·10	6·75

19 Dante House, Rhodes
20 Roman Wolf Statue 
21 Crown and Maltese Cross 
22 Savoia Marchetti S.M.75 over Statues, Rhodes Harbour 

(Des G. Rondini. Photo)

1940 (3 June). *Colonial Exhibition. T* **19/22** *and similar design inscr "TRIENNALE D'OLTREMARE". Wmk Crown. P* 14.

(a) POSTAGE.
203	**20**	5c. brown	30	65
204	**21**	10c. orange	30	65
205	**19**	25c. green	65	1·25
206	**20**	50c. violet	65	1·25
207	**21**	75c. carmine	65	1·25
208	**19**	1l.25 blue	65	1·25
209	**21**	2l.+75c. pink	65	1·25

(b) AIR.
210	**22**	50c. sepia	1·25	2·75
211	–	1l. violet	1·25	2·75
212	**22**	2l.+75c. deep blue	1·25	5·50
213	–	5l.+2l.50. red-brown	85	6·00
203/213 *Set of* 11			4·25	22·00

Design: *Horiz*—1, 5l. Savoia Marchetti S.M.75 airplane and Government House, Rhodes.

(23)
(E 24) 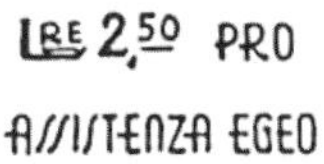

1943 (15 Nov). *Relief Fund.*

(a) POSTAGE. Nos. 17B/24B *surch with premium as T* **23**.
214	5c.+5c. claret	70	70
215	10c.+10c. sepia	70	70
216	20c.+20c. scarlet	70	70
217	25c.+25c. green	70	70
218	30c.+30c. deep blue (R.)	1·40	1·10
219	50c.+50c. chocolate	1·40	1·40
220	1l.25+1l.25 deep blue (R.)	1·75	1·75
221	5l.+5l. claret	70·00	70·00
214/221 *Set of* 8		70·00	70·00

(b) EXPRESS Surch with premium as Type E **24**.
E222	E **17**	1l.25+1l.25 green (R.)	35·00	20·00
E223		2l.50+2l.50 orange (R.)	40·00	27·00

(25)
(E 26) 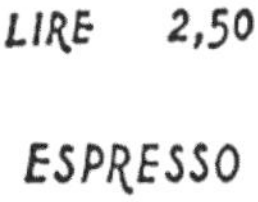

1944 (16 July). *War Victims' Relief. Nos.* 17/20B, 22/23B *surch with premium as T* **25**.
224	5c.+3l. claret	1·40	2·40
225	10c.+3l. sepia (R.)	1·40	2·40
226	20c.+3l. scarlet	1·40	2·40
227	25c.+3l. green (R.)	1·40	2·40
228	50c.+3l. chocolate (R.)	1·40	2·40
229	1l.25+5l. deep blue (R.)	21·00	25·00
224/229 *Set of* 6		25·00	35·00

1944. EXPRESS LETTER. *Nos.* 19/20B *surch as Type* E **26**.
E230	1l.25 on 25c. green	40	1·25
E231	2l.50 on 20c. scarlet	40	1·25

(27)
(28) 

1944 (11 Oct). *AIR. War Victims' Relief. Surch with premium as T* **27**, *in silver*.
232	**11**	50c. + 2l. black and yellow	6·75	2·50
233		80c. + 2l. black and carmine	8·25	5·00
234		1l. + 2l. black and turquoise-green	10·00	5·75
235		5l. + 2l. black and magenta	50·00	55·00
232/235 *Set of* 4			65·00	60·00

1945 (18 Feb). *Red Cross Fund. Nos.* 24B/25B *surch with premium as T* **28**.
236	+10on 5l. claret (R.)	6·75	10·00
237	+10on 10l. olive-green (R.)	6·75	10·00

In October 1944 the Dodecanese Islands were occupied by the British and Great Britain stamps overprinted "M.E.F." were used (see British Occupation of Former Italian Colonies in Part 1 (*British Commonwealth*) of this catalogue) until 31 March 1947 when they were transferred to Greek administration.

The islands are now known as Kalimnos, Kasos, Kos, Khalki, Lems, Lipsoi, Nisiros, Patmos, Tilos (Piskopi), Rhodes (Rodos), Karpathos, Simi and Astipalaia.

153

FIUME 1918

Fiume

1918. 100 Filler = 1 Krone

1919. 100 Centesimi = 1 Corona

1920. 100 Centesimi = 1 Lira

ALLIED OCCUPATION
17 November 1918–12 September 1919

The Hungarian port of Fiume (now known as Rijeka, in Croatia) was occupied by Allied troops after the First World War pending determination of its future.

FIUME
(1)

1918 (3 Dec)–**19**. Stamps of Hungary. 1913–18, optd as T **1** at Fiume by Kirchofer & Cia.

(a) Harvesters and Parliament.

1	18	2f. yellow-brown	2·50	1·25
2		3f. dull claret	2·50	1·25
3		5f. green	2·50	1·25
4		6f. blue-green	2·50	1·25
5		10f. rose-red	35·00	16·00
6	17	10f. rose-red (white figures)	50·00	24·00
7	18	15f. violet	2·50	1·25
8	17	15f. violet (white figures)	22·00	16·00
9	18	20f. grey-brown	2·50	1·25
10		25f. blue	1·60	1·50
11		35f. brown	4·50	2·50
12		40f. olive-green	23·00	13·00
13	19	50f. dull purple	3·25	1·90
14		75f. turquoise-blue	7·25	2·50
15		80f. yellow-green	7·25	2·50
16		1k. lake	19·00	5·75
17		2k. bistre-brown	3·25	1·90
18		3k. grey and dull violet	22·00	9·50
19		5k. pale brown and brown	50·00	13·00
20		10k. magenta and chocolate	£190	£140

(b) Charles and Zita.

21	27	10f. rose	1·90	1·60
22		20f. deep brown	1·25	1·25
23	28	40f. olive-green	14·50	5·00

(c) War Charity stamps.

24	20	10 + 2f. carmine	3·25	2·25
25	21	15 + 2f. deep violet	3·25	2·25
26	22	40 + 2f. lake	5·00	2·25

(d) Newspaper stamp.

27	N 9	(2f.) orange	2·40	95

(e) Express letter stamp.

28	E 18	2f. olive and red	2·40	95

See note below No. 31.

1918 (Dec). POSTAGE DUE. Postage Due stamps of Hungary optd as T**1**.

(a) On 1914 issue.

D29	D 9	6f. black and green	£225	85·00
D30		12f. black and green	£350	£140
D31		50f. black and green	70·00	55·00

(b) On 1915–18 issue.

D32	D 9	1f. red and green	80·00	70·00
D33		2f. red and green	50	40
D34		5f. red and green	3·25	3·25
D35		6f. red and green	50	40
D36		10f. red and green	6·40	1·90
D37		12f. red and green	65	50
D38		15f. red and green	14·50	13·00
D39		20f. red and green	65	50
D40		30f. red and green	14·50	11·00

Genuine overprints are in the second version of Type **1** with smudged letters and heavier impression (see note after No. 31). All values exist both overprinted by machine and handstamped.

1919 (1 Jan). Stamps of Hungary optd as T **1**, and surch "FRANCO" and new value.

(a) Savings Bank stamp (29 Jan).

29	B 17	15on 10f. dull purple	9·50	6·50

(b) Postage Due stamps (19 Jan)

30	D 9	45on 6f. red and green	6·50	6·50
31		45on 20f. red and green	16·00	6·50

With the exception of Nos. 5, 6, 20, D29, D32, D38 and D40 the prices for all the above are for stamps overprinted by machine. Nos. 5 (only with overprint inverted) and 20 exist machine-printed but are very rare but No. 6 does not exist thus There are two versions of the machine overprint Type **1**, one with the letters clear and lightly inked and the other with smudged letters and a heavier impression.

Six different types of handstamp have been used on these stamps, all with serifed letters, and in addition No. 9 exists with a bold sans-serif handstamp 8 mm long.

2 Liberty **3** Clock Tower over Market in Fiume **4**

5 Port of Fiume

(Des Rubinich. Litho Kirchofer & Cia, for the Italian National Council, Fiume)

1919 (28 Jan–Apr). Inscr "FIUME". P 11½.

I. *First printings, in sheets of* 70

(a) Thin toned paper, yellow shiny gum (Jan–Feb)

(b) Thin transparent paper, thin whitish gum (March)

32	2	2c. light blue (b)	50	50
33		3c. deep grey-brown (b)	50	50
34		5c. green (b)	50	50
35		5c. green (b)	50	50
36	3	10c. rose-red (a)	40	40
37		15c. reddish violet (a)	14·00	18·00
38		15c. violet (b)	50	50
39		20c. emerald (a)	1·25	50
40	4	25c. blue (a)	1·60	2·50
41		25c. blue (b)	1·10	20
43		40c. reddish brown (b)	80	80
44		45c. orange (a)	80	80
45		45c. orange (b)	80	95
46	5	60c. carmine-lake (c)	1·00	70
47		1cor. dull orange (a)	2·50	80
48		2cor. greenish blue (b)	2·50	1·10
49		3cor. red-orange (b)	3·25	1·25
50		5cor. chocolate (b)	16·00	11·50
51		10cor. olive-green (a)	13·00	32·00

II. *Second printing, in sheets of* 100. *Medium white paper, yellow or white gum (Apr).*

52	2	2c. light blue	50	50
53		3c. deep grey-brown	50	50
54		5c. green	65	50
56	3	10c. vermilion	22·00	14·50
57		15c. reddish violet	50	50
58		20c. emerald	60·00	65·00
59	4	25c. dull ultramarine	1·25	50
60	5	30c. blue-violet	80	50

154

FIUME   1919

61	**4**	40c. reddish brown	1·60	1·25
62		45c. bright orange	1·10	80
63	**5**	50c. yellow-green	80	50
64		60c. carmine-lake	80	50
65		1cor. orange-brown	1·10	50
66		2cor. greenish blue	2·50	80
67		3cor. orange-red	2·50	1·10
68		5cor. chocolate	3·25	1·25
69		10cor. dull olive-green	50·00	32·00
70		10cor. dull olive-green	55·00	28·00

See also Nos. 83/90.

6 Statue of Romulus, Remus and Wolf

7 13th-century Venetian War Galley

8 Piazza of St. Mark, Venice

D 9

(Des L. Meticovitz. Litho)

1919 (18 May). *Students' Education Fund* 200th *Day of Peace*. P 11½.

71	**6**	5c.+ 5l. green	8·75	5·00
72		10c.+ 5l. carmine	8·75	5·00
73		15c.+ 5l. grey	8·75	5·00
74		20c.+ 5l. orange	8·75	5·00
75	**7**	45c.+ 5l. pale olive	8·75	5·00
76		60c.+ 5l. carmine	8·75	5·00
77		80c.+ 5l. pale violet	8·75	5·00
78		1cor.+ 5l. slate	8·75	5·00
79	**8**	2cor.+ 5l. red-brown	8·75	5·00
80		3cor.+ 5l. grey-brown	8·75	5·00
81		5cor.+ 5l. yellow-brown	8·75	5·00
82		10cor.+ 5l. slate-violet	8·75	5·00

71/82 Set of 12 ... 95·00 55·00

All are overprinted faintly on the back "POSTA DI FIUME" three times, in black.

(Litho Zanardini & Co., Trieste)

1919 (28 July). T **2** to **5** *but inscr* "POSTA FIUME". P 11½.

83	**2**	5c. yellow-green	65	50
84	**3**	10c. rose	65	50
85	**5**	30c. violet	3·75	1·40
86	**4**	40c. brown	95	1·10
87		45c. orange	3·75	1·90
88	**5**	50c. yellow-green	3·75	2·25
89		60c. lake	3·75	2·25
90		10cor. olive	3·50	6·50

(Litho Zanardini & Co., Trieste)

1919 (28 July). *POSTAGE DUE*. P 11½.

D91	D **9**	2c. brown	1·10	95
D92		5c. brown	1·40	95

N 9A Trieste ptg

N 9

N 9B Milan ptg

(I. Litho Zanardini & Co., Trieste. II. Typo Bertieri and Vanzetti, Milan)

1919 (July–Sept). *NEWSPAPER*. P 11½.

N91	N **9**	2c. yellow-brown (**N9A**)	4·75	6·50
N92		2c. yellow-brown (**N9B**) (12 Sept)	4·75	6·50

No. N91 is on thinner paper than No. N92.
There are several other differences between the two types, as well as the illustrated figure of value. On N91 the legs of the eagle are not as clearly visible and the front curve of the "S" in "POSTA" is rounded whereas on N92 it is straight.

REGIME OF D'ANNUNZIO

12 September 1919–24 December 1920

On 12 September 1919 the Italian poet Gabriele d'Annunzio and some 300 volunteers seized Fiume, and on 8 September 1920 proclaimed it as the Italian Regency of the Carnaro (the present Kvarner Gulf). By the Treaty of Rapallo, between Italy and Yugoslavia, 24 November 1920, the Free State of Fiume was established, and on 24 December the town was occupied by Italian forces and D'Annunzio left.

9 Dr. Antonio Grossich

(10)

(Des L. Meticovitz. Litho)

1919 (20 Sept). *Dr. Grossich Foundation*. P 11½.
91 **9** 25c.(+2 cor.) blue ... 1·60 1·60
No. 91 is overprinted on the back as Nos. 71/82.

1919 (10 Oct)–**20**. *Surch as T* **10**.

(a) Inscr "FIUME".
92	**3**	5on 20c. emerald (58) (6.3.20)	30	30
		a. On No. 39	16·00	16·00
93	**4**	10on 45c. bright orange (62) (10.10.19)	30	35
		a. Imperf between (pair)	25·00	25·00
		b. On No. 44	16·00	16·00
		c. On No. 45	£190	£190
94		25on 50c. yellow-green (6.3.20)	9·50	14·50
95	**5**	55on 1cor. orange-brown (65) (24.12.19)	19·00	14·50
		a. On No. 47	£700	£700
96		55on 2cor. greenish blue (66) (24.12.19)	3·25	4·75
		a. On No. 48	£225	£225
97		55on 3cor. orange-red (67) (24.12.19)	3·25	3·75
		a. On No. 49	£160	£160
98		55on 5cor. chocolate (68) (24.12.19)	3·25	3·75
		a. On No. 50	£100	£160

(b) Inscr "POSTA FIUME".
99	**4**	5on 25c. blue (10.10.19)	35	50
100	**5**	15on 30c. violet (6.3.20)	35	50
101	**4**	15on 45c. orange (10.10.19)	35	50

155

FIUME   1919

102	**5**	15on 60c. lake (6.3.20)		50	50
103		25on 50c. yellow-green (6.3.20)		50	50
104		55on 10cor. olive (24.12.19)		14·50	13·00

Valore globale **Cent. 20** (11)   Valore globale **Cent. 60** (12)   **Valore globale Cent. 45** (13)

T **13** differs from T **12** in that the letters are thicker and the surcharge is heavier.

1919 (3 Dec)–**20**. *(a) Surch as T **11** or **12** (on T 7)*.

105	**6**	5c.on 5c. green		60	60
106		10c.on 10c. carmine		60	60
107		15c.on 15c. grey		60	60
108		20c.on 20c. orange		60	60
109	**7**	45c.on 45c. pale olive		80	80
110		60c.on 60c. rose-carmine		80	80
111		80c.on 80c. pale violet		1·10	1·10
112		1cor.on 1cor. slate		1·10	1·10
113	**8**	2cor.on 2cor. red-brown		1·10	1·10
114		3cor.on 3cor. grey-brown		2·50	2·50
115		5cor.on 5cor. yellow-brown		3·25	3·25

*(b) Surch with T **13** (5.4.20)*.

116	**7**	45c.on 45c. pale olive		90·00	70·00

Valore globale **Cent. 25** (14)   Valore globale **Cent. 80** (15)

1920 (5 Feb). *Surch as T **14** or **15** (on T 7)*.

118	**6**	5c.on 5c. green		30	30
119		10c.on 10c. carmine		30	30
120		15c.on 15c. grey		30	30
121		20c.on 20c. orange		30	30
122	**9**	25c.on 25c. blue		30	35
123	**7**	45c.on 45c. pale olive		50	50
124		60c.on 60c. carmine		50	50
125		80c.on 80c. pale violet		65	65
126		1cor.on 1cor. slate		50	50
127	**8**	2cor.on 2cor. red-brown		9·50	8·00
128		3cor.on 3cor. grey-brown		19·00	8·00
129		5cor.on 5cor. yellow-brown		11·00	24·00
130		10cor.on 10cor. slate-violet		1·10	1·10
118/130 *Set of 13*				40·00	40·00

The above surcharges were applied to cancel the charity premium.

16 Gabriele d'Annunzio

E **17**

(Des G. Marussig. Typo Bertieri and Vanzetti, Milan)

1920 (12 Sept). *New Currency. Background in ochre. P 11½*.

131	**16**	5c. bright green		50	50
132		10c. carmine		50	50
133		15c. slate		50	50
134		20c. orange		60	60
135		25c. indigo		80	80
136		30c. red-brown		90	90
137		45c. drab		1·40	1·40
138		50c. lilac		1·40	1·40
139		55c. yellow-ochre		1·40	1·40
140		1l. black		8·00	11·00
141		2l. deep claret		8·00	11·00
142		3l. myrtle-green		8·00	11·00

143		5l. bistre-brown		40·00	20·00
144		10l. slate-lilac		8·00	11·50
131/144 *Set of 14*				72·00	65·00

(Typo Zanardini & Co., Trieste)

1920 (12 Sept). *EXPRESS LETTER. P 11½*.

E145	E **17**	30c. blue-green		16·00	12·00
E146		50c. carmine		16·00	12·00

The 30c. in carmine and 50c. in blue-green are proofs.

N **17**

M **17** Severing the Gordian Knot

1920 (12 Sept). *NEWSPAPER. Litho. P 11½*.

N145	N **17**	1c. yellow-green		1·60	95

(Des A. de Carolis from sketches by D'Annunzio. Typo Danesi, Rome)

1920 (12 Sept). *MILITARY POST First Anniv of Capture of Frame by d'Annunzio's "legionaries" Type M **17** (and other types similarly inscribed). P 11½*.

M145	5c. green		35·00	16·00
M146	10c. carmine		21·00	13·00
M147	20c. bistre		35·00	13·00
M148	25c. blue		65·00	65·00
M145/148 *Set of 4*			£140	95·00

Designs:—10c. Arms of Fiume (blood pouring from a vase); 20c. "Crown of Thorns"; 25c. Daggers raised in clenched fists. These stamps were available for franking the correspondence of the "legionaries" on the day of issue only. Stamps of similar design inscribed "FIUME D'ITALIA" were not issued.

Reggenza Italiana del Carnaro

15 (17)

30 30 ESPRESSO (E **18**)

1920 (20 Nov). *(a) POSTAGE. Nos. M145/8 optd or surch as in T **17***.

146	1on 5c. green		95	40
147	2on 25c. blue (R.)		40	40
148	5c. green		13·00	1·10
149	10c. carmine		13·00	1·10
150	15on 10c. carmine		95	50
151	15on 20c. bistre		40	50
152	15on 25c. blue (R.)		50	65
153	20c. bistre		65	65
154	25c. blue (R.)		65	65
	a. Opt inverted		11·00	11·00
	b. Optd in black		90·00	90·00
155	25on 10c. carmine		1·60	1·90
156	50on 20c. bistre		3·50	1·25
157	55on 5c. green		13·00	2·25
158	1l.on 10c. carmine		21·00	13·00
159	1l.on 25c. blue (R.)		50·00	50·00
160	2l.on 5c. green		21·00	13·00
161	5l.on 10c. carmine		85·00	90·00

FIUME 1920

162 10l.on 20c. bistre ("10 LIRE 10" 22 mm) . . . £375 £275
    a. "10 LIRE 10" 20½ mm . . . £950 £550

(b) EXPRESS LETTER Nos. M147 and M145 optd as T 17 and additionally surch as Type E 18.
E163 30c.on 20c. bistre . . . 60·00 60·00
E164 50c.on 5c. green . . . 85·00 48·00

Nos. 154b. 158/62 and E163/4 have the "snake and stars" badge of the *Arditi* printed on the back over the gum.

No. 154b comes only from sheets overprinted for Arbe and Veglia (see note below No 6 of Arbe)

The price for No. 159 is for the unofficial printing in which "1 LIRA 1" was surcharged on No. 154. In the first, official, printing of 500 examples the complete overprint and value was applied in one operation to No M148 (*Price*. £250 *un* or £325 *used*).

FREE STATE

24 December 1920–22 February 1924

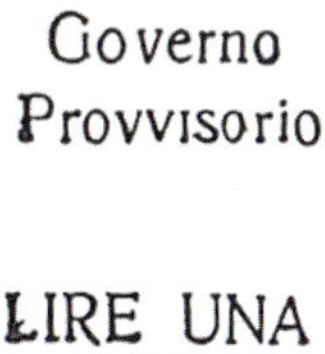

Governo Provvisorio

LIRE UNA
(18)

1921 (2 Feb). *Provisional Government Optd or surch as in T* **18**.

(a) POSTAGE. Background in ochre.

163	**16**	5c. bright green		30	30
164		10c. carmine		30	30
165		15c. slate		30	40
166		20c. orange		1·10	80
167		25c. indigo		1·10	80
168		30c. red-brown		1·10	80
169		45c. drab		65	65
170		50c. lilac		1·25	95
171		55c. yellow-ochre		1·10	75
172		1l. black		70·00	65·00
173		1l.on 30c. red-brown		65	65
174		2l. deep claret		16·00	14·50
175		3l. myrtle-green		16·00	14·50
176		5l. bistre-brown		16·00	14·50
177		10l. slate-lilac		16·00	14·50

(b) EXPRESS LETTER

E178	E **17**	30c. blue-green		6·50	8·00
E179		50c. carmine		9·50	8·00
163/E179 *Set of* 17				80·00	70·00

Segnatasse

Segnatasse

L. 0.05 (D **19**) L. 0.40 (D **20**)

1921 (21 Mar). *POSTAGE DUE. Surch as Types D* **19** *or D* **20**.

(a) On Nos. 105/115.

D178	**6**	2c.on 15c. grey		25·00	38·00
D179		4c.on 10c. carmine		£325	£225
D180		6c.on 20c. orange		95·00	95·00
D181		10c.on 20c. orange		6·50	7·25
D182	**7**	20c.on 45c. pale olive		2·25	2·50
D183		30c.on 1cor. slate		1·25	1·60
D184		40c.on 80c. pale violet		65	80
D185		50c.on 60c. carmine		65	80

D186		60c.on 45c. pale olive		3·25	3·75
D187	**8**	1l.on 2cor. red-brown		1·60	1·90

(b) On No. 116.

D188	**7**	20c.on 45c. pale olive		1·10	1·60
D189		60c.on 45c. pale olive		1·10	1·60
D190		80c.on 45c. pale olive		1·10	1·60

(c) On Nos. 118/30

D191	**6**	2c.on 15c. grey		80	80
D192		4c.on 10c. carmine		65	55
D193	**9**	5c.on 25c. blue		65	55
D194	**6**	6c.on 20c. orange		65	55
D195		10c.on 20c. orange		95	95
D196	**7**	20c.on 45c. pale olive		£225	£180
D197		30c.on 1cor. slate		8·00	4·75
D198	**7**	40c.on 80c. pale violet		£325	£180
D199		50c.on 60c. rose-carmine		13·00	11·00
D200		60c.on 45c. pale olive		£500	£325
D201	**8**	1l.on 2cor. red-brown		1·60	1·90

24 - IV - 1921
Costituente Fiumana
(19)

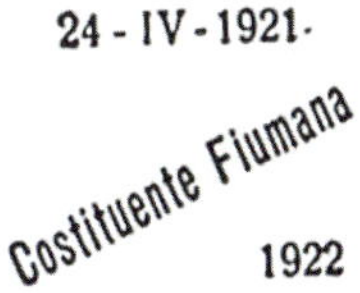

24 - IV - 1921·
Costituente Fiumana
1922
(20)

1921 (24 Apr). *New Constitution. Optd with T* **19** *(and "L" over "Cor." in high values).*

178	**6**	5c. green		1·60	1·60
179		10c. carmine		1·60	1·60
180		15c. grey		1·60	1·60
181		20c. orange		1·60	1·60
182	**7**	45c. pale olive		4·50	3·50
183		60c. carmine		4·50	3·50
184		80c. pale violet		5·75	4·75
185		1l.on 1cor. slate		3·75	6·50
186	**8**	2l.on 2cor. red-brown		35·00	95
187		3l.on 3cor. grey-brown		35·00	35·00
188		5l.on 5cor. yellow-brown		35·00	1·60
189		10l.on 10cor. slate-violet		42·00	40·00

1922 (12 Apr). *Optd as T* **20** *(and "L" over "Cor." in high values).*

190	**6**	5c. green		3·00	1·25
191		10c. carmine		30	30
192		15c. grey		10·00	4·50
193		20c. orange		95	95
194	**7**	45c. pale olive		7·75	4·75
195		60c. carmine		65	1·40
196		80c. pale violet		65	1·40
197		1l.on 1cor. slate		95	95
198	**8**	2l.on 2cor. red-brown		10·00	6·50
199		3l.on 3cor. grey-brown		95	1·25
200		5l.on 5cor. yellow-brown		65	1·25

21 Medieval Ship    E 25 Fiume in 16th Century

(Des G. Marussig. Typo Bertieri & Vanzetti, Milan)

1923 (Mar). *Pale buff background. P* 11½.

201		5c. green		30	35
202		10c. mauve		30	30
203		15c. brown		30	30
204		20c. vermilion		30	30
205		25c. grey		30	30
206		30c. myrtle-green		30	30
207		50c. pale blue		30	30
208		60c. rose		50	1·10

FIUME Arbe and Veglia 1923

209	1l. indigo	50	1·40
210	2l. chocolate	32·00	8·00
211	3l. olive-bistre	22·00	16·00
212	5l. yellow-brown	22·00	19·00

Designs:—5, 10, 15c. Type **21**; 20, 25, 30c. Roman arch: 50, 60c., 1l., St. Vitus; 2, 3, 5l. Tarsatic column.

(Des G. Maruscig. Typo)

1923 (23 Mar). *EXPRESS LETTER. Pale buff background. P* 11.

E213	E **25**	60c. carmine	12·00	7·25
E214		2l. blue	12·00	8·75

INCORPORATED IN ITALY

22 February 1924

By a treaty signed in Rome on 28 January 1924, Fiume was incorporated in Italy as from 22 February and the adjoining port of Susak, which had been in the Free State, was incorporated in Yugoslavia.

(25)   (E 26)

1924 (22 Feb). *Nos. 201/12 optd with T* **25**.

213	5c. green	65	3·00
214	10c. mauve	65	3·00
215	15c. brown	80	3·00
216	20c. vermilion	80	3·00
217	25c. grey	80	3·00
218	30c. myrtle-green	80	3·00
219	50c. pale blue	80	3·00
220	60c. rose	80	3·00
221	1l. indigo	80	3·00
222	2l. chocolate	2·10	7·00
223	3l. olive-bistre	3·25	8·25
224	5l. yellow-brown	3·25	8·25
213/224	*Set* of 12	14·00	45·00

1924 (22 Feb). *EXPRESS LETTER. Optd with Type E* **26**.

E225	E **25**	60c. carmine	80	4·00
E226		2l. blue	80	4·00

22 Febb 1924   22 Febbraio 1924
(26)   (E 27)

1924 (1 Mar). *Annexation. Nos. 201/12 optd with T* **26**.

225	5c. green	30	1·25
226	10c. mauve	30	1·25
227	15c. brown	30	1·25
228	20c. vermilion	30	1·25
229	25c. grey	30	1·25
230	30c. myrtle-green	30	1·25
231	50c. pale blue	30	1·25
232	60c. rose	30	1·25
233	1l. indigo	30	1·25
234	2l. chocolate	65	2·50
235	3l. olive-bistre	65	2·50
236	5l. yellow-brown	65	2·50
225/236	*Set* of 12	4·00	16·00

1924 (1 Mar). *EXPRESS LETTER. Optd with Type E* **27**.

E237	E **25**	60c. carmine	80	3·25
E238		2l. blue	80	3·25

In 1941 Italy re-occupied Susak and the surrounding area. Occupation issues are listed in Part 3 (*Balkans*) of this catalogue.

In 1945 the area was occupied by Yugoslav partisans (see VENEZIA GIULIA AND ISTRIA). In 1947 Fiume became part of Yugoslavia.

ARBE AND VEGLIA

During the period of D'Annunzio's Italian Regency of the Carnaro, separate issues were made for the islands of Arbe (now Rab) and Veglia (now Krk).

ARBE

1920 (Nov). *Nos. 148, etc, of Fiume optd "ARBE".*

A. Large letters measuring 15 mm. (18 Nov)

1A	5c. green	£150	95·00
2A	10c. carmine	£150	95·00
3A	20c. bistre	£150	95·00
4A	25c. blue	£400	95·00

B. Small letters measuring 12 mm. (28 Nov)

1B	5c. green	4·50	5·25
2B	10c. carmine	10·50	11·50
3B	20c. bistre	24·00	18·00
4B	25c. blue	14·50	18·00
5	50on 20c. bistre	26·00	18·00
6	55on 5c. green	26·00	18·00

Nos 1/E8 of Arbe and 1/E8 of Veglia were additionally overprinted on Nos 148/9, 153, 154b, 156/7 and E163/4 of Fiume. In each instance the first horizontal row of the sheet received no further overprint, the 2nd and 3rd rows the "ARBE" overprint and the 4th and 5th rows "VEGLIA". This arrangement results in vertical *se-tenant* pairs of Fiume and Arbe, and of Arbe and Veglia.

1920 (28 Nov). *EXPRESS LETTER. Nos. E163/4 of Fiume optd "ARBE" with small letters*

E7	30c.on 20c. bistre	95·00	55·00
E8	50on 5c. green	95·00	55·00

See note below No. 6.

VEGLIA

1920 (Nov). *Nos. 148, etc., of Fiume optd "VEGLIA".*

A. Large letters measuring 18 mm. (18 Nov)

1A	5c. green	£150	95·00
2A	10c. carmine	£150	95·00
3A	20c. bistre	£150	95·00
4A	25c. blue	£400	£140

B. Small letters measuring 15 mm. (28 Nov)

1B	5c. green	4·50	5·25
2B	10c. carmine	10·50	11·50
3B	20c. bistre	24·00	18·00
4B	25c. blue	14·50	18·00
5	50on 20c. bistre	26·00	18·00
6	55on 5c. green	26·00	18·00

See note below No. 6 of Arbe.

1920 (29 Nov). *EXPRESS LETTER. Nos. E163/4 of Fiume optd "VEGLIA" with small letters.*

E7	30c.on 20c. bistre	95·00	55·00
E8	50on 5c. green	95·00	55·00

See note below No. 6 of Arbe.

# TRIESTE 1947

Trieste

1947 (1 Oct)–**48**. *PARCEL POST. Contemporary Parcel Post stamps optd with Type P* **4** *on each half of the stamp.*

			Un pair	Used pair	Used half
P32	P **201**	1l. yellow-brown	30	40	15
P33		2l. turquoise-blue	40	50	15
P34		3l. red-orange	40	45	15
P35		4l. grey	45	65	15
P36		5l. bright purple (1.3.48)	2·40	4·25	60
P37		10l. violet	2·50	3·75	20
P38		20l. brown-purple	3·75	5·50	20
P39		50l. vermilion	4·75	8·50	20
P40		100l. blue	11·00	17·00	30
P41		200l. deep green (1.3.48)	£225	£275	3·75
P42		300l. deep claret	£170	£150	1·70
P43		500l. deep brown (1.3.48)	65·00	85·00	1·00
P32/43	Set of 12		£375	£500	11·00

See note on Parcel Post Stamps below No. PE98 of Italy.

A Free Territory of Trieste was created by the Treaty of Paris, 10 February 1947. It consisted of two zones: Zone A, including the city of Trieste and a coastal strip to the west, administered by a joint British and United States Military Government; and Zone B, including the villages of Koper, Pirran and Novigrad to the south of Trieste, administered by a Yugoslav Military Government

ZONE A
ALLIED MILITARY GOVERNMENT
100.Centesimi = 1 Lira
From 1945 to 1947 the stamps of Venezia Giulia (Italian stamps overprinted "A M.G. V.G.") were used in this area.

Stamps of Italy overprinted

A.M.G. F.T.T. (1)   **A.M.G. F.T.T.** (2)   **A.M.G. F.T.T.** (3)

1947 (1 Oct)–**48**. *Stamps of 1945–48 (T **192**/7) variously optd as T* **1** *to* **3**.

1	**1**	25c. greenish blue	15	70
2		50c. violet	15	70
3		1l. green	15	15
4		2l. purple-brown	15	15
5		3l. scarlet	15	15
6		4l. vermilion	15	15
7		5l. dull blue	15	15
8		6l. bluish violet	15	15
9		8l. blue-green (1.3.48)	1·80	1·90
10		10l. grey	15	15
11		10l. vermilion (1.3.48)	6·50	15
12		15l. pale blue	45	15
13		20l. purple	1·00	15
14	**2**	25l. deep green	2·30	2·20
15	**1**	30l. bright blue (1.3.48)	£120	3·25
16	**2**	50l. brown-purple	3·75	2·00
17	**3**	100l. carmine	24·00	10·00
1/17	Set of 17		£140	20·00

A.M.G. F.T.T. (3a)   **A.M.G. F.T.T.** (P 4)

1947 (1 Oct)–**48**. *AIR. Air stamps of 1945–48 optd with T* **3** *(1l. to 50l.) or T* **3a** *(others).*

18	**198**	1l. greenish slate	35	20
19	**199**	2l. dull ultramarine	35	20
20		5l. deep green	1·70	1·10
21	**198**	10l. carmine-red	2·00	1·10
22	**199**	25l. yellow-brown	4·25	2·00
23	**198**	50l. reddish violet	34·00	3·50
24	**204**	100l. deep bluish green (1.3.48)	80·00	3·00
25		300l. magenta (1.3.48)	8·00	10·00
26		500l. dull ultramarine (1.3.48)	12·00	14·00
27		1000l. purple-brown (24.9.48)	£110	£120
18/27	Set of 10		£225	£140

1947 (1 Oct)–**48**. *EXPRESS LETTER. Nos. E681/3 and E685 optd with T* **3**.

E28	E **201**	15l. lake	20	25
E29	E **200**	25l. red-orange (1.3.48)	28·00	6·00
E30		30l. violet	45	45
E31	E **201**	60l. carmine (1.3.48)	22·00	10·00
E28/31	Set of 4		45·00	15·00

1947 (1 Oct)–**49**. *CONCESSIONAL LETTER POST Optd with T* **1**. W **191**. P 14.

CL44	–	1l. brown (No. CL649)	15	55
CL45	CL **201**	8l. rose-red (29.10.47)	6·75	1·20
CL46	CL **220**	15l. violet (30.7.49)	35·00	5·50

1947 (1 Oct). *POSTAGE DUE Optd with T* **1**. W **191**. P. 14.

D44	D **192**	1l. orange	40	35
D45		5l. violet	3·50	35
		a. No wmk	£2500	£110
D46		10l. blue	5·75	1·20
D47		20l. carmine	17·00	1·40
D44/47	Set of 4		24·00	3·00

1947 (1 Oct)–**49**. *POSTAGE DUE Optd with T* **1**.

D48	D **201**	1l. red-orange (15.4.49)	30	35
D49		2l. blue-green	30	30
D50		3l. carmine (24.1.49)	90	3·25
D51		4l. sepia (24.1.49)	4·75	9·25
D52		5l. violet (15.4.49)	65·00	11·50
D53		6l. ultramarine (24.1.49)	16·00	18·00
D54		8l. mauve (24.1.49)	29·00	38·00
D55		10l. blue (15.4.49)	80·00	11·00
D56		12l. brown (24.1.49)	14·50	17·00
D57		20l. bright purple (15.4.49)	13·00	3·25
D58		50l. turquoise-green	1·20	45
D48/58	Set of 11		£200	£100

1947 (19 Nov). *AIR. 50th Anniv of Radio. Nos. 688/93 optd with T* 2.

59	**202**	6l. bluish violet	1·10	1·40
60	**203**	10l. deep carmine-red	1·10	1·40
61	–	20l. reddish orange	7·75	3·25
62	**202**	25l. turquoise-blue	1·20	1·50
63	**203**	35l. deep dull blue	1·20	1·90
64	–	50l. bright purple	7·00	2·20
59/64	Set of 6		17·00	10·50

A.M.G.-F.T.T. (4)   **A.M.G. F.T.T. 1948 TRIESTE** (5)   **A.M.G. F.T.T. 1948 TRIESTE** (5a)

1948 (1 July). *Centenary of 1848 Revolution. Nos. 706/17 optd with T* **4**.

65		3l. sepia	20	10
66		4l. bright purple	20	10
67		5l. blue	25	10
68		6l. green	30	10
69		8l. chocolate	20	10
70		10l. rose-red	25	10
71		12l. grey-green	1·40	80
72		15l. black	10·50	6·00
73		20l. carmine	14·50	6·25
74		30l. blue	1·00	1·30

159

TRIESTE   1948

75	50l. violet	7·00	11·50
76	100l. slate-blue	25·00	29·00
65/76	Set of 12	55·00	50·00

1948 (8 Sept). *Trieste Philatelic Congress.*
(a) POSTAGE Nos 661, 663 and 667 optd with T 5.

77	**192**	8l. blue-green (R.)	15	10
78	**193**	10l. vermilion (R.)	15	10
79	**194**	30l. bright blue (R.)	1·30	80

(b) AIR Nos 674, 676 and 678 optd with T 5a.

80	**198**	10l. carmine	25	10
81	**199**	25l. brown	45	50
82	**198**	50l. violet	45	50
77/82	Set of 6		2·50	1·90

1948 (24 Sept). *EXPRESS LETTER Centenary of 1848 Revolution No.* E718 *optd with T 4.*

E83	E **209**	35l. violet	1·90	1·70

1948 (15 Oct). *Bassano Bridge. No. 718 optd with T4.*

84	**209**	15l. deep blue-green (R.)	1·20	1·00

```
     AMG
     FTT
A.M.G. F.T.T.   AMG-FTT    fiera di Trieste
   (6)            (7)          1950
                               (8)
```

1948 (15 Nov). *Donizetti. No. 719 optd with T 6.*

85	**210**	15l. sepia (G.)	6·50	1·00

1949 (2 May). *25th Biennial Art Exhibition, Venice Nos. 721/4 optd with T 3a.*

86	**5l.** brown-red and flesh	75	70
87	**15l.** green and cream	6·00	6·00
88	**20l.** red-brown and buff	3·50	95
89	**50l.** blue and lemon	9·25	5·00
86/89	Set of 4	17·00	11·50

1949 (2 May). *27th Milan Fair. No. 720 optd with T 4.*

90	**211**	20l. sepia (R.)	6·75	1·50

1949 (2 May). *75th Anniv of Founding of Universal Postal Union. No. 725 optd with T 4.*

91	**213**	50l. ultramarine (R)	2·75	2·20

1949 (30 May). *Centenary of Roman Republic No. 726 optd with T 4.*

92	**214**	100l. brown (R.)	44·00	46·00

1949 (8 June). *First Trieste Free Election. No. 732 optd as T 7 (smaller).*

93	**218**	20l. lake (G.)	3·50	1·70

1949 (15 June). *European Recovery Plan. Nos 727/9 optd with T 3a.*

94	**215**	5l. blue-green	6·50	4·25
		a. Opt inverted	£1200	
95		15l. violet	8·50	8·75
96		20l. brown	8·50	7·25

1949 (8 July). *Second World Health Congress, Rome No. 733 optd with T 3a.*

97	**219**	20l. violet (R.)	10·00	3·75

1949 (16 July). *Honouring Giuseppe Mazzini (revolutionary) No. 730 optd with T 6.*

98	**216**	20l. grey-black (R.)	6·50	2·50

1949 (16 July). *Bicentenary of Birth of Vittorio Alfieri (poet). No. 731 optd with T 6.*

99	**217**	20l. sepia (R.)	6·50	2·50

1949 (27 27). *400th Anniv of Completion of Palladio's Basilica at Vicenza, No 734 optd with T 3a.*

100	**220**	20l. violet	8·50	6·50

1949 (27 Aug). *500th Anniv of Birth of Lorenzo de Medici ("The Magnificent") No. 735 optd with T 6.*

101	**221**	20l. violet-blue	10·00	5·25

1949 (10 Sept). *Thirteenth Bari Fair. No. 736 optd with T 4.*

102	**222**	20l. scarlet (G.)	6·25	3·00

1949 (21 Oct)–**50**. *Stamps of 1945–48 optd with T 7.*

103	**195**	1l. green (28.12.49)	20	55
104	—	2l. purple-brown (No. 656) (28.12.49)	20	10
105	**194**	3l. scarlet (21.10.49)	15	10
106	**193**	5l. dull blue (5.11.49)	15	10
107	**195**	6l. bluish violet (28.12.49)	15	10
108	**192**	8l. blue-green (28.12.49)	16·00	8·25
109	**193**	10l. vermilion (7.11.49)	20	10
110	**195**	15l. pale blue (28.11.49)	1·50	45
111	**194**	20l. purple (21.10.49)	80	10
112	**196**	25l. deep green (25.2.50)	16·00	1·40
113		50l. brown-purple (19.1.50)	27·00	1·50
114	**197**	100l. carmine (23.11.49)	75·00	9·75
103/114	Set of 12		£225	20·00

1949 (7 Nov)–**52**. *AIR. Air stamps of 1945–46 and 1948 optd with T 7.*

115	**198**	10l. carmine (28.12.49)	15	10
116	**199**	25l. brown (23.1.50)	20	10
117	**198**	50l. violet (5.12.49)	15	10
118	**204**	100l. blue-green (7.11.49)	85	10
119		300l. magenta (25.11.50)	11·50	7·00
120		500l. blue (25.11.50)	16·00	9·75
121		1000l. brown-purple (18.2.52)	25·00	23·00
115/121	Set of 7		48·00	36·00

1949 (7 Nov)–**52**. *CONCESSIONAL LETTER POST Nos. CL734/5 optd with T 7.*

CL122	CL **220**	15l. violet	1·10	30
CL123		20l. reddish violet (4.2.52)	5·75	30

1949 (7 Nov)–**52**. *POSTAGE DUE, Nos. D690/703 optd with T 7.*

D122	D **201**	1l. red-orange (22.11.49)	20	10
D123		2l. blue-green (28.12.49)	20	10
D124		3l. carmine (28.12.49)	20	20
D125		5l. violet (7.11.49)	85	20
D126		6l. ultramarine (7.11.49)	20	20
D127		8l. mauve (16.5.50)	20	35
D128		10l. blue (16.5.50)	85	20
D129		12l. brown (7.11.49)	1·30	35
D130		20l. bright purple (16.5.50)	3·75	15
D131		25l. brown-red (28.12.49)	5·00	1·50
D132		50l. turquoise-green (7.11.49)	5·00	20
D133		100l. brown-orange (25.11.50)	10·50	45
D134		500l. reddish pur & blue (11 2.52)	36·00	17·00
D122/134	Set of 13		55·00	19·00

1949 (7 Nov). *150th Anniv of Volta's Discovery of the Electric Cell. Nos. 737/8 optd with T 7.*

135	**223**	20l. carmine-red	3·25	2·40
136	**224**	50l. blue	10·00	9·75

1949 (7 Nov). *Rebuilding of Holy Trinity Bridge, Florence. No. 739 optd wish T 7.*

137	**225**	20l. green	3·50	2·00

1949 (7 Nov). *Bimillenary of Death of Catullus (poet). No. 740 optd with T 7.*

138	**226**	20l. blue	2·50	2·00

1949 (22 Nov)–**54**. *PARCEL POST. Contemporary Parcel Post stamps optd on each half of the stamps as T 7 but smaller.*

			Un pair	Used pair	Used half
P139	P **201**	1l. yellow-brn (7.10.50)	1·10	90	20

TRIESTE　　　　　　　　　　　　　　　　　　　　　　　　　　　　　　1949

P140	2l. turquoise-bl (1.8.51)	30	35	15
P141	3l. red-orange (1.8.51)	30	35	15
P142	4l. grey (1.8.51)	30	35	15
P143	5l. bright purple	30	35	15
P144	10l. violet	80	85	30
P145	20l. brown-purple	80	85	30
P146	30l. reddish pur (6.3.52)	55	55	20
P147	50l. vermilion (10.3.50)	90	75	20
P148	100l. blue (9.11.50)	2·00	1·90	20
P149	200l. deep green	18·00	19·00	50
P150	300l. deep claret (19.1.50)	70·00	70·00	50
P151	500l. dp brown (25.12.50)	42·00	43·00	75
P152　P 298	1000l. ultram (12.8.54)	£150	£170	5·00
P139/152 Set of 14		£250	£275	8·00

See note on Parcel Post Stamps below No. PE98 of Italy.

1949 (28 Dec). *Bicentenary of Birth of Domenico Cimarosa (composer) No. 741 optd with T 7.*
153　227　20l. slate-violet (R.) . . . . 3·25　1·60
　　　a. Opt double £700

1950 (12 Apr). *28th Milan Fair. No. 742 optd as T 7 (smaller).*
154　228　20l. brown (R.) . . . . 3·25　1·50

1950 (29 Apr). *32nd International Automobile Exhibition, Turin No. 743 optd as T 7 (smaller).*
155　229　20l. grey-violet (R.) . . . . 1·10　1·10

1950 (22 May). *Fifth General Conference of U.N.E.S.C.O. Nos. 744/5 optd as T 7 (smaller).*
156　—　20l. grey-green (R.) . . . . 1·70　65
157　230　55l. blue (R.) . . . . 10·50　8·50

1950 (29 May). *Holy Year. Nos. 746/7 optd with T 7.*
158　231　20l. violet . . . . 3·00　65
159　　　55l. blue . . . . 11·50　7·25

1950 (10 June). *Honouring Gaudenzio Ferrari (painter) No 748 optd as T 7 (smaller).*
160　232　20l. grey-green (R.) . . . . 2·00　1·70

1950 (15 July). *International Radio Conference Nos 749/50 optd as T 7 (smaller).*
161　233　20l. violet (R.) . . . . 4·75　3·75
162　　　55l. blue (R.) . . . . 19·00　16·00

1950 (22 July). *Bicentenary of Death of Ludovico Muratori (historian). No. 751 optd with T 7.*
163　234　20l. brown . . . . 3·25　1·70

1950 (29 July). *900th Anniv of Death of Guido D'Arezzo. No. 752 optd "AMG/FTT" in two lines.*
164　235　20l. green (R.) . . . . 3·25　1·70

1950 (21 Aug). *14th Levant Fair, Bari No. 753 optd as T 7 (smaller).*
165　236　20l. red-brown . . . . 1·90　1·50

1950 (27 Aug). *Second Trieste Fair. Nos, 664/5 optd with T 8.*
166　195　15l. pale blue . . . . 1·80　1·70
167　194　20l. purple . . . . 2·75　55
　　　a. Opt inverted . . . . £110　£110

1950 (11 Sept). *Wool Industry Pioneers No. 754 optd "AMG/FTT" in two lines.*
168　237　20l. deep blue (R.) . . . . 1·00　65

1950 (16 Sept). *European Tobacco Conference, Rome. Nos. 755/7 optd with T 7.*
169　238　5l. green and magenta . . . . 40　1·00
170　　　20l. green and brown . . . . 2·20　1·40
171　　　55l. brown and bright blue . . . . 20·00　17·00

1950 (16 Sept). *Bicentenary of Academy of Fine Arts. No. 758 optd with T 7.*
172　239　20l. red-brown and brown . . . . 2·40　1·50

1950 (16 Sept). *Centenary of Birth of Augusto Righi. No. 759 optd with T 7.*
173　240　20l. black and buff . . . . 3·00　1·50

1950 (27 Sept)–**52**. *EXPRESS LETTER. Nos. E684/5 optd as T 7 (smaller on 50l.)*
E174　E 200　50l. bright purple (4.2.52) . . . . 3·25　90
E175　E 201　60l. carmine . . . . 3·25　1·00

1950 (20 Oct). *Stamps of 1950 (Nos 760/78) optd as T 7, but smaller. (Nos. 176/92 12½ mm long. Nos. 193/4 10½ mm).*
176　　　50c. violet-blue . . . . 20　10
177　　　1l. blackish violet . . . . 30　10
178　　　2l. black-brown . . . . 90　10
179　　　5l. black . . . . 60　10
180　　　6l. purple-brown . . . . 20　10
181　　　10l. green . . . . 2·00　10
182　　　12l. turquoise-green . . . . 2·75　30
183　　　15l. slate-blue . . . . 2·75　10
184　　　20l. bright violet . . . . 2·75　10
185　　　25l. orange-brown . . . . 6·00　10
186　　　30l. bright purple . . . . 2·50　30
187　　　35l. carmine . . . . 1·70　1·40
188　　　40l. brown . . . . 1·20　30
189　　　50l. violet . . . . 65　10
190　　　55l. blue . . . . 20　20
191　　　60l. scarlet . . . . 5·75　3·00
192　　　65l. blue-green . . . . 35　40
193　　　100l. chestnut . . . . 3·00　40
194　　　200l. yellow-brown . . . . 1·80　2·50
176/194 Set of 19 . . . . 32·00　8·75

1951 (27 Mar). *Centenary of First Tuscan Stamp Nos 779/80 optd as T 7 (smaller).*
195　242　20l. scarlet and bright purple . . . . 3·00　1·50
196　　　55l. blue and ultramarine . . . . 36·00　26·00

1951 (2 Apr). *33rd International Automobile Exhibition. Turin No 781 optd as T 7 (smaller).*
197　243　20l. blue-green . . . . 1·10　1·20

1951 (11 Apr). *Consecration of Hall of Peace, Rome No. 782 optd as T 7 (smaller)*
198　244　20l. bright violet . . . . 1·60　1·30

1951 (12 Apr). *29th Milan Fair Nos 783/4 optd with T 7 (20l.) or smaller (55l.).*
199　245　20l. yellow-brown . . . . 1·80　1·20
200　246　55l. blue . . . . 2·10　2·10

1951 (26 Apr). *Tenth International Textiles Exhibition. Turin No. 785 optd as T 7 (smaller)*
201　247　20l. violet . . . . 1·60　1·40

1951 (5 May). *Fifth Centenary of Birth of Columbus No 786 optd with T 7.*
202　248　20l. turquoise-green . . . . 2·00　1·60

1951 (18 May). *Int Gymnastic Festival, Florence Nos 787/9 optd with T 7.*
203　249　5l. scarlet and sepia . . . . 4·50　10·50
204　　　10l. scarlet and turquoise-green . . . . 4·50　10·50
205　　　15l. scarlet and ultramarine . . . . 4·50　10·50

1951 (18 June). *Restoration of Montecassino Abbey Nos 790/1 optd as T 7 (smaller).*
206　250　20l. violet . . . . 60　45
207　　　55l. blue . . . . 1·30　1·10

161

TRIESTE   1951

```
      AMG-FTT          V FIERA DI
                         TRIESTE
       FIERA
         ⊕            A           F
                      M           T
         di           G           T
       TRIESTE                    ┼
        1951              1953
         (9)                (10)
```

1951 (24 June). *Third Trieste Fair Nos, 764, 768 and 774 optd with T* **9**.
208   6l. purple-brown 35   45
209   20l. bright violet 45   30
210   55l. blue . . . . 1·00   80

1951 (23 July). *500th Anniv of Birth of Perugino (painter). No. 792 optd "AMG/FTT" in two lines.*
211   **251**   20l. red-brown and sepia   70   55

1951 (23 July). *Triennial Art Exhibition, Milan. Nos. 793/4 optd "AMG/FTT" (in two lines, 20l.) or with T* **7** *(55l.).*
212   **252**   20l. black and grey-green (R.) . . . 1·10   90
213   —   55l. pink and blue (R.) . . . . . 1·60 1·70

1951 (23 Aug). *World Cycling Championship. No. 795 optd as T* **7** *(smaller).*
214   **253**   25l. grey-black (R.) . . . . 4·75 1·60

1951 (8 Sept). *Fifteenth Levant Fair, Bari. No. 796 optd as T* **7** *(smaller)*
215   **254**   25l. bright blue   80   55

1951 (15 Sept). *Centenary of Birth of F. P. Michetti. No. 797 optd with T* **7**.
216   **255**   25l. deep brown (R.)   80   55

1951 (11 Oct). *Sardinian Stamp Centenary. Nos 798/800 optd "AMG FTT" in blue.*
217   **256**   10l. black and sepia   30   50
218   —   25l. blue-green and carmine . . .   40   30
219   —   60l. orange-red and blue   80   80

1951 (31 Oct). *Industrial Census No. 801 optd "AMG FTT".*
220   **257**   10l. green   55   50

1951 (31 Oct). *National Census. No. 802 optd "AMG FTT".*
221   **258**   25l. violet-black   55   35

1951 (21 Nov). *Forestry Festival Nos 806/7 optd as T* **7** *(smaller).*
222   **260**   10l. deep green and olive-green . .   55   45
223   —   25l. deep green   75   40

1951 (23 Nov). *Verdi. Nos 803/5 optd "AMG FTT".*
224   —   10l. blue-green and purple   55   45
225   **259**   25l. sepia and reddish brown . . .   55   35
226   —   60l. deep blue and blue-green . . 1·00 1·30

1952 (28 Jan). *Bellini. No 808 optd "AMG FTT".*
227   **261**   25l. grey-black   70   40

1952 (1 Feb). *Caserta Palace. No. 809 optd as T* **7** *(smaller).*
228   **262**   25l. bistre and deep green   40   40

1952 (26 Mar). *Sports Stamps Exhibition No. 810 optd as T* **7** *(smaller).*
229   **263**   25l. brown and grey-black   50   40

1952 (12 Apr). *30th Milan Fair. No. 811 optd as T* **7** *(smaller).*
230   **264**   60l. bright blue (B.) . . . . . . 1·30 1·50

1952. *Leonardo da Vinci. Nos 812/4 optd as T* **7** *but smaller, in gold (60l.) or black.*
231   **265**   25l. orange (17 Apr)   15   20
232   **266**   60l. ultramarine (31 Dec) . . . . 1·00 1·20
233   **265**   80l. brown-red (31 Dec) . . . . . 1·20   40

1952 (7 June). *Overseas Fair, Naples No 817 optd as T* **7** *(smaller).*
234   **268**   25l. bright blue   70   40

1952 (14 June). *Modena and Parma Stamp Centenaries Nos. 815/6 optd "AMG FTT" in two vertical lines.*
235   **267**   25l. black and red-brown   35   25
236   —   60l. indigo and blue   75   70

1952 (14 June). *Art Exhibition, Venice No. 818 optd "AMG FTT".*
237   **269**   25l. black and cream   75   40

1952 (19 June). *Thirtieth Padua Fair. No. 819 optd "AMG/ FTT" in two lines, in red*
238   **270**   25l. red and slate-blue   50   40

1952 (28 June). *4th Trieste Fair. No. 820 optd "AMG/FTT" in two lines.*
239   **271**   25l. green, red and brown   50   40

1952 (6 Sept). *Sixteenth Levant Fair No 821 optd as T* **7** *(smaller).*
240   **272**   25l. deep green   60   40

1952 (20 Sept). *Savonarola. No. 822 optd as T* **7** *(smaller), in gold.*
241   **273**   25l. bluish violet   50   40

1952 (1 Oct). *Private Aeronautics Conference No 823 optd as T* **7** *(smaller).*
242   **274**   60l. blue and ultramarine (B.) . . 1·10 1·50

1952 (4 Oct). *Alpine Troops Exhibition. No 824 optd "AMG FTT".*
243   **275**   25l. grey-black   65   40

1952 (3 Nov). *Armed Forces Day. No. 825 optd as T* **7** *(smaller), and Nos, 826/7 optd "AMG FTT" in two vertical lines.*
244   **276**   10l. myrtle-green   10   20
245   **217**   25l. black-brown and grey-brown . .   30   10
246   —   60l. black and pale blue   50   45

1952 (21 Nov). *Ethiopia Mission. No 828 optd as T* **7** *(smaller).*
247   **278**   25l. brown and orange-brown . . .   80   40

1952 (6 Dec). *Centenary of Birth of Gemito (sculptor). No. 829 optd as T* **7** *but smaller.*
248   **279**   25l. red-brown   65   40

1952 (6 Dec). *Centenary of Birth of Mancini (painter). No. 830 optd as T* **7** *but smaller.*
249   **280**   25l. blackish green   65   40

1953 (5 Jan). *Centenary of Martyrdom of Belfiore No. 831 optd "AMG FTT".*
250   **281**   25l. deep blue and black (B) . . .   65   40

1953 (21 Feb). *Antonello Exhibition, Messina. No 832 optd as T* **7** *(smaller)*
251   **282**   25l. brown-red   60   40

1953 (24 Apr). *20th "Mille Miglia" Car Race. No 833 optd as T* **7** *(smaller).*
252   **283**   25l. bright violet   60   40

1953 (30 Apr). *Creation of Orders of Meritorious Labour. No 834 optd as T* **7** *(smaller)*
253   **284**   25l. bright violet   60   40

1953 (30 May). *Third Centenary of Birth of Corelli (composer). No. 835 optd as T* **7** *(smaller).*
254   **285**   25l. brown   60   40

TRIESTE   1953

1953 (16 June)–**54**. Stamps of 1953–54 (Nos 836/44) optd as T **7** (smaller).
255	**286**	5l. slate	10	20
256		10l. orange-red	10	10
257		12l. deep bluish green	10	10
258		13l. bright reddish purple (1.2.54)	10	55
259		20l. sepia	10	10
260		25l. reddish violet	10	10
261		35l. carmine-red	50	40
262		60l. blue	75	40
263		80l. orange-brown	1·00	55
255/263 Set of 9			2·50	2·25

1953 (27 June). Seventh Centenary of Death of St. Clare. No 847 optd as T **7** (smaller)
264	**287**	25l. brown-red and deep brown	85	40

1953 (27 June). Fifth Trieste Fair Nos 765, 769 and 775 optd with T **10**.
265		10l. green (R.)	30	25
266		25l. orange-brown (G.)	35	15
267		60l. scarlet (G.)	40	40

1953 (8 July). CONCESSIONAL PARCEL POST. Nos CP848/51 optd as T **7** (smaller).
			Un pair	Used left	Used right
CP268	CP **288**	40l. brown-orange	6·25	2·00	2·40
CP269		50l. blue	6·25	2·00	2·40
CP270		75l. sepia	9·00	2·75	3·75
CP271		110l. lilac-rose	9·75	2·75	3·75

Prices for used pairs are same as for unused. See note below No. 847 of Italy.

1953 (11 July). Mountains Festival No. 848 optd as T **7** (smaller).
272	**288**	25l. blue-green	1·10	40

1953 (16 July). International Agriculture Exhibition, Rome Nos. 849/50 optd as T **7** (smaller).
273	**289**	25l. sepia	30	10
274		60l. blue	45	40

1953 (6 Aug). Fourth Anniv of Atlantic Pact. Nos. 851/2 optd "AMG FTT".
275	**290**	25l. deep turquoise & yellow-orange	45	35
276		60l. violet-blue and mauve	1·50	1·60

1953 (13 Aug). Fifth Centenary of Birth of Signorelli (painter). No 853 optd as T **7** (smaller)
277	**291**	25l. grey-green and sepia	60	40

1953 (5 Sept). Sixth International Microbiological Congress No. 854 optd as T **7** (smaller).
278	**292**	25l. sepia and greenish black	75	40

1954 (26 Jan). Tourist Series. Nos 855/60 optd as T **7** (smaller).
279		10l. red-brown and sepia	15	20
280		12l. black and greenish blue	15	10
281		20l. reddish brown and brown-orange	15	10
282		25l. deep blue-green and pale blue	15	10
283		35l. brown and buff	35	45
284		60l. deep blue and turquoise-green	35	45
279/284 Set of 6			1·10	1·30

1954 (11 Feb). 25th Anniv of Lateran Treaty. Nos. 861/2 optd as T **7** (smaller).
285	**294**	25l. sepia and bistre-brown	25	10
286		60l. blue and bright blue	45	40

1954 (25 Feb). Introduction of Television in Italy Nos 863/4 optd "AMG/FTT" in two lines.
287	**295**	25l. bluish violet	25	10
288		60l. deep turquoise-green	55	40

1954 (20 Mar). Encouragement to Taxpayers No 865 optd as T **7** (smaller).

1954 (24 Apr). First Experimental Helicopter Mail Flight, Milan Turin No 866 optd "AMG FTT".
290	**297**	25l. blackish green	60	40

1954 (1 June). Tenth Anniv of Resistance Movement No. 867 optd as T **7** but smaller.
291	**298**	25l. grey-black and orange-brown	65	40

1954 (18 June). Sixth Trieste Fair Nos. 282 and 284 of Trieste additionally optd "FIERA DI/ TRIESTE/1954".
292		25l. deep blue-green and pale blue	35	20
293		60l. deep blue and turquoise-green	70	55

1954 (19 June). Centenary of Birth of Catalani (composer.). No 868 optd "AMG FTT".
294	**299**	25l. deep grey-green	60	40

1954 (8 July). Seventh Centenary of Birth of Marco Polo. Nos 869/70 optd as T **7** but smaller.
295	**300**	25l. brown	25	15
296		60l. slate-green	50	55

1954 (6 Sept). 60th Anniv of Italian Touring Club. No. 871 optd as T **7** (smaller).
297	**301**	25l. deep green and scarlet	50	35

1954 (30 Oct). International Police Congress, Rome. Nos. 872/3 optd as T **7** (smaller).
298	**302**	25l. carmine-red	35	40
299		60l. bright blue	15	55

The use of stamps of the Allied Military Government ceased on 15 November 1954

ZONE B

YUGOSLAV MILITARY GOVERNMENT

For Italian stamps surcharged "1 .V. 1945 TRIESTE/TRST", new value and star, see Venezia Giulia.

Stamps of Yugoslavia overprinted (unless otherwise Indicated)

PRINTERS. The "STT VUJA" overprints on Yugoslav stamps were printed in Belgrade and the stamps without overprints were printed by the "Ljuska" Printing works, Ljubjana.

Italian Currency

B **1**   B **2**

(Des Sakside. Litho)

1948   (1 May). Labour Day. P $10\frac{1}{2} \times 11\frac{1}{2}$.

A. Inscr In Slovene: "I. MAJ 1948 V STO"

B. Inscr In Italian. "I. MAGGIO 1948 NEL TILT"

TRIESTE 1948

C. Inscr in Croat. "I. SVIBANJ 1948 U STT"

B1	B 1	100l. carmine-red and stone (A)		6·50	3·75
		a. Strip of 3. Nos. B1/3		60·00	
B2		100l. carmine-red and stone (B.)		7·00	3·75
B3		100l. carmine-red and stone (C)		6·50	3·75

Nos 81/3 were issued together in *se-tenant* strips of three stamps within the sheet

1948 (23 May). *Red Cross No 545 (Roofless houses) surch* "VUJA/S.T.T." *and new value, in blue.*

B3a	131	2l. on 50p. brown and red		12·50	16·00

1948 (23 May). *POSTAGE DUE. Red Cross. No. D546 (Roofless houses, inscr* "PORTO") *surch* "VUJA STT" *and new value, in red*

BD4		2l. on 50p. green and red		£110	£120

(Des M. Strenar Typo)

1948 (17 Oct). AIR. *Economic Exhibition, Capodistria.* P 12½ × 11½.

B4	B 2	25l. grey		55	45
B5		50l. orange		55	45

B 3 Clasped Hands, Hammer and Sickle

B 4 Fishermen and Flying Boat

B 5 Man with Donkey

B 6 Mediterranean Gull over Chimneys

(Des M Strenar. Litho)

1949 (1 May). *Labour Day.* P 11½ × 12½.

B6	B 3	10l. blackish green		45	30

(Des M. Strenar (100 l.), R. Krošelj (others). Litho)

1949 (1 June). AIR. P 11½.

B 7	B 4	1l. turquoise		25	20
B 8	B 5	2l. red-brown		25	20
B 9	B 4	5l. blue		25	20
B10	B 5	10l. violet		1·70	1·10
B11	B 4	25l. yellow-brown		3·00	3·75
B12	B 5	50l. grey-green		2·50	3·00
B13	B 6	100l. purple-brown		4·75	5·00
B7/13 Set of 7				11·50	12·00

Yugoslav Currency

STT (B 7)   VUJA (B 8)   VUJA (B 9)   DIN 30

1949 (15 Aug–20 Sept). Nos. 502/3, 505, 508/9, 511 *and* 514/7 *optd with Type* B **7** *(2d. and 4d.) or as* B **8** *(others).*

B14	119	d.50, olive-grey (R.) (Partisan)		40	20
B15		1d. blue-green (R.)		40	30
		a. Opt inverted		65·00	65·00
B16	120	2d. scarlet (B.) (Tito)		50	20
B17	121	3d. vermilion (B.) (Jajce)		50	20

B18	120	4d. blue (R.) (20.9) (Tito)		65	35
B19	121	5d. blue (R.) (Jajce)		65	35
B20	–	9d. magenta (B.) (Girl with flag) (20.9)		1·40	1·20
B21	–	12d. ultramarine (R.) (Riflemen)		4·00	2·75
		a. Opt inverted		£225	£225
B22	119	16d. light blue (R.) (Partisans) (20.9)		7·25	5·50
B23		20d. vermilion (B.) (Riflemen)		9·00	6·25
B14/23 Set of 10				22·00	15·00

The space between the lines of overprint in Type B **8** varies. It is 1¼ *mm.* on No. B20, 2½ *mm.* on Nos, B14/15 and B21/3 and 4 *mm.* on Nos. B17 and B19.

1949 (8 Sept). *75th Anniv of Universal Postal Union. As Nos 612/13 on paper with network in colour of stamp, optd* "VUJA-STT" *in red.*

B24		5d. blue (Airplane, train and mail coach)		6·25	6·25
B25		12d. brown (Globe, letters and transport)		6·25	6·25

1949 (15 Sept). *POSTAGE DUE. Nos.* D527/31 *(Star and torches) optd with Type* B **8**.

BD26	D 126	50p. deep orange (B.)		70	35
BD27		1d. orange (B.)		45	35
BD28		2d. blue (R.)		50	35
BD29		3d. green (R.)		70	35
BD30		5d. violet (R.)		1·10	75
BD26/30 Set of 5				3·00	1·90

1949 (5 Nov). AIR. *Nos* B7/13 *optd* "DIN" *(B26/9) or surch as Type* B **9** *(others).*

B26	B 4	1d. turquoise		20	20
B27	B 5	2d. red-brown (Br.)		20	20
B28	B 4	5d. blue (B.)		25	20
B29	B 5	10d. violet (V.)		35	20
B30	B 4	15d.on 25l. yellow-brown (Br.)		11·50	11·00
B31	B 5	20d.on 50l. grey-green (G.)		2·20	3·50
B32	B 6	30d.on 100l. purple-brown		3·25	3·75
B26/32 Set of 7				16·00	17·00

1950 (21 Jan). *Centenary of Yugoslav Railways. Nos.* 631/33a *(various locomotives), all on paper with network in colour of stamp, optd* "VUJA-STT" *in red. (a) POSTAGE.*

B33		2d. green		95	70
B34		3d. carmine		1·40	75
B35		5d. blue		2·00	1·50
B36		10d. orange		9·75	5·50
		a. Opt inverted		£300	
B33/B36 Set of 4				12·50	7·50

(b) AIR. *No.* **MS**633b *with similar opt, in red.*

A. P 11½ × 12½.

MSB36A*a*	10d. purple		80·00	90·00
	b. Opt inverted		£450	—
	c. Opt double		£450	—

B. *Imperf*

MSB36B*a*	10d. purple		80·00	90·00
	b. Opt inverted		£450	—
	c. Opt double		£450	—

This sheet has an engine-turned background which is not present on the Yugoslav sheet

B 10 Girl on Donkey   B 11 Workers   BD 12 Fish

(Des M. Strenar. Photo)

1950 (7 Apr)–51. *Type* B **10** *and similar animal designs.* P 12½.

B37	50p. greenish slate		25	25
B38	1d. lake		25	25
B38*a*	1d. orange-brown (1.3.51)		75	30

164

TRIESTE 1950

B39	2d. blue		25	25
B39a	2d. light blue (1.3.51)		70	30
B40	3d. red-brown		30	25
B40a	3d. brown-red (1.3.51)		1·10	30
B41	5d. turquoise-green		1·10	30
B42	10d. brown		1·70	55
B43	15d. bluish violet		14·50	8·75
B44	20d. blackish green		4·25	3·75
B37/44	Set of 11		23·00	13·50

Designs:—1d. Cockerel; 2d. Geese; 3d. Bees on honeycomb; 5d. Oxen; 10d. Turkey; 15d. Kids; 20d. Silkworms on mulberry leaves.

1950 (1 May). *May Day.* P 12½.

B45	B 11	3d. violet	60	40
B46		10d. carmine	70	50

1950 (3 July). *Red Cross. No. 616 (Nurse and child) optd "VUJA/STT".*

B47	160	50p. brown and red	75	50

1950 (3 July). *POSTAGE DUE. Red Cross. No. D617 (Nurse and child, inscr "PORTO") optd "VUJA/STT".*

BD48	50p. bright purple and red		55	50

1950 (1 Nov). *POSTAGE DUE Type* BD **12** *and similar design.* P 12½.

BD49	—	50p. orange-brown	1·10	45
BD50	—	1d. grey-green	1·70	1·10
BD51	BD **12**	2d. greenish blue	2·00	1·50
BD52		3d. deep blue	2·20	1·50
BD53		5d. reddish purple	7·50	5·50
BD49/53	Set of 5		13·00	9·00

Design:—50p. and 1d. Two fishes

B **12** Worker

B **13** P. P. Vergerio, Jr.

(Des B. Jakac. Photo)

1951 (1 May). *May Day.* P 12½.

B48	B **12**	3d. red	55	50
B49		10d. olive	1·10	80

1951 (7 Oct). *Red Cross. No. 702 (Hoisting flag) optd "STT/VUJA".*

B49a	191	0d.50, ultramarine and red	10·00	10·00

1951 (7 Oct). *POSTAGE DUE. Red Cross. No. D703 (Hoisting flag, inscr "PORTO") optd "STT/VUJA".*

BD54	0d.50, emerald and red		£100	£100

(Des R. Krošelj. Litho)

1951 (21 Oct). *Festival of Italian Culture.* P 12½.

B50	B **13**	5d. blue	70	55
B51		10d. claret	70	55
B52		20d. blackish brown	70	55

(B **14**)

1951. *Cultural Anniversaries. As Nos. 698/9 but colours changed and optd with Type* B **14**.

B53	10d. brown-orange (B.) (P. Trubar) (4 Nov)		80	70
B54	12d. slate-black (R.) (M. Marulid) (29 Nov)		80	70

B **14a** Koper Square

B **15** Cyclists

(Des A. Jovanovic. Photo)

1952 (4 Feb). *AIR, 75th Anniv of Universal Postal Union. Type* B **14a** *and similar designs.* P 12½.

B54a	5d. yellow-brown		5·50	6·75
B54b	15d. blue		6·75	5·00
B54c	25d. myrtle-green		6·00	4·25

Designs: Vert—15 d. Lighthouse, Piran. Horiz—25 d. Hotel, Portoro?.

(Des J. Trpin. Photo)

1952 (26 Mar). *Physical Culture Propaganda. Type* B **15** *and similar horiz designs.* P 12½.

B55	5d. yellow-brown		15	15
B56	10d. green (Footballers)		20	15
B57	15d. carmine (Rowing Four)		20	15
B58	28d. deep ultramarine (Yachting)		70	70
B59	50d. lake (Netball-players)		1·60	1·90
B60	100d. deep slate-blue (Diver)		7·50	7·00
B55/60	Set of 6		9·50	9·00

1952 (25 May). *60th Birth Anniv of Marshal Tito. As Nos. 727/9 (portraits of Tito) but additionally inscr "STT VUJA".*

B61	196	15d. deep brown	1·80	1·20
B62	197	28d. brown-lake	1·90	1·60
B63		50d. deep green	2·50	2·20

1952 (22 June). *Children's Week. As No. 730 (child) but colour changed and optd "STT VUJA" reading upwards.*

B64	198	15d. carmine-pink (B.)	85	80

STT VUJNA
(B **16**)

1952 (26 July). *Fifteenth Olympic Games, Helsinki. As Nos. 731/6 but colours changed and optd with Type* B **16**, *in red*.

B65	5d. chocolate/flesh (Sal.) (Gymnastics)		70	40
B66	10d. deep green/cream (G.) (Running)		70	40
B67	15d. violet/mauve (B.) (Swimming)		70	40
B68	25d. chocolate/buff (Br.) (Boxing)		1·60	1·10
B69	50d. brown/yellow (O.) (Basketball)		8·25	5·00
B70	100d. ultramarine/pink (V.) (Football)		16·00	20·00
B65/70	Set of 6		25·00	25·00

1952 (13 Sept). *Navy Day. Nos. 737/9 optd "STT/VUJNA", in red.*

B71	15d. brown-purple (Split)		1·60	1·90
B72	28d. deep brown (Fishing boat)		1·70	2·70
B73	50d. greenish black (Sveti Stefan)		2·75	3·00

1952 (15 Oct). *POSTAGE DUE. Nos. D724/31 (Star and torches) optd "STT/VUJNA".*

BD74	D **126**	1d. chocolate (B.)	30	25
BD75		2d. emerald-green (R.)	30	25
BD76		5d. blue (R.)	30	25
BD77		10d. scarlet (B.)	30	25
BD78		20d. reddish violet (R.)	35	25
BD79		30d. orange (B.)	50	30
BD80		50d. ultramarine (R.)	2·00	80
BD81		100d. reddish purple (B.)	5·00	5·75
BD74/81	Set of 8		8·00	7·25

165

TRIESTE 1952

1952 (26 Oct). *Red Cross. No. 740 (Nurse) optd "STT VUJNA" reading upwards, in red.*
B74 **201** 50p. red, grey and black 30 25

1952 (26 Oct). *POSTAGE DUE. Red Cross. No. D741 (Cross) optd "STT VUJNA" reading upwards, in red.*
BD82 D **202** 50p. red and olive-grey 70 95

1952 (4 Nov). *Sixth Yugoslav Communist Party Congress. Nos. 741/4 (Workers in procession) optd "VUJNA STT".*
B75 **202** 15d. lake-brown (B.) 70 55
B76 15d. turquoise (R.) 60 55
B77 15d. chocolate (R.) 60 55
B78 15d. deep violet-blue (R.) 60 55
B75/78 Set of 4 . . . . 2·20 2·00

B **17** Starfish

(Des R. Kroselj. Photo)

1952 (29 Nov). *Philatelic Exhibition, Koper. P 11½.*
B78a B **17** 15d. red-brown . . . . 2·00 1·20
MSB78b 48 × 70 mm. B **17** 50d. blue-green.
 Imperf (sold at 85 d.) . . . . . . 18·00 17·00

1953 (3 Feb). *Tenth Death Anniv of Tesla (inventor). As Nos. 745/6 (Tesla) but colours changed and optd as Type B **16**.*
B79 **203** 15d. scarlet (B.) 25 10
B80 30d. violet-blue (R.) 75 35

1953 (23 Feb). *Stamps of Yugoslavia, some with colours, changed, optd "STT/VUJNA" without serifs*

(a) As Nos. 705/14. Recess (13 March).
B81 1d. grey (Electricity supply engineer) . . 5·75 5·25
B82 3d. scarlet (R.) (Harvester) . . . 35 30
B83 10d. green (G.) (Picking apples) . . 35 30
B84 30d. blue (B.) (Girl printer) . . . 4·00 4·00
B85 50d. turquoise (B.) (Dockers) . . 8·00 5·75

(b) As Nos. 718/23. Litho (25 Feb).
B86 2d. carmine-red (P.) (Harvester) . . 35 30
B87 5d. orange (Br.) (Fishing) . . . 30 30
B88 15d. scarlet (R.) (Picking sunflowers) . . 35 30
B81/88 Set of 8 . . . . 18·00 15·00
For overprint with serifs see Nos, B105/7

1953 (21 Apr). *United Nations Commemoration. Nos. 747/9 (Frescoes) opt "STT VUJNA".*
B89 15d. bronze-green (R.) 20 15
B90 30d. deep blue (R.) 30 25
B91 50d. brown-lake (B.) 65 45

1953 (2 June). *Adriatic Car and Motor Cycle Rally. As Nos. 750/3 (cars or motor cycle) but colours, changed and additionally inscr "STT/VUJNA".*
B92 15d. brown and yellow 30 15
B93 30d. bronze-green and pale emerald . . 30 15
B94 50d. deep magenta and salmon . . 30 20
B95 70d. deep blue and light blue . . . 1·40 90
B92/95 Set of 4 . . . . 2·10 1·30

1953 (18 July). *As No. 754 (Marshal Tito), but colour changed, optd as Type B **16**.*
B96 **206** 50d. deep grey-green (R.) . . . . 1·40 80

1953 (31 July). *38th Esperanto Congress, Zagreb. As Nos. 755/6 (Star, globe and flags) but colours changed, optd "STT/VUJNA", in red.*

(a) POSTAGE.
B97 **207** 15d. dull green and deep
 turquoise . . . . 1·80 2·75
(b) AIR.
B98 **207** 300d. green and violet £140 £150

1953 (5 Sept). *Tenth Anniv of Liberation of Istria and Slovene Coast. As No. 759 (Family), but colour changed, optd "STT/VUJNA".*
B99 **209** 15d. blue (R.) . . . . 2·00 1·20

1953 (3 Oct). *Death Centenary of Radicevic (poet) As No. 760 but colour changed. optd "STT/VUJNA".*
B100 **210** 15d. black (R.) . . . . 1·20 90

1953 (25 Oct). *Red Cross. As No. 761 (Blood transfusion) but colour changed and optd "STT/VUJNA".*
B101 **211** 2d. scarlet and bistre (B.) 35 15

1953 (25 25). *POSTAGE DUE. Red Cross. As No. D762 (Blood transfusion, inscr "PORTO") but colour changed and optd "STT/VUJNA".*
BD102 2d. scarlet and bright purple (B.) . . 40 40

1953 (29 Nov). *10th Anniv of First Republican Legislative Assembly. As Nos. 762/4 but colours changed and optd "STT/VUJNA", in the colour of the stamp.*
B102 15d. slate-violet (Jajce) 40 40
B103 30d. lake (Assembly building) . . . 90 55
B104 50d. deep turquoise-green (Tito) . . . 90 85

STT VUJNA
(B **18**)

1954 (5 Mar). *As Nos. 719, 721 and 723 but optd with Type B **18** (serifed capitals).*
B105 5d. orange (V.) (Fishing) 60 30
B106 10d. green (R.) (Picking apples) . . . 55 35
B107 15d. scarlet (G.) (Picking sunflowers) . . 60 35

1954 (16 Apr). *AIR. As Nos. 675/83c (airplane over tourist centres) but colours changed and optd "STT VUJNA".*
B108 1d. deep lilac ("Iron Gates",
 Danube) 20 20
B109 2d. blue-green (G.) (Plitvice) . . . 20 20
B110 3d. claret (Br.) (Mountain village) . . 20 20
B111 5d. deep brown (Plitvice) 20 20
B112 10d. turquoise (Ohrid) 20 20
B113 20d. brown (Br.) (Kotor Bay) . . . 30 25
B114 30d. blue (Dubrovnik) 30 25
B115 50d. olive-black (Bled) 35 25
B116 100d. scarlet (R.) (Mountain village) . . 2·20 1·70
B117 200d. blackish violet (V.) (Mostar) . . 2·75 2·00
B118 500d. orange (Br.) (Belgrade) (9 Oct) . . 13·00 9·00
B108/118 Set of 11 . . . . 18·00 13·00

1954 (30 June). *Animal designs as Nos. 765/76 but colours changed and optd "STT VUJNA", in red.*
B119 2d. slate, buff and Venetian red . . . 20 20
B120 5d. slate, buff and bluish grey . . . 20 20
B121 10d. brown and green 20 20
B122 15d. brown and deep turquoise-blue . . 20 20
B123 17d. sepia and black-brown 20 20
B124 25d. yellow, grey-blue & brown-
 ochre 30 25
B125 30d. sepia and violet-grey 35 25
B126 35d. slate-black and reddish purple . . 40 30
B127 50d. chocolate and yellow-green . . 75 60
B128 65d. slate-black and orange-brown . . 3·25 3·25
B129 70d. orange-brown and blue . . . . 3·75 3·25
B130 100d. black and pale blue . . . . 12·50 11·00
B119/130 Set of 12 . . . . 20·00 18·00

166

TRIESTE   1954

Designs: Horiz—2 d. European souslik; 5 d. Lynx; 10 d. Red deer; 15 d. Brown bear; 17 d. Chamois; 25 d Eastern white pelican. *Vert*—30 d. Lammergeier; 35 d. Black beetle; 50 d Grasshopper; 65 d. Black Dalmatian lizard, 70 d. Blind cave-dwelling salamander; 100 d. Trout

1954 (8 Oct). *150th Anniv of Serbian Insurrection. As Nos.* 778/81, *but colours changed and optd "STT VUJNA" in one line (*15, 50*d.) or two lines (others).*
B131	15d. red, blue, fawn and lake	35	20
B132	30d. brn-lake, flesh, turq-grn & bl (G.)	35	20
B133	50d. red, buff, red-brown & sepia (G.)	55	50
B134	70d. black-brown, turquoise-green, pale brown & deep blue-grn (R.)	90	80
B131/134 *Set of 4*		1·90	1·50

Designs:—15 d. Serbian flag, 1804; 30 d. Cannon, 1804; 50 d. Seal of insurgents' council; 70 d. Karageorge.

The use of stamps of the Yugoslav Military Government ceased on 25 October 1954.
On 26 October 1954, under a Four-Power Agreement, Zone A, except for three villages south of Trieste, was to be ruled by Italy, and Zone B, with the three villages, by Yugoslavia.
A final agreement between Italy and Yugoslavia, on the incorporation of these areas in the two countries was signed at Ancona on 10 November 1975.

VENEZIA GIULIA AND ISTRIA 1945

Venezia Giulia and Istria

100 Centesimi = 1 Italian Lira

A. YUGOSLAV OCCUPATION

Yugoslav Partisans, who had occupied much of the Istrian peninsula in 1943–44, attacked the cities of Venezia Guilia in the last days of the war. They entered Trieste on 30 April 1945 and on 2 May the German garrison surrendered to the New Zealand Division.
The following provisional issues were made by the Yugoslavs.

ISSUE FOR TRIESTE

1.V.1945
TRIESTE
★ L.2
TRST
(1)

1945 (15 June). *Stamps of the Italian Social Republic, 1944–45, surch as T* **1**.

(a) W **8** *of Italy (Crown).*

1	14	+1l. on 30c. brown (Drummer)	£325	£325
2	12	2+ 2l. on 25c. green (R.) (San Lorenzo)	15	40
3	14	10+ 10l. on 30c. brown	18·00	35·00

(b) Without wmk.

4	–	20c. + 1l. on 5c. brown (R.) (St. Ciriaco's Church)	15	40
5	13	+1l. on 25c. green (B.) (San Lorenzo)	15	40
6	14	+1l. on 30c. brown	15	40
7	15	+1l. on 50c. violet (Fascist allegory)	15	40
8	–	+1l. on 1l. violet (Montecassino Abbey)	15	40
9	–	+2l. on 1l.25, blue (R.) (St. Mary of Grace, Milan)	15	40
10	–	+2l. on 3l. green (R.) (St. Mary of Grace, Milan)	15	40
11	–	5+ 5l. on 1l. violet (R.)	15	40
12	14	10+ 10l. on 30c. brown (R.)	1·70	2·75
13	–	20+ 20l. on 5c. brown (B.)	5·00	7·25
2/13	Set of 12		24·00	44·00

A 1l. sepia and 1l. lilac-rose depicting San Giusto Cathedral, Trieste, were prepared but not issued.

ISSUE FOR ISTRIA

In June 1945 various stamps of Italy were overprinted "ISTRA" and further surcharged for use in Istria and Pola (now Pula) but they were not issued. However, four of these were further surcharged and issued on 1 July.

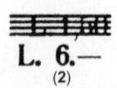

ISTRA
≡≡≡≡≡
L. 6.–
(2)

1945 (1 July). *Stamp of Italy (No. 14) or Italian Social Republic (others) surch as T* **2**.

14	99	4l.on 2l. on 1l. violet (249) (Julius Caesar)	60	80
15	14	6l.on 1,50l. on 75c. carmine (105)	3·75	5·25
16	–	10l.on 0, 10l. on 5c. brown (106)	21·00	16·00
17	103	20l.on 1l. on 50c. violet (59) (Victor Emmanuel III)	4·00	6·00

ISSUE FOR FIUME (Rijeka)

■3-V-1945■
FIUME RIJEKA
★
LIRE 16
(3)

1945 (26 July). *Stamps of Italian Social Republic. 1944–45, surch as T* **3**.

(a) W **8** *of Italy (Crown).*

18	12	2on 25c. green	15	40
19	14	16on 75c. carmine	£120	£150

(b) Without wmk.

20	–	4l.on l. violet	15	40
21	–	5l.on 10c. brown	15	40
22	–	6l.on 10c. brown	20	40
23	13	10l.on 25c. green	15	40
24	14	16l.on 75c. red	7·00	8·25

(c) On Express Letter stamp (Palermo Cathedral).

25	E 16	20l.on 1l.25 green	1·90	2·50
18/25	Set of 8		£110	£150

On No. 25 the surcharge is much larger to conform with the horizontal format of the design

On 9 June 1945 an agreement was signed in Belgrade under which Trieste and the roads and railways from there to Austria via Gorizia, Caporetto and Tarvisio, as well as Pola, should be under the control of the Supreme Allied Commander. The remainder of Venezia Giulia would be under Yugoslav control. The agreement formally came into effect on 12 June but the lines of demarcation were settled by an agreement signed by Lt.-Gen. Morgan and Gen, Jovanovic on 20 June.

B. ALLIED MILITARY GOVERNMENT

The area under British and United States control included Trieste, Pola, Gorizia and the Isonzo valley.

A.M.G.
V.G.
(4)

A.M.G.
V.G.
(5)

(= "Allied Military Government Venezia Giulia")

VENEZIA GIULIA AND ISTRIA 1945

1945 (22 Sept)–**47**. Stamps of Italy optd with T **4** or **5** (100l.).

(a) Imperial series.

26	100	10c. sepia (No. 241)		10	45
27		10c. sepia (No. 633) (25.9.45)		10	50
28	99	20c. carmine (No. 243) (9.12.46)		15	1·60
29		20c. carmine (No. 634) (25.9.45)		15	75
30		20c. carmine (No. 640)		35	3·00
31	101	60c. orange-verm (No. 636) (25.9.45)		15	85
32	103	60c. green (No. 641)		15	25
33	99	1l. violet (No. 642)		20	15
34	101	2l. brown-lake (No. 644)		30	15
35	98	5l. carmine (No. 645) (16.10.45)		70	25
36	101	10l. violet (No. 646)		80	40
37	99	20l. yellow-grn (No. 257) (10.7.46)		1·70	3·25
26/37 Set of 12				4·00	10·00

(b) Stamps of 1945–48 (Nos. 649, etc.).

38	194	25c. greenish blue (8.1.47)		15	55
39	–	2l. purple-brown (17.7.47)		55	40
40	194	3l. scarlet (8.1.47)		40	30
41	–	4l. vermilion (2.1.47)		55	30
42	195	6l. bluish violet (17.7.47)		1·30	1·70
43	194	20l. purple (23.7.47)		36·00	2·75
44	196	25l. deep green (10.7.46)		4·50	5·75
45	–	50l. brown-purple (10.7.46)		5·00	8·75
46	197	100l. carmine (13.9.46)		19·00	29·00
38/46 Set of 9				60·00	45·00

1945–47. AIR. Air stamps of Italy optd with T **4** (50c.) or **5** (others).

47	110	50c. sepia (22.9.45)		15	30
48	198	1l. slate (23.7.47)		40	3·25
49	199	2l. blue (16.1.47)		40	1·40
50	–	5l. deep green (23.1.47)		2·00	1·60
51	198	10l. carmine (23.1.47)		2·00	1·60
52	199	25l. blue (13.9.46)		2·50	2·00
53	–	25l. brown (23.7.47)		20·00	22·00
54	198	50l. deep green (13.9.46)		4·25	5·50
47/54 Set of 8				28·00	34·00

1946 (13 Sept). EXPRESS LETTER. Nos. E680 and E683 of Italy optd with T **5**.

E55	E 201	10l. blue		3·00	1·90
E56	E 200	30l. violet		7·25	11·50

C. YUGOSLAV MILITARY GOVERNMENT

The area under Yugoslav control included Fiume (Rijeka), all the Istrian peninsula except Pola (Pula), and former Italian territory to the N.E. of Trieste, including Postumia (Postojna).

6 Grapes

7 Roman Amphitheatre, Pula, and Istrian Fishing Vessel

8 Tunny

(Des M. Oražem. Photo Ljudska Ptg Wks, Ljubljana)

1945 (15 Aug). T **6/8** and similar designs. P 10½ × 11½.

57	6	0.25l. slate-green		90	90
58	–	0.50l. lake-brown		40	40
59	–	1l. scarlet (13.12)		40	40
60	–	1.50l. deep olive (24.12)		60	60

61	–	2l. deep blue-green		35	90
62	7	4l. light blue (24.12)		35	35
63	–	5l. slate (13.12)		60	60
64	–	10l. brown		1·50	1·50
65	8	20l. purple (13.12)		8·50	10·50
66	–	30l. bright magenta (24.12)		9·25	11·50
57/66 Set of 10				20·00	25·00

Designs: As T **6**—0.50l. Donkey and view; 1l. Rebuilding damaged homes; 1.50l. Olive branch; 2l. Duino Castle near Trieste. As T **7**—5l. Birthplace of Vladimir Gortan at Piran; 10l. Ploughing As T **8**—30l. Viaduct over the Solkan.
See also Nos. 74/83 and 98/101.

(D **9**) (D **10**)

1945–46. POSTAGE DUE. Stamps as last surch with value expressed in "Lit", by Tipografia Commerciale, Rijeka.

(a) As Type D **9** (31.12.45).

D67	1l.on 0.25l. slate-green		10·50	3·50
D68	4l.on 0.50l. lake-brown		1·40	1·30
D69	8l.on 0.50l. lake-brown		1·40	1·30
D70	10l.on 0.50l. lake-brown		9·25	3·25
D71	20l.on 0.50l. lake-brown		10·50	8·00

(b) Surch as Type D **10** (22.2.46).

D72	0.50l.on 20l. purple		1·30	1·60
	a. Straight top to "5" instead of curved		22·00	24·00
D73	2l.on 30l. bright magenta		2·50	3·25
	a. Curved bottom to "2" instead of straight		5·00	6·00
D67/73 Set of 7			34·00	20·00

(Photo Tipografija, Zagreb)

1946 (11 Feb–7 Mar). P 12 and some colours changed.

74	6	0.25l. grey-green (26.2)		25	35
75	–	0.50l. red-brown (18.2)		50	60
76	–	1l. green (26.2)		50	60
77	–	1.50l. deep olive (26.2)		25	35
78	–	2l. deep blue-green (18.2)		25	35
79	7	4l. scarlet (18.2)		25	35
80	–	5l. black		25	35
81	–	10l. brown (26.2)		90	1·00
82	8	20l. blue (7.3)		3·50	4·25
83	–	30l. bright magenta (7.3)		3·50	5·75
74/83 Set of 10				9·25	12·50

(D **11**) (D **12**)

1946 (25 Mar–11 May). POSTAGE DUE. Nos. 76 and 83 surch as Types D **11/12**, by Narodna Stamparija, Rijeka. Value expressed in "Lira".

D84	1l.on 1l. green		40	50
D85	2l.on 1l. green		40	60
D86	4l.on 1l. green		60	80
D87	10l.on 30l. bright magenta (11.5)		5·75	4·00
D88	20l.on 30l. bright magenta (11.5)		11·00	9·25
D89	30l.on 30l. bright magenta (11.5)		11·00	9·75
D84/89 Set of 6			26·00	22·00

169

VENEZIA GIULIA AND ISTRIA 1946

PORTO

1.-

■■ Lira ■■
(D 13)

PORTO

Lira

10.-
(D 14)

VENEZIA GIULIA. Stamps of Austria and Italy overprinted "Venezia Giulia" in 1918–19 are listed under Austrian Territories Acquired by Italy.

1946 (7 Sept). *POSTAGE DUE. Nos. 74 and 82 surch as Types D 13/14, respectively, by Tipografia Commerciale, Rijeka.*

D90	6	1l.on 0.25l. grey-green	60	50
		a. Thin "1"	42·00	22·00
D91		2l.on 0.25l. grey-green	95	70
		a. Thin "2"	20·00	19·00
D92		4l.on 0.25l. grey-green	60	50
		a. Thin "4"	20·00	19·00
D93	8	10l.on 20l. blue	5·00	4·00
		a. Thin "10"	70·00	55·00
D94		20l.on 20l. blue	11·00	9·25
		a. Thin "20"	£120	90·00
D95		30l.on 20l. blue	11·00	9·25
		a. Thin "30"	£140	£110
D90/95	Set of 6		26·00	22·00

In Nos. D90a/95a the figures of value are of various sizes but all are thinner with either very small serifs or none; the variety occurs on positions 94, 95, 99 and 100.

1946 (15 Nov). *Nos. 82/3 surch with new value and three bars over old value, by Urania, Rijeka.*

96		1on 20l. blue	1·40	1·50
97		2on 30l. bright magenta	1·40	1·50

(Photo State Ptg Wks, Belgrade)

1946 (30 Nov). *P 11½ and new values.*

98	–	1l. yellow-green (as 76)	90	90
99	–	2l. deep blue-green (as 78)	90	90
100	–	3l. rose-carmine (as 2l.)	4·00	3·25
101	7	6l. ultramarine	6·00	6·00
98/101	Set of 4		10·50	10·00

VOJNA UPRAVA JUGOSLAVENSKE ARMIJE

≡ L 1
(15)

Vojna Uprava Jugoslavenske Armije

≡ L 1 ≡
(D 16)

1947 (8 Feb). *As Nos. 514 (Girl with flag) and O540 (Torch) of Yugoslavia, but colours changed, optd with T 15, in Belgrade.*

102		1l.on 9d. pink	40	50
103		1.50l.on 0.50d. blue	40	50
104		2l.on 9d. pink	40	50
105		3l.on 0.50d. blue	40	50
106		5l.on 9d. pink	50	60
107		6l.on 0.50d. blue	35	45
108		10l.on 9d. pink	50	60
109		15l.on 0.50d. blue	70	80
110		35l.on 9d. pink	70	80
111		50l.on 0.50d. blue	90	1·00
102/111	Set of 10		4·75	5·50

1947 (8 Feb). *POSTAGE DUE. As No. D528 (Star and torches) of Yugoslavia, but colour changed, surch as Type D 16, in Belgrade.*

D112		1l.on 1d. blue-green	95	1·00
D113		2l.on 1d. blue-green	35	40
D114		6l.on 1d. blue-green	35	40
D115		10l.on 1d. blue-green	75	80
D116		30l.on 1d. blue-green	75	80
D112/116	Set of 5		2·75	3·00

By the Treaty of Paris, 10 February 1947, all former Italian territory in Venezia Giulia and Istria was included in Yugoslavia, except Gorizia and the area to be comprised in the Free Territory of Trieste (q.v.).

ERITREA 1893

Eritrea

100 Centesimi = 1 Lira

Between 1869 and 1880 an Italian shipping company bought the coastal territory round Assab from the local Sultan and this was transferred to the Italian State in 1882. Italian troops landed at Massawa in 1885 and Ethiopia recognised Italian sovereignty over possessions in the Red Sea by treaty on 2 May 1889.
Italian post offices were opened at Assab in 1883 and Massawa in 1885, using the general issues of Italian Post Offices in the Turkish Empire (q.v.) and unoverprinted stamps of Italy. Assab used the numeral cancellation "3840" and Massawa "3862" The Italian colony of Eritrea was proclaimed on 1 January 1890.

PRINTERS. All stamps of Eritrea were printed at the Italian Government Printing Works, *unless otherwise stated.*

WATERMARK CROWN. The Crown watermark, *W* **8** of Italy, is illustrated here.

Stamps of Italy overprinted except where otherwise stated.

Colonia Eritrea
(1)   (2)

1893 (1 Jan). *Stamps of 1863–91 optd with T* **1** *(*1c. to 5c.*) or* **2** *(others).*

1	4	1c. bronze-green	4·00	2·00
		a. Opt inverted	£325	£275
		b. Opt double	£1000	
2	5	2c. brown	1·40	85
		a. Opt inverted	£275	£250
		b. Opt double	£1000	
3	23	5c. green	45·00	2·75
		a. Opt inverted	£3500	£2000
4	12	10c. deep rose-red	55·00	2·75
5		20c. orange	£120	2·00
6		25c. blue	£400	14·50
7	14	40c. brown	4·50	6·50
8	14a	45c. dull green	4·50	9·75
9	15	60c. mauve	4·50	20·00
10	16	1l. brown and orange	13·00	20·00
11	29	5l. carmine and blue	£225	£160
1/11 *Set of* 11			£800	£425

1895–99. *Stamps of 1893–97 optd with T* **1** *(*1c. to 5c.*) or* **2** *(others).*

12	21	1c. brown (8 99)	8·00	4·75
13	22	2c. red-brown (8.99)	85	85
14	24	5c. green (7.97)	85	85
		a. Opt inverted	£225	£1700

15	25	10c. lake (6.98)	85	85
16	26	20c. orange (1.96)	1·25	1·00
17	27	25c. blue (1.96)	1·40	1·60
18	28	45c. pale green (10.95)	11·50	11·50
12/18 *Set of* 7			22·00	19·00

1903 (1 Apr). *Stamps of 1901 optd with T* **1**.

19	30	1c. brown	30	75
		a. Opt inverted	90·00	90·00
20	31	2c. orange-brown	30	45
21	32	5c. green	26·00	45
22	33	10c. lake	32·00	45
23		20c. orange	2·00	75
24		25c. blue	£200	9·00
		a. Opt double	£375	
25		40c. brown	£275	13·00
26		45c. grey-green	2·75	5·50
27		50c. mauve	80·00	15·00
		a. Violet	80·00	15·00
28	34	1l. brown and green	2·75	60
29		5l. blue and rose	16·00	21·00
19/29 *Set of* 11			£600	65·00

1903 (1 Apr). *POSTAGE DUE. Postage Due stamps of 1870–1903 optd with T* **1**. *at top of stamp.*

D30	D 12	5c. magenta and orange	8·00	20·00
		a. Opt double	£275	
D31		10c. magenta and orange	7·25	20·00
D32		20c. magenta and orange	7·25	11·50
D33		30c. magenta and orange	9·75	14·50
D34		40c. magenta and orange	26·00	32·00
D35		50c. magenta and orange	42·00	32·00
D36		60c. magenta and orange	11·50	14·50
D37		1l. magenta and blue	8·00	16·00
D38		2l. magenta and blue	80·00	65·00
D39		5l. magenta and blue	£160	£120
D40		10l. magenta and blue	£1500	£800
D30/39 *Set of* 10			£300	£300

For stamps with the overprint at bottom of stamp, see Nos. D53/63.

1905 (Nov). *POSTAGE DUE. Postage Due stamps of 1903 optd with T* **1**.

D41	D 13	50l. yellow	£375	£120
D42		100l. blue	£225	60·00

1905 (Nov). *Stamps of 1905 optd with T* **1**.

30	33	15c. on 20c. orange (73)	24·00	5·25

1907 (Sept). *EXPRESS LETTER. Inland Express Letter stamp of 1903 optd with T* **1**.

E31	E 35	25c. rose (E73)	14·50	11·50
		a. Opt double		

1908 (Dec)–**09**. *Stamps of 1906–08 optd with T* **1**.

31	37	5c. green	80	75
		a. Pair, one without opt	£400	
32	38	10c. rose (1909)	80	75
33	39	25c. blue (1909)	3·75	1·50

1909 (30 July). *EXPRESS LETTER. Foreign Express Letter stamp of 1908 optd with T* **1**.

E34	E 41	30c. blue and rose	75·00	90·00

171

ERITREA 1910

3 Ploughing   **4** Government Palace, Massawa   ERITREA (5)

1910–29. *T* **3/4** *(various frames). Recess.*

(a) P 13½ *(1910–14).*

34	3	5c. green (1.8.14)		65	1·60
35		10c. carmine (1.9.14)		3·00	2·40
36	4	15c. slate (16.10.10)		£160	9·00
37		25c. blue (1.3.10)		4·00	6·50

(b) P 11 *(1928–29).*

38	3	5c. green (10.28)		£110	29·00
39		10c. carmine (12.28)		13·00	23·00
40	4	15c. slate (4.29)		32·00	29·00

1916–21. *Stamps of 1906–20 optd with T* **5** *(20c.) or T* **1** *(others).*

41	37	15c. slate (104) (4.20)		13·00	5·75
42	41	20c. orange (105) (9.21)		3·00	7·25
		a. Opt double		£250	
43	40	40c. brown		24·00	21·00
44		50c. violet		8·00	1·60
45	39	60c. carmine-red (7 18)		16·00	14·00
46	44	10l. sage-green and pale rose		£225	£325
41/46	Set of 6			£250	£325

1916. *Red Cross Society stamps of 1915–16 optd with T* **5.**

47	53	10c.+ 5c. carmine (Apr)		2·00	8·00
		a. Opt inverted		£300	£300
		b. "EPITREA"		16·00	24·00
48	54	15c.+ 5c. slate (Nov)		10·50	18·00
49		20c.on 15c. + 5c. slate (Mar)		10·50	18·00
		a. Pair, one without opt		£800	
		b. "EPITREA"		40·00	60·00
50		20c.+ 5c. orange (June)		3·25	18·00
		a. Opt inverted		£300	£300
		b. Pair, one without opt		—	£1500
		c. "EPITREA"		23·00	35·00
47/50	Set of 4			23·00	55·00

Cent. 5   CENT. 20

(6)   (7)

1916. *No. 36 of Eritrea surch with T* **6** *or* **7.**

51	4	5c.on 15c. slate (R.) (Dec)		5·00	8·50
52		20c.on 15c. slate (June)		2·40	2·10
		a. Surch double, one inverted		£180	£180
		b. "CENT" counted		£130	£130
		c. "T" omitted		26·00	26·00

No. 52c occurs on position 65.

ERITREA   **ERITREA**   ERITREA

(8)   (9)   (10)

1916–24. *PARCEL POST. Parcel Post stamps of 1914–22 optd on each half of stamp.*

(a) With T **8** *(11.16).*

				Un pair	Used pair	Used half
P53	P **53**	5c. brown		60·00	90·00	3·75
P54		10c. blue		£1300	£2250	40·00
P55		25c. red		£120	£140	5·00
P56		50c. orange		38·00	95·00	4·00
P57		1l. violet		55·00	95·00	3·25
P58		2l. green		35·00	95·00	3·50
P59		3l. yellow		£425	£300	32·00
P60		4l. slate		£425	£300	32·00
P53, 55/60 Set of 7				£1000	£2750	75·00

(b) As T **5** *(12½ × 1½ mm) (1917–24).*

P61	P **53**	5c. brown		1·60	3·75	2·50
P62		10c. blue		1·60	3·75	2·50
P63		20c. black		1·60	3·75	2·50
P64		25c. red		1·60	3·75	2·50
P65		50c. orange		3·25	6·00	5·00
P66		1l. violet		3·25	6·00	5·00
P67		2l. green		3·25	6·00	5·00
P68		3l. yellow (1922)		3·25	6·00	5·00
P69		4l. slate		3·25	10·00	5·00
P70		10l. pale purple (9.24)		45·00	75·00	4·50
P71		12l. red-brown (9.24)		£110	£180	6·00
P72		15l. olive-green (9.24)		£110	£180	9·00
P73		20l. deep purple (9.24)		£110	£180	18·00
P61/73 Set of 13				£350	£600	45·00

1920–26. *POSTAGE DUE. As Nos. D30/40 but with opt at bottom of stamp.*

D53	D **12**	5c. magenta and orange		1·00	5·00
		a. Opt and centre inverted		£300	£300
D54		10c. magenta and orange		2·00	5·00
D55		20c. magenta and orange		£400	£160
D56		30c. magenta and orange		11·50	14·50
D57		40c. magenta and orange		26·00	18·00
D58		50c. magenta and orange		11·50	14·50
D59		60c. magenta and orange (1926)		13·50	18·00
D60		1l. magenta and blue (1923)		23·00	13·00
D61		2l. magenta and blue (1924)		£850	£425
D62		5l. magenta and blue		£200	£150
D63		10l. magenta and blue		29·00	38·00
D53/63 Set of 11				£1400	£800

1921 (Apr). *EXPRESS LETTER. Inland Express Letter stamp of 1920 optd with T* **1.**

E53	E **35**	50c. rose		2·00	13·00

1922 (Apr). *Victory stamps of 1921 optd as T* **5** *(13 mm long).*

53	**62**	5c. green		1·25	5·00
		a. Opt double		£225	
54		10c. carmine		1·25	5·00
55		15c. slate		1·25	6·50
56		25c. ultramarine		1·25	6·50
53/56 Set of 4				4·50	21·00

1922 (1 Nov). *Stamps of Somalia, 1906–16, optd with T* **9** *and bars (as T* **19** *of Somalia) in black.*

57		2c.on 1b. brown		3·75	9·75
		a. "C 2" omitted		£100	
		b. "C." omitted		40·00	
		c. Pair, one without "ERITREA"		£1000	
58		5c.on 2b. green		3·75	6·50
59		10c.on 1a. rose		3·75	1·60
		a. "10" omitted		50·00	
60		15c.on 2a. orange-brown		3·75	1·60
61		25c.on 22a. blue		3·75	1·60
		a. "C" omitted		32·00	
62		50c.on 5a. yellow-orange		11·50	6·50
		a. "C 50" omitted		£900	
		b. "ERITREA" double		—	£600
63		1l.on 10a. lilac		13·00	11·50
		a. "ERITREA" double		£550	£600
		b. Pair, one without "ERITREA"		£1400	
57/63 Set of 7				28·00	30·00

See also Nos 83/9 for stamps overprinted in different colours.

ERITREA   1923

1923 (24 Oct). *"Propaganda Fide" stamps optd with T* **10** *Centre in orange.*
64	**66**	20c. bronze-green		4·00	18·00
65		30c. carmine		4·00	18·00
66		50c. violet		2·75	20·00
67		1l. blue		2·75	20·00
64/67	Set of 4			12·00	70·00

ERITREA (11)   ERITREA (12)   E 13

1923 (29 Oct). *Fascist March on Rome stamps optd with T* **11**.
68	**73**	10c. deep green (R.)		4·25	7·25
69		30c. violet (R.)		4·25	7·25
70		50c. carmine-red		4·25	8·25
71	**74**	1l. light blue		4·25	21·00
72		2l. brown		4·25	24·00
73	**75**	5l. black and blue (R.)		4·25	35·00
68/73	Set of 6			23·00	95·00

1924 (1 Apr). *Manzoni stamps optd with T* **12**. *Centres in black or grey-black.*
74	10c. claret		5·00	20·00
75	15c. green		5·00	20·00
76	30c. black		5·00	20·00
77	50c. chestnut		5·00	20·00
78	1l. blue		40·00	£150
79	5l. dull purple		£400	£1300
74/79	Set of 6		£425	£1400

On Nos. 78/9 the surcharge reads up at left.

1924. *Stamps of 1901–06 optd with T* **8**.
80	**30**	1c. brown (May)		5·75	6·50
		a. Opt inverted		£200	
		b. Pair, one without opt		£550	
81	**31**	2c. brown-orange (July)		3·25	5·50
		a. Pair, one without opt		£550	
82	**37**	5c. green (July)		5·75	6·00

(Des A. Terzi. Recess)

1924 (1 July). EXPRESS LETTER. *Wmk Crown. P* 14.
E83	E **13**	60c. sepia and red		5·00	14·50
E84		2l. rose & slate-blue ("EXPRES")		18·00	17·50

1924 (July). *Stamps of Somalia optd as Nos. 57/63 but with "ERITREA" in different colours and bars in black.*
83	2c. on 1b. brown (B.)		12·00	18·00
	a. "C. 2" omitted			
84	5c. on 2b. green (R.)		10·50	11·50
	a. "C. 5" omitted		£450	£450
85	10c. on 1a. rose (B.)		5·25	9·25
86	15c. on 2a. orange-brown (B.)		5·25	9·25
	a. "ERITREA" inverted		£550	
	b. Pair, one without "ERITREA"		£900	
87	25c. on 2½a. blue (R.)		5·25	6·00
88	50c. on 5a. yellow-orange (B.)		5·25	11·50
	a. "C. 50" omitted		£550	
89	1l. on 10a. lilac (R.)		5·25	8·00
83/89	Set of 7		45·00	65·00

ERITREA (13)   ERITREA (14)

1925 (1 June). *Holy Year stamps cord with T* **13**.
90	20c.+ 10c. brown and myrtle-green		2·50	11·50
91	30c.+ 15c. brown and chocolate		2·50	13·00
92	50c.+ 25c. brown and violet		2·50	11·50
93	60c.+ 30c. brown and carmine		2·50	14·50
94	1l.+ 50c. purple and blue (R.)		2·50	20·00
95	5l.+2.50l. purple and orange-red (R.)		2·50	29·00
90/95	Set of 6		13·50	90·00

1925. *Portrait types optd with T* **1**.
96	**39**	20c. green (179) (1 Oct)		9·75	7·25
97		30c. slate (183) (July)		9·75	7·25
98	**34**	2l. myrtle and orange (111) (1 Oct)		45·00	42·00

1925 (Nov)–**26**. *Royal Jubilee stamps optd with T* **14**.
A. P 13½.
99A	**82**	60c. lake-red		6·00	13·00
100A		1l. blue		£1100	£2500
101A		1l.25 blue (7.26)		45	9·50

B. P 11.
99B	**82**	60c. lake-red		65	3·00
100B		1l. blue		65	5·00
101B		1l.25 blue (7.26)		4·00	16·00

ERITREA (15)   Eritrea (16)

1926 (12 Apr). *St. Francis of Assisi stamps optd with T* **15** *(centesimi values) or* **16** *(lire values).*
102	20c. dull green		1·50	6·50
103	40c. violet		1·50	6·50
104	60c. dull lake		1·50	11·50
105	1l.25 blue (*p* 11) (R.)		1·50	18·00
106	5l.+ 2.50l. olive (R.)		4·00	38·00
102/106	Set of 5		9·00	70·00

1926 (15 May). *Colonial Propaganda. As T* **6** *of Cyrenaica (Libya), but inset "ERITREA".*
107	5c.+ 5c. brown		60	4·00
108	10c.+ 5c. olive-green		60	4·00
109	20c.+ 5c. blue-green		60	4·00
110	40c.+ 5c. scarlet		60	4·00
111	60c.+ 5c. orange		60	4·00
112	1l.+ 5c. blue		60	4·00
107/112	Set of 6		3·25	22·00

70 Y.
(E 17)

1926 (1 June). EXPRESS LETTER. *Nos. E83/4 surch as Type E* **17** *(with four bars over old value on No. E114).*
E113	E **13**	70 on 60c. sepia and red (B.)		5·00	9·00
E114		2.50 on 2l. rose and slate blue (R.)		11·50	17·00

1926. *Portrait type optd with T* **5**.
113	**34**	75c. lake-red and carmine (185)		38·00	7·25
		a. Opt double		£200	
114		1l.25 blue and ultramarine (186)		23·00	7·25
115		2l.50 myrtle and orange (187)		75·00	21·00

1926. POSTAGE DUE. *No D31 of Italy optd at bottom as T* **1**.
D116	D **12**	60c. brown and orange		65·00	70·00

LIRE 1,25
(E 18)

Eritrea (17)

173

ERITREA 1927

1927 (Feb). EXPRESS LETTER. As No. E83, but perf 11, surch with Type E **18**.

E116	E **13**	1l.25 on 60c. sepia & carmine (B.)	9·00	2·25
		a. Black surch	£5500	£375
		b. Perf 14	65·00	8·00
		ba. Black surch	£160	20·00

1927 (21 Apr). First National Defence stamps optd with T **14**.

116		40c.+ 20c. black and brown	1·90	14·50
117		60c.+ 30c. brown and lake	1·90	14·50
118		1l.25 + 60c. black and blue	1·90	29·00
119		5l.+ 2l.50 black and blue-green	2·75	40·00
116/119	Set of 4		7·50	90·00

In Nos. 118/9 the original colours of the Italian issue are reversed, the 1l.25 being in the colour of the 5l. and vice versa. These two stamps exist overprinted on the original colours but were not issued.

1927 (10 Oct). Volta Centenary stamps optd with T **17**. Colours changed.

120	**90**	20c. bright violet	5·00	18·00
121		50c. orange	6·50	11·50
		a. Opt double	£130	
		b. Opt "Cirenaica" inverted with "Eritrea" normal	£275	
122		1l.25 blue	9·75	26·00

1927 (17 Oct)–**37**. PARCEL POST. Parcel Post stamps optd as T **5** (12½ × 1½ mm).

			On pair	Used pair	Used half
P123	P **92**	10c. deep blue (4.37)	£3500	£400	4·25
P124		25c. carmine (12.35)	£180	25·00	80
P125		30c. ultramarine (12.28)		85	10·00	60
P126		50c. orange (2.36)	£180	18·00	2·75
P127		60c. rose-scarlet (12.28)		80	18·00	1·25
P128		1l. violet (11.35)	£160	18·00	30
P129		2l. green (10.36)	£180	18·00	30
P130		3l. yellow-bistre	3·25	18·00	30
P131		4l. grey-black	3·25	18·00	30
P132		10l. purple (2.36)	£275	£325	6·00
P133		20l. dull purple (2.36)	£275	£325	9·50
P124/133	Set of 10		£1100	£700	17·00

1928–29. Portrait types optd.

(a) With T **1**.

123	**92**	7½c. brown (21.6.28)	11·50	38·00
124	**39**	20c. purple (180) (1.9.28)	3·25	2·75
125	**92**	50c. bright mauve (8.29)	38·00	23·00
126	**39**	60c. orange (184) (4.29)	65·00	75·00
127	**34**	75c. lake-red and carmine (185) (6.28)	48·00	4·50
128		1l.25 blue & ultram (186) (2.28)	23·00	2·75
129		2l.50 myrtle & orange (187) (8.28)	£100	32·00

(b) With T **17**.

130	**91**	50c. slate and brown (8 28)	10·50	3·25

(c) With T **5**.

131	**92**	50c. bright mauve (12.11.28)	29·00	23·00
132	**91**	1l.75 brown (28.1.29)	48·00	16·00
123/132	Set of 10		£350	£200

1928 (15 Oct). 45th Anniv of Italian–African Society. As T **8** of Cyrenaica (Libya), but inscr "POSTE ERITREA".

133	20c.+ 5c. blue green	1·60	5·25
134	30c.+ 5c. scarlet	1·60	5·25
135	50c.+ 10c. violet	1·60	9·00
136	1l.25 + 20c. blue	1·75	10·50
133/136 Set of 4		6·00	27·00

1929 (4 Mar). Second National Defence stamps optd with T **5**. colours changed.

137	30c.+ 10c. black and carmine	3·00	10·50
138	50c.+ 20c. slate-grey and lilac (R.)	3·00	12·00
139	1l.25 + 50c. blue and brown (R.)	3·75	20·00
140	5l.+ 2l. black and olive-green (R.)	3·75	38·00
137/140 Set of 4		12·00	75·00

ERITREA (18)	Eritrea (19)	ERITREA (20)

1929 (14 Oct). Montecassino stamps optd with T **19** (10l.) or T **18** (others). Colours changed.

141	20c. deep green (R.)	3·75	8·00
142	25c. orange-vermilion (B.)	3·75	8·00
143	50c.+ 10c. carmine-red (B.)	3·75	9·75
144	75c.+ 15c. sepia (R.)	3·75	9·75
145	1l.25 + 25c. deep purple (R.)	7·25	16·00
146	5l.+ 1l. blue (R.)	7·25	23·00
147	10l.+ 2l. deep brown (R.)	7·25	26·00
141/147 Set of 7		32·00	90·00

1930 (17 Mar). Marriage of Prince Humbert and Princess Marie José stamps optd with T **20**. Colours changed.

148	**109**	20c. green	1·00	3·00
149		50c.+ 10c. orange-vermilion	85	4·00
150		1l.25 + 25c. carmine-red	85	9·25

21 Telegraph Linesman

22

(Des Cossio. Litho)

1930 (1 Apr). T **21** and similar types. Wmk Crown. P 14.

151	2c. black and greenish blue	1·00	4·75
152	5c. black and violet	1·40	65
153	10c. black and brown	1·40	35
154	15c. black and blue-green	1·40	50
155	25c. black and yellow-green	1·40	35
156	35c. black and brown-red	4·50	8·75
157	1l. black and deep blue	1·40	35
158	2l. black and brown	4·50	8·75
159	5l. black and olive-green	8·00	14·50
160	10l. black and blue	11·50	26·00
151/160 Set of 10		32·00	60·00

Designs: Vert—2c., 35c. Lancer; 5c. and 10c. Postman; 25c. Rifleman. Horiz—1l. Massawa; 2l. Railway bridge; 5l. Asmara Deghe Selam; 10l. Camel transport.

1930 (26 July). Ferrucci stamps optd as T **5** (13 mm long) or with T **5** (5l.) Colours changed.

161	**114**	20c. bright violet (R.)	1·60	1·60
162	**115**	25c. green (R.)	1·60	1·60
163		50c. black (R.)	1·60	3·25
164		1l.25 blue (R.)	1·60	6·50
165	**116**	5l.+ 2l. carmine-red (B.)	5·00	13·00
161/165 Set of 5			10·00	24·00

1930 (20 Oct). Third National Defence stamps optd as T **5** (12 mm long). Colours changed.

166	30c.+ 10c. blue-green and deep green	15·00	13·00
167	50c.+ 10c. purple and deep green (R.)	15·00	13·00
168	1l.25 + 30c. red-brown and brown (R.)	15·00	13·00
169	5l.+ 1l.50 green and deep blue (R.)	42·00	65·00
166/169 Set of 4		85·00	95·00

(Des D Tofani. Photo)

1930 (27 Nov). 25th Anniv of Colonial Agricultural Institute. Wmk Crown. P 14.

170	**22**	50c.+ 20c. brown	2·25	9·75
171		1l.25 + 20c. blue	2·25	9·75
172		1l.75 + 20c. green	2·25	12·00
173		2l.55 + 50c. bright violet	3·25	20·00
174		5l.+ 1l. carmine-red	3·25	28·00
170/174 Set of 5			12·00	70·00

174

ERITREA 1930

ERITREA
(23)

24 King Victor Emmanuel III

1930 (4 Dec). *Virgil Bimillenary stamps optd with T 23. Colours changed.*
175	15c. violet-grey (R.)	85	4·00
	a. Opt omitted		
176	20c. red-brown (B.)	85	2·00
177	25c. blue-green (R.)	85	1·60
178	30c. brown (B.)	85	2·00
179	50c. purple (R.)	85	1·60
180	75c. rose-red (B.)	85	3·00
181	1l.25 greenish blue (R.)	85	4·00
182	5l.+ 1l.50 purple (R.)	3·00	21·00
183	10l.+ 2l.50 brown (B.)	3·00	32·00
175/183	Set of 9	11·00	75·00

Only one example of No. 175a is known.

1931 (7 May). *St. Anthony of Padua stamps optd with T 5. Colours changed.*
184	20c. brown (B.)	1·40	8·00
185	25c. green (R.)	1·40	3·25
186	30c. chocolate (B.)	1·40	3·25
187	50c. purple (B.)	1·40	3·25
188	75c. slate (R.)	1·40	8·00
	a. Opt 13 mm instead of 11 mm long	45·00	
189	1l.25 greenish blue (R.)	1·40	16·00
	a. Opt double	£450	
190	5l.+ 12l.50 sepia	3·75	38·00
184/190	Set of 7	11·00	70·00

No. 188a occurs on position 18.

(Des A. Calcagnadoro. Photo)

1931. *Wmk Crown. P 14.*
191	**24**	7½c. brown (8.7)	45	1·50
192		20c. carmine and blue (8.7)	35	10
193		30c. purple and olive-green (8.7)	45	10
194		40c. green and blue (8.7)	50	10
195		50c. deep green and brown (22.5)	10	10
		a. Deep green omitted	£1000	
		b. Brown omitted	£1000	
196		75c. carmine (7.7)	1·50	10
197		1l.25 blue and violet (8.7)	2·40	40
198		2l.50 green (8.7)	2·40	3·25
191/198	Set of 8		7·25	3·75

Stamps inscribed "CINQVANTENARIO ERITREO" will be found listed under Italian Colonies (General Issues) in this volume.

25 Dromedary

26 Fish Wharf

27 Ruins at Cholloe

28 Eritrean Woman

ONORANZE AL DUCA DEGLI ABRUZZI
(29)

(Des G. Rondini. Photo)

1933 (1 Dec). *T 25/28 and similar designs. Wmk Crown. P 14.*
199	**25**	2c. blue	50	2·25
200	**26**	5c. black	65	25
201	**25**	10c. brown	1·00	10
202	**26**	15c. orange-brown	1·25	1·25
203	–	25c. green	80	10
204	–	35c. bright violet	3·00	4·25
205	**27**	1l. blackish blue	10	10
206	–	2l. blackish green	11·50	2·00
207	–	5l. carmine	5·75	3·25
208	**28**	10l. orange-vermilion	8·00	13·00
199/208	Set of 10		30·00	24·00

Designs: *Horiz*—25c. Baobab tree; 35c. Native village; 2l. African elephant. *Vert*—5l. Eritrean man.

1934 (May). *Honouring the Duke of the Abruzzi. As Nos. 201/2 and 204/8 of Eritrea but colours changed and optd with T 29.*
209	**25**	10c. indigo (R.)	7·75	11·50
210	**26**	15c. blue	5·75	11·50
211	–	35c. green (R.)	3·75	11·50
212	**27**	1l. brown-lake	3·75	11·50
213	–	2l. carmine	10·50	11·50
214	–	5l. bright violet (R.)	6·00	16·00
215	**28**	10l. blackish green (R.)	6·00	20·00
209/215	Set of 7		32·00	85·00

1934 (12 12). POSTAGE DUE. *Postage Due stamps of 1934 optd with T 8.*
D216	**D 141**	5c. brown	25	3·25
D217		10c. deep blue	25	85
D218		20c. bright scarlet	2·00	1·60
D219		25c. green	2·00	2·00
D220		30c. orange-red	2·00	3·75
D221		40c. agate	2·00	3·75
D222		50c. violet	2·00	65
D223		60c. indigo	4·00	6·50
D224		1l. reddish orange	2·00	80
D225	**D 142**	2l. green	9·75	18·00
D226		5l. violet	21·00	21·00
D227		10l. blue	23·00	25·00
D228		20l. carmine-red	28·00	28·00
		a. Opt inverted	£275	
D216/228	Set of 13		90·00	£110

30 Grant's Gazelle

(Des G. Rondmi. Photo)

1934 (17 Oct). *Second International Colonial Exhibition, Naples. Wmk Crown. P 14.*

(a) POSTAGE.
216	**30**	5c. sepia and green	2·75	9·00
217		10c. black and brown	2·75	9·00
218		20c. blue and scarlet	2·75	7·25
219		50c. sepia and violet	2·75	7·25
220		60c. blue and brown	2·75	9·75
221		1l.25, green and blue	2·75	16·00
216/221	Set of 6		15·00	55·00

(b) AIR. As T 30, inscr "POSTA AEREA".
222		25c. orange and blue	2·75	9·00
223		50c. blue and green	2·75	7·25
224		75c. orange and sepia	2·75	7·25
225		80c. deep green and brown	2·75	9·00

175

ERITREA 1934

226	1l. deep green and scarlet		2·75	9·75
227	2l. sepia and blue		2·75	16·00
222/227 Set of 6			15·00	55·00

Designs:—25c. to 75c. Caproni Ca 101 airplane over landscape; 80c. to 2l. Savoia Marchetti S-66 flying boat over globe.

In the Second World War, British troops occupied Eritrea, after hard fighting at Keren, by 6 April 1941. Overprinted British stamps (listed in Part 1 (1840/1952) of this catalogue under British Occupation of Italian Colonies) were used in Eritrea from 1942 to 1952.

Eritrea was federated with Ethiopia on 15 September 1952.

31 King Victor Emmanuel III and Caproni Ca 101 Airplane

SERVIZIO DI STATO (O **32**)

(Des G. Rondini Photo)

1934 (5 Nov). *Rome-Mogadiscio Flight. Wmk Crown. P 14.*

(a) AIR.

228	**31**	25c.+ 10c. grey-green	3·25	5·00
229		50c.+ 10c. brown	3·25	5·00
230		75c.+ 15c. carmine	3·25	5·00
231		80c.+ 15c. brown-black	3·25	5·00
232		1l.+ 20c. lake-brown	3·25	5·00
233		2l.+ 20c. blue	3·25	5·00
234		3l.+ 25c. bright violet	16·00	40·00
235		5l.+ 25c. orange-vermilion	16·00	40·00
236		10l.+ 30c. purple	16·00	40·00
237		25l.+ 2l. green	16·00	40·00
228/237 Set of 10			75·00	£170

(b) OFFICIAL AIR. No. 237, colour changed, optd with Type O **32**.

O238	**31**	25l. + 2l. carmine	£1600

No. O238 is not known with original cancellation.

33 Macchi Castoldi MC-94 Flying Boat over Zebu–drawn Plough

34 Caproni Ca 101 Airplane over Massawa–Asmara Railway

(Des L. de Rosa (75 c.,10 l.), G. Rondini (others). Photo)

1936 (11 May–16 Sept). *T* **33/4** *and similar horiz designs. Wmk Crown. P 14.*

238	**33**	25c. blue-green (16.9)	85	2·25
239	**34**	50c. brown (June)	50	10
240	—	60c. orange-vermilion (16.9)	1·40	5·25
241	—	75c. red-brown (16.9)	1·25	1·00
242	—	1l. blue	10	10
243	**33**	1l.50 bright violet (16.9)	80	35
244	**34**	2l. slate-blue (16.9)	1·00	2·00
245	—	3l. brown-lake (16.9)	18·00	8·75
246	—	5l. yellow-green (16.9)	6·50	4·00
247	—	10l. carmine (16.9)	16·00	8·75
238/247 Set of 10			42·00	29·00

Designs:—60c., 5l. Savoia Marchetti S-74 airplane over Dom palm trees; 75c., 10l. Savoia Marchetti S-73 airplane over roadway through cactus trees; 1l., 3l. Caproni Ca 101 airplane over bridge.

1939 (June). *CONCESSIONAL LETTER POST. No. CL267 optd* "ERITREA".

CL248	**CL 109**	10c. reddish brown	13·00	16·00

No. CL248 is known used at Assab and Asmara.

In No. CL248 the overprint generally clips or is just above the figures of value. Stamps printed in a deeper brown with the overprint higher were not issued in Eritrea, and were sold only in Rome from 1941. These are almost worthless.

Eritrea was joined with Ethiopia and Italian Somaliland to form Italian East Africa, by a law approved on 1 June 1936, after the Italian conquest of Ethiopia For issues of this period see Italian East Africa.

ETHIOPIA 1936

Ethiopia

100 Centesimi = 1 Lira

ITALIAN ANNEXATION

Italian military operations against Ethiopia began on 3 October 1935 and Addis Ababa, from which the Emperor had departed for Europe, was captured on 5 May 1936. Ethiopia was annexed by Italy on 9 May 1936 and the King of Italy was proclaimed Emperor.

54 King Victor Emmanuel III   **55**

(Photo Govt Ptg Wks, Rome)

1936 (22 May–5 Dec). *Annexation of Ethiopia. As T* **54** *(portrait and various views) and T* **55**. *Wmk Crown. P* 14.

322a	54	10c. red-brown (5.12)	8·00	4·75
322b	–	20c. bright violet (5.12)	7·25	1·90
322c	55	25c. green	3·50	45
322d		30c. sepia	3·50	90
322e		50c. carmine-red	2·00	20
322f	–	75c. orange (5.12)	16·00	4·00
322g	–	1l.25 blue (5.12)	16·00	5·75
322a/g	Set of 7		50·00	16·00

Designs: *Horiz*—20c. Mountain scenery; 75c. Gondar Castle; 1l.25, Tomb of Scec Hussen and Dordola Hills.

By an Italian law approved on 1 June 1936 Ethiopia was incorporated with Eritrea and Italian Somaliland as Italian East Africa (see that country).

ITALY ALBUMS FROM DAVO

We carry a fine range of excellent Davo branded albums for Italy.

For full details ask for Davo brochure.

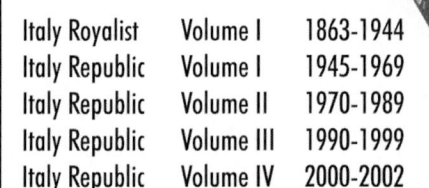

Italy Royalist	Volume I	1863-1944
Italy Republic	Volume I	1945-1969
Italy Republic	Volume II	1970-1989
Italy Republic	Volume III	1990-1999
Italy Republic	Volume IV	2000-2002

Stanley Gibbons Publications
7 Parkside, Christchurch Road, Ringwood
Hampshire, BH24 3SH, United Knigdom
Tel: +44 (0) 1425 472363 Fax: +44 (0) 1425 470247
Email: info@stanleygibbons.co.uk Internet: www.stanleygibbons.com

---

Looking beyond the catalogues for information?

THE ITALY & COLONIES STUDY CIRCLE

A SOCIETY COVERING ALL ASPECTS OF THE
PHILATELY & POSTAL HISTORY OF ITALY AND
THE ITALIAN AREA
THE PRIZE-WINNING JOURNAL FIL-ITALIA
REGULAR AUCTIONS OF SCARCE ITALIAN MATERIAL

Contact the Secretary:
L.R.HARLOW
7 Duncombe House, 8 Manor Road, Teddington, TW11 8BG

ITALIAN COLONIES 1932

Italian Colonies

GENERAL ISSUES

100 Centesimi = 1 Lira

In 1932–34 the following commemorative issues were made for use in Cyrenaica, Eritrea, Italian Somaliland and Tripolitania.

PRINTERS. The following were all printed at the Government Printing Works, Rome.

WATERMARK. The Crown watermark, used for all the following issues, is illustrated at the beginning of Eritrea.

1 Garibaldi and Victor Emmanuel
2 Garibaldi 
3 Caprera 
4 "Garibaldi" (statue), Savoia Marchetti S-55A Flying Boat and "Anita Garibaldi" (statue) 

(Des C. Mezzana (T **4**), F. Chiapelli (others). Photo)

1932 (1 July–6 Oct). *50th Death Anniv of Garibaldi*. Wmk Crown. P 14.

(a) POSTAGE. As T 1/2.

1	—	10c. green	2·30	5·75
2	1	20c. carmine-red	2·30	3·75
3	—	25c. green	2·30	3·75
4	1	30c. green	2·30	5·75
5	—	50c. carmine-red	2·30	3·75
6	—	75c. carmine-red	2·30	6·25
7	—	1l.25 blue	2·30	6·25
8	—	1l.75 + 25c. blue	4·00	11·50
9	—	2l.55 + 50c. sepia	4·00	18·00
10	2	5l.+ 1l. blue	4·00	21·00

Designs: *Horiz*—10c. Garibaldi's birthplace, Nice; 25c., 50c. "Here we make Italy or die"; 75c. Anita's death; 1l.25, Garibaldi's tomb; 1l.75, Quarto Rock. *Vert*—2l.55, Garibaldi statue, Rome.

(b) AIR. As T 3.

11	3	50c. carmine-red	2·30	5·75
12	—	80c. green	2·30	5·75
13	3	1l.+ 25c. sepia	4·75	13·50
14	—	2l.+ 50c. sepia	4·75	13·50
15	—	5l.+ 1l. sepia	4·75	13·50

Designs: *Vert*—80c. The Ravenna hut; 2l. Anita; 5l. Garibaldi.

(c) AIR EXPRESS (6 Oct).

E16	**4**	2l.25 + 1l. black and violet	4·75	13·50
E17		4l.50 + 1l.50 green and brown	4·75	17·00
1/E17	*Set of 17*		50·00	£150

5 Dante, 1265–1321
6 Leonardo Da Vinci's "Flying Man" 
7 Leonardo da Vinci 
8 Leonardo da Vinci 

(Postage des Chiapelli. Air des C. Mezzana. Recess (100l.), photo (others))

1932 (11 July–7 Sept). *Dante Alighieri Society*. Types of Italy optd "COLONIE ITALIANE" as in T **5/7** or so inscribed (T **8**). Wmk Crown. P 14.

(a) POSTAGE. As T 5.

18		10c. slate (R.)	55	1·20
19		15c. sepia (R.)	55	1·20
20		20c. grey-green (R.)	55	55
21		25c. green (R.)	55	55
22		30c. red-brown (R.)	55	70
23		50c. slate-blue (R.)	55	40
24		75c. carmine	90	1·60
25		1l.25 deep blue (R.)	90	2·10
26		1l.75 bright violet (R.)	1·10	4·25
27		2l.75 orange-vermilion	1·10	10·50
28		5l.+ 2l. olive-green (R.)	1·10	13·00
29		10l.+ 2l.50 blue (R.)	1·10	17·00

Designs:—10c. Giovanni Boccaccio; 15c. Niccolo Machiavelli; 20c. Fra Paola Sarpi; 25c. Vittorio Alfieri; 30c. Ugo Foscolo; 50c. Giacomo Leopardi; 75c. Giosue Carducci; 1l.25, Carlo Botta; 1l.75, Torquato Tasso; 2l.75, Francesco Petrarch; 5l. Ludovico Ariosto; 10l. Dante (*different*).

(b) AIR.

30	**6**	50c. slate (R.)	70	3·00
31	**7**	1l. slate-blue (R.)	70	3·00
32		3l. grey-green (R.)	1·40	4·00
33		5l. sepia (R.)	1·40	6·25
34	**6**	7l.70 + 2l. carmine-red	1·40	10·50
35	**7**	10l.+ 2l.50 orange-vermilion	1·40	16·00
36	**8**	100l. sepia and grey-green (7.9)	10·50	45·00
18/36	*Set of 19*		24·00	£130

9 Ploughing
10 Savoia Marchetti S-55X Flying Boat 

179

ITALIAN COLONIES 1933

(Des P Morbiducci (Postage) or L. Ferri (Air). Photo)

1933 (27 Mar–June). *50th Anniv of Foundation of Colony of Eritrea. Designs as T* **9** *and* **10**, *inscr* "CINQUANTENARIO ERITREO". *Wmk Crown. P 14.*

(a) POSTAGE.

37	**9**	10c. brown	4·50	5·75
38	–	20c. purple	4·50	5·75
39	–	25c. green	4·50	5·75
40	**9**	50c. bright violet	4·50	5·75
41	–	75c. carmine-red	4·50	7·75
42	–	1l.25 blue	4·50	7·75
43	**9**	2l.75 orange-vermilion	7·00	13·00
44	–	5l.+ 2l. deep blue-green	11·50	28·00
45	–	10l.+ 2l.50 red-brown	11·50	35·00

(b) AIR.

46	–	50c. red-brown	4·00	5·75
47	–	1l. black	4·00	5·75
48	**10**	3l. carmine-red	7·75	11·50
49	–	5l. brown	7·75	11·50
50	–	7l.70 + 2l. blackish green	11·50	28·00
51	**10**	10l.+ 2l.50 blue	11·50	28·00
52	–	50l. violet (12.6)	11·50	28·00
37/52 Set of 16			£100	£200

Designs: *Vert* (*Postage*)—20c., 75c., 5l. Camel transport; 25c., 1l.25, 10l. Lioness with star on left shoulder (Coat of Arms). *Horiz* (*Air*)—50c., 1l., 7l.70, Eagle; 50l. Savoia Marchetti S-55X flying boat over map of Eritrea.

Although the above stamps are inscribed "CINQUANTENARIO ERITREO", they were issued for general use throughout the Italian Colonies.

11 Agricultural Implements

12 Arab and Camel

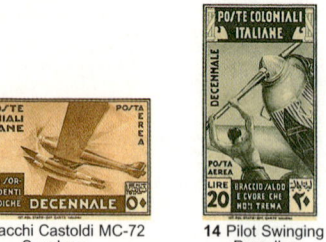

13 Macchi Castoldi MC-72 Seaplane

14 Pilot Swinging Propeller

(Des L. Ferri. Photo)

1933 (5 Oct–26 Dec). *10th Anniv of Fascist March on Rome. Designs as T* **11/14** *inscr* "DECENNALE". *Wmk Crown. P 14.*

(a) POSTAGE.

53	**11**	5c. orange-vermilion	4·75	5·25
54	**12**	25c. green	4·75	5·25
55	–	50c. bright violet	4·75	3·75
56	**11**	75c. carmine	4·75	7·75
57	**12**	1l.25 blue	4·75	7·75
58	–	1l.75 carmine-red	4·75	7·75
59	**11**	2l.75 deep blue	4·75	13·50
60	**12**	5l. brown-black	7·75	17·00
61	–	10l. slate-blue	7·75	20·00
62	–	25l. blackish green (26.12)	11·50	28·00

Designs: *Horiz*—50c., 1l.75, 10l. Tractor. *Vert*—25l. Soldier.

(b) AIR. *Inscr* "POSTA AEREA".

63	**13**	50c. red-brown	5·25	6·00
64	–	75c. purple	5·25	6·00
65	**13**	1l. brown	5·25	6·00
66	–	3l. olive-green	5·25	15·00
67	**13**	10l. deep violet	5·25	16·00
68	–	12l. blue-green	5·25	20·00
69	**14**	20l. blackish green	10·00	23·00
70	–	50l. blue (26.12)	17·00	23·00
53/70 Set of 18			£110	£200

Designs: *Horiz*—75c., 3l., 12l. Savoia Marchetti S-71 airplane. *Vert*—50l. Propeller.

15

16 Hailing Marina Fiat MF.5 Flying Boat

(Des M. Parrini. Photo)

1934 (18 Apr). *15th Milan Exhibition. Wmk Crown. P 14.*

71	**15**	20c. orange-vermilion	70	3·50
72	–	30c. green	70	3·50
73	–	50c. blue-black	70	3·50
74	–	1l.25 blue	70	7·00
71/74 Set of 4			2·50	16·00

(Des L. Ferri. Photo)

1934 (May). AIR. *Honouring the Duke of the Abruzzi (explorer). Wmk Crown. P 14.*

75	**16**	25l. olive-black	23·00	80·00

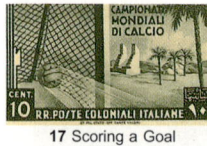

17 Scoring a Goal

18 Marina Fiat MF.5 Flying Boat over Stadium

(Des A. Ortona. Photo)

1934 (5 June). *World Football Championship. T* **17/18** *and similar types inscr* "CAMPIONATI MONDIALI DI CALCIO". *Wmk Crown. P 14.*

(a) POSTAGE.

76	**17**	10c. olive-green	18·00	22·00
77	–	50c. bright violet	35·00	14·00
78	–	1l.25 blue	35·00	55·00
79	–	5l. brown	44·00	£130
80	–	10l. grey-blue	44·00	£130

Design: *Vert*—5l., 10l. Fascist salute before the Kick-off.

(b) AIR. *Inscr* "POSTA AEREA".

81	**18**	50c. red-brown	8·75	22·00
82	–	75c. purple	8·75	22·00
83	–	5l. brown-black	32·00	44·00
84	–	10l. orange-vermilion	32·00	44·00
85	**18**	15l. carmine	32·00	44·00
86	–	25l. green	32·00	90·00
87	–	50l. blue-green	32·00	90·00
76/87 Set of 12			£325	£650

Designs: *Vert*—5, 10, 25l. "Saving a goal". *Horiz*—50l. Giant football and Marina Fiat MF.5 flying boat.

180

ITALIAN EAST AFRICA 1938

Italian East Africa

100 Centesimi = 1 Lira

A decree of 1 June 1936 combined Eritrea, Ethiopia and Italian Somaliland into the colony of Italian East Africa.

PRINTERS. The following were all printed at the Government Printing Works, Rome.

WATERMARK. The Crown watermark, used for all the following issues, is illustrated at the beginning of Eritrea.

1 Grant's Gazelle
2 R. Nile Statue and Lake Tsana 
3 Shadows on Road 
4 Italian Eagle and Lion of Judah 
5 Mussolini Monument and Mt. Amba Aradam
6 Bateleur 

(Des R. Maffei (25c. etc.), L. de Rosa (T **5**), G. Rondini (T **6** and 60c. etc.). Eng O. Mele (T **5**, 5l.), C. Mezzana (2l.). Photo (Nos. 21/25), recess (others))

1938 (7 Feb). *AIR. Designs as T* **5**/**6**. *Wmk Crown. P* 14.
21	–	25c. blue-green	1·80	2·30
22	**5**	50c. brown	39·00	10
23	–	60c. orange-vermilion	1·10	6·25
24	–	75c. chestnut	1·80	1·60
25	**6**	1l. slate-blue	10	10
26	**5**	1l.50 bright violet	70	35
27	–	2l. slate-blue	70	90
28	–	3l. lake	1·10	3·50
29	**6**	5l. red-brown	2·40	2·40
30	**5**	10l. purple	6·00	5·25
31	–	25l. slate-blue	12·00	12·50
21/31	*Set of 11*		60·00	32·00

Designs: *Horiz*—25, 75c., 3l., 25l. Savoia Marchetti S-73 airplane, rock sculpture of eagle and Mt. Amba Aradam; 60c., 2l. Savoia Marchetti S-73 airplane over Lake Tsana.

E **7** Plough and Native Huts
E **8** King Victor Emmanuel III 

(Des V. Retrosi. Recess)

1938 (7 Feb). *AIR EXPRESS. Wmk Crown. P* 14.
| E32 | E **7** | 2l. slate-blue | 90 | 2·75 |
| E33 | | 2l.50 sepia | 90 | 4·50 |

(Des C. Mezzana. Recess)

1938 (16 Apr). *EXPRESS. Wmk Crown. P* 14.
| E34 | E **8** | 1l.25 green | 90 | 2·75 |
| E35 | | 2l.50 scarlet (*inscr* "EXPRES") | 90 | 8·00 |

(Des. E. Castelli (T **1**), V. Retrosi (T **2**), G. Rondini (T **3**), G. Latini (T **4** and 15c. etc.), C. Mezzana (7½c. etc.). Eng V. Nicastro (T **2**/**4**), C. Mezzana (1l.25). Photo (2 to 50c.), recess (others))

1938 (7 Feb). *Designs as T* **1**/**4**. *Wmk Crown. P* 14.
1	**1**	2c. orange-vermilion	15	90
2	**4**	5c. brown	35	10
3	–	7½c. violet	55	2·30
4	**2**	10c. brown	1·60	10
5	–	15c. blue-green	35	35
6	–	20c. scarlet	35	10
7	**3**	25c. green	1·40	10
8	**1**	30c. brown	55	70
9	**4**	35c. blue	1·20	3·50
10	–	50c. bright violet	35	10
11	–	75c. lake	1·40	35
12	**3**	1l. grey-olive	90	10
13	–	1l.25 blue	1·20	35
14	**2**	1l.75 orange	18·00	10
15	**4**	2l. rose-carmine	1·10	35
16	**3**	2l.55 sepia	7·75	14·00
17	**1**	3l.70 bright violet	23·00	23·00
18	–	5l. blue	6·25	2·30
19	**4**	10l. red	7·75	7·00
20	**2**	20l. blue-green	14·00	14·00
1/20	*Set of 20*		45·00	65·00

Designs: *Vert*—7½c., 20c., 50c., 1l.25, Profile of King Victor Emmanuel III; 15c., 75c., 5l. Soldier implanting Fascist emblem.

9 Statue of Augustus
10 Eagle and serpent 

181

ITALIAN EAST AFRICA 1938

(Des C. Mezzana. Photo)
1938 (25 Apr). *Bimillenary of Birth of Augustus the Great. Wmk Crown. P 14.*

(a) POSTAGE. T **9** and similar vert design.
36	9	5c. brown	10	1·10
37	–	10c. brown-red	10	90
38	9	25c. green	80	90
39	–	50c. bright violet	80	70
40	9	75c. scarlet	80	1·80
41	–	1l.25 blue	80	3·50

Design:—10c., 50c., 1l.25, Statue of Goddess of Abundance.

(b) AIR.
42	10	50c. brown	35	1·80
43	–	1l. bright violet	55	2·75
36/43		Set of 8	3·75	12·00

11 Ethiopian Canoe

12 Soldier

(Des G. Rondini (**11**); L. De Rosa (**12**). Photo)
1940 (11 May). *Naples Exhibition. As T* **11/12**, *and similar design inscr "TRIENNALE D'OLTREMARE". Wmk Crown. P 14.*
44	11	5c. olive-brown	10	70
45	12	10c. red-orange	10	70
46	–	25c. green	80	1·20
47	11	50c. violet	80	70
48	12	75c. carmine	80	2·10
49	–	1l.25 blue	80	1·60
50	12	2l.+ 75c. lake	80	8·75
44/50		Set of 7	3·75	14·00

Design: Vert—25c., 1l.25, Allegory of Italian Conquest of Ethiopia.

13 Savoia Marchetti S-66 Flying Boat over Tractor

14 Savoia Marchetti S.M.83 Airplane over City

(Des L. De Rosa (**13**); G. Rondini (**14**). Photo)
1940 (11 May). *AIR. Naples Exhibition. Wmk Crown. P 14.*
51	13	50c. olive-grey	65	2·75
52	14	1l. violet	65	2·75
53	13	2l.+ 75c. grey-blue	80	
54	14	5l.+ 2l.50 red-brown	80	
51/54		Set of 4	2·50	

The Italian forces in East Africa surrendered to British and British African troops on 20 May 1941. The following issues were put on sale at the Philatelic Bureau in Rome but were not used in Italian East Africa

15 Hitler and Mussolini

(Des G. Rondini. Photo)
1941. *Axis Commemoration. Wmk Crown. P 14.*

(a) POSTAGE (19 June).
55	15	5c. orange-yellow	10
56		10c. chestnut	10
57		20c. black	1·10
58		25c. turquoise-green	1·10
59		50c. bright purple	1·10
60		75c. carmine	1·10
61		1l.25 ultramarine	1·10

(b) AIR. Inscr "POSTA AEREA" and with addition of Savoia Marchetti S.M.83 airplane.
62	15	1l. slate-blue (value at centre) (24.4)	26·00
63		1l. slate-blue (value at left) (20.5)	1·80
55/63		Set of 9	30·00

1941 (13 Aug). *POSTAGE DUE. Italian Postage Due stamps of 1934 optd "A.O.I." in sans-serif capitals.*
D64	D **141**	5c. brown	55
D65		10c. deep blue	55
D66		20c. bright scarlet	1·60
D67		25c. green	1·60
D68		30c. orange-red	4·00
D69		40c. agate	4·00
D70		50c. violet	4·00
D71		60c. indigo	7·00
D72	D **142**	1l. reddish orange	15·00
D73		2l. green	15·00
D74		5l. violet	15·00
D75		10l. blue	15·00
D76		20l. carmine-red	15·00
D64/76		Set of 13	90·00

In 1942 a set of postage due stamps, inscribed "A.O.I." and featuring a horse and rider, in eleven values (5c. to 10l.) and a 10 c. Concessional Letter Post stamp, inscribed "RECAPITO AUTORIZZATO" and depicting a lion, were prepared for use but not issued in Italian East Africa.

182

ITALIAN POST OFFICES IN CHINA 1917

Italian Post Offices in China

100 Cents = 1 Chinese Dollar

Italian troops were stationed in China from July 1900 and a concession was granted for their use of unoverprinted Italian stamps on 21 January 1901. On 20 September 1917 Italian Post Offices were opened in Peking and Tientsin for which the following stamps were issued. Their use was limited to legation and consular staff and Italian troops.

Stamps of Italy overprinted or surcharged

A. PEKING

PECHINO 2 CENTS (1)   **Pechino** (2)

1917 (Sept–Nov). *Stamps of 1901–16, surch locally by hand as T* **1**.

1	37	2c.on 5c. green	£120	70·00
		a. Surch inverted	£120	70·00
		b. Surch double, one inverted	£275	£190
		c. Error. 4c. on 5c.	£3500	
2	33	4c.on 10c. lake		
		a. Surch inverted		
3	38	4c. on 10c. rose	£225	£120
		a. Surch inverted	£250	£120
		b. Surch double, one inverted	£475	£275
4	36	6c.on 15c. slate	£475	£250
		a. Surch inverted	£475	£250
		b. Error 8c. on 15c.	£1900	£1500
5	49	8c.on 20c. on 15c. slate (No. 100)	£2250	£1100
		a. Surch inverted	£2250	£900
6	41	8c.on 20c. orange (No. 101)	£3750	£1200
		a. Surch inverted	£3250	£1200
7	40	20c.on 50c. violet (No. 70a)	£22000	£14000
		a. Surch inverted	£20000	£13000
		b. Error 40c. on 50c.	£8000	£7500
8	34	40c.on 1l. brown and green	£140000	£19000

1917 (1 Dec)–**18**. *Stamps of 1901–16 optd with T* **2**. *Typo at Turin*.

9	30	1c. brown	9·50	15·00
10	31	2c. red-brown	9·50	15·00
11	37	5c. green	3·00	4·00
12	38	10c. rose	3·00	4·00
13	41	20c. orange (No. 101)	90·00	75·00
14	39	25c. blue	3·00	6·75
15	40	50c. violet	3·00	8·25
16	34	1l. brown and green	6·75	13·50
17		5l. blue and rose	11·00	24·00
18	44	10l. sage-green and rose	90·00	£225
9/18	*Set of 10*		£200	£350

1917 (1 Dec). EXPRESS LETTER. *No. E80 optd with T* **2**.

E19	E 41	30c. blue and rose	6·75	19·00

1917 (1 Dec). POSTAGE DUE. *Optd with T* **2**.

D19	D 12	10c. magenta and orange	2·75	6·75
D20		20c. magenta and orange	2·75	6·75
D21		30c. magenta and orange	2·75	6·75
D22		40c. magenta and orange	5·50	6·75
D19/22	*Set of 4*		12·50	24·00

10 CENTS Pechino (3)   **2 dollari Pechino** (4)

1918–19. *Stamps of 1901–16 surch as T* **3** *or* **4** *(No. 27). Typo at Turin*.

19	30	½c.on 1c. brown	80·00	80·00
		a. "1 CENTS"	£350	£350
20	31	1c.on 2c. red-brown	3·00	5·25
		a. "1 CENTS"	£190	£190
21	37	2c.on 5c. green	3·00	5·25
22	38	4c.on 10c. rose	3·00	5·25
23	41	8c.on 20c. orange (No. 101)	13·50	11·00
24	39	10c.on 25c. blue	6·75	11·00
25	40	20c.on 50c. violet	8·25	11·00
26	34	40c.on 1l. brown and green	£100	£130
27		2d.on 5l. blue and rose	£190	£325
19/27	*Set of 9*		£375	£525

1918 (June). EXPRESS LETTER. *No. E80 surch as T* **3**.

E28	E 41	12c.on 30c. blue and rose	45·00	£140

1918 (July). POSTAGE DUE. *Surch as T* **3**.

D28	D 12	4c.on 10c. magenta and orange	£45000	£35000
D29		8c.on 20c. magenta and orange	13·50	21·00
D30		12c.on 30c. magenta and orange	41·00	60·00
D31		16c.on 40c. magenta and orange	£200	£300

A set of four postage due stamps (as D **12** of Italy), are known. The values are cancelled with four horizontal bars, overprinted - Pechino - and surcharged with new values. However these stamps were not issued.

2 dollari Pechino (5)   **2 DOLLARI Pechino** (6)   **10 CENTS Pechino** (7)

1918–19. *Stamps of 1901–08 surch locally by hand with T* **5/7**.

28	39	10c.on 25c. blue	3·50	9·50
29	34	2d.on 5l. blue and rose (T 6)	£6000	£4500
30		2d.on 5l. blue and rose (T 7)	£45000	£35000

B. TIENTSIN

1917 (Sept–Oct). *Stamps of 1901–16 surch locally by hand "TIENTSIN" and new value, as T* **1**.

31	37	2c.on 5c. green	£225	£190
		a. Surch inverted	£225	£190
		b. Surch double, one inverted	£275	£200
		c. Error, 4c. on 5c.	£5000	
32	38	4c.on 10c. rose	£400	£225
		a. Surch inverted	£400	£225
		b. Surch double, one inverted	£450	£275
33	36	6c.on 15c. slate	£950	£600
		a. Error. 4c. on 15c.	£2750	£2250
		b. Surch inverted	£950	£600

1917 (1 Dec)–**18**. *Stamps of 1901–16 optd "Tientsin" as T* **2**. *Typo at Turin*.

34	30	1c. brown	9·50	15·00
35	31	2c. red-brown	9·50	15·00
36	37	5c. green	3·00	4·00
37	38	10c. rose	3·00	4·00
38	41	20c. orange (No. 101)	90·00	75·00
39	39	25c. blue	3·00	6·75
40	40	50c. violet	3·00	6·75
41	34	1l. brown and green	6·50	13·50
42		5l. blue and rose	11·00	24·00
43	44	10l. sage-green and rose	90·00	£225
34/43	*Set of 10*		£200	£350

1917 (1 Dec). EXPRESS LETTER. *No E80 optd "Tientsin" as T* **2**.

E44	E 41	30c. blue and rose	6·75	19·00

183

ITALIAN POST OFFICES IN CHINA 1917

1917 (1 Dec). *POSTAGE DUE Optd "Tientsin" as T* **2**.
D44	D **12**	10c. magenta and orange	2·75	6·75
D45		20c. magenta and orange	2·75	6·75
D46		30c. magenta and orange	2·75	6·75
D47		40c. magenta and orange	5·50	6·75
D44/47 Set of 4			12·50	24·00

2
Dollari

Tientsin
(8)

1918–19. *Stamps of* 1901–16 *surch "Tientsin" and new value as T* **3** *or* **8** *(No. 52). Typo at Turin.*
44	**30**	2c.on 1c. brown	80·00	80·00
		a. "1 CENTS"	£350	£350
45	**31**	1c.on 2c. red-brown	3·00	5·25
		a. "1 CENTS"	£190	£190
46	**37**	2c.on 5c. green	3·50	5·25
47	**38**	4c.on 10c. rose	3·50	5·25
48	**41**	8c.on 20c. orange (No. 101)	13·50	11·00
49	**39**	10c.on 25c. blue	6·75	11·00
50	**40**	20c.on 50c. violet	8·25	11·00
51	**34**	40c.on 1l. brown and green	£100	£130
52		2d.on 5l. blue and rose	£190	£325
44/52 Set of 9			£325	£500

1918 (June). *EXPRESS LETTER. No.* E80 *surch "Tientsin" and new value as T* **3**.
E53	E **41**	12c.on 30c. blue and rose	45·00	£140

1918 (July). *POSTAGE DUE Surch "Tientsin" and new value as T* **3**.
D53	D **12**	4c.on 10c. magenta and orange	£1900	£2250
D54		8c.on 20c. magenta and orange	13·50	21·00
D55		12c.on 30c. magenta and orange	41·00	60·00
D56		16c.on 40c. magenta and orange	£200	£300

1919–21. *Stamps of* 1901 *surch locally by hand.*
(a) As T **8** *but with small "d"*
53	**34**	2d.on 5l. blue and rose (1919)	£6500	£5000

(b) In thin sans-serif letters and with capital "D"
54	**34**	2d. on 5l. blue and rose (1921)	£6000	£4500

The Italian offices were closed down on 31 December 1922.

ITALIAN POST OFFICES IN CRETE 1900

Italian Post Offices In Crete

1900. 40 Paras = 1 Piastre
1906. 100 Centesimi = 1 Lira

A military post office using unoverprinted Italian stamps operated in 1899. A civil post office opened 15 January 1900 and closed 31 December 1914.

Italian stamps surcharged or overprinted

LA CANEA

1 PIASTRA 1   **LA CANEA**
(1)   (2)

1900 (10 July). *Stamp of* 1893 *(Umberto I) surch as T* **1** *but without* "LA CANEA".
1   27   1pi. on 25c. blue (R.)   . . . .   5·50   34·00

1901 (1 July). *Stamp of* 1901 *(Victor Emmanuel III) surch with T* **1**.
2   33   1pi. on 25c. blue   . . . .   3·00   6·25

1906 (5 Nov). EXPRESS LETTER. *No* E73 *optd with T* **2**.
E1   E 35   25c. rose   . . . .   4·25   8·50

1906 (15 Nov). *Stamps of* 1901 *and* 1905 *(Arms (T* **30***) or portraits of Victor Emmanuel III (others)) optd with T* **2**.
3   30   1c. brown   50   1·20
4   31   2c. orange-brown   50   1·20
5   32   5c. green . . . .   1·00   1·50
6   33   10c. lake . . . .   £100 75·00
7   15c.on 20c. orange (73) . . . . .   1·20   1·70
8   25c. blue . . . .   5·75   5·75
9   40c. brown . . . .   5·25   5·75
10   45c. olive-green . . . .   4·50   5·75
11   50c. mauve . . . .   5·75   8·25
12   34   1l. brown and green . . . . 31·00 34·00
13   5l. blue and rose £150   £150
3/13 *Set of* 11 . . . .   £275   £250

1907–12. *Stamps of* 1906–09 *(portraits of Victor Emmanuel III) optd with T* **2**.
14   37   5c. green (7.07)   85   1·20
          a. Opt inverted £200
38   10c. rose-red (3.07)   85   1·20
16   41   15c. slate-black (V.) (1.12) . . . 1·70   3·00
17   39   25c. blue (4.09) . . . .   1·70   4·00
18   40   40c. brown (1910) . . . .   17·00 21·00
19   50c. violet (6.09) . . . .   1·70   4·00
14/19 *Set of* 6 . . . .   21·00 30·00

185

ITALIAN P.O.s IN THE TURKISH EMPIRE 1874

Italian Post Offices in the Turkish Empire

A. GENERAL ISSUES

100 Centesimi = 1 Lira

The following were in use in post offices in Alexandria (opened 1863, closed 1884; used numeral cancellation "234"), Assab (Eritrea, opened 1883, cancellation "3840"), La Goletta (Tunisia, 1879–97; cancellation "3336"), Massawa (Eritrea, opened 1885; cancellation "3862"), Susa (Tunisia, 1880–97; cancellation "3364"), Tripoli (opened 1869; cancellation "3051") and Tunis (1853–97; cancellation "235") and also at Consular post offices at Buenos Aires (1874–78) and Montevideo (1874–78). Alexandria, Tunis and Tripoli had previously used unoverprinted stamps of Sardinia and Italy.

In 1890 Eritrea became an Italian colony and had its own stamps from 1893. Stamps issued for Tripoli in 1909 are listed under Libya.

ESTERO
(1)

1c., 2c.   5c.   10c.   20c.

30c.   40c.   60c.   2l.

1874 (1 Jan). Stamps of 1863–77 with modified corners. optd with T **1**.

1	4	1c. olive-green	6·75	15·00
		a. Pale bronze-green	35·00	17·00
		b. Two square dots in lower right corner (pos. 61)	31·00	£140
		c. Three square dots in upper right corner (pos. 95)	£190	£900
		d. Corners altered, opt omitted	£38000	
		e. Opt inverted	£20000	
2	5	2c. brown	8·25	19·00
		a. Deep brown	9·25	19·00
		b. Corners altered, opt omitted	£38000	
3	6	5c. greenish grey	£450	19·00
		a. Lower right corner not altered (pos. 82)	£11000	£1400
4		10c. orange-buff	£1100	34·00
		a. Upper left corner not altered (pos. 16)	£14000	£750
		b. Two lower corners not altered (pos. 3, 39)		£5000
		c. All corners not altered (pos. 30)		£38000
5	10	20c. blue	£1000	19·00
6	6	30c. brown	1·40	10·50
		a. Chocolate	1·70	10·50
		b. Upper left and lower right corners not altered		£23000
		c. All corners not altered	1·40	9·50
7		40c. rose	3·50	75·00
8		60c. lilac	90·00	£400
9	7	2l. scarlet		

1878–79. Colours changed Optd with T **1**.

| 10 | 6 | 10c. blue (1879) | £225 | 12·50 |
| 11 | 10 | 20c. orange | £3750 | 9·50 |

5c.   10c.   20c.

25c.   50c.   2l.

1881–83. Stamps of 1879 with modified corners, optd with T **1**.

12	12	5c. green (2.82)	5·50	8·25
		a. Dots in lower right corner	£600	£700
13		10c. claret (3.83)	4·00	5·50
14		20c. orange (3.81)	4·00	4·75
15		25c. blue (3.81)	4·00	8·25
16		50c. mauve (5.81)	8·25	41·00
17		2l. orange-red	15·00	

No. 17 was prepared for use but not issued.

B. GENERAL OFFICES IN TURKISH EMPIRE

100 Paras = 1 Piastre

From 1901 new Italian post offices were opened in the Turkish Empire. At first general issues were made but later the individual offices had their own stamps. Opening and closing dates of each office are given under the appropriate headings in Section C.

Stamps of Italy surcharged

(a) ALBANIA

For use in post offices at Durazzo, Janina, Scutari and Valona.

ALBANIA
10 Para 10   **20 Para 20**
(2)   (3)

1902 (1 Sept). Stamps of 1901 surch as T **2**.

18	32	10pa.on 5c. green	2·20	1·00
19	33	35pa.on 20c. orange	3·75	3·00
20		40pa.on 25c. blue	7·75	3·00

1902 (Dec). As last, but without "ALBANIA" as T **3**.

21	32	10pa.on 5c. green	4·50	1·50
22	33	35pa.on 20c. orange	3·00	1·90
23		40pa.on 25c. blue	21·00	4·25

1907. Stamps of 1901–06 surch as T **2**.

24	37	10pa.on 5c. green (30 May)	27·00	34·00
25	38	20pa.on 10c. rose (1 Nov)	16·00	14·50
26	33	80pa.on 50c. mauve (1 Nov)	16·00	14·50

1907. As last but without "ALBANIA" as T **3**.

27	37	10pa.on 5c. green (30 June)	1·40	1·00
28	38	20pa.on 10c. rose (1 Nov)	1·40	1·25
29	33	80pa.on 50c. mauve (1 Nov)	29·00	18·00

From 1 June 1908 Nos. 27/28 were put on sale at all post offices in the Turkish Empire.

(b) GENERAL OFFICES IN EUROPE AND ASIA

For use in all post offices in the Turkish Empire.

1908 (1 June). Stamps of 1908 surch as T **3**.

| 30 | 39 | 40pa.on 25c. blue | 2·10 | 1·70 |
| 31 | 40 | 80pa.on 50c. mauve | 3·00 | 2·40 |

1908 (Dec). Stamp of 1906 surch as T **3**.

| 32 | 36 | 30pa.on 15c. slate (V) | 1·40 | 1·70 |

ITALIAN P.O.s IN THE TURKISH EMPIRE 1908

LEVANTE
1 PIASTRA 1
(E 4)

LEVANTE
60 Parà 60
(E 5)

1908–10. EXPRESS LETTER Nos. E73 and E80 surch with Types E **4** and E **5**.

E33	E **35**	1pi.on 25c. rose	2·10	2·40
E34	E **41**	60pa.on 30c. blue and rose (9.10)	3·00	3·75

C. INDIVIDUAL OFFICES IN TURKISH EMPIRE

100 Paras = 1 Piastre

Stamps of Italy overprinted or surcharged

(a) CONSTANTINOPLE (Istanbul)

The main post office was opened at Galata on 1 June 1908 and had sub-offices at Pera and Stamboul. These were closed from 1 October 1911 to December 1912 and from 30 November 1914. The office at Galata was reopened from 1 July 1921 to 25 November 1923.

10 PARA
(4)

2 PIASTRE
(5)

1908. Stamps of 1901–06 surch typo by "Levant Herald".

*(a) 1st Printing. Surch as T **4** and **5**. (1 June).*

33	**37**	10pa.on 5c. green	£140	£120
34	**38**	20pa.on 10c. rose	£140	£120
35	**36**	30pa.on 15c. slate	£400	£375
36	**39**	1pi.on 25c. blue	£400	£375
37	**40**	2pi.on 50c. mauve	£1200	£1100
38	**34**	4pi.on 1l. brown and green	£5500	£4000
39		20pi.on 5l. blue and rose	£18000	£11000

On No. 38 the "4" in the surcharge is of the normal type, the left-hand stroke joining the top of the vertical stroke.

10 PARA
(6)

1 PIASTRA
(7)

*(b) 2nd Printing Surch as T **6** and **7**. (1 June).*

40	**37**	10pa.on 5c. green	4·75	6·75
41	**38**	20pa.on 10c. rose	4·75	6·75
42	**36**	30pa.on 15c. slate	17·00	15·00
		a. Surch double	95·00	95·00
43	**39**	1pi.on 25c. blue	4·75	6·75
		a. "1 PIPSTRA"	80·00	80·00
		b. "1" omitted	80·00	80·00
		c. "PIASTRE" for "PIASTRA"	80·00	80·00
44	**40**	2pi.on 50c. mauve	41·00	41·00
		a. "2" and "PIASTRE" spaced	£170	£170
		b. "20" for "2"	£900	£900
		c. As b. but "0" partially erased	£275	£275
45	**34**	4pi.on 1l. brown and green	£600	£475
46		20pi.on 5l. blue and rose	£2500	£1500

On No. 45 the left-hand stroke of the "4" is prolonged beyond the top of the vertical stroke.

No. 43a occurs on position 13, 43b on position 31, 44a on position 5 and 44b/c on position 45.

30 PARA
(8)

4 PIASTRE
(9)

20 PIASTRE
(10)

*(c) 3rd Printing. Surch with T **8/10** (Aug).*

47	**36**	30pa.on 15c. slate (R.)	2·10	2·10
48	**34**	4pi.on 1l. brown and green	34·00	41·00
		a. "S" inverted	95·00	95·00
49		20pi.on 5l. blue and rose	£110	£120
		a. "S" inverted	£250	£250

Overprinted in stereotypes of 20, repeated five times in the sheet. The inverted "S" varieties occur on position 11 of the stereotype.

4 PIASTRE
(11)

20 PIASTRE
(12)

*(d) 4th Printing. Surch with T **11/12**. (Sept)*

50	**34**	4pi.on 1l. brown and green	34·00	41·00
		a. 20pi. on 1l.		£1000
51		20pi. on 5l. blue and rose	34·00	41·00

Costantinopoli
10 Parà 10
(13)

COSTANTINOPOLI
4 PIASTRE 4
(14)

1909 (Feb)–**11**. Stamps of 1901–10 surch at Turin as T **74** (4pi to 40pi) or **13** (others).

52	**37**	10pa.on 5c. green	1·00	1·50
53	**38**	20pa.on 10c. rose	1·00	1·50
54	**36**	30pa.on 15c. slate (V.)	1·00	1·50
55	**39**	1pi.on 25c. blue	1·00	1·50
		a. Surch double	£140	£140
56	**40**	2pi.on 50c. mauve	1·40	1·80
57	**34**	4pi.on 1l. brown and green	1·70	2·20
58		20pi.on 5l. blue and rose	41·00	39·00
59	**44**	40pi.on 10l. sage-green & rose (1911)	3·00	19·00
52/59		Set of 8	46·00	60·00

4 PIASTRE
(15)

10 PIASTRE
(16)

1921 (Nov). Stamps of 1906–19 surch locally as T **15** and **16** (10pi).

60	**37**	1pi.on 5c. green	£110	£200
61		2pi.on 15c. slate	4·00	6·75
62	**41**	4pi.on 20c. orange (105)	46·00	46·00
63	**39**	5pi.on 25c. blue	46·00	46·00
64		10pi.on 60c. carmine-lake	2·10	3·50
60/64		Set of 5	£190	£275

PIASTRE 3
PARÀ 20
(17)

PIASTRE 3
PARÀ 30
(18)

1921 (Dec)–**22**. Stamps of 1901–19 surch at Turin as T **17** or **18**.

65	**30**	10pa.on 1c. brown (2.22)	1·40	2·10
66	**31**	20pa.on 2c. orange-brown (2.22)	1·40	2·10
67	**37**	30pa.on 5c. green	3·00	3·75
68		1pi.20 on 15c. slate	4·75	2·10
69	**41**	3pi.on 20c. orange (105)	5·50	10·50
70	**39**	3pi.30 on 25c. blue (2.22)	2·40	2·10
71		7pi.20 on 60c. carmine-lake	4·75	3·75
72	**34**	15pi.on 1l. brown and green (3 22)	19·00	29·00
65/72		Set of 8	38·00	50·00

On No. 71 the lines of surcharge are 2 mm. apart. For similar surcharge but 1½ mm. apart see footnote below No. 108.

COSTANTINOPOLI
PIASTRE 3
PARÀ 30
(19)

Piastre
3,75
(20)

1922. Stamps of 1901–19 surch at Turin as T **19**.

73	**37**	20pa.on 5c. green (June)	12·50	17·00
74		1pi.20 on 15c. slate (May)	1·20	1·70
75	**39**	3pi.on 30c. orange-brown (Sept)	1·20	1·70
76	**40**	3pi 30 on 40c. brown (May)	1·20	1·70
77	**34**	7pi.20 on 1l. brown and green (May)	1·20	1·70
73/77		Set of 5	16·00	21·00

1922 (5 Aug). Stamp of 1908 surch locally with T **20**.

78	**39**	3,75pi.on 25c. blue	1·70	2·10

187

ITALIAN P.O.s IN THE TURKISH EMPIRE — 1922

30 PARÀ
(21)

PIASTRE 4.50
(22)

1922 (1 Aug). Stamps of 1901–20 surch locally as T **21** or **22**.

79	31	30pa.on 2c. orange-brown	1·50	2·75
80	37	30pa.on 5c. blue-green	3·50	8·25
81	41	1,50pi.on 20c. orange (105)	1·50	2·10
82	39	1,50pi.on 25c. blue	1·50	4·00
83	40	3,75pi.on 40c. brown	2·20	5·25
84		4,50pi.on 50c. mauve	6·75	12·50
85	39	7,50pi. on 60c. carmine-lake	5·50	9·50
86		15pi.on 85c. red-brown	10·50	19·00
87	34	18,75pi.on 1l. brown and green	4·75	15·00
88		45pi.on 5l. blue and rose	£275	£350
89	44	90pi.on 10l. sage-green and rose	£300	£400
79/89		Set of 11	£550	£750

On Nos. 81, 86, 88 and 89 the figures of value are above the word "PIASTRE" in the surcharge.
On No. 88 the figure "4" is open at the top and on No. 89 the tail of the figure "9" almost touches the oval. The lines of the surcharge are 2 mm. apart. For 15, 45 and 90pi with lines of surcharge 1½ mm. apart and figures "4" and "9" differently formed see footnote below No. 108.

1922 (Aug). EXPRESS LETTER. No. E118 surch locally as T **22** but with figure of value above "PIASTRE".

E90	E 41	15pi.on 1l.20 on 30c. blue & rose	17·00	34·00

30 PARA'
(23)

4½ PIASTRE
(24)

1922 (Oct–Nov). Stamps of 1901–20 surch locally as T **23** or **24**.

90	37	30pa.on 5c. yellow-green	1·00	2·10
91	38	1½pi.on 10c. rose	1·40	2·10
92	39	3pi.on 25c. blue	12·00	5·25
93	40	3¾pi.on 40c. brown	1·90	2·10
94		4½pi.on 50c. mauve	31·00	26·00
95	39	7½pi.on 85c. red-brown	5·25	6·00
96	34	7½pi.on 1l. brown and green (R.)	6·00	8·50
97		15pi.on 1l. brown and green	50·00	£100
98		45pi.on 5l. blue and rose	85·00	60·00
99	44	90pi.on 10l. sage-green and rose	60·00	£110
90/99		Set of 10	£225	£300

1922 (Nov). EXPRESS LETTER. No. E80 surch locally as T **24**.

E100	E 41	15pi.on 30c. blue and rose	£225	£375

COSTANTINOPOLI PIASTRE 3 PARÀ 30
(D 25) (25)

COSTANTINOPOLI 15 PIASTRE
(25a)

1922 (Dec). POSTAGE DUE. Optd with Type D **25**.

D100	D 12	10c. magenta and orange	34·00	48·00
D101		30c. magenta and orange	34·00	48·00
D102		60c. magenta and orange	34·00	48·00
D103		1l. magenta and blue	34·00	48·00
D104		2l. magenta and blue	£700	£1100
D105		5l. magenta and blue	£250	£350

Nos. D100/5 bear a control cachet applied over blocks of four so that a quarter of the circle falls on a corner of each stamp. It consists of two concentric circles, the inner enclosing the crest of the House of Savoy and between the circles appears the inscription "POSTE ITALIANE COSTANTINOPOLI".

1923 (Mar). Stamps of 1901–20 surch as T **25** or **25a**.

100	37	30pa.on 5c. green	1·70	1·90
101	39	1pi.on 25c. blue	1·70	1·90
102	40	3pi.30 on 40c. brown	1·70	1·50
103		4pi.20 on 50c. mauve	1·70	1·50
104	39	7pi.20 on 60c. carmine-lake	1·70	1·50
105		15pi.on 85c. red-brown	1·70	2·75
106	34	18pi.30 on 1l. brown and green	1·70	2·75
107		45pi.on 5l. blue and rose	2·50	5·50
108	44	90pi.on 10l. sage-green and rose	2·50	6·25
100/108		Set of 9	15·00	23·00

Nos. 101/8 also exist surcharged as T **25** or **25a** but with "COSTANTINOPOLI" omitted; these were not issued. The lines of overprint are 1½ mm apart; the 45pi. can also be distinguished from No. 88 by the figure "4", which is closed at the top, and the 90pi. from No. 89 by the tail of the figure "9" which is open. (Prices: 1pi.20, 3pi.30, 4p.20, 15pi., 18p.30, £8.25 each, 7pi.20 £24, 45pi. £24, 90pi. £22).

COSTANTINOPOLI
15 PIASTRE
(E 26)

1923 (Mar). EXPRESS LETTER. No. E130 surch with Type E **26**.

E109	E 41	15pi.on 1l.20 blue and rose	4·25	17·00

No. E130 surch as Type E **26** but without "COSTANTINOPOLI" was not issued (Price £8).

(b) DURAZZO (Durres)

Open 25 June 1902 to 1911 and 1913 to January 1923.

Durazzo 10 Parà 10
(26)

DURAZZO 4 PIASTRE 4
(27)

1909 (Feb)–**11**. Stamps of 1901–10 surch as T **26** or **27** (4pi to 40pi).

109	37	10pa.on 5c. green	70	1·20
110	38	20pa.on 10c. rose	70	1·20
111	36	30pa.on 15c. slate (V.)	31·00	2·10
112	39	1pi.on 25c. blue	1·40	1·70
113	40	2pi.on 50c. mauve	1·40	1·70
114	34	4pi.on 1l. brown and green	2·75	2·40
115		20pi.on 5l. blue and rose	£140	£140
116	44	40pi.on 10l. sage-grn & rose (1911)	6·75	60·00
109/116		Set of 8	£170	£190

1916 (Jan). No. 111 surch "CENT 20" and bars.

116a	36	20c.on 30pa. on 15c. slate	2·75	13·00

(c) JANINA (Ioannina)

Open 16 August 1902 to 1911 and 1913 to end 1914. From June to 20 November 1917 it reopened temporarily using unoverprinted Italian stamps.

Janina 10 Parà 10
(28)

JANINA 4 PIASTRE 4
(29)

1909 (Feb)–**11**. Stamps of 1901–10 surch as T **28** or **29** (4pi to 40pi).

117	37	10pa.on 5c. green	85	85
118	38	20pa.on 10c. rose	85	85
119	36	30pa.on 15c. slate (V.)	1·20	1·20
120	39	1pi.on 25c. blue	1·20	1·20
121	40	2pi.on 50c. mauve	1·20	1·40
122	34	4pi.on 1l. brown and green	2·40	1·70
123		20pi.on 5l. blue and rose	£170	£190
124	44	40pi.on 10l. sage-grn & rose (1911)	10·50	50·00
117/124		Set of 8	£170	£220

ITALIAN P.O.s IN THE TURKISH EMPIRE — 1909

(d) JERUSALEM

Open 1 June 1908 to 1 October 1911 and spring 1913 to 1 November 1914.

Gerusalemme 10 Parà 10 (30)
GERUSALEMME 4 PIASTRE 4 (31)

1909 (1 Feb)–**11**. Stamps of 1901–10 surch as T **30** or **31** (4pi to 40 pi).

125	37	10pa.on 5c. green	2·20	4·75
126	38	20pa.on 10c. rose	2·20	4·75
127	36	30pa.on 15c. slate (V.)	2·20	6·75
128	39	1pi.on 25c. blue	2·20	4·75
129	40	2pi.on 50c. mauve	10·50	13·50
130	34	4pi.on 1l. brown and green	13·50	27·00
131		20pi.on 5l. blue and rose	£650	£425
132	44	40pi.on 10l. sage-grn & rose (1911)	21·00	£200
125/132 Set of 8			£650	£600

(e) SALONIKA (Thessaloniki)

Open 25 May 1908 to 1 December 1911 and 1913 to December 1914.

Salonicco 20 Parà 20 (32)
SALONICCO 4 PIASTRE 4 (33)

1909 (Feb)–**11**. Stamps of 1901–10 surch as T **32** or **33** (4pi to 40pi).

133	37	10pa.on 5c. green	50	70
134	38	20pa.on 10c. rose	50	70
135	36	30pa.on 15c. slate (V.)	85	1·20
136	39	1pi.on 25c. blue	85	1·20
137	40	2pi.on 50c. mauve	1·00	1·40
138	34	4pi.on 1l. brown and green	1·40	1·70
139		20pi.on 5l. blue and rose	£250	£250
140	44	40pi.on 10l. sage-grn & rose (1911)	6·75	45·00
133/140 Set of 8			£250	£275

(f) SCUTARI (Shkodër)

Open 1 November 1901 to 1911 and 1913–15.

Scutari di Albania 10 Parà 10 (34)
SCUTARI DI ALBANIA 4 PIASTRE 4 (35)

1909 (Feb)–**15**. Stamps of 1901–10 surch as T **34** or **35** (4pi. to 40pi.).

141	31	4pa.on 2c. brown (1915)	1·70	3·50
142	37	10pa.on 5c. green	35	85
143	38	20pa.on 10c. rose	35	85
144	36	30pa.on 15c. slate (V)	17·00	3·50
145	39	1pi.on 25c. blue	35	1·40
146	40	2pi.on 50c. mauve	70	1·70
147	34	4pi.on 1l. brown and green	85	2·10
148		20pi.on 5l. blue and rose	19·00	27·00
149	44	40pi.on 10l. sage-grn & rose (1911)	45·00	90·00
141/149 Set of 9			75·00	£120

1916 (Jan). No. 144 surch "CENT. 20" and bars.

150	36	20c.on 30pa. on 15c. slate	3·00	15·00

(g) SMYRNA (Izmir)

Open 10 May 1908 to 1 October 1911 and 1913 to 1 October 1914. From May 1919 to 15 June 1923 a military post office functioned in Smyrna using unoverprinted Italian stamps.

Smirne 10 Parà 10 (36)
SMIRNE 4 PIASTRE 4 (37)

1909 (Feb)–**11**. Stamps of 1901–10 surch as T **36** or **37** (4pi to 40pi).

151	37	10pa.on 5c. green	35	60
152	38	20pa.on 10c. rose	35	60
153	36	30pa.on 15c. slate (V)	1·20	1·40
154	39	1pi.on 25c. blue	1·20	1·40
155	40	2pi.on 50c. mauve	1·70	2·10
156	34	4pi.on 1l. brown and green	2·40	2·50
157		20pi.on 5l. blue and rose	£100	£110
158	44	40pi.on 10l. sage-grn & rose (1911)	12·00	65·00
151/158 Set of 8			£110	£170

Stamps surch as T **19** but with "SMIRNE" in 1922 were not issued.

(h) VALONA (Vlórë)

Open 5 May 1908 to 1911 and 1913–23.

Valona 10 Parà 10 (38)
VALONA 4 PIASTRE 4 (39)
VALONA 30 PARA 30 (40)

1909 (Feb)–**11**. Stamps of 1901–10 surch as T **38** or **39** (4pi to 40pi).

159	37	10pa.on 5c. green	25	1·00
160	38	20pa.on 10c. rose	25	1·00
161	36	30pa.on 15c. slate (V)	12·00	3·50
162	39	1pi.on 25c. blue	85	1·20
163	40	2pi.on 50c. mauve	85	1·20
164	34	4pi.on 1l. brown and green	1·20	2·10
165		20pi.on 5l. blue and rose	33·00	38·00
166	44	40pi.on 10l. sage-grn & rose (1911)	38·00	90·00
159/166 Set of 8			75·00	£120

1915 (Sept). Stamp of 1911 surch with T **40**.

167	49	30pa. on 15c. slate (Mag.)	3·50	8·50

1916. No. 167 surch "CENT. 20" and bars.

168	49	20c. on 30pa. on 15c. slate	1·40	10·00

POST OFFICES IN AFRICA. For issues of Italian Post Offices in Benghazi and Tripoli, see under Libya.

LIBYA   1901

Libya

The area now called Libya, which had been more or less under Turkish rule since the 16th century, was organised as the vilayet of Tripoli in 1835.

Though by a law promulgated on 26 June 1927, Libya was divided into the two colonies of Cyrenaica and Tripolitania, definitive postage, air, express, parcel post and postage due stamps inscribed "Libia" were in use in the two colonies. Apart from some definitive air stamps only commemorative issues were made inscribed "Cirenaica" or "Tripolitania". On 3 December 1934, the two colonies were reunited as Libya.

100 Centesimi = 1 Lira

PRINTERS. All stamps of Italian Libya were printed at the Italian Government Printing Works.

A. LIBYA

I. ITALIAN POST OFFICES

BENGHAZI

An Italian Post Office was opened in Benghazi on 16 March 1901.

BENGASI

1 PIASTRA 1
(1)

1901 (July). *No. 67 of Italy surch with T* **1**.
169   33   1pi.on 25c. blue . . . .   27·00   80·00

1911 (Dec). *No. 77 of Italy surch with T* **1**.
170   39   1pi.on 25c. blue . . . .   31·00   80·00

Benghazi was occupied by Italian troops on 20 October 1911, in the Turco-Italian war.

TRIPOLI

An Italian Consular Post Office was opened in Tripoli in January 1869. At first unoverprinted Italian stamps were used, with the numeral cancellation "3051". From 1874 the General Issues for Italian Post Offices in the Turkish Empire (q.v.) were used. Overprints for Tripoli appeared in 1909.

Tripoli   **TRIPOLI**
di Barberia   **DI BARBERIA**
(1a)   (1b)

1909 (Dec). Stamps of Italy of 1901–08 optd with *T* **1b** (1l., 5l.) or **1a** (others).
171   30   1c. brown . . . .   3·00   2·75
          a. Opt inverted £180
173   31   2c. orange-brown . . . .   1·00   1·70
174   37   5c. green . . . .   70·00   6·25
175   38   10c. rose-red . . . .   2·10   1·70
176   41   15c. slate (V.) . . . .   2·50   3·00
177   39   25c. blue . . . .   1·70   1·70
178   40   40c. brown . . . .   4·25   3·75
179   50c. violet . . . .   6·00   5·25
180   34   1l. brown and green . . . .   75·00   50·00
181   5l. blue and rose . . . .   24·00   £130
171/181 Set of 10 . . . .   £170   £190

The 1 and 2c. with overprint Type **16** were not issued (Price: £2·50 each un).

1909 (Dec). EXPRESS LETTER. Nos. E73 and E80 of Italy optd with *T* **1b**.
E182   E 35   25c. rose . . . .   10·50   6·75
E183   E 41   30c. blue and rose . . . . . .   3·50   10·50

II. ITALIAN COLONY

On 29 September 1911 Italy declared war on Turkey and in October took the coastal town of Tripoli The outbreak of the Balkan War a year later forced Turkey to cede Tripoli to Italy on 18 October 1912, and the country was renamed Libya The conquest of the interior was not completed until 1932.

			Libia (2)	LIBIA (2a)	LIBIA (P 3)	LIBIA (3)

1912 (Dec)–22. Contemporary stamps of Italy optd with *T* **2a** (No. 5) or **2** (others).
1   30   1c. brown (11.15)   85   85
          a. Opt double £190   £190
2   31   2c. orange-brown   85   50
3   37   5c. green   85   35
          a. Opt inverted
          b. Opt double . . . .   75·00   75·00
          c. Pair, one without opt £250   £250
          d. Imperf (pair) £110   £110
4   38   10c. rose-red   85   35
          a. Opt double £100   £100
          b. Pair, one without opt £250   £250
5   49   15c. slate (V.) . . . .   £100   1·70
          a. Opt in blue-black (5.14) . . .   £9000   15·00
6   37   15c. slate (1.22) . . . .   3·50   3·50
7   33   20c. orange (11.15) . . . .   2·40   35
          a. Opt double £150   £150
          b. Pair, one without opt £400   £400
8   41   20c. orange (7.18) . . . .   2·75   3·50
          a. Opt double £120
          b. Pair, one without opt £400
9   39   25c. blue . . . .   2·75   35
10   40   40c. brown . . . .   5·25   1·00
11   33   45c. olive-green (4.17) . . . . .   22·00   17·00
          a. Opt inverted £275
12   40   50c. violet (12.15) . . . .   17·00   1·40
          a. Opt double £900
13   39   60c. carmine-red (8.18) . . . . .   12·00   13·50
          a. Opt double £500
14   34   1l. brown and green (12.15) . .   50·00   1·70
15   5l. blue and rose (12.15) £275   £200
16   44   10l. sage-green and pale rose
              (12.15) . . . .   24·00   80·00
1/16 Set of 16 . . . .   £475   £300

There are two types of the overprint, Type **2**. They vary in the shape of the letters and the second type has the letters thinner and more widely spaced.

1915 (Nov). EXPRESS LETTER. Express Letter stamps of Italy, optd with *T* **2**.
E17   E 35   25c. rose . . . .   19·00   8·50
E18   E 41   30c. blue and rose . . . . . .   5·25   22·00
The above exist with both types of the overprint

1915 (Nov)–24. PARCEL POST. Parcel Post stamps of Italy, optd with Type P **3**, on each half of the stamp.

				Un pair	Used pair	Used half
P17	P 53	5c. brown		85	3·50	85
P18		10c. deep blue		£250		
P19		20c. black (8.18)		1·50	3·50	1·20
		a. Opt back and		1·00	3·50	1·20
		front		£190		
		b. Opt on back only		£190		
P20		25c. red		1·00	3·50	1·20
P21		50c. orange		1·90	3·50	1·20
P22		1l. violet		1·90	5·25	1·20
P23		2l. green		2·75	5·25	1·20
P24		3l. yellow		3·50	5·25	1·20
P25		4l. slate		3·50	5·25	1·20
P26		10l. pale purple (9.24)		43·00	39·00	8·50
P27		12l. red-brown (9.24)		85·00	£110	9·50
P28		15l. olive-green (9.24)		85·00	£140	13·00
P29		20l. deep purple (9.24)		£110	£150	20·00
P17/29 Set of 13				£300	£425	55·00

See note on Parcel Post Stamps below No. PE98 of Italy.

LIBYA 1915

1915 (Nov)–**30**. POSTAGE DUE. *Postage Due stamps of Italy, optd with T* **2**.

D17	D **12**	5c. magenta and orange	1·40	4·25
D18		10c. magenta and orange	1·50	2·50
		a. Figures "10" and opt inverted		
D19		20c. magenta and orange	2·10	3·50
		a. Opt double	£275	
		b. Opt inverted	£275	
D20		30c. magenta and orange	2·50	4·25
D21		40c. magenta and orange	3·75	6·00
		a. Error Value in black (1930)	£2500	
D22		50c. magenta and orange	2·50	3·50
D23		60c. magenta and orange	4·00	7·75
D24		60c. brown and orange (1925)	60·00	85·00
D25		1l. magenta and blue	2·50	7·75
		a. Opt double	£3500	
D26		2l. magenta and blue	38·00	50·00
D27		5l. magenta and blue	50·00	75·00
D17/27 Set of 11			£150	£225

1915 (Dec)–**16**. *Red Cross Society stamps of Italy optd with T* **3**.

17	53	10c.+ 5c. carmine	2·10	8·50
		a. Opt double	£375	
18	54	15c.+ 5c. slate	11·00	19·00
19		20c.on 15c. + 5c. slate (3.16)	11·00	19·00
		a. Opt double	£375	
20		20c.+ 5c. orange (3.16)	3·50	19·00
17/20 Set of 4			25·00	60·00

1916 (Mar). *No. 100 of Italy optd with T* **2a**, *in violet*.

21	49	20c.on 15c. slate	18·00	5·00
		a. Optd in blue-black	40·00	6·00

WATERMARK CROWN. The crown watermark, Type **8** of Italy, is repeated here.

Wmk Crown

4 Roman Legionary

5 Goddess of Plenty

6 Roman Galley leaving Tripoli

7 Victory

(Des D. Cambellotti (**4**), V. Grassi (**5**). P. Paschetto (**6**) and G. Costantini (**7**). Recess)

1921 (July). *Wmk Crown*.

A. Perf 14¼ × 13¾.

22A	**4**	1c. sepia and black	35	2·50
23A		2c. red-brown and black	35	2·50
24A		5c. green and black	50	45
		a. Centre inverted	50·00	70·00
		b. Centre in red-brown (as 2c.)	£1200	
25A	**5**	10c. rose and black	50	25
		a. Centre inverted	50·00	70·00
26A		15c. brown-orange and sepia	55·00	1·00
		a. Centre inverted	£100	£190
27A		25c. blue and deep blue	50	15
		a. Centre inverted	17·00	21·00
28A	**6**	30c. sepia and black	6·75	50
		a. Centre inverted	£1500	£1500
29A		50c. olive and black	3·50	10
		a. Centre inverted		£2000
		b. Centre in sepia	£300	
30A		55c. violet and black	3·50	7·50
31A	**7**	1l. brown	13·50	15
		c. Wmk omitted	†	†
32A		5l. blue and black	21·00	13·50
33A		10l. olive and indigo	£150	75·00
		c. Wmk omitted	£350	£200
22A/33A Set of 12			£225	95·00

B. Perf 14¼ × 13¼.

22B	**4**	1c. sepia and black	1·00	5·25
23B		2c. red-brown and black	1·00	5·25
24B		5c. green and black	1·50	85
		a. Centre inverted	50·00	70·00
25B	**5**	10c. rose and black	1·50	50
		a. Centre inverted	50·00	70·00
26B		15c. brown-orange and sepia	£140	2·10
27B		25c. blue and deep blue	1·50	35
		a. Centre inverted	17·00	21·00
28B	**6**	30c. sepia and black	21·00	1·00
29B		50c. olive and black	10·50	35
30B		55c. violet and black	10·50	15·00
31B	**7**	1l. brown	41·00	35
		c. Wmk omitted	90·00	45·00
32B		5l. blue and black	50·00	21·00
33B		10l. olive and indigo	£375	95·00
		c. Wmk omitted	£375	£200
22B/33B Set of 12			£525	£500

There are numerous shades in this issue.

The lira values were printed in sheets of 50, the other values in sheets of 100. Both perforations appear in the same sheet, the 14¼ × 13¼ occurring in two horizontal rows: the 5th and 6th in the sheets of 100, the 2nd and 3rd for the 1 and 5l. and the 3rd and 4th for the 10l.

The 1l. with watermark omitted in the normal perforation cannot be distinguished from No. 58.

See also Nos. 47/62.

E 8

1921 (July). EXPRESS LETTER. *Wmk Crown. P* 14.

E34	E **8**	30c. red and blue	1·70	5·25
E35		50c. sepia and red	2·50	6·75

No. E34 is inscribed "EXPRES".
See also Nos. E42/3.

1922 (Apr). *1921 Victory stamps of Italy optd with T* **3**.

34	**62**	5c. green	1·20	5·25
		a. Opt double	£225	£225
35		10c. carmine	1·20	5·25
		a. Opt inverted	£300	£300
		b. Opt double	£225	£225
36		15c. slate	1·20	6·75
		a. Pair, one without opt	£700	
37		25c. ultramarine	1·20	6·75
34/37 Set of 4			4·25	22·00

C. 40 (8)   Cent. 60 (E 9)   1,60 LIRE 1,60 (E 10)

LIBYA 1922

1922 (1 June). Nos. 12 and 9 of Libya surch as T **8**.
38	**40**	40c.on 50c. mauve		2·20	1·70
39	**39**	80c.on 25c. blue		2·20	5·25

1922 (1 June). EXPRESS LETTER. Nos E17/18 surch with Types E **9/10**.
E40	60c.on 25c. rose	9·50	11·00
E41	1l.60on 30c. blue and rose	11·00	23·00

1923 (1 Sept). EXPRESS LETTER. P 14.
E42	E **8**	60c. sepia and red	5·25	10·50
E43		2l. red and blue	8·50	21·00

No E43 is inscribed "EXPRES".

9 "Libyan Sibyl" by Michelangelo

(Des A. Calcagnadoro. Eng A. Repettati. Recess)

1924 (Apr)–**31**. No wmk. P 14.
41	**9**	20c. green	70	10
		a. Perf 11 (1.26)	27·00	25
42		40c. brown	1·70	50
		a. Imperf (pair)	£400	£475
		b. Perf 11 (2.26)	24·00	2·10
43		60c. blue	70	10
		a. Perf 11 (4.26)	24·00	45
44		1l.75, orange (2.1.31)	25	10
45		2l. scarlet	2·10	85
		a. Imperf (pair)	£375	£400
		b. Perf 11 (1.29)	10·50	4·00
46		2l.55, violet (2.1.31)	4·00	5·75
41/46 Set of 6			8·50	6·75

There are numerous shades in this issue.

1924–40. Types as 1921. No wmk. P 14.
47	**4**	1c. sepia and black (10.24)	50	2·50
		a. Perf 11 (1930)	£150	
48		2c. brown and black (10.24)	70	2·50
		a. Perf 11 (1930)	£150	
49		5c. green and black (10.29)	1·40	70
		a. Perf 11 (10.29)	48·00	4·75
50		7½c. red-brown and black (3.31)	35	4·00
51	**5**	10c. rose and black (5.24)	35	25
		a. Perf 11 (4.26)	31·00	3·00
52		15c. orange and sepia (4.24)	4·25	1·00
		a. Perf 11 (6.26)	£170	13·50
53		25c. blue and deep blue (5.24)	55·00	50
54	**6**	30c. sepia and black (8.24)	25	50
		a. Perf 11 (1.27)	95·00	2·10
55		50c. olive and black (2.24)	25	50
		a. Perf 11 (9.27)	£500	10
56		55c. violet and black (3.25)	£200	£275
57	**7**	75c. scarlet and purple (2.31)	1·90	10
58		1l. brown (9.26)	6·00	35
		a. Perf 11 (6.26)	£120	35
59	**6**	1l.25, ultramarine and indigo (3.31)	25	10
60	**7**	5l. blue and black (1940)	90·00	55·00
		a. Perf 11 (12.36)	£1700	£200
61		10l. olive and indigo (p 11) (5.37)	£300	£250

There are numerous shades in this issue.

70 (E 11)

2.50 (E 12)

1926 (July). EXPRESS LETTER. Nos. E42/3 surch with Types E**11** or E**12**.
E62	70 on 60c. sepia and red (B.)	5·25	10·50
E63	2.50 on 2l. red and blue (R.)	8·50	21·00

See also No. E66.

LIRE 1,25 (E 13)

1927 (Feb)–**36**. EXPRESS LETTER. As Nos. E42/3, but perf 11, surch with Types E **13** or E **12**.
E64	1l.25 on 60c. sepia and red (B.)	4·25	1·50
	a. Surch inverted	£1500	£1000
	b. Perf 14 (4.36)	19·00	2·50
E65	1l.25 on 60c. sepia and red (Bk.) (1933)	£62000	£5500
E66	2l.50 on 2l. red and blue (R.)	95·00	£275

1927 (17 Oct)–**39**. PARCEL POST. Parcel Post stamps of Italy optd with Type P **3**, on each half of the stamp.
			Un pair	Used pair	Used half
P62	P **92**	5c. brown (1939)	£9000		
P63		10c. blue (2.36)	2·10	3·50	40
P64		25c. carmine (2.36)	2·10	3·50	40
P65		30c. ultramarine (1929)	35	1·70	40
P66		50c. orange	48·00	£100	10·00
		a. Opt 8½ mm instead of 9½ mm (12.31)	85·00	£170	17·00
P67	—	60c. rose-scarlet (value at right in figures) (1929)	35	1·70	40
P68	P **92**	1l. violet (2.36)	19·00	50·00	6·00
P69		2l. green (1937)	22·00	50·00	6·00
P70		3l. yellow-bistre	1·00	4·25	1·00
P71		4l. grey-black	1·00	7·75	2·00
P72		10l. magenta (2.36)	£180	£200	25·00
P73		20l. purple (2.36)	£180	£250	29·00

See note on Parcel Post Stamps below No. PE98 of Italy.

1928 (28 Oct)–**29**. AIR. Air stamps of Italy optd with T **2**.
63	**88**	50c. rose	6·75	8·50
64		80c. red-brown and purple (28.1.29)	21·00	33·00

1928–30. Stamps of Italy optd with T **3** (1l.75) or **2** (others).
65	**92**	7½c. brown (1.29)	5·25	26·00
66	**34**	1l.25 blue and ultramarine (1.29)	38·00	13·50
		a. Opt inverted	£1400	
67	**91**	1l.75 brown (p 11) (11.28)	43·00	1·70
		a. Perf 14 (1930)	—	£5000

LIBIA (CL 10)

10 Bedouin Woman

1929 (11 May). CONCESSIONAL LETTER POST. Nos. CL227/a of Italy optd with Type CL **10**.
CL68	CL **93**	10c. blue (p 14)	22·00	17·00
		a. Perf 11	75·00	75·00

LIBYA 1934

1934 (12 May). POSTAGE DUE. Postage Due stamps of Italy, optd as T 3.

D68	D 141	5c. brown	10	2·10
D69		10c. deep blue	10	2·10
D70		20c. bright scarlet	1·00	1·20
D71		25c. green	1·00	1·20
D72		30c. orange-red	1·00	4·25
D73		40c. agate	1·00	3·00
D74		50c. violet	1·20	35
D75		60c. indigo	1·50	10·50
D76	D 142	1l. reddish orange	1·40	35
D77		2l. green	38·00	10·50
D78		5l. violet	60·00	21·00
D79		10l. blue	10·50	31·00
		a. Pair, one without opt	£1700	
D80		20l. carmine-red	10·50	41·00
D68/80 Set of 13			£120	£120

1936 (11 May). Tenth Tripoli Trade Fair. Photo. Wmk Crown. P 14.

68	10	50c. bright violet	1·20	2·40
69		1l.25 blue	1·40	6·25

1936 (July)–**41**. AIR. Nos. 96 and 99 of Cyrenaica optd as T 3, but slightly larger.

70	16	50c. bright violet	1·70	35
		a. Opt inverted	£300	£300
		b. Opt double	£1400	
71	17	1l. grey-black (9.41)	3·50	17·00

1937 (Jan)–**41**. AIR. Air stamps of Tripolitania optd as T 3, but slightly larger.

72	18	50c. deep carmine	10	10
73		60c. orange-vermilion (31.10.41)	60	
74		75c. blue (4.41)	60	17·00
75		80c. purple (2.41)	60	31·00
		a. Opt double	£550	£750
76	19	1l. blue	1·50	85
		a. Pair, one without opt	£1200	
77		1l.20 brown (5.41)	60	38·00
78		1l.50 orange (31.10.41)	60	48·00
79		5l. green (31.10.41)	60	
72/79 Set of 8			4·75	

11 Triumphal Arch    **12** Roman Theatre, Sabrata

1937 (15 Mar). Inauguration of Coastal Highway. Photo. Wmk Crown. P 14.

(a) POSTAGE.

80	11	50c. brown-lake	2·20	3·50
81		1l.25 blue	2·20	7·75

(b) AIR.

82	12	50c. purple	2·20	4·25
83		1l. black	2·20	4·25
80/83 Set of 4			8·00	18·00

XI FIERA DI TRIPOLI
(13)

1937 (24 Apr). Eleventh Tripoli Trade Fair. Optd as T 13.

(a) POSTAGE.

84	11	50c. brown-lake	10·50	24·00
85		1l.25 blue	10·50	24·00

(b) AIR.

86	12	50c. purple	10·50	24·00
87		1l. black	10·50	24·00
84/87 Set of 4			20·00	85·00

14 Benghazi Waterfront    **15** Tripoli

1938 (20 Feb). Twelfth Tripoli Trade Fair. Inscr "XII FIERA CAMPIONARIA TRIPOLI". Photo. Wmk Crown. P 14.

(a) POSTAGE. As T 14.

88	14	5c. sepia	10	1·00
89	–	10c. olive-brown	10	70
90	14	25c. green	45	1·20
91	–	50c. bright violet	50	50
92	14	75c. carmine	85	1·70
93	–	1l.25 blue	95	3·50

Design:—10c., 50c., 1l.25, Fair Buildings

(b) AIR.

94	15	50c. olive-brown	1·00	1·90
95		1l. deep blue	1·00	4·00
88/95 Set of 8			4·50	13·00

16 Statue of Augustus    **17** Eagle and Serpent

(Des C. Mezzana. Photo)

1938 (25 Apr). Birth Bimillenary of Augustus the Great. T **16**/**17** and similar vert design. Wmk Crown. P 14.

(a) POSTAGE.

96	16	5c. bronze-green	10	1·00
97	–	10c. brown-red	10	1·00
98	16	25c. green	50	60
99	–	50c. mauve	50	45
100	16	75c. scarlet	1·50	3·25
101	–	1l.25 blue	1·50	2·20

Design:—10c., 50c., 1l.25, Statue of Goddess of Plenty.

(b) AIR.

102	17	50c. olive-brown	35	1·40
103		1l. mauve	50	3·00
96/103 Set of 8			4·50	11·50

18 Agricultural Landscape    **19** Buildings

(Des G. Rondini. Photo)

1939 (12 May). Thirteenth Tripoli Trade Fair. As T **18** (horiz designs inscr "XIII FIERA CAMPIONARIA DI TRIPOLI 1939 A. XVII"). Wmk Crown. P 14.

(a) POSTAGE.

104	18	5c. brown-olive	25	85
105	–	20c. brown-red	50	85

LIBYA Cyrenaica 1940

106	18	50c. mauve		55	85
107	—	75c. scarlet		55	1·70
108	18	1l.25 blue		55	2·50

Design:—20c., 75c. View of Ghadames.

(b) AIR. Inscr "POSTA AEREA".

109		25c. green	25	1·30
110		50c. bronze-green	35	1·30
111		1l. mauve	45	1·70
104/111	Set of 8		3·00	10·00

Designs: Fiat G18V airplane—25c., 1l. Arab and camel in desert; 50c. Fair Entrance.

(Des A. Ortona (25c., 1l.25); G. Rondini (others). Photo)

1940 (3 June). *Naples Exhibition. Designs as T* **19** *inscr "TRIENNALE D'OLTREMARE". Wmk Crown. P* 14.

(a) POSTAGE.

112		5c. brown	1·50	1·00
113		10c. red-orange	1·00	70
114		25c. green	60	1·00
115		50c. violet	60	70
116		75c. carmine	70	2·20
117		1l.25 ultramarine	85	3·75
118		2l.+ 75c. lake	85	13·00

Designs: *Vert*—25c., 1l.25, Mosque. *Horiz*—50c. T **19**; 10c., 75c., 2l. Oxen and plough.

(b) AIR. Inscr "POSTA AEREA".

119		50c. brownish black	50	85
120		1l. purple-brown	50	1·70
121		2l.+ 75c. indigo	85	5·25
122		5l.+ 2l.50, red-brown	85	7·75
112/122	Set of 11		8·00	34·00

Designs: *Horiz*—50c., 2l. Savoia Marchetti S.M.75 airplane over city; 1, 5l. Savora Marchetti S-73 airplane over oasis.

1941 (May). *CONCESSIONAL LETTER POST. No. CL267 of Italy optd "LIBIA" (as T* **3***). White gum.*

CL123	CL **109**	10c. brown	8·50	8·50

A similar stamp with larger opt and yellow gum was prepared for use in 1942 but was not issued in Libya.

19a Hitler and Mussolini

(Des G. Rondini. Photo)

1941 (16 May). *Rome-Berlin Axis Commemoration. Wmk Crown. P* 14.

(a) POSTAGE.

123	**19**a	5c. red-orange	10	2·75
124		10c. brown	10	2·75
125		20c. slate-purple	85	2·75
126		25c. green	85	2·75
127		50c. violet	85	2·75
128		75c. scarlet	85	8·50
129		1l.25 blue	85	8·50

(b) AIR. Inscr "POSTA AEREA".

130	**19**a	50c. slate-green	85	12·00
123/130	Set of 8		4·75	38·00

In 1942 a set of eleven postage due stamps, showing a camel and rider and inscribed "SEGNATASSE", and a 10c. Concessional Letter Post stamp, showing a stylized plant and inscribed "RECAPITO AUTORIZZATO", were prepared but not issued in Libya.

B. CYRENAICA

Commemorative stamps inscribed "Cirenaica" were issued before the separate colony was created on 26 June 1927.

100 Centesimi = 1 Lira

PRINTERS. All stamps of Italian Cyrenaica were printed at the Italian Government Printing Works.

Stamps of Italy overprinted, except where otherwise stated.

1923 (24 Oct). *"Propaganda Fide" stamps optd "CIRENAICA" (similar to T* **14***). Centres in orange.*

1	**66**	20c. bronze-green	4·00	18·00
2		30c. carmine	4·00	18·00
3		50c. violet	2·75	20·00
4		1l. blue	2·75	26·00
1/4	Set of 4		12·00	75·00

CIRENAICA	CIRENAICA	CIRENAICA
(1)	(2)	(3)

1923 (29 Oct). *Fascist March on Rome stamps optd with T* **1**.

5	**73**	10c. deep green (R.)	4·25	7·25
6		30c. violet (R.)	4·25	7·50
7		50c. carmine-red	4·25	8·25
8	**74**	1l. light blue	4·25	21·00
9		2l. brown	4·25	25·00
10	**75**	5l. black and blue (R.)	4·25	25·00
5/10	Set of 6		23·00	95·00

1924 (1 Apr). *Manzoni stamps optd "CIRENAICA" (similar to T* **1***), in red. Centres in black or grey–black.*

11	10c. claret	5·00	20·00
	a. Opt vert (reading up)	£300	
12	15c. green	5·00	20·00
	a. Opt vert (reading up)	£300	
	b. Opt vert (reading down)	£300	
13	30c. black	5·00	20·00
14	50c. chestnut	5·00	20·00
	a. Opt vert (reading up)	£300	
15	1l. blue	40·00	£150
16	5l. dull purple	£400	£1300

The overprint reads vertically upwards on Nos. 15 and 16.

1925 (1 June). *Holy Year stamps optd with T* **2**.

17	20c.+ 10c. brown and myrtle-green	2·50	11·50
18	30c.+ 15c. brown and chocolate	2·50	13·00
19	50c.+ 25c. brown and violet	2·50	11·50
20	60c.+ 30c. brown and carmine	2·50	15·00
21	1l.+ 50c. purple and blue (R.)	2·50	20·00
22	5l.+ 2.50l. purple and orange-red (R.)	2·50	30·00
17/22	Set of 6	13·50	90·00

1925 (Nov)–**26**. *Royal Jubilee stamps optd with T* **3**. *P* 11.

23	60c. lake-red	30	5·25
24	1l. blue	50	5·25
24a	1l.25 blue (7.26)	2·50	11·00
	b. Perf 13½ (7.26)	£150	£300

CIRENAICA	Cirenaica
(4)	(5)

1926 (12 Apr). *St. Francis of Assisi stamps optd with T* **5** *(Nos. 28/9) or* **4** *(others).*

25	20c. dull green	1·50	6·50
26	40c. violet	1·50	6·50
27	60c. dull lake	1·50	11·50
28	1l.25 blue (p 11) (R.)	1·50	18·00
29	5l.+ 2.50l. olive (R.)	4·25	35·00
	a. Optd double (R. + Bk.)	£1000	
25/29	Set of 5	9·25	70·00

LIBYA Cyrenaica 1926

Cirenaica (7)   **6**   **8**   **CIRENAICA** (12)   **13**

1926 (1 June). *Colonial Propaganda. Wmk Crown. P 14.*

30	6	5c.+ 5c. brown	60	4·00
31		10c.+ 5c. olive-green	60	4·00
32		20c.+ 5c. blue-green	60	4·00
33		40c.+ 5c. scarlet	60	4·00
34		60c.+ 5c. orange	60	4·00
35		1l.+ 5c. blue	60	6·50
30/35		Set of 6	3·25	24·00

1927 (21 Apr). *First National Defence stamps optd with T 3.*

36	40c.+ 20c. black and brown	1·75	15·00
37	60c.+ 30c. brown and lake	1·75	15·00
38	1l.25 + 60c. black and blue	1·75	30·00
	a. Opt double	£650	
39	5l.+ 2l.50 black and blue-green	2·75	40·00
36/39	Set of 4	7·25	90·00

In Nos. 38/9 the original colours of the Italian issue are reversed, the 1l.25 being in the colour of the 5l. and *vice versa*.

1927 (10 Oct). *Volta Centenary stamps optd with T 7 Colours changed.*

40	90	20c. violet	5·00	18·00
41		50c. orange	6·50	11·50
		a. Opt double	£130	
42		1l.25 blue	10·00	26·00

For 50c. overprinted "Cirenaica" inverted and "Eritrea", see No. 121b of Eritrea.

(Des A. Calcagnadoro. Litho)

1928 (15 Oct). *45th Anniv of Italian–African Society. Wmk Crown. P 14.*

43	8	20c.+ 5c. blue-green	1·60	5·25
44		30c.+ 5c. scarlet	1·60	5·25
45		50c.+ 10c. violet	1·60	9·25
46		1l.25 + 20c. blue	1·75	10·50
43/46		Set of 4	6·00	27·00

CIRENAICA (9)   **CIRENAICA** (10)   **Cirenaica** (11)

1929 (4 Mar). *Second National Defence stamps optd with T 9. Colours changed.*

47	30c.+ 20c. black and carmine	3·00	10·50
48	50c.+ 20c. slate-grey and lilac (R.)	3·00	12·50
49	1l.25 + 50c. blue and sepia (R.)	3·75	20·00
50	5l.+ 2l. black and olive-green (R.)	3·75	35·00
47/50	Set of 4	12·00	70·00

1929 (14 Oct). *Montecassino stamps optd with T 11 (10l.) or 10 (others). Colours changed.*

51	20c. deep green (R.)	3·75	8·25
52	25c. orange-red (B.)	3·75	8·25
53	50c.+ 10c. bright scarlet (B.)	3·75	10·00
54	75c.+ 15c. sepia (R.)	3·75	10·00
55	1l.25 + 25c. deep purple (R.)	7·25	16·00
56	5l.+ 1l. blue (R.)	7·25	20·00
57	10l.+ 2l. blackish brown (R.)	7·25	26·00
51/57	Set of 7	32·00	90·00

1930 (17 Mar). *Marriage of Prince Humbert and Princess Marie Jose stamps optd with T 12. Colours changed.*

58	109	20c. green	1·00	3·00
59		50c.+ 10c. orange-vermilion	80	4·00
60		1l.25 + 25c. carmine-red	80	9·25

1930 (26 July). *Ferrucci stamps optd as T 5 (12½ mm wide). Colours changed.*

61	20c. bright violet (R.)	1·60	1·60
62	25c. green (R.)	1·60	1·60
63	50c. black (R.)	1·60	3·25
64	1l.25 blue (R.)	1·60	6·50
65	5l.+ 2l. carmine-red (B)	2·75	5·00
61/65	Set of 5	9·00	23·00

1930 (20 Oct). *Third National Defence stamps optd with T 9. Colours changed.*

66	30c.+ 10c. blue-green and deep green	13·00	16·00
67	50c.+ 10c. purple and deep green (R.)	13·00	20·00
68	1l.25 + 30c. red-brown and brown (R.)	13·00	30·00
69	5l.+ 1l.50 green and deep blue (R.)	42·00	65·00
66/69	Set of 4	75·00	£120

(Des D. Tofani. Photo)

1930 (27 Nov). *25th Anniv (1929) of Italian Colonial Agricultural Institute. Wmk Crown. P 14.*

70	13	50c.+ 20c. brown	2·25	10·00
71		1l.25 + 20c. blue	2·25	10·00
72		1l.75 + 20c. green	2·25	12·00
73		2l.55 + 50c. bright violet	3·25	20·00
74		5l.+ 1l. carmine-red	3·25	28·00
70/74		Set of 5	12·00	70·00

CIRENAICA (14)   **CIRENAICA** (15)

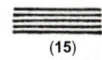

1930 (4 Dec). *Virgil Bimillenary stamps optd with T 14. Colours changed.*

75	15c. violet-grey (R.)	85	4·00
76	20c. red-brown (B.)	85	2·00
77	25c. blue-green (R.)	85	1·60
78	30c. brown (B.)	85	2·00
79	50c. purple (R.)	85	1·60
80	75c. rose-red (B.)	85	3·00
81	1l.25 greenish blue (R.)	85	4·00
82	5l.+ 1l.50 purple (R.)	3·00	21·00
83	10l.+ 2l.50 brown (B.)	3·00	32·00
75/83	Set of 9	11·00	65·00

1931 (7 May). *St. Antony of Padua stamps optd with T 9 or T 5. Colours changed.*

84	9	20c. brown (B.)	1·25	8·25
85		25c. green (R.)	1·25	3·25
		a. Optd on back		
86		30c. chocolate (B.)	1·25	3·25
87		50c. purple (B.)	1·25	3·25
88	5	75c. slate (R.)	1·25	8·25
		a. Opt 12½ instead of 14 mm long	40·00	55·00
89	9	1l.25, greenish blue (R.)	1·25	16·00

195

LIBYA Cyrenaica — 1932

90	5	5l.+ 2l.50, sepia	3·50	38·00
		a. Opt 12½ instead of 14 mm long	80·00	£120
84/90	Set of 7		10·00	70·00

No. 88a occurs on positions 25 and 27 and No. 90a on positions 49 and 50 in the sheet of 50.

1932 (7 Jan). AIR. T **18** of Tripolitania optd as T **5** (12½ mm wide).

91	50c. carmine-red (B.)	65	10
92	60c. orange-red (B.)	4·00	8·00
93	80c. deep purple (B.)	4·00	11·50

1932 (12 May). AIR. T **18** of Tripolitania optd with T **15**.

94	50c. carmine-red (B.)	1·00	1·00
95	80c. deep purple (B.)	5·25	12·00

The 60c. value was overprinted in 1943 but not issued in Cyrenaica.

16 Arab on Camel  **17** Columns of Leptis

(Des L. de Rosa. Photo)

1932 (8 Aug). AIR. Wmk Crown. P 14.

96	**16**	50c. bright violet	3·25	10
97		75c. brown-red	5·00	5·00
98		80c. blue	5·00	10·00
99	**17**	1l. grey-black	1·60	10
100		2l. green	2·00	5·00
101		5l. carmine-red	3·75	10·00
96/101	Set of 6		18·00	29·00

18 Graf Zeppelin  **19** Air Squadron

(Des G. Rondini. Photo)

1933 (5 May). AIR. Airship Graf Zeppelin. T **18** and similar horiz designs. Wmk Crown. P 14.

102	**18**	3l. brown	5·75	55·00
103		5l. bright violet	5·75	55·00
104		10l. green	5·75	£110
105		12l. blue	5·75	£120
106	**18**	15l. carmine-red	5·75	£120
107		20l. black	5·75	£140
102/107	Set of 6		30·00	£550

Designs:—5l.,12l. Graf Zeppelin and Roman galley: 10l., 20l. Graf Zeppelin and giant archer.

(Des C. Mezzana. Photo)

1933 (1 June). AIR. Balbo Transatlantic Mass Formation Flight of Savoia Marchetti S–55X Flying Boats. Wmk Crown. P 14.

108	**19**	19l.75 blue and deep green	11·50	£300
109		44l.75 steel-blue and scarlet	11·50	£300

(20)

1934 (20 Jan). AIR. Rome–Buenos Aires Flight. T **17** (new colours) surch or optd as T **20**. Wmk Crown. P 14.

110	**17**	2l.on 5l. red-brown	2·00	32·00
111		3l.on 5l. green	2·00	32·00
112		5l. yellow-brown	2·00	35·00
113		10l.on 5l. carmine-rose	2·25	35·00
110/113	Set of 4		7·50	£120

21 Arab Horseman

(Des G. Rondini. Photo)

1934 (16 Oct). Second International Colonial Exhibition, Naples. T **21** and similar designs inscr "II. MOSTRA...A. XII. 1934". Wmk Crown. P 14.

(a) POSTAGE.

114	**21**	5c. sepia and green	2·75	9·00
115		10c. black and brown	2·75	9·00
116		20c. blue and scarlet	2·75	7·50
117		50c. sepia and violet	2·75	7·50
118		60c. blue and brown	2·75	9·75
119		1l.25 green and blue	2·75	16·00

(b) AIR. Inscr "POSTA AEREA".

120		25c. orange and blue	2·75	9·00
121		50c. blue and green	2·75	9·00
122		75c. orange and sepia	2·75	9·00
123		80c. green and brown	2·75	9·00
124		1l. orange and scarlet	2·75	10·00
125		2l. sepia and blue	2·75	16·00
114/125	Set of 12		30·00	£110

Designs:—25c. to 75c. Arrival of Caproni Ca 101 mail plane; 80c. to 2l. Caproni Ca 101 airplane and Venus of Cyrene.

22 SERVIZIO DI STATO (O **23**)

(Des G. Rondini. Photo)

1934 (5 Nov). Rome–Mogadiscio Flight. Wmk Crown. P 14.

(a) AIR.

126	**22**	25c.+ 10c. grey-green	3·25	5·00
127		50c.+ 10c. brown	3·25	5·00
128		75c.+ 15c. carmine	3·25	5·00
129		80c.+ 15c. brown-black	3·25	5·00
130		1l.+ 20c. lake-brown	3·25	5·00
131		2l.+ 20c. blue	3·25	5·00
132		3l.+ 25c. bright violet	16·00	42·00
133		5l.+ 25c. orange	16·00	42·00

LIBYA Cyrenaica, Tripolitania 1923

134	22	10l.+ 30c. purple		16·00	42·00
135		25l.+ 2l. green		16·00	42·00
126/135 Set of 10				75·00	£180

(b) OFFICIAL AIR. No. 135, colour changed, optd with Type O 23.
O136 22 25l.+ 2l. carmine £1600 £1100

C. TRIPOLITANIA

Commemorative stamps inscribed "Tripolitania" were issued before the separate colony was created, on 26 June 1927.
The Tripoli Trade Fair issues from 1927 to 1935 were not inscribed "Tripolitania", but have the name of the town in which the fair was held, those issues from 1932 to 1934 were also inscribed "R. R. Poste Coloniali", which seems to indicate that they were general issues. For ease of reference these are all listed below The Tripoli Trade Fair issues of 1936 to 1939, which are (except for the 1938 issue), inscribed "Libia", are listed under Libya.

100 Centesimi = 1 Lira

PRINTERS. All stamps of Tripolitania were printed at the Italian Government Printing Works.

Stamps of Italy overprinted, except where otherwise stated.

1923 (24 Oct). *"Propaganda Fide" stamps optd "TRIPOLITANIA" (similar to T 10 but wider). Centres in orange.*
1	66	20c. bronze-green		4·25	19·00
2		30c. carmine		4·25	19·00
3		50c. violet		2·75	21·00
4		1l. blue		2·75	28·00
1/4 Set of 4				12·50	30·00

TRIPOLITANIA   TRIPOLITANIA
(1)   (2)

1923 (29 Oct). *Fascist March on Rome stamps optd with T 1.*
5	73	10c. deep green (R.)		5·00	7·75
6		30c. violet (R.)		5·00	7·75
7		50c. carmine-red		5·00	8·50
8	74	1l. light blue		5·00	22·00
9		2l. brown		5·00	26·00
10	75	5l. black and blue (R.)		5·00	38·00
5/10 Set of 6				27·00	£100

1924 (1 Apr). *Manzoni stamps optd "TRIPOLITANIA" (similar to T 12), in red (sideways, reading up, on Nos. 15/16). Centres in black or grey-black.*
11	10c. claret		5·25	21·00
12	15c. green		5·25	21·00
13	30c. black		5·25	21·00
14	50c. chestnut		5·25	21·00
15	1l. blue		41·00	£160
16	5l. dull purple		£425	£1400

1925 (1 June). *Holy year stamps optd with T 2.*
17	20c.+ 10c. brown and myrtle-green		2·50	12·00
18	30c.+ 15c. brown and chocolate		2·50	14·00
19	50c.+ 25c. brown and violet		2·50	12·00
20	60c.+ 30c. brown and carmine		2·50	10·00
21	1l.+ 50c. purple and blue (R.)		2·50	21·00
22	5l.+ 2.50l. purple and orange-red (R.)		1·00	31·00
17/22 Set of 6			13·50	95·00

TRIPOLITANIA   TRIPOLITANIA   Tripolitania
(3)   (4)   (5)

1925 (Nov)–**26**. *Royal Jubilee stamps optd with T 3. P 11.*
23	60c. lake-red		70	4·25
24	1l. blue		1·00	4·25
	a. Perf 13½		3·50	16·00
24b	1l.25 blue (7.26)		£750	£850
	c. Perf 13½		1·20	14·00

1926 (12 Apr). *St. Francis of Assisi stamps optd with T 4 or 5 (Nos 28/9).*
25	20c. dull green		1·60	7·00
	a. Pair, one without opt		£2000	
26	40c. violet		1·60	7·00

27	60c. dull lake		1·60	12·00
28	1l.25c. blue (p 11) (R.)		1·60	19·00
29	5l.+ 2.50l. olive (R.)		4·25	38·00
25/29 Set of 5			9·50	75·00

1926 (1 June). *Colonial Propaganda. As T 6 of Cyrenaica, but inscr "TRIPOLITANIA".*
30	5c.+ 5c. brown		60	4·25
31	10c.+ 5c. olive-green		60	4·25
32	20c.+ 5c. blue-green		60	4·25
33	40c.+ 5c. scarlet		60	4·25
34	60c.+ 5c. orange		60	4·25
35	1l.+ 5c. blue		60	7·00
30/35 Set of 6			3·25	25·00

6 Port of Tripoli   E 7 In the Desert

(Des N. D'Urso. Litho)

1927 (15 Feb). *First Tripoli Trade Fair. As T 6 and similar horiz types, inscr "PRIMA ESPOSIZIONE FIERA…TRIPOLI". Wmk Crown. P 14.*

(a) POSTAGE.
36	6	20c.+ 05c. black and purple		2·50	8·25
37		25c.+ 05c. black and blue-green		2·50	8·25
38	–	40c.+ 10c. black and sepia		2·50	8·25
39	–	60c.+ 10c. black and chestnut		2·50	8·25
40	–	75c.+ 20c. black and carmine-red		2·50	8·25
41	–	1l.25 + 20c. black and blue		13·00	21·00

Designs:—40c., 60c. Arch of Marcus Aurelius; 75c., 1l.25, View of Tripoli

(b) EXPRESS LETTER.
E42	E 7	1l.25 + 30c. black and violet		8·00	8·00
E43		2l.50 + 1l. black and yellow		8·00	8·00
36/E43 Set of 8				30·00	38·00

The 1 l. 25 is inscribed "ESPRESSO"

1927 (21 Apr). *First National Defence stamps optd with T 3.*
42	40c.+ 20c. black and brown		1·00	4·25
43	60c.+ 30c. brown and lake		1·00	4·25
44	1l.25+ 60c. black and blue		1·00	4·25
45	5l.+ 2l.50 black and blue-green		1·50	6·50
42/45 Set of 4			4·00	17·00

In Nos. 44/5 the original colours of the Italian issue are reversed, the 1l.25 being in the colour of the 5 l. and *vice versa*. These two stamps exist overprinted on the original colours but were not issued.

Tripolitania
8

TRIPOLITANIA
(10)   9 Palm Tree   11

1927 (10 Oct). *Volta Centenary stamps optd with T 8. Colours changed.*
46	90	20c. violet		4·25	19·00
47		50c. orange		7·00	12·00
		a. Opt double		£140	
48		1l.25 light blue		9·50	28·00

For 50c. orange overprinted "Tripolitania" inverted together with "Somalia Italiana" see No. 109b of Somalia.

LIBYA Tripolitania   1928

(Des A. Terzi. Litho)
1928 (20 Feb). *Second Tripoli Trade Fair. T* **9** *and similar types all inscr "SECONDA FIERA...TRIPOLI/1928". Wmk Crown. P 14.*

49	30c.+ 20c. sepia and maroon	2·10	9·50
50	50c.+ 20c. sepia and blue-green	2·10	9·50
51	1l.25+ 20c. sepia and scarlet	2·10	9·50
52	1l.75+ 20c. sepia and blue	2·10	9·50
53	2l.55+ 50c. sepia and brown	3·75	12·00
54	5l.+ 1l. sepia and violet	5·50	19·00
48/54	*Set of 6*	16·00	60·00

Designs: *Vert* as T **9**—30c. View of Tripoli; 1l.25, Camel riders. *Horiz* (38 × 22½ *mm*)—1l.75, Arab citadel; 2l.55, View of Tripoli; 5l. Desert outpost.

1928 (15 Oct). *45th Anniv of Italian-African Society. As T* **8** *of Cyrenaica, but inscr "POSTE TRIPOLITANIA".*

55	20c.+ 5c. blue-green	1·70	5·50
56	30c.+ 5c. carmine-red	1·70	5·50
57	50c.+ 10c. bright violet	1·70	9·75
58	1l.25+ 20c. blue	1·90	11·00
55/58	*Set of 4*	6·25	29·00

1929 (4 Mar). *Second National Defence stamps optd with T* **10**. *Colours changed.*

59	30c.+ 10c. black and carmine	3·00	5·50
60	50c.+ 20c. slate-grey (R.)	3·00	5·50
61	1l.25c.+ 50c. blue and brown (R.)	3·75	21·00
62	5l.+ 2l. black and olive-green (R.)	3·75	21·00
59/62	*Set of 4*	12·00	44·00

(Des A. Terzi. Litho)
1929 (7 Apr). *Third Tripoli Trade Fair. T* **11** *and similar types. Wmk Crown. P 14.*

63	30c.+ 20c. black and deep claret	7·00	12·00
64	50c.+ 20c. black and deep blue-green	7·00	12·00
65	1l.25+ 20c. black and scarlet	7·00	12·00
66	1l.75+ 20c. black and deep blue	7·00	12·00
67	2l.55+ 50c. black and brown	7·00	12·00
68	5l.+ 1l. black and violet	£100	£160
63/68	*Set of 6*	£120	£200

Designs: As T **11**—30c., 1l.25, Different trees; 50c. Dorcas gazelle. 38 × 22 *mm*—1l.75 Herd of goats; 2l.55 Camel caravan; 5l. Trees.

TRIPOLITANIA (12)   Tripolitania (13)

1929 (14 Oct). *Montecassino stamps optd with T* **13** *(10l.) or* **12** *(others) Colours changed.*

69	20c. deep green (R.)	3·75	8·50
70	25c. orange-red (B.)	3·75	8·50
71	50c.+ 10c. bright scarlet (B.)	3·75	10·50
72	75c.+ 15c. sepia (R.)	3·75	10·50
73	1l.25+ 25c. deep purple (R.)	7·50	17·00
74	5l.+ 1l. blue (R.)	7·50	21·00
75	10l.+ 2l. blackish brown (R.)	7·50	28·00
69/75	*Set of 7*	34·00	95·00

14 Gathering Bananas   **15** Water-carriers

(Des A. Terzi. Photo)
1930 (20 Feb). *Fourth Tripoli Trade Fair. T* **14/15** *and similar designs inscr "IV FIERA TRIPOLI.../1930". Wmk Crown. P 14.*

76	30c. sepia	1·60	6·00
77	50c. bright violet	1·60	6·00
78	1l.25 blue	1·60	6·00
79	1l.75+ 20c. scarlet	2·20	13·00
80	2l.55+ 45c. green	10·50	17·00

81	5l.+ 1l. orange-vermilion	10·50	26·00
82	10l.+ 2l. deep purple	10·50	29·00
76/82	*Set of 7*	35·00	95·00

Designs: As T **14**—50c. Tobacco plant; 1l.25, Venus of Cyrene. As T **15**—2l.55, Blackbucks; 5l. Motor and Camel transport, 10l. Rome pavilion, at exhibition entrance.

TRIPOLITANIA (16)   **17** Roman Arch

1930 (17 Mar). *Marriage of Prince Humbert and Princess Marie Jose stamps optd with T* **16**. *Colours changed.*

83	109	20c. green	1·00	3·00
84		50c.+ 10c. orange-vermilion	85	4·25
85		1l.25+ 25c. carmine-red	85	9·75

1930 (26 July). *Ferrucci stamps optd as T* **10** *(14½ mm wide) Colours changed.*

(a) POSTAGE.

86	114	20c. bright violet (R.)	1·70	1·70
87	115	25c. green (R.)	1·70	1·70
88		50c. black (R.)	1·70	3·50
89		1l.25 blue (R.)	1·70	7·00
90	116	5l.+ 2l. carmine-red (B.)	5·25	14·00

(b) AIR.

91	117	50c. purple (B.)	2·75	3·50
92		1l. deep blue (R.)	2·75	7·00
93		5l.+ 2l. carmine-red (B.)	10·00	21·00
86/93	*Set of 8*		25·00	55·00

1930 (20 Oct). *Third National Defence stamps optd with T* **10**. *Colours changed.*

94	30c.+ 10c. blue-green and deep green	14·00	17·00
95	50c.+ 10c. purple and deep green (R.)	14·00	21·00
96	1l.25+ 30c. red-brown and brown (R.)	14·00	31·00
97	5l.+ 1l.50 green and deep blue (R.)	45·00	70·00
94/97	*Set of 4*	80·00	£120

(Des M. A. Falorsi. Photo)
1930 (27 Nov). *25th Anniv (1929) of Italian Colonial Agricultural Institute. Wmk Crown. P 14.*

98	17	50c.+ 20c. brown	2·40	10·50
99		1l.25+ 20c. blue	2·40	10·50
100		1l.75+ 20c. green	2·40	12·50
101		2l.55+ 50c. bright violet	3·50	21·00
102		5l.+ 1l. carmine-red	3·50	29·00
98/102	*Set of 5*	13·00	75·00

1930 (4 Dec). *Virgil Bimillenary stamps optd as T* **10** *(28½ mm wide). Colours changed.*

(a) POSTAGE.

103	15c. violet-grey (R.)	85	4·25
104	20c. red-brown (B.)	85	2·10
105	25c. blue-green (R.)	85	1·70
106	30c. brown (B.)	85	2·10
107	50c. purple (R.)	85	1·70
108	75c. rose-red (B.)	85	3·00
109	1l.25 greenish blue (R.)	85	4·25
110	5l.+ 1l.50 purple (R.)	3·00	22·00
111	10l.+ 2l.50 brown (B.)	3·00	34·00

(b) AIR.

112	50c. blue-green (R.)	2·10	5·25
	a. Surch on back only		
113	1l. carmine (B.)	2·10	5·25
114	7l.70+ 1l.30 brown (R.)	4·25	24·00
115	9l.+ 2l. slate-blue (R.)	4·25	24·00
103/115	*Set of 13*	22·00	£120

LIBYA Tripolitania   1931

18 Columns of Leptis
19 
22 Savoia Marchetti S-55A Flying Boat over Ruins
23 Paw-Paw Tree

(Des L. de Rosa. Photo)

1931 (2 Jan)–**32**. AIR. Wmk Crown. P 14.
116	**18**	50c. carmine-red	50	15
117		60c. orange-red	1·90	6·00
117a		75c. blue (8.8.32)	1·90	4·75
118		80c. deep purple (16.11.31)	5·25	9·50
119	**19**	1l. blue (16.11.31)	85	15
120		1l.20 deep brown (16.11.31)	16·00	10·50
121		1l.50 orange-red (16.11.31)	5·25	10·50
122		5l. green (16.11.31)	17·00	16·00
116/122	Set of 8		44·00	50·00

1931 (Mar). CONCESSIONAL LETTER POST. No. CL267 optd "TRIPOLITANIA" (as T **1**).
CL123	CL **109**	10c. brown	8·50	8·50

(Des M. A. Falorsi. Photo)

1931 (7 Dec). AIR. 25th Anniv (1929) of Italian Colonial Agricultural Institute. Wmk Crown. P 14.
139	**22**	50c. blue	2·75	9·50
140		80c. bright violet	2·75	9·50
141		1l. black	2·75	14·00
142		2l. green	4·25	21·00
143		5l.+ 2l. carmine-red	5·25	30·00
139/143	Set of 5		16·00	80·00

(Des G. Rondini. Photo)

1932 (8 Mar). Sixth Tripoli Trade Fair. T **23** and similar types inscr "VI FIERA…TRIPOLI/1932". Wmk Crown. P 14.

(a) POSTAGE.
144	10c. brown	4·25	7·00
145	20c. lake-brown	4·25	7·00
146	25c. green	4·25	7·00
147	30c. blackish green	4·25	7·00
148	50c. deep violet	4·25	7·00
149	75c. carmine	5·25	7·00
150	1l.25 deep blue	5·25	10·50
151	1l.75+ 25c. brown	21·00	38·00
152	5l.+ 1l. blue	23·00	75·00
153	10l.+ 2l. purple	60·00	£140

Designs: Vert—10c. to 50c. Trees of various kinds; 75c. Roman mausoleum at Ghirza; 10l. Dorcas gazelle. Horiz—1l.25, Mogadiscio aerodrome; 1l.75, Lioness; 5l. Arab and camel.

(b) AIR. Inscr "POSTA AEREA".
154	50c. deep blue	7·00	19·00
155	1l. orange-brown	7·00	19·00
156	2l.+ 1l. black	19·00	48·00
157	5l.+ 2l. carmine	60·00	£100
144/157	Set of 14	£200	£450

Designs: Horiz. Marina Fiat MF.5 flying boat over—50c., 1l. Bedouin camp; 2, 5l. Tripoli.

20 Statue of Youth
E **21** War Memorial

(Des A. Terzi. Photo)

1931 (8 Mar). Fifth Tripoli Trade Fair. T **20** and similar designs all inscr "V FIERA…TRIPOLI/1931". Wmk Crown. P 14.

(a) POSTAGE.
123	10c. brown-black	3·00	4·25
124	25c. green	3·00	4·25
125	50c. bright violet	3·00	4·25
126	1l.25 blue	3·00	7·00
127	1l.75+ 25c. carmine	3·00	9·00
128	2l.75+ 45c. orange	3·00	10·50
129	5l.+ 1l. purple	8·25	17·00
130	10l.+ 2l. brown	29·00	38·00

Designs: Vert as T **20**—25c. Arab musician; 50c. View of Zeughet; 1l.25, Snake charmer; 1l.75, House and windmill; 2l.75, Libyan "Zaptie"; 5l. Arab horseman As Type E **21**—10l. Exhibition pavilion.

(b) AIR. Inscr "POSTA AEREA".
131	50c. blue	5·25	14·00

Design: As Type E **21**—50c. Airplane over desert.

(c) EXPRESS LETTER.
E132	E **21**	1l.25+ 20c. carmine	5·25	14·00
123/E132	Set of 10		60·00	£120

24 Arch of Marcus Aurelius
25 Mercury 

(Des G. Rondini. Photo)

1933 (2 Mar). Seventh Tripoli Trade Fair T **24** and similar designs inscr "VII FIERA…TRIPOLI/1933". Wmk Crown. P 14.

(a) POSTAGE.
158	10c. purple	22·00	17·00
159	25c. green	11·00	17·00
160	30c. orange-brown	11·00	17·00
161	50c. bright violet	9·50	17·00
162	1l.25 blue	25·00	38·00
163	5l.+ 1l. brown	47·00	75·00
164	10l.+ 2l.50 carmine	47·00	£110

1931 (7 May). St. Anthony of Padua stamps optd as T **10** (14½ mm wide), or T **5**. Colours changed.
132	**10**	20c. brown (B.)	1·40	3·50
133		25c. green (R.)	1·40	3·50
134		30c. brown-black (B.)	1·40	3·50
135		50c. purple (B.)	1·40	3·50
136	**5**	75c. slate (R.)	1·40	8·50
137	**10**	1l.25 greenish blue (R.)	17·00	17·00
138	**5**	5l.+ 2l.50 sepia	3·75	40·00
132/138	Set of 7		11·00	75·00

199

LIBYA Tripolitania 1933

Designs: Vert—10c. Ostrich, 25c. Type **24**, 50c. Arch of Marcus Aurelius. 1l.25, Golden eagle; 10l. Tripoli and the Fascist emblem. Horiz—30c. Arab drummer. 5l. Leopard.

(b) AIR Inscr "POSTA AEREA".

165	50c. green		6·00	11·00
166	75c. carmine		6·00	11·00
167	1l. blue		6·00	11·00
168	2l.+ 50c. bright violet		11·00	23·00
169	5l.+ 1l. orange-brown		20·00	38·00
170	10l.+ 2l.50, black		20·00	80·00
158/170	Set of 13		£225	£425

Designs: Horiz—50c., 2l. Seaplane over Tripoli, 75c., 10l. Caproni Ca 101 airplane over Tagiura; 1, 5l. Seaplane leaving Tripoli.

(Des C. Mezzana. Photo)

1933 (5 May). AIR. Airship Graf Zeppelin. T **25** and similar designs. Wmk Crown. P 14.

171	**25**	3l. brown	6·00	60·00
172	—	5l. bright violet	6·00	60·00
173	—	10l. green	6·00	£110
174	**25**	12l. blue	6·00	£120
175	—	15l. carmine-red	6·00	£120
176	—	20l. black	6·00	£150
171/176	Set of 6		32·00	£550

Designs:—5, 15l. Graf Zeppelin and Arch of Marcus Aurelius, 10, 20l. Graf Zeppelin and allegory of "dawn".

26 "Flight"    **27** Water Carriers

(Des C. Mezzana. Photo)

1933 (1 June). AIR. Balbo Transatlantic Mass Formation Flight. Wmk Crown. P 14.

177	**26**	19l.75 brown and black	12·00	£300
178		44l.75 green and blue	12·00	£300

1934 (20 Jan). AIR. Rome-Buenos Aires Flight. T **19** (new colours) surch or optd as T **20** of Cyrenaica. Wmk Crown. P 14.

179	**19**	2l.on 5l. red-brown	2·10	33·00
180		3l.on 5l. green	2·10	33·00
181		5l. yellow-brown	2·10	36·00
182		10l.on 5l. rose-carmine	2·10	36·00
179/182	Set of 4		7·75	£120

(Des G. Rondini. Photo)

1934 (17 Feb). Eighth Tripoli Trade Fair. T **27** and similar designs inscr "VIII FIERA...TRIPOLI/1934". Wmk Crown. P 14.

(a) POSTAGE.

183	10c. brown	3·00	9·50
184	20c. carmine	3·00	7·75
185	25c. green	3·00	7·75
186	30c. sepia	3·00	7·75
187	50c. bright violet	3·00	6·00
188	75c. carmine-red	3·00	12·00
189	1l.25 blue	34·00	44·00

Designs Horiz—30c, 1l.25, Moslem shrine, 75c. Ruins of Ghadamès Vert—20c. Arab, 25c. Minaret; 50c. Statue of Claudius.

(b) AIR Inscr "POSTA AEREA".

190	50c. grey-blue	5·25	14·00
191	75c. orange-vermilion	5·25	14·00
192	5l.+ 1l. green	80·00	£100
193	10l.+ 2l. purple	80·00	£100
194	25l.+ 3l. red-brown	85·00	£120

Designs: Horiz—50c., 5l. Marina Fiat MF.5 flying boat off port of Tripoli; 75c., 10l. Airplane over mosque with minaret. Vert—25l. Caproni Ca 101 airplane over desert.

(c) AIR EXPRESS. Inscr "POSTA AEREA ESPRESSO".

E195	2l.25, greenish black	21·00	34·00
E196	4l.50+ 1l. slate blue	21·00	34·00
183/E196	Set of 14	£250	£450

Design: Horiz—2l.25, 4l.50, Caproni Ca 101 airplane over Bedouins in desert.

(28) 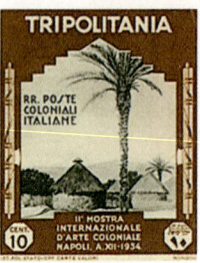   **29** Village

1934 (1 May). Oasis Flight As Nos. 190/E196, colours changed cold with T **28**.

(a) AIR.

197	50c. rosine	8·50	55·00
198	75c. olive-bistre	8·50	55·00
199	5l.+ 1l. bistre-brown	8·50	55·00
200	10l.+ 2l. grey-blue (R.)	£170	£350
201	25l.+ 3l. violet (R.)	£170	£350

(b) AIR EXPRESS.

E202	2l.25 orange-red	8·50	55·00
E203	4l.50+ 1l. lake	8·50	55·00
197/E203	Set of 7	£350	£900

(Des G. Rondini. Photo)

1934 (16 Oct). Second International Colonial Exhibition, Naples T **29** and, similar designs inscr "II MOSTRA INTERNAZIONALE" etc. Wmk Crown. P 14.

(a) POSTAGE.

204	**29**	5c. sepia and green	3·00	9·50
205		10c. black and brown	3·00	9·50
206		20c. blue and scarlet	3·00	7·75
207		50c. sepia and violet	3·00	7·75
208		60c. blue and brown	3·00	10·50
209		1l.25 green and blue	3·00	17·00

(b) AIR. Inscr "POSTA AEREA".

210	25c. orange and blue	3·00	9·50
211	50c. blue and green	3·00	7·75
212	75c. orange and sepia	3·00	7·75
213	80c. green and brown	3·00	9·50
214	1l. green and scarlet	3·00	10·50
215	2l. sepia and blue	3·00	17·00
204/215	Set of 12	32·00	£110

Designs:—25c. to 75c. Shadow of airplane over desert; 80c. to 2l. Arab camel corps and Caproni Ca 101 airplane.

30

(Des G. Rondini. Photo)

1934 (5 Nov). Rome—Mogadiscio Flight. Wmk Crown. P 14.

(a) AIR

216	**30**	25c.+ 10c. grey-green	3·50	5·25
217		50c.+ 10c. brown	3·50	5·25
218		75c.+ 15c. carmine	3·50	5·25
219		80c.+ 15c. brown-black	3·50	5·25
220		1l.+ 20c. lake-brown	3·50	5·25
221		2l.+ 20c. blue	3·50	5·25
222		3l.+ 25c. bright violet	16·00	44·00
223		5l.+ 25c. orange	16·00	44·00

LIBYA Tripolitania 1935

224	10l.+ 30c. purple		16·00	44·00
225	25l.+ 2l. green		16·00	44·00
216/225 *Set of* 10			75·00	£190

(b) OFFICIAL AIR. No. 225, colour changed, optd with Type O **23** *of Cyrenaica.*

O226	**30**	25l. + 2l. carmine	£1700	£2500

31 Arab in Burnous

32 Camel Transport

(Des G. Rondini. Photo)

1935 (16 Feb). *Ninth Tripoli Trade Fair. T* **31/2** *and similar designs inscr* "IX FIERA CAMPIONARIA TRIPOLI/1935 A.XIII". *Wmk Crown. P* 14.

(a) POSTAGE As T **31**.

226	–	10c.+ 10c. brown	85	3·00
227	–	20c.+ 10c. carmine	85	3·00
228	–	50c.+ 10c. bright violet	85	3·00
229	**31**	75c.+ 15c. carmine-red	85	3·00
230	–	1l.25+ 25c. blue	85	3·00
231	–	2l.+ 50c. blackish green	85	5·25

Designs *Vert*—10c., 20c. Pomegranate tree, 50c., 2l. Arab flute-player.

(b) AIR. As T **32**.

232	–	25c.+ 10c. blue-green	70	3·75
233	**32**	50c.+ 10c. grey-blue	70	3·75
234	–	1l.+ 25c. blue	70	3·75
235	**32**	2l.+ 30c. carmine	70	4·75
236	–	3l.+ 1l.50, brown	70	4·75
237	–	10l.+ 5l. purple	7·00	21·00
226/237 *Set of* 12			14·00	55·00

Designs *Vert*—25c. 3l. Watch-tower *Horiz*— 1l., 10l. Arab girl and airplane Caproni Ca 101.

On 10 June 1940, Italy declared war on the United Kingdom, and from 1940 to 1943, Libya was the scene of fluctuating warfare between the British Eighth Army and Italian troops reinforced by the German Afrika Korps. The Eighth Army finally cleared Libya on 16 February 1943. From 1943 to 1951 Libya was under British Military Administration. For the stamps issued in this period, see under "British Occupation of Italian Colonies" in Part 1 (1840–1952) of this catalogue.

SOMALIA 1903

Somalia

1903. 64 Besa = 16 Annas = 1 Rupia
1905. 100 Centesimi = 1 Lira
1922. 100 Besa = 1 Rupia
1926. 100 Centesimi = 1 Lira
1950. 100 Centesimi = 1 Somalo

The southern coast of what is now Somalia was known by the ancient name of Benadir, meaning landing places. From 1885 to 1889 the Italians made treaties with local sultans on the northern coast, who placed themselves under Italian protection. In 1892 the Sultan of Zanzibar, nominal ruler of the Benadir coast, leased to Italy the ports of Brava, Merka, Mogadishu and Uarsciek for 50 years. Administration was carried on first by the Filonardi Company and then, from 1898, by the Benadir Company

For a short period from 1876 to 1884 Egyptian Post Offices functioned at Berbera and Zeila, using unoverprinted stamps of Egypt. Details are given in Part 19 (*Middle East*) of this catalogue.

PRINTERS. *Except where otherwise stated*, all the following stamps were printed at the Government Printing Works, Turin (until 1928) or Rome (from 1929).

A. BENADIR

| | | 1 African Elephant | 2 Lion | 3 |

1903 (12 Oct). *Typo.* W **3** (sideways). P 14.
1	**1**	1b. brown	29·00	5·50
2		2b. blue-green	1·00	3·00
3	**2**	1a. carmine-red	1·00	4·75
4		2a. orange-brown	1·90	10·00
5		2½a. blue	1·00	10·00
6		5a. orange-yellow	1·90	21·00
7		10a. lilac	1·90	21·00
1/7	Set of 7		34·00	65·00

By an agreement of 13 January 1905 the Sultan of Zanzibar ceded sovereign rights in the Benadir ports to Italy for £144,000 and Italy assumed direct rule on 19 March 1905. A treaty with Ethiopia was made on 16 May 1908, by which the boundaries of the new Italian Colony were extended well inland in return for £120,000.

B. ITALIAN SOMALILAND

Centesimi
15 (3a)   C. (4)   5
C. 15 (5)   1 LIRA 1 (6)

1905 (29 Dec). Surch as T **3***a*, by Zanzibar Gazette.
| 8 | **2** | 15c.on 5a. orange-yellow | £2500 | £600 |
| 9 | | 40c.on 10a. lilac | £600 | £190 |

1906–16. Nos. 1/7 surch as T **4/6** (no bars at top of stamp).
10	**4**	2c.on 1b. brown (1.07)	6·50	11·00
		a. "C." omitted	£140	
11		5c.on 2b. blue-green (1.07)	6·50	7·50
		a. Surch double, one inverted	—	£2500
12	**5**	10c.on 1a. carmine-red (1.07)	6·50	7·50
13		15c.on 2a. orange-brown (3.06)	6·50	7·50
13*a*		20c.on 2a. orange-brown (11.16)	15·00	7·50
		b. Surch double	£300	
14		25c.on 2½a. blue (1907)	11·00	7·50
15		50c.on 5a. orange-yellow (1907)	19·00	19·00
16	**6**	1l.on 10a. lilac (1907)	19·00	26·00
10/16	Set of 8		45·00	65·00

For similar surcharge but with bars at top, see Nos. 68/75.

Somalia Italiana

Meridionale (D 7)   Somalia Italiana (D 8)

1906 (13 Apr)–**20**. POSTAGE DUE. Postage Due stamps of Italy optd with Type D **7**.
D17	D **12**	5c. magenta and orange	6·25	22·00
D18		10c. magenta and orange	34·00	28·00
D19		20c. magenta and orange	24·00	36·00
D20		30c. magenta and orange	21·00	40·00
D21		40c. magenta and orange	£170	40·00
D22		50c. magenta and orange	40·00	48·00
D23		60c. magenta and buff (22.3.08)	38·00	48·00
D24		1l. magenta and blue	£750	£190
D25		2l. magenta and blue	£700	£190
D26		5l. magenta and blue	£700	£225
D27		10l. magenta and blue	£120	£190
D17/27 Set of 11			£2250	£950

1909 (Jan)–**20**. POSTAGE DUE. Postage Due stamps of Italy optd with Type D **8**.
(a) Near top of stamp (1.09—6.19).
D28	D **12**	5c. magenta and orange	3·00	12·50
D29		10c. magenta and orange	3·00	12·50
D30		20c. magenta and orange	7·50	21·00
D31		30c. magenta and orange	22·00	21·00
D32		40c. magenta and orange	22·00	24·00
D33		50c. magenta and orange	22·00	40·00
D34		60c. magenta and orange (6.19)	32·00	34·00
D35		1l. magenta and blue	85·00	40·00
D36		2l. magenta and blue	£110	£100
D37		5l. magenta and blue	£140	£120
D38		10l. magenta and blue	22·00	44·00
D28/38 Set of 11			£425	£425

(b) Near bottom of stamp (10.20).
D39	D **12**	5c. magenta and orange	55·00	95·00
		a. Opt double	£275	
D40		10c. magenta and orange	55·00	95·00
D41		20c. magenta and orange	90·00	60·00
D42		30c. magenta and orange	£100	60·00
D43		40c. magenta and orange	£100	95·00
D44		50c. magenta and orange	90·00	85·00
D45		60c. magenta and orange	£100	85·00
D46		1l. magenta and blue	£100	£120
D47		2l. magenta and blue	£100	£120
D48		5l. magenta and blue	£110	£120
D39/48 Set of 10			£800	£850

1916 (May). Nos. 15/16 surch at top as T**4**, the old surch at foot cancelled by a continuous bar (20c.) or two short bars at both left and right (5c.).
17		5c.on 50c. on 5a. orange-yellow	31·00	30·00
		a. Lower bar at left omitted	85·00	
		b. Surch double, one inverted	£2250	
18		20c.on 1l. on 10a. lilac	5·50	21·00

These were surcharged at Mogadishu owing to loss of a consignment of stamps from Italy on board the *Giava*, sunk by a submarine.

SOMALIA (7)   SOMALIA ITALIANA (P 8)   SOMALIA (P 9)

202

SOMALIA 1916

1916 (July–Sept). *Red Cross stamps of Italy of 1915–16 optd with T* **7**.
19	53	10c.+ 5c. carmine		8·00	21·00
20	54	15c.+ 5c. slate (Sept)		25·00	26·00
21		20c.on 15c. + 5c. slate (Sept)		25·00	42·00
22		20c.+ 5c. orange		8·00	22·00
19/22		Set of 4		60·00	£100

Inverted overprints on Nos. 19 and 22 are forgeries.

1917–19. PARCEL POST. *Parcel Post stamps of Italy of 1914–22 optd with Type* **P 8** *on each half of stamp.*
			Un pair	Used pair	Used half
P23	P 53	5c. brown	1·50	21·00	60
		a. Opt double	£275		
P24		10c. deep blue	2·20	15·00	65
		a. Vert pairs, onewith "ITALIANA" only, the other with opt omitted	£1400		
P25		20c. black (1919)	£150	60·00	20·00
P26		25c. red	5·50	28·00	60
P27		50c. orange	75·00	38·00	12·00
P28		1l. violet	24·00	24·00	1·50
P29		2l. green	34·00	38·00	2·75
P30		3l. yellow	38·00	50·00	4·75
P31		4l. slate	45·00	50·00	12·00
P23/31		Set of 9	£325	£350	55·00

See note on Parcel Post Stamps below No. PE98 of Italy.
Double overprint on the 25c. is a forgery.
In Type **P 8** the "I" is to the left of "S" and the final letters "A" are not aligned. For similar types see Types **P 20/21**.
For unissued values overprinted with Type P 8 in red, see note after No. P92.
In 1941 the 50c. and 1, 2, 3 and 4l. values overprinted in black with Type **P 20** on each half were placed on sale in Rome only (*Price per set*: £850 *un*).

By a decree of 12 January 1921 a new printing of Nos. 1/7 was ordered and overprinted "SOMALIA ITALIANA" in one line but on 10 March they were ordered to be destroyed because the old monetary system of annas and rupias was no longer in use. 50 sets survived.

1921–23. PARCEL POST. *Parcel Post stamps of Italy of 1914–22 optd with Type* **P 9** *on each half of stamp.*
			Un pair	Used pair	Used half
P32	P 53	25c. red	38·00	60·00	10·00
P33		50c. orange (2.23)	48·00	60·00	3·00
P34		1l. violet (2.23)	48·00	75·00	3·00
P35		2l. green (2.23)	60·00	75·00	4·25
P36		3l. yellow (2.23)	75·00	75·00	10·00
P37		4l. slate (2.23)	75·00	75·00	12·00
P32/37		Set of 6	£300	£375	38·00

See note on Parcel Post Stamps below No. PE98 of Italy.

6 BESA 6
(8)

SOMALIA ITALIANA
BESA 15
(9)

1922 (1 Feb). *Stamps of Italian Somaliland of 1906–16 further surch at top as T* **8**.
23		3b.on 5c. on 2b. blue-green	9·25	15·00
24		6b.on 10c. on 1a. carmine-red	17·00	11·00
25		9b.on 15c. on 2a. orange-brown	17·00	15·00
26		15b.on 25c. on 2½a. blue	19·00	11·00
27		30b.on 50c. on 5a. orange-yellow	21·00	28·00
		a. Besa surch double	£600	
28		60b.on 1l. on 10a. lilac	21·00	50·00
23/28		Set of 6	95·00	£120

On No. 23 the surcharge consists of figures only, the word "BESA" being already inscribed on the stamp.

1922 (Apr). *Victory stamps of Italy of 1921 surch as T* **9**.
29	62	3b.on 5c. green	1·30	5·50
30		6b.on 10c. carmine	1·30	5·50
31		9b.on 15c. slate	1·30	7·50
32		15b.on 25c. ultramarine	1·30	7·50
29/32		Set of 4	4·75	23·00

18 BESA 18
(10)

2 2
(11)

1923 (1 July). *Stamps of Italian Somaliland of 1906–16 surch as T* **10/11** *(bars only on No. 33 and continuous bars on Nos. 42/3).*
33	–	barson 2c. on 1b. brown	7·50	21·00
34	10	2on 2c. on 1b. brown	7·50	21·00
35		3on 2c. on 1b. brown	7·50	12·00
		a. Surch double	£300	£275
		b. Surch triple	£300	£275
36	11	5b.on 50c. on 5a. orange-yellow	7·50	10·00
37	10	6on 5c. on 2b. blue-green	13·00	10·00
38	11	18b.on 10c. on 1a. carmine-red	13·00	10·00
39		20b.on 15c. on 2a. orange-brown	13·50	10·00
40		25b.on 15c. on 2a. orange-brown	16·00	10·00
41		30b.on 25c. on 2½a. blue	17·00	14·50
42	–	60b.on 1l. on 10a. lilac	17·00	30·00
43	–	1r.on 1l. on 10a. lilac	30·00	38·00
33/43		Set of 11	£130	£170

The bars on No. 33 cancel the "C. 2" surcharge.

Somalia Italiana
1
BESA 30 **Somalia Italiana** **B E S A**
(E 12)   (D 12)

60 BESA 60 **SOMALIA ITALIANA**
(E 13)

1923 (1 July). POSTAGE DUE. *As Type D* **12** *of Italy but without figures of value, surch as Type D* **12**, *in black.*
D49		1b. orange	95	3·50
D50		2b. orange	95	3·50
		a. Such inverted	£300	
D51		3b. orange	95	3·50
D52		5b. orange	1·90	3·50
D53		10b. orange	1·90	3·50
D54		20b. orange	1·90	3·50
D55		40b. orange	1·90	3·50
D56		1r. blue	3·00	19·00
D49/56		Set of 8	12·00	40·00

1923 (16 July). EXPRESS LETTER. *Nos.* E129/30 *of Italy surch.*
E44	E 12	30b.on 60c. rose-red	24·00	17·00
E45	E 13	60b.on 1l. 20, blue and rose	35·00	34·00

BESA SOMALIA   **SOMALIA BESA**
ITALIANA   **ITALIANA 10**
(P 12)

1923. PARCEL POST. *Parcel Post stamps of Italy surch as Type P* **12** *(No.* P44 *with figure at left and right).*
			Un pair	Used pair	Used half
P44	P 53	3b.on 5c. brown	5·50	13·00	3·50
		a. "3" omitted at left	£225		
P45		5b.on 5c. brown	5·50	13·00	3·50
P46		10b.on 10c. deep blue	5·50	11·00	2·00
P47		25b.on 25c. red	11·00	19·00	3·00
P48		50b.on 50c. orange	21·00	28·00	3·25
P49		1r.on 1l. violet	22·00	28·00	3·50
P50		2r.on 2l. green	38·00	37·00	6·50
P51	P 53	3r.on 3l. yellow	38·00	37·00	9·00
		a. Surch inverted	£300		
P52		4r.on 4l. slate	40·00	37·00	14·00
P44/52		Set of 9	£170	£200	45·00

203

SOMALIA 1923

See note on Parcel Post Stamps below No. PE98 of Italy.

SOMALIA ITALIANA

SOMALIA ITALIANA besa 20 (13)

BESA 13 (14)

SOMALIA ITALIANA besa 9

SOMALIA ITALIANA BESA 30 (15)

(16)

1923 (24 Oct). *"Propaganda Fide" stamps of Italy surch as T* **13**.
44	66	6b.on 20b. orange and bronze-green	4·50	20·00
45		13b.on 30c. orange and carmine	4·50	20·00
46		20b.on 50c. orange and violet	3·00	22·00
47		30b.on 1l. orange and blue	3·00	30·00
44/47 Set of 4			13·50	85·00

1923 (29 Oct). *Fascist March on Rome stamps of Italy surch as T* **14** (48/50) *or* **15** (51/3).
48	73	2c.on 10c. deep green (R.)	5·50	8·25
49		13b.on 30c. violet (R.)	5·50	8·25
50		20b.on 50c. carmine-red	5·50	9·00
51	74	30b.on 1l. light blue	5·50	24·00
52		1r.on 2l. brown	5·50	28·00
53	75	3r.on 5l. black and blue (R.)	5·50	40·00
48/53 Set of 6			30·00	£100

1924 (1 Apr). *Manzoni stamps of Italy (Nos. 155/60) surch as T* **76** *(sideways, reading up, on Nos. 58/9) Centres in black or grey-black.*
54	6b.on 10c. claret (R.)	5·50	22·00
55	9b.on 15c. green (R.)	5·50	22·00
56	13b.on 30c. black (R.)	5·50	22·00
57	20b.on 50c. chestnut (R.)	5·50	22·00
58	30b.on 1l. blue (R.)	45·00	£170
59	3r.on 5l. dull purple (R.)	£450	£1500
54/59 Set of 6		£475	£1600

E 17

(Des A. Terzi. Recess)

1924 (June). EXPRESS LETTER. W **3**. P.14.
E60	E **17**	30b. sepia and red	9·25	10·00
E61		60b. rose and slate-blue ("EXPRES")	14·00	18·00

SOMALIA ITALIANA Besa 30 (17)

Besa 15 SOMALIA ITALIANA (18)

1925 (1 June). *Holy Year stamps of Italy (Nos. 172/7) surch as T* **17**.
60	6b. + 3b. on 20c. + 10c. brown & green		3·00	13·00
61	13b. + 6b. on 30c. + 15c. brown & choc		3·00	15·00
62	15b. + 8b. on 50c. + 25c. brown & violet		3·00	13·00
63	18b. + 9b. on 60c. + 30c. brown & carm		3·00	17·00
64	30b. + 15b. on 1l. + 50c. purple & bl (R.)		3·00	22·00
65	1r. + 50b. on 5l. + 2.50l. purple and orange-red (R.)		3·00	34·00
60/65 Set of 6			16·00	£100

1925 (Nov)–**26**. *Royal Jubilee stamps of Italy optd with T* **18**.

A. Perf 13½.
66A	82	60c. lake-red	75	4·50
67A		1l. blue	5·50	24·00
67aA		1l.25, blue (7.26)	75	11·00

B. Perf 11.
66B	82	60c. lake-red	70·00	£100
67B		1l. blue	1·50	6·75
67aB		1l.25, blue (7.26)	£450	£500

SOMALIA ITALIANA (P **20**) "I" to left of "S"

SOMALIA ITALIANA (P **21**) "I" under "S"

(19)

1926 (1 Mar). *Stamps of Italian Somaliland 1906–16 optd at top with T* **19** *cancelling besa and anna currencies and reverting to Italian currency.*
68	2c.on 1b. brown	21·00	30·00
69	5c.on 2b. green	13·00	17·00
70	10c.on 1a. rose	8·25	5·50
71	15c.on 2a. orange-brown	8·25	7·50
72	20c.on 2a. orange-brown	9·50	7·50
73	25c.on 22a. blue	9·25	11·00
74	50c.on 5a. yellow-orange	13·00	19·00
75	1l.on 10a. lilac	21·00	24·00
68/75 Set of 8		95·00	£110

1926 (1 Mar). PARCEL POST. *Parcel Post stamps of Italy optd with Type P* **20** *on each half, in black.*
			Un pair	Used pair	Used half
P76	P **53**	10l. purple	65·00	42·00	8·50
P77		12l. red-brown	42·00	42·00	8·50
P78		15l. olive-green	42·00	42·00	8·50
P79		20l. dull purple	42·00	42·00	8·50
P76/79 Set of 4			£170	£150	30·00

See note on Parcel Post Stamps below No. PE98 of Italy. For unissued values in this type, see note after No. P31.

1926 (1 Mar)–**31**. PARCEL POST. *Parcel Post stamps of Italy optd with Type P* **21** *on each half, in red.*
			Un pair	Used pair	Used half
P80	P **53**	5c. brown	12·00	24·00	2·50
P81		10c. blue	12·00	24·00	2·50
P82		20c. black	34·00	24·00	7·50
P83		25c. red	34·00	24·00	5·75
P84		50c. orange	34·00	20·00	5·00
P85		1l. violet	40·00	24·00	6·00
P86		2l. green	75·00	24·00	7·50
P87		3l. yellow	10·00	24·00	8·00
P88		4l. slate	10·00	24·00	8·00
P89		10l. purple (11.30)	19·00	32·00	8·00
P90		12l. red-brown (7.31)	19·00	32·00	8·00
P91		15l. olive-green (7.31)	19·00	45·00	8·00
P92		20l. dull purple (7.31)	19·00	45·00	8·00
P80/92 Set of 13			£300	£400	85·00

See note on Parcel Post Stamps below No. PE98 of Italy.
In 1926–31 the 5, 10, 20, 25 and 50c. and 1 and 2l. were prepared with the overprint Type P **8** in red but were not issued.

1926 (1 Mar). POSTAGE DUE. *As Type D* **12** *of Italy but without figures of value, surch as Type D* **12** *but without "BESA", in black.*
D76	5c. orange		15·00	17·00
D77	10c. orange		15·00	9·00
	a. Surch inverted		£140	
D78	20c. orange		15·00	17·00
	a. Surch inverted		£375	
D79	30c. orange		15·00	9·25
	a. Surch inverted		£140	

SOMALIA 1926

D80	40c. orange		15·00	9·25
	a. Surch inverted		£140	
D81	50c. orange		19·00	9·25
	a. Surch inverted		£140	
D82	60c. orange		19·00	9·25
	a. Surch inverted		£140	
D83	1l. blue		32·00	17·00
D84	2l. blue		45·00	17·00
D85	5l. blue		50·00	25·00
D86	10l. blue		48·00	32·00
D76/86 Set of 11			£250	£150

SOMALIA ITALIANA (20)   Somalia (20a)   SOMALIA ITAL 21

1926 (12 Apr). *St. Francis of Assisi stamps of Italy (Nos. 191/6) optd with T **20** (centesimi values) or **20a** (lire values)*

76	20c. dull green	1·70	7·75
77	40c. violet	1·70	7·75
78	60c. dull lake	1·70	13·00
79	1l.25 blue (p 11) (R.)	1·70	21·00
80	5l.+ 2.50l. olive (R.)	4·75	40·00
76/80 Set of 5		10·50	80·00

(Des A Calcagnadoro. Typo)

1926 (1 June). *Italian Colonial Institute. W **3**. P 14.*

81	21	5c. + 5c. brown	70	4·50
82		10c. + 5c. olive-green	70	4·50
83		20c. + 5c. blue-green	70	4·50
84		40c. + 5c. scarlet	70	4·50
85		60c. + 5c. orange	70	4·50
86		1l. + 5c. blue	70	7·50
81/86 Set of 6			3·75	27·00

CENT 70 (22)   (E 23)

SOMALIA ITALIANA

1926 (July)–**30**. *Various contemporary stamps of Italy optd with T **22**.*

87	31	2c. orange-brown (2.27)	1·00	3·50
		a. Pair, one without opt	£900	
88	37	5c. green (2.27)	1·90	3·50
89	92	7½c. brown (12.28)	17·00	30·00
		a. Opt double	£300	
90	38	10c. rose (2.27)	1·30	40
91	39	20c. purple (2.27)	1·30	1·50
92	34	25c. green and yellow-green (2.27)	1·30	1·20
92a	39	30c. slate-black (9.30)	10·50	19·00
93	91	50c. slate and brown (R.) (6.28)	18·00	5·50
94	92	50c. bright mauve (7.30)	26·00	32·00
95	39	60c. orange (2.27)	3·00	5·25
		a. Opt double	—	£2000
96	34	75c. lake-red and carmine	90·00	19·00
		a. Pair, one without opt	£1300	
97		1l. brown and green (2.27)	3·00	75
98		1l.25 blue and ultramarine	7·50	1·90
99	91	1l.75 brown (p 11) (12.28)	60·00	13·00
100	34	2l. myrtle and orange	21·00	10·00
101		2l.50 myrtle and orange	21·00	13·00
102		5l. blue and rose	55·00	28·00
103	44	10l. sage-green and pale rose	55·00	45·00
87/103 Set of 18			£350	£210

1926 (Oct). *EXPRESS LETTER. Nos. E60/1 surch as Type E **23**.*

E104		70c.on 30b. sepia and red	10·00	13·00
		a. Arabic figure "0" omitted	60·00	70·00
E105		2l.50 on 60b. rose & slate-blue (R.)	13·00	15·00
		a. Arabic figure "0" omitted	70·00	85·00
		b. Arabic figure "5" omitted		

No. E104a occurs on position 30 and No. E105a on position 18 in the sheets of 50.

1927 (Feb)–**40**. *EXPRESS LETTER. As No. E 60 but perf 11, surch as Type E **23**.*

E106		1l.25 on 30b. sepia and red (B.)	12·00	9·25
		a. Perf 14 (5 40)	£140	£300

1927 (21 Apr). *First National Defence stamps of Italy (Nos. 204/7), colours of lira values changed. optd with T **18**.*

104		40c.+ 20c. black and brown	2·10	17·00
105		60c.+ 30c. brown and lake	2·10	17·00
106		1l.25 + 60c. black and blue	2·10	35·00
		a. Opt double	£750	
107		5l.+ 2l. 50 black and blue green	3·75	45·00
104/107 Set of 4			9·00	£100

Somalia Italiana (23)   24   SOMALIA ITALIANA (25)

1927 (10 Oct). *Volta Centenary stamps of Italy, colours changed, optd with T **23**.*

108	90	20c. bright violet	4·75	21·00
109		50c. orange	7·50	13·00
		a. Opt double	£150	
		b. Optd "Tripolitania" inverted and T **23** normal	£325	
110		1l.25 blue	10·00	30·00

1928 (Dec)–**41**. *PARCEL POST. Parcel Post stamps of Italy optd on each half of stamp.*

*(a) With Type P **8**, to black.*

			Un pair	Used pair	Used half
P111	P **92**	5c. brown (2.40)	1·20	3·75	1·30
P112		10c. blue (2.40)	1·50	3·75	1·20
P113		25c. scarlet (1941)	30·00	13·00	6·25
P114		30c. ultramarine	60	1·50	80
P115		50c. orange (11.40)	£12000	—	95·00
P116		60c. red	60	1·90	80
P117		1l. violet (10.31)	£350	—	£100
P118		2l. green (2.40)	£350		£100
P119		3l. yellow	1·90	6·75	1·90
P120		4l. grey-black	1·90	6·75	2·10
		a. Opt double, one inverted	£100		
P121		10l. mauve (2.36)	£300	£300	27·00
P122		20l. purple (2.34)	£300	£300	27·00

*(b) With Type P **8**, in red.*

P123	P **92**	5c. brown (12.37)	13·00		
P124		3l. yellow (1.30)	22·00	40·00	5·00
P125		4l. grey-black (1.30)	22·00	40·00	5·25

*(c) With Type P **20**, in black.*

P126	P **92**	25c. scarlet (1.12.31)	50·00	60·00	8·00
P127		1l. violet (1.12.31)	32·00	28·00	3·25
P128		2l. green (1.12.31)	32·00	28·00	3·25

See note on Parcel Post Stamps below No. PE98 of Italy.

(Des A. Calcag Calcagnadoro. Typo)

1928 (15 Oct). *45th Anniv of Italian–African Society. W **3**. P 14.*

111	24	20c.+ 5c. blue-green	1·90	6·00
112		30c.+ 5c. scarlet	1·90	6·00
113		50c.+ 10c. violet	1·90	10·50
114		1l.25 + 20c. blue	2·10	12·00
111/114 Set of 4			7·00	32·00

205

SOMALIA 1929

1929 (4 Mar). *Second National Defence stamps of Italy, colours changed, optd with T **25**.*
115	30c.+ 10c. black and carmine	3·50	12·00
116	50c.+ 20c. slate-grey and lilac (R.)	3·50	14·00
117	1l.25 + 50c. blue and brown (R.)	4·25	22·00
118	5l.+ 2l. black and olive-green (R.)	4·25	40·00
115/118 Set of 4		14·00	80·00

SOMALIA ITALIANA (26)   Somalia Italiana (27)   SOMALIA ITALIANA (28)

1929 (14 Oct). *Montecassino Abbey stamps of Italy, colours changed, optd with T **27** (10l.) or **26** (others).*
119	20c. deep green (R.)	4·25	10·00
120	25c. orange-red (B.)	4·25	10·00
121	50c.+ 10c. bright scarlet (B.)	4·25	11·00
122	75c.+ 15c. sepia (R.)	4·25	11·00
123	1l.25 + 25c. deep purple (R.)	8·00	19·00
124	5l.+ 1l. blue (R.)	8·00	22·00
125	10l.+ 2l. blackish brown (R.)	8·00	30·00
119/125 Set of 7		38·00	£100

1930 (17 Mar). *Marriage of Prince Humbert and Princess Marie Jose stamps of Italy, colours changed, optd with T **28**.*
126	**109**	20c. green	1·20	3·50
127		50c.+ 10c. orange-vermilion	1·00	4·75
128		1l.25 + 25c. carmine-red	1·00	10·50

1930 (26 July). *Ferrucci stamps of Italy, colours changed, cold similar to T **22** but larger (4 mm deep and 10½ mm long).*
129	**114**	20c. bright violet (R.)	1·90	2·00
130	**115**	25c. green (R.)	1·90	1·90
131		50c. black (R.)	1·90	3·75
132		1l.25 blue (R.)	1·90	7·50
133	**116**	5l.+ 2l. carmine-red (B.)	5·50	15·00
129/133 Set of 5			12·00	27·00

1930 (20 Oct). *Third National Defence stamps of Italy, colours changed, optd with T **25**.*
134	30c.+ 10c. blue-green and deep green	15·00	19·00
135	50c.+ 10c. purple and deep green (R.)	15·00	22·00
136	1l.25 + 30c. red-brown and brown (R.)	15·00	35·00
137	5l.+ 1l. 50 green and deep blue (R.)	48·00	75·00
134/137 Set of 4		24·00	80·00

29 Irrigation Canal   S O M A L I A (30)

1930 (27 Nov). *25th Anniv (1929) of Italian Colonial Agricultural Institute. Photo. W 3.*
138	**29**	50c.+ 20c. brown	2·75	11·00
139		1l.25 + 20c. blue	2·75	11·00
140		1l.75 + 25c. green	2·75	13·50
141		2l.55 + 50c. bright violet	3·75	22·00
142		5l.+ 1l. carmine-red	3·75	32·00
138/142 Set of 5			14·00	80·00

1930 (4 Dec). *Virgil Bimillenary stamps of Italy, colours changed, optd with T **30**.*
143	15c. violet-grey (R.)	1·00	4·50
144	20c. red-brown (R.)	1·00	2·20
145	25c. blue-green (R.)	1·00	1·90
146	30c. brown (B.)	1·00	2·20
147	50c. purple (R.)	1·00	1·90
148	75c. rose-red (B.)	1·00	3·50
149	1l.25 greenish blue (R.)	1·00	4·50
150	5l.+ 1l.50 purple (R.)	3·50	24·00
151	10l.+ 2l.50 brown (B.)	3·50	38·00
143/151 Set of 9		12·50	75·00

1931 (Feb–Dec). *Stamps of Italy optd as T **22**, in red.*
152	**102**	25c. green (1 Dec)	9·25	11·00
153	**103**	50c. bright violet	9·25	3·75

1931 (7 May). *St. Antony of Padua stamps of Italy, colours changed optd with T **20a** (75c., 5l.) or **30** (others).*
154	20c. brown (B.)	1·50	9·25
155	25c. green (R.)	1·50	3·75
156	30c. blackish brown (B.)	1·50	3·75
157	50c. plum (B.)	1·50	3·75
158	75c. deep slate (R.)	1·50	9·25
159	1l.25, slate-blue (R.)	1·50	19·00
160	5l. + 2l.50, sepia	4·25	42·00
154/160 Set of 7		12·00	95·00

32 Tower at Mnara-Ciromo   **33** Hippopotamus   ONORANZE AL DUCA DEGLI ABRUZZI (**34**)

1932 (1 Mar)–**38**. *T **32/33** and similar designs. Photo. W **3**. P 12.*
161	–	5c. chestnut (27.4.32)	2·10	3·50
		a. Perf 14 (11.35)	60	50
162	–	7½c. bright violet (27.4.32)	11·00	8·00
		a. Perf 14 (12.36)	60	11·00
		b. Perf 12 × 14	65·00	70·00
163	–	10c. black (7.7.32)	4·50	35
		a. Perf 14 (6.35)	60	35
164	–	15c. olive-green (7.7.32)	1·50	95
		a. Perf 14 (9.36)	60	1·90
165	**32**	20c. carmine	£170	25
		a. Perf 14 (4.35)	60	25
		b. Perf 14 × 12	£1000	£450
		c. Perf comp of 12 and 14	£375	£375
166		25c. green	1·50	35
		a. Perf 14 (4.35)	60	35
		b. Perf 14 × 12	£120	45·00
		c. Perf comp of 12 and 14	£120	£120
167	–	30c. brown (27.4.32)	15·00	1·00
		a. Perf 14 (4.35)	1·20	40
		b. Perf 12 × 14		
168	–	35c. blue (27.4.32)	2·75	4·50
		a. Perf 14 (1937)	1·20	40
		b. Perf 12 × 14	70·00	85·00
169	–	50c. bright violet	£250	4·50
		a. Perf 14 (4.35)	13·00	35
		b. Perf 12 × 14	45·00	22·00
170	–	75c. carmine	1·90	60
		a. Perf 14 (2.36)	19·00	40
		b. Perf 14 × 12	70·00	55·00
		c. Perf comp of 12 and 14	£1000	£450
171	–	1l.25 blue	9·25	50
		a. Perf 14 (12.35)	30·00	75
		b. Perf 14 × 12	–	£500
172	–	1l.75 orange-vermilion (27.4.32)	4·50	60
		a. Perf 14 (11.35)	75·00	9·25
		b. Perf 14×12	£300	£300
173	–	2l. carmine (27.4.32)	1·90	40
		a. Perf 14 (4.36)	30·00	60
		b. Perf 14 × 12	£275	£250
174	–	2l.55 slate-blue (27.4.32)	15·00	38·00
		a. Perf 14 (3.38)	£140	£275
175	–	5l. carmine (27.4.32)	8·75	3·50
		a. Perf 14 (3.38)	7·50	2·30
176	**33**	10l. bright violet (27.4.32)	19·00	11·00
		a. Perf 14 (4.37)	£120	22·00
		b. Perf 12 × 14	55·00	60·00
177	–	20l. green (27.4.32)	48·00	48·00
		a. Perf 14 (12.37)	£10000	£850
178	–	25l. blue (7.7.32)	48·00	75·00
		a. Perf 14 (5.38)	£650	£275
161/178 Set of 18 (cheapest)			£160	£180

206

SOMALIA 1934

Designs: *Horiz*—5c. to 15c. Francesco Crispi Lighthouse, Cape Guardafui; 35c. to 75c. Governor's Residence, Mogadishu; 25l. Lioness. *Vert*—1l.25 to 2l. Termitarium (ant-hill); 2l.55, 5l. Ostrich; 20l. Lesser kudu.

1934 (May). *Honouring the Duke of the Abruzzi. As Nos. 163, 166, 169, 171 and 175/8 but colours changed and optd with T* **34**.

179	–	10c. brown	7·00	12·00
180	**32**	25c. green (R.)	6·75	12·00
181	–	50c. purple	4·50	12·00
182	–	1l.25 blue (R.)	4·50	12·00
183	–	5l. black (R.)	6·75	12·00
184	–	10l. carmine	6·75	19·00
185	–	20l. grey-blue (R.)	6·50	19·00
186	–	25l. green (R.)	6·50	19·00
179/186 *Set of 8*			45·00	£110

1934 (12 May). *POSTAGE DUE. Postage Due stamps of Italy of 1934 optd with T* **22**.

D187	D **141**	5c. chocolate	60	1·90
D188		10c. blue	60	1·90
D189		20c. carmine red	2·20	3·75
D190		25c. green	2·20	3·75
D191		30c. orange-vermilion	5·50	6·75
D192		40c. sepia	5·50	9·25
D193		50c. bright violet	11·00	2·75
D194		60c. slate-blue	15·00	21·00
D195	D **142**	1l. orange	17·00	7·50
D196		2l. green	32·00	21·00
D197		5l. bright violet	45·00	38·00
D198		10l. blue	45·00	40·00
D199		20l. carmine	40·00	48·00
D187/199 *Set of 13*			£200	£190

35 Woman and Child    **36**

🜲 SERVIZIO DI STATO
(O **36a**)

(Des G. Rondini. Photo)

1934 (17 Oct). *Second International Colonial Exhibition, Naples.* W **3**. P 14.

(a) POSTAGE.

187	**35**	5c. green and sepia	3·50	10·50
188		10c. brown and black	3·50	10·00
189		20c. scarlet and blue	3·50	8·25
190		50c. violet and sepia	3·50	8·25
191		60c. brown and blue	3·50	11·00
192		1l.25 blue and green	3·50	19·00
187/192 *Set of 6*			19·00	60·00

(b) AIR. As T **35**, *inscr "POSTA AEREA".*

193		25c. blue and orange	3·50	10·00
194		50c. green and blue	3·50	10·00
195		75c. sepia and orange	3·50	8·25
196		80c. brown and green	3·50	8·25
197		1l. scarlet and green	3·50	11·00
198		2l. blue and sepia	3·50	19·00
193/198 *Set of 6*			19·00	60·00

Designs:—25c. to 75c. Caproni Ca 101 airplane over River Juba; 80c. to 2l. Cheetahs watching Caproni Ca 101 airplane.

(Des G. Rondini. Photo)

1934 (5 Nov). *Rome-Mogadishu Flight.* W **3**. P 14.

(a) AIR.

199	**36**	25c.+ 10c. grey-green	3·50	5·50
200		50c.+ 10c. brown	3·50	5·50
201		75c.+ 10c. carmine	3·50	5·50
202		80c.+ 15c. brown-black	3·50	5·50
203		1l.+ 20c. lake-brown	3·50	5·50
204		2l.+ 20c. blue	3·50	5·50
205		3l.+ 25c. bright violet	18·00	48·00
206		5l.+ 25c. orange-vermilion	18·00	48·00
207		10l.+ 30c. purple	18·00	48·00
208		25l.+ 2l. green	18·00	48·00
199/208 *Set of 10*			95·00	£200

(b) OFFICIAL AIR. No. 208, colour changed, optd with Type O **36a**.

O209	**36**	25l. + 2l. rose	£1900	£2750

11 NOV. 1934-XIII
SERVIZIO AEREO
SPECIALE
(O **37**)

1934 (11 Nov). *OFFICIAL AIR. No. 193 optd with Type* O **37**.

O210		25c. blue and orange	£2000 £2500
		a. Error "1943" for "1934"	£2500

Forgeries exist.

37 King Victor Emmanuel III 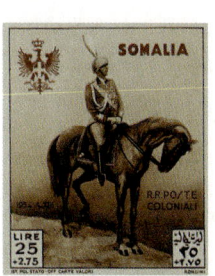   **38** King Victor Emmanuel III

(Des G. Rondini. Photo)

1935 (1 Jan). *King of Italy's Visit to Italian Somaliland.* W **3**. P 14.

209	**37**	5c.+ 5c. brown-black	1·90	11·00
210		7½c.+ 7½c. purple	1·90	11·00
211		15c.+ 10c. blackish green	1·90	11·00
212		20c.+ 10c. scarlet	1·90	11·00
213		25c.+ 10c. green	1·90	11·00
214		30c.+ 10c. sepia	1·90	11·00
215		50c.+ 10c. bright violet	1·90	11·00
216		75c.+ 15c. carmine	1·90	11·00
217		1l.25 + 15c. blue	1·90	11·00
218		1l.75 + 25c. orange	1·90	11·00
219		2l.75 + 25c. grey-blue	12·50	38·00
220		5l.+ 1l. claret	12·50	38·00
221		10l.+ 1l. 80 lake-brown	12·50	38·00
222	**38**	25l.+ 2l. 75 sepia and red-brown	£120	£190
209/222 *Set of 14*			£160	£375

38a Native Girl and Macchi Castoldi MC-94 Flying Boat

207

SOMALIA jubaland 1936

(Des G. Rondini. Photo)
1936. AIR. T **38**a and similar types. W **3**. P 14.
223	25c. blue-green (11.8)	1·25	3·00
224	50c. brown (3.7)	25	25
225	60c. orange (11.8)	1·90	5·50
226	75c. chestnut (11.8)	1·20	1·50
227	1l. bright blue (10.5)	25	25
228	1l.50 bright violet (11.8)	1·20	75
229	2l. grey-blue (11.8)	4·25	1·20
230	3l. lake (11.8)	13·00	5·00
231	5l. green (11.8)	15·00	9·25
232	10l. carmine (11.8)	19·00	15·00
223/232	Set of 10	50·00	38·00

Designs:—25c., 1l.50, Banana trees; 50c., 2l. Woman in cotton plantation; 60c., 5l. Orchard; 75c., 10l. Women harvesting; 1l. Type **38a**. (The 25c. and 1l.50 also show a Macchi Castoldi MC-94 flying boat and the 50 to 75c. and 2 to 10l. show a Caproni Ca 101 airplane.)

Italian Somaliland was joined with Eritrea and Ethiopia to form Italian East Africa, by a law approved on 1 June 1936. It then became officially known as the Government of Somalia The stamps of Italian East Africa (q.v.) were used in Somalia from 1938 until 1942. In 1939 a 10 c. Concessional Letter Post Stamp (No. CL267 of Italy overprinted "SOMALIA ITALIANA") was prepared for use but was not issued.
In the Second World War, British, British African and South African troops occupied Somalia in February 1941. Overprinted British stamps (listed in 1840/1952 *British Commonwealth*) of this catalogue under British Occupation of Italian Colonies) were used in Somalia from 1942 to 1950.

C. JUBALAND

Under an Anglo–Italian agreement of 15 July 1924, a strip of territory from 50 to 100 miles wide was ceded to Italy on the Kenyan side of the Juba River, in fulfilment of the secret Treaty of London, 1915.

OLTRE GIUBA (1)   OLTRE GIUBA (P 2)   **OLTRE GIUBA** (D 3)

1925 (29 June). *Contemporary stamps of Italy optd with T* **1**.
1	30	1c. brown	2·50	8·75
		a. Opt inverted	£250	
2	31	2c. orange-brown	1·80	8·75
3	37	5c. green	1·50	4·50
4	38	10c. rose	1·50	4·50
5	37	15c. slate	1·50	6·25
6	41	20c. orange (105)	1·50	6·25
7	39	25c. blue	1·80	6·25
8		30c. orange-brown	2·50	7·00
9	40	40c. pale brown	3·75	5·50
10		50c. mauve	3·75	5·50
11	39	60c. carmine-lake	3·75	7·00
12	34	1l. brown and green	7·00	8·75
13		2l. myrtle and orange	47·00	24·00
14		5l. blue and rose	75·00	35·00
15	44	10l. sage-green and pale rose	9·00	39·00
1/15		Set of 15	£150	£160

1925 (29 June). PARCEL POST. *Parcel Post stamps of Italy of 1914–22 optd with Type* P **2** *on each half of stamp.*
			Un	Used pair	Used half
P16	P 53	5c. brown	4·50	12·00	1·50
P17		10c. blue	2·75	12·00	1·50
P18		20c. black	2·75	12·00	1·50
P19		25c. red	2·75	12·00	1·50
P20		50c. orange	4·50	12·00	1·50
P21		1l. violet	3·75	28·00	5·50
		a. Opt double	£300		
P22		2l. green	7·00	28·00	5·50
P23		3l. yellow	20·00	38·00	9·00
P24		4l. slate	6·25	38·00	8·00
P25		10l. pale purple	39·00	55·00	9·00
P26		12l. red-brown	85·00	90·00	12·00
P27		15l. olive-green	75·00	90·00	12·00
P28		20l. deep purple	75·00	90·00	12·00
P16/28		Set of 13	£300	£475	75·00

See note on Parcel Post Stamps below No. PE98 of Italy.

1925 (29 June). POSTAGE DUE. *Postage Due stamps of Italy optd with Type* D **3**.
D29	D 12	5c. magenta and orange	8·00	7·00
D30		10c. magenta and orange	8·00	7·00
D31		20c. magenta and orange	8·00	11·00
D32		30c. magenta and orange	8·00	11·00
D33		40c. magenta and orange	8·00	12·50
D34		50c. magenta and orange	10·00	16·00
D35		60c. maroon and orange	10·00	18·00
D36		1l. magenta and blue	14·00	25·00
D37		2l. magenta and blue	65·00	90·00
D38		5l. magenta and blue	80·00	90·00
D29/38	Set of 10		£200	£275

OLTRE GIUBA (4)   **OLTRE GIUBA** (5)

1925 (Oct)–**26**. *Contemporary stamps of Italy optd with T* **4**.
39	39	20c. green	5·00	10·00
40		30c. slate	6·50	11·00
41	34	75c. lake-red and carmine (6.26)	30·00	35·00
42		1l.25 blue and ultramarine (6.26)	42·00	44·00
43		2l.50 myrtle and orange (6.26)	47·00	24·00
39/43	Set of 5		£120	£160

1925 (Nov)–**26**. *Royal Jubilee stamps of Italy optd with T* **5**.
A. Perf 13½.
44A	82	60c. lake-red		£5000
45A		1l. blue	£250	£650
46A		1l.25, blue (7.26)	2·50	18·00

B. Perf 11.
44B	82	60c. lake-red	75	6·25
45B		1l. blue	75	10·75
46B		1l.25, blue	2·20	15·00

OLTRE GIUBA (6)   Oltre Giuba (7)   8 Map of Jubaland

1926 (12 Apr). *St. Francis of Assisi stamps of Italy optd with T* **20** *(centesimi values) or* **21** *(lire values).*
47		20c. dull green	1·60	12·50
48		40c. violet	1·60	12·50
49		60c. dull lake	1·60	18·00
50		1l.25 blue (p 11) (R.)	1·60	27·00
51		5l.+ 2l.50 olive (R.)	4·50	39·00
47/51	Set of 5		10·00	£100

1926 (12 Apr). EXPRESS LETTER. *Express Letter stamps of Italy optd with T* **5**.
E52	E 35	70c. rose-red	18·00	25·00
E53	E 41	2l.50, blue and rose	27·00	55·00

1926 (21 Apr). *First Anniv of Italian Acquisition of Jubaland. Typo. W* **3** *(see Benadir,* 1903*). P* 14.
54	8	5c. brown-orange	75	8·00
55		20c. green	75	8·00
56		25c. brown	75	8·00
57		40c. carmine	75	8·00
58		60c. purple	75	8·00
59		1l. blue	75	8·00
60		2l. grey green	75	8·00
54/60	Set of 7		4·75	50·00

Nos. 54/60 have a coloured background in a paler tone of the colour of the stamp.

208

SOMALIA Jubaland, somalia — 1926

1926 (1 June). *Italian Colonial Institute.* As T **21** of Italian Somaliland.

61	5c. + 5c. brown		65	4·25
62	10c. + 5c. olive-green		65	4·25
63	20c. + 5c. green		65	4·25
64	40c. + 5c. scarlet		65	4·25
65	60c. + 5c. orange		65	4·25
66	1l. + 5c. blue		65	4·25
61/66	*Set of* 6		3·50	25·00

Jubaland was incorporated in Italian Somaliland on 30 June 1926.

D. SOMALIA (ITALIAN TRUST TERRITORY)

On 21 November 1949 the former Italian colony of Somalia was placed under United Nations Trusteeship, with Italy as trustee, and on the understanding that the territory should become an independent state in ten years.

39 Winged Wheel
40 Tower at Mnara-Ciromo 
41 Ostrich 
42 Governor's Residence, Mogadishu 
43 River Scene 

(Des L. Gasbarra (T **40**), G. Savini (T **41**), R. De Sanctis (T **42**) Photo)

1950 (1 Apr). *New Currency.* W **39**. P 14.

233	**40**	1c. black	1·70	2·75
234	**41**	5c. carmine	10	10
235	**42**	6c. blue-violet	1·30	1·30
236	**40**	8c. dull green	1·30	1·30
237	**42**	10c. green (24 Apr)	10	10
238	**41**	20c. turquoise-green	10	10
239	**40**	35c. vermilion	2·10	2·20
240	**42**	55c. blue	1·70	75
241	**41**	60c. reddish violet	1·70	75
242	**40**	65c. chocolate	3·00	1·20
243	**42**	1s. brown-orange	3·75	15
233/243		*Set of* 11	15·00	10·50

(Des G. Savim. Photo)

1950 (24 Apr)–**51**. *AIR.* W **39**. P 14.

244	**43**	30c. yellow-brown	75	40
245		45c. carmine	75	40
246		65c. blackish violet	75	40
247		70c. deep blue	75	60
248		90c. brown	75	60
249		1s. bright purple	1·20	40
250		1s.35 violet	1·90	1·20
251		1s.50 turquoise-green	1·90	1·90
252		3s. blue (5.12.50)	22·00	10·50
253		5s. chocolate (5.12.50)	22·00	10·50
254		10s. red-orange (6.3.51)	32·00	5·25
244/254		*Set of* 11	75·00	32·00

E **44** Grant's Gazelle

(Des R. De Sanctis Photo)

1950 (24 Apr). *EXPRESS LETTER.* W **39**. P 14.

E255	E **44**	40c. turquoise-green	5·00	3·50
E256		80c. violet	8·00	6·00

P **44**  D **44**

(Des E. Pizzi. Photo)

1950 (16–30 May). *PARCEL POST.* W **39**. P 14 × 13.

			Un pair	Used pair	Used half
P255	P **44**	1c. carmine (30.5)	1·50	1·50	30
P256		3c. blackish violet	1·50	1·50	30
P257		5c. bright purple (30.5)	1·50	1·50	30
P258		10c. orange (30.5)	1·50	1·50	30
P259		20c. brown	1·50	1·50	30
P260		50c. turquoise-green (30.5)	3·75	3·75	60
P261		1s. violet	15·00	15·00	1·50
P262		2s. yellow-brown	19·00	19·00	3·00
P263		3s. blue (30.5)	30·00	30·00	6·00
P255/263		*Set of* 9	65·00	65·00	10·00

See note on Parcel Post Stamps below No. PE98 of Italy.

(Des E Pizzi Photo)

1950 (16 May). *POSTAGE DUE.* W **39**. P 14.

D255	D **44**	1c. blackish violet	75	75
D256		2c. blue	75	75
D257		5c. turquoise-green	75	75
D258		10c. bright purple	75	75
D259		40c. violet	4·50	4·50
D260		1s. brown	6·75	6·75
D255/260		*Set of* 6	13·00	13·00

44 Councillors
45 Symbol of Fair 

(Des R. Pierbattista. Photo)

1951 (4 Oct). *First Territorial Council.* W **39**. P 14.

(a) POSTAGE.

255	**44**	20c. brown and deep green	3·00	1·90
256		55c. violet and sepia	7·50	8·25

(b) AIR. Inscr "PRIMO CONSIGLIO TERRITORIALE".

257	—	1s. blue and violet	3·00	95
258	—	1s.50 orange-brown & bronze-green	7·50	5·50
255/258		*Set of* 4	19·00	15·00

Design: *Vert*—1s., 1s.50, Flags and Savoia Marchetti S.M.95C airliner over Mogadishu.

209

SOMALIA somalia 1952

(Des G. Ricci. Photo)

1952 (14 Sept). *First Somali Fair, Mogadishu.* W **39**. P 14.

(a) POSTAGE.

259	45	25c. sepia and brown-red	2·20	2·40
260		55c. sepia and bright blue	2·20	3·25

(b) AIR Inscr "POSTA AEREA".

| 261 | – | 1s.20 blue and bistre | 3·00 | 3·75 |

Design:—1s.20, Palm tree, Douglas DC-4 airliner and minaret.

46 Mother and Baby

47 Somali and Entrance to Fair

(Des G. Ricci. Photo)

1953 (27 May). *Anti-Tuberculosis Campaign.* W **39**. P 14.

(a) POSTAGE.

262	46	5c. sepia and reddish violet	60	1·50
263		25c. sepia and red	60	1·50
264		50c. sepia and blue	75	1·50

(b) AIR Inscr "SOMALIA" and aeroplane.

265	46	1s.20 sepia and deep green	1·90	3·00
262/265		Set of 4		3·50	6·75

(Des A. Calselli. Photo Courvoisier)

1953 (28 Sept). *Second Somali Fair, Mogadishu.* T **47** and similar design. P 11½.

(a) POSTAGE.

266	47	25c. bluish green and grey	40	60
267		60c. blue and blue-grey	95	1·30

(b) AIR. Inscr "POSTA AEREA".

268		1s. 20 lake and flesh	60	75
269		1s. 50 brown and buff	75	1·20
266/269		Set of 4		2·40	3·50

Design:—1s.20, 1s.50, Palm, airplane and entrance.

48 Stamps of 1903 and Map

49 Airplane and Constellations

(Des A. Calselli. Eng V. Nicastro. Recess)

1953 (16 Dec). *50th Anniv of First Stamps of Italian Somaliland.* W **39**. P 14.

(a) POSTAGE.

270	48	25c. bistre brown, carmine red & lake	40	95
271		35c. bistre brown, carmine red & grn	40	95
272		60r. bistre brown, carmine red & orge	40	1·90

(b) AIR Inscr "POSTA AEREA" and airplane on map.

273	48	60c. bistre brn, carm red & orge brn	60	1·50
274		1s. bistre brown, carmine-red & black	60	2·25
270/274		Set of 5		2·20	6·75

(Des A. Calselli. Photo Courvoisier)

1953 (16 Dec). *AIR. 75th Anniv of Universal Postal Union.* P 11½.

275	49	1s.20 scarlet and buff	40	1·20
276		1s.50 brown and huff	75	1·20
277		2s. blue green and light blue	75	1·20

50 Somali Bush Country

51 Alexander Island and River Juba

(Des G. Massa. Photo)

1954 (1 June). *Leprosy Relief Convention.* P 12½ × 13 *(horiz)* or 13 × 12½ *(vert)*.

(a) POSTAGE.

278	50	25c. deep grey-green and bright blue	75	1·50
279		60c. sepia and chestnut	75	1·50

(b) AIR Inscr "POSTA AEREA".

280	51	1s.20 brown and deep blue green	95	1·20
281		2s. purple and carmine red	1·30	1·90
278/281		Set of 4		3·50	5·50

52 Somali Flag

52a Adenium somalense

53 Stars

E 54 Gardenia lutea

(Des A. Calselli. Litho)

1954 (12 Oct). *Institution of Somali Flag.* W **39**. P 13½ × 13.

(a) POSTAGE.

282	52	25c. turquoise-bl, emer red, yell & blk	35	35

(b) AIR. Inscr "POSTA AEREA".

283	52	1s. 20, turq bl, emer, red, yell & brn	35	45

(Des R. De Sanctis (1c., 10c.), L. Gasbarra (5c.), F. Caruso (25c., 1s.), G. Savini (60c., 1s.20), D. Mancini (lettering all values). Photo)

1955 (26 Feb)–**59**. T **52a** and similar vent designs. P 13½ × 13.

*(a) W **39** sideways.*

284		1c. red, black and light blue	10	10
285		5c. mauve, green and pale blue	10	10
286		10c. yellow, green and deep lilac	50	10
287		25c. yellow, green and chocolate	1·30	75

210

SOMALIA somalia 1955

288	60c. red, green and black		10	10
289	1s. yellow, green and brown purple		10	75
290	1s.20 yellow, green and blackish brown		10	1·50

(b) W 53.

290a	1c. red, black and light blue (1.7.56)		25	25
290c	10c. yellow, green & deep lilac (19.6.59)		10	10
290d	15c. yellow, green blk & scar (25.3.58)		35	25
290e	25c. yellow. green & choc (19.6.59)		10	40
290f	50c. red, green yellow & blue (25.3.58)		35	60
284/290f Set of 12			3·00	4·50

Designs. 5c. Blood lily (*Haemanthus multiflorus*); 10c. *Grinum scabrum*; 15c. Baobab (*Adansonia digitata*); 25c. *Poinciana elata*; 50c. Glory lily (*Gloriosa virescens*); 60c. *Calatropis procera*; 1s. Sea lily (*Pancratium trainthum*); 1s.20, *Sesamothamnus bussernus*.

(Des R. De Sanctis (50c.), L. Gasbarra (1s.), D. Mancini (lettering, both values). Photo)

1955 (27 Feb). *EXPRESS LETTER. Type E 54 and similar horiz floral design.* W **39**. P 13 × 13½.

E291	50c. yellow, green and lilac		40	85
E292	1s. red, green and pale blue		75	1·10

Design:—1s. Coral tree (*Eryhrina melanocantha*).

54 Oribi

54a Lesser Kudu

(Des F. Caruso (35c., 45c.) L. Gasbarra (50c., 75c.), R. Mura (1s. 20, 1s.50), G. Funaioli (3s.), D. Mancini (lettering, all values). Photo)

1955 (12 Apr)–**59**. AIR.

(a) T 54 and similar designs. W **39** sideways. P 13½.

291	35c. black, orange and myrtle-green		10	75
292	45c. black, orange and grey-violet		2·75	1·20
293	50c. brown black, orange & reddish vio		10	75
294	75c. brown black orange and rose red		1·90	75
295	1s.20 black, orange & dp bluish green		1·90	75
296	1s.50 black, orange and blue		2·75	2·20

(b) T 54a and similar design. W **53**. P 14.

296a	3s. slate-purple & yellow-brn (4.10.58)		1·90	2·20
296b	5 s. yellow and black (2.2.59)		1·90	2·20
291/296b Set of 8			12·00	12·50

Designs:—45c. Salt's dik-dik; 50c. Speke's gazelle; 75c. Gerenuk; 1s.20, Soemmering's gazelle; 1s.50, Waterbuck; 5s. Hunter's hartebeest.

55 Native Weaver

(Des R. Pierbattista. Photo)

1955 (24 Sept). *Third Somali Fair. T 55 and similar horiz designs.* W **53**. P 14.

(a) POSTAGE.

297	25c. sepia		50	70
298	30c. deep green		50	70

(b) AIR Inscr "POSTA AEREA".

299	45c. bistre-brown and orange		40	70
300	1s.20 blue and pink		60	70
297/300 Set of 4			1·80	2·50

Designs:—30c. Cattle fording river; 45c. Camels around well; 1s.20, Native women at well.

56 Voters and Map

57 Somali Arms

(Des G. Ricci. Photo)

1956 (30 Apr). *First Legislative Assembly.* W **53**. P 14.

(a) POSTAGE.

301	**56**	5c. sepia and grey green	10	10
302		10c. sepia and olive brown	10	10
303		25c. sepia and brown red	10	40

(b) AIR. Inscr "POSTA AEREA"

304	**56**	60c. sepia and blue	35	60
305		1s.20 sepia and orange	35	60
301/305 Set of 5			90	1·60

(Des R. Pierbattista. Photo)

1957 (6 May). *Inauguration of National Emblem. Arms in greenish blue and ochre.* W **53**. P 13½.

(a) POSTAGE.

306	**57**	5c. brown	10	40
307		25c. carmine	10	40
308		60c. blue violet	10	75

(b) AIR. Inscr "POSTA AEREA".

309	**57**	45c. blue	35	60
310		1s.20 deep bluish green	35	60
306/310 Set of 5			90	2·50

58 Falchiero Barrage

59 Somali Nurse with Baby

1957 (28 Sept). *Fourth Somali Fair. T 58 and similar designs. Photo.* W **53**. P 14.

(a) POSTAGE.

311	5c. deep lilac and brown		10	10
312	10c. deep bluish green and bistre		10	10
313	25c. blue and carmine red		10	75

(b) AIR. Inscr "POSTA AEREA".

314	60c. sepia and deep blue		70	75
315	1s.20 black and red		70	75
311/315 Set of 5			1·50	2·20

211

SOMALIA somalia 1957

Designs: *Horiz*—10c. Juba River bridge, 25c. Silos at Margherita, 60c. Irrigation canal. *Vert*—1s.20. Oil well.

1957 (30 Nov). *Tuberculosis Relief Campaign. Photo. W* **53**. *P* 14.

(a) POSTAGE.
316	59	10c.+ 10c. sepia and red	40	40
317		25c.+ 10c. sepia and green	40	40

(b) AIR. Inscr "POSTA AEREA".
318	59	55c.+ 20c. sepia and blue	40	60
319		1s.20 + 20c. sepia and violet	40	60
316/319 *Set of 4*			1·40	1·80

1958 (28 Apr). *Sports. Various designs as T* **60**. *W* **53**. *P* 14.

(a) POSTAGE.
320	2c. lilac	10	10
321	4c. green	10	10
322	5c. vermilion	10	10
323	6c. grey-black	10	10
324	8c. ultramarine	10	10
325	10c. orange	10	10
326	25c. deep green	10	10

(b) AIR. Inscr "POSTA AEREA".
327	60c. brown	10	10
328	1s.20, blue	10	35
329	1s.50, carmine red	10	35
320/329 *Set of 10*		90	1·40

Designs: *Horiz*—4c. Football; 6c. Motorcycle racing; 10c. Archery; 25c. Boxing. *Vert*—5c. Throwing the discus; 8c. Fencing; 60c. Running; 1s.20, Cycling; 1s.50, Basketball

(Des C. Mancioli. Photo)

1958 (4 Oct). *AIR. EXPRESS. W* **53**. *P* 14.
E330	E **61**	1s. 70 orange-red and black	1·90	1·50

(Des C. Mancioli Photo)

1959 (19 June). *Opening of Constituent Assembly. T* **61** *and similar design inscr "ASSEMBLEA CONSTITUENTE". W* **53**. *P* 14.

(a) POSTAGE.
330	61	5c. ultramarine and green	10	10
331		25c. ultramarine and yellow-brown	10	10

(b) AIR. Inscr "POSTA AEREA".
332	—	1s.20, ultramarine and yellow-brown	30	40
333	—	1s.50, ultramarine and olive-green	30	40
330/333 *Set of 4*			70	90
MS333a 150 × 200 mm. Nos. 330/3 (sold at 4s.50)			1·90	2·75

Design: *Horiz*—1s.20, 1s.50, Police bugler.

62 White Stork  **63** Incense Tree

(Des C. Mancioli. Photo)

1959 (4 Sept). *Somali Water Birds. T* **62** *and similar designs. W* **53**. *P* 14.

(a) POSTAGE.
334	5c. black, red and yellow	10	10
335	10c. red, yellow and red-brown	10	10
336	15c. black and orange	10	10
337	25c. black, yellow-orange and crimson	10	10

(b) AIR. Inscr "POSTA AEREA".
338	1s.20, black, red and violet	30	40
339	2s. red and blue	35	60
334/339 *Set of 6*		95	1·20

Designs: *Vert*—10c. Saddle-bill stork; 15c. Sacred ibis; 25c. Pink-backed pelicans. *Horiz*—1s.20, Marabou stork; 2s. Great egret.

(Des C. Mancioli. Photo)

1959 (28 Sept). *Fifth Somali Fair. T* **63** *and similar designs. W* **53**. *P* 14.

(a) POSTAGE.
340	20c. black and Yellow-orange	10	30
341	60c. black, carmine and yellow-orange	10	30

(b) AIR. Inscr "POSTA AEREA".
342	1s.20, black and red	35	45
343	2s. black, orange-brown and blue	50	60
340/343 *Set of 4*		95	1·50

Designs: *Vert*—60c. Somali child with incense-burner. *Horiz*—1s.20, Ancient Egyptian transport of incense; 2s. Incense-burner and Mogadishu Harbour.

E **61** Young Gazelles

61 The Constitution, and Assembly Building, Mogadishu

64 Institute Badge

65 "The Horn of Africa"

212

SOMALIA somalia

(Des C. Mancioli. Photo)

1960 (14 Jan). *Opening of University Institute of Somalia. Mogadishu. T* **64** *and similar designs. W* **53**. *P* 14.

(a) POSTAGE.
344	5c. orange-red and brown	10	10
345	50c. brown and violet-blue	10	10
346	80c. black and scarlet	10	10

(b) AIR. Inscr "POSTA AEREA".
347	45c. brown, black and deep green	10	10
348	1s.20, blue, black and light blue	40	50
344/348 *Set of* 5		70	80

Designs: *Horiz*—45c., 1s.20, Institute buildings. 50c. Map of Africa. *Vert*—80c. Institute emblem.

(Des C. Mancioli. Photo)

1960 (7 Apr). *World Refugee Year. T* **65** *and similar designs inscr* "ANNO MONDIALE DEL RIFUGIATO 1959-1960". *W* **53**. *P* 14.

(a) POSTAGE.
349	10c. green, black and light brown	10	25
350	60c. yellow-brown, ochre and black	10	25
351	80c. bluish green, black and rose-pink	10	25

(b) AIR Inscr "POSTA AEREA".
352	1s.50, red, blue and green	40	60
349/352 *Set of* 4		65	1·25

Designs. *Horiz*—60c. Design similar to T **65**. *Vert*—80c. Palm; 1s.50, White stork.

In May 1960 the British Government arranged for the British Somaliland Protectorate to be united with the former Italian colony. British Somaliland became independent on 26 June 1960, and the union of the two territories as the independent Republic of Somalia took place on 1 July 1960. Subsequent issues are listed in Part 14 (*Africa since Independence N—Z*) of this catalogue.

LIECHTENSTEIN 1912

Liechtenstein

Austrian stamps were valid in Liechtenstein up to 31 January 1921

1912. 100 Heller = 1 Krone
1921. 100 Rappen = 1 Franc (Swiss)

The principality of Liechtenstein, founded in 1719, achieved sovereignty in 1806 and became fully independent in 1866.

I. ISSUES OF THE AUSTRIAN POST OFFICE

Prince John II
12 November 1858–11 February 1929

The first post office in Liechtenstein was opened at Balzers in 1818. Austria took responsibility for the postal service in the principality and from 1850, when postage stamps were first issued in Austria, unoverprinted stamps of Austria were sold for use there. Even after the introduction of special stamps for Liechtenstein in 1912, Austrian stamps continued to be used until 1921 either alone or in conjunction with those stamps.

Such usage can only be identified by the cancellation. During the period of the Austrian postal administration only the following post offices operated in Liechtenstein: Balzers. Vaduz (opened 1845). Nendeln (1864–1912). Schaan (1872), Triesen (1890) and Eschen (transferred from Nendeln in 1912). Early single-line cancellers for Vaduz were inscribed "VADUTZ".

The Austrian administration ended in February 1920.

1 Prince John II   2   3

(T **1** to **3** des K. Moser. Die eng F. Shirnbock. Typo Austrian Govt Wks, Vienna)

1912–15. P 12½ × 13.

(a) Thick surfaced paper (2.2.12).
1	1	5h. green	10·50	6·50
2		10h. rose	40·00	6·00
3		25h. blue	40·00	20·00

(b) Thin unsurfaced paper (April 1915).
4	1	5h. green	8·75	6·00
5		10h. red	55·00	15·00
6		25h. blue	£1100	80·00

Nos. 1/3 with a circular cancellation inscribed "VADUZ" and the letter "b" and dated during February 1912 were supplied cancelled-to-order by the Philatelic Bureau in Vienna. At the end of February the canceller was sent to Vaduz for normal use.

A 15h. red was prepared in 1917 but was not issued.

Nos. 1/12 imperforate were sold only in Vienna.

1917 (15 June)–**18**. P 12½ × 13.
7	2	3h. violet	75	55
8		5h. yellow-green	75	55
9	3	10h. claret	95	85
10		15h. red-brown	95	75
11		20h. deep green (11.18)	95	85
12		25h. blue	95	75
7/12	Set of 6		4·75	4·00

See note under No. 6.

1918 (12 Nov). 60th Anniv of Prince John's Accession. As T **3** but dated "1858–1918" in upper corners. P 12½ × 13.
| 13 | 3 | 20h. deep green | 60 | 1·00 |

1920 (3 Mar).

*(a) Optd with T **4**.*
14	2	5h. yellow-green	1·60	4·50
15	3	10h. claret	1·60	4·50
16		25h. blue	1·60	4·50

*(b) Surch as T **5** or **6**.*
17	2	40on 3h. violet	1·60	4·50
18	3	1kr.on 15h. red-brown	1·60	4·50
19		2½kr.on 20h. deep green	1·60	4·50
14/19	Set of 6		8·75	25·00

II. ISSUES OF PRINCIPALITY OF LIECHTENSTEIN

The constitution was adopted on 5 October 1921.

7   8 Castle of Vaduz

(T **7** to **11** and D **11**. Des L. Kasimir. Recess Paulussen & Co. Vienna)

1920 (from July). Imperf.
20	7	5h. olive-bistre	15	2·40
21		10h. orange	15	2·40
22		15h. indigo	15	2·40
23		20h. brown	15	2·40
24		25h. olive-green	15	2·40
25		30h. slate-grey	15	2·40
26		40h. carmine	15	2·40
27	8	1k. blue	15	2·40
20/27	Set of 8		1·10	17·00

9 Prince John I   **10** Arms   D **11**

1920 (from July). P 12½.
28	7	5h. olive-bistre	10	35
29		10h. orange	10	35
30		15h. indigo	10	35
31		20h. red-brown	10	35

1920 (July). P 12½.
28	7	5h. olive-bistre	15	40
29		10h. orange	15	40
30		15h. indigo	15	40
31		20h. red-brown	15	40

LIECHTENSTEIN 1920

32	–	25h. olive-green		10	35
33	7	30h. slate-grey		10	35
34	–	40h. claret		10	35
35	–	50h. apple-green		10	35
36	–	60h. red-brown		10	35
37	–	80h. bright rose		10	35
38	8	1k. lilac		20	55
39	–	2k. light blue		25	60
40	9	5k. grey-black		40	70
41	–	7½k. slate		55	90
42	10	10k. ochre		60	1·00
28/42 Set of 15				2·75	6·50

Designs: As T **8**—25h. Chapel of St. Mamertus; 40h. Gutenberg Castle; 50h. Courtyard of Vaduz Castle; 60h. Red House, Vaduz; 80h. Church Tower at Schaan; 2k. Bendern. As T **9**—7½k. Prince John II.

1920 (July). POSTAGE DUE. P 12½.

D43	D **11**	5h. red		20	35
D44	–	10h. red		20	35
D45	–	15h. red		20	35
D46	–	20h. red		20	35
D47	–	25h. red		20	35
D48	–	30h. red		20	35
D49	–	40h. red		20	35
D50	–	50h. red		20	35
D51	–	80h. red		20	35
D52	–	1k. blue		20	35
D53	–	2k. blue		20	35
D54	–	5k. blue		20	35
D43/54 Set of 12				2·10	3·75

11 Madonna 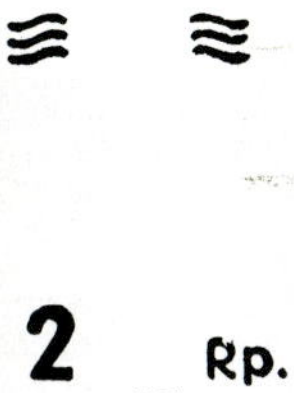   (12)   (13)

(Des T. and L. Kasimir. Recess Paulussen & Co, Vienna)

1920 (5 Oct). *Prince John's 80th Birthday.*

A. P 12½.

43A	**11**	50h. olive-green		50	1·80
44A	–	80h. rose-red		50	1·80
45A	–	2k. blue		50	1·80

B. Imperf.

43B	**11**	50h. olive-green		1·40	—
44B	–	80h. rose-red		2·40	—
45B	–	2k. blue		2·40	—

1921. *No. 21 surch in Swiss currency, in violet.*

46	**12**	2r. on 10h. orange (1 Feb)		65	22·00
47	**13**	2r. on 10h. orange (10 Mar)		40	13·50

14 Arms    **15** St. Mamertus Chapel    **16** Vaduz

(Des L. Kasimir. Recess Paulussen & Co, Vienna)

1921 (Feb–Nov). *Swiss Currency.*

A. P 12½.

47aA	**14**	2r. olive-yellow		†	
48A	–	2½r. black-brown		55	8·00
49A	–	3r. orange		55	8·00
50A	–	5r. olive		7·50	1·25
51A	–	7½r. indigo		3·75	25·00
52A	–	10r. yellow-green		50·00	28·00
53A	–	13r. red-brown		7·50	60·00
54A	–	15r. deep violet		16·00	26·00

B. P 9½.

47aB	**14**	2r. olive-yellow		75	80
48B	–	2½r. black-brown		65	39·00
49B	–	3r. orange		£275	£3250
50B	–	5r. olive		50·00	8·00
51B	–	7½r. indigo		£275	£850
52B	–	10r. yellow-green		20·00	4·00
53B	–	13r. red-brown		£120	£1600
54B	–	15r. deep violet		10·50	11·50

1921. P 12½.

55	**15**	20r. black and violet		30·00	85
56	–	25r. black and rose-red		1·90	3·00
57	–	30r. black and deep green		38·00	5·75
58	–	35r. black and brown		2·75	6·25
59	–	40r. black and blue		4·75	2·50
60	–	50r. black and deep green		5·75	3·25
61	–	80r. black and grey		16·00	38·00
62	**16**	1f. black and lake		31·00	23·00
47a/62 Set of 16 (cheapest)				£170	£160

Designs: As T **15**—25r. Vaduz Castle; 30r. Bendern; 35r. Prince John II; 40r. Church Tower at Schaan; 50r. Gutenberg Castle; 80r. Red House, Vaduz.

See also Nos. 65/6.

10 (18)

1924 (Mar–Apr). *Nos. 51 and 53 surch as T* **18**, *in red.*

A. P 12½.

63A	**14**	5 on 7½r. indigo		75	1·10
64A	–	10 on 13r. red-brown		55	1·60

B. P 9½.

63B	**14**	5 on 7½r. indigo		15·00	7·50
64B	–	10 on 13r. red-brown		55	1·60

(Recess Mint Berne)

1924–25. *Granite paper. Wmk Cross (T* **13** *of Switzerland). P* 11½.

65	**14**	10r. yellow-green (6.24)		14·00	3·00
66	–	30r. black and blue (1925)		9·75	90

Design:—30r. Bendern (as No. 57)

19 Vine-dresser    **20** Castle of Vaduz    **21** Government Bldg and Church, Vaduz

(Des E. Verling. Eng K. Sprenger. T **19**, typo, Mint, Berne; T **20**, recess, Landestopographie, Berne; T **21** recess, Mint, Berne)

1924–27. *Granite Paper. Wmk Cross. P* 11½.

67	**19**	2½r. magenta & sage green (20.12.27)		85	3·50
68	–	5r. blue and brown (9.24)		1·20	55
69	–	7½r. brown and green (20.12.27)		90	4·00
70	**20**	10r. green (4.25)		8·50	50
71	**19**	15r. blue-green and maroon (20.12.27)		4·75	17·00
72	**20**	20r. red (3.26)		20·00	60
73	**21**	1½f. blue (4.25)		60·00	50·00
67/73 Set of 7				90·00	70·00

215

LIECHTENSTEIN 1925

The 10 and 20r. were each issued both in sheets and in coils (from 1930).

22 Prince John II
23 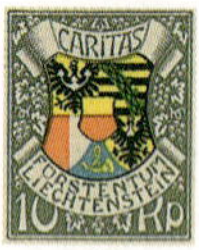
24 Salvage Work by Austrian Soldiers 

(Des E. Verling. Eng K. Sprenger. Recess Landestopographie, Berne)

1925 (5 Oct). *85th Birthday of Prince John. Granite paper.* Wmk Cross. P 11½.
74	**22**	10r.+5r. green	21·00	9·25
75		20r.+5r. carmine-red	15·00	9·25
76		30r.+5r. blue	4·75	2·00

(Des by E. Verling. Typo Mint, Berne)

1927 (5 Oct). *87th Birthday of Prince John. Granite paper.* Wmk Cross. P 11½.
77	**23**	10r.+5r. green	5·75	13·50
78		20r.+5r. maroon	5·75	13·50
79		30r.+5r. blue	5·50	12·50

The arms are in black, yellow, red, green and pale blue in each case.

(Des E. Verling. Litho Orell Füssli, Zürich)

1928 (6 Feb). *Flood Relief.* T **24** *(and similar types).* P 11½.
80		5r.+5r. brown and plum	13·50	18·00
81		10r.+10r. brown and green	13·00	16·00
82		20r.+10r. brown and scarlet	13·00	16·00
83		30r.+10r. brown and blue	8·75	16·00
80/83	*Set of 4*		44·00	60·00

Designs:—5r. Railway bridge between Buchs and Schaan; 10r. Village of Ruggell; 30r. Salvage work by Swiss soldiers.

D 25
25 Prince John II 
26 Prince John II, 1858–1928 

(Des E. Verling. Typo Mint, Berne)

1928 (2 Apr). POSTAGE DUE. *Granite paper.* Wmk Cross. P 12.
D84	**D 25**	5r. vermilion and violet	60	1·90
D85		10r. vermilion and violet	1·20	1·70
D86		15r. vermilion and violet	2·50	10·00
D87		20r. vermilion and violet	2·10	1·90
D88		25r. vermilion and violet	2·10	7·50
D89		30r. vermilion and violet	5·00	9·25
D90		40r. vermilion and violet	6·75	10·50
D91		50r. vermilion and violet	6·75	15·00
D84/91	*Set of 8*		24·00	50·00

(Des E. Verling. T **25**, Typo, Mint, Berne; T **26**, Recess Orell Füssli, Zürich)

1928 (12 Nov). *70th Anniv of the Accession of Prince John II.* P 11½.
(a) Wmk Cross. Granite paper.
84	**25**	10r. olive and red-brown	2·10	2·30
85		20r. olive and vermilion	4·75	5·75
86		30r. olive and dull blue	11·00	13·00

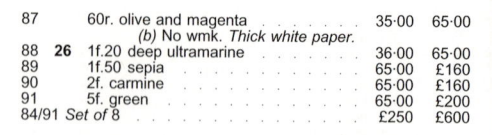

87		60r. olive and magenta	35·00	65·00

(b) No wmk. Thick white paper.
88	**26**	1f.20 deep ultramarine	36·00	65·00
89		1f.50 sepia	65·00	£160
90		2f. carmine	65·00	£160
91		5f. green	65·00	£200
84/91	*Set of 8*		£250	£600

Prince Francis I
11 February 1929–25 July 1938

27 Prince Francis I as a boy
28 Prince Francis I 

(Des H. C. Kosel. Photo Wiener Kunstdruck, Vienna)

1929 (2 Dec). *Accession of Prince Francis I.* T **27** *and* **28** *(and similar types).* P 11½.
92		10r. green	50	1·60
93		20r. scarlet	75	2·10
94		30r. blue	1·10	12·00
95		70r. brown	10·50	60·00
92/95	*Set of 4*		11·50	70·00

Designs:—30r. Princess Elsa; 70r. Prince Francis and Princess Elsa.

31 Girl Vintager
32 Prince Francis I and Princess Elsa 

(Des H. C. Kosel. Photo Rosenbaum Bros. Vienna)

1930. T **31** *and similar designs.*
A. Perf 10½.
96A		3r. lake (1.7)	45	65
97A		5r. deep green (12.8)	1·00	75
98A		10r. deep reddish lilac (12.8)	1·00	50
99A		20r. scarlet (12.8)	21·00	80
100A		25r. slate-green (10.9)	5·00	18·00
101A		30r. blue (12.8)	5·00	1·10
105A		60r. blackish green (12.8)	60·00	18·00
106A		90r. maroon (12.8)	60·00	£100
107A		1f.20 sepia (10.9)	80·00	£160
108A		1f.50 deep violet-blue (10.9)	34·00	42·00
109A		2f. red-brown and deep bluish green (10.9)	48·00	75·00

B. Perf 11½.
97B		5r. deep green (12.8)	2·10	1·10
98B		10r. deep reddish lilac (12.8)	3·00	55
99B		20r. scarlet (12.8)	65·00	75
100B		25r. slate-green (10.9)	£200	£275
101B		30r. blue (12.8)	16·00	1·40
102B		35r. grey-green (10.9)	6·25	10·50
104B		50r. brownish black (12.8)	60·00	9·50
105B		60r. blackish-green (12.8)	£200	18·00
106B		90r. maroon (12.8)	£200	£110
107B		1f. 20 sepia (10.9)	£250	£200
108B		1f.50 deep violet-blue (10.9)	£110	60·00
109B		2f. red-brown and deep bluish green (10.9)	£180	£110

C. Perf 11½ × 10½.
98C		10r. deep reddish lilac (12.8)	13·00	25·00
101C		30r. blue (12.8)	£1400	£2000

216

LIECHTENSTEIN   1930

102C	35r. grey-green (10.9)	25·00	11·50
103C	40r. brown (12.8)	6·25	3·50
104C	50r. brownish black (12.8)	£250	15·00
107C	1f.20 sepia (10.9)	£10000	£11000
109C	2f. red-brown and deep bluish green (10.9)	£6500	£6500

D. Perf compound of 10½ and 11½.

98D	10r. deep reddish lilac (12.8)	35·00	£120
99D	20r. scarlet (12.8)	85·00	£200
101D	30r. blue (12.8)	£110	£250
105D	60r. blackish green (12.8)	£150	£325
109D	2f. red-brown and deep bluish green (10.9)	£375	£1100

Designs: *Vert*—5r. Mt. Three Sisters—Edelweiss; 10r. Alpine Cattle—Alpine roses; 20r. Courtyard of Vaduz Castle; 25r. Mt. Naafkopf; 30r. Valley of Samina; 35r. Rofenberg Chapel; 40r. St. Mamertus' Chapel; 50r. Kurhaus at Malbun; 60r. Gutenberg Castle; 90r. Schellenberg Monastery; 1f.20, Vaduz Castle; 1f.50, Pfälzer club hut.

*The stamps with compound perfs have three sides 10½, and one side 11½, or three sides 11½ and one side 10½. The 10r. also exists perf 10½ × 11½ and 10½ × 11½ × 11½ × 10½ (same prices as No. 98D).

34 Monoplane over Vaduz Castle and Rhine Valley

35 Airship *Graf Zeppelin* over Alps

(Des H. C. Kosel. Photo Rosenbaum Bros, Vienna)

1930 (12 Aug). AIR. T **34** *(and similar types). Backgrounds of grey wavy lines.* P 10½ × 11½ (1f.) or 10½ (others).

110	15r. sepia	4·50	6·00
111	20r. deep blue-green	11·50	12·00
112	25r. brown	5·75	19·00
113	35r. blue	9·00	13·00
114	45r. deep green	25·00	44·00
115	1f. claret	40·00	30·00
110/115	Set of 6	85·00	£110

Designs: *Vert*—15, 20r. Biplane over snowy mountain peak. *Horiz*—25, 35r. Biplane over Vaduz Castle; 1f. Type **34**.

(Des H. C. Kosel. Photo Wiener Kunstdruck, Vienna)

1931 (1 June). AIR. T **35** *(and similar type)*. P 11½.

116	1f. blackish green	28·00	24·00
117	2f. deep slate-blue	80·00	£225

Design:—2f. Different view of *Graf Zeppelin* over Alps.

REGIERUNGS DIENSTSACHE
(O **36**)

36

37 Princess Elsa

1932 (1 Apr). OFFICIAL. Nos. 97, etc. optd with Type O **36**.

A. Perf 10½.

O118A	5r. (Bk.)	8·00	6·25
O119A	10r. (R.)	40·00	40·00
O120A	20r. (B.)	40·00	6·25
O121A	30r. (R.)	8·75	8·00
O124A	60r. (R.)	7·50	21·00

O125A	1f.20 (G.)	90·00	£225

B. Perf 11½.

O118B	5r. (Bk.)	11·50	6·00
O119B	10r. (R.)	£100	6·00
O120B	20r. (B.)	£110	6·00
O121B	30r. (R.)	21·00	7·00
O122B	35r. (Bk.)	6·25	16·00
O123B	50r. (B.)	36·00	10·00
O124B	60r. (R.)	18·00	20·00
O125B	1f.20 (G.)	£250	£225

C. Perf 11½ × 10½.

O119C	10r. (R.)	£550	£1000
O122C	35r. (Bk.)	15·00	15·00
O123C	50r. (B.)	90·00	10·00

D. Perf compound.

O119D	10r. (R.)	£140	£300
O123D	50r. (B.)	£160	£375

*No. O119D has three sides perf 10½ and one side 11½. No O123D three sides 11½ and one side 10½.

(Des H. C. Kosel. Photo Chwala, Vienna)

1932 (19 Dec). *Youth Charities.* T **36** *and* **37** *(different medallion portraits).* P 11½.

118	10r.+5r. deep green	14·50	22·50
119	20r.+5r. rose-scarlet	15·00	23·00
120	30r.+10r. blue (Prince Francis)	17·00	27·00

38 Mt. Naafkopf

(O **39**)

39 Prince Francis I

(Des H.C. Kosel. Photo Elbemühl, Vienna)

1933 (23 Jan). T **38** *and similar designs.* P 14½.

121	25r. bright orange	£190	60·00
122	90r. deep green	6·50	48·00
123	1f.20 red-brown	48·00	£180

Designs:—90r. Gutenberg Castle; 1f.20, Vaduz Castle.

1933 (24 Jan). OFFICIAL. Nos. 121 and 123 optd with Type O **39**.

O126	25r. bright orange	25·00	25·00
O127	1f.20 red-brown	55·00	£170

(Des H. Kosel. Photo Courvoisier)

1933 (28 Aug). *Prince Francis's 80th Birthday, Granite paper.* P 11.

124	**39**	10r. bright violet	13·00	33·00
125		20r. scarlet	13·00	33·00
126		30r. bright blue	13·00	33·00

40

41 "Three Sisters"

42 Vaduz Castle

217

LIECHTENSTEIN   1933

43 Pfälzer Hut, Bettlerjoch 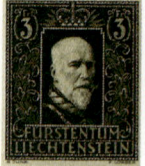   **44** Prince Francis I

45 Arms of Liechtenstein    **46** Golden Eagle

GRILLED GUM. A gum breaker was used on some of the paper between 1933 and 1942, to prevent curling. The machinery impressed a grill into the gum with enough force to transfer the pattern to the paper and we therefore quote prices for both unused and used examples.

(3r. to 1f.50 des H. Kosel and H. Sieger, photo Courvoisier. 2f. des H. Kosel, 3f., 5f. des R. Junk; eng F. Lorber; recess Govt Ptg Wks, Vienna)

1933–35. T **40/45** *and similar designs. Granite paper (3r. to 1f.50). Grilled gum (15, 30, 35, 40r., 1f.50).* P 12½ (2f. to 5f.) or 11½ (others).

127	3r. brown-red (17.12.34)	20	45
128	5r. emerald (17.12.34)	2·50	45
	a. Grilled gum	2·75	6·50
129	10r. reddish violet (17.12.34)	65	35
	a. Grilled gum	40	5·00
130	15r. reddish orange (9.12.35)	25	85
131	20r. red (1.1.35)	60	45
132	25r. yellow-brown (1.1.35)	15·00	40·00
133	30r. blue (9.12.35)	3·25	85
134	35r. bronze green (9.12.35)	85	3·50
135	40r. sepia (9.12.35)	95	2·40
136	50r. brown (18.6.34)	17·00	11·00
137	60r. dull purple (18.6.34)	1·70	4·00
138	90r. deep green (18.6.34)	5·25	13·50
139	1f.20 deep blue (18.6.34)	1·90	12·50
140	1f.50 red-brown (9.12.35)	2·30	16·00
141	2f. red-brown (19.8.35)	42·00	£130
142	3f. blue (15.12.33)	55·00	£130
143	5f. dull purple (6.5.35)	£300	£650
127/143	Set of 17	£400	£950

Designs: As T **41**—10r. Schaan Church; 15r. Bendern am Rhein; 20r. Town Hall, Vaduz; 25r. Saminatal. As T **42**—30r. Saminatal (*different*); 35r. Schellenberg ruins; 40r. Government Building, Vaduz; 60r. Vaduz Castle (*different*); 90r. Gutenberg Castle. As T **43**—1f.50, Valüna. As T **44**—2f. Princess Elsa. The 10 and 20r. were each issued both in sheets and in coils. See also Nos. **MS**144, **MS**153, 174, 225/6 and 258.

1934 (29 Sept). *Vaduz First Liechtenstein Philatelic Exhibition. Sheet 105 × 125 mm. Granite paper.* P 12.
MS144 **45** 5f. chocolate   £1100   £1700

(Des L. Hesshaimer. Photo Courvoisier)

1934–35. AIR. T **46** *and similar vert designs. Granite paper.* P 11½.
145	10r. bright reddish violet (1.4.35)	5·25	13·50
	a. Grilled gum	8·00	14·00
146	15r. red-orange (1.4.35)	13·00	30·00
	a. Grilled gum	18·00	35·00
147	20r. scarlet (1.4.35)	14·00	30·00
	a. Grilled gum	18·00	35·00

148	30r. greenish blue (1.4.35)	14·00	30·00
	a. Grilled gum	18·00	35·00
149	50r. emerald (17.12.34)	20·00	25·00
	a. Grilled gum	14·00	28·00
145/149	Set of 5 (*cheapest*)	60·00	£120

Designs:—10r. to 20r. Golden eagles in flight; 30r. Ospreys in nest; 50r. Golden eagle on rock.

1934–35. OFFICIAL.

*(a) Nos. 128/32 optd with Type O **39**.*
O150	5r. emerald (R.) (1.4.35)	1·00	1·20
O151	10r. reddish violet (1.4.35)	2·50	95
O152	15r. reddish orange (V.) (9.12.35)	30	1·50
O153	20r. red (1.4.35)	35	95
O154	25r. yellow-brown (R.) (3.1.35)	20	13·50
O155	25r. yellow-brown (Bk.) (17.12.35)	1·90	9·25

*(b) Nos. 133, 136, 138, 140 optd as Type O **39**, but 17 mm in diameter.*
O156	30r. blue (R.) (9.12.35)	2·50	5·00
O157	50r. brown (V.) (17.12.34)	1·00	1·90
O158	90r. deep green (1.4.35)	5·50	25·00
O159	1f.50 red-brown (B.) (9.12.35)	32·00	£110
O150/159	Set of 10	60·00	£190

60   **Rp**
(48)

49 Hindenburg and Schaan Church

1935 (24 June). AIR. *Surch with* T **48**.
150   **34**   60r.on 1f. claret (No. 115)   21·00   32·00

(Des L. Hesshaimer. Photo Courvoisier)

1936 (1 May). AIR. T **49** *and similar horiz design. Granite paper. Grilled gum.* P 11½.
151	1f. carmine	26·00	65·00
152	2f. bright violet	22·00	55·00

Design:—2f. *Graf Zeppelin over Schaan Airport.*

1936 (24 Oct). *Second Liechtenstein Philatelic Exhibition and Opening of Postal Museum, Vaduz. Sheet 165 × 119 mm containing two each of Nos. 131 and 133. Imperf.*
MS153   Sold at 2 fr.   35·00   35·00

51 Masescha am Triesenberg    **52** Schellenberg Castle

(Des M. Schiestl. Photo Courvoisier)

1937–38. T **51/52** *and similar designs Granite paper. Grilled gum (3 to 50r., 1f.).* P 11½.
154	3r. red-brown (24.7.37)	20	35
155	5r. emerald-green and buff (15.9.37)	15	20
156	10r. violet and buff (15.6.37)	15	15
157	15r. black and buff (15.11.37)	40	50
158	20r. red and buff (4.10.37)	25	30
159	25r. brown and buff (15.10.37)	60	2·20
160	30r. bright blue and buff (2.12.37)	1·40	55
161	40r. dull green and buff (13.8.37)	1·40	1·20
162	50r. brown and buff (15.6.37)	95	1·80
163	60r. claret and buff (1.2.38)	1·40	1·70
164	90r. slate-violet and buff (1.2.38)	7·50	8·75
165	1f. deep claret and buff (13.8.37)	1·30	8·25
166	1f.20 purple-brown & buff (1.4.38)	6·00	11·50
167	1f.50 bluish slate and buff (15.2.38)	3·00	12·00
154/167	Set of 14	22·00	55·00

218

LIECHTENSTEIN   1937

Designs: *As T* **51**—3r. Schalun ruins; 10r. Knight and Vaduz Castle; 15r. Upper Saminatal; 20r. Church and bridge at Bendern; 25r. Steg Chapel and girl. *As T* **52**—30r. Farmer and orchard, Triesenberg; 50r. Knight and Gutenberg Castle; 60r. Baron von Brandis and Vaduz Castle; 90r. "Three Sisters" mountain; 1f. Boundary-stone on Luzensteig; 1f.20 Minstrel and Gutenberg Castle; 1f.50 Lawena (Schwarzhorn).

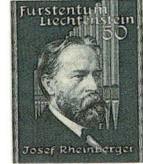

53 Roadmakers at Triesenberg   **54** Josef Rheinberger

(Des H. Raebiger. Photo Courvoisier)

1937 (30 June). *Workers' Issue.* T **53** *and similar horiz designs. Granite paper. Grilled gum.* P 11½.
168	10r. mauve	80	45
169	20r. scarlet	1·10	75
170	30r. blue	1·50	1·60
171	50r. brown	95	2·10
168/171	Set of 4	4·00	4·50

Designs:—10r. Bridge at Malbun; 30r. Binnen Canal Junction; 50r. Francis Bridge near Planken.

1937–38. OFFICIAL. Nos. 155/6, 158/60, 162, 165 and 167 optd as Type O **39**, but 17 mm in diameter.
O174	5r. emerald-green and buff (29.9.37)	20	20
O175	10r. violet and buff (R.) (17.7.37)	35	60
O176	20r. red and buff (V.) (6.10.37)	95	1·10
O177	25r. brown and buff (26.11.37)	55	1·40
O178	30r. bright blue and buff (6.12.37)	1·10	1·40
O179	50r. brown and buff (R.) (17.7.37)	60	1·10
O180	1f. deep claret and buff (20.8.37)	75	5·50
O181	1f.50 bluish slate & buff (P.) (16.2.38)	2·20	8·00
O174/181	Set of 8	6·00	17·00

1938 (30 July). *Third Liechtenstein Philatelic Exhibition, Vaduz. Sheet 100 × 135 mm containing stamps as No. 175 in different colour in a block of four.* P 12.
MS173 **54** 50r. slate-blue ... 35·00   21·00

Prince Francis Joseph II
25 July 1938–13 November 1989

(Des R. Junk. Eng F. Lorber. Recess Govt Ptg Wks, Vienna)

1938 (15 Aug). *Death of Prince Francis I.* P 12½.
174 **44** 3f. black/yellow ... 6·25   49·00

(Des W. Dachauer. Eng F. Lorber. Recess Govt Ptg Wks, Vienna)

1939 (17 Mar). *Birth Centenary of Rheinberger (composer).* P 12½.
175 **54** 50r. greenish slate ... 55   2·75
See No. **MS**173.

55 Black-headed gulls   **56** Offering Homage to First Prince

(Des L. Hesshaimer. Photo Courvoisier)

1939 (3 Apr). *AIR. T* **55** *and similar horiz designs. Granite paper. Grilled gum.* P 11½.
176	10r. reddish violet (Barn swallows)	25	50
	a. Smooth gum	30	50
177	15r. red-orange	40	1·40
178	20r. brown-red (Herring gulls)	80	45
179	30r. blue (Common buzzard)	80	1·10
180	50r. emerald (Northern goshawk)	2·75	1·70
181	1f. carmine (Lammergeier)	2·20	11·00
182	2f. reddish violet (Lammergeier)	1·90	11·50
176/182	Set of 7	8·25	25·00

(Des and eng E. Zotow. Recess Govt Ptg Wks, Vienna)

1939 (29 May). *Homage to Francis Joseph II.* P 12.
183	**56**	20r. lake	75	1·20
184		30r. blue	75	1·20
185		50r. blue-green	75	1·30

57 Francis Joseph II   D **58**

(Des J. Troyer. Eng F. Lorber. Recess Govt Ptg Wks, Vienna)

1939. *As T* **57** *(various types).* P 12.
186	2f. blue-green/*cream* (18.12)	5·00	25·00
187	3f. deep violet/*cream* (18.12)	4·50	25·00
188	5f. brown/*cream* (29.5)	10·50	21·00

Designs:—2f. Cantonal Arms; 3f. Arms of the Principality. No. 188 was issued in sheetlets of four stamps.

(Des J. Troyer. Eng A. Yersin. Design recess; value typo. PTT Bureau, Berne)

1940 (1 July). *POSTAGE DUE.* P 11½.
D189	D **58**	5r. carmine and blue	1·20	2·50
D190		10r. carmine and blue	50	1·00
D191		15r. carmine and blue	60	5·00
D192		20r. carmine and blue	75	1·20
D193		25r. carmine and blue	1·40	2·75
D194		30r. carmine and blue	2·75	5·00
D195		40r. carmine and blue	2·75	4·25
D196		50r. carmine and blue	3·00	5·00
D189/196	*Set of 8*		12·00	24·00

Postage Due stamps were no longer used after 31 December 1958.

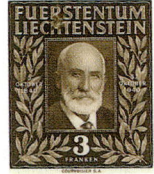

58 Prince John when a Child   **59** Prince John II

(Des K. Gessner (3f.), J. Troyer (others). Photo Courvoisier)

1940 (10 Aug–5 Oct). *Birth Centenary of Prince John II. T* **58** *and similar horiz designs. Granite paper. Grilled gum.* P 11½.
189	20r. brown-red	50	1·40
190	30r. indigo	70	2·20
191	50r. slate-green	1·10	5·75
192	1f. brown-violet	6·50	43·00

219

LIECHTENSTEIN 1940

193	1f.50 violet-black	5·25	42·00
194	3f. brown (5 Oct)	3·50	12·00
189/194	Set of 6	15·00	£100

Designs:—Portraits in early manhood (30r.), in middle age (50r.), and in later life (1f.). Memorial tablet (1f.50).

60 Wine Press

61 Madonna and Child

64 Prince John Charles

65 Princess Georgina

(T **64/5**. Des J. Troyer. Photo Courvoisier)

1942 (5 Oct). T **64** and similar vert designs. Granite paper. Grilled gum. P 11½.

210	20r. rose	25	75
211	30r. blue (Francis Joseph I)	45	1·40
212	1f. purple (Alois I)	1·40	9·50
213	1f.50 brown (John I)	1·40	9·50
210/213	Set of 4	3·25	19·00

(Des C. Liner. Photo Courvoisier)

1941 (7 Apr). Agricultural Propaganda. T **60** and similar horiz designs. Granite paper. Grilled gum. P 11½.

195	10r. brown	45	40
196	20r. claret	65	75
197	30r. blue	75	1·40
198	50r. myrtle-green	2·30	10·50
199	90r. violet	2·30	11·50
195/199	Set of 5	5·75	22·00

Designs: 10r. Harvesting maize; 30r. Sharpening scythe; 50r. Milkmaid and cow; 90r. Girl wearing traditional headdress.

1943 (5 Mar). Marriage of Prince Francis Joseph II and Countess Georgina von Wildczek. As T **65** (various portraits). P 11½.

214	10r. purple	50	70
215	20r. brown-red	50	1·10
216	30r. slate-blue	50	1·10

Portraits: Vert—10r. Francis Joseph II. Horiz (44 × 25 mm.)—30r. Prince and Princess.

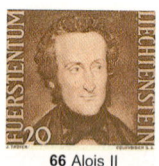

(Des J. Troyer. Eng E. Zotow. Recess PTT Bureau, Berne)

1941 (7 July). Granite paper. P 11½.
200 **61** 10f. brown-purple/yellow-ochre ... 33·00 70·00
Issued in sheetlets of four stamps.

66 Alois II

67 Marsh Land

(Des J. Troyer. Photo Courvoisier)

1943 (5 July). As T **66** (portraits of Princes). P 11½.

217	20r. red-brown	50	50
218	30r. ultramarine (John II)	80	95
219	1f. blackish brown (Francis I)	1·30	5·50
220	1f.50 slate-green (Francis Joseph II)	1·30	5·50
217/220	Set of 4	3·50	11·50

62 Prince Hans Adam

63 St Lucius preaching

(Des E. Zotow (centres), J. Troyer (frames). Photo Courvoisier)

1943 (6 Sept). Completion of Irrigation Canal. Various designs as T **67**. P 11½.

221	10r. blackish violet	20	35
222	30r. blue	35	1·70
223	50r. blue-green	65	6·25
224	2f. olive-brown	1·60	9·75
221/224	Set of 4	2·50	16·00

Designs:—30r. Draining the canal; 50r. Ploughing reclaimed land; 2f. Harvesting crops.

(Des J. Troyer. Photo Courvoisier)

1941 (18 Dec). T **62** and similar horiz designs. Granite paper. Grilled gum. P 11½.

201	20r. brown-red	35	1·20
202	30r. blue	65	1·90
203	1f. violet-grey	1·90	1·90
204	1f.50 green	1·90	11·50
201/204	Set of 4	4·25	23·00

Portraits:—30r. Prince Wenzel; 1f. Prince Anton Florian; 1f.50, Prince Joseph

(Des M. Schiestl and J. Troyer. Photo Courvoisier)

1943 (27 Dec). New designs as T **41**. P 11½.

| 225 | 10r. violet-grey (Vaduz Castle) | 40 | 55 |
| 226 | 20r. red-brown (Gutenberg Castle) | 35 | 70 |

Each issued both in sheets and in coils.

(Des and eng E. Zotow. Recess PTT Bureau, Berne)

1942 (22 Apr). 600th Anniv of Separation from Estate at Montfort. T **63** and similar horiz designs. Granite paper. P 11½.

205	20r. brown-red/flesh	75	65
206	30r. blue/flesh	70	1·40
207	50r. olive-green/flesh	1·60	5·00
208	1f. sepia/flesh	2·00	9·75
209	2f. dull violet/flesh	2·30	9·75
205/209	Set of 5	6·75	24·00

Designs:—30r. Count of Montfort replanning Vaduz; 50r. Counts of Montfort-Werdenberg and Sargans signing treaty; 1f. Battle of Gutenberg; 2f. Homage to Prince of Liechtenstein.

69 Planken

70 Prince Francis Joseph II

72

220

LIECHTENSTEIN 1944

(Des J. Troyer. Photo Courvoisier)

1944 (17 April)—**49**. *Views as T 69. Buff backgrounds.* P 11½.

227	3r. brown (Planken)	20	20
228	5r. green (Bendern)	20	15
228a	5r. brown (Bendern) (1.12.49)	10·00	45
229	10r. violet-grey (Triesen) (11.9.44)	12·00	45
230	15r. blue-grey (Ruggell) (11.9.44)	40	55
231	20r. brown-red (Vaduz)	40	35
232	25r. violet-brown (Triesenberg)	45	55
233	30r. blue (Schaan)	50	40
234	40r. brown (Balzers) (11.9.44)	65	1·10
235	50r. slate-blue (Mauren)	1·50	1·70
236	60r. light green (Schellenberg) (11.9.44)	4·25	3·25
237	90r. olive-green (Eschen) (11.9.44)	4·25	3·50
238	1f. claret (Vaduz Castle) (11.9.44)	3·00	3·75
239	1f.20 red brown (Valuna Valley) (16.11.44)	3·25	4·00
240	1f.50 blue (Lawena) (16.11.44)	3·25	3·75
227/240 *Set of 15*		40·00	22·00

(Des F. Lorber. Photo Courvoisier)

1944 (22 Dec). *Buff backgrounds.* P 11½.

241	**70**	2f. brown	4·00	10·00
242	–	3f. green (Princess Georgina)	3·50	8·00

See also Nos. 302/3.

(Des J. Troyer. Photo Courvoisier)

1945 (9 April). *Birth of Crown Prince Johann Adam Pius (now known as Prince Hans Adam).* P 11½.

243	**72**	20r. lake, yellow and gold	65	40
244	–	30r. blue yellow and gold	80	1·00
245	–	100r. grey, yellow and gold	2·10	4·00

73
74 First Aid
75 St. Lucius

(Des J. Troyer. Eng K. Bickel. Recess PTT Bureau, Berne)

1945 (3 Sept)—**47**. P 11½.

246	**73**	5f. grey-blue/*buff*	16·00	18·00
247		5f. red-brown/*buff* (20.3.47)	17·00	27·00

(Des J. Seger. Photo Courvoisier)

1945 (27 Nov). *Red Cross. As T 74 and similar vert designs. Cross in red. Buff backgrounds.* P 11½.

248	10r.+10r. purple (Mother and children)	1·40	1·40
249	20r.+20r. claret	1·40	2·00
250	1f.+1f.40 blue (Nurse and invalid)	6·25	18·00

(Des J. Troyer. Eng K. Bickel. Recess PTT Bureau, Berne)

1946 (14 Mar). P 11½.

251	**75**	10f. grey/*buff*	24·00	22·00

Issued in sheetlets of four stamps.

(Des E. Verling. Photo Courvoisier)

1946 (10 Aug). *Fourth Liechtenstein Philatelic Exhibition, Vaduz and 25th Anniv of Postal Agreement with Switzerland. Sheet 84 × 60 mm.* P 11½.

MS251a	10r. (×2) Old Postal Coach (*horiz*), violet, brown and buff (sold at 3f.)	28·00	38·00

76 Red Deer Stag
(O **77**)

(Des J. Seger. Photo Courvoisier)

1946 (10 Dec). *As T 76 (various designs).* P 11½.

252	20r. brown-red	1·20	1·30
253	30r. greenish blue (Arctic hare)	1·60	2·10
254	1f.50 brown-olive (Capercaillie)	5·75	8·50

1947 (3 July). OFFICIAL. *Nos. 228, etc optd with Type O* **77**.

O255	5r. green (Bendern)	1·10	75
O256	10r. violet-grey (Triesen)	1·10	95
O257	20r. brown-red (Vaduz)	1·60	1·00
O258	30r. blue (Schaan)	1·70	1·40
O259	50r. slate-blue (Mauren)	1·70	2·75
O260	1f. claret (Vaduz Castle)	7·50	9·25
O261	1f.50 blue (Lawena)	7·50	9·25
O255/261 *Set of 7*		20·00	23·00

77 Chamois
78 Princess Elsa

(Des J. Seger. Photo Courvoisier)

1947 (15 Oct). *As T 77 (various designs).* P 11½.

255	20r. brown-lake	2·00	2·10
256	30r. greenish blue (Alpine marmot)	3·00	2·75
257	1f.50 sepia (Golden eagle)	6·75	12·00

See also Nos. 283/5.

(Des H. C. Kosel. Eng F. Lorber. Recess State Printing Wks, Vienna)

1947 (15 Dec). *Death of Princess Elsa.* P 14½.

258	**78**	2f. black/*yellow*	2·20	9·25

79 Wilbur Wright
80 "Ginevra de Benci" (Da Vinci)
(**81**)

(Des J. Troyer. Photo Courvoisier)

1948. AIR. *Pioneers of Flight. As T 79 (various portraits).* P 11½.

259	10r. blue-green (6.4)	65	20
260	15r. violet (6.4)	65	1·00
261	20r. red-brown (6.4)	80	25
262	25r. brown-lake (6.4)	1·10	1·25

221

LIECHTENSTEIN   1948

263	40r. violet-blue (15.7)	1·30	1·60
264	50r. greenish blue (15.7)	1·70	1·60
265	1f. brown-purple (15.7)	3·50	2·40
266	2f. claret (15.7)	4·00	3·75
267	5f. olive-green (6.4)	5·25	4·75
268	10f. black (12.10)	28·00	14·00
259/268	Set of 10	43·00	28·00

Portraits:—10r. Leonardo da Vinci; 15r. Joseph Montgolfier; 20r. Jakob Degen; 25r. Wilhelm Kress; 40r. Etienne Robertson; 50r. William Henson; 1f. Otto Lilienthal; 2f. Salomon Andrée; 10f. Icarus.

(Des J. Troyer. Photo Courvoisier)

1949. As T 80 *(paintings).* P 11½.

269	10r. green (15.3)	45	25
270	20r. brown-red (15.3)	95	50
271	30r. sepia (23.5)	2·50	1·20
272	40r. light blue (23.5)	5·25	60
273	50r. violet (15.3)	4·50	5·25
274	60r. grey (23.5)	9·25	4·75
275	80r. orange-brown (15.3)	2·30	3·25
276	90r. olive-green (23.5)	9·25	4·00
277	120r. magenta (15.3)	2·30	4·00
269/277	Set of 9	34·00	22·00

Designs:— 20r. "Portrait of a Young Girl" (Rubens); 30r. Self-portrait of Rembrandt in plumed hat; 40r. "Stephan Gardiner, Bishop of Winchester" (Quentin Massys); 50r. 'Madonna and Child' (Hans Memling); 60r. "Franz Meister in 1456" (Jehan Fouquet); 80r. "Lute Player" (Orazio Gentileschi); 90r. "Portrait of a Man" (Bernhardin Strigel); 120r. "Portrait of a Man (Duke of Urbino)" (Raphael).
See also No. **MS**279a.

1949 (14 Apr). *No 227 surch with T 81.*

278	69	5r. on 3r. brown and buff (Br.)	50	35

82 Posthorn and Map of World

83 Rossauer Castle

(Des P. Châtillon. Photo Courvoisier)

1949 (23 May). *75th Anniv of Universal Postal Union.* P 11½.

279	82	40r. blue	2·75	3·25

1949 (6 Aug). *Fifth Liechtenstein Philatelic Exhibition, Vaduz. Sheet 122 × 70 mm containing paintings as 1949 issue in new colours. Imperf.*
MS279a 10r. blue-green (as 10r.); 20r. magenta (as 80r.); 40r. blue (as 120r.). Sold at 3f. ... 90·00 £110

(Des J. Seger. Eng H. Ranzoni (1f.50), F. Lorber (others).
Recess Govt Ptg Wks, Vienna)

1949 (15 Nov). *250th Anniv of Acquisition of Domain of Schellenberg. T 83 and similar designs.* P 14½.

280	20r. purple	1·50	1·40
281	40r. deep blue	5·25	6·00
282	1r.50 brown-red	8·00	7·50

Designs: *Horiz*—40r. Bendern Church. *Vert*—1f.50, Prince Johann Adam I.

84 Roebuck

(85)

(Des J. Seger. Photo Courvoisier)

1950 (7 Mar). *As T 84 (animals).* P 11½.

283	20r. brown-lake	7·75	2·30
284	30r. blue-green (Black grouse)	13·50	7·75
285	80r. sepia (Eurasian badger)	27·00	30·00

1950 (7 Nov). *No 279 surch with T 85.*

286	82	100r. on 40r. blue	19·00	31·00

O **86**

86 Boy cutting Loaf

(Des K. Bickel. Design recess, value typo PTT Bureau, Berne)

1950 (7 Nov)–**68**. OFFICIAL. Buff paper. P 11½.

O287	O **86**	5r. bright purple and grey	10	10
O288		10r. green and magenta	10	10
O289		20r. brown and blue	25	25
O290		30r. brown-purple and scarlet	35	35
O291		40r. blue and red-brown	50	50
O292		55r. grey-green and scarlet	85	1·00
		a. White granite paper	38·00	£120
O293		60r. blue-grey and magenta	1·40	1·10
		a. White granite paper (5.68)	3·75	14·00
O294		80r. red-orange and grey	95	95
O295		90r. sepia and blue	1·00	1·00
O296		1f.20 turquoise and orange	1·40	1·40
O287/296	Set of 10		5·50	5·50

See also Nos. O495/506.

(Des M. Hausle. Photo Courvoisier)

1951 (3 May). *Designs as T 86.* P 11½.

287	5r. magenta	25	10
288	10r. green	50	10
289	15r. chestnut	4·25	4·75
290	20r. sepia	95	20
291	25r. claret	4·25	4·75
292	30r. grey-green	2·50	50
293	40r. turquoise-blue	7·50	4·25
294	50r. brown-purple	6·50	3·00
295	60r. brown	6·25	3·00
296	80r. red-brown	6·25	6·75
297	90r. yellow-olive	13·00	4·50
298	1f. violet-blue	42·00	5·50
287/298	Set of 12	85·00	35·00

Designs:—10r. Man whetting scythe; 15r. Mowing; 20r. Girl with sweet corn; 25r. Haywain; 30r. Gathering grapes; 40r. Man with scythe, 50r. Herdsman with cows; 60r. Ploughing; 80r. Girl carrying basket of fruit; 90r. Women gleaning; 1f. Tractor hauling load.
The 10 and 20r. were each issued both in sheets and in coils.

87 "Lock on the Canal" (Aelbert Cuyp)

88 "Willem von Heythuysen, Burgomaster of Haarlem" (Frans Hals)

222

LIECHTENSTEIN 1951

(Frames des A. Frommelt. Photo Courvoisier)
1951 (24 July). *Paintings. T* **87/88** *and similar design.* P 11½.
299	87	10r.+10r. olive-green	7·50	5·25
300	88	20r.+10r. blackish brown	8·00	10·50
301	—	40r.+10r. blue	6·75	7·00

Design: As *T* **87**—40r. "Landscape" (Jacob van Ruysdael).

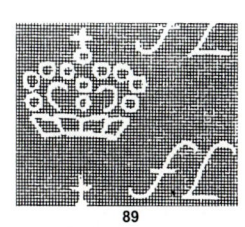

89

90 Vaduz Castle

(Des and eng F. Lorber. Recess State Ptg Works, Vienna)
1951 (20 Nov)–**52**. *As Nos. 241/2 but redrawn and T* **90**. *Buff granite paper.* W **89** (sideways).

A. P 12½ × 12.
302A	70	2f. deep blue	12·50	22·00
303A	—	3f. lake-brown	£110	75·00

B. Perf 14½.
302B	70	2f. deep blue	£600	£130
303B	—	3f. lake-brown	95·00	£160
304	90	5f. bronze-green (25.9.52)	£130	£110

Design:—3f. Princess Georgina.

91 "Portrait" (Giovanni Savoldo)

92 "Madonna and Child" (Sandro Botticelli)

(93)

(Frames des A. Frommelt. Photo Courvoisier)
1952 (27 Mar). *Paintings. T* **91/2** *and similar design.* P 11½.
305	91	20r. plum	25·00	2·20
306	92	30r. brown-olive	17·00	5·75
307	—	40r. deep blue	9·00	3·75

Design: As *T* **91**—40r. "St John" (Andrea del Sarto).

1952 (25 Sept). *No. 281 surch with T* **93**, *in carmine.*
308	1f.20 on 40r. deep blue	17·00	37·00

94 "Portrait of a Young Man" (A.G.)

95 "St Nicholas" (Bartholomäus Zeitblom)

(Frames des A. Frommelt. Photo Courvoisier)
1953 (5 Feb). *Paintings from Prince's Collection. T* **94/5** *and similar designs.* P 11½.
309	94	10r. bronze-green	1·00	65
310	95	20r. bistre-brown	11·00	1·70
311	—	30r. chocolate	22·00	5·25
312	—	40r. deep Prussian blue	24·00	34·00
309/312	Set of 4		55·00	37·00

Designs: As *T* **95**—30r. "St. Christopher" (Lucas Cranach, the elder). As *T* **94**—40r. "Leonhard, Count of Hag" (Hans von Kulmbach).

96 Lord Baden-Powell

(Des A. Frommelt. Recess Waterlow & Sons)
1953 (4 Aug). *Fourteenth International Scout Conference.* P 13½.
313	96	10r. green	1·40	90
314	—	20r. deep brown	9·50	1·50
315	—	25r. scarlet	9·00	15·00
316	—	40r. deep blue	8·75	3·25
313/316	Set of 4		26·00	19·00

97 Alemannic Ornamental Disc (c. A.D. 600)

98 Prehistoric Walled Settlement, Borscht

(Des A. Hild. Photo Courvoisier)
1953 (26 Nov). *Opening of National Museum, Vaduz. T* **97** *and similar vert design and T* **98**. P 11½.
317	97	10r. deep orange-brown	7·00	8·25
318	98	20r. bronze-green	7·00	8·00
319	—	1f.20 indigo	36·00	24·00

Design:—1f.20, Rössen jug (c. 3000 B.C.).

99 Footballers

(99a)

(Des J. Seger. Photo Courvoisier)
1954 (18 May). *Football. T* **99** *and similar horiz designs.* P 11½.
320	10r. red-brown and pale rose-red	1·60	75
321	20r. bronze-green and sage-green	5·75	2·00
322	25r. deep brown and yellow-brown	13·00	21·00
323	40r. blackish violet and grey	11·50	7·25
320/323	Set of 4	29·00	28·00

Designs:—20r. Footballer kicking ball; 25r. Goal-keeper; 40r. Two footballers.
For similar sporting designs see Nos. 332/5, 340/3, 351/4, 363/6.

LIECHTENSTEIN 1954

1954 (28 Sept). *Nos. 299/301 surch as T* **99***a*.
324	35r. on 10r.+10r. olive-green (G.)		3·00	1·60
325	60r. on 20r.+10r. blackish brown (Br.)		11·00	8·25
326	65r. on 40r.+10r. blue (B.)		6·50	5·75

100 Madonna and Child
101 Princess Georgina 
102 Crown Prince John Adam Pius 

(Des and eng K. Bickel. Recess PTT Bureau, Berne)

1954 (16 Dec). *Termination of Marian Year.* P 11½.
327	**100**	20r. chestnut	2·50	2·75
328		40r. greenish black	13·00	14·00
329		1f. sepia	14·00	13·50

(Des H. Schütz (2f.), L. Pfeffer (3f.). Eng H. T. Schimek. Recess State Ptg Works, Vienna)

1955 (5 Apr). *T* **101** *and similar vert portrait. Buff paper.* P 14½.
330	2f. dp brn (Prince Francis Joseph II)	55·00	31·00
331	3f. blackish green	55·00	31·00

(Des J. Seger. Photo Courvoisier)

1955 (14 June). *Mountain Sports. Horiz designs as T* **99**. P 11½.
332	10r. plum and turquoise-blue	1·70	75
333	20r. myrtle-green and olive-bistre	4·00	75
334	25r. blackish brown and cobalt	13·00	12·50
335	40r. blackish olive and pale brown-red	11·50	3·50
332/335	Set of 4	28·00	16·00

Designs:—10r. Slalom racer; 20r. Mountaineer hammering in piton; 25r. Skier; 40r. Mountaineer resting on summit.

(Des A. Frommelt. Photo Courvoisier)

1955 (14 Dec). *Tenth Anniv of Liechtenstein Red Cross. T* **102** *and similar vert portraits inscr "1945 1955". Cross in red.* P 11½.
336	10r. blackish violet	1·30	40
337	20r. slate-green (Prince Philip)	3·00	1·20
338	40r. bistre-brown (Prince Nicholas)	5·00	5·25
339	60r. brown-lake (Princess Nora)	5·00	3·50
336/339	Set of 4	13·00	9·50

See also No. 350.

(Des J. Seger. Photo Courvoisier)

1956 (21 June). *Athletics. Horiz designs as T* **99**. P 11½.
340	10r. bronze-green and pale red-brown	90	50
341	20r. deep purple and pale olive-green	2·50	75
342	40r. chocolate and pale blue	3·75	4·25
343	1f. deep olive-brown & pale vermilion	7·50	8·75
340/343	Set of 4	13·00	13·00

Designs:—10r. Throwing the javelin; 20r. Hurdling; 40r. Pole vaulting; 1f. Running.

103
104 Prince Francis Joseph II 
105 Norway Spruce 

(Des A. Frommelt. Photo Courvoisier)

1956 (21 Aug). *150th Anniv of Sovereignty of Liechtenstein.* P 11½.
344	**103**	10r. deep dull purple and gold	2·00	60
345		1f.20 blackish blue and gold	8·50	3·25

(Des from painting by Max Poebing-Mylot. Photo Courvoisier)

1956 (21 Aug). *50th Birthday of Prince Francis Joseph II.* P 11½.
346	**104**	10r. green	1·30	35
347		15r. deep ultramarine	2·10	2·10
348		25r. deep purple	2·10	2·10
349		60r. deep brown	6·00	2·10
346/349	Set of 4		10·50	6·00

1956 (21 Aug). *Sixth Philatelic Exhibition, Vaduz. As T* **102** *but inscr* "6 BRIEFMARKEN-AUSSTELLUNG". *Photo.* P 11½.
350	20r. deep olive-green	2·30	40

(Des J. Seger. Photo Courvoisier)

1957 (14 May). *Gymnastics. Horiz designs as T* **99**. P 11½.
351	10r. bronze-green and rose-pink	2·00	70
352	15r. plum and pale bluish green	4·25	4·75
353	25r. deep bluish green and pale drab	5·00	6·25
354	1f.50 sepia and bistre-yellow	13·00	11·00
351/354	Set of 4	22·00	21·00

Designs showing gymnast:—10r. somersaulting; 15r. vaulting; 25r. exercising with rings; 1f.50, somersaulting on parallel bars.

(Des A. Frommelt. Photo Courvoisier)

1957 (10 Sept). *Liechtenstein Trees and Bushes. T* **105** *and similar vert designs.* P 11½.
355	10r. deep slate-purple	2·75	1·40
356	20r. brown-lake (Wild rose bush)	3·00	50
357	1f. green (Silver birch)	5·00	5·00

For similar designs see Nos. 369/71, 375/7 and 401/3.

106 Lord Baden-Powell
107 St. Mamertus Chapel 

(Des A. Frommelt. Photo Courvoisier)

1957 (10 Sept). *50th Anniv of Boy Scout Movement and Birth Centenary of Lord Baden-Powell (founder). T* **106** *and similar vert design.* P 11½.
358	10r. deep violet blue	1·00	1·00
	a. Pair. Nos. 358/9	2·25	
359	20r. deep brown	1·00	1·00

Design:—10r. Torchlight procession.
Nos. 358/9 were issued together in *se-tenant* pairs within sheets of 12 stamps.

(Des A. Frommelt. Photo Courvoisier)

1957 (16 Dec). *Christmas. Vert designs as T* **107**. P 11½.
360	10r. sepia	70	20
361	40r. deep blue	2·20	5·00
362	1f.50 brown-purple	7·75	8·00

Designs: (from St. Mamertus Chapel)—40r. Altar shrine; 1f.50, "Pietà" (sculpture).
For similar designs see Nos. 372/4 and 392/4.

(Des J. Seger. Photo Courvoisier)

1958 (18 Mar). *Sports. Horiz designs as T* **99**. P 11½.
363	15r. reddish violet and light blue	90	1·00
364	30r. deep olive and pale reddish purple	3·00	5·25

224

LIECHTENSTEIN 1958

365	40r. blackish green and salmon		5·00	5·50
366	90r. sepia and light yellow-green		2·75	3·50
363/366	Set of 4		10·50	14·00

Designs:—15r. Swimmer; 30r. Fencers; 40r. Tennis player; 90r. Racing cyclists.

108 Relief Map of Liechtenstein

109

(Des J. Seger. Photo Courvoisier)

1958 (18 Mar). *Brussels International Exhibition.* P 11½.
367	**108**	25r. slate-purple, yell-ochre & verm	50	50
368		40r. slate-purple, greenish bl & verm	65	55

(Des A. Frommelt. Photo Courvoisier)

1958 (12 Aug). *Liechtenstein Trees and Bushes.* Vert designs as T **105**. P 11½.
369	20r. sepia (Sycamore)	2·30	50
370	50r. deep olive (Holly)	9·00	3·75
371	90r. blackish violet (Yew)	2·30	2·50

(Des A. Frommelt. Photo Courvoisier)

1958 (4 Dec). *Christmas* Vert designs as T **107**. P 11.
372	20r. slate-green	2·20	1·90
373	35r. blackish violet	2·20	2·50
374	80r. sepia	2·50	2·10

Designs:—20r. "St Maurice and St. Agatha"; 35r. "St. Peter"; 80r. St. Peter's Chapel, Mals-Balzers.

(Des M. Frommelt. Photo Courvoisier)

1959 (15 Apr). *Liechtenstein Trees and Bushes.* Vert designs as T **105**. P 11½.
375	20r. deep lilac (Red-berried larch)	3·75	1·90
376	50r. brown-red (Red-berried elder)	3·50	2·10
377	90r. deep myrtle green (Linden)	3·00	2·50

(Des M. Frommelt. Photo Courvoisier)

1959 (15 Apr). *Pope Pius XII Mourning.* P 11½.
378	**109**	30r. purple and gold	60	60

110 Flags of Vaduz Castle and Rhine Valley

111 Harvester

(Des J. Seger (5r. to 60r.), A. Ender (75r. to 1f.50). Photo Courvoisier)

1959 (23 July)–**64**. *Various horiz views as T* **110** *and scenes as T* **111**. P 11½.
379	5r. olive-brown (30.5.61)	10	10
380	10r. deep slate-purple	10	10
381	20r. deep magenta	25	10
382	30r. brown-red	35	25
383	40r. bronze-green (30.5.61)	70	40
384	50r. deep blue	50	40
385	60r. turquoise-blue	65	50
386	75r. yellow-brown (19.9.60)	95	1·10
387	80r. olive-green (3.10.61)	85	65
388	90r. purple (3.10 61)	1·00	95
389	1f. brown (3.10.61)	1·00	80
390	1f.20 deep orange-red (7.4.60)	1·30	1·20
390a	1f.30 bluish green (15.4.64)	1·30	1·40
391	1f.50 greenish blue (7.4.60)	1·50	1·50
379/391	Set of 14	9·50	8·50

Designs: *Horiz*—5r. Bendern Church; 20r. Rhine Dam; 30r. Gutenberg Castle; 40r. View from Schellenberg; 50r. Vaduz Castle; 60r. Naafkopf-Falknis Mountains (view from the Bettlerjoch); 1f.20, Harvesting apples; 1f.30, Farmer and wife; 1f.50, Saying grace at table. *Vert*—80r. Alpine haymaker; 90r. Girl in vineyard; 1f. Mother in kitchen.

(Des M. Frommelt. Photo Courvoisier)

1959 (2 Dec). *Christmas.* Various vert designs similar to T **107**. P 11½.
392	5r. deep myrtle-green	50	20
393	60r. olive-brown	5·00	3·75
394	1f. brown-purple	3·00	2·00

Designs:—5r. Bendern Church belfry; 60r. Relief on bell of St. Theodul's Church; 1f. Sculpture on tower of St. Lucius's Church.

112 Bell 47J Ranger Helicopter

(113)

(Des M. Frommelt. Photo Courvoisier)

1960 (7 Apr). AIR. *30th Anniv of First Liechtenstein Airmail Stamps.* T **112** and similar horiz designs. P 11½.
395	30r. orange-red	1·80	1·90
396	40r. deep blue	4·00	1·90
397	50r. brown-purple	6·00	3·75
398	75r. olive-green	2·00	2·00
395/398	Set of 4	12·50	8·75

Designs:—40r. Boeing 707 jetliner; 50r. Convair Coronado jetliner; 75r. Douglas DC-8 jetliner.

1960 (7 Apr). *World Refugee Year. Nos* 367/8 *surch as T* **113**.
399	**108**	30r.+10r. on 40r.	80	80
400		50r.+10r. on 25r.	1·20	1·20

(Des M. Frommelt. Photo Courvoisier)

1960 (19 Sept). *Liechtenstein Trees and Bushes.* Vert designs as T **105**. P 11½.
401	20r. yellow-brown	5·50	5·25
402	30r. reddish purple	6·25	8·00
403	50r. deep bluish green	18·00	10·00

Designs:—20r. Beech tree; 30r. Juniper; 50r. Mountain pines.

114 Europa "Honeycomb"

115 Princess Gina

225

LIECHTENSTEIN 1960

(Des L. Jäger. Photo Harrison & Sons)

1960 (19 Sept). *Europa*. P 14.
404 114 50r. multicoloured . . . . . . 65·00 44·00

(Des J. Seger. Eng H. Ranzoni. Recess State Printing Works, Vienna)

1960 (6 Dec)—**64**. T **115** *and similar portraits*. P. 14.
404a   1f.70 violet (15.4.64) . . . . . . 1·40 1·00
405   2f. deep blue . . . . 1·90 1·60
406   3f. deep brown . . . . 2·40 1·60
Portraits:—1f.70, Crown Prince Hans Adam; 3f. Prince Francis Joseph II.

116 Heinrich von Frauenberg
117 "Power Transmission"

(Photo Courvoisier)

1961 (30 May). *Minnesingers (1st issue)*. Vert designs as T **116**. P 11½.
407   15r. multicoloured 30 30
408   25r. multicoloured 50 45
409   35r. multicoloured 70 60
410   1f. multicoloured . . . . . . 1·10 1·00
411   1f.50 multicoloured . . . . . 4·75 7·25
407/411 *Set of 5* . . . . 9·00 8·75
Designs (reproductions from the Manessian Manuscript of Songs):—25r. Ulrich von Liechtenstein; 35r. Ulrich von Gutenberg; 1f. Konrad von Altstätten: 1f.50, Walther von der Vogelweide. See also Nos. 415/8, 428/31 and **MS**525.

(Des L. Jäger. Photo Harrison)

1961 (3 Oct). *Europa*. P 13½.
412 **117** 50r. multicoloured 30 30

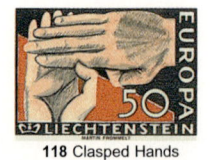

117a Prince John II
118 Clasped Hands

(Des J Seger, Photo Courvoisier)

1962 (2 Aug). *50th Anniv of First Liechtenstein Postage Stamps*. Sheet 133 × 118 mm. T **117a** *and similar horiz designs*. P 11½.
MS412a 5r. myrtle-green; 10r. rose-carmine;
25r. grey-blue. Sold at 2f.50 . . . . 8·25 4·50
Designs:—10r. Prince Francis I; 25r. Prince Francis Joseph II.

(Des M. Frommelt. Photo Courvoisier)

1962 (2 Aug). *Europa*. P 11½.
413 **118** 50r. red and indigo 40 40

119 Campaign Emblem
120 Pietà

(Des L. Jäger. Eng K. Bickel, Jr. Recess PTT Bureau, Berne)

1962 (2 Aug). *Malaria Eradication*. P 11½.
414 **119** 50r. deep turquoise-blue 35 35

(Photo Courvoisier)

1962 (6 Dec). *Minnesingers (2nd issue)*. *Multicoloured designs as T* **116**. P 11½.
415   20r. King Konradin 25 25
416   30r. Kraft von Toggenburg . . . 65 70
417   40r. Heinrich von Veldig 65 70
418   2f. Tannhäuser . . . . 1·90 2·00
415/418 *Set of 4* . . . . 3·00 3·25

(Des M. Frommelt. Photo Courvoisier)

1962 (6 Dec). *Christmas*. Vert designs as T **120**. P 11½.
419   30r. deep magenta 40 45
420   50r. orange-red 55 55
421   1f.20 deep blue . . . . 1·20 1·20
Designs:—50r. Fresco with Angel; 1f.20, View of Mauren. See also Nos. 438/40.

121 Prince Francis Joseph II
122 Milk and Bread

(Des J. Seger. Eng H. Ranzoni. Recess State Ptg Wks, Vienna)

1963 (3 Apr). *25th Anniv of Reign of Prince Francis Joseph II*. P 13½ × 14.
422 **121** 5f. deep grey-green . . . . . 3·50 2·50

(Des G. Malin. Photo Courvoisier)

1963 (26 Aug). *Freedom from Hunger*. P 11½.
423 **122** 50r. brown, purple and carmine-red 35 40

123 "Angel of Annunciation"
124 "Europa"

(Des L. Jäger. Photo Courvoisier)

1963 (26 Aug). *Red Cross Centenary*. T **123** *and similar vert designs. Cross in red; background pale grey*. P 11½.
424   20r. olive-yellow and emerald-green . . 25 25
425   80r. reddish violet and pale mauve . . 40 55
426   1f. grey-blue and ultramarine . . . 95 75
Designs:—80r. "The Epiphany"; 1f. "Family".

LIECHTENSTEIN   1963

(Des G. Malin. Photo Courvoisier)

1963 (26 Aug). *Europa*. P 11½.
427 **124** 50r. multicoloured 60   50

(Photo Courvoisier)

1963 (5 Dec). *Minnesingers (3rd issue). Multicoloured designs as T* **116**. P 11½.
428   25r. Heinrich von Sax 20   20
429   30r. Kristen von Hamle 35   35
430   75r. Werner von Teufen 60   60
431   1f.70 Hartmann von Aue . . . . . . 1·40 1·40
428/431 Set of 4 . . . . 2·20 2·20

125 Olympic Rings and Flags

126 Arms of Counts of Werdenberg, Vaduz

(Des J. Seger. Photo Courvoisier)

1964 (15 Apr). *Olympic Games, Tokyo*. P 11½.
432 **125** 50r. red, black and greenish blue   35   40

(Photo Courvoisier)

1964 (1 Sept). *Arms (1st issue). T* **126** *and similar vert designs. Multicoloured*. P 11½.
433   20r. Type **126** 20   20
434   30r. Barons of Brandis 25   25
435   80r. Counts of Sulz 70   70
436   1f.50 Counts of Hohenems 90   95
433/436 Set of 4 . . . . 1·90 1·90
See also Nos. 443/6.

127 Roman Castle, Schaan

128 P. Kaiser

(Des G. Malin. Photo Enschedé)

1964 (1 Sept). *Europa*. P 13 × 14.
437 **127** 50r. multicoloured 65   45

(Photo Courvoisier)

1964 (9 Dec). *Christmas. Vert designs as T* **120**. P 11½.
438   10r. deep slate-purple 10   10
439   40r. deep blue 20   20
440   1f.30 reddish purple 85   85
Designs:—10r. Masescha Chapel; 40r. "Mary Magdalene" (altar painting); 1f.30, "St. Sebastian, Madonna and Child, and St. Rochus" (altar painting).

(Des and eng K. Bickel. Recess PTT Bureau, Berne)

1964 (9 Dec). *Death Centenary of Peter Kaiser (historian)*. P 11½.
441 **128** 1f. bluish green/*cream* 55   45

129 "Madonna" (wood sculpture, c. 1700)

130 Europa "Links" (ancient belt-buckle)

(Des and eng K. Bickel. Recess PTT Bureau, Berne)

1965 (22 Apr). P 11½.
442 **129** 10f. vermilion . . . . 7·25 3·00
Issued in sheetlets of four stamps.

1965 (31 Aug). *Arms (2nd issue). As T* **126** *(vert designs). Multicoloured*. P 11½.
443   20r. Von Schellenberg 20   20
444   30r. Von Gutenberg 30   20
445   80r. Von Frauenberg 80   70
446   1f. Von Ramschwag 80   70
443/446 Set of 4 . . . . 1·90 1·50

(Des G. Malin. Photo Courvoisier)

1965 (31 Aug). *Europa*. P 11½.
447 **130** 50r. chocolate, pale grey & ultram 45   35

131 "Jesus in the Temple"

132 Princess Gina and Prince Franz (after painting by Pedro Leitao)

(Des L. Jäger, after painting by Nigg. Photo Courvoisier)

1965 (7 Dec). *Birth Centenary of Ferdinand Nigg (painter). T* **131** *and similar designs*. P 11½.
448   10r. bronze-green and yellow-green . . . 15   15
449   30r. lake-brown and orange 20   20
450   1f.20 deep bluish green & bright blue   85   85
Designs: *Vert*—10r. "The Annunciation"; 30r. "The Magi".

(Photo Courvoisier)

1965 (7 Dec). *Special Issue*. P 11½.
451 **132** 75r. black, flesh, gold & light grey 45   45
See also No. 457.

133 Telecommunications Symbols

134 Tree ("Wholesome Earth")

227

LIECHTENSTEIN   1965

(Des G. Malin. Photo Courvoisier)

1965 (7 Dec). *Centenary of International Telecommunications Union.* P 11½.
452 133 25r. multicoloured 20 25

(Des L. Jäger. Photo Courvoisier)

1966 (26 Apr). *Nature Protection.* T **134** *and similar horiz designs.* P 11½.
453 10r. myrtle-green and greenish yellow . . . 10 10
454 20r. Prussian blue and light blue . . . 10 10
455 30r. ultramarine and blue-green . . . 10 10
456 1f.50 red and yellow 55 55
453/456 Set of 4 . . . . 75 75
Designs:—20r. Bird ("Pure Air"); 30r. Fish ("Clean Water"); 1f.50, Sun ("Protection of Nature").

(Photo by Atelier Dita Herein, Vaduz. Photo Courvoisier)

1966 (26 Apr). *Prince Franz Joseph II's 60th Birthday. As* T **132** *but with portrait of Prince Franz and inscr "1906–1966".* P 11½.
457 1f. agate, light brown, gold & light grey 45 45

135 Arms of Herren von Richenstein

136 Europa "Ship"

(Des L. Jäger. Photo Courvoisier)

1966 (6 Sept). *Arms of Triesen Families.* T **135** *and similar vert designs. Multicoloured.* P 11½.
458 20r. Type **135** 10 10
459 30r. Jinker Vaistli 15 15
460 60r. Edle von Trisun 40 40
461 1f.20 Die von Schiel 55 55
458/461 Set of 4 . . . . 1·10 1·10

(Des G. and J. Bender, and G. Malin. "Autotype" process (photo) Enschedé)

1966 (6 Sept). *Europa.* P 14½ × 13½.
462 **136** 50r. multicoloured 35 35

137 Vaduz Parish Church

138 Cogwheels

(Des J. Seger. Photo Courvoisier)

1966 (6 Dec). *Restoration of Vaduz Parish Church.* T **137** *and similar vert designs.* P 11½.
463 5r. light yellow-green and orange-red . . . 10 10
464 20r. purple and light bistre . . . 10 10
465 30r. Prussian blue and pale brown-red . . . 10 15
466 1f.70 lake-brown and pale green . . . 65 70
463/466 Set of 4 . . . . 85 95
Designs:—20r. St. Florin; 30r. Madonna; 1f.70, God the Father.

(Des O. Bonnevalle. Photo Courvoisier)

1967 (20 Apr). *Europa.* P 11½.
467 **138** 50r. multicoloured 35 35

139 "The Man from Malanser"

140 Crown Prince Hans Adam

(Des L. Jäger. Photo Courvoisier)

1967 (20 Apr). *Liechtenstein Sagas (first issue).* T **139** *and similar horiz designs. Multicoloured.* P 11½.
468 20r. Type **139** 10 15
469 30r. "The Treasure of Gutenberg" . . . 25 25
470 1f.20 "The Giant of Guflina" . . . 70 60
See also Nos. 492/4 and 516/18.

(Des A. Pilch. Eng A. Nefe and R. Toth. Recess State Ptg Wks, Vienna)

1967 (29 June). *Royal Wedding Sheet (86 × 95 mm) comprising* T **140** *and similar vert design.* P 14 × 13½.
MS471 1f.50 indigo and light blue (T **140**);
 1f.50, red-brn & lt red-brn (Princess Marie) 2·50 2·20

141 "Alpha and Omega"

142 Father J. B. Büchel (educator, historian and poet)

(Des G Malin. Photo Courvoisier)

1967 (25 Sept). *Christian Symbols.* T **141** *and similar vert designs. Multicoloured.* P 11½.
472 20r. Type **141** 10 10
473 30r. "Tropaion" (Cross as victory symbol) 10 10
474 70r. Christ's monogram 75 55

(Des and eng H. Heüsser. Recess and photo PTT, Berne)

1967 (25 Sept). *Büchel Commemoration. Phosphorescent paper.* P 11½.
475 **142** 1f. lake and pale green 60 50

143 "E.F.T.A."

144 "Peter and Paul", Mauren

(Des J. Seger. Photo Courvoisier)

1967 (25 Sept). *European Free Trade Association.* P 11½.
476 **143** 50r. multicoloured 35 30

LIECHTENSTEIN 1967

(Des G. Malin. Photo Courvoisier)

1967–71. T **144** *and similar vert designs showing "Patrons of the Church". Multicoloured.* P 11½.
477	5r. "St Joseph", Planken (29.8.68)	10	10
478	10r. "St Lawrence", Schaan (25.4.68)	10	10
479	20r. Type **144** (7.12.67)	20	10
480	30r. "St Nicholas", Balzers (7.12.67)	25	15
480a	40r. "St Sebastian", Nendeln (11.6.71)	50	25
481	50r. "St George", Schellenberg (25.4.68)	60	30
482	60r. "St Martin", Eschen (25.4.68)	60	35
483	70r. "St Fridolin", Ruggell (7.12.67)	60	45
484	80r. "St Gallus", Triesen (25.4.68)	75	55
485	1f. "St Theodolus", Triesenberg (25.4.68)	85	55
486	1f.20 "St Anna", Vaduz Castle (7.12.67)	1·20	80
487	1f.50 "St Marie", Bendern-Camprin (8.3.68)	1·70	1·10
488	2f. "St Lucius" (patron saint of Liechtenstein) (5.12.68)	1·90	1·30
477/488 *Set of* 13		8·25	5·50

The 10 and 20r. were each issued both in sheets and in coils.

145 Campaign Emblem

146 Europa "Key"

(Des J. Seger. Photo Courvoisier)

1967 (7 Dec). *"Technical Assistance".* P 11½.
489	**145** 50r.+20r. multicoloured	50	35

(Des H. Schwarzenbach and J. Schädler. Photo Courvoiser)

1968 (25 Apr). *Europa.* P 11½.
490	**146** 50r. gold, black, ultram & bright red	35	35

147 Arms of Liechtenstein and Wilczek

148 Sir Rowland Hill

(Des L. Jäger. Photo Courvoisier)

1968 (29 Aug). *Silver Wedding Anniversary of Prince Francis Joseph II and Princess Gina.* P 11½.
491	**147** 75r. multicoloured	50	55

(Des L. Jäger. Photo Courvoisier)

1968 (29 Aug). *Liechtenstein Sagas (second issue). Horiz designs as* T **139***. Multicoloured.* P 11½.
492	30r. "The Treasure of St Mamerten"	10	10
493	50r. "The Hobgoblin in the Bergerwald"	25	25
494	80r. "The Three Sisters"	70	60

(Des K. Bickel. Design recess, value typo PTT Bureau, Berne)

1968 (29 Aug)**–69**. OFFICIAL. *As Nos. O287/96. Colours changed and new values. White granite paper.* P 11½.
O495	O 86	5r. olive-brown and orange	10	10
O496		10r. violet and red	10	10
O497		20r. red and emerald	25	25
O498		30r. green and red	35	35
O499		50r. deep blue and red	60	60
O500		60r. orange and blue	60	60
O501		70r. deep claret and emerald	75	75
O502		80r. grey-green and red	75	75
O503		95r. slate-green and red (24.4.69)	1·20	1·20
O504		1f. reddish purple and turquoise	1·00	1·00
O505		1f.20 chestnut and turquoise	1·20	1·20
O506		2f. agate and orange (24.4.69)	2·50	2·50
O495/506 *Set of* 12			8·25	8·25

(Des A. Pilch. Eng A. Nefe. Recess State Ptg Wks, Vienna)

1968 (5 Dec). *"Pioneers of Philately" (first issue).* T **148** *and similar vert designs.* P 14 × 13½.
495	20r. bronze-green	15	10
496	30r. red-brown (Philippe de Ferrary)	10	10
497	1f. black (Maurice Burrus)	85	70

See also Nos. 504/5 and 554/6.

150 Arms of Liechtenstein

151 Colonnade

(Des A. Pilch. Eng A. Fischer. Recess State Ptg Wks, Vienna)

1969 (24 Apr). P 14 × 13½.
498	**150** 3f.50 blackish brown	2·50	1·20

(Des L. Gasbarra, G. Belli and J. Seger. Photo Harrison)

1969 (24 Apr). *Europa.* P 14½.
499	**151** 50r. multicoloured	60	40

152 "Biology"

153 Arms of St. Luzi Monastery

(Des H. Erni. Photo Courvoisier)

1969 (28 Aug). *250th Anniv of Liechtenstein.* T **152** *and similar horiz designs. Multicoloured.* P 11½.
500	10r. Type **152**	10	10
501	30r. "Physics"	10	15
502	50r. "Astronomy"	35	30
503	80r. "Art"	60	60
500/503 *Set of* 4		1·10	1·10

(Des A. Pilch. Eng A. Nefe. Recess State Ptg Wks, Vienna)

1969 (28 Aug). *"Pioneers of Philately" (second issue). Vert portraits as* T **148**. P 14 × 13½.
504	80r. blackish brown (Carl Lindenberg)	50	50
505	1f.20 deep blue (Theodore Champion)	1·10	85

229

LIECHTENSTEIN 1969

(Des L. Jäger. Photo Courvoisier)

1969–71. *Arms of Church Patrons.* T **153** *and similar vert designs showing arms. Multicoloured.* P 11½.

506	20r. St. Johann's Abbey (3.12.70)		20	25
507	30r. Type **153** (4.12.69)		30	25
508	30r. Ladies' Priory, Schänis (3.12.70)		25	20
509	30r. Knights Hospitalers, Feldkirch (2.9.71)		35	25
510	50r. Pfäfers Abbey (4.12.69)		30	40
511	50r. Weingarten Abbey (2.9.71)		40	45
512	75r. St. Gallen Abbey (3.12.70)		55	65
513	1f.20 Ottobeuren Abbey (2.9.71)		1·40	1·00
514	1f.50 Chur Episcopate (4.12.69)		1·30	1·20
506/514	*Set of* 9		4·75	5·75

154 Symbolic "T"

155 Orange Lily

(Des J. Seger. Photo State Ptg Wks, Vienna)

1969 (4 Dec). *Centenary of Liechtenstein Telegraph System.* P 13½.

515	**154** 30r. multicoloured		25	25

(Des L. Jäger. Photo Courvoisier)

1969 (4 Dec). *Liechtenstein Sagas (third issue). Horiz designs as* T **139**. *Multicoloured.* P 11½.

516	20r. "The Cheated Devil"		10	10
517	50r. "The Fiery Red Goat"		40	35
518	60r. "The Grafenberg Treasure"		60	50

(Des G. Malin. Photo Courvoisier)

1970 (30 Apr). *Nature Conservation Year.* T **155** *and similar vert floral designs. Multicoloured.* P 11½.

519	20r. Type **155**		20	10
520	25r. Wild orchid		25	20
521	50r. Ranunculus		40	35
522	1f.20 Bog bean		85	85
519/522	*Set of* 4		1·60	1·50

See also Nos. 532/5 and 548/51.

156 "Flaming Sun"

157 Prince Wenzel

(Des L. le Brocquy and J. Schädler. Litho State Ptg Wks, Berlin)

1970 (30 Apr). *Europa.* P 14.

523	**156** 50r. yellow, deep blue & light green		45	35

(Des from photo by W. Wachter. Photo Courvoisier)

1970 (30 Apr). *25th Anniv of Liechtenstein Red Cross.* P 11½.

524	**157** 1f. multicoloured		85	70

(Photo Courvoisier)

1970 (27 Aug). *800th Anniv of Wolfram von Eschenbach. Sheet* 73 × 96 *mm containing vert designs similar to* T **116** *from the "Codex Manesse". Multicoloured.* P 11½.

MS525	30r. Wolfram von Eschenbach; 50r. Reinmar the Fiddler; 80r. Hartmann von Starkenberg; 1f.20 Friedrich von Hausen. Sold for 3f.		2·75	2·75

158 Prince Francis Joseph II

159 "Mother and Child" (sculpture, R. Schädler)

(Des A. Pilch. Eng A. Nefe (2f.50, 3f.). Des W. Wachter. Eng W. Pfeiler (1f.70,). Recess State Ptg Wks, Vienna)

1970–74. T **158** *and similar vert portraits.* P 14 × 13½.

526	1f.70 bottle green (5.12.74)		2·00	1·50
526a	2f.50 deep ultramarine (11.6.71)		2·10	1·70
527	3f. black (3.12.70)		2·50	1·80

Designs:—1f.70, Prince Hans Adam, 2f.50, Princess Gina.

(Photo Courvoisier)

1970 (3 Dec). *Christmas.* P 11½.

528	**159** 30r. multicoloured		30	20

160 Bronze Boar (La Tène period)

161 Europa Chain

(Des L. Jäger. Photo Courvoisier)

1971 (11 Mar). *Inauguration of National Museum.* T **160** *and similar horiz designs.* P 11½.

529	25r. black, dull violet-blue & ultramarine		20	20
530	30r. bright green and sepia		25	20
531	75r. multicoloured		55	50

Designs:—30r. Ornamental peacock (Roman, 2nd-century); 75r. Engraved bowl (13th-century).

(Des G. Malin. Photo Courvoisier)

1971 (11 Mar). *Liechtenstein Flowers (second issue). Vert designs similar to* T **155**. *Multicoloured.* P 11½.

532	10r. Cyclamen		20	10
533	20r. Moonwort		20	20
534	50r. Superb pink		40	35
535	1f.50 Alpine columbine		1·30	1·00
532/535	*Set of* 4		1·90	1·50

(Des H. Haflidason, adapted J. Schädler. Litho State Ptg Wks, Vienna)

1971 (11 June). *Europa.* P 13½.

536	**161** 50r. yellow, light blue and black		40	40

LIECHTENSTEIN   1971

162 Part of Text

163 Cross-country Skiing

(Des L. Jäger. Photo Courvoisier)

1971 (2 Sept). *50th Anniversary of 1921 Constitution. T* **162** *and similar square design. Multicoloured.* P 11½.
537	70r. Type **162**		65	55
538	80r. Princely crown		70	60

(Des H. Erni. Photo Courvoisier)

1971 (9 Dec). *Winter Olympic Games, Sapporo, Japan (1972). T* **163** *and similar vert designs. Multicoloured.* P 11½.
539	15r. Type **163**		20	10
540	40r. Ice hockey		35	30
541	65r. Downhill skiing		60	35
542	1f.50 Figure skating		1·60	1·10
539/542	Set of 4		2·20	1·60

164 "Madonna and Child" (sculpture, Andrea della Robbia)

165 Gymnastics

(Photo Courvoisier)

1971 (9 Dec). *Christmas.* P 11½.
543	**164**	30r. multicoloured	30	20

(Des H. Erni. Photo Courvoisier)

1972 (16 Mar). *Olympic Games, Munich. T* **165** *and similar horiz designs. Multicoloured.* P 11½.
544	10r. Type **165**		10	10
545	20r. High jumping		15	10
546	40r. Running		30	25
547	60r. Throwing the discus		45	35
544/547	Set of 4		90	75

(Des G. Malin. Photo Courvoisier)

1972 (16 Mar). *Liechtenstein Flowers (third issue). Vert designs similar to T* **155**. *Multicoloured.* P 11½.
548	20r. Sulphur anemone		15	10
549	30r. Turk's-cap lily		25	15
550	60r. Alpine centaury		50	40
551	1f.20 Reed-mace		95	75
548/551	Set of 4		1·60	1·20

166 "Communications"

167 Bendern

(Des P. Huovinen, adapted J. Schädler. Photo Courvoisier)

1972 (16 Mar). *Europa.* P 11½.
552	**166**	40r. multicoloured	30	30

(Des J. Seger. Eng H. Ranzoni. Recess State Ptg Wks, Vienna)

1972 (8 June). *"Liba '72" Stamp Exhibition, Vaduz. Sheet* 101 × 65 *mm containing T* **167** *and similar horiz design.* P 13½.
MS553	1f. slate-violet; 2f. rose-red		2·50	2·50

Design:—2f. Vaduz castle.

(Des A. Pilch. Eng A. Nefe. Recess State Ptg Wks, Vienna)

1972 (7 Sept). *"Pioneers of Philately" (3rd series). Vert portraits as T* **148**. P 14 × 13½.
554	30r. slate-green		25	25
555	40r. maroon		30	30
556	1f.30 deep ultramarine		1·10	85

Portraits:—30r. Emilio Diena; 40r. Andre de Cock; 1f.30,Theodore E. Steinway.

168 "Faun"

169 "Madonna with Angels" (F. Nigg)

(Des R. Schädler. Photo Courvoisier)

1972 (7 Sept). *"Natural Art". Motifs fashioned from roots and branches. T* **168** *and similar vert designs. Multicoloured.* P 11½.
557	20r. Type **168**		10	10
558	30r. "Dancer"		20	20
559	1f.10 "Owl"		85	80

(Photo Courvoisier)

1972 (7 Dec). *Christmas.* P 11½.
560	**169**	30r. multicoloured	30	20

170 Lawena Springs

171 Europa "Posthorn"

(Des L. Jäger Eng H. Heusser. Recess PTT Bureau, Berne)

1972 (7 Dec)–73. *Landscapes. T* **170** *and similar horiz designs. Phosphorescent paper.* P 11½.
561	5r. purple and pale yellow (6.12.73)		15	10
562	10r. slate green and pale sage-green		10	10
563	15r. chestnut and pale yellow-olive		10	10
564	25r. plum and pale blue (6.12.73)		30	20
565	30r. plum and pale ochre (8.3.73)		35	30
566	40r. plum and pale cinnamon (6.12.73)		45	30
567	50r. deep blue and pale lilac (7.6.73)		40	35
568	60r. myrtle-green and pale greenish yellow (7.6.73)		60	50
569	70r. deep blue and pale cobalt (7.6.73)		70	60
570	80r. deep bluish green & pale sage-green		80	60
571	1f. red-brown and pale apple-green		1·00	75
572	1f.30 deep blue and pale apple-green (8.3.73)		1·10	1·00
573	1f.50 sepia and light blue		1·40	1·20
574	1f.80 bistre-brown & pale brn (8.3.73)		1·70	1·50
575	2f. sepia & pale turquoise-bl (6.12.73)		2·20	1·50
561/575	Set of 15		10·00	8·00

231

LIECHTENSTEIN 1972

Designs: 5r. Silum; 15r. Ruggeller Reed; 25r. Steg, Kirchlispitz; 30r. Feld Schellenberg; 40r. Rennhof Mauren; 50r. Tidrüfe; 60r. Eschner Riet; 70r. Mittagspitz; 80r. Schaan Forest; 1f. St. Peter's Chapel, Mals; 1f.30, Frommenhaus; 1f.50, Ochsenkopf; 1f.80, Hehlawangspitz; 2f. Saminaschlucht.
The 50r. was issued both in sheets and in coils.

(Des J. Schädler, after L. F. Anisdahl. Photo Courvoisier)
1973 (8 Mar). *Europa*. P 11½.
| 576 | 171 | 30r. multicoloured | 35 | 20 |
| 577 | | 40r. multicoloured | 40 | 30 |

172 Chambered Nautilus Goblet
173 Arms of Liechtenstein 

(Des W. Wachter. Photo Courvoisier)
1973 (7 June). *Treasures from Prince's Collection (1st series). Drinking Vessels*. T **172** and similar vert designs. Multicoloured. P 11½.
578		30r. Type **172**	25	20
579		70r. Ivory tankard	60	45
580		1f.10 Silver cup	85	70

See also Nos. 589/92.

(Des A. Pilch. Eng W. Seidel. Recess and photo State Ptg Works, Vienna)
1973 (6 Sept). P 14.
| 581 | 173 | 5f. multicoloured | 4·75 | 3·00 |

174 False Ringlet
175 "Madonna" (Bartolomeo di Tommaso da Foligno) 

(Des L. Jäger. Photo Courvoisier)
1973 (6 Dec). *Small Fauna of Liechtenstein*. T **174** and similar horiz designs. Multicoloured. P 11½.
582		30r. Type **174**	20	20
583		40r. Curlew	90	35
584		60r. Edible frog	35	40
585		80r. Grass snake	70	55
582/585		Set of 4	2·00	1·40

See also Nos. 596/9.

(Des K. Gessner. Eng A. Nefe. Recess and photo State Ptg Wks, Vienna)
1973 (6 Dec). *Christmas*. P 13½.
| 586 | 175 | 30r. multicoloured | 30 | 25 |

176 "Shouting Horseman" (sculpture, Andrea Riccio)
177 Footballers 

(Des W. Wachter. Photo Courvoisier)
1974 (21 Mar). *Europa*. T **176** and similar vert design. Multicoloured. P 11½.
| 587 | | 30r. Type **176** | 30 | 20 |
| 588 | | 40r. "Squatting Aphrodite" (sculpture, Antonio Susini) | 45 | 35 |

(Des W. Wachter. Photo Courvoisier)
1974 (21 Mar). *Treasures from Prince's Collection (2nd series). Chinese Porcelain*. Vert desig.ns, similar to T **172**, but dated "1974". Multicoloured. P 11½.
589		30r. Vase, 19th-century	20	20
590		50r. Vase, 1740	40	25
591		60r. Vase, 1830	45	35
592		1f. Vase, *circa* 1700	75	65
589/592		Set of 4	1·60	1·30

(Des B. Kaufmann. Photo Courvoisier)
1974 (21 Mar). *World Cup Football Championship, West Germany*. P 11½.
| 593 | 177 | 80r. multicoloured | 75 | 50 |

178 Posthorn and U.P.U. Emblem
179 Bishop Marxer 

(Des B. Kaufmann. Photo State Ptg Wks, Vienna)
1974 (6 June). *Centenary of Universal Postal Union*. P 13½.
| 594 | 178 | 40r. black, bright green and gold | 35 | 25 |
| 595 | | 60r. black, vermilion and gold | 45 | 35 |

(Des L. Jäger. Photo Courvoisier)
1974 (6 June). *Small Fauna of Liechtenstein (2nd series)*. Horiz designs as T **174**. Multicoloured. P 11½.
596		15r. Mountain newt	10	10
597		25r. Adder	10	10
598		70r. Cynthia's fritillary (butterfly)	80	55
599		1f.10 Three-toed woodpecker	1·20	80
596/599		Set of 4	2·00	1·40

(Des A. Pilch. Eng A. Fischer. Recess and photo State Ptg Wks, Vienna)
1974 (6 June). *Death Bicentenary of Bishop Franz Marxer*. P 13½.
| 600 | 179 | 1f. multicoloured | 75 | 50 |

LIECHTENSTEIN 1974

180 Prince Francis Joseph II and Princess Gina
181 "St. Florian" 

(Des K. Gessner. Eng W. Pfeiler. Recess and photo State Ptg Wks Vienna)

1974 (5 Sept). P 13½ × 14.
601   **180**   10f. agate and gold . . . . 9·25   6·25
No. 601 was issued in sheetlets of four stamps.

(Des W. Wachter. Photo Courvoisier)

1974 (5 Dec). *Christmas. Glass Paintings.* T **181** *and similar vert designs. Multicoloured.* P 11½.
602   30r. Type **181** 25   15
603   50r. "St Wendelin" 50   30
604   60r. "St Mary, Anna and Joachim" . 65   35
605   70r. "Jesus in Manger" . . . 85   55
602/605 *Set of 4* . . . . . 2·00   1·00

182 Prince Constantin
183 "Cold Sun" (M. Frommelt) 

(Des L. Jäger. Photo Courvoisier)

1975 (13 Mar). *Liechtenstein Princes.* T **182** *and similar horiz designs.* P 11½.
606   70r. myrtle-green and gold . . . 55   50
607   80r. brown-purple and gold . . . 70   70
608   1f.20 deep violet-blue and gold . 1·00   90
Designs:—80r. Prince Maximilian; 1f.20, Prince Alois.

(Photo Courvoisier)

1975 (13 Mar). *Europa. Paintings.* T **183** *and similar horiz design. Multicoloured.* P 11½.
609   30r. Type **183** 25   20
610   60r. "Village" (L. Jäger) . . . 70   55

184 Imperial Cross
185 "Red Cross" 

(Des O. Zeiller. Eng W. Seidel (30r., 2f.), A. Fischer (60r., 1f., 1f.30.). Recess and photo State Ptg Wks, Vienna)

1975 (5 June–4 Sept). *Imperial Insignia (1st series).* T **184** *and similar multicoloured designs.* P 14.
611   30r. Type **184** 30   20
612   60r. Imperial Sword 45   35
613   1f. Imperial Orb 90   65
614   1f.30 Imperial Robe (50 × 32 *mm*) (4.9) . . . . . . 6·25   4·75
615   2f. Imperial Crown . . . . 2·75   1·90
611/615 *Set of 5* . . . . . 9·75   7·00
No. 614 was issued in sheets of 8.

See also Nos. 670/3.

(Des Regina Marxer. Photo Courvoisier)

1975 (5 June). *30th Anniv of Liechtenstein Red Cross.* P 11½.
616   **185**   60r. multicoloured . . . 75   45

186 St. Mamerten, Triesen
187 Speed Skating 

(Des G. Malin. Photo Courvoisier)

1975 (4 Sept). *European Architectural Heritage Year.* T **186** *and similar horiz designs. Multicoloured.* P 11½.
617   40r. Type **186** 30   25
618   50r. Red House, Vaduz . . . 35   30
619   70r. Prebendary buildings, Eschen . 60   55
620   1f. Gutenberg Castle, Balzers . . 90   80
617/620 *Set of 4* . . . . . 1·90   1·70

(Des B. Kaufmann. Photo Courvoisier)

1975 (4 Dec). *Winter Olympic Games, Innsbruck.* T **187** *and similar horiz designs. Multicoloured.* P 11½.
621   20r. Type **187** 20   10
622   25r. Ice hockey 25   20
623   70r. Skiing (downhill) . . . 65   55
624   1f.20 Skiing (slalom) . . . 1·10   90
621/624 *Set of 4* . . . . . 2·00   1·50

188 "Daniel in the Lions' Den"
189 "Mouflon" 

(Des A. Pilch. Recess and photo State Ptg Wks, Vienna)

1975 (4 Dec). *Christmas and Holy Year. Capitals in Chur Cathedral.* T **188** *and similar vert designs.* P 13½.
625   30r. deep reddish violet and gold . 25   20
626   60r. deep green and gold . . . 50   35
627   90r. brown-lake and gold . . . 70   85
Designs:—60r. "Madonna"; 90r. "St Peter".

(Des W. Wachter. Photo Courvoisier)

1976 (11 Mar). *Europa. Ceramics by Prince Hans von Liechtenstein.* T **189** *and similar vert design. Multicoloured.* P 11½.
628   40r. Type **189** 50   30
629   80r. "Ring-necked Pheasant and Brood" 75   70

233

LIECHTENSTEIN   1976

190 Crayfish

191 Roman Fibula

(Des L. Jäger. Photo Courvoisier)

1976 (11 Mar). *World Wildlife Fund.* T **190** *and similar vert designs. Multicoloured.* P 11½.
630	25r. Type **190**	30	30
631	40r. Turtle	60	30
632	70r. European otter	85	70
633	80r. Lapwing	1·70	90
630/633	Set of 4	3·25	2·00

(Des G. Malin. Photo Courvoisier)

1976 (11 Mar). *75th Anniv of National Historical Society.* P 11½.
634	**191** 90r. multicoloured	85	60

192 Obverse of 50f. Coin depicting portrait of Prince

193 Judo

(Des L. Jäger, Photo Courvoisier)

1976 (10 June). *70th Birthday of Prince Francis Joseph II. Sheet 102 × 65 mm containing T **192** and similar horiz design. Multicoloured. Imperf.*
MS635 1f. Type **192**; 1f. Reverse of 50f. coin depicting Arms of Liechtenstein .... 1·70   2·00

(Des L. Jäger. Photo Courvoisier)

1976 (10 June). *Olympic Games, Montreal.* T **193** *and similar vert designs. Multicoloured.* P 11½.
636	35r. Type **193**	30	25
637	50r. Volleyball	35	40
638	80r. Relay	60	50
639	1f.10 Long jumping	85	75
636/639	Set of 4	1·90	1·70

194 "Singing Angels"

195 "Pisces"

(Des K. Gessner. Eng W. Seidel (50r., 70r.), A. Fischer (1f.). Recess and photo State Ptg Wks, Vienna)

1976 (9 Sept). *400th Birth Anniv (1977) of Peter Paul Rubens (painter).* T **194** *and similar multicoloured designs.* P 14 (1f.) or 13½ × 14 (others).
640	50r. Type **194**	60	65
641	70r. "Sons of the Artist"	90	85
642	1f. "The Daughters of Cecrops" (49 × 39 mm)	3·50	3·50

(Des M. Hunziker. Photo Courvoisier)

1976 (9 Sept). *Signs of the Zodiac (1st series).* T **195** *and similar vert designs. Multicoloured.* P 11½.
643	20r. Type **195**	20	20
644	40r. "Aries"	30	25
645	80r. "Taurus"	60	55
646	90r. "Gemini"	85	70
643/646	Set of 4	1·70	1·60

See also Nos. 666/9 and 710/3.

196 "Child Jesus of Prague"

197 Sarcophagus Statue, Chur Cathedral

(Des and photo Courvoisier)

1976 (9 Dec). *Christmas. Monastic Wax Sculptures.* T **196** *and similar multicoloured designs.* P 11½.
647	20r. Type **196**	20	10
648	50r. "The Flight into Egypt" (vert)	60	35
649	80r. "Holy Trinity" (vert)	90	55
650	1f.50 "Holy Family"	1·40	1·00
647/650	Set of 4	2·70	1·90

(Des A. Pilch. Eng W. Seidel. Recess and photo State Ptg Wks, Vienna)

1976 (9 Dec). *Bishop Ortlieb von Brandis of Chur Commemoration.* P 13½ × 14.
651	**197** 1f.10 chestnut and gold	1·00	70

O 198 Government Building, Vaduz

199 Map of Liechtenstein, 1721 (J. Heber)

(Des O. Zeiller. Eng A. Fischer. Recess and typo State Ptg Wks, Vienna)

1976 (9 Dec)–**89**. OFFICIAL. P 13½ × 14.
O652	O **198** 10r. brown and bluish violet	10	10
O653	20r. carmine and greenish blue	10	25
O654	35r. deep blue and vermilion	20	60
O655	40r. reddish violet and emerald	30	30
O656	50r. slate-green and cerise	35	30
O657	70r. brown-purple & blue-green	45	50

234

LIECHTENSTEIN   1976

O658	80r. blue-green and bright purple	50	60
O659	90r. bluish violet & turquoise-bl	55	60
O660	1f. olive-grey and bright purple	60	50
O661	1f.10 chocolate and bright blue	75	1·20
O662	1f.50 myrtle green and scarlet	95	75
O663	2f. red-orange and greenish blue	1·20	60
O664	5f. reddish purple and yellow-orange (4.9.89)	8·75	7·50
O652/664 Set of 13		13·00	12·00

(Des and photo Courvoisier)

1977 (10 Mar). *Europa. T* **199** *and similar horiz design. Multicoloured.* P 12½ × 12.
664	40r. Type **199**	25	25
665	80r. "View of Vaduz, 1815" (F. Bachmann)	60	60

(Des M. Hunziker. Photo Courvoisier)

1977 (10 Mar). *Signs of the Zodiac (2nd series). Vert designs as T* **195**. *Multicoloured.* P 11½.
666	40r. "Cancer"	30	25
667	70r. "Leo"	60	55
668	80r. "Virgo"	75	70
669	1f.10 "Libra"	85	90
666/669 Set of 4		2·20	2·10

(Des O. Zeiller. Eng W. Seidel (40, 80r.), A. Fischer (50, 90r.) Recess and photo State Ptg Wks, Vienna)

1977 (8 June). *Imperial Insignia (2nd series). Vert designs as T* **184**. *Multicoloured.* P 14.
670	40r. Holy Lance and Reliquary with Particle of the Cross	30	25
671	50r. "St. Matthew" (Imperial Book of Gospels)	35	50
672	80r. St. Stephen's Purse	50	50
673	90r. Tabard of Imperial Herald	70	75
670/673 Set of 4		1·60	1·70

200 Coin of Emperor Constantine II

201 Frauenthal Castle, Styria

(Des L. Jäger, Photo Courvoisier)

1977 (8 June). *Coins (1st series). T* **200** *and similar vert designs. Multicoloured.* P 11½.
674	35r. Type **200**	30	30
675	70r. Lindau Brakteat	55	55
676	80r. Coin of Ortlieb von Brandis	65	55

See also Nos. 707/9.

(Des O. Stefferl. Eng W. Seidel (20, 80r.), A. Fischer (50, 90r.). Recess and photo State Ptg Wks, Vienna)

1977 (8 Sept). *Castles. T* **201** *and similar horiz designs.* P 13½ × 14.
677	20r. bronze-green and gold	25	20
678	50r. crimson and gold	50	40
679	80r. blackish lilac and gold	75	60
680	90r. indigo and gold	80	70
677/680 Set of 4		2·00	1·60

Designs:—50r. Gross-Ullersdorf, Moravia; 80r. Liechtenstein Castle, near Mödling, Austria; 90r. Palais Liechtenstein, Alserbachstrasse, Vienna.

202 Children in Costume

203 Princess Tatjana

(Des A. Pilch. Photo Courvoisier)

1977 (8 Sept). *National Costumes. T* **202** *and similar vert designs. Multicoloured.* P 11½.
681	40r. Type **202**	30	25
682	70r. Two girls in traditional costume	45	45
683	1f. Woman in festive costume	65	65

(Des L. Jäger. Photo Courvoisier)

1977 (7 Dec). *Princess Tatjana.* P 11½.
684	**203** 1f.10 yellowish brown, reddish brown and gold	95	95

204 "Angel"

205 Palais Liechtenstein, Bankgasse, Vienna

(Des J. Seger. Photo Courvoisier)

1977 (7 Dec). *Christmas Sculptures by Erasmus Kern. T* **204** *and similar vert designs. Multicoloured.* P 11½.
685	20r. Type **204**	15	15
686	50r. "St. Rochus"	40	35
687	80r. "Madonna"	65	60
688	1f.50 "God the Father"	1·00	1·00
685/688 Set of 4		1·90	1·90

(Des O. Stefferl. Eng W. Seidel (40r.). A. Fischer (80r.). Recess and photo State Ptg Wks, Vienna)

1978 (2 March). *Europa. T* **205** *and similar horiz design.* P 14.
689	40r. Prussian blue and gold	35	30
690	80r. brown-lake and gold	80	60

Design:—80r. Feldsberg Castle.

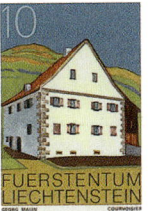

206 Farmhouse, Triesen

207 Vaduz Castle

235

LIECHTENSTEIN   1978

(Des G. Malin. Photo Courvoisier)

1978 (2 March–1 June). *Buildings.* T **206** *and similar vert designs. Multicoloured.* P 12 × 11½.
691	10r. Type **206** (1.6)	10	10
692	20r. Upper village of Triesen (1.6)	15	15
693	35r. Barns, Balzers (1.6)	30	30
694	40r. Monastery building, Bendern (1.6)	30	25
695	50r. Rectory tower, Balzers-Mäls	40	40
696	70r. Rectory, Mauren	55	55
697	80r. Farmhouse, Schellenberg	65	65
698	90r. Rectory, Balzers	75	85
699	1f. Rheinberger House, Vaduz	80	80
700	1f.10 Vaduz Mitteldorf	85	90
701	1f.50 Town Hall, Triesenberg (1.6)	1·20	1·20
702	2f. National Museum and Administrator's residence, Vaduz (1.6)	1·70	1·60
691/702	*Set of 12*	7·00	7·00

(Des O. Stefferl. Eng W. Seidel (40, 70r.), A. Fischer (50, 80r.). Recess and photo State Ptg Wks, Vienna)

1978 (1 June). *40th Anniv of Prince Francis Joseph II's Accession.* T **207** *and similar horiz designs. Multicoloured.* P 13½ × 14.
703	40r. Type **207**	35	35
704	50r. Courtyard	35	35
705	70r. Hall	65	55
706	80r. High altar, Castle chapel	70	60
703/706	*Set of 4*	1·90	1·60

208 Coin of Prince Charles
209 "Portrait of a Piebald" (J. G. von Hamilton and A. Faistenberger) 
210 "Adoration of the Shepherds" 

(Des L. Jäger. Photo Courvoisier)

1978 (7 Sept). *Coins (2nd series).* T **208** *and similar vert designs. Multicoloured.* P 11½.
707	40r. Type **208**	30	30
708	50r. Coin of Prince John Adam	40	35
709	80r. Coin of Prince Joseph Wenzel	65	60

(Des M. Hunziker. Photo Courvoisier)

1978 (7 Sept). *Signs of the Zodiac (3rd series). Vert designs as* T **195**. *Multicoloured.* P 11½.
710	40r. "Scorpio"	30	25
711	50r. "Sagittarius"	40	35
712	80r. "Capricorn"	65	55
713	1f.50 "Aquarius"	1·10	1·00
710/713	*Set of 4*	2·20	2·00

(Des A. Böcskör. Eng A. Fischer (1f.10), W. Seidel (others). Recess and photo State Ptg Wks, Vienna)

1978 (7 Dec). *Paintings.* T **209** *and similar designs. Multicoloured.* P 12 (1f.10) or 13½ (others).
714	70r. Type **209**	60	60
715	80r. "Portrait of a Blackish-brown Stallion" (J. G. von Hamilton)	80	80
716	1f.10 "Golden Carriage of Prince Joseph Wenzel" (Martin von Meytens) (48½ × 38 *mm*)	1·00	1·00

(Des and photo Courvoisier)

1978 (7 Dec). *Christmas. Church Windows of Triesenberg.* T **210** *and similar vert designs. Multicoloured.* P 11½.
717	20r. Type **210**	15	15
718	50r. "Enthroned Madonna with St. Joseph"	40	40
719	80r. "Adoration of the Magi"	70	75

211 Comte AC-8 Mail Plane St. Gallen over Schaan
212 Child Drinking 

(Des O. Stefferl. Photo Courvoisier)

1979 (8 Mar). *Europa.* T **211** *and similar horiz design. Multicoloured.* P 11½.
720	40r. Type **211**	55	50
721	80r. Airship *Graf Zeppelin* over Vaduz Castle	95	75

(Des R. Altmann. Photo Courvoisier)

1979 (8 Mar). *International Year of the Child.* T **212** *and similar vert designs. Multicoloured.* P 11½.
722	80r. Type **212**	50	60
723	90r. Child eating	55	70
724	1f.10 Child reading	1·00	85

213 Ordered Wavefield
214 Abstract Composition

(Des J. Schädler. Photo Courvoisier)

1979 (7 June). *50th Anniv of International Radio Consultative Committee (CCIR).* P 11½.
725	**213** 50r. blue and black	40	35

(Des L. Jäger. Photo Courvoisier)

1979 (7 June). *Liechtenstein's Entry into Council of Europe.* P 11½.
726	**214** 80r. multicoloured	70	60

215 Sun rising over Continents
216 Arms of Carl Ludwig von Sulz 

236

LIECHTENSTEIN 1979

(Des H. P. Gassner. Photo Courvoisier)
1979 (7 June). *Development Aid.* P 11½.
727 **215** 1f. multicoloured 85 75

(Des A. Böcskör. Eng A. Fischer (70r.), W. Seidel (others).
Recess and photo State Ptg Wks, Vienna)
1979 (7 June). *Heraldic Windows in Liechtenstein National Museum.* T **216** *and similar vert designs. Multicoloured.* P 13½.
728 40r. Type **216** 35 30
729 70r. Arms of Barbara von Sulz 70 60
730 1f.10 Arms of Ulrich von Ramschwag
 and Barbara von Hallwil . . . 90 80

217 Sts. Lucius and Florian (fresco, Waltensberg-Vuorz Church)
218 Base of Ski-slope, Valüna 

(Des A. Pilch. Eng A. Fischer. Recess and photo State Ptg Wks, Vienna)
1979 (6 Sept). *Patron Saints.* P 13½ × 12½.
731 **217** 20f. multicoloured . . . . . 16·00 11·00
Issued in sheets of four.

(Des B. Kaufmann. Photo Courvoisier)
1979 (6 Dec). *Winter Olympics, Lake Placid.* T **218** *and similar horiz designs. Multicoloured.* P 11½.
732 40r. Type **218** 30 25
733 70r. Malbun and Ochsenkopf . . . 65 60
734 1f.50 Ski-lift, Sareis . . . . . 1·20 1·00

219 "The Annunciation"
220 Maria Leopoldine von Esterhazy (bust by Canova) 

(Des A. Böcskör. Eng W. Seidel (80r.), A. Fischer (others).
Recess and photo State Ptg Wks, Vienna)
1979 (6 Dec). *Christmas.* T **219** *and similar horiz designs showing embroideries by F. Nigg. Multicoloured.* P 13½.
735 20r. Type **219** 20 40
736 50r. "Christmas" 40 35
737 80r. "Blessed are the Peacemakers" . . 60 75

(Des L. Jäger. Photo Courvoisier)
1980 (10 Mar). *Europa.* T **220** *and similar vert design.* P 11½.
738 40r. dull yellow-green, dp bl-grn & gold 50 50
739 80r. brown, deep carmine-red and gold 80 75

Design:—80r. Maria Theresia von Liechtenstein (after Martin von Meytens).

221 Arms of Andreas Büchel, 1690
222 3r. Stamp of 1930 

(Des H. P. Gassner. Photo Courvoisier)
1980 (10 Mar). *Arms of Bailiffs (1st series).* T **221** *and similar horiz designs. Multicoloured.* P 11½.
740 40r. Type **221** 30 25
741 70r. Georg Marxer, 1745 . . . . 60 55
742 80r. Luzius Frick, 1503 . . . . 70 85
743 1f.10 Adam Oehri, 1634 . . . . 85 75
740/743 *Set of 4* . . . . 2·20 2·10
See also Nos. 763/6 and 788/91.

A set of three stamps, 40, 70r., 1f.10, for Olympic Games, Moscow, was prepared but not issued.

(Des H. P. Gassner. Photo Courvoisier)
1980 (8 Sept). *50th Anniv of Postal Museum.* P 11½.
744 **222** 80r. brown-lake, deep bluish green
 and grey 70 65

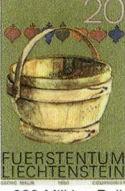

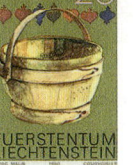

223 Milking Pail
224 Crossbow 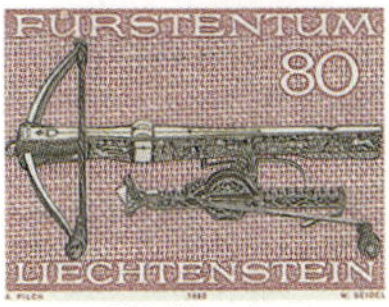

(Des G. Malin. Photo Courvoisier)
1980 (8 Sept). *Alpine Dairy Farming Implements.* T **223** *and similar vert designs. Multicoloured.* P 11½.
745 20r. Type **223** 20 10
746 50r. Wooden heart dairy herd descent
 marker 40 35
747 80r. Butter churn 65 60
The 20 and 50r. were each issued both in sheets and in coils.

(Des A. Pilch. Eng W. Seidel (80r.), A Fischer (others). Recess and photo State Ptg Wks, Vienna)
1980 (8 Sept). *Hunting Weapons.* T **224** *and similar horiz designs.* P 13½ × 14.
748 80r. blackish brown & brown-lilac . . 65 60
749 90r. black and blue-green 75 65
750 1f.10 brownish blk & dp yellow-ochre . 90 80
Designs:—90r. Spear and knife; 1f.10, Rifle and powder horn.

237

LIECHTENSTEIN   1980

225 Triesenberg Costumes

226 Beech Trees, Matrula (spring)

229 Prince Alois and Princess Elisabeth with Francis Joseph

230 Scout Emblems

(Des A. Pilch. Photo Courvoisier)

1980 (8 Sept). *Costumes.* T **225** and similar horiz designs. Multicoloured. P 11½.
751	40r. Type **225**	30	30
752	70r. Dancers, Schellenberg	65	60
753	80r. Brass band, Mauren	75	70

(Des H. P. Gassner. Photo Courvoisier)

1981 (9 June). *75th Birthday of Prince Francis Joseph II. Sheet 120 × 87 mm containing T **229** and similar vert designs. Multicoloured. P 11½.*
MS767	70r. Type **229**; 80r. Princes Alois and Francis Joseph; 150r. Prince Francis Joseph II	3·00	3·00

(Des W. Wachter. Eng W. Seidel (40r., 1f.50), A Fischer (others). Recess and photo State Ptg Wks, Vienna)

1980 (9 Dec). *The Forest through the Four Seasons.* T **226** and similar vert designs. Multicoloured. P 13½.
754	40r. Type **226**	30	30
755	50r. Firs in the Valorsch (summer)	40	35
756	80r. Beech trees, Schaan (autumn)	65	55
757	1f.50 Edge of forest, Oberplanken (winter)	1·10	1·20
754/757	Set of 4	2·20	2·10

(Des L. Jäger. Photo Courvoisier)

1981 (9 June). *50th Anniv of Liechtenstein Boy Scout and Girl Guide Movements.* P 11½.
768	**230** 20r. multicoloured	45	35

227 Angel bringing Shepherds Good Tidings

228 National Day Procession

231 Symbols of Disability

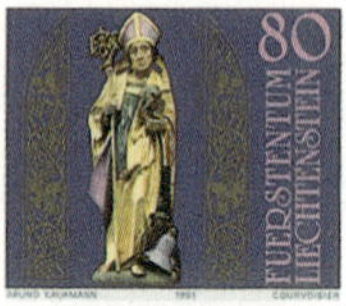

232 St. Theodul (sculpture)

(Des G. Malin. Photo Courvoisier)

1980 (9 Dec). *Chnstmas.* T **227** and similar vert designs. Multicoloured. P 11½.
758	20r. Type **227**	20	45
759	50r. Crib	40	35
760	80r. Epiphany	60	60

(Des G. Malin. Photo Courvoisier)

1981 (9 June). *International Year of Disabled Persons.* P 11½.
769	**231** 40r. multicoloured	35	35

(Des B. Kaufmann. Photo Courvoisier)

1981 (9 June). *1600th Birth Anniv of St. Theodul.* P 11½.
770	**232** 80r. multicoloured	65	60

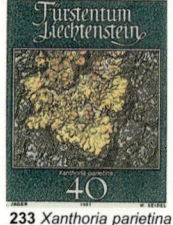

(Des Regina Marxer. Photo Courvoisier)

1981 (9 Mar). *Europa.* T **228** and similar vert design. Multicoloured. P 12 × 12½.
761	40r. Fireworks at Vaduz Castle	35	25
762	80r. Type **228**	80	70

233 *Xanthoria parietina*

234 Gutenberg Castle

(Des L. Jäger. Eng W. Seidel. Recess and photo State Ptg Wks, Vienna)

(Des H. P. Gassner. Photo Courvoisier)

1981 (9 Mar). *Arms of Bailiffs (2nd series). Horiz designs as T **221**.* Multicoloured. P 11½.
763	40r. Anton Meier, 1748	25	25
764	70r. Kaspar Kindle, 1534	55	45
765	80r. Hans Adam Negele, 1600	65	55
766	1f.10 Peter Matt, 1693	80	75
763/766	Set of 4	2·00	1·80

1981 (7 Sept). *Mosses and Lichens.* T **233** and similar vert designs. Multicoloured. P 14 × 13½.
771	40r. Type **233**	25	25
772	50r. *Parmelia physodes*	50	40
773	70r. *Sphagnum palustre*	65	60
774	80r. *Amblystegium serpens*	75	70
771/774	Set of 4	1·90	1·70

LIECHTENSTEIN   1981

(Des O. Zeiller. Eng W. Seidel (20, 40r.), A Fischer (others)
Recess and photo State Ptg Wks, Vienna)

1981 (7 Sept). *Gutenberg Castle. T* **234** *and similar horiz designs.
Multicoloured.* P 13½.

775	20r. Type **234**		20	20
776	40r. Courtyard		25	30
777	50r. Parlour		45	35
778	1f.10 Great Hall		1·00	90
775/778 Set of 4			1·70	1·60

235 Cardinal Karl Borromäus von Mailand

236 St. Nicholas blessing Children

(Des A. Böcskör. Eng Maria Laurent (40r., 1f.), W. Seidel
(others). Recess and photo State Ptg Wks, Vienna)

1981 (7 Dec). *Famous Visitors to Liechtenstein (1st series). T* **235** *and similar square designs. Multicoloured.* P 14.

779	40r. Type **235**		30	30
780	70r. Johann Wolfgang von Goethe (writer)		70	75
781	80r. Alexandre Dumas, the younger (writer)		75	65
782	1f. Hermann Hesse (writer)		85	75
779/782 Set of 4			2·30	2·20

See also Nos. 804/7 and 832/5.

(Des B. Kaufmann. Photo Courvoisier)

1981 (7 Dec). *Christmas. T* **236** *and similar vert designs.
Multicoloured.* P 11½.

783	20r. Type **236**		20	20
784	50r. Adoration of the Kings		40	40
785	80r. Holy Family		75	65

237 Peasant Revolt, 1525

238 Triesenberg Sports Ground

(Des A. Pilch. Photo Courvoisier)

1982 (8 Mar). *Europa. T* **237** *and similar horiz design.
Multicoloured.* P 11½.

786	40r. Type **237**		35	35
787	80r. King Wenceslaus with Counts (Imperial direct rule, 1396)		75	70

(Des H. P. Gassner. Photo Courvoisier)

1982 (8 Mar). *Arms of Bailiffs (3rd series). Horiz designs as T* **221**. *Multicoloured.* P 11½.

788	40r. Johann Kaiser, 1664		35	25
789	70r. Joseph Anton Kaufmann, 1748		65	50
790	80r. Christoph Walser, 1690		75	60
791	1f.10 Stephan Banzer, 1658		1·00	95
788/791 Set of 4			2·50	1·80

(Des B. Kaufmann. Photo Courvoisier)

1982 (7 June). *World Cup Football Championship, Spain. T* **238** *and similar horiz designs. Multicoloured.* P 11½.

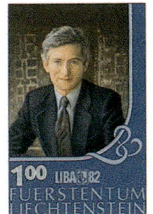

792	15r. Type **238**		15	60
793	25r. Eschen/Mauren playing fields		25	25
794	1f.80 Rheinau playing fields, Balzers		1·50	1·40

239 Crown Prince Hans Adam

240 Tractor (agriculture)

(Des D. Constantine and Cornelia Eberle. Photo Courvoisier)

1982 (7 June). *"Liba 82" Stamp Exhibition. T* **239** *and similar vert design. Multicoloured.* P 11½.

795	1f. Type **239**		85	85
796	1f. Princess Marie Aglaë		85	85

(Des H. P. Gassner. Photo Courvoisier)

1982 (20 Sept). *Rural Industries T* **240** *and similar horiz designs. Multicoloured.* P 11½.

797	30r. Type **240**		25	20
798	50r. Cutting flowers (horticulture)		45	35
799	70r. Worker and logs (forestry)		60	55
800	150r. Worker and milk (dairy farming)		1·30	1·20
797/800 Set of 4			2·40	2·10

241 "Neu Schellenberg"

242 Angelika Kauffmann (artist, self-portrait)

(Des and eng W.Seidel. Recess and photo State Ptg Wks, Vienna)

1982 (20 Sept). *150th Birth Anniv of Moritz Menzinger (artist). T* **241** *and similar horiz designs. Multicoloured.* P 13½ × 14.

801	40r. Type **241**		30	30
802	50r. "Vaduz"		60	45
803	100r. "Bendern"		95	90

(Des A. Böcskör. Eng W. Seidel (40, 70r.), M. Laurent (others). Recess and photo State Ptg Wks, Vienna)

1982 (6 Dec). *Famous Visitors to Liechtenstein (2nd series). T* **242** *and similar square designs. Multicoloured.* P 14.

804	40r. Emperor Maximilian I (after Bernhard Strigel)		25	25
805	70r. Georg Jenatsch (liberator of Grisons)		55	50
806	80r. Type **242**		65	55
807	1f. St. Fidelis of Sigmaringen		85	80
804/807 Set of 4			2·10	1·90

239

LIECHTENSTEIN   1982

243 Angel playing Lute

244 Notker Balbulus of St. Gall

(Des H. P. Gassner. Photo Courvoisier)

1982 (6 Dec). *Christmas.* T **243** *and similar vert designs showing details from Chur Cathedral High Altar by Jakob Russ. Multicoloured.* P 11½.

808	20r. Type **243**		15	15
809	50r. Madonna and child		45	35
810	80r. Angel playing organ		70	65

(Des G. Gloser. Photo Courvoisier)

1983 (7 Mar). *Europa.* T **244** *and similar vert design. Multicoloured.* P 11½.

811	40r. Type **244**		30	25
812	80r. Hildegard of Bingen		80	55

245 Shrove Thursday

246 River Bank

(Des Regina Marxer. Eng W. Seidel. Recess and photo State Ptg Wks, Vienna)

1983 (7 Mar). *Shrovetide and Lent Customs.* T **245** *and similar vert designs. Multicoloured.* P 14.

813	40r. Type **245**		30	25
814	70r. Shrovetide carnival		70	50
815	1f.80 Lent Sunday bonfire		1·70	1·40

(Des H. P. Gassner. Photo Courvoisier)

1983 (6 June). *Anniversaries and Events.* T **246** *and similar square designs. Multicoloured.* P 11½.

816	20r. Type **246** (Council of Europe river and coasts protection campaign)		35	20
817	40r. Montgolfier Brothers' balloon (bicentenary of manned flight)		50	35
818	50r. Airmail envelope (World Communications Year)		55	45
819	80r. Plant and hands holding spade (overseas aid)		75	65
816/819	Set of 4		1·90	1·50

247 "Schaan"

248 Princess Gina

(Photo Courvoisier)

1983 (6 June). *Landscape Paintings by Anton Ender.* T **247** *and similar square designs. Multicoloured.* P 11.

820	40r. Type **247**		35	25
821	50r. "Gutenberg Castle"		60	45
822	200r. "Steg Reservoir"		2·50	1·90

(Des W. Wachter. Photo Courvoisier)

1983 (5 Sept). T **248** *and similar vert design. Multicoloured.* P 11½.

823	2f.50 Type **248**		2·75	2·50
824	3f. Prince Francis Joseph II		3·25	3·00

249 Pope John Paul II

250 Snowflake and Stripes

(Des J. A. Slominski (Slomi). Photo Courvoisier)

1983 (5 Sept). *Holy Year.* P 11½.
825 **249** 80r. multicoloured . . . . 1·20 80

(Des H. Leupin. Photo Courvoisier)

1983 (5 Dec). *Winter Olympic Games, Sarajevo.* T **250** *and similar vert designs. Multicoloured.* P 11½.

826	40r. Type **250**		30	25
827	80r. Snowflake		85	75
828	1f.80 Snowflake and rays		1·70	1·70

251 Seeking Shelter

252 Aleksandr Vassilievich Suvorov (Russian general)

(Des H. P Gassner. Photo Courvoisier)

1983 (5 Dec). *Christmas.* T **251** *and similar horiz designs. Multicoloured.* P 11½.

829	20r. Type **251**		15	20
830	50r. Infant Jesus		55	35
831	80r. Three Kings		80	70

(Des A. Böcskör. Eng M. Laurent (40, 80r.), W. Seidel (others) Recess and photo State Ptg Wks, Vienna)

1984 (12 Mar). *Famous Visitors to Liechtenstein (3rd series).* T **252** *and similar square designs. Multicoloured.* P 14.

832	40r. Type **252**		40	30
833	70r. Karl Rudolf von Buol-Schauenstein, Bishop of Chur		70	60
834	80r. Carl Zuckmayer (dramatist)		80	65
835	1f. Curt Goetz (actor)		95	90
832/835	Set of 4		2·50	2·20

240

LIECHTENSTEIN 1984

253 Bridge

254 The Warning Messenger

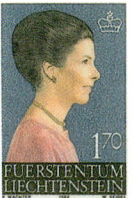

257 Princess Marie

258 Annunciation

(Des J. Larrivière and E. Frick. Photo Courvoisier)

1984 (12 Mar). *Europa. 25th Anniv of European Posts and Telecommunications Conference.* P 11½.
836	253	50r. greenish blue and deep new blue	55	40
837		80r. rose and lake-brown	80	80

(Des B. Gassner. Eng W. Seidel. Recess and photo State Ptg Wks, Vienna)

1984 (12 June). *Liechtenstein Legends. The Destruction of Trisona.* T **254** *and similar vert designs, each sepia, olive-grey and new blue.* P 14.
838	35r. Type **254**	25	25
839	50r. The buried town	55	40
840	80r. The spared family	80	70

255 Pole Vaulting

256 Currency (trade and banking)

(Des Cornelia Eberle. Photo Courvoisier)

1984 (12 June). *Olympic Games, Los Angeles.* T **255** *and similar horiz designs. Multicoloured.* P 11½.
841	70r. Type **255**	65	65
842	80r. Throwing the discus	80	80
843	1f. Putting the shot	1·00	1·00

(Des H. P. Gassner. Photo Courvoisier)

1984 (10 Sept). *Occupations* T **256** *and similar horiz designs. Multicoloured.* P 11½.
844	5r. Type **256**	10	10
845	10r. Plumber adjusting pipe (building trade)	10	10
846	20r. Operating machinery (industry–production)	25	25
847	35r. Draughtswoman (building trade–planning)	35	35
848	45r. Office worker and world map (industry–sales)	50	50
849	50r. Cook (tourism)	50	25
850	60r. Carpenter (building trade–interior decoration)	60	50
851	70r. Doctor injecting patient (medical services)	70	70
852	80r. Scientist (industrial research)	80	75
853	100r. Bricklayer (building trade)	1·00	85
854	120r. Flow chart (industry–administration)	1·20	1·40
855	150r. Handstamping covers (post and communications)	1·90	1·40
844/855 *Set of* 12		7·25	6·50

(Des W. Wachter. Eng W. Seidel. Recess and photo State Ptg Wks, Vienna)

1984 (10 Dec). T **257** *and similar vert design. Multicoloured.* P 14.
856	1f.70 Type **257**	1·40	1·40
857	2f. Crown Prince Hans Adam	1·40	1·70

(Des Helga Hilti. Photo Courvoisier)

1984 (10 Dec). *Christmas* T **258** *and similar vert designs. Multicoloured.* P 11½.
858	35r. Type **258**	40	30
859	50r. Holy Family	35	40
860	80r. The three kings	65	70

259 Apollo and the Muses playing Music

260 St. Elisabeth Convent, Schaan

(Des Cornelia Eberle. Photo Courvoisier)

1985 (11 Mar). *Europa. Music Year.* T **259** *and similar horiz designs showing details from 18th-century harpsichord lid. Multicoloured.* P 11½.
861	50r. Type **259**	60	50
862	80r. Apollo and the Muses playing music (*different*)	85	75

(Des O. Zeiller. Eng M. Laurent (1f.), W. Seidel (others). Recess and photo State Ptg Wks, Vienna)

1985 (11 Mar). *Monasteries.* T **260** *and similar horiz designs. Multicoloured.* P 13½ × 14.
863	50r. Type **260**	60	45
864	1f. Schellenberg Convent	1·10	1·00
865	1f.70 Gutenberg Mission, Balzers	1·50	1·50

261 Princess Gina and handing out of Rations

262 Justice

(Des Cornelia Eberle. Photo Courvoisier)

1985 (10 June). *40th Anniv of Liechtenstein Red Cross.* T **261** *and similar horiz designs. Multicoloured.* P 11½.
866	20r. Type **261**	30	25
867	50r. Princess Gina and Red Cross ambulance	55	60
868	120r. Princess Gina with refugee children	95	1·20

241

LIECHTENSTEIN   1985

(Des G. Gloser. Photo Courvoisier)

1985 (10 June). *Cardinal Virtues.* T **262** *and similar vert designs. Multicoloured.* P 11½.
869	35r. Type **262**	35	30
870	50r. Temperance	55	50
871	70r. Prudence	70	65
872	1f. Fortitude	75	85
869/872	*Set of 4*	2·10	2·10

263 Papal Arms

264 "Portrait of a Canon" (Quentin Massys)

(Des G. Malin. Photo Courvoisier)

1985 (2 Sept). *Papal Visit. Sheet 100 × 67 mm containing* T **263** *and similar vert designs. Multicoloured.* P 11½.
MS873 50r. Type **263**; 80r. St Maria zum Trost Chapel; 170r. "Our Lady of Liechtenstein" (statue) (29 × 43 *mm*) .... 3·25 3·25

(Des Cornelia Eberle. Eng M. Laurent (1f.), W Seidel (others). Recess and photo State Ptg Wks, Vienna)

1985 (2 Sept). *Paintings in Metropolitan Museum, New York.* T **264** *and similar vert designs. Multicoloured.* P 13½ × 14.
874	50r. Type **264**	70	60
875	1f. "Clara Serena Rubens" (Rubens)	1·10	1·10
876	1f.20 "Duke of Urbino" (Raphael)	70	1·20

265 Halberd used by Charles I's Bodyguard

266 Frankincense

(Des O. Zeiller. Eng W. Seidel. Recess and photo State Ptg Wks, Vienna)

1985 (9 Dec). *Guards' Weapons and Armour.* T **265** *and similar horiz designs. Multicoloured.* P 13½ × 14.
877	35r. Type **265**	45	35
878	50r. Morion used by Charles I's bodyguard	55	50
879	80r. Halberd used by Carl Eusebius's bodyguard	75	70

(Des J. Schädler. Photo Courvoisier)

1985 (9 Dec). *Christmas.* T **266** *and similar vert designs. Multicoloured.* P 11½.
880	35r. Type **266**	40	30
881	50r. Gold	65	60
882	80r. Myrrh	65	75

267 Puppets performing Tragedy

268 Courtyard

(Des P. Flora. Eng W. Seidel. Recess and photo State Ptg Wks, Vienna)

1985 (9 Dec). *Theatre.* T **267** *and similar horiz designs. Multicoloured.* P 14.
883	50r. Type **267**	65	65
884	80r. Puppets performing comedy	85	80
885	1f.50 Opera	1·30	1·20

(Des G. Malin. Photo Courvoisier)

1986 (10 Mar)–**89**. *Vaduz Castle.* T **268** *and similar vert designs. Multicoloured.* P 11½.
886	20r. Type **268**	25	20
887	25r. Keep (6.3.89)	40	35
888	50r. Castle	60	55
889	90r. Inner gate (9.3.87)	90	75
890	1f.10 Castle from gardens	1·20	1·00
891	1f.40 Courtyard (*different*) (9.3.87)	1·50	1·30
886/891	*Set of 6*	4·50	3·75

The 20 and 50r. were each issued both in sheets and in coils.

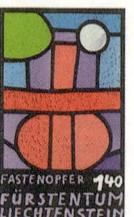

269 Barn Swallows

270 "Offerings"

271 Palm Sunday

(Des L. Jäger. Photo Courvoisier)

1986 (10 Mar). *Europa, Birds.* T **269** *and similar vert design. Multicoloured.* P 11½.
892	50r. Type **269**	60	55
893	90r. European robin	95	85

(Des F Gehr. Photo Courvoisier)

1986 (10 Mar). *Lenten Fast.* P 11½.
894 **270** 1f.40 multicoloured .... 1·40 1·40

(Des Regina Marxer. Eng W. Seidel. Recess and photo State Ptg Wks, Vienna)

1986 (9 June). *Religious Festivals.* T **271** *and similar vert designs. Multicoloured.* P 14.
895	35r. Type **271**	45	30
896	50r. Wedding	55	35
897	70r. Rogation Day procession	80	55

LIECHTENSTEIN 1986

272 Karl Freiherr Haus von Hausen

273 Francis Joseph II

(Des E. Frick. Photo Courvoisier)

1986 (9 June). *125th Anniv of Liechtenstein Land Bank.* P 11½.
898   **272**   50r. dp chocolate. brown-ochre & buff 55   55

(Des O. Zeiller. Eng W. Seidel. Recess and photo State Ptg Wks, Vienna)

1986 (9 June). *80th Birthday of Prince Francis Joseph II.* P 13½.
899   **273**   3f.50 multicoloured . . . . 3·25   3·00

274 Roebuck in Ruggeller Riet

275 Cabbage and Beetroot

(Des W. Oehry. Eng W. Seidel. Recess and photo State Ptg Wks, Vienna)

1986 (9 Sept). *Hunting. T* **274** *and similar vert designs. Multicoloured.* P 13 × 13½.
900   35r. Type **274** 45   45
901   50r. Chamois at Rappenstein 70   70
902   1f.70 Stag in Lawena . . . . 1·50   1·50

(Des P. Kindle. Photo Courvoisier)

1986 (9 Sept). *Field Crops. T* **275** *and similar horiz designs. Multicoloured.* P 11½.
903   50r. Type **275** 50   50
904   80r. Red cabbages 85   85
905   90r. Potatoes, onions and garlic 95   95

276 Archangel Michael

277 Silver Fir

278 Gamprin Primary School

(Des L. Schnüriger. Photo Courvoisier)

1986 (9 Dec). *Christmas. T* **276** *and similar vert designs. Multicoloured.* P 11½.
906   35r. Type **276** 30   30
907   50r. Archangel Gabriel 65   65
908   90r. Archangel Raphael 90   90

(Des L. Jäger. Photo Courvoisier)

1986 (9 Dec). *Tree Bark. T* **277** *and similar vert designs. Multicoloured.* P 11½.
909   25r. Type **277** 30   30
910   90r. Norway spruce 95   95
911   1f.40 Pedunculate oak . . . . 1·50   1·50

(Des H. P. Gassner. Photo Courvoisier)

1987 (9 Mar). *Europa. T* **278** *and similar vert design. Multicoloured.* P 11½.
912   50r. Type **278** 60   55
913   90r. Schellenberg parish church 95   90

280 Niklaus von Flüe

281 Miller's Thumb (*Cottus gobio*)

(Des G. Gloser. Photo Courvoisier)

1987 (9 Mar). *500th Death Anniv of Niklaus von Flüe (martyr).* P 11½.
914   **280**   1f.10 multicoloured . . . . 1·20   1·20

(Des L. Jäger. Photo Courvoisier)

1987 (9 June). *Fishes (1st series). T* **281** *and similar horiz designs. Multicoloured.* P 11½.
915   50r. Type **281** 55   55
916   90r. Brook trout (*Salmo trutta fario*) . . 85   85
917   1f.10 European grayling (*Thymallus thymallus*) . . . . 1·40   1·40
See also Nos. 959/61.

282 Prince Alois (frame as in first stamps)

283 Staircase

(Des O. Zeiller and K. Moser. Eng W. Seidel. Recess and photo State Ptg Wks, Vienna)

1987 (9 June). *75th Anniv of First Liechtenstein Stamps.* P 14.
918   **282**   2f. multicoloured . . . . 2·20   2·20

(Des O. Zeiller. Photo Courvoisier)

1987 (7 Sept). *Liechtenstein City Palace, Vienna. T* **283** *and similar vert designs. Multicoloured.* P 11½.
919   35r. Type **283** 35   35
920   50r. Minoritenplatz doorway 75   70
921   90r. Staircase (*different*) . . . . 1·00   1·00

243

LIECHTENSTEIN 1987

284 Arms

285 Constitution Charter, 1862

(Des G. Malin. Photo Courvoisier)

1987 (7 Sept). *275th Anniv of Transfer of County of Vaduz to House of Liechtenstein.* P 11½.
922   **284**   1f.40 multicoloured   1·50   1·50

(Des E. Frick. Photo Courvoisier)

1987 (7 Sept). *125th Anniv of Liechtenstein Parliament.* P 11½.
923   **285**   1f.70 multicoloured   1·80   1·80

286 St. Matthew

287 "The Toil of the Cross-Country Skier"

(Des Cornelia Eberle. Eng W. Seidel. Recess and photo State Ptg Wks, Vienna)

1987 (7 Dec). *Christmas.* T **286** *and similar vert designs showing illuminations from Golden Book of Pfäfers Abbey. Multicoloured.* P 14.
924   35r. Type **286**   40   35
925   50r. St. Mark   60   60
926   60r. St. Luke   65   65
927   90r. St. John   1·20   1·20
924/927 *Set of 4*   2·50   2·50

(Des P. Flora. Eng W. Seidel. Recess and photo State Ptg Wks, Vienna)

1987 (7 Dec). *Winter Olympic Games, Calgary (1988).* T **287** *and similar horiz designs. Multicoloured.* P 14 × 13½.
928   25r. Type **287**   35   35
929   90r. "The Courageous Pioneers of Skiing"   1·00   1·00
930   1f.10 "As Our Grandfathers used to Ride on a Bobsled"   1·40   1·40

288 Dish Aerial

289 Agriculture

(Des H. P. Gassner. Photo Courvoisier)

1988 (7 Mar). *Europa. Transport and Communications.* T **288** *and similar vert design. Multicoloured.* P 11½.
931   50r. Type **288**   40   40
932   90r. Maglev monorail   1·10   1·00

(Des L. Jäger. Photo Courvoisier)

1988 (7 Mar). *European Campaign for Rural Areas.* T **289** *and similar horiz designs. Multicoloured.* P 11½.
933   80r. Type **289**   80   80
934   90r. Village centre   1·20   1·20
935   1f.70 Road   1·90   1·90

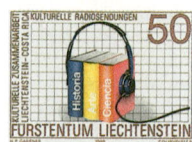

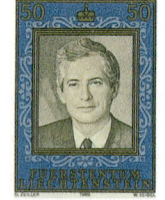

290 Headphones on Books (radio broadcasts)

291 Crown Prince Hans Adam

(Des H. P. Gassner (50c.), E. J. Hidalgo (1f.40). Photo Courvoisier)

1988 (6 June). *Costa Rica-Liechtenstein Cultural Co-operation.* T **290** *and similar horiz design.* P 11½.
936   50r. multicoloured   60   60
937   1f.40 carm-red, brn ochre & myrtle grn   1·50   1·50
Design:—1f.40, Man with pen and radio (adult education).

(Des O. Zeiller. Eng W. Seidel. Recess and photo State Ptg Wks Vienna)

1988 (6 June). *50th Anniv of Accession of Prince Francis Joseph II. Sheet* 100 × 68 *mm containing* T **291** *and similar vert designs. Multicoloured.* P 14 × 13½.
MS938 50r. Type **291**; 50r. Prince Alois; 2f. Prince Francis Joseph II   4·50   4·25

292 St. Barbara's Shrine, Balzers

293 Cycling

(Des G. Gloser. Photo Courvoisier)

1988 (5 Sept). *Wayside Shrines.* T **292** *and similar vert designs. Multicoloured.* P 11½.
939   25r. Type **292**   35   35
940   35r. Shrine containing statues of Christ, St. Peter and St. Paul at Oberdorf, Vaduz   40   40
941   50r. St. Anthony of Egypt's shrine, Fallagass, Ruggel   50   50

(Des P. Flora. Eng W. Seidel. Recess and photo State Ptg Wks, Vienna)

1988 (5 Sept). *Olympic Games, Seoul.* T **293** *and similar horiz designs. Multicoloured.* P 14 × 13½.
942   50r. Type **293**   45   45
943   80r. Gymnastics   80   85
944   90r. Running   1·00   1·10
945   1f.40 Equestrian event   1·80   1·90
942/945 *Set of 4*   5·00   5·00

LIECHTENSTEIN   1988

294 Joseph and Mary

295 Letter beside Footstool (detail)

(Des G. Gloser. Photo Courvoisier)

1988 (5 Dec). *Christmas. T* **294** *and similar vert designs. Multicoloured.* P 11½.
946	35r. Type **294**	35	30
947	50r. Baby Jesus	65	70
948	90r. Wise Men presenting gifts to Jesus	1·10	1·10

(Des Cornelia Eberle. Eng W. Seidel. Recess and photo State Ptg Wks, Vienna)

1988 (5 Dec). *"The Letter" (portrait of Marie-Thérèse, Princesse de Lamballe by Anton Hickel). T* **295** *and similar vert designs. Multicoloured.* P 13 × 13½.
949	50r. Type **295**	65	75
950	90r. Desk and writing materials (detail)	1·00	1·10
951	2f. "The Letter" (complete painting)	2·10	2·40

296 "Cat and Mouse"

298 Rheinberger and Score

(Des E. Bermann. Photo Courvoisier)

1989 (6 Mar). *Europa. Children's Games. T* **296** *and similar vert design. Multicoloured.* P 11½.
| 952 | 50r. Type **296** | 65 | 65 |
| 953 | 90r. "Hide and Seek" | 1·20 | 1·20 |

(Des H. P. Gassner. Eng W. Seidel. Recess and photo State Ptg Wks, Vienna)

1989 (6 Mar). *150th Birth Anniv of Josef Gabriel Rheinberger (composer).* P 14 × 13½.
| 954 | **298** | 2f.90 black, chalky blue & brt purple | 3·50 | 3·75 |

299 Little Ringed Plover (*Charadrius dubius*)

300 Northern Pike (*Esox lucius*)

(Des L. Jäger. Photo Courvoisier)

1989 (5 June). *Endangered Animals. T* **299** *and similar vert designs. Multicoloured.* P 11½.
955	25r. Type **299**	65	30
956	35r. Green tree frog (*Hyla arborea*)	45	45
957	50r. *Libelloides coccajus* (lace-wing)	65	60
958	90r. Polecat (*Putorius putorius*)	1·30	1·20
955/958	Set of 4	2·75	2·30

(Des L. Jäger. Photo Courvoisier)

1989 (5 June). *Fishes (2nd series). T* **300** *and similar horiz designs. Multicoloured.* P 11½.
959	50r. Type **300**	50	55
960	1f.10 Lake trout (*Salmo trutta lacustris*)	1·20	1·30
961	1f.40 Stone loach (*Noemacheilus barbatulus*)	1·70	1·90

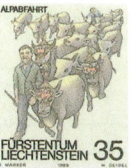

301 Return of Cattle from Alpine Pastures

302 Falknis

(Des Regina Marxer. Eng W. Seidel. Recess and photo State Ptg Wks, Vienna)

1989 (4 Sept). *Autumn Customs. T* **301** *and similar vert designs. Multicoloured.* P 14.
962	35r. Type **301**	40	45
963	50r. Peeling corn cobs	70	75
964	80r. Cattle market	80	80

(Photo Courvoisier)

1989 (4 Sept)–93. *Mountains. T* **302** *and similar horiz designs showing watercolours by Josef Schädler.* P 11½.
965	5r. multicoloured (5.6.90)	10	10
966	10r. multicoloured (3.9.90)	10	10
967	35r. multicoloured (3.9.90)	30	35
968	40r. multicoloured (3.6.91)	40	50
969	45r. multicoloured (5.6.90)	45	55
970	50r. multicoloured	45	55
971	60r. multicoloured (3.9.90)	55	60
972	70r. multicoloured (5.6.90)	65	75
973	75r. multicoloured	70	80
974	80r. bluish violet, cinnamon and black	75	85
975	1f. multicoloured (5.6.90)	90	1·10
976	1f.20 multicoloured (3.9.90)	1·10	1·20
977	1f.50 multicoloured	1·50	1·40
978	1f.60 multicoloured (2.3.92)	1·90	1·70
979	2f. multicoloured (1.3.93)	1·60	1·75
965/979	Set of 15	10·50	11·00

Designs:—5r. Augstenberg; 10r. Hahnenspiel; 35r. Nospitz; 40r. Ochsenkopf; 45r. Three Sisters; 60r. Kuhgrat; 70r. Galinakopf; 75r. Plassteikopf; 80r. Naafkopf; 1f. Schönberg; 1f.20, Bleikaturm; 1f.50, Garsellitürm; 1f.60, Schwarzhorn; 2f. Scheienkopf.
No. 980 *is vacant.*

245

LIECHTENSTEIN   1989

Prince Hans Adam II
13 November 1989

303 "Melchior and Balthasar"

304 Mace Quartz

(Des Cornelia Eberle. Eng W. Seidel. Recess and photo State Ptg Wks, Vienna)

1989 (4 Dec). *Christmas. T* **303** *and similar multicoloured designs showing details of triptych by Hugo van der Goes.* P 13½ (50r.) or 13½ × 14 (others).
981	35r. Type **303**	55	45
982	50r. "Kaspar and Holy Family" (27 × 34 mm)	55	65
983	90r. "St. Stephen"	90	90

(Des Ursula Kühne. Eng W. Seidel. Recess and photo State Ptg Wks, Vienna)

1989 (4 Dec). *Minerals. T* **304** *and similar horiz. designs. Multicoloured.* P 13½ × 13.
984	50r. Type **304**	60	60
985	1f.10 Globe pyrite	1·50	1·50
986	1f.50 Calcite	1·90	1·90

305 Nendeln Forwarding Agency, 1864

306 Penny Black

(Des H. P. Gassner. Photo Courvoisier)

1990 (5 Mar). *Europa. Post Office Buildings. T* **305** *and similar vert design. Multicoloured.* P 11½.
987	50r. Type **305**	65	65
988	90r. Vaduz post office, 1976	1·00	1·00

(Des H. P. Gassner. Photo Courvoisier)

1990 (5 Mar). *150th Anniv of the Penny Black.* P 11½.
989	**306** 1f.50 multicoloured	1·90	1·80

307 Footballers

308 Tureen, Oranges and Grapes

(Des R. Sprenger. Photo Courvoisier)

1990 (5 Mar). *World Cup Football Championship, Italy.* P 12 × 11½.
990	**307** 2f. multicoloured	2·30	2·20

(Des Cornelia Eberle. Eng W. Seidel. Recess and photo State Ptg Wks, Vienna)

1990 (5 June). *Ninth Death Anniv of Benjamin Steck (painter). T* **308** *and similar square designs. Multicoloured.* P 14.
991	50r. Type **308**	75	75
992	80r. Apples and pewter bowl	1·00	1·00
993	1f.50 Basket, apples, cherries and pewter jug	1·50	1·50

309 Princess Gina

310 Ring-necked Pheasant

(Des H. P. Gassner. Photo Courvoisier)

1990 (5 June). *Prince Francis Joseph II and Princess Gina Commemoration. T* **309** *and similar horiz design. Multicoloured.* P 11½.
994	2f. Type **309**	2·10	2·10
995	3f. Prince Francis Joseph II	3·25	3·25

(Des W. Oehry. Eng W. Seidel. Recess and photo State Ptg Wks, Vienna)

1990 (3 Sept). *Game Birds. T* **310** *and similar vert designs. Multicoloured.* P 13 × 13½.
996	25r. Type **310**	35	35
997	50r. Black grouse	65	65
998	2f. Mallard	2·40	2·40

311 Annunciation

312 St. Nicholas

(Photo Courvoisier)

1990 (3 Dec). *Christmas. T* **311** *and similar vert designs. Multicoloured.* P 12.
999	35r. Type **311**	45	45
1000	50r. Nativity	55	60
1001	90r. Adoration of the Magi	1·00	1·00

(Des Regina Marxer. Eng W. Seidel. Recess and photo State Ptg Wks, Vienna)

1990 (3 Dec). *Winter Customs. T* **312** *and similar vert designs. Multicoloured.* P 14.
1002	35r. Type **312**	45	45
1003	50r. Awakening on New Year's Eve	55	55
1004	1f.50 Giving New Year greetings	1·60	1·60

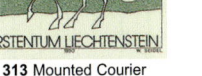

LIECHTENSTEIN   1990

313 Mounted Courier

314 "Olympus 1" Satellite

(Des P. Flora. Eng W. Seidel. Recess and photo State Ptg Wks, Vienna)

1990 (3 Dec). *500th Anniv of Regular European Postal Services.* P 13½ × 14.
1005 **313** 90r. multicoloured . . . . 1·00 1·00

(Des H. P. Gassner. Photo Courvoisier)

1991 (4 Mar). *Europa. Europe in Space. T* **314** *and similar vert design. Multicoloured.* P 11½.
1006   50r. Type **314** 60   60
1007   90r. "Meteosat" satellite . . . . 1·00 1·00

315 St. Ignatius de Loyola (founder of Society of Jesus)

316 U.N. Emblem and Dove

(Des Martha Griebler. Photo Courvoisier)

1991 (4 Mar). *Anniversaries. T* **315** *and similar horiz design. Multicoloured.* P 11½.
1008   80r. Type **315** (500th birth anniv) 95   90
1009   90r. Wolfgang Amadeus Mozart (composer, death bicentenary) . . . 1·00 1·00

(Des Cornelia Eberle. Photo Courvoisier)

1991 (4 Mar). *Admission to United Nations Membership (1990).* P 11½.
1010 **316** 2f.50 multicoloured . . . . 2·75 2·75

317 Non-Commissioned Officer and Private

318 "Near Maloja" (Giovanni Giacometti)

(Des P. Flora, eng W. Seidel (70r.). Des and eng W. Seidel (others). Recess and photo State Ptg Wks, Vienna)

1991 (3 June). *125th Anniv of Last Mobilization of Liechtenstein's Military Contingent (to the Tyrol). T* **317** *and similar horiz designs. Multicoloured.* P 13½ × 14.
1011   50r. Type **317** 55   60
1012   70r. Tunic, chest and portrait 75   70
1013   1f. Officer and private . . . . 1·20 1·20

(Des Ursula Kühne. Photo Courvoisier)

1991 (3 June). *700th Anniv of Swiss Confederation. T* **318** *and similar vert designs, showing paintings by Swiss artists. Multicoloured.* P 11½.
1014   50r. Type **318** 55   55
1015   80r. "Rhine Valley" (Ferdinand Gehr) . . . 90   85
1016   90r. "Bergell" (Augusto Giacometti) . . . 95   95
1017   1f.10 "Hoher Kasten" (Hedwig Scherrer) . . . . 1·20 1·20
1014/1017 *Set of 4* . . . . 3·25 3·25

319 Stampless and Modern Covers

320 Princess Marie

(Des E. Frick. Photo Courvoisier)

1991 (2 Sept). *"Liba 92" National Stamp Exhibition, Vaduz.* P 11½.
1018 **319** 90r. multicoloured . . . . 1·00 1·00

(Des H. P. Gassner. Eng W. Seidel. Recess and photo State Ptg Wks, Vienna)

1991 (2 Sept). *T* **320** *and similar vert design. Multicoloured.* P 13 × 13½.
1019   3f. Type **320** . . . . 3·25 3·25
1020   3f.40 Prince Hans Adam II . . . . 3·50 3·50

321 Virgin of the Annunciation (exterior of left wing)

322 Cross-country Skiers and Testing for Drug Abuse

(Des Ursula Kühne. Eng W. Seidel. Recess and photo State Ptg Wks, Vienna)

1991 (3 Dec). *Christmas. T* **321** *and similar vert designs showing details of the altar from St. Mamertus Chapel, Triesen. Multicoloured.* P 13½ × 14.
1021   50r. Type **321** 55   55
1022   80r. Madonna and Child (wood-carving attr. Jörg Syrlin, inner shrine) . . . 85   85
1023   90r. Angel Gabriel (exterior of right wing) 95   90

(Des H. Anderegg. Photo Courvoisier)

1991 (3 Dec). *Winter Olympic Games, Albertville. T* **322** *and similar vert designs. Multicoloured.* P 11½.
1024   70r. Type **322** 80   80
1025   80r. Ice hockey player tackling opponent and helping him after fall 85   85
1026   1f.60 Downhill skier and fallen skier caught in safety net . . . . 1·90 1·80

247

LIECHTENSTEIN 1992

323 Relay Race, Drugs and Shattered Medal

324 Aztecs

(Des H. Anderegg. Photo Courvoisier)

1992 (2 Mar). *Olympic Games. Barcelona. T 323 and similar vert designs. Multicoloured.* P 11½.
1027	50r. Type 323		50	55
1028	70r. Cycling road race		95	90
1029	2f.50 Judo		2·75	2·75

(Des H. von Vogelsang. Photo Courvoisier)

1992 (2 Mar). *Europa. 500th Anniv of Discovery of America by Columbus. T 324 and similar horiz design. Multicoloured.* P 12.
1030	80r. Type 324		80	80
1031	90r. Statue of Liberty and New York skyline		95	90

325 Clown in Envelope ("Good Luck")

326 Arms of Liechtenstein–Kinsky Alliance

(Des Martha Griebler; photo Courvoisier (1032/3). Des P. Flora, eng W. Seidel; recess and photo State Ptg Wks, Vienna (1034/5))

1992 (1 June). *Greetings Stamps. T 325 and similar horiz designs. Multicoloured.* P 12½ (1032/4) or 14 × 13½ (1034/5).
1032	50r. Type 325		50	50
1033	50r. Wedding rings in envelope and harlequin violinist		50	50
1034	50r. Postman blowing horn (31 × 21 *mm*)		50	50
1035	50r. Flying postman carrying letter sealed with heart (31 × 21 *mm*)		50	50
1032/1035	Set of 4		1·80	1·80

(Photo Courvoisier)

1992 (1 June). *"Liba '92" National Stamp Exhibition. Silver Wedding Anniv of Prince Hans Adam and Princess Marie. Sheet 100 × 67 mm containing T 326 and similar vert design. Multicoloured.* P 11½.
MS1036 2f. Type **326**; 2f.50, Royal couple (photo by Anthony Buckley) .... 5·50 5·25

327 Blechnum spicant

328 Reading Edict

(Des Cornelia Eberle. Eng W. Seidel. Recess and photo State Ptg Wks, Vienna)

1992 (7 Sept). *Ferns. T 327 and similar square designs. Multicoloured.* P 14.
1037	40r. Type 327		40	40
1038	50r. Maidenhair spleenwort (*Asplenium trichomanes*)		55	50
1039	70r. Hart's-tongue (*Phyllitis scolopendrium*)		75	70
1040	2f.50 *Asplenium ruta-muraria*		2·40	2·50
1037/1040	Set of 4		3·75	3·50

(Des P. Flora. Eng W. Seidel. Recess and photo State Ptg Wks, Vienna)

1992 (7 Sept). *650th Anniv of County of Vaduz.* P 13½ × 14.
1041 **328** 1f.60 multicoloured .... 1·70 1·70

329 Chapel of St. Mamertus, Triesen

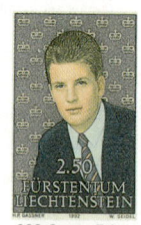

330 Crown Prince Alois

(Des G. Gloser. Photo Courvoisier)

1992 (7 Dec). *Christmas. T 329 and similar vert designs.* P 11½.
1042	50r. Type 329		55	50
1043	90r. Crib, St. Gallus's Church, Triesen		95	95
1044	1f.60 St. Mary's Chapel, Triesen		1·70	1·70

(Des H. P. Gassner. Eng W. Seidel. Recess and photo State Ptg Wks, Vienna)

1992 (7 Dec). P 13 × 13½.
1045 **330** 2f.50 multicoloured .... 2·50 2·40

248

LIECHTENSTEIN 1993

331 "Nafkopf and Huts, Steg"
332 "910805" (Bruno Kaufmann) 

(Des Ursula Kühne. Photo Courvoisier)
1993 (1 Mar). *140th Birth Anniv of Hans Gantner (painter).* T **331** and similar horiz designs. Multicoloured. P 11½.
1046	50r. Type **331**	40	40
1047	60r. "Hunting Lodge, Sass"	70	70
1048	1f.80 "Red House, Vaduz"	2·20	2·20

(Des S. Bockmühl. Photo Courvoisier)
1993 (1 Mar). *Europa. Contemporary Art.* T **332** and similar vert design. Multicoloured. P 11½.
1049	80r. Type **332**	1·00	1·00
1050	1f. "The little Blue" (Evi Kliemand)	1·20	1·20

333 "Tale of the Ferryman" (painting)
334 "Tree of Life" 

(Des H. P. Gassner. Photo Courvoisier)
1993 (7 June). *Tibetan Collection in the National Museum.* T **333** and similar vert designs. Multicoloured. P 11½.
1051	60r. Type **333**	75	70
1052	80r. Religious dance mask	75	90
1053	1f. "Tale of the Fish" (painting)	1·10	1·40

(Des Cornelia Eberle. Photo Courvoisier)
1993 (7 June). *Missionary Work.* P 11½.
1054	**334** 1f.80 multicoloured	2·20	2·00

335 "The Black Hatter"
336 Crown Prince Alois and Duchess Sophie of Bavaria 

(Des F. Hundertwasser. Eng W. Seidel. Recess and photo State Ptg Wks, Vienna)
1993 (7 June). *Homage to Liechtenstein.* P 14 × 13½.
1055	**335** 2f.80 multicoloured	3·75	3·75

(Des H. P. Gassner (from photograph by Klaus Schädler). Photo Courvoisier)
1993 (7 June). *Royal Wedding.* Sheet 100 × 67 mm. P 11½.
MS1056	**336** 4f. multicoloured	5·00	5·00

337 Origanum
338 Eurasian Badger 
339 "Now that the Quiet Days are Coming..." (Rainer Maria Rilke) 

(Des Cornelia Eberle. Eng W. Seidel. Recess and photo State Ptg Wks, Vienna)
1993 (6 Sept). *Flowers.* T **337** and similar vert designs showing illustrations from Hortus Botanicus Liechtensteinensis. Multicoloured. P 13 × 13½.
1057	50r. Type **337**	75	65
1058	60r. Meadow sage	85	70
1059	1f. Seseli annuum	1·40	1·10
1060	2f.50 Large self-heal	2·20	2·75
1057/1060	Set of 4	4·50	4·50

(Des W. Dehry. Eng W. Seidel. Recess and photo State Ptg Wks, Vienna)
1993 (6 Sept). *Animals.* T **338** and similar vert designs. Multicoloured. P 13 × 13½.
1061	60r. Type **338**	70	75
1062	80r. Beech marten	1·00	1·00
1063	1f. Red fox	1·30	1·30

(Des F. Neugebauer and Ursula Kühne. Photo Courvoisier)
1993 (6 Dec). *Christmas* T **339** and similar vert designs. Multicoloured. P 11½.
1064	60r. Type **339**	70	70
1065	80r. "Can You See the Light..." (Th. Friedrich)	1·00	1·00
1066	1f. "Christmas, Christmas..." (R. A. Schröder)	1·10	1·10

340 Ski Jump
341 Seal and Title Page 

(Des H. Anderegg. Photo Courvoisier)
1993 (6 Dec). *Winter Olympic Games, Lillehammer, Norway (1994).* T **340** and similar vert designs. Multicoloured. P 11½.
1067	60r. Type **340**	90	90
1068	80r. Slalom	1·10	1·10
1069	2f.40 Bobsleighing	2·50	2·50

249

LIECHTENSTEIN   1994

(Des Cornelia Eberle (60r.), Ursula Kühne (1f.80). Photo Courvoisier)

1994 (7 Mar). *Anniversaries.* T **341** *and similar horiz design. Multicoloured.* P 11½.
| 1070 | 60r. Type **341** (275th anniv of Principality) | 75 | 75 |
| 1071 | 1f.80 State, Prince's and Olympic flags (centenary of International Olympic Committee) | 2·10 | 2·10 |

342 Andean Condor (*Vultur gryphus*)

343 Football Pitch and Hopi Indians playing Kickball

(Des H. P. Gassner. Eng W. Seidel. Recess and photo State Ptg Wks, Vienna)

1994 (7 Mar). *Europa. Discoveries of Alexander von Humboldt.* T **342** *and similar vert design. Multicoloured.* P 13 × 13½.
| 1072 | 80r. Type **342** | 95 | 95 |
| 1073 | 1f. *Rhexia cardinalis* (plant) | 1·20 | 1·20 |

(Des E. Frick, Photo Courvoisier)

1994 (7 Mar). *World Cup Football Championship, U.S.A.* P 11½.
| 1074 | **343** 2f.80 multicoloured | 3·25 | 3·25 |

344 Elephant with Letter

345 "Eulogy of Madness" (mobile, Jean Tinguely)

(Des Regina Marxer. Photo Courvoisier)

1994 (6 June). *Greetings Stamps.* T **344** *and similar horiz designs. Multicoloured.* P 12½.
1075	60r. Type **344**	75	75
1076	60r. Cherub with flower and hearts	75	75
1077	60r. Pig with four-leaf clover	75	75
1078	60r. Dog holding bunch of tulips	75	75
1075/1078	Set of 4	2·75	2·75

(Eng W. Seidel. Recess and photo State Ptg Wks, Vienna)

1994 (6 June). *Homage to Liechtenstein.* P 13½ × 14.
| 1079 | **345** 4f. black, rose and reddish violet | 5·00 | 5·00 |

346 Spring

347 Strontium

(Des Martha Griebler. Photo Courvoisier)

1994 (5 Sept). *Seasons of the Vine.* T **346** *and similar horiz designs. Multicoloured.* P 11½.
1080	60r. Type **346**	75	75
	a. Block of 4. Nos. 1080/3	2·50	
1081	60r. Vine leaves (Summer)	75	75
1082	60r. Trunk in snowy landscape (Winter)	75	75
1083	60r. Grapes (Autumn)	75	75
1080/1083	Set of 4	2·75	2·75

Nos. 1080/3 were issued together in *se-tenant* blocks of four stamps within the sheet, each block forming a composite design.

(Des Ursula Kühne. Eng W. Seidel. Recess and photo State Ptg Wks, Vienna)

1994 (5 Sept). *Minerals.* T **347** *and similar horiz designs. Multicoloured.* P 13½ × 13.
1084	60r. Type **347**	85	90
1085	80r. Quartz	1·10	1·10
1086	3f.50 Iron dolomite	4·00	3·75

348 "The True Light"

349 Earth

(Des Anne Frommelt. Photo Courvoisier)

1994 (5 Dec). *Christmas.* T **348** *and similar vert designs. Multicoloured.* P 11½.
1087	60r. Type **348**	70	70
1088	80r. "Peace on Earth"	95	95
1089	1f. "Behold, the House of God"	1·20	1·20

(Des E. Steiner. Eng W. Seidel. Recess and photo State Ptg Wks, Vienna)

1994 (5 Dec). *The Four Elements.* T **349** *and similar square designs. Multicoloured.* P 14.
1090	60r. Type **349**	75	75
1091	80r. Water	95	95
1092	1f. Fire	1·20	1·20
1093	2f.50 Air	2·75	2·75
1090/1093	Set of 4	5·00	5·00

350 "The Theme of all our Affairs must be Peace"

351 U.N. Flag and Bouquet of Flowers

(Des Cornelia Eberle. Photo Courvoisier)

1995 (6 Mar). *Europa. Peace and Freedom.* T **350** *and similar horiz design, showing quotations of Franz Josef II. Multicoloured.* P 11½.
| 1094 | 80r. Type **350** | 95 | 95 |
| 1095 | 1f. "Through Unity comes Strength and the Bearing of Sorrows" | 1·30 | 1·30 |

250

LIECHTENSTEIN   1995

(Des Ursula Kühne (60r.), Regina Marxer (1f.80), L. Jäger (3f.50). Photo Courvoisier).

1995 (6 Mar). *Anniversaries and Event.* T **351** *and similar multicoloured designs.* P 11½.
1096	60r. Princess Marie with children (50th anniv of Liechtenstein Red Cross) (horiz)	75	75
1097	1f.80 Type **351** (50th anniv of United Nations Organization)	2·20	2·20
1098	3f.50 Alps (European Nature Conservation Year)	4·25	4·25

352 "Falknis Mountains"
353 "One Heart and One Soul"

(Des M. Frommelt. Photo Courvoisier).

1995 (6 June). *Birth Centenary of Anton Frommelt (painter).* T **352** *and similar horiz designs. Multicoloured.* P 11½.
1099	60r. Type **352**	75	75
1100	80r. "Three Oaks"	1·00	1·00
1101	4f.10 "The Rhine"	4·75	4·75

(Des Nico. Photo Courvoisier).

1995 (6 June). *Greetings Stamps.* T **353** *and similar horiz designs. Multicoloured.* P 12½.
1102	60r. Type **353**	75	75
	a. Vert strip of 4. Nos. 1102/5	3·00	
1103	60r. Bandage round sunflower ("Get Well")	75	75
1104	60r. Baby arriving over rainbow ("Hurrah! Here I am")	75	75
1105	60r. Delivering letter by hot-air balloon ("Write again")	75	75
1102/1105	Set of 4	2·75	2·75

Nos. 1102/5 were issued together in vertical *se-tenant* strips of four stamps within the sheet.

354 Coloured Ribbons woven through River
355 Arnica (*Arnica montana*)

(Des Cornelia Eberle. Eng P. Schopfer. Recess and litho PTT, Berne).

1995 (5 Sept). *Liechtenstein-Switzerland Co-operation.* P 13½.
1106	**354**	60r. multicoloured	75	75

No. 1106 was valid for use in both Liechtenstein and Switzerland (see No. 1308 of Switzerland).

(Des Cornelia Eberle. Eng W. Seidel. Recess and litho State Ptg Wks, Vienna).

1995 (5 Sept). *Medicinal Plants.* T **355** *and similar vert designs. Multicoloured.* P 13 × 13½.
1107	60r. Type **355**	70	75
1108	80r. Giant nettle (*Urica dioica*)	95	75
1109	1f.80 Common valerian (*Valeriana* sp.)	2·20	2·20
1110	3f.50 Fig-wort (*Ranunculus* sp.)	3·50	3·75
1107/1110	Set of 4	6·50	6·75

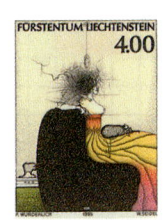

356 Angel (detail of painting)
357 "Lady with Lapdog" (Paul Wunderlich)

(Des Marianne Siegl. Eng W. Seidel. Recess and photo State Ptg Wks, Vienna).

1995 (4 Dec). *Christmas* T **356** *and similar vert designs showing painting by Lorenzo Monaco. Multicoloured.* P 14 × 13½.
1111	60r. Type **356**	70	70
1112	80r. "Virgin Mary with Infant and Two Angels"	95	95
1113	1f. Angel facing left (detail of painting)	1·20	1·20

(Des and eng W. Seidel. Recess and photo State Ptg Wks, Vienna).

1995 (4 Dec). *Homage to Liechtenstein.* P 14 × 13½.
1114	**357**	4f. multicoloured	4·75	4·75

358 Eschen
359 Crucible

(Des O. Zeiller (10r.), O. Zeiller and Marianne Siegl (others). Photo Courvoisier).

1996 (4 Mar)–**2001**. *Scenes.* T **358** *and similar horiz design. Multicoloured.* P 11½.
1115	10r. Type **358**	10	10
1116	20r. Planken (3.3.97)	25	25
1117	50r. Ruggell (6.3.00)	55	55
1117a	60r. Balzers (6.3.00)	60	60
1118	80r. Ruggell (1.3.99)	85	85
1120	1f. Nendeln (1.3.99)	1·10	1·10
1120a	1f. Eschen (6.3.00)	1·20	1·20
1122	1f.20 Triesen (1.3.99)	1·30	1·30
1123	1f.30 Triesen (3.3.97)	1·40	1·40
1124	1f.40 Mauren (6.3.00)	1·50	1·50
1125	1f.70 Schaanwald (3.3.97)	1·80	1·80
1125a	1f.80 Malbun (5.6.01)	1·90	1·90
1125b	1f.90 Schaan (6.3.00)	2·10	2·10
1126	2f. Gamprin (2.6.98)	2·10	2·10
1127	4f. Triesenburg (2.6.98)	4·25	4·25
1127a	4f.50 Bendern (5.6.01)	4·75	4·75
1128	5f. Vaduz Castle (4.3.01)	5·25	5·25
1115/1128	Set of 17	28·00	28·00

Numbers have been left for additions to this series.

(Des L. Jäger. Photo Courvoisier).

1996 (4 Mar). *Bronze Age in Europe.* P 11½.
1130	**359**	90r. multicoloured	1·10	1·10

251

LIECHTENSTEIN 1996

360 Kinsky and Diary Extract, 7 March 1917

(Des H. P. Gassner. Photo Courvoisier)

1996 (4 Mar). *Europa. Famous Women. Nora, Countess Kinsky (mother of Princess Gina of Liechtenstein).* T **360** and similar horiz design. P 11½.
1131	90r. brownish grey, deep reddish purple and deep turquoise-blue	1·00	1·00
1132	1f.10 brownish grey, deep turquoise-blue and deep reddish purple	1·20	1·20

Design:—1f.10, Kinsky and diary extract for 28 February 1917

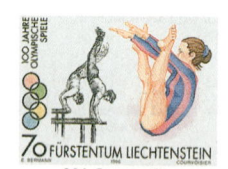

361 Gymnastics

(Des E. Bermann. Photo Courvoisier)

1996 (3 June). *Centenary of Modern Olympic Games.* T **361** and similar horiz designs. Multicoloured. P 11½.
1133	70r. Type **361**	75	75
1134	90r. Hurdling	95	95
1135	1f.10 Cycling	1·30	1·30

362 "Primroses"

(Des Ursula Kühne. Photo Courvoisier)

1996 (3 June). *Birth Centenary of Ferdinand Gehr (painter).* T **362** and similar horiz designs. Multicoloured. P 11½.
1136	70r. Type **362**	80	80
1137	90r. "Daisies"	1·00	1·00
1138	1f.10 "Poppy"	1·20	1·20
1139	1f.80 "Buttercups" (33 × 23 mm)	2·00	2·00
1136/1139	Set of 4	4·50	4·50

363 State Arms

(Des Cornelia Eberle. Eng W. Seidel. Recess photo and embossed)

1996 (2 Sept). P 14.
1140	**363** 10f. multicoloured	10·50	10·50

364 Veldkirch, 1550   **365** "Poltava"

(Des and eng W. Seidel. Recess and photo State Ptg Wks, Vienna)

1996 (2 Sept). *Millenary of Austria.* P 13½.
1141	**364** 90r. multicoloured	1·10	1·10

(Des Cornelia Eberle. Eng W. Seidel. Recess and photo State Ptg Wks, Vienna)

1996 (2 Dec). *43rd Death Anniv of Eugen Zotow (painter).* T **365** and similar square designs. Multicoloured. P 14.
1142	70r. Type **365**	75	75
1143	1f.10 "Three Brothers in a Berlin Park"	75	75
1144	1f.40 "Vaduz"	1·00	1·00

366 St. Matthew   **367** Schubert

(Des Karin Beck. Eng W. Seidel. Recess and photo State Ptg Wks, Vienna)

1996 (2 Dec). *Christmas.* T **366** and similar vert designs showing illustrations from illuminated manuscript Liber Viventium Fabariensis. Multicoloured. P 14.
1145	70r. Type **366**	80	75
1146	90r. Emblems of St. Mark	1·00	95
1147	1f.10 Emblems of St. Luke	1·20	1·20
1148	1f.80 Emblems of St. John	2·00	2·00
1145/1148	Set of 4	4·50	4·50

(Des Martha Griebler. Eng W. Seidel. Recess and photo State Ptg Wks, Vienna)

1997 (3 Mar). *Birth Bicentenary of Franz Schubert (composer).* P 13½.
1149	**367** 70r. multicoloured	85	85

368 The Wild Gnomes

(Des Regina Marxer. Photo Courvoisier)

1997 (3 Mar). *Europa. Tales and Legends.* T **368** and similar square design. Multicoloured. P 12 × 11½.
1150	90r. Type **368**	90	90
1151	1f.10 Man, pumpkin and rabbit (The Foal of Planken)	1·20	1·20

LIECHTENSTEIN 1997

369 "Madonna and Child with St. Lucius and St. Florinus" (Gabriel Dreher)

370 *Phaeolepiota aurea*

(Des Marianne Siegl. Eng W. Seidel. Recess and photo State Ptg Wks, Vienna).
1997 (2 June). *National Patron Saints.* P 13½ × 13.
| 1152 | **369** | 20f. multicoloured | 17·00 | 17·00 |

(Des Iris Heeb. Eng W. Seidel. Recess and photo State Ptg Wks, Vienna)
1997 (22 Aug). *Fungi.* T **370** and similar square designs. Multicoloured. P 14.
1153	70r. Type 370		70	70
1154	90r. *Helvella silvicola*		90	90
1155	1f.10 Orange peel fungus (*Aleuria aurantia*)		1·20	1·20

371 Steam Train, Schaanwald Halt

372 "Girl with Flower" (Enrico Baj)

(Des J. Schädler. Photo Courvoisier)
1997 (22 Aug). *125th Anniv of Liechtenstein Railways.* T **371** and similar horiz designs. Multicoloured. P 11½.
1156	70r. Type **371**		75	75
1157	90r. Diesel-electric train, Nendeln station		95	95
1158	1f.80 Electric train, Shaan-Vaduz station		1·90	1·90

(Des W. Seidel. Photo Courvoisier)
1997 (22 Aug). *Homage to Liechtenstein.* P 11½.
| 1159 | **372** | 70r. multicoloured | 75 | 75 |

373 Basket of Roses

374 Cross-country

(Des H. Preute. Eng W. Seidel. Recess and photo Austrian State Ptg Wks, Vienna)
1997 (1 Dec). *Christmas. Glass Tree Decorations.* T **373** and similar square designs. Multicoloured. P 14.
1160	70r. Type 373		70	70
1161	90r. Bell		90	90
1162	1f.10 Bauble		1·10	1·10

(Des P. Sinawehl. Photo Courvoisier)
1997 (1 Dec). *Winter Olympic Games, Nagano, Japan (1998). Skiing.* T **374** and similar horiz designs. Multicoloured. P 12½.
1163	70r. Type **374**		70	70
1164	90r. Slalom		95	95
1165	1f.80 Downhill		1·90	1·90

375 "Verano (The Summer)"

376 Prince's Festival Procession, Vaduz

(Photo Courvoisier)
1998 (2 Mar). *Homage to Liechtenstein. Paintings by Heinz Mack.* T **375** and similar vert designs. Multicoloured. P 11½.
1166	70r. Type **375**		70	70
	a. Vert strip of block of 4. Nos. 1166/9		2·75	
1167	70r. "Homage to Liechtenstein"		70	70
1168	70r. "Between Day and Dream"		70	70
1169	70r. "Salute Cirico!"		70	70
1166/69	Set of 4		2·50	2·50

Nos. 1166/9 were issued together in *se-tenant* blocks of four stamps plus one vertical *se-tenant* strip within sheets of 20.

(Des Evelyne Bermann. Photo Courvoisier)
1998 (2 Mar). *Europa. National Festivals.* T **376** and similar horiz design. Multicoloured. P 11½.
| 1170 | 90r. Type **376** | | 95 | 95 |
| 1171 | 1f.10 Music Societies Festival, Gutenberg Castle, Balzers | | 1·20 | 1·20 |

377 National Flags on Bridge

378 Goalkeeper

(Des H. P. Gassner. Photo Courvoisier)
1998 (2 Mar). *75th Anniv of Liechtenstein—Switzerland Customs Treaty.* P 11½.
| 1172 | **377** | 1f.70 multicoloured | 1·80 | 1·80 |

(Des L. Jäger. Photo Courvoisier)
1998 (2 Mar). *World Cup Football Championship, France.* P 12.
| 1173 | **378** | 1f.80 multicoloured | 1·90 | 1·90 |

253

LIECHTENSTEIN 1998

379 Clown with Queen of Hearts

(Des P. Flora. Recess and photo State Ptg Wks, Vienna)
1998 (2 June). *Greeting Stamps. Clowns.* T **379** and similar horiz designs. Multicoloured. P 14½ × 14.
1174	70r. Type **379**	70	70
	a. Vert strip of 4. Nos. 1174/7	2·75	
1175	70r. Clown holding four-leaf clovers	70	70
1176	70r. Clown raising hat	70	70
1177	70r. Clown holding heart	70	70
1174/77	Set of 4	2·50	2·50

Nos. 1174/7 were issued together in vertical *se-tenant* strips of four stamps within the sheet.

380 Wooden Milk Vat

381 Expelling of Johann Langer from Liechtenstein

(Des J. Schädler. Photo Couvoisier)
1998 (7 Sept). *Traditional Crafts.* T **380** and similar square designs. Multicoloured. P 11½.
1178	90r. Type **380**	90	90
1179	2f.20 Clog	2·20	2·20
1180	3f.50 Wheel	3·50	3·50

(Des Regina Marxer. Photo Couvoisier)
1998 (7 Sept). *150th Anniv of 1848 Revolutions in Europe.* P 11½.
1181	**381**	1f.80 multicoloured	1·90	1·90

382 Virgin Mary

383 Zum Löwen Guest House

(Des Marianne Siegl. Recess and photo Austrian State Ptg Wks, Vienna)
1998 (7 Dec). *Christmas.* T **382** and similar multicoloured designs. P 14.
1182	70r. Type **382**	75	75
1183	90r. "The Nativity" (35 × 26 mm)	90	90
1184	1f.10 Joseph	1·20	1·20

Nos. 1182 and 1184 show details of the complete relief depicted on No. 1183.

(Des G. Malin. Photo Couvoisier)
1998 (7 Dec). *Preservation of Historical Environment. Hinterschellenberg.* T **383** and similar multicoloured designs. P 11½.
1185	90r. Type **383**	90	95
1186	1f.70 St. George's Chapel (*vert*)	1·90	1·90
1187	1f.80 Houses	1·90	1·90

384 Automatic and Manual Switchboards

385 Eschen

(Des Karin Beck. Photo Courvoisier)
1998 (7 Dec). *Centenary of Telephone in Liechtenstein.* P 11½.
1188	**384**	2f.80 multicoloured	3·00	3·00

(Des L. Jäger. Photo Courvoisier)
1999 (1 Mar). *300th Anniv of Purchase of the Unterland by Prince Johann Adam.* Sheet 107 × 68 mm containing T **385** and similar horiz designs. Multicoloured. P 11½.
MS1189 90r. × 5 plus label, Composite design of the Unterland showing the villages of Eschen, Gamprin, Mauren, Ruggell and Schellenberg 4·50 4·50

386 Smooth Snake and Schwabbrünnen-Aescher Nature Park

387 Council Anniversary Emblem and Silhouettes

(Des Cornelia Eberle. Photo Courvoisier)
1999 (1 Mar). *Europa. Parks and Gardens.* T **386** and similar vert design. Multicoloured. P 11½.
1190	90r. Type **386**	1·00	1·00
1191	1f.10 Corncrake and Ruggell marsh	1·10	1·10

(Des Rapallo. Photo Courvoisier)
1999 (25 May). *Anniversaries and Event.* T **387** and similar vert designs. Multicoloured. P 12 × 11½.
1192	70r. Type **387** (50th anniv of Council of Europe and European Convention on Human Rights)	75	75
1193	70r. Bird with envelope in beak (125th Anniv of Universal Postal Union)	75	75
1194	70r. Heart in hand (75th Anniv of Caritas Liechtenstein (welfare organization))	75	75

388 Judo

389 "Herrengasse"

254

LIECHTENSTEIN 1999

(Des P. Sinawehl (1200/3), A. Tuma (others). Photo Courvoisier)

1999 (25 May). *Eighth European Small States Games, Liechtenstein. T* **388** *and similar horiz designs. Multicoloured.* P 11½.

1195	70r. Type **388**		70	70
1196	70r. Swimming		70	70
1197	70r. Throwing the Javelin		70	70
1198	90r. Cycling		95	95
1199	90r. Shooting		95	95
1200	90r. Tennis		95	95
1201	90r. Squash		95	95
1202	90r. Table tennis		95	95
1203	90r. Volleyball		95	95
1195/1203	Set of 9		7·00	7·00

(Des and eng W. Seidel. Recess and photo Austrian State Ptg Wks, Vienna)

1999 (9 Sept). *Paintings by Eugen Verling. T* **389** *and similar horiz designs.* P 14.

1204	70r. Type **389**		85	85
1205	2f. "Old Vaduz with Castle"		1·20	1·20
1206	4f. "House in Fürst-Franz-Josef Street, Vaduz"		5·00	5·00

390 Scene from *Faust*, Act I

391 "The Annunciation"

(Des Martha Griebler. Eng W. Seidel. Recess and photo Austrian State Ptg Wks, Vienna)

1999 (9 Sept). *250th Birth Anniv of Johann Wolfgang Goethe (poet and playwright). T* **390** *and similar horiz design. Multicoloured.* P 14.

1207	1f.40 Type **390**		1·50	1·50
1208	1f.70 Faust and the Devil sealing wager		1·80	1·80

(Des Ursula Kühne. Eng W. Seidel. Recess and photo Austrian State Ptg Wks, Vienna)

1999 (6 Dec). *Christmas. Paintings by Joseph Walser from Chapel of Our Lady of Comfort, Dux. T* **391** *and similar horiz designs. Multicoloured.* P 13½ × 14.

1209	70r. Type **391**		75	75
1210	90r. "Nativity"		95	95
1211	1f.10 "Adoration"		1·20	1·20

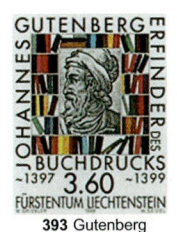

392 Identification Mark on Door, Übersaxen

393 Gutenberg

(Des H. Fritsch. Photo Courvoisier)

1999 (6 Dec). *Walser Identification Marks. T* **392** *and similar vert designs. Multicoloured.* P 11½.

1212	70r. Type **392**		75	75
1213	90r. Mark on mural		95	95
1214	1f.80 Mark on axe		1·90	1·90

(Des Martha Griebler. Eng W. Seidel. Recess and photo Austrian State Ptg Wks, Vienna)

1999 (6 Dec). *600th Birth Anniv of Johannes Gutenberg (inventor of printing press).* P 13½.

1215	393	3f.60 multicoloured	2·75	2·75

394 "The Adoration of the Shepherds" (Matthias Stomer)

395 Emblem

(Des Karin Beck. Photo Courvoisier)

2000 (1 Jan). *2000 Years of Christianity. Sheet* 108 × 68 mm *containing T* **394** *and similar square design. Multicoloured.* P 12.

MS1216	70r. Type **394**; 1f.10, "Three Kings" (Ferdinand Gehr)		1·75	1·75

(Des H. P. Gassner. Photo Courvoisier)

2000 (1 Jan). *Provision of Postal Services by Liechtenstein Post in Partnership with Swiss Post.* P 11½.

1217	395	90r. multicoloured	95	95

396 "Mars and Rhea Silvia" (Peter Paul Rubens)

397 "Fragrance of Humus"

(Des Cornelia Eberle. Eng W. Seidel. Recess and photo Austrian State Ptg Wks, Vienna)

2000 (6 Mar). *Paintings. T* **396** *and similar horiz design. Multicoloured.* P 13½ × 13.

1218	70r. Type **396**		75	75
1219	1f.80 "Cupid with Soap-Bubble" (Rembrandt)		1·90	1·90

(Eng W. Seidel. Recess and photo Austrian State Ptg Wks, Vienna)

2000 (9 May). *"EXPO 2000" World's Fair, Hanover, Germany. T* **397** *and similar vert designs showing paintings by Friedensreich Hundertwasser. Multicoloured.* P 14 × 13½.

1220	70r. Type **397**		75	75
1221	90r. "Do Not Wait Houses-Move"		1·00	1·00
1222	1f.10 "The Car: a Drive Towards Nature and Creation"		1·20	1·20

255

LIECHTENSTEIN   2000

398 "Building Europe"

399 "Dove of Peace" (Antonio Martini)

(Des J.-P. Cousin. Photo Courvoisier)

2000 (9 May). *Europa.* P $11\frac{1}{2} \times 12$.
1223   398   1f.10 multicoloured . . . . 1·10   1·10

(Des Marianne Siegl. Photo Courvoisier)

2000 (9 May). *"Peace 2000".* T **399** *and similar horiz designs showing paintings by members of Association of Mouth and Foot Painting Artists. Multicoloured.* P $12 \times 11\frac{1}{2}$.
1224   1f.40 Type **399** . . . . 1·50   1·50
1225   1f.70 "World Peace" (Alberto Alvarez) . . . . 1·80   1·80
1226   2f.20 "Rainbow" (Eiichi Minami) . . . . 2·30   2·30

400 Koalas on Rings (Gymnastics)

401 "The Dreaming Bee" (Joan Miró)

(Des Rapello. Photo Courvoisier)

2000 (4 Sept). *Olympic Games Sydney.* T **400** *and similar horiz designs. Multicoloured.* P 12.
1227   80r. Type **400** 80   80
1228   1f. Joey leaping over crossbar (High jump) 95   95
1229   1f.30 Emus approaching finish line (Athletics) . . . . 1·40   1·40
1230   1f.80 Duckbill platypuses in swimming race . . . . 1·90   1·90

(Des Cornelia Eberle. Eng W. Seidel (2 f.). Recess. State Ptg Wks, Vienna (2 f.) or photo Courvoisier (others))

2000 (4 Sept). *Inauguration of Art Museum.* T **401** *and similar vert designs. Multicoloured.* P $14 \times 13\frac{1}{2}$ (2 f.) or 12 (others).
1231   80r. Type **401** 85   85
1232   1f.20 "Cube" (Sol LeWitt) . . . . 1·30   1·30
1233   2f. "Bouquet of Flowers" (Roelant Savery) (31 × 46 mm) . . . . 2·00   2·00

402 "Peace Doves"

403 Root Crib

(Des H. P. Gassner. Photo Courvoisier)

2000 (4 Sept). *25th Anniv of Organization for Security and Co-operation in Europe.* P $12 \times 11\frac{1}{2}$.
1234   **402**   1f.30 multicoloured . . . . 1·40   1·40

(Des Ursula Kühne. Eng W. Seidel. Recess and photo State Ptg Wks, Vienna)

2000 (4 Dec). *Christmas. Cribs.* T **403** *and similar horiz designs. Multicoloured.* P 14.
1235   80r. Type **403** 80   80
1236   1f.30 Oriental crib . . . . 1·40   1·40
1237   1f.80 Crib with cloth figures . . . . 1·90   1·90

(Des Iris Heeb. Eng. W. Seidel. Recess and photo State Ptg Wks, Vienna)

2000 (4 Dec). *Fungi. Square designs as* T **370**. *Multicoloured.* P 14.
1238   90r. *Mycena adonis* 90   90
1239   1f.10 *Chalciporus amarellus* . . . . 1·20   1·20
1240   2f. Pink waxcap (*Hygrocybe calyptriformis*) . . . . 2·10   2·10

404 Postman delivering Parcel

405 Silver Easter Egg

(Des Rapallo. Photo Courvoisier)

2001 (5 Mar). *Greetings Stamps.* T **404** *and similar horiz design. Multicoloured. Granite paper.* P $12 \times 11\frac{1}{2}$.
1241   70r. Type **404** 75   75
1242   70r. Postman delivering flowers 75   75
Nos. 1241/2 are for the stamps with the parcel (1241) and flowers (1242) intact. The parcel and flowers can be scratched away to reveal a greetings message.

(Des Silvia Ruppen. Eng W.Seidel. Recess and photo State Ptg Wks, Vienna)

2001 (5 Mar). *Decorated Easter Eggs.* T **405** *and similar vert designs. Multicoloured.* P $13\frac{1}{2} \times 14$.
1243   1f.20 Type **405** . . . . 1·30   1·30
1244   1f.80 Cloissonné egg . . . . 2·00   2·00
1245   2f. Porcelain egg . . . . 2·00   2·00

406 Mountain Spring

407 Emblem

(Des J. Schädler. Photo Courvoisier)

2001 (5 Mar). *Europa. Water Resources. Granite paper.* P $11\frac{1}{2} \times 12$.
1246   **406**   1f.30 multicoloured . . . . 1·40   1·40

LIECHTENSTEIN 2001

(Des H. P. Gassner. Photo Courvoisier)

2001 (5 Mar). *Liechtenstein Presidency of Council of Europe. Granite paper.* P 11½ × 11½.
1247 407 1f.80 multicoloured . . . . . . 1·90 1·90

408 Carolingian Cruciform Fibula

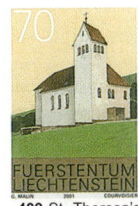

409 St. Theresa's Chapel, Schaanwald

(Des G. Malin. Photo Courvoisier)

2001 (5 June). *Centenary of Historical Association.* T **408** and similar vert designs. Multicoloured. Granite paper. P 11½ × 12.
1248 70r. Type **408** 75 75
1249 70r. "Mars of Gutenberg" (statue) . . . 75 75

(Des G. Malin. Photo Courvoisier)

2001 (3 Sept). *Preservation of Historical Environment.* T **409** and similar vert designs. Multicoloured. P 11½.
1250 70r. Type **409** 75 75
1251 90r. St. Johann's Torkel (wine press), Mauren . . . . . . 1·00 1·00
1252 1f.10 Pirsch Transformer Station, Schaanwald . . . . . . 1·10 1·10

410 Mary and kneeling Votant (Chapel of Our Lady, Dux, Schann)

411 Rheinberger and Scene from *Zauberwort* (song cycle)

(Des Marianne Siegl. Eng W. Seidel. Recess and photo State Ptg Wks, Vienna)

2001 (3 Sept). *Votive Paintings.* T **410** and similar vert designs. Multicoloured. P 13½.
1253 70r. Type **410** 70 70
1254 1f.20 Mary and Jesus, St. George among other Saints, and text of vow (St. George's Chapel, Schellenberg) . . . . . . 1·20 1·20
1255 1f.30 Mary, St. Joseph of Arimathea, St. Christopher, Johann Christoph Walser (votant) and text of vow (Chapel of Our Lady, Dux, Schann) . . . . . . 1·50 1·50

(Des Martha Griebler. Eng W. Seidel Recess and photo State Ptg Wks, Vienna)

2001 (3 Sept). *Death Centenary of Josef Gabriel Rheinberger (composer).* P 14.
1256 **411** 3f.50 multicoloured . . . . . . 3·75 3·75

(Des J. Schädler. Photo Courvoisier)

2001 (3 Dec). *Traditional Crafts (2nd series). Square designs as* T **380**. *Multicoloured.* P 12.
1257 70r. Agricultural implements and horseshoe 75 75
1258 90r. Rake . . . . . . 1·00 1·00
1259 1f.20 Harness . . . . . . 1·30 1·30

412 "Annunciation"

413 Square

2001 (3 Dec). *Christmas.* T **412** and similar vert designs showing medallions from The Joyful, Sorrowful and Glorious Rosary Cycle. Multicoloured. P 12.
1260 70r. Type **412** 70 70
1261 90r. Nativity 90 90
1262 1f.30 Presentation of Jesus at the Temple . . . . . . 1·50 1·50

(Photo Courvoisier)

2001 (3 Dec). *Paintings by Gottfried Honeggar.* T **413** and similar vert design. Multicoloured. P 11½.
1263 1f.80 Type **413** . . . . . . 2·00 2·00
1264 2f.20 Circle . . . . . . 2·20 2·20

414 Mountains and River

415 "Schellenberg"

(Des L. Jäger. Photo State Ptg Wks, Vienna)

2002 (4 Mar). *International Year of Mountains and 50th Anniv of the International Commission of Alpine Protection.* T **414** and similar vert design. Multicoloured. P 14 × 13½.
1265 70r. Type **414** 65 65
1266 1f.20 Stylized mountains . . . . . . 1·10 1·10

(Des Marianne Siegl. Photo State Ptg Wks, Vienna)

2002 (4 Mar). *30th Death Anniv of Friedrich Kaufmann (artist).* T **415** and similar horiz designs. Multicoloured. P 13½ × 14.
1267 70r. Type **415** 65 65
1268 1f.30 "Schaan" . . . . . . 1·20 1·20
1269 1f.80 "Steg" . . . . . . 3·50 3·50

416 Space Shuttle and Bee

417 Man on Tightrope

(Des Silvia Ruppen. Photo State Ptg Wks, Vienna)

2002 (4 Mar). *Liechtenstein's participation in NASA Space Technology and Research Students Project.* P 13½ × 14.
1270 **416** 90r. multicoloured 85 85

The project submitted by the Liechtenstein Gymnasium concerned the study of the effects of space on carpenter bees.

257

LIECHTENSTEIN 2002

(Des P. Flora. Eng W. Seidel. Recess and photo State Ptg Wks, Vienna)

2002 (4 Mar). *Europa. Circus.* T **417** and similar horiz design. Multicoloured. P 14½ × 14.
| 1271 | 90r. Type **417** | 85 | 85 |
| 1272 | 1f.30 Juggler | 1·20 | 1·20 |

418 Emblem
419 Houses, Popers

(Des Cornelia Eberle. Photo State Ptg Wks, Vienna)

2002 (4 Mar). *"Liba '02" National Stamp Exhibition, Vaduz* (1st issue). P 14 × 13½.
| 1273 | **418** | 1f.20 multicoloured | 1·10 | 1·10 |

(Des G. Malin. Photo State Ptg Wks, Vienna)

2002 (3 June). *Preservation of Historical Environment* (2nd series). T **419** and similar horiz design. Multicoloured. P 14 × 13½.
| 1274 | 70r. Type **419** | 65 | 65 |
| 1275 | 1f.20 House, Weiherring | 1·10 | 1·10 |

420 Footballers
421 Princess Marie

(Des S. Bockmühl. Photo State Ptg Wks, Vienna)

2002 (3 June). *World Cup Football Championship, Japan and South Korea.* P 13½ × 14.
| 1276 | **420** | 1f.80 multicoloured | 1·70 | 1·70 |

(Des Marianne Siegl. Photo State Ptg Wks, Vienna)

2002 (3 June). *The Royal Couple.* T **421** and similar horiz design. Multicoloured. P 13½.
| 1277 | 3f. Type **421** | 2·75 | 2·75 |
| 1278 | 3f.50 Prince Hans-Adam II | 3·25 | 3·25 |

422 Ghost Orchid (*Epipogium aphyllum*)
423 Stamps and Emblem

(Des Regina Marxer. Photo State Ptg Wks, Vienna)

2002 (8 Aug). *Orchids.* T **422** and similar vert designs. Multicoloured. P 13½.
1279	70r. Type **422**	65	65
1280	1f.20 Fly orchid (*Ophrys insectifera*)	1·10	1·10
1281	1f.30 Black vanilla orchid (*Nigritella nigra*)	1·20	1·20

(Des Cornelia Eberle. Photo State Ptg Wks, Vienna)

2002 (8 Aug). *"Liba 02" National Stamp Exhibition, Vaduz* (2nd issue). 90th Anniv of First Liechtenstein Stamps. T **423** and similar vert design. Multicoloured. P 13½.
| 1282 | 90r. Type **423** | 85 | 85 |
| 1283 | 1f.30 Stamps showing royal family | 1·20 | 1·20 |

424 Princess Sophie
425 Mary and Joseph

(Des Marianne Siegl. Photo State Ptg Wks, Vienna)

2002 (8 Aug). *Prince Alois and Princess Sophie.* T **424** and similar horiz design. Multicoloured. P 13½.
| 1284 | 2f. Type **424** | 1·90 | 1·90 |
| 1285 | 2f.50 Prince Alois | 2·30 | 2·30 |

(Des Regina Hassler. Photo State Ptg Wks, Vienna)

2002 (25 Nov). *Christmas. Batik.* T **425** and similar vert designs. Multicoloured. P 14 × 13½.
1286	70r. Type **425**	65	65
1287	1f.20 Nativity	1·10	1·10
1288	1f.80 Flight into Egypt	1·70	1·70

426 The Eagle, Vaduz
427 St. Fridolin Parish Church

(Des S. Scherrer. Eng W. Seidel Recess and photo State Ptg Wks, Vienna)

2002 (25 Nov). *Inn Signs.* T **426** and similar horiz designs. Multicoloured. P 13½ × 14.
1289	1f.20 Type **426**	1·10	1·10
1290	1f.80 The Angel, Balzers	1·70	1·70
1291	3f. The Eagle, Bendern	2·75	2·75

(Des G. Malin. State Ptg Wks, Vienna)

2003 (3 Mar). *Preservation of Historical Environment* (3rd series). T **427** and similar multicoloured design. P 13½.
| 1292 | 70r. Type **427** | 65 | 65 |
| 1293 | 2f.50 House, Spidach (*horiz*) | 2·30 | 2·30 |

428 Postal Emblem
429 Pruning Vines

LIECHTENSTEIN 2003

(Des Karin Beck. Litho State Ptg Wks, Vienna)
2003 (3 Mar). *Europa. Poster Art.* P 13½ × 13.
| 1294 | **428** | 1f.20 multicoloured | 1·10 | 1·10 |

(Des Martha Griebler. Litho State Ptg Wks, Vienna)
2003 (3 Mar). *Viticulture.* T **429** *and similar square designs.* Multicoloured. P 14.
1295	1f.30 Type **429**	1·20	1·20
1296	1f.80 Tying up vines	1·70	1·70
1297	2f.20 Hoeing	2·00	2·00

MACHINE LABELS

A   B

From 4 December 1995 pre-printed gummed labels in eleven designs as Type A were available from automatic machines, the value being overprinted at the tune of purchase according to the customer's requirements. Values from 10r. to 99f.90, in 10r. steps, could be dispensed.

The eleven labels, designed by E Frick and printed in photogravure by Courvoisrer on granite paper, show the following commune arms: Vaduz, Planken, Ruggell, Schaan, Sehellenberg, Balzers, Eschen, Gamprin, Mauren, Triesen and Triesenberg.

A new issue was released on 2 June 2003, as type B, the twelve labels, designed by Marianne Siegel illustrated streets and buildings from Nerdeln, Ruggell, Schaanwald, Vaduz, Eschen, Mauren, Triesen, Triesenburg, Schellenburg, Balzers, Schaan, and Gamprin- Bendern. The labels were printed by Flexography.

SAN MARINO 1865

San Marino

100 Centesimi = 1 Lira

REPUBLIC

According to tradition, the Republic of San Marino was founded in the 4th century by Marinus, a stonecutter from the island of Arbe (now Rab), who had fled from Rimini to escape religious persecution.

Early letters from San Marino were taken to Rimini for posting. A separate receiving office was opened in the Republic during 1833, but the mail continued to be routed via Rimini where, from 1852, stamps of the Papal States, Romagna or Sardinia were applied There were no postal markings during this period to distinguish mail from San Marino.

From 1862 Sardinian and then Italian stamps were affixed at San Marino. A boxed straight-line "S. MARINO" handstamp was applied to the front or back of covers but the stamps continued to be cancelled with the Rimini datestamp (although some adhesives are known with both markings).

In 1865 a postal convention with Italy was signed under which San Marino processed its own mail. Italian stamps continued to be used until 1877. Such use can be identified by the cancellations of which there were two types:

A   B

PRICES. Prices of Nos Z1/12 are for loose examples with full San Marino cancellation in the cheapest version (usually with Type B). Poor cancels are worth less, stamps on piece with exceptionally clear postmarks and stamps on cover are worth more.

1865–77. Stamps of Italy cancelled with Type A or B.

(a) Nos. 8/15.

Z1	4	1c. green	£190
Z2	5	2c. brown	£140
Z3	6	5c. grey	35·00
Z4		10c. buff	35·00
Z5		15c. blue	—
Z6		30c. brown	£130
Z7		40c. rose	£140
Z8		60c. mauve	£275

(b) Nos 17/19.

Z9	6	20c.on 15c. dull blue (I)	46·00
Z10		20c.on 15c. dull blue (II)	£100
Z11		20c.on 15c. dull blue (III)	32·00

(c) No 20/a.

Z12	10	20c. pale blue	55·00
		a. Bright blue	19·00

Only three examples of No. Z5 are known.

PRINTERS. Until 1926 the stamps of San Marino were printed at the Italian Government Printing Works, Turin, *except where otherwise stated*.

1   2

(Des and eng E. Repettati, Turin. Typo)

1877 (1 Aug)–**90**. Wmk Crown, T **8** of Italy (sideways). P 14.

1	1	2c. green	17·00	3·00
2	2	5c. yellow (1.4.90)	£130	8·00
3		10c. ultramarine	£140	8·00
3a		10c. blue (1.4.90)	£200	22·00
4		20c. pale red	7·00	1·70
5		25c. claret (1.4.90)	£150	7·25
6		30c. brown	£1100	36·00
7		40c. mauve	£1100	36·00

See also Nos. 18/28 and 32/37.

$C\underline{\underline{mi.}}$ 5 (3) $C\underline{\underline{mi.}}$ 5 (4)

$C\underline{\underline{mi.}}$ 5 (5) $C\underline{\underline{mi.}}$ 5 (6)

$C\underline{\underline{mi.}}$ 10 (7) $C\underline{\underline{mi.}}$ 10 (8)

$C\underline{\underline{mi.}}$ 10 (9) $C\underline{\underline{mi.}}$ 10 (10)

$C\underline{\underline{mi.}}$ 10   10 (11)   (12) 10

1892. T **2** surch, by Angeli and Co., San Marino.

8	3	5c.on 10c. ultramarine (27.6)	£22000	£3500
9	4	5c.on 10c. ultramarine (27.6)	£19000	£2750
10	5	5c.on 10c. ultramarine (27.6)	£19000	£2750
10a	6	5c.on 10c. ultramarine (27.6)	£19000	£2750
10b	3	5c.on 10c. blue (27.6)	55·00	12·50
10c	4	5c.on 10c. blue (27.6)	49·00	11·50
10d	5	5c.on 10c. blue (27.6)	49·00	11·50
10e	6	5c.on 10c. blue (27.6)	49·00	11·50
11	3	5c.on 30c. brown (16.6)	£375	48·00
12	4	5c.on 30c. brown (16.6)	£325	35·00
		a. "Gmi." for "Cmi."	£475	65·00
13	5	5c.on 30c. brown (16.6)	£325	44·00
14	6	5c.on 30c. brown (16.6)	£325	44·00
14a	7	10c.on 20c. vermilion (10.7)	21·00	2·75
15	8	10c.on 20c. vermilion (10.7)	21·00	2·75
16	9	10c.on 20c. vermilion (10.7)	21·00	2·75
16a	10	10c.on 20c. vermilion (10.7)	21·00	2·75
16b	11	10c.on 20c. vermilion (10.7)	21·00	2·75
17	12	10c.on 20c. vermilion (17.9)	£475	4·50

There are also many other minor varieties.

All of the above exist with surcharge *inverted* and are worth about 25% more than the corresponding normal stamps.

1892 (10 July)–**94**. Colours changed and new values. Wmk Crown (sideways). P 14.

18	1	2c. blue (1.4.94)	11·50	2·75
19	2	5c. olive-green	3·00	1·70
20		10c. blue-green (1.4.94)	7·00	1·70
21		15c. lake (1.4.94)	85·00	22·00
22		30c. yellow	7·00	6·25
23		40c. brown	7·00	2·75
24		45c. yellow-green	7·00	3·00
25		65c. chestnut (1.4.94)	7·00	2·50
26		1l. red and yellow	£2000	£325
27		2l. brown and buff (1.4.94)	£2000	£275
28		5l. lake and blue (1.4.94)	£190	£100

The lire values have value tablets in upper corners.

SAN MARINO 1894

13 Government Palace

14 Government Palace

15 Interior of Government Palace

16

17 Statue of Liberty

18

19 Mt. Titano

(T **17/19** des C. Carpaneto. Typo)

1899 (5 Feb). *For internal use.* Wmk Crown. P 14.
38	**17**	2c. brown	2·00	75
39		5c. brown-orange	4·25	1·40

See also Nos. 86/91.

1903 (1 Apr). Wmk Crown (sideways). P 14.
40	**18**	2c. lilac	9·50	2·00
41	**19**	5c. blue-green	6·00	1·10
42		10c. carmine-pink	5·50	85
43		20c. brown-orange	£110	15·00
44		25c. blue	12·00	2·20
45		30c. lake	6·50	4·25
46		40c. vermilion	9·50	5·25
47		45c. yellow	9·50	5·50
48		65c. deep brown	9·50	5·50
49		1l. olive-green	23·00	7·50
50		2l. bright violet	£375	£130
51		5l. steel blue	£225	95·00
40/51	*Set of* 12		£700	£250

See also Nos. 73/85 and 111/22.

Medallions show the Captains-Regent Pietro Tonnini and Francesco Marcucci.

(Des F. Azzurri. Litho Grand Didier and Bruno, Turin)

1894 (30 Sept). *Opening of Government Palace and Installation of Captains-Regent.* W **16** (sideways on 1l.). P 15½ × 15 or 15 × 15½ (1l.).
29	**13**	25c. maroon and blue	4·50	70
30	**14**	50c. maroon and red	18·00	2·40
31	**15**	1l. maroon and green	14·50	3·25

1894 (30 Dec)–**99**. *Colours changed.* Wmk Crown (sideways). P 14.
32	**1**	2c. claret	9·50	3·25
33	**2**	5c. blue-green (15.6.99)	5·25	1·70
34		10c. brown-lake (15.6.99)	5·25	2·20
35		20c. lilac	6·00	2·75
36		25c. blue (15.6.99)	5·25	2·50
37		1l. pale ultramarine	£2000	£275

1905

15 (20)

1905

15 (21)

E **22** Mt. Titano and "Liberty"

1905 (1 Sept). *No.* 43 *surch with T* **20**.
52	**19**	15c.on 20c. brown-orange	10·50	2·75
		a. Larger "5" in "1905" (T **21**)	70·00	35·00

(Recess Officina Calcografica Italiana, Rome)

1907 (25 Apr). *EXPRESS LETTER.* P 12.
E53	E **22**	25c. rose	19·00	6·75

D 17

D 18

22

23

(Des and eng E. Repettati. Typo)

1897 (1 Apr)–**1919**. *POSTAGE DUE. Values in brown.* Wmk Crown (sideways).
D38	D **17**	5c. green	20	25
D39	D **18**	10c. green	20	25
		a. Centre inverted	£100	
D40		30c. green	1·40	60
D41		50c. green	3·00	1·20
		a. Centre inverted	£100	
D42		60c. green	14·50	4·50
D43	D **17**	1l. rose	5·75	2·75
D44		3l. rose (15.9.19)	19·00	10·50
D45		5l. rose	70·00	29·00
D46	D **18**	10l. rose	26·00	19·00
D38/46	*Set of* 9		£130	60·00

See also Nos. D102/10, D111/29 and D164/78.

(Des Ortolani. Recess Officina Calcografica Italiana, Rome)

1907 (1 May)–**10**. *Yellowish background.* P 12.
  I. Heavy printing. Clear lines of shading 18½ × 25 mm.
  II. Fine printing. Faint lines of shading 19 × 25 mm.
53	**22**	1c. brown (I)	11·00	1·40
		a. Type II (10.5.10)	3·75	1·10
54	**23**	15c. slate (I)	15·00	1·80
		a. Type II (22.5.10)	£425	11·00

SAN MARINO 1917

1917 Cent. 20

Pro combattenti

Cent. 50 1918
(24)   (25)

1917 (15 Dec). *For Combatants. Surch as T* **24**.
55	18	25c.on 2c. lilac	7·00	2·00
		a. "ro" widely spaced	8·25	8·00
		b. "en" of "enti" widely spaced	8·25	8·00
		c. "17" widely spaced	8·25	8·00
56	19	50c.on 2l. violet	39·00	20·00
		a. "19" widely spaced	80·00	85·00

1918 (15 Mar). *Surch with T* **25**.
57	23	20c.on 15c. slate (R)	3·25	1·40
		a. Capital "I" for first figure "1" of "1918" (pos. 49)	17·00	14·50

26 Statue of Liberty

27 View of San Marino

(Des C. Carpeneto. Typo)

1918 (1 June). *War Casualties Fund. Centres in black.* Wmk Crown (sideways on T **26**). P12.
58	26	2c. (+5 c.) dull lilac	1·20	40
59		5c. (+5 c.) blue-green	1·20	40
60		10c. (+5 c.) carmine	1·20	40
61		20c. (+5 c.) brown-orange	1·20	40
62		25c. (+5 c.) bright ultramarine	1·40	40
63		45c. (+5 c.) brown	1·40	40
64	27	1l. (+5 c.) blue-green	14·00	10·00
65		2l. (+5 c.) lilac	15·00	6·75
66		3l. (+5 c.) carmine	15·00	6·75
58/66	*Set of 9*		46·00	23·00

3 Novembre

1918   3 Novembre 1918
(28)   (29)

1918 (12 Dec). *Italian Victory over Austria and War Casualties Fund. Optd with T* **28** *(with two bars at foot) or* **29**. *Centres in black.*
67	26	20c. (+5c.) brown-orange	2·20	1·40
68		25c. (+5c.) bright ultramarine	2·20	1·40
69		45c. (+5c.) brown	2·20	1·40
70	27	1l. (+5c.) blue-green	6·00	2·50
71		2l. (+5c.) lilac	13·50	6·75
72		3l. (+5c.) carmine	13·50	6·25
67/72	*Set of 6*		36·00	18·00

1921 (31 Oct)–**23**. *Colours changed.* Wmk Crown (sideways). P 14.
73	18	2c. chestnut	1·30	40
74	19	5c. olive-green	2·10	40
75		10c. brown-orange	1·50	40
76		15c. blue-green	1·30	40
77		20c. brown	1·50	40
78		25c. slate (2.22)	1·50	40
79		30c. magenta	1·30	40
80		40c. rose	1·20	40
81		50c. dull purple (5.23)	1·90	60
82		80c. blue (8.22)	2·50	1·60
83		90c. brown (5.23)	3·00	1·60
84		1l. pale ultramarine	1·60	65
85		2l. orange-red	13·50	10·50
73/85	*Set of 13*		31·00	16·00

1922 (Feb–Aug). *Colours changed.* Wmk Crown. P 14.
86	17	2c. purple (Feb)	25	20
87		5c. olive-green (Feb)	35	20
88		10c. orange-brown	35	20
89		20c. chocolate	35	20
90		25c. pale ultramarine	75	40
91		45c. lake	1·70	80
86/91	*Set of 6*		3·25	1·80

ESPRESSO   Cent. 60
(E 30)   (E 31)

1923 (30 May). *EXPRESS LETTER. Optd with Type E* **30**. Wmk Crown. P 14.
E92	19	60c. violet	50	40

1923 (26 July). *EXPRESS LETTER. Surch with Type E* **31**. Wmk Crown. P 14.
E93	E 22	60c. on 25c. rose	50	40

Nos. E92/3 were not issued without overprint or surcharge.

30 Arbe (Rab)

31 St. Marinus

(Des V. Moraldi. Eng A. Blasi. Typo Petiti, Rome)

1923 (6 Aug). *Delivery to San Marino of Italian flag flown on Arbe, after the island returned to Yugoslavia.* Wmk Crown. P 14.
92	30	50c. olive-green	45	30

Names of designer, etc. printed on the back.

(Des M. Fucci. Eng A. Blasi. Typo Petiti. Rome)

1923 (11 Aug). *San Marino Mutual Aid Society.* Wmk Crown (sideways). P 14.
93	31	30c. chocolate	45	25

32 Mt. Titano

33 "Liberty"

E **34**

(Des E. Federici. Recess Petiti. Rome)

1923 (20 Sept). *Red Cross Fund.* Wmk Crown (sideways on No. E101). P14.

(a) POSTAGE.
94	32	5c.+ 5c. olive-green	55	20
95		10c.+ 5c. orange	75	20
96		15c.+ 5c. deep green	55	20
97		25c.+ 5c. lake	75	40
98		40c.+ 5c. brown-purple	7·00	1·20
99		50c.+ 5c. grey	3·75	20
100	33	1l.+ 5c. blue and black	8·25	2·75

SAN MARINO   1923

		(b) EXPRESS LETTER.		
E101	E 34	60c.+ 5c. deep red	1·10	1·20
94/E101	Set of 8		20·00	5·75

34   **35** Garibaldi   **36**

(Des U. Amaducci. Typo Petiti, Rome)

1923 (29 Sept). *San Marino Volunteers in Great War.* Wmk Crown (sideways). P 14.
101	34	1l. chocolate	11·50	6·00

1924 (17 July). *POSTAGE DUE. As Nos D38/46 but colours reversed. Values in brown.*
D102	D 17	5c. carmine	20	40
D103	D 18	10c. carmine	20	40
D104		30c. carmine	25	40
D105		50c. carmine	1·50	80
D106		60c. carmine	7·50	40
D107	D 17	1l. green	10·50	6·25
D108		3l. green	22·00	21·00
D109		5l. green	34·00	24·00
D110	D 18	10l. green	£300	£200
D102/110	Set of 9		£350	£225

In these and Nos. D111/29 the letters "C" or "L" of the value differ considerably in several denominations.

(Des M. Fucci. Litho Petiti, Rome)

1924 (25 Sept). *75th Anniv of Garibaldi's Refuge in San Marino.* Wmk Crown (sideways). P 14.
102	35	30c. deep purple	2·20	70
103		50c. brown	3·75	1·60
104		60c. carmine-lake	5·50	2·00
105	36	1l. blue	6·50	3·50
106		2l. green	8·75	4·00
102/106	Set of 5		24·00	10·50

(37)   (38)   60

1924 (9 Oct). *T 26 surch as T 37 (bars over inscr at foot), and T 27 surch as T 38.*
107	26	30c.on 45c. black and brown	1·50	60
108	27	60c.on 1l. black and blue-green	3·00	3·25
109		1l.on 2l. black and lilac	13·50	8·75
110		2l.on 3l. black and carmine	14·50	7·25
107/110	Set of 4		29·00	18·00

C.5 (I)   C.5 (II)

1925 (2 Apr)–**39**. *POSTAGE DUE. As Nos D102/10 but colours changed and new values. Values in brown.*
D111	D 17	5c. blue (I)	25	20
		a. Centre inverted	£110	
D112		5c. blue (II) (9.39)	20	20
D113	D 18	10c. blue	25	20
		a. Centre inverted	£110	
D114		15c. blue (1.5.39)	20	20
D115		20c. blue (1.5.39)	25	20
D116		25c. blue (1.5.39)	30	40
D117		30c. blue	70	20
D118		40c. blue (1.5.39)	4·00	1·60
D119		50c. blue	50	40
		a. Centre inverted	£110	
D120		60c. blue	1·50	60
D121	D 17	1l. orange	7·25	
D122		2l. orange (1.5.39)	1·30	1·20
D123		3l. orange	95·00	21·00
D124		5l. orange	24·00	4·00
D125	D 18	10l. orange	36·00	6·25
D126		15l. orange (22.1.27)	1·00	20
D127		25l. orange (22.1.27)	60·00	12·50
D128		30l. orange (11.6.28)	9·00	5·25
D129		50l. orange (22.1.27)	12·00	6·50
D111/129	Set of 19		£225	55·00

1925 (8 Apr). Wmk Crown (sideways). P 14.
111	19	5c. claret	60	20
112		10c. olive-green	60	20
113		15c. purple	60	20
114		20c. blue-green	60	20
115		25c. bright violet	60	20
116		30c. orange	24·00	65
117		40c. brown	60	20
118		50c. slate	60	20
119		60c. carmine	1·00	20
120		1l. blue	1·00	40
121		2l. yellow-green	9·00	3·00
122		5l. blue	24·00	10·25
111/122	Set of 12		55·00	14·50

Cent. 75   (39)   40 A. Onofri

1926 (1 July). *Stamps of 1921–23 surch as T 39.*
123	19	75c.on 80c. blue	1·60	60
124		1l.20 on 90c. brown	1·60	60
125		1l.25 on 90c. brown (R.)	3·50	1·60
126		2l.50 on 80c. blue (R.)	8·25	4·00
123/126	Set of 4		13·50	6·00

(Des E. Federici. Recess)

1926 (29 July). *Death Centenary of Antonio Onofri, "Father of the Country". P 11.*
127	40	10c. black and indigo	30	20
128		20c. black and grey-olive	95	50
129		45c. black and violet	55	60
130		65c. black and olive-green	55	60
131		1l. black and orange	4·25	2·40
132		2l. black and magenta	4·25	2·40
127/132	Set of 6		9·75	6·00

Lire 1,85 (41)   1,25 (42)

1926 (25 Nov). *No. E92 surch with T 41 for ordinary use.*
133	19	1l.85 on 60c. violet	45	40

1926 (25 Nov). *EXPRESS LETTER. No. E92 surch as in T 41.*
E134	19	1l.25 on 60c. violet	90	60

1927 (10 Mar). *Surch as T 42.*
134	40	"1.25" on 1l. black and orange	5·50	2·00
135		"2.50" on 2l. black and magenta	8·50	4·00
136		"5" on 2l. black and magenta	33·00	28·00

SAN MARINO   1927

(43) 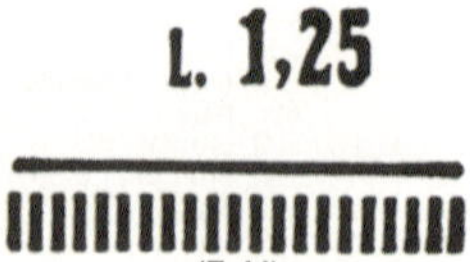   (E 44)

1927 (15 Sept). *Unissued Express stamp (No 115 surch "ESPRESSO" as Type E 30 and "50") surch as in T 43.*
137   19   1l.75on 50 on 25c. bright violet   95   60

1927 (15 Sept). EXPRESS LETTER. *No E93 further surch with Type E 44.*
E138   E 22   1l.25on 60c. on 25c. rose   65   55

PRINTERS, etc.—The following issues to No. **MS**232*b* were designed by E. Federici, and engraved and recess-printed by Bradbury, Wilkinson & Co., *unless otherwise stated.*

44 San Marino War Memorial

45 Franciscan Convent and Capuchin Church

1927 (28 Sept). *War Cenotaph Commemoration.* P 12.
138   44   50c. plum . . . .   1·40   80
139   —   1l.25, blue . . . .   2·50   1·20
140   —   10l. blackish violet . . . .   24·00   12·50

1928 (2 Jan). *700th Death Anniv of St. Francis of Assisi.* T **45** *and similar type inscr* "VII CENTENARIO FRANCESCANO". P 12.
141   45   50c. scarlet . . . .   23·00   1·90
142   —   1l.25 blue . . . .   9·50   2·50
143   —   2l.50 chocolate . . . .   9·50   3·00
144   —   5l. dull violet . . . .   27·00   18·00
141/144 *Set of* 4 . . . .   60·00   23·00
Design:—2l.50, 5l. Death of St Francis.

P 46

(Des E. Federici. Recess (values typo) Staderini, Rome)
1928 (22 Nov). *PARCEL POST.* P 12.
P145   P 46   5c. brown-purple and blue   30   20
P146   —   10c. blue and light blue   30   20
P147   —   20c. black and blue   30   20
P148   —   25c. crimson and blue   30   20
P149   —   30c. ultramarine and blue   30   20
P150   —   50c. orange and blue   30   20
P151   —   60c. carmine and blue   30   20
P152   —   1l. violet and red   30   20
P153   —   2l. blue-green and red   85   40
P154   —   3l. bistre and red . . . .   1·00   80
P155   —   4l. grey and red . . . .   1·20   1·00
P156   —   10l. magenta and red . . . .   4·00   1·60
P157   —   12l. brown-lake and red . . . .   14·00   5·75
P158   —   15l. olive-green and red . . . .   23·00   12·50
P159   —   20l. purple and red . . . .   30·00   19·00
P145/159 *Set of* 15 . . . .   70·00   38·00
Both unused and used prices are for complete pairs.
See also Nos. P309/25, P454/5, P522/6 and P770/5.

46 La Rocca Fortress    47 Government Palace    48 Statue of Liberty

49    E 50 Statue of Liberty and View of San Marino

1929 (28 Mar)–**35**. W **49**. P 12.
145   46   5c. ultramarine and maroon . . . .   1·40   40
146   —   10c. mauve and greenish blue . . . .   2·00   40
147   —   15c. emerald and orange . . . .   1·70   40
148   —   20c. red and blue . . . .   1·70   40
149   —   25c. black and green . . . .   1·70   40
150   —   30c. vermilion and grey . . . .   1·70   40
151   —   50c. grey-green and purple . . . .   1·70   40
152   —   75c. grey and scarlet . . . .   1·70   40
153   47   1l. emerald and chocolate . . . .   2·00   40
154   —   1l.25 black and blue . . . .   2·00   40
155   —   1l.75 orange and emerald . . . .   3·25   80
156   —   2l. scarlet and grey-blue . . . .   2·50   80
157   —   2l.50 ultramarine and crimson . . . .   2·50   80
158   —   3l. blue and orange . . . .   2·50   80
159   —   3l.70 maroon & grey-grn (14.4.35) . . . .   2·50   1·00
160   48   5l. myrtle-green and violet . . . .   2·75   1·00
161   —   10l. blue and bistre-brown . . . .   9·25   4·00
162   —   15l. purple and myrtle-green . . . .   46·00   48·00
163   —   20l. scarlet and deep ultramarine £300   £200
145/163 *Set of* 19 . . . .   £350   £250

1929 (29 Aug). EXPRESS LETTER. W **49**. P 12.
(a) Type E **50** *(but without* "UNION POSTALE UNIVERSELLE" *and inscr* "ESPRESSO").
E164   —   1l.25, green   20   15
(b) Optd "UNION POSTALE UNIVERSELLE" *as in Type* E **50**.
E165   E **50**   2l.50 blue (R.)   75   65

(D 50)    50 Mt. Titano

1931 (18 May). *POSTAGE DUE Nos. D111, D113 and D117 with centres obliterated, in black, and new values superimposed in silver, as Type* D **50**.
D164   D 17   15c.on 5c. blue   25   20
D165   D 18   15c.on 10c. blue   25   20
D166   —   15c.on 30c. blue   25   20
D167   D 17   20c.on 5c. blue   25   20
D168   D 18   20c.on 10c. blue   25   20
D169   —   20c.on 30c. blue   25   20
D170   D 17   25c.on 5c. blue . . . .   1·50   40
D171   D 18   25c.on 10c. blue . . . .   1·30   40
D172   —   25c.on 30c. blue . . . .   16·00   4·00
D173   D 17   40c.on 5c. blue . . . .   1·30   20
D174   D 18   40c.on 10c. blue . . . .   1·50   20

SAN MARINO 1946

84 U.N.R.R.A. Aid for San Marino

(Des F. Martelli. Recess, background litho)

1946 (14 Mar). *United Nations Relief and Rehabilitation Administration.* P 14.
324 84 100l. red, purple and orange 8·00 3·50

85 Airplane and Mt. Titano (86)

(Des G. Zani)

1946 (8 Aug)–**47**. *AIR.* T **85** *and similar designs.* P 14.

(a) Photo. No wmk.
325	–	25c. blue-grey	15	15
326	85	75c. orange-red	15	15
327	–	1l. brown	15	15
328	85	2l. grey-green	15	15
329	–	3l. violet	15	15
330	–	5l. royal blue	15	15
331	–	10l. rose-red	15	15
332	–	35l. vermilion (11.46)	3·50	3·25
333	–	100l. deep brown (27.3.47)	1·10	1·20

(b) Recess. Wmk Winged Wheel.
334	–	20l. claret	65	1·60
335	–	50l. bronze green	7·50	5·25
325/335		Set of 11	11·50	10·00

Designs: *Horiz*—25c., 1, 10l. Wings over Mt. Titano; 100l. Airplane over globe. *Vert*—5, 20, 35, 50l. Four aircraft over Mt. Titano.

1946 (28 Aug). *Stamp Day. No. 323 surch with T* **86** *(additional premium).*
336 83 50l. + 10l. blue and brown-olive (R.) 14·00 8·25

E **87** Pegasus and Mt. Titano (86a)

(Eng L. Orestano. Recess)

1946 (21 Nov). *EXPRESS LETTER.* P 14.
E337 E **87** 30l. ultramarine 4·75 3·75
See also No. E420.

1946 (30 Nov). *National Philatelic Convention. Nos. 329/31 but in new colours and without "POSTA AEREA" surch as T* **86a** *in red.*
336a	3l. + 25l. sepia	55	80
336b	5l. + 25l. orange	55	80
336c	10l. + 50l. blue	6·75	6·25

87 Quotation from F.D.R. on Liberty

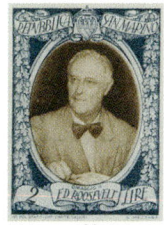

88 Franklin D. Roosevelt

(Des C. Mezzana)

1947 (3 May). *In Memory of President Franklin D. Roosevelt.* T **87**/**8** *and other portrait designs.* Wmk Winged Wheel. P 14.

(a) POSTAGE.
336d	87	1l. brown and ochre	10	20
336e	88	2l. sepia and blue	10	20
336f	–	5l. multicoloured	10	20
336g	–	15l. multicoloured	10	20
336h	87	50l. sepia and vermilion	65	20
336i	88	100l. sepia and violet	1·10	80
336d/i		Set of 6	1·90	1·60

Design: *Horiz*—5l., 15l. Roosevelt and flags of San Marino and U.S.A.

(b) AIR. Inscr "POSTA AEREA".
336j		1l. sepia and ultramarine	10	20
336k		2l. sepia and vermilion	10	20
336l		5l. multicoloured	10	20
336m		20l. sepia and brown-purple	25	20
336n		31l. sepia and orange	75	30
336o		50l. sepia and carmine	1·20	55
336p		100l. sepia and blue	3·25	1·00
336q		200l. multicoloured	26·00	13·50
336j/q		Set of 8	28·00	14·50

Designs: *Horiz*—1l., 31l., 50l. Roosevelt and eagle; 2l., 20l., 100l. Roosevelt and San Marino arms. *Vert*—5l., 200l. Roosevelt and flags of San Marino and U.S.A.

1947 (16 June). *As last but surch.*

(a) POSTAGE.
336r	87	3l.on 1l. brown and ochre	20	25
336s	88	4l.on 2l. sepia and blue (R.)	20	25
336t	–	6l.on 5l. multicoloured	20	25

(b) AIR.
336u		3l.on 1l. sepia and ultramarine (R.)	20	30
336v		4l.on 2l. sepia and vermilion	20	30
336w		6l.on 5l. multicoloured	20	30
336r/w		Set of 6	1·10	1·50

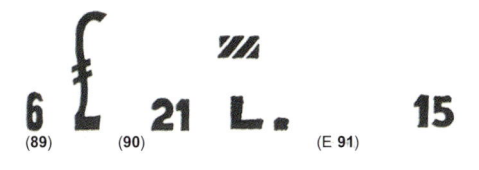

(89) (90) (E 91)

(E 92)

91 St. Marinus Founding Republic

269

SAN MARINO 1947

1947 (16 June). *No 317a surch with T* **89** *or* **90**.
337		6l.on 4l. red-orange	10	20
338		21l.on 4l. red-orange	50	60

1947 (16 June–13 Nov). EXPRESS LETTER. *Nos. E309/10 and E337 surch with Types* E **91/2**.
E339	E 79	15l.on 5l. carmine	15	25
E340		15l.on 10l. blue	15	25
E341	E 87	60l.on 30l. ultramarine (R) (13.11)	2·30	3·50

(Recess Bradbury, Wilkinson & Co.)

1947 (18 July). *Reconstruction.* W **49** (sideways). P 12.

(a) POSTAGE.
339	91	1l. mauve and emerald-green	10	20
340		2l. olive-green and mauve	10	20
341		4l. blue-green and purple-brown	10	20
342		10l. slate-blue and orange	10	20
343		25l. mauve and red	50	1·00
344		50l. brown and deep green	21·00	10·50

(b) AIR. Inscr "POSTA AEREA".
345	91	25l. blue and orange	1·50	1·60
346		50l. blue and brown	2·10	2·40
339/346		*Set of 8*	23·00	14·50

Nos. 339/42 measure 22½ × 30 mm. Nos. 343/6 measure 24½ × 32 mm. and have two rows of ornaments forming the frame.

Giornata Filatelica
Rimini - San Marino
18 Luglio 1947   +   1
(92)   (93)

1947 (18 July). AIR. *Rimini Philatelic Exhibition. No. 333 optd with T* **92**.
347		100l. sepia (R.)	1·10	85

1947 (13 Nov). *Reconstruction. Nos. 339/41 surch as T* **93**.
348	91	1l.+ 1l. mauve and emerald-green	10	20
		a. Horiz strip of 5. Nos. 348/52	60	
349		1l.+ 2l. mauve and emerald-green	10	20
350		1l.+ 3l. mauve and emerald-green	10	20
351		1l.+ 4l. mauve and emerald-green	10	20
352		1l.+ 5l. mauve and emerald-green	10	20
353		2l.+ 1l. olive-green and mauve	10	20
		a. Horiz strip of 5. Nos. 353/7	60	
354		2l.+ 2l. olive-green and mauve	10	20
355		2l.+ 3l. olive-green and mauve	10	20
356		2l.+ 4l. olive-green and mauve	10	20
357		2l.+ 5l. olive-green and mauve	10	20
358		4l.+ 1l. blue-green and purple-brown	2·75	2·10
		a. Pair. Nos. 358/9	5·75	4·25
359		4l.+ 2l. blue-green and purple-brown	2·75	2·10
348/359		*Set of 12*	5·50	5·50

Nos. 348/52 and 353/7 respectively were issued together in horizontal *se-tenant* strips of 5 within their sheets; Nos. 358/9 were issued in vertical and horizontal *se-tenant* pairs within the sheet.

94 Mt. Titano, Statue of Liberty and 1847 U.S.A. stamp

95 Mt. Titano and 1847 U.S.A. stamp

(Des R. Franzoni)

1947 (24 Dec). *Centenary of First U.S.A. Postage Stamp. Designs as T* **94/5** *inscr* "CENTENARIO DEL FRANCOBOLLO U.S.A.". Wmk Winged Wheel.

(a) POSTAGE. Photo. P 14 × 13½ (3l.) *or* 14 (others).
360	94	2l. sepia and purple	10	20
361	—	3l. grey, scarlet and blue	10	20
362	94	6l. green and blue	10	20
363	—	15l. violet, scarlet and blue	30	35
364	—	35l. sepia, scarlet and blue	1·40	1·10
365	—	50l. green, scarlet and blue	1·40	1·10

(b) AIR. Recess. P 13½ × 14.
366	95	100l. chocolate and violet	9·25	7·00
360/366		*Set of 7*	11·50	10·00

Designs: 3l., 35l. U.S.A. stamps, 5c. and 10c. of 1847, 90c. of 1869, and flags of U.S.A. and San Marino; 15l., 50l. similar stamps but differently arranged.

96 Worker and San Marino Flag   **L.100** (**97**)

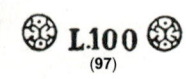

(Des R. Garrasi. Eng. M. Canfarini; recess (100l.) Photo (5 to 50l.))

1948 (3 June). *Workers Issue.* Wmk Winged Wheel. P 14.
367	96	5l. brown	10	20
368		8l. green	10	20
369		30l. carmine	25	20
370		50l. brown and rosy mauve	1·60	1·60
371		100l. deep blue and violet	49·00	28·00
367/371		*Set of 5*	46·00	27·00

For designs as Type **96** but with additional inscriptions, see Nos 506/7.

1948 (9 Oct). *No 217 surch with T* **97**.
372	59	100l. on 15c. black and carmine	48·00	30·00

POSTA AEREA 200   ≡ 35
(98)   (E 99)

1948 (9 Oct). AIR. *No. 343 surch with T* **98**.
373	91	200l. on 25l. mauve and red	32·00	14·00

1948 (9 Oct). EXPRESS LETTER. *No. E337 stitch with Type* E **99** *and similar type in red.*
E374	E 87	35l.on 30l. ultramarine	41·00	29·00
E375		80l.on 30l. ultramarine	20·00	15·00

The surcharge on No. E375 has the value and four short bars.

100   *100*
(P 99)

1948 (9 Oct)–**50**. PARCEL POST. *Nos. P324/5 surch as Type* P **99**.
P374	P 46	100l. on 50l. yellow and red	85·00	65·00
P375		200l.on 25l. carm & bl (27.2.50)	£250	£180

SAN MARINO   1949

99 Faetano   **100** Mt. Titano

Giornata Filatelica
San Marino-Riccione
28·6·1949
(102)

(Des G. Campestrini. Recess (Nos. 386/7), photo (others))

1949 (27 Jan)–**50**. T **99/100** and similar views. Wmk Winged Wheel. P 14.

374	–	1l. blue and black	10	20
375	–	2l. rose-red and purple	10	20
376	**99**	3l. ultramarine and violet	10	20
377	–	4l. violet and black	15	20
378	–	5l. yellow-brown and purple	15	20
379	**99**	6l. black and blue	50	20
380	**100**	8l. orange-brown and deep brown	30	20
381	–	10l. blue and black	30	20
382	–	12l. violet and rose-red	65	40
383	–	15l. rose-red and violet	3·75	2·10
383a	**99**	20l. yellow-brown & ultram (27.2.50)	21·00	1·20
384	–	35l. violet and green	9·25	2·40
385	–	50l. orange-brown and rose-red	3·75	2·10
385a	–	55l. blue-green and blue (27.2.50)	48·00	17·00
386	**100**	100l. green and blackish brown	70·00	40·00
387	–	200l. brown and deep blue	70·00	50·00
374/387 Set of 16			£200	£100

Designs. *Horiz*—1l., 5l., 35l. Guaita Tower and walls; 2l., 12l., 50l. Serravalle and Mt. Titano; 4l., 15l., 55l. Franciscan Convent and Capuchin Church. *Vert*—10l., 200l. Guaita Tower.
For similar stamps see Nos. 491/5, 522a/7a and 794/9.

1949 (28 June). Stamp Day. Nos 339/40 optd with T **102**.

388	**91**	1l. mauve and emerald-green	20	20
389	–	2l. olive-green and mauve	20	20

104 Garibaldi   **105** Garibaldi in San Marino

(Des R. Franzoni)

1949. Centenary of Garibaldi's Retreat from Rome. Wmk Winged Wheel (sideways on Nos. 394/400). P 14.

(a) POSTAGE. T **104** and similar vert portraits (31 July).

390	–	1l. rose carmine and black	35	20
391	–	2l. blue and brown	35	20
392	**104**	3l. green and rose-red	35	20
393	–	4l. sepia and blue	35	20
394	–	5l. sepia and mauve	35	20
395	–	15l. greenish blue and rose-red	55	80
396	–	20l. rose carmine and violet	1·10	1·40
397	**104**	50l. violet and claret	15·00	11·50

Portraits:—1l., 20l. Francesco Nullo; 2l., 5l. Anita; 4l.; 15l. Ugo Bassi.

Nos. 390/3 measure 22 × 28 mm. and Nos 394/7, 27 × 37 mm.

(b) AIR (28 June).

398	**105**	2l. blue and claret	15	20
399	–	3l. brownish black & deep green	15	20
400	–	5l. blue-green and blue	15	20
401	–	25l. violet and green	3·25	1·90
402	–	65l. grey-black and blackish green	13·50	5·75
390/402 Set of 13			32·00	20·00

Nos. 398/400 measure 28 × 22 mm, and 401/2, 37 × 27 mm.

106 Mail Coach and Mt. Titano   **107** Mt. Titano from Serravalle

108 Second and Guaita Towers   **109** Guaita Tower

(Des R. Franzoni. Eng V. Nicastro. Recess)

1949–51. 75th Anniv of Universal Postal Union. Wmk Winged Wheel. P 14.

(a) POSTAGE.

403	**106**	100l. purple and blue (29.12.49)	10·50	7·50

(b) AIR. Inscr "POSTA AEREA".

404	**106**	200l. blue (9.2.50)	1·20	1·30
405	–	300l. brown, orange-brown and brown-purple (31.1.51)	23·00	12·50

Nos. 403/5 were each printed in sheets of six; the 200l. also exists in sheets of 25.

(Des G. Campestrini. No. 415 eng V.E. Filippi)

1950 (12 Apr)–**51**. AIR. Views. P 13½ × 14 (No. 414) or 14 (others).

(a) Photo Wmk Winged Wheel.

(i) Size 22 × 28 mm (5l.) or 28 × 22 mm (others).

406	**107**	2l. green and violet	20	20
407	–	3l. brown and blue	20	25
408	**108**	5l. carmine and brown	20	25
409	–	10l. blue and deep green	1·20	60
410	–	15l. violet and black	1·30	80

(ii) Size 27 × 37 mm (55l. & 250l.) or 37 × 27 mm (others).

411	–	55l. green and blue	20·00	12·00
412	**107**	100l. grey-black and carmine	15·00	6·75
413	**108**	250l. brown and violet	70·00	28·00
414	**109**	500l. brown & grey-grn (28.4.51)	65·00	55·00

(b) Recess. No wmk. Size 47 × 33 mm.

415	**109**	500l. purple, green and blue	90·00	65·00
406/415 Set of 10			£225	£150

Designs:—3l. Distant view of Domagnano; 10l. Domagnano; 15l. San Marino from St. Mustiola; 55l. Borgo Maggiore.

SAN MARINO 1950

XXVIII FIERA
INTERNAZIONALE
DI MILANO
APRILE 1950
(110)

111 Government Palace

1950 (12 Apr). AIR. 28th Milan Fair. As Nos. 408 and 410/11, but colours changed, optd with T **110** (in six lines on 5l.)
416	5l. green and blue	15	20
417	15l. grey-black and carmine (B.)	60	55
418	55l. brown and violet	3·75	2·75

1950 (11 Dec). EXPRESS LETTER. Wmk Winged Wheel. P 14.
E419	E 79	60l. carmine-lake	7·25	5·50
E420	E **87**	80l. blue	9·25	5·50

(Des R. Franzoni. Eng V. Nicastro (25l.), T. Cionini (75l.), M. Colombati (100l.) Recess)

1951 (15 Mar). Red Cross. T **111** and similar national scenes inscr "CROCE ROSSA SAMMARINESE". Cross in red. Wmk Winged Wheel. P 13½ × 14.
419	25l. reddish purple, scarlet & deep brn	6·25	4·75
420	75l. brown, scarlet and yellow-brown	8·75	6·00
421	100l. black, scarlet and deep brown	9·50	7·25

Designs: Horiz—75l. Archway of Murata Nuova. Vert—100l. Guaita Tower.

Giornata Filatelica San Marino - Riccione

20-8-1951

L. 300

(112)

1951 (20 Aug). AIR. Stamp Day. No. 415 surch with T **112**.
422	**109**	300l. on 500l. purple, green & blue	38·00	28·00

Pro-alluvionati
italiani
1951

L. 100

113 Flag, Douglas DC-6 Airliner and Mt. Titano

(114)

(Des R. Franzoni. Eng T. Cionini. Recess)

1951 (22 Nov). AIR. Wmk Winged Wheel. P 13½ × 14.
423	**113**	1000l. blue and blackish brown	£375	£325

1951 (6 Dec). AIR. Italian Flood Relief Fund. No. 413 surch with T **114**.
424	**108**	100l. on 250l. brown and violet	3·25	3·25

115 "Columbus at the Council of Salamanca" (after Barabino)

FIERA DI TRIESTE
1952
(116)

(Des R. Franzoni. Eng M. Canfarini (20l.), A. Quieti (25l.), E. Donnini (60l.), M. Colombati (80l.), S. Vana (No. 436) and T. Cionini (No. 437). Recess (Nos. 432/7), photo (others))

1952 (28 Jan). 500th Birth Anniv (1951) of Christopher Columbus. T **115** and similar horiz designs. Wmk Winged Wheel. P 14.

(a) POSTAGE.
425	1l. brown-orange and bronze-green	20	20
426	2l. sepia and violet	20	20
427	3l. violet and brown	20	20
428	4l. blue and chestnut	20	20
429	5l. green and blue-green	45	20
430	10l. sepia and black	70	40
431	15l. carmine and black	95	60
432	20l. blue and blue-green	1·40	1·00
433	25l. purple and purple-brown	5·75	3·50
434	60l. reddish brown and violet	8·00	6·25
435	80l. grey and black	24·00	15·00
436	200l. blue-green and blue	49·00	31·00

(b) AIR Inscr "POSTA AEREA".
437	200l. blue and black	29·00	19·00
425/437 Set of 13		£110	70·00

Designs:—2, 25l. Columbus and his fleet; 3, 10, 20l. Landing in America; 4, 15, 80l. Red Indians and American settlers; 5, 200l. (No. 436); Columbus and Map of America; 60l. Type **115**; 200l. (No. 437), Columbus, Statue of Liberty (New York) and skyscrapers.

1952 (29 June). Trieste Fair. As Nos. 425/31 and 437, but colours changed. Optd with T **116**.

(a) POSTAGE.
438	1l. violet and brown	10	20
439	2l. carmine and black	10	25
440	3l. green and blue-green (R.)	10	25
441	4l. sepia and black	10	30
442	5l. reddish violet and violet	15	40
443	10l. blue and red-brown (R.)	85	75
444	15l. red-brown and blue	3·00	2·50

(b) AIR.
445	200l. brown and black (R.)	36·00	26·00
438/445 Set of 8		36·00	28·00

117 Rose

SAN MARINO 1952

118 Cyclamen, Douglas DC-6 Airliner, Rose, San Marino and Riccione

(Des R. Franzoni. Eng M. Canfarini (200l.). Recess (200l.), photo (others))

1952 (23 Aug). *AIR. Stamp Day and Philatelic Exhibition. T* **117** *and similar designs and* **118**. Wmk Winged Wheel. P 14 × 10 (Nos. 446/8), 14 (others).

446	–	1l. bright purple and violet	10	20
447	–	2l. blue-green and blue	10	20
448	117	3l. vermilion and sepia	10	20
449	118	5l. brown and bright purple	10	20
450		25l. deep green and violet	35	80
451		200l. blue-green, blue, claret, purple and red	60·00	26·00
446/451 Set of 6			55·00	25·00

Designs: As *T* **117**—1l. Cyclamen; 2l. Views of San Marino and Riccione.

119 Airplane over San Marino

(Des G. Zanzoni)

1952 (17 Nov). *AIR. Aerial Survey of San Marino. T* **119** *and similar design inscr "RILIEVO FOTOGRAMMETRICO"*. Wmk Winged Wheel. P 14.

452		25l. bronze-green and yellow	1·70	1·60
453		75l. bluish violet and brown	5·25	3·25

Design:—75l. Airplane over Mt. Titano.

1953 (5 Mar). *PARCEL POST.* Wmk Winged Wheel. P 14.
P454	P **46**	10l. grey and violet	45·00	12·50
P455		300l. violet and lake	£110	£110

Both unused and used prices are for complete pairs.

120 "The Discus Thrower"

121 Tennis

(122)

GIORNATA FILATELICA
S. MARINO - RICCIONE
24 AGOSTO 1953

(Des R. Franzoni. Eng M. Canfarini (200l.). Recess (200l.), photo (others))

1953 (20 Apr). *Sports (designs as T* **120/1***)*. P 14.

(a) POSTAGE.
454		1l. black and deep brown	10	20
455		2l. brown and black	10	20
456		3l. turquoise-blue and black	10	20
457		4l. deep bright blue & blackish green	10	20
458		5l. blackish green and sepia	10	20
459		10l. carmine-red and deep bright blue	25	20
460		25l. deep brown and brown-black	1·90	1·00
461		100l. grey-black and blackish brown	6·50	3·50

(b) AIR. Inscr "POSTA AEREA".
462		200l. blue-green and green	46·00	34·00
454/462 Set of 9			50·00	36·00

Designs: As *T* **120**—3l. Running. As *T* **121**: *Horiz*—4l. Cycling; 5l. Football; 100l. Roller skating; 200l. Skiing. *Vert*—10l. Model glider flying; 25l. Shooting.
See also No. 584.

1953 (24 Aug). *Stamp Day and Philatelic Exhibition As No. 461, but colours changed, optd with T* **122**.
463		100l. deep green and deep turquoise	15·00	11·00

123 Narcissus

124 Douglas DC-6 Airliner over Mt. Titano and Arms

(Des R. Franzoni)

1953 (28 Dec). *As T* **123** *(flowers)*. Wmk Winged Wheel. P 13 (25l., 80l., 100l.) or 14 (others).
464		1l. blue, green and yellow	10	20
465		2l. blue, green and yellow	10	20
466		3l. blue, green and yellow	10	20
467		4l. blue, green and yellow	10	20
468		5l. deep green and scarlet	10	20
469		10l. pale blue, green and yellow	10	20
470		25l. blue, green and rose	1·80	1·60
471		80l. blue, green and vermilion	14·00	14·50
472		100l. blue, green and rose	22·00	55·00
464/472 Set of 9			35·00	65·00

Floral designs:—2l. "Parrot" tulip; 3l. Oleander; 4l. Cornflower; 5l. Carnation; 10l. Iris; 25l. Cyclamen; 80l. Geranium; 100l. Rose.

(Des R. Franzoni. Eng V. Nicastro. Recess)

1954 (5 Apr). *AIR.* Wmk Winged Wheel. P 14.
473	**124**	1000l. sepia and deep blue	75·00	70·00

125 Walking

126 Statue of Liberty

(Des R. Franzoni. Eng V. Nicastro (250l.))

1954–55. *Sports (designs as T* **125***)*. Wmk Winged Wheel.

(a) Photo. P 14 (28.8.54).
474		1l. magenta and bluish violet	10	15
475		2l. bluish violet and blackish green	10	15
476		3l. chestnut and brown	10	15
477		4l. blue and greenish blue	10	15
478		5l. sepia and deep blue-green	10	15
479		8l. deep lilac and bright purple	10	20
480		12l. carmine-red and black	10	20
481		25l. deep bluish green and blue	60	25

SAN MARINO   1954

482	80l. deep turquoise-green and deep blue		1·50	45
483	200l. brown and deep lilac		7·00	2·40

(b) Recess. P 13 (10.3.55).

484	250l. black, chestnut, brn-pur & sepia		39·00	30·00
474/484	Set of 11		44·00	31·00

Designs: *Vert*—1l., 80l. T **125**; 4l., 200l. (27 × 37 mm), 250l. (28 × 37½ mm), Gymnastics; 25l. Wrestling. *Horiz*—2l. Fencing; 3l. Boxing; 5l. Motor-cycle racing; 8l. Throwing the javelin; 12l. Car racing.

(Des R. Franzoni)

1954 (16 Dec). Wmk Winged Wheel (sideways). P 13.

(a) POSTAGE.

485	**126**	20l. blue and chocolate	20	25
486		60l. deep green and carmine	65	45

(b) AIR. Inscr "POSTA AEREA".

487	**126**	120l. red-brown and deep blue	1·10	75

127 Hurdling   **128** Yacht

(Des C. Mancioli)

1955 (26 June). *AIR. First International Exhibition of Olympic Stamps. T* **127** *and similar horiz design. Wmk Mult Stars (T* **307** *of Italy). P 14.*

488	80l. black and scarlet	75	60
489	120l. red and deep turquoise-green	1·20	1·40

Design:—120l. Relay racing.

(Des C. Mancioli)

1955 (27 Aug). *Seventh International Philatelic Exhibition. Wmk Mult Stars. P 14.*

490	**128**	100l. black and blue	2·75	2·40

See also No. 518.

(Des R. Franzoni)

1955 (15 Nov). *Views as T* **99** *but new designs and colours. Wmk Mult Stars. P 14.*

491	5l. deep brown and blue	10	10
492	10l. deep bluish green and red-orange	10	10
493	15l. carmine-red and slate-green	10	10
494	25l. bluish violet and sepia	25	15
495	35l. brown-red and lilac	20	15
491/495	Set of 5	65	55

Designs: *Horiz*—5l., 25l. Archway of Murata Nuova. *Vert*—10l., 35l. Guaira Tower; 15l. Government Palace.
For similar stamps see Nos. 519/21 and 797/9.

129 Ice Skating   **130** Pointer

1955 (15 Dec). *Winter Olympic Games, Cortina D'Ampezzo. T* **129** *and similar designs inscr "CORTINA 1956". Wmk Mult Stars. P 14.*

(a) POSTAGE.

496	1l. sepia and yellow	20	15
497	2l. greenish blue and red	10	10
498	3l. black and brown	10	10
499	4l. sepia and myrtle-green	10	10
500	5l. ultramarine and pale red	10	10
501	10l. bright blue and pink	10	15
502	25l. black and red	60	50
503	50l. sepia and grey-blue	1·20	1·00
504	100l. black and turquoise-green	4·00	3·00

(b) AIR. Inscr "POSTA AEREA".

505	200l. black and red-orange	19·00	13·00
496/505	Set of 10	23·00	16·00

Designs: *Horiz*—2l., 25l. Skiing; 3l., 50l. Bobsleighing; 5l., 100l. Ice hockey; 200l. Ski jumping. *Vert*—4l. Slalom racing; 10l. Figure skating.

1956 (24 Mar). *Winter Relief Fund. As T* **96** *but additionally inscr "ASSISTENZA INVERNALE". Wmk Mult Stars. P 14.*

506	50l. deep green	4·75	5·25

1956 (24 Mar). *50th Anniv of "Arengo" (San Marino Parliament). As T* **96** *but additionally inscr "50 ANNIVERSARIO/ARENGO/ 25 MARZO 1906". Wmk Mult Stars. P 14.*

507	50l. blue	5·75	5·25

(Des R. Franzoni)

1956 (8 June). *Dogs (horiz designs as T* **130***). Multicoloured centres (25l. to 100l.). Wmk Mult Stars. P 14.*

508	1l. bistre-brown and deep bright blue	10	20
509	2l. grey and brown-red	10	20
510	3l. bistre-brown and deep blue	10	20
511	4l. grey and turquoise-blue	10	20
512	5l. sepia and carmine-red	10	20
513	10l. deep brown and deep bright blue	10	20
514	25l. grey-blue	75	60
515	60l. brown-red	5·75	3·00
516	80l. grey-blue	8·25	3·75
517	100l. deep rose-red	13·50	8·50
508/517	Set of 10	26·00	15·00

Dogs:—2l. Borzoi; 3l. Sheepdog; 4l. Greyhound; 5l. Boxer; 10l. Great Dane; 25l. Irish Setter; 60l. Alsatian; 80l. Rough collie; 100l. Foxhound.

1956 (25 Aug). *Philatelic Exhibition. As T* **128** *but inscr "1956". Wmk Mult Stars. P 14.*

518	**128**	100l. sepia & deep turquoise-green	1·10	1·20

1956 (6 Oct). *International Philatelic Congress. As Nos 491/5 but larger size and new values inscr "CONGRESSO INTERNAZ. PERITI FILATELICI SAN MARINO SALSO-MAGGIORE 6–8 OTTOBRE 1956".*

519	20l. sepia and blue	55	20
520	80l. brown-red and violet	1·50	1·00
521	100l. deep bluish green and orange	2·10	1·60

Designs (26½ × 37 mm)—20l. Guaita Tower; 100l. Government Palace. (36½ × 27 mm)—80l. Archway of Murata Nuova.

1956 (19 Nov)–**61**. *PARCEL POST. Wmk Mult Stars. P 13.*

P522	P **46**	10l. grey-green and lake	20	40
P523		50l. yellow and red	80	1·00
P524		100l. on 50l. yellow and red	60	45
P525		300l. violet and brown (6.60)	55·00	35·00
P526		500l. sepia and carmine (16.2.61)	1·90	3·75
P522/526	Set of 5		50·00	36·00

Both unused and used prices are for complete pairs.

274

SAN MARINO 1956

(131) POSTA AEREA
132 Marguerites
133 Anita Garibaldi 

1956 (10 Dec). *AIR. No. 504 optd with T* **131**.
522   100l. black and turquoise-green . . . . 1·40   1·40

(Des A. Frailich (500l.), E. L'Orchera (others). Recess (125l., 500l.), photo (others))

1957 (9 May)–**61**. *Views as T* **99** *but new designs and colours.* Wmk Mult Stars. P 14.
522a	1l. dp bluish grn & blksh grn (16.2.61)	10	10
523	2l. carmine-red & deep grey-green	10	10
524	3l. deep brown and blue	10	10
524a	4l. grey-blue and deep sepia (16.2.61)	10	15
525	20l. deep bluish grn & blackish grn	10	10
525a	30l. bright violet & bistre-brn (16.2.61)	60	80
526	60l. bright violet and sepia	60	80
526a	115l. deep brown and blue (16.2.61)	20	40
527	125l. deep blue and black	40	25
527a	500l. black and green (27.2.58)	65·00	50·00
522a/527a	Set of 10	60·00	47·00

Designs: *Vert*—2l. Borgo Maggiore Church; 3l., 30l. Town gate, San Marino; 4l., 125l. View of San Marino from southern wall; 20l., 115l. Borgo Maggiore market-place. *Horiz*—1l., 60l. View of San Marino from Hospital Avenue. (37½ × 28 mm) 500l. Panorama of San Marino.
See also Nos. 794/6.

(Des R. Franzoni)

1957 (31 Aug). *Flowers as T* **132**. *Multicoloured.* Wmk Mult Stars. P 14.
528	1l. Type **132**	10	15
529	2l. Polyanthuses	10	15
530	3l. Lilies	10	15
531	4l. Orchid	10	15
532	5l. Lilies of the Valley	10	15
533	10l. Poppies	10	15
534	25l. Pansies	10	15
535	60l. Gladiolus	30	45
536	80l. Wild roses	65	65
537	100l. Anemones	1·10	1·10
528/537	Set of 10	2·50	3·00

(Des R. Franzoni)

1957 (12 Dec). *150th Birth Anniv of Garibaldi Portraits as T* **133**. Wmk Mult Stars. P 14.

(a) As T **133**.
538	2l. deep blue and bluish violet	15	15
539	3l. myrtle green and deep rose-red	15	15
540	5l. drab and brown	15	15

(b) Size 26½ × 37 mm.
541	15l. violet and blue	15	20
542	25l. black and deep bluish green	15	25
543	50l. deep brown and bluish violet	95	1·20
	a. Pair Nos. 543/4	2·00	2·50
544	100l. bluish violet and deep brown	95	1·20
538/544	Set of 7	2·40	3·00

Portraits:—5l., 100l. Garibaldi; 3l., 25l. Francesco Nullo; 15l. Ugo Bassi; 50l. As Type **133**.
Nos. 543/4 were issued together in *se-tenant* pairs within the sheet.

L.75 (E **134**)   (E **135**) L.100

1957 (12 Dec). *EXPRESS LETTER Nos. E419/20 surch with Types E* **134/5**.
E545	E **79**	75l.on 60l. carmine-lake	1·90	1·90
E546	E **87**	100l.on 80l. blue	1·90	1·80

134 St. Marinus and Fair Entrance
135 Exhibition Emblem, Atomium and Mt. Titano 

(Des C. Mancioli)

1958 (12 Apr). *Thirty-sixth Milan Fair. Designs as T* **134**, *inscr* "XXXVI FIERA DI MILANO". Wmk Mult Stars. P 14.

(a) POSTAGE.
545	15l. yellow and blue	20	10
546	60l. green and rose-red	30	35

(b) AIR. Inscr "POSTA AEREA".
547	125l. pale blue and sepia	2·40	2·50

Designs: *Horiz*—60l. Italian pavilion. *Vert*—125l. Bristol 173 Rotocoach helicopter and airplane over fair.

(Des C. Mancioli)

1958 (12 Apr). *Brussels International Exhibition.* Wmk Mult Stars. P 14.
548	**135**	40l. sepia and deep yellow-green	10	20
549		60l. brown-lake and light blue	25	30

136 View of San Marino
137 Wheat 

(Des R. Franzoni. Eng E. Donnini. Recess)

1958 (23 June). *AIR. T* **136** *and similar horiz design.* Wmk Mult Stars. P 13½.
550	200l. deep blue and brown	2·75	1·90
	a. Strip Nos. 550/1 plus label	6·50	
551	300l. violet and bright crimson	2·75	1·90

Design:—300l. Mt. Titano.
Nos. 550/1 were issued together with intervening half stamp-size label showing San Marino arms.

(Des R. Franzoni)

1958 (1 Sept). *Fruit and Agricultural Products. Vert designs as T* **137**. Wmk Mult Stars. P 14.
552	**137**	1l. yellow-ochre and blue	10	15
553	—	2l. orange-red and deep green	10	15
554	—	3l. yellow-orange and blue	10	15
555	—	4l. carmine and green	10	15
556	—	5l. orange-yellow, bronze grn & bl	10	15

275

SAN MARINO 1958

557	**137**	15l. yellow, brown and blue	10	15
558	–	25l. multicoloured	10	15
559	–	40l. multicoloured	40	25
560	–	80l. multicoloured	55	50
561	–	125l. multicoloured	2·75	2·10
552/561	Set of 10		4·00	3·50

Designs:—2l., 125l. Maize; 3l., 80l. Grapes; 4l., 25l. Peaches; 5l., 40l. Plums.

138 Naples 10 grana stamp of 1858, and Bay of Naples

139 Mediterranean Gull

(Des R. Franzoni)

1958 (8 Oct). *Centenary of First Naples Postage Stamps.* Wmk Mult Stars. P 14.

(a) POSTAGE.
| 562 | **138** | 25l. red-brown and blue | 25 | 20 |

(b) AIR. Inscr "POSTA AEREA".
| 563 | **138** | 125l. red-brown and bistre-brown | 1·80 | 1·40 |

The Naples stamp inset on No. 563 is the 50 grana value.

(Des R. Franzoni)

1959 (12 Feb). *AIR. Native Birds. Various horiz designs as T* **139**. Wmk Mult Stars. P 14.

564	5l. black and deep bluish green	20	15
565	10l. orange-brown, black and blue	20	15
566	15l. multicoloured	20	15
567	120l. multicoloured	85	40
568	250l. black, yellow and deep green	1·90	1·60
564/568	Set of 5	3·00	2·20

Birds:—10l. Common kestrel; 15l. Mallard; 120l. Feral rock pigeon; 250l. Barn swallow.

140 P. de Coubertin (founder)

141 Vickers Viscount 700 Airliner over Mt. Titano

(Des A. Vicini, R. Mura. Eng E. Donnini. Recess (120l.), photo (others))

1959 (19 May). *Pre-Olympic Games Issue. T* **140** *and similar portraits of committee executives.* Wmk Mult Stars. P 13½ (120l.) or 14 (others).

(a) POSTAGE.
569	2l. black and orange-brown	10	15
570	3l. sepia and reddish violet	10	15
571	5l. deep bluish green and ultramarine	10	15
572	30l. black and violet	10	15
573	60l. sepia and deep bluish green	10	15
574	80l. deep bluish green and lake	10	15

(b) AIR Inscr "POSTA AEREA".
| 575 | 120l. brown | 2·40 | 1·60 |
| 569/575 | Set of 7 | 2·70 | 2·20 |

Designs: *Vert*—2l. T **140**; 3l. A. Bonacossa; 5l. A. Brundage; 30l. C Montu; 60l. J. S. Edström; 80l. De Baillet-Latour. *Horiz* (35 × 21½ mm)—120l. De Coubertin and Olympic Flame.

(Des A. Vicini and R. Mura)

1959 (1 June). *AIR. Alitalia Inaugural Flight, Rimini-London.* Wmk Mult Stars. P 14.
| 576 | **141** | 120l. violet | 1·10 | 1·20 |

142 Abraham Lincoln and Scroll

143 1859 Romagna ½b. stamp and Arch of Augustus, Rimini

(Des R. Franzoni. Eng V. Nicastro (70l.), M. Colombati (200l.), recess. Photo (others))

1959 (1 July). *150th Birth Anniv of Lincoln. Portraits as T* **142** *inscr "ABRAMO LINCOLN 1809–1959".* Wmk Mult Stars. P 13 × 14 (70l.), 14 × 13 (200l.) or 14 (others).

(a) POSTAGE.
577	5l. brown and sepia	10	15
578	10l. bright green and deep turquoise-blue	10	15
579	15l. grey and deep bluish green	10	15
580	70l. violet	20	25

(b) AIR. Inscr "POSTA AEREA".
| 581 | 200l. deep blue | 3·25 | 1·90 |
| 577/581 | Set of 5 | 3·50 | 2·40 |

Designs: Portraits of Lincoln with: *Horiz*—10l. Map of San Marino; 15l. Government Palace, 200l. Mt. Titano. *Vert*—70l. Mt. Titano.

(Des R. Franzoni)

1959 (29 Aug). *Centenary of First Romagna Postage Stamps. T* **143** *and similar horiz design inscr "1859–1959".* Wmk Mult Stars. P 14.

(a) POSTAGE.
| 582 | 30l. brown and sepia | 15 | 20 |

(b) AIR. Inscr "POSTA AEREA".
| 583 | 120l. deep bluish green & greenish blk | 1·10 | 1·20 |

Design:—120l. 1859 Romagna 3b. stamp and view of Bologna.

(Des R. Franzoni)

1959 (29 Aug). *World University Games, Turin. Design as T* **120** *but additionally inscr "UNIVERSIADE TORINO 1959".* P 14.
| 584 | 30l. orange-red | 30 | 45 |

144 Portal of Messina Cathedral and ½gr. Sicily stamp

145 Golden Oriole

(Des A. Vicini, G. Tiberi (1l.), A. Morena (2l.), R. Pierbattista (3l.), R. Mura (4l.), R. Franzoni (others))

1959 (16 Oct). *Centenary of First Sicilian Postage Stamps. Designs as T* **144**. Wmk Mult Stars. P 14.
585	1l. deep brown and orange-yellow	10	10
586	2l. brown-red and olive-green	10	10
587	3l. deep slate-blue and blue	10	10

SAN MARINO 1959

588	4l. brown and brown-red	10	10
589	5l. reddish purple and deep grey-blue	10	10
590	25l. multicoloured	10	15
591	60l. multicoloured	10	20

(b) AIR. Inscr "POSTA AEREA".

592	200l. multicoloured	1·10	90
585/592 *Set of 8*		1·60	1·60

Designs: *Vert*—2l. Selinunte Temple (1gr.); 3l. Erice Church (2gr.); 4l. "Concordia" Temple, Agrigento (5gr.); 5l. "Castor and Pollux" Temple, Agrigento (10gr.); 25l. "St. John of the Hermits" Church, Palermo (20gr.). *Horiz*—60l. Taormina (50gr.); 200l. Bay of Palermo (50gr.).

(Des R. Franzoni)

1960 (28 Jan). *Birds. Designs as T 145.* Wmk Mult Stars. P 14.

593	1l. yellow-orange, olive and blue	10	15
594	2l. brown, red and green	10	15
595	3l. carmine, brown and green	10	15
596	4l. black, red-brown and bluish green	10	20
597	5l. carmine, brown and green	10	15
598	10l. multicoloured	10	20
599	25l. multicoloured	35	20
600	60l. multicoloured	95	1·00
601	80l. multicoloured	2·75	2·10
602	110l. multicoloured	3·00	3·00
593/602 *Set of 10*		7·00	6·50

Birds: *Vert*—2l. Nightingale; 4l. Hoopoe; 10l. Eurasian goldfinch; 25l. River kingfisher; 80l. Green woodpecker; 110l. Red-breasted flycatcher. *Horiz*—3l. Eurasian woodcock; 5l. Red-legged partridge; 60l. Common pheasant.

146 Putting the Shot

147 Melvin Jones (founder) and Lions International H.Q.

(Des C. Mancioli)

1960 (23 May). *Olympic Games. Sports designs as T 146* inscr "ROMA 1960". P 14.

(a) POSTAGE.

603	1l. violet and crimson	10	10
604	2l. orange and grey-black	10	10
605	3l. reddish violet and bistre-brown	10	10
606	4l. brown and rose-red	10	10
607	5l. blue and brown	10	10
608	10l. blue and chestnut	10	10
609	15l. reddish violet and green	10	15
610	25l. red-orange and blue-green	10	15
611	60l. orange-brown and green	10	15
612	110l. red, black and green	10	20

(b) AIR. Inscr "POSTA AEREA".

613	20l. reddish violet	10	15
614	40l. carmine-red and yellow-brown	10	15
615	80l. orange-yellow and blue	10	15
616	125l. sepia and red	25	25
603/616 *Set of 14*		1·40	1·75

Designs: *Vert*—2l. Gymnastics; 3l. Long-distance walking; 4l. Boxing; 10l. Cycling; 20l. Handball; 40l. Breasting the tape; 60l. Football. *Horiz*—5l. Fencing; 15l. Hockey; 25l. Rowing; 80l. Diving; 110l. Horse-jumping; 125l. Rifleshooting.

(c) SHEETS (27 Aug). Comprising Nos. 603/616 in new colours, imperf.

MS616*a* 90 × 125 mm. 1, 2, 3, 60l. orange-brown, myrtle-green and pale grey-green	2·10	1·60
MS616*b* 90 × 127 mm. 4, 10, 20, 40l. orange-brown, red and pale-red	2·10	1·60
MS616*c* 145 × 100 mm. 5, 15, 25, 80, 110, 125l. orange-brown, deep brown, bright & pale grn	3·25	3·50

(Des A. Vicini)

1960 (1 July). *Lions International. T 147 and similar designs.* Wmk Mult Stars. P 14.

(a) POSTAGE.

617	30l. red-brown and bluish violet	10	20
618	45l. orange-brown and slate-violet	35	20
619	60l. brown-red and blue	10	20
620	115l. bluish green and black	40	40
621	150l. bistre-brown and slate-violet	1·40	2·10

(b) AIR. inscr "POSTA AEREA".

622	200l. ultramarine and grey-green	4·00	5·50
617/622 *Set of 6*		5·75	7·75

Designs (with Lions emblem): *Vert*—30l. Mt. Titano; 60l. San Marino Government Palace. *Horiz*—115l. Pres. Clarence Sturm; 150l. Vice-Pres. Finis E. Davis; 200l. Globe.

148 Riccione

149 "Youth with Basket of Fruit"

(Des R. Franzoni)

1960 (27 Aug). *12th Riccione–San Marino Stamp Day. Centres multicoloured: frame colours given.* Wmk Mult Stars. P 14.

(a) POSTAGE.

623	**148**	30l. brown-red	15	20

(b) AIR. Inscr "POSTA AEREA".

624	**148**	125l. blue	85	80

1960 (29 Dec). *350th Death Anniv of Caravaggio (painter).* Wmk Mult Stars. P 14.

625	**149**	200l. multicoloured	4·75	5·00

150 Hunting Roe Deer

151 Bell 47J Ranger Helicopter near Mt. Titano

(Des C. Mancioli)

1961 (4 May). *Hunting (1st issue)—Historical scenes. T 150 and similar designs.* Wmk Mult Stars. P 14.

626	1l. ultramarine and deep magenta	10	10
627	2l. red and sepia	10	10
628	3l. black and orange-red	10	10
629	4l. brown-red and blue	10	10
630	5l. brown and yellow-green	10	10

277

SAN MARINO   1961

631	10l. slate-violet and red-orange	10	10
632	30l. blue and yellow	10	10
633	60l. red-brown, brown-orange and black	10	15
634	70l. red, purple and green	10	15
635	115l. blue, bright purple and black	30	25
626/635	*Set of* 10	1·10	1·10

Hunting scenes: *Vert*—2l. 16th-cent falconer; 10l. 16th-cent falconer (mounted); 60l. 17th-cent hunter with rifle and dog. *Horiz*—3l. 16th-cent boar hunt; 4l. Duck-shooting with crossbow (16th-cent); 5l. 16th-cent stag-hunt with bow and arrow; 30l. 17th-cent huntsman with horn and dogs; 70l. 18th-cent hunter and beater; 115l. Duck-shooting with bow and arrow (18th-cent).
See also Nos. 679/88.

(Des C. Mancioli. Eng S. Vana. Recess)

1961 (6 July). *AIR*. Wmk Mult Stars. P 14.

636	**151**	1000l. crimson	30·00	29·00

152 Guaita Tower, Mt Titano and 1858 Sardinian Stamp

1961 (5 Sept). *Italian Independence Centenary Philatelic Exhibition, Turin, Litho and embossed.* Wmk Mult Stars. P 13½.

637	**152**	30l. ochre, orange, pale bl & deep bl	35	35
638		70l. ochre, orange, black & pale blue	50	40
639		200l. ochre, orange, pale blue & blk	40	55

153 Mt. Titano

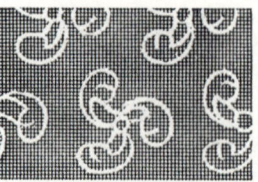

154 Three Feathers

1961 (20 Oct). *Europa*. W **154**. P 13.

640	**153**	500l. blue-green and brown	28·00	9·00

155 King Enzo's Palace, Bologna

156 Duryea—U.S.A., 1892

(Des P. Vicenzi)

1961 (25 Nov). *Bologna Stamp Exhibition*. T **155** and similar vert designs inscr "BOLOGNA". W **154**. P 14.

641	30l. black and greenish blue	10	10
642	70l. black and bronze-green	10	15
643	100l. black and red-brown	10	20

Designs:—70l. Gateway of Merchant's Palace; 100l. Towers of Garisenda and Asinelli, Bologna.

(Des C. Mancioli)

1962 (23 Jan). *Veteran Motor Cars*. Designs as T **156**. Wmk Mult Stars. P 14.

644	1l. light blue and brown	10	15
645	2l. orange and bright blue	10	15
646	3l. orange and black	10	15
647	4l. carmine-red and black	10	15
648	5l. orange and violet	10	15
649	10l. orange and black	10	15
650	15l. rose-red and black	10	15
651	20l. blue and black	10	20
652	25l. orange and grey-black	10	20
653	30l. yellow-brown and black	15	20
654	50l. bright purple and black	15	20
655	70l. blue-green and black	15	20
656	100l. red, yellow and black	15	35
657	115l. blue-green, orange and black	20	40
658	150l. yellow, orange and black	45	60
644/658	*Set of* 15	1·80	3·00

Motor Cars: *Horiz*—2l. Panhard and Levassor, 1895; 3l. Peugeot "Vis-à-vis", 1895; 4l. Daimler, 1899; 10l. Decauville 1900; 15l. Wolseley, 1901; 20l. Benz, 1902; 25l. Napier, 1903; 50l. Oldsmobile, 1904; 100l. Isotta Fraschini, 1908; 115l. Bianchi, 1910; 150l. Alfa, 1910. *Vert*—5l. F.I.A.T., 1899; 30l. White, 1903; 70l. Renault, 1904.

157 Wright Type A Biplane

158 Roping Down

(Des C. Mancioli)

1962 (4 Apr). *Vintage Aircraft*. T **157** and similar horiz designs. W **154**. P 14.

659	1l. black and yellow	10	15
660	2l. brown and green	10	15
661	3l. orange-brown and grey-green	10	15
662	4l. black and yellow-brown	10	15
663	5l. carmine and blue	10	15
664	10l. orange-brown and blue-green	10	15
665	30l. yellow-brown and blue	10	20
666	60l. yellow-brown and deep slate-violet	10	25
667	70l. black and red-orange	20	30
668	115l. yellow-brown, black and green	50	60
659/668	*Set of* 10	1·40	2·00

278

SAN MARINO   1962

Designs:—2l. Archdeacon-Voisin "Boxkite" float glider; 3l. Albert and Emile Bonnet-Labranche biplane; 4l. Glenn Curtiss *June Bug*; 5l. Henri Farman H.F.III biplane; 10l. Blériot XI; 30l. Hubert Latham's Antoinette IV; 60l. Alberto Santos-Dumont's biplane *14 bis*; 70l. Alliott Verdon-Roe Triplane II; 115l. Faccioli's airplane.

(Des P. Vicenzi)

1962 (14 June). *Mountaineering.* T **158** *and similar vert designs.* W **154**. P 14.

669	1l. yellow-brown and black	10	15
670	2l. deep bluish green and black	10	15
671	3l. bright purple and black	10	15
672	4l. blue and black	10	15
673	5l. red-orange and black	10	15
674	15l. orange-yellow and black	10	15
675	30l. rose-carmine and black	10	15
676	40l. greenish blue and black	10	15
677	85l. light green and black	15	20
678	115l. violet-blue and black	20	40
669/678 *Set of 10*		1·00	1·60

Designs:—2l. View of Sassolungo; 3l. Mt. Titano; 4l. Three Lavaredo peaks; 5l. The Matterhorn; 15l. Skier; 30l. Climber negotiating overhang; 40l. Step-cutting in ice; 85l. Aiguille du Géant; 115l. Citadel on Mt. Titano.

159 Hunter and Retriever

160 Arrows encircling "Europa"

(Des C. Mancioli)

1962 (25 Aug). *Hunting (2nd Issue)—Modern Hunting.* T **159** *and similar designs.* W **154**. P 14.

679	1l. dull purple and yellow-green	10	15
680	2l. deep blue and yellow-orange	10	15
681	3l. black and light blue	10	15
682	4l. sepia and light brown	10	15
683	5l. deep chocolate and yellow-green	10	15
684	15l. black and orange-brown	10	15
685	50l. sepia and green	10	20
686	70l. bluish green and orange-red	10	20
687	100l. black and orange-red	20	20
688	150l. green and reddish lilac	20	35
679/688 *Set of 10*		1·10	1·60

Designs: *Vert*—2l. Huntsman and hounds; 150l. Hunter shooting pheasant. *Horiz*—Hunting: 3l. Marsh ducks (with decoys); 4l. Roe deer; 5l. Grey partridge; 15l. Northern lapwing; 50l. Partridge; 70l. Marsh geese; 100l. Wild boar.

(Des A. Vicini, L. Gasbarra)

1962 (25 Oct). *Europa.* W **154**. P 14.
689 **160** 200l. carmine-red and black 75 80

161 Egyptian Merchant Ship, 2000 B.C.

162 "The Fornarina" (or "The Veiled Woman")

(Des C. Mancioli)

1963 (10 Jan). *Ancient Ships.* T **161** *and similar designs.* W **154**. P 14.

690	1l. grey-blue and yellow-orange	10	15
691	2l. sepia and reddish purple	10	15
692	3l. sepia and bright mauve	10	15
693	4l. dull purple and light grey	10	15
694	5l. sepia and lemon	10	15
695	10l. chocolate and bright green	10	15
696	30l. sepia and greenish blue	45	35
697	60l. dull ultramarine and yellow-green	50	35
698	70l. rose-red and black	40	35
699	115l. red-brown and new blue	1·10	1·20
690/699 *Set of 10*		2·75	2·75

Ships: *Horiz*—2l. Greek trier, 5th century B.C.; 3l. Roman trireme, 1st century B.C.; 4l. Viking longship, 10th century; 5l. The *Santa Maria*; 30l. Galley, *circa* 1600; 115l. Duncan Dunbar (full-rigged merchantman), 1850. *Vert*—10l. Carrack, *circa* 1550; 60l. Sovereign of the Seas (English galleon), 1637; 70l. *Fyn* Danish ship of the line, *circa* 1750.

1963 (28 Mar). *Paintings by Raphael.* T **162** *and similar vert designs. Multicoloured.* W **154**. P 14.

700	30l. Type **162**	10	20
701	70l. Self-portrait	10	15
702	100l. Sistine Madonna (detail of woman praying)	10	20
703	200l. "Portrait of a Young Woman" (Maddalena Strozzi) (27 × 44 mm)	10	25
700/703 *Set of 4*		35	75

163 Saracen Game, Arezzo

164 Peacock

(Des C. Mancioli)

1963 (22 June). *Ancient Tournaments.* T **163** *and similar designs.* W **154**. P 14.

704	1l. magenta	10	15
705	2l. slate-black	10	15
706	3l. black	10	15
707	4l. violet	10	15
708	5l. reddish violet	10	15
709	10l. grey-green	10	15
710	30l. Venetian red	10	15
711	60l. slate-blue	10	15
712	70l. bistre-brown	10	20
713	115l. black	15	25
704/713 *Set of 10*		95	1·50

Tournaments: *Horiz*—2l. 14th-century, French cavaliers; 4l. 15th-century, Presenting arms to an English cavalier; 30l. Quintana game, Foligno; 70l. 15th-century, Cavaliers (from castle mural, Malpaga). *Vert*—3l. Cross-bow Championships, Gubbio; 5l. 16th-century, Cavaliers, Florence; 10l. Quintana game, Ascoli Piceno; 60l. Palio (horse-race), Siena; 115l. 13th-century. The Crusades: cavaliers' challenge.

(Des Ziveri)

1963 (31 Aug). *Butterflies.* T **164** *and similar multicoloured designs.* W **154**. P 14.

714	25l. Type **164**	15	15
715	30l. *Nessaea obrinus*	15	15
716	60l. Large tortoiseshell	15	15
717	70l. Peacock (*horiz*)	15	30
718	115l. *Papilio blumei* (*horiz*)	25	35
714/718 *Set of 5*		75	1·00

SAN MARINO 1963

165 Corner of Government Palace, San Marino

166 Pole Vaulting

(Des A. Vicini, A. Carrarini (No. 719); A. Vicini, R. Pierbattista (No. 720))

1963 (31 Aug). *San Marino–Riccione Stamp Fair.* T **165** and similar vert design. W **154**. P 14.
719	**165**	100l. black and blue	15	15
720	—	100l. blue and sepia	15	15

Design:—No. 720, Fountain, Riccione.

(Des C. Mancioli)

1963 (21 Sept). *Olympic Games. Tokyo (1964) (1st issue). Sports designs as* T **166**. W **154**. P 14.
721	1l. brown-purple and yellow-orange	10	10
722	2l. sepia and yellow-green	10	10
723	3l. sepia and light blue	10	10
724	4l. sepia and blue	10	10
725	5l. sepia and red	10	10
726	10l. brown-purple and bright purple	10	10
727	30l. brown-purple and grey	10	10
728	60l. sepia and light yellow	10	10
729	70l. sepia and greenish blue	10	10
730	115l. sepia and green	10	10
721/730	Set of 10	90	90

Designs: *Horiz*—1l. Hurdling; 3l. Relay-racing; 4l. High jumping (men); 5l. Football; 10l. High jumping (women); 60l. Throwing the javelin; 70l. Water-polo; 115l. Throwing the hammer. *Vert*—30l. Throwing the discus.

See also Nos. 743/52.

167 "E" and Flag of San Marino

168 Tupolev TU-104A Jetliner

(Des C. Mancioli)

1963 (21 Sept). *Europa.* W **154**. P 14.
731	**167**	200l. blue and orange-brown	45	30

(Des Arseni)

1963 (5 Dec)–**65**. *AIR. Contemporary Aircraft.* T **168** and similar designs. W **154**. P 14.
732	5l. brown-purple, chocolate and turquoise-blue	10	10
733	10l. blue and orange-red	10	15
734	15l. red, reddish violet & bluish violet	10	10
735	25l. carmine, reddish vio & bluish vio	10	10
736	50l. red and turquoise-blue	10	10
737	75l. red-orange and emerald-green	10	10
738	120l. red and ultramarine	10	20
739	200l. black and green	10	10
740	300l. black and orange	10	25
741	500l. multicoloured (4.3.65)	3·00	3·00
742	1000l. multicoloured (12.3.64)	1·50	1·50
732/742	Set of 11	5·00	5·00

Designs: *Horiz*—15l. Douglas DC-8 jetliner; 25, 1000l. Boeing 707 jetliner (different views); 50l. Vickers Viscount 837 airliner; 120l. Vickers VC-10 jetliner; 200l. Hawker Siddeley Comet 4C jetliner; 300l. Boeing 727-100 jetliner. *Vert*—10l. Boeing 707 jetliner; 75l. Sud Aviation Caravelle jetliner; 500l. Rolls Royce Dart 527 turboprop engine.

169 Running

170 Murray Blenkinsop Locomotive (1812)

(Des C. Mancioli)

1964 (25 June). *Olympic Games, Tokyo (2nd Issue).* T **169** and similar designs. W **154**. P 14.
743	1l. brown and yellow-green	15	10
744	2l. red-brown and sepia	15	10
745	3l. yellow-brown and black	15	10
746	4l. slate-blue and orange-red	15	10
747	5l. sepia and light blue	15	10
748	15l. purple and yellow-orange	15	10
749	30l. deep violet-blue and light blue	15	10
750	70l. orange-brown and green	15	10
751	120l. orange-brown and blue	15	10
752	150l. black-purple and red	15	20
743/752	Set of 10	1·40	1·00

Designs: *Vert*—2l. Gymnastics; 3l. Basketball; 120l. Cycling; 150l. Fencing. *Horiz*—4l. Pistol-shooting; 15l. Long jumping; 30l. Diving; 70l. Sprinting.

1964 (25 June). *"Towards Tokyo" Sports Stamp Exhibition, Rimini.* As Nos. 749/50, but inscr "VERSO TOKIO" and colours changed.
753	30l. deep grey-blue and reddish violet	10	10
754	70l. orange-brown and turquoise-blue	10	10

(Des C. Mancioli)

1964 (29 Aug). *"Story of the Locomotive".* T **170** and similar horiz designs. W **154**. P 14.
755	1l. black and buff	10	10
756	2l. black and light bluish green	10	10
757	3l. black and light violet	10	10
758	4l. black and light yellow	10	10
759	5l. black and light salmon-red	10	10
760	15l. black and yellow-green	15	10
761	20l. black and pink	15	15
762	50l. black and light violet-blue	30	15
763	90l. black and yellow-orange	35	15
764	110l. black and light blue	35	35
755/764	Set of 10	1·75	1·25

Locomotives:—2l. *Puffing Billy* (1813); 3l. *Locomotion No 1* (1825); 4l. *Rocket* (1829); 5l. *Lion* (1838); 15l. *Bayard* (1839); 20l. Crampton type (1849); 50l. *Little England* (1851); 90l. *Spitfire* (c. 1855); 110l. *Rogers* (c. 1765).

171 Baseball Players

172 "E" and part of Globe

280

SAN MARINO 1964

(Des C. Mancioli)

1964 (29 Aug). *Seventh European Baseball Championships, Milan.* T **171** *and similar horiz design.* W **154**. P. 14.
765	30l. sepia and emerald green		10	15
766	70l. black and cerise		10	25

Design:—70l. Player pitching ball.

(Des E. Arseni)

1964 (15 Oct). *Europa.* W **154**. P. 14.
767	**172**	200l. red, blue and light blue	25	45

173 Pres. Kennedy giving Inaugural Address

174 Cyclists at Government Palace

(Des E. Arseni)

1964 (22 Nov). *First Death Anniv of John F. Kennedy (President of United States of America).* T **173** *and similar multicoloured design.* W **154**. P. 14.
768	70l. Type **173**		10	10
769	130l. Pres. Kennedy and U.S. flag (vert)		10	30

1965 (Jan)–**72**. PARCEL POST. W **154**. P. 13.
P770	P **46**	10l. grey-green and lake		20	15
P771		50l. yellow and red		25	40
P772		100l.on 50l. yellow and red		90	90
P773		300l. violet and brown		30	35
P774		500l. sepia and red (8.72)		6·75	6·75
P775		1000l. green and red-brown (5.5.67)		55	1·00
P770/775 *Set of 6*				8·00	8·50

Both unused and used prices are for complete pairs.

(Des E. Arseni)

1965 (15 May). *Cycle Tour of Italy.* T **174** *and similar vert designs.* W **154**. P. 14.
770	30l. sepia		15	10
771	70l. reddish purple		15	10
772	200l. rosine		15	10

Designs: Cyclists passing "The Rock" (70l.); Mt. Titano (200l.).

175 Brontosaurus

176 Rooks on Chessboard

(Des E. Arseni)

1965 (30 June). *Prehistoric Animals.* T **175** *and similar designs.* W **154**. P. 14.
773	1l. brown-purple and green		10	15
774	2l. black and grey-blue		10	15
775	3l. orange-yellow and deep bluish grn		10	15
776	4l. blackish brown and blue		10	15
777	5l. deep brown-purple and green		10	15
778	10l. deep brown-purple and green		10	15
779	75l. deep blue and turquoise-green		25	15
780	100l. deep brown-purple and green		40	25
781	200l. deep brown-purple and green		70	40
773/781 *Set of 9*			1·80	1·50

Animals: *Vert*—2l. Brachyosaurus. *Horiz*—3l. Pteranodon; 4l. Elasmosaurus; 5l. Tyrannosaurus; 10l. Stegosaurus; 75l. Thamatosaurus Victor; 100l. Iguanodon; 200l. Triceratops.

(Des C. Mancioli)

1965 (28 Aug). *Europa.* W **154**. P. 14.
782	**176**	200l. multicoloured	45	35

(E **177**)

1965 (28 Aug). EXPRESS LETTER. *Nos. E800 and E802 surch as Type E* **177**.
E783	–	120l.on 75l. blk & greenish yell	15	15
E784	E **180**	135l.on 100l. black & red-orange	15	15

177 Dante

178 Mt. Titano and Flags

(Eng E. Vangelli (40l.), S. Vana (90l.), A. Quieti (130l.), M. Colombati (140l.). Recess and photo)

1965 (20 Nov). *700th Anniv of Dante's Birth.* T **177** *and similar designs.* W **154**. P. 14.
783	40l. sepia and indigo		10	15
784	90l. sepia and carmine-red		10	15
785	130l. sepia and red-brown		10	15
786	140l. sepia and bright blue		10	25
783/786 *Set of 4*			35	65

Designs:—90l. "Hell"; 130l. "Purgatory"; 140l. "Paradise".

(Des A. Vicini and E. Fabiani)

1965 (25 Nov). *Visit of President Saragat of Italy.* W **154**. P. 14.
787	**178**	115l. multicoloured	15	25

179 Trotting

E **180** Crossbow and Three "Castles"

SAN MARINO   1965

(Des E. Arseni)

1966 (28 Feb). *Equestrian Sports.* T **179** *and similar designs. Multicoloured.* W **154**. P 14 × 13 (*horiz*) or 13 × 14 (*vert*).
788	10l. Type **179**	15	15
789	20l. Cross-country racing (*vert*)	15	15
790	40l. Horse-jumping	15	15
791	70l. Horse-racing	15	15
792	90l. Steeple-chasing	15	20
793	170l. Polo (*vert*)	15	20
788/793	*Set of 6*	80	90

1966 (29 Mar). *New values in old designs.* W **154**. P 14.
794	5l. brown and blue (as 522a)	15	10
795	10l. deep bluish green & black (as 524)	15	10
796	15l. violet and sepia (as 524a)	15	10
797	40l. brown-red and slate-lilac (as 491)	15	10
798	90l. grey-blue and black (as 492)	15	10
799	140l. red-orange and bluish vio (as 493)	15	10
794/799	*Set of 6*	80	55

(Des C. Mancioli)

1966 (29 Mar). EXPRESS LETTER. *Type* E **180** *and similar horiz design.* W **154**. P 14.
E800	— 75l. black and greenish yellow	10	10
E801	E **180** 80l. black and light purple	10	10
E802	— 100l. black and red-orange	10	10

Design:—75l. As Type E **180**, but crossbow in white without "shadows".

180 "La Bella"    **181** Stone Bass (*Cernia Bruna*)

182 Our Lady of Europe   **183** Peony

(Des J. Pedreira)

1966 (24 Sept). *Europa.* W **154**. P 14.
814	**182** 200l. multicoloured	30	25

(Des R. Bergamo)

1967 (12 Jan). *Flowers.* T **183** *and similar vert designs. Multicoloured.* W **154**. P 14.
815	5l. Type **183**	10	15
816	10l. Campanula	10	15
817	15l. Pyrenean poppy	10	15
818	20l. Purple deadnettle	10	15
819	40l. Hemerocallis	10	15
820	140l. Gentian	10	15
821	170l. Thistle	10	20
815/821	*Set of 7*	65	1·00

Each flower has a different background view of Mt. Titano.

184 St. Marinus   **185** Map of Europe   **186** Caesar's Mushroom (*Amanita caesarea*)

(Des T. Vecellio)

1966 (16 June). *Paintings by Titian.* T **180** *and similar vert designs. Multicoloured.* W **154**. P 14.
800	40l. Type **180**	10	15
801	90l. "The Three Graces"	10	15
802	100l. "The Three Graces"	10	20
803	170l. "Sacred and Profane Love"	10	25
800/803	*Set of 4*	35	65

The 90l. and 100l. show different details from the picture.

(Des R. Bergamo)

1966 (27 Aug). *Sea Animals.* T **181** *and similar designs. Multicoloured.* W **154**. P 14 × 13 (*horiz*) or 13 × 14 (*vert*).
804	1l. Type **181**	15	15
805	2l. Cuckoo Wrasse	15	15
806	3l. Common Dolphin (*Labro Pavone*)	15	15
807	4l. John Dory (*Pesce San Pietro*)	15	15
808	5l. Octopus (*vert*)	15	15
809	10l. Red Scorpionfish (*Scorpena Rossa*)	15	15
810	40l. Eyed Electric Ray (*Torpedine*) (*vert*)	15	15
811	90l. Medusa (*vert*)	15	15
812	115l. Long-snouted Seahorse (*Cavalluccio Marino*) (*vert*)	15	20
813	130l. Dentex Seabream (*Dentia*)	15	25
804/813	*Set of 10*	1·40	1·50

1967 (16 Mar). *Paintings by Francesco Barbieri (Guercino).* T **184** *and similar multicoloured designs.* W **154**. P 14.
822	40l. Type **184**	10	20
	a. Horiz strip of 3. Nos. 822/4	50	
823	170l. "St Francis"	15	20
824	190l. "Return of the Prodigal Son" (45 × 37 mm)	15	20

Nos. 822/4 were issued in horizontal *se-tenant* strips of 3 within the sheet.

1967 (5 May). *Europa.* W **154**. P 14.
825	**185** 200l. grey-green & light brown-orge	40	30

(Des E. Arseni)

1967 (15 June). *Fungi.* T **186** *and similar vert designs. Multicoloured.* W **154**. P 13 × 14.
826	5l. Type **186**	15	10
827	15l. The miller (*Clitopilus prunulus*)	15	10
828	20l. Parasol mushroom (*Lepiota procera*)	15	10
829	40l. Cep (*Boletus edulis*)	15	10
830	50l. Russula paludosa	15	10
831	170l. St. George's mushroom (*Lyophyllum georgii*)	15	20
826/831	*Set of 6*	80	65

SAN MARINO 1967

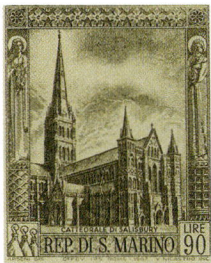

187 Salisbury Cathedral

188 Cimabue Crucifix, Florence

(Des E. Arseni. Eng T. Mele (20l.), S. Vana (40l.), M. Colombati (80l.), V. Nicastro (90l.), E. Donnini (170l.). Recess)

1967 (21 Sept). *Gothic Cathedrals.* T **187** *and similar vert designs.* W **154**. P 14.

832	20l. violet/*cream* (Amiens)		15	15
833	40l. blackish green/*cream* (Siena)		15	10
834	80l. greenish blue/*cream* (Toledo)		15	10
835	90l. sepia/*cream*		15	10
836	170l. carmine/*cream* (Cologne)		15	15
832/836 Set of 5			70	55

(Des T. Mele. Recess and photo)

1967 (5 Dec). *Christmas.* W **154**. P 14.

837	**188**	300l. red-brown and bluish violet	30	40

189 Arms of San Marino

190 Europa "Key"

(Des Martelli. Litho)

1968 (14 Mar). *Arms of San Marino Villages.* T **189** *and similar vert designs. Multicoloured.* W **154**. P 13½.

838	2l. Type **189**		10	15
839	3l. Penna Rossa		10	15
840	5l. Fiorentino		10	15
841	10l. Montecerreto		10	15
842	25l. Serravalle		10	15
843	35l. Montegiardino		10	15
844	50l. Faetano		10	15
845	90l. Borgo Maggiore		10	15
846	180l. Montelupo		10	20
847	500l. State crest		20	30
838/847 Set of 10			1·00	1·50

(Des H. Schwarzenbach. Eng S. Vana. Recess)

1968 (29 Apr). *Europa.* W **154**. P 14 × 13.

848	**190**	250l. brown	40	35

191 "The Battle of San Romano" (detail)

(Des E. Vangelli. Eng A. Quieti. Recess)

1968 (27 June). *671st Birth Anniv of Paolo Uccello (painter).* T **191** *and similar designs, showing details from his three paintings titled "The Battle of San Romano".* W **154**. P 14.

849	50l. black/*pale lilac*		10	15
850	90l. black/*pale lilac* (vert)		10	15
851	130l. black/*pale lilac*		10	20
852	230l. black/*pale pink*		10	30
849/852 Set of 4			35	70

192 "The Nativity" (detail, Botticelli)

193 "Peace"

(Des and eng T. Mele. Recess)

1968 (5 Dec). *Christmas.* W **154**. P 14.

853	**192**	50l. deep ultramarine	10	15
854		90l. deep claret	10	15
855		180l. blackish brown	10	25

(Eng A. Quieti (50l., 90l.), E. Donnini (80l.), R. Di Giuseppe (180l.). Recess)

1969 (13 Feb). *"The Good Government" (frescoes) by Ambrogio Lorenzetti.* T **193** *and similar designs.* W **154**. P 14.

856	50l. deep blue		10	10
857	80l. sepia		10	10
858	90l. slate-violet		10	10
859	180l. claret		10	15
856/859 Set of 4			35	40

Designs: Vert—80l. "Justice"; 90l. "Temperance". Horiz—180l. View of Siena.

194 "Young Soldier" (Bramante)

283

SAN MARINO 1969

1969 (28 Apr). *525th Birth Anniv of Donato Bramante (architect and painter).* T **194** and similar horiz painting. Multicoloured. W **154**. P 14.
860 50l. Type **194** 15 15
861 90l. "Old Soldier" (Bramante) 15 15

195 Colonnade

196 Benched Carriage ("Char-a-banc")

199 "Aries"

200 "Flaming Sun"

(Des L. Gasparra, G. Belli and A. Ponsiglione. Eng G. Denza. Recess)

1969 (28 Apr). *Europa.* W **154**. P 14 × 13.
862 **195** 50l. myrtle-green 25 15
863 180l. reddish purple 25 15

(Des D. Vangelli (Nos. 877/82), L. Vangelli (Nos. 883/8))

1970 (18 Feb). *Signs of the Zodiac.* T **199** and similar horiz designs. Multicoloured. P 14 × 13.
877 1l. Type **199** 10 15
878 2l. "Taurus" 10 15
879 3l. "Gemini" 10 15
880 4l. "Cancer" 10 15
881 5l. "Leo" 10 15
882 10l. "Virgo" 10 15
883 15l. "Libra" 10 15
884 20l. "Scorpio" 10 15
885 70l. "Sagittarius" 10 15
886 90l. "Capricorn" 15 25
887 100l. "Aquarius" 15 25
888 180l. "Pisces" 20 35
877/888 Set of 12 . . . . . 1·30 2·00

(Photo Harrison & Sons)

1969 (25 June). *Horses and Carriages.* T **196** and similar horiz designs. Multicoloured. P 14½ × 14.
864 5l. Type **196** 10 15
865 10l. Barouche 10 15
866 25l. Private drag 10 15
867 40l. Hansom cab 10 15
868 50l. Curricle 10 15
869 90l. Wagonette 10 15
870 180l. Spider phaeton 10 20
864/870 Set of 7 . . . . . 65 1·00

(Des L. le Brocquy)

1970 (30 Apr). *Europa.* P 14 × 13.
889 **200** 90l. red and yellow-green 15 20
890 180l. red and yellow 30 25

201 "The Fleet in the Bay of Naples" (Pieter Brueghel, the elder)

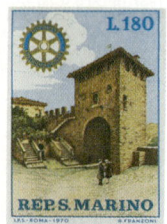

202 St. Francis' Gate

1970 (30 Apr). *10th "Europa" Stamp Exhibition, Naples.* P 14.
891 **201** 230l. multicoloured 15 25

(Des R. Franzoni)

1970 (25 June). *65th Anniv of Rotary International and 10th Anniv of San Marino Rotary Club.* T **202** and similar vert design. Multicoloured. P 13 × 14.
892 180l. Type **202** 10 20
893 220l. "Rocco" Fort, Mt. Titano 25 40

197 Mt. Titano

198 "Faith"

1969 (17 Sept). *Paintings by R. Viola.* T **197** and similar multicoloured designs. P 14.
871 20l. Type **197** 15 15
872 180l. "Pier at Rimini" (*vert*) 15 25
873 200l. "Pier at Riccione" (*horiz*) 15 25

(Eng M. Colombati (20l.). A. Quieti (180l.). T. Mele (200l.) Recess and photo)

1969 (10 Dec). *Christmas.* T **198** and similar vert designs, showing "The Theological Virtues" by Raphael. W **154**. P 13 × 14.
874 20l. deep violet and orange 10 15
875 180l. deep violet and green ("Hope") 10 25
876 200l. deep violet and buff ("Charity") 10 25

203 "Girl with Mandolin"

204 Black Pete

SAN MARINO 1970

1970 (10 Sept). *Death Bicentenary of Giambattista Tiepolo (painter).* T **203** *and similar multicoloured designs.* P 14.
894	50l. Type **203**		15	20
	a. Horiz strip of 3. Nos 894/6		60	
895	180l. "Girl with Parrot"		15	25
896	220l. "Rinaldo and Armida Surprised" (57 × 37 mm)		15	15

Nos. 894/6 were issued together in horizontal *se-tenant* strips of 3 within the sheet.

(Des Walt Disney Studios)

1970 (22 Dec). *Fourth Death Anniv of Walt Disney (film producer). Cartoon Characters.* T **204** *and similar multicoloured designs.* P 14 × 13 (220l.) or 13 × 14 (others).
897	1l. Type **204**		15	15
898	2l. Gyro Gearloose		15	15
899	3l. Pluto		15	15
900	4l. Minnie Mouse		15	15
901	5l. Donald Duck		15	15
902	10l. Goofy		15	15
903	15l. Scrooge McDuck		10	20
904	50l. Hewey, Dewey and Louie		35	25
905	90l. Mickey Mouse		60	65
906	220l. Walt Disney and scene from *The Jungle Book* (horiz)		3·75	2·50
897/906 *Set of 10*			5·00	3·25

205 "Customs House, Venice"

1971 (23 Mar). *"Save Venice" Campaign. Paintings by Canaletto.* T **205** *and similar horiz designs. Multicoloured.* P 14.
907	20l. Type **205**		10	15
908	180l. "Grand Canal, Balbi Palace and Rialto Bridge"		15	35
909	200l. "St Mark's and Doge's Palace"		20	40

206 Congress Building and San Marino Flag

207 Europa Chain

1971 (29 May). *Italian Philatelic Press Union Congress, San Marino.* T **206** *and similar multicoloured design.* P 12.
910	20l. Type **206**		10	10
911	90l. Government Palace door and emblems (*vert*)		10	10
912	180l. Type **206**		10	15

(Des H. Haflidason)

1971 (29 May). *Europa.* P 13½.
913	**207**	50l. new blue and yellow-orange	20	15
914		90l. yellow-orange and new blue	20	20

208 "Duck" Jug with "Lasa" Decoration

209 Day Lily (*Hemerocallis hybrida*)

(Eng V. Nicastro (50l.), E. Donnini (180l.), T. Mele (others). Recess and photo)

1971 (16 Sept). *Etruscan Art (1st series).* T **208** *and similar designs.* P 14.
915	50l. black and flesh		10	15
916	80l. black and pale olive-green		10	15
917	90l. black and pale blue-green		10	20
918	180l. black and flesh		10	20
915/918 *Set of 4*			70	55

Designs: *Vert*—80l. Head of Hermes (bust); 90l. Man and wife (relief from sarcophagus). *Horiz*—180l. Chimera (bronze).
See also Nos. 1018/21.

(Des Anne Marie Trechslin. Photo Courvoisier)

1971 (2 Dec). *Flowers.* T **209** *and similar vert designs. Multicoloured. Granite paper.* P 11½.
919	1l. Type **209**		10	10
920	2l. *Phlox paniculata*		10	10
921	3l. Wild pink (*Dianthus plumarius*)		10	10
922	4l. Globe flower (*Trollius europaeus*)		10	10
923	5l. *Centaurea dealbata*		10	10
924	10l. Peony (*Paeonia lactiflora*)		10	10
925	15l. Christmas rose (*Helleborus niger*)		10	10
926	50l. Pasque flower (*Anemone pulsatilla*)		10	10
927	90l. *Gaillardia aristata*		10	10
928	220l. *Aster dumosus*		15	15
919/928 *Set of 10*			95	95

210 "Allegory of Spring" (detail)

211 "Communications"

1972 (23 Feb). *"Allegory of Spring" by Sandro Botticelli.* T **210** *and similar designs, showing different details of the painting. Multicoloured.* P 13 × 14 (180l.) or 14 (others).
929	50l. Type **210**		10	15
930	180l. The Three Graces (27 × 37 mm)		15	25
931	220l. Flora		25	25

(Des P. Huovinen. Photo Courvoisier)

1972 (27 Apr). *Europa. Granite paper.* P 11½.
932	**211**	50l. multicoloured	20	10
933		90l. multicoloured	20	10

285

SAN MARINO 1972

212 "Taming the Bear"

(Des and eng V. Nicastro. Recess and photo)

1972 (27 Apr). *"Life of St. Marinus"* 16th-century Paintings from former Government Palace. T **212** and similar horiz designs. P 14 × 13.

934	25l. black and buff		10	10
935	55l. black and salmon		10	10
936	100l. black and cobalt		10	10
937	130l. black and olive-yellow		10	10
934/937	Set of 4		35	35

Designs:—55l. "The Conversion of Donna Felicissima"; 100l. "Hostile archers turned to stone"; 130l. "Mt. Titano given to St. Marinus".

215 Veterans Emblem

216 Plane over Mt. Titano

1972 (26 Aug). *"Veterans of Philately"* Award of Italian Philatelic Federation. P 13 × 14.

950	**215**	25l. gold and ultramarine	10	20

(Des A. Vicini. Photo Courvoisier)

1972 (25 Oct). AIR. Granite paper. P 11½.

951	**216**	1000l. multicoloured	1·00	1·00

213 House Sparrow (*Passer italine*)

214 "Healthy Man"

217 Five-cent Coin of 1864

219 Printing Press

218 New York, 1673

(Des A. M. Trechslin. Photo Courvoisier)

1972 (30 June). *Birds.* T **213** and similar vert designs. Multicoloured. Granite paper. P 11.

938	1l. Type **213**		15	10
939	2l. Firecrest (*Regulus ignicapillus*)		15	10
940	3l. Blue tit (*Parus caeruleus*)		15	10
941	4l. Ortolan bunting (*Emboriza Lortulana*)		15	10
942	5l. Bluethroat (*Luscinia Svecica*)		15	10
943	10l. Bullfinch (*Pyrrhula pyorhula*)		15	10
944	25l. Northern linnet (*Carduelis cannabina*)		15	10
945	50l. Black-eared wheatear (*Oenanthe hispanica*)		15	10
946	90l. Sardinian warbler (*Sylvia melanocephala*)		15	10
947	220l. Western greenfinch (*Carduelis chloris*)		15	10
938/947	Set of 10		1·40	90

(Des O. Sabbatini. Litho)

1972 (15 Dec). *San Marino Coinage.* T **217** and similar horiz designs. P 12½ × 13.

952	5l. bronze, black and light grey	45	10
953	10l. bronze, black and orange	45	10
954	15l. silver, black and cerise	45	10
955	20l. silver, black and light purple	45	10
956	25l. silver, black and deep violet-blue	45	15
957	50l. silver, black and new blue	10	10
958	55l. silver, black and yellow-ochre	15	10
959	220l. gold, black and bright green	20	10
952/959	Set of 8	2·40	75

Coins (obverse and reverse on each stamp):—10l. 10c. of 1935; 15l. 1l. of 1906; 20l. 5l. of 1898; 25l. 5l. of 1937; 50l. 10l. of 1932; 55l. 20l. of 1938; 220l. 20l. of 1925.

(Photo Courvoisier)

1973 (9 Mar). *"Interpex" Stamp Exhibition and Important Cities of the World (1st series).* New York. T **218** and similar horiz design. Granite paper. P 11½.

960	200l. brown-ochre, blush grey and black	25	20
	a. Pair. Nos. 960/1	60	50
961	300l. new blue, lilac and deep reddish lilac	35	30

Design:—300l. New York, 1973.
Nos. 960/1 were issued together in *se-tenant* horizontal and vertical pairs within the sheet.

(Des F. Filanci)

1972 (26 Aug). *World Heart Month.* T **214** and similar multicoloured design. P 13 × 14 (50l.) or 14 × 13 (90l.).

948	50l. Type **214**	15	10
949	90l. "Sick Man" (*horiz*)	15	10

286

SAN MARINO 1973

See also Nos. 1032/3, 1075/6, 1144/5, 1160/1, 1197/8, 1215/16, 1230/1, 1259/60, 1271/2, 1306/7, 1331/2, 1358/9, 1524/5 and **MS**1590.

(Des R. Cantiani)

1973 (10 May). *Tourist Press Congress*. P 13 × 14.
962   219   50l. multicoloured 10   20

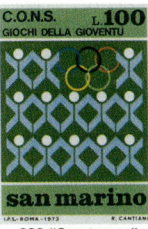

220 "Sportsmen"
221 Europa "Posthorn"

(Des R. Cantiani)

1973 (10 May). *Youth Games*. P 13 × 14.
963   220   100l. multicoloured 15   20

(Des L. F. Anisdahl. Photo Courvoisier)

1973 (10 May). *Europa. Granite paper*. P 11½.
964   221   20l. bright green, ultramarine &
                  flesh 35   20
965   180l. mauve, carmine and pale
                  blue 35   40

222 Grapes
223 Couzinet 70 *Arc-en-Ciel*

(Des A. M. Trechslin. Photo Courvoisier)

1973 (11 July). *Fruits*. T **222** and similar vert designs. Multicoloured. Granite paper. P 11½.
966   1l. Type **222** 10   10
967   2l. Mandarines 10   10
968   3l. Apples 10   10
969   4l. Plums 10   10
970   5l. Strawberries 10   10
971   10l. Pears 10   15
972   25l. Cherries 10   10
973   50l. Pomegranate 10   10
974   90l. Apricots 10   10
975   220l. Peaches 25   20
966/975 *Set of 10* .... 1·00 1·00

(Des E. Vangelli)

1973 (31 Aug). *Aircraft*. T **223** and similar horiz designs. P 14 × 13.
976   25l. deep blue, orange-yellow and
             gold 10   15
977   55l. deep blue, lavender-grey and
             gold 10   10
978   60l. deep blue, rose and gold 10   10
979   90l. deep blue, bistre and gold ... 10   10
980   220l. deep blue, orange and gold .. 10   15
976/980 *Set of 5* 45   55
Aircraft:—55l. Macchi Castoldi MC-72-181 seaplane; 60l. Tupolev ANT-9; 90l. Ryan NYP Special *Spirit of St. Louis* (Charles Lindbergh's plane), 1927; 220l. Handley Page H.P.42.

224 Crossbowman, Serravalle Castle
225 "Adoration of the Magi" (detail)

(Des J. Seger. Photo State Ptg Works, Vienna)

1973 (7 Nov). *San Marino's Victory in Crossbow Tournament, Massa Marittima*. T **224** and similar vert designs. Multicoloured. P 13½.
981   5l. Type **224** 10   10
982   10l. Crossbowman, Pennarossa
             Castle 10   10
983   15l. Drummer, Montegiardino Castle .. 10   10
984   20l. Trumpeter, Fiorentino Castle ... 10   10
985   30l. Crossbowman, Montecerreto
             Castle 10   10
986   40l. Trumpeter, Borgo Maggiore
             Castle 10   10
987   50l. Trumpeter, Guaita Castle 10   10
988   80l. Crossbowman, Faetano Castle .. 10   10
989   200l. Crossbowman, Montelupo Castle . 10   15
981/989 *Set of 9* 80   85

(Photo Courvoisier)

1973 (19 Dec). *Christmas. 600th Birth Anniv of Gentile da Fabriano*. T **225** and similar vert designs, showing different details of Fabriano's altarpiece "Adoration of the Magi". Granite paper. P 12 × 11½.
990   5l. multicoloured 10   10
991   30l. multicoloured 10   10
992   115l. multicoloured 10   10
993   250l. multicoloured 10   20
990/993 *Set of 4* 35   45

226 Combat Shield (16th century)
227 "The Joy of Living" (Emilio Greco)

(Des and eng C. Slania. Recess and litho State Bank Note Ptg Works, Helsinki)

1974 (12 Mar). *Ancient Weapons from "Cesta" Museum, San Marino*. T **226** and similar vert designs. P 13.
994   5l. black, cinnamon & light turq-grn .. 10   10
995   10l. black, cobalt and pale cinnamon .. 10   10
996   15l. black, violet-blue and light blue . 10   10
997   20l. black, violet-blue and cinnamon .. 10   10
998   30l. black, brown and light cobalt 10   10
999   30l. black, cobalt and pink 10   10
1000   80l. black, turq-bl & pale reddish
             lilac 10   10
1001   250l. black and greenish yellow 10   10
994/1001 *Set of 8* 75   75

287

SAN MARINO 1974

Designs:—10l. German armour (16th-century); 15l. Crested morion (16th century); 20l. Horse head-armour (15th–16th century); 30l. Italian morion with crest (16th–17th century); 50l. Gauntlets and sword pommel (16th century); 80l. Sallet helmet (16th century); 250l. Sforza shield (16th century).

(Eng V. Nicastro (100l.), R. di Giuseppe (200l.). Recess and litho)

1974 (9 May). *Europa. Sculpture.* T **227** and similar vert design. P 13 × 14.
| 1002 | 100l. black and pale buff | 35 | 20 |
| 1003 | 200l. black and pale green | 35 | 25 |

Design:—200l. "The Joy of Living" (complete sculpture).

228 "Sea and Mountains"
229 Arms of Sansepolcro

(Des G. Cumo. Photo Courvoisier)

1974 (18 July). *San Marino-Riccione Stamp Fair.* Granite paper. P 11½.
| 1004 | **228** 50l. multicoloured | 15 | 20 |

(Photo State Ptg Works, Vienna)

1974 (18 July). *9th Crossbow Tournament, San Marino.* T **229** and similar vert designs, showing arms. Multicoloured. P 12.
1005	15l. Type **229**	35	15
	a. Horiz strip of 5. Nos. 1005/9	1·75	
1006	20l. Massa Marittima	35	15
1007	50l. San Marino	35	15
1008	115l. Gubbio	35	25
1009	300l. Lucca	35	10
1005/1009	*Set of 5*	1·60	75

Nos. 1005/9 were issued together in horizontal *se-tenant* strips of 5 within the sheet.

230 U.P.U. Emblem and Shadow

(Des and photo Courvoisier)

1974 (9 Oct). *Centenary of Universal Postal Union.* Granite paper. P 11½.
| 1010 | **230** 50l. multicoloured | 10 | 10 |
| 1011 | 90l. multicoloured | 10 | 10 |

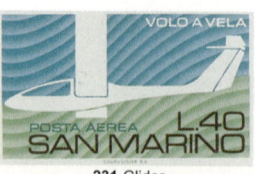

231 Glider
232 Mt. Titano and Verses of Hymn

(Des and photo Courvoisier)

1974 (9 Oct). *AIR. 50th Anniv of Gliding in Italy.* T **231** and similar horiz designs showing gliders in "air currents". Granite paper. P 11½.
1012	40l. turquoise-blue, lt grn & reddish brn	15	10
1013	120l. ultram, greenish bl & dp reddish pur	15	15
1014	500l. bluish violet, dp mauve & dp carm	25	40

(Des T. Mele)

1974 (12 Dec). *Death Centenary of Niccolò Tommaseo (writer).* T **232** and similar vert design. P 13½ × 14.
| 1015 | 50l. black, pale green and red | 10 | 10 |
| 1016 | 150l. black, lemon and blue | 10 | 15 |

Design:—150l. Portrait of Tommaseo.

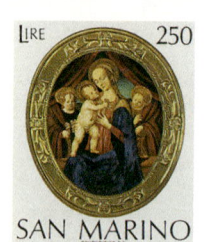

233 "Madonna and Child" (4th-century painting)

(Des and photo Courvoisier)

1974 (12 Dec). *Christmas.* Granite paper. P 11½.
| 1017 | **233** 250l. multicoloured | 25 | 30 |

234 "Dancing Scene", Tomb of the Leopards, Tarquinia
235 "Escape Tunnel"

(Des Italian Govt Ptg Wks, Rome. Eng A. Quieti, (20l., 220l.). M Ramassotto (30l.), T. Mele (180l.). Recess and litho)

1975 (20 Feb). *Etruscan Art (2nd series). Tomb Paintings.* T **234** and similar horiz designs. Multicoloured. P 14.
1018	20l. Type **234**	10	10
1019	30l. "Chariot Race", Tomb of the Hill, Chiusi	10	10
1020	180l. "Achilles and Troillus", Tomb of the Bulls, Tarquinia	15	15
1021	220l. "Dancers" Tomb of the Triclinium, Tarquinia	15	25
1018/1021	*Set of 4*	45	55

(Des E. Morri)

1975 (20 Feb). *30th Anniv of Escape of One Hundred Thousand Italian War Refugees to San Marino.* P 13½ × 14.
| 1022 | **235** 50l. multicoloured | 10 | 20 |

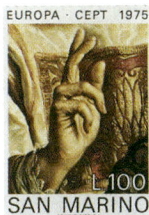

SAN MARINO   1975

236 "The Blessing"
237 "The Virgin Mary" 

(Des and photo Courvoisier)

1975 (14 May). *Europa. Details from "St Marinus" by Guercino.* T **236** and similar vert design. Multicoloured. Granite paper. P 12 × 11½.
| 1023 | 100l. Type **236** | 35 | 15 |
| 1024 | 200l. "St Marinus" | 40 | 25 |

(Des and photo Courvoisier)

1975 (10 July). *Holy Year. Details from Frescoes by Giotto from Scrovegni Chapel, Padua.* T **237** and similar multicoloured designs. Granite paper. P 12 × 11½.
1025	10l. Type **237**	10	15
1026	40l. "Virgin and Child"	10	15
1027	50l. "Heads of Angels"	10	15
1028	100l. "Mary Magdalene" (*horiz*)	10	15
1029	500l. "Heads of Saints" (*horiz*)	15	35
1025/1029	Set of 5	50	85

238 "Aphrodite" (sculpture)
239 Congress Emblem 

(Des and photo Courvoisier)

1975 (19 Sept). *15th Europa Stamp Exhibition, Naples.* Granite paper. P 11½.
| 1030 | **238** | 50l. black, pale greenish grey and reddish violet | 10 | 20 |

(Des G. Valentini. Photo Courvoisier)

1975 (19 Sept). *"Eurocophar" International Pharmaceutical Congress, San Marino.* Granite paper. P 11½.
| 1031 | **239** | 100l. multicoloured | 15 | 20 |

240 Tokyo, 1835
241 "Woman on Balcony" 

(Des and photo Courvoisier)

1975 (19 Sept). *Important Cities of the World (2nd series). Tokyo.* T **240** and similar horiz design. Multicoloured. Granite paper. P 11½.
1032	200l. Type **240**	20	20
	a. Pair Nos. 1032/3	55	70
1033	300l. Tokyo, 1975	30	45

Nos. 1032/3 were issued together in *se-tenant* horizontal and vertical pairs within the sheet.

(Des and photo Courvoisier)

1975 (3 Dec). *International Women's Year. Paintings by Gentilini.* T **241** and similar multicoloured designs. Granite paper. P 11½ × 12 (150l.) or 12 × 11½ (others).
1034	70l. Type **241**	10	10
1035	150l. "Heads of Two Women" (*horiz*)	15	15
1036	230l. "Profile of Girl"	15	30

242 "Head of the Child" (detail)
243 "Modesty" 

(Des and photo Courvoisier)

1975 (3 Dec). *Christmas and 500th Birth Anniv of Michelangelo. Painting "Doni Madonna" and details.* T **242** and similar vert designs. Multicoloured. Granite paper. P 11½.
1037	50l. Type **242**	10	10
	a. Strip of 3 Nos. 1037/9	45	
1038	100l. Head of the Virgin (detail)	10	15
1039	250l. "Doni Madonna"	20	25

Nos. 1037/9 were issued together in *se-tenant* strips of three within the sheet.

(Des and photo Courvoisier)

1976 (4 Mar)–**78**. *"The Civil Virtues". Sketches by Emillo Greco.* T **243** and similar vert designs. Granite paper. P 11½.
1039a		5l. black and pale lavender (28.9.78)	10	10
1040		10l. black and pale stone	10	10
1041		20l. black and pale rose-lilac	10	15
1041a		35l. black and pale stone (28.9.78)	10	10
1042		50l. black and yellow-green	10	10
1043		70l. black and pale rose (14.4.77)	10	10
1044		90l. black & pale grey-pink (14.4.77)	10	10
1045		100l. black and pale pink	10	10
1046		120l. black and pale blue (14.4.77)	10	10
1047		150l. black and pale lilac	10	10
1048		160l. black & pale turq-grn (14.4.77)	10	10
1049		170l. black and pale flesh (14.4.77)	10	10
1050		220l. black and pale grey	10	15
1051		250l. black and pale greenish yellow	10	20
1052		300l. black and pale greenish grey	15	25
1053		320l. black and pale mauve (14.4.77)	15	25
1054		500l. black and stone	20	40
1055		1000l. black and pale azure	40	80
1055a		2000l. black and cream (28.9.78)	1·30	1·80
1039a/1055a	Set of 19		3·25	4·50

Designs:—5l. "Wisdom"; 20, 160l. "Temperance"; 35l. "Love"; 50, 70l. "Fortitude"; 90, 220l. "Prudence"; 100, 120l. "Altruism"; 150, 170l. "Hope"; 250l. "Justice"; 300, 320l. "Faith"; 500l. "Honesty"; 1000l. "Industry"; 2000l. "Faithfulness".

289

SAN MARINO   1976

244 Capitol, Washington
245 Emblem and Maple Leaf. 

(Des and photo Courvoisier)

1976 (29 May). *Bicentenary of American Revolution and "Interphil 1976" International Stamp Exhibition, Philadelphia.* T **244** *and similar vert designs. Multicoloured. Granite paper.* P 11½.
1056	70l. Type **244**		10	10
1057	150l. Statue of Liberty, New York		10	15
1058	180l. Independence Hall, Philadelphia		15	25

(Des and photo Courvoisier)

1976 (29 May). *Olympic Games, Montreal. Granite paper.* P 11½.
1059	**245**	150l. black and rosine	15	25

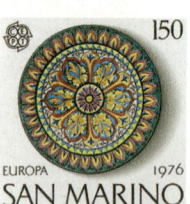

246 Polychrome Plate (U. Bruno)
247 S.U.M.S. Emblem 

(Des and photo Courvoisier)

1976 (8 July). *Europa Handicrafts.* T **246** *and similar square design. Multicoloured. Granite paper.* P 11½.
1060	150l. Type **246**		40	20
1061	180l. Silver plate (A. Ruscelli)		40	25

(Des G. Valentini)

1976 (8 July). *Centenary of San Marino Social Welfare Union.* P 13½ × 14.
1062	**247**	150l. vermilion, greenish yell & lilac	15	25

248 Children of Different Races
249 "San Marino" 

(Des and photo Courvoisier)

1976 (14 Oct). *30th Anniv of United Nations Educational, Scientific and Cultural Organization. Granite paper.* P 11½ × 12.
1063	**248**	180l. sepia, orange and deep blue	10	20
1064		220l. deep brown, buff and sepia	15	35

(Des G. Valentini)

1976 (14 Oct). *"Italia 1976" International Stamp Exhibition, Milan.* P 13½ × 14.
1065	**249**	150l. multicoloured	15	25

250 "The Annunciation"
251 Mount Titano and Emblem 

(Des and eng A. Quieti. Recess and litho)

1976 (15 Dec). *Christmas and 400th Death Anniv of Titian.* T **250** *and similar vert design. Multicoloured.* P 13½ × 14.
1066	150l. Type **250**		20	15
	a. Pair. Nos. 1066/7		55	55
1067	300l. "The Nativity"		30	35

Nos. 1066/7 were issued together in *se-tenant* pairs within the sheet.

(Des and photo Courvoisier)

1977 (9 Feb). *"San Marino 1977" International Stamp Exhibition (1st issue). Granite paper.* P 11½ × 12.

(a) POSTAGE.
1068	**251**	80l. rose-red, green & yellow-olive	10	10
1069		170l. lemon, reddish vio & bright bl	10	15
1070		200l. reddish orange, dull ultramarine & bright greenish blue	15	20

(b) AIR Inscr "POSTA AEREA".
1071	**251**	200l. yellow-ochre, bronze-grn & bl	15	75
1068/1071 Set of 4			45	1·10

See also No. 1082.

252 "San Marino" (Ghirlandaio)
253 Leonardo da Vinci's Drawing of "Helicopter" 

(Des and photo Courvoisier)

1977 (14 Apr). *Europa. Landscapes.* T **252** *and similar horiz design. Multicoloured. Granite paper.* P 11½ × 12.
1072	170l. Type **252**		45	25
1073	200l. "San Marino" (Guercino)		45	35

(Eng G. Verdelocco. Recess and litho)

1977 (15 June). *Centenary of Enrico Forlanini's First Vertical Flight Experiment.* P 13 × 14.
1074	**253**	120l. multicoloured	15	20

SAN MARINO 1977

254 University Square, 1877
255 Design of First San Marino Stamp 

(Des and photo Courvoisier)

1977 (15 June). *Centenary of Rumanian Independence and Important Cities of the World (3rd series). Bucharest.* T **254** and similar horiz design. P 11½.
1075	200l. deep blue-green and pale blue		25	20
	a. Pair. Nos. 1075/6		65	55
1076	400l. brown and stone		35	30

Design:—400l. City centre, 1977.
Nos. 1075/6 were issued together in *se-tenant* horizontal and vertical pairs within the sheet.

(Des F. Filanci. Eng A. Fischer. Recess State Ptg Wks, Vienna)

1977 (15 June). *Centenary of San Marino Postage Stamps.* P 15 × 14½.
1077	**255**	40l. bottle-green	10	10
1078		70l. deep ultramarine	10	10
1079		170l. vermilion	10	15
1080		500l. light brown	35	40
1081		1000l. deep rose-lilac	50	75
1077/1081	*Set of 5*		1·00	1·40

256 "St. Marinus Blessing" (Retrosi)
257 Medicinal Plants 

(Des and photo Courvoisier)

1977 (28 Aug). *"San Marino 1977" International Stamp Exhibition (2nd issue).* P 11½.
1082	**256**	1000l. multicoloured	90	1·20

No. 1082 was issued in small sheets of five stamps.

(Des and photo Courvoisier)

1977 (19 Oct). *Italian Pharmacists' Union Congress. Granite paper.* P 12 × 11½.
1083	**257**	170l. multicoloured	15	25

258 Woman gripped by Octopus
259 Angel 

(Des B. Caruso. Photo Courvoisier)

1977 (19 Oct). *World Rheumatism Year. Granite paper.* P 11½.
1084	**258**	200l. multicoloured	15	30

(Des E. Greco. Photo Courvoisier)

1977 (15 Dec). *Christmas.* T **259** and similar vert designs. Granite paper. P 11½.
1085	170l. slate-black, pale brownish grey and silver	15	15
	a. Strip of 3. Nos. 1085/7	60	
1086	230l. slate-black, pale brownish grey and silver	15	20
1087	300l. slate-black, pale brownish grey and silver	25	25

Designs:—230l. Palm tree and olive; 300l. The Virgin.
Nos. 1085/7 were issued in *se-tenant* strips of three within the sheet.

260 Baseball Player
261 San Francesco Gate 

(Photo Courvoisier)

1978 (30 May). *World Baseball Championships. Granite paper.* P 11½.
1088	**260**	90l. brownish black, turquoise-blue and ultramarine	10	15
1089		120l. brownish-black, bright yellow-green and green	10	20

(Photo Courvoisier)

1978 (30 May). *Europa. Architecture.* T **261** and similar vert design. Granite paper. P 11½.
1090		170l. deep grey-blue & pale blue	45	25
1091		200l. sepia and stone	50	30

Design:—200l. Ripa Gate.

262 Feather
263 Mt. Titano and Antenna 

291

SAN MARINO 1978

(Photo Courvoisier)

1978 (30 May). *World Hypertension Month. Granite paper.* P 11½.
1092 262 320l. black, turquoise-blue & brt scar 20 40

(Photo Courvoisier)

1978 (26 July). *San Marino's Admission to International Telecommunications Union. Granite paper.* P 12 × 11½.
1093 263 10l. yellow and deep rose-red 10 10
1094   200l. pale blue and bluish violet 20 15

264 Hawk and Slender-billed Gull

265 Wright Brothers' Flyer 1

(Des G. Cumo. Photo Courvoisier)

1978 (26 July). *30th San Marino-Riccione Stamp Fair. Granite paper.* P 11½ × 12.
1095 264 120l. multicoloured 10 15
1096   170l. multicoloured 20 25

(Photo Courvoisier)

1978 (28 Sept). *AIR. 75th Anniv of First Powered Flight. Granite paper.* P 11½.
1097 265 10l. multicoloured 15 10
1098   50l. multicoloured 15 10
1099   200l. multicoloured 15 10

266 Allegory of Human Rights

267 Holly

(Des R. Guttuso. Photo Courvoisier)

1978 (10 Dec). *30th Anniv of Declaration of Human Rights. Granite paper.* P 11½.
1100 266 200l. multicoloured 15 25

1978 (10 Dec). *Christmas.* T **267** and similar horiz designs. *Multicoloured.* P 14 × 13.
1101 10l. Type 267 .... 10 10
1102 120l. Star 10 10
1103 170l. Snowflakes 10 15

268 Albert Einstein

269 Motor-coach, 1915

(Photo Courvoisier)

1979 (29 Mar). *Birth Centenary of Albert Einstein (physicist). Granite paper.* P 11½.
1104 268 120l. grey-brown, sepia and pale grey 15 25

(Photo Courvoisier)

1979 (29 Mar). *Europa.* T **269** and similar horiz design. *Multicoloured. Granite paper.* P 11½.
1105 170l. Type 269 .... 30 40
1106 220l. Horse-drawn stage-coach 40 55

270 San Marino Crossbowmen Federation Emblem

271 Maigret (G. Simenon)

(Eng. M. Ramassotto. Recess and litho)

1979 (12 July). *14th Crossbow Tournament.* P 14 × 13½.
1107 270 120l. multicoloured 15 15

(Eng G. Toffoletti. Recess and litho)

1979 (12 July). *Fictional Detectives.* T **271** and similar vert designs. *Multicoloured.* P 13 × 14.
1108 10l. Type 271 .... 10 15
1109 80l. Perry Mason (S. Gardner) 10 15
1110 150l. Nero Wolfe (R. Stout) 10 15
1111 170l. Ellery Queen (F. Dannay and M. B. Lee) 10 20
1112 220l. Sherlock Holmes (A. Conan Doyle) 10 25
1108/1112 *Set of* 5 .... 45 80

272 Water Skiing

273 St. Apollonia

(Des G. Consilvio. Photo Courvoisier)

1979 (6 Sept). *Water Skiing Championships, Castelgandolfo. Granite paper.* P 11½.
1113 272 150l. myrtle green, light blue and black 15 25

(Photo Courvoisier)

1979 (6 Sept). *13th International Stomatology Congress. Granite paper.* P 11½.
1114 273 170l. multicoloured 15 25

292

SAN MARINO 1979

274 "Knowledge"

275 Horse Chestnut (*Aesculus hippocastanum*) and Red Deer

(Des M. Busignani Reffi. Photo Courvoisier)

1979 (6 Sept). *International Year of the Child. T 274 and similar vert designs. Multicoloured. Granite paper.* P 11½.
1115	20l. Type **274**	15	10
1116	120l. "Friendship"	15	10
1117	170l. "Equality"	15	15
1118	220l. "Love"	15	25
1119	350l. "Existence"	25	35
1115/1119	*Set of 5*	75	85

(Des A. M. Trechslin. Photo Courvoisier)

1979 (25 Oct). *Environmental Protection. Trees and Animals. T 275 and similar vert designs. Multicoloured. Granite paper.* P 11½.
1120	5l. Type **275**	20	10
1121	10l. Cedar of Lebanon (*Cedrus libani*) and golden eagle	20	10
1122	35l. Flowering dogwood (*Cornus florida rubra*) and racoon	20	15
1123	50l. Banyan (*Ficus benghalensis*) and tiger	20	10
1124	70l. Stone pine (*Pinus pinea*) and hoopoe	20	10
1125	90l. Larch (*Larix sibirica*) and yellow-throated marten	20	10
1126	100l. Tasmanian blue gum (*Eucalyptus globulus*) and koala	20	10
1127	120l. Date palm (*Phoenix dactylifera*) and dromedary	20	10
1128	150l. Silver maple (*Acer saccharum*) and American beaver	20	10
1129	170l. Baobab (*Adansonia digitata*) and African elephant	20	15
1120/1129	*Set of 10*	1·80	1·00

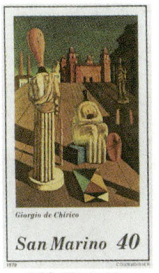

276 "Disturbing Muses"

277 St. Joseph

(Photo Courvoisier)

1979 (6 Dec). *First Death Anniv of Giorgio de Chirico (painter) T 276 and similar vert designs. Multicoloured. Granite paper.* P 11½.
1130	40l. Type **776**	10	10
1131	150l. "Ancient Horses"	10	15
1132	170l. "Self-portrait"	10	20

(Photo Courvoisier)

1979 (6 Dec). *Christmas. T 277 and similar vert designs showing "The Holy Family" (fresco) by Antonio Alberti or details from it. Multicoloured. Granite paper.* P 11½.
1133	80l. Type **277**	15	15
1134	170l. Infant Jesus	15	15
1135	220l. Magus	15	25
1136	320l. "The Holy Family"	20	35
1133/1136	*Set of 4*	60	80

278 St. Benedict of Nursia

279 Cigarette Ends

(Photo Courvoisier)

1980 (27 Mar). *15th Birth Centenary of St. Benedict of Nursia. Granite paper.* P 11½.
1137	**278**	170l. multicoloured	15	25

(Des G. Consilvio. Photo Courvoisier)

1980 (27 Mar). *Anti-smoking Campaign. T 279 and similar vert designs. Multicoloured. Granite paper.* P 11½.
1138	120l. Type **279**	15	20
1139	220l. Face hidden by cigarettes	15	25
1140	520l. Face wreathed in smoke	25	45

280 Naples

281 Giovanbattista Belluzzi (military architect)

1980 (27 Mar). *"Europa" International Stamp Exhibition, Naples.* P 14 × 13.
1141	**280**	170l. multicoloured	15	25

(Des G. Macina. Photo Courvoisier)

1980 (8 May). *Europa. T 281 and similar vert design. Multicoloured. Granite paper.* P 11½.
1142	170l. Type **281**	50	25
1143	220l. Antonio Orafo (silver and goldsmith)	60	30

293

SAN MARINO   1980

282 London, 1850  **283** Cycling **286** City Fortifications **287** "The Annunciation" (detail)

(Photo Courvoisier)

1980 (8 May). *"London 1980" International Stamp Exhibition and Important Cities of the World (4th series). London.* T **282** and similar horiz design. Granite paper. P 11½.
1144	200l. brown-ochre and blackish green		15	25
	a. Pair Nos. 1144/5		60	65
1145	400l. light new blue & deep reddish lilac		40	35

Design:—400l. London, 1980.
Nos. 1144/5 were issued together in *se-tenant* horizontal and vertical pairs within the sheet.

(Eng. E. Donnini. Recess and litho)

1980 (18 Sept). *World Tourism Conference, Manila.* P 13 × 14.
1153	**286**	220l. multicoloured	15	30

(Des A. Böcskör. Eng W. Seidel (180l.), A. Fischer (others). Recess and photo State Ptg Wks, Vienna)

1980 (11 Dec). *Christmas.* T **287** and similar vert designs showing paintings by Andrea del Sarto. Multicoloured. P 13½.
1154	180l.	"Madonna of the Harpies" (detail)	15	25
1155	250l.	Mary (detail, "The Annunciation")	25	25
1156	500l.	Type **287**	40	50

(Des G. Porzano. Photo Courvoisier)

1980 (10 July). *Olympic Games, Moscow.* T **283** and similar vert designs. Granite paper. P 11½.
1146	70l. black, emerald and myrtle green		10	15
1147	90l. black, yellowish orge & orge-brown		10	15
1148	170l. black, carmine-red & dp magenta		10	20
1149	350l. black, greenish blue & deep dull blue		20	35
1150	450l. black, bluish violet & deep ultram		25	45
1146/1150	Set of 5		70	1·20

Designs:—90l. Basketball; 170l. Running; 350l. Gymnastics; 450l. High jump.

288 St. Joseph's Eve Bonfire **289** Hands holding Broken Branch

(Photo Courvoisier)

1981 (24 Mar). *Europa.* T **288** and similar vert design. Multicoloured. Granite paper. P 11½.
1157	200l. Type **288**		45	25
1158	300l. National Day fireworks		70	35

284 Stolz and Score of *Philatelic Waltz*  **285** Weightlifter

(Des A. Böcskör. Eng A. Fischer. Recess and photo State Ptg Wks, Vienna)

1980 (18 Sept). *Birth Centenary of Robert Stolz (composer).* P 14.
1151	**284**	120l. dull ultramarine and black	15	20

(Photo Courvoisier)

1981 (15 May). *International Year of Disabled Persons.* Granite paper. P 11½.
1159	**289**	300l. orange-yellow, myrtle green and yellow-green	10	40

(Des G. Porzano)

1980 (18 Sept). *European Junior Weightlifting Championship.* P 14 × 13½.
1152	**285**	170l. carmine, black and deep turq	15	25

290 "St. Charles's Square, 1817" (Jakob Alt)  **291** Motor Cyclist

SAN MARINO   1981

(Photo Courvoisier)

1981 (15 May). *"WIPA 1981" International Stamp Exhibition and Important Cities of the World (5th series). Vienna.* T **290** and similar horiz design. Multicoloured. Granite paper. P 11½.
1160   200l. Type **290**   10   20
    a. Pair. Nos. 1160/1   35   60
1161   300l. St. Charles's Square, 1981   20   35
Nos. 1160/1 were issued together in *se-tenant* horizontal and vertical pairs within the sheet.

(Litho Harrison)

1981 (10 July). *San Marino Motor Cycle Grand Prix.* P 14 × 14½.
1162   **291**   200l. multicoloured   15   35

292 Girl playing Pipes    **293** House

(Des E. Greco. Photo Courvoisier)

1981 (10 July). *Birth Bimillenary of Virgil (poet).* T **292** and similar vert designs, each greenish slate and silver. Granite paper. P 11½.
1163   300l. Type **292**   35   35
1164   550l. Soldier   45   55
1165   1500l. Shepherd   70   1·40
MS1166   128 × 100 mm. Nos. 1163/5 . . . . .   2·50   2·75

(Photo Courvoisier)

1981 (22 Sept). *Urban Development Scheme.* T **293** and similar vert designs. Multicoloured. Granite paper. P 11½.
1167   20l. Type **293**   10   15
1168   80l. Tree (provision of green belts) . . .   10   15
1169   400l. Gas flame (power plants)   15   40

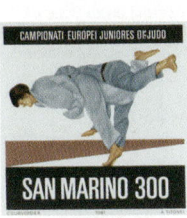

294 Judo    **295** "Girl with Dove" (Picasso)

(Des A. Titonel. Photo Courvoisier)

1981 (22 Sept). *European Junior Judo Championships, San Marino.* Granite paper. P 11½.
1170   **294**   300l. multicoloured   20   40

(Photo Courvoisier)

1981 (23 Oct). *Birth Centenary of Pablo Picasso (artist).* T **295** and similar vert design. Multicoloured. Granite paper. P 11½.
1171   150l. Type **295**   15   25
1172   200l. "Homage to Picasso" (detail, Renato Guttuso)   15   30

296 Bread    **297** King Presenting Gift

(Des B. Caruso. Photo Courvoisier)

1981 (23 Oct). *World Food Day.* Granite paper. P 11½.
1173   **296**   300l. multicoloured   20   40

(Des A. Böcskör. Eng W. Seidel. Recess and photo State Ptg Wks, Vienna)

1981 (15 Dec). *Christmas and 500th Birth Anniv of Benvenuto Tisi da Garofalo (artist).* T **297** and similar vert designs showing details from "Adoration of the Magi and St. Bartholomew". Multicoloured. P 13½.
1174   200l. Type **297**   15   15
1175   300l. Kneeling King   20   25
1176   600l. Virgin and Child   35   60

298 Cancellation and "San Marino 82" Emblem    **299** "The Cicada and the Ant" (Aesop fable)

(Des G. Valentini. Photo Courvoisier)

1982 (19 Feb). *Centenary of Postal Stationery.* Granite paper. P 11½.
1177   **298**   200l. multicoloured   10   25

(Photo Courvoisier)

1982 (19 Feb). *Centenary of Savings Bank.* Granite paper. P 11½.
1178   **299**   300l. multicoloured   20   40

300 Assembly of Heads of Families, 1906    **301** Archimedes

295

SAN MARINO 1982

(Des R. Martelli. Photo Courvoisier)

1982 (21 Apr). *Europa. T* **300** *and similar vert design. Multicoloured. Granite paper.* P 11½.
1179　300l. Type **300** . . . . 2·10　55
1180　450l. Napoleon at the border of San
　　　Marino, 1797 . . . . 1·60　75

(Des A. Titonel. Eng P. Arghittu (200 to 450l.), F. Pedacchia (1000l.), M. Robiati (1400l.), A. Ciaburro (5000l.). Photo (20 to 150l., 250, 350, 400l.), recess and litho (200, 300, 450l.) or recess (1000 to 5000l.))

1982 (21 Apr)–**83**. *Pioneers of Science. T* **301** *and similar vert designs.* P 14 × 13½.
1181　20l. carmine and black . . . . 10　10
1182　30l. deep turquoise-blue and black . . 10　10
1183　40l. deep yellow-brown and black . . 10　10
1184　50l. emerald and black . . . . 10　10
1185　60l. dull vermilion and black . . . . 10　10
1186　100l. blackish brown and black . . . 10　10
1187　150l. dp yellow-brown & black
　　　(24.2.83) . . . . 10　15
1188　200l. flesh and black . . . . 20　15
1189　250l. Venetian red and black
　　　(24.2.83) . . . . 45　15
1190　300l. apple green and black . . . . . 15　20
1191　350l. blue-green and black (24.2.83) . 25　20
1192　400l. deep claret and black
　　　(24.2.83) . . . . 35　30
1193　450l. bright rose and black . . . . . 30　40
1194　1000l. bright carmine and black
　　　(24.2.83) . . . . 55　60
1195　1400l. venetian red and black
　　　(24.2.83) . . . . 75　1·00
1196　5000l. indigo and ultramarine . . . . 2·50　3·75
1181/1196 *Set of* 16 . . . . 5·50　6·75

Designs:—30l. Copernicus; 40l. Isaac Newton; 50l. Antoine Lavoisier; 60l. Marie Curie; 100l. Robert Koch; 150l. Alexander Fleming; 200l. Thomas Edison; 250l. Alessandro Volta; 300l. Guglielmo Marconi; 350l. Evangelista Torricelli; 400l. Carl Linnaeus; 450l. Hippocrates; 1000l. Pythagoras; 1400l. Leonardo da Vinci; 5000l. Galileo.

302 "Notre Dame, 1806" (J. Hill)

(Photo Courvoisier)

1982 (10 June). *"Philexfrance 82" International Stamp Exhibition and Important Cities of the World (6th series). Paris. T* **302** *and similar horiz design. Granite paper.* P 11½.
1197　300l. buff and black . . . . 25　25
　　　a. Pair. Nos. 1197/8 . . . . . . 60　65
1198　450l. multicoloured . . . . 30　35

Design:—Notre Dame and Ile de Cité, 1982.
Nos. 1197/8 were issued together in *se-tenant* horizontal and vertical pairs within the sheet.

(Des R. Guttuso. Photo Courvoisier)

1982 (10 June). *800th Birth Anniv of St. Francis of Assisi. Granite paper.* P 11½.
1199　**303**　200l. multicoloured . . . . . . 10　30

304 Pope John Paul II

305 Globe encircled by Flag Stamps

(Des G. Cumo. Litho)

1982 (29 Aug). *Visit of Pope John Paul II to San Marino.* P 13½ × 14.
1200　**304**　900l. dull purple, myrtle green and
　　　　　dull blue-green . . . . 60　95

(Photo Courvoisier)

1982 (1 Sept). *Fifth Anniv of International Association of Philatelic Catalogue Editors (ASCAT). Granite paper.* P 11½.
1201　**305**　300l. multicoloured . . . . . . 20　40

306 Face besplattered with Blood

307 "Accipe Lampadam Ardentem" (detail)

(Des B. Caruso. Photo Courvoisier)

1982 (1 Sept). *15th International Congress of Amnesty International, Rimini. Granite paper.* P 11½.
1202　**306**　700l. bright scarlet and black . . 45　75

(Des and eng W. Pfeiler. Recess and photo State Ptg Wks, Vienna)

1982 (15 Dec). *Christmas. T* **307** *and similar vert designs showing paintings by Gregorio Sciltian. Multicoloured.* P 13¼.
1203　200l. Type **307** . . . . 15　15
1204　300l. "Madonna della Città" (detail) . . 25　35
1205　450l. Angel (detail, "Accipe Sal
　　　Sapientiae") . . . . 30　50

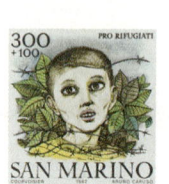

308 Refugee

309 Begni Building and Quill

(Des B. Caruso. Photo Courvoisier)

1982 (15 Dec). *"For Refugees". Granite paper.* P 11½.
1206　**308**　300l. + 100l. multicoloured . . . 20　40

SAN MARINO 1983

(Des T. Mele)
1983 (24 Feb). *Centenary of Secondary School.* P 13½ × 14.
1207 **309** 300l. multicoloured 20 40

310 Formula One Racing Cars

311 Auguste Piccard and Stratosphere Balloon *F.N.R.S.*

(Des A. de Giusti)
1983 (20 Apr). *San Marino Formula One Grand Prix.* P 14 × 13½.
1208 **310** 50l. multicoloured 10 10
1209 350l. multicoloured 30 50

(Photo Courvoisier)
1983 (20 Apr). *Europa.* T **311** *and similar vert design. Multicoloured. Granite paper.* P 11½.
1210 400l. Type **311** . . . . 1·50 1·00
1211 500l. Piccard and bathyscaphe . . 1·70 1·30

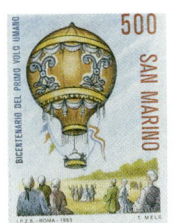

312 Amateur Radio Operator

313 Montgolfier Balloon

(Des T. Mele. Eng F. Pedacchia (400l.), M. Robiati (500l.) Recess)
1983 (20 Apr). *World Communications Year.* T **312** *and similar horiz design.* P 14 × 13½.
1212 400l. black, ultramarine and scarlet . . . 30 45
1213 500l. black, chestnut and rose-red . . . 30 60
Design:—500l. Postman on bicycle.

(Des T. Mele. Recess and litho)
1983 (22 May). *Bicentenary of Manned Flight.* P 13½ × 14.
1214 **313** 500l. multicoloured 35 60

314 "Rio de Janeiro, 1845" (Richard Bate)

(Photo Courvoisier)
1983 (29 July). *"Brasiliana '83" International Stamp Exhibition and Important Cities of the World (7th series). Rio de Janeiro.* T **314** *and similar horiz design. Multicoloured. Granite paper.* P 11½.
1215 400l. Type **314** 30 35
 a. Pair. Nos. 1215/16 . . . . . 1·40 1·40
1216 1400l. Rio de Janeiro, 1983 . . . . 1·00 1·10

Nos. 1215/16 were issued together in *se-tenant* horizontal and vertical pairs within the sheet.

315 Feeding Colt

316 "Madonna of the Grand Duke"

(Des A. Sassu)
1983 (29 Sept). *World Food Programme.* P 14 × 13½.
1217 **315** 500l. multicoloured 35 60

(Des A. Böcskör. Eng W. Seidel. Recess and photo State Ptg Wks, Vienna)
1983 (1 Dec). *Christmas. 500th Birth Anniv of Raphael.* T **316** *and similar vert designs. Multicoloured.* P 13½.
1218 300l. Type **316** 25 25
 a. Strip of 3. Nos. 1218/20 . . . 1·10
1219 400l. "Madonna of the Goldfinch" (detail) 35 35
1220 500l. "Madonna of the Chair" (detail) . . 45 40
Nos. 1218/20 were issued together in *se-tenant* strips of three within the sheet.

317 Demetrius Vikelas

318 Bridge

1984 (8 Feb). *90th Anniv of International Olympic Committee.* T **317** *and similar vert designs showing I.O.C. Presidents.* P 14 × 13½.
1221 300l. brownish black & deep bluish green 40 40
1222 400l. dull claret and new blue . . . 50 45
1223 550l. slate-lilac and deep bluish green 60 60
Designs:—400l. Lord Killanin, 550l. Juan Samaranch.

(Des J. Larrivière. Photo Courvoisier)
1984 (27 Apr). *Europa. 25th Anniv of European Posts and Telecommunications Conference. Granite paper.* P 11½.
1224 **318** 400l. chrome yellow, bluish violet and black . . . . 1·30 90
1225 550l. chrome yellow, deep carmine and black . . . . 2·00 1·20

SAN MARINO 1984

319 Flag Waver
320 Male Athlete 

(Des R. Martelli. Eng G. Lancia (300l.), R. Sabbatucci (400l.). Recess and litho)

1984 (27 Apr). *Flag Wavers.* T **319** and similar vert design. Multicoloured. P $13\frac{1}{2}$ × 14.
1226	300l. Type **319**	20	35
1227	400l. Waver with two flags	55	50

(Des T. Mele. Eng T. Cipriano. Recess and litho)

1984 (14 June). *Olympic Games, Los Angeles.* Sheet 151 × 110 mm, containing T **320** and similar vert design. Multicoloured. P $13\frac{1}{2}$ × 14.
MS1228 550l. Type **320**; 1000l. Female athlete . . . . 1·60   1·60

321 Motocross
322 Collins Street, 1839 

(Des A. de Giusti)

1984 (14 June). *World Motocross Championship.* P $13\frac{1}{2}$ × 14.
1229	**321**	450l. multicoloured	35	60

(Photo Courvoisier)

1984 (21 Sept). *"Ausipex 84" International Stamp Exhibition and Important Cities of the World (8th series). Melbourne.* T **322** and similar horiz design. Multicoloured. Granite paper. P$11\frac{1}{2}$.
1230	1500l. Type **322**	1·20	1·20
	a. Pair. Nos. 1230/1	2·75	3·00
1231	2000l. Flinders Street Station, 1984	1·50	1·60

Nos. 1230/1 were issued together in *se-tenant* horizontal and vertical pairs within the sheet.

323 Pres. Pertini and San Marino City
324 "Universe" 

1984 (20 Oct). *Visit of President Sandro Pertini of Italy.* P 14 × $13\frac{1}{2}$.
1232	**323**	1950l. multicoloured	1·30	1·60

(Des B. Jacovitti)

1984 (30 Oct). *Youth Philately.* T **324** and similar vert designs. Multicoloured. P $13\frac{1}{2}$ × 14.
1233	50l. Type **324**	10	15
1234	100l. Caveman and modern man framed by television ("The Evolution of Life")	15	15
1235	150l. Pipe smoker driving car ("The World in which we Live")	15	15
1236	200l. Man with fig leaf and snake with apple ("Mankind")	15	20
1237	450l. Scientist with H-bomb ("Science")	20	50
1238	550l. Man in barrel with books and candle ("Philosophy")	30	60
1233/1238	*Set of 6*	1·00	1·60

325 Angel with Book
326 Johann Sebastian Bach and Score 

(Des E. Mossini. Eng R. Sabbatucci. Recess and litho)

1984 (5 Dec). *Christmas.* T **325** and similar vert designs showing details of "Madonna of San Girolamo" by Correggio. Multicoloured. P $13\frac{1}{2}$ × 14.
1239	400l. Type **325**	40	55
	a. Strip of 3. Nos. 1239/41	1·60	
1240	450l. Virgin and child	50	60
1241	550l. Attendant	60	75

Nos. 1239/41 were issued together in *se-tenant* strips of three within the sheet.

(Photo Courvoisier)

1985 (18 Mar). *Europa.* T **326** and similar vert design. Granite paper. P 12.
1242	450l. grey-black and yellow	1·30	95
1243	600l. blackish brown and bright green	2·00	1·30

Design:—600l. Vincenzo Bellini and score.

327 State Flags, Stadium and Swimming Pictogram
328 Sunset and Birds 

(Des G. Macina)

1985 (16 May). *First European Small States Games.* T **327** and similar vert designs. Multicoloured. P $13\frac{1}{2}$ × 14.
1244	50l. Type **327**	10	10
1245	350l. Flags, stadium and running pictogram	20	25
1246	400l. Flags, stadium and shooting pictogram	25	35

SAN MARINO   1985

1247	450l. Flags, stadium and cycling pictogram	30	40
1248	600l. Flags, stadium and handball pictogram	40	55
1244/1248	Set of 5	1·10	1·50

(Des F. Martelli, Jnr)

1985 (16 May). *Emigration.* P 13½ × 14.
1249	328	600l. multicoloured	45	60

333 Common Carp

334 Cat (after Pompeian mosaic)

(Photo Harrison)

1985 (11 Sept). *World Angling Championships, River Arno, Florence.* P 14 × 15.
1257	333	600l. multicoloured	45	60

(Photo Courvoisier)

1985 (25 Oct). *International Feline Federation Congress. Granite paper.* P 12 × 11½.
1258	334	600l. multicoloured	45	60

329 Face and Hand holding Dove

330 Camera and San Marino Palace

(Des G. Oikonomoy. Photo Courvoisier)

1985 (24 June). *International Youth Year. T* **329** *and similar vert design, each orange-yellow, greenish blue and gold. Granite paper.* P 12 × 11½.
1250	400l. Type **329**	30	40
1251	600l. Girl's face, dove and horse's head	40	60

1985 (24 June). *18th International Federation of Photographic Art Congress.* P 13½ × 14.
1252	330	450l. multicoloured	35	50

335 Colosseum, 85 A.D.

(Photo Courvoisier)

1985 (25 Oct). *"Italia 85" International Stamp Exhibition and Important Cities of the World (9th series). Rome. T* **335** *and similar horiz design. Multicoloured. Granite paper.* P 11½.
1259	1000l. Type **335**	65	80
	a. Pair. Nos. 1259/60	1·60	2·10
1260	1500l. Colosseum, 1985	90	1·20

Nos. 1259/60 were issued together in *se-tenant* horizontal and vertical pairs within the sheet.

331 Sun breaking through Clouds and Sapling

332 Don Abbondio and Don Rodrigo's Henchmen

1985 (24 June). *Tenth Anniv of Helsinki European Security and Co-operation Conference.* P 13½ × 14.
1253	331	600l. multicoloured	45	65

336 Flying Angel

(Des A. Tuma. Eng W. Seidel. Recess and photo State Ptg Wks, Vienna)

1985 (3 Dec). *Christmas. T* **336** *and similar horiz designs. Multicoloured.* P 14 × 13½.
1261	400l. Type **336**	55	50
	a. Strip of 3. Nos. 1261/3	2·20	
1262	450l. Madonna and child	75	55
1263	600l. Angel resting	85	75

Nos. 1261/3 were issued together in *se-tenant* strips of three within the sheet.

(Eng F. Serandrea (400l.), R. Sabbatucci (450l.), F. Pedacchia (600l.). Recess)

1985 (11 Sept). *Birth Bicentenary of Alessandro Manzoni (writer). T* **332** *and similar horiz designs showing scenes from* I Promessi Sposi. P 14 × 13½.
1254	400l. green	25	35
1255	450l. reddish brown	30	45
1256	600l. blue	40	60

Designs:—450l. Forcing curate to bless wedding; 600l. Plague in Milan.

299

SAN MARINO 1986

337 Aerial View of Cailungo Hospital

338 "Giotto" Space Probe

(Photo Courvoisier)

1986 (6 Mar). *World Health Day (650l.) and 30th Anniv of Social Security Institute (450l.). T **337** and similar horiz design. Multicoloured. Granite paper.* P 11½.
1264   450l. Type **337** 30   55
1265   650l. Front view of Cailungo hospital . .   40   70

(Photo Courvoisier)

1986 (6 Mar). *Appearance of Halley's Comet. T **338** and similar horiz design. Multicoloured. Granite paper.* P 11½.
1266   550l. Type **338** 45   60
1267   1000l. "Adoration of the Magi" (Giotto) 75   1·20

339 Player and Emblem

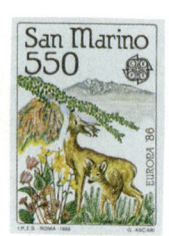

340 Deer

(Des M. R. Pasquali. Eng G. Lancia. Recess)

1986 (22 May). *World Table Tennis Championships, Rimini.* P 13½ × 14.
1268   **339**   450l. Prussian blue, ultramarine and crimson 35   65

(Des G. Ascari)

1986 (22 May). *Europa. T **340** and similar vert design. Multicoloured.* P 13½ × 14.
1269   550l. Type **340** . . . . 6·75   4·50
1270   650l. Common kestrel . . . . . . 9·00   5·00

341 Water Tower, 1870 (lithograph, Charles Shober)

342 Swallows

(Photo Courvoisier)

1986 (22 May). *"Ameripex" International Stamp Exhibition and Important Cities of the World (10th series). Chicago. T **341** and similar horiz designs. Multicoloured. Granite paper.* P 11½.
1271   2000l. Type **341** . . . . 1·50   1·60
    a. Pair. Nos. 1271/2 . . . . . . 3·50
1272   3000l. Water tower, 1986 . . . . . 1·90   2·50
Nos. 1271/2 were issued together in *se-tenant* pairs within the sheet.

(Des L. Minguzzi. Photo Courvoisier)

1986 (10 July). *International Peace Year. Granite paper.* P 11½.
1273   **342**   550l. multicoloured 40   70

343 Head of Soldier

344 "Apollo dancing with the Muses" (detail, Giulio Romano)

(Eng F. Pedacchia (550l.), F. Sarandrea (650l.), M. Robiati (2000l.). Recess and litho)

1986 (10 July). *15th Anniv of Establishment of Diplomatic Relations with Chinese People's Republic. Terracotta Figures from Qin Shi Huang's Tomb. Sheet 153 × 95 mm, containing T **343** and similar designs.* P 13½.
MS1274   550l. black and light blue; 650l. black and deep brown; 2000l. black and magenta . . . . 3·50   3·50
Designs: *Horiz*—650l. Head of horse. *Vert*—2000l. Head of soldier (*different*).

(Photo Harrison)

1986 (16 Sept). *25th Anniv of San Marino Choral Society.* P 14 × 15.
1275   **344**   450l. multicoloured 35   50

345 Boules Player

346 Boy

(Photo Harrison)

1986 (16 Sept). *European Boules Championships, San Marino.* P 14 × 15.
1276   **345**   550l. multicoloured 40   60

(Des B. Caruso. Photo Courvoisier)

1986 (16 Sept). *40th Anniv of United Nations Children's Fund. Child Survival Campaign. Granite paper.* P 12.
1277   **346**   650l. multicoloured 45   80

SAN MARINO   1986

347 "St. John the Baptist"
348 Motor Car and Route Map (Paris-Peking Rally, 1907) 
351 "Chromatic Invention" (Corrado Cagli)
352 Baroudeur Microlight, San Marino Air Club

(Des Maria Schulz. Eng W. Seidel. Recess and photo State Ptg Wks, Vienna)

1986 (26 Nov). Christmas. Triptych by Hans Memling. T **347** and similar vert designs. Multicoloured. P 14.
1278	450l. Type **347**		55	60
	a. Strip of 3. Nos. 1278/80		2·10	
1279	550l. "Madonna and Child"		70	65
1280	650l. "St. John the Evangelist"		75	80

Nos 1278/80 were issued together in *se-tenant* strips of three within the sheet.

(Des E. Zangheri. Photo Courvoisier)

1987 (12 Mar). Motor Rallies. T **348** and similar horiz designs. Multicoloured. Granite paper. P 11½.
1281	500l. Type **348**		35	45
1282	600l. Peugeot "205" (15th San Marino Rally)		35	55
1283	700l. Motor car and crowds (60th anniv of Mille Miglia)		55	65

349 Sketch of Church
350 Modern Sculpture (Reffi Busignani) 

(Photo Courvoisier)

1987 (12 Mar). Europa. Architecture. Our Lady of Consolation Church, Borgomaggiore (Giovanni Michelucci). T **349** and similar vert design. Granite paper. P 12.
1284	600l. black and carmine-red		7·75	3·50
1285	700l. brownish black and yellow		9·00	4·50

Design:—700l. Church interior.

(Des F. Filanci)

1987 (13 June). Modern Sculptures in San Marino. T **350** and similar vert designs showing works by artists named. Multicoloured. P 14 × 13½.
1286	50l. Type **350**		10	15
1287	100l. Bini		10	15
1288	200l. Guguianu		15	20
1289	300l. Berti		15	35
1290	400l. Crocetti		30	40
1291	500l. Berti		30	55
1292	600l. Messina		40	65
1293	1000l. Minguzzi		55	1·10
1294	2200l. Greco		1·20	2·30
1295	10000l. Sassu		7·25	11·50
1286/1295	Set of 10		9·50	16·00

Nos. 1296/9 are vacant.

(Photo Courvoisier)

1987 (13 June). Art Biennale. T **351** and similar vert design. Granite paper. P 11½.
1300	500l. blue, black and vermilion		35	55
1301	600l. multicoloured		40	70

Design:—500l. "From My Brazilian Diary — Virgin Forest" (Emilio Vedova).

(Des A. de Giusti. Photo Courvoisier)

1987 (13 June). Granite paper. P 11½.
1302	**352** 600l. multicoloured		45	65

353 Bust of Mahatma Gandhi in Gandhi Square, San Marino
354 Olympic Rings and Hurdler in "Stamp" 

(Des F. Filanci)

1987 (29 Aug). "A Society based on Non-violence". P 14 × 13½.
1303	**353** 500l. multicoloured		40	60

(Photo Courvoisier)

1987 (29 Aug). "Olymphilex" Olympic Stamps Exhibition and World Light Athletics Championships, Rome. Granite paper. P 12.
1304	**354** 600l. multicoloured		50	90

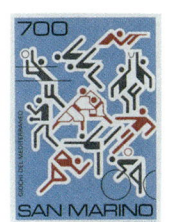

355 Sports Pictograms
356 "View from Round Tower, 1836" (anon) 

(Photo Courvoisier)

1987 (29 Aug). Mediterranean Games, Syria. Granite paper. P 12.
1305	**355** 700l. scar-verm, dull ultram & bl-blk		50	80

301

SAN MARINO 1987

(Photo Courvoisier)

1987 (16 Oct). *"Hafnia 87" International Stamp Exhibition, Copenhagen, and Important Cities of the World (11th series)*. T **356** *and similar horiz designs. Multicoloured.* P 11½.
1306	120 Type **356**	1·10	1·20
	a. Pair. Nos. 1306/7	3·25	3·75
1307	220 View from Round Tower, 1987	2·00	2·30

Nos. 1306/7 were issued together in *se-tenant* horizontal and vertical pairs within the sheet.

357 "The Annunciation" (detail)

358 1923 30c., 1944 20l.+10l. and 1975 200l. Stamps of St. Marinus

(Des P. Sinawehl. Eng W. Seidel. Recess and photo State Ptg Wks, Vienna)

1987 (12 Nov). *Christmas. 600th Birth Anniv of Fra Giovanni of Florence (Beato Angelico)*. T **357** *and similar vert designs. Multicoloured.* P 13½.
1308	600l. Type **357**	85	60
	a. Strip of 3. Nos. 1308/10	2·75	
1309	600l. Madonna and Child (detail, Triptych of Cortona)	90	60
1310	600l. Saint (detail, "The Annunciation")	90	60

Nos 1308/10 were issued together in *se-tenant* strips of three within the sheet.

(Des F. Filanci. Photo Courvoisier)

1988 (17 Mar). *Thematic Collecting*. T **358** *and similar square designs. Multicoloured. Granite paper.* P 11½.
1311	50l. Type **358**	10	10
1312	150l. Aerogramme and 1933 3l. *Graf Zeppelin* stamp (transport)	10	15
1313	300l. 1954 5l. and 1981 200l. motor cycle racing stamps and 1986 meter mark showing motor cycle (sport)	20	35
1314	350l. 1978 200l. human rights stamp on cover and 1982 200l. St. Francis of Assisi stamp (art)	25	35
1315	1000l. 1949 50l. Garibaldi stamp, 1985 450l. Europa stamp and 1952 1l. Columbus stamp (famous people)	70	1·10
1311/1315	Set of 5	1·20	1·90

See also Nos. 1340/4 and 1393/7.

359 Maglev Monorail "Bullet" Train and Globe

360 Carlo Malagola and Palazzo della Mercanzia

(Photo Courvoisier)

1988 (17 Mar). *Europa Transport and Communication*. T **359** *and similar vert design. Multicoloured. Granite paper.* P 12½.
1316	600l. Type **359**	4·50	2·30
1317	700l. Optical fibres and globe	7·25	3·00

(Des A. Merlanti. Photo)

1988 (7 May). *900th Anniv of Bologna University*. T **360** *and similar vert designs. Multicoloured.* P 13½ × 14.
1318	550l. Type **360**	45	45
1319	650l. Pietro Ellero and Palazzo del Podestà	50	55
1320	1300l. Giosuè Carducci and Pala dei Mercanti	80	1·20
1321	1700l. Giovanni Pascoli and Atheneum	95	1·50
1318/1321	Set of 4	2·50	3·25

361 La Strada

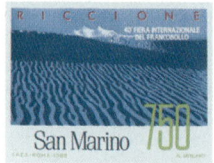

362 Mt. Titano from Beach

1988 (8 July). *Award of Celebrities of Showbusiness Prize to Federico Fellini (film director)*. T **361** *and similar vert designs showing film posters. Multicoloured.* P 13½ × 14.
1322	300l. Type **361**	20	40
1323	900l. *La Dolce Vita*	70	1·00
1324	1200l. *Amarcord*	80	1·40

(Des A. Merlanti)

1988 (8 July). *40th Riccione Stamp Fair*. P 14 × 13½.
1325	**362** 750l. royal blue, brt green & magenta	50	80

363 Healthy Tree with Diseased Roots

364 Man running

(Des W. Baiocchi and E. di Carlo (250, 1000l.), W. Baiocchi (350l.), E. di Carlo (650l.))

1988 (19 Sept). *Present Day Problems. International AIDS Congress, San Marino*. T **363** *and similar horiz designs.* P 14 × 13½.
1326	250l. multicoloured	25	25
1327	350l. rose-carmine and black	25	30
1328	650l. multicoloured	50	60
1329	1000l. multicoloured	75	95
1326/1329	Set of 4	1·60	1·90

Designs:—350l. "AIDS" crumbling; 650l. Knotted cord and emblem of virus; 1000l. Printed information.

302

SAN MARINO 1988

(Des G. Porzano. Litho)

1988 (19 Sept). *Olympic Games, Seoul. Sheet 118 × 103 mm containing T 364 and similar vert designs, each black, bright magenta and greenish yellow.* P 13½ × 14.
MS1330 650l. Type **364**; 750l. Hurdling; 1300l.
Woman running . . . . 2·75 2·75

365 "Kurhaus, Scheveningen, 1885" (anon)
366 "Angel with Violin" 

(Photo Courvoisier)

1988 (18 Oct). *"Filacept" International Stamp Exhibition, The Hague, and Important Cities of the World (12th series). T 365 and similar horiz designs. Multicoloured. Granite paper.* P 11½.
1331 1600l. Type **365** . . . . 1·20 1·20
    a. Pair. Nos. 1331/2 . . . . 3·50 3·75
1332 3000l. Kurhaus, Scheveningen, 1988 . 2·10 2·50
Nos. 1331/2 were issued together in *se-tenant* horizontal and vertical pairs within the sheet.

(Eng P. Arghittu (1334), E. Donnini (others). Recess and photo)

1988 (9 Dec). *Christmas. 550th Birth Anniv of Melozzo da Forli. T 366 and similar vert designs. Multicoloured.* P 14 (1334) or 13½ × 14 (others).
1333 650l. Type **366** 85 60
    a. Strip of 3. Nos. 1333/5 . . . . . . 2·75 1·90
1334 650l. "Angel of the Annunciation" (20 × 37 mm) 85 60
1335 650l. "Angel with Mandolin" 85 60
Nos. 1333/5 were issued together in *se-tenant* strips of three within the sheet.

(Des F. Filanci)

1989 (31 Mar). *Europa. Children's Games. Sheet 115 × 80 mm containing T 368 and similar vert design. Multicoloured.* P 13½ × 14.
MS1339 650l. Type **368**; 750l. Hopscotch . . 5·50 5·50

(Des F. Filanci. Photo Courvoisier)

1989 (13 May). *Postal History. Square designs as T 358. Multicoloured. Granite paper.* P 11½.
1340 100l. "San Marino 1977" Exhibition 1000l. stamp on cover (postal tariffs) 10 10
1341 200l. 1988 350l. stamp on cover (cancellations) 10 20
1342 400l. Parcel receipt (parcel post) . . . 30 35
1343 500l. Essay by Martin Riester, 1865 . . 40 45
1344 1000l. 1862 handstamp on cover (pre-stamp period) . . . . 1·40 95
1340/1344 Set of 4 . . . . 3·50 1·90

369 Emblem
370 Oath of the Tennis Court 

(Des Studio Azimut Int. Photo Courvoisier)

1989 (13 May). *Sport. T 369 and similar horiz designs. Multicoloured. Granite paper.* P 12.
1345 650l. Type **369** (30th anniv of San Marino Olympic Committee) . . . 70 70
1346 750l. Emblems (admission of San Marino Football Federation to UEFA and FIFA) 75 75
1347 850l. Tennis racquet and ball (San Marino championships) 55 75
1348 1300l. Formula 1 racing car (San Marino Grand Prix, Imola) . . . . . . 80 1·40
1345/1348 Set of 4 . . . . 2·30 3·25

(Des R. Marcenaro. Litho State Ptg Wks, Paris)

1989 (7 July). *Bicentenary of French Revolution. T 370 and similar vert designs. Multicoloured.* P 12½ × 13.
1349 700l. Type **370** 55 75
1350 1000l. Arrest of Louis XVI 80 90
1351 1800l. Napoleon's army . . . . . . 1·40 1·60

367 Bird in Tree (Federica Sparagna)
368 Sledging

1989 (31 Mar). *"Nature is Beautiful. Nature is Useful. Nature is...". T 367 and similar horiz designs. Multicoloured.* P 14 × 13½.
1336 200l. Type **367** 20 20
1337 500l. Birds beneath tree (Giovanni Monteduro) 50 55
1338 650l. Landscape (Rosa Mannarino) . . 70 70
Nos. 1336/8 depict the first three winning entries in a children's drawing competition.

371 Marguerite and Armand
372 "Angel of the Annunciation" 

1989 (18 Sept). *Award of Celebrities of Show Business Prize to Rudolph Nureyev (ballet dancer). T 371 and similar vert designs. Multicoloured.* P 13½ × 14.
1352 1200l. Type **371** . . . . 70 1·40
1353 1500l. *Apollo Musagète* . . . . . . 1·10 1·60
1354 1700l. Ken Russell's film *Valentino* . . 1·40 1·90

303

SAN MARINO 1989

(Photo Courvoisier)

1989 (17 Nov). *Christmas.* T **372** *and similar multicoloured designs showing details of the polyptych in Church of the Servants of Mary. Granite paper.* P 11½.

1355	650l. Type **372**	55	60
	a. Strip of 3. Nos. 1355/7		1·70
1356	650l. "Nativity" (50 × 40 mm)	55	60
1357	650l. Mary ("Annunciation")	55	60

Nos. 1355/7 were issued together in *se-tenant* strips of three within the sheet.

373 Capitol, 1850

(Photo Courvoisier)

1989 (17 Nov). *"World Stamp Expo '89" International Stamp Exhibition. Washington D.C. and Important Cities of the World (13th series).* T **373** *and similar horiz design. Multicoloured. Granite paper.* P 11½.

1358	2000l. Type **373**	1·60	1·20
	a. Pair. Nos. 1358/9	3·75	3·25
1359	2500l. Capitol, 1989	1·90	1·90

Nos. 1358/9 were issued together in *se-tenant* horizontal and vertical pairs within the sheet.

374 Old Post Office

375 "Martyrdom of St. Agatha" (Tiepolo) and Cardinal Alberoni leaving City

(Des F. Violi)

1990 (22 Feb). *Europa Post Office Buildings.* T **374** *and similar vert designs. Multicoloured.* P 13½ × 14.

1360	700l. Type **374**	1·20	95
1361	800l. Dogana Post Office	1·60	1·20

(Des F. Filanci. Photo Courvoisier)

1990 (22 Feb). *250th Anniv of End of Cardinal Alberoni's Occupation of San Marino. Granite paper.* P. 12.

1362	**375** 3500l. multicoloured	2·40	3·00

376 Map pinpointing San Marino

377 Statue, Government Palace

(Des F. Filanci. Photo Courvoisier)

1990 (23 Mar–June). *European Tourism Year. Multicoloured. Granite paper.*

(*a*) *Sheet stamps.* T **376** *and similar vert designs.* P 11½.

1363	600l. Type **376**	35	65
1364	600l. Aerial view showing villages	35	65
1365	600l. First Tower	35	65

(*b*) *Booklet stamps.* T **377** *and similar horiz designs* (Nos. 1366/9) *and vert designs as Nos. 1363/5 (others).* P 11½ (3 sides) (1366/9) or imperf × p 11½ (1370/2) (11 June).

1366	50l. Type **377**	10	10
	a. Booklet pane. Nos. 1366/72 plus label		2·40
1367	50l. Liberty Statue and English inscription	10	10
1368	50l. Government Palace and German inscription	10	10
1369	50l. Man with flag and French inscription	10	10
1370	600l. Type **376**	65	65
1371	600l. As No. 1364	65	65
1372	600l. As No. 1365	65	65
1363/1372	*Set of* 10	3·00	4·00

The booklet pane has its outer edges imperforate.
See also Nos. 1424/7.

378 West Germany (winners 1954, 1974)

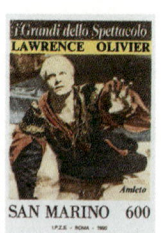

379 Olivier in *Hamlet*

(Des Studio Azimut Int)

1990 (23 Mar). *World Cup Football Championship, Italy. Previous Winners. Sheet* 120 × 114 *mm containing* T **378** *and similar vert designs. Multicoloured.* P 13½ × 14.
MS1373 700l. Type **378**; 700l. Italy (1934, 1938, 1982); 700l. England (1966); 700l. Uruguay (1930, 1950); 700l. Brazil (1958, 1962, 1970); 700l. Argentina (1978, 1986) . . . . 4·25 4·25

1990 (3 May). *Award of Celebrities of Show Business Prize to Laurence Olivier (actor).* T **379** *and similar vert designs. Multicoloured.* P 13½ × 14.

1374	600l. Type **379**	55	80
1375	700l. Richard III	65	1·00
1376	1500l. The Runner	1·30	1·90

Nos. 1374/6 are wrongly inscribed "Lawrence".

380 Mt. Titano and State Flags

381 Pinocchio

(Des G. Ascari. Litho State Ptg Wks, Paris)

1990 (11 June). *Visit of President Francesco Cossiga of Italy.* P 13½ × 12.

1377	**380** 600l. multicoloured	40	60

304

SAN MARINO 1990

(Des B. Jacovitti. Photo Courvoisier)

1990 (6 Sept). *Death Centenary of Carlo Collodi (writer).* T **381** and similar vert designs showing characters from Pinocchio. Multicoloured. Granite paper. P 11½.

1378	250l. Type **381**	25	25
1379	400l. Geppetto	25	40
1380	450l. Blue fairy	40	55
1381	600l. Cat and wolf	40	70
1378/1381	*Set of 4*	1·20	1·70

382 Pre-Columbian Civilizations

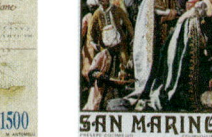

383 Mary and Two Kings

(Des Mariella Antomelli. Litho State Ptg Wks, Paris)

1990 (6 Sept). *500th Anniv (1992) of Discovery of America by Columbus (1st issue).* T **382** and similar horiz design. Multicoloured. P 13 × 12½.

1382	1500l. Type **382**	1·10	1·20
1383	2000l. Produce of the New World	1·40	1·90

See also Nos. 1401/2 and 1417/18.

(Photo Courvoisier)

1990 (31 Oct). *Christmas.* T **383** and similar vert design showing details of Cuciniello Crib. Multicoloured. Granite paper. P 11½.

1384	750l. Type **383**	85	75
	a. Horiz pair. Nos. 1384/5	1·70	1·60
1385	750l. Baby Jesus in manger and third King	80	75

Nos. 1384/5 were issued together in *se-tenant* pairs within the sheet, each pair forming a composite design.

384 Swallowtail (*Papilio machaon*) on *Ephedra major*

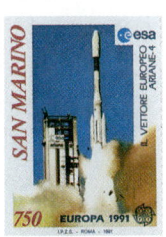

385 Launch of "Ariane–4"

(Des M. Demma (200, 300l.), F. Testa (others))

1990 (31 Oct). *Flora and Fauna.* T **384** and similar vert designs. Multicoloured. P 14 × 13½.

1386	200l. Type **384**	15	15
1387	300l. *Apoderus coryli* (weevil) and hazelnut (*Corylus avellana*)	25	30
1388	500l. Garden dormouse (*Eliomys quercinus*) and acorns of holm oak (*Quercus ilex*)	40	55
1389	1000l. Green lizard (*Lacerta viridis*) and *Ophrys bertolonii* (orchid)	70	1·00
1390	2000l. Firecrest (*Regulus ignicapillus*) on black pine (*Pinus nigra*)	1·40	2·10
1386/1390	*Set of 5*	2·75	3·75

1991 (12 Feb). *Europa. Europe in Space.* T **385** and similar vert design. Multicoloured. P 13½ × 14.

1391	750l. Type **385**	2·30	1·90
1392	800l. "E.R.S.-1" survey satellite	2·30	2·30

(Des F. Filanci. Photo Courvoisier)

1991 (12 Feb). *World of Stamps.* Square designs as T **358**. Multicoloured. Granite paper. P 11½.

1393	100l. Stamp shop	15	10
1394	150l. Stamp club	15	15
1395	200l. Exhibition	15	20
1396	450l. Stamp album and catalogues	95	40
1397	1500l. Philatelic publications (25th anniv of Italian Philatelic Press Union)	1·10	1·40
1393/1397	*Set of 5*	2·30	2·00

386 Torch Bearer leaving Athens

387 Cat

(Des Marzia Fulchieri. Litho B.D.T. Int Security Ptg Ltd, Dublin)

1991 (22 Mar). *Olympic Games, Barcelona (1992) (1st issue).* T **386** and similar horiz designs. Multicoloured. P 15 × 14.

1398	400l. Type **386**	30	40
1399	600l. Torch bearer passing through San Marino	40	60
1400	2000l. Torch bearer arriving in Barcelona	1·80	2·10

See also No. **MS**1434.

(Des Mariella Antomelli. Litho State Ptg Wks, Paris)

1991 (22 Mar). *500th Anniv (1992) of Discovery of America by Columbus (2nd issue).* Horiz designs as T **382**. Multicoloured. P 13 × 12½.

1401	750l. Navigational dividers, quadrant, hour-glass, compass and route map	70	80
1402	3000l. *Santa Maria, Niña* and *Pinta*	2·75	2·75

(Des F. Filanci)

1991 (4 June). *Pets.* T **387** and similar vert designs. Multicoloured. P 14 × 13½.

1403	500l. Type **387**	30	45
1404	550l. Hamster on wheel	30	55
1405	750l. Great Dane and Pomeranian	50	75
1406	1000l. Aquarium fishes	80	1·10
1407	1200l. Canaries in cage	90	1·30
1403/1407	*Set of 5*	2·50	3·75

388 Players, Balls and Baskets

389 James Clerk-Maxwell (physicist)

305

SAN MARINO 1991

(Des F. Testa)

1991 (4 June). *Centenary of Basketball.* T **388** *and similar vert design. Multicoloured.* P 13½ × 14.
| 1408 | 650l. Type **388** | 55 | 70 |
| 1409 | 750l. James Naismith (inventor) and players | 60 | 95 |

(Des A. Ciaburro)

1991 (24 Sept). *One Hundred Years of Radio (1st issue).* P 14 × 13½.
| 1410 | **389** | 750l. multicoloured | 45 | 1·10 |

Clerk-Maxwell formulated the theory of electromagnetic radiation.
See also Nos. 1431, 1452, 1479 and 1521/2.

390 Dove and Broken Chain (unification of Germany)

391 Keep

(Des P. Effert. Litho State Ptg Wks, Berlin)

1991 (24 Sept). *"Birth of a New Europe". Sheet 120 × 72 mm containing* T **390** *and similar vert designs. Multicoloured.* P 14 × 13½.
MS1411 1500l. Type **390**; 1500l. Pres. Gorbachev of Soviet Union, Pres. Bush of United States and rainbow (stategic arms talks); 1500l. Flower breaking through barbed wire (Eastern European democracy) .... 4·00 3·75

(Des F. Filanci. Litho Questa)

1991 (13 Nov). *Christmas.* T **391** *and similar vert designs showing La Rocca fortress. Multicoloured.* P 14½.

(a) POSTAGE.
| 1412 | 600l. Type **391** | 55 | 60 |
| 1413 | 750l. Inland view of fortress | 70 | 75 |

(b) AIRMAIL. Inscr "Posta Aerea".
| 1414 | 1200l. Fortress on crag | 95 | 1·30 |

392 Bianca and Falliero (Pesaro production)

393 Roses

(Des T.P.A., Parma)

1992 (3 Feb). *Birth Bicentenary of Gioachino Rossini (composer).* T **392** *and similar horiz design showing scenes from productions of his operas. Multicoloured.* P 14 × 13½.
| 1415 | 750l. Type **392** | 60 | 80 |
| 1416 | 1200l. The Barber of Seville (La Scala Theatre, Milan) | 90 | 1·20 |

(Des Mariella Antomelli. Litho State Ptg Wks, Paris)

1992 (3 Feb). *500th Anniv of Discovery of America by Columbus (3rd issue). Horiz designs as* T **382***. Multicoloured.* P 12.
| 1417 | 1500l. Amerindians watching fleet | 90 | 1·60 |
| 1418 | 2000l. Route map of the four voyages | 1·40 | 2·10 |

(Des Marzia Fulchieri. Litho B.D.T. Int Security Ptg Ltd. Dublin)

1992 (26 Mar). *Plants.* T **393** *and similar vert designs. Multicoloured.* P 13½ × 13.
1419	50l. Type **393**	10	15
1420	200l. Ficus as house plant	10	15
1421	300l. Orchid in conservatory	20	30
1422	450l. Cacti in pots	30	40
1423	5000l. Pelargoniums in trough	3·75	5·00
1419/1423	Set of 5	4·00	5·50

394 Courting Couple

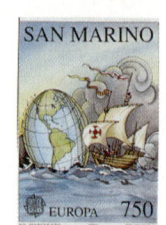

395 Egg-shaped Globe and Caravel

(Des F. Filanci. Litho Enschedé)

1992 (26 Mar). *Tourism. Booklet stamps. Multicoloured.*

(a) Horiz designs as T **377***.* P 14½ × 13 (3 sides).
1424	50l. Man with crossbow and Italian inscription	10	10
	a. Booklet pane. Nos. 1424/30 plus label		1·90
1425	50l. Tennis player and English inscription	10	10
1426	50l. Motor cycle rider and French inscription	10	10
1427	50l. Ferrari racing car and German inscription	10	10

(b) T **394** *and similar vert designs. Imperf × p 13½.*
1428	600l. Type **394**	45	55
1429	600l. Man in restaurant	45	55
1430	600l. Woman reading on veranda	45	55
1424/1430	Set of 7	1·60	1·90

(Des A. Ciaburro)

1992 (26 Mar). *One Hundred Years of Radio (2nd issue). Horiz design as* T **389***. Multicoloured.* P 14 × 13½.
| 1431 | 750l. Heinrich Rudolf Hertz (physicist) | 45 | 90 |

Hertz proved Clerk-Maxwell's theory.

(Des R. Marcenaro. Photo Courvoisier)

1992 (22 May). *Europa. 500th Anniv of Discovery of America.* T **395** *and similar vert design. Multicoloured. Granite paper.* P 12.
| 1432 | 750l. Type **395** | 70 | 80 |
| 1433 | 850l. Caravel and island inside broken egg | 70 | 1·00 |

SAN MARINO   1992

396 Football
397 Inedible Mushrooms 
400 Tennis Player
401 Stars

(Des Marzia Fulchieri. Litho State Ptg Wks, Berlin)
1992 (22 May). *Olympic Games, Barcelona (2nd issue). Sheet 137 × 105 mm containing T **396** and similar multicoloured designs.* P 14.
MS1434 1250l. Type **396**; 1250l. Shooting (*horiz*); 1250l. Swimming; 1250l. Running . . 5·00 4·75

(Des M. Fulchieri. Photo Courvoisier)
1992 (18 Sept). *Third Titano Mycological Exhibition, Borgo Maggiore. T **397** and similar vert designs. Multicoloured. Granite paper.* P 11½.
1435	250l. Type **397**	25	35
	a. Horiz pair. Nos. 1435/6		60
1436	250l. Inedible mushrooms (*different*)	25	35
1437	350l. Edible mushrooms in bowl	35	40
	a. Horiz pair. Nos. 1437/8		80
1438	350l. Edible mushrooms on cloth	35	40
1435/1438 *Set of 4*		1·10	1·30

Stamps of the same value were issued together in horizontal *se-tenant* pairs within their sheets, each pair forming a composite design.

398 View and Arms of San Marino
399 "La Sacra Conversazione" 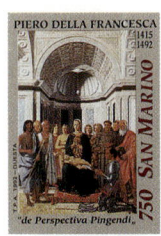

(Des P. Effert. Litho Enschedé)
1992 (18 Sept). *Admission of San Marino to United Nations Organization. T **398** and similar vert design. Multicoloured.* P 12 × 12½.
1439	1000l. Type **398**	70	80
	a. Pair. Nos. 1439/40	1·50	
1440	1000l. View of San Marino (*different*) and United Nations emblem	70	80

Nos 1439/40 were issued together in *se-tenant* pairs within the sheet.

(Litho Questa)
1992 (16 Nov). *Christmas. 500th Death Anniv of Piero della Francesca (artist). T **399** and similar vert designs. Multicoloured.* P 14½.
1441	750l. Type **399**	70	60
	a. Strip of 3. Nos. 1441/3	1·50	
1442	750l. Close-up of Madonna	70	70
1443	750l. Close-up of shell decoration	70	60

Nos 1441/3 were issued together in *se-tenant* strips of three within the sheet.

(Des N. Tedeschi. Litho)
1993 (29 Jan). *Sporting Events. T **400** and similar vert designs. Multicoloured.* P 13½ × 14.
1444	300l. Type **400** (Italian and San Marino Youth Games)	15	25
1445	400l. Cross-country skiers (European Youth Olympic Days (winter), Aosta, Italy)	20	40
1446	500l. Runners (European Youth Olympic Days (summer), Eindhoven, Netherlands)	30	45
1447	600l. Fisherman (Freshwater Angling Clubs World Championship, Ostellato, Italy)	35	55
1448	700l. Runners breasting tape (Small States Games, Malta)	55	70
1449	1300l. Sprinters (Mediterranean Games, Roussillon, France)	80	1·20
1444/1449 *Set of 6*		2·10	3·25

(Des N. de Maria (750l.), M. Paladino (850l.). Litho Courvoisier)
1993 (29 Jan). *Europa. Contemporary Art. T **401** and similar horiz design.* P 11½.
1450	750l. multicoloured	65	90
1451	850l. ultramarine and orange	80	1·00

Design:—850l. Silhouette.

(Des A. Ciaburro)
1993 (26 Mar). *One Hundred Years of Radio (3rd issue). Horiz design as T **389**. Multicoloured.* P 14 × 13½.
1452	750l. Edouard Branly (physicist) and his "radioconductor"	65	95

Branly developed method of revealing Hertzian waves.

402 Finish of World Championship 100 Metres Race, Tokyo, 1991
404 Scarce Swallowtail (*Iphiclides podalirius*) on Wild Apple 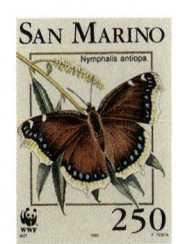

307

SAN MARINO 1993

(Des F. Ramberti. Litho and hologram Setec Oy, Helsinki)

1993 (26 Mar). *Inauguration of State Television.* Sheet 140 × 70 mm containing T **402** and similar horiz designs. Multicoloured. P 13½.
MS1453 2000l. Type **402**; 2000l. Hologram of satellite over San Marino by night; 2000l. Neil Armstrong on the Moon, 1969 . . . . . . 5·75   5·75

(Des F. Testa. Litho B.D.T. Int Security Ptg Ltd, Dublin)

1993 (26 May). *Butterflies.* T **404** and similar vert designs. Multicoloured. P 14 × 14½.
1454   250l. Type **404** 20   25
 a. Block or horiz strip of 4. Nos. 1454/7 90
1455   250l. Clouded yellow (*Colias crocea*) on wild vetch 20   25
1456   250l. Glanville's fritillary (*Melitaea cinxia*) 20   25
1457   250l. Camberwell beauty (*Nymphalis antiopa*) on white willow 20   25
1454/1457 Set of 4 75   90

Nos. 1454/7 were issued together in *se-tenant* blocks and horizontal strips of four stamps within the sheet.

405 Denmark    **406** Carlo Goldoni

(Des R. Marcenaro. Litho Enschedé)

1993 (26 May). *"The European Village"* Sheet 145 × 170 mm containing T **405** and similar vert designs, each representing a European Community member. Multicoloured. P 13½ × 14.
MS1458 750l. Type **405**; 750l. England; 750l. Eire; 750l. Luxembourg; 750l. Germany; 750l. Netherlands; 750l. Belgium; 750l. Portugal; 750l. Italy; 750l. Spain; 750l. France; 750l. Greece . . . . 9·00   9·00

(Des D. Fo (550l.), R. Marcenaro (650l.), P. Pizzi (850l.), F. Filanci (1850l.). Litho Enschedé)

1993 (17 Sept). *Death Anniversaries.* T **406** and similar multicoloured designs. P 14 × 13½ (vert) or 13½ × 14 (horiz).
1459   550l. Type **406** (dramatist, bicentenary) 30   40
1460   650l. Horace (*Quintus Horatius Flaccus*) (poet, 2000th anniv) . . 30   50
1461   850l. Scene from opera *Orpheus* by Claudio Monteverdi (composer, 350th anniv) (*horiz*) 55   70
1462   1850l. Guy de Maupassant (writer, centenary) (*horiz*) . . . . . . 1·10   1·50
1459/1462 Set of 4 . . . . 2·00   2·75

(Des F. Filanci. Litho Questa)

1993 (12 Nov). *Christmas.* T **407** and similar multicoloured designs. P 14½.
1463   600l. Type **407** 30   55
1464   750l. "Adoration of the Child" (Gerrit van Honthorst) (*horiz*) 45   65
1465   850l. "Adoration of the Shepherds" (Van Honthorst) 65   80

(Des F. Testa. Litho B.D.T. Int Security Ptg Ltd, Dublin)

1994 (31 Jan). *Tenth International Dog Show.* T **408** and similar horiz designs. Multicoloured. P 15 × 14.
1466   350l. Type **408** 25   25
1467   400l. Afghan hound 25   40
1468   450l. Belgian tervuren shepherd dog 25   40
1469   500l. Boston terrier 25   40
1470   550l. Mastiff 30   50
1471   600l. Malamute 35   55
1466/1471 Set of 6 . . . . 1·50   2·20

409 Ernst Vettori (90 metre ski jumping) 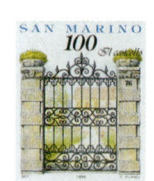   **410** Gate

(Des W. Toni. Litho B.D.T. Int Security Ptg Ltd, Dublin)

1994 (31 Jan). *Winter Olympic Games, Lillehammer, Norway, 1992 Gold Medal Winners.* Sheet 164 × 112 mm containing T **409** and similar square designs. Multicoloured. P 13½.
MS1472 750l. × 2, Type **409**; 750l. × 2, Patrick Ortlieb (downhill skiing); 750l. × 2, Alberto Tomba (giant slalom); 750l. Natalia Mishkutionok and Arthur Dmitriev (pairs figure skating) . . . . 5·50   5·50

(Des F. Filanci. Litho B.D.T. Int Security Ptg Ltd, Dublin)

1994 (11 Mar). *Gardens.* T **410** and similar vert designs. Multicoloured. P 13½ × 13.
1473   100l. Type **410** 10   15
1474   200l. Pergola 10   20
1475   300l. Well 20   25
1476   450l. Gazebo 20   40
1477   1850l. Pond 95   1·60
1473/1477 Set of 5 . . . . 1·40   2·40

411 Olympic Flags    **412** Players

(Des W. Toni)

1994 (11 Mar). *Centenary of International Olympic Committee.* P 14 × 13½.
1478   411   600l. multicoloured 55   70

407 San Marino   **408** Long-haired Dachshund

308

SAN MARINO 1994

(Des A. Ciaburro)

1994 (11 Mar). *One Hundred Years of Radio (4th issue)*. Horiz design as *T* **389**. Multicoloured. P 14 × 13½.
1479   750l. Aleksandr Stepanovich Popov   50   80
Popov was the first to use a suspended wire as an aerial.

(Des Mariella Antomelli. Litho Questa)

1994 (23 May). *World Cup Football Championship, U S A*. *T* **412** and similar vert designs. Multicoloured. P 14.
1480   600l. Type **412**   30   50
      a. Horiz strip of 5. Nos. 1480/4 . . . 1·60
1481   600l. Player kicking ball   30   50
1482   600l. Player heading ball   30   50
1483   600l. Players tackling   30   50
1484   600l. Goalkeeper saving goal   30   50
1480/1484 *Set of 5* . . . . 1·40 2·30
Nos. 1480/4 were issued together in horizontal *se-tenant* strips of five stamps within the sheet.

413 Route Map   **414** Government Palace

(Litho Questa)

1994 (23 May). *Europa. Discoveries. Exploration of Sun by "Ulysses" Space Probe*. *T* **413** and similar vert design. Multicoloured. P 14½.
1485   750l. Type **413**   40   85
1486   850l. "Ulysses" approaching Sun . . . .   50 1·10

(Des F. Filanci. Litho Enschedé)

1994 (30 Sept). *Centenary of Government Palace*. *T* **414** and similar multicoloured designs. P 13½ × 14 (1000l.) or 14 × 13½ (others).
1487   150l. Type **414**   10   20
1488   600l. Tower and view of San Marino
      from ramparts   30   50
1489   650l. Clock-tower   30   60
1490 1000l. Government chamber (*horiz*) . . .   55   90
1487/1490 *Set of 4* . . . . 1·10 2·00

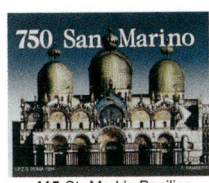

415 St. Mark's Basilica   **416** Angels playing Musical Instruments

(Des F. Ramberti)

1994 (8 Oct). *900th Anniv of Dedication of St Mark's Basilica, Venice*. P 14 × 13½.
1491   **415**   750l. multicoloured . . . . . 2·75   4·00
      a. Tête-bêche (vert pair) . . . 8·50
MS1492 80 × 115 mm. No. 1491 together with
No. 2276 of Italy . . . . 1·30 2·75
No. 1491 was issued in vertical *tête-bêche* pairs within sheets of twenty, each stamp *se-tenant* with a half stamp-size inscribed label.

No. **MS**1492 was issued simultaneously in San Marino and Italy. Each stamp bears an inscription on the back, over the gum, limiting its validity to the appropriate country.

(Des Marzia Fulchieri. Litho B.D.T. Int Security Ptg Ltd, Ireland)

1994 (18 Nov). *Christmas. 500th Death Anniv of Giovanni Santi (painter)*. *T* **416** and similar vert designs showing details of "The Enthroned Madonna and Child with Saints". Multicoloured. P 14 × 15.
1493   600l. Type **416**   30   50
1494   750l. Madonna and child   40   65
1495   850l. Angel playing harp   45   75

417/420 "Italy on the Road in a Sea of Flowering Greenery"

(Des R. Marcenaro. Litho Enschedé)

1994 (18 Nov). *Centenary of Italian Touring Club*. P 14 × 13½.
1496   **417**   1000l. multicoloured   50   60
      a. Block of 4. Nos. 1496/9 . . . 2·10
1497   **418**   1000l. multicoloured   50   60
1498   **419**   1000l. multicoloured   50   60
1499   **420**   1000l. multicoloured   50   60
1496/1499 *Set of 4* . . . . 1·80 2·20
Nos. 1496/9 were issued together in *se-tenant* blocks of four stamps within the sheet, each block forming the composite design illustrated.

421 Cyclist   **422** Flora and Fauna

309

SAN MARINO 1995

(Des A. Rinnaudo. Litho)

1995 (10 Feb). *Sporting Events.* T **421** *and similar vert designs. Multicoloured.* P 13½ × 14.

1500	100l. Type **421** (Junior World Cycling Championships, Italy and San Marino)		10	20
1501	500l. Volleyball (centenary)		30	40
1502	650l. Skater (Men's Speed-skating Championships, Baselga di Piné, Italy)		30	55
1503	850l. Sprinter (World Athletics Champion-ships, Gothenburg, Sweden)		50	75
1500/1503	Set of 4		1·10	1·70

(Des Cheryl Harness. Litho)

1995 (10 Feb). *European Nature Conservation Year.* T **422** *and similar vert designs. Multicoloured.* P 13½ × 14.

1504	600l. Type **422**		30	45
	a. Horiz strip of 5. Nos. 1504/8		1·60	
1505	600l. Frog, lizard and water lily		30	65
1506	600l. Water lily, bird and ladybirds		30	40
1507	600l. Butterfly, white-headed duck (young) and frog		30	40
1508	600l. Mandarin and duckling		30	40
1504/1508	Set of 5		1·40	2·10

Nos. 1504/8 were issued together in horizontal *se-tenant* strips of five stamps within the sheet, each strip forming a composite design of river life.

423 U.N. Emblem

424 Mute Swans over Coastline

(Des F. Filanci. Litho B.D.T. Int Security Ptg Ltd, Dublin)

1995 (24 Mar). *50th Anniv of United Nations Organization.* T **423** *and similar vert designs. Multicoloured.* P 14 × 15.

1509	550l. Type **423**		35	45
1510	600l. Rose with emblem		30	50
1511	650l. Hourglass		35	60
1512	1200l. Rainbow and emblem forming "50"		65	1·10
1509/1512	Set of 4		1·50	2·40

(Des M. Pollard. Litho B.D.T. Int Security Ptg Ltd, Dublin)

1995 (24 Mar). *Europa. Peace and Freedom.* T **424** *and similar horiz design. Multicoloured.* P 15 × 14.

1513	750l. Type **424**		35	75
1514	850l. Landscape		40	85

425 Basilica and "Legend of the True Cross" (detail of fresco, Agnolo Gaddi)

426 Eye and Airplane

(Des F. Filanci. Litho B.D.T. Int Security Ptg Ltd, Dublin)

1995 (5 May). *700th Anniv of Santa Croce Basilica, Florence.* T **425** *and similar horiz design. Multicoloured.* P 15 × 14.

1515	1200l. Type **425**		75	1·00
1516	1250l. Pazzi Chapel and "Madonna and Child with Saints" (Andrea della Robbia)		75	1·10

(Des F. Guiol. Litho B.D.T. Int Security Ptg Ltd, Dublin)

1995 (5 May). *20th Anniv of World Tourism Organization.* T **426** *and similar horiz designs. Multicoloured.* P 15 × 14.

1517	600l. Type **426**		30	50
1518	750l. Five ribbons (continents) around La Rocca fortress		40	65
1519	850l. Airplane and postcards circling globe		50	75
1520	1200l. Five ribbons around globe		75	95
1517/1520	Set of 4		1·70	2·50

427 Guglielmo Marconi and Transmitter

(Des E. Jünger (1521), F. Ramberti (1522). Litho State Ptg Works, Berlin)

1995 (8 June). *One Hundred Years of Radio (5th issue). Centenary of First Radio Transmission.* T **427** *and similar horiz design. Multicoloured.* P 14.

1521	850l. Type **427**		50	60
	a. Pair. Nos. 1521/2		1·10	
1522	850l. Radio frequency dial		50	60

Nos. 1521/2 were issued together in *se-tenant* pairs within the sheet.

428 The General, 1928 (1)

(Des F. Filanci. Litho B.D.T. Int Security Ptg Ltd, Dublin)

1995 (14 Sept). *Centenary of Motion Pictures. Sheet 187 × 120 mm containing* T **428** *and similar horiz designs. Black* (The General) *or multicoloured (others).* P 15 × 14.

MS1523	250l. × 4, Buster Keaton in *The General*; 250l. × 4, Burt Lancaster and Claudia Cardinale in *The Leopard*; 250l. × 4, Bruno Bozzetto's *Allegro non Troppo* (animated film); 250l. × 4, Mel Gibson in *Braveheart* . . . . 3·75 3·75

Each film is represented by four different frames, numbered from 1 to 4.

429 Qianmen Complex, 1914

310

SAN MARINO 1995

(Des Wu Jiankun. Litho Questa)

1995 (14 Sept). *"Beijing 1995" International Stamp and Coin Exhibition, Peking, and Important Cities of the World (14th series).* T **429** and similar horiz design. Multicoloured. P 13½ × 14.
1524	1500l. Type **429**		90	1·30
	a. Pair. Nos. 1524/5		1·90	
1525	1500l. Qianmen complex, 1995		90	1·30

Nos. 1524/5 were issued together in *se-tenant* pairs within the sheet.

430 "The Annunciation" (detail of illuminated MS)

431 Reindeer pulling Sleigh

(Des F. Filanci. Litho B.D.T. Int Security Pig Ltd, Dublin)

1995 (6 Nov). *"Neri of Rimini" Art and Literature Exhibition.* P 14 × 15.
1526	**430**	650l. multicoloured	50	55

(Des R. Marcenaro and A. Mariani. Litho B.D.T. Int Security Ptg Ltd, Dublin)

1995 (6 Nov). *Christmas.* T **431** and similar vert designs. Multicoloured. P 14 × 15.
1527	750l. Type **431**	55	75
	a. Horiz strip of 3. Nos. 1527/9	1·70	
1528	750l. Children dancing around Christmas tree	55	75
1529	750l. Wise Men approaching stable with crib	55	75

Nos. 1527/9 were issued together in horizontal *se-tenant* strips of three stamps within the sheet, each strip forming a composite design.

432 Cheetah

433 Throwing the Discus

(Des F. Filanci. Litho B.D.T. Int Security Ptg Ltd, Dublin)

1995 (6 Nov). *Inauguration of San Marino Express Mail Service.* P 15 × 14.
1530	**432**	6000l. multicoloured	3·75	5·25

(Des F. Filanci. Litho B.D.T. Int Security Ptg Ltd, Dublin)

1996 (12 Feb). *Centenary of Modern Olympic Games.* T **433** and similar vert designs. Multicoloured. P 14 × 15.
1531	100l. Type **433**	10	15
1532	500l. Wrestling	35	40
1533	650l. Long jumping	35	55
1534	1500l. Throwing the javelin	65	1·30
1535	2500l. Running	1·00	2·00
1531/1535	Set of 5	2·20	4·00

434 Dolphin swimming

435 Mother Teresa of Calcutta

(Des F. Filanci. Photo Courvoisier)

1996 (22 Mar). *Third "Nature World" Exhibition, Rimini.* T **434** and similar horiz designs. Multicoloured. Granite paper. P 12.
1536	50l. Type **434**	10	15
1537	100l. Frog on leaf	10	15
1538	150l. Emperor penguins	10	30
1539	1000l. Butterfly on flower	55	80
1540	3000 l. Mallard	1·70	2·50
1536/1540	Set of 5	2·30	3·50

(Des Gina Lollobrigida. Photo Courvoisier)

1996 (22 Mar). *Europa. Famous Women.* Granite paper. P 12.
1541	**435**	750l. multicoloured	1·00	1·00

436 Marco Polo and Palace in the Forbidden City

437 Great Wall of China

(Des Cristina Bruscaglia. Photo)

1996 (22 Mar). *700th Anniv (1995) of Marco Polo's Return from Asia and "China '96" International Stamp Exhibition, Peking.* P 14 × 13½.
1542	**436**	1250l. multicoloured	1·20	1·10

(Des Tian Liming. Litho Postage Stamp Ptg Wks, Peking, China)

1996 (6 May). *25th Anniv of San Marino–China Diplomatic Relations.* T **437** and similar horiz design. Multicoloured. P 12.
1543	750l. Type **437**	60	50
	a. Horiz pair. Nos. 1543/4	1·30	
1544	750l. Walled rampart, San Marino	60	50
MS1545	110 × 75 mm. Nos. 1543/4	1·50	1·50

Nos. 1543/4 were issued together in horizontal *se-tenant* pairs within the sheet, each pair forming a composite design.

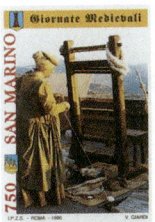

438 Traditional Weaving

439 Front Page

311

SAN MARINO   1996

(Des F. Filanci. Litho)

1996 (6 May). *"Medieval Days" Traditional Festival. Booklet stamps.* T **438** *and similar multicoloured designs. Imperf × p 14 (vert) or p 14 × imperf (horiz).*
1546	750l. Type **438**	45	60
	a. Booklet pane. Nos. 1546/53	3·75	
1547	750l. Potter	45	60
1548	750l. Traditional craftswoman	45	60
1549	750l. Playing traditional game	45	60
1550	750l. Trumpeters (*horiz*)	45	60
1551	750l. Flag display (*horiz*)	45	60
1552	750l. Crossbow tournament (*horiz*)	45	60
1553	750l. Dancing and playing musical instruments (*horiz*)	45	60
1546/1553 Set of 8		3·25	4·25

(Des F. Filanci. Photo Courvoisier)

1996 (25 May). *Centenary of* La Gazzetta dello Sport *(newspaper). Granite paper.* P 12.
| 1554 | **439** | 1850l. multicoloured | 1·30 | 1·60 |

(Des E. Innocenti. Litho)

1996 (25 May). *33rd "Festivalbar" Song Festival.* P 14 × 13½.
| 1555 | **440** | 2000l. multicoloured | 1·75 | 1·30 |

(Des F. Filanci. Photo Courvoisier)

1996 (25 May). *Italian Music.* T **441** *and similar horiz designs showing singers and their songs Multicoloured. Granite paper.* P 12 × 11½.
1556	750l. Type **441**	45	55
	a. Sheetlet of 12. Nos. 1556/67	5·50	
1557	750l. Armando Gill and "Come Pioveva"	45	55
1558	750l. Ettore Petrolini and "Gastone"	45	55
1559	750l. Vittorio De Sica and "Parlami d'amore Mariú"	45	55
1560	750l. Odoardo Spadaro and "La porti un bacione a Firenze"	45	55
1561	750l. Alberto Rabagliati and "O mia bela Madonina"	45	55
1562	750l. Beniamino Gigli and "Mamma"	45	55
1563	750l. Claudio Villa and "Luna rossa"	45	55
1564	750l. Secondo Casadei and "Romagna Mia"	45	55
1565	750l. Renato Rascel and "Arrivederci Roma"	45	55
1566	750l. Fred Buscaglione and "Guarda che luna"	45	55
1567	750l. Domenico Modugno and "Nel blu, dipinto di blu"	45	55
1556/1567 Set of 12		5·00	6·00

Nos. 1556/67 were issued together in *se-tenant* sheetlets of 12 stamps.

440 Applauding Crowd

441 Enrico Caruso and "O Sole Mio"

442 Yellowstone National Park, United States

443 Hen and Chicks

(Photo Courvoisier)

1996 (20 Sept). *50th Anniv of United Nations Educational, Scientific and Cultural Organization. World Heritage Sites.* T **442** *and similar horiz designs. Multicoloured. Granite paper.* P 11½.
1568	450l. Type **442**	25	35
1569	500l. Prehistoric cave paintings, Vézère Valley, France	40	40
1570	650l. San Gimignano, Italy	50	55
1571	1450l. Wies Pilgrimage Church, Germany	95	1·20
1568/1571 Set of 4		1·90	2·20

(Des R. Marcenaro. Photo Courvoisier)

1996 (20 Sept). *50th Anniv of United Nations Children's Fund.* T **443** *and similar horiz design. Multicoloured. Granite paper.* P 11½.
| 1572 | 550l. Type **443** | 35 | 45 |
| 1573 | 1000l. Chicks in nest | 70 | 85 |

444 Playing Lotto

445 Hong Kong, 1897

(Des Mariella Antomelli. Photo Courvoisier)

1996 (8 Nov). *Christmas.* T **444** *and similar vert designs. Multicoloured. Granite paper.* P 14½.
1574	750l. Type **444**	40	55
	a. Sheetlet of 16. Nos. 1574/89	6·75	
1575	750l. Hanging decoration	40	55
1576	750l. Father Christmas on sleigh and child reading book	40	55
1577	750l. Christmas tree	40	55
1578	750l. Bowls of fruit and nuts	40	55
1579	750l. Snowflakes and shooting star	40	55
1580	750l. Children's toys	40	55
1581	750l. Presents	40	55
1582	750l. Hanging Father Christmas decoration	40	55
1583	750l. Nativity scene	40	55
1584	750l. Mistletoe	40	55
1585	750l. Stocking hanging on mantelpiece	40	55
1586	750l. Family celebrating	40	55
1587	750l. Christmas tree outside window and party	40	55
1588	750l. Snowman outside window and party	40	55
1589	750l. Calendar pages and bottle of champagne (New Year's celebrations)	40	55
1574/1589 Set of 16		5·75	8·00

Nos. 1574/89 were issued together in *se-tenant* sheetlets of 16 stamps forming a composite design.

(Des Huang Li. Litho Postage Stamp Ptg Wks, Peking)

1997 (12 Feb). *Important Cities of the World (15th series). Sheet 84 × 94 mm containing* T **445** *and similar horiz design. Multicoloured.* P 12½.
MS1590 750l. Type **445**; 750l. Hong Kong, 1997 . . . . 1·50 1·50

312

SAN MARINO 1997

446/449 Championship Races

452 Bicycle and Stopwatch

453 Scanning the Heavens

(Des R. Marcenaro. Photo Courvoisier)

1997 (12 Feb). *World Skiing Championships, Sestriere.* Granite paper. P 12.

1591	446	1000l. multicoloured	55	80
		a. Block of 4. Nos. 1591/4	2·30	
1592	447	1000l. multicoloured	55	80
1593	448	1000l. multicoloured	55	80
1594	449	1000l. multicoloured	55	80
1591/1594 Set of 4			2·00	3·00

Nos. 1591/4 were issued together in *se-tenant* blocks of four within the sheet, each block forming the composite design illustrated.

450 Acquaviva

451 St. Marinus tames the Bear

(Des Mariella Antomelli. Photo Courvoisier)

1997 (21 Mar). *Communes.* T **450** and similar horiz designs. Granite paper. P 12.

1595	100l. Type 450	10	10
1596	200l. Borgomaggiore	10	15
1597	250l. Chiesanuova	10	20
1598	400l. Domagnano	25	35
1599	500l. Faetano	30	40
1600	550l. Fiorentino	35	45
1601	650l. Montegiardino	45	55
1602	750l. Serravalle	50	60
1603	5000l. San Marino	2·75	4·00
1595/1603 Set of 9		4·50	6·00

(Des F. Filanci. Photo Courvoisier)

1997 (21 Mar). *Europa. Tales and Legends.* T **451** and similar vert design. Granite paper. P 12.

1604	650l. Type **451**	45	75
1605	750l. Felicissima begs St. Marinus to cure her son Verissimus	55	80

(Des V. Pradal. Photo Courvoisier)

1997 (19 May). *Sporting Events in San Marino.* T **452** and similar horiz designs, each with Mt. Titano in the background. Multicoloured. Granite paper. P 12.

1606	500l. Type **452** (80th Giro d'Italia cycle race)	20	40
1607	550l. Tennis racket and ball (men's tennis championships)	30	45
1608	750l. Ferrari Formula One racing car (17th San Marino Grand Prix)	30	60
1609	850l. Juventus badge, football and trophy (Republic of San Marino Trophy football championship)	45	70
1610	1000l. Boules (World Pétanque Championship)	55	80
1611	1250l. Motor cycle (World 250cc Motocross Championship)	80	1·00
1612	1500l. Car dashboard (Mille Miglia (classic car rally))	1·10	1·20
1606/1612 Set of 7		3·25	4·75

(Des F. Filanci. Photo Courvoisier)

1997 (19 May). *Fifth International Symposium on Unidentified Flying Objects and Associated Phenomena, San Marino.* Granite paper. P 12.

1613	**453**	750l. multicoloured	45	60

454 Stone Pine (*Pinus pinea*)

455 Count Giovanni Barbavera di Grevellona

(Des Studio Expansion. Photo Courvoisier)

1997 (27 June). *Trees.* T **454** and similar vert designs. Multicoloured. Granite paper. P 12.

1614	50l. Type **454**	15	10
1615	800l. White oak (*Quercus pubescens*)	50	65
1616	1800l. Walnut (*Juglans regia*)	1·10	1·60
1617	2000l. Pear (*Pirus communis*)	1·30	1·80
1614/1617 Set of 4		2·75	3·75

313

SAN MARINO   1997

(Des F. Filanci. Photo Courvoisier)

1997 (27 June). *120th Anniv of First San Marino Postage Stamp.* T **455** *and similar horiz designs. Granite paper.* P 11½.
1618	800l. reddish brown and emerald	50	60
	a. Block or horiz strip of 4. Nos. 1618/21	2·10	
1619	800l. reddish brown and bright blue	50	60
1620	800l. reddish brown and deep mauve	50	60
1621	800l. reddish brown and rosine	50	60
1618/1621	Set of 4	1·80	2·20

Designs:—No. 1618, Type **455** (Director-General of Italian Post Office and co-signatory of postal convention between Italy and San Marino); 1619, Italian Government Printing Works, Turin, and Enrico Repettati (chief engraver); 1620, San Marino-Philatelist (monthly magazine) and Otto Bickel (collectables dealer) holding illustrated envelopes; 1621, Alfredo Reffi (stamp dealer and postcard publisher) and postcard.

Nos. 1618/21 were issued together in *se-tenant* blocks and horizontal strips of four stamps within the sheet, the frames of the stamps reproducing the design of the first San Marino stamps.

458 St. Francis of Assisi and Dove

459 "Adoration of the Magi" (detail of altarpiece by Giorgio Vasari, San Fortunato Abbey, Rimini)

(Des G. Covili. Photo Courvoisier)

1997 (14 Nov). *Voluntary and Charitable Service.* T **458** *and similar horiz designs. Multicoloured. Granite paper.* P 12.
1639	550l. Type **458** (voluntary aid after Assisi earthquake)	30	45
1640	650l. Mariele Ventre (organizer of Zecchino d'Oro) and children (40th anniv of Antoniano in Bologna (charitable organization))	40	55
1641	800l. Children around globe (40th anniv of Zecchino d'Oro (children's song festival))	45	70

456 First Tower and Dal Monte

457 Quadratino (Antonio Rubino)

(Des L. Mattei. Photo Courvoisier)

1997 (18 Sept). *Beatification of Father Bartolomeo Maria dal Monte. Granite paper.* P 12.
1622	**456**	800l. multicoloured	50	65

(Des V. Pradal and M. Dotta. Photo Courvoisier)

1997 (14 Nov). *Christmas. Granite paper.* P 12.
1642	**459**	800l. multicoloured	55	70

460 Beetle

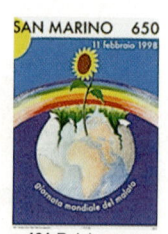

461 Rainbow over Grass and Sunflower erupting from Globe

(Des F. Filanci. Photo Courvoisier)

1999 (18 Sept). *Italian Comic Strips.* T **457** *and similar horiz designs. Multicoloured. Granite paper.* P 12.
1623	800l. Type **457**	50	65
	a. Sheetlet of 16. Nos. 1623/38	8·25	
1624	800l. Signor Bonaventura (Sergio Tofano)	50	65
1625	800l. Kit Carson (Rino Albertarelli)	50	65
1626	800l. Cocco Bill (Benito Jacovitti)	50	65
1627	800l. Tex Willer (Gian Bonelli and Aurelio Galleppini)	50	65
1628	800l. Diabolik (Angela and Luciana Giussani and Franco Paludetti)	50	65
1629	800l. Valentina (Guido Crepax)	50	65
1630	800l. Corto Maltese (Hugo Pratt)	50	65
1631	800l. Sturmtruppen (Franco Bonvicini)	50	65
1632	800l. Alan Ford (Max Bunker)	50	65
1633	800l. Lupo Alberto (Guido Silvestri)	50	65
1634	800l. Pimpa (Francesco Tullio Altan)	50	65
1635	800l. Bobo (Sergio Staino)	50	65
1636	800l. Zanardi (Andrea Pazienza)	50	65
1637	800l. Martin Mystére (Alfredo Castelli and Giancarlo Alessandrini)	50	65
1638	800l. Dylan Dog (Tiziano Sclavi and Angelo Stano)	50	65
1623/1638	Set of 16	7·25	9·50

Nos. 1623/38 were issued together in *se-tenant* sheetlets of 16 stamps.

(Des Volkswagen. Photo Courvoisier)

1997 (14 Nov). *60th Anniv of Volkswagen (motor manufacturer). Sheet 154 × 115 mm containing* T **460** *and similar horiz designs. Multicoloured. Granite paper.* P 12.
MS1643	800l. Type **460**; 800l. Golf Mk I; 800l. New Beetle; 800l. Golf Mk IV	3·00	3·00

No. **MS**1643 includes a tear-off entry coupon for a prize draw for a new Beetle.

(Des Maddalena Medas and Michela Mangani. Litho BDT Int Security Ptg Ltd, Dublin)

1998 (11 Feb). *World Day of the Sick.* T **461** *and similar vert design. Multicoloured.* P 14 × 15.
1644	650l. Type **461**	40	55
1645	1500l. Dove and rainbow over waves and globe	85	1·20

314

SAN MARINO 1998

462 125S Racing Car, 1947
463 Verse of "Infinity", 1819 

(Des Studio Bagarre. Litho BDT Int Security Ptg Ltd, Dublin)
1998 (11 Feb). *Birth Centenary of Enzo Ferrari (motor manufacturer). Racing Cars.* T **462** and similar horiz designs. Multicoloured. P 13.
1646	800l. Type **462**	50	65
	a. Sheetlet of 12. Nos. 1646/57	6·25	
1647	800l. Model 375, 1950 (wrongly inscr "500 F2, 1952")	50	65
1648	800l. Lancia D50, 1956 (wrongly inscr "801")	50	65
1649	800l. Racing car (wrongly inscr "246 Dino")	50	65
1650	800l. Model 156, 1961	50	65
1651	800l. John Surtees' 158, 1964	50	65
1652	800l. Niki Lauda's 312T, 1975	50	65
1653	800l. Jody Scheckter's 312T4, 1979	50	65
1654	800l. Model 126C, 1981	50	65
1655	800l. Michelo Alboreto's 156/85, 1985	50	65
1656	800l. Model 639, 1989	50	65
1657	800l. Michael Schumacher's F310, 1996	50	65
1646/1657	Set of 12	5·50	7·00

Nos. 1646/57 were issued together in *se-tenant* sheetlets of 12 stamps.

(Des F. Filanci. Litho B.D.T. Int Security Ptg Ltd, Dublin Ireland)
1998 (31 Mar). *Birth Bicentenary of Giacomo Leopardi (poet).* T **463** and similar horiz designs. Multicoloured. P 15 × 14.
1658	550l. Type **463**	40	65
1659	650l. "A Village Saturday", 1829	40	60
1660	900l. "Nocturne of a Wandering Asian Shepherd", 1822–30	60	75
1661	2000l. "To Sylvia", 1828	1·30	1·60
1658/1661	Set of 4	2·50	3·00

464 Installation of Captains Regent
465 Emigrant Ship, Passport and Ticket 

(Des F. Filanci. Litho B.D.T. Int Security Ptg Ltd, Dublin Ireland)
1998 (31 Mar). *Europa. National Festivals.* T **464** and similar vert design. Multicoloured. P 14 × 15.
1662	650l. Type **464**	45	60
1663	1200l. Religious procession (Feast Day of Patron Saint)	75	1·10

(Des TPA. Photo Courvoisier)
1998 (28 May). *Museum of the Emigrant,* T **465** and similar horiz design. Multicoloured. Granite paper. P 12.
1664	800l. Type **465**	65	65
1665	1500l. Emigrants working, restaurant, work permit, pay slip, money and residency permit	1·10	1·20

466 Goalkeeper reaching for Ball
467 Launch of Space Shuttle, Cape Canaveral 

(Des V. Pradal and M. Dotta. Photo Courvoisier)
1998 (28 May). *World Cup Football Championship, France. Booklet stamps.* T **466** and similar vert designs. Multicoloured. Granite paper. P 12.
1666	650l. Type **466**	60	60
	a. Booklet pane. No. 1666 × 4	2·40	
1667	800l. Two players challenging for ball	90	80
	a. Booklet pane. No. 1667 × 4	3·75	
1668	900l. Three players challenging for ball	1·10	85
	a. Booklet pane. No. 1668 × 4	4·50	

(Des V. Pradal. Photo Courvoisier)
1998 (28 May). *San Marino Flag in Space. Sheet 140 × 70 mm containing* T **467** and similar horiz designs. Multicoloured. Granite paper. P 12.
MS1669 2000l. Type **467**; 2000l. Space capsule in orbit and San Marino flag; 2000l. Space shuttle returning to Earth ... 5·00 5·00

468 *20,000 Leagues Under the Sea* (Jules Verne)
469 Sailing Dinghy and Factory Chimneys 

(Des F. Filanci. Photo Courvoisier)
1998 (28 Aug). *Science Fiction Novels.* T **468** and similar vert designs. Multicoloured. Granite paper. P 14½.
1670	800l. Type **468**	45	65
	a. Sheetlet of 16. Nos. 1670/85	7·25	
1671	800l. *War of the Worlds* (H. G. Wells) (centenary of publication)	45	65
1672	800l. *Brave New World* (Aldous Huxley)	45	65
1673	800l. *1984* (George Orwell)	45	65
1674	800l. *Foundation Trilogy* (Isaac Asimov)	45	65
1675	800l. *City* (Clifford D. Simak)	45	65
1676	800l. *Fahrenheit 451* (Ray Bradbury)	45	65
1677	800l. *The Seventh Victim* (Robert Sheckley)	45	65
1678	800l. *The Space Merchants* (Frederik Pohl and Cyril Kornbluth)	45	65
1679	800l. *The Coming Dark Age* (Roberto Vacca)	45	65
1680	800l. *Stranger in a Strange Land* (Robert Heinlein)	45	65
1681	800l. *A Clockwork Orange* (Anthony Burgess)	45	65
1682	800l. *The Drowned World* (James Ballard)	45	65
1683	800l. *Dune* (Frank Herbert)	45	65

315

SAN MARINO 1998

1684	800l.	*2001 A Space Odyssey* (Arthur Clarke)	45	65
1685	800l.	*Do Androids Dream of Electric Sheep?* (Philip K. Dick)	45	65
1670/1685	Set of 16		6·50	9·50

Nos. 1670/85 were issued together in *se-tenant* sheetlets of 16 stamps.

(Des M. Medas and M. Mangani. Photo Courvoisier)

1998 (28 Aug). *International Stamp Fair, Riccione.* T **469** and similar vert design. Multicoloured. Granite paper. P 12 × 11½.
| 1686 | 800l. Type **469** | 45 | 65 |
| 1687 | 1500l. Dolphin jumping through stamp and factory chimneys | 90 | 1·20 |

470 Pope John Paul II

471 Boy and Tree of Santa Clauses

(Des I. Fantini. Photo)

1998 (23 Oct). *"Italiá 98" International Stamp Exhibition, Milan (1st issue).* P 14.
| 1688 | **470** | 800l. multicoloured | 70 | 65 |

(Des R. Marcenaro. Photo Courvoisier)

1998 (23 Oct). *Christmas.* T **471** and similar vert designs. Multicoloured. Granite paper. P 12 × 11½.
1689	800l. Type **471**	50	75
	a. Block of 4. Nos. 1689/92	2·10	
1690	800l. Pacific Island child	50	75
1691	800l. Boy in clogs and rabbit	50	75
1692	800l. Girl and dog	50	75
1689/1692	Set of 4	1·90	2·75

Nos. 1689/92 were issued together in *se-tenant* blocks of four stamps within the sheet, each block forming a composite design of a tree of Santa Clauses bearing gifts.

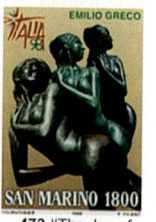

472 Woman

473 "The Joy of Living" (Emilio Greco)

(Des R. Marcenaro. Photo Courvoisier)

1998 (23 Oct). *50th Anniv of Universal Declaration of Human Rights.* T **472** and similar vert design. Multicoloured. Granite paper. P 12 × 11½.
1693	900l. Type **472**	65	75
	a. Horiz pair. Nos. 1693/4	1·40	1·60
1694	900l. Man	65	75

Nos. 1693/4 were issued together in *se-tenant* pairs within the sheet, each pair forming a composite design.

(Des F. Filanci. Photo Courvoisier)

1998 (23 Oct). *"Italiá 98" International Stamp Exhibition (2nd issue). Art Day.* Granite paper. P 12 × 11½.
| 1695 | **473** | 1800l. multicoloured | 1·10 | 1·50 |

DENOMINATION. From No. 1696 San Marino stamps are denominated both in lira and in euros. The Catalogue listings use the forum until the introduction of the euro notes and coins on 1 January 2002.

474 The Coronation of Poppea (Claudio Monteverdi)

475 Hand writing with Quill Pen

(Des F. Filanci. Litho Cartor)

1999 (12 Feb). *400 Years of Opera.* T **474** and similar horiz designs. Multicoloured. P 13 × 13½.
1696	800l. Type **474**	50	65
	a. Sheetlet of 16. Nos. 1696/1711	8·25	
1697	800l. Dido and Aeneas (Henry Purcell)	50	65
1698	800l. Orpheus and Eurydice (Christoph Willibald Gluck)	50	65
1699	800l. Don Juan (Wolfgang Amadeus Mozart)	50	65
1700	800l. The Barber of Seville (Gioacchino Rossini)	50	65
1701	800l. Norma (Vincenzo Bellini)	50	65
1702	800l. Lucia di Lammermoor (Gaetano Donizetti)	50	65
1703	800l. Aida (Giuseppe Verdi)	50	65
1704	800l. Faust (Charles Gounod)	50	65
1705	800l. Carmen (Georges Bizet)	50	65
1706	800l. The Ring of the Nibelung (Richard Wagner)	50	65
1707	800l. Boris Godunov (Modest Musorgsk)	50	65
1708	800l. Tosca (Giacomo Puccini)	50	65
1709	800l. The Love for Three Oranges (Sergei Prokofiev)	50	65
1710	800l. Porgy and Bess (George Gershwin)	50	65
1711	800l. West Side Story (Leonard Bernstein)	50	65
1696/1711	Set of 16	7·25	9·50

Nos. 1696/1711 were issued together in *se-tenant* sheetlets of 16 stamps.

(Des Maddalena Medas. Litho Cartor)

1999 (12 Feb). *12th World Hang-gliding Championship, Montecucco, Italy.* T **475** and similar vert design. Multicoloured. P 13½ × 13.
| 1712 | 800l. Type **475** | 45 | 65 |
| 1713 | 1800l. Hang-glider with balloon | 1·10 | 1·50 |

476 Mountain Pine (*Pinus mugo*)

477 Eastern Slopes of Mount Titano

(Des F. Testa. Litho Cartor)

1999 (27 Mar). *San Marino Bonsai Exhibition.* T **476** and similar horiz designs. Multicoloured. P 13 × 13½.
| 1714 | 50l. Type **476** | 15 | 10 |
| 1715 | 300l. Olive (*Olea europaea*) | 15 | 25 |

316

SAN MARINO 1999

1716	35 0l. Scots pine (*Pinus silvestris*)		20	30
1717	500l. Pedunculate oak (*Quercus robur*)		25	40
1714/1717	Set of 4		65	95

(Des TPA. Litho Cartor)

1999 (27 Mar). *Europa. Parks and Gardens.* T **477** *and similar horiz design. Multicoloured.* P 13 × 13½.

1718	650l. Type **477**		45	65
1719	1250l. Cesta Tower, Mount Titano		70	1·20

478 Emblem and Town Hall, Treviso

479 Article 1 of First Treaty (1874) and Swiss Parliament Building

(Des V. Pradal. Litho Cartor)

1999 (27 Mar). *World Cycling Championships, Treviso and Verona, Italy.* T **478** *and similar horiz design. Multicoloured.* P 13 × 13½.

1720	900l. Type **478**		55	75
1721	3000l. Emblem and amphitheatre, Verona		1·80	2·50

(Des F. Filanci. Litho Cartor)

1999 (12 May). *125th Anniv of Universal Postal Union.* T **479** *and similar horiz design. Multicoloured.* P 13 × 13½.

1722	800l. Type **479**		50	65
1723	3000l. World map highlighting original UPU signatories, 1875		1·80	2·50

480 Garibaldi (after Lorusso) and Crowds in front of the Quirinale, Rome

481 "50" and People climbing Ladder to Council Emblem

(Des F. Filanci. Litho Cartor)

1999 (12 May). *150th Anniv of Garibaldi's Refuge in San Marino after Fall of the Roman Republic.* P 13 × 13½.

1724	480	1250l. multicoloured	75	1·00

(Des F. Filanci. Litho Cartor)

1999 (12 May). *50th Anniv of Council of Europe.* P 13½ × 13.

1725	481	1300l. multicoloured	80	1·10

482 European Brown Hare (*Lepus europaeus*)

483 Pilgrimage Route Map and Canterbury Cathedral

(Des V. Fogato. Litho Cartor)

1999 (5 June). *Animals.* T **482** *and similar horiz designs. Multicoloured.* P 13 × 13½.

1726	500l. Type **482**		30	40
1727	650l. Eurasian red squirrel (*Sciurus vulgaris*)		45	55
1728	1100l. Eurasian badger (*Meles meles*)		65	90
1729	1250l. Red fox (*Vulpes vulpes*)		70	1·00
1730	1850l. North African crested porcupine (*Hystrix cristata*)		1·10	1·50
1726/1730	Set of 5		3·00	4·00

(Des F. Filanci. Litho Cartor)

1999 (5 June). *Holy Year 2000.* T **483** *and similar horiz designs. Multicoloured.* P 13 × 13½.

1731	650l. Type **483**		45	55
1732	800l. Priest blessing pilgrim (fresco, Novales Abbey) and Rheims Cathedral		50	65
1733	900l. Hospice welcoming pilgrims (fresco, St. James's Chapel, Brian on) and Pavia Cathedral		55	75
1734	1250l. Pilgrims on the road (bas-relief, Fidenza Cathedral) and Fidenza Cathedral		70	1·00
1735	1500l. "Mount of Joy" (Sir Charles Eastlake) and St. Peter's Cathedral, Rome		85	1·20
1731/1735	Set of 5		2·75	3·75

484 Fregoso Castle, Sant'Agata Feltria

(Des TPA. Litho Cartor)

1999 (20 Sept). *Architecture of Montefeltro.* T **484** *and similar horiz designs. Multicoloured.* P 13 × 13½.

1736	50l. Type **484**		10	10
1737	250l. Feltresca Castle, San Leo		15	30
1738	650l. Ducal Palace, Urbino		40	65
1739	1300l. Ubaldinesca Castle, Sassocorvaro		75	1·30
1740	6000l. Il Montale and La Rocca fortress, San Marino		3·50	5·50
1736/1740	Set of 5		4·50	7·00

485 St. Martin tearing Cloak in Half

(Des L. Blanco. Litho Cartor)

1999 (20 Sept). *50th Anniv of San Marino Red Cross.* P 13 × 13½.

1741	485	800l. multicoloured	50	75

317

SAN MARINO   1999

486 Team Photograph (Italian championship, 1901)

(Des Studio Expansion. Litho Cartor)

1999 (20 Sept). *Centenary of A.C. Milan Football Club*. Sheet 155 × 115 mm containing T **486** and similar horiz designs. Multicoloured. P 13 × 13½.
MS1742 800l. Type **486**; 800l. Players Gren, Nordahl and Liedholm, 1950s; 800l. Team photograph, Wembley (goalkeeper in front row) (European Championship, 1963); 800l. Team photograph, Vienna (goalkeeper in back row), 1990; 800l. Team and children celebrating Italian Championship, 1994; 800l. Team with trophy (Italian Championship, 1999) . . . . 3·75 3·50

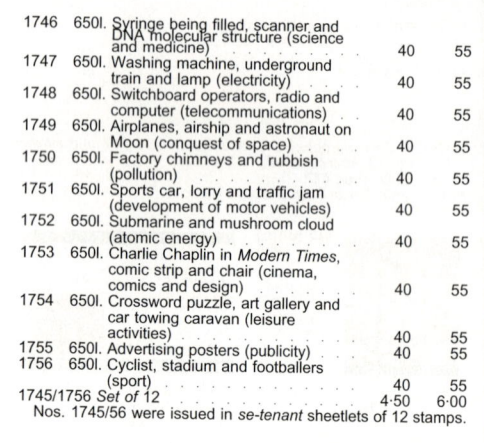

487 Nativity

(Des Sivia Guidi. Litho Cartor)

1999 (5 Nov). *Christmas*. P 13 × 13½.
1743 **487** 800l. multicoloured 50 75

488 18/50 h.p. Horch

(Ds Verba Srl. Litho Cartor)

1999 (5 Nov). *Centenary of Audi (car manufacturer)*. Sheet 155 × 115 mm containing T **488** and similar horiz designs. Multicoloured. P 13 × 13½.
MS1744 1500l. Type **488**; 1500l. Audi TT; 1500l. Audi A8; 1500l. Auto Union racing car . . . . 4·50 4·50
No. **MS**1744 includes a tear-off entry coupon for a prize draw for an Audi A3.

489 Tank, Soldiers and Civilians (First and Second World Wars)

(Des F. Filanci. Litho Cartor)

2000 (2 Feb). *The Twentieth Century*. T **489** and similar horiz designs. Multicoloured. P 13 × 13½.
1745 650l. Type **489** 40 55
     a. Sheetlet of 12. Nos. 1745/56 . . . 5·00
1746 650l. Syringe being filled, scanner and DNA molecular structure (science and medicine) 40 55
1747 650l. Washing machine, underground train and lamp (electricity) . . . 40 55
1748 650l. Switchboard operators, radio and computer (telecommunications) . . . 40 55
1749 650l. Airplanes, airship and astronaut on Moon (conquest of space) . . . 40 55
1750 650l. Factory chimneys and rubbish (pollution) 40 55
1751 650l. Sports car, lorry and traffic jam (development of motor vehicles) . . 40 55
1752 650l. Submarine and mushroom cloud (atomic energy) 40 55
1753 650l. Charlie Chaplin in *Modern Times*, comic strip and chair (cinema, comics and design) 40 55
1754 650l. Crossword puzzle, art gallery and car towing caravan (leisure activities) 40 55
1755 650l. Advertising posters (publicity) . . 40 55
1756 650l. Cyclist, stadium and footballers (sport) 40 55
1745/1756 Set of 12 . . . . . . 4·50 6·00
Nos. 1745/56 were issued in *se-tenant* sheetlets of 12 stamps.

490 St. John Lateran Basilica, Rome, Pilgrim (detail of engraving by G. Perugino) and Mt. Titano

491 Emblem and La Rocca Fortress

(Des Mariella Antomelli. Litho Cartor)

2000 (2 Feb). *Holy Year 2000*. Sheet 155 × 115 mm containing T **490** and similar horiz designs. P 13 × 13½.
MS1757 1000l. Type **490**; 1000l. St. Paul without the Walls Basilica, Rome, St. Marinus (statue) and La Rocca fortress; 1000l. St. Mary Major Basilica, Rome, with Madonna and Child; 1000l. St. Peter's Basilica, Rome, and St. Marinus (detail of painting by Pompeo Batoni) . . . . 3·00 3·00

(Des C. Ceccaroni. Litho Cartor)

2000 (27 Apr). *40th Anniv of San Marino Rotary Club*. T **491** and similar vert design. Multicoloured. P 13½ × 13.
1758 650l. Type **491** 35 65
1759 800l. Government Palace, Arms and Statue of Liberty, San Marino . . . 55 75

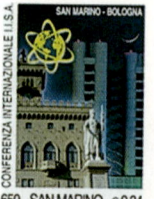

492 IISA Emblem, Government Palace, Fiera di Bologna Towers and Statue of Liberty, San Marino

493 Vincenzo Muccioli (founder of San Patrignano Community) and Drug Addict

SAN MARINO   2000

(Des V. Pradal and M. Dotta. Litho Cartor)

2000 (27 Apr). *International Institute of Administrative Science Conference, Bologna (1760) and European City of Culture (others).* T **492** *and similar vert designs. Multicoloured.* P 13½ × 13.
1760	650l. Type **492**		30	65
1761	800l. Guglielmo Marconi's workbench, radio aerial, San Pietro Cathedral, clock tower, Tubertini dome and St. Petronius Basilica		40	75
1762	1200l. Microchip, musical instruments, St. Petronius Basilica, Santa Maria della Vita Church and Asinelli and Garisenda Towers		65	1·10
1763	1500l. Books, detail of still life by Giorgio Morandi, campanile and apse of St. Giacomo Maggiore and St. Francis Churches and Arengo Tower		1·10	1·40
1760/1763 *Set of 4*			2·20	3·50

(Des San Patrignano Community. Litho Cartor)

2000 (27 Apr). *Fifth Anniv of Rainbow International Association Against Drugs.* T **493** *and similar horiz designs. Multicoloured.* P 13 × 13½.
1764	650l. Type **493**	35	55
1765	1200l. Blocks spelling "rainbow" in sky	65	1·10
1766	2400l. Mucciolli and reformed addicts	1·60	2·20

494 "Building Europe"

495 "2000"

(Des J.-P. Cousin. Litho Cartor)

2000 (27 Apr). *Europa.* P 13½ × 13.
| 1767 | **494** | 800l. multicoloured | 30 | 75 |

(Des Laura Carattoni. Litho Cartor)

2000 (31 May). *"Stampin the Future". Winning Entries in Children's International Painting Competition.* P 13 × 13½.
| 1768 | **495** | 800l. multicoloured | 50 | 75 |

496 Dog and Butterfly

497 Bicycles

(Des F. Altan. Litho Cartor)

2000 (31 May). *Olympic Games, Sydney. Multicoloured.* P 13½ × 13.
1769	1000l. Type **496**		70	95
	a. Block of 4. Nos. 1769/72		3·00	
1770	1000l. Hippopotamus and penguin		70	95
1771	1000l. Elephant and ladybird		70	95
1772	1000l. Rabbit and snail		70	95
1769/1772 *Set of 4*			2·50	3·50

Nos. 1769/72 were issued together in *se-tenant* blocks of four.

(Des V. Pradal. Litho Cartor)

2000 (31 May). *Centenary of International Cycling Union.* P 13 × 13½.
| 1773 | **497** | 1200l. multicoloured | 70 | 1·10 |

498 Child hiding beneath Soldier's Helmet

(Des Nicoletta Ceccoli. Litho Cartor)

2000 (15 Sept). *Tenth Anniv of International Convention on Children's Rights.* T **498** *and similar horiz designs. Multicoloured.* P 13 × 13½.
1774	650l. Type **498**	40	55
1775	800l. Child cowering away from frightening shadow	50	75
1776	1200l. Child in flower	75	1·10
1777	1500l. Childhood fantasies tumbling from book	90	1·50
1774/1777 *Set of 4*		2·30	3·50

499 Council Emblem and Child's face

(Des V. Pradal. Litho Cartor)

2000 (15 Sept). *50th Anniv of European Convention on Human Rights.* P 13 × 13½.
| 1778 | **499** | 800l. multicoloured | 50 | 75 |

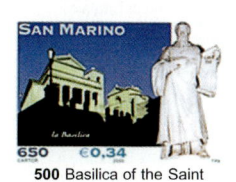

500 Basilica of the Saint

(Des TPA. Litho Cartor)

2000 (15 Sept). *Churches of Montefeltro.* T **500** *and similar horiz designs. Multicoloured.* P 13 × 13½.
1779	650l. Type **500**		40	55
1780	800l. Church of St. Mary of Antico, Maiolo		55	75
1781	1000l. St. Lawrence's Church, Talamello		60	95
1782	1500l. Parish Church, San Leo		90	1·40
1783	1800l. Sanctuary of Our Lady of Graces, Pennabilli		1·10	1·70
1779/1783 *Set of 5*			3·25	4·75

319

SAN MARINO   2000

501 "Virgin and Child" (Ludovico Carracci)

502 Melchiorre Delfico (author of History of the Republic of San Marino) and Title Page

(Des F. Filanci. Litho Cartor)

2000 (14 Nov). *Christmas.* P 13.
| 1784 | **501** | 800l. multicoloured | 1·90 | 75 |

(Des F. Filanci. Photo Courvoisier)

2000 (14 Nov). *1700th Anniv of San Marino (1st issue). Booklet stamps.* T **502** and similar vert designs. Multicoloured. P 12.
1785	800l. Type **502**	50	75
	a. Booklet pane. Nos. 1785/8	2·00	
1786	800l. Giuseppe Garibaldi (painting)	50	75
1787	800l. Abraham Lincoln and passage from his letter to the Captains Regent, 1861	50	75
1788	800l. Refugees arriving in San Marino, 1943–45	50	75
1789	800l. Roman jewels	50	75
	a. Booklet pane. Nos. 1789/92	2·00	
1790	800l. 1463 map of San Marino	50	75
1791	800l. Napoleon Bonaparte	50	75
1792	800l. "L'Arengo" (detail) (postcard, 1906)	50	75
1793	800l. Child, class and swimming pool	50	75
	a. Booklet pane. Nos. 1793/6	2·00	
1794	800l. Young man, construction site and computers	50	75
1795	800l. Woman, street scene and church	50	75
1796	800l. Man, dancers and building	50	75
1797	1200l. St. Marinus (detail) (Francesco Manzocchi de Forl)	75	1·20
	a. Booklet pane. Nos. 1797/1800	3·00	
1798	1200l. 15th-century painting of St. Marinus	75	1·20
1799	1200l. St. Marinus (painting, School of Guercino)	75	1·20
1800	1200l. "St. Marinus in glory" (anon)	75	1·20
1801	1200l. Double throne of Captains Regent	75	1·20
	a. Booklet pane. Nos. 1801/4	3·00	
1802	1200l. Title page of 17th-century edition of Republican Statutes	75	1·20
1803	1200l. Parade of Palace guards	75	1·20
1804	1200l. Flags	75	1·20
1785/1804	Set of 20	9·45	15·00

See also Nos. 1846/9

503 Michael Schumacher and Ferrari Racing Car

(Des Bolaffi S.p.A. Litho)

2001 (10 Jan). *Michael Schumacher, Drivers' Champion and Ferrari, Constructors' Champion (2000). Sheet 110 × 75 mm containing T* **503** *and similar horiz design. Multicoloured.* P 13 × 13½.
| **MS**1805 | 1500l. Type **503**; 1500l. Schumacher, racing car and engineers | 2·50 | 2·50 |

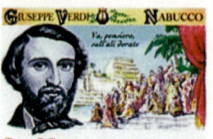

504 Verdi and Scene from Nabucco

(Des F. Filanci. Litho Cartor)

2001 (19 Feb). *Death Centenary of Guiseppe Verdi (composer).* T **504** and similar horiz designs showing scenes from named operas. Multicoloured. P 13 × 13½.
1806	800l. Type **504**	50	75
	a. Sheetlet of 12. Nos. 1806/17	6·25	
1807	800l. Ernani	50	75
1808	800l. Rigoletto	50	75
1809	800l. Il Trovatore	50	75
1810	800l. La Traviata	50	75
1811	800l. I Vespri Siciliani	50	75
1812	800l. Un Ballo in Maschera	50	75
1813	800l. La Forza del Destino	50	75
1814	800l. Don Carlos	50	75
1815	800l. Aida	50	75
1816	800l. Otello	50	75
1817	800l. Falstaff	50	75
1806/1817	Set of 12	5·50	8·00

Nos. 1806/17 were issued together in *se-tenant* sheetlets of 12 stamps with an enlarged margin in the bottom right-hand corner bearing portrait of Verdi.

505 Malatestian Temple (by Leon Battista Alberti), Rimini

506 Yacht

(Des TPA, Parma. Litho Cartor)

2001 (19 Feb). *Commemoration of Malatesta Family (Lords of Rimini).* T **505** and similar horiz design. Multicoloured. P 13 × 13½.
| 1818 | 800l. Type **505** | 50 | 75 |
| 1819 | 1200l. "Christ's Devotion" (Giovanni Bellini) | 70 | 1·10 |

(Des Maddalena Medas. Litho Cartor)

2001 (19 Feb). *Tenth Anniv of "San Marino 24 Hour Yacht Race".* T **506** and similar vert designs. Multicoloured. P 13.
1820	1200l. Type **506**	70	1·10
	a. Block or strip of 4. Nos. 1820/3	3·00	
1821	1200l. Yacht with green and purple spinnaker	70	1·10
1822	1200l. Yacht with brown and white sails	70	1·10
1823	1200l. Yacht with white spinnaker	70	1·10
1820/1823	Set of 4	2·50	4·00

Nos. 1820/3 were issued together in *se-tenant* blocks or strips of four stamps within the sheet.

SAN MARINO 2001

507 Bowls and Athletics	508 Safe containing Water and Forest
511 Early Stringed Instrument and Ceramics	512 Figure reaching Downwards

(Des V. Pradal and M. Dotta. Litho Cartor)

2001 (17 Apr). *Ninth European Small States Games. T* **507** *and similar vert designs. Multicoloured.* P 13½ × 13.
1824	800l. Type **507**	50	75
	a. Sheetlet of 8. Nos. 1824/31	4·25	
1825	800l. Swimming	50	75
1826	800l. Cycling	50	75
1827	800l. Target and skeet shooting	50	75
1828	800l. Judo	50	75
1829	800l. Tennis and table tennis	50	75
1830	800l. Basketball and volleyball	50	75
1831	800l. RASTA (mascot)	50	75
1824/1831 Set of 8		3·75	5·50

Nos. 1824/31 were issued together in *se-tenant* sheetlets of eight stamps.

(Des TPA, Parma. Litho Cartor)

2001 (17 Apr). *Europa. Water Resources. T* **508** *and similar vert design. Multicoloured.* P 13½ × 13.
1832	800l. Type **508**	55	75
1833	1200l. Mountain, tap and running water	80	1·10

509 Santa Maria and Dahlia variabilis

510 Ellis Island Immigration Museum, New York

(Des Maddalena Medas. Litho Cartor)

2001 (17 Apr). *"Euroflora 2001" International Flower Show, Genoa. T* **509** *and similar vert designs. Multicoloured.* P 13½ × 13.
1834	800l. Type **509**	50	75
1835	1200l. *Santa Maria* and *Zantedeschia aethiopica*	70	1·10
1836	1500l. *Santa Maria* and rose "Helen Troubel"	90	1·40
1837	2400l. Faro Tower, Genoa and *Amaryllis hippeastrum*	1·40	2·30
1834/1837 Set of 4		3·25	5·00

(Des F. Filanci. Litho Cartor)

2001 (17 Apr). *"Emigration of the Sammarinese" Exhibition, New York and 25th Anniv of San Marino Social Club, Detroit. T* **510** *and similar horiz design. Multicoloured.* P 13 × 13½.
1838	1200l. Type **510**	70	1·10
1839	2400l. San Marino Social Club, Detroit	1·40	2·20

(Des F. Filanci. Litho Cartor)

2001 (23 June). *Inauguration of State Museum. T* **511** *and similar horiz designs. Multicoloured.* P 13 × 13½.
1840	550l. Type **511**	35	45
1841	800l. Painting and gallery	50	75
1842	1500l. Ancient ceramics	90	1·40
1843	2000l. European artifacts	2·75	1·90
1840/1843 Set of 4		4·00	4·00

(Des L. Mattotti. Litho Cartor)

2001 (23 June). *50th Anniv of United Nations High Commissioner for Refugees. T* **512** *and similar vert design. Multicoloured.* P 13½ × 13.
1844	1200l. Type **512**	70	1·10
	a. Horiz pair. Nos. 1844/5	1·50	2·30
1845	1200l. Figure reaching upwards	70	1·10

Nos. 1844/5 were issued together in *se-tenant* pairs within the sheet, each pair forming a composite design.

513 Mount Titan

(Des T. Pericoli. Litho Cartor)

2001 (23 June). *1700th Anniv of San Marino (2nd issue). Scenes of Mount Titan. T* **513** *and similar horiz designs. Multicoloured.* P 13 × 13½.
1846	1200l. Type **513**	70	1·10
	a. Block of 4. Nos. 1846/9	3·00	
1847	1200l. Three Towers, Mount Titan	70	1·10
1848	1200l. Fields below Mount Titan	70	1·10
1849	1200l. Urban infrastructure below Mount Titan	70	1·10
1846/1849 Set of 4		2·50	4·00

Nos. 1846/9 were issued together in *se-tenant* blocks of four stamps within the sheet.

514 Old Bakery Mill Silo and Woman surrounded by People

SAN MARINO 2001

(Des F. Filanci. Litho Cartor)

2001 (10 Sept). *125th Anniv of San Marino Social Welfare Union (S.U.M.S.).* T **514** *and similar horiz design. Multicoloured.* P 13 × 13½.
1850	1200l. Type **514**		70	70
	a. Horiz pair. Nos. 1850/1		1·50	1·50
1851	1200l. New Bakery Mill Silo headquarters and woman giving sheaves of corn to crowd		70	70

Nos. 1850/1 were issued together in *se-tenant* pairs within the sheet.

515 Banner

516 Children encircling Globe

(Des F. Filanci. Litho Cartor)

2001 (10 Sept). *"Defence of Nature" Exhibition of Works by Joseph Beuys (artist), San Marino.* P 13½ × 13½.
1852	**515**	2400l. multicoloured	1·40	2·30

(Des Urska Golob. Litho Cartor)

2001 (10 Sept). *United Nations Year of Dialogue among Civilizations.* P 13½ × 13.
1853	**516**	2400l. multicoloured	1·40	2·30

517 Angel playing Lute

518 Coins and Map of Euro Zone

(Des Nicoletta Ceccoli. Litho Cartor)

2001 (18 Oct). *Christmas.* T **517** *and similar horiz designs. Multicoloured.* P 13.
1854	800l. Type **517**		50	45
	a. Sheet of 16. Nos. 1854/69		8·25	
1855	800l. Woman with basket and king riding on camel		50	45
1856	800l. King riding camel, woman leading sheep, and woman with parcel		50	45
1857	800l. Man with parcel and Holy Family on Mount Titano		50	45
1858	800l. Sheep, birds and man with lantern		50	45
1859	800l. Ascending angel with trumpet		50	45
1860	800l. Angel with lyre		50	45
1861	800l. King with blue crown riding camel		50	45
1862	800l. Women with parcel, basket and dog		50	45
1863	800l. Shepherd and sheep		50	45
1864	800l. Descending angel with trumpet		50	45
1865	800l. Woman with parcel and angel with trumpet		50	45
1866	800l. Angel playing violin		50	45
1867	800l. Man with parcels on sledge		50	45
1868	800l. Woman with parcel in right hand		50	45
1869	800l. Angel playing drum		50	45
1854/1869	Set of 16		7·25	6·50

Nos. 1854/69 were issued together in *se-tenant* sheetlets of 16 stamps, each sheetlet forming a composite design.

(Des F. Filanci. Litho Cartor)

2001 (18 Oct). *Introduction of Euro Coins and Banknotes (2002).* T **518** *and similar horiz design. Multicoloured.* P 13 × 13½.
1870	1200l. Type **518**		50	70
1871	2400l. Banknotes and map of Euro Zone		1·40	1·40

New Currency 100 cents = 1 euro

519 Rabbits

520 Hippopotamus Ice Skating

(Des F. Filanci (2c., 50c.) or P. Candelari (others). Litho Cartor)

2002 (16 Jan). *New Currency.* T **519** *and similar vert designs. Multicoloured.* P 13½ × 13.
1872	1c. Type **519**	10	10
1873	2c. Sunset	10	10
1874	5c. Cactus flower	10	10
1875	10c. Field of grain	15	15
1876	25c. Alpine landscape	40	40
1877	50c. Olive leaves	75	75
1878	€1 Sparrows	1·40	1·40
1879	€5 Baby	7·25	7·25

Numbers have been left for additions to this series.

(Des F. Altan. Litho Cartor)

2002 (16 Jan). *Winter Olympic Games, Salt Lake City.* T **520** *and similar vert designs. Multicoloured.* P 13½ × 13.
1885	41c. Type **520**	60	60
	a. Block of 4. Nos. 1885/8	2·50	
1886	41c. Dog skiing	60	60
1887	41c. Elephant playing ice hockey	60	60
1888	41c. Rabbit cross-country skiing	60	60
1885/1888	Set of 4	2·20	2·20

Nos. 1885/8 were issued together in *se-tenant* blocks of four.

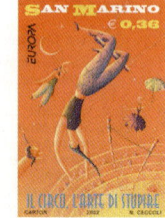

521 Poggiali racing

522 Trapeze Artist

(Litho Cartor)

2002 (16 Jan). *Manuel Poggiali–2001 125 cc. Motorcycle World Champion.* T **521** *and similar horiz design. Multicoloured.* P 13 × 13½.
1889	62c. Type **521**		90	90
	a. Horiz pair. Nos. 1889/90		1·90	1·90
1890	62c. Side view of Poggiali racing		90	90

Nos. 1889/90 were issued together in horizontal *se-tenant* pairs within the sheet.

SAN MARINO 2002

(Des Nicoletta Ceccoli. Litho Cartor)

2002 (22 Mar). *Europa. Circus.* T **522** and similar vert design. Multicoloured. P 13½ × 13.
1891	36c. Type **522**	55	55
1892	62c. Equestrienne performer	90	90

523 Players and Ball (finals, 1934)

(Des V. Pradal and M. Dotta. Litho Cartor)

2002 (22 Mar). *World Cup Football Championship, Japan and South Korea.* Winning Italian Teams. Sheet 155 × 116 mm containing T **523** and similar horiz designs. Multicoloured. P 13 × 13½.
MS1893 41c. Type **523** (score wrongly inscr as 4–2, instead of 2–1); 41c. Player heading ball (finals, 1938) (score wrongly inscr as 1–0, instead of 4–2); 41c. Players jumping (semi-finals, 1970); 41c. Italy and Brazil players at goal mouth (finals, 1982); 41c. Player tackling (third-place playoff, 1990); 41c. Italy and Nigeria No. 10 players at goal (second round, 1994) ... 3·75   3·50

524 Cyclist

(Des F. Filanci. Litho Cartor)

2002 (22 Mar). *Priority Mail Stamps.* T **524** and similar horiz design. Multicoloured. P 13 × 13½.
1894	62c. Type **524**	90	90
1895	€1.24 Hurdler	1·80	1·80

Nos. 1894/5 were issued in sheets of ten stamps each with a label, inscribed "POSTA PRIORITARIA PRIORITY MAIL" attached either at top or foot.

525 Three Towers, Mount Titano

526 Map of Europe as Tree

(Des G. Zani. Litho Cartor)

2002 (3 June). *International Year of Mountains.* T **525** and similar vert designs. Multicoloured. P 13½ × 13.
1896	41c. Type **525**	60	60
	a. Horiz strip of 3. Nos. 1896/8	1·90	
1897	41c. Tower and wall on Mount Titano	60	60
1898	41c. Tower on peak	60	60

Nos. 1896/8 were issued together in horizontal *se-tenant* strips of three stamps within the sheet.

(Des Mariella Antomelli. Litho Cartor)

2002 (3 June). *Tenth Anniv of Maastricht Treaty.* P 13 × 13½.
1899	**526**	€1.24 multicoloured	1·80	1·80

527 1877 2c. and 10c. Stamps

528 Blacksmith working at Anvil

(Des V. Pradal and M. Dotta. Litho Cartor)

2002 (3 June). *125th Anniv of First San Marino Stamps.* Sheet 140 × 71 mm containing T **527** and similar square designs depicting stamps issued in 1877. Multicoloured. P 13½.
MS1900 €1.24, Type **527**; €1.24, 10c. and 20c. stamps; €1.24, 20c. and 30c. stamps; €1.24, 30c. and 40c. stamps ... 10·00   10·00

(Des M. Medas. Litho Cartor)

2002 (19 Sept). *Traditional Crafts.* T **528** and similar vert designs. Multicoloured. P 13½ × 13.
1901	26c. Type **528**	40	40
1902	36c. Broom-maker tying grass bundle	55	55
1903	41c. Chair-mender repairing chair seat	60	60
1904	77c. Scribe writing at table	1·10	1·10
1905	€1.24 Knife-grinder sharpening knife at wheel	1·80	1·80
1906	€1.55 Charcoal burner and wood clamp	2·20	2·20
1901/1906	Set of 6	6·00	6·00

529 Emblems, World Map, Aerial and Morse Code Notation

530 Government Palace

(Des V. Pradal and M. Dotta. Litho Cartor)

2002 (19 Sept). *International Amateur Radio Union Region 1 Conference.* T **529** and similar vert design. Multicoloured. P 13½ × 13.
1907	36c. Type **529**	55	55
1908	62c. Emblems, national flag, world map, aerial and Morse code notation	90	90

323

SAN MARINO 2002

(Des A. Giuffrida and Studio Avalon. Litho Cartor)

2002 (19 Sept). *Tourism*. Sheet 155 × 116 mm containing T **530** and similar multicoloured designs showing places of interest. P 12½.
MS1909 62c. Type **530**; 62c. Guaita (First Tower), Mount Titan (44 × 30 mm); 62c. Cesta (Second Tower) and Montale (Third Tower), Mount Titan (44 × 30 mm); 62c. Basilicia del Santo and San Pietro Church (44 × 30 mm); 62c. Capuchin Church (44 × 30 mm); 62c. St. Francis Gate (39 × 39 mm) . . . . . . 5·25 5·25

531 Woman's Mouth

532 Child's and Adult's Hands

(Des F. Filanci. Litho Cartor)

2002 (31 Oct). *Greetings Stamps*. T **531** and similar vert designs. Multicoloured. P 13½ × 13.
1910	41c. Type **531**	60	60
1911	41c. Child's face and "Hello"	60	60
1912	41c. Man's face and "best wishes"	60	60
1913	41c. Baby's face and "Ehi"	60	60
1914	41c. Man's perplexed face	60	60
1915	41c. Hand covering smiling face and "sorry"	60	60
1910/1915	Set of 6	3·25	3·25

(Des I. Fantini. Litho Cartor)

2002 (31 Oct). *Christmas*. Sheet 185 × 144 mm containing T **532** and similar vert designs. Multicoloured. P 12½.
MS1916 41c. Type **532**; 41c. Mother wearing earrings and baby; 41c. Baby at breast; 41c. Mother and baby sleeping; 41c. Adult hands holding baby; 41c. Mother and baby wrapped in shawl; 41c. Wakeful baby against mother's shoulder; 41c. Baby with finger in mouth laughing with mother; 41c. Baby asleep against mother's shoulder; 41c. Baby looking away from smiling mother; 41c. Baby with arm extended towards mother's face; 41c. Two babies . . . . 7·00 7·00

533 Mushrooms and Artichokes

(Des F. Filanci. Litho Cartor)

2003 (24 Jan). *Italian Cuisine*. T **533** and similar square designs. Multicoloured. P 12½.
1917	41c. Type **533**	60	60
	a. Sheetlet. Nos. 1917/32	9·75	
1918	41c. Cooked meats	60	60
1919	41c. Spaghetti	60	60
1920	41c. Cappelletti	60	60
1921	41c. Prawns	60	60
1922	41c. Mixed seafood	60	60
1923	41c. Ravioli	60	60
1924	41c. Tagliatelle	60	60
1925	41c. Chicken and potatoes	60	60
1926	41c. Fish	60	60
1927	41c. Fruit tart	60	60
1928	41c. Chocolate pudding	60	60
1929	41c. Scrambled eggs	60	60
1930	41c. Pancetta	60	60
1931	41c. Pastries	60	60
1932	41c. Brandy snap basket	60	60
1917/1932	Set of 16	8·50	8·50

Nos. 1917/32 were issued together in *se-tenant* sheetlets of 16 stamps, the stamps arranged in blocks of four to form plates.

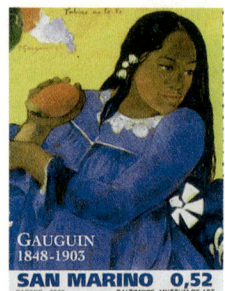

534 "Woman with Mango" (Paul Gauguin)

(Des F. Filanci. Litho Cartor)

2003 (24 Jan). *Artists' Anniversaries*. T **534** and similar vert designs. Multicoloured. P 13½ × 13.
1933	52c. Type **534** (death centenary)	75	75
1934	62c. "Wheat-field with flight of crows" (Vincent Van Gogh) (150th birth anniv)	90	90
1935	€1.55 "Portrait of a young woman" (Parmigianino) (500th birth anniv)	2·20	2·20

535 Combination Skiing

(Des Pradal-Doter-Pojer. Litho Cartor)

2003 (24 Jan). *World Nordic Skiing Championship, Val di Femme*. Sheet 156 × 116 mm containing T **535** and similar vert designs. Multicoloured. P 13½ × 13.
MS1936 77c. Type **535**; 77c. Ski jumping; 77c. Cross Country Skiing . . . . 3·50 3·50

324

SAN MARINO

STAMP BOOKLETS

The following checklist covers, in simplified form, booklets issued by San Marino. It is intended that it should be used in conjunction with the main listings and details of stamps and panes listed there are not repeated.

Prices are for complete booklets.

Booklet No.	Date	Contents and Cover Price	Price
SB1	16.5.85	*Small States Games* 1 pane, No. 1246 × 10 (400ol.)	3·50
SB2	11.6.90	*European Tourism Year* 1 pane. No. 1366a (2000l.)	2·40
SB3	26.3.92	*Tourism* 1 pane, No. 1424a (2000l.)	1·90
SB4	6.5.96	"*Medieval Days*" 1 pane, No. 1546a (6000l.)	3·50
SB5	28.5.98	*World Cup Football Championship, France* 3 panes, Nos. 1666a, 1667a and 1668a (9400l.)	10·50
SB6	14.11.00	*1700th Anniv of San Marino* 4 panes, Nos. 1785a, 1789a, 1793a and 1801a (plus 800l. postcard 120000l.)	12.50

SWITZERLAND + LIECHTENSTEIN

Our large stocks of both countries (also Austria) from the earliest Classics to the latest new issues are always at your disposal – please consult us for anything Swiss!

Not only can we help with most of the stamps listed, used, mint or unmounted mint, as singles or in sets, but we have interesting stocks of additional material, such as **MILITARY STAMPS, POSTAL STATIONERY, FRAMAS, LABELS,** and, of course, a large stock of **COVERS and POSTAL HISTORY,** including pre-stamp, excellent airmails, Postage Due items, T.P.Os, Bundesfeier and Pro Juventute Cards etc. etc.

Detailed price lists against 4 x 1st class stamps, or avail yourself of our many services such as: Mail Order to all parts of the world – Wants List service – Regular monthly supplies – Approvals for early issues – Photocopy offers – Mailing list for special offers – Catalogue and literature supplies.

LEO BARESCH LTD. PTS
P.O. Box 791, HASSOCKS, W. Sussex, BN6 8PZ
Tel. 01273 845501 – Fax 01273 842411
e-mail: leo@baresch.plus.com

SWITZERLAND ALBUMS FROM DAVO

We carry a fine range of excellent Davo branded albums for Switzerland.

For full details ask for Davo brochure.

Switzerland Volume I   1845-1944
Switzerland Volume II   1945-1969
Switzerland Volume III   1970-1999
Switzerland Volume IV   2000-2002

Stanley Gibbons Publications
7 Parkside, Christchurch Road, Ringwood
Hampshire, BH24 3SH, United Knigdom
Tel: +44 (0) 1425 472363 Fax: +44 (0) 1425 470247
Email: info@stanleygibbons.co.uk Internet: www.stanleygibbons.com

SWITZERLAND

Switzerland

100 Rappen = 1 Franken
100 Centimes = 1 Franc
100 Centesimi = 1 Franco

These are expressions of the same currency in three languages

CONDITION. The condition of all issues of the Cantonal Administrations and Federal stamps up to No. 51 is an important factor in establishing catalogue value. The prices are for stamps in good condition with four margins, but the stamps in very fine condition with large margins all round are worth very much more, whilst medium and close-cut copies are supplied at lower prices.

I. CANTONAL ADMINISTRATIONS

ZURICH

C **1**    C **2**

(Litho Orell, Fussli & Co, Zurich)

1843 (1 Mar). *Types* C **1** *(inscr "Local-Taxe") and* C **2** *(inscr "Cantonal-Taxe")*. Imperf.
(a) Ground of horizontal red lines.

			Un.	Used	On Cover
Z1	C **1**	4r. black	£13000	£16000	£36000
Z2	C **2**	6r. black	£1400	£1100	£2500

Variety Retouched background.
Z3 C **2** 6r. black £7000 £3500 £7000

(b) Ground of vertical red lines.
Z4 C **1** 4r. black £14000 £14000 £33000
Z5 C **2** 6r. black £4500 £1200 £3000

There are five varieties of type of each value. In October, 1862, reprints were made of both values on thinner paper and *without red lines.*

A 4r. and a half of a 4r. are known used On Cover for a 6r.

GENEVA

C **3**    C **4**    C **5**

(Litho C. A. Schmid, Geneva)

1843 (30 Sept). *Black impression.* Imperf.
G1   C **3**   5+5c. on *yellow-green* . . £42000 £28000 £44000
Varieties. (i) Half-stamp used separately as 5c.
G2   C **3**   5c. on *yellow-green* . . . £17000 £7000 £12000
(ii) Pairs cut wrong way.
G2a C **3**   5+5c. on *yell-grn (horiz)* . £59000 £46000 £80000
G2b   5+5c. on *yell-grn (vert)* . . . £74000

No. G2a is a horizontal pair with right half at left and left half at right. No. G2b is a vertical pair comprising either two left halves or two right halves.

(Litho C. A. Schmid, Geneva)

1845 (1 April). *Small Eagle. Black Impression.* Imperf.
G3   C **4**   5c. on *yellow-green* £2000 £1300 £2500

1847–48. *Large Eagle. Black impression.* Imperf.
G4   C **5**   5c. on *yellow green* £1500 £1300 £3000
G5   5c. on *blue green*
             (22.8.48) £3000 £2250 £3750

1849. *Similar design, printed on white paper.*
G6   C **5**   5c. yellow-green £350 £2500 £22000

This is an envelope stamp cut out and used as an adhesive, as there was little demand for the entire envelopes.

BASEL
TOWN POST

C **6** Dove of Basel

(Des M Berri. Eng (eagle embossed), Krebs, Frankfurt-a-M.)

1845 (1 July). Imperf.
B1   C **6**   2½r. carmine, black and
              blue £9500 £9500 £14000
The stamp with *vermilion* centre, and *green* background in the four corners, is a proof (*Price* £3500).

II. TRANSITIONAL PERIOD

GENEVA

T **1**    T **2**    T **3**

(Types T **1/3**. Litho C. A. Schmid, Geneva)

1849 (Oct). Imperf.
L1   T **1**   4c. black and red £27000 £16000 £32000

1850 (22 Jan). Imperf.
L2   T **2**   5c. black and red £1800 £1400 £2250
The numeral of each stamp on the plate of the 4c. was altered by hand into a "5"; there are consequently 100 varieties of the numeral of the higher value. Both these stamps were formerly attributed to Vaud.

1850 (Aug). Imperf.
L3   T **3**   5c. black and red £7000 £3000 £5000
This stamp was formerly attributed to Neuchâtel. In Nos. L1 to L3 the background of the central portion of the stamp is in the second colour.

ZURICH

T **4**

327

SWITZERLAND Switzerland　　　　　　　　　　　　　　　　　　　　　　1850

(Drawn by F. Muller. Typo)
1850 (Mar). *Background in second colour. Imperf.*
L4　T **4**　2½r. black and red £4750 £2750 £28000
This stamp was formerly attributed to Winterthur.

III. FEDERAL ADMINISTRATION

1　　　　　　2　　　　　　3

(T **1/3**. Litho M. Durheim, Berne)

(a) Central cross with black trance (or blue frame on No. 12a)
(b) Central cross without frame

1850 (May). *40 varieties in the plate. Imperf.*

(i) *Inscr* "ORTS POST".

			Un	Used
1	**1**	2½r. black and red (a)	£2000	£1000
2		2½r. black and red (b)	£4000	£1900

(ii) *Inscr* "POSTE LOCALE".

| 3 | **2** | 2½r. black and red (a) | £1600 | £950 |
| 4 | | 2½r. black and red (b) | £38000 | £19000 |

1850 (1 Oct). *40 varieties in the plate. Imperf.*

(i) *Inscr* "RAYON I".

5	**3**	5r. red, black and blue (a)	£3750	£850
6		5r. red, black and blue (b)	£1200	£325
7		5r. red, black and deep blue (a)	£4000	£850
8		5r. red, black and deep blue (b)	£2500	£550

(ii) *Inscr* "RAYON II".

9		10r. red, black and orange-yellow (a)	—	£70000
10		10r. red, black and yellow (b)	£700	80·00
11		10r. red, black and orange yellow (b)	£1900	£225
		a. Carton paper	£1800	£250
12		10r. red black and brownish yellow (b)	£2000	£400

1851 (30 Mar). *Colours changed. Imperf. Inscr* "RAYON I".

12a	**3**	5r. red and pale blue (a)	—	£84000
13		5r. red and pale blue (b)	£425	85·00
14		5r. red and deep blue (b)	£1200	£160

4　　　　　　5　　　　　　6

(T **4/5**. Litho M. Durheim, Berne)

1852 (1 Jan). *Inscr* "RAYON III". *Small figures of value. 10 varieties in the plate. Imperf.*

20	**4**	15r. vermilion	£8500	£425
21		15c. rose	£8000	£500
22		15c. vermilion	£9000	£650

1852 (Apr). *Ten new varieties of the 15r. with larger figures of value. Imperf.*

23	**5**	15r. rose	£1600	80·00
24		15r. vermilion	£1600	75·00
		a. Printed both sides		

PRINTINGS OF TYPE 6.
Munich　Details of background clear, with the lines of the lozenges distinctly visible, especially beneath the right arm of Helvetia.
Berne　Printing of background far less distinct than in Munich printings, lines in lozenges tend to run together, especially beneath the right arm. The figure is surrounded by a band of thick colour, not present on the Munich printings.

(Eng E. Vogt, Munich Embossed)

1854 (15 Sept). *Printed by J. G. Weiss, Munich. Thin paper. Emerald-green silk thread. Imperf.*

25	**6**	5r. yellow-brown	£500	60·00
		a. Orange-brown	£4250	£1100
		b. Error 5r. blue		
26		10r. bright blue	£500	31·00
27		15r. rose	£700	£110
28		40r. pale green	£800	£180
		a. Pale yellow-green	£6000	£750

No. 25b is on paper with silk thread.
The 5r. in blue on paper without thread is from a trial printing.

1854 (14 Oct)–**62**. *Printed at Mint Berne. Imperf.*

A. *Green silk thread. Medium paper.*

29	**6**	5r. grey-brown (4.11.54)	£375	95·00
30		10r. milky blue (29.5.56)	£850	85·00
31		15r. pale rose (29.1.55)	£700	75·00
32		20r. orange (14.10.54)	£900	£100

B. *Different coloured threads for each value.*

(a) *Thick paper.*

33	**6**	5r. yellow brown (*yellow thread*) (5.55)	£300	80·00
		a. Deep brown (*yellow thread*)	£300	85·00
34		5r. pale brown (*black thread*) (1.56)	£250	23·00
		a. Deep brown (*black thread*)	£200	24·00
35		10r. blue (*carmine thread*) (9.56)	£190	28·00
		a. Pale blue (*carmine thread*)	£200	55·00
36		15r. rose (*blue thread*) (7.57)	£325	42·00
		a. Pale rose (*blue thread*)	£350	48·00
37		40r. yellow-green (*red thread*) (4.55)	£600	65·00
38		1f. grey lilac (*black thread*) (2.55)	£850	£650
		a. Lilac (*black thread*)	£800	£600
39		1f. grey-lilac (*yellow thread*) (1856)	£950	£650
		a. Lilac (*yellow thread*)	£850	£600

(b) *Thin paper.*

40	**6**	10r. blue (*carmine thread*) (1857)	£2750	£300
41		1f. grey-lilac (*yellow thread*) (1857)	£12000	£5000
		a. Lilac (*yellow thread*)	£14000	£5500

C. *Bright green silk thread.*

(a) *Thin paper.*

42	**6**	5r. grey-brown (6.56)	£2750	£700
43		10r. blue (1857)	£3750	£600
44		15r. rose (4.57)	£1900	£190
45		20r. orange (6.56)	£1900	£160

(b) *Thick paper.*

46	**6**	2r. grey (1.1.62)	£140	£300
		a. Bisected and used with No. 45 (on piece)	†	£2750
47		5r. brown (4.58)	£120	10·50
		a. Deep brown	£120	10·50
		b. Purple-brown	£170	22·00
		c. Bisected (on piece)	†	£1000
48		10r. blue (6.59)	£130	8·00
		a. Deep blue	£140	9·75
49		15r. rose (1858)	£225	29·00
		a. Pale rose	£225	29·00
50		20r. orange (26.8.57)	£275	38·00
51		40r. green (1858)	£250	36·00
		a. Yellow-green	£325	38·00

No. 46a was allowed to do duty as a 1r. value to make-up the printed matter rate to Italy Most known examples were used to frank newspapers.
No. 47c was accepted by the Geneva postal authorities from mid-1861 to June 1862 as payment for printed matter in excess of 20 copies which was charged at half rate (2½r.).

SWITZERLAND Switzerland 1862

| 7 |    8 |  8a |  I |  II (normal) |  II (inverted) |

WATERMARK. There are two types of the impressed watermark. In Type **8a** the arms of the cross are longer and narrower while the oval frame lines are so close that they usually appear to be one.

D Two types of frame.
10.
  I. Corner triangles complete below winged wheel in all corners.
  II. Corner triangle broken below wheel in one corner. This type is found normal with broken triangle in top right-hand corner, or inverted with broken triangle in bottom left-hand corner.

FOR WELL CENTRED COPIES ADD 35%

(Des J. Riess, Munich. Typo Berne)

1862 (1 Oct)–**64**. Wmk **8** (impressed). P11½.
52	7	2c. grey	44·00	1·70
53		3c. black	6·25	47·00
54		5c. brown (8.12.62)	2·00	30
		a. Yellow-brown	60·00	1·30
		b. Purple-brown	1·70	25
		c. Blackish brown	65·00	11·00
		d. Double impression, one inverted	£2750	£170
55		10c. blue	£225	25
		a. Deep blue	£225	30
		b. Double impression, one inverted	—	£5000
56		20c. orange-yellow (5.3.63)	£200	2·50
		a. Pale orange	1·40	1·10
		b. Deep orange	1·40	1·20
57		30c. vermilion	£750	18·00
58		40c. green (30.6.63)	£750	27·00
59		60c. copper-bronze (18.5.63)	£500	65·00
60		1f. bronze-gold (18.5.63)	£700	£180
		a. Gold (1864)	12·00	45·00

See also Nos. 61/7 and 105/13.

1867 (Mar)–**78**. Colours changed and new values. W **8** (impressed). P 11½.
61	7	2c. light bistre-brown (1.2.74)	1·60	65
		a. Bistre	1·60	60
		b. Red-brown	£400	85·00
62		10c. rose	1·90	35
		a. Pale rose	2·50	30
63		15c. lemon-yellow (1.1.75)	2·20	18·00
64		25c. blue-green (1.9.68)	1·30	1·20
		a. Deep green	6·50	12·00
		b. Yellow-green	28·00	18·00
		c. Double impression, one inverted	—	£475
65		30c. blue	£1500	£160
		a. Ultramarine	£300	5·25
66		40c. grey (5.4.78)	1·50	60·00
		a. Pale grey	1·50	60·00
67		50c. purple	35·00	18·00
		a. Deep purple	35·00	21·00

Nos 68/88 are vacant.

| D 9 |  D 10 |

(Des and eng J. Durussel. Typo Stampfli & Co, Berne until 1906 and then at the Mint)

1878 (1 July)–**80**. *POSTAGE DUE. White paper. Figures in deep blue.* W **8** (impressed). P 11½.

(a) Frame Type I.
D89	D **9**	1c. blue	2·00	75
D90	D **10**	2c. blue	1·40	65
D91		3c. blue (31.1.80)	12·00	8·75
D92		5c. blue	14·50	5·00
D92a	D **9**	5c. blue	†	—
D93	D **10**	10c. blue	£140	5·00
D94		20c. blue	£180	3·25
D95		50c. blue	£350	13·50
D96		100c. blue	£450	5·00
D97		500c. blue	£400	8·50

(b) Frame Type II.
A. *Normal.*
D 98 A	D **10**	3c. blue (31.1.80)	8·75	4·75
D 99 A		5c. blue	13·00	7·50
D100A		10c. blue	£150	4·00
D101A		20c. blue	£180	1·70
D102A		50c. blue	£350	7·25
D103A		100c. blue	£1000	80·00
D104A		500c. blue	£425	47·00

B. *Inverted.*
D 98 B	D **10**	3c. blue (31.1.80)	8·00	4·50
D 99 B		5c. blue	12·00	4·75
D100B		10c. blue	£150	2·50
D101B		20c. blue	£200	5·00
D102B		50c. blue	£350	14·50
D103B		100c. blue		£1600
D104B		500c. blue	£400	42·00

There are many shades of Nos. D89/D104.
A single cancelled example of No. D92a with rayed background is known.

FOR WELL CENTRED COPIES ADD 30%
(Nos. 111/13 only)

1881. *Granite paper.* W **8** (impressed). P 11½.
105	7	2c. ochre	30	10·00
		a. Double impression, one inverted	£275	
106		5c. black-brown	20	2·30
		a. Double impression, one inverted	13·00	£300
107		10c. bright rose	2·40	2·50
108		15c. lemon-yellow	4·50	£275
109		20c. brown-orange	20	75·00
110		25c. green	20	50·00
111		40c. slate	25	£2250
112		50c. purple	8·50	£275

329

SWITZERLAND Switzerland 1882

	a. Double impression, one inverted		£200	£2750
113	1f. gold		10·00	£850
	Stamps of this issue are found with forged postmarks.			

1882. POSTAGE DUE. *Granite paper. Figures In deep blue.* W **8** (impressed). P 11½.

A. Frame Type II (normal).

D116A	D **10**	10c. blue (7.1)	£140	25·00
D117A		20c. blue (6.3)	£350	33·00
D118A		50c. blue (2.5)	£2000	£350
D119A		100c. blue (2.5)	£650	£275
D120A		500c. blue (12.6)	£12000	£160

B. Frame Type II (inverted).

D116B	D **10**	10c. blue (7.1)	£150	30·00
D117B		20c. blue (6.3)	£375	44·00
D118B		50c. blue (2.5)	£2000	£375
D119B		100c. blue (2.5)	£700	£300
D120B		500c. blue (12.6)	£13000	£180

See also Nos. D188/95 and D268/73.

9 **10** 40c. Nos. 136, 142, 149, 158

FOR WELL CENTRED COPIES ADD:
35% for Nos. 121/5; 30% for Nos. 126/33

(Des C. Hasert. Eng E. Burger. Typo Stämpfli & Co, Berne)

1882 (1 Apr)–**99.** Impressed watermark. P11½.

(a) Plain wove paper. W **8**.

121	**9**	2c. olive-bistre	£275	£190
122		5c. maroon	£650	55·00
123		10c. pink	£1700	43·00
124		12c. pale ultramarine	£110	20·00
125		15c. orange-yellow	£180	£190

The 15c. was formerly listed *tête-bêche* but it is doubtful if this is a genuine variety.

(b) Granite paper. A. W **8a** (1882–93).

126A	**9**	2c. olive-bistre	13·00	95
		c. Bronze-brown	16·00	65
		d. Olive-brown	19·00	1·20
127A		3c. purple-brown	17·00	17·00
		c. Drab	22·00	20·00
128A		5c. maroon	29·00	25
		c. Tête-bêche (pair)	—	—
130A		10c. pink	£110	95
		c. Rose	50·00	95
		d. Carmine (1893)	35·00	10·00
131A		12c. pale ultramarine	47·00	1·90
		c. Ultramarine	65·00	3·50
132A		15c. lemon	95·00	9·75
		b. Deep yellow	£140	13·00
		ba. Tête-bêche (pair)	—	—
		c. Orange-yellow	£12000	£2750
133A		15c. purple (15.12.89)	£130	7·75

B. W **8a** (1884–99).

126B	**9**	2c. olive-bistre	65	30
		c. Bronze-brown	1·60	40
		d. Olive-brown	65	10
127B		3c. purple-brown	6·50	3·25
		c. Drab	1·10	1·60
128B		5c. maroon	30·00	2·20
		d. Claret (1894)		11·50
129B		5c. deep green (1899)	8·50	20
		c. Pale green	2·75	10
130B		10c. rose	8·00	1·60
		d. Carmine (1893)	8·75	2·40
		e. Scarlet (1897)	2·30	15

131B		12c. ultramarine	4·00	10
		d. Dull blue (1894)	£140	16·00
		e. Bright blue (1894)	4·00	10
133B		15c. dull violet (1894)	31·00	1·00
		c. Deep violet (1894)	31·00	85

See also Nos. 194/9.

FOR WELL CENTRED COPIES ADD:
30% for Nos. 134/9
40% for Nos. 140/4
30% for Nos. 145/54

(Des and eng and recess printed until 1886 by Müllhaupt & Son. Berne; from 1886 by Max Girardet, Berne)

1882–1903. *Plain wove paper. Impressed watermark.*

(a) Perf 11¾. W **8** (1882–1901).

134	**10**	20c. yellow-orange	£110	2·40
		a. Orange	£100	2·40
135		25c. blue-green	£110	1·40
		a. Pale yellow-green	55·00	85
		b. Deep yellow-green	55·00	85
136		40c. grey	65·00	19·00
137		50c. pale blue	£100	10·50
		a. Deep blue	85·00	8·75
138		1f. maroon	£140	2·00
		a. Claret	£180	2·40
139		3f. yellow-brown (1891)	£120	6·25
		a. Brown-orange	£170	9·50
		b. Wmk **8a** (1901)	—	£3250

(b) Perf 9½. W **8** (1888).

140	**10**	20c. yellow-orange	£600	49·00
		a. Orange	£650	55·00
141		25c. deep yellow-green	£110	6·25
		a. Green	95·00	4·75
142		40c. grey	£475	£325
143		50c. pale blue	£950	£150
		a. Deep blue	£850	£200
144		1f. maroon	£700	46·00
		a. Claret	£650	32·00

(c) Perf 11½ × 11. A. W **8** (1891–98).

145A	**10**	20c. orange	£350	4·00
146A		25c. yellow-green	£200	1·10
		c. Green	£160	95
148A		30c. deep brown (1892)	£275	23·00
		c. Pale brown	£325	23·00
149A		40c. grey	£650	75·00
150A		50c. pale blue	£300	9·00
		c. Deep blue	£350	11·00
152A		1f. maroon	£550	8·25
		c. Claret	£600	12·00
154A		3f. yellow-brown (1898)	—	£12000

B. W **8a** (1894–1902).

145B	**10**	20c. orange	24·00	60
		c. Yellow-orange (1895)	32·00	1·00
146B		25c. yellow-green	8·25	55
		c. Green	13·00	30
		d. Grey-green	24·00	2·40
147B		25c. blue (1899)	7·00	45
148B		30c. deep brown (1892)	55·00	1·80
		c. Pale brown	55·00	2·40
149B		40c. grey	35·00	3·00
150B		50c. pale blue	30·00	2·20
		c. Deep blue	40·00	2·50
151B		50c. yellow-green (1899)	38·00	5·00
		c. Grey-green	38·00	5·00
152B		1f. maroon	41·00	1·80
		c. Claret	43·00	1·90
		d. Rosy mauve (1895)	60·00	2·40
153B		1f. carmine (1902)	£170	6·25
		c. Rose-carmine	£275	7·50
		d. Bright carmine	£325	8·75
154B		3f. yellow-brown (1898)	£120	15·00

(d) Perf 11½ × 12. W **8a** (1901–03).

155	**10**	20c. orange	17·00	45
		a. Yellow-orange	29·00	1·00
156		25c. deep blue	36·00	2·40
		a. Blue	6·50	35

330

SWITZERLAND Switzerland 1882

157	30c. deep brown		60·00	2·30
	a. Pale brown		22·00	65
	b. Lake-brown		22·00	55
158	40c. grey		55·00	14·50
159	50c. green		28·00	2·20
160	1f. claret		£1300	£100
161	1f. carmine (1903)		£300	14·50
162	3f. brown (1902)		£130	10·50

The 25c. is known imperforate but this is probably an essay. See also Nos. 193 and 200/24.

1883–1908. POSTAGE DUE. Granite paper. Impressed watermark. P 11½. A. Frame Type I. B. Frame Type II (normal). C. Frame Type II (inverted).

(a) Pale blue green. Figures in carmine W 8 (1883).

D163B	D 10	5c.	£100	70·00
D164B		10c.	£150	55·00
D165B		20c.	£275	55·00
D166B		50c.	£325	£160
D167B		100c.	£900	£850
D168B		500c.	£1800	£400
D163C		5c.	36·00	21·00
D164C		10c.	55·00	15·00
D165C		20c.	£100	13·00
D166C		50c.	£120	45·00
D167C		100c.	£350	£225
D168C		500c.	£700	£120

(b) Dull greenm Figures in carmine W 8 (1884–87).

D169B	D 10	5c.	24·00	17·00
D170B		10c.	32·00	3·75
D171B		20c.	36·00	4·75
D172B		50c.	80·00	40·00
D173B		100c.	£160	95·00
D174B		500c.	£300	50·00
D169C		5c.	22·00	10·00
D170C		10c.	30·00	4·00
D171C		20c.	32·00	4·50
D172C		50c.	70·00	39·00
D173C		100c.	£150	85·00
D174C		500c.	£275	36·00

(c) Yellow-green (shades). Figures in carmine W 8 (1887–88).

D175A	D 10	5c.	£350	£275
D176A		10c.	£350	£275
D177A		20c.	£900	£250
D178A		50c.	£850	£600
D179A		100c.	£850	£600
D180A		500c.	£1700	£800
D175B		5c.	32·00	6·75
D176B		10c.	32·00	4·00
D177B		20c.	£110	5·50
D178B		50c.	£225	75·00
D179B		100c.	£250	90·00
D180B		500c.	£475	13·50
D175C		5c.	24·00	6·25
D176C		10c.	28·00	5·50
D177C		20c.	£110	4·75
D178C		50c.	£225	60·00
D179C		100c.	£225	70·00
D180C		500c.	£550	21·00

(d) Olive-green (shades). Figure in carmine (I) W 8 (1889–93).

D181A	D 10	3c.	£300	£225
D182A		5c.	£200	£170
D183A		10c.	£200	£170
D184A		20c.	£180	£150
D185A		50c.	£300	£200
D186A		100c.	£300	£200
D187A		500c.	£700	£300
D181B		3c.	4·50	1·90
D182B		5c.	18·00	1·80
D183B		10c.	26·00	90
D184B		20c.	24·00	70
D185B		50c.	80·00	5·25
D186B		100c.	£100	8·50
D187B		500c.	£120	12·00
D181C		3c.	7·25	4·75
D182C		5c.	22·00	2·10
D183C		10c.	26·00	1·70
D184C		20c.	22·00	1·40
D185C		50c.	80·00	3·50
D186C		100c.	90·00	11·50

D187C		500c.	£140	13·00

II. W **8a** (1894–96).

D188A	D 10	5c.	£200	£190
D189A		10c.	£275	£180
D190A		20c.	£250	£250
D191A		50c.	£650	£350
D192A		100c.	£700	£400
D188B		5c.	16·00	2·20
D189B		10c.	20·00	2·50
D190B		20c.	20·00	3·75
D191B		50c.	£100	29·00
D192B		100c.	£250	90·00
D188C		5c.	10·00	1·10
D189C		10c.	14·50	1·00
D190C		20c.	16·00	1·70
D191C		50c.	50·00	9·00
D192C		100c.	80·00	27·00

(e) Olivish green to grass-green. Figures in vermillion W 8 (1897).

D193A	D 10	1c.	£450	£425
D194A		5c.	£300	£250
D195A		10c.	£450	£275
D196A		20c.	£450	£275
D197A		50c.	£500	£250
D198A		100c.	£900	£800
D199A		500c.	£1500	£900
D193B		1c.	32·00	11·00
D194B		5c.	20·00	7·50
D195B		10c.	90·00	8·25
D196B		20c.	90·00	7·25
D197B		50c.	90·00	24·00
D198B		100c.	90·00	65·00
D199B		500c.	£120	22·00
D193C		1c.	90·00	65·00
D194C		5c.	80·00	36·00
D195C		10c.	£180	70·00
D196C		20c.	£200	70·00
D197C		50c.	£225	90·00
D198C		100c.	£200	£140
D199C		500c.	£225	£120

(f) Olive-green (shades). Figures in vermillion W 8a (1897–1908).

D200A	D 10	1c.	£180	£200
D201A		5c.	£120	£130
D202A		10c.	£120	90·00
D203A		20c.	£130	90·00
D204A		50c.	£250	£170
D205A		100c.	£250	£170
D206A		500c.	£1400	£850
D200B		1c.	40	40
D201B		5c.	1·30	30
D202B		10c.	3·25	45
D203B		20c.	8·00	65
D204B		50c.	11·00	1·90
D205B		100c.	12·00	1·70
D206B		500c.	£140	£130
D200C		1c.	45	60
D201C		5c.	1·30	50
D202C		10c.	3·25	75
D203C		20c.	8·00	1·10
D204C		50c.	11·00	1·80
D205C		100c.	12·00	2·30
D206C		500c.	£140	£120

Some of the shades of Nos. D200/6 can only be distinguished from the true shade of Nos. D193/9 by the worn appearance of the print and the generally faint and dull colours of the numeral. Dated cancellations prior to 9.11.97 indicate stamps belonging to Nos. D193/9.

11   A   B

331

SWITZERLAND Switzerland — 1900

FOR WELL CENTRED COPIES ADD 30%

(Des E. Grasset. Eng F. Florian, Paris. Recess M. Girardet. Berne)

1900. 25th Anniv of Universal Postal Union. W **8**a (impressed). P 12 × 11½ (harrow or line).

(a) Figures of value solid, as A (2 July).

188	**11**	5c. green	26·00	1·50
189		10c. reside	7·00	65
190		25c. blue	13·00	8·50

(b) Re-engraved. Horizontally-lined background clearer. Figures of value lined, as B. Top telegraph wire thinner than in the original plate.

191	**11**	5c. green (1 Aug)	2·75	60
192		10c. rosine (Oct)	35·00	20·00

The 25c. was also re-engraved, but was not issued for use, although a few specimens were obtained by favour. Price £700 un.

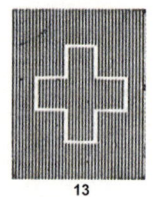

1904. T **12** (T **10** redrawn). W8a (Impressed). P 11¾.

193	**12**	40c. pearl-grey	32·00	10·00

The 40c., T **12**, may be distinguished from Type **10** by the shape and size of the figures of value (see illustration above No. 121).

(Typo Stampfli & Co, Berne and after summer 1906 by The Mint, Berne)

1905–07. W **13**.

I. Granite paper. P 11½ (Aug 1906).

194	**9**	2c. olive-brown	3·25	80
195		3c. drab	3·25	30·00
196		5c. pale green	3·50	15
		a. Yellow-green	3·50	10
197		10c. red-orange	3·50	15
		a. Vermilion	8·75	1·10
198		12c. blue	4·75	80
		a. Deep blue	7·25	2·40
199		15c. purple	47·00	7·00

II. Plain white paper (printed by Gicardet, Berne).

(a) P 11 × 11 (Aug 1905–6).

200	**10**	20c. orange	3·00	1·20
201		25c. blue	4·25	3·25
202		30c. brown	4·75	1·10
		a. Pale brown	9·50	2·00
203	**12**	40c. pearl-grey	70·00	65·00
204	**10**	50c. grey-green	26·00	3·00
205		1f. deep carmine	60·00	1·40
206		3f. bistre-brown (8.06)	£170	65·00

(b) Redrawn. P 11½ × 11 (1906).

207	**14**	25c. pale blue	5·00	60

(c) Redrawn. P 11½ (1906).

208	**14**	25c. blue	60·00	2·75
209	**12**	40c. pearl-grey	23·00	4·00

The 25c., Type **14**, is Type **10** redrawn, the stars in the frame are larger, the background under "FRANCO" is netted instead of being composed of straight and curved lines, and the numerals in the upper corners are altered in shape.

(d) P 11½ × 12 (1907).

210	**10**	20c. orange	6·75	3·50
211		50c. grey-green	36·00	6·75
212		1f. carmine	90·00	50·00
213		3f. bistre-brown	£250	£130

Nos. 200/213 on plain white paper are also found in many shades on a kind of oiled paper.

III. Granite paper (printed by Benziger & Co. Einsiedeln) (1907).

(a) P 11½ × 12.

214	**10**	20c. orange-yellow	1·70	1·10
		a. Red-orange	22·00	18·00
215	**14**	25c. blue	7·75	3·75
216	**10**	30c. brown	4·75	4·75
217	**12**	40c. pearl-grey	18·00	19·00
218	**10**	50c. green	5·50	1·00
		a. Deep green	8·00	2·00
219		1f. carmine	21·00	3·25

(b) P 11½ × 11.

220	**14**	25c. blue	9·00	3·00
221	**10**	30c. brown	£140	£275
222	**12**	40c. pearl-grey	—	£13000
223	**10**	1f. carmine	£11000	£4500
224		3f. bistre-brown	£100	15·00

15 Tell's Son   **16**   **17**

(a)   (b)

(Des A. Welti (T **14**), C. L'Eplattenier (T **15**). Typo Mint, Berne)

1907 (11 Nov). *Granite paper.* W **13**. P 11½.

225	**15**	2c. olive-yellow	30	25
226		3c. cinnamon	20	5·00
227		5c. green	2·30	15
228	**16**	10c. rose-red	1·40	15
229		12c. ochre	30	1·70
230		15c. mauve	3·75	7·00
225/230		Set of 6	8·50	13·00

GRILLED GUM. Some of the paper used during the period 1932 to 1944 was passed through a gum breaker, prior to printing, to prevent subsequent curling. The machinery used impressed a grill into the gum by means of patterned rollers. Sufficient force was exerted for this grill to be transferred to the paper beneath the gum and, in consequence, we quote prices for both unused and used examples.

(Des C. L'Eplattenier. Typo Mint, Berne)

1908 (Aug)–**40**. *Granite paper (ordinary).* W **13**. P 11½.

(i) Designer's name in full on rock (a).

231	**17**	40c. orange-yellow and purple	5·75	60·00

(ii) Initials "C.L." only on rock (b).

232	**17**	20c. yellow and red	1·10	30
233		25c. light blue and deep blue	1·90	20
		a. Tête-bêche (pair)	28·00	£110
		b. pale green and pale blue		
234		30c. pale green and yellow-brown	1·90	20
235		35c. yellow and green	1·90	2·20
		a. Chalk-surfaced paper. Grilled gum (1933)	1·70	9·75
236		40c. orange-yellow and purple	9·75	30
237		40c. light blue (3.21)	3·25	25
238		40c. blue (4.22)	1·50	15
239		40c. yellow-green & dp magenta (1.25)	23·00	20
		a. Chalk-surfaced paper. Grilled gum (1933)	27·00	55

SWITZERLAND Switzerland 1908

240	50c. yellow-green and deep green		6·25	15
	a. Chalk-surfaced paper. Grilled gum (1933)		5·00	35
	b. Chalk-surfaced paper. Smooth gum (1940)		12·00	31·00
241	60c. orange-brown (11.18)		6·50	20
	a. Chalk-surfaced paper. Grilled gum (1933)		7·75	85
	b. Chalk-surfaced paper. Smooth gum (1940)		18·00	25·00
242	70c. orange-yellow and chocolate		50·00	5·00
243	70c. buff and violet (10.24)		13·00	1·00
	a. Chalk-surfaced paper. Grilled gum (1934)		12·00	2·50
244	80c. buff and olive-grey (11.16)		7·00	40
	a. Chalk-surfaced paper. Grilled gum (1933)		8·00	2·40
	b. Chalk-surfaced paper. Smooth gum (1933)		18·00	£250
245	1f. pale green and claret		4·75	25
	a. Chalk-surfaced paper. Grilled gum (1933)		14·00	4·00
246	3f. pale yellow and yellow-bistre		£170	85
231/246	Set of 16 (*cheapest*)		£275	65·00

BOOKLET PANES. Those panes which have two values *se-tenant*, or include *se-tenant* labels, are now listed and can be found under the lowest value stamp included in each pane.

Most booklet panes were also available to collectors as uncut sheets. Many combinations not occurring in normal panes can be found from such sheets but, with the exception of *tête-bêche* pairs of the same value, these are not listed.

A checklist of booklets is given at the end of the country.

Type **18a**. Cord passes in front of crossbow stock
Type **18b**. Cord is behind stock; loop at top is thin
Type **18c**. Cord is behind stock; loop is thick, also other differences

(Des A. Welti (T **18**), C. L'Eplattenier (T **19**). Typo Mint)

1908–33. *Granite paper*. W **13**. P 11½–12.

(a) T **18/19** (1908–09).

247	**18a**	2c. bistre (28.12.08)	20	50
		a. Tête-bêche (pair)	1·90	24·00
248		3c. deep violet (1.09)	20	6·75
249		5c. green (1.09)	2·00	15
		a. Tête-bêche (pair)	14·00	43·00
250	**19**	10c. carmine (1.09)	55	15
		a. Tête-bêche (pair)	2·30	8·00
251		12c. yellow-brown (1.09)	70	25
252		15c. mauve (1.09)	16·00	45
		a. Deep mauve	24·00	50

(b) T **18b** (1910–33).

253	**18b**	2c. bistre (3.10)	8·00	3·50
254		3c. deep violet (3.11)	10	15
		a. Tête-bêche (pair)	2·50	6·00
255		3c. orange-brown (1.17)	10	20
		a. Tête-bêche (pair)	4·75	11·50
256		3c. ultramarine/*buff* (7.30)	2·40	4·50
		a. Grilled gum (8.23)	5·00	12·00

257		5c. green (7.10)	13·00	2·75
		a. Tête-bêche (pair)	85·00	£250
258		7½c. grey (7.18)	1·40	20
		a. Tête-bêche (pair)	14·00	43·00
259		7½c. green/*buff* (6.27)	30	1·90

(c) *Redrawn T* **18c** (1911–33).

260	**18c**	2c. ochre (9.11)	10	15
		a. Tête-bêche (pair)	2·30	7·25
261		2½c. claret (12.17)	15	65
262		2½c. bistre/*buff* (1.28)	30	1·60
263		5c. green (3.11)	1·10	15
		a. Tête-bêche (pair)	4·25	11·00
264		5c. orange/*buff* (10.21)	10	20
		a. Booklet pane. Nos. 264 × 5 and 280 (1921)	24·00	
265		5c. violet-grey/*buff* (6.24)	10	15
		a. Booklet pane. Nos. 265 × 5 and 280 (1924)	21·00	
266		5c. deep claret/*buff* (6.27)	10	20
		a. Booklet pane. Nos. 266 × 5 and 280 (1927)	48·00	
		b. Booklet pane. Nos. 266 × 5 and 281 (1928)	12·00	
267		5c. deep green/*buff* (7.30)	30	20
		a. Booklet pane. Nos. 267 × 5 and 282 (1930)	20·00	
		b. Grilled gum (1933)	70	1·60
		ba. Booklet pane. Nos. 267b × 5 and 282b (1933)	42·00	
268		7½c. grey (1.18)	3·50	1·70

See note on grilled gum below No. 230.

1908–10. *POSTAGE DUE*. *Granite paper*. *Figures in vermilion*. W **13**. P 11½.

I. *Frame Type II (normal)* II. *Frame Type II (Inverted)*.

A. Greenish olive (1908).

D269IA	D **10**	5c.	1·60	95
D270IA		10c.	2·50	1·60
D271IA		20c.	6·75	7·75
D272IA		50c.	34·00	£130
D269IIA		5c.	1·60	85
D270IIA		10c.	2·50	1·60
D271IIA		20c.	6·75	8·25
D272IIA		50c.	34·00	£130

B. Brown-olive (shades) (1909–10).

D268I	D **10**	1c.	15	60
D269IB		5c.	80	85
D270IB		10c.	2·50	1·90
D271IB		20c.	2·50	3·00
D272IB		50c.	22·00	70
D273I		100c.	42·00	1·40
D268II		1c.	15	60
D269IIB		5c.	80	85
D270IIB		10c.	2·50	1·90
D271IIB		20c.	4·75	4·50
D272IIB		50c.	21·00	80
D273II		100c.	40·00	1·40

D **21**    F **21**    **21** William Tell

(Des C L'Eplattenier. Die eng A. Geel Typo PTT Printing Bureau, Berne)

1910 (1 Sept). *POSTAGE DUE*. *Value, shield and flowers in red*. *Granite paper*. W **13**. P 11½.

D274	D **21**	1c. blue-green	10	15
D275		3c. blue-green	10	15
D276		5c. blue-green	10	10
D277		10c. blue-green	10·00	10
D278		15c. blue-green	50	70
D279		20c. blue-green	12·00	10
D280		25c. blue-green	95	40

333

SWITZERLAND 1911

D281	30c. blue-green		85	25
D282	50c. blue-green		1·20	45
D274/282 Set of 9			23·00	2·20

22 The Myth   **23** The Rutli

24 The Jungfrau

21A Small Figures   **21B** Large Figures

(Des C. L'Eplattenier. Typo Mint)

1911–26. FRANK. Blue granite paper. W **13**. P 11½.

(a) Small black control figures at top.

F268	F **21**	2c. red and olive-green	10	10
F269		3c. red and olive-green (1916)	2·40	25
F270		5c. red and olive-green	85	10
F271		10c. red and olive-green	1·00	10
F272		15c. red and olive-green (1919)	20·00	2·75
F273		20c. red and olive-green (1921)	2·50	40
F268/273 Set of 6			24·00	3·25

(b) Large control figures at top (1.26).

F274	F **21**	5c. red and olive-green	12·50	2·75
F275		10c. red and olive-green	9·25	3·00
F276		20c. red and olive-green	10·00	3·00

These stamps were issued to charity hospitals for the free transmission of their mails, and are generally found with black control numbers at the top. They were also made available to collectors, both mint and cancelled-to-order, either numbered or without control number (*Price for set of 6 without control numbers:* £20 *un,* £225 *us*).

See also Nos. F335/7.

(Des E. Grasset. Eng A. Burkhard (5f.), J. Sprenger (others). Recess Survey Dept, Berne)

1914 (July)–**18.** Granite paper. W **13**. P 11½ (comb).

294	**22**	3f. deep blue-green	£550	2·75
295		3f. rose-carmine (2.18)	70·00	45
296	**23**	5f. deep ultramarine	30·00	1·10
297	**24**	10f. deep mauve	£110	1·50

For T **23** redrawn see No 336. See also No. 337.

1 (25)   **13** (26)   **13** (27)   **80** (28)   **80** (—)

1915 (26 Jan–Oct). Surch as T **25** to **28**.

298	**20b**	1c. on 2c. ochre	10	55
299	**19**	13c. on 12c. yellow-brown	10	5·25
300	**21**	13c. on 12c. yellow-brown/buff	15	60
301	**17**	80c. on 70c. orange-yell & choc (Oct)	23·00	8·50
298/301 Set of 4			21·00	13·50

(Des R. Kissling. Die eng J. Springer. Typo Mint)

1914 (July)–**33.** Granite paper. W **13**. P 11½.

278	**21**	10c. red/buff (a)	2·20	18·00
279		10c. red/buff (b)	35	20
		a. Tête-bêche (pair)	2·10	6·50
		b. Booklet pane. Nos. 279 × 5 and 285 (1918)	25·00	
280		10c. green/buff (2.21)	10	15
		a. Tête-bêche (pair)	75	1·20
281		10c. blue-green/buff (6.27)	70	15
		a. Tête-bêche (pair)	1·30	2·30
282		10c. reddish violet/buff (7.30)	1·20	20
		a. Tête-bêche (pair)	5·75	2·30
		b. Grilled gum (1933)	4·00	50
		ba. Tête-bêche (pair)	19·00	33·00
283		12c. yellow-brown/buff	35	2·40
284		13c. olive-green/buff (9.15)	1·20	20
285		15c. purple/buff	2·00	15
		a. Tête-bêche (pair)	75·00	£100
		b. Deep violet/buff	28·00	3·00
286		15c. brown-lake/buff (6.27)	2·50	1·40
		a. Grilled gum (1933)	34·00	39·00
287		20c. purple/buff (1.21)	1·80	15
		a. Tête-bêche (pair)	4·75	8·00
288		20c. orange-red/buff (7.24)	65	20
		a. Tête-bêche (pair)	4·50	9·25
289		20c. scarlet/buff (3.25)	20	15
		a. Tête-bêche (pair)	2·00	80
		b. Grilled gum (1932)	5·50	85
		ba. Tête-bêche (pair)	£750	£1800
290		25c. orange-red/buff (1.21)	1·40	1·10
291		25c. scarlet/buff (10.22)	60	35
292		25c. yellow-brown/buff (9.25)	4·25	80
		a. Grilled gum (1933)	80·00	27·00
293		30c. blue/buff (10.24)	6·50	15
		a. Grilled gum (1932)	60·00	1·60

There are two dies of the 10c.: in (*a*) the bar of the "H" is exactly half way, in (*b*) it is nearer the top.

See note on grilled gum below No. 230.

10 (29)   **Industrielle Kriegswirtschaft** (O 29)   **Industrielle Kriegswirtschaft** (O 30)   (30)

1916–24. POSTAGE DUE. Old values cancelled with fancy pattern in red on which new value as T **29** is surch in black.

D299	D **21**	5on 3c. red and blue-green	10	15
D300		10on 1c. red & blue-green (1924)	25	5·00
D301		10on 3c. red & blue-green (1924)	25	90
D302		20on 50c. red & blue-grn (1924)	70	90
D299/302 Set of 4			1·20	6·25

1918. OFFICIAL. Contemporary stamps optd by Hermann Stolz, Berne.

(a) With Type O **29** *(23 July).*

O299	**18b**	3c. orange-brown	£130	£200
O300	**18c**	5c. green	7·75	30·00
O301	**18b**	7½c. grey	£400	£500
O302	**18c**	7½c. grey	£750	£950
O303	**21**	10c. red/buff (b)	10·50	37·00
O304		15c. purple/buff	10·50	43·00
O305	**17**	20c. yellow and red	£140	£350
O306		25c. light blue and deep blue	£140	£350
O307		30c. pale green and yellow-brown	£140	£350

(b) With Type O **30** *(3 Sept).*

O308	**18b**	3c. orange-brown	4·00	24·00
O309	**18c**	5c. green	16·00	42·00
O310	**18b**	7½c. grey	4·00	18·00
O311	**21**	10c. red/buff (b)	65·00	70·00

SWITZERLAND Switzerland 1919

O312		15c. purple/*buff*	£140	
O313	**17**	20c. yellow and red	8·00	42·00
O314		25c. light blue and blue	8·00	42·00
O315		30c. pale green and yellow-brown	13·50	70·00
O308/315 *Set of* 8			£225	

The above stamps were for the use of the official departments dealing with the import and export of war material. No. O312 was not issued, the stock being sold with the remainders of the other values. Forgeries exist.

Stamps used on cover are worth considerably more than the used prices quoted.

1919 (30 Apr)–**20**. AIR. Optd with T **30** *in red*.

302	**17**	30c. pale green & yellow-brown (11.20)	£100	£900
303		50c. yellow-green and deep green	32·00	95·00

Beware of forgeries.

31 32 33 (34)

(Des E. Vallet, P. Robert and O. Baumberger. Eng J. Sprenger, Typo Mint)

1919 (1 Aug). *Peace Celebration*. P 11½.

304	**31**	7½c. grey-olive and black	60	1·20
305	**32**	10c. yellow and red	90	5·25
306	**33**	15c. yellow and reddish violet	1·70	1·20

1921 (Jan)–**30**. Surch as T **25** or **27** or with T **34** (No. 315).

307	**18b**	2½on 3c. orange-brown	10	25
		a. Tête-bêche (pair)	90	3·25
308	**18c**	3on 2½c. bistre/*buff* (6.30)	10	1·50
309		5on 2c. ochre (R.)	10	2·40
310	**18b**	5on 7½c. grey (R.)	10	25
		a. Tête-bêche (pair)	4·50	60·00
311	**18c**	5on 7½c. grey (R.)	£3500	£4500
312	**18b**	5on 7½c. green/*buff* (6.30)	15	5·25
313	**21**	10on 13c. olive-green/*buff* (R.)	15	1·40
314		20on 15c. purple/*buff* (B.)	6·25	3·25
		a. Surch in black	80	1·30
		b. Do. Tête-bêche (pair)	2·50	65·00
315	**17**	20on 25c. light blue and deep blue	15	25
		a. Tête-bêche (pair)	1·20	7·50

307/315 (exc. 311) *Set of* 8 (*cheapest*) 1·50 11·50

35 Monoplane  36 Pilot

37 38 Biplane  39 Icarus  40

(Des K. Bickel (317/19, 320, 321/2). P. Vibert (others). Typo PTT Printing Bureau, Berne)

1923 (1 Mar)–**40**. AIR. *Granite paper (ordinary)*. W **13**. P 11½.

316	**35**	15c. yellow-green and dull scarlet	2·50	4·50
317		20c. green and deep green (5.25)	70	4·25
		a. Chalk-surfaced paper. Grilled gum (6.37)	40	30
		b. Chalk-surfaced paper. Smooth gum (1940)	85	35·00
318		25c. bluish grey and deep dull blue	7·50	12·00
		a. Chalk-surfaced paper. Grilled gum (1.34)	5·75	38·00
319	**36**	36c. cinnamon and light brown	16·00	34·00
320	**37**	35c. lake-brown & brown-ochre (1.7.29)	15·00	32·00
		a. Chalk-surfaced paper. Grilled gum (11.33)	7·25	34·00
321	**36**	40c. slate-lilac and dull violet	10·50	34·00
322	**37**	40c. blue and apple green (1.7.29)	39·00	55·00
		a. Chalk-surfaced paper. Grilled gum (11.33)	33·00	37·00
323	**38**	45c. red and indigo	1·40	4·25
		a. Chalk-surfaced paper. Grilled gum (8.37)	2·75	37·00
324		50c. black and red	11·00	10·50
		a. Deep grey green and red (chalk-surfaced paper, grilled gum) (6.35)	1·70	75
325	**39**	65c. slate-blue & dp turq-bl (13.5.24)	7·25	10·00
		a. Chalk-surfaced paper. Grilled gum (1937)	1·70	4·75
326		75c. red-orange and claret (13.5.24)	14·00	42·00
		a. Chalk-surfaced paper. Grilled gum (1936)	32·00	£140
327		1f. reddish lilac and purple (13.5.24)	36·00	25·00
		a. Chalk-surfaced paper Grilled gum (1933)	3·25	1·60
328	**40**	2f. chestnut, sepia & grey-brn (5.7.30)	60·00	55·00
		a. Chalk-surfaced paper. Grilled gum (7.35)	11·50	6·00
316/328 *Set of* 13 (*cheapest*)			£100	£200

See note on grilled gum below No. 230.

D 41  41

(Des L. Salzmann. Typo PTT Printing Bureau, Berne)

1924–34. POSTAGE DUE. *Granite paper (ordinary)*. W **13**. P 11½.

D329	D **41**	5c. red and olive-green	50	10
		a. Grilled gum (1934)	70	40

335

SWITZERLAND Switzerland 1924

D330	10c. red and olive-green		2·10	10
	a. Grilled gum (1934)		2·50	70
D331	15c. red and olive-green ('26)		1·60	35
D332	20c. red and olive-green		5·25	10
	a. Grilled gum (1934)		4·25	80
D333	25c. red and olive-green		2·10	25
	a. Grilled gum (1934)		6·50	50·00
D334	30c. red and olive-green		2·10	40
D335	40c. red and olive-green ('26)		2·75	35
D336	50c. red and olive-green		3·25	40
D329/336 Set of 8			17·00	2·50

Printings with grilled gum (see note below No. 230) are on chalk-surfaced paper.

(Des L. Salzmann. Typo)

1924 (1 Oct)–**40.** *Shield and value in red. Granite paper (ordinary).* W **13**. P 11½.

329	41	90c. deep green and green	10·50	35
		a. Chalk-surfaced paper. Grilled gum (1933)	17·00	80
		b. Chalk-surfaced paper. Smooth gum (1940)	32·00	30·00
330		1f.20 brown-lake and salmon-pink	5·75	1·40
		a. "HELVETIA"	20·00	60·00
		b. Chalk-surfaced paper. Grilled gum (1934)	50·00	2·50
		c. Chalk-surfaced paper. Smooth gum (1940)	32·00	50·00
331		1f.50 blue and greenish blue	25·00	1·50
		a. Chalk-surfaced paper. Grilled gum (1934)	28·00	3·25
		b. Chalk-surfaced paper Smooth gum (1940)	18·00	£475
332		2f. black and olive-grey	55·00	1·70
		a. Chalk-surfaced paper. Grilled gum (1933)	27·00	3·50
329/332 Set of 4 (*cheapest*)			60·00	6·00

See note on grilled gum below No. 230.

42 Seat of First U.P.U. Congress

43 The Mythen

(Des A. Tieche (20c.), W. Stettler (30c.). Eng J. Sprenger. Recess Survey Dept, Berne (20c.), Orell, Fussli & Co, Zurich (30c.).)

1924 (9 Oct). *50th Anniv of Universal Postal Union. Granite paper.* T **42** *and similar vert design.* W **13**. P 11½.

333		20c. red	45	90
334	42	30c. deep blue	95	4·00

Design:—20c. Similar to Type **42** but with different frame.

1927 (Jan)–**34.** *FRANK. Large control figures. White granite paper.* W **13**. P 11½.

F335	F **21**	5c. orange-red and light green	4·50	10
F336		10c. orange-red and light green	2·10	10
		a. Grilled gum (1934)	£450	£700
F337		20c. orange-red and light green	3·25	15

10c. with grilled gum (see note below No. 230) is on chalk-surfaced paper. This was placed on sale at the National Stamp Exhibition post office.

See note below No. F276.

(Des E. Cardinaux (3f.), E. Grasset (others). Eng J. Sprenger. Recess)

1928–31. *Granite paper.* W **13**. P 11½.

335	43	3f. red-brown (1931)	41·00	1·60
336	23	5f. deep blue	£120	3·25
337	24	10f. deep grey-green (12.2.30)	£200	29·00

On No. 336 the engraver's name, "J. Sprenger", appears at right bottom corner instead of "A. BURKHARD" as in Type **23**. The whole design is redrawn.

PRINTERS. Early in 1932 the stamp printing department of the Mint was taken over by the PTT Printing Bureau.

44 Symbol of Peace

45 "After the Darkness, Light"

(Des M. Barraud; eng G. Matter, typo PTT Printing Bureau, Berne (T **44**). Des G. Fustier, photo Courvoisier (T **45**).)

1932 (2 Feb). *International Disarmament Conference. Granite paper with grilled gum.* P 11½.

(a) W **13**.

338	44	5c. blue-green	15	15
339		10c. bright orange	20	10
340		20c. magenta	25	10
341		30c. bright blue	2·10	60
342		60c. bistre-brown	14·50	3·00

(b) No wmk.

343	45	1f. olive-grey and blue	15·00	4·50
338/343 Set of 6			29·00	7·50

46 Peace and the Air Post

47 Louis Favre (engineer)

48 Staubbach Falls

(Des O. Braumberger. Typo PTT Printing Bureau, Berne.)

1932 (2 Feb). *AIR. International Disarmament Conference. Granite paper with grilled gum.* W **13**. P 11½.

344	46	15c. light green and green	40	1·60
345		20c. flesh and scarlet	1·00	2·20
346		90c. light blue and blue	5·75	24·00

(Des and eng K. Bickel, Recess Orell Fussli, Zurich)

1932 (31 May). *50th Anniv of St. Gotthard Railway.* T **47** *and similar vert portraits. Granite paper.* W **13**. P 11½.

347		10c. chestnut	10	15
348		20c. orange-red	20	15
349		30c. royal blue	40	1·10

Designs:—20c. Alfred Escher (President of Railway): 30c. Emil Welti (founder).

(Des E. Jordi. Typo PTT Printing Bureau, Berne)

1934 (2 July). *As T* **48** *(landscapes). Granite paper with grilled gum.* W **13**. P 11½.

350		3c. yellow-olive	25	1·70
351		5c. blue-green	20	10
		a. Tête-bêche (pair)	1·40	2·40
352		10c. deep mauve	45	10
		a. Tête-bêche (pair)	2·40	1·60
353		15c. orange	40	1·30
		a. Tête-bêche (pair)	2·50	4·75

SWITZERLAND Switzerland 1934

354	20c. bright scarlet		50	10
	a. Tête-bêche (pair)		3·00	3·50
355	25c. orange-brown		6·50	4·25
356	30c. ultramarine		20·00	45
350/356	Set of 7		26·00	7·25

Designs:—5c. Mt. Pilatus; 10c. Chillon Castle and Dents du Midi; 15c. Grimsel Pass; 20c. Landwasser Viaduct, Filisur (St. Gotthard Railway); 25c. Viamala Gorge; 30c. Rhine Falls near Schaffhausen.

1934 (29 Sept). *National Philatelic Exhibition, Zunch ("NABA"). Sheet 62 × 72 mm.*
MS357 Nos. 351/4 .... £350 £500

F 49 Deaconess    (49)    (50)    51 Freiburg Cowherd

(Des K. Bickel. Typo PTT Printing Bureau, Berne)

1935 (1 Jan)–**43**. *FRANK. Designs as Type F **49**. W 13. A. Granite paper will, grilled gum (1935). B. Granite paper (ordinary) (1943).* P 11½.

(a) With large control figures.

F358A	5c. green		4·00	20
F359A	10c. violet		4·00	15
F360A	20c. scarlet		4·50	25
F358B	5c. green		2·75	4·75
F359B	10c. violet		1·80	3·75
F360B	20c. scarlet		2·75	5·75

(b) Without control figures.

F361A	5c. green		14·00	1·20
F362A	10c. violet		14·00	1·20
F363A	20c. scarlet		14·00	1·20
F361B	5c. green		1·70	3·75
F362B	10c. violet		1·70	3·75
F363B	20c. scarlet		1·70	3·75

Designs:—10c. Sister of the Ingenbohl Order, 20c. Henri Dunant (founder of Red Cross).
See note on grilled gum below No. 230.

1935–37. *AIR. Nos. 316 and 344/6 surch.*

(a) Surch with T 49.

358	35	10on 15c. yellow-green and dull scarlet	5·75	32·00

(b) Surch as T 50.

359	46	10on 15c. light green and green	50	35
		a. Surch inverted	£8000	£8500
360		10on 20c. flesh & scarlet (9.9.36)	55	1·60
361		30on 90c. light blue & blue (9.9.36)	3·00	9·50
362		40on 20c. flesh and scarlet ('37)	4·00	10·50
363		40on 50c. light bl & bl (R.) (1.8.36)	3·00	10·50
358/363	Set of 6		15·00	60·00

(Des from picture by F. Hodler. Photo Courvoisier)

1936 (1 Oct). *National Defence Fund. Granite paper (No. MS367 with grilled gum).* P 11½.

364	51	10c.+5c. reddish violet	35	55
365		20c.+10c. orange-red	65	2·50

366		30c.+10c. ultramarine	3·00	13·00
MS367	109 × 102 mm. Nos. 364/6 (26 Oct)		33·00	£170

52 Staubbach Falls    52A I    52A II

I. No diagonal lines through "o".
II. Two diagonal lines through "o" and railway track heavier.

52B I 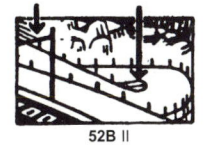   52B II

In Type I, the kerbstone beneath the gantry does not touch the crossbar, in Type II it does. All the kerbstones in Type II are larger and bolder than in Type I.

(Des and eng K. Bickel. Recess PTT Printing Bureau, Berne)

1936 (Nov)–**42**. *As T 52 (landscapes as 1934 issue but redrawn with figure of value in line with "HELVETIA" at bottom).*

A. Smooth white non granite paper. P 11½.

368A	3c. yellow-olive		15	15
369A	5c. blue-green		15	10
	c. Tête-bêche (pair)		30	40
370A	10c. bright purple (I)		1·40	15
	c. Tête-bêche (pair)		4·00	4·25
	d. Type II (1938)		60	15
	dc. Tête-bêche (pair)		2·40	1·60
371A	10c. red-brown (1939)		20	10
	c. Tête-bêche (pair)		1·30	1·40
372A	10c. chestnut (1942)		10	10
	c. Tête-bêche (pair)		50	40
373A	15c. orange		30	45
374A	20c. scarlet (St. Gotthard) (I)		80·00	21·00
	d. Type II (1937)		4·75	15
	dc. Tête-bêche (pair) (II)		21·00	31·00
375A	20c. scarlet (17.9.38) (Lugano)		20	10
	c. Tête-bêche (pair)		85	55
376A	25c. yellow-brown		65	90
377A	30c. dull ultramarine		1·20	15
378A	35c. bright green		1·30	1·10
379A	40c. grey		7·75	15
368A/379A	Set of 12 (cheapest)		14·00	3·25

B. Non granite paper with grilled gum.

368B	3c. yellow-olive		85	4·00
369B	5c. blue-green		15	15
	c. Tête-bêche (pair)		65	1·20
370B	10c. bright purple (I)		75	10
	c. Tête-bêche (pair)		3·25	2·75
	d. Type II (1937)		75	10
	dc. Tête-bêche (pair)		2·00	2·50
371B	10c. red-brown (1939)		1·80	19·00
373B	15c. orange		45	40
374B	20c. scarlet (St. Gotthard) (I)		5·50	60
	d. Type II (1937)		5·00	15
	dc. Tête-bêche (pair) (II)		18·00	30·00
375B	20c. scarlet (17.9.32)		35	15
	c. Tête-bêche (pair)		2·20	12·00
376B	25c. yellow-brown		9·25	3·50
377B	30c. dull ultramarine		1·00	15
378B	35c. bright green		1·20	1·80
379B	40c. grey		7·50	20

Designs:—5c. Mt. Pilatus; 10c. (370/2) Chillon Castle and Dents du Midi; 15c. Grimsel Pass; 20c. (374), Landwasser Viaduct, Filisur (St. Gotthard Railway); 20c. (375), Lake Lugano and Mt. San Salvatore; 25c. Viamala Gorge; 30c. Rhine Falls; 35c. Mt. Neufakenstein and Klus; 40c. Mt. Santis and Lake Seealp.

337

SWITZERLAND Switzerland 1936

Nos. 368A, 369A, 370dA, 371A, 372, 373A, 375A and 376A/9A were also issued in coils. The 5, 10 (all colours), 20 and 30c. values had a control letter and figures on the back of every fifth stamp in the roll.
See note on grilled gum below No. 230.
See also Nos. 489/94 and No. **MS**387a.
Copies of No. 374 are known with a worn impression, these are from printings using worn dies of Type I, and were previously listed as No. 347c. The die was re-engraved in 1937, see No. 374d.

(D 53) 53 Mobile P.O.

1937 (1 June). *POSTAGE DUE.* Nos. D334, D337 and D339 surch as Type **D 53**.

D380	D 41	5 on 15c. red and olive-green	65	2·75
D381		10 on 30c. red and olive-green	65	95
D382		20 on 50c. red and olive-green	1·20	3·00
D383		40 on 50c. red and olive-green	1·90	7·50
D380/383 Set of 4			4·00	13·00

(Des B. Reber. Photo Courvoisier)

1937 (5 Sept). *Granite paper.* P 11½.
380 53 10c. yellow and black 25 20
This stamp was for use on mail posted at mobile post offices. For redrawn type, issued in 1946, see No 471.

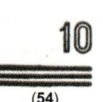

D 54   (O 54)   (54)

(Des W. Weiskonig. Eng G. Matter. Recess PTT Printing Bureau, Berne)

1938 (1 Feb). *POSTAGE DUE.*

A. *Smooth white non granite paper.* P 11½.

D384A	D 54	5c. scarlet	30	10
D385A		10c. scarlet	45	10
D386A		15c. scarlet	95	2·00
D387A		20c. scarlet	90	10
D388A		25c. scarlet	1·10	1·80
D389A		30c. scarlet	1·20	80
D390A		40c. scarlet	1·20	25
D391A		50c. scarlet	1·60	1·60
D384A/391A Set of 8			7·00	6·00

B. *White non granite paper with grilled gum.*

D384B	D 54	5c. scarlet	70	1·00
D385B		10c. scarlet	70	80
D386B		15c. scarlet	1·30	2·40
D387B		20c. scarlet	75	15
D388B		25c. scarlet	1·40	6·25
D389B		30c. scarlet	1·20	1·40
D390B		40c. scarlet	1·50	1·20
D391B		50c. scarlet	2·40	2·10
D384B/391B Set of 8			9·00	13·50

See note on grilled gum below No. 230.
From 1954 ordinary postage stamps were used in place of Postage Due stamps and Nos. D384/91 were withdrawn in March 1956.

1938. *OFFICIAL. Various issues optd as Type* O **54**.

(a) As T **52** (Landscape types. Recess).
A. *Smooth white non-granite paper.*

O381A	3c. yellow-olive		10	25
O382A	5c. blue-green		10	20
O383A	10c. bright purple (II)		95	35
O384A	15c. orange		40	1·20
O385A	20c. scarlet (No. 375)		45	20
O386A	25c. yellow-brown		45	1·10
O387A	30c. dull ultramarine		55	55
O388A	35c. bright green		55	1·20
O389A	40c. grey		55	35

B. *Non-granite paper with grilled gum.*

O381B	3c. yellow-olive		5·25	40
O382B	5c. blue-green		1·50	35
O383B	10c. bright purple (II)		1·80	50
O384B	15c. orange		3·50	1·20
O385B	20c. scarlet (No. 375)		3·50	
O386B	25c. yellow-brown		85·00	7·50
O387B	30c. dull ultramarine		3·00	95
O388B	35c. bright green		2·40	1·70
O389B	40c. grey		3·00	70

(b) *Helvetia seated.*

O390	17	50c. yellow-green and deep green	95	1·10
O391		60c. orange-brown	1·30	1·80
O392		70c. buff and violet	1·30	3·25
O393		80c. buff and olive-grey	1·40	2·30
O394		1f. pale green and claret	1·50	2·30

(c) *Arms type Shield and value in vermilion.*

O395	41	90c. deep green and green	1·50	2·75
O396		1f.20, brown-lake and salmon-pink	1·50	3·25
O397		1f.50, blue and greenish blue	2·50	4·75
O398		2f. black and olive-grey	3·00	5·25
O381/398 Set of 18			17·00	27·00
O381B/389B Set of 9			90·00	10·00

See note on grilled gum below No. 230.

1938 (Apr). *AIR.* No. 325a surch with T **54**.
381 39 10 on 65c. slate-blue & dp turquoise-blue 30 35
See also No. **MS**387a.

55 International Labour Bureau

(Des H. Fischer. Photo Courvoisier)

1938 (2 May). T **55** *and similar horiz designs. Granite paper.* P 11½.

382	20c. red and buff		20	15
383	30c. blue and pale blue		30	15
384	60c. brown and buff		1·50	1·30
385	1f. black and buff		6·25	10·00
382/385 Set of 4			7·50	10·50

Designs:—30c. Palace of League of Nations (inscr "S.D.N."); 60c. Inner Courtyard of Palace of League of Nations (inscr "S.D.N."); 1f. International Labour Bureau (*different*).

(59)

338

SWITZERLAND Switzerland　　　　　　　　　　　　　　　　1938

1938 (22 May). *AIR. Special Flights. No. 324a surch with T* **59**.
386　**38**　75c. on 50c. deep grey-green and
　　　　　red　　　　　　　　　　　　　　　†　　4·75
　　This stamp was affixed to letters handed to Post Offices, or sold cancelled but not unused.

60 William Tell's Chapel

(Des H. Thoni. Photo Courvoisier)

1938 (15 June). *National Fête. Fund for Swiss Subjects abroad. Yellow borders. Granite paper.* P 11½.
387　60　10c.+10c. violet　　　　　　　　40　　45
　　　　a. Grilled gum*　　　　　　　20·00　65·00
*See note below No 230.

1938 (17 Sept). *National Philatelic Exhibition, Aarau and 25th Anniv of Swiss Air Mail Service. Sheet 74 × 87 mm Granite paper.*
MS387a Nos. 375 (pair) and 381 (sold at
　　1f.50)　　　　　　　　　　　　　30·00　25·00

61 First Act of Federal Parliament

62 Symbolical of Swiss Culture

(Des and ring K. Bickel. Recess PTT Printing Bureau, Berne)

1938 (17 Sept)–**54**. *As T* **61** *(symbolic designs). Granite paper with black and red fibres. Yellowish gum.* P 11½. *A. Buff paper with bluish surface coating B. Buff paper (May 1942) C. White paper with blue and red fibres (July 1954).*
388A　3f. red-brown　　　　　　　　10·50　4·00
　　B　　　　　　　　　　　　　　　19·00　　30
　　C　　　　　　　　　　　　　　　 6·50　　30
389A　5f. slate-blue　　　　　　　　　11·00　2·50
　　B　　　　　　　　　　　　　　　13·00　　30
　　C　　　　　　　　　　　　　　　 5·25　　30
390A　10f. green　　　　　　　　　　47·00　　25
　　B　　　　　　　　　　　　　　　23·00　　90
　　C　　　　　　　　　　　　　　　 9·25　1·10
Designs:—5f. "The Assembly at Stans"; 10f. A polling booth.
　　On the first issue the bluish coating is sensitive to light and water and has often disappeared, particularly on used examples.
　　The third issue, which appeared in July 1954, is on white paper with blue and red fibres, a yellowish surface coating and white gum, this coating is also prone to disappearance.

(Nos. 391/2. Des and ring K. Bickel. Design recess; coat of arms photo PTT, Berne. No. 393. Des V. Surbek. Photo Courvoisier)

1939 (1 Feb). *National Exhibition, Zurich. T* **62** *and similar types. Inscr in French* (F), *German* (G), *or Italian* (I). *Coat of arms in scarlet Grilled gum* (20, 30c.) P 11½.
391F　10c. deep violet　　　　　　　　30　　15
　　G　　　　　　　　　　　　　　　　35　　10
　　I　　　　　　　　　　　　　　　　30　　15
392F　20c. carmine　　　　　　　　　　60　　15
　　G　　　　　　　　　　　　　　　　50　　10
　　I　　　　　　　　　　　　　　　　2·50　　30
393F　30c. blue and buff　　　　　　　3·25　3·75
　　G　　　　　　　　　　　　　　　2·30　1·20
　　I　　　　　　　　　　　　　　　2·75　5·75
Designs:—10c. Group symbolic of Swiss Industry and Agriculture; 30c. Piz Rosegg and Tschirva Glacier.

64 Crossbow and Floral Branch

65 Laupen Castle

(Des V. Surbek. Photo Courvoisier)

1939 (6 May). *National Exhibition, Zurich. Inscr In French* (F), *German* (G) *or Italian* (I). *Smooth white granite paper.* P 11½.
394F　5c. emerald　　　　　　　　　 1·10　2·75
　　G　　　　　　　　　　　　　　　　85　2·75
　　I　　　　　　　　　　　　　　　 1·10　3·25
　　Fa　grilled gum　　　　　　　　　　70　　60
　　Ga　grilled gum　　　　　　　　　　45　1·60
　　Ia　grilled gum　　　　　　　　　　50　2·20
395F　10c. blackish-brown　　　　　　1·50　3·25
　　G　　　　　　　　　　　　　　　　90　3·25
　　I　　　　　　　　　　　　　　　 1·50　3·25
　　Fb　grilled gum　　　　　　　　　　70　1·30
　　Ga　sheet stamp　　　　　　　　　　40　　80
　　Ib　grilled gum　　　　　　　　　　70　1·40
396F　20c. scarlet　　　　　　　　　 3·50　24·00
　　G　　　　　　　　　　　　　　　2·50　24·00
　　I　　　　　　　　　　　　　　　3·50　24·00
　　Fa　grilled gum　　　　　　　　　1·30　1·90
　　Ga　grilled gum　　　　　　　　　　95　1·20
　　Ia　grilled gum　　　　　　　　　　65　2·50
397F　30c. royal blue　　　　　　　　3·50　6·25
　　G　　　　　　　　　　　　　　　2·75　5·50
　　I　　　　　　　　　　　　　　　2·40　7·25
394F/397F *Set of 4* (*cheapest*)　　　 5·50　10·00
394G/397G *Set of 4* (*cheapest*)　　　 4·00　8·00
394I/397I *Set of 4* (*cheapest*)　　　 4·00　12·00
　　No. 395aG, the 30c. and all grilled gum varieties were issued in sheets, the remainder in coils. The coils were issued both with and without control numbers on the back of every fifth stamp in the roll.
　　No. 395aG can be distinguished by the length of "COURVOISIER S A" which is longer and extends to beyond the base of the "V" of "HELVETIA", whereas in the coil stamps the imprint extends to just before the "V".
　　See note on grilled gum below No. 230.

(Des P. Bosch. Photo Courvoisier)

1939 (15 June). *National Fete. Fund for Destitute Mothers. Coat of arms In scarlet. Granite paper.* P 11½.
398　65　10c.+10c. brown and grey　　　25　　40

66 Geneva

67 "Les Rangiers"

(Des A. Yersin. Photo Courvoisier)

1939 (22 Aug). *75th Anniv of Geneva (Red Cross) Convention. Cross In scarlet. Granite paper.* P 11½.
399　66　20c. red and buff　　　　　　30　　20
400　　　30c. bright blue and grey　　　45　1·10

339

SWITZERLAND Switzerland 1940

(Des C. Liner (5c.), B. Reber (10c., 20c.), Ch. L'Eplattenier (30c.) Photo Courvoisier)

1940 (20 Mar). *National Fete and Red Cross Fund. As T 67 (memorial types inscr "FETE NATIONALE 1940" in German (5c., 20c.), Italian (10c.), and French (30c.)). Coat-of arms in scarlet. Granite paper.* P 11½.

401	5c.+5c. black and green	25	90
402	10c.+5c. black and orange	25	30
403	20c.+5c. black and red	2·20	60
	a. Redrawn design	8·75	4·25
404	30c.+10c. black and blue	1·30	4·75
401/404 Set of 4		4·00	6·25
MS404*a* 125 × 65 mm. Nos. 401/2, 403*a*/4			
Imperf (sold at 5f.) (16 July)		£190	£550

Battle memorials:—Sempach (5c.), Giornico (10c.), and Calven (20c.).

No. 403. The inscription at the base of the statue is enclosed in a white rectangular tablet.

No 403*a*. The inscription is on a grey background forming part of the statue.

68 "William Tell" (Ferdinand Hodler)

69 Ploughing

(Des and eng Karl Bickel. Recess PTT, Berne)

1941 (15 Jan)–**59**. *As T 68 (historical types). Granite paper.* P 11½.

405	50c. deep violet-blue/*blue-green*	4·25	10
406	60c. reddish-brown/*cinnamon*	6·25	10
407	70c. deep reddish purple/*mauve*	2·75	45
408	80c. black/*olive-grey*	1·10	10
408*a*	80c. black/*mauve* (29.10.58)	2·30	30
409	90c. scarlet/*pink*	1·10	10
409*a*	90c. scarlet/*buff* (22.6.59)	3·25	95
410	1f. myrtle green/*blue-green*	1·40	10
411	1f.20 plum/*olive-grey*	1·90	10
411*a*	1f.20 purple/*reddish lilac* (29.10.58)	3·25	55
412	1f.50 indigo/*buff*	2·00	40
413	2f. brown-lake/*pink*	2·75	40
413*a*	2f. brown-lake/*cream* (22.6.59)	6·00	30
405/413*a* Set of 13		35·00	3·75

Designs: (*Works of art*)—50c. "Oath of Union (James Vibert); 70c. "Kneeling Warrior" (Ferdinand Hodler); 80c. "Dying Ensign" (Hodler); 90c. "Standard-bearer" (Niklaus Deutsch). (*Portraits*)—1f. Col Louis Pfyffer; 1f.20, George Jenatsch; 1f.50, Lt-Gen Francois de Reynold; 2f. Col Joachim Forrer.

(Des A. Patocchi. Photo Courvoisier)

1941 (21 Mar). *Agricultural Development Plan. Granite paper.* P 11½.

| 414 | **69** | 10c. chocolate and buff | 10 | 15 |

70 The Jungfrau

71 Chemin Creux, near Kussnacht

(Des and eng A. Yersin. Recess PTT, Berne)

1941 (1 May)–**48**. *AIR. T 70 (landscapes). Granite paper.* P 11½.

415	30c. ultramarine/*salmon*	85	15
415*a*	30c. slate-blue/*salmon* (1.10.48)	7·25	9·00
416	40c. grey/*salmon*	85	15
416*a*	40c. ultramarine/*salmon* (1.10.48)	36·00	1·50
417	50c. olive/*salmon*	1·10	15
418	60c. yellow-brown/*salmon*	1·50	15
419	70c. violet/*salmon*	1·20	30
420	1f. blue-green/*buff*	2·30	35
421	2f. lake/*buff*	7·25	1·70
422	5f. deep blue/*buff*	24·00	9·25
415/422 Set of 10		75·00	20·00

Designs:—40c. Valais; 50c. Lac Lemon; 60c. Alpstein; 70c. Ticino; 1f. Vierwaldstattersee (*Lake Lucerne*); 2f. Engadin; 5f. Churfirsten.

1941 (12 May). *AIR. Special (Buochs-Payerne) Flights. No. 420 with "PRO AERO/28.V.1941" added.*

| 423 | 1f. blue-green/*buff* | 5·75 | 16·00 |

(Des P. Bösch and C. L'Eplattenier. Photo Courvoisier)

1941 (15 June). *National Fête and 650th Anniv of Foundation of Swiss Confederation. T 71 and another design dated "1291–1941". Granite paper.* P 11½.

| 424 | 10c.+10c. blue, scarlet and yellow | 30 | 50 |
| 425 | 10c. scarlet, brown-red and buff | 50 | 70 |

Premium in aid of Public Utility Funds.
Design:—10c. Relief map of Lake Lucerne with Arms of Uri, Schwyz and Unterwalden around it.

72 Arms of Berne, Masons laying Corner-stone and Knight

(O **73**)

(Des P. Bösch. Photo Courvoisier)

1941 (6 Sept). *750th Anniv of Foundation of Berne. Granite paper.* P 11½.

| 426 | **72** | 10c. black, yellow, scarlet and olive | 10 | 30 |

1942 (25 Feb)–**43**. *OFFICIAL. (a) Nos. 368/79 optd with Type O 73 Smooth white non-granite paper.*

O427	3c. yellow-olive	30	1·25
O428	5c. blue-green	30	15
O429	10c. red-brown (No. 371)	60	40
O430	10c. chestnut (No. 372) (1943)	25	30
O431	15c. orange	60	1·25
O432	20c. scarlet (No. 375)	60	20
O433	25c. yellow-brown	60	1·75
O434	30c. dull ultramarine	1·75	60
O435	35c. bright green	1·75	2·00
O436	40c. grey	1·10	45

(b) Nos. 405/13 with larger opt.

O437	50c. deep violet-blue/*blue-green*	4·50	3·25
O438	60c. reddish-brown/*cinnamon*	4·75	2·25
O439	70c. deep reddish purple/*mauve*	5·00	6·00
O440	80c. black/*olive-grey*	1·25	1·10
O441	90c. scarlet/*pink*	1·50	1·00
O442	1f. myrtle green/*blue-green*	1·75	1·50
O443	1f.20 plum/*olive-grey*	1·90	1·75
O444	1f.50 indigo/*buff*	2·25	2·75
O445	2f. brown-lake/*pink*	3·00	3·00
O427/445 Set of 19		30·00	28·00

73 "To survive, collect salvage"

SWITZERLAND Switzerland 1942

(Des A. Yersin. Photo Courvoisier)
1942 (21 Mar). *Salvage Campaign. As T 73. Inscr in French (F), German (G). or Italian (I). Value and coat of arms in scarlet, tablets In blue. Granite paper. P 11½.*
427F	10c. brown		45	30
	G		20	20
	I		7·50	2·50

Inscriptions:—"Zum Durchhalten/Altstoffe sammeln" (G); "PER RESISTERE/RACCOGLIETE/LA ROBA VECCHIA" (I).

74 View of Old Geneva

75 Soldiers' Memorial at Forch, near Zurich

(Des A. Yersin and O. Rüegg. Photo Courvoisier)
1942 (15 June). *National Fête. National Relief Fund and Second Millenary of Geneva Coat of Arms in scarlet. Granite paper. P 11½.*
428	74	10c.+10c. black and yellow	35	45
429	75	20c.+10c. red and yellow	45	85
MS429a	105 × 62 mm. Nos. 428/9 Imperf (sold at 2f.)		40·00	£200

76 **76a**

(Eng A. Yersin. Recess PTT Printing Bureau, Berne)
1943 (26 Feb). *Centenary of First Swiss Cantonal Postage Stamps. Background of horiz red lines. P 11½.*
430	76	10c. (4+6) black	10	10

Miniature Sheets.
MS430a 164 × 140 mm. No. 430 (block of 12) Imperf (sold at 5f.) .... 46·00 43·00

(Litho Orell Fussli, Zurich)
MS430b 70 × 75 mm. T **76a** 4 and 6 (c.) black Imperf (sold at 3f.) .... 50·00 47·00

77 Intragna (Ticino)   **77a** "Double Geneva"

(Des A. Yersin and P. Burkhard. Photo Courvoisier)
1943 (15 June). *National Fête and Youth's Vocational Training Fund. T 77 (and another design inscr "FESTA NAZIONALE 1943") Coat of arms and values in scarlet. Granite paper. P 11½.*
431		10c.+10c. grey-black and buff	35	50
432		20c.+10c. brown-red and buff	40	80

Design:—20c. Federal Palace, Berne.

1943 (13 July). AIR. *Special Flights 30th Anniv of First Flight across Alps by Oscar Bider. As No. 432, but optd "PRO AERO/13.VII.1943" and value in black.*
433		1f. brown-red and buff	2·20	8·00

(Des B. Reber. Photo Courvoisier)
1943 (17 Sept). *National Philatelic Exhibition, Geneva ("GEPH") and Centenary of Geneva Cantonal Stamp. Sheet 72 × 73 mm. Imperf.*
MS433a	77a 5c. black and yellow green (sold at 3f.)		34·00	31·00

78 Apollo of Olympia

79 Heiden

(Des Mme Maya Allenbach (after H. R. von der Mühl). Photo Courvoisier)
1944 (21 Mar). *Olympic Games Jubilee. Granite paper. P 11½.*
434	78	10c. black and orange	20	45
435		20c. black and carmine	30	45
436		30c. black and light blue	75	6·75

There were two printings, first on paper with yellowish gum and long granite threads and then paper with thick white gum and short granite threads.

(Des O. Rüegg (5c.), W. Koch (10c.), A. Juon (20c.), P. and B. Artaria (30c.). Photo Courvoisier)
1944 (15 June). *National Fête and Red Cross Fund. As T 79 (views, inscr "FESTA NAZIONALE 1944/BUNDES FEIER 1944/FÊTE NATIONALE", or similar inscr). Coat of arms in scarlet. Granite paper. P 11½.*
437		5c.+5c. green and buff	35	1·50
438		10c.+10c. grey and buff	35	35
439		20c.+10c. carmine and buff	35	55
440		30c.+10c. blue and buff	2·40	12·00
437/440	Set of 4		3·00	13·00

Designs:—10c. St. Jacques on the R. Birs; 20c. Castle ruins, Mesocco; 30c. Basel.

80 Haefeli DH-3 Biplane

(Des O. Baumberger (10c. to 30c.), H. R. von der Mühl (1f.50). Photo Courvoisier)
1944 (1 Sept). AIR. *25th Anniv of National Air Post. T 80 and similar horiz designs. Granite paper. P 11½.*
441		10c. bistre-brown and sage green	10	20
442		20c. rosine and stone	25	20
443		30c. ultramarine and blue	50	65
444		1f.50, agate, grey brown and vermilion	7·25	14·50
441/444	Set of 4		7·25	14·00

Aircraft:—20c. Fokker F.VIIb/3m; 30c. Lockheed 9B Orion; 1f.50, Douglas DC-3.

No. 444 was only on sale until 18 September and was only valid for use on the special commemorative flight from Zurich to Geneva and back on 20 September.

SWITZERLAND Switzerland 1945

81 Symbolical of Faith, Hope and Charity

81a Lifeboat

(Des N. Stoecklin (T **81**), V. Surbek (T **81** a). Photo Courvoisier)

1945 (20 Feb). *War Relief Fund. Granite paper.* P 11½.
445 **81** 10c.+10c. blackish olive, black & grey 50 30
446 20c.+60c. scarlet, black and grey . . . 2·50 4·75
MS446a 70 × 110 mm. Imperf . T **81a** 3f.+7f. indigo £180 £170

81b "Basel Dove"

(Des E. and M. Lenz. Typo and dove embossed. PTT, Berne)

1945 (14 Apr). *Centenary of Basel Cantonal Stamp Issue. Sheet 71 × 63 mm. Granite paper. Imperf.*
MS446b **81**b 10 (c.) grey-green, red and black (sold at 3f.) . . . . . . £120 80·00

82 *Trans* "Peace to men of good will"

83 Olive Branch

(Des N. Stoecklin (5 to 40c.), A. Patocchi and H. Steiner (50c. to 2f.); photo Courvoisier. Des and eng K. Bickel, recess PTT, Berne (3 to 10f.))

1945 (9 May). *Peace Granite paper.* As T **82/3** (*symbolic designs inscr "PAX"*). P 11½.
447 5c. green and grey 10 20
448 10c. brown and grey 35 15
449 20c. carmine and grey 45 15
450 30c. ultramarine and grey . . . 80 2·30
451 40c. orange and grey . . . 3·00 8·25
452 50c. brown red and buff . . . 4·25 16·00
453 60c. dark and light grey . . . 4·75 5·75
454 80c. green and buff . . . 8·75 60·00
455 1f. blue and buff . . . 11·00 65·00
456 2f. brown and buff . . . 42·00 £130
457 3f. green/*buff* . . . 49·00 46·00
458 5f. red-brown/*buff* . . . £150 £225
459 10f. violet/*buff* . . . £150 90·00
447/459 Set of 13 . . . £375 £600
Designs: As T **82**—5c. to 40c., Numerals. As T **83**, 38 × 22½ mm—60c. Keys, 80c. Horn of Plenty; 1f. Dove; 2f. Spade and flowers in ploughed field As T **83**, but 38 × 21 *mm* and "PAX" in large outlined capital letters—3f. Crocuses; 5f. Clasped hands; 10f. Aged couple.

84

85 Silk weaving

(Des N. Stoecklin. Photo Courvoisier)

1945 (9 May). *Red Cross. Cross and premium in red. Granite paper.* P 11½.
460 **84** 5c.+10c. green 75 60

(Des P. Boesch, eng A. Yersin; recess and photo PTT Berne (5c.) Des Faustina Iselin (10c.), H. Zaugg (20c.), F. Deringer (30c.); photo Courvoisier)

1945 (15 June). *National Fête. T* **85** *and similar horiz designs. Coat-of-arms in scarlet. Granite paper (10 to 30c.).* P 11½.
461 5c.+5c. blue-green . . . 90 1·50
462 10c.+10c. brown and grey . . . 80 40
463 20c.+10c. brown-red and buff . . . 1·00 45
464 30c.+10c. blue and grey . . . 10·50 21·00
461/464 Set of 4 . . . 12·00 21·00
Designs:—10c. and 20c. Jura and Emmental farmhouses; 30c. Timbered house.

86 J. H. Pestalozzi

87 Zoglig Instructional Glider

(Des and eng Karl Bickel, from a relief by J. M. Christen. Recess, PTT Berne)

1946 (12 Jan). *Bath Bicemtenary of J. H. Pestalozzi (educational reformer).* P 11½.
465 **86** 10c. purple 20 15

(Des O. Baumberger. Photo Courvoisier)

1946 (1 May). *AIR. Special (Lausanne, Lucerne, Locarno) Flights. Granite paper.* P 11½.
466 **87** 1f.50 red and grey . . . 23·00 22·00
No. 466 was valid for postage only on the special postal flights of 22nd and 23rd May, 1946.

88 Cheese-making

89 Chalet in Appenzell

(No. 467. Des P. Boesch. Eng A. Yersin. Design recess; coat-of-arms photo, plain paper, PTT, Berne Des No. 468, F. Iselin, Nos. 469/70 des W. Koch. Photo Granite paper Courvoisier)

1946 (15 June). *National Fête and Fund for Swiss Citizens Abroad. T* **88** *and designs as T* **89***, inscr "I. VIII 1946". Coat-of-arms in scarlet.* P 11½.
467 5c.+5c. green . . . 70 2·00
468 10c.+10c. sepia and buff . . . 65 55
469 20c.+10c. red and buff . . . 65 55
470 30c.+10c. blue and blue-grey . . . 5·75 7·25
467/470 Set of 4 . . . 5·75 9·25
Designs:—Châlets in Vaud (10c.) and Engadine (30c.).

SWITZERLAND Switzerland   1946

1946 (6 July). T **53** *redrawn. Granite paper.* P 11½.
471   10c. yellow and black .... 3·00   15
   No. 471 measures 38 × 22½ mm. as against No. 380's 37 × 21 mm. The most outstanding difference is that in No. 471 there are eight lines of horizontal shading above the highest white peak at the top right of the design, whereas in No. 380 there are only three.

95 Sun of St. Moritz    **96** Ice Hockey

(Des 5c., 10c. A. Diggelmann; 20c., 30c. W. Weiskönig. Photo Courvoisier.)

1948 (15 Jan). *Fifth Winter Olympic Games. As T* **95/6** *(designs inscr* "ST. MORITZ OLYMPIA 1948") *Granite paper.* P 11½.
481   5c.+5c. brown, yellow and green 50   1·40
482   10c.+10c. blue, light blue and brown ... 55   85
483   20c.+10c. yellow, black and claret 85   1·60
484   30c.+10c. black, light blue and blue .. 2·30 5·00
481/484 Set of 4 .... 3·75 8·00
Designs:—10c. Snow crystals; 30c. Ski-runner.

90 Douglas DC-4 Airliner, Statue of Liberty and St. Peter's Cathedral, Geneva

(Des B. Reber. Photo Courvoisier.)

1947 (17 May). AIR. *First Geneva—New York "Swissair" Flight. Granite paper.* P 11½.
472   **90**   2f.50, deep blue, pale blue and
               red .... 11·50 15·00
   No. 472 was valid for postage only on 2nd May for use on the first "Swissair" flight between Geneva and New York.

97 Johann Rudolf Wettstein    **99** Frontier Guard

(Des 5c., 10c., 20c., Hermann Eidenbenz; 30c. Maya Allenbach. Photo Courvoisier.)

1948 (27 Feb). *Tercentenary of the Treaty of Westphalia and Centenaries of the Neuchatel Revolution and Swiss Federation. T* **97** *and designs inscr* "1848–1948". *Granite paper.* P 11½.
485   5c. green and dark green 20   30
486   10c. grey-black and grey 20   15
487   20c. carmine and rose 30   15
488   30c. blue, grey-blue and brown 75   1·10
485/488 Set of 4 .... 1·30 1·50
Designs:—10c. Neuchatel Castle; 20c. Symbol of Helvetia; 30c. Symbol of Federal State.
See also No. **MS**498a.

91 Platelayers   **92** Rorschach Station

(5c. des P. Boesch, eng A. Yersin; recess PTT, Berne 10c., 20c. des W. Koch, 30c. des H. Thöni; photo Courvoisier.)

1947 (14 June). *National Fête Professional Education of Invalids and Anti-Cancer Funds. As T* **91/2** (horiz designs inscr "1. VIII 1947"). *Granite paper. Coat-of-arms in scarlet.* P 11½.
473   5c.+15c. green 70   1·90
474   10c.+10c. black and buff 80   50
475   20c.+10c. carmine and buff .... 1·20 50
476   30c.+10c. blue and grey .... 6·00 8·75
473/476 Set of 4 .... 8·00 10·50
Designs:—20c. Luen-Castiel and 30c. Fluelen Railway Stations.

1948 (1 Mar–1 Oct). *As Nos. 369/79, but colours changed and new design (25 c).*
489   5c. reddish brown 25   10
   a. Tête-bêche (pair) (1.10.48) .... 1·60 1·30
490   10c. green 30   10
   a. Tête-bêche (pair) (1.10.48) .... 1·60 1·30
491   20c. chestnut 30   10
   a. Tête-bêche (pair) (1.10.48) .... 2·20 2·30
492   25c. scarlet .... 1·80 1·40
493   30c. deep turquoise-blue .... 12·00 3·25
494   40c. deep blue .... 30·00 30
489/494 Set of 6 .... 40·00 6·75
Designs:—5c. Mt. Pilatus; 10c. Chillon Castle and Dents du Midi; 20c. Lake Lugano and Mt. San Salvatore; 25c. National Park; 30c. Rhine Falls; 40c. Mt. Sands and Lake Seealp.
   The 5, 10, 20 and 30c. values were also issued in coils with a control letter and figures on the back of every fifth stamp in the roll. The 40c. was also issued in coils but without control numbers.

93 Limmat, First Swiss Steam Locomotive

(Des 5c. B. Reber. 10c. O. Baumberger, 20c., 30c. O. Rüegg. Photo Courvoisier.)

1947 (6 Aug). *Centenary of Swiss Railways. As T* **93** *(horiz designs Inscr* "1847–1947"). *Granite paper.* P 11½.
477   5c. green, yellow and black 25   30
478   10c. black and brown 30   15
479   20c. scarlet, buff and lake 35   15
480   30c. blue, grey and light blue ..... 1·40 1·30
477/480 Set of 4 .... 2·20 1·70
Designs:—10c. Steam freight locomotive, 20c. Electric train crossing Melide causeway; 30c. Railway bridge.

(5c. des and eng, K. Lieven. Recess Plain paper PTT, Berne, 10c. des F. Iselin, 20c. W. Koch, 30c. P. Chatillon. Photo Granite paper. Courvoisier.)

1948 (15 June). *National Fête and Anti-Tuberculosis Fund. T* **99** *and horiz designs inscr* "1. VIII 1948". *Coat of arms in scarlet.* P 11½.
495   5c.+5c. green 55   85
496   10c.+10c. slate and grey 50   45
497   20c.+10c. brown-red and buff 50   50
498   30c.+10c. ultramarine and grey ..... 3·50 4·25
495/498 Set of 4 .... 4·50 5·50
Designs (Typical houses in):—10c. Fribourg; 20c. Valais; 30c. Ticino.

343

SWITZERLAND Switzerland   1948

1948 (21 Aug). *National Philatelic Exhibition. Basel ("IMABA").* Sheet 110×61 mm. T **97**. Granite paper. P 11½.
MS498*a* 10c. reddish purple and grey; 20c.
  bluish grey & grey (sold at 3f.) . . . . 75·00 49·00

101 Glider

102 Posthorn

(Des H. Erni. Eng A. Yersin. Design recess, background typo PTT, Berne)

1949 (11 Apr). *AIR. Special (La Chaux de-Fonds, St. Gallen, Lugano) Flights.* P 11½.
499 **101** 1f.50 purple and yellow . . . . . 32·00 34·00
  No. 499 was valid for postage only on the special postal flights of 27 and 28 April, 1949.

(Des W. Weiskonig. Photo Courvoisier)

1949 (16 May). *Centenary of Federal Post.* T **102** *and similar types inscr "1849/1949" Granite paper.* P 11½.
500 5c. yellow pink and grey 20 30
501 20c. yellow, violet and grey 40 20
502 30c. yellow, brown and grey . . . . 60 5·75
  Designs:—20c. Mail coach drawn by five horses; 30c. Postal motor coach and trailer.

107A I.

107B II.

Type II: (a) Two clear horizontal lines instead of three between shore and top of rocks. (b) horizontal line inserted to mark base of building. (c) Cross-hatching extended above "20 H".

(Des and eng Karl Bickel. Recess PTT, Berne)

1949 (1 Aug)–**50**. T **106/7** *and similar designs.* P 11½.
510   3c. grey-black . . . . 3·75 3·75
511   5c. orange 45 10
   a. Tête-bêche (pair) (1.3.50) . . . . 1·10 15
512   10c. yellow-green 30 10
   a. Tête-bêche (pair) (1.3.50) 90 20
513   15c. turquoise 45 15
514   20c. maroon (I) . . . . £4750 55·00
   a. Type II 75 10
   b. Tête-bêche (pair) (II) (1.3.50) . . . . . 2·00 70
515   25c. scarlet 60 10
516   30c. olive 75 10
517   35c. brown . . . . 1·70 55
518   40c. blue . . . . 1·70 10
519   50c. bluish grey . . . . 2·75 10
520   60c. blue-green . . . . 7·50 10
521   70c. violet . . . . 2·75 20
510/521 Set of 12 (*cheapest*) . . . . 21·00 5·00
  Designs:—10c. Mountain cog railway, Rochers de Naye; 15c. Rotary snowplough; 20c. Grimsel reservoir; 25c. Lake Lugano and Melide railway causeway; 30c. Verbois hydro-electric power station; 35c. Alpine road (Val d'Anniviers); 40c. Rhine harbour, Basel; 50c. Suspension railway, Säntis; 60c. Railway viaduct. Landwasser; 70c. Survey mark. Finsteraarhorn.
  The 5, 10, 25, 30 and 40c. values were also issued in coils with a control letter and figures on the back of every fifth stamp in the roll and the 20c. Type II in coils with or without controls.

103 Main Motif of U.P.U. Monument, Berne

104 Postman

(Des H. Thöni. Photo Granite Paper. Courvoisier)

1949 (16 May). *75th Anniv of Universal Postal Union.* T **103** *and similar horiz designs.* P 11½.
503   10c. green 20 20
504   25c. claret (Globe and ribbon) . . . . . . 55 6·25
505   40c. blue (Globe and pigeons) . . . . . . 80 2·30

(5c. des W. Koch, Eng K. Lieven Recess Plain paper. PTT, Berne. 10c. des F. Deringer, 20c. H. Zaugg, 40c. W. Koch, Photo Granite paper. Courvoisier.)

1949 (15 June). *National Fête and Aid to Youth Fund.* T **104** *and various horiz designs as* T **89**, *inscr "1. VIII. 1949". Coat-of-arms in scarlet.* P 11½.
506   5c.+5c. purple . . . . 65 1·20
507   10c.+10c. blue-green and buff 40 55
508   20c.+10c. brown and buff 75 60
509   40c.+10c. blue and light blue . . . . 4·25 7·00
506/509 Set of 4 . . . . 4·50 9·00
  Designs (Typical houses in):—10c. Basel; 20c. Lucerne, 40c. Prättigau.

1950 (1 Feb). *OFFICIAL. Nos.* 511/21 *optd with Type O* **73**.
O522   5c. orange 50 40
O523   10c. yellow-green 90 40
O524   15c. turquoise . . . . 9·25 11·00
O525   20c. maroon (II) . . . . 2·75 25
O526   25c. scarlet . . . . 4·50 6·00
O527   30c. olive . . . . 3·50 1·90
O528   35c. brown . . . . 4·75 8·25
O529   40c. blue . . . . 3·50 1·00
O530   50c. bluish grey . . . . 5·75 4·50
O531   60c. blue-green . . . . 7·50 4·75
O532   70c. violet . . . . 19·00 16·00
O522/532 Set of 11 . . . . 55·00 50·00

110 First Federal Postage Stamps

111 Putting the Weight

(5c. des B. Reber, eng. K. Bickel. Recess (coat-of-arms photo) Plain paper PTT, Berne. Others des H. Fischer. Photo Granite paper Courvoisier)

1950 (1 June). *National Fête, Red Cross Fund, and Centenary of First Federal Postage stamps.* T **110** *and sporting types as* T **111** *inscr "1.VIII 1950" Coat-of-arms in scarlet.* P 11½.
522   5c.+5c. black 60 65
523   10c.+10c. green and greenish grey . . . . . 1·10 60

106 High-tension Pylons

107 Sitter Viaducts near St. Gall

344

SWITZERLAND Switzerland   1951

524	20c.+10c. brown-olive and grey		1·10	65
525	30c.+10c. magenta and grey		6·25	15·00
526	40c.+10c. blue and grey		7·50	8·00
522/526 Set of 5			15·00	23·00

Designs:—20c. Wrestling; 30c. Sprinting; 40c. Ritle-shooting.

112 Arms of Zurich

113 Valaisan Polka   **114** "Telegraph"

(5c. Des P. Boesch. Eng A. Yersin. Recess (coat-of-arms photo). Plain paper. PTT, Berne. Others, Des H. Fischer. Photo Granite paper Courvoisier)

1951 (1 June). *National Fête. Mothers' Fund and Sixth Centenary of Zürich.* T **112** and national activities as T **113** inscr "I.VIII 1951". *Coat-of-arms in scarlet.* P 11½.

527	5c.+5c. black		55	45
528	10c.+10c. green and grey		85	50
529	20c.+10c. brown-olive and grey		1·20	65
530	30c.+10c. magenta and grey		6·25	11·00
531	40c.+10c. blue and grey		7·75	7·50
527/531 Set of 5			15·00	18·00

Designs:—20c. Flag-swinging; 30c. Homussen (national game); 40c. Blowing alphorn.

1951 (29 Sept). *National Philatelic Exhibition, Lucerne* ("*LUNABA*"). *Sheet* 74 × 57 *mm. As No.* 529. *Imperf.*
MS531*a* 40c. multicoloured (sold at 3f.)   £200   £120

(Des P. Gauchat. Photo Granite paper. Courvoisier)

1952 (1 Feb). *Swiss Telecommunications Centenary. Designs as* T **114** *inscr* "1852 1952". P 11½.

532	5c. red-orange and yellow		40	45
533	10c. emerald and pink ("Telephone")		50	10
534	20c. magenta and lavender ("Radio")		75	10
535	40c. blue and pale blue ("Television")		3·00	2·75
532/535 Set of 4			4·25	3·00

115 Arms of Glarus and Zug   **116** River Doubs

(5c. Des P. Boesch. Eng A. Yersin. Recess (coat-of-arms photo). Plain paper, PTT, Berne Others. Des O. Baumberger. Photo Granite paper. Courvoisier)

1952 (31 May). *Pro Patria. Cultural Funds and 600th Anniv of Glarus and Zug joining Confederation.* T **115** *and horiz designs as* T **116**. P 11½.

536	5c.+5c. scarlet and black		50	70
537	10c.+10c. blue-green and cream		45	40
538	20c.+10c. claret and pink		50	40
539	30c.+10c. brown and buff		4·25	5·25
540	40c.+10c. blue and pale blue		5·00	4·75
536/540 Set of 5			9·75	10·50

Designs:—20c. St Gotthard Lake; 30c. River Moesa; 40c. Marjelen Lake.

117 Arms of Berne   **118** Rapids, R. Reuss

(5c. Des P. Boesch. Eng A. Yersin. Recess (coat-of-arms, photo). Plain paper. PTT, Berne, Others. Des O. Baumberger. Photo Granite paper. Courvoisier)

1953 (1 June). *Pro Patria. Emigrants' Fund and 600th Anniv of Berne joining Confederation.* T **117** *and various horiz designs as* T **118**. P 11½.

541	5c.+5c. scarlet and black		70	75
542	10c.+10c. blue-green and cream		30	35
543	20c.+10c. claret and pink		40	40
544	30c.+10c. brown and buff		2·75	6·75
545	40c.+10c. blue and pale blue		3·75	4·75
541/545 Set of 5			7·00	12·00

Designs:—20c. Lake Sihl; 30c. Aqueduct Bisse; 40c. Lac Léman.

119 Zürich Airport   **120** Alpine Postal Coach and Winter Landscape

(Des E. and M. Lenz. Photo Granite paper. Courvoisier.)

1953 (29 Aug). *Inauguration of Zurich Airport.* P 11½.
546   **119**   40c. blue, grey-blue, grey and scarlet   3·50   4·75

(Des H. Thöni. Photo Granite paper. Courvoisier.)

1953 (8 Oct). *Mobile P.O. Issue.* T **120** *and similar horiz design.* P 11½.

547	10c. yellow, grey-green and emerald		20	10
548	20c. yellow, brown-lake and scarlet		35	10

Design:—20c. Alpine postal coach and summer landscape.

121 Ear of Wheat and Flower   **122** Map of Rhine

(Des H. Hartmann (10c.), B. Reber (20c.), N. Stoecklin (25c.), H. Schwarzenbach (40c.). Photo Granite paper. Courvoisier.)

1954 (15 Mar). *Publicity Issue. Designs as* T **121/2**, *inscr* "1954". P 11½.

549	10c. yellow, cerise, bronze-green & grn		65	15
550	20c. buff, slate-blue, black & brown-lake		95	15
551	25c. bronze-green, pale blue & verm		1·60	2·00
552	40c. blue, yellow and black		2·75	1·20
549/552 Set of 4			5·25	3·25

Designs: *Horiz*—10c. T **121** (Agricultural Exhibition, Lucerne); 20c. Winged spoon (Cookery Exhibition, Berne); 40c. Football and world map (World Football Championship). *Vert*—25c. T **122** (50th Army of Navigation of R. Rhine).

345

SWITZERLAND Switzerland   1954

123 Opening Bars of "Swiss Hymn"

(5c. Des and eng K. Lieven. Recess Plain paper. PTT. Berne. Others. Des P. Chatillon. Photo Granite paper. Courvoisier)

1954 (1 June). *Pro Patria. Youth Fund and Centenary of Death of Father Zwyssig (composer of "Swiss Hymn"). T* **123** *and horiz designs as T* **118** *but inscr "1954". P* 11½.
553	5c.+5c. deep turquoise-green	65	75
554	10c.+10c. blue-green and turquoise	30	35
555	20c.+10c. maroon and cream	40	35
556	30c.+10c. brown and buff	2·75	6·75
557	40c.+10c. deep blue and pale blue	5·25	4·75
553/557 *Set of 5*		8·50	11·50

Designs:—10c. Lake Neuchâtel; 20c. R. Maggia; 30c. Taubenloch Gorge Waterfall, R. Scliuss; 40c. Lake Sils.

124 Lausanne Cathedral
125 Alphorn Blower 

(Des A. Rosselet (5c.), M. Allenbach (10c.), P. Boesch (20c.), K. Wirth (40c.) Photo Granite paper. Courvoisier)

1955 (15 Feb). *Publicity Issue. Designs as T* **124**/5, *inscr "1955". P* 11½.
558	5c. black, scarlet, yellow & bistre-brown	75	20
559	10c. yellow, red, bistre and emerald	75	10
560	20c. sepia and red	1·00	10
561	40c. rose, black and blue	1·90	1·20
558/561 *Set of 4*		4·00	1·40

Designs: *Horiz*—5c. T **124** (National Philatelic Exhibition, Lausanne); 10c. Vaud girl's hat (Vevey Winegrowers' Festival); 40c. Car steering-wheel (25th International Motor Show, Geneva). *Vert*—20c. T **125** (Alpine Herdsman and Costume Festival, Interlaken).

1955 (15 Feb). *National Philatelic Exhibition, Lausanne. Sheet* 103 × 52 *mm. T* **124**. *Imperf.*
MS561a 10c. and 20c. multicoloured (sold at 2f.) . . . £150 80·00

126 Federal Institute of Technology, Zurich

(5c. Des E. and M. Lenz Eng A. Yersin. Recess Plain paper. PTT, Berne. Others. Des F. Fedier. Photo Granite paper. Courvoisier)

1955 (1 June). *Pro Patria. Mountain Population Fund and Centenary of Federal Institute of Technology T* **126** *and horiz designs as T* **118** *but inscr "1955". P* 11½.
562	5c.+5c. slate	75	70
563	10c.+10c. deep blue green and cream	75	35
564	20c.+10c. lake and pink	80	35

565	30c.+10c. deep brown and buff	6·00	4·75
566	40c.+10c. deep bright blue and pale blue	6·00	4·00
562/566 *Set of 5*		13·00	9·25

Designs:—10c. Grandfey railway viaduct, River Saane; 20c. Lake Aegeri; 30c. Grappelensee; 40c. Lake Bienne.

127 "Road Safety"
128 Fokker F.VIIb/3m and Douglas DC-6 Aircraft 

(Des B. Reber (5c.), U. Huber-Bavier (10c.) E. Hauri (20c.), P. Gauchat (40c.). Photo Granite paper. Courvoisier)

1956 (1 Mar). *Publicity Issue. Designs as T* **127**/8, *inscr "1956". P* 11½.
567	5c. yellow, black and grey-olive	50	20
568	10c. grey-black, emerald and red	80	10
569	20c. yellow, black, vermilion & carm red	90	10
570	40c. blue and red	3·00	1·00
567/570 *Set of 4*		4·75	1·30

Designs: *Horiz*—5c. First postal motor coach (50th anniv of postal motor coach service); 10c. Electric train emerging from Simplon Tunnel and Stockalper Palace (50th anniv of opening of Simplon Tunnel); 20c. Type **127** *Vert*—40c. Type **128** (25th anniv of "Swissair").

129 Rose, Scissors and Tape-measure
130 Printing Machine's Inking Rollers 

(5c. Des E. and M. Lenz. Eng A. Yersin. Recess Plain paper. PTT, Berne. Others. Des P. Togni. Photo Granite paper. Courvoisier)

1956 (1 June). *Pro Patria. Swiss Women's Fund. T* **129** *and horiz designs as T* **118** *but inscr "1956". P* 11½.
571	5c.+5c. deep turquoise-green	65	75
572	10c.+10c. deep emerald and pale green	60	30
573	20c.+10c. claret and pink	65	50
574	30c.+10c. deep brown and light brown	4·25	4·75
575	40c.+10c. deep bright blue and pale blue	4·25	3·75
571/575 *Set of 5*		8·50	9·00

Designs:—10c. R. Rhone at St. Maurice; 20c. Katzensee; 30c. R. Rhine at Trin; 40c. Walensee.

(Des E. Witzig (5c.), W. Muhlemann (10c.), E. and M. Lenz (20c.), D. Brun (40c.) Photo Granite paper. Courvoisier)

1957 (27 Feb). *Publicity Issue. Designs as T* **130**, *inscr "1957". P* 11½.
576	5c. carmine, yellow, blue, black & grey	35	10
577	10c. brown, deep bluish grn & turq-grn	2·30	10
578	20c. deep grey and orange-red	70	10
579	40c. yellow-olive, maroon, green & blue	2·00	70
576/579 *Set of 4*		4·75	90

SWITZERLAND Switzerland   1957

Designs:—5c. T **130** ("Graphic 57" International Exhibition, Lausanne): 10c. Electric train crossing bridge (75th Anniv of St. Gotthard Railway), 20c. Civil Defence shield and coat-of-arms ("Civil Defence"), 40c. Munatius Plancus, Basel and Rhine (2,000th Anniv of Basel).

131 Shields of Switzerland and the Red Cross

132 "Charity"

(Des 5c. E. and M. Lenz. Eng A. Yersin. Recess Plain paper. PTT. Berne. Others. Des P. Gauchat and K. Mannhart Photo Granite paper. Courvoisier)

1957 (1 June). *Pro Patria. Swiss Red Cross and National Cancer League Funds.* Designs as T **131/2**. P 11½.

580	**131**	5c.+5c. red and deep slate	50	60
581	**132**	10c.+10c. dull purple, deep emerald green and carmine	50	25
582		20c.+10c. grey, red and carmine	65	25
583		30c.+10c. grey-blue brown & carm	3·50	4·00
584		40c.+10c. ochre, blue and carmine	3·50	3·25
580/584 Set of 5			7·75	7·50

133 Symbol of Unity

134 Nyon Castle

(Des W. Weiskonig. Eng H. Heusser. Recess PTT, Berne)

1957 (15 July). *Europa.* P 11½.

| 585 | **133** | 25c. scarlet | 75 | 20 |
| 586 | | 40c. blue | 3·25 | 45 |

(Des P. Perret (5c.), M. Allenbach 10c., 40c.), R. Bircher (20c.) Photo Granite paper. Courvoisier)

1958 (5 Mar). *Publicity issue.* Horiz designs as T **134**, inscr "1958". P 11½.

587	5c. blackish vio, pale buff & yellow olive	35	15
588	10c. blackish green, red and green	35	10
589	20c. carmine, lilac and vermilion	70	10
590	40c. indigo, crimson, deep bl & light bl	3·00	95
587/590 Set of 4		4·00	1·20

Designs:—5c. T **134** (2000th Anniv of Nyon), 10c. Woman's head with unions (Saffa Exhibition, Zurich); 20r. Crossbow (25th Anniv as symbol of Swiss manufacture); 40c. Salvation Army bonnet (75th Anniv of Salvation Army in Switzerland).

135 "Needy Mother"

136 Fluorite

(Des D. Brun. Eng A. Yersin. Recess Plain paper. PTT. Berne (5c.). Des N. Stoecklin. Photo Granite Paper. Courvoisier (others))

1958 (31 May). *Pro Patria. For Needy Mothers.* T **135** and horiz designs of minerals, rocks and fossils as T **136**, inscr "PRO PATRIA 1958". P 11½.

591	5c.+5c. brown-purple	60	45
592	10c.+10c. yellow green and black	60	25
593	20c.+10c. bistre, red and black	65	45
594	30c.+10c. bright purple, ochre and black	3·25	3·50
595	40c.+10c. pale turq-blue, ultram & blk	3·25	2·50
591/595 Set of 5		7·50	6·50

Designs:—20c. *Lytoceras fimbriatus* (ammonite); 30c. Garnet; 40c. Rock crystal.

137 Atomic Symbol

138 Modern Transport

(Des H. Schwarzbachner. Photo Granite paper. Courvoisier)

1958 (25 Aug). *Second United Nations Atomic Conference, Geneva.* P 11½.

| 596 | **137** | 40c. orange-red, blue and cream | 50 | 25 |

(Des C. Piatti (5c., 20c.), E. and M. Lenz (10c.). B. Cuendet (50c.) Photo Granite paper. Courvoisier)

1959 (9 Mar). *Publicity issue.* Horiz designs as T **138**, inscr "1959". P 11½.

597	5c. red, green, yellow, black & slate-pur	35	15
598	10c. yellow, pale drab and green	45	10
599	20c. blue, black, bistre-brown and red	90	10
600	50c. blue, violet and light blue	1·30	85
597/600 Set of 4		2·75	1·10

Designs:—5c. T **138** (Opening of "The Swiss House of Transport and Communications"); 10c. Lictor's fasces of the Coat-of-Arms of St. Gall and posthorn (NABAG National Philatelic Exhibition, St. Gall); 20c. Owl, hare and fish (Protection of Animals); 50c. J. Calvin, Th. de Beze and University building (Fourth centenary of University of Geneva).

1959 (9 Mar). *National Philatelic Exhibition St. Gallen* ("NABAG") Sheet 94 × 57 mm. As No. 598. Imperf.
MS600a 10c. and 20c. multi (sold at 2f.) 12·00 12·50

139 "Swiss Citizens Abroad"

140 "Europa"

(141)

(Des B. Reber. Eng K. Bickel, jun. Recess Plain paper. PTT Berne (5c.). Des N. Stoecklin. Photo Granite paper. Courvoisier (others))

1959 (1 June). *Pro Patria. For Swiss Citizens Abroad.* T **139** and horiz designs of minerals, rocks and fossils as T **136**, inscr "PRO PATRIA 1959". P 11½.

601	5c.+5c. red and greenish grey	45	50
602	10c.+10c. red, orange, yellow grn & blk	70	30
603	20c.+10c. turquoise, yellow, mag & blk	80	35
604	30c.+10c. bluish violet, brown & blk	2·40	2·10
605	40c.+10c. grey-blue greenish bl & blk	2·40	2·00
601/605 Set of 5		6·00	4·75

Designs:—10c. Agate; 20c. Tourmaline; 30c. Amethyst; 40c. Fossilized giant salamander.

347

SWITZERLAND Switzerland 1959

(Des H. Schwarzenbach. Eng H. Heusser. Recess PTT, Berne)
1959 (22 June). *Europa*. P 11½.
| 606 | **140** | 30c. red | 65 | 10 |
| 607 | | 50c. blue | 75 | 15 |

1959 (22 June). *European P.T.T. Conference, Montreux*. No. 606/7 optd with Type **141**.
| 608 | **140** | 30c. red (B.) | 26·00 | 7·75 |
| 609 | | 50c. blue (R.) | 26·00 | 7·75 |

Postal validity of the above stamps was restricted to mail posted at special post offices in the Conference Hall and at Palace Hotel, Montreux, for the duration of the Conference, and also at the Philatelic Agency Berne, until 31 July, 1959.

142 "Campaign against Cancer"

(Des E. Ruder (10c.). M. Allenbach (20c.), P. Jacopin (50c.), E. and M. Lenz (75c.) Photo Granite paper. Courvoisier)
1960 (7 Apr). *Publicity Issue. Horiz designs as T **142**, inscr "1460–1960" (20c.) or "1960" (others). P 11½.
610		10c. red, pale green and green	75	15
611		20c. yellow, black, brown and cerise	90	15
612		50c. yellow, ultramarine and blue	90	55
613		75c. red, black and light blue	4·00	4·75
610/613		Set of 4	6·00	5·00

Designs:—10c. Type **142** (50th anniv of Swiss National League for Cancer Control); 20c. Charter and sceptre (500th anniv of Basel University); 50c. "Uprooted tree" (World Refugee Year); 75c. Douglas DC-8 jetliner ("Swissair enters the jet age").

143 15th-century Schwyz Cantonal Messenger

143a Lausanne Cathedral

143b 614   **143c** 615   **143d** 617   **143e** 622

I. Sheet stamps

143f 614b   **143g** 615c   **143h** 617b   **143i** 622b

II. Coil stamps

PHOSPHORESCENT PAPER. In 1963 phosphorescent paper, which reacts under a UV lamp, was introduced. Up to 1973 these can be distinuished without a lamp by the violet fibres in the paper. Non-phosphorescent granite paper has red and blue fibres.

(Des W. Weisskonig (5c., 10c., 15c., 20c., 25c., 40c., 70c., 80c., 1f.20); H. Hartmann (others). Eng H. Heusser (5c. to 20c.), A. Yersin (others). Recess PTT, Berne)
1960 (10 May)–**76**. *As T **143** (postal history) and T **143a** ("Architectural Monuments" (1st series)).* P 11½.

(a) Ordinary paper (10.5.60).
614	5c. new blue (I)	10	10
	a. Tête-bêche (pair) (24.10.60)	30	25
	p. Phosphor granite paper (3.10.63)	10	15
	pa. Tête-bêche (pair) (24.6.68)	30	30
	b. Type II (coils) (6.60)	90	1·10
	bp. Phosphor granite paper* (1.65)	1·00	1·20
615	10c. bluish green (I)	15	10
	a. Tête-bêche (pair)	45	25
	p. Phosphor granite paper (3.10.63)	15	10
	pa. Tête-bêche (pair) (24.6.68)	25	25
	pb. Booklet pane. No. 615p × 2 plus two labels (1968)	75	
	c. Type II (coils)	50	30
	cp. Phosphor granite paper* (1.65)	50	25
616	15c. Venetian red	10	10
	p. Phosphor granite paper (3.10.63)	50	35
617	20c. cerise (I)	30	10
	a. Tête-bêche (pair) (24.10.60)	65	45
	p. Phosphor granite paper (3.10.63)	25	10
	pa. Tête-bêche (pair) (24.6.68)	60	35
	b. Type II (coils) (6.60)	60	55
	bp. Phosphor granite paper* (1.65)	65	30
618	25c. emerald	45	10
	p. Phosphor granite paper (3.10.63)	30	10
619	30c. vermilion	35	10
	p. Phosphor granite paper (3.10.63)	45	10
	pa. Tête-bêche (pair) (24.6.68)	60	35
620	35c. orange-red	90	75
621	40c. purple	50	10
	p. Phosphor granite paper (1967)	70	10
	pa. Tête-bêche (pair) (1976)	1·10	1·00
622	50c. ultramarine (I)	90	10
	a. Tête-bêche (pair)	2·10	2·20
	p. Phosphor granite paper (3.10.63)	65	10
	b. Type II (coils) (6.60)	3·50	3·75
	bp. Phosphor granite paper* (1.65)	3·75	4·00
623	60c. bright rose-red	70	10
	p. Phosphor granite paper (1967)	70	15
624	70c. orange	1·20	45
625	75c. greenish blue	1·50	60
	p. Phosphor granite paper (1968)	95	75
626	80c. brown-purple	90	10
	p. Phosphor granite paper (3.10.63)	1·60	10
627	90c. deep yellow-green	1·10	10
	a. Double print	£750	£750
	p. Phosphor granite paper (1967)	1·60	10
628	1f. yellow-orange	1·70	10
	p. Phosphor granite paper (1967)	1·30	25
629	1f.20 brown-red	1·90	15
	p. Phosphor granite paper (1968)	2·10	1·90
630	1f.50 bright emerald	2·40	25
	p. Phosphor granite paper (1968)	2·10	1·90
631	2f. blue	4·00	50

(b) Non phosphorescent granite paper (blue and red fibres) (4.2.63).
632	1f.30 orange-brown/*lilac*	1·40	15
633	1f.70 purple/*lilac*	1·80	15
634	2f.20 blue-green/*green*	2·40	40
635	2f.80 red-orange/*pale orange*	3·00	35
614/635	Set of 22 (non-phosphorescent)	25·00	4·50
614/19p, 621/3p, 625/30p Set of 15 (phosphorescent)		12·00	5·50

Designs: (Postal History) *Horiz*—5c. 17th-century Fribourg Cantonal Messenger; 15c. 17th-century mule-driver; 20c. 19th-century mounted postman. (Monuments) *Vert*—30c. Grossmunster, Zürich; 35c., 1f.30, Woodcutters Guildhall, Bienne; 40c. St. Peter's Cathedral, Geneva; 50c. Spalentor (gate): Basel; 60c. Zeaglockenturm (clock tower), Berne; 70c. Collegiate Church of St. Peter and St. Stephen, Bellinzona; 75c. Kapellbrucke (bridge) and Wasserturm, Lucerne; 80c. St Gall Cathedral; 90c. Munot Fort, Schaffhausen; 2f.80, as 70c. but redrawn without belltower on Collegiate Church. *Horiz*—1f. Fribourg Town Hall; 1f.20, Basel Gate, Solothurn; 1f.50, Ital Reding's House, Schwyz; 1f.70, 2f., 2f.20, Abbey Church, Emsiedeln.

*These phosphorescent stamps in Type II were first issued in coils only (numbered on the back of every fifth stamp). In 1966

SWITZERLAND Switzerland 1960

they were reissued in the coil printing-sheets (with every fifth row or column numbered on the back) but can only be distinguished thus in blocks or with sheet margins.

The 40, 60, 90c., 1f. and Nos 623/5, on both ordinary and phosphor granite paper, were also issued in coils with control figures on the back of every fifth stamp in the roll.

For similar Buildings see Nos. 698/713 and 1276.

144 Symbols of Occupational Trades

144a Conference Emblem

(Des H. Kumpel. Eng H. Heusser. Photo, background recess PTT, Berne (50c.). Des N. Stoecklin. Photo Courvoisier (others). Granite paper)

1960 (1 June). *Pro Patria. For Swiss Youth.* T **144** *and horiz designs inscr "PRO PATRIA 1960".* P 11½.

636	5c.+5c. yellow-brn, pale bl, bl & sepia	75	60
637	10c.+10c. salmon-pink, green & black	75	30
638	20c.+10c. olive-yellow, brt purple & blk	80	30
639	30c.+10c. blue, orange-brown & black	3·50	2·75
640	50c.+10c. gold and blue	3·25	2·75
636/640	Set of 5	8·25	6·00

Designs:—5c. Smoky quartz; 10c. Orthoclase (feldspar); 20c. Devil's toenail (fossilized shell); 30c. Azurite; 50c. Type **144** ("50 Years of the National Day Collection").

1960 (1 June). *50th Anniv of Pro Patria Chanty Fund. Sheet 85 × 75 mm. As No.* 640. *Imperf.*

MS641	**144** 50c.+10c. gold and blue (block of 4) (sold at 3f.)	29·00	16·00

(Des P. Rahikamen. Eng H. Heusser Recess PTT, Berne)

1960 (19 Sept). *Europa.* P 11½.

642	**144a** 30c. red	45	10
643	50c. blue	70	20

145 "Aid for Development"

146 "Cultural Works of Eternity"

(Des E. & M. Lenz (5c.), H. Neuberg (10c.), J. & L. Ongaro (20c.), B. Reber (50c.) Photo Granite paper. Courvoisier)

1961 (20 Feb). *Publicity Issue. Horiz designs as T* **145** *inscr "MARS 1961" (20c.) or "1961" (others).* P 11½.

644	5c. red, turquoise-blue and grey	60	20
645	10c. yellow and greenish blue	60	10
646	20c. greenish yellow, dp brn, grey & car	1·20	20
647	50c. carmine, grey-green and ultramarine	2·20	75
644/647	Set of 4	4·25	1·10

Designs:—5c. Type **145** ("Aid to countries in process of development"); 10c. Circular emblem ("Hyspa" Exhibition of 20th-century Hygiene. Gymnastics and Sport, Berne); 20c. Hockey stick (World and European Ice Hockey Championships, Geneva and Lausanne); 50c. Map of Switzerland with telephone centres as wiring diagram (inauguration of Swiss fully automatic telephone service).

(Des H. Schwarzenbach. Eng K. A. Bickel jun. Recess Plain paper. PTT, Berne (5c.). Des N. Stoecklin. Photo Courvoisier (others). Granite paper)

1961 (1 June). *Pro Patria. For Swiss Cultural Works.* T **146** *and horiz designs of minerals, rocks and fossils inscr "PRO PATRIA 1961".* P 11½.

648	5c.+5c. blue	45	40
649	10c.+10c. bright purple, green & black	60	30
650	20c.+10c. bright carmine, grey-bl & blk	60	30
651	30c.+10c. turquoise-blue, orange & blk	1·70	2·30
652	50c.+10c. bistre, blue and black	1·70	2·20
648/652	Set of 5	4·50	5·00

Designs:—10c. Fluorite; 20c. Fossilized fish (Glarone Rabbitfish); 30c. Lazulite; 50c. Fossilized fern.

147 Doves

148 St. Matthew

(Des T. Kurpershoek and H. Thöni. Eng K. Bickel, jun. Recess PTT, Berne)

1961 (18 Sept). *Europa.* P 11½.

653	**147** 30c. red	40	10
654	50c. bright blue	50	20

(Des Agathe Bagnoud. Eng H. Heusser. Recess Granite paper. PTT, Berne)

1961 (18 Sept). T **148** *and similar vert designs showing wood carvings from St. Oswald's Church, Zug.* P 11½.

655	3f. crimson	4·00	20
656	5f. Prussian blue (St. Mark)	6·00	10
657	10f. sepia (St. Luke)	9·00	45
658	20f. brown-red (St. John)	17·00	1·90
655/658	Set of 4	32·00	2·40

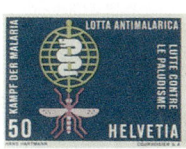

149 World Health Organization Emblem and Mosquito

150 Rousseau

151 Obwalden Silver Half-taler

(Des P. Perret (5c.), H. Hartmann (50c.). D. Brun (others) Photo Granite paper, Courvoisier)

1962 (19 Mar). *Publicity issue Horiz designs as T* **149**. P 11½.

659	5c. red, buff, black and grey-black	70	20
660	10c. bistre, bright purple and blue-green	50	10
661	20c. slate, violet-grey, bistre and mauve	80	15
662	50c. green, magenta and deep blue	85	45
659/662	Set of 4	2·50	80

Designs:—5c. Electric train (introduction of Trans-Europe Express); 10c. Oarsman (World Rowinq Championship Lucerne); 20c. Jungfraujoch and Mönch (50th anniv of Jungfraujoch Railway Station); 50c. Type **149** (malaria eradication).

(Des and eng K. Bickel. Recess Plain paper. PTT, Berne (5c.). Des C. Piatti. Photo Granite paper. Courvoisier (others)

1962 (1 June). *Pro Patria. For Old People's Homes and Swiss Cultural Works.* T **150** *and vert designs of old Swiss coins as T* **151**, *inscr "PRO PATRIA 1962".* P 11½.

663	5c.+5c. blue	15	20
664	10c.+10c. grey-blue, black and green	25	25

349

SWITZERLAND Switzerland 1962

665	20c.+10c. olive-yellow, black & carm	35	35
666	30c.+10c. green, grey-blue & orge-red	70	1·60
667	50c.+10c. slate-violet, black & bright bl	75	1·40
663/667	Set of 5	2·00	3·50

Coins:—20c. Schwyz gold ducat; 30c. Uri batzen; 50c. Nidwalden batzen.

152 Europa "Tree"  **153** Campaign Emblem (Freedom from Hunger)

(Des Lex Weyer. Photo Granite paper. Courvoisier)

1962 (17 Sept). *Europa.* P 11½.
668	152	30c. orge-yell, greenish yell & red-brn	60	30
669		50c. blue, lt turq-green & red-brown	65	40

(Des E. Poncy (5c.), H. Auchli (10c.), H. Thöni (20c.), E. & M. Lenz (30c.), W. Baumberger (50c. No. 674), H. Hartmann (50c. No. 675). Photo Granite paper. Courvoisier)

1963 (21 Mar). *Publicity Issue.* Horiz designs as T **153**. P 11½.
670	5c. yellow-brn, carmine-red & grey-bl	70	20
671	10c. carmine-red, grey and bronze-green	40	10
672	20c. lake, carmine-red and pale grey	1·50	15
673	30c. pale yellow, ochre and dull green	1·40	1·10
674	50c. red, silver and blue	1·00	55
675	50c. grey, rose, greenish yell & ultram	1·00	60
670/675	Set of 6	5·50	2·40

Designs:—5c. Boy scout (50th Anniv of Swiss Bay Scout League); 10c. Badge (Centenary of Swiss Alpine Club); 20c. Luegelkinn Viaduct (50th Anniv of Lötschberg Railway); 50c. (No. 674), Jubilee emblem (Red Cross Centenary); 50c. (No. 675), Hôtel des Pastes, Paris, 1863 (Paris Postal Conference).

1963 (21 Mar). *International Red Cross Centenary.* Sheet 100 × 80 mm. As No. 674. Imperf.
MS675a 50c. fluorescent blue, red, deep blue and cobalt (block of four) (sold at 3f.)   4·50   4·00

154 Dr. Anna Heer (nursing pioneer) 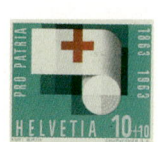   **155** Roll of Bandage

(Des and eng K. Bickel. Recess Plain paper. PTT, Berne (5c.). Des K. Wirth. Photo Granite paper, Courvoisier (others))

1963 (1 June). *Pro Patria. For Swiss Medical and Refugee Aid.* T **154** and horiz designs of Red Cross activities as T **155**, inscr "PRO PATRIA 1963". P 11½.
676	5c.+5c. blue	20	25
677	10c.+10c. red grey and blue-green	25	15
678	20c.+10c. red grey, deep violet & pink	30	20
679	30c.+10c. red, carmine, sepia & orange	90	1·20
680	50c.+10c. red, indigo and light blue	1·10	1·20
676/680	Set of 5	2·50	2·75

Designs:—20c. Gilt parcel; 30c. Blood plasma; 50c. Red Cross brassard.

156 Glider and Jet Aircraft    **157** "Co-operation"

(Des R. Gerbig. Photo Granite paper. Courvoisier)

1963 (1 June). *AIR. 25th Anniv of Swiss "Pro Aero" Foundation, and Special Flights.* P 11½.
681	156	2f. yellow, red, blue and silver	3·00	3·25

No. 681 was valid for postage only on the special Berne-Locarno or Langenbruck-Berne (helicopter feeder) flights of July 13th, 1963.

(Des A. Holm, B. Reber. Photo Granite paper. Courvoisier)

1963 (16 Sept). *Europa.* P 11½.
582	157	50c. ochre and blue	55	25

158 Exhibition Emblem    **159** Great St. Bernard Tunnel

(Des P. Monnerat (T **158**), A. Hofmann (others). Photo Courvoisier)

1963 (16 Sept). *Swiss National Exhibition, Lausanne.* T **158** and similar horiz designs. Granite paper. P 11½.
683	158	10c. emerald and deep olive	20	10
684		20c. red and lake-brown	15	10
685	—	50c. ultramarine, grey and red	45	25
686	—	75c. reddish violet, grey and red	55	45
683/686	Set of 4		1·20	80

Designs:—50c. "Outlook" (emblem on globe and smaller globe); 75c. "Insight" (emblem on large globe).

(Des B. Reber (5c.), H. Erni (10c.), E. & M. Lenz (20c.), W. Grandjean ("Bodjol") (50c.) Photo Granite paper. Courvoisier)

1964 (9 Mar). *Publicity Issue.* Horiz designs as T **159**. P 11½.
687	5c. blue, vermilion and yellow olive	20	15
688	10c. turquoise-green and blue	25	10
689	20c. multicoloured	50	10
690	50c. multicoloured	85	45
687/690	Set of 4	1·60	70

Designs:—5c. T **159** (Opening of Great St. Bernard Road Tunnel); 10c. Ancient "god of the waters" (Protection of water supplies); 20c. Swiss soldiers of 1864 and 1964 (Centenary of Swiss Association of Non-commissioned Officers); 50c. Standards of Geneva and Swiss Confederation (150th Anniv of arrival of Swiss in Geneva).

PHOSPHORESCENT PAPER. See note after T **143**.

160 J G. Bodmer (inventor)    **161** Europa "Flower"

350

SWITZERLAND Switzerland 1964

(Des and eng K. Bickel. Recess PTT, Berne (5c.). Des J. F. Liengme. Photo Courvoisier (others))

1964 (1 June). *Pro Patria. For Swiss Mountain Aid and Cultural Funds.* T **160** *and vert designs of old Swiss coins as T* **151**. *Non-phosphorescent granite paper (50c.), phosphorescent paper (others).* P 11½.
691	5c.+5c. greenish blue	10	15
692	10c.+10c. drab, black and bluish green	15	15
693	20c.+10c. grey-blue, black & magenta	25	20
694	30c.+10c. grey-blue, black and orange	35	55
695	50c.+10c. olive-yellow, brown and blue	70	75
691/695 Set of 5		1·40	1·60

Coins:—10c. Zürich copper; 20c. Basel "doppeldicken"; 30c. Geneva silver cater; 50c. Berne half gold florin.

(Des G. Bétemps and E. Witzig. Eng K. Bickel jun. Recess PTT, Berne)

1964 (14 Sept). *Europa. Phosphorescent paper.* P 11½.
696	**161**	20c. red	35	10
697		50c. blue	55	20

(Des W. Weiskönig (10c., 15c., 20c., 50c.), H. Hartmann (others) Eng A. Yersin. Recess PTT, Berne)

1964–73. As T **143**a *("Architectural Monuments", Second Series). Phosphorescent, slightly greyish toned paper.* P 11½.
698	5c. cerise (12.9.68)	10	10
699	10c. ultramarine (12.9.68)	10	10
	a. Tête-bêche (pair) (18.6.70)	30	25
	b. Booklet pane. No 699 × 2 plus two labels (1970)	30	
700	15c. bright chestnut (12.9.68)	20	10
	a. Tête-bêche (pair) (8.1.73)	40	40
701	20c. blue green (12.9.68)	25	10
	a. Tête-bêche (pair) (18.6.70)	55	50
702	30c. vermilion (12.9.68)	30	10
	a. Tête-bêche (pair) (18.6.70)	85	90
703	50c. new blue (12.9.68)	50	10
704	70c. brown (18.9.67)	75	10
705	1f. bluish green (12.9.68)	1·00	10
706	1f.20 brown lake (12.9.68)	1·20	15
707	1f.30 ultramarine (21.2.66)	1·50	55
708	1f.50 emerald (12.9.68)	1·60	20
709	1f.70 dull vermilion (21.2.66)	1·90	70
710	2f. orange (18.9.67)	2·10	20
711	2f.20 blue-green (14.9.64)	2·75	55
712	2f.50 blue-green (18.9.67)	2·75	25
713	3f.50 purple (18.9.67)	3·75	30
698/713 Set of 16		19·00	3·25

Buildings: *Horiz*—5c. Lenzburg Castle; 10c. Freuler Mansion, Näfels; 15c. Mauritius Church, Appenzell; 20c. Planta House, Samedan; 30c. Town Square, Gais; 50c. Neuchâtel Castle and Collegiate Church. *Vert*—70c. Lussy "Höchhus', Wolfen-schiessen; 1f. Riva San Vitale Church; 1f.20, Payerne Abbey Church; 1f.30, St. Pierre-de-Clages Church; 1f.50, Gateway, Porrentruy; 1f.70, Frauenfeld Castle; 2f. Castle Seedorf (Uri); 2f.20, Thomas Tower and Arch, Liestal; 2f.50, St. Oswald's Church, Zug; 3f.50, Benedictine Abbey, Engelberg.

The 15c. was also issued in coils with a control number on the back of every fifth stamp.

162 Swiss 5r. Stamp of 1854 with "Lozenge" Cancellation
163 Father T. Florentini 
164 Fish-tailed Goose ("Evil") 

(Des E. & M. Lenz (5c.), A. Flückiger (10c.), A. Oertle (20c.), H. Thöni (50c.). Photo Courvoisier)

1965 (8 Mar). *Publicity Issue.* T **162** *and similar horiz designs. Non-phosphorescent granite paper (50c), phosphorescent paper (others).* P 11½.
714	5c. black, red and light brown	10	10
715	10c. brown, blue and emerald	10	10
716	20c. multicoloured	25	10
717	50c. red, black and greenish blue	50	35
714/717 Set of 4		85	60

Designs:—5c. Nurse and patient ("Nursing"); 10c. T **162** "NABRA 1965" National Stamp Exhibition, Berne), 20c. WAC officer (25th anniv of Women's Army Corps); 50c. World telecommunications map (centenary of International Telecommunications Union).

(Des A. Fluckiger. Photo Courvoisier)

1965 (8 Mar). *National Philatelic Exhibition, Berrie ("NABRA"). Sheet 94 × 61 mm. As T* **162**. *Granite paper.* Imperf.
MS718 10c. orange, blue and green (20r.) 20c. green blue & caret (40r.) (sold at 3f.) .... 1·20 1·30

(Des and eng H. Heusser. Recess PTT, Berne (5c.) Des H. Schwarzenbach. Photo Courvoisier (others))

1965 (1 June). *Pro Patria. For Swiss Abroad and Art Research.* T **163** *and vert designs as T* **164**, *inscr* "PRO PATRIA 1965". *Phosphorescent paper.* P 11½.
719	**163**	5c.+5c. blue	10	10
720	**164**	10c.+10c. multicoloured	10	10
721	–	20c.+10c. multicoloured	25	10
722	–	30c.+10c. brown and blue	40	35
723	–	50c.+10c. blue and orange brown	55	40
719/723 Set of 5			1·30	95

Designs:—Ceiling paintings in St. Martin's Church, Zillis (Grisons)—20c. One of Magi Journeying to Herod; 30c. Fishermen; 50c. The temptation of Christ.

165 Swiss Emblem and Arms of Cantons
166 Matterhorn 

(Des A. Rosselet. Photo Courvoisier)

1965 (1 June). *150th Anniv of Entry of Valais. Neuchatel and Geneva into Confederation. Granite paper.* P 11½.
724 **165** 20c. multicoloured 25 10

(Des E. Hauri. Photo Courvoisier)

1965 (1 June). *Mobile P.O. Issue Non-phosphorescent granite (10c.) or phosphorescent (30c.) paper.* P 11½.
725 **166** 10c. black, grey bluish green & red 25 10
726 30c. black, grey, red & bluish green 65 60
No. 726 is inscribed "CERVIN".

162 Swiss 5r. Stamp of 1854 with "Lozenge" Cancellation
163 Father T. Florentini
164 Fish-tailed Goose ("Evil")
167 Europa "Sprig"
168 I.T.U Emblem and Satellites 

(Des W. Muhlemann, after H. Karlsson. Photo Courvoisier)

1965 (14 Sept). *Europa Phosphorescent paper.* P 11½.
727 **167** 50c. emerald and light blue 60 20

351

SWITZERLAND Switzerland 1965

(Des A. Rosselet. Photo Courvoisier)
1965 (14 Sept). *International Telecommunications Union Centenary Congress, Montreux.* T **168** *and similar horiz design phosphorescent (10c.) or non-phosphorescent granite (30c.) paper. Multicoloured.* P 11½.
728	10c. Type **168**		10	10
729	30c. Symbols of world telecommunications		30	25

PHOSPHORESCENT PAPER. All stamps from No. 730 to No. 926 are printed on phosphorescent paper, with violet fibres, *unless otherwise stated.*

169 Figure Skating   **170** River Kingfisher

(Des W. Haettenschweiler. Photo Courvoisier)
1965 (14 Sept). *World Figure Skating Championships, Davos.* P 11½.
730	**169**	5c. multicoloured	10	10

(Des B. Waltenspül (10c.), D. Brun (20c.). H. Kümpel (50c.) Photo Courvoisier)
1966 (21 Feb). *Publicity Issue. Horiz designs as* T **170**. *Multicoloured.* P 11½.
731	10c. Type **170**		20	10
732	20c. Mercury's helmet and laurel twig		25	10
733	50c. Phase in nuclear fission and flags		45	20

Publicity events: 10c. Preservation of natural beauty; 20c. 50th Swiss Industrial Fair, Basel (MUBA); 50c. International Institute for Nuclear Research (CERN).

171 H. Federer (author)   **172** Society Emblem   **173** Europa Ship

(Des and eng K. Lievin. Recess PTT, Berne (5c.). Des H. Schwarzenbach. Photo Courvoisier (others))
1966 (1 June). *Pro Patria. For Aid to Mothers.* T **171** *and vert designs as* T **164**, *inscr "PRO PATRIA 1966" Nos. 735/8 multicoloured.* P 11½.
734	5c.+5c. greenish blue		10	10
735	10c.+10c. Joseph's dream		10	10
736	20c.+10c. Joseph on his way		25	15
737	30c.+10c. Virgin and Child		40	35
738	50c.+10c. Angel pointing the way		55	40
734/738 Set of 5			1·25	1·00

The designs of Nos. 735/8 represent the Flight into Egypt and are taken from ceiling paintings in St. Martin's Church, Zillis (Grisons).

(Des A. Flückiger. Photo Courvoisier)
1966 (1 June). *50th Anniv of New Helvetic Society for Swiss Abroad.* P 11½.
739	**172**	20c. vermilion and bright blue	20	10

(Des G. and J. Bender. Eng A. Yersin. Recess PTT, Berne)
1966 (26 Sept). *Europa.* P 11½.
740	**173**	20c. rose red	25	10
741		50c. blue	50	20

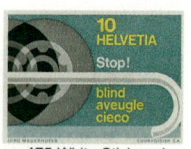

174 Finsteraarhorn   **175** White Stick and Motorcar Wheel (Welfare of the Blind)

(Des H. Thöni. Photo Courvoisier)
1966 (26 Sept). *"Swiss Alps".* P 11½.
742	**174**	10c. multicoloured	10	10

(Des J. Mauerhofer (10c.), R. Mumprecht (20c.). Photo Courvoisier)
1967 (13 Mar). *Publicity Issue.* T **175** *and similar horiz design.* P 11½.
743	10c. multicoloured		10	10
744	20c. multicoloured		25	10

Designs:—20c. Flags of European Free Trade Area countries (abolition of E.F.T.A. tariffs).

176 C.E.P.T. Emblem and Cogwheels   **177** Theodor Kocher (surgeon)   **178** Cogwheel and Swiss Emblem

(Des J. Mauerhofer, after O. Bonnevalle. Eng A. Yersin. Recess PTT, Berne)
1967 (13 Mar). *Europa.* P 11½.
745	**176**	30c. grey-blue	30	10

(Des and eng K. Lieven Recess PTT, Berne (5c.). Des H. Schwarzenbach. Photo Courvoisier (others))
1967 (1 June). *Pro Patria. For National Day Collection.* T **177** *and vert designs as* T **164** *inscr "PRO PATRIA 1967".* P 11½.
746	5c.+5c. new blue		10	10
747	10c.+10c. multicoloured		10	10
748	20c.+10c. multicoloured		25	10
749	30c.+10c. multicoloured		40	35
750	50c.+10c. multicoloured		55	40
746/750 Set of 5			1·30	95

Designs: Ceiling paintings in St. Martin's Church, Zillis (Grisons)—10c. Annunciation to the shepherds; 20c. Christ and the woman of Samaria; 30c. Adoration of the Magi; 50c. Joseph seated on a throne.

(Des H.-R. Lauterburg (10c.), H. Kümpel (20c.), B. Waltenspül (30c.), W. Muhlemann (50c.) Photo Courvoisier)
1967 (18 Sept). *Publicity Issue.* T **178** *and similar horiz designs. Multicoloured.* P 11½.
751	10c. Type **178**		10	10
752	20c. Hour-glass and Sun		20	10
753	30c. San Bernardino highway		35	10
754	50c. "OCTI" emblem		50	20
751/754 Set of 4			1·00	45

Publicity events: 10c. 50th anniv of Swiss Week; 20c. 50th Anniv of Aged People Foundation; 30c. Opening of San Bernardino road tunnel; 50c.75th Anniv of Central Office for International Railway Transport (OCTI).

352

SWITZERLAND Switzerland   1968

179 "Mountains" and Swiss Emblem
180 "Maius" 

(Des A. Flückiger (10c.), H. Schwarzenbach (20c.), R. Geiser (30c.), M. Gallay (50c.). Photo Courvoisier)

1968 (14 Mar). *Publicity issue* T **179** *and similar horiz designs.* P 11½.
755	10c. red, cobalt, dp grn, grn & light grn	10	10
756	20c. yellow, brown and greenish blue	25	10
757	30c. bright ultram, ochre & yell-brn	30	10
758	50c. red, deep greenish bl & light bl	55	20
755/758	*Set of* 4	1·10	45

Designs and events:—10c. Type **179** (50th anniv of Swiss Women's Alpine Club); 20c. Europa "key" (Europa); 30c. Staunton rook and chessboard (18th Chess Olympiad Lugano); 50c. Dispatch "satellites" and aircraft tail fin (inauguration of new Geneva Air Terminal).

(Des E. Witzig. Photo Courvoisier)

1968 (30 May). *Pro Patria. For National Day Collection.* T **180** *and similar vert designs, inscr* "PRO PATRIA 1968". *Multicoloured.* P 11½.
759	10c.+10c. Type **180**	10	10
760	20c.+10c. "Leo"	25	15
761	30c.+10c. "Libra"	35	10
762	50c.+20c. "Pisces"	55	50
759/762	*Set of* 4	1·10	75

The designs of Nos. 759/62 are symbols of months and the signs of the zodiac taken from stained-glass panels in the rose window, Lausanne Cathedral.

181 Protective Helmet
182 Guide Camp and Emblem 

(Des E. Küng (10c.), P. Birkhäuser (20c.), B. La Roche (30c.), J. Mauerhofer (50c.). Photo Courvoisier)

1968 (12 Sept). *Publicity Issue.* T **181** *and similar horiz designs. Multicoloured.* P 11½.
763	10c. Type **181**	10	10
764	20c. Geneva and Zurich stamps of 1843	25	10
765	30c. Part of Swiss map	30	10
766	50c. "Six Stars" (countries) and anchor	45	25
763/766	*Set of* 4	1·00	50

Events:—10c. 50th Anniv of Swiss Accident Insurance Company; 20c. 125th Anniv of Swiss stamps; 30c. 25th Anniv of Swiss Territorial Planning Society; 50c. Centenary of Rhine Navigation Act.

(Des E. Meier (10c.), H. Erni (20c.), P. Monnerat (30c.), H. Leupin (50c.), E. and M. Lenz (2f.). Photo Courvoisier)

1969 (13 Feb). *Publicity issue.* T **182** *and similar horiz designs Multicoloured.* P 11½.
767	10c. Type **182**	25	10
768	20c. Pegasus constellation	25	10
769	30c. Emblem of Comptoir Suisse	30	10
770	50c. Emblem of Gymnaestrade	45	30
771	2f. Haefeli DH-3 biplane and Douglas DC-8 jetliner	2·00	1·40
767/771	*Set of* 5	1·10	55

Events:—10c. 50th Anniv of Swiss Girl Guides' Federation; 20c. Opening of first Swiss Planetarium, Lucerne; 30c. 50th Anniv of Compton Suisse, Lausanne; 50c. Fifth Gymnaestrada, Basel; 2f. 50th Anniv of Swiss Airmail Services.

183 Colonnade
184 "St. Francis of Assisi preaching to the Birds" (Abbey-church, Königsfelden) 

(Des L. Gasbarra, G. Belli and H. Hartmann. Photo Courvoisrer)

1969 (28 Apr). *Europa.* P 11½.
| 772 | **183** | 30c. multicoloured | 35 | 10 |
| 773 | | 50c. multicoloured | 50 | 40 |

(Des E. Witzig. Photo Courvoisier)

1969 (29 May). *Pro Patria. For National Day Collection.* T **184** *and similar vert designs, showing stained-glass windows. Multicoloured.* P 11½.
774	10c.+10c. Type **184**	10	10
775	20c.+10c. "The People of Israel drinking" (Berne Cathedral)	25	15
776	30c.+10c. "St Christopher" (Läufel-fingen Church, Basel)	35	20
777	50c.+20c. "Madonna and Child" (St. Jacob's Chapel, Gräppling, Flums)	55	45
774/777	*Set of* 4	1·10	80

185 Kreuzberge
186 Huldrych Zwingli (Protestant reformer) 

(Des H. Thöni (50c.), E. Hauri (others). Photo Courvoisier)

1969 (18 Sept). *Publicity and "Swiss Alps" (20c.) Issue.* T **185** *and similar horiz designs.* P 11½.
778	20c. Type **185**	30	10
779	30c. Children crossing road	30	10
780	50c. Hammersmith	45	25

Events:—30c. Road Safety campaign for children; 50c. 50th Anniv of International Labour Organization.

(Des G. Humair. Eng H. Heusser. Recess PTT, Berne)

1969 (18 Sept). *Swiss Celebrities.* T **186** *and similar horiz designs.* P 11½.
781	10c. reddish violet	10	10
782	20c. emerald	25	10
783	30c. carmine	35	10
784	50c. new blue	45	35
785	80c. chestnut	80	80
781/785	*Set of* 5	1·80	1·30

Designs:—20c. General Henri Guisan; 30c. Francesco Borromini (architect); 50c. Othmar Schoeck (composer); 80c. Germaine de Stael (writer).

353

SWITZERLAND Switzerland 1970

187 Telex Tape

188 "Flaming Sun"

(Des E. & M. Lenz (20c.), E. Bosshart (30c. No. 787), D. Brun (30c. No. 788), H. Thöni (50c.), H. Hartmann (80c.) Photo Courvoisier)

1970 (26 Feb). *Publicity Issue. T* **187** *and similar horiz designs. Multicoloured.* P 11½.
786	20c. Type **187**		20	10
787	30c. Fireman saving child		45	10
788	30c. "Chained wing" emblem		30	10
789	50c. U.N. emblem		50	25
790	80c. New U.P.U. Headquarters		90	95
786/790	Set of 5		2·10	1·40

Events:—20c. 75th anniv of Swiss Telegraphic Agency; 30c. (No. 787) Centenary of Swiss Firemen's Assocation; 30c. (No. 788) 50th anniv of "Pro Infirmis" Foundation; 50c. 25th anniv of United Nations Organization; 80c. inauguration of new Universal Postal Union headquarters, Berne.

(Des L. le Brocquy, adapted P. Kräuchi. Eng A. Yersin. Recess PTT, Berne)

1970 (4 May). *Europa.* P 11½.
791	**188**	30c. red	30	10
792		50c. new blue	55	25

(Des C. Piatti. Photo Courvoisier)

1970 (29 May). *Pro Patria. For National Day Collection. Vert designs similar to T* **184***, but showing glass by contemporary artists and Inscr "1970". Multicoloured.* P 11½.
793	10c.+10c. "Sailor" (G. Casty)		10	15
794	20c.+10c. Architectonic composition (C. Piatti)		25	15
795	30c.+10c. "Bull", symbol of Marduk, from "The Four Elements" (H. Stocker)		35	15
796	50c.+20c. "Man and Woman" (M. Hunziker & K. Ganz)		55	45
793/796	Set of 4		1·10	80

189 Footballer (75th Anniv of Swiss Football Association)

190 Numeral

(Des B. Schorderet (10c.), H. Burgin (20c.), A. Diggelmann (30c.), J. Mauerhofer (50c.) Photo Courvoisier)

1970 (17 Sept). *Publicity and "Swiss Alps" (30c.) Issue. T* **189** *and similar horiz designs. Multicoloured.* P 11½.
797	10c. Type **189**		25	10
798	20c. Census form and pencil (Federal Census)		20	10
799	30c. Piz Palu, Grisons		35	10
800	50c. Conservation Year Emblem (Nature Conservation Year)		45	35
797/800	Set of 4		1·10	60

(Des A. Hofmann. Eng M. Muller. Recess PTT, Berne)

1970 (17 Sept). *Coil Stamps.* P 11½.
801	**190**	10c. carmine	10	10
802		20c. bronze-green	25	10
803		50c. bright blue	55	30

These stamps were also available in sheets of 50 from philatelic sales counters. All stamps in such sheets, and every fifth stamp in the coils, bear control numbers on the reverse, at first this number was in the colour of the stamp but from 1987 the 10 and 50c. were issued with black numbers. The 50c. exists on both phosphorescent (coloured numbers) and fluorescent (black numbers) paper, unnumbered stamps can only be distinguished under a U.V. lamp. The 10 and 20c. values were issued on phosphorescent paper only.

191 Female Gymnasts ("Youth and Sport")

192 "Rayon I" Stamp of 1850

(Des A. Diggelmann (Nos. 804/5), H. Bauer (20c.), H. Hartmann (50c.), A. Flückiger (others). Photo Courvoisier)

1971 (11 Mar). *Publicity Issue. T* **191** *and similar horiz designs.* P 11½.
804	10c. multicoloured		20	25
	a. Pair Nos. 804/5		50	50
805	10c. multicoloured		20	25
806	20c. multicoloured		25	10
807	30c. multicoloured		30	10
808	50c. ochre and royal blue		50	25
809	80c. multicoloured		85	65
804/809	Set of 6		2·10	1·40

Designs and events:—10c. (No. 804) Type **191**, (No. 805) Male athletes ("Youth and Sport" constitutional amendment); 20c. Stylized rose (child welfare); 30c. "Rayon II" stamp of 1850 and basilisk ("NABA" Philatelic Exhibition, Basel); 50c. "Co-operation" symbol (aid for technical development); 80c. "Intelsat 4" (International Telecommunications Union Space Conference).
Nos. 804/5 were issued together in *se-tenant* pairs within the sheet.

(Des E. Schnell Typo PTT, Berne)

1971 (11 Mar). *"NABA 1971" Stamp Exhibition. Basel Sheet* 61 × 75 mm. *Imperf.*
MS810	**192** 50c. × 4 red black and blue (sold at 3f.)		1·80	1·70

Issued with tri-lingual inscription on the reverse.

193 Europa Chain

194 "Telecommunication Services" (50th Anniv of Radio-Suisse)

(Des H. Haflidason, adapted W. Muhlemann. Eng A. Yersin. Recess PTT, Berne)

1971 (3 May). *Europa.* P 11½.
811	**193**	30c. orange-yellow and magenta	30	10
812		50c. orange-yellow and new blue	50	20

(Des C. Piatti. Photo Courvoisier)

1971 (27 May). *Pro Patria. For National Day Collection. Vert designs similar to T* **184***, but showing glass by contemporary artists and inscr "1971". Multicoloured.* P 11½.
813	10c.+10c. "Religious Abstract" (J.-F. Comment)		10	10
814	20c.+10c. "Cockerel" (J. Prahin)		25	15
815	30c.+10c. "Fox" (K. Volk)		35	15
816	50c.+20c. Christ's Passion" (B. Schorderet)		60	55
813/816	Set of 4		1·20	85

SWITZERLAND Switzerland 1971

(Des E. Hauri (30c.) H. Thöni (40c.). Photo Courvoisier)

1971 (23 Sept). *Publicity and "Swiss Alps" (30c.) Issue.* T **194** and similar horiz design. P 11½.
817   30c. plum, blue-grey and mauve   35   10
818   40c. multicoloured   40   35
Design:—30c. Les Diablerets, Vaud.

195 Alexandre Yersin (bacteriologist)
196 Warning Triangle and Wrench (75th Anniv of Motoring Organizations) 

(Des G. Humair. Eng M. Muller. Recess PTT, Berne)

1971 (23 Sept). *Famous Physicians.* T **195** and similar horiz portraits. P 11½.
819   10c. deep olive   10   10
820   20c. blue green   20   10
821   30c. carmine red   30   10
822   40c. new blue   45   45
823   80c. purple   80   80
819/823 Set of 5   1·70   1·40
Portraits:—20c. Auguste Forel (psychiatrist); 30c. Jules Gonin (ophthalmologist); 40c. Robert Koch (German bacteriologist); 80c. Frederick Banting (Canadian physiologist).

(Des H. Lauterburg (10c.), H. Auchli (20c.), R. Hirter (30c.), C. Piatti (40c.). Photo Courvoisier)

1972 (17 Feb). *Publicity Issue.* T **196** and similar horiz designs. P 11½.
824   10c. multicoloured   10   10
825   20c. multicoloured   25   10
826   30c. yellow-orange, orge-red & carm-red   30   10
827   40c. reddish violet, green and new blue   50   30
824/827 Set of 4   1·00   55
Designs and events:—20c. Signal-box switch-table (125th Anniversary of Swiss Railways); 30c. Stylized radio waves and girl's face (50th anniv of Swiss Broadcasting); 40c. Symbolic tree (50th "Swiss Citizens Abroad" Congress).

197 Swissair Boeing 747-100 Jetliner
198 "Communications" 

(Des B. Waltenspul. Photo Courvoisier)

1972 (17 Feb). *AIR. Pro Aero Foundation and 50th Annivs of North Atlantic and International Airmail Services.* P 11½.
828   **197**   2f.+1f. multicoloured   2·50   1·90
Issued for compulsory use on the special Geneva–New York and Geneva–Zurich–Nurnberg flights. The stamp could also be used for other mail.

(Des P. Huovinen and C. Piatti. Photo Courvoisier)

1972 (2 May). *Europa.* P 11½.
829   **198**   30c. multicoloured   30   10
830   40c. multicoloured   45   20

199 Late Stone Age Harpoon Heads
200 Civil Defence Emblem 

(Des E. and M. Lenz. Photo Courvoisier)

1972 (1 June). *Pro Patria. For National Day Collection. Archaeological Discoveries (1st series).* T **199** and similar vert designs. Multicoloured. P 11½.
831   10c.+10c. Type **199**   20   15
832   20c.+10c. Bronze water vessel, c 570 B.C.   35   15
833   30c.+10c. Gold Bust of Marcus Aurelius, 2nd-cent A.D.   50   20
834   40c.+20c. Alemannic disc, 7th cent A.D.   55   65
831/834 Set of 4   1·40   1·00
See also Nos. 869/72, 887/90 and 901/4.

(Des J. Mauerhofer (10c.), E. Hauri (20c.), R. Gerbig (30c.), M. Hunziker and C. Piatti (40c.) Photo Courvoisier)

1972 (21 Sept). *Publicity and "Swiss Alps" (20c.) issue.* T **200** and similar horiz designs. Multicoloured. P 11½.
835   10c. Type **200**   10   10
836   20c. Spannörter   30   15
837   30c. Sud Aviation Alouette III rescue helicopter   40   10
838   40c. The "Four Elements" (53 × 31 mm)   45   30
835/838 Set of 4   1·10   60
Subjects:—10c. Swiss Civil Defence; 20c. Tourism; 30c. Swiss Air Rescue Service; 40c. Protection of the environment.

201 Alberto Giacometti (painter)
202 Dish Aerial 

(Des H. Erni. Eng K. A. Bickel. Recess & photo PTT, Berne)

1972 (21 Sept). *Swiss Celebrities.* T **201** and similar vert portraits. P 11½.
839   10c. black and buff   10   10
840   20c. black and pale bistre   25   10
841   30c. black and pink   30   10
842   40c. black and pale blue   45   25
843   80c. black and pale reddish purple   50   50
839/843 Set of 5   1·70   1·20
Portraits:—20c. Charles Ramuz (novelist); 30c. Le Corbusier (architect); 40c. Albert Einstein (physicist); 80c. Arthur Honegger (composer).

(Des H. Thöni (15c.); E. and M. Lenz (30c.); J. Mauerhofer (40c.). Photo Courvoisier)

1973 (15 Feb). *Publicity Issue.* T **202** and similar horiz designs. Multicoloured. P 11½.
844   15c. Type **202**   20   20
845   30c. Quill pen   30   10
846   40c. Interpol emblem   45   25
Events:—15c. Construction of Satellite Earth Station, Leuk-Brentjong; 30c. Centenary of Swiss Association of Commercial Employees; 40c. 50th anniversary of International Criminal Police Organization (Interpol).

355

SWITZERLAND Switzerland 1973

203 Sottoceneri

204 Toggenburg Inn Sign

(Des H. Wetli (Nos. 847/857). H. Hartmann (others). Eng H. Heusser (Nos. 847, 849/51, 854), P. Schopfer (848, 853, 855/7) K. Bickel, jun (852, 866a), M. Muller (866b), A. Yersin (others). Recess and photo (Nos. 847/857) or recess PTT. Berne)

1973 (15 Feb)—80. *Phosphorescent paper.* P 11½.

(a) T **203** *and similar vert designs. Fibre-less paper.*
847	5c. blue and yellow-ochre (30.8.73)	10	10
848	10c. bronze-grn & bright pur (30.8.73)	10	10
849	15c. ultramarine and salmon (30.8.73)	20	10
850	25c. bluish violet & bright grn (30.8.73)	25	20
851	30c. deep violet and red (30.8.73)	30	10
852	35c. bluish violet & red-orge (27.11.75)	50	30
853	40c. deep greenish grey and new blue (30.8.73)	40	10
854	50c. deep green and light orange	50	10
855	60c. yellow-brown and grey (30.8.73)	65	10
856	70c. myrtle-grn & dull pur (30.8.73)	75	10
857	80c. rose-red & bright emer (30.8.73)	85	15

(b) T **204** *and similar horiz designs. Fibre-less paper (3f., 3f.50) or paper with fibres (others).*
858	1f. deep purple (19.9.74)	1·10	10
	a. Fibre-less paper (24.8.78)	1·20	25
859	1f.10, deep green-blue (27.11.75)	1·20	15
860	1f.20, rose-red (19.9.74)	1·30	1·00
861	1f.30, yellow-orange	1·60	25
862	1f.50, emerald (19.9.74)	1·70	15
863	1f.70, slate	1·90	40
864	1f.80, orange-red	2·00	20
865	2f. blue (19.9.74)	2·20	20
	a. Fibre-less paper (24.8.78)	2·75	35
866	2f.50, light brown (11.9.75)	3·25	40
866a	3f. brown-lake (6.9.79)	3·75	70
866b	3f.50, deep olive (21.2.80)	3·00	25
847/866b	Set of 22 (*cheapest*)	24·00	4·75

Designs:—*Vert*—10c. Grisons; 15c. Central Switzerland; 25c. Jura; 30c. Simmental; 35c. Houses, Central Switzerland; 40c. Vaud; 50c. Valais; 60c. Engadine; 70c. Sopraceneri; 80c. Eastern Switzerland. *Horiz*—1f. Rose window, Lausanne Cathedral; 1f.10, Gallus portal, Basel Cathedral; 1f.20, Romanesque capital, St-Jean-Baptiste Church, Grandson; 1f.50, Medallion, St. Georgen Monastery, Stein am Rhein; 1f.70, Roman Capital, Jean-Baptiste Church, Grandson; 1f.80, Gargoyle, Berne Cathedral; 2f. Oriel, Schaffhausen; 2f.50, Weathercock, St. Ursus Cathedral, Solothurn; 3f. Font, St. Maurice Church, Saanen; 3f.50, Astronomical clock, Berne.

The 2f.50 was issued on non-phosphorescent paper with violet fibres in 1984.

205 Europa "Posthorn"

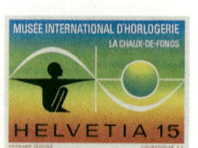

206 Horological Emblem

(Des L. F. Anisdahl. Eng K. A. Bickel. Recess PTT, Berne)

1973 (30 Apr). *Europa.* P 11½.
867	**205**	25c. yellow and lake	30	25
868		40c. yellow and ultramarine	40	20

(Des E. and M. Lenz. Photo Courvoisier)

1973 (29 May). *Pro Patria. For National Day Collection. Archaeological Discoveries (2nd series).* Designs as T **199**, but horiz. Multicoloured. P 11½.
869	15c.+5c. Rauraric jar	25	25
870	30c.+10c. Head of a Gaul (bronze)	40	15
871	40c.+20c. Almannic "Fish" brooches	65	65
872	60c.+20c. Gold bowl	1·00	95
869/872	Set of 4	2·10	1·80

(Des B. Jéquier (15c.), L. Grendene (30c.), P. Ferret (40c.). Photo Courvoisier)

1973 (30 Aug). *Publicity Issue.* T **206** *and similar horiz designs. Multicoloured.* P 11½.
873	15c. Type **206**	20	20
874	30c. Skiing emblem	30	10
875	40c. Face of child	40	20

Subjects:—15c. Inauguration of International Horological Museum, Neuchatel (1974); 30c. World Alpine Skiing Championships, St. Moritz (1974); 40c. "Terre des Hommes" (Child-care organisation).

207 Global Hostels

208 Cantonal Messenger (Basel)

(Des C. Piatti (15c.), H. Schelbert (30c.), H. Bürgin (40c.). Photo Courvoisier)

1974 (29 Jan). *Publicity Issue.* T **207** *and similar horiz designs. Multicoloured.* P 11½.
876	15c. Type **207**	15	10
877	30c. Gymnast and hurdlers	30	10
878	40c. Pistol and target	40	25

Subjects:—15c. "50 Years of Swiss Youth Hostels"; 30c. Centenary of Swiss Workmen's Gymnastics and Sports Association (S.A.T.U.S.); 40c. World Shooting Championships, 1974.

(Des F. Boscovits. Photo Courvoisier)

1974 (29 Jan). *"Internaba 1974" Stamp Exhibition, Basel. Sheet 83 × 73 mm containing T **208** and similar vert designs, showing cantonal messengers. Multicoloured.* P 11½.
MS879	30c. Type **208**; 30c. Zug; 60c. Uri; 80c. Schwyz (sold at 3f.)	3·75	4·25

209 "Continuity" (Max Bill)

210 Eugene Borel (first Director of International Bureau U.P.U.)

(Des M. Bill. Photo Courvoisier)

1974 (28 Mar). *Europa. Swiss Sculptures.* T **209** *and similar vert design.* P 11½.
880	30c. black and red	30	10
881	40c. brown, blue and black	45	35

Design:—40c. "Amazone" (Carl Burckhardt).

SWITZERLAND Switzerland 1974

(Des E. Kassner. Eng M. Müller. Recess and photo PTT, Berne)

1974 (28 Mar). *Centenary of Universal Postal Union. T* **210** *and similar vert portraits.* P 11½.
882	30c. black and pink		30	15
883	40c. black and light grey		45	25
884	80c. black and pale yellow-green		85	75

Portraits:—40c. Heinrich von Stephan (founder of U.P.U.); 80c. Montgomery Blair (U.S. Postmaster-General and initiator of 1863 Paris Postal Conference).

211 View of Berne

212 "Oath of Allegiance" (sculpture) (W. Witschi) (Centenary of Federal Constitution)

(Des F. Witzig. Photo Courvoisier)

1974 (28 Mar). *17th Universal Postal Union Congress, Lausanne. T* **211** *and similar horiz design. Multicoloured.* P 11½.
885	30c. Type **211**		30	20
	a. Pair Nos. 885/6		65	45
886	30c. View of Lausanne		30	20

Nos. 885/6 were issued together in *se-tenant* pairs within the sheet.

(Des E. and M. Lenz. Photo Courvoisier)

1974 (30 May). *Pro Patria. For National Day Collection. Archaeological Discoveries (3rd series). Designs as T* **199**, *but horiz. Multicoloured.* P 11½.
887	15c.+5c. Glass bowl		25	25
888	30c.+10c. Bull's head (bronze)		40	15
889	40c.+20c. Gold brooch		65	60
890	60c.+20c. "Bird" vessel (clay)		95	90
887/890 Set of 4			2·00	1·70

(Des H. Hartmann (No. 891), H. Scheller (892), E. Bosshart (893). Photo Courvoisier)

1974 (19 Sept). *Publicity Issue. T* **212** *and similar horiz designs.* P 11½.
891	15c. deep brown-olive, yell-ol & lilac		20	15
892	30c. multicoloured		30	10
893	30c. multicoloured		30	10

Designs:—No. 892, Foundation emblem (Aid for Swiss Sports Foundation): 893, Posthorn and "postal transit" arrow (125th anniv of Federal Posts).

No. 893 was issued on fibre-less paper.

213 "Metre" and Krypton Line (Centenary of Metre Convention)

214 "The Mönch" (F. Hodler)

(Des R. Hirter (15c.), H. Erni (30c.), H. Hartmann (60c.), B. Waltenspül (90c.). Photo Courvoisier)

1975 (13 Feb). *Publicity Issue. T* **213** *and similar horiz designs. Fibre-less paper.* P 11½.
894	15c. orange, ultramarine & deep green		20	25
895	30c. red-brown, claret and yellow		30	10
896	60c. vermilion, black and bright blue		60	40
897	90c. multicoloured		1·00	70
894/897 Set of 4			1·90	1·30

Designs:—30c. Heads of women (International Women's Year); 60c. Red Cross flag and barbed-wire (Humanitarian International Law Conference, Geneva); 90c. Astra airship *Ville de Lucerne* ("Aviation and Space Travel" exhibition, Transport and Communications Museum, Lucerne).

(Des H. Kümpel. Photo Courvoisier)

1975 (28 Apr). *Europa Paintings T* **214** *and similar vert designs. Multicoloured. Fibre-less paper.* P 12 × 11½.
898	30c. Type **214**		35	15
899	50c. "Still Life with Guitar" (R. Auberjonois)		55	40
900	60c. "L'effeuilleuse" (M. Barraud)		70	50

(Des E. and M. Lenz. Photo Courvoisier)

1975 (30 May). *Pro Patria. Archaeological Discoveries (4th series). Vert designs as T* **199**. *Multicoloured. Fibre-less paper.* P 11½.
901	15c.+10c. Gold brooch, Oron-le-Châtel		25	25
902	30c.+20c. Bacchus (bronze statuette), Avenches		45	25
903	50c.+20c. Bronze daggers, Bois-de-Vaux, Lausanne		70	80
904	60c.+25c. Coloured glass decanter, Maralto		85	75
901/904 Set of 4			2·00	1·80

215 Disabled Person in Wheelchair being dragged up Steps ("Eliminate Obstacles!")

216 Forest Scene (Centenary of Federal Forest Laws)

(Des C. Piatti (15c.), W. Beutter (30c.), P. Besson (50c.), Courvoisier (60c.). Photo Courvoisier)

1975 (11 Sept). *Publicity Issue. T* **215** *and similar horiz designs. Fibre-less paper.* P 11½.
905	15c. black, bright green and lilac		20	20
906	30c. black, rosine and orange-red		30	10
907	50c. reddish brown and yellow-bistre		60	45
908	60c. multicoloured		70	40
905/908 Set of 4			1·60	1·10

Designs:—30c. Organisation emblem (Interconfessional Pastoral care by Telephone Organisation); 50c. E.A.H.Y. emblem (European Architectural Heritage Year); 60c. Beat Fischer von Reichenbach (founder) (300th anniv of Fischer postal service).

(Des A. Rosselet (No. 909), B. Kühne (910). C. Piatti (911), A. Cserno and J.-J Chevalley (912). Recess PTT, Berne (912) Photo Courvoisier (others))

1976 (12 Feb). *Publicity Issue. T* **216** *and similar horiz designs.* P 11½.
909	20c. multicoloured		20	20
910	40c. multicoloured		40	20
911	40c. black, salmon and claret		40	20
912	80c. black and pale blue		85	75
909/912 Set of 4			1·70	1·20

Designs:—No. 910, Fruit and vegetables (campaign to promote nutriments as opposed to alcohol); 911, African child (fight against leprosy); 912, Early and modern telephones (telephone centenary).

Nos. 909/11 were issued on fibre-less paper.

SWITZERLAND Switzerland   1976

217 Floral Embroidery
218 Kyburg Castle, Zurich 
221 Blue Cross (Centenary of Swiss Blue Cross (society for care of alcoholics))
222 St. Ursanne

(Des H. Hartmann. Eng M. Müller. Recess PTT, Berne)

1976 (3 May). *Europa. Handicrafts.* T **217** *and similar vert design.* P 11½.
913	40c. yellow, red-brown and pink		40	15
914	80c. blue, rose-red and yellow-ochre		80	55

Design:—80c. Decorated pocket watch.
No. 914 was issued on fibre-less paper.

(Des C. Mojonnet (20c.). Bornand, Gaeng and Monod (40c.), D. Froidevaux (80c.). Photo Courvoisier)

1977 (27 Jan). *Publicity Issue.* T **221** *and similar horiz designs.* P 11½.
927	20c. blue and grey-brown		20	15
928	40c. multicoloured		40	10
929	80c. multicoloured		80	55

Designs:—40c. Festival emblem (Vevey vintage festival); 80c. Balloons carrying letters ("Juphilex 1977" youth stamp exhibition, Berne).

(Des A. Oertle. Photo Courvoisier)

1976 (28 May). *Pro Patria. Swiss Castles (1st series).* T **218** *and similar horiz designs. Multicoloured. Fibre-less paper.* P 11½.
915	20c.+10c. Type **218**		30	30
916	40c.+20c. Grandson castle, Vaud		60	25
917	40c.+20c. Murten castle. Fribourg		60	35
918	80c.+40c. Bellinzona castle, Ticino		1·40	1·50
915/918	Set of 4		2·75	2·20

See also Nos. 932/5, 955/8 and 977/80.

(Des and eng K. Oberli (40c.), K. Bickel, jun (80c.), Recess and photo PTT, Berne)

1977 (2 May). *Europa. Landscapes.* T **222** *and similar horiz design. Multicoloured.* P 11½.
930	40c. Type **222**		40	15
931	80c. Sils-Baselgia		80	60

(Des A. Oertle. Photo Courvoisier)

1977 (23 May). *Pro Patria. Swiss Castles (2nd series). Horiz designs as* T **218**. *Multicoloured.* P 11½.
932	20c.+10c. Aigle, Vaud		30	30
933	40c.+20c. Pratteln, Basel-Landschaft		55	25
934	70c.+30c. Sargans, St. Gallen		90	1·00
935	80c.+40c. Hallwil, Aargau		1·10	1·10
932/935	Set of 4		2·50	2·40

219 Roe Deer Fawn, Frog and Barn Swallow (World Federation for Protection of Animals)
220 Oskar Bider and Blériot XI 

(Des P. Bergmaier (No. 919), U. Knoblauch (920), E. Hauri (921), W. Haettenschweiler (922). Photo Courvoisier)

1976 (16 Sept). *Publicity Issue.* T **219** *and similar horiz designs. Fibre-less paper.* P 11½.
919	20c. black, deep brown & yellow-green		25	25
920	40c. black, yellow and rosine		45	15
921	40c. multicoloured		45	15
922	80c. rosine, deep violet and blue		90	55
919/922	Set of 4		1·80	1·00

Designs:—No. 920, "Sun" and inscription ("Save Energy" campaign); 921. St. Gotthard mountains (Swiss Alps); 922, Skater (World Speed Skating Championships, Davos).

223 Factory Worker
224 Sternsingen, Bergün

(Des R. Hirter (20c.), W. Muhlemann (40c.), H. Bürgin (80c.). Photo Courvoisier)

1977 (25 Aug). *Publicity Issue.* T **223** *and similar horiz designs. Multicoloured.* P 11½.
936	20c. Type **223**		20	20
937	40c. Ionic capital		40	15
938	80c. Association emblem and butterfly		85	55

Subjects:—20c. Centenary of Federal Factories Act; 40c. Protection of cultural monuments; 80c. Swiss Footpaths Association.

(Des K. Wirth. Eng K. Bickel, jun. Recess PTT, Berne)

1977 (27 Jan). *Swiss Aviation Pioneers.* T **220** *and similar horiz designs.* P 11½.
923	40c. black, magenta and red		45	15
924	80c. black, deep reddish pur & new bl		80	60
925	100c. black, grey-olive and bistre		1·00	80
926	150c. black, brown and blue-green		1·50	1·40
923/926	Set of 4		3·25	2·50

Designs:—80c. Eduard Spelterini and balloon basket; 100c. Armand Dufaux and Dufaux IV biplane; 150c. Walter Mittelholzer and Dormer Do-B Merkur seaplane *Switzerland*.

(Des S. Moser. Eng H. Heusser (30, 40, 70, 90c.); P. Schopfer (others). Recess PTT, Berne)

1977 (25 Aug)–**84**. *Regional Folk Customs.* T **224** *and similar horiz designs.* P 11½.
939	5c. deep blue-green		10	10
	a. Perf two or three sides. Booklets (1.2.84)		95	70
	ab. Booklet pane. No. 939a × 4		4·00	
940	10c. red		10	10
	a. Perf two sides. Booklets (5.1.79)		70	70
	ab. Booklet pane. No. 940a × 2 plus two labels (5.1.79)		1·40	
	ac. Booklet pane. No. 940a × 4 (1.2.84)		2·80	

PHOSPHORESCENT PAPER. *All stamps from No. 927 are printed on phosphorescent, fibre-less paper, unless otherwise stated.*

SWITZERLAND Switzerland 1977

941	20c. red-orange	20	10
	a. Perf two or three sides. Booklets (5.1.79)	35	30
	ab. Booklet pane. No. 941a × 4 (5.1.79)	1·40	
941b	25c. reddish brown (11.9.84)	40	25
941c	30c. emerald (25.11.82)	35	15
942	35c. deep olive	45	20
	a. Perf two or three sides. Booklets (1.2.84)	1·50	1·20
	ab. Booklet pane. No 942a × 4 (1.2.84)	1·40	
943	40c. deep claret	50	10
	a. Perf two or three sides. Booklets (5.1.79)	55	50
	ab. Booklet pane. No 943a × 4 (5.1.79)	1·40	
	b. Granite paper (24.8.78)	85	65
943c	45c. indigo (11.9.84)	65	50
944	50c. brown-red	55	10
	a. Perf two or three sides Booklets (1.2.84)	1·10	95
	ab. Booklet pane. No. 944a × 4 (1.2.84)	4·50	
	ac. Booklet pane. No. 944a × 2 plus two labels (1.2.84)	2·20	
944b	60c. sepia (11.9.84)	80	55
945	70c. deep rose-lilac	80	10
946	80c. Prussian blue	95	25
947	90c. purple-brown	1·00	30
939/947	Set of 13	6·25	2·75

Designs:—10c. Sechseläuten, Zurich; 20c. Silvesterkläuse, Herisau; 25c. Chesstete, Solothurn; 30c. Röllelibutzen, Alstätten; 35c. Gansabhauet, Sursee; 40c. Escalade, Geneva; 45c. Klausjagen, Küssnacht; 50c. Achetringele, Laupen; 60c. Schnabelgeissen, Offenbach; 70c. Processions storiche, Mendrisio; 80c. Vogel Gryff, Basel; 90c. Roitschäggätä, Lötschental.

The booklet panes have their outer three edges imperforate, giving stamps with one or two adjacent sides imperf.

40c. printed in litho is a forgery.

225 Mailcoach Route Plate, Vaud Canton

226 *La Suisse*, Lake Geneva

(Des E. Witzig (20c.), A. Flückiger (40c.), A. M. Petitmaitre (70c.), J. Hägeli (80c.) Photo Courvoisier)

1978 (9 Mar). *Publicity Issue. T 225 and similar horiz designs. Multicoloured. P 11½.*

948	20c. Type 225	25	10
949	40c. View of Lucerne	40	10
950	70c. Title page of book *Mélusine*	75	60
951	80c. Stylised camera and lens	85	60
948/951	Set of 4	2·20	1·30

Events:—20c. "Lemanex 78" National Stamp Exhibition; 40c. 800th Anniv of Lucerne; 70c. 500th Anniv of Printing in Geneva; 80c. Second International Triennial Exhibition of Photography, Fribourg.

(Des C. Piatti. Photo Courvoisier)

1978 (9 Mar). *"Lemanex 78" National Stamp Exhibition, Lausanne. Sheet 133 × 149 mm containing T 226 and similar horiz designs, showing lake steamers, with 4 labels. Multicoloured. P 11½.*

MS952	20c. Type **226**; 20c. *Il Verbano*; 40c. *Gotthard*; 40c. *Ville de Neuchâtel*; 40c. *Romanshorn*; 40c. *Le Winkelried*; 70c. *Loetschberg*; 80c. *Waedenswil* (sold at 5f.)	4·50	4·75

227 Stockalper Palace, Brig

228 Abbé Joseph Bovet (composer)

(Des K. Oberli. Eng M. Müller. Recess and photo PTT. Berne)

1978 (2 May). *Europa. T 227 and similar horiz design. P 11½.*

953	40c. multicoloured	45	10
954	80c. cobalt, yellow-brown and black	90	60

Design:—80c. Old Diet Hall, Berne.

(Des A. Oertle. Photo Courvoisier)

1978 (26 May). *Pro Patria. Swiss Castles (3rd series). Horiz designs as T 218. Multicoloured. P 11½.*

955	20c.+10c. Hagenwil, Thurgau	35	30
956	40c.+20c. Bergdorf, Berne	50	20
957	70c.+30c. Tarasp, Graubünden	1·00	1·10
958	80c.+40c. Chilton, Vaud	1·30	1·30
955/958	Set of 4	2·75	2·50

(Des M. Boegli Eng K. Bickel, jun. Recess PTT, Berne)

1978 (14 Sept). *Celebrities. T 228 and similar vert designs. P 11½.*

959	20c. dull green	25	15
960	40c. brown-purple	45	10
961	70c. olive-grey	75	55
962	80c. grey-blue	85	55
959/962	Set of 4	2·10	1·20

Designs:—40c. Henri Dunant (founder of Red Cross); 70c. Carl Gustav Jung (psychiatrist); 80c. Auguste Piccard (physicist).

229 Worker wearing Goggles

230 Arms of Switzerland and Jura

(Des B. Mäder. Photo Courvoisier)

1978 (14 Sept). *Safety at Work. T 229 and similar horiz designs. Multicoloured. P 11½.*

963	40c. Type **229**	45	20
	a. Strip of 3 Nos. 963/5	1·40	
964	40c. Worker wearing respirator	45	20
965	40c. Worker wearing safety helmet	45	20

Nos. 963/5 were issued together in *se-tenant* strips of three within the sheet.

(Des and photo Courvoisier)

1978 (25 Sept). *Creation of Canton of Jura. P 11½.*

966	**230** 40c. bright scarlet, black & yellow-ochre	45	10

359

SWITZERLAND Switzerland   1979

231 Rainer Maria Rilke (writer)

232 Othmar H. Ammann and Verrazano Narrows Bridge

(Des H. Erni. Eng P. Schopfer. Recess PTT, Berne)

1979 (21 Feb). *Celebrities. T* **231** *and similar vert designs.* P 11½.
967	20c. deep dull green	25	15
968	40c. red	45	10
969	70c. red-brown	75	55
970	80c. Prussian blue	85	55
967/970	Set of 4	2·10	1·20

Designs:—40c. Paul Klee (artist), 70c. Herman Hesse (novelist and poet); 80c. Thomas Mann (novelist).

(Des H. Thöni (20c.), W. Haettenschweiler (40c.), K. Wirth (70c.), H. Burgin (80c.). Photo Courvorsier)

1979 (21 Feb). *Publicity Issue. T* **232** *and similar horiz designs. Multicoloured.* P 11½.
971	20c. Type **232**	20	15
972	40c. Target and marker	45	10
973	70c. Hot-air balloon *Esperanto*	75	60
974	80c. Aircraft tail fins	85	55
971/974	Set of 4	2·00	1·30

Subjects:—20c. Birth centenary of O.H. Ammann (engineer); 40c. 50th Federal Riflemen's Festival, Lucerne; 70c. World Esperanto Congress, Lucerne; 80c. Basel-Mulhouse Airport.

233 Old Letter Box, Basel

234 Gold Stater

(Des K. Oberli. Eng M. Müller. Recess and photo PTT, Berne)

1979 (30 Apr). *Europa. T* **233** *and similar vert design.* P 11½.
975	40c. multicoloured	45	15
976	80c. deep grey-blue, pale blue & yellow-ochre	85	65

Design:—80c. Alpine relay station on Jungfrauloch.

(Des A. Oertle. Photo Courvoisier)

1979 (25 May). *Pro Patria. Swiss Castles (4th series). Horiz designs as T* **218**. *Multicoloured.* P 11½.
977	20c.+10c. Oron, Vaud	30	30
978	40c.+20c. Spiez, Berne	50	25
979	70c.+30c. Porrentruy, Jura	80	95
980	80c.+40c. Rapperswil, St. Gallen	1·10	1·20
977/980	Set of 4	2·40	2·40

(Des E. and M. Lenz (20c.), F. Bauer (40c.), R. Gerbig (70c.), H. Auchli (80c.). Photo Courvoisier)

1979 (6 Sept). *Publicity Issue. T* **234** *and similar designs. Multicoloured.* P 11½.
981	20c. Type **234**	25	15
982	40c. Child on a dove (*horiz*)	45	10
983	70c. Morse key and satellite (*horiz*)	75	50
984	80c. "Ariane" rocket	85	50
981/984	Set of 4	2·10	1·10

Subjects:—20c. Centenary of Swiss Numismatic Society; 40c. International Year of the Child; 70c. 50th Anniv of Swiss Radio Amateurs; 80c. European Space Agency.

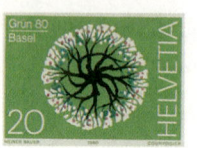

235 Tree in Blossom

236 Johann Konrad Kern (politician)

(Des H. Bauer (20c.), E. and M. Lenz (40c.), A. Flückiger (70c.), J. Ongaro (80c.). Photo Courvoisier)

1980 (21 Feb). *Publicity Issue. T* **235** *and similar horiz designs. Multicoloured.* P 11½.
985	20c. Type **235**	25	10
986	40c. Carved milk vessel	45	10
987	70c. Town Hall, Winterthur	70	55
988	80c. Pic-Pic car	80	60
985/988	Set of 4	2·00	1·20

Subjects:—20c. Horticultural and Landscape Gardening Exhibition, Basel; 40c. 50th anniv of Arts and Crafts Centre; 70c. Centenary of Society for Swiss Art History; 80c. 50th International Motor Show, Geneva.

(Des and eng P. Schopfer. Recess PTT, Berne)

1980 (28 Apr). *Europa. T* **236** *and similar horiz design. Granite paper.* P 11½.
989	40c. flesh black and rose	45	10
990	80c. flesh, black and blue	85	55

Design:—80c. Gustav Adolf Hasler (communications pioneer).

237 Mason and Carpenter

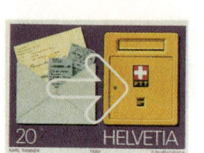

238 Girocheque and Letter Box

(Des P. Schiegg (20, 80c.), G. Rimensberger (others). Photo Courvoisier)

1980 (29 May). *Pro Patria. Trade and Craft Signs. T* **237** *and similar vert designs. Multicoloured.* P 11½.
991	20c.+10c. Type **237**	30	30
992	40c.+20c. Barber	65	30
993	70c.+30c. Hatter	1·00	1·20
994	80c.+40c. Baker	1·20	1·00
991/994	Set of 4	2·75	2·40

(Des A. Flückiger, eng M. Müller; recess and photo PTT Berne (70c). Des K. Tanner; photo Courvoisier (others))

1980 (5 Sept). *Swiss PTT Services. T* **238** *and similar horiz designs.* P 11½.
995	20c. multicoloured	25	20
996	40c. multicoloured	50	10
997	70c. drab, black and lavender	70	50
998	80c. multicoloured	80	55
995/998	Set of 4	2·00	1·20

Designs:—40c. Postbus; 70c. Transfer roller (50th anniv of PTT postage stamp printing office); 80c. Telephone and flowers (Centenary of telephone in Switzerland).

SWITZERLAND Switzerland 1980

239 Weather Chart
240 Granary from Kiesen 

(Des P. Kräuchi (20c.), R. Hirter (40c.), W. Haettenschweiler (80c.). Photo Courvoisier)

1980 (5 Sept). *Publicity Issue. T* **239** *and similar horiz designs. Multicoloured.* P $11\frac{1}{2}$.
999	20c. Type **239** (Centenary of Swiss Meteorological Office)	25	20
1000	40c. Figures and cross (Centenary of Swiss Trade Union Federation)	45	25
1001	80c. Motorway sign (Opening of St. Gotthard road tunnel)	90	85

(Des A. Wittmer (20c.), R. Mösch (40c.), E. Hauri (80c.), K. Wirth (110c.). Photo Courvoisier)

1981 (9 Mar). *Publicity Issue. T* **240** *and similar multicoloured designs.* P $11\frac{1}{2}$.
1002	20c. Type **240** (Ballenberg Open-air Museum)	25	15
1003	40c. Disabled figures (International Year of Disabled Persons)	45	10
1004	70c. "The Parish Clerk" (Albert Anker, 150th birth anniv) (*vert*)	75	65
1005	80c. Theodolite and rod (16th International Federation of Surveyors Congress, Montreux)	80	55
1006	110c. Tail of DC-9-81 (50th anniv of Swissair)	1·10	85
1002/1006 *Set of 5*		3·00	2·10

241 Figure leaping from Earth
242 Dancing Couple 

(Des H. Erni. Photo Courvoisier)

1981 (9 Mar). *AIR. 50th Anniv of Swissair.* P $11\frac{1}{2}$.
1007	**241** 2f.+1f. reddish lilac, deep dull violet and lemon	2·40	2·10

No. 1007, printed in sheets of eight, was for compulsory use on Swissair Jubilee flights to Chicago, Helsinki, Djakarta and Buenos Aires; it was also valid on other mail.

(Des W. Haettenschweiler. Photo Courvoisier)

1981 (4 May). *Europa. T* **242** *and similar vert design. Multicoloured.* P $11\frac{1}{2}$.
1008	40c. Type **242**	45	10
1009	80c. Stone putter	90	60

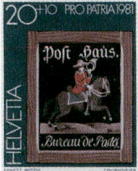

243 Aarburg Post Office Sign, 1685
244 Seal of Fribourg 

(Des E. Witzig. Photo Courvoisier)

1981 (27 May). *Pro Patria. Postal Signs. T* **243** *and similar vert designs. Multicoloured.* P $11\frac{1}{2}$.
1010	20c.+10c. Type **243**	35	40
1011	40c.+20c. Mail coach sign of Fribourg Cantonal Post	65	25
1012	70c.+30c. Gondola post office sign (Ticino Cantonal Post)	1·00	1·30
1013	80c.+40c. Splugen post office sign	1·20	1·10
1010/1013 *Set of 4*		2·75	2·75

(Des E. Witzig. Eng M. Müller (80c.), K. Bickel, jun (others). Recess and photo PTT, Berne)

1981 (3 Sept). *500th Anniv of Covenant of Stans. T* **244** *and similar horiz designs.* P $11\frac{1}{2}$.
1014	40c. brown-red, black & orange-brown	45	15
1015	40c. myrtle-green, black and claret	45	15
1016	40c. reddish brown, black & lt grey-blue	85	60

Designs:—No. 1015, Seal of Solothurn; 1016, Old Town Hall, Stans.

245 Voltage Regulator from Jungfrau Railway's Power Station
246 "C4/5" Class Steam Locomotive 

(Des A. Flückiger (20c.), G. Rimensberger (40c.), K. Baumgartner (70c.), R. Hirter (1f.10). Photo Courvoisier)

1981 (3 Sept). *Publicity Issue. T* **245** *and similar horiz designs. Multicoloured.* P $11\frac{1}{2}$.
1017	20c. Type **245**	25	15
1018	40c. Crossbow quality seal	45	10
1019	70c. Group of young people	75	60
1020	1f.10, Mosaic	1·20	80
1017/1020 *Set of 4*		2·40	1·50

Subjects:—20c. Opening of Technorama of Switzerland, Winterthur (museum of science and technology); 40c. 50th anniv of Organization for Promotion of Swiss Products and Services; 70c. 50th anniv of Swiss Association of Youth Organizations; 1f.10, Restoration of St. Peter's Cathedral, Geneva.

(Des C. Piatti. Photo Courvoisier)

1982 (18 Feb). *Centenary of St. Gotthard Railway. T* **246** *and similar horiz design.* P $11\frac{1}{2}$.
1021	40c. black and reddish purple	45	15
	a. Horiz strip. Nos. 1021/2 plus label	90	30
1022	40c. multicoloured	45	15

Design:—No. 1022, "Re 6/6" class electric locomotive.
Nos. 1021/2 were issued together in sheets of 10 stamps, with *se-tenant* intervening labels showing a detail of the workers' memorial by Vincenzo Vela at Airolo station.

247 Hoteliers Association Emblem
248 "Swearing Oath of Eternal Fealty, Rütli Meadow" (detail of mural, Heinrich Danioth)

SWITZERLAND Switzerland   1982

(Des P. Schiegg (20c.), K. Kaiser (40c.), A. Bovey (70c.), C. Kuhn-Klein (80c.), E. Hauri (110c.). Photo Courvoisier)

1982 (18 Feb). *Publicity Issue.* T **247** *and similar horiz designs. Multicoloured.* P 11½.
1023	20c. Type **247**	25	15
1024	40c. Flag formed from four Fs	45	10
1025	70c. Gas flame encircling emblem	75	55
1026	80c. Lynx and scientific instruments	80	55
1027	110c. Retort	1·10	80
1023/1027	*Set of 5*	3·00	1·90

Subjects:—20c. Centenary of Swiss Hoteliers Association; 40c.150th anniv of Swiss Gymnastic Society; 70c. 50th anniv of International Gas Union; 80c. 150th anniv of Natural History Museum, Berne; 110c. Centenary of Swiss Society of Chemical Industries.

(Des C. Piatti. Photo Courvoisier)

1982 (3 May). *Europa.* T **248** *and similar horiz design. Multicoloured.* P 11½.
1028	40c. Type **248**	45	20
1029	80c. Treaty of 1291 founding Swiss Confederation	85	55

249 "The Sun", Willisau   **250** "Aquarius" and Old Berne

(Des A. Bovey. Photo Courvoisier)

1982 (27 May). *Pro Patria. Inn Signs (1st series). Multicoloured.* P 11½.
1030	20c.+10c. Type **249**	25	30
1031	40c.+20c. "On the Wave", St. Saphorin	65	15
1032	70c.+30c. "The Three Kings", Rheinfelden	85	1·10
1033	80c.+40c. "The Crown", Winterthur	1·00	95
1030/1033	*Set of 4*	2·75	2·50

See also Nos. 1056/9.

(Des E. and M. Lenz. Eng K. Bickel, jun (1f.20, 1f.50, 1f.70, 1f.80, 4f., 4f.50), P. Schopfer (others). Recess and photo PTT, Berne)

1982 (23 Aug)–**86**. *Signs of the Zodiac and Landscapes.* T **250** *and similar vert designs.* P 11½.
1034	1f. multicoloured	1·00	10
1035	1f.10, brown, dull blue and dull violet-blue	1·10	10
1036	1f.20, myrtle green, cobalt and grey-brown	1·30	20
1036a	1f.40, multicoloured (11.2.86)	1·70	1·30
1037	1f.50, deep blue, azure and salmon	1·60	20
1038	1f.60, multicoloured	1·90	85
1039	1f.70, cobalt, brown-ochre and deep turquoise-blue (17.2.83)	1·80	15
1040	1f.80, grey-brown, green and blackish green (17.2.83)	2·10	1·10
1041	2f. cobalt, brown-ochre and deep blue (17.2.83)	2·50	1·80
1042	2f. cobalt, brown-ochre and deep blue (24.11.83)	2·10	30
1042a	2f.50, red, dull green and bronze green (19.2.85)	2·75	50
1043	3f. Indian red, grey-green and greenish black (19.2.85)	3·00	30
1044	4f. bright yellow-green, violet and brown-purple (21.2.84)	4·25	60
1045	4f.50, brown-ochre and chocolate (21.2.84)	4·75	1·20
1034/1045	*Set of 14*	29·00	8·00

Designs:—1f.10, "Pisces" and Nax, near Sion; 1f.20, "Aries" and the Graustock, Obwalden, 1f.40, "Gemini" and Bischofszell; 1f.50, "Taurus" and Basel Cathedral; 1f.60, "Gemini" and Schönengrund; 1f.70, "Cancer" and Wetterhorn; 1f.80, "Leo" and Areuse Gorge; 2f. (1041), "Virgo" and Aletsch Glacier; 2f. (1042), "Virgo" and Schwarzsee above Zermatt; 2f.50, "Libra" and Féchy; 3f. "Scorpio" and Corippo; 4f. "Sagittarius" and Glarus; 4f.50, "Capricorn" and Schuls.

251 Articulated Tram   **252** Eurasian Perch

(Des K. Tanner (20c.), A. Koella (40c.), H. Schelbert (70c.), W. Mühlemann (80c.). Photo Courvoisier)

1982 (23 Aug). *Publicity Issue.* T **251** *and similar horiz designs. Multicoloured.* P 11½.
1046	20c. Type **251**	40	15
1047	40c. Salvation Army singer and guitarist	50	10
1048	70c. Dressage rider	75	65
1049	80c. Emblem	80	60
1046/1049	*Set of 4*	2·20	1·40

Subjects:—20c. Centenary of Zurich trams; 40c. Centenary of Salvation Army in Switzerland; 70c. World Dressage Championship, Lausanne; 80c. 14th Congress of International Water Supply Association, Zurich.

(Des E. Witzig (20c.), E. and M. Lenz (40c.), R. Hirter (70c.), R.-V. Geiser (80c.). Photo Courvoisier)

1983 (17 Feb). *Publicity Issue.* T **252** *and similar horiz designs. Multicoloured.* P 11½.
1050	20c. Type **252**	30	15
1051	40c. University of Zurich	45	10
1052	70c. Teleprinter tape forming "JP"	75	65
1053	80c. Micrometer and cycloidal computer drawing	85	55
1050/1053	*Set of 4*	2·10	1·30

Subjects:—20c. Centenary of Swiss Fishing and Pisciculture Federation; 40c. 150th anniv of University of Zurich; 70c. Centenary of Swiss Journalists' Federation; 80c. Centenary of Swiss Machine Manufacturers' Association.

253 Jost Bürgi's Celestial Globe, 1594   **254** Seal, 1832–48

(Des H. Hartmann. Eng M. Müller. Recess and photo PTT, Berne)

1983 (3 May). *Europa.* T **253** *and similar vert design.* P 11½.
1054	40c. pale orange, rose-pink and purple-brown	45	15
1055	80c. yellowish green, azure and blue-black	90	70

Design:—80c. Niklaus Riggenbach's rack and pinion railway, 1871.

(Des B. Scarton. Photo Courvoisier)

1983 (26 May). *Pro Patria. Inn Signs (2nd series). Horiz designs as* T **249**. *Multicoloured.* P 11½.
1056	20c.+10c. "The Lion", Heimiswil	35	35
1057	40c.+20c. "The Cross", Sachsein	65	20

SWITZERLAND Switzerland   1983

1058	70c.+30c. "The Jug", Lenzburg Castle	1·00	1·20
1059	80c.+40c. "The Cavalier", St. George	1·20	1·10
1056/1059	Set of 4	2·75	2·50

(Des C. Piatti. Photo Courvoisier)

1983 (26 May). *150th Anniv of Basel-Land Canton.* P 11½.
1060 254 40c. multicoloured 45 15

255 Gallo-Roman Capital, Martigny

256 Pre-stamp Cover, 1839

(Des P. Ferret (20c.). Eleonore Schmid (40c.), W. Haettenschweiler (70c.). H.-J. Bolzhauser (80c.). Photo Courvoisier)

1983 (22 Aug). *Publicity Issue.* T **255** and similar horiz designs. P 11½.
1061	20c. pale orange and black	25	15
1062	40c. multicoloured	60	10
1063	70c. multicoloured	85	70
1064	80c. multicoloured	85	55
1061/1064	Set of 4	2·30	1·40

Designs:—20c. Type **255** (2000th anniv of Octodurus/Martigny); 40c. Bernese shepherd-dog and Schwyz hunting dog (Centenary of Swiss Kennel Club); 70c. Cyclists (Centenary of Swiss Cyclists and Motor Cyclists Federation); 80c. Carrier pigeon and world map (World Communications Year).

(Des H.-J. Bolzhauser (25c.), M. Dayer (50c.), L. Pizzotti (80c.). Photo Courvoisier)

1984 (21 Feb). *Publicity Issue.* T **256** and similar horiz designs. Multicoloured. P 11½.
1065	25c. Type **256**	30	20
1066	50c. Collegiate Church clock and buildings	55	15
1067	80c. Olympic rings and Lausanne	1·00	65

Subjects:—25c. National Stamp Exhibition, Zurich; 50c. 1100th anniv of Saint-Imier; 80c. Permanent headquarters of International Olympic Committee at Lausanne.

257 Bridge

258 Hexagonal Stove from Rosenburg Mansion, Stans

(Des J. Larrivière. Photo Courvoisier)

1984 (2 May). *Europa. 25th Anniv of European Posts and Telecommunications Conference.* P 11½.
1068	**257**	50c. bright claret, deep carmine and crimson	60	20
1069		80c. dull ultramarine, deep bright blue and royal blue	95	65

(Des E. Witzig. Photo Courvoisier)

1984 (24 May). *Pro Patria. Tiled Stoves.* T **258** and similar vert designs. Multicoloured. P 11½.
1070	35c.+15c. Type **258**	50	50
1071	50c.+20c. Winterthur stove (by Hans Heinrich Pfau), Freuler Palace, Nafels	70	40

1072	70c.+30c. Box-stove (by Rudolf Stern) from Plaisance, Riaz	95	1·10
1073	80c.+40c. Frame-modelled stove (by Leonard Racle)	1·30	1·20
1070/1073	Set of 4	3·00	2·75

259 Bauschänzli, City Hall and Fraumunster

260 Burning Match

(Des K. Oberli. Photo Courvoisier)

1984 (24 May). *"Naba Züri 84" National Stamp Exhibition, Zurich. Sheet 145 × 70 mm containing T **259** and similar vert designs forming panorama of Zurich. Multicoloured.* P 11½.
MS1074 50c. Type **259**; 50c. St. Peter's; 50c. Town Hall, Helmhaus and Wasser Church; 50c. Cathedral (sold at 3f.) .... 4·25 4·00

(Des E. Hauri. Photo Courvoisier)

1984 (11 Sept). *Fire Prevention.* P 11½.
1075 **260** 50c. multicoloured 55 15

261 Railway Conductor's Equipment

262 Ernest Ansermet (orchestral conductor)

(Des U. Grünig (35c.), A. Wittmer (50c.), K. Wirth (70c.), E. Hauri (80c.)). Photo Courvoisier)

1985 (19 Feb). *Publicity Issue.* T **261** and similar horiz designs. Multicoloured. P 11½.
1076	35c. Type **261** (centenary of Train Staff Association)	65	25
1077	50c. Stone with Latin inscription (2000 years of Rhaeto-Romanic culture)	15	15
1078	70c. Rescue of man (centenary of International Lake Geneva Rescue Society)	80	60
1079	80c. Grande Dixence dam (International Large Dams Congress, Lausanne)	95	65
1076/1079	Set of 4	2·10	1·25

(Des H. Erni. Photo Courvoisier)

1985 (7 May). *Europa. Music Year.* T **262** and similar vert design. Multicoloured. P 11½.
1080	50c. Type **262**	65	20
1081	80c. Frank Martin (composer)	90	75

363

SWITZERLAND Switzerland 1985

263 Music Box, 1895    **264** Baker   **267** Woman's Head   **268** "Bridge in the Sun" (Giovanni Giacometti)

(Des K. Tanner. Photo Courvoisier)

1985 (28 May). *Pro Patria. Musical Instruments.* T **263** and similar horiz designs. Multicoloured. P 11½.
1082	25c.+10c. Type **263**	50	50
1083	35c.+15c. 18th-century box rattle	65	60
1084	50c.+20c. Emmental necked zither (by Peter Zaugg), 1828	80	25
1085	70c.+30c. Drum, 1571	1·10	1·20
1086	80c.+40c. 20th-century diatonic accordion	1·30	1·20
1082/1086	*Set of 5*	4·00	3·25

(Des A. Bovey (50c.), R.-V. Geiser (70c.). W. Wermelinger (80c.). Photo Courvoisier)

1985 (10 Sept). *Publicity Issue.* T **264** and similar horiz designs. Multicoloured. P 11½.
1087	50c. Type **264** (centenary of Swiss Master Bakers' and Confectioners' Federation)	60	15
1088	70c. Cross on abstract background (50th anniv of Swiss Radio International)	80	65
1089	80c. Geometric pattern and emblem (Postal, Telegraph and Telephone International World Congress, Interlaken)	85	60

FLUORESCENT PAPER. All stamps from No. 1090 were printed on fluorescent paper, *unless otherwise stated.*

265 Intertwined Ropes    **266** Sportsmen

(Des R. Naef (35 c), H. Auchli (50c.), E. and M. Lenz (80c.). Harriet Höppner (90c.). F. Bauer (1f.10). Photo Courvoisier)

1986 (11 Feb). *Publicity Issue.* T **265** and similar horiz designs. P 11½.
1090	35c. multicoloured	45	25
1091	50c. deep brown, drab & dull vermilion	35	15
1092	80c. reddish orange, dull green & black	90	65
1093	90c. multicoloured	1·00	65
1094	1f.10, multicoloured	1·20	1·20
1090/1094	*Set of 5*	3·25	2·25

Designs:—35c. Type **265** (50th anniv of Swiss Workers' Relief Organization); 50c. Battle site on 1698 map (600th anniv of Battle of Sempach); 80c. Statuette of Mercury (2000th anniv of Roman Chur); 90c. Gallic head (2000th anniv of Vindonissa); 1f.10, Roman coin of Augustus (2000th anniv of Zurich).

(Des K. Wirth. Photo Courvoisier)

1986 (11 Feb). *Pro Sport.* P 11½.
1095	**266** 50c.+20c. multicoloured	85	65

(Des H. Erni. Eng K. Bickel, jun. Recess and litho PTT, Berne)

1986 (27 May). *Europa.* T **267** and similar vert design. Multicoloured. P 13½.
1096	50c. Type **267**	55	20
1097	90c. Man's head	1·10	75

(Des H.-J. Bolzhauser. Photo Courvoisier)

1986 (27 May). *Pro Patria. Paintings.* T **268** and similar horiz designs. Multicoloured. P 11½.
1098	35c.+15c. Type **268**	60	65
1099	50c.+20c. "The Violet Hat" (Cuno Amiet)	90	25
1100	80c.+40c. "After the Funeral" (Max Buri)	1·40	1·40
1101	90c.+40c. "Still Life" (Félix Vallotton)	1·50	1·30
1098/1101	*Set of 4*	4·00	3·25

269 Franz Mail Van    **270** Stylized Doves (International Peace Year)

(Des K. Oberli Eng P. Schopfer (5, 45 to 60, 80c.), M. Müller (others). Recess and litho PTT, Berne)

1986 (9 Sept)–89. *The Post Past and The Present.* T **269** and similar vert designs. P 13½ × 13.
1102	5c. yellow, dp reddish purple & dp carm	55	15
1103	10c. dp bluish green, blue-grn & salmon	50	10
1104	20c. dull orange, brn & pale bl (10.3.87)	20	15
1105	25c. dp turquoise-bl, greenish bl & yell	55	40
1106	30c. greenish slate, black and lemon (10.3.87)	40	15
1107	35c. lake, rosine and lemon	70	25
1108	45c. pale blue, black & dp brn (10.3.87)	50	30
1109	50c. slate-violet, bright yellow-green and slate-purple (10.3.87)	55	15
	a. Perf 3 sides (8.9.88)	1·10	55
	ab. Booklet pane No. 1109a × 10	11·00	
1110	60c. red-orange, lemon and reddish brown (10.3.87)	65	30
1111	75c. apple green, bronze green and carmine (7.3.89)	85	70
1112	80c. indigo, bright blue and brown	1·50	50
1113	90c. dp olive, yellow-brown & apple grn	1·70	80
1102/1113	*Set of 12*	7·75	3·50

Designs:—10c. Mechanized parcel sorting; 20c. Mule post; 25c. Letter cancelling machine; 30c. Stagecoach; 35c. Post Office counter clerk; 45c. Paddle-steamer *Stadt Luzern*, 1830s; 50c. Postman; 60c. Loading mail bags onto airplane; 75c. 17th-century mounted courier; 80c. Town postman, 1900s; 90c. Interior of railway sorting carriage.

SWITZERLAND Switzerland   1986

The 5, 10, 25, 35, 80 and 90c. were issued on both phosphorescent and fluorescent paper, the other values on fluorescent paper only.
The 25, 35, 80 and 90c. were also issued in coils.

No. 1114 *is vacant.*

(Des Michèle Berri (35c.). A. Flückiger (50c.). P. Baur (80c.), P. Bataillard (90c.) Photo Courvoisier)

1986 (9 Sept). *Publicity Issue. T 270 and similar horiz designs. Multicoloured.* P 11½.

1115	35c. Type **270**	45	40
1116	50c. Sun behind snow-covered tree (50th anniv of Swiss Winter Relief Fund)	55	15
1117	80c. Symbols of literature and art (centenary of Berne Convention for protection of literary and artistic copyright)	1·00	75
1118	90c. Red Cross, Red Crescent and symbols of aggression (25th International Red Cross Conference meeting, Geneva)	95	70
1115/1118 Set of 4		2·75	1·80

271 Mobile Post Office

272 "Scarabaeus" (Bernhard Luginbühl)

(Des K. Tanner (35c.), P. Bataillard (50c.), S. Bundi (80c.), H. Hartmann (90 c.). Michèle Berri (1f.10) Photo Courvoisier)

1987 (10 Mar). *Publicity Issue. T 271 and similar horiz designs. Multicoloured.* P 11½.

1119	35c. Type **271** (50th anniv of mobile post offices)	50	25
1120	50c. Lecturers of the seven faculties (450th anniv of Lausanne University)	55	15
1121	80c. Profile, maple leaf and logarithmic spiral (150th anniv of Swiss Engineers' and Architects' Association)	95	65
1122	90c. Boeing 747-300/400 jetliner and electric train (Geneva Airport rail link)	1·20	75
1123	1f.10, Symbolic figure and water (2000th anniv of Baden thermal springs)	1·30	1·20
1119/1123 Set of 5		4·00	2·75

(Des C. Piatti. Photo Courvoisier)

1987 (26 May). *Europa. Sculpture T 272 and similar horiz design. Multicolored.* P 11½.

1124	50c. Type **272**	55	20
1125	90c. "Carnival Fountain", Basel (Jean Tinguely)	1·20	85

273 Wall Cabinet, 1764

274 Butcher cutting Chops

(Des E. and M. Lenz. Photo Courvoisier)

1987 (26 May). *Pro Patria. Rustic Furniture. T 273 and similar horiz designs. Multicoloured.* P 11½.

1126	35c.+15c. Type **273**	60	65
1127	50c.+20c. 16th-century chest	80	30
1128	80c.+40c. Cradle, 1782	1·40	1·50
1129	90c.+40c. Wardrobe, 1698	1·50	1·40
1126/1129 Set of 4		3·75	3·50

(Des K. Tanner (35c.), Lilian Perrin (50c.). A. Wittmer (90c.). Photo Courvoisier)

1987 (4 Sept). *Publicity Issue. T 274 and similar horiz designs. Multicoloured.* P 11½.

1130	35c. Type **274** (centenary of Swiss Master Butchers' Federation)	45	45
1131	50c. Profiles on stamps (50th anniv of Stamp Day)	60	20
1132	90c. Cheesemaker breaking up curds (centenary of Swiss Dairying Association)	1·00	70

275 Zug Clock Tower   (**276**)

(Des H. Schelbert. Photo Courvoisier)

1987 (4 Sept). *Bicentenary of Tourism. T 275 and similar vert designs. Multicoloured. Phosphorescent paper (**MS**1137) or fluorescent paper (others).* P 11½.

1133	50c. Type **275**	60	15
1134	80c. St. Charles's church, Negrentino, Prugiasco/Blenio valley	90	65
1135	90c. Witches Tower, Sion	1·00	70
1136	1f.40, Jörgenberg Castle, Waltensburg/Vuorz, Surselva	1·60	1·70
1133/1136 Set of 4		3·75	2·75
MS1137 78 × 102 mm. Nos. 1133/6		4·00	4·00

(Optd PTT, Berne)

1987 (7 Sept). *Flood Victims Relief Fund. No.* 1109 *surch with T* **276** *in bright rose.*

1138	50c.+50c. slate-violet, bright yellow-green and slate-purple	1·60	1·00

277 Society Emblem

278 Junkers Ju 52/3m *Auntie Ju* flying past Matterhorn

(Des Bernadette Baltis (25c.). V. Wyss (35c.), H. Paoli (50c.), A. Wittmer (80c.), H. Erni (90c.) Photo Courvoisier)

1988 (8 Mar). *Publicity Issue. T 277 and similar horiz designs. Multicoloured.* P 11½.

1139	25c. Type **277** (centenary of Swiss Women's Benevolent Society)	30	25
1140	35c. Brushing woman's hair (centenary of Swiss Master Hairdressers' Association)	40	40
1141	50c. St. Fridolin banner and detail of Aegidius Tschudy's manuscript (600th anniv of Battle of Naefels)	60	15

365

SWITZERLAND Switzerland   1988

1142	80c. Map and farming country seen from Beromünster radio tower (European Campaign for Rural Areas)		95	75
1143	90c. Girl playing shawm (50th anniv of Lucerne International Music Festival)		1·00	70
1139/1143	Set of 5		3·00	2·00

(Des H. Hartmann. Photo Courvoisier)

1988 (3 Mar). *50th Anniv of Pro Aero Foundation*. P 11½.
1144	278	140c.+60c. multicoloured		2·50	2·50

279 Rudolf von Neuenburg

280 Arrows on Map of Europe

(Des E. and M. Lenz Photo Courvoisier)

1988 (24 May). *Pro Patria. Minnesingers*. T **279** and similar vert designs. Multicoloured. P 11½.
1145	35c.+15c. Type **279**		65	70
1146	50c.+20c. Rudolf von Rotenburg		90	40
1147	80c.+40c. Johannes Hadlaub		1·40	1·40
1148	90c.+40c. Hardegger		1·50	1·50
1145/1148	Set of 4		4·00	3·50

(Des S. Bundi. Photo Courvoisier)

1988 (24 May). *Europa, Transport and Communications*. T **280** and similar vert design. P 11½.
1149	50c. olive-bistre, brt emerald & blue-grn		55	20
1150	90c. rose-lilac, lt green & reddish violet		1·10	70

Design:—90c. Computer circuit on map of Europe.

281 Snap Link

(Des J. Zwyer (35c.), E. and M. Lenz (50c.), B. la Roche (80c.), E. Kellenberger (90c.). Photo Courvoisier)

1988 (13 Sept). *Publicity Issue*. T **281** and similar horiz designs. Multicoloured. P 11½.
1151	35c. Type **281** (50th anniv of Swiss Accident Prevention Office)		45	35
1152	50c. Drilling letters (centenary of Swiss Metalworkers' and Watchmakers' Association)		55	20
1153	80c. Triangulation pyramid, theodolite and map (150th anniv of Swiss Federal Office of Topography)		95	80
1154	90c. International Red Cross Museum, Geneva (inauguration)		1·10	80
1151/1154	Set of 4		2·75	1·90

282 "Meta" (Jean Tinguely)

(Photo French Govt Ptg Wks)

1988 (25 Nov). *Modern Art*. P 13 × 12½.
1155	282	90c. multicoloured		2·75	2·10

283 Army Postman

284 King Friedrich II presenting Berne Town Charter (Bendict Tschachtlan Chronicle)

(Des J. Ongaro (25c.), Bernadette Baltis (35c.), U. Stuber (50c.), H. Inderbitzi (80c.), J.-O. Bercher (90c.) Photo Courvoisier)

1989 (7 Mar). *Publicity Issue*. T **283** and similar horiz designs. Multicoloured. P 11½.
1156	25c. Type **283** (centenary of Swiss Army postal service)		35	30
1157	35c. Fontaine du Sauvage and Porte au Loup, Delémont (700th anniv of granting of town charter)		45	45
1158	50c. Eye and composite wheel (centenary of Public Transport Association)		65	20
1159	80c. Diesel train on viaduct (centenary of Rhaetian railway)		1·20	95
1160	90c. St. Bernard dog and hospice (2000th anniv of Great St. Bernard Pass)		1·00	70
1156/1160	Set of 5		3·25	2·30

(Des Lilian Perrin. Photo Courvoisier)

1989 (23 May). *Pro Patria. Medieval Chronicles*. T **284** and similar horiz designs. Multicoloured. P 11½.
1161	35c.+15c. Type **284**		65	70
1162	50c.+20c. Adrian von Bubenberg watching troops entering Murten (Diebold Schilling's Berne Chronicle)		90	35
1163	80c.+40c. Messenger presenting missive to Council of Zurich (Gerold Edlibach Chronicle)		1·40	1·60
1164	90c.+40c. Schilling presenting Chronicle to Council of Lucerne (Diebold Schilling's Lucerne Chronicle)		1·60	1·60
1161/1164	Set of 4		4·00	3·75

285 Hopscotch

286 Bricklayer

SWITZERLAND Switzerland　　　　　　　　　　　　　　　　1989

(Des A. Bovey. Photo Courvoisier)

1989 (23 May). *Europa. Children's Games.* T **285** *and similar vert design. Multicoloured.* P 11½.

1165	50c. Type **285**	60	25
1166	90c. Blind-man's buff	1·20	90

(Des W. Haettenschweiler. Eng P. Schopfer. Recess and litho PTT, Berne)

1989 (25 Aug)–**2001**. *Occupations.* T **286** *and similar horiz designs.* P 13 × 13½.

1168	2f.75, slate-purple, black & greenish yell	2·75	1·60
1169	2f.80, orange-yellow, reddish brown and dull ultramarine (24.1.92)	3·25	1·30
1170	3f. brt blue, dp brown & lt brown (5.7.94)	3·00	1·30
1171	3f.60, yell-orge, pur-brn & pur (24.1.92)	3·75	2·40
1173	3f.75, bottle grn, bl-grn & brt grn (6.3.90)	3·75	2·75
1174	4f. multicoloured (15.3.94)	4·00	1·40
1175	5f. dp ultram, yell-ochre & brt bl (7.9.93)	6·25	1·40
	a. Paper with flourescent fibres (15.2.01)	5·50	5·50
1176	5f.50, grey, crimson and cerise	5·50	3·00
1168/1176	*Set of 8 (cheapest)*	32·00	14·00

Designs:—2f.80, Cook; 3f. Carpenter; 3f.60, Pharmacist; 3f.75, Fisherman; 4f. Vine grower; 5f. Cheesemaker; 5f.50, Dressmaker. Numbers have been left for additions to this series.

287 Testing Device 　　**288** Exercises

(Des E. and M. Lenz (35c.). W. Weber (50c.), F. Bauer (80c.). R. Somazzi (90c.). R. Zoellig (1f.40). Photo Courvoisier)

1989 (25 Aug). *Publicity Issue.* T **287** *and similar horiz designs. Multicoloured.* P 11½.

1181	35c. Type **287** (centenary of Swiss Electrotechnical Association)	45	35
1182	50c. Family on butterfly (50th anniv of Swiss Travel Fund)	55	15
1183	80c. "Wisdom" and "Science" (bronze statues) (centenary of Fribourg University)	95	70
1184	90c. Audio tape (1st anniv of National Sound Archives)	1·00	70
1185	140c. Bands of colour forming bridge (centenary of Interparliamentary Union)	1·60	1·50
1180/1185	*Set of 5*	4·00	3·00

(Des V. Wyss. Photo Courvoisier)

1989 (25 Aug). *Pro Sport.* P 11½.

1186	**288**	50c.+20c. multicoloured	1·00	95

289 1882 5c. and 50c. Stamps and Emblem 　　**290** Cats

(Des B. Waltenspül (25c.). B. la Roche (35c.), Bernadette Baltis (50c.). R. Hirter (90c.). Photo Courvoisier)

1990 (6 Mar). *Publicity Issue.* T **289** *and similar horiz designs. Multicoloured.* P 11½.

1187	25c. Type **289** (centenary of Union of Swiss Philatelic Societies)	35	20
1188	35c. Locomotive and control car (inauguration of Zurich Rapid Transit System)	50	35
1189	50c. Mountain farmer (50th anniv of Assistance for Mountain Communities)	55	15
1190	90c. Ice hockey players (A-series World Ice Hockey Championships, Berne and Fribourg)	1·00	70
1187/1190	*Set of 4*	2·20	1·30

(Des C. Piatti. Eng M. Müller Recess and litho PTT, Berne)

1990 (6 Mar)–**95**. *Animals.* T **290** *and similar vert designs. Multicoloured.* P 13½ × 13.

1192	10c. Cow (24.1.92)	10	10
1193	50c. Type **290**	55	10
1194	70c. Rabbit (15.1.91)	80	25
	a. Perf 3 sides. Booklets (28.11.95)	95	90
	ab. Booklet pane. No. 1194a × 10	9·50	
1195	80c. Barn owls (15.1.91)	90	25
1196	100c. Horse and foal (16.3.93)	1·10	25
1197	110c. Geese (29.11.95)	1·20	35
1198	120c. Dog (16.3.93)	1·30	65
1199	140c. Sheep (29.11.95)	1·60	90
1200	150c. Goats (5.7.94)	1·70	90
1201	160c. Turkey (24.1.92)	1·80	1·20
1202	170c. Donkey (28.11.95)	1·90	90
1203	200c. Chickens (5.7.94)	1·90	85
1192/1203	*Set of 12*	13·50	6·00

The 70 and 80c. were also issued in coils.
Numbers have been left for additions to this series.

291 Flyswats and Starch Sprinklers Seller 　　**292** Lucerne Post Office

(Des E. Witzig. Photo Courvoisier)

1990 (22 May). *Pro Patria. Street Criers.* T **291** *and similar vert designs showing engravings by David Herrliberger. Multicoloured.* P 11½.

1205	35c.+15c. Type **291**	65	70
1206	50c.+20c. Clock seller	90	30
1207	80c.+40c. Knife grinder	1·40	1·50
1208	90c.+40c. Couple selling pinewood sticks	1·60	1·60
1205/1208	*Set of 4*	4·00	3·75

(Des K. Oberli. Eng M. Müller Recess and litho PTT, Berne)

1990 (22 May). *Europa. Post Office Buildings.* T **292** *and similar horiz design. Multicoloured.* P 13½.

1209	50c. Type **292**	65	20
1210	90c. Geneva Post Office	1·00	60

367

SWITZERLAND Switzerland   1990

293 Conrad Ferdinand Meyer (writer)

294 Anniversary Emblem and Crosses

(Des H. Erni. Eng P. Schopfer. Recess and litho PTT. Berne.)
1990 (5 Sept). *Celebrities.* T **293** *and similar vert designs.* P 13½.
1211	35c. black and sage-green	45	35
1212	50c. black and blue	55	15
1213	80c. black and yellow	85	75
1214	90c. black and salmon-pink	1·00	65
1211/1214	Set of 4	2·50	1·70

Designs:—50c. Angelika Kauffmann (painter): 80c. Blaise Cendrars (writer); 90c. Frank Buchser (painter).

(Des Rüttimann & Haas. Photo Courvoisier)
1990 (5 Sept). *700th Anniv (1991) of Swiss Confederation (1st issue).* T **294** *and similar horiz design.* P 11½.
1215	50c. Type **294**	60	20
1216	90c. Emblem and crosses (*different*)	1·10	85

See also Nos. 1219/22 and 1224.

295 Geneva Cantonal Post Drivers' Brass Badge

296 Figures on Jigsaw Pieces

(Des F. Bauer. Photo Courvoisier)
1990 (5 Sept). *"Helvetia Genève 90" National Stamp Exhibition.* Sheet 102 × 78 mm *containing* T **295** *and similar horiz designs.* Multicoloured. P 11½.
MS1217	50c.+25c. Type **295.** 50c.+25c. Place du Bourg-de-Four, Geneva, 50c.+25c. Rousseau Island, Geneva, 50c.+25c. Geneva 1843 5+5c. stamp on cover	4·75	5·00

(Des H. Bürgin. Photo Courvoisier)
1990 (20 Nov). *Population Census.* P 11½.
1218	**296**	50c. multicoloured	60	20

297 "700 JAHRE"

298 Alps and City Skyline

(Des A. Bovey. Photo Courvoisier)
1991 (22 Feb). *700th Anniv of Swiss Confederation (2nd issue).* T **297** *and similar horiz designs, each showing a section of the Swiss cross.* Multicoloured. P 11½.
1219	50c. Type **297**	70	40
	a. Block of 4 Nos. 1219/22	2·75	
1220	50c. "700 ONNS"	70	40
1221	50c. "700 ANS"	70	40
1222	50c. "700 ANNI"	70	40
1219/1222	Set of 4	2·50	1·40

Nos. 1219/22 were issued together in *se-tenant* blocks of four within the sheet, each block having a composite design of the cross in the centre.

(Des F. Bauer. Photo Courvoisier)
1991 (22 Feb). *800th Anniv of Berne.* P 11½.
1223	**298**	80c. multicoloured	95	50

299 Federal Palace, Berne, and Capitol, Washington

300 Jettison of "Ariane" Rocket Friction Protection Jacket

(Des H. Hartmann. Photo Courvoisier)
1991 (22 Feb). *700th Anniv of Swiss Confederation (3rd issue). Swiss Emigration to U.S.A.* P 12.
1224	**299**	160c. multicoloured	1·70	1·00

(Des E. and M. Lenz. Photo Courvoisier)
1991 (14 May). *Europa. Europe in Space.* T **300** *and similar horiz design.* Multicoloured. P 11½.
1225	50c. Type **300**	60	35
1226	90c. Orbit of Halley's Comet, "Giotto" space probe and its trajectory	1·10	85

301 Abstract

302 Stone Bridge, Lavertezzo

(Des W. Barth (50c.), H. Federle (70c.), M. Bosshart (80c.), W. Leuenberger (90c.) Photo Courvoisier)
1991 (14 May). *Pro Patria. Modern Art.* T **301** *and similar horiz designs.* Multicoloured. P 11½.
1227	50c.+20c. Type **301**	80	35
1228	70c.+30c. Artist's mongram	1·10	1·30
1229	80c.+40c. "Labyrinth"	1·40	1·40
1230	90c.+40c. "Man and Beast"	1·50	1·60
1227/1230	Set of 4	4·25	4·25

(Des P. Baur. Photo Courvoisier)
1991 (10 Sept). *Bridges.* T **302** *and similar horiz designs.* Multicoloured. P 11½.
1231	50c. Type **302**	55	15
1232	70c. Wooden Neubrügg, Bremgarten	80	70
1233	80c. Koblenz-Felsenau iron truss railway bridge	1·00	65
1234	90c. Garter concrete bridge, Simplon Pass	1·00	65
1231/1234	Set of 4	3·00	1·90

SWITZERLAND Switzerland 1991

303 P.T.T. Employees

304 Lake Moesola

(Des R. Mühlemann. Photo Courvoisier)

1991 (10 Sept). *Centenary of Swiss Postal, Telephone and Telegraph Officials' Union.* P 11½.
1235 **303** 80c. multicoloured 90   50

(Des H. Schelbert. Litho PTT, Berne)

1991 (16 Dec). *Mountain Lakes.* T **304** *and similar vert design.* P 13½ × 13.
1236   50c. multicoloured 50   10
1237   80c. purple-brown, rose-red and claret 85   20
Design:—80c. Fishing boat moored at jetty on Melchsee. See also No. 1257.

305 Mouth of River Rhine and Caspian Tern

306 Map of Americas and *Santa Maria*

(Des A. Wittmer (50c.), W. Weber (80c.), B. Waltenspül (90c.). Photo Courvoisier)

1992 (24 Mar). *Publicity Issue.* T **305** *and similar horiz designs. Multicoloured.* P 11½.
1238   50c. Type **305** (centenary of Treaty for International Regulation of the Rhine) 55   40
1239   80c. Family (50th anniv of Pro Familia) 85   35
1240   90c. Chemical formula and model of difluorobutane molecule (centenary of International Chemical Nomenlature Conference, Geneva) 90   85

(Des O. Galli. Photo Courvoisier)

1992 (24 Mar). *Europa. 500th Anniv of Discovery of America by Columbus.* T **306** *and similar vert design. Multicoloured.* P 11½.
1241   50c. Type **306** 60   25
1242   90c. Route map of first voyage and sketch for statue of Columbus (Vincenzo Vela) . . . . . 1·20   80

307 Skier

308 1780s Earthenware Plate, Heimberg

(Des B. Cosendai (50c.), P. Chappuis (80c.), Y. Robellaz (90c.). Photo Courvoisier)

1992 (22 May). *Sierre International Comics Festival.* T **307** *and similar horiz designs. Multicoloured.* P 11½.
1243   50c. Type **307** 60   25
1244   80c. Mouse-artist drawing strip . . 1·00   70
1245   90c. Love-struck man holding bunch of stamp flowers behind back . . 1·20   90

(Des D. Traversi. Photo Courvoisier)

1992 (22 May). *Pro Patria. Folk Art.* T **308** *and similar vert designs. Multicoloured.* P 11½.
1246   50c.+20c. Type **308** 80   40
1247   70c.+30c. Paper cut-out by Johann Jakob Hauswirth . . . . . 1·20   1·30
1248   80c.+40c. Maplewood cream spoon, Gruyères . . . . 1·40   1·30
1249   90c.+40c. Carnation from 1780 embroidered saddle cloth, Grisons . . . . 1·50   1·50
1246/1249 Set of 4 . . . . 4·50   4·00

309 Flags and Alps

310 Clowns on Trapeze

(Des F. Dorner. Photo Courvoisier)

1992 (22 May). *Alpine Protection Convention.* P 12.
1250 **309** 90c. multicoloured . . . . . 1·00   65

(Des R. Knie. Photo Courvoisier)

1992 (25 Aug). *The Circus.* T **310** *and similar horiz designs. Multicoloured.* P 11½.
1251   50c. Type **310** 60   25
1252   70c. Sealion with Auguste the clown . . 95   70
1253   80c. Chalky the clown and elephant . . 1·00   45
1254   90c. Harlequin and horse . . . . 1·20   85
1251/1254 Set of 4 . . . . 3·25   2·00

311 Sport Pictograms

312 Train and Map

(Des J. Tinquely. Photo Courvoisier)

1992 (25 Aug). *Pro Sport.* P 11½ × 12.
1255 **311** 50c.+20c. black & brt greenish blue . . . . 1·30   85

(Des L. Pizzotti. Photo Courvoisier)

1992 (24 Nov). *Centenary (1993) of Central Office for International Rail Carnage.* P 11½.
1256 **312** 90c. multicoloured . . . . . 1·10   85

369

SWITZERLAND Switzerland 1993

313 "A" (first class) Mail
314 Zürich and Geneva 1843 Stamps 
315 Paracelsus (after Augustin Hirschvogel) (500th birth anniv) 
318 Appenzell Dairyman's Earring
319 "Work No. 095" (Emma Kunz)

(Des H. Schelbert. Eng M. Müller. Recess and litho PTT, Berne)

1993 (19 Jan). T **313** and similar vert design. P 13½ × 13.
1257	60c. dp blue, greenish yellow & new bl		60	20
1258	80c. dull vermilion, yellow-orange & scar		85	20

Design:—60c. Lake Tanay.

(Des H. Billharz. Photo Courvoisier)

1993 (16 Mar). 150th Anniv of Swiss Postage Stamps. T **314** and similar vert designs. Multicoloured. P 11½.
1259	60c. Type **314**		70	30
1260	80c. Postal cancellation (stamps for postage)		95	65
1261	100c. Magnifying glass (stamp collecting)		1·30	80

(Des G. Ducimetiere (60c.), P. Scholl (80c.), J. Ongaro (180c.). Photo Courvoisier)

1993 (16 Mar). Publicity Issue. T **315** and similar designs. P 11½.
1262	60c. sepia, grey and blue		70	30
1263	80c. multicoloured		1·00	60
1264	180c. multicoloured		2·10	2·00

Designs: Vert—80c. Discus thrower (from Greek vase) (inauguration of Olympic Museum, Lausanne). Horiz—180c. Worker's head (centenary of International Metalworkers' Federation).

316 Hohentwiel (lake paddle-steamer) and Flags
317 Interior of Media House, Villerbanne, France 

(Des A. Wittmer. Photo Courvoisier)

1993 (5 May). Lake Constance European Region. P 12.
1265 **316** 60c. multicoloured ... 85 45

(Des M. Botta. Eng P. Schopfer. Recess and litho PTT, Berne)

1993 (5 May). Europa. Contemporary Architecture. T **317** and similar vert design. P 13½.
1266	60c. ultramarine, black & turquoise-blue		70	25
1267	80c. vermilion, black and slate		1·00	80

Design:—80c. House, Breganzona, Ticino.

(Des B. Scarton. Photo Courvoisier)

1993 (5 May). Pro Patria. Folk Art. T **318** and similar horiz designs. Multicoloured. P 11½.
1268	60c.+30c. Type **318**		1·00	75
1269	60c.+30c. Flühli enamelled glass bottle, 1738		1·00	75
1270	80c.+40c. Driving cows to summer pasture (detail of mural, Sylvestre Pidoux)		1·40	1·50
1271	100c.+40c. Straw hat ornaments		1·50	1·70
1268/1271	Set of 4		4·50	4·25

(Des Bernadette Baltis. Photo Courvorsier)

1993 (7 Sept). Paintings by Swiss Women Artists. T **319** and similar square designs. Multicoloured. P 11½.
1272	60c. Type **319**		75	35
1273	80c. "Great Singer Lilas Goergens" (Aloïse) (33 × 33 mm)		1·00	60
1274	100c. "Under the Rain Cloud" (Meret Oppenheim) (33 × 33 mm)		1·20	90
1275	120c. "Four Spaces with Horizontal Bands" (Sophie Taeuber-Arp) (33 × 33 mm)		1·50	1·50
1272/1275	Set of 4		4·00	3·00

320 Kapell Bridge and Water Tower, Lucerne
321 Hieroglyphic, Cuneiform and Roman Scripts 

(Des H. Hartmann. Litho PTT, Berne)

1993 (7 Sept). Kapell Bridge, Lucerne, Restoration Fund. P 13½ × 13.
1276 **320** 80c.+20c. dp carmine & orange-red ... 1·70 1·70

(Des F. Bauer. Photo Courvorsier)

1994 (15 Mar). "Books and the Press" Exhibition, Geneva. T **321** and similar horiz designs Multicoloured. P 11½.
1277	60c. Type **321**		70	35
1278	80c. Gothic letterpress script		95	60
1279	100c. Modern electronic fonts		1·20	1·00

322 Athletes
323 Footballers 

370

SWITZERLAND Switzerland   1994

(Des R. Hirter (60c.), B. Waltenspül (80c.), A. Wittmer (100c.), A. Bovey (180c.). Photo Courvoisier)

1994 (15 Mar). *Publicity Issue.* T **322** *and similar horiz designs. Multicoloured.* P 11½.
1280	60c. Type **322** (50th Anniv of National Sports School, Magglingen)	70	45
1281	80c. Jakob Bernoulli (mathematician) (after Nicolas Bernoulli) and formula and diagram of the law of large numbers (International mathematicians Congress, Zürich)	95	65
1282	100c. Heads, Unisource emblem, globe and flags (collaboration of Swiss, dutch and Swedish telecommunications companies)	1·10	85
1283	180c. Radar image, airliner and globe (50th anniv of International Civil Aviation Organization)	2·10	1·80
1280/1283	Set of 4	4·25	3·50

(Des H. Schelbert. Photo Courvoisier)

1994 (15 Mar). *World Cup Football Championship, U.S.A., and Centenary (1995) of Swiss Football Association.* P 11½.
| 1284 | **323** | 80c. multicoloured | 90 | 55 |

324 *Trieste* (bathyscaphe)

325 Neuchâtel Weight-driven Clock (Jacques Matthey-Jonais)

(Des P. Baur. Photo Courvoisier)

1994 (17 May). *Europa. Discoveries and Inventions.* T **324** *and similar vert design showing vehicles used by Auguste Piccard in deep-sea and stratospheric explorations. Multicoloured.* P 12.
| 1285 | 60c. Type **324** | 80 | 45 |
| 1286 | 100c. F.N.R.S. (stratosphere balloon) | 1·70 | 1·20 |

(Des D. Traversi. Photo Courvoisier)

1994 (17 May). *Pro Patria. Folk Art.* T **325** *and similar vert designs. Multicoloured.* P 11½.
1287	60c.+30c. Type **325**	1·00	75
1288	60c.+30c. Embroidered pomegranate on linen	1·00	55
1289	80c.+40c. Mould for Kräfli pastry	1·40	1·60
1290	100c.+40c. Paper-bird cradle mobile	1·60	1·80
1287/1290	Set of 4	4·50	4·25

326 Symbolic Condom

327 Simenon and his Home, Echandens Castle, Lausanne

(Des N. de Saint Phalle. Photo Courvoisier)

1994 (15 Oct). *Anti-AIDS Campaign.* P 11½.
| 1291 | **326** | 60c. multicoloured | 85 | 30 |

(Des P. Schopfer and D. Roegiest. Eng P. Schopfer. Recess and litho PTT, Berne)

1994 (15 Oct). *Fifth Death Anniv of Georges Simenon (novelist).* P 13½.
| 1292 | **327** | 100c. multicoloured | 1·10 | 75 |

328 "Swiss Electricity"

329 Eurasian Beaver

(Des G. Staehelin (1293), R. Mirer (1294), P. Scholl (1295), R. Zollig (1296). Photo Courvoisier)

1995 (7 Mar). *Publicity Issue.* T **328** *and similar designs.* P 11½.
1293	60c. multicoloured	75	30
1294	60c. bright blue and black	75	30
1295	80c. multicoloured	1·00	70
1296	180c. multicoloured	2·20	1·60
1293/1296	Set of 4	4·25	2·50

Designs: *Horiz*—No. 1293, Type **328** (centenary of Swiss Association of Electricity Producers and Distributors), 1295, "(sda ats)" (centenary of Swiss News Agency), 1296, "ONU UNO" and emblem (50th anniv of United Nations Organization). *Vert*—No. 1294, Wrestlers (centenary of Swiss Wrestling Association and National Wrestling and Alpine Herdsmen's Festival, Chur).

(Des Sibylle Erni. Photo Courvoisier)

1995 (7 Mar). *Endangered Animals.* T **329** *and similar vert designs. Multicoloured.* P 12.
1297	60c. Type **329**	80	30
1298	80c. Map butterfly	1·10	60
1299	100c. Green tree frog	1·40	90
1300	120c. Little owl	1·70	1·60
1297/1300	Set of 4	4·50	3·00

330 Cream Pail, 1776

331 Couple and Dove

(Des R. Hirter. Photo Courvoisier)

1995 (16 May). *Pro Patria. Folk Art.* T **330** *and similar horiz designs. Multicoloured.* P 11½.
1301	60c.+30c. Type **330**	1·10	55
1302	60c.+30c. Neuchâtel straw hat	1·10	75
1303	80c.+40c. Detail of chest lock, 1580	1·40	1·60
1304	100c.+40c. Langnau ceramic sugar bowl	1·60	1·80
1301/1304	Set of 4	4·75	4·25

(Des H. Erni. Recess, embossed and litho PTT, Berne)

1995 (16 May). *Europa. Peace and Freedom.* T **331** *and similar horiz design.* P 13½.
| 1305 | 60c. deep blue and cobalt | 75 | 45 |
| 1306 | 100c. reddish brown and brown-ochre | 1·20 | 90 |

Design:—100c. Europa with Zeus as bull.

371

SWITZERLAND Switzerland 1995

332 Basel (right-hand part)
333 Coloured Ribbons woven through River 

(Des Bernadette Baltis. Photo Courvoisier)

1995 (16 May). *"Basler Taube 1995" Stamp Exhibition, Basel.* Sheet 100 × 131 mm containing T **332** and similar vert designs. P 13 × 14.
MS1307 60c.+30c. black, deep violet-blue &
new blue; 80c.+30c. multicoloured;
100c.+50c. black, dp violet-blue & new blue;
100c.+50c. black, dp violet-blue & new
blue . . . . . . 6·50 6·50
Designs:—80c.+30c. Basel 2½r. Dove stamp (150th anniv of issue); 60c.+30c., 100c.+50c. (2) Panorama of Basel by Matthäus Merian (composite design).

(Des Cornelia Eberle. Eng P. Schopfer. Recess and litho PTT, Berne)

1995 (5 Sept). *Switzerland–Liechtenstein Co-operation.* P 13½.
1308 **333** 60c. multicoloured . . . 70 40
No. 1308 was valid for use in both Switzerland and Liechtenstein (see No. 1106 of Liechtenstein).

334 The Vocation of André Carrel (1925)
335 Ear, Eye and Mouth 

(Des W. Jeker. Photo Courvoisier)

1995 (5 Sept). *Centenary of Motion Pictures.* T **334** and similar horiz designs. P 11½.
1309 60c. Type **334** 85 35
1310 80c. *Anna Göldin - The Last Witch* . 95 55
1311 150c. *Pipilotti's Mistakes - Absolution* . 1·80 1·50

(Des R. Bittel. Photo Courvoisier)

1995 (5 Sept). *"Telecom 95" International Telecommunications Exhibition, Geneva.* P 11½.
1312 **335** 180c. multicoloured . . . 1·90 1·10

336 "A" (first class) Mail
337 Emblem 

(Des J.-B. Lévy. Litho PTT, Berne)

1995 (28 Nov). P 13½ × 13.
1313 **336** 90c. new blue, orange-verm &
lemon . . . . . . 1·00 35
a. Perf 3 sides. Booklets . . . 1·00 80
ab. Booklet pane.
No. 1313a × 10 . . . . . 10·00

On 29 July 1999 this stamp was issued printed on paper which is bluish with glowing fibres when viewed under a U.V. lamp. It appears bright white under the lamp.

(Des N. Lehr (1314), W. Henkel (1315), N. Troxler (1316), Jenny Leibundgut (1317), Sibylle von Fischer (1318). Photo Courvoisier)

1996 (12 Mar). *Publicity Issue.* T **337** and similar horiz designs. Multicoloured. P 11½.
1314 70c. Type **337** (centenary of Touring
       Club of Switzerland) . . . 80 45
1315 70c. Heart (50th anniv of charity
       organizations) 95 55
1316 90c. Brass band (30th Federal Music
       Festival, Interlaken) . . . 1·10 70
1317 90c. Young girls (centenary of Pro Filia
       (girls' aid society)) . . . 1·00 70
1318 180c. Jean Piaget (child psychologist,
       birth centenary) . . . . 2·10 1·80
1314/1318 Set of 5 . . . . . . 5·25 3·75

338 Coloured Ribbons and "Bern 96" Gymnastic Festival Emblem
339 Corinna Bille (writer) 

(Des B. La Roche. Photo Courvoisier)

1996 (12 Mar). *Pro Sport.* P 11½.
1319 **338** 70c.+30c. multicoloured . . 1·00 1·20

(Des and eng P. Schopfer. Recess and litho PTT, Berne)

1996 (14 May). *Europa. Famous Women.* T **339** and similar vert design. Multicoloured. P 13½.
1320 70c. Type **339** 80 45
1321 110c. Iris von Roten-Meyer (feminist
       writer) . . . . . . 1·70 1·00

340 Magdalena Chapel, Wolfenschiessen, and Cross
341 Olympic Rings 

(Des H. Schelbert. Photo Courvoisier)

1996 (14 May). *Pro Patria. Heritage.* T **340** and similar vert designs. Multicoloured. P 11½.
1322 70c.+35c. Type **340** . . . 1·10 75
1323 70c.+35c. Underground sawmill and
       workshop, Col-des-Roches . . 1·10 95
1324 90c.+40c. Baroque baths, Pfäfers . 1·50 1·60
1325 110c.+50c. Roman road and milestone,
       Great St. Bernhard . . . 1·70 1·90
1322/1325 Set of 4 . . . . . . 5·00 4·75

SWITZERLAND Switzerland 1996

(Des A. Wittmer. Litho PTT, Berne)

1996 (14 May). *Centenary of Modern Olympic Games.* P 13½.
1326 **341** 180c. multicoloured ...... 2·00 1·70

342 Representation of 1995 "A" Mail Stamp

343 Musical Movement and Mechanical Ring (Isaac-Daniel Piguet)

(Des J.-B. Lévy. Litho PTT, Berne)

1996 (27 June). *Guinness World Record for Largest "Living" Postage Stamp (arrangement of people to represent stamp design).* P 13½.
1327 **342** 90c. multicoloured ...... 1·50 1·10

(Des B. Brüsch. Photo Courvoisier)

1996 (10 Sept). *Bicentenary of Antoine Favre-Salomon's Invention of the Metal Teeth System for Music Boxes.* T **343** and similar horiz designs. Multicoloured. P 11½.
1328 70c. Type **343** 85 40
1329 90c. "Basso-piccolo mandolin" cylinder music box (Eduard Jaccard) ... 1·10 65
1330 110c. Station automaton (Paillard & Co) ..... 1·40 1·00
1331 180c. Kalliope disc music box ..... 2·20 1·90
1328/1331 Set of 4 .... 5·00 3·50

344 Pattern

345 "The Golden Cow" (Daniel Ammann)

(Des B. Müller-Meyer. Photo Heusser AG, Gümligen)

1996 (10 Sept). *Greetings Stamps. Booklet stamps.* T **344** and similar horiz designs. Multicoloured. Self-adhesive. Die-cut straight edge × wavy edge.
1332 90c. Type **344** ...... 1·30 1·20
1333 90c. Mottled pattern ...... 1·30 1·20
1334 90c. Coil pattern ...... 1·30 1·20
1335 90c. Flower and leaf pattern ...... 1·30 1·20
1332/1335 Set of 4 .... 4·75 4·25

Nos. 1332/5 are peeled directly from the cover of the booklet. It is not therefore possible to collect these as booklet panes.

(Photo Courvoisier)

1996 (26 Nov). *Winning Entries in Stamp Design Competition.* T **345** and similar vert designs. P 11½.
1336 70c. gold and bright blue 80 50
1337 90c. multicoloured ...... 1·10 70
1338 110c. multicoloured ...... 1·30 95
1339 180c. brown, black and new blue ...... 2·10 2·00
1336/1339 Set of 4 ...... 4·75 3·75

Designs:—90c. "Wake with a Smile" (Max Sprick); 110c. "Leaves" (Elena Emma-Pugliese); 180c. "Dove" (René Conscience).

346 Globi delivering Mail

347 Venus of Octodurus

(Des H. Schmid. Litho PTT, Berne)

1997 (11 Mar). *Globi (cartoon character by Robert Lips).* P 13½.
1340 **346** 70c. multicoloured 75 40

(Des B. Scarton. Photo Courvoisier)

1997 (11 Mar). *Gallo-Romam Works of Art,* T **347** and similar vert designs. Multicoloured. P 11½.
1341 70c. Type **347** (from Forum Claudii Vallensium (now Martigny)) ... 80 55
1342 90c. Bust of Bacchus (from Augusta Raurica (now August)) .... 1·10 85
1343 110c. Ceramic fragment showing "Victory" (from Iulio Magus (now Schleitheim)) ..... 1·20 1·10
1344 180c. Mosaic showing female theatrical mask (from Vallon) ...... 2·10 2·10
1341/1344 Set of 4 ...... 4·75 4·25

Each stamp is inscribed with the name of the Foundation bearing responsibility for the preservation of the respective archaeological sites.

348 Class 460 Series 2000 Locomotive

349 Douglas DC-4 Grand Old Lady over Globe

(Des Michèle Berri. Photo Courvoisier)

1997 (11 Mar). *150th Anniv of Zurich–Baden Rail link.* T **348** and similar horiz designs. Multicoloured. P 11½.
1345 70c. Type **348** 80 55
1346 90c. "Red Arrow" railcar ...... 1·10 90
1347 1f.40, Pullman coach ...... 1·60 1·70
1348 1f.70, Limmat (first Swiss steam locomotive) ...... 2·20 2·20
1345/1348 Set of 4 ...... 5·00 4·75

(Des A. Wittmer. Litho PTT, Berne)

1997 (11 Mar). *50th Anniv of Swissair's North Atlantic Service.* P 13½.
1349 **349** 180c. multicoloured ...... 2·00 1·70

SWITZERLAND Switzerland 1997

350 Farmland

351 "Devil and the Goat" (painting by Heinrich Danioth on rock face of Schöllenen Gorge)

(Des Rosmarie Tissi. Litho PTT, Berne)

1997 (13 May). *Publicity Issue.* T **350** and similar horiz design. Multicoloured. P 13½.
1350	70c. Type **350** (centenary of Swiss Farmers' Union)	80	55
1351	90c. Street plan (centenary of Swiss Municipalities' Union)	1·00	85

(Des P. Zimmermann. Eng H. Baldauf. Recess and litho PTT, Berne)

1997 (13 May). *Europa. Tales and Legends. The Devil's Bridge.* P 13½.
1352	**351**	90c. bright rose-red and blackish brown and yellow	95	75

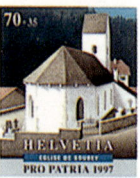

352 St. Valbert's Church, Soubey (Jura)

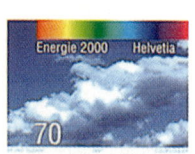

353 Clouds (Air)

(Des Bernadette Baltis. Photo Courvoisier)

1997 (13 May). *Pro Patria. Heritage and Landscapes.* T **350** and similar vert designs. Multicoloured. P 11½.
1353	70c.+35c. Type **352**	1·10	90
1354	70c.+35c. Culture mill, Lützelflüh (Berne)	1·10	90
1355	90c.+40c. Ittingen Charterhouse (Thurgau)	1·40	1·60
1356	110c.+50c. Casa Patriziale, Russo (Ticino)	1·80	1·90
1353/1356	Set of 4	5·00	4·75

(Des B. Oldani. Photo Courvoisier)

1997 (12 Sept). *Energy 2000 (energy efficiency programme). The Elements.* T **353** and similar horiz designs. Multicoloured. P 12 × 11½.
1357	70c. Type **353**	80	55
1358	90c. Burning wood (Fire)	1·10	90
1359	110c. Water droplets (Water)	1·30	1·10
1360	180c. Pile of soil (Earth)	2·10	2·10
1357/1360	Set of 4	4·75	4·25

354 King Rama V and President Adolf Deucher

355 Paul Karrer and Molecular Structure of Vitamin A

(Des R. Hirter. Litho PTT, Berne)

1997 (12 Sept). *Centenary of Visit of King Rama V of Siam. Non-phosphorescent paper.* P 13½.
1361	**354**	90c. multicoloured	95	85

(Des C. Reuterswärd. Eng C. Slania. Recess and litho PTT, Berne)

1997 (13 Nov). *The Nobel Prize.* T **355** and similar horiz design. Non-phosphorescent paper. P 13½ × 13½.
1362	90c. black and grey	1·10	90
1363	110c. black and dull purple	1·30	1·10

Designs:—90c. Type **355** (Chemistry Prize, 1937); 110c. Alfred Nobel (founder of Prize Fund).

356 Woman and Boy (German)

357 Postal Service Emblem

(Des D. Rhyner. Litho PTT, Berne)

1997 (20 Nov). *"The Post keeps Us in Touch".* T **356** and similar horiz designs. Non-phosphorescent paper. P 13½ × 13.
1364	70c. black, scarlet-vermilion and new blue	95	70
	a. Horiz strip of 4. Nos. 1364/7	4·00	
1365	70c. black, lemon and new blue	95	70
1366	70c. black, lemon and bright green	95	70
1367	70c. black, bright green and scarlet-vermilion	95	70
1364/1367	Set of 4	3·50	2·50

Designs:—No. 1365, Boy wearing baseball cap with woman (French); 1366, Young couple (Italian); 1367, Girl and man (Romansch).

Nos. 1364/7 were issued in horizontal *se-tenant* strips of four stamps within the sheet.

(Des K. Wälti and A. Frutiger (1368), Wirú Identity, Zurich (1369). Litho PTT, Berne)

1998 (7 Jan). *Separation of Swiss Post and Swisscom (telecommunications).* T **357** and similar horiz design. P 13½.
1368	90c. black, yellow and magenta	90	70
1369	90c. royal blue, new blue and vermilion	90	70

Design:—No. 1369, Swisscom emblem.

358 Arrows

359 Winter Olympics, 2006

SWITZERLAND Switzerland   1998

(Des Brigit Herrmann. Photo Courvoisier)

1998 (7 Jan). *Bicentenary of Declaration of Helvetic Republic and 150th Anniv of Swiss Federal State.* T **358** *and similar horiz designs. Multicoloured.* P 11½.
1370	90c. Type **358**	85	85
	a. Block of 4. Nos. 1370/3	3·50	
1371	90c. Face value at bottom right	85	85
1372	90c. Face value at top left	85	85
1373	90c. Face value at top right	85	85
1370/1373	Set of 4	3·00	3·00

Nos. 1370/3 were issued together in *se-tenant* blocks of four stamps within the sheet.

(Des Candidacy Committee. Litho PTT, Berne)

1998 (12 Feb). *Swiss Candidacy for Winter Olympic Games, 2006.* P 13½.
1374	**359**	90c. multicoloured	1·00	85

360 Elderly Couple
361 "On Top of the Simplon Pass" 

(Des Marianne Brügger (1375), P. Scholl (1376), J. Müller (1377). Photo Courvoisier)

1998 (10 Mar). *Publicity Issues.* T **360** *and similar horiz designs. Multicoloured.* P 11½.
1375	70c. Type **360** (Old Age and Survivor's Insurance)	80	60
1376	70c. National Museum, Prangins Castle (centenary of Swiss National Museum, Zurich, and inauguration of Prangins branch)	80	55
1377	90c. Fingerprints (centenary of St. Gallen University)	1·10	75

(Des Margret Schnyder. Litho PTT, Berne)

1998 (10 Mar). *Paintings by Jean-Frédéric Schnyder.* T **361** *and similar horiz designs. Multicoloured.* P 13 × 13½.
1378	10c. Type **361** (10.3.98)	15	15
1379	20c. "Snowdrift near Neuthal" (10.3.98)	25	20
1380	50c. "Franches Montagnes" (10.3.98)	55	50
1381	70c. "Two Horses" (10.3.98)	80	40
1382	90c. "En Route" (10.3.98)	90	25
1383	110c. "Winter Morning by the Alpnachersee"	1·20	55
1385	140c. "Zug" (8.9.98)	1·60	1·10
1386	170c. "Olive Grove" (8.9.98)	1·70	1·20
1387	180c. "Near Reutigen" (8.9.98)	1·90	1·40
1378/1387	Set of 9	8·25	5·25

362 St. Gall, Rhine Valley
363 Lanterns 

(Des M. Bucher. Photo Courvoisier)

1998 (12 May). *Pro Patria. Heritage and Landscapes.* T **362** *and similar horiz designs. Multicoloured.* P 11½.
1390	70c. + 35c. Type **362**	1·10	95
1391	70c. + 35c. Round church, Saas Balen	1·10	95
1392	90c. + 40c. Forest, Bödmeren	1·50	1·50
1393	90c. + 40c. The old refuge (museum), St. Gotthard	1·50	1·50
1394	110c. + 50c. Smithy, Corcelles	1·80	2·00
1390/1394	Set of 5	6·25	6·25

(Des W. Henkel. Litho PTT, Berne)

1998 (12 May). *Europa. National Festivals. National Day.* P 13 × 13½.
1395	**363**	90c. multicoloured	1·00	85

364 In-line Skating
365 Bridge 24, Slender West Lake, Yangzhou, China 

(Des M. Eherhard. Photo Courvoisier)

1998 (8 Sept). *Sports. Booklet stamps.* T **364** *and similar square designs. Multicoloured. Self-Adhesive. Die-cut straight edge × wavy edge.*
1396	70c. Type **364**	60	60
1397	70c. Snow-boarding	60	60
1398	70c. Mountain biking	60	60
1399	70c. Basketball	60	60
1400	70c. Beach volleyball	60	60
1396/1400	Set of 5	2·75	2·75

Nos. 1396/1400 are peeled directly from the cover of the booklet and cannot therefore be collected as separate panes. The booklet also contains two labels giving the Post Office's web-site address.

(Des Xu Yan Bo (20c.), Bernadette Baltis (70c.), H. Anderegg (90c.). Eng P. Schopfer (20c.). Recess and litho (20c.) or litho (70c.). PTT Berne photo Courvoisier (90c.))

1998 (25 Nov). *Lakes.* T **365** *and similar horiz design. Multicoloured.* P 13½.
1401	20c. Type **365**	55	55
	a. Pair. Nos. 1401/2	1·10	1·20
1402	70c. Chillon Castle, Lake Geneva	55	60
MS1403	96 × 70 mm. 90c. Chillon Castle and Bridge 24 (52 × 44 mm). P 11½	1·00	1·10

Nos. 1401/2 were issued together in *se-tenant* pairs within the sheet.

In 1999 No. **MS**1403 was issued for the "China 99" World Philatelic Exhibition. It was overprinted in gold **China 1999** with emblem and with a gold/silver hologram and only occurs on cover.

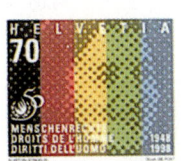

366 Emblem and Face
367 Christmas Wrapping 

(Des Esther Stingelin and B. Scarton. Litho PTT, Berne)

1998 (25 Nov). *50th Anniv of Universal Declaration of Human Rights.* P 13½.
1404	**366**	70c. multicoloured	85	80

(Des B. Brüsch. Litho PTT, Berne)

1998 (25 Nov). *Christmas.* P 13½.
1405	**367**	90c. multicoloured	1·00	90

375

SWITZERLAND Switzerland　　　　　　　　　　　　　　　　　　　　1999

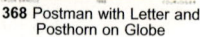

368 Postman with Letter and Posthorn on Globe

369 Little Pingu carrying Parcel

Design: 55 × 29 mm—70c. UPU emblem on card in envelope. Nos. 1415/16 were issued together in *se-tenant* pairs within sheetlets of eight stamps, each pair forming a composite design.

373 Jester and Clown

374 Chestnuts from Malcantone

(Des C. Sandoz. Photo Courvoisier)

1999 (21 Jan). *150th Anniv of Swiss Postal Service*. P 11½ × 12.
1406　368　90c. multicoloured　　　　　　85　　80

(Des O. Gutmann. Litho PTT, Berne)

1999 (9 Mar). *Youth Stamps. Pingu (cartoon character). T* **369** *and similar horiz design. Multicoloured.* P 13½.
1407　70c. Type **369**　　　　　　　　　85　　65
1408　90c. Papa Pingu driving snowmobile　1·10　90

(Des R. Knie (1417), J.-C. Maret and J.-P. Arlaud (1418), J. Wandfluh (1420); litho PTT Berne. Des A. Wittmer; photo Courvoisier (1419))

1999 (5 May). *Publicity Issue. T* **373** *and similar horiz designs. Phosphorescent paper (1419) or paper with fluorescent fibres (others).* P 11½ (1419) or 13½ (others).
1417　70c. multicoloured　　　　　　95　　70
1418　90c. multicoloured　　　　　　1·00　90
1419　90c. multicoloured　　　　　　1·00　90
1420　1f.10, orange-vermilion and black　1·20　1·10
1417/1420 Set of 4　　　　　　　　3·75　3·20
Designs:—No. 1417, Type **373** (50th anniv of SOS Children's Villages); 1418, Sketch of giant puppets (Wine-growers' Festival, Vevey); 1419, Flags of member countries and emblem (50th anniv of Council of Europe); 1420, Red Cross and emblem (50th anniv of Geneva Conventions).

370 Vieux Bois falls in Love at First Sight

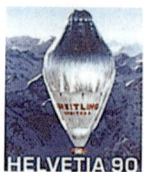

371 Breitling Orbiter 3

(Des Suzanne Rivier. Litho Guhl & Scheibler, Aesch)

1999 (9 Mar). *Birth Bicentenary of Rodolphe Töpffer (cartoonist). Booklet stamps. T* **370** *and similar horiz designs showing scenes from The Love of Monsieur Vieux Bois. Multicoloured. Self-adhesive. Die-cut straight edge × wavy edge.*
1409　90c. Type **370**　　　　　　　　80　　85
1410　90c. Vieux Bois declares his love　　80　　85
1411　90c. Vieux Bois jumps in air from joy, knocking over furniture　　　　80　　85
1412　90c. Vieux Bois helping his love over wall　　　　　　　　　　　80　　85
1413　90c. Wedding of Vieux Bois　　　80　　85
1409/1413 Set of 5　　　　　　　　3·50　3·75

Nos. 1409/13 are peeled directly from the cover of the booklet. It is not therefore possible to collect these as booklet panes.

(Litho PTT, Berne)

1999 (24 Mar). *First World Circumnavigation by Balloon, by Bertrand Piccard and Brian Jones.* P 13½.
1414　371　90c. multicoloured　　　　　1·00　70

(Des M. Bucher. Litho PTT, Berne)

1999 (5 May). *Pro Patria. Heritage and Landscapes. T* **374** *and similar vert designs. Multicoloured. Paper with fluorescent fibres.* P 13½.
1421　70c.+35c. Type **374**　　　　　　1·10　95
1422　70c.+35c. La Sarraz Castle　　　1·10　95
1423　90c.+40c. *Uri* (lake steamer)　　1·50　1·50
1424　110c.+50c. St. Christopher carrying Baby Jesus (detail of fresco, St. Paul's Chapel, Rhäzüns)　1·90　1·90
1421/1424 Set of 4　　　　　　　　5·00　4·75

375 Ibex Horns (National Park, Engadine)

376 Roofs of Buildings

(Des N. Vital. Litho PTT, Berne)

1999 (5 May). *Europa. Parks and Gardens. Paper with fluorescent fibres.* P 13½.
1425　375　90c. black and ultramarine　1·00　80

372 Envelope Flap

(Des I. Moscatelli. Photo Courvoisier)

1999 (5 May). *125th Anniv of Universal Postal Union. T* **372** *and another design.* P 12.
1415　20c. Lemon and black　　　　　35　　35
　　a. Pair. Nos. 1415/16　　　　　1·30　1·30
1416　70c. black, vermilion and lemon　　95　　95

(Des Susanne Huber and M. Schmid. Photo Courvoisier)

1999 (9 Sept). *"naba 2000" National Stamp Exhibition, St. Gallen. Sheet 66 × 85 mm containing T* **376** *and similar vert designs. Multicoloured.* P 11½.
MS1426 20c.+10c. Type **376**; 70c.+30c. Spire of St. Laurenzen's Church; 90c.+30c. Oriel window　　　　　　　　　　　2·50　2·50

376

SWITZERLAND Switzerland   1999

377 Children holding Pictures

378 Schöllenen Gorge Monument, Suvorov and Soldiers

(Des Dinhard School (70c.), R. Hirter (90c.), Michéle Berri (1f.10). Litho PTT, Berne)

1999 (24 Sept). *Publicity Issue*. T **377** *and similar horiz designs. Multicoloured. Paper with fluorescent fibres.* P 13½.
1427	70c. Type **377** (Children's Rights)		75	55
1428	90c. Carl Lutz (Swiss diplomat in Budapest during Second World War, 24th death anniv)		1·00	75
1429	1f.10, Chemical model of ozone and globe (birth bicentenary of Christian Schönbein (chemist))		1·20	1·00
1430	180c. "Midday in the Alps" (death centenary of Giovanni Segantini (painter))		2·00	1·90
1427/1430	Set of 4		4·50	3·75

(Des B. Ilyukhin (1431). Photo Courvoisier)

1999 (24 Sept). *Bicentenary of General Aleksandr Suvorov's Crossing of the Alps.* T **378** *and similar horiz design. Multicoloured.* P 12.
1431	70c. Type **378**		70	65
1432	110c. Suvorov vanguard (after engraving by L. Hess) passing Lake Klöntal		1·20	1·10

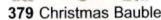

379 Christmas Bauble

380 "2000" around Globe

(Des W. Henkel and Gigi Schmid. Litho PTT, Berne)

1999 (23 Nov). *Christmas.* P 13½.
1433	**379**	90c. multicoloured	1·00	80

(Des L. Marx. Photo Courvoisier)

1999 (23 Nov). *Year 2000.* P 11½.
1434	**380**	90c. multicoloured	1·80	1·30

381 Cyclist

382 Alphorn Player

(Des R. Hirter. Litho PTT Berne)

2000 (7 Mar). *Centenary of International Cycling Union.* P 13½.
1435	**381**	70c. multicoloured	80	70

(Des R. Bissig. Litho)

2000 (7 Mar). *Snow Storms.* T **382** *and similar horiz designs. Multicoloured.* P 13 × 13½.
1436	10c. Type **382**		10	10
1437	20c. Fondue		25	25
1438	30c. Jugs and grapes on tray		40	40
1439	50c. Mountain goat		60	55
1440	60c. Clock		70	70
1441	70c. St. Bernard dogs		80	80
1436/1441	Set of 6		2·50	2·50

The 50c. was also issued in coils.

383 "ON I"

384 "frau" and Emblem

(Des Susanne Huber and M. Schmid. Photo Courvoisier)

2000 (10 May). *"naba 2000" National Stamp Exhibition, St. Gallen (2nd issue). Sheet* 65 × 85 *mm containing* T **383** *and similar vert designs. Multicoloured.* P 11½ × 12.
MS1442	20c.+10c. Type **383** (top right-hand corner); 20c.+10c. "5" (bottom left-hand corner); 70c.+35c. "RAY" (top left-hand corner); 90c.+45c. "Rp" (bottom right-hand corner)	3·25	3·25

The four stamps in No. **MS**1448 were issued together to form a composite design depicting a modern representation of a 1850 5r. Federal Administration stamp.

(Des Jenny Leibundgut. Litho PTT, Berne)

2000 (10 May). *Centenary of National Council of Women. Paper with fluorescent fibres.* P 13½.
1443	**384**	70c. multicoloured	80	50

385 "Building Europe"

386 Town Square, Nafels

(Des J.-P. Cousin. Litho PTT, Berne)

2000 (10 May). *Europa. Paper with fluorescent fibres.* P 13½.
1444	**385**	90c. multicoloured	95	95

(Des K. Oberli. Eng H. Baldauf. Recess and litho PTT, Berne)

2000 (10 May). *Pro Patria. "Townscapes 2000" (rejuvenation projects).* T **386** *and similar horiz designs. Multicoloured. Paper with fluorescent fibres.* P 13½.
1445	70c.+35c. Type **386**		1·20	1·10
1446	70c.+35c. Main road, Tengia		1·20	1·10
1447	90c.+40c. Main road, Brugg		1·60	1·40
1448	90c.+40c. Marketplace, Carouge		1·60	1·40
1445/1448	Set of 4		5·00	4·50

377

SWITZERLAND Switzerland 2000

387 Payerne Church and Violin

(Des Marina Ott. Litho PTT, Berne)

2000 (21 June). *Tourism. T* **387** *and similar horiz designs. Multicoloured. Paper with fluorescent fibres.* P 13 × 13½.
1449	387	90c. multicoloured (20.9.01)	1·10	45
1450		100c. multicoloured (20.9.01)	1·20	70
1451		110c. deep blue, deep turquoise and vermilion (20.9.01)	1·70	1·50
1452		120c. multicoloured (21.6.00)	1·40	1·00
1453		130c. multicoloured (21.6.00)	1·40	15
1454		180c. multicoloured (21.6.00)	2·00	1·30
1455		200c. multicoloured (21.11.00)	2·20	90
1456		220c. multicoloured (13.3.01)	2·50	1·90
1457		300c. multicoloured (21.11.00)	3·25	65
1459		400c. multicolourred (13.3.01)	4·50	3·25
1449/1459	Set of 10		19·00	10·50

Designs:—90c. Willisan farm house and horse; 100c. La Suisse (lake stream) and woman looking over Lake Geneva; 110c. Kleine Matterhorne glacier and skier; 120c. Type **387**; 130c. St. Saphorin Church and bottle of wine; 180c. National spring and bather, Vals; 200c. Landscape and walker; 220c. Bus and children; 300c. Stone bridge and mountain bike; 400c. Airplane fin and man with suitcase.

388 Embroidery

(Des P. Hostteller. Embroidered Bischoff Textil AG, St. Gallen)

2000 (21 June). *St. Gallen Embroidery. Self-adhesive. Imperf.*
1460	**388**	5f. cobalt and slate-blue	8·75	8·75
MS1461	158 × 132 mm. No. 1460 × 4		£110	£110

389 Emblem

(Des O. Galli. Litho PTT, Berne)

2000 (15 Sept). *Population Census. Paper with fluorescent fibres.* P 13½.
1462	389	70c. multicoloured	80	65

(Litho Flexoprint Permapack, Rorschach)

2000 (15 Sept). *"Stampin the Future". Winning Entries in Children's International Painting Competition. Booklet stamps. T* **390** *and similar horiz designs. Multicoloured. Self-adhesive. Paper with fluorescent fibres. Die-cut straight edge × wavy edge.*
1463		70c. Type **390**	50	65
1464		70c. "Looks below the Sun" (Charlotte Bättig)	50	65
1465		70c. "The Perfect World" (Sandra Dobler)	50	65
1466		70c. "My Town" (Stephanie Aerschmann)	50	65
1463/1466	Set of 4		1·80	2·30

Nos. 1463/6 are peeled directly from the cover of the booklet. It is not therefore possible to collect these as booklet panes.

391 Swimming    **392** Cathedral and Horsemen

(Des B. Leuenberger. Photo Questa)

2000 (15 Sept). *Olympic Games, Sydney. Booklet stamps. T* **391** *and similar circular designs. Multicoloured. Paper with fluorescent fibres. Self-adhesive. Die-cut straight edge.*
1467		90c. Type **391**	95	95
1468		90c. Cycling	95	95
1469		90c. Running	95	95

Nos. 1467/9 are peeled directly from the cover of the booklet. It is not therefore possible to collect these as booklet panes.

(Des M. Eberhard. Litho PTT, Berne)

2000 (21 Nov). *Stamp Day. Paper with fluorescent fibres.* P 13½.
1470	**392**	70c. multicoloured	80	65

393 Dresden-style Tree Decoration    **394** Alice Rivaz

(Des Bernadette Baltis. Photo Courvoisier)

2000 (21 Nov). *Christmas. Granite paper.* P 11½.
1471	**393**	90c. multicoloured	1·20	80

(Des P. Schopfer (70c.), R. Hirter (90c.), Y. Fidalgo (110c.), A. Wittmer (130c.). Litho PTT, Berne)

2001 (13 Mar). *Anniversaries. T* **394** *and similar horiz designs. Paper with fluorescent fibres.* P 13½.
1472		70c. multicoloured	80	60
1473		90c. multicoloured	1·00	80
1474		110c. vermilion, grey and black	1·20	1·30
1475		130c. multicoloured	1·40	1·50
1472/1475	Set of 4		4·00	3·75

Designs: As Type **394**—70c. Type **394** (writer, birth centenary); 110c. "CARITAS" and jigsaw pieces (centenary of Caritas Christian charity organization); 130c. Refugees (50th anniv of United Nations High Commissioner for Refugees). Size 39 × 30 mm—90c. Airplane (centenary of Aero-Club of Switzerland).

SWITZERLAND Switzerland   2001

395 Flowers and Envelope
396 Woman's Head 
399 Blue Rainbow Fish
400 Straits Rhododendron (*Melastoma malabathricum*)

(Des M. Eberhard. Litho PTT, Berne)

2001 (13 Mar). *Greetings Stamp. Paper with fluorescent fibres.* P 13½.
1476 **395** 90c. multicoloured 95 50

(Des Sabina Oberholzer (70c.), R. Schraivogel and Y. Netzhammer (90c.). Litho PTT, Berne (70c.), photo Courvoisier (90c.))

2001 (9 May). *Anniversary and Event. T* **396** *and similar horiz design. Multicoloured. Paper with fluorescent fibres (70c.) or granite paper (90c.).* P 13½ (70c.) or 11¾ (90c.).
1477 70c. Type **396** (re-opening of Vela Museum, Ligornetto) 80 80
1478 90c. Chocolate segment (centenary of Chocosuisse) . . . . 1·00 1·00
No. 1478 is printed in sheetlets of 15 stamps and is impregnated with the scent of chocolate.

2001 (9 May). *Self-adhesive booklet stamps. Litho SNP Ausprint (70c.), Guhl & Scheibler, Aesch (90c.). Phosphorescent markings (70c.) or paper with fluorescent fibres (90c.). Die-cut wavy line × imperf (70c.) or imperf × die-cut wavy line (90c.).*
1479 70c. multicoloured 80 80
1480 90c. new blue, orange vermilion and lemon . . . . 95 1·00
Design:—70c. As No. 1441; 90c. Type **336**.
Nos. 1479/80 are peeled directly from the covers of the booklets. It is not therefore possible to collect these as booklet panes.
Nos. 1479/80 were also available as coil stamps in rolls of 100 with the self-adhesive paper around each stamp removed.
The phosphorescent markings on No. 1479, which appear pink under U.V. light, form two short bars on the left and right-hand side of the stamp.

397 Italian Theatre, La Chaux-de-Fonds
398 Water 

(Des V. Wyss. Litho PTT, Berne)

2001 (9 May). *Pro Patria. Cultural Heritage. T* **397** *and similar horiz designs. Paper with fluorescent fibres.* P 13½.
1481 70c.+35c. black, dull orange-red and red . . . . 1·20 1·20
1482 70c.+40c. black, grey-brown and light green . . . . 1·20 1·20
1483 90c.+40c. black, reddish brown and lemon . . . . 1·60 1·60
1484 90c.+40c. multicoloured . . . . . . 1·60 1·60
1481/1484 Set of 4 . . . . 5·00 5·00
Designs:—No. 1482, Hauterive Monastery; 1483, Leuk Castle; 1484, Rorschach Granary.

(Des Jenny Leibundgut. Litho PTT, Berne)

2001 (9 May). *Europa. Water Resources. Paper with fluorescent fibres.* P 13½.
1485 **398** 90c. multicoloured 95 95

(Des M. Pfister. Photo Enschedé)

2001 (20 Sept). *Illustrations from Rainbow Fish (book by Martin Pfister). T* **399** *and similar horiz design. Multicoloured.* P 13 × 14.
1486 70c. Type **399** 65 25
1487 90c. Purple rainbow fish 80 50

(Des N. Loh and Suzanne Potterat. Litho Enschedé)

2001 (20 Sept). *Switzerland–Singapore Joint Issue. Flowers. Sheet 98 × 68 mm containing T* **400** *and similar horiz designs. Multicoloured.* P 13½ × 13.
MS1488 70c. Type **400**; 90c. *Saraca cauliflora*; 110c. Edelweiss (*Leontopodium alpinum*); 130c. Gentian (*Gentiana clusii*) . . . . . . 3·75 3·75

401 "The Birth of Venus"
402 Buildings (Beat Kehrli) 

(Des T. Wetter. Litho PTT, Berne)

2001 (20 Sept). *Death Centenary of Arnold Böcklin (artist). Paper with fluorescent fibres.* P 13½.
1489 **401** 180c. multicoloured . . . . . . 1·70 1·50

(Litho PTT, Berne)

2001 (20 Nov). *Stamp Day. Winning entry in stamp design competition. Paper with fluorescent fibres.* P 13½.
1490 **402** 70c. multicoloured 65 25

403 Gablonz-style Christmas Tree Ornament
404 Ladder, Wall and Stars 

(Des Bernadette Baltis. Litho Questa)

2001 (20 Nov). *Christmas. Granite paper.* P 11½.
1491 **403** 90c. multicoloured 65 25

(Des J. Wandflüh. Litho PTT, Berne)

2002 (12 Mar). *Escalade (festival) (celebrating 400th anniv of defeat of Savoyard attack on the city), Geneva. Paper with fluorescent fibres.* P 13½.
1492 **404** 70c. multicoloured 65 25

379

SWITZERLAND Switzerland 2002

405 "E" and Towers, Biel
406 RABDe 500 InterCity Tilting Train (ICN) 

(Des T. Steineman. Photo Questa)

2002 (12 Mar). "Expo '02" National Exhibition, Biel, Murten, Neuchâtel and Yverdon-les-Bains (1st issue). T **405** and similar horiz designs, each featuring "Arteplage" (exhibition platform) of each host town. Multicoloured. Granite paper. P 14 × 14½.

1493	70c. Type **405**	65	25
	a. Block of 4. Nos. 1493/6	2·75	
1494	70c. Reversed "P" and Monolith, Murten	65	25
1495	70c. "O", pebble-shaped construction over water, Neuchâtel	65	25
1496	70c. "2" and artificial cloud, Yverdon-les-Bains	65	25
1493/1496	Set of 4	2·40	90

Nos. 1493/6 were issued together in *se-tenant* blocks of four stamps.
See also No. **MS**1509.

(Des B. Kehrli. Photo Enschedé)

2002 (12 Mar). Centenary of Swiss Federal Railways (SBB) (national railway operator). T **406** and similar horiz designs. Multicoloured. P 13 × 14.

1497	70c. Type **406**	65	25
1498	90c. Inter-city 2000 double-deck train	80	50
1499	120c. Railcar, Lucerne–Lenzburg Seetal line	1·10	1·00
1500	130c. 119 Re 460 locomotive	1·20	1·00
1497/1500	Set of 4	3·50	2·50

407 Fa ade
408 Augusta A-109-K2 Helicopter and Hawker 800B Air Ambulance 

(Des M. Gnehm. Litho PTT, Berne)

2002 (12 Mar). Centenary of Federal Parliament Building. Paper with fluorescent fibres. P 13½.
1501 **407** 90c. multicoloured ... 80 50

(Des R. Schenker. Litho and holography Cartor)

2002 (12 Mar). 50th Anniv of Swiss Air Rescue (Rega). P 13 × 13½.
1502 **408** 180c. multicoloured ... 1·70 1·50

409 Clown
410 Bruzella, Ticino Canton 

(Des H. Falk. Litho PTT, Berne)

2002 (15 May). Europa. Circus. T **409** and similar horiz design. Multicoloured. Paper with fluorescent fibres. P 13½.
1503	70c. Type **409**	65	25
1504	90c. Clown (different)	80	50

(Des T. Fluri. Litho Cartor)

2002 (15 May). Pro Patria. Water Mills Preservation. T **410** and similar horiz designs showing water mills. Multicoloured. P 13½.

1505	70c.+35c. Type **410**	95	50
1506	70c.+35c. Oberdorf, Basel Canton	95	50
1507	90c.+40c. Lussery-Villars, de Vaud Canton	1·20	1·20
1508	90c.+40c. Büren a. d. Aare, Berne Canton	1·20	1·20
1505/1508	Set of 4	4·00	3·00

411 "X"
412 Two Teddies (Switzerland, c. 1950) 

(Des T. Steineman. Photo Questa)

2002 (15 May). "Expo '02", Sixth National Exhibition, Biel, Murten, Neuchâtel and Yverdon-les-Bains (2nd issue). Sheet 95 × 70 mm. P 14 × 14½.
MS1509 **411** 90c. multicoloured ... 85 85

(Des U. Fueter and U. Hungerbühler. Litho Enschedé)

2002 (15 May). Centenary of the Teddy Bear. Booklet stamps. T **412** and similar multicoloured designs. Self-adhesive. Die-cut straight edge.

1510	90c. White Teddy with pink bow (France, 1925) (26 × 26 mm, round)	80	50
1511	90c. Type **412**	80	50
1512	90c. Teddy with grey-brown bow (Germany, 1904) (22 × 32 mm, oval)	80	50
1513	90c. "Philibert", Swiss Post Teddy (Switzerland, 2002) (26 × 22 mm, rectangle)	80	50
1514	90c. Teddy with grey paws (England, c. 1920) (26 × 26 mm, round)	80	50
1510/1514	Set of 5	3·50	2·30

Nos. 1510/14 are die-cut around the shape of the frame. The stamps peeled directly from the cover of the booklet. It is not therefore possible to collect these as booklet panes.

413 Emblem
414 Emperor Dragonfly (*Anax imperator*) 

(Des R. Pfund. Litho Enschedé)

2002 (11 Sept). Membership of the United Nations. Ordinary paper. P 14 × 14½.
1515 **413** 90c. multicoloured ... 80 50

380

# SWITZERLAND Switzerland 2002

(Des Bernadette Baltis. Litho Enschedé)
2002 (17 Sept). *Insects. T* **414** *and similar horiz designs. Multicoloured. Ordinary paper.* P 14 × 14½.
1516	10c. Type **414**	10	10
1517	20c. Dark green fritillary (*Mesoacidalia aglaja*)	20	10
1518	50c. Alpine longhorn beetle (*Rosalia alpina*)	45	20
1519	100c. Striped bug (*Graphosoma lineatum*)	90	50
1516/1519	Set of 4	1·50	85

415 Printing Press (copper engraving, Abraham Bosse)
416 Ladybird on Leaf

(Des and eng P. Schopfer. Recess and litho PTT, Berne)
2002 (17 Sept). *Swiss Post Stamp Printers, Berne Commemoration. Paper with fluorescent fibres.* P 13½.
1520   **415**   70c. multicoloured   65   20
No. 1520 was the last stamp printed by Swiss Post Stamp Printers.

(Des Bernadette Baltis. Litho Enschedé)
2002 (17 Sept). *Greeting Stamp. Self-adhesive. Die-cut straight edge × p* 12½.
1521   **416**   90c. multicoloured   80   50
No. 1521 was issued *se-tenant* with a label and was available both as a single stamp or in booklets of 10 stamps plus 10 *se-tenant* labels.

417 Quartz
418 Kingfisher and Jura Water Engineering System (Michèle Berri)

(Des SchottMerz, Berne. Litho German State Ptg Wks, Berlin)
2002 (17 Sept). *Minerals. T* **417** *and similar horiz design. Multicoloured. Paper with fluorescent fibres.* P 13½.
1522   200c. Type **417**   1·90   1·60
1523   500c. Titanite   4·50   4·25
Numbers have been left for additions to this series.

(Des Michèle Berri. Litho Walsall Security Printers Ltd)
2002 (19 Nov). *Stamp Day. Winning Entry in Stamp Design Competition.* P 14.
1535   **418**   70c. multicoloured   65   25

419 Bohemian Cardboard Tree Decoration, c. 1900
420 Skier

(Des Bernadette Baltis. Photo Questa)
2002 (19 Nov). *Christmas. Granite paper.* P 11½.
1536   **419**   90c. multicoloured   80   50

(Des C. Spahr and E. Iseli. Litho Walsall Security Printers Ltd)
2002 (19 Nov). *World Alpine Skiing Championship, St. Moritz.* P 14.
1537   **420**   90c. multicoloured   80   50

421 "70"
422 Hypericum (*Hypericum perforatum*)

(Des Sandra di Salvo. Litho and embossed Questa)
2003 (6 Mar). *Centenary of Swiss National Association of the Blind and Library for the Blind and Visually Impaired. Paper with fluorescent fibres.* P 14½.
1538   **421**   70c. orange-vermilion   65   25
No. 1538 was embossed with 70 in Braille.

(Des Suzanne Potterat. Litho Walsall)
2003 (6 Mar). *Medicinal Plants. T* **422** *and similar vert designs. Multicoloured.* P 14.
1539	70c. Type **422**	65	25
1540	90c. Periwinkle (*Vinca minor*)	80	50
1541	110c. Valerian (*Valeriana officinalis*)	1·00	60
1542	120c. Arnica montana	1·10	65
1543	130c. Centaury (*Centaurium minus*)	1·20	70
1544	180c. Mallow (*Malva sylvestris*)	1·60	1·00
1545	220c. Chamomile (*Matricaria chamomilla*)	2·00	1·80
1539/1545	Set of 7	8·50	5·00

423 Waterfall

(Des R. Schenker. Litho Cartor)
2003 (6 Mar). *International Year of Water.* P 13 × 13½.
1546   **423**   90c. multicoloured   80   50

424 Contour Lines, Compass and Runner

(Des T. Dätwyler. Litho Cartor)
2003 (6 Mar). *World Orienteering Championships, Rapperswil-Jona.* P 13½.
1547   **424**   90c. multicoloured   80   50

381

SWITZERLAND Switzerland, Switzerland 2003

425 Horse's Head

(Des L. Cocchi. Litho Cartor)
2003 (6 Mar). *Centenary of Marché-Concours (horse show and market), Saignelégier.* P 13½.
1548 **425** 90c. multicoloured 80 50

426 *Alinghi* (yacht)

(Des R. Hirter. Litho Cartor)
2003 (7 Mar). *Switzerland, America's Cup Winners, 2003.* P 13 × 13½.
1549 **426** 90c. multicoloured 80 50

POSTCARD STAMPS

P **1** Tourism Emblem

(Des Martine Chatagny. Litho Enschedé)
2002 (19 Nov). *Self-adhesive gum. No value expressed.* Imperf × die-cut perf 13½.
P1 P **1** (1f.30) multicoloured . . . . 1·20 50
P2 (1f.80) multicoloured . . . . 1·70 85
No. P1 was for use only on postcards sent to countries within Europe and No. P2 to overseas countries. They were not valid for use on other mail or in combination with other stamps.

MACHINE LABELS

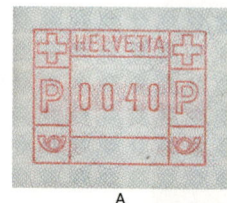

A    B

From 9 August 1976 gummed labels were available from automatic machines, the value, from 5c. to 99f.95, being printed at the time of purchase.
At first only four machines were installed and these dispensed labels similar to Type A but with an additional letter and number in the bottom frame, indicating the issuing machine: A1, Zurich main railway station; A2, Berne; A3, Grindelwald; A4, Geneva.

From June 1978 these code letters were removed and many more machines were installed. Five different types of label without code letters have been identified: A. Similar to illustration but with narrow letters about 4 mm high, value printed in bright purple on granite paper (26.6.78). B. As illustrated, with broader letters about 3½ mm high, value printed in bright purple on granite paper (26.2.79). C. As illustrated, printed in deep carmine on granite paper (15.6.81). D. As illustrated, printed in bright purple on fibreless paper (20.7.81). E. As D but printed in deep carmine (20.7.81).
Type A was printed from 1976–87 on phosphorescent paper with an overall grey-blue pattern. From 1987 fluorescent paper was used, at first with the same pattern. The overall background pattern was changed to yellow crosses in November 1990, and again in November 1993 to outline maps of Switzerland in yellow-olive.
Type B, printed on the "maps" paper, was issued 17 June 1995 for the "Basler Taube 1995" stamp exhibition.

C

On 14 May 1996 four new designs, as Type C, were introduced, depicting the seasons of the year and printed on fluorescent paper with a short silver bar in the left margin. The illustrations show: Spring, Jura (daisies in foreground); Summer, Grisons (Type C); Autumn, Tessin (multicoloured trees and shrubs in foreground); Winter, Alps (dull ultramarine forest in foreground).

D

20.9.01 A set of four designs featuring transport was issued. The designs featured a train, lorry, car and airplane.

EXPRESS MAIL SERVICE (EMS) LABELS

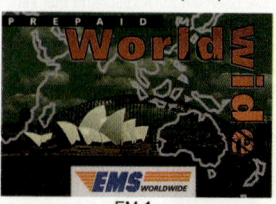

EM **1**

From 4 August 1997 these labels were available from post offices to pre-pay letters weighing not more than 500 grams. Three designs were issued, showing Tower Bridge, Golden Gate Bridge and Sydney Harbour Bridge with the Opera House. These labels were for use to Europe, North America and Worldwide destinations respectively.
They are cancelled by a portion of the label being torn off by postal staff.

SWITZERLAND Switzerland

STAMP BOOKLETS

The following checklist covers, in simplified form, booklets issued by Switzerland. It is intended that it should be used in conjunction with the main listings and details of stamps and panes listed there are not repeated.

Nos. SB19/25 were sold at 5c. over face value. Booklets prepared for use in automatic machines have the suffix S.

Some booklets exist in more than one version, differing in advertisements on the cover; such differences are not covered by this list.

Booklets containing the 1986, 1989 and 1992 "Pro Sport" stamps were privately produced by the Swiss Sports Federation.

Booklets containing "Pro Patria" stamps are listed at the end of this section; those containing "Pro Juventute" stamps are listed after that section.

Prices are for complete booklets

Booklet No.	Date	Contents and Face Value	Price
SB1	1904	Cross and Numeral (T **9**). W **8** 4 panes, No. 129 × 6 (1f.20)	£600
SB2	1904	Cross and Numeral (T **9**). W **8** 4 panes, No. 130B × 6 (2f.40)	£2250
SB3	1905	Cross and Numeral (T **9**). W **13** 4 panes, No. 196 × 6 (1f.20)	£1000
SB4	1905	Cross and Numeral (T **9**). W **13** 4 panes, No. 197 × 6 (2f.40)	£850
SB5	1907	Tell's Son (T **15**) 4 panes, No. 227 × 6 (1f.20)	£400
SB6	1907	Helvetia (T **16**) 4 panes, No. 228 × 6 (2f.40)	£325
SB7	1909	Sitting Helvetia (T **17**) 4 panes, No. 233 × 6 (3f.)	£300
SB8	1909	Tell's Son (T **18**) 5 panes, No. 247 × 6 (60c.)	£180
SB9	1909	Tell's Son (T **18**) 5 panes, No. 249 × 6 (1f.50)	£425
SB10	1909	Helvetia (T **19**) 5 panes, No. 250 × 6 (3f.)	£200
SB11	1910	Tell's Son (T **20**a) 5 panes, No. 257 × 6 (1f.50)	£3500
SB12	1911	Tell's Son (T **20**b) 5 panes, No. 260 × 6 (60c.)	£500
SB13	1911	Tell's Son (T **20**b) 5 panes, No. 263 × 6 (1f.50)	£200
SB14	1915	Tell's Son (T **20**a) 5 panes, No. 254 × 6 (90c.)	£200
SB15	1915	Tell (T **21**) 5 panes, No. 279 × 6 (3f.)	£180
SB16	1917	Tell's Son (T **20**a) 5 panes, No. 255 × 6 (90c.)	£180
SB17	1917	Tell's Son (T **20**b) and Tell (T **21**) 4 panes, No. 263 × 6, 3 panes, No. 279 × 6 (3f.)	£180
SB18	1918	Tell's Son (T **20**a) and Tell (T **21**) 1 pane, No. 258 × 6; 1 pane, No. 279 × 6; 1 pane, No. 2796, 2 panes, No. 285 × 6 (3f.50)	£200
SB19	1921	Tell's Son (T **20**a) and Tell (T **21**) 1 pane, No. 310 × 6; 1 pane, No. 279 × 6; 1 pane, No. 279b; 2 panes, No. 314a × 6 (3f.95+5c.)	£150
SB20	1921	Tell's Son (T **20**b) and Tell (T **21**) 1 pane, No. 264a; 2 panes, No. 280 × 6; 2 panes, No. 287 × 6 (3f.95+5c.)	£190
SB21	1924	Tell's Son (T **20**b) and Tell (T **21**) 1 pane, No. 265a; 2 panes, No. 280 × 6; 2 panes, No. 287 × 6 (3f.95+5c.)	£200
SB22	1925	Tell's Son (T **20**b) and Tell (T **21**) 1 pane, No. 265a; 2 panes, No. 280 × 6; 2 panes, No. 289 × 6 (3f.95+5c.)	£250
SB23	1927	Tell's Son (T **20**b) and Tell (T **21**) 1 pane, No. 266a; 2 panes, No. 280 × 6; 2 panes, No. 289 × 6 (3f.95+5c.)	£250
SB24	1928	Tell's Son (T **20**b) and Tell (T **21**) 1 pane, No. 266b; 2 panes, No. 281 × 6; 2 panes, No. 289 × 6 (3f.95+5c.)	£250
SB25	1930–33	Tell's Son (T **20**b) and Tell (T **21**) 1 pane, No. 267a; 2 panes, No. 282 × 6; 2 panes, No. 289 × 6 (3f.95+5c.)	£250
		a. Grilled gum Nos. 267ba, 282b and 289b (1933)	£600
SB26	1935	Landscapes (as T **48**) 1 pane, No. 352 × 6; 1 pane, No. 353 × 6, 1 pane, No. 354 × 6 (3f.)	£250
SB27	1936	Landscapes (as T **48**) 2 panes, No. 351 × 6; 2 panes, No. 352 × 6; 1 pane, No. 354 × 6 (3f.)	£250
SB28	1936	Landscapes (as T **48**) 1 pane, No. 351 × 6; 3 panes, No. 352 × 6, 2 panes, No. 354 × 6 (4f.50)	£275
SB29S	1936	Landscapes (as T **52**) 1 pane, No. 351 × 10 (50c.)	£225
SB30	1936	Landscapes (as T **48** and **52**) 2 panes, No. 369B × 6; 2 panes, No. 352 × 6; 1 pane, No. 354 × 6 (3f.)	£250
SB31	1937	Landscapes (as T **52**) 2 panes, No. 369A × 6, 2 panes, No. 370A × 6, 1 pane, No. 374dA × 6 (3f.)	£225
		a. Grilled gum. Nos. 369B, 370B and 374dB	£300
SB32	1937	Landscapes (as T **52**) 1 pane, No. 369A × 6, 3 panes, No. 370A × 6, 2 panes, No. 374dA × 6 (4f.50)	£400
		a. Grilled gum. Nos. 369B, 370B and 374dB	£400
SB33	1937–39	Landscapes (as T **52**) 2 panes, No. 369A × 6; 2 panes, No. 370dA × 6, 1 pane, No. 375A × 6 (1939) (3f.)	£160
		a. Grilled gum. Nos. 369B, 370dB and 375B (1937) (3 f.)	£225
		b. Mixed gum. Nos. 369A, 370dB and 375A (1939)	£400
SB34S	1939	National Exhibition, Zurich (T **64**) 1 pane, No. 394G × 10 (50c.)	£225
SB35	1939	Landscapes (as T **52**) 1 pane, No. 369A × 6; 3 panes, No. 370dA × 6, 2 panes, No. 375A × 6 (4f.50)	£180
		a. Grilled gum. Nos. 3696, 370dB and 375B	£250
SB36	1942	Landscapes (as T **52**) 2 panes, No. 369A × 6, 2 panes, No. 371A × 6; 1 pane, No. 375A × 6 (3f.)	£130
SB37	1942	Landscapes (as T **52**) 1 pane, No. 369A × 6; 3 panes, No. 371A × 6; 2 panes, No. 375A × 6 (4f.50)	£140

383

SWITZERLAND Switzerland

SB38	1943	Landscapes (as T **52**) 2 panes, No. 369A × 6; 2 panes, No. 372A × 6; 1 pane, No. 375A × 6 (3f.)	95·00
SB39	1943	Landscapes (as T **52**) 1 pane, No. 369A × 6; 3 panes, No. 372A × 6, 2 panes, No. 375A × 6 (4f.50)	£140
SB40	1948	Landscapes (as T **52**) 2 panes, No. 489 × 6; 2 panes, No. 490 × 6; 1 pane, No. 491 × 6 (3f.)	£130
SB41	1948	Landscapes (as T **52**) 1 pane, No. 489 × 6; 3 panes, No. 490 × 6; 2 panes, No. 491 × 6 (4f.50)	£160
SB42S	1948	Landscapes (as T **52**) 1 pane, No. 489 × 10 (50c.)	£140
SB43S	1949	Technology (T **107**) 1 pane, No. 511 × 10 (50c.)	£150
SB44	1950	Technology (as T **106**/7) 1 pane, No. 511 × 4; 3 panes, No. 512 × 4; 2 panes, No. 514a × 4 (3f.)	£130
SB45	1950	Technology (as T **106**/7) 3 panes, No. 511 × 4; 5 panes, No. 512 × 4; 3 panes, No. 514a × 4 (5f.)	£130
SB46S	1960	Postal History 1 pane, No. 614 × 10 (50c.)	27·00
SB47	1960–66	Postal History 1 pane, No. 614 × 4; 3 panes, No. 615 × 4; 2 panes, No. 617 × 4 (3f.)	46·00
		a. Phosphor. Nos. 614p, 615p and 617p (1966)	46·00
SB48	1960–66	Postal History and Monuments 2 panes, No. 614 × 4; 3 panes, No. 615 × 4; 3 panes, No. 617 × 4; 1 pane, No. 622 × 4 (6f.)	50·00
		a. As above but containing Nos. 614p, 615p, 617p and 622 (1966)	45·00
		b. As above but containing Nos. 614, 615p, 617p and 622 (1966)	36·00
SB49	1962–66	Postal History 2 panes, No. 614 × 4; 2 panes, No. 615 × 4; 1 pane, No. 617 × 4 (2f.)	26·00
		a. Phosphor. Nos. 614p, 615p and 617p (1966)	46·00
SB50	1962–67	Postal History 3 panes, No. 614 × 4; 5 panes, No. 615 × 4, 3 panes, No. 617 × 4 (5f.)	34·00
		a. Phosphor. Nos. 614p, 615p and 617p (1967)	26·00
		b. Mixed. 3 panes, No. 614p × 4; 3 panes, No. 615p × 4; 2 panes, No. 617 × 4 (1967)	20·00
SB51S	1967	Postal History 1 pane, No. 615 × 10 (1f.)	36·00
SB52	1968	Postal History and Monuments 2 panes, No. 615p × 4; 1 pane, 2 panes, No. 615pb; 2 panes, No. 617p × 4; No. 619p × 4 (5f.)	22·00
SB53S	1970	Monuments (2nd series) 1 pane, No. 699 × 10 (1f.)	30·00
SB54	1970	Monuments (2nd series) 2 panes, No. 699 × 4; 1 pane, No. 699b; 2 panes, No. 701 × 4; 2 panes, No. 702 × 4 (5f.)	20·00
SB55	1973	Monuments (2nd series) 2 panes, No. 699 × 4; 1 pane, No 700 × 4; 3 panes, No. 702 × 4 (5f.)	22·00
SB56	5.1.76–78	Monuments (1st and 2nd series) 1 pane, No. 699b; 2 panes, No. 701 × 4; 2 panes, No. 621p × 4 (5f.) Green cover. Contents on front overprinted	17·00
		a. Orange cover. Contents on front overprinted (1976)	17·00
		b. Green cover. Correct contents printed on front and PTT posthorn emblem (1976)	17·00
		c. Green cover. New PTT emblem (cross over "PTT") (1978)	16·00
SB57	5.1.79–83	Folk Customs 1 pane, No. 940ab; 2 panes, No. 941ab, 2 panes, No. 943ab (5f.) Couple dancing on front. Orange cover	8·50
		a. As above but blue cover (1980)	18·00
		b. As above but green cover (1981)	25·00
		c. Couple with whips on front. Grey cover (1.4.82)	30·00
		d. As c. but blue cover (18.4.83)	42·00
SB58	1.2.84–85	Folk Customs 1 pane, No. 939ab; 1 pane, No. 940ac; 1 pane, No. 942ab; 1 pane, No. 944ab, 1 pane, No. 944ac (5f.) Yellow cover	14·50
		a. Orange cover (2.9.85)	60·00
SB59	2.9.85	Folk Customs 1 pane, No. 939ab; 1 pane, No. 940ac; 1 pane, No. 942ab; 4 panes, No. 944ab (10f.)	14·50
SB60	8.9.88	The Post Past and Present 1 pane, No. 1109ab (5f.)	9·50
SB61	22.2.91	700th Anniv of Swiss Confederation 1 pane, No. 1219a × 2 (4f.)	9·00
SB62	19.1.93	Lake Taney 1 pane, No. 1257 × 10 (6f.)	11·50
SB63	30.6.94	"A" Mail (T **313**) 1 pane, No. 1258 × 10 (8f.)	10·00
SB64	28.11.94	Rabbit 1 pane, No. 1194ab (7f.)	8·50
SB65	28.11.94	"A" Mail (T **336**) 1 pane, No. 1313ab (9f.)	11·50
SB66	12.3.96	Pro Sport (T **338**) 1 pane, No. 1319 × 10 (10f.)	13·00
SB67	10.9.96	Greetings Stamps. Self-adhesive Nos. 1332/5, each × 2 (7f.20)	7·75
SB68	8.9.98	Sports Self-adhesive Nos. 1396/1400, each × 2 (7f.)	6·50
SB69	9.3.99	Rodolphe Topffer Self-adhesive Nos. 1409/13, each × 2 plus 4 labels (9f.)	9·50
SB70	29.7.00	Publicity Issue 1 pane, No. 1418 × 10 (9f.)	8·50
SB71	15.9.00	"Stampin the Future" Nos. 1463/6, each × 2 (5f.60)	6·00
SB72	15.9.00	Olympic Games, Sydney Nos. 1467/9, (2f.70)	1·40
SB73	9.5.01	St. Barnard. Self-adhesive No. 1479 × 12 (8f.40)	8·00
SB74	9.5.01	"A" Mail (T **336**). Self-adhesive No. 1480 × 2 (10f.80)	10·50
SB75	15.5.02	Centenary of the Teddy Bear. Self-adhesive Nos. 1510/14, each × 2 (9f.)	8·50

SWITZERLAND 1913

| SB76 | 17.9.02 | Greeting stamp. Self-adhesive No. 1522 × 10, plus 10 labels (9f.) | | 8·50 |

PRO PATRIA STAMP BOOKLETS

The premium on the stamps was for the benefit of the Swiss National Day Fund. The booklets were sold at a further premium above face value to defray the cost of making them up. In 1990 and 1991 this premium was 50c.; from 1992 it was 80c.

In 1989 a booklet containing No. 1162 × 10 was produced by the National Day Committee as an experiment and sold in selected localities by schoolchildren; it cannot therefore be considered a Post Office issue.

Booklet No.	Date	Contents	Price
PSB1	1990	1 pane, No. 1206 × 10	8·50
PSB2	1991	1 pane, No. 1227 × 10	7·50
PSB3	1992	1 pane, No. 1246 × 10	7·00
PSB4	1993	1 pane, No. 1268 × 10	8·00
PSB5	1994	1 pane, No. 1289 × 10	10·00
PSB6	1995	1 pane, No. 1303 × 10	10·00
PSB7	1996	1 pane, No. 1324 × 10	11·00
PSB8	1997	1 pane, No. 1355 × 10	18·00
PSB9	1998	1 pane, No. 1392 × 10	13·00
PSB10	1999	1 pane, No. 1423 × 10	13·00
PSB11	2000	1 pane, No. 1448 × 10	11·00
PSB12	2001	1 pane, No. 1483 × 10	11·00
PSB13	2002	1 pane, No. 1508 × 10	11·00

"PRO JUVENTUTE" CHARITY STAMPS

As a special exception these have not been included in chronological order in the general list as to do so effectively would entail renumbering so many stamps.

PREMIUMS. All "Pro Juventute" stamps are sold at an additional premium which goes to Benevolent Societies. Until 1937 these premiums were not shown on the stamps, but were as follows:—

2c. for all 3c. franking values, 5c. for all 5c., 7½c., 10c., 15c. and 20c. values; and 10c. for all 30c. and 40c. values.

From 1937, when the premium first appeared on the designs, we show it in the catalogue listing.

PRINTING PROCESSES AND DESIGNS. The issues from 1913 to 1926 are typographed at the Mint and the designs show the costumes or arms of the cantons named. Thenceforward printing processes and designs varied as described below.

INSCRIPTIONS. All the following are inscribed "PRO JUVENTUTE" and the year of issue, except Nos. J1a/8 which are undated.

C 1 Helvetia and Matterhorn
C 2 Appenzell 
C 4 
C 6 

(Des A. Grasset)

1913 (1 Dec). W **13**. P 12 × 11½.
| J1 | C 1 | 5c. green | | 2·50 | 4·25 |

(Nos. J1a to J8. Des W. Balmer. Eng J. Sprenger)

1915 (1 Dec). Type C **2** and similar type. Buff paper. W **13**. P 11½.
J1a		5c. green	2·75	5·50
	b.	Tête-bêche (pair)	70·00	
J2		10c. red (Girl from Lucerne)	80·00	55·00

1916 (1 Dec). Type C **4** and similar portraits. Buff paper. W **13**. P 11½.
J3	3c. violet (Freiburg)	5·75	23·00
J4	5c. green (Berne)	9·25	6·25
J5	10c. red (Vaud)	39·00	42·00

1917 (1 Dec). Type C **6** and similar types. Buff paper. W **13**. P 11½.
J6	3c. violet (Valais)	4·25	33·00
J7	5c. green (Unterwalden)	7·25	4·00
J8	10c. red (Ticino)	18·00	17·00

C 9 Uri
C 11 Nidwalden 
C 14 Schwyz 

(This and the following issues to 1926 were designed by R. Munger. The shield is in all cases outlined in black.)

1918 (1 Dec). Type C **9** and similar type. Buff paper. W **13**. P 11½.
| J 9 | 10c. red, yellow and black | 6·75 | 11·00 |
| J10 | 15c. violet, red, yellow & black (Geneva) | 9·00 | 6·50 |

1919 (1 Dec). Type C **11** and similar types. Cream paper. W **13**. P 11½.
J11	7½c. red, grey and black	2·75	7·75
J12	10c. green, red and black (Vaud)	2·75	7·50
J13	15c. red, violet and black (Obwalden)	3·75	3·75

1920 (1 Dec). Type C **14** and similar types. Cream paper. W **13**. P 11½.
J14	7½c. red, grey and black	2·75	7·25
J15	10c. blue, red and black (Zürich)	4·50	7·75
J16	15c. red, blue, violet and black (Ticino)	2·30	3·25

C 17 Valais
C 20 Zug 
C 24 Basel 

1921 (1 Dec). Type C **17** and similar types. Cream paper. W **13**. P 11½.
J17	10c. red, black and green	60	1·60
J18	20c. black, orange, red & violet (Berne)	2·00	2·00
J19	40c. red and blue (Switzerland)	6·75	26·00

1922 (1 Dec). Type C **20** and similar types. Cream paper. W **13**. P 11½.
J20	5c. brown-orange, pale blue and black	70	3·75
J21	10c. sage-green and black	75	1·30
J22	20c. violet, pale blue and black	80	1·30
J23	40c. blue, scarlet and black	8·25	31·00
J20/23	Set of 4	9·50	34·00

Arms:—10c. Freiburg; 20c. Lucerne; 40c. Switzerland.

1923 (1 Dec). Type C **24** and similar types. Cream paper. W **13**. P 11½.
J24	5c. brown-orange and black	40	2·50
J25	10c. sage-green, red, black and yellow	40	1·10
J26	20c. violet, green, red and black	40	1·10
J27	40c. blue, red and black	7·25	24·00
J24/27	Set of 4	7·50	26·00

Arms:—10c. Glarus; 20c. Neuchâtel; 40c. Switzerland.

385

SWITZERLAND Switzerland 1924

C 28 Appenzell    **C 32** St. Gall    **C 36** Thurgau

1924 (1 Dec). *Type C 28 and similar types. Cream paper.* W **13**. P 11½.

J28	5c. black and lilac		25	90
J29	10c. red, green and black		25	60
J30	20c. black, yellow and carmine		35	55
J31	30c. red, blue and black		1·30	6·25
J28/31	*Set of 4*		1·90	7·50

Arms:—10c. Solothurn; 20c. Schaffhausen; 30c. Switzerland.

1925 (1 Dec). *Type C 32 and similar types. Cream paper.* W **13**. P 11½.

J32	5c. green, black and violet		20	75
J33	10c. black and green		25	60
J34	20c. black, blue, yellow and red		35	60
J35	30c. red, blue and black		1·20	5·25
J32/35	*Set of 4*		1·10	8·00

Arms:—10c. Appenzell–Ausser-Rhoden; 20c. Graubunden; 30c. Switzerland.

1926 (1 Dec). *Type C 36 and similar types. Cream paper.* W **13**. P 11½.

J36	5c. purple, green, bistre and black		20	65
J37	10c. green, black and carmine		20	55
J38	20c. carmine, black and blue		25	55
J39	30c. blue, carmine and black		1·10	5·75
J36/39	*Set of 4*		1·60	6·75

Arms—10c. Basel; 20c. Aargau; 30c. Switzerland and Lion of Lucerne.

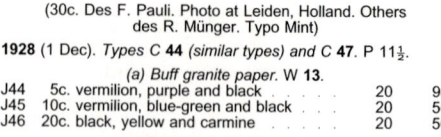

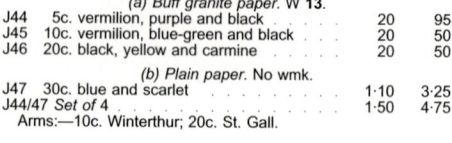

C 40 Forsaken Orphan    **C 42** J. H. Pestalozzi   **C 43** J. H. Pestalozzi

(Des K. Bickel (20c.), E. G. Ruegg (others). 5c., 10c. typo, Mint. 20c. recess, Survey Dept. 30c. photo, at Leiden (Holland))

1927 (1 Dec). *Types C 40 (and similar type), C 42 and C 43.* P 11½.

(a) Granite paper. W **13**.

J40	5c. maroon and yellow/*greyish*		15	85
J41	10c. green and rose/*greenish*		15	40
J42	20c. scarlet		15	40

(b) Plain paper. No wmk.

J43	30c. blue and black		1·00	3·25
J40/43	*Set of 4*		1·30	4·50

Design:—10c. Orphan at Pestalozzi School.

C 44 Lausanne    **C 47** J. H. Dunant

(30c. Des F. Pauli. Photo at Leiden, Holland. Others des R. Münger. Typo Mint)

1928 (1 Dec). *Types C 44 (similar types) and C 47.* P 11½.

(a) Buff granite paper. W **13**.

J44	5c. vermilion, purple and black		20	95
J45	10c. vermilion, blue-green and black		20	50
J46	20c. black, yellow and carmine		20	50

(b) Plain paper. No wmk.

J47	30c. blue and scarlet		1·10	3·25
J44/47	*Set of 4*		1·50	4·75

Arms:—10c. Winterthur; 20c. St. Gall.

C 48 Mt. San Salvatore Lake Lugano    **C 49** Nicholas de Flüe

(Des F. Gos (5c.), E. Boss (10c., 20c.), A. Stockmann (30c.).Photo Enschedé, Haarlem)

1929 (1 Dec). *Types C 48 (similar types) and C 49. Plain paper.* No wmk. P 11 × 11½.

J48	5c. vermilion and violet		10	60
J49	10c. grey-blue and bistre-brown		15	35
J50	20c. blue and carmine		20	35
J51	30c. indigo		1·00	5·75
J48/51	*Set of 4*		1·20	6·25

Designs:—10c. Mt. Titlis, Lake Engstlen; 20c. Mt. Lyskamm from Riffelberg.

C 50 Freiburg    **C 51** A. Bitzius—"Jeremias Gotthelf"

(30c. Des F. Pauli. Recess Survey Dept. Others des P. Boesch. Typo Mint)

1930 (1 Dec). *Types C 50 (similar types) and C 51. Granite paper.* W **13**. P 11½.

J52	5c. ultramarine, black and green/*buff*		15	65
J53	10c. yellow, vermilion, black & vio/*buff*		15	35
J54	20c. yellow, green, black & carmine/*buff*		20	40
J55	30c. slate-blue		1·10	3·25
J52/55	*Set of 4*		1·60	4·25

Designs:—10c. Arms of Altdorf; 20c. Arms of Schaffhausen.

C 52 St. Moritz and Silvaplana Lakes    **C 53** Alexandre Vinet

SWITZERLAND Switzerland 1931

(30c. Des G. Matter. Recess Survey Dept. Others des E. Jordi. Photo Courvoisier)

1931 (1 Dec). Types **C 52** (similar views) and **C 53**. Granite paper. P 11½.

(a) No wmk.

J56	5c. green	30	70
J57	10c. violet (Wetterhorn)	25	40
J58	20c. brown-lake (Lac Léman)	40	40

(b) W 13.

J59	30c. ultramarine	4·00	8·75
J56/59 Set of 4		4·50	9·25

C 54 Flag swinging
C 55 Eugen Huber 

(30c. Des and eng K. Bickel. Recess Orell Füssli. Others des H. B. Wieland. Typo PTT, Berne)

1932 (1 Dec). Types **C 54** (similar types) and **C 55**. Granite paper. P 11½.

(a) No wmk.

J60	5c. scarlet and green	50	90
J61	10c. orange (Putting the Weight)	60	90
J62	20c. scarlet (Wrestlers)	65	85

(b) W 13.

J63	30c. ultramarine	1·90	3·75
J60/63 Set of 4		3·25	6·50

PRINTERS. All Swiss Girl types from 1933 to 1936 were designed by Jules Courvoisier, Nos. J82/3, J85, J87, 93/5, J97/9 and J101/3 by C. Liner and Nos. J86 and J89/91 by H. Zaugg. They were all printed in photogravure by L. Courvoisier, La Chaux-de-Fonds.
Types C 57, C 59, C 61, C 62, C 64 (and No. J 81), C 67, C 69, C 71 and C 73/4 were designed and engraved by K. Bickel and all recess-printed by Orell Fussli, Zürich, except Types C 64 (and No. J81), C 67, C 69, C 71 and C 73/4 which were recessprinted at the PTT Printing Bureau, Berne.

C 56 Vaud
C 57 P. Gregoire Girard 
C 59 A. von Haller 

1933 (1 Dec). Types **C 56** (similar types) and **C 57**. Granite paper. P 11½. 30c. W 13, others unwmkd.

J64	5c. green and buff	30	80
J65	10c. violet and buff (Berne)	30	40
J66	20c. scarlet and buff (Ticino)	45	50
	a. Buff background inverted		
J67	30c. blue	1·80	4·00
J64/67 Set of 4		2·50	5·25

1934 (1 Dec). Type **C 59** and designs as Type **C 56**. Granite paper (Nos. J68/70 with grilled gum). P 11½. 30c. W 13, others unwmkd.

J68	5c. green and buff (Appenzell)	30	95
J69	10c. violet and buff (Valais)	35	40
J70	20c. scarlet and buff (Graubunden)	40	45
J71	30c. blue	1·70	4·00
J68/71 Set of 4		2·50	5·25

C 61 Stefano Franscini
C 62 H. G. Nägeli 

1935 (1 Dec). Type **C 61** and designs as Type **C 56**. Granite paper (Nos. J72/5 with grilled gum). P 11½. 30 c. W 13, others unwmkd.

J72	5c. green and buff (Basel)	25	95
J73	10c. violet and buff (Lucerne)	30	40
J74	20c. scarlet and buff (Geneva)	35	65
J75	30c. blue	2·00	4·25
J72/75 Set of 4		2·75	5·75

1936 (1 Dec). Type **C 62** and similar designs as Type **C 56**. Granite paper (Nos. J77/9 with grilled gum). P 11½. 5c. W 13, others unwmkd.

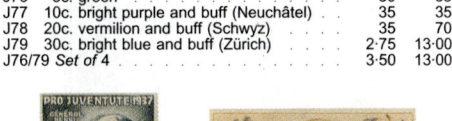

J76	5c. green	30	35
J77	10c. bright purple and buff (Neuchâtel)	35	35
J78	20c. vermilion and buff (Schwyz)	35	70
J79	30c. bright blue and buff (Zürich)	2·75	13·00
J76/79 Set of 4		3·50	13·00

C 64 Gen. Henri Dufour
C 66 "Youth" 

1937 (1 Dec). Types **C 64** and **C 66** and similar types. No wmk. P 11½.

(a) Plain paper.

J80	5c.+5c. blue-green	10	15
J81	10c.+5c. bright purple	10	15

(b) Granite paper.

J82	20c.+5c. vermilion, buff and silver	60	30
J83	30c.+10c. ultramarine, buff and silver	95	3·25
J80/83 Set of 4		1·60	3·50

Designs: As Type **C 64**—10c. Nicholas de Flüe; 30c. as Type **C 66**, but with girl's head facing reverse direction.

1937 (20 Dec). 25th Anniv of "Pro Juventute" Stamp Issues. Sheet 105 × 55 mm. As Nos. J82/3. Imperf.
MSJ83a 20c.+5c. red and silver; 30c.+10c. ultramarine and silver ... 4·50 37·00

C 67 Salomon Gessner
C 69 Gen. Herzog 
C 71 Gottfried Keller 

1938 (1 Dec). Type **C 67** and similar designs as Type **C 56**. P 11½.

(a) Plain paper.

J84	5c.+5c. emerald-green	20	20

(b) Granite paper

J85	10c.+5c. violet and buff (St. Gall)	20	20
J86	20c.+5c. scarlet and buff (Uri)	20	20
J87	30c.+10c. blue and buff (Aargau)	1·00	2·50
J84/87 Set of 4		1·50	2·75

SWITZERLAND Switzerland 1939

1939 (1 Dec). *Type C* **69** *and similar designs as Type C* **56**. P 11½.

(a) Plain paper
J88	5c.+5c. emerald-green	15	20

(b) Granite paper.
J89	10c.+5c. violet and buff (Freiburg)	25	20
J90	20c.+5c. scarlet and buff (Nidwalden)	30	45
J91	30c.+10c. blue and buff (Basel)	1·30	4·25
J88/91	Set of 4	1·80	4·50

1940 (30 Nov). *Type C* **71** *and similar designs as Type C* **56**. P 11½.

(a) Plain paper.
J92	5c.+5c. green	15	15

(b) Granite paper
J93	10c.+5c. brown and buff (Thurgau)	20	15
J94	20c.+5c. scarlet and buff (Solothurn)	30	20
J95	30c.+10c. blue and buff (Zug)	1·00	5·25
J92/95	Set of 4	1·50	5·25

First printing of No. J92 was inscribed "1818–1890" instead of "1819". This was corrected before issue but previously distributed examples of the error exist.

C **73** Johann Kasper Lavater

C **74** Niklaus Riggenbach (rack railway pioneer)

1941 (1 Dec). *200th Anniversaries (a) of Birth of Lavater (philosopher) and (b) of Death of Richard (clockmaker). Type C* **73** *and similar designs as Type C* **56**. P 11½.
J96	5c.+5c. green	15	15
J97	10c.+5c. brown and buff	20	20
J98	20c.+5c. scarlet and buff	25	20
J99	30c.+10c. blue	90	3·50
J96/99	Set of 4	1·40	3·75
MSJ99a	75 × 70 mm. Nos. J97/8. Imperf	55·00	£325

Designs:—10c. and 20c. Girls in the national costumes of Schaffhausen and Obwalden; 30c. Daniel Jean Richard.

(Nos. J100 and J103. Des and eng K. Bickel. Recess Plain paper. Mint, Berne. Nos. J102/3. Des C. Liner. Photo Granite paper. Courvoisier, La Chaux-de-Fonds)

1942 (1 Dec). *Type C* **74** *and similar designs as Type C* **56**. P 11½.
J100	5c.+5c. green	15	20
J101	10c.+5c. brown and buff	25	25
J102	20c.+5c. scarlet and buff	25	20
J103	30c.+10c. blue	1·10	3·25
J100/103	Set of 4	1·50	3·50

Designs:—10c., 20c. Girls in the national costumes of Appenzell Ausser–Rhoden and Glarus; 30c. Conrad Escher von der Linth (statesman).

PRINTERS. All Alpine flowers designs from 1943 to 1949 were designed by H. Fischer and printed in photogravure by Courvoisier on granite paper. Types C **75**, C **77/82** and No. J113 were designed and engraved by K. Bickel and recess-printed at the PTT Printing Bureau, Berne on plain paper.

C **75** Emanuel von Fellenberg

C **76** Silver Thistle

C **77** Numa Droz

1943 (1 Dec). *Death Centenary of Philip Emanuel von Fellenberg (economist). Type C* **75** *and alpine flower designs as Type C* **76**. P 11½.
J104	5c.+5c. green	15	20
J105	10c.+5c. blackish olive, buff and grey	20	25
J106	20c.+5c. lake, yellow and pink	25	25
J107	30c.+10c. blue, pale blue and black	1·10	6·00
J104/107	Set of 4	1·50	6·00

Flowers:—20c. "Ladies' Slipper"; 30c. Gentian.

1944 (1 Dec). *Birth Centenary of Numa Droz (statesman). Type C* **77** *and alpine flower designs as Type C* **76**. P 11½.
J108	5c.+5c. green	10	15
J109	10c.+5c. olive, yellow and green	25	20
J110	20c.+5c. red, yellow and grey	35	20
J111	30c.+10c. blue, grey and light blue	1·00	6·00
J108/111	Set of 4	1·50	6·00

Flowers:—10c. Edelweiss; 20c. Martagon lily; 30c. *Aquilegia alpina*.

C **78** Ludwig Forrer

C **79** Rudolf Toepffer

C **80** Jacob Burckhardt (historian)

1945 (1 Dec). *Centenary of Births of Ludwig Forrer (statesman) and Susanna Orelli (social reformer). Type C* **78** *and similar portrait type and alpine flower designs as Type C* **76**. P 11½.
J112	5c.+5c. green	20	20
J113	10c.+10c. red-brown	25	15
J114	20c.+10c. rose-red, pink and yellow	65	20
J115	30c.+10c. blue, mauve and grey	2·30	4·75
J112/115	Set of 4	3·00	4·75

Designs:—10c. Susanna Orelli; 20c. *Rosa alpina* (Alpine Dog Rose); 30c. *Crocus albiflorus* (Spring crocus).

1946 (30 Nov). *Death Centenary of Rudolf Toepffer (author and painter). Type C* **79** *and alpine flower designs as Type C* **76**. P 11½.
J116	5c.+5c. green	20	15
J117	10c.+10c. green, grey and orange	40	20
J118	20c.+10c. lake, grey and yellow	50	25
J119	30c.+10c. blue, grey and mauve	2·10	4·25
J116/119	Set of 4	3·00	4·50

Flowers:—10c. Narcissus; 20c. Houseleek; 30c. Blue Thistle.

1947 (1 Dec). *Type C* **80** *and Alpine flower designs as Type C* **76**. P 11½.
J120	5c.+5c. green	25	15
J121	10c.+10c. grey-black, yellow and grey	40	15
J122	20c.+10c. red-brown orange and grey	50	15
J123	30c.+10c. blue, pink and grey	1·70	4·25
J120/123	Set of 4	2·50	4·25

Flowers:—10c. Alpine Primrose; 20c. Orange-Lily; 30c. Cyclamen.

C **81** Gen. U. Wille

C **82** Nicholas Wengi

1948 (1 Dec). *Type C* **81** *and Alpine flower designs as Type C* **76**. P 11½.
J124	5c.+5c. purple	25	15
J125	10c.+10c. green, yellow and grey	50	15

SWITZERLAND Switzerland   1948

J126	20c.+10c. brown, carmine and buff	50	20
J127	40c.+10c. blue, yellow and grey	2·10	4·25
J124/127	Set of 4	3·00	4·25

Flowers:—10c. Foxglove; 20c. Rust-leaved Alpine rose; 40c. Lily of Paradise.

1949 (1 Dec). *Type C 82 and Alpine flower designs as Type C 76.* P 11½.

J128	5c.+5c. brown-lake	30	15
J129	10c.+10c. blue-green, grey and yellow	40	20
J130	20c.+10c. brown, light blue and buff	50	20
J131	40c.+10c. blue, mauve and green	2·40	3·25
J128/131	Set of 4	3·25	3·50

Flowers:—10c. *Pulsatilla alpina*; 20c. Alpine clematis; 40 c. Superb pink.

C 83 General Theophil Sprecher von Bernegg

C 84 Red Admiral Butterfly

C 85 Johanna Spyri (authoress)

(No. J132 des and eng Karl Bickel. Recess PTT, Berne. Nos. J133/6 des Niklaus Stoecklin. Photo Granite paper. Courvoisier)

1950 (1 Dec). *Type C 83 and insect designs as Type C 84.* P 11½.

J132	C 83	5c.+5c. purple-brown	30	20
J133	C 84	10c.+10c. brown, ver, blk & turq	60	25
J134	—	20c.+10c. blk, vio-blue & red-orge	65	20
J135	—	30c.+10c. brown, grey & mag	4·50	11·50
J136	—	40c.+10c. yell, blkish brn & lt bl	4·25	7·00
J132/136		Set of 5	9·25	17·00

Designs:—20c Clifden's nonpareil (moth); 30c. Honey bee; 40c. Moorland clouded yellow (butterfly).

(No. J137 des and eng K. Bickel. Recess PTT, Berne. Nos. J138/41 des H. Fischer. Photo Granite paper. Courvoisier)

1951 (1 Dec). *Type C 85 and insect designs as Type C 84.* P 11½.

J137	5c.+5c. claret	35	15
J138	10c.+10c. deep blue and light green	45	20
J139	20c.+10c. black, cream and magenta	60	20
J140	30c.+10c. black, orange and olive	3·00	7·75
J141	40c.+10c. brown, red & light ultram	3·50	6·25
J137/141	Set of 5	7·25	13·00

Designs:—10c. Banded agrion (dragonfly); 20c. Scarce swallowtail (butterfly); 30c. Orange-tip (butterfly); 40c. Viennese emperor moth.

C 86 "Portrait of a Boy" (Anker)

C 87 "Portrait of a Girl" (Anker)

C 88 Jeremias Gotthelf (novelist) (after Albert Bitzius)

(No. J142 des and eng K. Bickel. Recess PTT, Berne. Nos. J143/6 des N. Stoecklin. Photo Granite paper. Courvoisier)

1952 (1 Dec). *Type C 86 and insect designs as Type C 84.* P 11½.

J142	5c.+5c. lake	30	10
J143	10c.+10c. red-orange, blk & pale bl-grn	45	20
J144	20c.+10c. cream, black and mauve	50	20
J145	30c.+10c. light blue, black & bistre-brn	3·25	6·00
J146	40c. +10c. buff, brown & pale vio-blue	3·25	5·00
J142/146	Set of 5	7·00	10·50

Designs:—Seven-spotted ladybird; 20c. Marbled white (butterfly); 30c. Chalk-hill blue (butterfly); 40c. Oak eggar moth.

(Nos. J147, J151 des and eng K. Bickel. Recess PTT, Berne. Nos. J148/50 des H. Fischer. Photo Granite paper. Courvoisier)

1953 (1 Dec). *Type C 87 and similar portrait and insect designs as Type C 84.* P 11½.

J147	5c.+5c. lake	30	15
J148	10c.+10c. rose, sepia & pale blue-grn	40	25
J149	20c.+10c. black, buff & rose-magenta	45	25
	a. Booklet pane. Nos. J149 × 4 and J150 × 2	50·00	
J150	30c.+10c. black, scarlet & yellow-olive	3·75	5·50
J151	40c.+10c. blue	4·00	4·25
J147/151	Set of 5	8·00	9·50

Designs:—10c. Black arches moth; 20c. Camberwell beauty (butterfly); 30c. *Purpureus kaehleri* (longhorn beetle); 40c. F. Hodler (self-portrait).

Nos. J149/50 were also issued together in sheets comprising 16 of the 20c. and 8 of the 30c. and sold at 8f. The composition of the sheet produces horizontal and vertical *se-tenant* pairs and also horizontal *tête-bêche* pairs of the two values. (*Price per sheet un*, £250).

(No. J152 Eng K. Bickel (after Dietler). Recess PTT, Berne. Nos. J153/6. Des N. Stoecklin. Photo Granite paper. Courvoisier)

1954 (1 Dec). *Type C 88 and insect designs as Type C 84.* P 11½.

J152	5c.+5c. purple-brown	30	15
J153	10c.+10c. multicoloured	40	20
J154	20c.+10c. multicoloured	85	30
J155	30c.+10c. multicoloured	4·00	5·00
J156	40c.+10c. blk, yell, red & pale blue	4·00	4·50
J152/156	Set of 5	8·50	9·25

Designs:—10c. Garden tiger moth; 20c. Buff-tailed bumble bee; 30c. *Ascalaphus libelluloides* (owl-fly); 40c. Swallowtail (butterfly).

C 89 C. Pictet de-Rochemont

C 90 Carlo Maderno (architect)

C 91 L. Euler (mathematician)

(No. J157. Eng K. Bickel. Recess PTT, Berne. Nos. J158/61. Des H. Fischer. Photo Granite paper. Courvoisier)

1955 (1 Dec). *Type C 89 and insect designs as Type C 84.* P 11½.

J157	5c.+5c. brown-purple	30	15
J158	10c.+10c. brown-purple, sepia, yellow, blue and yellow-green	45	20
J159	20c.+10c. black, dp blue, yell & red	60	20
J160	30c.+10c. black, red, cream & yell-brn	3·75	4·00
J161	40c.+10c. black, carmine & pale blue	3·75	3·75
J157/161	Set of 5	8·00	7·50

Designs:—10c. Peacock (butterfly); 20c. Great horntail; 30c. Yellow tiger moth; 40c. Apollo (butterfly).

(No. J162. Eng K. Bickel. Recess PTT, Berne. Nos. J163/66. Des N. Stoecklin. Photo Granite paper. Courvoisier)

1956 (1 Dec). *Type C 90 and insect designs as Type C 84.* P 11½.

J162	5c.+5c. brown-purple	30	15
J163	10c.+10c. deep green, carm-red & grn	40	15
J164	20c.+10c. violet, sepia, yell & rose-carm	45	15

SWITZERLAND Switzerland   1956

J165	30c.+10c. blue, indigo & olive-yellow	2·40	3·50
J166	40c.+10c. pale yellow, sepia & cobalt	2·50	3·00
J162/166	Set of 5	5·25	6·25

Designs:—10c. Common burnet (moth); 20c. Lesser purple emperor (butterfly); 30c. Blue ground beetle; 40c. Large white (butterfly).

(No. J167. Eng K. Bickel, after painting by E. Handmann. Recess PTT, Berne. Nos. J168, J171. Des N. Stoecklin. Nos. J169/70. Des H. Fischer. Photo Granite paper. Courvoisier)

1957 (30 Nov). *Type C* **91** *and insect designs as Type C* **84**. P 11½.

J167	5c.+5c. claret	30	15
J168	10c.+10c. yell-orge, brn, grnsh yell & ol	40	15
J169	20c.+10c. yellow, deep brn & mag	50	15
J170	30c.+10c. emer, dp bl-grn & lt brn-pur	3·25	3·25
J171	40c.+10c. brown, red, sepia & cobalt	3·00	2·10
J167/171	Set of 5	6·75	5·25

Designs:—10c. Clouded yellow (butterfly); 20c. Magpie moth; 30c. Rose chafer (beetle); 40c. Rosy underwing (moth).

C 92 Albrecht von Haller (naturalist)

C 93 Pansy

C 94 Karl Hilty (lawyer)

(No. J172 Eng K. Bickel, after painting by S. Freudenberger. Recess PTT, Berne. Nos. J173/6. Des H. Schwarzenbach. Photo Granite paper. Courvoisier)

1958 (1 Dec). *Type C* **92** *and wild flowers as Type C* **93**. P 11½.

J172	5c.+5c. claret	25	15
J173	10c.+10c. yellow, brown and green	35	15
J174	20c.+10c. yell, cerise, grn & carm-lake	50	15
J175	30c.+10c. yell, blue, grn & bistre-brn	2·40	2·30
J176	40c.+10c. yell, grey, gm & deep blue	2·40	2·00
J172/176	Set of 5	5·50	4·25

Designs:—20c. Chinese aster; 30c. Morning Glory; 40c. Christmas rose.

(No. J177. Eng K. Bickel, after photo in Swiss National Library, Berne. Recess PTT, Berne. Nos. J178/81. Des H. Schwarzenbach. Photo Granite paper. Courvoisier)

1959 (1 Dec). *Type C* **94** *and wild flower types as Type C* **93**. P 11½.

J177	5c.+5c. claret	25	15
J178	10c.+10c. yell, light brn, grn & blue-grn	40	15
J179	20c.+10c. scarlet, green and purple	50	15
J180	30c.+10c. yellow, orange, green & olive	2·20	2·00
J181	50c.+10c. mag, yell, grn, grey & ultram	2·20	2·20
J177/181	Set of 5	5·00	4·25

Designs:—10c. Marsh marigold; 20c. Poppy; 30c. Nasturtium; 50c. Sweet pea.

C 95 A. Calame (painter)

C 96 J. Furrer (First President of Swiss Confederation)

(No. J182. Eng K. Bickel, after lithograph by J. Hébert. Recess PTT, Berne. Nos. J183/6. Des H. Schwarzenbach. Photo Granite paper. Courvoisier)

1960 (1 Dec). *Type C* **95** *and wild flowers as Type C* **93**. P 11½.

J182	5c.+5c. greenish blue	35	10
J183	10c.+10c. yell, yell-grn, drab & dp grn	35	15
J184	20c.+10c. yell-green, sepia & magenta	40	15
J185	30c.+10c. yellow-green, bl & orge-brn	2·20	2·50
J186	50c.+10c. grnsh yell, yell-grn & ultram	2·30	2·50
J182/186	Set of 5	5·00	5·00

Designs:—10c. Dandelion; 20c. Phlox; 30c. Larkspur; 50c. Thorn apple.

(No. J187. Eng K. Bickel, after lithograph by J. Hasler. Recess PTT, Berne. Nos. J188/191. Des H. Schwarzenbach. Photo Granite paper. Courvoisier)

1961 (1 Dec). *Type C* **96** *and wild flowers as Type C* **93**. P 11½.

J187	5c.+5c. deep blue	15	15
J188	10c.+10c. yell, red, yell-grn & dp grn	25	15
J189	20c.+10c. yellow, grey, green and red	30	15
J190	30c.+10c. violet, yell, green & purple	1·10	1·80
J191	50c.+10c. yellow, green, brn & blue	1·60	1·70
J187/191	Set of 5	3·00	3·50

Designs:—10c. Sunflower; 20c. Lily-of-the-Valley; 30c. Iris; 50c. Silverweed.

C 97 "Child's World"

C 98 Mother and Child

C 98a Mother and Child

(Des P. Roshardt (5c., 50c.), H. Steiner (10c., 30c.), F. Iselin (20c.), E. Renggli (100c.). Photo Granite paper. Courvoisier)

1962 (1 Dec). *50th Anniv of Pro Juventute Foundation. Type C* **97** *and similar designs inscr "PRO JUVENTUTE 1912–1962" and Type C* **98**/*a*. P 11½ *or imperf.* (No. **MSJ**196*a*).

J192	5c.+5c. rose, green, yell & slate-violet	20	15
J193	10c. +10c. carmine-red and green	25	15
J194	20c.+10c. lt grn, sepia, pink & orge-red	50	30
J195	30c.+10c. red, magenta and yellow	85	1·80
J196	50c.+10c. yellow, brown and blue	85	1·70
J192/196	Set of 5	2·40	3·75
MSJ196*a* 82 × 62 mm. 100c.+20c. mult (× 2) (sold at 3f.)		4·00	4·25

Designs: *Horiz as Type C* **97**—5c. Apple blossom; 30c. "Child's World" (child in meadow); 50c. Forsythia.

PHOSPHORESCENT PAPER. All stamps from No. J197 to J248 are printed on phosphorescent paper with violet fibres, *unless otherwise stated*. See note below T **143**.

SWITZERLAND Switzerland   1963

C 99 "Portrait of a Boy" (Anker)
C 100 "Portrait of a Girl" (Anker) 
C 101 West European Hedgehogs 

(5c. des and eng K. Bickel. Recess PTT, Berne. Others des W. Weiskönig. Photo Courvoisier.)

1963 (30 Nov). *Type C **99** and wild flowers as Type C **93**.* P 11½.
J197	5c.+5c. greenish blue	10	20
	a. Ordinary white paper	70	1·20
J198	10c.+10c. yell, yell-brn, light blue & grn	80	1·20
	a. Ordinary granite paper	95	55
J199	20c.+10c. orange-red, yell-grn & carm	1·10	1·10
	a. Ordinary granite paper	95	55
J200	30c.+10c. rose, light bl, yell-grn & brn	1·10	1·30
J201	50c.+10c. bright pur, yell grn & blue	1·20	1·20
J197/201 Set of 5 (*cheapest*)		4·00	4·50

Designs:—10c. Oxeye daisy; 20c. Geranium; 30c. Cornflower; 50c. Carnation.

(5c. des and eng K. Bickel. Recess. Plain paper. PTT, Berne. Others des W. Weiskönig. Photo Courvoisier.)

1964 (1 Dec). *Type C **100** and wild flowers as Type C **93**.* P 11½.
J202	5c.+5c. turquoise-blue	10	10
J203	10c.+10c. orange, yellow and green	15	10
J204	20c.+10c. rose-red, green and carmine	20	10
J205	30c.+10c. bright purple, grn & brn	45	50
J206	50c.+10c. red, yell, grey-brn, grn & bl	60	50
J202/206 Set of 5		1·40	1·20

Designs:—10c. Daffodil; 20c. Rose; 30c. Red clover; 50c. White water-lily.

(Des H. Erni. Photo Courvoisier.)

1965 (1 Dec). *Type C **101** and similar vert animal designs.* P 11½.
J207	5c.+5c. ochre, chocolate and red	10	10
J208	10c.+10c. ochre, brn, blk & grnsh blue	10	10
J209	20c.+10c. grey-blue, brown & orge-brn	20	10
J210	30c.+10c. deep blue, black & yellow	45	40
J211	50c.+10c. black, brown & bright blue	50	40
J207/211 Set of 5		1·20	1·00

Animals:—10c. Alpine marmots; 20c. Red deer; 30c. Eurasian badgers; 50c. Arctic hares.

(Des H. Erni. Photo Courvoisier.)

1966 (1 Dec). *Vert animal designs as Type C **101**. Multicoloured.* P 11½.
J212	5c.+5c. Stoat	10	10
J213	10c.+10c. Eurasian red squirrel	10	10
J214	20c.+10c. Red fox	20	10
J215	30c.+10c. Brown hare	45	40
J216	50c.+10c. Chamois	50	40
J212/216 Set of 5		1·20	1·00

C 102 Roe Deer
C 103 Capercaeillie 
C 104 "McGredy's Sunset" Rose 

(Des C. Piatti. Photo Courvoisier.)

1967 (1 Dec). *Vert animal designs as Type C **102**. Multicoloured.* P 11½.
J217	10c.+10c. Type C**102**	15	10
J218	20c.+10c. Pine marten	20	10
J219	30c.+10c. Ibex	45	10
J220	50c.+20c. European otter	55	50
J217/220 Set of 4		1·20	70

(Des W. Wehinger. Photo Courvoisier.)

1968 (28 Nov). *Type C **103** and similar vert bird designs, Multicoloured.* P 11½.
J221	10c.+10c. Type C **103**	20	10
J222	20c.+10c. Northern bullfinch	30	10
J223	30c.+10c. Woodchat shrike	40	25
J224	50c.+20c. Firecrest	70	40
J221/224 Set of 4		1·50	75

(Des W. Wehinger. Photo Courvoisier.)

1969 (1 Dec). *Vert bird designs as Type C **103**. Multicoloured.* P 11½.
J225	10c.+10c. Eurasian goldfinch	20	15
J226	20c.+10c. Golden oriole	30	15
J227	30c.+10c. Wallcreeper	45	30
J228	50c.+20c. Jay	70	55
J225/228 Set of 4		1·50	1·00

(Des R. Gerbig. Photo Courvoisier.)

1970 (1 Dec). *Vert bird designs as Type C **103**. Multicoloured.* P 11½.
J229	10c.+10c. Blue tits	20	10
J230	20c.+10c. Hoopoe	30	15
J231	30c.+10c. Great spotted woodpecker	45	20
J232	50c.+20c. Great crested grebes	65	65
J229/232 Set of 4		1·40	1·00

(Des R. Gerbig. Photo Courvoisier.)

1971 (1 Dec). *Vert bird designs as Type C **103**. Multicoloured.* P 11½.
J233	10c.+10c. Common redstarts	20	10
J234	20c.+10c. Bluethroats	30	15
J235	30c.+10c. Peregrine falcon	45	15
J236	40c.+20c. Mallards	65	60
J233/236 Set of 4		1·40	90

(Des A. M. Trechslin. Photo Courvoisier.)

1972 (1 Dec). *Vert rose designs as Type C **104**. Multicoloured.* P 11½.
J237	10c.+10c. Type C **104**	25	15
J238	20c.+10c. "Miracle"	30	15
J239	30c.+10c. "Papa Meilland"	50	25
J240	40c.+20c. "Madame Dimitriu"	80	80
J237/240 Set of 4		1·70	1·20

C 105 Chestnut
C 106 Arms of Aarburg 
C 107 Letter Balance 

(Des K. Baumgartner. Photo Courvoisier.)

1973 (29 Nov). *"Fruits of the Forest". Type C **105** and similar vert designs. Multicoloured.* P 11½.
J241	15c.+5c. Type C **105**	20	10
J242	30c.+10c. Cherries	40	10
J243	40c.+20c. Blackberries	60	45
J244	60c.+20c. Bilberries	80	95
J241/244 Set of 4		1·80	1·40

391

SWITZERLAND Switzerland 1974

(Des H. Schwarzenbach. Photo Courvoisier)

1974 (29 Nov). *"Fruits of the Forest". Vert designs as Type C* **105**. *Multicoloured.* P 11½.
J245	15c.+10c. Daphne	25	10
J246	30c.+20c. Belladonna	45	10
J247	50c.+20c. Laburnum	75	80
J248	60c.+25c. Mistletoe	90	75
J245/248	Set of 4	2·10	1·60

Nos. J245 and J247 were issued on fibre-less paper.

PHOSPHORESCENT PAPER. All stamps from No. J249 are printed on phosphorescent, fibre-less paper, *unless otherwise stated*.

(Des Courvoisier (10c.), K. Baumgartner (15c., 30c., 50c.). V. Wyss-Fischer (60c.). Photo Courvoisier)

1975 (27 Nov). *Vert designs as Type C* **105**. *Multicoloured.* P 11½.
J249	10c.+5c. "Post-Brent" (postman's hamper)	20	15
J250	15c.+10c. Hepatica	25	15
J251	30c.+20c. Rowan	45	10
J252	50c.+20c. Yellow deadnettle	70	75
J253	60c.+25c. Sycamore	85	75
J249/253	Set of 5	2·20	1·70

(Des V. Wyss-Fischer (20c., 80c.). H. Schwarzenbach (40c.). Photo Courvoisier)

1976 (29 Nov). *"Fruits of the Forest". Vert designs as Type C* **105**. *Multicoloured.* P 11½.
J254	20c.+10c. Barberry	30	15
J255	40c.+20c. Black elder	55	20
J256	40c.+20c. Lime	55	20
J257	80c.+40c. Lungwort	1·10	1·00
J254/257	Set of 4	2·20	1·40

(Des A. M. Trechslin. Photo Courvoisier)

1977 (28 Nov). *Roses. Vert designs as Type C* **104**. *Multicoloured.* P 11½.
J258	20c.+10c. *Rosa foetida bicolor*	30	10
J259	40c.+20c. "Parfum de I' Hay"	55	10
J260	70c.+30c. *R. foetida persiana*	1·00	1·10
J261	80c.+40c. *R. centifolia muscosa*	1·10	1·00
J258/261	Set of 4	2·75	2·10

(Des G. Cambin. Photo Courvoisier)

1978 (28 Nov). *Arms of the Communes. Type C* **106** *and similar vert designs. Multicoloured.* P 11½.
J262	20c.+10c. Type C **106**	25	10
J263	40c.+20c. Gruyères	55	10
J264	70c.+30c. Castasegna	95	1·00
J265	80c.+40c. Wangen	1·00	90
J262/265	Set of 4	2·50	1·90

(Des G. Cambin. Photo Courvoisier)

1979 (28 Nov). *Arms of the Communes. Vert designs as Type C* **106**. *Multicoloured.* P 11½.
J266	20c.+10c. Cadro	25	10
J267	40c.+20c. Rüte	50	10
J268	70c.+30c. Schwamendingen	95	1·10
J269	80c.+40c. Perroy	1·00	90
J266/269	Set of 4	2·40	2·00

(Des G. Cambin. Photo Courvoisier)

1980 (26 Nov). *Arms of the Communes. Vert designs as Type C* **106**. *Multicoloured.* P 11½.
J270	20c.+10c. Cortaillod	25	10
J271	40c.+20c. Sierre	55	10
J272	70c.+30c. Scuol	95	1·10
J273	80c.+40c. Wolfenschiessen	1·10	90
J270/273	Set of 4	2·50	2·00

(Des G. Cambin. Photo Courvoisier)

1981 (26 Nov). *Arms of the Communes. Vert designs as Type C* **106**. *Multicoloured.* P 11½.
J274	20c.+10c. Uffikon	25	20
J275	40c.+20c. Torre	55	20

J276	70c.+30c. Benken	95	1·10
J277	80c.+40c. Préverenges	1·10	95
J274/277	Set of 4	2·50	2·20

(Des E. Witzig (10c.), Anne Marie Trechslin (others). Photo Courvoisier)

1982 (25 Nov). *Type C* **107** *and vert rose designs as Type C* **104**. *Multicoloured.* P 11½.
J278	10c.+10c. Type C **107**	20	20
J279	20c.+10c. "La Belle Portugaise"	30	20
J280	40c.+20c. "Hugh Dickson"	55	20
J281	70c.+30c. "Mermaid"	1·00	1·10
J282	80c.+40c. "Madame Caroline"	1·20	85
J278/282	Set of 5	3·00	2·30

C **108** Kitchen Stove, c. 1850

C **109** Heidi and Goat (Johanna Spyri)

(Des G. Rimensberger. Photo Courvoisier)

1983 (24 Nov). *Children's Toys. Type C* **108** *and similar horiz designs. Multicoloured.* P 11½.
J283	20c.+10c. Type C **108**	30	15
J284	40c.+20c. Rocking horse, 1826	60	15
J285	70c.+30c. Doll, c. 1870	95	1·10
J286	80c.+40c. Steam locomotive, c. 1900	1·10	1·00
J283/286	Set of 4	2·75	2·20

(Des G. Rimensberger. Photo Courvoisier)

1984 (26 Nov). *Characters from Children's Books. Type C* **109** *and similar horiz designs. Multicoloured.* P 11½.
J287	35c.+15c. Type C **109**	55	50
J288	50c.+20c. Pinocchio and kite (Carlo Callodi)	65	20
J289	70c.+30c. Pippi Longstocking (Astrid Lindgren)	1·10	1·20
J290	80c.+40c. Max and Moritz on roof (Wilhelm Busch)	1·20	1·00
J287/290	Set of 4	3·25	2·40

(Des G. Rimensberger. Photo Courvoisier)

1985 (26 Nov). *Characters from Children's Books. Horiz designs as Type C* **109**. *Multicoloured.* P 11½.
J291	35c.+15c. Hansel, Gretel and Witch	50	50
J292	50c.+20c. Snow White and the seven dwarves	70	20
J293	80c.+40c. Red Riding Hood and wolf	1·10	1·10
J294	90c.+40c. Cinderella and Prince Charming	1·20	1·20
J291/294	Set of 4	3·25	2·75

C **110** Teddy Bear

C **111** Girl carrying Pine Branch and Candle

(Des E. Witzig. Photo Courvoisier)

1986 (25 Nov). *Children's Toys. Type C* **110** *and similar vert designs. Multicoloured.* P 11½.
J295	35c.+15c. Type C **110**	65	60
J296	50c.+20c. Spinning top	75	25

SWITZERLAND Switzerland 1987

J297	80c.+40c. Steamroller	1·20	1·40
J298	90c.+40c. Doll	1·30	1·20
J295/298	Set of 4	3·50	3·00

(Des Eleonore Schmid. Photo Courvoisier)

1987 (24 Nov). *Child Development Pre-school Age.* Type C **111** and similar vert designs. Multicoloured. P 11½.

J299	25c.+10c. Type C **111**	45	35
J300	35c.+15c. Mother breast-feeding baby	60	65
J301	50c.+20c. Toddler playing with bricks	75	25
J302	80c.+40c. Children playing in sand	1·20	1·20
J303	90c.+40c. Father with child on his shoulders	1·30	1·10
J299/303	Set of 5	4·00	2·25

C **112** Learning to Read

C **113** Community Work

(Des Harriet Höppner. Photo Courvoisier)

1988 (25 Nov). *Child Development School Age.* Type C **112** and similar vert designs. Multicoloured. P 11½.

J304	35c.+15c. Type C **112**	60	65
J305	50c.+20c. Playing triangle	75	25
J306	80c.+40c. Learning arithmetic	1·30	1·40
J307	90c.+40c. Drawing	1·40	1·20
J304/307	Set of 4	3·75	3·25

(Des R. Mühlemann. Photo Courvoisier)

1989 (24 Nov). *Child Development Adolescence.* Type C **113** and similar vert designs. Multicoloured. P 11½.

J308	35c.+15c. Type C **113**	60	65
J309	50c.+20c. Young couple (friendship)	65	30
J310	80c.+40c. Boy at computer screen (vocational training)	1·30	1·40
J311	90c.+40c. Girl in laboratory (higher education and research)	1·40	1·20
J308/311	Set of 4	3·50	3·25

C **114** Building Model Ship (hobbies)

C **115** Ramsons

(Des F. Bauer. Photo Courvoisier)

1990 (20 Nov). *Child Development. Leisure Activities.* Type C **114** and similar horiz designs. Multicoloured. P 11½.

J312	35c.+15c. Type C **114**	60	60
J313	60c.+20c. Youth group	65	30
J314	80c.+40c. Sport	1·40	1·50
J315	90c.+40c. Music	1·50	1·30
J312/315	Set of 4	3·75	3·25

(Des V. Wyss-Fischer. Photo Courvoisier)

1991 (26 Nov). *Woodland Flowers.* Type C **115** and similar vert designs. Multicoloured. P 11½.

J316	50c.+25c. Type C **115**	80	30
J317	70c.+30c. Wood cranesbill	1·10	1·10
J318	80c.+40c. Nettle-leaved bellflower	1·30	1·10
J319	90c.+40c. Few-leaved hawkweed	1·40	1·40
J316/319	Set of 4	4·25	3·50

C **116** Melchior (wood puppet)

C **117** Christmas Wreath

(Des Bernadette Baltis. Photo Courvoisier)

1992 (24 Nov). *Christmas* (J320) *and Trees* (others). Type C **116** and similar horiz designs showing silhouette of tree and close-up of its leaves and fruit. Multicoloured. P 11½.

J320	50c.+25c. Type C **116**	80	40
J321	50c.+25c. Beech	80	40
J322	70c.+30c. Norway maple	1·20	1·30
J323	80c.+40c. Pedunculate oak	1·20	1·20
J324	90c.+40c. Norway spruce	1·40	1·30
J320/324	Set of 5	5·00	4·25

(Des Bernadette Baltis. Photo Courvoisier)

1993 (23 Nov). *Christmas* (J325) *and Woodland Plants* (others). Type C **117** and similar vert designs. Multicoloured. P 11½.

J325	60c.+30c. Type C **117**	95	65
J326	60c.+30c. Male fern	95	65
J327	80c.+40c. Guelder rose	1·40	1·30
J328	100c.+50c. Mnium punctatum	1·70	1·80
J325/328	Set of 4	4·50	4·00

C **118** Candles

C **119** Detail of "The Annunciation" (Bartolomé Murillo)

(Des B. Brusch. Photo Courvoisier)

1994 (28 Nov). *Christmas* (J329) *and Fungi* (others). Type C **118** and similar horiz designs. Multicoloured. P 11½.

J329	60c.+30c. Type C **118**	95	70
J330	60c.+30c. Wood blewit (*Lepista nuda*)	95	70
J331	80c.+40c. Red boletus (*Leccinum sp.*)	1·40	1·40
J332	100c.+50c. Shaggy pholiota (*Pholiota squarrosa*)	1·70	1·70
J329/332	Set of 4	4·50	4·00

(Des G. Forster. Photo Courvoisier)

1995 (28 Nov). *Christmas* (J333) *and Wildlife* (others). Type C **119** and similar horiz designs. Multicoloured. P 11½.

J333	60c.+30c. Type C **119**	95	80
J334	60c.+30c. Brown trout	95	80
J335	80c.+40c. Grey wagtail	1·40	1·50
J336	100c.+50c. Spotted salamander	1·70	1·80
J333/336	Set of 4	4·50	4·50

C **120** Shooting Star and Constellations

C **121** Mistletoe

393

SWITZERLAND Switzerland 1996

(Des B. Struchen. Photo Courvoisier)

1996 (26 Nov). *Christmas (J337) and Wildlife (others). Type C* **120** *and similar horiz designs. Multicoloured. P 11½.*

J337	70c.+35c. Type C **120**	1·20	95
J338	70c.+35c. European grayling	1·20	95
J339	90c.+45c. Crayfish	1·40	1·40
J340	110c.+55c. European otter	1·80	1·70
J337/340 Set of 4		5·00	4·50

(Des Eleonore Schimd. Photo Courvoisier)

1997 (20 Nov). *Christmas (J341) and Wildlife (others). Type C* **121** *and similar horiz designs. Multicoloured. P 11½.*

J341	70c.+35c. Type C **121**	1·20	1·10
J342	70c.+35c. Three-spined stickleback	1·20	1·10
J343	90c.+45c. Yellow-bellied toad	1·40	1·30
J344	110c.+55c. Ruff	1·80	1·60
J341/344 Set of 4		5·00	3·50

C **122** Christmas Bell

C **123** Children and Snowman (Margaret Strub)

(Des B. Struchen. Photo Courvoisier)

1998 (8 Nov). *Christmas (J345) and Wildlife (others). Type C* **122** *and similar horiz designs. Multicoloured. P 11½.*

J345	70c.+35c. Type C **122**	1·20	1·10
J346	70c.+35c. Ramshorn snail	1·20	1·10
J347	90c.+45c. Great crested grebe	1·50	1·30
J348	110c.+55c. Pike	1·80	1·60
J345/348 Set of 4		5·25	4·50

(Litho PTT, Berne)

1999 (23 Nov). *Christmas (J349) and Illustrations from* Nicolo the Clown *(picture book by Verena Pavoni) (others). Type C* **123** *and similar vert designs. Multicoloured. P 13½.*

J349	70c.+35c. Type C **123**	1·10	1·00
J350	70c.+35c. Nicolo holding guitar	1·10	1·00
J351	90c.+45c. Nicolo with his father	1·40	1·40
J352	110c.+55c. Nicolo with donkey	1·70	1·70
J349/352 Set of 4		4·75	4·50

C **124** Santa Claus

C **125** Santa Claus and Cat

(Litho PTT, Berne)

2000 (21 Nov). *Christmas. Illustrations from* Little Albert *(book) by Albert Manser. Type C* **124** *and similar horiz designs. Multicoloured. Paper with fluorescent fibres. P 13½.*

J353	70c.+35c. Type C **124**	1·30	1·20
J354	70c.+35c. Boys sitting on fence and girl	1·30	1·20
J355	90c.+45c. Little Albert with umbrella	1·60	1·60
J356	90c.+45c. Children sledging	1·60	1·60
J353/356 Set of 4		5·25	5·00

(Des Gabi Fluck (J357) and Stephan Brülhart (others) Litho PTT, Berne)

2001 (20 Nov). *Illustrations from Children's Books. Type C* **125** *and similar vert designs. Multicoloured. Paper with fluorescent fibres. P 13½.*

J357	70c.+35c. Type C **125** ("What's Santa Claus Doing?" (text Karin von Oldersausen, illustrations Gabi Fluck))	1·00	50
J358	70c.+35c. Leopold the leopard in tree ("Leopold and the Sun" by Stephan Brülhart)	1·00	50
J359	90c.+45c. Bear on scooter ("Honey Bear" by S. Brülhart)	1·25	1·25
J360	90c.+45c. Tom the monkey in tree ("Leopold and the Sun")	1·25	1·25
J357/360 Set of 4		4·00	3·25

C **126** "Christmas rose"

(Des Anne Marie Trechslin. Litho Enschedé)

2002 (19 Nov). *Roses. Type C* **126** *and similar vert designs. Multicoloured. P 13½.*

J361	70c.+35c. Type C **126**	1·00	50
J362	70c.+35c. "Ingrid Bergman"	1·00	50
J363	90c.+45c. "Belle Vaudoise"	1·25	1·25
J364	90c.+45c. "Charmian"	1·25	1·25
J365	130c.+65c. "Frühlingsgold"	1·80	1·80
J361/365 Set of 5		5·75	4·75

No. J361 is impregnated with the fragrance of cinnamon and cloves and Nos. J362/5 with the perfume of roses.

"PRO JUVENTUTE" STAMP BOOKLETS

The following checklist covers booklets containing "Pro Juventute" stamps. It is intended that it should be used in conjunction with the main listings so that details of stamps and panes listed there are not repeated.

With the exception of No. JSB1, all these booklets were sold at above face value, the premium being used to defray the costs of making up the booklets. From 1953–66 inclusive this premium was 20c.; from 1967–72, 40c.; from 1973–89, 60c.; and from 1990 onwards, 1f.

Prices are for complete booklets

Booklet No.	Date	Contents	Price
JSB1	1915	5 panes, No. J1a × 6	£1300
JSB2	1953	1 pane, No. J147 × 6; 1 pane, J148 × 6; 1 pane, J149a. Text On Cover in French	£130
JSB3	1953	As No. JSB2, but text On Cover in German	60·00
JSB4	1954	3 panes, No. J152 × 4; 3 panes, J153 × 4; 1 pane, J154 × 4	46·00
JSB5	1955	3 panes, No. J157 × 4; 3 panes, J158 × 4; 1 pane, J159 × 4	41·00
JSB6	1956	3 panes, No. J162 × 4; 3 panes, J163 × 4; 1 pane, J164 × 4	27·00
JSB7	1957	3 panes, No. J167 × 4; 3 panes, J168 × 4; 1 pane, J169 × 4	80·00
JS88	1958	3 panes, No. J172 × 4; 3 panes, J173 × 4; 1 pane, J174 × 4	23·00
JSB9	1959	3 panes, No. J177 × 4; 3 panes, J178 × 4;	

SWITZERLAND Switzerland

JSB10	1960	1 pane, J179 × 4 3 panes, No. J182 × 4; 3 panes, J183 × 4;	23·00
JSB11	1961	1 pane, J184 × 4 3 panes, No. J187 × 4; 3 panes, J188 × 4;	19·00
JSB12	1962	1 pane, J189 × 4 4 panes, No. J192 × 4; 4 panes, J193 × 4	20·00 20·00
JSB13	1963	3 panes, No. J197 × 4; 3 panes, J198 × 4;	
JSB14	1964	1 pane, J199 × 4 3 panes, No. J202 × 4; 3 panes, J203 × 4;	18·00
JSB15	1965	1 pane, J204 × 4 3 panes, No. J207 × 4; 3 panes, J208 × 4;	11·00
JSB16	1966	1 pane, J209 × 4 3 panes, No. J212 × 4; 3 panes, J213 × 4;	7·75
JSB17	1967	1 pane, J214 × 4 2 panes, No. J217 × 4; 2 panes, J218 × 4,	7·75
JSB18	1968	1 pane, J219 × 4 2 panes, No. J221 × 4; 2 panes, J222 × 4;	7·75
JSB19	1969	1 pane, J223 × 4 2 panes, No. J225 × 4; 2 panes, J226 × 4;	8·00
JSB20	1970	1 pane, J227 × 4 2 panes, No. J229 × 4; 2 panes, J230 × 4;	7·50
JSB21	1971	1 pane, J231 × 4 2 panes, No. J233 × 4; 2 panes, J234 × 4;	9·50
JSB22	1972	1 pane, J235 × 4 2 panes, No. J237 × 4; 2 panes, J238 × 4;	9·50
JSB23	1973	1 pane, J239 × 4 3 panes, No. J241 × 4; 1 pane, J242 × 4;	9·25
JSB24	1974	1 pane, J243 × 4 2 panes, No. J245 × 4, 2 panes, J246 × 4	8·75 7·00
JSB25	1975	2 panes, No. J249 × 4; 1 pane, J250 × 4, 2 panes, J251 × 4	7·00
JSB26	1976	2 panes, No. J254 × 4; 1 pane, J255 × 4;	
JSB27	1977	1 pane, J256 × 4 2 panes, No. J258 × 4; 2 panes, J259 × 4	7·25 8·25
JSB28	1978	2 panes, No. J262 × 4; 2 panes, J263 × 4	7·75
JSB29	1979	2 panes, No. J266 × 4; 2 panes, J267 × 4	7·25
JSB30	1980	2 panes, No. J270 × 4; 2 panes, J271 × 4	6·50
JSB31	1981	2 panes, No. J274 × 4; 2 panes, J275 × 4	7·75
JSB32	1982	2 panes, No. J279 × 4; 2 panes, J280 × 4	8·25
JSB33	1983	2 panes, No. J283 × 4; 2 panes, J284 × 4	9·00
JSB34	1984	1 pane, No. J287 × 4; 3 panes, J288 × 4	10·50
JSB35	1985	3 panes, No. J292 × 4	10·50
JSB36	1986	3 panes, No. J296 × 4	10·50
JSB37	1987	2 panes, No. J299 × 4, 2 panes, J301 × 4	11·00
JSB38	1988	3 panes, No. J306 × 4	11·00
JSB39	1989	3 panes, No. J309 × 4	11·00
JSB40	1990	1 pane, No. J313 × 10	11·00
JSB41	1991	1 pane, No. J316 × 10	10·50
JSB42	1992	1 pane, No. J321 × 10	10·50
JSB43	1993	1 pane, No. J326 × 10	10·50
JSB44	1994	1 pane, No. J330 × 10	10·50
JSB45	1995	1 pane, No. J334 × 10	11·00
JSB46	1996	1 pane, No. J338 × 10	12·50
JSB47	1997	1 pane, No. J342 × 10	12·50
JSB48	1998	1 pane, No. J345 × 6; 1 pane, J347 × 4	13·00
JSB49	1999	1 pane, No. J350 × 6; 1 pane, J351 × 4	14·00
JSB50	2000	1 pane, No. J354 × 6; 1 pane, 355 × 4	14·00
JSB51	2001	1 pane, No. J358 × 6; 1 pane, J359 × 4	15·00
JSB52	2002	1 pane, No. J362 × 6; 1 pane, 363 × 4	15·00

POSTCARD STAMP BOOKLET

PSB1	19.11.02	Tourism Emblem (Type P **1**) No. P1 × 6 (7f.20)	7·00
PSB2	19.11.02	Tourism Emblem No. P2 × 6 (10f.)	9·50

SWITZERLAND

Design Index

INDEX TO STAMP DESIGNS

This index provides in a condensed form a key to designs and subjects of Swiss stamps. In all sections, where the same design, or subject, appears more than once in a set only the first number is given.

Portraits are listed under surnames only; those without surnames (e.g. rulers and some saints) are under forenames. Works of art and inventions are indexed under the artist's, or inventor's, name, where this appears on the stamp. Other issues appear under the main subject or part of the inscription. The Pro Juventute stamp designs are also included in this index.

A 1258, 1313, 1327, 1480	B.F.U. 1151	Chimney. J290
Aarburg J262	Bicycle 1457	Chine-Suisse 1401
Aargau J87	Bider. 923	Chocolate. 1478
Academia 1120	Bienne 620	Christmas decoration. 1433
Accordion 1086	Birds 341, 343, 731, 1200, 1238, 1339,	Christmas wreath. J325
Agence Télégraphique Suisse. 786	J193, J221, J225, J229, J233, J335,	Cinderella J294
A.H.V 1375	J344, J347	Cinquieme Suisse 739
Aide aux pays...de développement 644	Blair 884	Clock 1287
Aigle. 932	Blind. 743	Clowns 1251, J351
Aircraft . . 317, 349, 362, 415, 441, 466,	Blind-man's bluff. 1166	Club de Femmes Alpinistes. 755
472, 499, 546, 570, 597, 613, 681,	Blue Cross 927	C.N.A. 964
758, 771, 828, 923, 974, 1006, 1110,	Bodmer 691	Coach. . . 380, 502, 547, 567, 597, 1119
1122, 1144, 1349, 1473	Borel. 882	Coach and horses 501
Airport 974	Borromini 783	Cogwheel. 751
Airship 897	Bovet 959	Coins 664, 692, 981, 1094
Aloise. 1273	Boy holding crossbow . . 257, 292, 325b	Comic strips. 1243, 1251, 1340
Alphirtenfest. 560	Boy with guitar J350	Comptoir 769
Altstätten 941c	Boy with umbrella. J355	Computer. J310
Ammann. 971	Brandver Hütung 1075	Confoederatio 424, 428, 431, 437, 461,
Angel J333	Breastfeeding. J300	467, 473, 495, 506, 522, 527, 536, 541
Anker 1004	Breitling Orbiter 1414	Constitution fédérale 891
Année de l'Enfant 982	Bricklayer. 1168	Corbusier 841
Année de l'Handicapé 1003	Brickwall. 644	Cortaillod J270
Année de la femme 895	Bridges. 1231	Counting. J306
Année de la Nature 800	Brig. 953	Cow 1192, 1336
Année Intern de la Paix 1145	Buchser 1214	Crayfish J339
Année Mondiale des	Burckhardt J120	Crossbow. 589, 1018
Communications 1064	Burgdorf 956	C.S.A.J. 1019
Année Mondiale du Réfugie 612	Bus 380, 471, 502, 549, 996, 1454	Cycling 1063, 1398, 1435, 1468
Anni per la Gioventu. MS196a	Butcher. 1130	
Ansermet 1080	Butterflies 938, 1298, J133, J136, J139,	Dancing 1008
Appenzell. 700, J101	J144, J149, J156, J158, J161, J164,	Davos. 730, 922
Architectural heritage 907	J168	Deer 919, J209, J217
Ariane (rocket) 984, 1225	Buxhundpresse 1277	Delemont 1157
Armée du Salut . . . . see Salvation Army		Desarmement 343, 349
Arms. 724, J262, J266, J270, J274	Cadro J266	Développement 808
Army postman 1156	Calame. J182	Diablerets. 817
A.S.S.O. 689	Calven 403	Discus thrower. 1263
Astronomical clock. 866b	Campagne éuropéene pour le monde	Dish aerial 844
Automatic telephone service 647	rural 1142	Dogs 1062, 1160, 1198
	Cancer 610	Doll J285, J298
Baden. 1123	Candels J329	Donkey 1202, J352
Badgers J210	Capital 860, 937	Doorways 859
Bahnstation 661	Carpenter 1170	Dove 1139
Baker 1087	Cars 988	Dragonfly J138
Ballenberg 1002	Carving. 986	Drawing J307
Banting. 823	Castasegna J264	Dressage 1048
Barramini 783	Cats 1193	Dressmaker 1176
Barrel J249	Cendrars 1213	Drilling 1152
Basel 579, 622, 732, 770, 807, MS810,	Centenadium 430	Droz J108
MS879, 946, 985, 1060, J91	C.E.R.N. 733	Druckerei PTT 997
Basel—Mulhouse Airport 974	Cervin. 726	Drum 1085
Basel University 611	Cheesemaker 1132, 1175	Dufaux 925
Basketball 1399	Chef 1169	Dufour J80
Bather 1451	Chemins de fer. . . . . see Railways	Dunant 960, J47
Beach Volleyball 1400	Cherries J242	
Beaver 1297	Chess. 757	"Economise energy". 921
Bees. J134, J154	Chestnut. J241	E.F.T.A. 744
Beetles J150, J165, J170	Chickens 1203	Einsiedeln 631
Bell J345	Child 911, J40, J142, J147, J193,	Einstein 842
Bellinzona 624, 918	J197, J202	Elephant. 1253
Benken J276	Child and branches J82	Embroidery 1460, MS1461
Bergün 939	Child in field J195	Energie 2000 1357
Bern. . . . . see Berne	Child playing with bricks J301	Engelberg. 713
Berne . . . 426, 550, 623, 645, 672, 690,	Children 1427, J354	Escher 353
MS718, 790, 827, 885, 929, 954, 1026,	Children crossing road. 569, 779	Esperanto. 973
1223	Children playing in sand J302	Esposizione Nazionale . . see Exposition
Berne convention 1117	Children's book characters J287, J291	Nationale
Berneg J132	Childreńs paintings 1463	E.T.V. 1024
Berries J343	Chillon 958	Euler. J167

396

SWITZERLAND Design Index

Europa . . 585, 606, 642, 653, 668, 682, 696, 727, 740, 745, 756, 772, 791, 811, 829, 867, 880, 898, 913, 930, 953, 975, 989, 1008, 1028, 1054, 1068, 1080, 1096, 1124, 1149, 1165, 1209, 1225, 1241, 1266, 1285, 1305, 1320, 1352, 1395, 1425, 1444, 1485
Exposition Nationale 394
Eye 1158

Fabrikgesetz 936
Father with child on shoulders J303
Favre 352
Federer 734
Fellenberg J104
Fern J326
Fétes des Vignerons 1418
F.H.D.S.C.F. 716
Finsteraarhorn 742
Fireman 787
Fischer 908
Fisherman 1173
Fishes . . . 599, 1050, J334, J338, J342, J348
Flags 744, 1250, J60
Florentini 719
Flowers J105, J109, J114, J117, J121, J125, J129, J173, J178, J183, J188, J192, J198, J203, J237, J250, J258, J279, J316
Flüe J51, J81
Fondation Pierre Glanadda 1341
Fonoteca nazionale Lugano 1184
Font 866*a*
Football 552, 797, J314
Forel 820
Formula 1240
Forrer, J. 413
Forrer, L. J112
Fossils 605, 638, 650
Fox J214
Franscini J75
Frau 1443
Frauenfeld 709
Fribourg 628, 951, 1014, J89
Fribourg University 1183
Frog 1299
Fruit 910, J242, J254
Fungi J330,
Furrer J187
Fürstentum Leichtenstein 1308

Gais 702
Gargoyle 864
Geese 1197
Gemeinnütziger 1139
Geneva . . 399, 428, 561, 596, 621, 646, 690, 724, 733, 896, 943, 950, 988, 1020, 1118, 1122, 1154, **MS**1217
Geneva Airport 758
Geneva University 600
Genève . . . . *see* Geneva
Gessner J84
Giacometti 839
Giornico 402
Giotto (space probe) 1226
Girard J67
Girl carrying candle J299
Glarus J102
Glider 681
Goat 1200, J287
Gonin 821
Gotthelf J55, J152
Grand-St-Bernard 687, 1160
Grandson 916
Graphic 576
Gruyères J263
Guelder rose J327
Guinness record 1327
Guisan 782
Gun 878
Gymnastics 804, 877

Hagenwil 955
Hairdressing 1140
Haller J71, J172
Hallwil 935
Hansel and Gretel J291
Harbour 518
Hares 599, J211, J215
Hasler 990
Hat 559, 1302
Heart 1315
Hedgehogs J207
Heer 676
Heidi J287
Heimatwerk 986
Helicopter 837
Helmet 763
"Helvetia" 487
Herisau 941
Herzog J88
Hesse 969
Hilty J177
Hockey stick 646
Hodler J151
Honegger 843
Hopscotch 1165
Horse 1196, 1254
Horsemen 1470
Hot-air balloon 924, 973
Hoteliers Society 1023
Hour-glass 752
Huber J63
Hunger 673
Hurdling 877
Hydro-electric power station 516

Ice hockey 483, 1190
I.G.U. 1025
I.N.S.A.I. 965
Insects . . J133, J138, J143, J148, J153, J158, J163, J168
Interlaken 560, 1089
Internaba **MS**879
Internationale Rheinregulierung . . . 1238
Interparliamentary Union 1185
Interpol 846
Ioannes . . . . *see* John, St.
I.T.U. 717, 728

Jahr der Frau 895
Jenatsch 411
Jigsaw pieces 1218, 1474
John, St. 658
JP 1052
Jung 961
Jungfrau 415
Jungfraujoch 661
"Juphilex 1977" 929
Jura 966

Karrer 1362
Kauffman 1212
Keller J92
Kern 989
King J320
Kingfisher 731
Kite J288
Klee 968
Koch 822
Kocher 746
Kreuzberge 778
Kulturgüterschutz 937
Kunz 1272
Küssnacht 943*c*
Kyburg 915

Ladybird 1515, J143
Lake 515, 1236, 1257
Lake Steamer 1265
Landesausstellung 394
Landestopographie 1153
Landscapes . . 355, 371, 415, 847, 1034
La Poste 1368
Laupen 398, 944
Lausanne 434, 558, 576, 617, 646, 683, 769, 886, 948, 1048, 1067, 1079
Lausanne University 1120
Lavater J96
Leaves 1338
"Lemanex 78" 948, **MS**952
Lenzburg 698
Leprosy 911
Les Diablerets 817
Les Rangiers 401
Letter balance J278
Letterbox 995
Letter cancelling 1105
Letter sorting 1113
Leuk 844
Libro 1279
Liestal 711
Lighted match 1075
Link 1151
Linth J103
Livre 1278
Lizard J336
Logs J308
Loi sur les fabriques 936
Lötschberg 672
Lötschental 947
Lucas . . . . *see* Luke, St.
Lucerne 549, 625, 660, 768, 897, 949, 972, 1143, 1276
Lugano 757, 1184
Luke, St. 657
Lutz 1428
Luzern . . . . *see* Lucerne

Maderno J162
Malaria 662
Mammals 599, 919, 1252, J207, J212, J217
Mann 970
Maps 551, 765, 999, 1091, 1142, 1149, 1241, 1256
Marcus . . . . *see* Mark, St.
Mark, St. 656
Martigny 1061
Martin 1081
Mathematica 1281
Matterhorn 725
Matthaeus . . . . *see* Matthew, St.
Matthew, St. 655
Medallion 862
Melchior J320
Mendrisio 945
Men linking hands 300
Menschenrechte 1404
Messenger 614
Meta 1155
Meteorology 999
Metres convention 894
Meyer 1211
Microscope J311
Minerals 602, 636, 649
Mistletoe J341
Mittelholzer 926
Mobile Post Office 380, 471, 547, 1119
Molecular diagram 1240
Montreaux 1005
Morse key 983
Mosaic 1020
Mother and child J194, **MS**J196*a*
Moths . . . J134, J141, J146, J148, J153, J160, J163, J169, J171
Mountains 284, 298, 338, 342, 355, 371, 489, 1236, 1257, J48, J56
Mouse 1244
Mule driver 616
Mule post 1104
Murten 917
Musée Internationale d'Horlogerie . . 873
Music 1117, J315
Musikfest 1316

Naba Zuri '84' **MS**1074
Nabag **MS**600*a*
Nabra **MS**718, **MS**810
Näfels 699, 1141
Nägeli J76
Nature protection 838
Neuchâtel 486, 703, 724
Nidwalden J90
Nobel 1363
Nomenclatutre Chimique 1240
Numeral 801

SWITZERLAND Design Index

Numeral within circle of stars ... D105
Numismatic Society ... 981
Nursing ... 714
Nyon ... 587

Obwalden ... J98
O.C.T.I. ... 754
Olympics ... 434, 481, 1067, 1326, 1374
Oppenheim ... 1274
Orelli ... J113
Organisation de l'Aviation ... 1283
Organisation International du Travail ... 780
Oriel ... 865
Oron ... 977
Ottenbach ... 944*b*
Otter ... J220, J340
Owls ... 599, 640, **MS**641, 1195, 1200, 1300

Paracelsus ... 1262
Paral bow ... 1405
Parcel sorting ... 1103
Paris ... 675
Parrainage pour communes de montagne ... 1189
Patrimoine architectural *see* Architectural heritage
Payerne ... 706
Pax ... 302, 447, 460
Pedestrian crossing ... 569
Pegasus ... 768
"Per registere raccogliete la roba vecchia" ... 427
Perroy ... J269
Pestalozzi ... 465
Pfyffer ... 410
Pharmacist ... 1171
Photography ... 951
Piaget ... 1318
Piccard ... 962
Pictet-de-Rochemont ... J157
Pilot wearing goggles ... 319
Pingu ... 1407
Pinocchio ... J288
Pistol ... 878
Piz Palu ... 799
Plants ... J245, J254
Ploughing ... 414
Pompiers ... *see* Fire Service
Population census ... 798
Porrentury ... 708, 979
Post ... 1364, 1406
Postbox ... 995, J289
Postbus ... 567
Posthorn ... 500, 893
Postman ... 617, 1109
Post Office counter ... 1107
Post van ... 471, 1102
"Pour tenir récuperéz les matières usagées" ... 427
Prangins Museum ... 1376
Pratteln ... 933
Préverenges ... J277
Prince ... J294
Pro Aero 423, 433, 466, 499, 681, 828, 1007, 1144
Pro Aqua ... 688, 1049
Pro Augusta ... 1342
Pro Familia ... 1239
Pro Fauna ... 599
Pro Filia ... 1317
Pro Infirmis ... 788
Pro Ivliomayo ... 1343
Pro Natura ... 731
Pro Patria ... 537, 542, 553, 562, 571, 580, 591, 601, 636, **MS**641, 648, 663, 676, 691, 719, 734, 746, 759, 774, 793, 813, 831, 869, 887, 901, 915, 932, 955, 977, 991, 1010, 1030, 1049, 1056, 1070, 1082, 1098, 1126, 1145, 1161, 1205, 1227, 1246, 1268, 1287, 1301, 1322, 1390, 1421, 1445, 1481
Prospect ... 1085
Pro Sport ... 1095, 1186, 1255, 1319
Protection civile ... 578, 835
"Protect the Alps" ... 1250
Pro Vallon ... 1344
PTT Union ... 1235
Putting the Shot ... 523, 1009, J61
Pylons ... 510

Quill pen ... 845

Rabbit ... 1194
Radio ... 818, 826, 1088
Railway bridge ... 480
Railways 477, 512, 577, 597, 659, 672, 825, 1021, 1046, 1122, 1159, 1188, 1256, J286, 1345
Ramuz ... 840
Rapperswil ... 980
Reading ... J304
Red Cross ... 460, 674, **MS**675*a*, 1118, 1420
Red Cross Museum ... 1154
Red Riding Hood ... J293
Reka ... 1182
Ret-Romania ... 1077
Reynold ... 412
RhB ... 1159
Rheinreguilerung ... 1238
Rheinschiffahrt ... 551
Rheinschiffahrtsakte ... 766
Richard ... J99
Rifle-shooting ... 526
Riggenbach ... J100
Rilke ... 967
Riva San Vitale ... 705
Rivaz ... 1472
Road ... 517
Rocking horse ... J284
Romisch-Chur ... 1092
Ropes ... 1090
Roses ... 806, 1476, J237, J258, J278
Rousseau ... 663
Rowing ... 660
Running ... 525, 805, 1007, 1469
Rüte ... J267

S.A.C. ... 671
St. Bernard ... 1160
St. Bernard tunnel ... 687
St. Gall ... 598, **MS**600*a*, 626, J85
St. Gallen University ... 1377
St. Gallen ... *see* St. Gall
St. Gotthard ... 352, 577, 920, 1001
Safety helmets ... 1264
Saffa ... 588
Saint-Imier ... 1066
S.B.R.V. ... 1087
St. Moritz ... 481, 874
St. Peters Cathedral ... 1020
St. Pierre-de-Clages Church ... 707
S.A.J.V. ... 1019
Salut ... *see* Salvation Army
Salvation Army ... 590, 1047
Samedan ... 701
San Bernardino ... 753
San Gottardo ... *see* St. Gotthard
Sargans ... 934
S.A.T.U.S. ... 877
Satellite ... 983
S.C.F. ... 716
Schaffhausen ... 627, J97
Schoeck ... 784
Schönbein ... 1429
Schwamendingen ... J268
Schwyz ... 630
Scissors ... 571
S.C.M.V. ... 1140
Scout ... 670
Scuol ... J272
Seal ... 1014, 1060
Sea-Lion ... 1252
Seedorf Uri ... 710
Segantini ... 1430
Semaine Suisse ... *see* Swiss Week
Sempach ... 401, 1091
S.E.V. ... 1181
"700 Anni" ... 1222
"700 Ans" ... 1221
"700 Jahre" ... 1219
"700 Onns" ... 1220
7.9.87 (overprint) ... 1138
S.F.G. ... 1024
S.F.V. ... 1050
S.G.B. ... 1000
S.G.C.I. ... 1027
Sheep ... 1199
Shield, flowers and mountains ... D274, F268
Shield over mountains ... 332
Shields ... J9, J11, J14, J17, J24, J28, J32, J36, J44, J52
Ships ... 597, 1078, 1108, 1241, J312
S.I.A. ... 1121
Sierre ... J271
Sign ... 861
Simenon ... 1292
Simplon ... 568
S.I.S.L. ... 1078
S.J.H. ... 878
Skating ... 730, 922, 1396
Skiing ... 484, 874, 1243
S.K.V. ... 845
Sledging ... J356
Sleigh ... J353
S.M.U.V. ... 1152
S.M.V. ... 1132
Snail ... J346
Snowboarding ... 1397
Snowman ... J349
Snowplough ... 513
Snowstorms ... 1436, 1479
Snow White and the Seven Dwarfs ... J292
Société d'Histoire de l'Art ... 987
Société d'Utilité Publique des Femmes ... 1139
Soldiers ... 689
Solothurn ... 629, 941*b*, 1015, J94
Spannörter ... 836
Spelterini ... 924
Spiez ... 978
Spinning top ... J296
Sport ... 1280
Sprick ... 1337
Spyri ... J137
Squirrels ... J213
S.R.B. ... 1063
S.S.I.C. ... 1027
Staël ... 785
Stagecoach ... 1106
Stained glass windows ... 774, 813
Stamp printing press ... 997
Stamps ... 715, 764, 807, 1131, 1187, 1259
Stans ... 1016
Stars ... 532, J337
Steam Roller ... J297
Stephan ... 883
Stop Aids ... 1291
Stove ... J283
Sun ... 752, 861
Sursee ... 942
Survey mark ... 521
Suspension railway ... 519
S.U.V.A. ... 763, 963
Suvorov ... 1431
Swimming ... 1467
Swissair ... 1006
Swisscore ... 1369
Swiss Electricity ... 1293
Swiss Sports Federation ... 892
Swiss week ... 751
Symbol ... 445

Taeuber-Arp ... 1275
Tarasp ... 957
T.C.S. ... 1314
Techorama ... 1017
Teddy bear ... J295
Telecom '95' ... 1312
Telecommunications ... 809, 818
Telephone ... 906, 912, 998
Tell ... 295
Tents ... 767
Terre des Hommes ... 875

SWITZERLAND   Design Index

Thun.........................878	Valais.........................724	Winged envelope...............339
Thurgau......................J93	Vegetables....................910	Winged figure..................323
Tinguely.....................1155	Vela Museum 1477	Winterthur 1017
Toad........................J343	Vevey....................559, 928	Winterhilfe 1116
Toepffer J116, 1409	Viaducts.......................511	Witch........................J291
Topography 1153	Viellesse......................752	Wolfenschiessen 704, J273
Torre........................J275	*Ville de Lucerne* (airship).........897	Woman and mountains 286
Tourism 1133, **MS**1137	Vindonissa...................1093	Women in traditional costumes.... J64,
Tourisme pédestre..............938	Vine grower 1174	J68, J72, J77
Toys J283, J295	Vinet J59	Worker........................780
Trains..... J286, 477, 659, 672, 1021,	Violin 1449	World Cup '94'................1284
1159, 1188, 1256,	Visite 1361	Wrench.......................824
Transport 597, 1122, 1256	V.S.J........................1052	Wrestling 524, J62
Transports publics 1158	V.S.M..................1053, 1130	
Tree and scroll................488		Year '2000'...................1434
Trees .. 612, 827, 909, 985, 1116, J321		Yersin........................819
Triangle (instrument)...........J305	Walker 1453	Young couple J309
Tunnel S. Bernardino...........753	Wanderwege 938	Youths J313
Turkey 1203	Wangen J265	
"1291–1991" 1215, 1224	Warning triangle...............824	Zodiac signs..................1034
	Waterfalls.....................493	Z.P.V........................1076
Uffikon J274	Weathervane..................866	Zug....................712, J95
U.I.T.....................see I.T.U	Welti.........................354	"Zum Durchhalten Altstoffe
U.N.I.C.E.F. 982	Wengi.......................J128	sammeln"..................427
Union 1350	Wettstein 485	Zürich 391, 588, 619, 940, 1046, 1065,
Union Interparlementaire 1185	Wheat........................673	1094
Unisource 1295	Wheelchair....................905	Zürich airport 546
U.N.O. 789	Wille........................J124	Zürich University 1051
U.P.U. 336, 503, 790, 885, 1415	Window 858	Zurigo ....see Zürich
Uri..........................J86	Wine........................1450	Zwingli 781
U.S.K.A......................983	Wing.........................788	

399

SWITZERLAND INTERNATIONAL ORGANIZATIONS 1922

International Organizations situated in Switzerland

The stamps listed under this heading were issued by the Swiss Post Office primarily for the use of officials of the Organizations named.

PRICES FOR UNUSED STAMPS. Prior to 1 February 1944 the stamps listed were not available unused to collectors but only postally used. On that date the stamps then in use were made available to collectors in unused condition. We therefore quote unused prices only for those issues which have been on sale to the public, although others do exist unused.

A. LEAGUE OF NATIONS

SOCIÉTÉ DES NATIONS
(LN 1)   (LN 2)

Various issues optd with Type LN 1

1922–44. *(I) T* **17**, **20** *to* **24**, **41** *and* **43**.

LN1	20b	2½c. bistre/*buff* (1928)	—	40
LN2	20a	3c. ultramarine/*buff* (1930)	—	4·50
		a. Grilled gum (1933)	—	7·25
LN3	20b	5c. orange/*buff*	—	2·10
LN4		5c. violet-grey/*buff* (1925)	—	2·10
LN5		5c. deep claret/*buff* (1927)	—	1·20
LN5 *a*		5c. deep green/*buff* (1931)	—	13·00
		ab. Grilled gum (1933)	—	14·00
LN6	20a	7½c. green/*buff* (1927)	—	30
LN7	21	10c. green/*buff*	—	35
LN8		10c. blue-green/*buff* (1928)	—	95
LN8 *a*		10c. reddish violet/*buff* (1931)	—	1·80
LN9		15c. brown-lake/*buff* (1927)	—	70
LN10		20c. purple/*buff*	—	3·75
LN11		20c. scarlet/*buff* (1925)	—	1·50
LN12		25c. orange-red/*buff*	—	6·00
LN13		25c. scarlet/*buff*	—	75
LN14		25c. yellow-brown/*buff* (1928)	—	9·25
LN15	17	30c. pale green and yellow-brown	—	7·25
LN16	21	30c. blue/*buff* (1924)	—	4·25
		a. Grilled gum (1932)	—	£325
LN17	17	35c. yellow and green	—	3·75
LN18		40c. blue	—	1·00
LN19		40c. yellow-green & dp mag (1925)	—	6·50
LN20		50c. yellow-green and deep green	—	6·25
		a. Chalk-surfaced paper. Grilled gum (1935)	50	1·30
LN21		60c. orange-brown	23·00	80
		a. Chalk-surfaced paper. Grilled gum (1944)	26·00	£160
LN22		70c. buff and violet (1924)	—	14·00
		a. Chalk-surfaced paper. Grilled gum (1936)	1·50	35
LN23		80c. buff and olive-grey	—	1·90
		a. Chalk-surfaced paper. Grilled gum (1942)	1·20	1·70
LN24	41	90c. scarlet, dp green & grn (1924)	—	9·25
		a. Chalk-surfaced paper. Grilled gum (1936)	—	3·00
LN25	17	1f. pale green and claret	—	5·00
		a. Chalk-surfaced paper. Grilled gum (1942)	—	3·75
LN26	41	1f.20 scarlet, brown-lake and salmon-pink (1924)	—	3·50
		a. "HFLVETIA"	—	£200
		b. Chalk-surfaced paper. Grilled gum (1936)	2·50	2·30
LN27		1f.50 scarlet, blue and greenish blue (1924)	—	9·25
		a. Chalk-surfaced paper. Grilled gum (1935)	2·50	2·50
LN28		2f. scarlet, black & ol-grey (1924)	—	9·00
		a. Chalk-surfaced paper. Grilled gum (1936)	3·00	3·00
LN29	22	3f. rose-carmine	—	17·00
LN29*a*	43	3f. red-brown (1937)	—	£100
LN30	23	5f. deep ultramarine	—	38·00
LN31		5f. deep blue (No. 336) (1928)	—	70·00
LN32	24	10f. deep mauve	—	75·00
LN33		10f. deep grey-green (1928)	—	85·00

1932. *(II) International Disarmament Conference.*

LN34	44	5c. blue-green	—	10·50
LN35		10c. bright orange	—	95
LN36		20c. magenta	—	95
LN37		30c. bright blue	—	31·00
LN38		60c. bistre-brown	—	9·00
LN39	45	1f. olive-grey and blue	—	7·50
LN34/39 *Set of 6*			—	55·00

1934–35. *(III) As T* **48** *(Landscape types. Typo).*

LN40	3c. yellow-olive	—	30
LN41	5c. blue-green (1935)	—	40
LN42	15c. orange (1935)	—	80
LN43	25c. orange-brown	—	11·00
LN44	30c. ultramarine	—	95
LN40/44 *Set of 5*		—	12·00

1937–43. *(IV) As T* **52** *(Landscape types. Recess).*

A. Smooth white non-granite paper.

LN45A	3c. yellow-olive	10	20
LN46A	5c. blue-green	20	20
LN47A	10c. bright purple (I) (No. 370)	—	11·50
	c. Type (II) (No. 370d)	—	70
LN48A	10c. red-brown (1942)	—	65
LN49	10c. chestnut (1943)	50	45
LN50A	15c. orange	30	40
LN51A	20c. scarlet (II) (No. 374Ad)	—	1·20
LN51c	20c. scarlet (II) (No. 375) (1942)	55	75
LN52A	25c. yellow-brown	45	65
LN53A	30c. dull ultramarine	45	55
LN54A	35c. bright green	45	65
LN55A	40c. grey	75	90
LN45/55 *Set of 12*		—	6·50

B. Non-granite paper with grilled gum.

LN45B	3c. yellow-olive	—	35
LN46B	5c. blue-green	—	35
LN47B	10c. bright purple (I) (No. 370)	—	11·50
	c. Type (II) (No. 370d)	—	5·25
LN50B	15c. orange	—	60
LN51B	20c. scarlet (II) (No. 3745Bd)	—	1·70
LN52B	25c. yellow-brown	—	95
LN53B	30c. dull ultramarine	—	90
LN54B	35c. bright green	—	3·00
LN55B	40c. grey	—	2·40

1938. *(V) Nos. 382/5.*

(a) Optd with Type LN **1**.

LN56	20c. red and buff	—	1·20
LN57	30c. blue and pale blue	—	1·90
LN58	60c. brown and buff	—	3·50
LN59	1f. black and buff	—	6·00
LN56/59 *Set of 4*		—	11·50

(b) Optd with Type LN **2**.

LN60	20c. red and buff	—	1·40
LN61	30c. blue and pale blue	—	2·50
LN62	60c. brown and buff	—	4·50
LN63	1f. black and buff (R.)	—	7·50
LN60/63 *Set of 4*		—	14·50

SWITZERLAND INTERNATIONAL ORGANIZATIONS 1938

1939. *(VI) Nos. 388B/390B.*

LN64	3f. red-brown	3·00	6·25
LN65	5f. slate-blue	5·00	8·50
LN66	10f. green	8·00	19·00

COURRIER DE LA SOCIÉTÉ DES NATIONS

(LN 3)

1944. Optd as Type LN 3; as shown on Nos. LN67/75, *larger type on LN76/84, or in two lines (still larger type) on LN85/7.*

(a) As T 52 (Landscape types. Recess. Smooth white paper).

LN67	3c. yellow-olive	20	25
LN68	5c. blue-green	20	25
LN69	10c. chestnut	20	20
LN70	15c. orange	30	30
	a. Grilled gum	£1900	£2000
LN71	20c. scarlet (No. 375)	45	55
	a. Grilled gum	£1900	£2000
LN72	25c. yellow-brown	55	70
	a. Grilled gum	£1900	£2000
LN73	30c. dull ultramarine	60	75
LN74	35c. bright green	60	1·00
LN75	40c. grey	65	1·30
	a. Grilled gum	£1900	£2000

(b) Nos. 405 to 413.

LN76	50c. deep violet-blue/*blue-green*	1·10	2·00
LN77	60c. reddish brown/*cinnamon*	1·40	2·40
LN78	70c. deep reddish purple/*mauve*	1·50	2·20
LN79	80c. black/*olive-grey*	1·30	2·00
LN80	90c. scarlet/*pink*	1·30	2·00
LN81	1f. myrtle green/*blue-green*	1·50	2·30
LN82	1f.20 plum/*olive-grey*	2·00	3·25
LN83	1f.50 indigo/*buff*	2·20	3·75
LN84	2f. brown-lake/*pink*	2·75	4·75

(c) Nos. 388B/390B.

LN85	3f. red-brown	4·50	8·75
LN86	5f. slate-blue	7·00	12·00
LN87	10f. green	12·50	23·00
LN67/87 Set of 21		40·00	70·00

B. INTERNATIONAL LABOUR OFFICE

S.d.N. Bureau international du Travail
(LB 1)

(LB 2)

Various issues optd with Type LB **1**

1923–44. *(I) T* **17, 20** *to* **24, 41** *and* **43.**

LB1	**20b**	2½c. bistre/*buff* (1927)	—	20
LB2	**20a**	3c. ultramarine/*buff* (1930)	—	70
LB3	**20b**	5c. orange/*buff*	—	35
LB4		5c. deep claret/*buff* (1927)	—	15
LB5	**20a**	7½c. green/*buff* (1927)	—	20
LB6	**21**	10c. green/*buff*	—	30
LB7		10c. blue-green/*buff* (1928)	—	55
LB8		15c. brown-lake/*buff* (1928)	—	70
LB9		20c. purple/*buff*	—	7·00
LB10		20c. scarlet/*buff* (1927)	—	3·00
LB11		25c. scarlet/*buff*	—	65
LB12		25c. yellow-brown/*buff* (1928)	—	1·60
LB13	**17**	30c. pale green and yellow-brown	—	31·00
LB14	**21**	30c. blue/*buff* (1925)	—	1·10
LB15	**17**	35c. yellow and green	—	5·00
LB16		40c. blue	—	65
LB17		40c. yellow-green & dp mag (1928)	—	7·25
LB18		50c. yellow-green and deep green	—	3·25
		a. Chalk-surfaced paper. Grilled gum (1942)	1·20	1·20
LB19		60c. orange-brown	90	1·20
LB20		70c. buff and violet (1924)	—	19·00
		a. Chalk-surfaced paper. Grilled gum (1937)	1·20	1·70
LB21		80c. buff and olive-grey	6·25	1·00
		a. Chalk-surfaced paper. Grilled gum (1944)	22·00	£130
LB22	**41**	90c. scarlet, dp green & grn (1925)	—	2·50
		a. Chalk-surfaced paper. Grilled gum (1942)	—	7·75
LB23	**17**	1f. pale green and claret	—	1·40
		a. Chalk-surfaced paper. Grilled gum (1942)	—	3·00
LB24	**41**	1f.20 scarlet, brown-lake and salmon-pink (1925)	—	3·25
		a. "HFLVETIA"	—	£700
		b. Chalk-surfaced paper. Grilled gum (1942)	10·50	2·50
LB25		1f.50 scar, bl & greenish bl (1925)	—	8·25
		a. Chalk-surfaced paper. Grilled gum (1937)	2·00	2·00
LB26		2f. scarlet, black & of-grey (1925)	—	22·00
		a. Chalk-surfaced paper. Grilled gum (1936)	2·50	3·25
LB27	**22**	3f. rose-carmine	—	14·00
LB27*a*	**43**	3f. red-brown (1937)	—	£120
LB28	**23**	5f. deep ultramarine	—	22·00
LB29		5f. deep blue (No. 336) (1928)	—	60·00
LB30	**24**	10f. deep mauve	—	90·00
LB31		10f. deep grey-green (1930)	—	90·00

1932. *(II) International Disarmament Conference.*

LB32	**44**	5c. blue-green	—	70
LB33		10c. bright orange	—	60
LB34		20c. magenta	—	85
LB35		30c. bright blue	—	4·25
LB36		60c. bistre-brown	—	4·25
LB37	**45**	1f. olive-grey and blue	—	6·00
LB32/37 Set of 6			—	15·00

1937. *(III) T* **48** *(Landscape type. Typo).*

LB38	**48**	3c. yellow-olive	—	3·00

1937–43. *(IV) As T* **52** *(Landscape types. Recess.)*

A. Smooth white non-granite paper.

LB39A	3c. yellow-olive	20	25
LB40A	5c. blue-green	20	25
LB41A	10c. bright purple (I) (No. 370)	—	1·20
	c. Type II (No. 370d)	—	3·25
LB41Ad	10c. red-brown (1942)	—	65
LB41Ae	10c. chestnut (1943)	30	30
LB42A	15c. orange	30	25
LB43A	20c. scarlet (III) (No. 374d)	—	1·10
LB43Ac	20c. scarlet (No. 375) (1942)	55	75
LB44A	25c. yellow-brown	50	65
LB45A	30c. dull ultramarine	50	60
LB46A	35c. bright green	50	85
LB47A	40c. grey	80	90
LB39A/47A Set of 12		—	7·00

B. Non-granite paper with grilled gum.

LB39B	3c. yellow-olive	—	80
LB40B	5c. blue-green	—	65
LB41B	10c. bright purple (I) (No. 370)	—	1·20
LB42B	15c. orange	—	1·30
LB43B	20c. scarlet (III) (No. 374d)	—	95
LB44B	25c. yellow-brown	—	1·60
LB45B	30c. dull ultramarine	—	1·60
LB46B	35c. bright green	—	2·00
LB47B	40c. grey	—	1·70

1938. *(V) Nos. 382/5.*

(a) Optd with Type LB **1.**

LB48	20c. red and buff	—	75
LB49	30c. blue and pale blue	—	1·40
LB50	60c. brown and buff	—	2·75
LB51	1f. black and buff	—	4·50
LB48/51 Set of 4		—	8·50

(b) Optd with Type LB **2.**

LB52	20c. red and buff	—	2·00
LB53	30c. blue and pale blue	—	1·70

SWITZERLAND INTERNATIONAL ORGANIZATIONS 1938

LB54	60c. brown and buff	—	3·75
LB55	1f. black and buff (R.)	—	3·75
LB52/55	Set of 4	—	10·50

1939. (VI) Nos. 388B/390B.
LB56	3f. red-brown	3·00	5·50
LB57	5f. slate-blue	4·00	9·75
LB58	10f. green	6·75	14·50

1944. *Various issues optd "COURRIER DU BUREAU INTERNATIONAL DU TRAVAIL," as Type LN 3; in three lines on Nos. LB59/76 or in two lines on LB77/9.*

(a) As T 52 (Landscape types. Recess. Smooth white paper).
LB59	3c. yellow-olive	20	20
LB60	5c. blue-green	20	25
LB61	10c. chestnut	30	30
LB62	15c. orange	40	50
LB63	20c. scarlet (No. 375)	45	60
LB64	25c. yellow-brown	50	70
LB65	30c. dull ultramarine	75	1·00
LB66	35c. bright green	80	1·20
LB67	40c. grey	85	1·40

(b) Nos. 405/13.
LB68	50c. deep violet-blue/*blue-green*	2·30	3·75
LB69	60c. reddish brown/*cinnamon*	2·30	3·00
LB70	70c. deep reddish purple/*mauve*	2·75	2·50
LB71	80c. black/*olive-grey*	65	70
LB72	90c. scarlet/*pink*	65	70
LB73	1f. myrtle green/*blue-green*	85	75
LB74	1f.20 plum/*olive-grey*	1·00	80
LB75	1f.50 Indigo/*buff*	1·20	85
LB76	2f. brown-lake/*pink*	1·70	1·20

(c) Nos. 388B/390B.
LB77	3f. red-brown	3·75	3·00
LB78	5f. slate-blue	5·50	5·00
LB79	10f. green	11·50	14·00
LB59/79	Set of 21	35·00	38·00

BUREAU INTERNATIONAL DU TRAVAIL
(LB 3)

LB 4 Miners (bas-relief)

Visite du Pape Paul VI Genève 10 juin 1969
(LB 5)

1950 (1 Feb). *Nos. 511/21 optd with Type LB 3.*
LB80	5c. orange	2·75	2·75
LB81	10c. yellow-green	2·75	4·75
LB82	15c. turquoise	3·50	3·00
LB83	20c. maroon (II)	3·50	5·75
LB84	25c. scarlet	3·75	4·50
LB85	30c. olive	4·00	5·75
LB86	30c. brown	4·00	5·00
LB87	40c. blue	4·00	5·25
LB88	50c. bluish grey	5·50	5·25
LB89	60c. blue-green	6·50	7·00
LB90	70c. violet	8·00	9·50
LB80/90	Set of 11	45·00	55·00

(Des H. Thoni. Eng K. Bickel, jun. Recess PTT, Berne)

1956 (22 Oct)—**60**. *Type LB 4 and similar design inscr "BUREAU INTERNATIONAL DU TRAVAIL". P 11½.*
LB91	LB 4	5c. slate-purple	10	10
LB92		10c. green	10	10
LB93	—	20c. scarlet	2·00	2·00
LB94	—	20c. carmine (24.10.60)	30	25
LB95	—	30c. orange (24.10.60)	45	35
LB96	LB 4	40c. blue	1·40	1·20
LB97		50c. blue (24.10.60)	20	30
LB98	—	60c. brown	30	25
LB99	—	2f. reddish purple	80	70
LB91/99	Set of 9		5·00	4·50

Design: *Horiz*—20c. (2), 30c., 60c., 2f. Globe, flywheel and factory chimney.

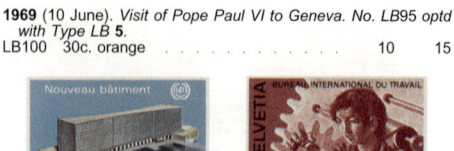

1969 (10 June). *Visit of Pope Paul VI to Geneva. No. LB95 optd with Type LB 5.*
LB100	30c. orange	10	15

LB 6 New Headquarters Building

LB 7 Man at Lathe

(Photo Courvoisier)

1974 (30 May). *Inauguration of New I.L.O. Headquarters, Geneva. Phosphorescent granite paper. P 11½.*
LB101	LB 6	80c. multicoloured	70	60

(Des H. Ernie. Photo Courvoisier)

1975 (15 Feb)—**88**. *Type LB 7 and similar horiz designs. Granite paper (30, 60, 100c.). Phosphorescent paper. P 11½.*
LB102	30c. lake-brown	25	25
LB103	60c. deep ultramarine	45	40
LB104	90c. red-brown, dull vermilion and dull green (13.9.88)	70	65
LB105	100c. green	80	65
LB106	120c. ochre & reddish brown (22.8.83)	60	75
LB102/106	Set of 5	2·50	2·75

Designs:—60c. Woman at drilling machine; 90c. Welder and laboratory assistant; 100c. Surveyor with theodolite; 120c. Apprentice and instructor with slide gauge.

LB 8 Keys

(Des M. Pastore. Litho PTT, Berne)

1994 (17 May). *75th Anniv of International Labour Organization. Phosphorescent paper. P 13½.*
LB107	LB 8	180c. multicoloured	1·40	1·60

C. INTERNATIONAL EDUCATION OFFICE

(Des M. Pastore. Litho PTT, Berne)

1944 (15 May). *Various issues optd "COURRIER DU BUREAU INTERNATIONAL D'EDUCATION", as Type LN 3, in black, in three lines on Nos. LE1/18, or in two lines on Nos. LE19/21.*

(a) As T 52 (Landscape types. Recess. Smooth white paper).
LE1	3c. yellow-olive	20	40
LE2	5c. blue-green	50	95
LE3	10c. chestnut	55	1·20
LE4	15c. orange	50	1·10
LE5	20c. scarlet (No. 375)	50	1·10
LE6	25c. yellow-brown	50	1·10
LE7	30c. dull ultramarine	85	1·50
LE8	35c. bright green	75	1·40
LE9	40c. grey	95	1·70

(b) Nos. 405/13.
LE10	50c. deep violet-blue/*blue-green*	5·25	7·25
LE11	60c. reddish brown/*cinnamon*	5·25	7·25
LE12	70c. deep reddish purple/*mauve*	5·25	7·25
LE13	80c. black/*olive-grey*	55	1·20
LE14	90c. scarlet/*pink*	65	1·30
LE15	1f. myrtle green/*blue-green*	75	1·50
LE16	1f.20 plum/*olive-grey*	95	1·80

402

SWITZERLAND INTERNATIONAL ORGANIZATIONS 1944

LE17	1f.50 indigo/*buff*	1·20	3·00
LE18	2f. brown-lake/*pink*	1·90	2·75

(c) Nos. 388B/390B.

LE19	3f. red-brown	4·50	12·00
LE20	5f. slate-blue	6·75	19·00
LE21	10f. green	10·00	27·00
LE1/21	Set of 21	46·00	95·00

(LE 1)   (LE 2)   LE 3 Globe on Books

1946 (12 Jan). *No. 465 optd with Type LE* **1**.

LE22	**86**	10c. purple (R.)	15	25

1948 (1 Oct). *Nos. 489/94 optd with Type LE* **2**.

LE23	5c. reddish brown	1·70	2·00
LE24	10c. green	1·90	2·10
LE25	20c. chestnut	1·70	2·00
LE26	25c. scarlet	1·70	2·00
LE27	30c. deep turquoise-blue	1·90	2·10
LE28	40c. deep blue	1·70	2·00
LE23/28	Set of 6	9·50	11·00

1950 (1 Feb). *Nos. 511/21 optd with Type LE* **2**.

LE29	5c. orange	70	75
LE30	10c. yellow-green	90	90
LE31	15c. turquoise	90	95
LE32	20c. maroon (II)	3·00	3·00
LE33	25c. scarlet	6·75	8·75
LE34	30c. olive	6·75	7·75
LE35	35c. brown	4·50	6·00
LE36	40c. blue	4·75	5·75
LE37	50c. bluish grey	5·50	6·00
LE38	60c. blue-green	6·50	7·50
LE39	70c. violet	7·50	8·75
LE29/39	Set of 11	43·00	50·00

(Des D. Brun. Eng K. Lieven (Type LE 3). Des H. Hartmann. Eng K. Bickel (others). Recess PTT, Berne)

1958 (22 Sept)–**60**. *Type LE* **3** *and similar vert design inscr "BUREAU INTERNATIONAL D'EDUCATION". P* 11½.

LE40	LE **3**	5c. slate-purple	10	10
LE41		10c. green	10	10
LE42	–	20c. scarlet	1·80	1·80
LE43	–	20c. carmine (24.10.60)	20	15
LE44	–	30c. orange (24.10.60)	30	25
LE45	LE **3**	40c. blue	2·20	1·80
LE46		50c. blue (24.10.60)	45	35
LE47	–	60c. brown	55	45
LE48	–	2f. purple	1·50	1·30
LE40/48	Set of 9		6·50	5·75

Design:—20c. (2), 30c., 60c., 2f. Pestalozzi Monument, Yverdon.

D. WORLD HEALTH ORGANIZATION

(LH 1)

1948 (24 June). *Nos. 489/92 and 494 optd with Type LH* **1**.

LH1	5c. reddish brown	2·00	1·20
LH2	10c. green	2·50	2·50
LH3	20c. chestnut	2·30	2·50
LH4	25c. scarlet	2·50	2·75
LH5	40c. deep blue	3·00	2·40
LH1/5	Set of 5	11·00	10·50

1948 (24 June)–**50**. *Various issues optd as Type LH* **1** *but larger*.

(a) Nos. 511/21.

LH6	5c. orange	70	35
LH7	10c. yellow-green	1·40	1·20
LH8	15c. turquoise	1·80	90
LH9	20c. maroon (II)	5·25	3·50
LH10	25c. scarlet	5·50	5·50
LH11	30c. olive	2·50	3·25
LH12	35c. brown	2·75	4·50
LH13	40c. blue	2·50	1·10
LH14	50c. bluish grey	3·50	3·75
LH15	60c. blue-green	3·50	3·75
LH16	70c. violet	5·50	3·25

(b) Nos. 408/13 and 388B/390.

LH17	80c. black/*olive-grey*	1·10	1·40
LH18	90c. scarlet/*pink*	6·25	3·00
LH19	1f. myrtle green/*blue-green*	1·30	1·60
LH20	1f.20 plum/*olive-grey*	7·75	7·75
LH21	1f.50 indigo/*buff*	17·00	8·50
LH22	2f. brown-lake/*pink*	3·50	2·40
LH23	3f. red-brown	36·00	21·00
LH24	5f. slate-blue	7·75	5·50
LH25	10f. green	75·00	38·00
LH6/25	Set of 20	£170	£110

Dates of issue—The 80c., 1f., 2f. and 5f. were issued on 24.6.48 and the remainder on 1.2.50.

LH **2** Staff of Aesculapius   (LH 3)

(Des H. Thoni. Eng A. Yersin. Recess PTT, Berne)

1957 (16 Sept)–**60**. *P* 11½.

LH26	LH **2**	5c. slate-purple	10	10
LH27		10c. green	10	10
LH28		20c. scarlet	1·80	1·80
LH29		20c. carmine (24.10.60)	15	15
LH30		30c. orange (24.10.60)	25	25
LH31		40c. blue	1·60	1·60
LH32		50c. blue (24.10.60)	35	35
LH33		60c. brown	40	40
LH34		2f. reddish purple	1·20	1·20
LH26/34	Set of 9		5·75	5·00

1962 (19 Mar). *Malaria Eradication. No. LH32 optd with type LH* **3**.

LH35	LH **2**	50c. blue	15	25

LH **4** Staff of Aesculapius

(Des H. Thoni. Litho (140c.) or typo (others) PTT, Berne)

1975 (15 Feb)–**86**. *Phosphorescent granite paper (30 to 100c.). P* 11½.

LH36	LH **4**	30c. pale yellowish green, brown-purple and rose	25	25
LH37		60c. lemon, blue and pale blue	50	45
LH38		90c. greenish yellow, violet and bright reddish violet	75	65
LH39		100c. pale blue, red-brown & orge	80	75
LH40		140c. light green, turquoise and rosine (27.5 86)	1·20	1·20
LH36/40	Set of 5		3·25	3·25

403

SWITZERLAND INTERNATIONAL ORGANIZATIONS 1995

LH 5 Staff of Aesculapius

(Litho PTT, Berne)

1995 (28 Nov). *Phosphorescent paper.* P 13.
LH41	LH **5**	180c. olive-yellow, yell-brn & rosine	1·50	1·60

E. INTERNATIONAL REFUGEES ORGANIZATION

ORGANISATION INTERNATIONALE POUR LES RÉFUGIÉS

(LR 1)

(Litho PTT, Berne)

1950 (1 Feb). *Various issues optd with Type LR **1**.*

(a) Nos. 511/2, 514/5 and 518.
LR1	5c. orange	10·00	7·25
LR2	10c. yellow-green	11·00	8·00
LR3	20c. maroon (II)	10·00	7·50
LR4	25c. scarlet	11·00	8·00
LR5	40c. blue	10·50	7·50

(b) Nos. 408, 410 and 413.
LR6	80c. black/*olive-grey*	10·00	11·50
LR7	1f. myrtle green/*blue-green*	9·50	6·00
LR8	2f. brown-lake/*pink*	9·50	6·00
LR1/8	Set of 8	75·00	50·00

F. WORLD METEOROLOGICAL ORGANIZATION

LM **1** "The Elements"   LM **2** WMO Emblem

(Des D. Brun (Type LM **1**), E. Poncy (20c., 60c., 2f.). Eng À. Yersin. Recess PTT Berne)

1956 (22 Oct)–**60**. *Type LM **1** and similar design inscr* "ORGANISATION METEOROLOGIQUE MONDIALE". P 11½.
LM1	LM **1**	5c. slate-purple	10	10
LM2	–	10c. green	10	10
LM3	–	20c. scarlet	1·30	1·80
LM4	–	20c. carmine (24.10.60)	15	15
LM5	–	30c. orange (24.10.60)	25	25
LM6	LM **1**	40c. blue	1·30	1·80
LM7	–	50c. blue (24.10.60)	35	35
LM8	–	60c. brown	40	40
LM9	–	2f. reddish purple	1·40	1·20
LM1/9	Set of 9		5·00	5·75

Design: Horiz—20c. (2), 30c., 60c., 2f. Weathervane.

(Des H. Hartmann. Eng K. Bickel-Courtin. (Type LM **2**). Photo Courvoisier (80c.) or recess PTT, Berne (others))

1973 (30 Aug). *Centenary of World Meteorological Organization. Type LM **2** and similar horiz design inscr* "OMI OMM 1873 1973". *Granite paper.* P 11¾.
LM10	LM **2**	30c. rose-carmine	25	25
LM11	–	40c. new blue	35	35

LM12	–	80c. violet and gold	65	60
LM13	LM **2**	1f. yellow-brown	80	70
LM10/13	Set of 4		1·80	1·70

G. UNIVERSAL POSTAL UNION

LP **1** U.P.U. Monument Berne   LP **2** "Letter Post"

(Des H. Thorn (5c., 40c., 2f.); E. Poncy (others). Eng K. Bickel. Recess PTT, Berne)

1957 (16 Sept)–**60**. *Type LP **1** and similar horiz design inscr* "UNION POSTALE UNIVERSELLE". P 11½.
LP1	LP **1**	5c. slate-purple	10	10
LP2	–	10c. green	10	10
LP3	–	20c. scarlet	1·30	1·80
LP4	–	20c. carmine (24.10.60)	15	15
LP5	–	30c. orange (24.10.60)	25	25
LP6	LP **1**	40c. blue	1·30	1·70
LP7	–	50c. blue (24.10.60)	35	35
LP8	–	60c. brown	40	50
LP9	LP **1**	2f. reddish purple	1·40	1·70
1/9	Set of 9		4·75	6·00

Design:—10c., 20c. (2), 30c., 60c. Pegasus (sculpture).

(Des B. Waltenspul. Photo Courvoisier)

1976 (16 Sept)–**89**. *Type LP **2** and similar horiz designs. Phosphorescent paper.* P 11½.
LP10	40c. dp reddish pur, greenish bl & clar	35	35
LP11	80c. multicoloured	60	60
LP12	90c. multicoloured	75	75
LP13	100c. multicoloured	75	75
LP14	120c. multicoloured (22.8.83)	1·00	1·00
LP15	140c. slate, royal blue & verm (7.3.89)	1·30	1·30
LP10/15	Set of 6	4·25	4·25

Designs:—80c. Parcel Post"; 90c. "Financial Services"; 100c. "Technical Co-operation"; 120c. Carrier pigeon, international reply coupon and postal money order; 140c. Express Mail Service. The 120 and 140c. are additionally inscribed "TIMBRE DE SERVICE".

LP **3** Computer, Mail Sacks and Globe

(Des B. Waltenspul. Litho PTT, Berne)

1995 (28 Nov). *Phosphorescent paper.* P 13½.
LP16	LP **3**	180c. multicoloured	1·60	1·60

LP **4** Hand reaching for Rainbow

404

SWITZERLAND INTERNATIONAL ORGANIZATIONS 1999

(Des J.-M. Folon. Litho PTT, Berne)

1999 (9 Mar). *125th Anniv of Universal Postal Union. Type LP* **4** *and similar horiz design. Multicoloured.* P 13½.
LP17	20c. Type LP **4**		20	20
	a. Block. Nos. 1416/17 plus 2 labels		85	
LP18	70c. Hand holding rainbow		65	65

Nos. LP17/18 were issued together in sheets containing two blocks, each consisting of the two values arranged in chessboard fashion with two labels, one showing the U.P.U. emblem and the other giving the anniversary dates.

H. UNITED NATIONS
NATIONS UNIES
OFFICE EUROPÉEN
(LU **1**)

1950 (1 Feb). *Various issues optd with Type LU* **1**.

(a) Nos. 511/21.
LU1	5c. orange	55	1·30
LU2	10c. yellow-green	70	1·10
LU3	15c. turquoise	1·20	1·50
LU4	20c. maroon (II)	1·60	2·30
LU5	25c. scarlet	2·50	3·50
LU6	30c. olive	2·50	3·50
LU7	35c. brown	5·25	7·25
LU8	40c. blue	3·25	2·75
LU9	50c. bluish grey	4·25	6·25
LU10	60c. blue-green	5·00	7·50
LU11	70c. violet	6·00	7·25

(b) Nos. 408/13 and 388B/390B.
LU12	80c. black/olive-grey	8·25	6·25
LU13	90c. scarlet/pink	8·25	6·25
LU14	1f. myrtle green/blue-green	8·25	6·25
LU15	1f.20 plum/olive-grey	8·25	6·25
LU16	1f.50 indigo/buff	8·75	14·00
LU17	2f. brown-lake/pink	8·75	10·50
LU18	3f. red-brown	75·00	60·00
LU19	5f. slate-blue	75·00	60·00
LU20	10f. green	£100	95·00
LU1/20	*Set of 20*	£325	£300

LU **2**   LU **3**   LU **4**

(Des H. Thoni. Photo Courvoisier)

1955 (24 Oct). *Tenth Anniv of U. N.* P 11½.
LU21	LU **2**	40c. blue and yellow	1·80	2·10

(Des H. Thoni. Eng A. Yersin (Type LU **3**), K. Bickel (Type LU **4**). Recess, PTT Berne)

1955 (24 Oct)–**59**. P 11½.
LU22	LU **3**	5c. slate-purple	10	10
LU23		10c. green	10	10
LU24	LU **4**	20c. vermilion	2·40	3·00
LU25		20c. carmine (24.10.59)	15	15
LU26		30c. orange (24.10.59)	25	20
LU27	LU **3**	40c. blue	2·20	2·30
LU28		50c. blue (24.10.59)	40	25
LU29	LU **4**	60c. brown	35	35
LU30		2f. purple	90	90
LU22/30	*Set of 9*		6·25	6·50

ANNÉE MONDIALE DU RÉFUGIÉ

1959   1960
(LU **5**)

LU **6** Palace of Nations, Geneva

1960 (7 Apr). *World Refugee Year Nos. LU25 and LU28 optd as Type LU* **5**.
LU31	LU **4**	20c. carmine	10	15
LU32	LU **3**	50c. blue (R.)	15	25

(Des H. Hartmann. Eng A. Yersin. Recess PTT, Berne)

1960 (24 Oct). *15th Anniv of U. N. Granite paper.* P 11½.
LU33	LU **6**	5f. greenish blue	2·30	3·00

LU **7**   LU **8** UNCSAT Emblem

(Des H. Them. Eng A. Yersin (10c., 50c.), K. Bickel jun (others). Recess PTT, Berne)

1962 (24 Oct). *Opening of U.N. Philatelic Museum. Geneva. Type LU* **7** *and similar design.* P 11½.
LU34	LU **7**	10c. green and red	10	10
LU35	–	30c. orange and blue	10	15
LU36	LU **7**	50c. blue and red	15	25
LU37	–	60c. brown and green	15	30
LU34/37	*Set of 4*		45	75

Designs: *Horiz*—30c., 60c. As Type LU **4** but inscr "ONU MUSÉE PHILATELIQUE".

(Des H. Them. Eng A. Yersin (50c.), .K. Bickel jun (2f.). Recess; emblem typo PTT, Berne)

1963 (4 Feb). *U. N. Scientific and Technological Conference, Geneva (UNCSAT). Type LU* **8** *and similar design.* P 11½.
LU38	50c. carmine and blue	25	30
LU39	2f. yellow-green and purple	60	1·10

Design: *Horiz*—2f. As Type LU **4** but with emblem.

Under the terms of a postal agreement between the Swiss Post Office and the United Nations the Swiss issues for the Palais des Nations at Geneva were withdrawn on 4 October 1969 and replaced by United Nations issues with face value in Swiss currency. These are listed in this volume under United Nations, Geneva Headquarters.

I. INTERNATIONAL TELECOMMUNICATION UNION

LT **1** Transmitting Aerial   LT **2** New Headquarters Building

405

SWITZERLAND INTERNATIONAL ORGANIZATIONS 1958

(Des D. Brun. Eng H. Heusser (Type LT **1**). Des H. Thoni. Eng A. Yersin (others). Recess PTT, Berne)

1958 (22 Sept)–**60**. *Type LT 1 and similar vert design inscr* "UNION INTERNATIONALE DES TELECOMMUNICA-TIONS". P 11½.

LT1	LT **1**	5c. slate-purple	10	10
LT2	–	10c. green	10	10
LT3	–	20c. scarlet	1·30	1·50
LT4	–	20c. carmine (24.10.60)	20	15
LT5	–	30c. orange (24.10.60)	30	25
LT6	LT **1**	40c. blue	1·50	1·70
LT7	–	50c. blue (24.10.60)	45	35
LT8	–	60c. brown	55	45
LT9	–	2f. purple	1·80	1·30
LT1/9	Set of 9		6·75	6·50

Design:—20c., (2), 30c., 60c., 2f. Receiving aerials.

(Des A. Cserno and J.-J. Chevalley. Photo Courvoisier)

1973 (30 Aug). *Inauguration of New I.T.U. Headquarters, Geneva.* P 11½.
LT10　LT **2**　80c. black and light blue　　65　　60

LT **3** Boeing 747 Jetliner and Ocean-liner

LT **4** Optical Fibre Cables

(Des A. Cserno and J.-J. Chevalley. Eng H. Heusser. Recess and photo PTT, Berne)

1976 (12 Feb). *World Telecommunications Network. Type LT 3 and similar horiz designs. Phosphorescent granite paper.* P 11½.
LT11	40c. deep ultramarine and orange-red	35	30
LT12	90c. violet, cobalt and lemon	75	65
LT13	1f. brown-red, blue-green and orange-yellow	80	80

Designs:—40c. "Sound waves"; 1f. Face and microphone in television screen.

(Des J.-J. Chevalley and P. Langlois. Litho PTT, Berne)

1988 (13 Sept). P 11½.
LT14　LT **4**　1f.40 . multicoloured　　1·20　1·30

LT **5** Emblem emitting Radio Signals

(Des J.-J. Chevalley. Litho PTT, Berne)

1994 (17 May). *One Hundred Years of Radio. Phosphorescent paper.* P 13½.
LT15　LT **5**　1f.80, multicoloured　　1·50　1·60

LT **6** "a b c" and X-ray of Bone Joint ("Teleeducation")

(Des A. Baldinger. Photo Courvoisier)

1999 (9 Mar). *Type LT 6 and similar horiz design. Multicoloured.* P 11½.
LT16	10c. Type LT **6**	10	10
LT17	100c. Arrow and x-ray of bone joint ("Telemedicine")	90	90

J. WORLD INTELLECTUAL PROPERTY ORGANIZATION

LV **1** WIPO Seal

(Des R. Hirter. Litho PTT, Berne)

1982 (27 May)–**85**. *Type LV 1 and similar horiz designs. Multicoloured.* P 11½.
LV1	40c. Type LV **1**	45	40
LV2	50c. Face and symbolic representation of intellect (10.9.85)	60	55
LV3	80c. WIPO building, Geneva	90	85
LV4	100c. Hand pressing buttons, retort and cogwheel (industrial property)	1·20	1·10
LV5	120c. Head, ballet dancer, cello and book (Copyright)	1·40	1·30
LV1/5	Set of 5	4·00	3·75

K. INTERNATIONAL OLYMPIC COMMITTEE

LW **1** Olympic Rings

(Des J. Folon. Photo)

2000 (15 Sept). *Olympic Games, Sydney. Self-adhesive booklet stamps. Die-cut.*
LW1	LW **1**	20c. multicoloured	20	20
LW2		70c. multicoloured	60	60

STAMP BOOKLETS

LWSB1　15.9.00 Olympic Games, Sydney Nos. LW1/2 (90c.)　　1·30

UNITED NATIONS 1969

United Nations

The following issues, many in the designs of the stamps for the New York Headquarters but with values in Swiss currency, can only be used on mail from the Palais des Nations, Geneva.

They differ from those listed after Switzerland by being issues of the United Nations Postal Administration, and not the Swiss P.T.T.

G 9 "Birds" in Flight

G 10 Emblem and New York Headquarters

G 12 U.N. Emblem

G 1 U.N. Headquarters, New York, and World Map

G 2 U.N. Flag

G 11 Flags

G 13 Globe and Weather Vane

G 3 Three Figures on Globe ("Races United")

G 4 Palms des Nations, Geneva

G 14 Starcke's Statue

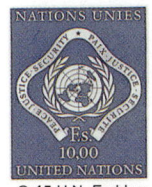

G 15 U.N. Emblem

G 5 Palais des Nations, Geneva

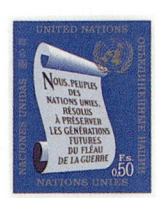

G 6 Opening Words of U.N. Charter

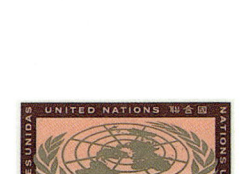

G 7 U.N. Emblem across Globe

G 8 "UN" and Emblem

(Des J. Vertel (5c.), G. Hannon (20c.), O. Mathesen (50, 60c.), L. Holdandwicz and M. Freudenreich (70c.), V. PierreNoel (80c.), H. Sanborn (90c.), Rashid-ud-Din (1f.), M. El Mekki (2f.), Adapted from statue (3f.), J. Doeve (10f.), O. Hamann (others) Litho and embossed West German State Pig Wks, Berlin (1f.). Recess State Bank Note Ptg Wks, Helsinki (10f.), Photo State Bank Note Ptg Wks, Helsinki (5, 70, 80, 90c., 2f.), Austrian State Pig Wks, Vienna (75c.) or Courvoisier (others))

1969 (4 Oct)–**72**. P 13 (5, 70, 90c.), 12½ (10c.), 11½ × 12 (75c., 10f.), 14 (80c, 1f.), 12 × 11½ (2f), 11½ (others).

G1	G 1	5c. multicoloured	10	10
		a. Yellow-green omitted		
G2	G 2	10c. multicoloured	10	10
G3	G 3	20c. multicoloured	20	10
G4	G 4	30c. multicoloured	25	15
G5	G 5	40c. multicoloured (5.1.72)	30	25
G6	G 6	50c. multicoloured	40	25
G7	G 7	60c. gold, orange-red and deep red brown (17.4.70)	40	25
G8	G 8	70c. red, gold and black (22.9.70)	50	35
G9	G 9	75c. multicoloured	50	45
G10	G 10	80c. multicoloured (22.9.70)	55	45
G11	G 11	90c. multicoloured (22.9.70)	65	50
G12	G 12	1f. deep blue-green & lt blue-grn	75	40
G13	G 13	2f. multicoloured (22.9.70)	1·50	1·20
G14	G 14	3f. multicoloured	2·40	2·10
G15	G 15	10f. deep ultramarine (17.4.70)	7·75	7·25
G1/15	Set of 15		15·00	13·00

407

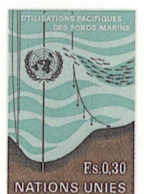

UNITED NATIONS 1971

G 16 U.N. Emblem on Sea-bed

G 17 "Refugees"

G 22 "Maia" (Picasso)

G 23 "X" over Atomic Explosion

(Des P. Rahikainen. Recess and photo State Bank Note Ptg Wks, Helsinki)

1971 (25 Jan). *Peaceful Uses of the Sea-bed.* P 13.
G16   G **16**   30c. multicoloured 35   35

(Des O. Hamann. Photo Courvoisier)

1971 (19 Nov). *United Nations International Schools.* P 11½.
G22   G **22**   1f.10 multicoloured 85   75

(Des A. Johnson. Photo Heraclio Fournier, Spain)

1972 (14 Feb). *Non-Proliferation of Nuclear Weapons.* P 13½.
G23   G **23**   40c. multicoloured 65   65

(Des K. Nygaard and M. Weber. Litho Enschedé)

1971 (12 Mar). *United Nations Work with Refugees.* P 13 × 12½.
G17   G **17**   50c. black, orange and carmine-red 55   55

G 18 Wheatsheaf on Globe

G 19 New U.P.U. Headquarters Building

G 24 "Proportions of Man" (Leonardo da Vinci)

G 25 Environmental Emblem

(Des G. Hamori. Recess and litho State Bank Note Ptg Wks, Helsinki)

1972 (7 Apr). *World Health Day.* P 13.
G24   G **24**   80c. multicoloured 75   75

(Des R. Perrot. Litho and embossed Enschedé)

1972 (5 June). *U.N. Environmental Conservation Conference, Stockholm.* P 12½ × 14.
G25   G **25**   40c. multicoloured 45   45
G26   G **26**   80c. multicoloured 70   70

(Des O. Mathiesen. Photo Heracho Fournier, Spain)

1971 (13 Apr). *World Food Programme.* P 14.
G18   G **18**   50c. multicoloured 55   55

(Des O. Mathiesen. Photo Courvoisier)

1971 (28 May). *Opening of New Universal Postal Union Headquarters Building, Berne.* P 11½.
G19   G **19**   75c. multicoloured 85   85

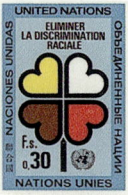

G 20 Four-leafed Clover

G 21 Linked Globes

G 26 Europe "Flower"

G 27 "World United" (part of Sert mural, Geneva)

(Des A. Medina. Litho Japanese Govt Ptg Wks, Tokyo)

1972 (11 Sept). *Economic Commission for Europe (E.C.E.).* P 13 × 13½.
G27   G **27**   1f.10 multicoloured . . . . . . 1·30   1·30

(Des O. Hamann. Photo Courvoisier)

1972 (17 Nov). *United Nations Art.* P 12½.
G28   G **28**   40c. multicoloured 45   45
G29   G **29**   80c. multicoloured 80   80

(Des D. Gonzague (30c.), O. Hamann (50c.). Photo Japanese Govt Ptg Wks, Tokyo)

1971 (21 Sept). *Racial Equality Year.* P 13½.
G20   G **20**   30c. multicoloured 40   35
G21   G **21**   50c. multicoloured 40   35

UNITED NATIONS 1973

G 28 Laurel and Broken Sword

G 29 Skull on Poppy

(Des K. Plowitz. Litho Ajans-Türk Matbaasi, Ankara)
1973 (9 Mar). *Disarmament Decade.* P. 13.
G30 G **30** 60c. multicoloured 50 50
G31   1f.10 multicoloured 85 85

(Des G. Hamori. Photo Heraclio Fournier, Spain)
1973 (13 Apr). *"No Drugs" Campaign.* P 14 × 13½.
G32 G **29** 60c. multicoloured 60 60

G 30 Emblems with Honeycomb

G 31 "Namibia"

(Des Courvoisier staff artists. Photo Heraclio Fournier, Spain)
1973 (25 May). *U.N. Volunteers Programme.* P 14.
G33 G **30** 80c. multicoloured 70 70

(Des G. Hamori. Photo Heraclio Fournier, Spain)
1973 (1 Oct). *"Namibia" (South West Africa).* P 14
G34 G **31** 60c. multicoloured 60 60

G 32 Human Rights Flame

G 33 Headquarters Building

(Des A. Guerra. Photo Japanese Govt Ptg Wks, Tokyo)
1973 (16 Nov). *25th Anniv of Declaration of Human Rights.* P 13 × 13½.
G35 G **32** 40c. multicoloured 30 30
G36   80c. multicoloured 70 70

(Des H. Bencsath. Photo Heraclio Fournier, Spain)
1974 (11 Jan). *Inauguration of New International Labour Organization Headquarters, Geneva.* P. 14.
G37 G **33** 60c. multicoloured 40 40
G38   80c. multicoloured 90 90

(Des A. Johnson. Photo Ashton-Potter, Canada)
1974 (22 Mar). *Centenary of Universal Postal Union.* P 12½.
G39 G **34** 30c. multicoloured 25 25
G40   60c. multicoloured 50 50

(Des adapted by O. Hamann. Photo Heraclio Fournier, Spain)
1974 (6 May). *Brazilian Peace Mural* P 14
G41 G **35** 60c. multicoloured 55 55
G42   1f. multicoloured 80 80

G 36 Young Children with Globe

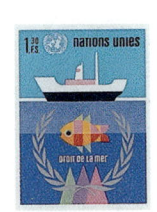

G 37 Ship and Fish

(Des H. Bencsath. Photo Heraclio Fournier, Spain)
1974 (18 Oct). *World Population Year.* P 14.
G43 G **36** 60c. multicoloured 70 70
G44   80c. multicoloured 75 75

(Des A. Kalderon. Photo Heraclio Fournier, Spain)
1974 (22 Nov). *U.N. Conferences on "Law of the Sea".* P. 14.
G45 G **37** 1f.30 multicoloured . . . . . . 1·20 1·20

G 38 Satellite, Globe and Symbols

G 39 "Sex Equality"

(Des H. Bencsath. Litho State Bank Note Ptg Wks, Helsinki)
1975 (14 Mar). *Peaceful Uses of Outer Space.* P. 13.
G46 G **38** 60c. multicoloured 50 50
G47   90c. multicoloured 90 90

(Des E. Kurti and A. Kalderon. Litho Questa)
1975 (9 May). *International Women's Year.* P 14.
G48 G **39** 60c. multicoloured 55 55
G49   90c. multicoloured 80 80

G 34 Globe within Posthorn

G 35 "Children's Choir" (Candido Portinari)

G 40 "The Hope of Mankind"

G 41 Cupped Hand

409

UNITED NATIONS 1975

(Des A. Kalderon. Litho Ashton-Potter, Toronto)

1975 (26 June). *30th Anniv of United Nations Organization.* P 13 × 13½.
G50 G 40 60c. multicoloured 45 45
G51 90c. multicoloured 70 70
MSG52 92 × 70mm. Nos. G50/1, Imperf ... 1·10 1·10

(Des H. Bencsath. Photo Heraclio Fournier)

1975 (22 Sept). *"Namibia–U.N. Direct Responsibility".* P 13½.
G53 G 41 50c. multicoloured 45 45
G54 1f.30 multicoloured 85 85

G 42 Wild Rose and Barbed Wire
G 43 Linked Ribbands 

(Des E. Olvio. Recess State Bank Note Ptg Wks, Helsinki)

1975 (21 Nov). *U.N. Peace-keeping Operations* P 12½.
G55 G 42 60c. turquoise-blue 80 80
G56 70c. reddish violet 65 65

(Des G. Hannon. Photo Heraclio Fournier)

1976 (12 Mar). *World Federation of U.N. Associations.* P 14.
G57 G 43 90c. multicoloured 75 75

G 44 Globe and Crate
G 45 Houses bordering Globe 

(Des H. Bencsath. Photo Courvoisier)

1976 (23 Apr). *U.N. Trade and Development Conference.* P 11½.
G58 G 44 1f.10 multicoloured 95 95

(Des E. Weisshoff. Photo Heraclio Fournier)

1976 (28 May). *U.N. Human Settlements Conference.* P 14.
G59 G 45 40c. multicoloured 35 35
G60 1f.50 multicoloured .... 1·20 1·20

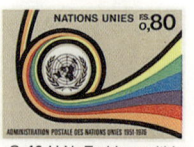

G 46 U.N. Emblem within Posthorn
G 47 Stylised Ear of Wheat 

(Des H. Viola. Photo Courvoisier)

1976 (8 Oct). *25th Anniv of U.N. Postal Administration* P 11½.
G61 G 46 80c. multicoloured .... 2·25 2·00
G62 1f.10 multicoloured .... 2·25 2·10

(Des E. Weishoff. Litho Questa)

1976 (19 Nov). *World Food Council Publicity.* P 14½.
G63 G 47 70c. multicoloured 55 55

G 48 W. I. P. O. Headquarters
G 49 Rain Drop and Globe 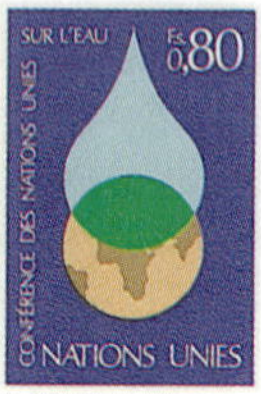

(Des E. Weishoff. Photo Heraclio Fournier)

1977 (11 Mar). *World Intellectual Property Organisation Publicity.* P 13½ × 14.
G64 G 48 80c. multicoloured 70 70

(Des E. Tomei. Photo Japanese Govt Ptg Wks, Tokyo)

1977 (22 Apr). *U.N. Water Conference* P 13.
G65 G 49 80c. multicoloured 70 70
G66 1f.10 multicoloured 90 90

G 50 Protective Hands
G 51 "Intertwining of Races" 

(Des G. Hamori. Photo Heraclio Fournier)

1977 (27 May). *Security Council Commemoration.* P 14.
G67 G 50 80c. multicoloured 70 70
G68 1f.10 multicoloured 90 90

(Des M. A. Munnawar. Litho State Bank Note Ptg Wks, Helsinki)

1977 (19 Sept). *"Combat Racism".* P 13½ × 13.
G69 G 51 40c. multicoloured 30 30
G70 1f.10 multicoloured 90 90

G 52 Atoms and Laurel Leaf
G 53 Tree and Birds

(Des W. Janowski and M. Freudenreich. Photo Heraclio Fournier)

1977 (18 Nov). *"Peaceful Uses for Atomic Energy".* P 14.
G71 G 52 80c. multicoloured 70 70
G72 1f.10 multicoloured 90 90

UNITED NATIONS 1977

(Des M. Hioki. Litho Questa)
1978 (29 Jan). P 14½.
G73   G **53**   35c. multicoloured 30   30

G **54** Smallpox Bacilli and Globe
G **55** Broken Manacle

(Des E. Weishoff. Photo Courvoisier)
1978 (31 Mar). *Global Eradication of Smallpox.* P 11½.
G74   G **54**   80c. multicoloured 70   70
G75   1f.10 multicoloured 90   90

(Des C. Tomei. Photo State Ptg Wks. Vienna)
1978 (5 May). *"Namibia. Liberation, Justice, Co-operation".* P 12.
G76   G **55**   80c. multicoloured 70   70

G **56** Aircraft Flight Paths
G **57** Globe, Flags and General Assembly Interior

(Des T. R. Savrda. Photo Heraclio Fournier)
1978 (12 June). *International Civil Aviation Organization– Safety in the Air.* P 14.
G77   G **56**   70c. multicoloured 55   55
G78   80c. multicoloured 65   65

(Des H. Bencsath. Photo Mitsubishi Corporation, Japan)
1978 (15 Sept). *General Assembly.* P 13.
G79   G **57**   70c. multicoloured 55   55
G80   1f.10 multicoloured 90   90

G **58** Hemispheres within Cogwheels
G **59** "Disaster"

(Des S. Keter and D. Pesach. Photo Heraclio Fournier)
1978 (17 Nov). *Technical Co-operation among Developing Countries.* P 14.
G81   G **58**   80c. multicoloured 80   80

(Des M. Klutmann. Photo Heraclio Fournier)
1979 (9 Mar). *U.N. Disaster Relief Co-ordinator.* P 14.
G82   G **59**   80c. multicoloured 65   65
G83   1f.50 multicoloured . . . . 1·40   1·40

G **60** Children and Rainbow
G **61** Olive Branch and Map of Namibia

(Des A. Glaser. Photo Heraclio Fournier)
1979 (4 May). *International Year of the Child.* P 14.
G84   G **60**   80c. multicoloured 75   75
G85   1f.10 multicoloured . . . . 1·10   1·10

(Des E. Weishoff. Litho Ashton-Potter)
1979 (5 Oct). *"For a Free and Independent Namibia".* P 13.
G86   G **61**   1f.10 multicoloured . . . . 1·00   1·00

G **62** International Court of Justice and Scales
G **63** Key symbolizing Unity of Action

(Des K. Maeno. Litho State Bank Note Ptg Wks, Helsinki)
1979 (9 Nov). *International Court of Justice.* P 13.
G87   G **62**   80c. multicoloured 70   70
G88   1f.10 multicoloured 95   95

(Des J.-P. Meuer. Litho Questa)
1980 (11 Jan). *New International Economic Order.* P 14½.
G89   G **63**   80c. multicoloured 70   70

G **64** Emblem
G **65** Helmet

(Des M. A. Munnawar. Litho Questa)
1980 (7 Mar). *U.N. Decade for Women.* P 14½.
G90   G **64**   40c. multicoloured 30   30
G91   70c. multicoloured 50   50

(Des B. Wiese. Litho Enschedé)
1980 (16 May). *Peace-keeping Operations.* P 14 × 12½.
G92   G **65**   1f.10 new blue and blue-green . . 95   95

411

UNITED NATIONS　　　　　　　　　　　　　　　　　　　　　　　　　　1980

G **66** Dove and "35" 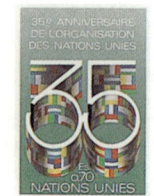　　G **67** "35" composed of Flags　　G **73** "Sebastocrator Kaloyan and hisWife Desislava" (13th-cent Bulgarian fresco)　　G **74** Sun and Sea

(Des G. Sagi (40c.), C. Mutver (70c.), O. Hamann (**MS**). Litho Ashton-Potter, Toronto)

1980 (26 June). *35th Anniv of United Nations.* P 13.
G93	G **66**	40c. grey-black and turquoise-blue	35	35
G94	G **67**	70c. multicoloured	60	60
MSG95		92 × 73 mm. Nos. 693/4 Imperf	90	90

(Des O. Hamann. Photo Courvoisier)

1981 (15 Apr). *Art.* P 11½.
G101	G **73**	80c. multicoloured	70	70

(Des U. Dreyer. Litho State Bank Note Ptg Wks, Helsinki)

1981 (29 May). *New and Renewable Sources of Energy.* P.13.
G102	G **74**	1f.10 multicoloured	95	95

G **68** Various Emblems forming Bunch of Flowers 　　G **69** Figures ascending Graph　　G **75** Grafted Plant　　G **76** Emblems of Science, Agriculture and Industry

(Des D. Kowall (40c.), A. Medina (70c.). Litho Ashton-Potter, Toronto)

1980 (21 Nov). *Economic and Social Council.* P 13.
G96	G **68**	40c. multicoloured	35	35
G97	G **69**	70c. blue, dull vermilion and black	60	60

(Des G. Nussgen (40c.). B. Mirbach (70c.). Litho Walsall Security Printers)

1981 (13 Nov). *Tenth Anniv of U.N. Volunteers Programme.* P 13½ × 13.
G103	G **75**	40c. multicoloured	35	35
G104	G **76**	70c. multicoloured	60	60

G **70** Text and U.N. Emblem

(Des D. Dewhurst. Photo Courvoisier)

1981 (30 Jan). *Inalienable Rights of the Palestinian People.* P 11½.
G98	G **70**	80c. multicoloured	70	70

G **77** "Anti-apartheid"　　G **78** Flags

(Des T. Savrda (30c.), D. Kowall (1f.). Photo Courvoisier)

1982 (22 Jan). P 11½.
G105	G **77**	30c. multicoloured	30	30
G106	G **78**	1f. multicoloured	85	85

G **71** Disabled Person 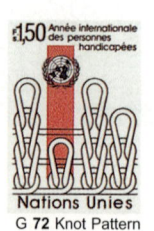　　G **72** Knot Pattern　　G **79** Leaves　　G **80** Hand holding Seedling

(Des G. P. van der Hyde (40c.), S. van Heeswyck (1f.50). Photo Heraclio Fournier)

1981 (6 Mar). *International Year of Disabled Persons.* P 14.
G99	G **71**	40c. black and greenish blue	40	40
G100	G **72**	1f.50 black and bright scarlet	1·30	1·30

412

UNITED NATIONS 1982

(Des S. Brunner (40c.), P. Hartert (1f.20). Litho Enschedé)
1982 (19 Mar). *Human Environment.* P 13½ × 13.
G107 G **79** 40c. multicoloured 35 35
G108 G **80** 1f.20 multicoloured . . . . 1·10 1·10

G **81** Olive Branch and U.N. Emblem
G **82** Satellite and Emblems 

(Des W. C. Nerwinski (80c.), G. Hamori (1f.). Litho Enschedé)
1982 (11 June). *Second United Nations Conference on Exploration and Peaceful Uses of Outer Space.* P 13½.
G109 G **81** 80c. brt violet, rose-pink & lt green 70 70
G110 G **82** 1f. multicoloured 80 80

G **83** Bird
G **84** Snake (reptiles) 

(Des G. Hamori. Photo Heraclio Fournier)
1982 (19 Nov). *Conservation and Protection of Nature.* P 14.
G111 G **83** 40c. multicoloured 35 35
G112 G **84** 1f.50 multicoloured . . . . 1·30 1·30

G **85** Cable Network

(Des L. Berengo. Litho Walsall Security Printers Ltd)
1983 (28 Jan). *World Communications Year.* P 13½ × 13.
G113 G **85** 1f.20 multicoloured . . . . 1·10 1·10

G **86** Ship and Buoy
G **87** Radar Screen within Lifebelt 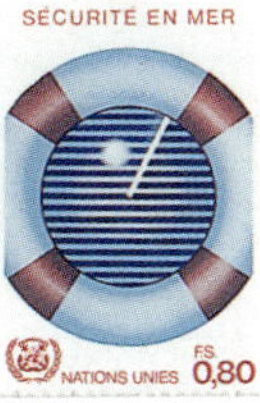

(Des J. M. Lenfant (40c.), V. Wurnitsch (80c.). Litho Questa)
1983 (18 Mar). *Safety at Sea: International Maritime Organization.* P 14½.
G114 G **86** 40c. multicoloured 35 35
G115 G **87** 80c. multicoloured 80 80

G **88** Giving Food

(Des M. Kwiatkowski. Recess Govt Ptg Wks, Tokyo)
1983 (22 Apr). *World Food Programme.* P 13½.
G116 G **88** 1f.50 blue . . . . 1·40 1·40

G **89** Coins and Cogwheels
G **90** Exports 

(Des D. Braklow (80c.), W. Brykczynski (1f.10). Litho Carl Ueberreuter, Vienna)
1983 (6 June). *Trade and Development.* P 14.
G117 G **89** 80c. multicoloured 75 75
G118 G **90** 1f.10 multicoloured . . . . 1·00 1·00

G **91** "Homo Humus Humanitas"
G **92** "Droit de Creer" 

(Des F. Hundertwasser. Recess and photo State Ptg Wks, Vienna)
1983 (9 Dec). *35th Anniv of Universal Declaration of Human Rights.* P 14.
G119 G **91** 40c. multicoloured 50 50
G120 G **92** 1f.20 multicoloured . . . . 1·20 1·20

G **93** World Housing

(Des Marina Langer-Rosa and H. Langer. Litho State Ptg Wks, Berlin)
1984 (3 Feb). *International Conference on Population, Mexico City.* P 14.
G121 G **93** 1f.20 multicoloured . . . . 1·10 1·10

413

UNITED NATIONS 1984

G 94 Fish in net

G 95 Planting Saplings

(Des A. Vanooijen. Litho Walsall Security Printers Ltd)
1984 (15 Mar). *World Food Day.* P 14½.
G122   G 94   50c. multicoloured   65   65
G123   G 95   80c. multicoloured   75   75

G 96 Fort St. Angelo, Malta

G 97 Los Glaciares, Argentina

(Des R. J. Callan and T. Lee. Litho Harrison)
1984 (18 Apr). *World Heritage—U.N. Educational, Scientific and Cultural Organization.* P 14½.
G124   G 96   50c. multicoloured   55   55
G125   G 97   70c. multicoloured   65   65
No. G124 is wrongly described as Valetta.

G 98 Man and Woman

G 99 Head of Woman

(Des H. Erni. Photo Courvoisier)
1984 (29 May). *Future for Refugees.* P 11½.
G126   G 98   35c. black and yellow-olive . . .   35   35
G127   G 99   1f.50 black and reddish
              brown . . . .   1·40   1·40

G 100 Heads

(Des E. Weishoff. Litho J. W.)
1984 (15 Nov). *International Youth Year.* P 13½.
G128   G 100   1f.20 multicoloured . . . .   1·20   1·20

G 101 Turin Centre Emblem

G 102 U Thant Pavilion

(Des R. J. Callari and T. Lee. Eng M. Iwakuni and H. Ozaki (80c.), H. Sasaki and K. Uematsu (1f.20). Recess Govt Ptg Wks, Tokyo)
1985 (1 Feb). *20th Anniv of Turin Centre of International Labour Organization.* P 13½.
G129   G 101   80c. brown-red   75   75
G130   G 102   1f.20 deep blue-green . . . .   1·10   1·10

G 103 Ploughing and Group of People

(Des H. Geluda and M. Pereg. Photo Courvoisier)
1985 (15 Mar). *Tenth Anniv of United Nations University, Tokyo Granite paper.* P 11½.
G131   G 103   50c. multicoloured   65   65
G132   80c. multicoloured   80   80

G 104 Postman

G 105 Doves

(Des A. Glaser (20c.), K. Sliwka (1f.20). Litho Carl Ueberreuter, Vienna)
1985 (10 May). P 14.
G133   G 104   20c. multicoloured   20   20
G134   G 105   1f.20 new blue and black . . .   95   95

G 106 "Snow Scene" (Andrew Wyeth)

G 107 "Harvest Scene" (Andrew Wyeth)

414

UNITED NATIONS 1985

(Photo Courvoisier)
1985 (26 June). *40th Anniv of United Nations Organization. Granite paper.* P 11½.
G135	G 106	50c. multicoloured	50	50
G136	G 107	70c. multicoloured	65	65
MSG137	76 × 81 mm. Nos. 6135/6 *Imperf*		1·80	1·80

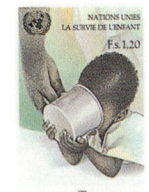

G 108 Children
G 109 Child Drinking

(Des M. Harris (50c.). A. Vanooijen (1f.20). Recess and photo Govt Ptg Wks, Tokyo)
1985 (22 Nov). *U.N.I.C.E.F. Child Survival Campaign.* P 13½.
G138	G 108	50c. multicoloured	40	40
G139	G 109	1f.20 multicoloured	1·30	1·30

G 110 Children raising Empty Bowls to Weeping Mother
G 111 Herring Gulls

(Des Alemayehou Gabremedhiu. Photo Courvoisier)
1986 (31 Jan). *Africa in Crisis. Granite paper.* P 11½.
G140	G 110	1f.40 multicoloured	1·50	1·50

(Des R. Alcantara Rodriguez. Litho Questa)
1986 (14 Mar). P 15 × 14½.
G141	G 111	5c. multicoloured	15	15

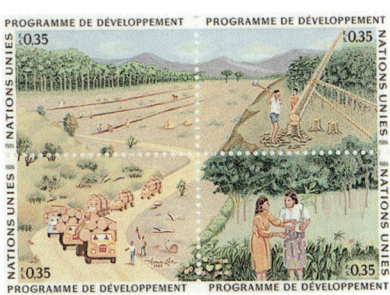

G 112/15 Timber Production

(Des T. Lee. Photo Govt Ptg Wks, Tokyo)
1986 (14 Mar). *Development Programme.* P 13½.
G142	G 112	35c. multicoloured	2·50	2·30
		a. Block of 4 Nos. 6142/5	10·50	
G143	G 113	35c. multicoloured	2·50	2·30
G144	G 114	35c. multicoloured	2·50	2·30
G145	G 115	35c. multicoloured	2·50	2·30
G142/145	*Set of* 4		9·00	8·25

Nos. G142/5 were issued together in *se-tenant* blocks of four within the sheet, each block forming the composite design illustrated.

G 116 Magnifying Glass and Stamp
G 117 United Nations Stamps

(Des I. Axelsson. Eng C. Slania. Recess Swedish Stamp Ptg Office)
1986 (22 May). *Philately.* P 12½.
G146	G 116	50c. slate-green & scarlet-verm	55	55
G147	G 117	80c. black and orange	95	95

G 118 Ribbon forming Dove
G 119 "Peace" and Olive Branch

(Des R. Ferrini (45c.), S. Kanidinc (1f.40). Photo and embossed Govt Ptg Wks, Tokyo)
1986 (20 June). *International Peace Year.* P 13½.
G148	G 118	45c. multicoloured	55	55
G149	G 119	1f.40 multicoloured	1·50	1·60

G 120 (½ size illustration)

(Litho Enschedé)
1986 (14 Nov). *40th Anniv of World Federation of United Nations Associations. Sheet* 120 × 65*mm. Multicoloured.* P 13 × 13½.
MSG150 G 120 35c. Birds (Benigno Gomez); 45c. Circle and prisms (Alexander Calder); 50c. "Eye" (Joan Miró); 70c. Dove and musical instruments (Ole Hamann) . . . . . 6·25 7·50

G 121 Trygve Lie (after Harald Dal)

(Eng W. Seidel. Recess and photo State Ptg Wks, Vienna)
1987 (30 Jan). *Ninth Death Anniv of Trygve Lie (first U. N. Secretary-General).* P 13½ × 14
G151	G 121	1f.40 multicoloured	1·50	1·50

UNITED NATIONS 1987

G **122** Abstract

G **123** Armillary Sphere, Geneva Centre

(Des G. Mathieu: photo Courvoisier (90c.). Recess and photo Govt Ptg Wks, Tokyo (1f.40).)

1987 (30 Jan). P 11½ × 12 (90c.) or 13½ (1f.40).
G152 G **122** 90c. multicoloured . . . 90 90
G153 G **123** 1f.40 multicoloured . . . 1·40 1·40

G **124** Mixing Cement and Carrying Bricks

G **125** Fitting Windows and Painting

(Des W. Brykczynski. Litho Enschedé.)

1987 (13 Mar). *International Year of Shelter for the Homeless.* P 13½ × 12.
G154 G **124** 50c. deep olive and black . . . 60 60
G155 G **125** 90c. blue, greenish blue and black . . . 1·10 1·10

G **126** Mother and Baby

G **127** Workers in Paddy-field

(Des Susan Borgen, N. Werret and C. M. Dudash. Litho Questa.)

1987 (12 June). *Anti-drugs Campaign.* P 14½ × 15.
G156 G **126** 80c. multicoloured . . . 1·10 1·10
G157 G **127** 1f.20 multicoloured . . . 1·60 1·60

G **128** People in Boat and Palms des Nations, Geneva

G **129** Dancers

(Des Elisabeth von Janota-Bzowski (35c.), F. H. Oerter (50c.). Litho Questa)

1987 (23 Oct). *United Nations Day.* P 14½ × 15.
G158 G **128** 35c. multicoloured . . . 45 45
G159 G **129** 50c. multicoloured . . . 75 75

G **130** Whooping Cough

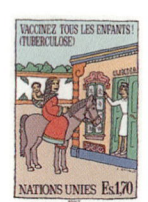

G **131** Tuberculosis

(Des S. Chwast. Litho Questa.)

1987 (20 Nov). *"Immunize Every Child".* P 15 × 14½.
G160 G **130** 90c. multicoloured . . . 1·00 1·00
G161 G **131** 1f.70 multicoloured . . . 1·90 1·90

G **132** Goatherd

G **133** Women and Baskets of Fruit

(Des S. Arolas. Litho CPE Australia Ltd, Melbourne)

1988 (29 Jan). *International Fund for Agricultural Development "For a World Without Hunger" Campaign.* P 13½.
G162 G **132** 35c. multicoloured . . . 55 55
G163 G **133** 1f.40 multicoloured . . . 1·50 1·50

G **134** People

G **135/136** Pine Forest (½-size illustration)

UNITED NATIONS 1988

(Des B. Wiinblad. Photo Heraclio Fournier)
1988 (29 Jan). P. 14.
G164 G **134** 50c. multicoloured 50 50

(Des B. Bralds. Litho Questa)
1988 (18 Mar). *"Survival of the Forests"*. P. 14 × 15.
G165 G **135** 50c. multicoloured . . . . . 4·75 4·50
         a. Vert pair Nos. G165/6 . . 10·00 10·00
G166 G **136** 1f.10 multicoloured . . . . . 4·75 4·50
Nos. G165/6 were issued together in sheetlets of 12 stamps comprising six vertical *se-tenant* pairs, each pair forming the composite design illustrated.

G **137** Instruction in Fruit Growing
G **138** Teaching Animal Husbandry

(Des C. Magadini. Litho Enschedé)
1988 (6 May). *International Volunteer Day*. P. 13 × 14 (80c.) or 14 × 13 (90c.).
G167 G **137** 80c. multicoloured 80 80
G168 G **138** 90c. multicoloured 95 95

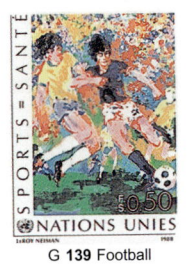

G **139** Football
G **140** Swimming

(Des L. Neiman. Litho Govt Ptg Wks, Tokyo)
1988 (17 June). *"Health in Sports"*. P. 13½ × 13 (50c.) or 13 × 13½ (1f.40).
G169 **50c.** multicoloured 55 55
G170 1f.40 multicoloured . . . . . 1·60 1·60

G **141** Flame

(Des R. Callari. Photo Courvoisier)
1988 (9 Dec). *40th Anniv of Declaration of Human Rights. Granite paper.* P. 11½.
G171 G **141** 90c. multicoloured . . . . . 1·00 1·00
MSG172 120 × 79mm. G **141** 2f. multicoloured . . . . . 1·60 1·80

G **142** Communications
G **143** Industry
G **144** "Blue Helmet" Soldier

(Des S. Lumboy. Litho Enschedé)
1989 (27 Jan). *World Rank*. P. 13 × 14.
G173 80c. multicoloured 85 85
G174 1f.40 multicoloured . . . . . 1·50 1·50

(Des T. Bland. Litho CPE Australia Ltd. Melbourne)
1989 (17 Mar). *Award of Nobel Peace Prize to United Nations Peace-keeping Forces.* P. 14 × 13½.
G175 90c. multicoloured . . . . . 1·10 1·10

G **145** Cold Arctic Air over Europe
G **146** Surface Temperatures of Kattegat

(Des R. Callari and R. Stein. Litho Enschedé)
1989 (21 Apr). *25th Anniv of World Weather Watch*. P. 13 × 14.
G176 G **145** 90c. multicoloured . . . . . 1·00 1·00
G177 G **146** 1f.10 multicoloured . . . . . 1·30 1·30

G **147** Tree and Birds
G **148** Woman and Flower

(Des A. Lehmden (50c.) Des A. Brauer, eng W. Seidel (2f.) Photo (50c.) or recess and photo (2f.) State Ptg Wks, Vienna)
1989 (23 Aug). *Tenth Anniv of United Nations Vienna International Centre.* P. 14.
G178 G **147** 50c. multicoloured 75 75
G179 G **148** 2f. multicoloured . . . . . 2·10 2·10

417

UNITED NATIONS   1989

G **149** "Young Mother sewing" (Mary Cassatt) (Article 3)
G **150** "Runaway Slave" (Albert Mangones) (Article 4)  
G **155** Frangipani (Plumena rubra)
G **156** Cinchona officinalis

(Des R. Callari, R. Stein and A. Gaines. Litho Enschedé)

1989 (17 Nov). *Universal Declaration of Human Rights (1st series)*. P 13½.
G180 G **149**   35f. multicoloured   80   80
G181 G **150**   80f. multicoloured   1·80 1·80

Nos. G180/1 were each issued with *se-tenant* label giving the text of the Article in English, French or German, in sheets of 12 stamps and 12 labels.
See also Nos. G193/4, G209/10, G224/5 and G234/5.

(Photo Courvoisier)

1990 (4 May). *Medicinal Plants. Granite paper.* P 11½.
G186 G **155**   90c. multicoloured   1·00 1·00
G187 G **156**   1f.40 multicoloured   1·60 1·60

G **151** Port Activities
G **152** Palais des Nations 

(Des R. Bernstein. Litho Questa)

1990 (2 Feb). *International Trade Centre*. P 14½ × 15.
G182 G **151**   1f.50 multicoloured   1·80 1·80

G **157** Projects forming "45"

G **158** Dove and "45"

(Des G. Breniaux and Elizabeth White. Photo Heraclio Fournier)

1990 (2 Feb). P 14.
G183 G **182**   5f. multicoloured   5·00 5·00

(Des Ruth Schmidthammer (90c.), M. Mertens (1f.10), R. Stein (**MS**.) Litho Enschedé)

1990 (26 June). *45th Anniv of United Nations Organization.* P 14½ × 13.
G188 G **157**   90c. multicoloured   1·10 1·10
G189 G **158**   1f.10 multicoloured   1·50 1·50
MSG190 100 × 73 mm. Nos. G188/9   3·25 3·25

G **153** "AIDS"

G **154** "Man" (Leonardo da Vinci)

G **159** Men making Deal over Painting 
G **160** Man spilling Waste from Cart

(Des J. Tofil (50c.), Lee Keun Moon (80c.). Litho Enschedé)

1990 (16 Mar). *Anti-AIDS Campaign.* P 13½ × 12½.
G184 G **153**   50c. multicoloured   65   65
G185 G **154**   80c. multicoloured   1·10 1·10

(Des J. Ryzec. Litho Heraclio Fournier)

1990 (13 Sept). *Crime Prevention.* P 14.
G191 G **159**   50c. multicoloured   65   65
G192 G **160**   2f. multicoloured   2·50 2·50

418

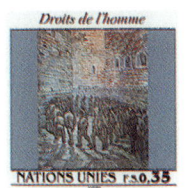

UNITED NATIONS   1990

G **161** "Prison Courtyard" (Vincent van Gogh) (Article 9)
G **162** "Katho's Son Redeems the Evil Doer from Execution" (Albrecht Dürer) (Article 10) 

(Des R. Callari, R. Stein and A. Gaines. Litho Enschedé)
1990 (16 Nov). *Universal Declaration of Human Rights (2nd serves)*. P 13½.
G193 G **161** 35c. multicoloured 1·20 1·20
G194 G **162** 90c. black and pale flesh 3·00 3·00
   Nos. G193 and G194 were each issued with *se-tenant* label giving the text of the Article in English, French or German, in sheets of 12 stamps and 12 labels.

G **169** Papers and Ballot Box
G **170** U.N. Emblem

(Des R. Mawilmada (80c.). M. Goujou (1f.50). Litho Questa)
1991 (10 May). P 15 × 14½.
G201 G **169** 80c. multicoloured 90 90
G202 G **170** 1f.50 multicoloured 1·70 1·70

G **163/166** Lake

(Des C. Ochagavia. Litho Heraclio Fournier)
1991 (15 Mar). *Economic Commission for Europe. "For a Better Environment"*. P 14.
G195 G **163** 90c. multicoloured 2·00 2·00
           a. Block of 4 Nos. 6195/8 8·50
G196 G **164** 90c. multicoloured 2·00 2·00
G197 G **165** 90c. multicoloured 2·00 2·00
G198 G **166** 90c. multicoloured 2·00 2·00
G195/198 *Set of* 4 7·25 7·25
   Nos. G195/8 were issued together in *se-tenant* blocks of four within the sheet, each block forming the composite design illustrated.

G **171** Baby in Open Hands (Ryuta Nakalima)
G **172** Children playing amongst Flowers (David Popper) 

(Litho Questa)
1991 (14 June). *30th Anniv (1989) of U.N. Declaration on the Rights of the Child and 1990 World Summit on Children. New York Children's Drawings*. P 14½.
G203 G **171** 80c. multicoloured 1·00 1·00
G204 G **172** 1f.10 multicoloured 1·20 1·20

G **173** Bubble of Toxin, City and Drums

G **174** Hand pushing back Gas Mask

G **167** Mountains
G **168** Baobab

(Des R. Callari and R. Stein. Litho Heraclio Fournier)
1991 (10 May). *First Anniv of Namibian independence*. P 14.
G199 G **167** 70c. multicoloured 85 75
G200 G **168** 90c. multicoloured 1·00 95

(Des O. Asboth (80c.), M. Granger (1f.40). Litho Heraclio Fournier)
1991 (11 Sept). *Banning of Chemical Weapons*. P 13½ × 14.
G205 G **173** 80c. multicoloured 95 95
G206 G **174** 1f.40 multicoloured 1·50 1·50

UNITED NATIONS   1991

G 175 U.N. (New York) 1951 15c. Stamp
G 176 U.N. (New York) 1951 50c. Stamp 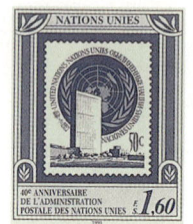

(Des R. Callari. Litho Questa)

1991 (24 Oct). *40th Anniv of United Nations Postal Administration.* P $14\frac{1}{2} \times 15$.
G207	G 175	50c. blue and deep lilac/cream	60	60
G208	G 176	1f.60 indigo/cream	1·90	1·90

G 181 U.N. Headquarters, New York
G 182/183 Sea Life ($\frac{1}{2}$-size illustration) 

(Des N. Martin. Litho Questa)

1992 (24 Jan). P $15 \times 14\frac{1}{2}$.
G213	G 181	3f. multicoloured	3·00	3·00

(Des B. Bralds. Litho Questa)

1992 (13 Mar). *"Clean Oceans".* P 14×15.
G214	G 182	80c. multicoloured	1·40	1·40
		a. Vert pair. Nos. G214/15	3·00	3·00
G215	G 183	80c. multicoloured	1·40	1·40

Nos. G214/15 were issued together in sheetlets of 12 stamps comprising six vertical *se-tenant* pairs, each pair forming the composite design illustrated.

G 177 "Early Morning in Ro, 1925" (Paul Klee) (Article 15)
G 178 "The Marriage of Arnolfini" (Jan van Eyck) (Article 16)

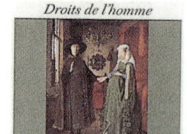

(Des R. Callari, R. Stein and A. Gaines. Litho Enschedé)

1991 (20 Nov). *Universal Declaration of Human Rights (3rd series).* P $13\frac{1}{2}$.
G209	G 177	50c. multicoloured	1·70	1·70
G210	G 178	90c. multicoloured	3·25	3·25

Nos. G209/10 were each issued with *se-tenant* label giving the text of the Article in English, French or German, in sheets of 12 stamps and 12 labels.

G 184/187 Planet Earth

(Des P. Max. Photo Courvoisier)

1992 (22 May). *Second United Nations Conference on Environment and Development, Rio de Janeiro. Granite paper.* P $11\frac{1}{2}$.
G216	G 184	75c. multicoloured	1·10	1·10
		a. Block of 4 Nos. G216/19	4·50	
G217	G 185	75c. multicoloured	1·10	1·10
G218	G 186	75c. multicoloured	1·10	1·10
G219	G 187	75c. multicoloured	1·10	1·10
G216/219		Set of 4	4·00	4·00

Nos. G216/19 were issued together in *se-tenant* blocks of four within the sheet, each block forming the cornposite design illustrated.

G 179 Sagarmatha National Park, Nepal
G 180 Stonehenge, United Kingdom

(Des R. Stein. Litho Cartor)

1992 (24 Jan). *20th Anniv of U.N.E.S.C.O. World Heritage Convention.* P 13.
G211	G 179	50c. multicoloured	60	60
G212	G 180	1f.10 multicoloured	1·70	1·70

G 188/189 "Mission Planet Earth"

UNITED NATIONS 1992

(Des A. Hejja. Photo Courvoisier)

1992 (4 Sept). *International Space Year. Granite paper. Rouletted.*
G220	G **188**	1f.10 multicoloured	1·60	1·60
		a. Horiz pair Nos. G220/1	3·25	
G221	G **189**	1f.10 multicoloured	1·60	1·60

Nos G220/1 were issued together in horizontal *se-tenant* pairs within the sheet, each pair forming the composite design illustrated.

G **190** Women in Science and Technology

G **191** Graduate using V.D.U.

(Des S. Mandel. Litho Unicover Corp, Cheyenne, U.S.A.)

1992 (2 Oct). *Commission on Science and Technology for Development.* P 13½ × 14.
G222	G **190**	90c. multicoloured	1·10	1·10
G223	G **191**	1f.60 multicoloured	1·90	1·90

G **192** "The Oath of the Tennis Court" (Jacques Louis David) (Article 21)

G **193** "Rocking Chair I" (Henry Moore) (Article 22)

(Des R. Stein and A. Gaines. Litho Enschedé)

1992 (20 Nov). *Universal Declaration of Human Rights (4th series).* P 13½.
G224	G **192**	50c. multicoloured	1·70	1·70
G225	G **193**	90c. multicoloured	3·25	3·25

Nos. G224/5 were each issued with *se-tenant* label giving the text of the Article in English, French or German, in sheets of 12 stamps and 12 labels.

G **194** Voluntary Work

G **195** Security of Employment

(Des C. Dudash. Litho Cartor)

1993 (5 Feb). *"Ageing. Dignity and Partrcipatron". Tenth Anniv (1992) of International Plan of Action on Ageing.* P 13.
G226	G **194**	50c. multicoloured	60	60
G227	G **195**	1f.60 multicoloured	1·80	1·80

G **196** Gorilla

G **197** Peregrine Falcon (*Falco peregrinus*)

G **198** Amazon Manatee (*Trichechus inungurts*)

G **199** Snow Leopard (*Panthers, uncia*)

(Des Betina Ogden. Litho Enschedé)

1993 (3 Mar). *Endangered Species (1st series).* P 12½.
G228	G **196**	80c. multicoloured	90	90
		a. Block of 4. Nos. 6228/31	3·75	
G229	G **197**	80c. multicoloured	90	90
G230	G **198**	80c. multicoloured	90	90
G231	G **199**	80c. multicoloured	90	90
G228/231		Set of 4	3·25	3·25

Nos. G228/31 were issued together in *se-tenant* blocks of four within the sheet.

See also Nos. G246/9, G264/7, G290/3, G308/11, G333/6, G372/5, G389/92, G409/12 and G433/6.

G **200** Neighbourhood and Community Environment

G **201** Urban Environment

(Des M. Glaser. Litho Leigh-Mardon Pty Ltd, Melbourne)

1993 (7 May). *45th Anniv of World Health Organization.* P 15 × 14½.
G232		60c. multicoloured	75	75
G233		1f. multicoloured	1·20	1·20

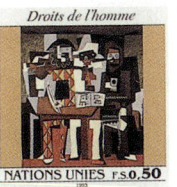

G **202** "Three Musicians" (Pablo Picasso) (Article 27)

G **203** "Voice of Space" (Rene Magritte) (Article 28)

421

UNITED NATIONS 1993

(Des A. Gaines and R. Stein. Litho Enschedé)
1993 (11 June). *Declaration of Human Rights (5th series)*. P 13½.
G234   G 202   50c. multicoloured   1·70   1·70
G235   G 203   90c. multicoloured   3·25   3·25
    Nos. G234/5 were each issued with *se-tenant* label giving the text of the Article in English, French or German, in sheets of 12 stamps and 12 labels.

G 204/207 Peace

(Des H. Erni. Recess and litho PTT, Berne)
1993 (21 Sept). *International Peace Day. Rouletted.*
G236   G 204   60c. multicoloured   95   95
           a. Block of 4 Nos. 6236/9   4·00
G237   G 205   60c. multicoloured   95   95
G238   G 206   60c. multicoloured   95   95
G239   G 207   60c. multicoloured   95   95
G236/239 *Set of* 4   3·50   3·50
    Nos. G236/9 were issued together in *se-tenant* blocks of four within the sheet, each block forming the composite design illustrated.

G 208 Polar Bears 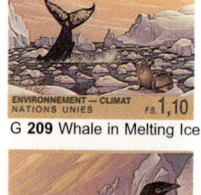   G 209 Whale in Melting Ice

G 210 Elephant Seal    G 211 Adelie Penguins

(Des B. Bralds. Litho Questa)
1993 (29 Oct). *The Environment—Climate.* P 14½.
G240   G 207   1f.10 multicoloured   1·60   1·60
           a. Horiz strip of 4. Nos.
             G240/3   6·50
G241   G 209   1f.10 multicoloured   1·60   1·60
G242   G 210   1f.10 multicoloured   1·60   1·60
G243   G 211   1f.10 multicoloured   1·60   1·60
G240/243 *Set of* 4   5·75   5·75
    Nos. G240/3 were issued together in horizontal *se-tenant* strips of four within the sheet, each strip forming a composite design.

G 212 Father calling Child    G 213 Three Generations

(Des R. Callari. Litho Cartor)
1994 (4 Feb). *International Year of the Family.* P 13.
G244   G 212   80c. multicoloured   85   85
G245   G 213   1f. multicoloured   1·20   1·60

G 214 Mexican Prairie Dogs (*Cynomys mexicanus*)    G 215 Jabiru (*Jabiru mycteria*)

G 216 Blue Whale (*Balaenoptera musculus*)    G 217 Golden Lion Tamarin (*Leontopithecus rosalia*)

(Des L. Parson. Litho Enschedé)
1994 (18 Mar). *Endangered Species (2nd series).* P 12½.
G246   G 214   80c. multicoloured   90   90
           a. Block of 4. Nos.
             G246/9   3·75
G247   G 215   80c. multicoloured   90   90
G248   G 216   80c. multicoloured   90   90
G249   G 217   80c. multicoloured   90   90
G246/249 *Set of* 4   3·25   3·25
    Nos. G246/9 were issued together in *se-tenant* blocks of four within the sheet.

G 218 Hand delivering Refugee to New Country

(Des Francoise Peyroux. Litho Leigh-Mardon Pty Ltd, Melbourne)
1994 (29 Apr). *United Nations High Commissioner for Refugees.* P 14½ × 15.
G250   G 218   1f.20 multicoloured   1·50   1·50

UNITED NATIONS 1994

G 219/222 Shattered Globe and "Evaluation"

(Des K. Koga. Litho Questa)

1994 (24 May). *International Decade for Natural Disaster Reduction.* P 14 × 14½.
G251	G 219	60c. multicoloured	1·00	1·00
		a. Block of 4. Nos. G251/254	4·25	
G252	G 220	60c. multicoloured	1·00	1·00
G253	G 221	60c. multicoloured	1·00	1·00
G254	G 222	60c. multicoloured	1·00	1·00
G251/254 Set of 4			3·50	3·50

Nos. G251/4 were issued together in *se-tenant* blocks of four stamps within the sheet, each block forming the composite design illustrated.

G 223 Mobilization of Resources in Developing Countries

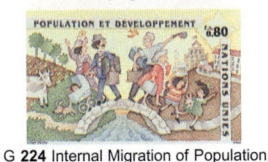

G 224 Internal Migration of Population

(Des J. Smath. Litho Enschedé)

1994 (1 Sept). *International Population and Development Conference, Cairo.* P 13½ × 14.
G255	G 223	60c. multicoloured	65	65
G256	G 224	80c. multicoloured	85	85

G 225 Palais des Nations, Geneva

G 226 "Creation of the World" (detail of tapestry, Oili Mäki)

G 227 Palais des Nations

(Des R. Callari. Litho Questa)

1994 (1 Sept). P 14½ × 15.
G257	G 225	60c. multicoloured	70	70
G258	G 226	80c. multicoloured	95	95
G259	G 227	1f.80 multicoloured	1·90	1·90

G 228 Map and Linked Ribbons

G 229 Map and Ribbons

(Des L. Sardá. Litho Enschedé)

1994 (28 Oct). *30th Anniv of United Nations Conference or Trade and Development.* P 13½ × 14.
G260	G 228	80c. multicoloured	1·00	1·00
G261	G 229	1f. multicoloured	1·20	1·20

G 230 Anniversary Emblem

G 231 "Social Summit 1995"

(Des R. Callari. Recess and litho PTT, Berne)

1995 (1 Jan). *50th Anniv of United Nations Organization (1st issue).* P 13½.
G262	G 230	80c. multicoloured	95	95

See also Nos. G270/**MS**G272 and G275/86.

(Des F. Hundertwasser. Eng W. Seidel. Recess and photo State Ptg Wks, Vienna)

1995 (3 Feb). *World Summit for Social Development, Copenhagen.* P 13½ × 14.
G263	G 231	1f. multicoloured	1·40	1·40

G 232 Crowned Lemur (*Lemur coronatus*)

G 233 Giant Scops Owl (*Otus gurneyi*)

423

UNITED NATIONS 1995

G **234** Painted Frog
(*Atelopus varius zeteki*)

G **235** American Wood Bison
(*Bison bison athabascae*)

(Des Sibylle Erni. Litho Enschedé)

1995 (24 Mar). *Endangered Species (3rd series)*. P 13 × 12½.
G264	G **232**	80c. multicoloured		90	95
		a. Block of 4. Nos.			
		G264/7		3·75	
G265	G **233**	80c. multicoloured		90	95
G266	G **234**	80c. multicoloured		90	95
G267	G **235**	80c. multicoloured		90	95
G264/267	*Set of 4*			3·25	3·50

Nos. G264/7 were issued together in *se-tenant* blocks of four stamps within the sheet.

G **236** Field in Summer

G **237** Field in Winter

(Des G. Kumpf. Litho Questa)

1995 (26 May). *"Youth Our Future"*. *Tenth Anniv of International Youth Year*. P 14½ × 15.
G268	G **236**	80c. multicoloured		95	95
G269	G **237**	1f. multicoloured		1·20	1·20

G **238** Signing U.N. Charter

G **239** Veteran's Memorial Hall and Opera House, San Francisco (venue for signing of Charter)

(Des P. and C. Calle. Eng Inge Madlé Recess (G270/1) or recess and litho (**MS**G272) Enschedé)

1995 (26 June). *50th Anniv of United Nations Organization (2nd issue)*. P 13½ × 14.
G270	G **238**	60c. maroon		75	75
G271	G **239**	1f.80 blackish green		1·90	1·90
MSG272	92 × 70 mm. Nos. G270/1. Imperf			2·75	2·75

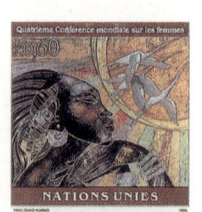

G **240** Woman and Cranes

G **241** Women Worshipping

(Des Ting Shao Kuang. Photo Postage Stamp Ptg Wks, Peking)

1995 (5 Sept). *Fourth World Conference on Women, Peking*. P 12½.
G273	G **240**	60c. multicoloured		80	80
G274	G **241**	1f. multicoloured		1·20	1·20

G **242/244**

G **245/247**

424

UNITED NATIONS 1995

G 248/250

G 251/253

(Des B. Verkaaik. Litho Questa)

1995 (24 Oct). *50th Anniv of United Nations Organization (3rd issue).* P 14.

G275	G 242	30c. multicoloured	40	40
		a. Sheetlet of 12 Nos. G275/86	5·00	
		b. Booklet pane. Nos. G275/7	90	
G276	G 243	30c. multicoloured	40	40
G277	G 244	30c. multicoloured	40	40
G278	G 245	30c. multicoloured	40	40
		a. Booklet pane. Nos. G278/80	90	
G279	G 246	30c. multicoloured	40	40
G280	G 247	30c. multicoloured	40	40
G281	G 248	30c. multicoloured	40	40
		a. Booklet pane. Nos. G281/3	90	
G282	G 249	30c. multicoloured	40	40
G283	G 250	30c. multicoloured	40	40
G284	G 251	30c. multicoloured	40	40
		a. Booklet pane Nos. G284/6	90	
G285	G 252	30c. multicoloured	40	40
G286	G 253	30c. multicoloured	40	40
G275/286 *Set of* 12			4·25	4·25

Nos. G275/7 and G278/80 form the left and right halves respectively of a composite design, and Nos. G281/3 and G284/6 another composite design, the two composites being issued together (separated by a gutter) in a *se-tenant* sheetlet of 12 stamps.

The booklet panes have a perforated white margin on three sides of the block.

G 254 Catching Fish

(Des R. Mirer. Litho Enschedé)

1996 (2 Feb). *50th Anniv of World Federation of United Nations Associations.* P13 × 13½.
G287 G 254 80c. multicoloured . . . . 1·10 1·10

G 255 "Galloping Horse treading on a Flying Swallow" (Chinese bronze sculpture, Han Dynasty)

G 256 Palais des Nations, Geneva

(Des L. Bianco (40c.). Catherine Charbonnier Casile (70c.). Litho Questa)

1996 (2 Feb). P 14½ × 15.
G288	G 255	40c. multicoloured	40	45
G289	G 256	70c. multicoloured	75	85

G 257 *Paphropedilum delenatii*

G 258 *Pachypodium baronii*

G 259 Yellow Amaryllis (*Sternbergia lutea*)

G 260 Cobra Plant (*Darlingtonia californica*)

(Des Diane Bruyninckx. Litho Enschedé)

1996 (14 Mar). *Endangered Species (4th series).* P 13 × 12½.
G290	G 257	80c. multicoloured	85	85
		a. Block of 4 Nos. G290/3	3·75	
G291	G 258	80c. multicoloured	85	85
G292	G 259	80c. multicoloured	85	85
G293	G 260	80c. multicoloured	85	85
G290/293 *Set of* 4			3·00	3·00

Nos. G290/3 were issued together in *se-tenant* blocks of four stamps within the sheet.

425

UNITED NATIONS 1996

G **261** Family on Verandah of House

G **262** Women in Traditional Dress in Gardens

G **263** Produce Seller and City

G **264** Boys playing on Riverside

G **265** Elderly Couple reading Newspaper

(Des Teresa Fasolino. Litho Enschedé)

1996 (3 June). *"Habitat II" Second United Nations Conference on Human Settlements, Istanbul, Turkey.* P 14 × 13½.
G294	G **261**	70c. multicoloured	1·10	1·10
		a. Horiz strip of 5. Nos. G294/8	4·00	
G295	G **262**	70c. multicoloured	1·10	1·10
G296	G **263**	70c. multicoloured	1·10	1·10
G297	G **264**	70c. multicoloured	1·10	1·10
G298	G **265**	70c. multicoloured	1·10	1·10
G294/298	Set of 5		4·75	4·75

Nos. G294/8 were issued together in horizontal *se-tenant* strips of five stamps within the sheet, each strip forming a composite design.

(Des L. Neiman. Litho Questa)

1996 (19 July). *Sport and the Environment Centenary of Modern Olympic Games.* P 14 × 14½ (70c.) or 14½ × 14 (1f.10).
G299	G **266**	70c. multicoloured	75	75
G300	G **267**	1f.10 multicoloured	1·30	1·30
MSG301	88 × 78mm. Nos. G299/300		1·60	1·60

G **268** Birds in Treetop

G **269** Flowers growing from Bomb

(Des Chen Yu (90c.). Zhou Jing (1f.10). Litho Questa)

1996 (17 Sept). *"A Plea for Peace". Winning Entries in China Youth Design Competition.* P 15 × 14½.
G302	G **268**	90c. multicoloured	95	95
G303	G **269**	1f.10 multicoloured	1·30	1·30

G **270** "The Sun and the Moon" (South American legend)

G **271** "Ananse" (African spider tale)

(Des Walt Disney Co. Litho Questa)

1996 (20 Nov). *50th Anniv of United Nations Children's Fund Children's Stories.* P 14½ × 15.
G304	G **270**	70c. multicoloured	80	80
G305	G **271**	1f.80 multicoloured	1·70	1·70

Each issued in sheets of eight stamps and one label bearing the anniversary emblem.

G **272** U.N. Flag

G **273** "Building Palais des Nations" (detail of fresco, Massimo Campigli)

(Litho Questa)

1997 (12 Feb). P 14½ × 15.
G306	10c. multicoloured	15	15
G307	1f.10 multicoloured	1·10	1·10

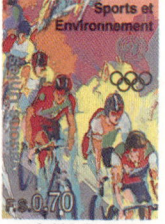

G **266** Cycling

G **267** Running

G **274** Polar Bear (*Ursus maritimus*)

G **275** Blue Crowned Pigeon (*Goura cristata*)

UNITED NATIONS 1997

G **276** Marine Iguana (*Amblyrhynchus cristatus*)

G **277** Guanaco (*Lama guanicoe*)

(Des Daniela Costa. Litho Enschedé)

1997 (13 Mar). *Endangered Species (5th series)*. P 13 × 12½.
G308	G **274**	80f. multicoloured	85	85
		a. Block of 4. Nos. G308/11	3·50	
G309	G **275**	80f. multicoloured	85	85
G310	G **276**	80f. multicoloured	85	85
G311	G **277**	80f. multicoloured	85	85
G308/311 Set of 4			3·00	3·00

Nos. G308/11 were issued together in *se-tenant* blocks of four within the sheet.

G **278/281** Sunrise over Mountains

(Des P. Max. Photo Courvoisier)

1997 (30 May). *"Earth Summit + 5"*. Fifth Anniv of United Nations Conference on Environment and Development. Granite paper. P 11½.
G312	G **278**	45f. multicoloured	60	60
		a. Block of four. Nos. G312/15	2·50	
G313	G **279**	45f. multicoloured	60	60
G314	G **280**	45f. multicoloured	60	60
G315	G **281**	45f. multicoloured	60	60
G312/315 Set of 4			2·25	2·25

MSG316 90 × 75 mm. 1f.10, Motifs as Nos. G312/15. Imperf . . . . 1·25 1·25

Nos. G312/15 were issued together in *se-tenant* blocks of four stamps within the sheet, each block forming the composite design illustrated.

G **282** Fokker F.7 Trimotor and Airship

G **283** Lockheed Constellation and Boeing 314 Flying Boat

G **284** De Havilland D.H.106 Comet and Boeing 747 Jetliners

G **285** Ilyushin and Boeing 747 and Jetliners

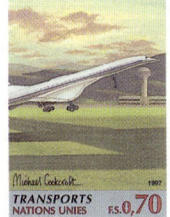

G **286** Concorde Supersonic Jetliner

(Des M. Cockcroft. Litho Questa)

1997 (29 Aug). *50th Anniversaries of Economic Commission for Europe and Economic and Social Commission for Asia and the Pacific*. P 14 × 14½.
G317	G **282**	70f. multicoloured	1·00	1·00
		a. Horiz strip of 5. Nos. 317/21	5·00	
G318	G **283**	70f. multicoloured	1·00	1·00
G319	G **284**	70f. multicoloured	1·00	1·00
G320	G **285**	70f. multicoloured	1·00	1·00
G321	G **286**	70f. multicoloured	1·00	1·00
G317/321 Set of 5			4·50	4·50

Nos. 317/21 were issued together in horizontal *se-tenant* strips of five stamps within the sheet, each strip forming a composite design.

G **287** 1986 50c. Philately Stamp

G **288** 1986 80c. Philately Stamp

(Des R. Stein. Litho Enschedé)

1997 (14 Oct). *"Tribute to Philately"*. P 13½ × 14.
G322	G **287**	70c. multicoloured	85	85
G323	G **288**	1f.10 multicoloured	1·20	1·20

427

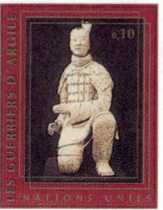

UNITED NATIONS   1997

G **289** Kneeling Warrior

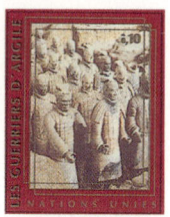

G **290** Ranks of Armoured Warriors

G **291** Head

G **292** Group in Wrap-over Tunics

G **293** Head and Shoulders

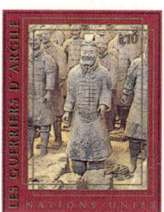

G **294** Group in Armour

G **295** Palais des Nations, Geneva

(Litho Questa)

1998 (13 Feb). P 14½ × 15.
G332   G **295**   2f. multicoloured . . . .   2·10   2·10

G **296** Tibetan Stump-tailed Macaques (*Macaca thibetana*)

G **297** Greater Flamingoes (*Phoenicopterus ruber*)

G **298** Queen Alexandra's Birdwings (*Ornithoptera alexandrae*)

G **299** Fallow Deer (*Cervus dama*)

(Des R. Stein. Litho Austrian State Ptg Wks, Vienna)

1997 (19 Nov). *25th Anniv of World Heritage Convention. Terracotta Warriors from Emperor Qin Shi Huang's Tomb, Xian, China.* P 13½.

(*a*) *Booklet stamps.*

G324	G **289**	10c. multicoloured	35	35
		a. Booklet pane. No. G324 × 4	1·40	
G325	G **290**	10c. multicoloured	55	55
		a. Booklet pane. No. G325 x 4	2·20	
G326	G **291**	10c. multicoloured	25	25
		a. Booklet pane. No. G326 × 4	1·00	
G327	G **292**	10c. multicoloured	25	25
		a. Booklet pane. No. G327 × 4	1·00	
G328	G **293**	10c. multicoloured	25	25
		a. Booklet pane. No. G328 × 4	1·00	
G329	G **294**	10c. multicoloured	25	25
		a. Booklet pane. No. G329 × 4	1·00	

(*b*) *Sheet stamps.*

G330	G **291**	45c. multicoloured	50	50
G331	G **292**	70c. multicoloured	70	70
G324/331 *Set of 8*			2·75	2·75

(Des Suzanne Duranceau. Litho Enschedé)

1998 (13 Mar). *Endangered Species (6th series).* P 13 × 12½.

G333	G **296**	80c. multicoloured	85	85
		a. Block of 4. Nos. G333/6	3·50	
G334	G **297**	80c. multicoloured	85	85
G335	G **298**	80c. multicoloured	85	85
G336	G **299**	80c. multicoloured	85	85
G333/336 *Set of* 4			3·00	3·00

Nos. G333/6 were issued togther in *se-tenant* blocks of four stamps within the sheet.

UNITED NATIONS 1998

G 300 Walrus

(Des J. Ellis. Litho Enschedé)

1998 (20 May). *International Year of the Ocean.* Type G **300** and similar horiz designs. Multicoloured. P 14 × 13½.
G337	45c. Type G **300**		50	50
	a. Sheetlet of 12. Nos G337/48		6·25	
G338	45c. Polar bears		50	50
G339	45c. Polar bear, musk oxen, penguins and seal on ice		50	50
G340	45c. Diver		50	50
G341	45c. Seals		50	50
G342	45c. Narwhale		50	50
G343	45c. Fishes and shark		50	50
G344	45c. Shark's tail, seal and puffin		50	50
G345	45c. Fishes and penguin's back		50	50
G346	45c. Fish and jellyfishes		50	50
G347	45c. Seal, penguin and squid		50	50
G348	45c. Penguin hunting fishes		50	50
G337/348 *Set of 12*			5·50	5·50

Nos. G337/48 were issued together in *se-tenant* sheetlets of 12 stamps.

G 304 Birds

G 305 Hand releasing Birds

(Des J.-M. Folon. Litho Cartor)

1998 (27 Oct). *50th Anniv of Universal Declaration of Human Rights.* P 13½ × 13.
G353	G **304**	90c. multicoloured	1·00	1·00
G354	G **305**	1f.80 multicoloured	2·00	2·00

G 306 Palace Façade

G 301 Orang-utan with Young

(Des R. Garcia. Litho Govt Ptg Wks, Tokyo, Japan)

1998 (19 June). *Rainforest Preservation.* P 13 × 13½.
G349	G **301**	70c. multicoloured	85	85
MSG350	82 × 70 mm. G **301** 3f. multicoloured		3·00	3·00

G 307 Great Palm House

G 302 Soldier with Children

G 303 Soldier holding Baby

(Des A. Davidson. Photo Courvoisier)

1998 (15 Sept). *50 Years of United Nations Peacekeeping.* Granite paper. P 12.
G351	G **302**	70c. multicoloured	75	75
G352	G **303**	90c. multicoloured	1·00	1·00

G 308 Gloriette

429

UNITED NATIONS 1998

G **309** Blue and White Vase (Mirror Room)

G **310** Detail of Wall Hanging (Johann Wenzl Bergl)

G **311** Porcelain Stove

(Des R. Stein. Litho Questa.)

1998 (4 Dec). *World Heritage Site. Schönbrunn Palace, Vienna.* P 14 × 13½ (horiz) or 13½ × 14 (vert).

G355	G 306	10c. multicoloured	50	55
		a. Booklet pane. No. G355 × 4	2·00	
G356	G 307	10c. multicoloured	60	60
		a. Booklet pane. No. G356 × 4	2·40	
G357	G 308	10c. multicoloured	30	30
		a. Booklet pane. No. G357 × 4	1·20	
G358	G 309	30c. multicoloured	40	45
		a. Booklet pane. No. G358 × 3	1·60	
G359	G 310	30c. multicoloured	40	45
		a. Booklet pane. No. G359 × 3	1·60	
G360	G 311	30c. multicoloured	40	45
		a. Booklet pane. No. 360 × 3	1·60	
G361	G 307	70c. multicoloured	60	60
G362	G 309	1f.10 multicoloured	1·20	1·30
G355/362	Set of 8		4·00	4·25

G **312** Palais Wilson, Geneva

(Photo Courvoisier)

1999 (5 Feb). *Headquarters of United Nations High Commissioner for Human Rights. Granite paper.* P 11½.

G363	G 312	1f.70 brown-red	1·90	1·90

G **313** Tasmanian Wilderness

G **314** Wet Tropics, Queensland

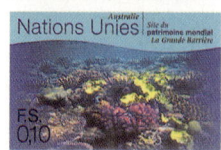

G **315** Great Barrier Reef

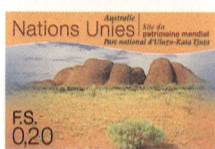

G **316** Uluru-Kata Tjuta National Park

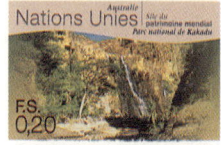

G **317** Kakadu National Park

G **318** Willandra Lakes Region

(Des Passmore Design. Litho Questa)

1999 (19 Mar). *World Heritage Sites in Australia.* P 13.

G364	G 313	10c. multicoloured	25	25
		a. Booklet pane. No. G364 × 4	1·00	
G365	G 314	10c. multicoloured	20	20
		a. Booklet pane. No. G365 × 4	80	
G366	G 315	10c. multicoloured	20	20
		a. Booklet pane. No. G366 × 4	80	
G367	G 316	20c. multicoloured	30	30
		a. Booklet pane. No. G367 × 4	1·20	
G368	G 317	20c. multicoloured	30	30
		a. Booklet pane. No. G368 × 4	1·20	
G369	G 318	20c. multicoloured	30	30
		a. Booklet pane. No. G369 × 4	1·20	

UNITED NATIONS 1999

G370	G 317	90c. multicoloured		1·10	1·10
G371	G 315	1f.10 multicoloured		1·30	1·30
G364/371	*Set of* 8			3·50	3·50

G **319** Asiatic Wild Ass (*Equus hemionus*)

G **320** Hyacinth Macaw (*Anodorhynchus hyacinthinus*)

G **321** Jamaican Boa (*Epicrates subflavus*)

G **322** Bennett's Tree Kangaroo (*Dendrolagus bennettianus*)

(Des T. Barrall. Litho Enschedé)

1999 (22 Apr). *Endangered Species (7th series).* P 13 × 12½.

G372	G 319	90c. multicoloured		95	95
		a. Block of 4. Nos. G372/5		4·00	
G373	G 320	90c. multicoloured		95	95
G374	G 321	90c. multicoloured		95	95
G375	G 322	90c. multicoloured		95	95
G372/375	*Set of* 4			3·50	3·50

Nos. G372/5 were issued together in *se-tenant* blocks of four stamps within the sheet.

G **323/324** Satellite-aided Agriculture

(Des A. Hejja. Litho Courvoisier)

1999 (7 July). *Third Conference on Exploration and Peaceful Uses of Outer Space, Vienna. Granite paper. Rouletted.*

G376	G 323	45c. multicoloured		60	60
		a. Horiz pair. Nos. G376/7		1·25	1·25
G377	G 324	45c. multicoloured		60	60
MSG378	90 × 75 mm. 2f. Combined design as Nos. G376/7 (71 × 29 mm). P 14½			1·90	1·90
MSG379	90 × 75 mm. 2f. As No. **MS**G378 but additionally inscr "PHILEXFRANCE 99 LE MONDIAL DU TIMBRE PARIS 2 AU 11 JUILLET 1999" in bottom margin			2·00	2·00

Nos. G376/7 were issued together in horizontal *se-tenant* pairs within the sheet, each pair forming the composite design illustrated.

G **325/328** Early 20th-century Mail Transport

(Des M. Hess. Litho Courvoisier)

1999 (23 Aug). *125th Anniv of Universal Postal Union. Granite paper.* P 11½.

G380	G 325	70c. multicoloured		85	85
		a. Block of 4. Nos. G380/3		3·50	
G381	G 326	70c. multicoloured		85	85
G382	G 327	70c. multicoloured		85	85
G383	G 328	70c. multicoloured		85	85
G380/383	*Set of* 4			3·00	3·00

Nos. G380/3 were issued together in *se-tenant* blocks of four stamps within the sheet, each block forming the composite design illustrated.

G **329** Palais des Nations, Geneva

G **330** (⅔-*size illustration*)

431

UNITED NATIONS   1999

(Des R. Stein. Litho Walsall Security Printers Ltd)
1999 (21 Sept). *"In Memoriam: Fallen in the Cause of Peace"*.
P 14½ × 14.
G384   G 329   1f.10 multicoloured   . . . . .   1·30   1·30
MSG385 90 × 75 mm. **G 330** 2f.
multicoloured   . . . .   2·10   2·10

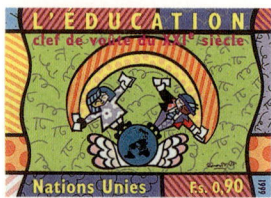

G **331** Couple on Globe

G **332** "Environment"

(Des R. Britto. Litho Austrian State Ptg Wks, Vienna)
1999 (18 Nov). *Education: Keystone to the 21st Century*.
P 13½ × 14.
G386   G 331   90c. multicoloured   . . . . .   1·00   1·00
G387   G 332   1f.80 multicoloured   . . . . .   2·10   2·10

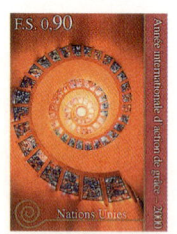

G **333** Glory Window (Gabrielle Loire), Chapel of Thanksgiving, Dallas

(Des R. Katz. Litho and thermography Cartor)
2000 (1 Jan). *International Year of Thanksgiving*. P 13½.
G388   G 333   90c. multicoloured   . . . . .   1·30   1·30

G **334** Hippopotamus (*Hippopotamus amphibius*)

G **335** Coscoroba Swan (*Coscoroba coscoroba*)

G **336** Emerald Monitor (*Varanus prasinus*)

G **337** Sea Otter (*Enhydra lutris*)

(Des R. Hynes. Litho Enschedé)
2000 (6 Apr). *Endangered Species (8th series)*. P 13 × 12½.
G389   G 334   90c. multicoloured   . . . . .   1·40   1·40
   a. Block of 4. Nos.
      G389/92   . . . . .   5·75
G390   G 335   90c. multicoloured   . . . . .   1·40   1·40
G391   G 336   90c. multicoloured   . . . . .   1·40   1·40
G392   G 337   90c. multicoloured   . . . . .   1·40   1·40
G389/392 **Set of** 4   . . . .   5·00   5·00
   Nos. G389/92 were issued together in *se-tenant* blocks of four stamps within the sheet.

G **338** "The Embrace" (Rita Adaïmy)

G **339** "Living Single" (Richard Kimanthi)

(Des R. Stein. Litho Cartor)
2000 (30 May). *"Our World 2000" International Art Exhibition, New York. Entries in Millennium Painting Competition*. P 13 × 13½ (90c.) or 13½ × 13 (1f.10).
G393   G 338   90c. multicoloured   . . . . .   1·30   1·30
G394   G 339   1f.10 multicoloured   . . . . .   1·30   1·30

432

UNITED NATIONS 2000

G **340** Corner Stone Dedication, 1949

G **341** Window Cleaner, Secretariat Building, 1951

(Des R. Katz. Litho Cartor)

2000 (7 July). *55th Anniv of the United Nations and 50th Anniv of Opening of U.N. Headquarters, New York.* P $13\frac{1}{2} \times 13$.
G395 G **340** 90c. scarlet-vermilion, cobalt
and yellow-ochre . . . . . 1·20 1·20
G396 G **341** 1f.40 scarlet-vermilion, cobalt
and yellow-ochre . . . . . 1·50 1·50
MSG397 67 × 86 mm. Nos. G395/6 . . . . . . 2·75 2·75

G **342** Two Women

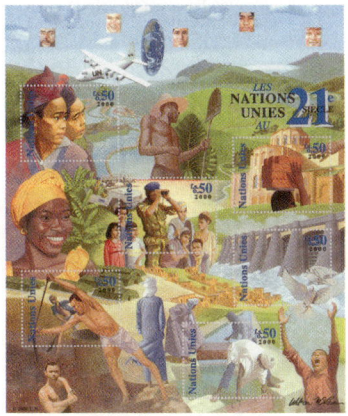

G **343** ($\frac{1}{3}$-*size illustration*)

(Des W. McLean. Litho Austrian State Ptg Wks, Vienna)

2000 (15 Sept). *"The United Nations in the 21st Century".* Sheet 141 × 165 mm containing Type **G 342** and similar horiz designs, forming an overall design Type **G 343**. Multicoloured. P 14.
MSG398 50c. Type **G 342**; 50c. Man carrying bricks on head; 50c. Soldier and villagers; 50c. Dam and doves; 50c. Men digging; 50c. Men damming irrigation channel . . . . . . 2·75 2·75

G **344** Granada

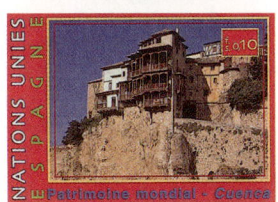

G **345** Cliff-top Houses, Cuenca

G **346** Roman Aqueduct, Segovia

G **347** Archaeological Site, Mérida

G **348** Toledo

433

UNITED NATIONS 2000

G 349 Güell Park, Barcelona

(Des R. Stein. Litho Questa)
2000 (6 Oct). *World Heritage Sites in Spain.* P 15 × 14½.

		(a) Booklet stamps.		
G399	G 344	10c. multicoloured	25	25
		a. Booklet pane. No. G399 × 4	1·10	
G400	G 345	10c. multicoloured	25	25
		a. Booklet pane. No. G400 × 4	1·10	25
G401	G 346	10c. multicoloured	25	
		a. Booklet pane. No. G401 × 4	1·10	25
G402	G 347	20c. multicoloured	25	25
		a. Booklet pane. No. G402 × 4	1·10	
G403	G 348	20c. multicoloured	25	25
		a. Booklet pane. No. G403 × 4	1·10	
G404	G 349	20c. multicoloured	25	25
		a. Booklet pane. No. G404 × 4	1·10	
		(b) Sheet stamps.		
G405	G 345	1f. multicoloured	1·10	1·10
G406	G 348	1f.20 multicoloured	1·20	1·20
G399/406		Set of 8	3·50	3·50

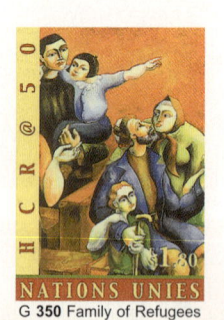

G 350 Family of Refugees

G 351 (½-size illustration)

(Des Yu. Georgian. Litho Enschedé)
2000 (9 Nov). *50th Anniv of United Nations High Commissioner for Refugees.* P 13½ × 13.

G407	G 350	80c. multicoloured	1·10	1·10
MSG408	121 × 82 mm. **G 351** 1h.80, multicoloured		1·75	1·75

G 352 Lynx (*Felis lynx canadensis*)

G 353 Green Peafowl (*Pavo muticus*)

G 354 Galapagos Tortoise (*Geochelone elephantopus*)

G 355 Lemur (*Lepilemur sp.*)

(Des Higgins Bond. Litho Enschedé)
2001 (1 Feb). *Endangered Species (9th series).* P 13 × 12½.

G409	G 352	90c. multicoloured	1·10	1·10
		a. Block of 4. Nos. G409/12	4·50	
G410	G 353	90c. multicoloured	1·10	1·10
G411	G 354	90c. multicoloured	1·10	1·10
G412	G 355	90c. multicoloured	1·10	1·10
G409/412		Set of 4	4·00	4·00

Nos. G409/12 were issued together in *se-tenant* blocks of four stamps within the sheet.

G 356 Hands forming Heart (Ernest Pignon-Ernest)

G 357 Women's Head and White Dove (Paul Siché)

UNITED NATIONS 2001

(Des R. Stein and Rorie Katz. Litho Enschedé)

2001 (29 Mar). *United Nations International Year of Volunteers.* P 13½.
G413	G 356	90c. multicoloured	1·10	1·10
G414	G 357	1f.30 multicoloured	1·20	1·20

G 358 Pagoda, Kyoto

G 359 Imperial Palace, Nara

G 360 Himeji Castle

G 361 Shirakawa-go and Gokayama Villages

G 362 Itsukushima Shinto Shrine

G 363 Temple, Nikko

(Des R. Katz. Litho Enschedé)

2001 (1 Aug). *World Heritage Sites in Japan.* P 13 × 13½.

(a) Booklet stamps.
G415	G 358	10c. multicoloured	20	20
		a. Booklet pane. No. G415 × 4	85	
G416	G 359	10c. multicoloured	20	20
		a. Booklet pane. No. G416 × 4	85	
G417	G 360	10c. multicoloured	20	20
		a. Booklet pane. No. G417 × 4	85	
G418	G 361	30c. multicoloured	40	40
		a. Booklet pane. No. G418 × 4	1·60	
G419	G 362	30c. multicoloured	40	40
		a. Booklet pane. No. G419 × 4	1·60	
G420	G 363	30c. multicoloured	40	40
		a. Booklet pane. No. G420 × 4	1·60	

(b) Sheet stamps.
G421	G 359	1f.10 multicoloured	1·20	1·20
G422	G 362	1f.30 multicoloured	1·00	1·60
G415/422	Set of 8		3·50	4·25

G 364 Hammarskjöld

(Des O. Mathiesen. Recess Banknote Corporation of America Inc)

2001 (18 Sept). *40th Death Anniv of Dag Hammarskjöld (United Nations Secretary General, 1953–61).* P 11 × 11½.
G423	G 364	2f. deep carmine	1·30	1·30

G 365 Postman and "Stamps"

G 366 Trumpets and "Stamps"

435

UNITED NATIONS 2001

G 367 Emblem

(Des R. Katz. Litho Enschedé)
2001 (18 Oct). 50th Anniv of United Nations Postal Administration. P 13½.
G424 G 365 90c. multicoloured 95   95
G425 G 366 1f.30 multicoloured . . . . . 1·40 1·40
MSG426 102 × 102 mm. G 367 1f.30, 1f.80, cobalt and bright carmine. P 13 . . . . . 3·00 3·00

G 368 Flowers and Coastline

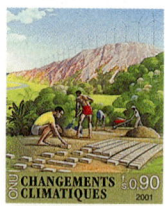

G 369 Wind-powered Generators and Brick Making

G 370 Power Station inside Glass Dome

G 371 Couple sitting beside Lake

(Des R. Giusti. Litho Walsall Security Printers Ltd)
2001 (16 Nov). Climate Change. P 13½.
G427 G 368 90c. multicoloured 95   95
              a. Horiz strip of 4. Nos. G427/30 . . . . . 4·00
G428 G 369 90c. multicoloured 95   95
G429 G 370 90c. multicoloured 95   95
G430 G 371 90c. multicoloured 95   95
G427/430 Set of 4 . . . . . 3·50 3·50
    Nos. G427/30 were issued together in horizontal se-tenant strips of four stamps, each strip forming a composite design.

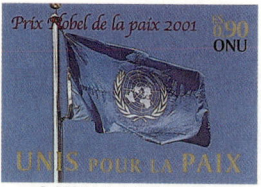

G 372 United Nations Flag

(Des R. Stein. Litho Cartor)
2001 (10 Dec). Kofi Annan, Winner of Nobel Peace Prize, 2001. P 13½.
G431 G 372 90c. multicoloured 95   95

G 373 Armillary Sphere, Ariana Park

(Des R. Stein. Litho Austrian State Ptg Wks, Vienna)
2002 (1 Mar). P 14.
G432 G 373 1f.30 multicoloured . . . . . 1·00 1·00

G 374 Bald Uakari (Cacajao calvus)

G 375 Ratel (Mellivora capensis)

G 376 Pallas's Cat (Otocolobus manul)

G 377 Savannah Monitor (Varanus exanthematicus)

(Des Lori Anzalone. Litho Enschedé)
2002 (4 Apr). Endangered Species (10th series). P 13 × 12½.
G433 G 374 90c. multicoloured 95   95
              a. Block of 4. Nos. G433/6 . . . . . 4·00
G434 G 375 90c. multicoloured 95   95
G435 G 376 90c. multicoloured 95   95
G436 G 377 90c. multicoloured 95   95
G433/436 Set of 4 . . . . . 3·50 3·50
    Nos. G433/6 were issued together in se-tenant blocks of four stamps within the sheet.

UNITED NATIONS 2002

G **378** Wooden Statue

G **379** Carved Wooden Container

(Des Karen Kelleher. Litho Questa)

2002 (20 May). *East Timor Independence.* P 14 × 14½.
G437 G **378** 90c. multicoloured 75 75
G438 G **379** 1f.30 multicoloured . . . . . . 1·10 1·10

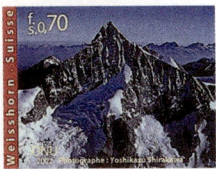

G **380** Weisshorn, Switzerland

G **381** Mount Fuji, Japan

G **382** Vinson Massif, Antarctica

G **383** Kamet, India

(Des R. Stein and R. Katz. Litho Cartor)

2002 (24 May). *International Year of Mountains.* P 13 × 13½.
G439 G **380** 70c. multicoloured 55 55
    a. Block or vert strip of 4.
       Nos. G439/42 . . . . . . 3·25
G440 G **381** 70c. multicoloured 55 55
G441 G **382** 1f.20 multicoloured 95 95
G442 G **383** 1f.20 multicoloured 95 95
G439/442 *Set of* 4 . . . . 2·75 2·75
   Nos. G439/42 were issued together either in *se-tenant* blocks or vertical strips of four stamps within sheetlets of twelve.

G **384** Sun, Water, Birds and Flowers

G **385** Figure's wearing Fashionable Dress

G **386** Women's Profile

G **387** Yacht

(Des P. Max. Litho Questa)

2002 (27 June). *World Summit on Sustainable Development, Johannesburg.* P 14½ × 14.
G443 G **384** 90c. multicoloured 75 75
G444 G **385** 90c. multicoloured 75 75
    a. Block or vert strip of 4.
       Nos. G443/6 . . . . . . 4·50
G445 G **386** 1f.80 multicoloured . . . . . . 1·50 1·50
G446 G **387** 1f.80 multicoloured . . . . . . 1·50 1·50
G443/446 *Set of* 4 . . . . 4·00 4·00
   Nos. G443/6 were issued together either in *se-tenant* blocks or vertical strips of four stamps in sheetlets of twelve.

UNITED NATIONS 2002

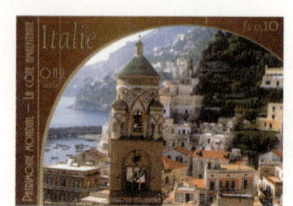

G 388 Duomo di Sant'Andrea, Amalfi Coast

G 389 View across Islands, Aeolian Islands

G 390 Del Moro Fountain, Rome

G 391 Santa Maria del Fiore, Florence

G 392 Leaning Tower, Pisa

G 393 The Forum, Pompeii

(Des R. Katz. Litho Cartor)
2002 (30 Aug). *World Heritage Sites in Italy.* P $13\frac{1}{2} \times 13$.

(a) Booklet stamps.

G447	G 388	10c. multicoloured	10	10
		a. Booklet pane. No. G447 × 4	45	
G448	G 389	10c. multicoloured	10	10
		a. Booklet pane. No. G448 × 4	45	
G449	G 390	10c. multicoloured	10	10
		a. Booklet pane. No. G449 × 4	45	
G450	G 391	20c. multicoloured	20	20
		a. Booklet pane. No. G450 × 4	85	
G451	G 392	20c. multicoloured	20	20
		a. Booklet pane. No. G451 × 4	85	
G452	G 393	20c. multicoloured	20	20
		a. Booklet pane. No. G452 × 4	85	

(b) Sheet stamps.

G453	G 392	90c. multicoloured	80	80
G454	G 389	1f.30 multicoloured	1·20	1·20
G447/454 Set of 8			2·50	2·50

G 394 A.I.D.S. Symbol on U.N. Secretariat Building, New York

G 395 A.I.D.S. Symbol on U.N. Secretariat Building, New York at Night ($\frac{1}{2}$-size illustration)

(Des R. Katz. Litho Walsall Security Printers Ltd)
2002 (24 Oct). *A.I.D.S. Awareness Campaign.* P $13\frac{1}{2}$.
G455 G 394 1f.30 multicoloured   1·20 1·20
MSG456 80 × 80 mm. G 395 90c. + 30c.
P $14\frac{1}{2}$ 1·20 1·20
The premium was for A.I.D.S. charities.

G 396 Doves

(Des T. Clauson. Litho Questa)
2002 (24 Oct). P $14\frac{1}{2} \times 15$.
G457 G 396 3f. multicoloured   2·75 2·75

438

UNITED NATIONS   2002

G **397** Artefacts

(Des R. Katz and R. Stein. Litho Questa)

2003 (31 Jan). *Indigenous Art. Sheet 125 × 97 mm. Multicoloured.* P 14½.
MSG458 90c. Inca poncho, Peru; 90c. Bahia statue, Brazil; 90c. Blanket, Ecuador; 90c. Mayan stone sculpture, Xunantunich, Belize; 90c. Embroidered fabric, Guatemala; 90c. Colima terracotta sculpture, Mexico . . . . . . 5·00   5·00

G **398** Headquarters Building

(Des C. Wursten. Litho Questa)

2003 (20 Feb). *Inauguration of New Inter-Parliamentary Union Headquarters, Geneva.* P 14½ × 14.
G459   G **398**   90c. multicoloured   80   80

STAMP BOOKLETS

The following checklist covers, in simplified form, booklets issued by the United Nations Geneva Headquarters. It is intended that it should be used in conjunction with the main listings and details of stamps and panes listed there are not repeated.

Prices are for complete booklets

Booklet No	Date	Contents and Face Value	Price
SBG1	24 Oct 1995	50th Anniv of U.N.O. 4 panes, Nos. G275b, G278a, G281a and G284a (3f.60)	3·00
SBG2	19 Nov 1997	Terracotta Warriors 6 panes, Nos. G324a, G325a, G326a, G327a, G328a and 329a (2f.40)	7·75
SBG3	4 Dec 1998	Schönbrunn Palace 6 panes, Nos. G355a, G356a, G357a, G358a, G359a and G360a (3f.90)	10·50
SBG4	19 Mar 1999	Australia 6 panes, Nos. G364a, G365a, G366a, G367a, G368a and G369a (3f.60)	6·25
SBG5	6 Oct 2000	Spain 6 panes, Nos. G399a, G400a, G401a, G402a, G403a and G404a (3f.60)	6·75
SBG6	1 Aug 2001	Japan 6 panes, Nos. G415a, G416a, G417a, G418a, G419a and G420a (4f.80)	7·50
SBG7	30 Aug	Italy 6 panes, Nos. G447a, G448a, G449a, G450a, G451a and G452a (3f.60)	4·00

439

VATICAN CITY 1929

Vatican City

1929. 100 Centesimi = 1 Lira
2002. 100 cents = 1 Euro

By the Lateran Treaty of 11 February 1929, the temporal power of the Papacy, lost in 1870, was restored by the creation of the state of Vatican City, an area of one-sixth of a square mile in the heart of Rome, around St. Peter's and the Vatican Palace.

PRINTERS. All the stamps of Vatican City were printed at the Italian Government Printing Works, Rome, except where otherwise stated.

1 Papal Tiara and St. Peter's Keys
2 Pope Pius XI 
E 3 

(Des E. Federici. T **1** recess with background typo, T **2** photo)

1929 (1 Aug). T **1** (with a repetition of minute white letters reading "POSTEVATICANE" in horizontal rows on a tinted background) and T **2**. P 14.

1	1	5c. brown/rose	20	25
2		10c. grey-green/green	30	35
3		20c. violet/lilac	75	55
4		25c. blue/azure	90	55
5		30c. black/yellow	1·10	70
6		50c. black/salmon	1·60	70
7		75c. carmine/grey	2·20	1·30
8	2	80c. carmine	1·60	40
9		1l.25 blue	2·50	95
10		2l. sepia	5·00	1·90
11		2l.50 vermilion	4·25	2·75
12		5l. green	5·00	9·75
13		10l. olive-black	11·00	14·50

(Des E. Federici. Photo)

1929 (1 Aug). EXPRESS LETTER. P 14.

E14	E 3	2l. carmine	20·00	14·50
E15		2l.50 blue	16·00	18·00
1/E15	Set of 15		55·00	55·00

(3) C. = **(P 4)** 25 PER PACCHI **(D 4)** LIRE 1,10 SEGNATASSE

1931 (30 Sept). Surch with T **3** in red.
14 1 25c. on 30c. black/yellow ... 2·75 1·20

1931 (1 Oct). PARCEL POST. Variously optd as Type P **4**.

P15	1	5c. brown/rose	20	55
P16		10c. grey-green/green	20	55
P17		20c. violet/lilac	1·60	2·50
P18		25c. blue/azure	7·25	5·75
P19		30c. black/yellow	8·00	5·75
P20		50c. black/salmon	12·50	5·75
P21		75c. carmine/grey	1·50	5·75
P22	2	80c. carmine	1·10	5·75
P23		1l.25 blue	1·50	5·75
P24		2l. sepia	1·10	5·75
P25		2l.50 vermilion	2·00	5·75
P26		5l. green	2·20	5·75
P27		10l. olive-black	1·80	5·75
P15/27	Set of 13		37·00	55·00

On T **2** the overprint is sideways in two lines "PER" reading upwards at left. "PACCHI" downwards at right.

1931 (1 Oct). PARCEL POST EXPRESS. Optd as Type P **4** reading vertically upwards at left, the letters shaped to avoid encroaching on the portrait.

PE15		2l. carmine	1·50	5·75
PE16		2l.50 blue	1·50	5·75

1931 (1 Oct). POSTAGE DUE. Surch or optd only, as Type D **4**.

D15	1	5c. brown/rose	20	55
D16		10c. grey-green/green	20	55
D17		20c. violet/lilac	1·50	1·80
D18		40c. on 30c. black/yellow	2·50	4·25
D19	2	60c on 2l. sepia	33·00	26·00
D20		1l.10 on 2l.50 vermilion	6·50	18·00
D15/20	Set of 6		40·00	46·00

In addition to they actual overprint, these Postage Due stamps bear an overprinted frame, in brown, composed of two lines and the letter "T" repeated around, and inside, its borders. This frame is larger than the design of the stamps and in practically all cases is cut into on one or more sides by the perforations.

4  **5**

(Des E. Federici. Recess Institut de Gravure, Paris)

1933 (3 Apr). "Holy Year" (1933-1934). P 13.

15	4	25c.+10c. green	6·75	4·75
16		75c.+15c. scarlet	14·00	15·00
17	5	80c.+20c. red-brown	36·00	22·00
18		1l.25+25c. ultramarine	10·50	16·00
15/18	Set of 4		60·00	50·00

6 Arms of Pope Pius XI 
7 Wing of Vatican Palace 
8 Vatican Gardens and Dome of St. Peter's

9 Pope Pius XI

10 St. Peter's Basilica
11 St. Peter's Keys 

440

VATICAN CITY 1933

(Eng F. Schirnböck (10 to 80c.), F. Federici (others). Recess)
1933 (31 May). W **11**. P 14.

19	**6**	5c. lake	10	10
20	**7**	10c. black and sepia	10	10
21		12½c. black and green	10	10
22		20c. black and orange	10	10
23		25c. black and olive	10	10
24	**8**	30c. chocolate and black	10	10
25		50c. chocolate and purple	10	10
26	**8**	75c. chocolate and lake	10	10
27		80c. chocolate and carmine-rose	10	10
28	**9**	1l. black and violet	4·25	2·75
29		1l.25 black and blue	15·00	5·50
30		2l. black and brown	36·00	22·00
31		2l.75 black and purple	44·00	45·00
32	**10**	5l. green and sepia	20	30
33		10l. deep green and blue	20	35
34		20l. green and black	35	45

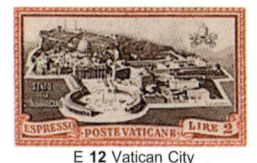

E **12** Vatican City
≡ 2,55 ≡ (12)

(Eng E. Federici and F. Schirnböck. Recess)
1933 (31 May). *EXPRESS LETTER*. W **11**. P 14.

E35	E **12**	2l. chocolate and carmine	35	35
E36		2l.50 chocolate and blue	35	65
19/E36 Set of 18			90·00	70·00

See also Nos. E107/8.

1934 (18 June). *Surch as T* **12** *by Tipografia Camerale Vaticana*. P 14.

35	**2**	40c.on 80c. carmine	3·75	2·20
36		1l.30 on 1l.25 blue	65·00	46·00
37		2l.05 on 2l. sepia	£150	16·00
		a. No comma between "2" and "05"	£300	26·00
38		2l.55 on 2l.50 vermilion	95·00	£180
		a. No comma between "2" and "5"	£160	£200
39		3l.05 on 5l. green	£300	£250
40		3l.70 on 10l. olive-black	£300	£475
35/40 Set of 6			£800	£850

There were two printings for all values; the surcharges of the second printing are generally wider than those of the first. In both printings there are variations in spacing and font e.g. three types of "5" exist in the surcharge on No 38, occurring in various combinations.
No. 37a occurs on positions 25 and 28 and No. 38a on position 1, both in the first printing.

13 Tribonian presenting Pandects to Justinian

14 Pope Julius II

15 Doves and Bell

(Des E. Federici. Photo)
1935 (1 Feb). *International Juridical Congress, Rome, 1934. Frescoes by Raphael*. P 14.

41	**13**	5c. orange	1·80	1·40
42		10c. violet	1·80	1·40

43		25c. green	6·25	4·75
44	**14**	75c. carmine	42·00	21·00
45		80c. brown	30·00	18·00
46		1l.25 blue	34·00	10·50
41/46 Set of 6			£200	50·00

Type **14** is erroneously inscribed as representing Pope Gregory IX.

(Des C. Mezzana, Photo)
1936 (22 June). *Catholic Press Exhibition, Rome. As T* **15** *(Inscr "ESPOSIZIONE MONDIALE DELLA STAMPA CATTOLICA 1936")*. P 14.

47	**15**	5c. blue-green	1·10	1·00
48		10c. black	1·10	1·00
49		25c. yellow-green	26·00	6·25
50	**15**	50c. purple	1·00	1·00
51	–	75c. carmine	26·00	24·00
52	–	80c. red-brown	1·40	2·10
53	–	1l.25 blue	1·25	2·10
54	–	5l. bistre-brown	1·25	5·75
47/54 Set of 8			55·00	39·00

Designs:—10c, 75c. Church and Bible, 25c., 80c. St. John Bosco; 1l.25, 5l. St. Francis of Sales.

16 Statue of St Peter

17 Ascension of Elijah

18 Crypt of Basilica of St. Cecilia

(Des C. Mezzana Recess)
1938 (22 June). *AIR. T* **16/17** *and similar designs*. W **11**. P 14.

55	**16**	25c. chocolate	10	10
56		50c. green	10	10
57	**17**	75c. lake	20	30
58		80c. deep blue	20	45
59	**16**	1l. violet	35	55
60	–	2l. bright blue	75	90
61	**17**	5l. black	1·80	2·00
62		10l. purple	1·80	2·00
55/62 Set of 8			4·75	5·75

Designs:—50c., 2l. Dove carrying olive branch and St. Peter's Square: 80c, 10l. Transportation of the Holy House.

(Des C. Mezzana. Photo)
1938 (12 Oct). *International Christian Archaeological Congress, Rome. T* **18** *and similar type*. P 14.

63	**18**	5c. sepia	20	25
64		10c. orange-vermilion	20	25
65		25c. green	30	30
66	–	75c. scarlet	7·25	6·25
67		80c. bright violet	22·00	19·00
68		1l.25 blue	29·00	24·00
63/68 Set of 6			50·00	45·00

Design:—75c. to 1l.25, Basilica of Saints Nereus and Achilles in the catacombs of Domitilla.

SEDE VACANTE
MCMXXXIX
(19)

441

VATICAN CITY   1939

20 Coronation    **21** Arms of Pope Pius XII    **22** Pope Pius XII

1939 (20 Feb). *Death of Pope Pius XI. Optd with T* **19** *("See Vacant")*.
69	**1**	5c. brown/*rose*	31·00	7·25
70		10c. grey-green/*green*	35	25
71		20c. violet/*lilac*	35	25
72		25c. blue/*azure*	3·75	3·50
73		30c. black/*yellow*	75	20
74		50c. black/*salmon*	75	25
75		75c. carmine/*grey*	75	25
69/75	Set of 7		34·00	10·50

(Des C. Mezzana. Photo)

1939 (2 June). *Coronation of Pope Pius XI.* P 14.
76	**20**	25c. green	1·30	35
77		75c. carmine-red	30	50
78		80c. blight violet	3·75	2·75
79		1l.25 blue	30	50
76/79	Set of 4		5·00	3·50

(Des C. Mezzana. Portraits eng Nicastro and Richelli. Recess)

1940 (12 Mar). *First Anniv of Coronation of Pope Pius XII. T* **21** *and portraits as T* **22**. W **11**. P 14.
80	**21**	5c. lake	10	10
81	**22**	1l. black and violet	20	10
82		1l.25 black and blue	20	10
83	**22**	2l. black and brown	75	1·10
84		2l.75 black and purple	1·30	2·20
80/84	Set of 5		2·25	3·25

Design:—1l.25, 2l.75; as T **22**, but showing portrait of the Pope facing left.
For other values and colours in T **21**/2, see Nos. 99/106.

23    **24** Consecration of Archbishop Pacelli    **25** Raphael (painter self-portrait)

(Des G. Rondini. Photo)

1942 (1 Sept). *Prisoners of War Relief Fund (1st series).* Inscr "MCMXLII". P 14.
85	**23**	25c. blue-green	10	20
86		80c. chestnut-brown	10	20
87		1l.25 blue	10	20

See also Nos. 92/4 and 107/9.

(Des C. Mezzana. Photo)

1943 (16 Jan). *Pope's Episcopal Silver Jubilee.* P 14.
88	**24**	25c. blue-green and grey-green	10	10
89		80c. chocolate and yellow-brown	10	20
90		1l.25 blue and ultramarine	10	20
91		5l. indigo and olive-black	15	35
88/91	Set of 4		40	80

1944 (31 Jan). *Prisoners of War Relief Fund (2nd series). As T* **23**, *but inscr* "MCMXLIII". P 14.
92	**23**	25c. blue-green	10	10
93		80c. chestnut-brown	10	10
94		1l.25 blue	10	15

(Des C. Mezzana. Photo)

1944 (21 Nov). *Fourth Centenary of Pontifical Academy of the Virtuosi of the Pantheon. As T* **25** *(inscr "1543–1943").* W **11**. P 14.
95		25c. olive and deep green	20	20
96		80c. violet and red-lilac	30	35
97		1l.25 blue and deep violet	30	30
98		10l. bistre and brownish yellow	55	1·80
95/98	Set of 4		1·20	2·40

Designs:—80c Antonio da Sangallo (architect); 1l.25, Carlo Maratti (painter) (after Francesco Maratta); 10l. Antonio Canova (sculptor, self-portrait).

1945 (5 Mar). *T* **21** *and portraits as T* **22**. Recess. P 14.
99	**21**	5c. grey	10	10
100		30c. brown	10	10
101		50c. green	10	10
102	–	1l. black and brown	15	10
103	–	1l.50 black and red	10	10
104	–	2l.50 black and blue	15	15
105	**22**	5l. black and lilac	20	25
106		20l. black and green	35	40

Design:—1l. to 2l.50, as T **22**, but portrait of the Pope facing left.

1945 (5 Mar). EXPRESS LETTER. Recess. P 14.
E107	E **12**	3l.50 blue and carmine	45	55
E108		5l. green and blue	75	1·00
99/E108	Set of 10		2·25	2·50

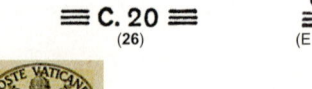

≡ C. 20 ≡
(26)

6
(E 27)

≡ C.25 ≡   ≡ C. 25 ≡
D 26   A   B

≡ L. 1 ≡   ≡ L. 1 ≡
       C   D

(Des C. Mezzana. Recess, background litho)

1945 (20 Aug). POSTAGE DUE. *Printed in black on burelage background in colour given.* P 14.

A, 1st Printing.
D107A	D **26**	5c. *yellow*	10	10
D108A		20c. *violet*	10	10
D109A		80c. *red*	10	10
D110A		1l. *green*	10	10
D111A		2l. *blue*	10	10
D112A		5l. *grey*	15	15
D107A/112A	Set of 6		60	60

B, 2nd Printing.
D107B	D **26**	5c. *yellow*	15·00	13·00
D108B		20c. *violet*	60·00	15·00
D109B		80c. *red*	2·00	1·30
D110B		1l. *green*	2·50	2·10
D111B		2l. *blue*	2·50	2·10
D112B		5l. *grey*	90·00	42·00
D107B/112B	Set of 6		£150	70·00

In the 1st printing the lines of the background are narrower than the white spaces in between and in the 2nd printing they are wider than the white spaces.

1945 (1 Sept). *Prisoners of War Relief Fund (3rd series). As T* **23**, *but inscr* "MCMXLIV". Wmk Winged Wheel. P 14.
107	**23**	1l. green	10	15
108		3l. carmine	10	15
109		5l. blue	10	15

VATICAN CITY   1946

1946 (9 Jan). *Nos. 99/106 surch as T* **26**.
110	**21**	20c.on 5c. grey	10	10
111		25c.on 30c. brown (A)	10	10
		a. Type B	10	10
112		1l.on 50c. green (C)	10	10
		a. Type D	4·75	4·50
113	—	1l.50 on 1l. black & brown (B)	10	10
114	—	3l.on 1l.50 black and red	30	10
115	—	5l.on 21.50 black and blue	45	25
116	**22**	10l.on 5l. black and lilac	1·60	65
117		30l.on 20l. black and green	4·25	2·20

The two types of the 25c. and 1l. come from different printings.

1946 (9 Jan). EXPRESS LETTER. *Nos. E107/8 surch as Type E* **27**.
E118	**E 12**	6l.on 3l.50 blue and carmine	5·50	2·75
E119		12l.on 5l. green and blue	5·50	2·75
110/E119	Set of 10		10·00	5·50

27 St. Ignatius of Loyola

E 28 Matthew Giberti, Bishop of Verona

(Des C. Mezzana. Photo)

1946 (20 Feb). *Fourth Centenary of Inauguration of Council of Trent.* P 14.

(*a*) POSTAGE As *T* **27** (*inscr* "CONCILIVM OECVMENICVM XIX" *etc.*).
118		5c. sepia and olive-bistre	25	25
119		25c. sepia and violet	25	25
120		50c. sepia and orange-brown	25	25
121		75c. sepia and black	25	25
122		1l. sepia and purple	25	25
123		1l.50 sepia and vermilion	25	25
124		2l. sepia and green	25	25
125		2l.50 sepia and blue	25	25
126		3l. sepia and scarlet	25	25
127		4l. sepia and yellow-bistre	25	25
128		5l. sepia and ultramarine	25	25
129		10l. sepia and carmine	25	25

Designs:— 5c. Trent Cathedral; 25c. St. Angela Marini; 50c. St. Anthony Maria Zaccaria; 1l. St. Caletan of Thiene; 1l.50, St. John Fisher, Bishop of Rochester; 2l. Cristoforo Madrussi, Bishop of Trent; 2l.50. Reginald Pole, Archbishop of Canterbury; 3l. Marcello Cervini; 4l. Giovanni Maria Del Monte; 5l. Emperor Charles V; 10l. Pope Paul III Farnese.

(*b*) EXPRESS LETTER. Type *E* **28** *and similar horiz design.*
E130		6l. sepia and green	20	20
E131		12l. sepia and red-brown	20	20
118/E131	Set of 14		3·00	3·00

Design:— 12l. Cardinal Gaspare Contarini Bishop of Belluno.

28 Dove with Olive Branch over St. Peter's Forecourt

29 Barn Swallows circling Spire of St. Peter's Basilica

(Des C. Mezzana. Photo)

1947 (10 Nov). AIR. *T* **28/29** *and similar designs.* W **11**. P 14.
130	**28**	1l. carmine	10	10
131	—	4l. sepia	10	10
132	**28**	5l. blue	10	10
133	**29**	15l. violet	1·30	1·10
134	—	25l. blue-green	4·50	2·40
135	**29**	50l. black	6·50	4·25
136		100l. red-orange	31·00	8·00
130/136	Set of 7		39·00	14·00

Design:—4l., 25l. Transportation of the Holy House.

30 "Raphael accompanying Tobias" (after Botticelli)

(Des M. Canfarini. Eng C. Mezzana. Recess)

1948 (28 Dec). AIR. W **11**. P 14.
137	**30**	250l. violet-black	36·00	7·25
138		500l. ultramarine	£550	£350

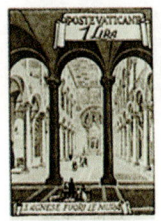

31 St. Agnes's Basilica

32 Pope Pius XII

(Des C. Mezzana. Eng M. Canfarini (100l.). Recess (100l.), photo (others))

1949 (7 Mar). As *T* **31** *(1l. to 40l.) and T* **32**. W **11**.

A. P 14.
139A		1l. drab	10	10
140A		3l. deep violet	10	10
141A		5l. red-orange	10	10
142A		8l. deep blue-green	15	15
143A		13l. deep dull green	3·25	3·25
144A		16l. olive-grey	30	30
145A		25l. rosine	6·50	85
146A		35l. bright mauve	36·00	16·00
147A		40l. blue	30	20
148A		100l. black	4·00	4·00
139A/148A	Set of 10		46·00	28·00

B. P 14 × 13 (1 to 8l.) or 13 × 14 (others).
139B		1l. drab	20	20
140B		3l. deep violet	20	20
141B		5l. red-orange	18·00	8·50
142B		8l. deep blue-green	20	20
143B		13l. deep dull green	6·00	3·50
144B		16l. olive-grey	40	25
145B		25l. rosine	8·50	85
146B		35l. bright mauve	38·00	17·00
147B		40l. blue	40	25
139B/147B	Set of 9		65·00	28·00

Basilicas: *Vert*—3l. St Clement; 5l. St. Praxedes; 8l. St. Mary in Cosmedin *Horiz*—13l. Holy Cross; 16l. St. Sebastian; 25l. St. Laurence's; 35l. St. Paul's; 40l. Sta. Maria Maggiore.

443

VATICAN CITY   1949

E **33** St John's Basilica    **33** Angels over Globe

(Des C. Mezzana. Photo)

1949 (7 Mar). *EXPRESS LETTER. Type E **33** and similar type.*
W **11**. P 14 or 13 × 14.
E149   40l. grey . . . .   14·50   4·50
E150   80l. red-brown . . . .   50·00   28·00
Design:—40l. St Peter's Basilica.

(Des N. Ena. Eng M. Colombati. Recess)

1949 (3 Dec). *AIR. 75th Anniv of Universal Postal Union.* W **11**.
P 14.
149   **33**   300l. ultramarine . . . .   27·00   11·00
150   —   1000l. green . . . .   £130   90·00

34 "I will Give You the Keys of the Kingdom"    **35** Guards Marching    **36** Pope Proclaiming Dogma

(Des C. Mezzana (6l., 8l., 25l., 30l.), N. Ena (10l., 60l.). Photo)

1949 (24 Dec). *"Holy Year". T **34** and similar types inscr "ANNO SANTO MCML".* Wmk Winged Wheel (sideways). P 14.
151   **34**   5l. brown and red-brown   10   10
152   —   6l. yellow-brown and black   10   10
153   —   8l. blue-green and blue   90   50
154   —   10l. grey-blue and green   30   10
155   **34**   20l. red-brown and blue-green . .   1·50   35
156   —   25l. bright blue and brown   75   35
157   —   30l. bright purple and blue-green   1·80   1·10
158   —   60l. scarlet and deep brown . . .   1·20   1·10
151/158 Set of 8 . . . .   6·00   3·25
Designs:—6l., 25l. Four Basilicas; 8l., 30l. Pope Boniface VIII; 10l., 60l. Pope Pius XII opening the Holy Door.

(Des C. Mezzana. Photo)

1950 (12 Sept). *Centenary of Papal Guard.* Wmk Winged Wheel (sideways). P 14.
159   **35**   25l. sepia . . . .   5·75   4·00
160   —   35l. blue-green . . . .   3·25   4·00
161   —   55l. red-brown . . . .   1·80   4·00

(Des C. Mezzana. Photo)

1951 (8 May). *Proclamation of Dogma of the Assumption. T **36** and similar type inscr "GAVDENT ANGELI".* P 14.
162   —   25l. brown-purple . . . .   10·00   90
163   —   55l. blue . . . .   4·25   13·50
Design:— 55l. Angels over St Peter's.

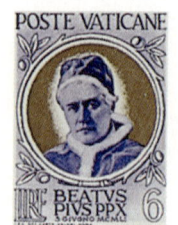

37 Pope Pius X    **38** Final Session of Council (fresco)

(Des C. Mezzana. Photo)

1951 (3 June). *Beatification of Pope Pius X. T **37** and similar portrait inscr "BEATVS PIVS PPX".* W **11**. P 14 × 13.
164   **37**   6l. gold and violet   10   15
165   —   10l. gold and green   15   15
166   —   60l. gold and light blue . . . . .   7·25   7·25
167   —   115l. gold and brown . . . .   22·00   22·00
164/167 Set of 4 . . . .   26·00   26·00
Designs:—60l., 115l. Pope looking left.

(Des C. Mezzana. Eng M. Colombati (T **38**), and T. Cionini (others). Recess)

1951 (31 Oct). *1500th Anniv of Council of Chalcedon. T **38** and similar horiz type inscr "CONCILIO DI CALCEDONIA", etc.* W **11**. P 14 × 13.
168   **38**   5l. slate   35   35
169   —   25l. brown-lake . . . .   3·00   2·40
170   **38**   35l. carmine . . . .   5·75   4·50
171   —   60l. blue . . . .   18·00   14·50
172   **38**   100l. brown . . . .   55·00   36·00
168/172 Set of 5 . . . .   70·00   50·00
Design:—25l., 60l. "Pope Leo I meeting Attila" (Raphael).

39 Gratian   **(40)**

(Des C. Mezzana. Eng V. Nicastro. Recess)

1951 (20 Dec). *AIR. 8th Centenary of Decree of Gratian.* W **11**. P 14 × 13.
173   **39**   300l. reddish purple £300   £200
174   —   500l. blue . . . .   36·00   18·00

1952 (7 Mar). *No. 143, surch with T **40**.*
175   12l. on 13l. dull green (R.) . . . .   1·60   95

41 Mail Coach and First Stamp    **42** St. Maria Goretti

444

VATICAN CITY 1952

(Des C. Mezzana. Eng M. Canfarini. Recess)
1952 (9 June). *Centenary of First Papal States' Stamp.* W **11**. P 13 × 13½ or 13 × 12½ (No **MS**176a).
176 41 50l. black and blue/*cream* . . . . . 4·25 4·25
MS176a 112 × 121 mm. No. 176 (block of four) £170 £170

(Des C. Dabrowska. Photo)
1953 (12 Feb). *50th Anniv of Martyrdom of St. Maria Goretti.* W **11**. P 14.
177 42 15l. violet and brown . . . . . 4·25 2·50
178   35l. brown and carmine-red . . . 3·00 2·20

43 St. Peter and Inscription
44 Dome of St. Peter's 

(Des C. Mezzana. Eng T. Cionini (5l., 100l.), S. Vana (12l., 25l.), M. Colombati (20l., 35l.), F. Pagani (45l.) and V. Nicastro (others). Recess)
1953 (23 Apr). *St. Peter's Basilica.* T **43** and similar vert designs. W **11**. P 14 (5, 12, 35, 60l) or 13½ (others).
179 3l. black and brown-lake 10 10
180 5l. black and deep slate 10 10
181 10l. black and green 10 10
182 12l. black and orange-brown . . . 10 10
183 20l. black and violet 20 10
184 25l. black and deep red-brown . . 10 10
185 35l. black and carmine-red 10 10
186 45l. black and sepia 20 20
187 60l. black and deep blue 10 10
188 65l. black and carmine 30 20
189 100l. black and plum 10 10
Designs:—5l. Pius XII and Roman sepulchre, 10l. St. Peter's tomb. 12l. St. Sylvester I and Constantine's basilica (previous building), 20l. Julius II and Bramante's design, 25l. Paul III and apse. 35l. Sixtus V and cupola; 45l. Paul V and fa ade, 60l. Urban VIII and baldaquin, 65l. Alexander VII and colonnade, 100l. Pius VI and sacristy.

(Des C. Mezzana. Eng V. Nicastro (50l). T. Cionini (85l.) Recess)
1953 (23 Apr). *EXPRESS LETTER. As T* **43** *but inscr* "ESPRESSO". W **11**. P 14.
E190 50l. deep red-brown & deep turquoise 20 20
E191 85l. deep red-brown and orange . . . 35 25
179/E191 *Set of 13* . . . . 1·80 1·60
Designs:—50l. St. Peter and tomb; 85l. Pius XII and sepulchre.

(Des E. Pizzi. Eng M. Colombati. Recess)
1953 (10 Aug)—60. *AIR.* W **11**.
190 44 500l. red-brown & dp brown (*p* 13) . . . . 24·00 8·25
190a   500l. green and deep turquoise-green (*p* 13) (31.1.58) . 7·25 3·75
         b. Perf 14 ('60) £900 £600
191   1000l. blue and deep blue (*p* 13) 65·00 15·00
191a   1000l. carmine and lake (*p* 14) (31.1.58) 75 75
         b. Perf 13 ('60) . . . . 1·00 1·00

45 St. Clare of Assisi (after Grotto)
46 "St. Bernard" (after Lippi) 

(T **45/6** des E. Pizzi. Photo)
1953 (12 Aug). *700th Death Anniv of St. Clare (founder of Poor Clares Order).* P 13.
192 45 25l. dp brown, yellow-brown & turq-bl . . . . . . 1·80 1·80
193   35l. brown, yellow-brown & brown-red . . . . . 18·00 16·00

1953 (10 Nov). *800th Death Anniv of St. Bernard of Clairvaux.* P 13.
194 46 20l. brown-purple & deep olive-green 75 75
195   60l. bronze-green and blue . . . 7·25 6·50

47 Lombard's Episcopal Seal
48 Pope Pius XI and Vatican City 

(T **47/8** des F. Pizzi. Photo)
1953 (29 Dec). *800th Anniv of Libri Sententiarium (theological treatise by Peter Lombard, Bishop of Paris).* P 13.
196 47 100l. greenish yellow, blue and crimson . . . . 44·00 33·00

1954 (12 Feb). *25th Anniv of Lateran Treaty.* W **11**. P 13.
197 48 25l. brown lake, buff and pale blue . . . . . . 1·10 90
198   60l. deep blue, grey & yellow brown . . . . . . 3·25 3·00

D **49** State Arms

(Des B. Anderlini. Recess, background litho)
1954 (30 Apr). *POSTAGE DUE. Burelage background in colours shown in brackets.* W **11**. P 14.
D199 D **49** 4l. black (*red*) 10 10
D200   6l. black (*green*) 15 15
D201   10l. black (*yellow*) 10 10
D202   20l. black (*blue*) 30 30
D203   50l. black (*sepia*) 10 10
D204   70l. black (*chocolate*) . . 10 10
D199/204 *Set of 6* 75 75

445

VATICAN CITY 1954

49 Pope Pius XII
50 St. Pius X 

(Des E. Pizzi. Eng M. Canfarini (T **49**), V. Nicastro (others). Recess)

1954 (26 May). *Marian Year and Centenary of Dogma of the Immaculate Conception.* T **49** and similar portrait inscr "1854–1954". W **11**. P 13.
199	–	3l. violet	10	10
200	**49**	4l. carmine	10	10
201	–	6l. crimson	10	10
202	**49**	12l. turquoise green	1·10	90
203	–	20l. brown	90	90
204	**49**	35l. bright blue	1·80	1·60
199/204	*Set of 6*		3·75	3·25

Portrait:— 3l., 6l., 20l., Pope Pius IX facing right.

(Des E. Pizzi. Photo)

1954 (29 May). *Canonization of Pope Pius X.* W **11**. P 13.
205	**50**	10l. yellow, lake and sepia	20	20
206		25l. yellow, lake and dull violet	2·75	2·00
207		35l. yellow, lake and grey black	4·25	3·75

51 Basilica of St. Francis of Assisi
52 "St. Augustine" (after Botticelli) 

(Des P.G. Lerario. Photo)

1954 (1 Oct). *200th Anniv of Elevation of Basilica of St. Francis of Assisi to Papal Chapel.* W **11**. P 14.
208	**51**	20l. violet-black and cream	1·80	1·10
209		35l. deep brown and cream	1·50	1·80

(Des E. Pizzi Photo)

1954 (13 Nov). *1600th Anniv of Birth of St. Augustine.* W **11**. P 14.
210	**52**	35l. deep turquoise-green	90	75
211		50l. brown	1·60	1·50

53 Madonna of Ostra Brama, Vilna
54 St. Boniface and Fulda Cathedral 

(Des C. Dabrowska. Photo)

1954 (7 Dec). *Termination of Marian Year.* W **11**. P 13.
212	**53**	20l. yellow, blue, sepia and carmine	1·30	90
213		35l. yellow, sepia, carmine and blue	9·75	8·25
214		60l. yellow, carmine, blue and sepia	16·00	14·50

(Des E. Pizzi. Eng M. Canfarini. Recess)

1955 (28 Apr). *1200th Anniv of Martyrdom of St. Boniface.* W **11**. P 13.
215	**54**	10l. slate-green	10	10
216		35l. violet	55	45
217		60l. deep turquoise-green	85	75

55 "Pope Sixtus II and St. Lawrence" (fresco, Niccolina Chapel)
56 Pope Nicholas V 
57 St. Bartholomew 

(Des R. Pierbattista. Photo)

1955 (27 June). *Fifth Death Centenary of Fra Giovanni da Fiesole, "Fra Angelico" (painter).* W **11** (sideways). P 14.
218	**55**	50l. carmine-red and azure	4·25	2·75
219		100l. blue and flesh	3·00	2·75

(Des E. Pizzi (after Fra Angelico). Photo)

1955 (28 Nov). *Fifth Death Centenary of Pope Nicholas V.* W **11** (sideways). P 14.
220	**56**	20l. sepia and turquoise-blue	30	20
221		35l. sepia and carmine rose	35	30
222		60l. sepia and bright green	65	65

(Des M. Melis. Photo)

1955 (29 Dec). *Ninth Death Centenary of St. Bartholomew the Young.* W **11**. P 14.
223	**57**	10l. black and sepia	10	10
224		25l. black and carmine-red	45	35
225		100l. black and deep bluish green	2·20	1·70

58 "Annunciation" (Melozzo da Forlì)
59 Corporal of the Guard

(Des C. Dabrowska. Eng V. Nicastro (T **58**), F. Pagani (10l., 35l., 100l.), M. Colombati (15l., 50l., 300l.). Recess)

1956 (22 Feb). *AIR.* T **58** and similar vert designs showing paintings. W **11** (sideways). P 13.
226	**58**	5l. black	10	10
227	–	10l. deep turquoise-green	10	10

VATICAN CITY   1956

228	—	15l. orange	...	30	30
229	58	25l. carmine	...	10	10
230	—	35l. carmine-red	...	3·00	3·00
231	—	50l. sepia	...	10	10
232	58	60l. deep bright blue	...	55	55
233	—	100l. orange-brown	...	10	10
234	—	300l. slate-violet	...	65	65
226/234 Set of 9				4·50	4·50

Designs:—10l., 35l., 100l., "Annunciation" (P. Cavallini); 15l., 50l., 300l. "Annunciation" (Leonardo da Vinci).

(Des C. Dabrowska. Eng T. Cionini (4l., 35l.), V. Nicastro (6l., 50l.), M. Colombati (10l., 60l.). Recess)

1956 (27 Apr). *450th Anniv of Swiss Guard.* T **59** *and similar vert designs inscr* "GUARDIA SVIZZERA PONTIFICIA". W **11** (sideways). P 13.

235	—	4l. carmine	...	15	10
236	59	6l. red-orange	...	15	10
237	—	10l. deep blue	...	15	10
238	—	35l. deep brown	...	55	55
239	59	50l. bluish violet	...	75	75
240	—	60l. deep turquoise-green	...	85	85
235/240 Set of 6				2·30	2·20

Designs:—4l., 35l. Captain Roust; 10l., 60l. Two drummers.

60 St. Rita

61 St. Ignatius presenting Jesuit Constitution to Pope Paul III

(Des C. Dabrowska. Photo)

1956 (19 May). *Fifth Death Centenary of St. Rita at Cascia.* W **11**. P 14.

241	60	10l. greenish grey	...	10	10
242	—	25l. sepia	...	55	55
243	—	35l. blue	...	40	40

(Des C. Dabrowska. Eng M. Canfarini. Recess)

1956 (31 July). *Fourth Death Centenary of St. Ignatius of Loyola.* W **11** (sideways). P 13.

244	61	35l. brown	...	55	55
245	—	60l. slate	...	90	90

62 St. John of Capistrano

63 Madonna and Child

(Des C. Dabrowska. Eng V. Nicastro. Recess)

1956 (30 Oct). *Fifth Death Centenary of St. John of Capistrano.* W **11** (sideways). P 14.

246	62	25l. green and slate-black	...	2·00	2·00
247	—	35l. deep brown and brown-purple	...	75	75

(Des C. Dabrowska. Eng M. Colombati. Recess)

1956 (20 Dec). *"Black Madonna" of Czestochowa Commemoration.* W **11** (sideways). P 14.

248	63	35l. black and deep blue	...	35	35
249	—	60l. ultramarine and grey-green	...	45	45
250	—	100l. claret and sepia	...	65	60

64 St. Domenico Savio

65 Cardinal D. Capranica (founder) and Capranica College

(Des C. Dabrowska. Eng M. Colombati. Recess)

1957 (21 Mar). *Death Centenary of St. Domenico Savio.* T **64** *and similar design.* W **11** (sideways). P 13.

251	64	4l. brown	...	10	10
252	—	6l. carmine	...	10	10
253	64	25l. green	...	20	20
254	—	60l. ultramarine	...	1·20	85
251/254 Set of 4				1·40	1·10

Designs:—6l., 60l. St. Domenico Savio and St. John Bosco.

(Des Veroi. Eng V. Nicastro (5l., 35l.) Des C. Dabrowska. Eng E. Donnini (10l., 100l.), Recess)

1957 (27 June). *Fifth Centenary of Capranica College.* T **65** *and similar horiz design.* W **11**. P 13.

255	65	5l. crimson-lake	...	10	10
256	—	10l. brown	...	10	10
257	65	35l. deep slate	...	10	10
258	—	100l. bright blue	...	65	65
255/258 Set of 4				85	85

Design:—10l., 100l. Pope Pius XII and plaque.

66 Pontifical Academy of Science

(Des Andreina Grassellini. Photo)

1957 (9 Oct). *20th Anniv of the Pontifical Academy of Science.* W **11**. P 14.

259	66	35l. myrtle-green and deep blue	...	55	45
260	—	60l. blue and deep bistre-brown	...	55	55

67 Mariazell Basilica

68 Apparition of Virgin Mary

447

VATICAN CITY   1957

(Des C. Dabrowska. Eng V. Nicastro (T **67**). M. Canfarini (Nos. 262, 264). Recess)

1957 (14 Nov). *800th Anniv of Mariazell Basilica. T* **67** *and similar horiz design.* W **11**. P 13.

261	67	5l. green	10	10
262	–	15l. slate-black	10	10
263	67	60l. ultramarine	85	85
264	–	100l. violet	1·00	1·00
261/264		Set of 4	1·80	1·80

Design:—15l., 100l. Statue of the Virgin of Mariazell within Sanctuary.

(Des C. Dabrowska. Eng S. Vana (T **68**), F. Pagani (10l., 35l.), V. Nicastro (15l., 100l.) Recess)

1958 (21 Feb). *Centenary of the Apparition of the Virgin Mary at Lourdes. T* **68** *and similar vert designs.* W **11**. P 13 × 14.

265	68	5l. deep blue	10	10
266	–	10l. deep turquoise-green	10	10
267	–	15l. brown	10	10
268	68	25l. carmine	10	10
269	–	35l. sepia	10	10
270	–	100l. violet	10	10
265/270		Set of 6	55	55

Designs:—10l., 35l. Invalid at Lourdes, 15l., 100l. St. Bernadette.

69 "Civtas Dei" ("City of God" at Exhibition)

70 Pope Clement XIII (from sculpture by A. Canova)

(Des C. Dabrowska. Eng F. Tulli (T **69**), A Quieti (others). Recess)

1958 (19 June). *Brussels International Exhibition. T* **69** *and similar vert design.* W **11**. P 13 (35l.) or 13 × 14 (others).

271	–	35l. deep claret	30	30
272	69	60l. deep orange-red	65	65
273	–	100l. violet	1·60	1·50
274	–	300l. ultramarine	1·10	1·30
271/274		Set of 4	3·25	3·25
MS274a		91 × 149 mm. Nos. 271/4. P 13	20·00	20·00

Design:—35l., 300l. Pope Pius XII.

(Des C. Dabrowska. Eng A. Quieti (5l.), M. Canfarini (10l.), M. Colombati. (35l.), V. Mastrangelo (100l.). Recess)

1958 (2 July). *Birth Bicentenary of Antonio Canova (sculptor). T* **70** *and similar vert designs.* W **11**. P 14.

275		5l. brown	10	10
276		10l. carmine	10	10
277		35l. slate-green	30	20
278		100l. deep blue	90	90
275/278		Set of 4	1·25	1·20

Designs: (from sculptures by A Canova)—10l. Pope Clement XIV; 35l. Pope Pius VI; 100l. Pope Pius VII.

71 St. Peter's Keys

(Des A. Grassellini. Photo)

1958 (21 Oct). *"Vacant See".* W **11**. P 14.

279	71	15l. sepia/*yellow*	1·40	75
280		25l. sepia	10	10
281		60l. sepia/*lavender*	10	10

72 Pope John XXIII

73 St. Lawrence

(Des A. Grassellini. Photo)

1959 (2 Apr). *Coronation of Pope John XXIII. T* **72** *and similar vert design inscr "IV-XI MCMLVIII".* W **11** (sideways). P 14.

282	72	25l. multicoloured	10	10
283	–	35l. multicoloured	10	10
284	72	60l. multicoloured	10	10
285	–	100l. multicoloured	10	10
282/285		Set of 4	35	35

Design:—35l., 100l. Arms of Pope John XXIII.

(Des A. Grassellini. Photo)

1959 (25 May). *1700th Death Anniv (15 to 100l. in 1958) of Martyrs under Valerian. Vert portraits as T* **73**. W **11** (sideways). P 14.

286		15l. red-brown, yellow and red	10	10
287		25l. red-brown, yellow & reddish lilac	10	10
288		50l. red-brown, yellow, black & turn-bl	10	15
289		60l. red-brown, yellow & bronze-green	10	15
290		100l. red-brown, yellow & brown-purple	10	15
291		300l. sepia and yellow-brown	35	35
286/291		Set of 6	75	90

Portraits:—25l. Pope Sixtus II; 50l. St. Agapitus, 60l. St. Filisissimus; 100l. St. Cyprian; 300l. St. Fructuosus.

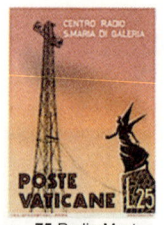

74 Pope Pius XI

75 Radio Mast

(Des A. Grassellini. Photo)

1959 (25 May). *30th Anniv of Lateran Treaty.* W **11** (sideways). P 14.

292	74	30l. deep brown	10	10
293		100l. deep violet-blue	20	20

(Des A. Grassellini Photo)

1959 (27 Oct). *2nd Anniv of St. Maria di Galeria Radio Station Vatican City.* W **11** (sideways). P 14.

294	75	25l. rose, yellow and black	10	10
295		60l. yellow, red and blue	15	25

448

VATICAN CITY   1959

76 Obelisk and St. John Lateran Basilica

77 St. Casimir, Vilna Palace and Cathedral

80 Transept of St. John Lateran Basilica

81 "The Flight into Egypt" (after Beato Angelico)

(Des Andreina Grassellini. Eng R. Di Giuseppe (5, 50l.), S Mattei (10, 60l.). A. Quieti (15, 100l.), O. Torcolini (25, 200l.), F. Pagani (35, 500l.). Recess)

1959 (27 Oct). *AIR. Roman Obelisks. Various vert designs as T* **76**. W **11**. P 13 × 14.

296	76	5l. violet	10	10
297	–	10l. blue-green	10	10
298	–	15l. sepia	10	10
299	–	25l. deep bronze-green	10	10
300	–	35l. ultramarine	10	10
301	76	50l. green	10	10
302	–	60l. crimson	10	10
303	–	100l. indigo	15	10
304	–	200l. brown	20	15
305	–	500l. orange-brown	35	35
296/305		*Set of* 10	1·30	1·20

Designs:— 10, 60l. Obelisk and Church of Sta. Maria Maggiore, 15, 100l. Vatican Obelisk and Apostolic Palace; 25, 200l. Obelisk and Churches of St. Mary in Montesanto and St Mary of the Miracles, Piazza del Popolo; 35, 500l. Sallustian Obelisk and Trinita dei Monti Church.

(Des V. K. Jonynas. Eng A. Quieti. Recess)

1959 (14 Dec). *Fifth Birth Centenary of St. Casimir (patron saint of Lithuania).* W **11**. P 14.

| 306 | 77 | 50l. brown | 10 | 10 |
| 307 | – | 100l. myrtle-green | 20 | 20 |

78 "Christ Adored by the Magi" (after Raphael)

79 "St. Antoninus" (after Dupré)

(Des C. Dabrowska. Eng M. Colombati. Recess)

1959 (14 Dec). *Christmas.* W **11**. P 13 × 14.

308	78	15l. black	10	10
309	–	25l. crimson	10	10
310	–	60l. ultramarine	20	25

(Des A. Grassellini. Eng M. Canfarini (T **79**), A. Quieti (others). Recess)

1960 (29 Feb). *5th Death Centenary of St. Antoninus of Florence. T* **79** *and similar vert design inscr* "S. ANTONINUS MCDLIX MCMLIX". W **11**. P 13 × 14.

311	79	15l. ultramarine	10	10
312	–	25l. deep turquoise-green	10	10
313	79	60l. deep brown	30	25
314	–	110l. claret	45	45
311/314		*Set of* 4	85	80

Design:—25l., 110l. "St Antoninus preaching sermon" (after Portigiani).

(Des A. Grassellini. Photo)

1960 (29 Feb). *Roman Diocesan Synod.* W **11**. P 14.

| 315 | 80 | 15l. sepia | 10 | 10 |
| 316 | – | 60l. black | 15 | 20 |

(Des A. Grassellini)

1960 (7 Apr). *World Refugee Year. Vert designs as T* **81** *inscr* "ANNO MONDIALE DEL RIFUGIATO". W **11** (sideways). P 14.

317	81	5l. deep green	10	10
318	–	10l. sepia	10	10
319	–	25l. carmine-red	20	15
320	81	60l. reddish violet	30	30
321	–	100l. ultramarine	1·10	95
322	–	300l. deep bluish green	1·00	85
317/322		*Set of* 6	2·50	2·20

Designs:—10, 100l. "St. Peter giving Alms" (Masaccio). 25, 300l. "Madonna of Mercy" (Piero della Francesca).

82 Cardinal Sarto (Pius X) leaving Venice for Conclave in Rome

83 "Feeding the Hungry"

(Des C. Dabrowska. Eng M. Colombati (15l.), M. Canfarini (35l.), V. Nicastro (60l.). Recess)

1960 (11 Apr). *First Anniv of Transfer of Relics of Pope Pius X from Rome to Venice. T* **82** *and similar vert designs inscr* "XI. IV MCMLIX" (35l.) *or* "XII-IV-MCMLIX" (60l.). W **11** (sideways). P 13 × 14 (35l.) or 13 (others).

323	82	15l. light brown	20	25
324	–	35l. crimson	75	65
325	–	60l. deep turquoise-green	1·40	1·20

Designs:—35l. Pope John XXIII kneeling before relics of Pope Pius X; 60l. Relics in procession across St. Mark's Square, Venice.

(Des A. Grassellini (after Delia Robbia). Photo)

1960 (8 Nov). *"Corporal Works of Mercy".* W **11**. P 14.

(a) POSTAGE. *Horiz designs as T* **83**.

326		5l. sepia and red-brown	10	10
327		10l. sepia and deep bluish-green	10	10
328		15l. sepia and black	10	10
329		20l. sepia and crimson	10	10
330		30l. sepia and bluish violet	10	10
331		35l. sepia and chocolate	10	10
332		40l. sepia and red-orange	10	10
333		70l. sepia and yellow-ochre	10	10

VATICAN CITY   1960

Designs:—10l. "Giving drinks to the thirsty"; 15l. "Clothing the naked"; 20l. "Sheltering the homeless"; 30l. "Visiting the sick"; 35l. "Visiting the imprisoned"; 40l. "Burying the dead"; 70l. Pope John XXIII between "Faith" and "Charity".

(b) EXPRESS LETTER. As T **83** inscr "ESPRESSO".
E334	75l. sepia and scarlet		10	10
E335	100l. sepia and deep blue		10	10
326/E335	Set of 10		90	90

Design:—75l., 100l. Papal Arms between "Justice" and "Hope".

84 "The Nativity" after Gerard Honthorst (Gherardo delle Notte)

85 St. Vincent de Paul

(Des Grassellini. Photo)

1960 (6 Dec). *Christmas.* W **11**. P 14.
334	84	10l. black and grey-green	10	10
335		15l. deep olive-brown & bistre-brown	10	10
336		70l. blue and turquoise-blue	10	15

(Des L. Gasbarra and E. Pizzi (40l., 70l.), R. Mura and E. Pizzi (100l.) Photo)

1960 (6 Dec). *Tercentenary of Deaths of St. Vincent de Paul and St. Louise de Marillac.* T **85** and similar vert designs. W **11** (sideways). P 14.
337	40l. slate-violet	20	15
338	70l. black	20	20
339	100l. brown	40	35

Designs:—70l. St. Louise de Marillac; 100l. St. Vincent giving child to care of St. Louise.

86 St. Meinrad

87 "Pope Leo I meeting Attila" (Algardi)

(Des P. Grassellini (100l.) C. Dabrowska (others). Photo)

1961 (28 Feb). *11th Death Centenary of St. Meinrad.* T **86** and similar designs inscr "861–IUBILAEUM S MEINRADI-1961". W **11** (sideways on vert designs). P 14.
340	30l. black	35	35
341	40l. deep lilac	75	65
342	100l. bistre-brown	1·50	1·30

Designs: *Vert*—40l. "Black Madonna", Einsiedeln Abbey. *Horiz*—100l. Einsiedeln Abbey, Switzerland.

(Des A. Grassellini. Photo)

1961 (6 Apr). *15th Death Centenary of Pope Leo I.* W **11** (sideways). P 14.
343	87	15l. lake-red	10	15
344		70l. deep bluish green	55	50
345		300l. sepia	1·50	1·20

88 Route of St. Paul's Journey to Rome

(Des A. Grassellini (15l., 75l..), P. Grassellini (others). Photo)

1961 (13 June). *19th Centenary of St. Paul's Arrival in Rome.* T **88** and similar horiz designs inscr "LXI-MCMLXI". W **11**. P 14.
346		10l. deep bluish green	10	10
347		15l. black and purple-brown	10	10
348		20l. black and orange-red	20	10
349		30l. blue	30	25
350		75l. black and orange-brown	35	30
351		200l. black and blue	1·30	1·00
346/351	Set of 6		2·10	1·70

Designs:—15l., 75l. St. Paul's arrival in Rome (after Maraini); 20l., 200l. Basilica of St. Paul-outside-the-Walls, Rome; 30l. T **88**.

89 L 'Osservatore Romano, 1861 and 1961

90 St. Patrick (ancient sculpture)

(Des P. Grassellini. Photo)

1961 (4 July). *Centenary of L 'Observatore Romano (Vatican newspaper).* T **89** and similar horiz designs. W **11**. P 14.
352	40l. black and chocolate	20	25
353	70l. black and light blue	55	50
354	250l. black and yellow	1·70	1·30

Designs:—70l. L' Observatore Romano offices; 250l. Printing machine.

(Des E. Pizzi. Photo)

1961 (6 Oct). *Fifteenth Death Centenary of St. Patrick.* T **90** and similar vert design. W **11** (sideways). P 14.
355	90	10l. grey-green and buff	10	10
356	–	15l. sepia and blue	10	10
357	90	40l. deep bluish green & light yellow	10	10
358	–	150l. red-brown and turquoise-blue	40	35
355/358	Set of 4		65	60

Design:—15l., 150l. St Patrick's Sanctuary, Lough Derg.

91 Arms of Roncalli family

92 "The Nativity"

450

VATICAN CITY 1961

(Des P. Grassellini (10l., 115l.), E. Pizzl (others). Photo)

1961 (25 Nov). *80th Birthday of Pope John XXIII.* T **91** *and similar vert designs inscr* "LXXX AETATIS ANNO IOANNIS XXIII" *etc.* W **11** (sideways). P 14.

359	10l. brown and black	10	10
360	25l. grey-green and bistre-brown	10	10
361	30l. reddish violet and violet-blue	10	10
362	40l. grey-blue and reddish violet	10	10
363	70l. light brown and greenish grey	10	15
364	115l. black and brown	20	25
359/364	*Set of 6*	65	70

Designs:—25l. Church of St. Mary, Sotto il Monte; 30l. Church of St. Mary, Monte Santo; 40l. Church of Saints Ambrose and Charles, Rome; 70l. St. Peter's Chair, Vatican Basilica; 115l. Pope John XXIII.

(Des Luca Ch'en. Photo)

1961 (25 Nov). *Christmas Centres multicoloured, frame colours below.* W **11** (sideways). P 14.

365	92	15l. bluish green	10	10
366		40l. grey-black	10	10
367		70l. reddish purple	15	20

93 "Annunciation" (after F. Valle)
94 Land Reclamation' Medal of 1588 

(Des C. Dabrowska. Eng M. Colombati. Recess)

1962 (13 Mar). AIR. W **11** (sideways). P 13 × 14.

368	93	1000l. brown	1·10	95
369		1500l. blue	1·60	1·50

1962 (6 Apr). *Malaria Eradication.* T **94** *and similar vert design.* Photo. W**11** (sideways). P 14.

370	94	15l. deep violet	10	10
371	–	40l. carmine	10	10
372	94	70l. brown	10	10
373	–	300l. green	30	30
370/373	*Set of 4*		55	55

Design:—40l., 300l. Map of Pontine Marshes reclamation project (at time of Pope Pius VI).

95 "The Good Shepherd" (statue, Lateran Museum)
96 St. Catherine (after Il Sodoma (Bazzi)) 

1962 (12 June). *Religious Vocations.* T **95** *and similar vert design.* Photo. W **11** (sideways). P 14.

374	95	10l. black and reddish violet	10	10
375	–	15l. orange-brown and blue	10	10
376	95	70l. black and green	20	20
377	–	115l. orange-brown and brown-red	1·30	1·10
378	95	200l. black and brown	1·30	1·10
374/378	*Set of 5*		2·75	2·30

Design:—15l., 115l. Wheatfield ready for harvest.

1962 (12 June). *Fifth Centenary of Canonization of St. Catherine of Siena.* Photo. W **11** (sideways). P 14.

379	96	15l. light brown	10	10
380		60l. reddish violet	20	25
381		100l. ultramarine	30	30

97 Paulina M. Jaricot
98 St. Peter and St. Paul (from graffito on child's tomb) 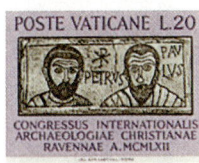

1962 (5 July). *Death Centenary of Paulina M. Jaricot (founder of Society for the Propagation of the Faith). Centres multicoloured; frame colours below.* Photo. W **11** (sideways). P 14.

382	97	10l. lilac	10	10
383		50l. bluish green	20	20
384		150l. grey	25	30

1962 (25 Sept). *Sixth international Christian Archaeology Congress, Ravenna.* T **98** *and similar horiz design.* Photo. W **11**. P 14.

385	98	20l. sepia and reddish violet	10	10
386	–	40l. deep grey-green and brown	10	10
387	98	70l. sepia and turquoise	10	10
388	–	100l. deep grey-grn & brown red	10	10
385/388	*Set of 4*		35	35

Design:—40l., 100l. "The Passion" (from bas relief on tomb in Domitilla cemetery, near Rome).

99 "Faith" (after Raphael)
100 "The Nativity" 

(Des L. B. Barriviera (30l., 115l.) Eng M. Colombati. Recess and photo (30l.) or photo (others))

1962 (30 Oct). *Ecumenical Council* T **99** *and similar vert designs.* W **11** (sideways). P 14.

389		5l. sepia and blue	10	10
390		10l. deep sepia and green	10	10
391		15l. sepia and red	10	10
392		25l. greenish grey and red	10	10
393		30l. black and mauve	10	10
394		40l. deep sepia and carmine	10	10
395		60l. orange brown and green	10	10
396		115l. carmine red	10	10
389/396	*Set of 8*		70	70

Designs:—Divine Virtues 10l. "Hope": 15l. "Charity" (both after Raphael) 25l. Arms of Pope John XXIII and symbols of Evangelists (frontispiece of *Humanae Salutis* by Arrigo Bravi), 30l. Central Nave, St Peter's (council venue), 40l. Pope John XXIII, 60l. "St Peter" (bronze in Vatican Basilica). 115l. The Holy Ghost in form of dove.

451

VATICAN CITY   1962

(Des M. Topno. Photo)

1962 (4 Dec). *Christmas. Centres multicoloured, frame colours below.* W **11**. P 14.
397	**100**	10l. grey		10	10
398		15l. drab		10	10
399		90l. greyish green		10	10

105 "The Nativity" (African terracotta statuette)

106 St. Cyril

101 "Miracle of the Loaves and Fishes" (after Murillo)

102 Pope John XXIII

1963 (21 Mar). *Freedom from Hunger. T* **101** *and similar vert design. Photo.* W **11** (sideways). P 14.
400	**101**	15l. sepia and brown		10	10
401	–	40l. deep bronze green & rose red		10	10
402	**101**	100l. deep sepia and blue		10	10
403	–	200l. deep bronze-green & turq		20	15
400/403	Set of 4			45	40

Design:—40, 200l. "Miracle of the Fishes" (Raphael).

(Des A. Bukuru. Photo)

1963 (22 Nov). *Christmas.* W **11** (sideways). P 14.
413	**105**	10l. brown and yellow-brown		10	10
414		40l. brown and blue		10	10
415		100l. brown and olive		10	10

1963 (22 Nov). *1,100th Anniv of Conversion of Slavs by Saints Cyril and Methodius. T* **106** *and similar vert designs. Photo.* W **11** (sideways). P 14.
416		30l. slate-purple		10	10
417		70l. brown		10	10
418		150l. reddish purple		10	15

Designs:—70l. Map of Moravia; 150l. St. Methodius.
The Saints' portraits are taken from frescoes in the Basilica of St. Clements, Rome, and the map from a fresco in the third "Loggia" of the Vatican Palace.

1963 (8 May). *Award of Balzan Peace Prize to Pope John XXIII. Photo.* W **11** (sideways). P 14.
404	**102**	15l. red brown		10	10
405		160l. black		15	20

107 Pope Paul VI

108 St. Peter, Pharaoh's Tomb, Wadi-es-Sebua

103 St. Peter's Keys

104 Pope Paul VI

1963 (20 June). *"Vacant See". Photo.* W **11** (sideways). P 14.
406	**103**	10l. sepia		10	10
407		40l. sepia/yellow		10	10
408		100l. sepia/bluish violet		10	10

1964 (4 Jan). *Pope Paul's Visit to the Holy Land. T* **107** *and similar vent designs. Photo.* W **11** (sideways). P 14.
419		15l. black		10	10
420		25l. brown-red		10	10
421		70l. sepia		10	10
422		160l. bright blue		10	10
419/422	Set of 4			35	35

Designs:—25l. Church of the Nativity, Bethlehem; 70l. Church of the Holy Sepulchre, Jerusalem; 160l. Well of the Virgin Mary, Nazareth.

(Des C. Dabrowska. Eng V. Nicastro, M. Colombati. Recess)

1963 (16 Oct). *Coronation of Pope Paul VI. T* **104** *and similar vert design.* W **11** (sideways). P 14.
409	**104**	15l. black		10	10
410	–	40l. carmine		10	10
411	**104**	115l. brown		15	15
412	–	200l. grey		15	20
409/412	Set of 4			45	50

Design:—40l., 200l. Arms of Pope Paul VI.

1964 (10 Mar). *Nubian Monuments Preservation. Photo.* W **11**. P 14.
423	**108**	10l. brown and blue		10	10
424	–	20l. multicoloured		10	10
425	**108**	70l. brown and olive-brown		10	10
426	–	200l. multicoloured		10	10
423/426	Set of 4			35	35

Design:—20l., 200l. Philae Temple.

VATICAN CITY 1964

109 Pope Paul VI
110 Michelangelo 
113 Cues's Birthplace
114 Pope Paul at prayer

1964 (22 Apr). *Vatican City's Participation in New York World's Fair.* T **109** *and similar vert designs. Photo.* W **11** *(sideways).* P 14.
427	**109**	15l. deep violet-blue		10	10
428	–	50l. sepia		10	10
429	**109**	100l. slate-blue		10	10
430		250l. brown		10	15
427/430 *Set of 4*				35	35

Designs:—50l. Michelangelo's "Pietà", 250l. Detail of Madonna's head from "Pietà".

(Des C. Dabrowska. Eng A. Quieti (10l.), M. Canfarini (25l.), T. Mele (30l.), V. Nicastro (40l.), S. Vana (150l.). Recess)
1964 (16 June). *400th Death Anniv of Michelangelo.* T **110** *and similar vert designs.* W **11** *(sideways).* P 14.
431		10l. black		10	10
432		25l. claret		10	10
433		30l. olive		10	10
434		40l. violet		10	10
435		150l. deep bronze-green		10	10
431/435 *Set of 5*				45	45

Designs: Michelangelo's paintings, Sistine Chapel—25l. Prophet Isaiah; 30l. Delphic Sibyl; 40l. Prophet Jeremiah; 150l. Prophet Joel.

111 "The Good Samaritan" (after Emilio Greco)
112 "Christmas Scene" (after Kimiko Koseki) 

(Eng A. Quieti. Recess, Cross photo)
1964 (22 Sept). *Red Cross Centenary (1963). Cross in red.* W **11** (sideways). P 14.
436	**111**	10l. red-brown		10	10
437		30l. blue		10	10
438		300l. sepia		20	20

1964 (16 Nov). *Christmas. Photo.* W **11** (sideways). P 14.
439	**112**	10l. multicoloured		10	10
440		15l. multicoloured		10	10
441		135l. multicoloured		10	10

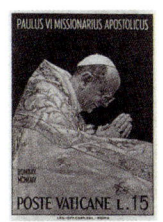

(Des C. Dabrowska. Eng M. Colombati (4l.), V. Nicastro (200l.). Recess)
1964 (16 Nov). *500th Death Anniv of Nicholas Cues (Cardinal Cusanus).* T **113** *and similar horiz design.* W **11** (sideways). P 14.
442	40l. deep bluish green		10	10
443	200l. carmine-red		10	15

Design:—200l. Cardinal Cusanus's sepulchre, St. Peter's (relief by A. Bregno).

1964 (2 Dec). *Pope Paul's Visit to India.* T **114** *and similar designs. Photo.* W **11** (sideways on vert stamps). P 14.
444	15l. black-purple		10	10
445	25l. green		10	10
446	60l. sepia		10	10
447	200l. black-purple		10	15
444/447 *Set of 4*			35	40

Designs: *Horiz*— 25l. Public altar. "The Oval". Bombay; 60l. "Gateway to India". Bombay. *Vert*—200l. Pope Paul walking across map of India.

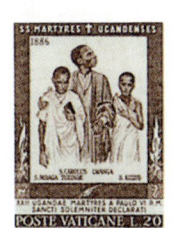

115 Sts. Mbaga Tuzinde, Carolus Lwanga and Kizito
116 Dante (after Raphael) 

(Des C. Dabrowska. Eng E. Donnini (15l.), M. Colombati (20l.), V. Nicastro (30l.), S. Vana (75l.), F. Pagani (100l.), T. Mele (160l.). Recess).
1965 (16 Mar). *Ugandan Martyrs.* T **115** *and similar vert portrait designs.* W **11**. P 13 × 14.
448	15l. turquoise		10	10
449	20l. brown		10	10
450	30l. ultramarine		10	10
451	75l. black		10	10
452	100l. scarlet		10	10
453	160l. violet		10	10
448/453 *Set of 6*			55	55

Designs:—15l. St Joseph Mukasa and six other martyrs, 30l. Sts Matthias Mulumba, Noe Mawagalli, and Lucas Banabakintu, 75l. Sts. Gonzaga Gonza, Athanasius Bazzekuketta, Pontianus Ngondwe and Bruno Serunkuma, 100l. Sts. Anatolius Kinggwajjo, Andreas Kaggwa and Adulphus Mukasa, 160l. Sts Mukasa Kinwananvu and Gyavria.

(Des C. Dabrowska. Eng A. Quieti (10l.), C. Denza (40l.), B. Soccorsi (70l.), E. V. de Cresci (200l.) Recess and photo)
1965 (18 May). *700th Anniv of Dante's Birth.* T **116** *and similar vert designs.* W **11** (sideways). P 13 × 14.
454	10l. brown and yellow-brown		10	10
455	40l. brown and rose-red		10	10

453

VATICAN CITY   1965

456	70l. brown and yellow-green		10	10
457	200l. brown and light blue		10	15
454/457	Set of 4		35	35

Designs: After drawings by Botticelli—40l. "Inferno"; 70l. "Purgatory"; 200l. "Paradise".

117 St. Benedict (after Perugino)

118 Pope Paul

1965 (2 July). *Declaration of St. Benedict as Patron Saint of Europe. T* **117** *and similar vert design. Photo. W* **11** *(sideways). P* 14.

458	40l. bistre-brown		10	10
459	300l. deep bluish green		20	20

Design:—300l. Montecassino Abbey.

1965 (4 Oct). *Pope Paul's Visit to the United Nations, New York. T* **118** *and similar vert design. Photo. W* **11** *(sideways). P* 14.

460	**118**	20l. bistre-brown		10	10
461	—	30l. blue		10	10
462	—	150l. bronze-green		10	10
463	**118**	300l. purple		20	20
460/463	Set of 4			45	45

Design:—30l., 150l. U.N.O. Headquarters, New York.

119 "The Nativity" (Peruvian setting)

120 Pope Paul

(Des C. Dabrowska Eng M. Colombati. Recess)

1965 (25 Nov). *Christmas. W* **11**. *P* 13 × 14.

464	**119**	20l. lake	10	10
465		40l. brown	10	10
466		200l. green	10	15

(Des after bronze relief by E. Manfrini (5l.) or sculptures by M. Rudelli (others). Photo)

1966 (8 Mar). *Vert designs as T* **120**. *W* **11**. *P* 14.

467	5l. bistre-brown	10	10
468	10l. violet	10	10
469	15l. brown	10	10
470	20l. bronze-green	10	10
471	30l. lake-brown	10	10
472	40l. turquoise	10	10
473	55l. grey-blue	10	10
474	75l. brown-purple	10	10
475	90l. magenta	10	10
476	130l. blackish olive	10	10

Designs: (sculptures):—10l. "Music"; 15l. "Science", 20l. "Painting"; 30l. "Sculpture", 40l. "Building"; 55l. "Carpentry", 75l. "Agriculture", 90l. "Metallurgy", 130l. "Learning".

1966 (8 Mar). *EXPRESS LETTER. T* **120** *and similar vert design inscr* "ESPRESSO". *W* **11**. *P* 14.

E477	—	150l. blackish brown	10	10
E478	**120**	180l. light brown	15	15
467/E478	Set of 12		1·10	1·10

Design:—150l. Arms of Pope Paul VI.

121 Queen Dabrowka and King Mieszko I

122 Pope John XXIII and St Peter's, Rome

(Des C. Dabrowska Eng T. Mere (15l.). E. Uonnini (25l.) V. Nicastro (40l.), E. Vangelli (50l.), M. Colombati (150l.), A. Quieti (220l.) Recess)

1966 (3 May). *Poland's Christian Millenium. T* **121** *and similar horiz designs. W* **11** *(sideways). P* 14 × 13.

477	15l. black	10	10
478	25l. violet	10	10
479	40l. orange-red	10	10
480	50l. crimson	10	10
481	150l. slate	10	10
482	220l. brown	10	15
477/482	Set of 6	55	60

Designs:—25l. Adalbert (Wojciech), and Wroclaw and Gniezno Cathedrals; 40l. St. Stanislas, Skalka Cathedral and Wawel Royal Palace, Cracow, 50l. Queen Jadwiga (Hedwig), Ostra Brama Gate with Mater Miserrcordiae, Wilno, and Jagellon University Library, Cracow; 150l. "Black Madonna", Jasna Gora Monastery (Czestochowa) and St John's Cathedral, Warsaw; 220l. Pope Paul VI greeting Poles.

1966 (11 Oct). *Fourth Anniv of Opening of Ecumenical Council. T* **122** *and similar vert designs. Photo. W* **11** *(sideways). P* 14.

483	10l. black and scarlet	10	10
484	15l. deep green and brown	10	10
485	55l. magenta and blackish brown	10	10
486	90l. black and deep green	10	10
487	100l. orange-yellow and green	10	10
488	130l. sepia and brown	10	10
483/488	Set of 6	55	55

Designs:—15l. Book of Prayer, 5t Peter's, 55l. Mass, 90l. Pope Paul with Patriarch Athenagoras, 100l. Episcopal ring; 130l. Pope Paul at closing ceremony (12.10.65).

123 "The Nativity" (after sculpture by Scorzelli)

124 Jetliner over St. Peter's

(Des R. Scorzelli. Photo)

1966 (24 Nov). *Christmas. W* **11** *(sideways). P* 14.

489	**123**	20l. plum	10	10
490		55l. bronze-green	10	10
491		225l. yellow-brown	10	15

VATICAN CITY 1967

(Des after painting by Peppino Piccolo (T **124**). Photo)
1967 (7 Mar). *AIR. T* **124** *and similar vert designs.* W **11** (sideways). P 14.
492	**124**	20l. violet	10	10
493	–	40l. deep slate-lilac and light pink	10	10
494	–	90l. deep slate-blue and grey	10	10
495	**124**	100l. black and pale salmon-red	10	10
496	–	200l. deep slate-lilac and pale bluish grey	10	15
497	–	500l. deep purple-brown and light brown	35	30
492/497 *Set of 6*			75	75

Designs:—40l., 200l. Radio mast and St. Gabriel's statue; 90l., 500l. Aerial view of St. Peter's.

125 St. Peter

126 "The Three Shepherd Children" (sculpture)

1967 (15 June). *1,900th Anniv of Martyrdom of Saints Peter and Paul.* T **125** *and similar vert designs. Multicoloured. Photo.* W **11** (sideways). P 13 × 14.
498		15l. Type **125**	10	10
499		20l. St. Paul	10	10
500		55l. The two Saints	10	10
501		90l. Bernini's baldachin, St. Peter's	10	10
502		220l. Arnolfo di Cambio's tabernacle, St. Paul's Basilica	15	15
498/502 *Set of 5*			50	50

(Des Chiavi. Photo)
1967 (13 Oct). *50th Anniv of Fatima Apparitions.* T **126** *and similar vert designs. Multicoloured.* W **11** (sideways). P 13 × 14.
503		30l. Type **126**	10	10
504		50l. Basilica of Fatima	10	10
505		200l. Pope Paul VI praying before Virgin's statue at Fatima	20	20

127 Congress Emblem

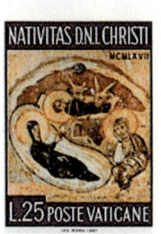

128 "The Nativity" (Byzantine carving)

(Des G. Gervasi. Photo)
1967 (13 Oct). *Third World Apostolic Laity Congress, Rome.* W **11**. P 14.
506	**127**	40l. rose-carmine	15	15
507		130l. new blue	15	15

1967 (28 Nov). *Christmas. Photo. No wmk.* P 14.
508	**128**	25l. multicoloured	10	10
509		55l. multicoloured	10	10
510		180l. multicoloured	10	15

129 "Angel Gabriel" (detail from "The Annunciation" by Fra Angelico)

D 130

130 Pope Paul VI

(Des E. Vangelli. Eng T. Mele. Recess and litho)
1968 (12 Mar). *Air.* W **11**. P 13 × 14.
511	**129**	1000l. lake/*cream*	85	65
512		1500l. black/*cream*	1·20	1·00

(Des R. Scorzelli. Eng F. Tulli. Recess and photo)
1968 (28 May). *POSTAGE DUE.* W **11**. P 14.
D513		10l. black/*pale grey*	10	10
D514		20l. black/*pale blue*	10	10
D515		50l. black/*pale pink*	10	10
D516		60l. black/*pale green*	10	10
D517		100l. black/*pale buff*	10	10
D518		180l. black/*pale mauve*	10	10
D513/518 *Set of 6*			55	55

(Des A. Grassellini (55l.). Photo)
1968 (22 Aug). *Pope Paul's Visit to Colombia.* T **130** *and similar vert designs.* W **11**. P 14.
513		25l. reddish brown and black	10	10
514		55l. ochr, light grey and black	10	10
515		220l. sepia, pale blue and black	10	15

Designs:—55l. Monstrance (Raphael's "Disputa"); 220l. Map of South America.

131 "The Holy Child of Prague"

132 "The Resurrection" (Fra Angelico)

(Des C. Dabrowska. Eng M. Colombati. Recess)
1968 (28 Nov). *Christmas.* W **11**. P 13 × 14.
516	**131**	20l. purple and light red	10	10
517		50l. violet and light lilac	10	10
518		250l. blue and light blue	20	20

(Des and eng E. Donnini. Recess and photo)
1969 (6 Mar). *Easter. Background of vert buff lines.* W **11**. P 13 × 14.
519	**132**	20l. carmine	10	10
520		90l. green	10	10
521		180l. ultramarine	10	10

455

VATICAN CITY 1969

133 Colonnade
134 Pope with Young Africans 
137 Commemorative Medal of Pius IX
138 "Christ" (Simone Martini)

(Des L. Gasbarra, G. Belli and A. Ponsiglione. Photo)

1969 (28 Apr). *Europa.* W **11**. P 14.

522	**133**	50l. yellow-brown and slate	10	10
523		90l. yellow-brown and vermilion	15	15
524		130l. yellow-brown and olive green	15	20

(Eng M. Colombati (20l.). V. Nicastro (180l.). Photo (50l.) or recess and photo (others))

1970 (29 Apr). *Centenary of First Vatican Council.* T **137** and similar vert designs. P 13 × 14.

536	20l. chocolate and yellow orange	10	10
537	50l. multicoloured	10	10
538	180l. brown purple and red	10	15

Designs:—50l. Arms of Pius IX; 180l. Council souvenir medal.

(Des L. Bianchi-Barriviera. Photo)

1969 (31 July). *Pope Paul's Visit to Uganda.* T **134** and similar vert designs. W **11** (sideways). P 13 × 14.

525	25l. brown and deep ochre	10	10
526	55l. brown and brown red	10	10
527	250l. multicoloured	10	15

Designs:—55l. Pope with African bishops. 250l. Map of Africa and olive branch.

1970 (29 May). *50th Anniv of Pope Paul's Ordination as Priest.* T **138** and similar horiz designs. Multicoloured. Photo. P 14 × 13.

539	15l. Type **138**	10	10
540	25l. Christ (R. v. d. Weyden)	10	10
541	50l. Christ (A. Dürer)	10	10
542	90l. Christ (El Greco)	10	10
543	180l. Pope Paul VI	10	10
539/543	Set of 5	45	45

135 Pope Pius IX
136 "Expo 70" Emblem
139 "Adam" (Michelangelo)
140 Pope Paul VI 

(Des C. Dabrowska. Eng A. Quieti (30l.), F. Pagani (50l.), V. Nicastro (220l.) Recess)

1969 (18 Nov). *Centenary of St Peter's Circle Society.* T **135** and similar vert designs. W **11**. P 13 × 14.

528	30l. brown-red	10	10
529	50l. deep slate	10	10
530	220l. reddish purple	10	15

Designs:—50l. Monogram of Society, 220l. Pope Paul VI.

(Des T. Gismondi (220l.) Photo)

1970 (8 Oct). *25th Anniversary of United Nations.* T **139** and similar vert designs. Multicoloured. P 13 × 14.

544	20l. Type **139**	10	10
545	90l. "Eve" (Michelangelo)	10	10
546	220l. Olive branch	10	15

(Des T. Ogata. Photo)

1970 (16 Mar). *"Expo 70" World's Fair, Osaka* T **136** and similar vert designs. Multicoloured. P 13 × 14.

531	25l. Type **136**	10	10
532	40l. Osaka Castle	10	10
533	55l. "Madonna and Child" (Domoto)	10	10
534	90l. Vatican pavilion	10	10
535	110l. Mt. Fuji	10	10
531/535	Set of 5	45	45

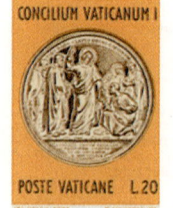

1970 (26 Nov). *Pope's Visit to Asia and Oceania.* T **140** and similar vert designs. Multicoloured. Photo. P 13 × 14.

547	25l. Type **140**	10	10
548	55l. "Holy Child of Cebu" Philippines	10	10
549	100l. "Madonna and Child", Darwin Cathedral (G. Hamori)	10	10
550	130l. Manila Cathedral	10	10
551	220l. Sydney Cathedral	10	15
547/551	Set of 5	45	50

VATICAN CITY 1971

141 "Angel with Lectern"
142 "Madonna and Child" (F. Gnissi) 
145 "St. Stephen" (from chasuble, Székesfehérvár Church, Hungary)
146 Bramante's Design for Cupola, St. Peter's

1971 (2 Feb). *Racial Equality Year. Sculptures by C. Ruffini.* T **141** *and similar vert design. Multicoloured. Photo.* P 13 × 14.
552	20l. Type **141**	10	10
553	40l. "Christ Crucified, and Doves"	10	10
554	50l. Type **141**	10	10
555	130l. As 40l.	10	10
552/555	Set of 4	35	35

(Photo Austrian State Ptg Wks, Vienna)

1971 (26 Mar). *Easter Religious Paintings* T **142** *and similar vert designs. Multicoloured.* P 14.
556	25l. Type **142**	10	10
557	40l. "Madonna and Child" ("Sassetta", S. di Giovanni)	10	10
558	55l. "Madonna and Child" (C. Crivelli)	10	10
559	90l. "Madonna and Child" (C. Maratta)	10	10
560	180l. "The Holy Family" (G. Ceracchini)	10	15
556/560	Set of 5	45	50

143 "St Dominic Guzman" (Sienese School)
144 "St. Matthew" 

1971 (25 May). *800th Birth Anniv of St. Dominic Guzman (founder of Preaching Friars Order).* T **143** *and similar vert paintings. Multicoloured.* P 13 × 14.
561	25l. Type **143**	10	10
562	55l. Portrait by Fra Angelico	10	10
563	90l. Portrait by Titian	10	10
564	180l. Portrait by El Greco	10	15
561/564	Set of 4	35	40

(Eng V. Nicastro (200l.), E. Donnini (500l.), A. Quieti (others). Recess and photo)

1971 (30 Sept). AIR. *Ceiling Frescoes of the Four Evangelists by Fra Angelico, Niccolina Chapel, Vatican.* T **144** *and similar horiz designs.* P 14 × 13.
565	200l. black and pale green	20	20
566	300l. black and pale ochre	30	25
567	500l. black and pale pink	55	45
568	1000l. black and pale mauve	65	55
565/568	Set of 4	1·50	1·30

Designs:—300l. "St. Mark"; 500l. "St. Luke"; 1000l. St. John.

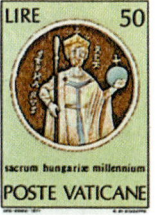

(Des R. di Giuseppe (50l.), A. Quieti (180l.). Photo)

1971 (25 Nov). *Millennium of St. Stephen, King of Hungary.* T **145** *and similar vert design.* P 13 × 14.
569	50l. multicoloured	10	10
570	180l. black and yellow	10	15

Design:—180l. "Madonna, Patroness of Hungary" (sculpture, c 1511).

(Des and eng R. di Giuseppe, Recess and photo)

1972 (22 Feb). *Bramante Celebrations.* T **146** *and similar vert designs.* P 13 × 14.
571	25l. black and light yellow	10	10
572	90l. black and light yellow	10	10
573	130l. black and light yellow	15	15

Designs:—90l. Donato Bramante (architect) from medal; 130l. Spiral staircase, Innocent VIII's Belvedere, Vatican.

147 "St. Mark at Sea" (mosaic)

(Des E. Vangelli (180l.) Photo)

1972 (6 June). *U.N.E.S.C.O. "Save Venice" Campaign.* T **147** *and similar horiz designs. Multicoloured.* P 14 × 13 (Nos. 575/8) or 14 (others).
574	25l. Type **147**	20	20
575	50l. Venice (top left-hand section)	15	20
	a. Block of 4 Nos 575/8	60	
576	50l. Venice (top right-hand section)	15	20
577	50l. Venice (bottom left-hand section)	15	20
578	50l. Venice (bottom right-hand section)	15	20
579	180l. St Mark's Basilica	90	70
574/579	Set of 6	1·50	1·50
MS580	113 × 161 mm. Nos. 574/9	1·75	1·75

Nos. 575/8 are smaller, 39 × 28 mm and were issued in se-tenant blocks of four within the sheet, forming a composite design of a 1581 fresco showing a panoramic map of Venice.

148 Gospel of St. Mark (from codex Biblia dell' Aracoeli)

457

VATICAN CITY 1972

1972 (11 Oct). *International Book Year. Illuminated Manuscripts. T* **148** *and similar horiz designs. Multicoloured. Photo.* P 14 × 13.

581	30l. Type **148**	10	10
582	50l. Gospel of St. Luke ("Biblia dell' Aracoeli")	10	10
583	90l. 2nd Epistle of St. John (Bologna codex)	10	10
584	100l. Revelation of St. John (Bologna codex)	10	10
585	130l. Epistle of St. Paul to the Romans (Italian codex)	15	15
581/585	*Set of 5*	50	50

149 Luigi Orione (founder of "Caritas")

150 Cardinal Bassarione (Roselli fresco, Sistine Chapel)

(Des T. Mele. Photo)

1972 (28 Nov). *Birth Centenaries T* **149** *and similar horiz design. Multicoloured.* P 14 × 13.

586	50l. Type **149**	10	10
587	180l. Lorenzo Perosi (composer)	10	15

(Des and eng A. Quieti (40l.), E. Donnini (90l.), M. Ramassotto (130l.) Recess)

1972 (28 Nov). *500th Death Anniv of Cardinal Bassarione. T* **150** *and similar vert designs.* P 13 × 14.

588	40l. bluish green	10	10
589	90l. brown-lake	10	10
590	130l. black	15	15

Designs:—40l. "Reading of Bull of Union" (relief) 130l. Arms of Cardinal Bassarione.

153 Torun (birthplace)

154 "St. Wenceslas"

(Des O. Zeiller. Eng A. Fischer (20l., 100l.), A. Nefe (others). Recess Austrian State Ptg Wks, Vienna)

1973 (19 June). *500th Birth Anniv of Copernicus. T* **153** *and similar vert design.* P 14.

597	**153**	20l. deep bluish green	10	10
598	—	50l. brown	10	10
599	**153**	100l. reddish purple	15	15
600	—	130l. indigo	15	20
597/600		*Set of 4*	45	50

Design:—50l., 130l. Copernicus.

1973 (25 Sept). *Millenary of Prague Diocese. T* **154** *and similar vert designs. Multicoloured. Photo.* P 14.

601	20l. Type **154**	10	10
602	90l. Arms of Diocese	10	10
603	150l. Tower of Prague Cathedral	20	15
604	220l. "St. Adalbert"	20	20
601/604	*Set of 4*	55	50

151 Congress Emblem

152 St. Theresa's Birthplace

(Des P. Blizzard (25l.). Photo)

1973 (27 Feb). *International Eucharistic Congress. Melbourne. T* **151** *and similar vert designs. Multicoloured.* P 13 × 14.

591	25l. Type **151**	10	10
592	75l. Michelangelo's "Pietà"	10	10
593	300l. Melbourne Cathedral	20	20

(Des and eng M. Ramassotto (25l.), T. Mele (55l.) A. Quieti (220l.). Recess and photo)

1973 (23 May). *Birth Centenary of St Theresa of Lisieux. T* **152** *and similar yen designs.* P 13 × 14.

594	25l. black and pink	10	10
595	55l. black and light yellow	10	10
596	220l. black and light blue	20	15

Designs:—55l. St. Theresa; 220l. Basilica di Lisieux.

155 Church of St. Hripsime

156 "Angel" (porch of St. Mark's, Venice)

(Des and eng G. Verdelocco (25l.), M. Ramassotto (90l.), V. Nicastro (180l.) Recess and litho)

1973 (27 Nov). *800th Death Anniv of St. Narsete Shnorali (Armenian patriarch). T* **155** *and similar vert designs.* P 13 × 14.

605	25l. blackish brown and light ochre	10	10
606	90l. black and pale lavender	10	10
607	180l. blackish purple and pale green	15	20

Designs:—90l. Armenian "khatchkar" (stone stele) inscribed "Victory", 180l. St Narsete Shnorali.

(Des and eng A. Quieti. Recess and litho)

1974 (21 Feb). *AIR.* P 13 × 14.

608	**156**	2500l. multicoloured	2·00	1·50

VATICAN CITY 1974

157 "And There was Light"
158 Noah's Ark and Dove 
161 Christus Victor
162 Fountain. St. Peter's Square

(Designs selected from students' competition entries. Photo)

1974 (23 Apr). *International Book Year* (1973). *"The Bible". T* **157** *and similar multicoloured designs illustrating biblical texts.* P 13 × 14.

609	15l. Type **157**	10	10
610	25l. "Noah entrusts himself to God" (horiz)	10	10
611	50l. "The Annunciation"	10	10
612	90l. "The Nativity"	10	10
613	180l. "The Lord feeds His People" (horiz)	15	20
609/613	*Set of 5*	50	55

1974 (23 Apr). *Centenary of Universal Postal Union Mosaics. T* **158** *and similar horiz design. Multicoloured. Litho.* P 13 × 14.

614	50l. Type **158**	10	10
615	90l. Sheep in landscape	20	20

159 Pupils
160 "Civita" (medieval quarter), Bagnoregio 

(Des and eng T. Mele. Recess and litho)

1974 (18 June). *700th Death anniv of St. Thomas Aquinas (founder of Fra Angelico school). "The School of St. Thomas" (painting, St. Mark's Convent, Florence). T* **159** *and similar designs in agate and gold.* P 14.

616	50l. Type **159**	10	10
	a. Horiz strip of 3. Nos. 616/18		35
617	90l. St. Thomas and pupils (24 × 40 mm)	15	15
618	220l. Pupils (*different*)	20	15

Nos. 616/18 were issued together in horizontal *se-tenant* strips of three within the sheet, each strip forming a composite design.

(Des T. Mele. Photo)

1974 (26 Sept). *700th Death Anniv of St. Bonaventura of Bagnoregro Wood-carvings. T* **160** *and similar vert designs. Multicoloured.* P 13 × 14.

619	40l. Type **160**	10	10
620	90l. "Tree of Life"	10	10
621	220l. "St. Bonaventura" (B. Gozzoli)	15	20

(Des L. Bianchi-Barriviera (250l.). Photo)

1974 (18 Dec). *Holy Year (1975). Religious Art. T* **161** *and similar vert designs. Multicoloured.* P 13 × 14.

622	10l. Type **161**	10	10
623	25l. Christ	10	10
624	30l. Christ (different)	10	10
625	40l. Cross and dove	10	10
626	50l. Christ enthroned	10	10
627	55l. St. Peter	10	10
628	90l. St. Paul	10	10
629	100l. St. Peter	10	10
630	130l. St. Paul	10	10
631	220l. Arms of Pope Paul VI	15	20
632	250l. Pope Paul VI giving blessing	15	20
622/32	*Set of 11*	1·10	1·20

(Des L. Bianchi-Barriviera. Recess)

1975 (22 May). *European Architectural Heritage Year. Fountains. T* **162** *and similar horiz designs.* P 14.

633	20l. black and pale cinnamon	10	10
634	40l. black and pale lilac	10	10
635	50l. black and pale salmon	10	10
636	90l. black and pale yellow-green	10	10
637	100l. black and pale green	10	10
638	200l. black and pale blue	20	15
633/638	*Set of 6*	65	60

Designs:—40l. Piazza St. Martha; 50l. Del Forno; 90l. Belvedere courtyard; 100l. Academy of Sciences; 200l. Galley fountain.

163 "Pentecost"(El Greco)
164 Miracle of Loaves and Fishes (gilt glass) 

(Des and eng V. Nicastro. Recess)

1975 (22 May). *Pentecost.* P 13½ × 14.

639	**163**	300l. orange and carmine	25	25

1975 (25 Sept). *9th International Christian Archaeological Congress. 4th-century Art. T* **164** *and similar horiz designs. Multicoloured. Photo.* P 14 × 13½.

640	30l. Type **164**	20	10
641	150l. Christ (painting)	20	10
642	200l. Raising of Lazarus (gilt glass)	20	20

459

VATICAN CITY   1975

165 Pope Sixtus IV investing Bartolomeo Sacchi as First Librarian (fresco)
166 Passionists' House, Argentario 

(Des and eng V. Nicastro (250l.). A. Quieti (others). Recess and litho)

1975 (25 Sept). *500th Anniv of Apostolic Library*. T **165** and similar designs. P 13½ (150 l.) or 14 × 13½ (others).
643   70l. carmine and pale violet 10   10
644   100l. bottle grn & pale yellowish grn 10   10
645   250l. orange-red and pale blue 20   20
Designs:—Vert—100l. Pope Sixtus IV (codex). Horiz—250l. Pope Sixtus IV visiting library (fresco).

(Des E. Vangelli. Photo)

1975 (27 Nov). *Death Bicentenary of St. Paul of the Cross (founder of Passionist religious order)*. T **166** and similar multicoloured designs. P 13½ (150l.) or 14 × 13½ (others).
646   50l. Type **166** 10   10
647   150l. "St. Paul" (D. della Porta) (26 × 31 mm) 15   15
648   300l. Basilica of St. John and St. Paul 20   20

167 Detail from Painting
168 "The Last Judgement" (detail) 

1975 (27 Nov). *International Women's Year. Painting by Fra Angelico*. T **167** and similar vert design. Multicoloured. Photo. P 13½ × 14.
649   100l. Type **167** 20   15
650   200l. Detail from painting (different) 20   20

(Des and eng A. Quieti. Recess)

1976 (19 Feb). *AIR*. T **168** and similar vert designs showing detail from "The Last Judgement" by Michelangelo. P 13½ × 14.
651   500l. red-brown & deep ultramarine 90   75
652   1000l. red-brown & deep ultramarine .... 1·00   75
653   2500l. red-brown & deep ultramarine .... 1·40   1·00

(Des and eng V. Nicastro. Recess)

1976 (13 May). *400th Death Anniv of Titian*. T **169** and similar horiz design showing detail from "Madonna in Glory with with the Child Jesus and Six Saints". P 14 × 13½.
654   100l. lake 20   20
655   300l. lake 25   25

(Des T. Male. Photo)

1976 (2 July). *41st International Eucharistic Congress, Philadelphia*. T **170** and similar vert designs. P 13½ × 14.
656   150l. multicoloured 20   15
657   200l. gold and blue 20   20
658   400l. gold and deep green 35   30
Designs:—200l. Eucharist within protective hands. 400l. Adoration of the Eucharist.

171 "Transfiguration" (detail)
172 St. John's Tower and Fountain 

1976 (30 Sept). *"Transfiguration" by Raphael*. Multicoloured. T **171** and similar vert designs showing details from the painting Photo. P 13½ × 14.
659   30l. Type **171** ("Moses") 10   10
660   40l. "Christ Transfigured" 10   10
661   50l. "Prophet Elijah" 10   10
662   100l. "Two Apostles" 10   10
663   150l. "The Relative" 15   10
664   200l. "Landscape" 20   20
659/664   Set of 6 70   65

(Des C. Bianchi-Barrivieva Eng E. Donnini (50l., 100l., 300l.). F. Tulli (120l., 250l.). G. Verdelocco (180l.). Recess and litho)

1976 (23 Nov). *Architecture*. T **172** and similar horiz designs. P 14.
665   50l. agate and pale lilac 10   10
666   100l. sepia and pale brown 10   10
667   120l. greenish blk & pale yellowish grin 10   10
668   180l. black and pale brownish grey 20   15
669   250l. deep brown & pale yell-ochre 20   20
670   300l. brown-purple 20   20
665/670   Set of 6 80   75
Designs:—100l. Fountain of the Sacrament; 120l. Fountain at entrance to Gardens; 180l. Cupola of St. Peter's and Sacristy Basilica; 250l. Borgia Tower, Sistine Chapel and Via della Fondamenta; 300l. Apostolic Palace, Courtyard of St. Damasius.

169 "Madonna in Glory with the Child Jesus and Six Saints" (detail)
170 Eucharist Ear of Wheat and Globe 
173 "Canticles of Brother Sun" (detail) 
174 Detail from Fresco 

460

VATICAN CITY 1977

(Des D. Cambellotti. Photo)

1977 (10 Mar). *750th Death Anniv of St. Francis of Assisi. Multicoloured. T 173 and similar horiz designs showing details from "Canticles of Brother Sun" by D. Cambellotti.* P 14 × 13½.
671	50l. Type **173**	10	10
672	70l. "Brother Sun"	10	10
673	100l. "Sister Moon and Stars"	10	10
674	130l. "Sister Water"	10	15
675	170l. "Praise in Infirmities and Tribulations"	15	15
676	200l. "Praise for Bodily Death"	20	15
671/676	Set of 6	70	70

(Des and eng F. Tulli. Recess)

1977 (20 May). *600th Anniv of Return of Pope Gregory from Avignon. Fresco by G. Vasari. T 174 and similar vert design in black.* P 14.
677	170l. Type **174**	20	20
	a. Pair Nos 677/8	60	50
678	350l. Detail from fresco (*different*)	35	25

Nos. 677/8 were issued together in *se-tenant* pairs within the sheet.

175 "Death of the Virgin"

176 "God of the Nile"

1977 (4 July). *Festival of Assumption. Miniatures from Apostolic Library. T 175 and similar vert design. Multicoloured. Photo.* P 13½ × 14.
679	200l. Type **175**	20	20
680	400l. "Assumption of Virgin into Heaven"	35	30

(Des T. Mele. Photo)

1977 (29 Sept). *Classical Sculpture in Vatican Museums (1st series). Statues. T 176 and similar horiz designs. Multicoloured.* P 14 × 13½.
681	50l. Type **176**	10	10
682	120l. "Pericles"	10	10
683	130l. "Husband and Wife with joined Hands"	15	15
684	150l. "Belvedere Apollo"	15	15
685	170l. "Laocoon"	15	20
686	350l. "Belvedere Torso"	20	25
681/686	Set of 6	75	85

See also Nos. 687/92.

177 "Creation of the Human Race"

178 'Madonna with the Parrot' (detail)

(Des T. Mele. Photo)

1977 (9 Dec). *Classical Sculpture in Vatican Museums (2nd series). Paleo-Christian Sarcophagi Carvings. T 177 and similar horiz designs. Multicoloured.* P 14 × 13½.
687	50l. Type **177**	10	10
688	70l. "Three Youths in the Fiery Furnace"	10	10
689	100l. "Adoration of the Magi"	10	10
690	130l. "Christ raising Lazarus from the Dead"	15	15
691	200l. "The Good Shepherd"	20	20
692	400l. "Resurrection"	30	30
687/692	Set of 6	85	85

(Des M. Tuccelli. Photo)

1977 (9 Dec). *400th Birth Anniv of Rubens.* P 13½ × 14.
693	**178** 350l. multicoloured	30	30

179 "The Face of Christ"

180 Arms of Pope Pius IX

(Des P. Fazzini. Photo)

1978 (9 March). *80th Birthday of Pope Paul VI. T 179 and similar horiz design. Multicoloured.* P 14 × 13.
694	350l. Type **179**	30	25
695	400l. Portrait of Pope Paul VI (drawing by L.B. Barriviera)	35	30

(Eng P. N. Arghittu. Recess and litho)

1978 (9 May). *Death Centenary of Pope Pius IX. T 180 and similar vert designs. Multicoloured.* P 13 × 14.
696	130l. Type **180**	10	10
697	170l. Seal of Pius IX	15	15
698	200l. Portrait of Pius IX	20	20

181 Microwave Antenna and Radio Vatican Emblem

182 St. Peter's Keys

(Des and eng A. Morena. Recess)

1978 (11 July). *AIR. Tenth World Telecommunications Day.* P 14 × 13.
699	**181** 1000l. multicoloured	85	65
700	2000l. multicoloured	1·70	1·40
701	3000l. multicoloured	2·50	1·90

(Des E. Vangelli. Photo)

1978 (23 Aug). *"Vacant See".* P 14.
702	**182** 120l. pale blue and reddish violet	20	15
703	150l. flesh and reddish violet	20	15
704	250l. greenish yellow and reddish violet	20	20

461

VATICAN CITY   1978

183 St. Peter's Keys    **184** Pope John Paul I

(Des E. Vangelli. Photo)

1978 (12 Oct). *"Vacant See".* P 14.
705	183	120l. greenish yellow, light blue and black	20	15
706		200l. pale yellow, rose-red and black	20	15
707		250l. multicoloured	20	20

1978 (11 Dec). *Pope John Paul I Commemoration.* T **184** and similar designs. Multicoloured. Photo. P 14 × 13 (350l.) or 13 × 14 (others).
708	70l. Type **184**	10	10
709	120l. The Pope smiling	15	15
710	250l. The Pope in Vatican Gardens	20	20
711	350l. The Pope giving blessing (*horiz*)	20	20
708/711 Set of 4		60	60

185 Arms of Pope John Paul II    **186** The Martyrdom (14th century Latin codex)

(Eng F. Tulli (400l.), A. Quieti (others). Recess and litho)

1979 (22 Mar). *Inauguration of Pontificate of Pope John Paul II.* T **185** and similar horiz designs. Multicoloured. P 14 × 13.
712	170l. Type **185**	20	15
713	250l. The Pope giving his blessing	20	20
714	400l. "Christ handing the Keys to St. Peter" (relief, A. Buonvicino)	35	30

1979 (18 May). *900th Death Anniv of St. Stanislaus.* T **186** and similar vert designs. Multicoloured. Photo. P 14.
715	120l. Type **186**	20	15
716	150l. St. Stanislaus appears to the people (14th century Latin codex)	20	15
717	250l. Gold reliquary	20	20
718	500l. Cracow Cathedral	40	35
715/718 Set of 4		90	75

187 Meteorograph

(Eng P. Arghittu. Recess and litho)

1979 (25 June). *Death Centenary of Angelo Secchi (astronomer).* T **187** and similar horiz designs. Multicoloured. P 13 × 14.
719	180l. Type **187**	20	15
720	220l. Spectroscope	20	20
721	300l. Telescope	25	25

188 St. Basil and Vignette "Handing Monastic Laws to a Hermit"   **189** Aerial View of Vatican City

(Eng M. Tuccelli. Recess and litho)

1979 (25 June). *1600th Death Anniv of St. Basil the Great.* T **188** and similar vert design. Multicoloured. P 13½ × 14.
| 722 | 150l. Type **188** | 20 | 15 |
| 723 | 520l. St. Basil and vignette "Caring for the Sick" | 40 | 35 |

(Des A. Ciaburro. Photo)

1979 (11 Oct). *50th Anniv of Vatican City State.* T **189** and similar horiz designs showing Popes and their arms. P 14 × 13½.
724	50l. chestnut, black and bright rose	10	10
725	70l. multicoloured	10	10
726	120l. multicoloured	10	10
727	150l. multicoloured	10	10
728	170l. multicoloured	20	15
729	250l. multicoloured	20	20
730	450l. multicoloured	35	40
724/730 Set of 7		1·00	1·00

Designs:—70l. Pius XI; 120l. Pius XII; 150l. John XXIII; 170l. Paul VI; 250l. John Paul I; 450l. John Paul II.

190 Child in Swaddling Clothes (relief, Foundling Hospital, Florence)

(Eng V. Puliti. Recess)

1979 (27 Nov). *International Year of the Child.* T **190** and similar vert designs. P 13½ × 14.
731	50l. multicoloured	15	15
732	120l. multicoloured	20	15
733	200l. multicoloured	20	20
734	350l. multicoloured	25	30
731/734 Set of 4		70	70

462

VATICAN CITY   1980

191 Abbot Desiderius offering Codices to St. Benedict

1980 (21 Mar). *1500th Birth Anniv of St. Benedict of Nursia (founder of Benedictine Order).* T **191** *and similar horiz designs. Multicoloured. Photo.* P 14 × 13½.
735	80l. Type **191**		10	10
736	100l. Writing the rules of the Order		10	10
737	150l. Page from the rules		15	15
738	220l. Death of St. Benedict		20	15
739	450l. Montecassino Abbey (after Paul Bril)		35	35
735/739 *Set of 5*			80	70

192 Hands reaching out to Pope and Arms of Santo Domingo

193 Bernini (self-portrait) and Medallion showing Baldacchino, St. Peter's

(Des I. Bianchi-Barriviera (3000l.) Eng F. Tulli. Recess and litho)

1980 (24 June). AIR. *Pope John Paul II's Journeys (1st series).* T **192** *and similar horiz designs.* P 14 × 13½.
740	200l. multicoloured		20	15
741	300l. multicoloured		30	20
742	500l. bluish violet, red and black		45	35
743	1000l. multicoloured		90	70
744	1500l. multicoloured		1·40	95
745	2000l. red, new blue and black		1·80	1·50
746	3000l. brownish black, carmine-red and deep blue (18.9.80)		2·75	2·10
740/746 *Set of 7*			7·00	5·25

Designs:—300 to 2000l. As T **192** but different coats of arms; 300l. Mexico; 500l. Poland; 1000l. Ireland; 1500l. United States; 2000l. United Nations. 3000 l. Pope John Paul II, Archbishop Dimitrios, and arms of Turkey.
See also Nos. 768/78, 814/25, 862/9, 886/93, 912/16, 940/4, 963/6, 992/6, 1019/22, 1049/51, 1076/80, 1113/14, 1136/41 and 1174/9, 1206/11, 1236/40, 1284/8 and 1312/16.

(Des Maria M. Tuccelli. Litho)

1980 (16 Oct). *300th Death Anniv of Gian Lorenzo Bernini (artist and architect).* T **193** *and similar horiz designs. Multicoloured.* P 14 × 13.
747	80l. Type **193**		10	10
748	170l. Bernini and medallion showing his plan for St. Peter's		20	15
749	250l. Bernini and medallion showing bronze chair and group "Doctors of the Church", St. Peter's		20	20
750	350l. Bernini and medallion showing Apostolic Palace stairway		30	30
747/750 *Set of 4*			70	70

194 St.Albertus on Mission of Peace

195 Communion of the Saints

(Des A. Canevari. Photo)

1980 (18 Nov). *700th Death Anniv of St. Albertus Magnus.* T **194** *and similar vert design. Multicoloured.* P 13½ × 14.
751	300l. Type **194**		25	25
752	400l. St. Albertus as Bishop		35	30

(Des G. Hajnal. Photo)

1980 (18 Nov). *Feast of All Saints.* T **195** *and similar horiz design. Multicoloured.* P 14x13½.
753	250l. Type **195**		20	20
754	500l. Christ and saints		40	40

196 Marconi, Pope Pius XI and Radio Emblem

(Des I. Fantini. Photo)

1981 (12 Feb). *50th Anniv of Vatican Radio.* T **196** *and similar horiz designs. Multicoloured.* P 14 × 13½.
755	100l. Type **196**		10	10
756	150l. Microphone		15	15
757	200l. Antenna of Santa Maria di Galeria Radio Centre and statue of Archangel Gabriel		20	20
758	600l. Pope John Paul II		45	40
755/758 *Set of 4*			80	75

197 Virgil and his Writing-desk

(Des V. Puliti. Litho and die-stamped)

1981 (23 Apr). *Death Bimillenary of Virgil (Roman poet).* T **197** *and similar horiz design. Multicoloured.* P 14.
759	350l. Type **197**		35	40
760	600l. As Type **197** but inscribed "P. VERGILI / MARONIS / AENEIDOS / LIBRI"		55	55

Nos. 759/60 were each issued in sheets of 16 stamps and 9 labels depicting a drawing from *Bucolica*, the labels forming a cross.

463

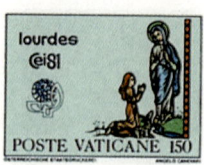

VATICAN CITY 1981

198 Congress Emblem and Apparition of Virgin to St. Bernadette

199 Jan van Ruusbroec writing Treatise

202 Agnes handing Church to Grand Master of the Crosiers of the Red Star

203 "Pueri Cantores" (left panel)

(Des A. Canevari. Photo State Ptg Wks, Vienna)

1981 (22 June). *42nd International Eucharistic Congress, Lourdes*. T **198** *and similar horiz designs. Multicoloured*. P 14.
761	80l. Congress emblem		10	10
762	150l. Type **198**		15	15
763	200l. Emblem and pilgrims going to Lourdes		20	20
764	500l. Emblem and Bishop with faithful venerating Virgin		45	40
761/764	*Set of 4*		80	75

(Eng F. Tulli. Recess and litho)

1981 (29 Sept). *600th Death Anniv of Jan van Ruusbroec (Flemish mystic)*. T **199** *and similar vert design. Multicoloured*. P 13½ × 14.
765	200l. Type **199**		20	20
766	300l. Ruusbroec		25	30

200 Turin Shroud and I.Y.D.P. Emblem

201 Arms of John Paul II

(Des G. Hajnal. Photo)

1981 (29 Sept). *International Year of Disabled Persons*. P 14 × 13.
767	**200** 600l. multicoloured		45	45

(Des A. Canevari. Photo)

1981 (3 Dec). *Pope John Paul II's Journeys (2nd series)*. T **201** *and similar horiz designs. Multicoloured*. P 13½ × 14.
768	50l. Type **201**		10	10
769	100l. Crucifix and map of Africa		10	10
770	120l. Hands holding crucifix		15	15
771	150l. Pope performing baptism		15	15
772	200l. Pope embracing African bishop		20	20
773	250l. Pope blessing sick man		25	25
774	300l. Notre-Dame Cathedral, Paris		30	25
775	400l. Pope addressing U.N.E.S.C.O., Paris		35	35
776	600l. "Christ of the Andes", Rio de Janeiro		55	50
777	700l. Cologne Cathedral		65	60
778	900l. Pope giving blessing		85	75
768/778	*Set of 11*		3·25	3·00

1982 (16 Feb). *700th Death Anniv of Blessed Agnes of Prague*. T **202** *and similar vert design. Multicoloured*. P 13½ × 14.
779	700l. Type **202**		65	55
780	900l. Agnes receiving letter from St. Clare		80	70

(Eng F. Tulli. Recess and litho)

1982 (21 May). *500th Death Anniv of Luca della Robbia (sculptor)*. T **203** *and similar designs*. P 14.
781	1000l. pale sage green and indigo		90	75
	a. Horiz strip of 3. Nos. 781/3		2·75	
782	1000l. multicoloured		90	75
783	1000l. pale sage green and indigo		90	75

Designs: As T **203**—No. 783, "Pueri Cantores" (right panel). 44 × 36 mm—No. 782. "Virgin Mary in Prayer".
Nos. 781/3 were issued together in horizontal *se-tenant* strips of three within the sheet.

204 Virgin Mary and St. Joseph clothe St. Theresa

205 Examining Globe

(Des R. Tommasi. L. Ferroni. Photo)

1982 (23 Sept). *400th Death Anniv of St. Theresa of Avila*. T **204** *and similar vert designs*. P 13½ × 14.
784	200l. pale orange, brownish grey & scar		20	15
785	600l. brownish grey, pale orange & blue		55	45
786	1000l. brownish grey, pale orge & dp mve		90	75

Designs:—600l. Ecstasy of St. Theresa; 1000l. St. Theresa writing *The Interior Castle*.

(Eng A. Ciaburro. Recess)

1982 (23 Nov). *400th Anniv of Gregorian Calendar*. T **205** *and similar vert designs showing details from Pope Gregory XIII's tomb*. P 13½ × 14.
787	200l. bottle green		20	15
788	300l. black		30	25
789	700l. deep magenta		65	60
MS790	159 × 109 mm. Nos. 787/9		2·00	1·75

Designs:—300l. Presenting proposals to Pope Gregory XIII; 700l. Kneeling figures.

464

VATICAN CITY   1982

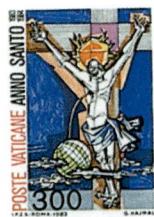

206 "Nativity" (Veit Stoss)

207 Crucifixion

(Des A. Böcskör. Eng D. Leitgeb. Recess and photo State Ptg Wks, Vienna)

1982 (23 Nov). *Christmas.* T **206** and similar vert design. P 14.
| 791 | 300l. stone, sepia and gold | 30 | 25 |
| 792 | 450l. pale rose-lilac, brown-purple & silver | 35 | 35 |

Design:—450l. "Nativity with Pope John Paul II" (Enrico Manfrini).

(Des G. Hajnal. Photo)

1983 (10 Mar). *Holy Year.* T **207** and similar vert designs. Multicoloured. P 13½ × 14.
793	300l. Type **207**	30	25
794	350l. Christ the Redeemer	35	25
795	400l. Pope bringing message of redemption to world	40	30
796	2000l. Dove of the Holy Spirit passing through Holy Door	1·80	1·50
793/796	Set of 4	2·50	2·10

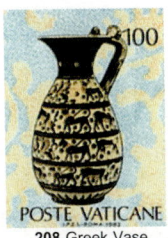

208 Greek Vase

209 "Theology"

1983 (10 Mar). *"The Vatican Collections; The Papacy and Art—U.S.A. 1983" Exhibition (1st issue).* 125 × 170 mm containing T **208** and similar vert designs. Multicoloured. Litho. P 13½ × 14.
MS797 100l. Type **208**, 200l. Italianate vase, 250l. Terracotta female bust, 300l. Bust of Emperor Marcus Aurelius, 350l. Bird (fresco fragment), 400l. Sacred vestment of Pope Clement VIII ...... 2·30 2·30
See also Nos. **MS802** and **MS803**.

(Eng V. Puliti. Recess)

1983 (14 June). *500th Birth Anniv of Raphael (artist).* T **209** and similar vert designs showing allegories on the Segnatura Room ceiling. P 13½ × 14.
798	50l. deep blue and ultramarine	10	10
799	400l. deep reddish purple and magenta	35	35
800	500l. brown and chestnut	50	40
801	1200l. blackish green & deep blue-green	1·10	95
798/801	Set of 4	2·00	1·60

Designs:—400l. "Poetry"; 500l. "Justice"; 1200l. "Philosophy".

1983 (14 June). *"The Vatican Collections: The Papacy and Art—U.S.A. 1983" Exhibition (2nd issue).* Sheet 124 × 171 mm containing vert designs as T **208**. Multicoloured. Recess and litho. P 13½ × 14.
MS802 100l. Etruscan terracotta horse's head; 200l. Greek relief of horseman; 300l. Etruscan head of man; 400l. Head of Apollo Belvedere; 500l. Fresco of Moses 1000l. "Madonna and Child" (Bernardo Daddi) ...... 2·50 2·50

1983 (10 Nov). *"The Vatican Collections: The Papacy and Art—U.S.A. 1983" Exhibition (3rd issue).* Sheet 124 × 171 mm containing vert designs as T **208**. Multicoloured. Recess and litho. P 13½ × 14.
MS803 150l. Oedipus and Sphinx (Greek cup); 200l. Votive statue of child (Etruscan bronze); 350l. Statue of Emperor Augustus; 400l. Statue of Good Shepherd; 500l. "St. Nicholas saving Ship" (Gentile Fabriano); 1200l. "The Holy Face" (Georges Rouault) ...... 3·00 3·00

210 "Moses explaining the Law to the People" (Luca Signorelli)

(Des D. Vangelli. Photo)

1983 (10 Nov). *AIR. World Communications Year.* T **210** and similar horiz design. Multicoloured. P 14.
| 804 | 2000l. Type **210** | 1·80 | 1·30 |
| 805 | 5000l. "St. Paul preaching in Athens" (Raphael) | 4·00 | 3·25 |

211 Mendel and Hybrid Experiment

212 St. Casimir and Vilna Cathedral and Castle

(Des M. Codoni. Photo)

1984 (28 Feb). *Death Centenary of Gregor Johann Mendel (geneticist).* P 14 × 13½.
| 806 | **211** | 450l. multicoloured | 55 | 50 |
| 807 | | 1500l. multicoloured | 1·50 | 1·20 |

(Des R. Viesulas. Photo)

1984 (28 Feb). *500th Death Anniv of St. Casimir (patron saint of Lithuania).* P 14.
| 808 | **212** | 550l. multicoloured | 55 | 50 |
| 809 | | 1200l. multicoloured | 1·30 | 1·10 |

465

VATICAN CITY 1984

213 Pontifical Academy of Sciences
214 Pope in Karachi 

(Des L. Bianchi-Barriviera. Eng G. Verdelocco (150l.), V. Puliti (550l.). F. Borrelli (1500l.). Photo (450l.), recess and litho (others))

1984 (18 June). *Cultural and Scientific Institutions.* T **213** and similar horiz designs. P. 14.
810	150l. light yellow and deep brown	20	20
811	450l. multicoloured	50	40
812	550l. light yellow and deep violet	60	50
813	1500l. light yellow and Prussian blue	1·50	1·20
810/813	Set of 4	2·50	2·10

Designs:—450l. Seals and document from Vatican Secret Archives; 550l. Entrance to Vatican Apostolic Library; 1500l. Vatican Observatory, Castelgandolfo.

(Des A. Canavari. Photo)

1984 (2 Oct)–**85**. *Pope John Paul II's Journeys (3rd series).* T **214** and similar horiz designs. Multicoloured. P 13½ × 14.
814	50l. Type **214**	10	10
815	100l. Pope and image of Our Lady of Peñafrancia, Philippines	10	10
	a. Booklet pane. Nos. 815 × 4, 818 × 4, 819 × 4, 820 × 4 plus four labels (14.3.85)	5·00	
816	150l. Pope with crucifix (Guam)	15	15
817	250l. Pope and Tokyo Cathedral	35	30
818	300l. Pope at Anchorage, Alaska	20	20
819	400l. Crucifix, crown and map of Africa	30	25
820	450l. Pope and image of Our Lady of Fatima (Portugal)	35	25
821	550l. Pope, Archbishop of Westminster and Canterbury Cathedral	90	65
822	1000l. Pope and image of Our Lady of Lujan (Argentina)	1·60	1·10
823	1500l. Pope, Lake Leman and Geneva	2·40	1·70
824	2500l. Pope and Mount Titano (San Marino)	4·00	2·75
825	4000l. Pope and Santiago de Compostela Cathedral (Spain)	6·25	4·50
814/825	Set of 12	15·00	11·00

215 Damasus and Sepulchre of Sts. Marcellinus and Peter
216 More (after Holbein) and Map 

(Des Patrizia Gabriele. Photo)

1984 (27 Nov). *1600th Death Anniv of Pope St. Damasus.* T **215** and similar horiz designs. Multicoloured. P 14 × 13½.
826	200l. Type **215**	20	20
827	500l. Damasus and epigraph from St. Januarius's tomb	55	55
828	2000l. Damasus and basilica ruins	1·80	1·70

(Eng A. Ciaburro. Recess and litho)

1985 (7 May). *450th Death Anniv of St. Thomas More.* T **216** and similar honz designs. Multicoloured. P 14 × 13½.
829	250l. Type **216**	30	30
830	400l. More and title page of *Utopia*	45	45
831	2000l. More and title page of *Life of Thomas More* by Domenico Regi	2·00	1·80

217 St. Methodius holding Religious Paintings
218 Cross on Map of Africa 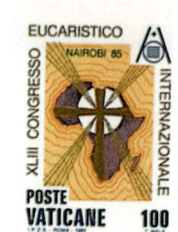

(Des G. Hajnal. Photo)

1985 (7 May). *1100th Death Anniv of Saint Methodius.* T **217** and similar vert designs. Multicoloured. P 13½ × 14.
832	500l. Type **217**	55	50
833	600l. Sts. Cyril and Methodius with Pope Clement I's body	75	65
834	1700l. Sts. Benedict, Cyril and Methodius	1·60	1·50

(Des T. Mele. Photo)

1985 (18 June). *43rd International Eucharistic Congress, Nairobi.* T **218** and similar vert designs. Multicoloured. P 13½ × 14.
835	100l. Type **218**	20	15
836	400l. Assembly of bishops	45	40
837	600l. Chalice	70	50
838	2300l. Family gazing at cross	2·75	2·10
835/838	Set of 4	3·75	2·75

219 Eagle (from Door, St. Paul's Basilica, Rome)
220 Mosaic Map of Italy and Symbol of Holy See 

(Des Patrizia Gabriele. Photo)

1985 (18 June). *900th Death Anniv of Pope Gregory VII.* T **219** and similar multicoloured designs. P 13½ × 13½ (2500l.) or 13½ × 14 (others).
839	150l. Type **219**	20	20
840	450l. Pope Gregory VII	55	50
841	2500l. Pope Gregory's former sarcophagus (*horiz*)	3·00	2·40

(Des Laura Bedetti. Photo)

1985 (15 Oct). *Ratification of Modification of 1929 Lateran Concordat.* P 14 × 13½.
842	**220** 400l. multicoloured	45	40

466

VATICAN CITY   1985

221 Carriage

222 "Nation shall not Lift up Sword against Nation..."

229 St. Camillus saving Invalid from Flood (after Pierre Subleyras)

230 "The Philosophers"

(Eng L. Vangelli. Recess and litho)

1985 (15 Oct). *"Italia '85" International Stamp Exhibition, Rome.* T **221** *and similar horiz design.* P 14 × 13½.
843	450l. bright carmine and new blue		35	40
844	1500l. deep blue and bright magenta		1·20	1·10
MS845	161 × 108mm. Nos. 843/4		2·75	2·50

Design:—1500l. Carriage (*different*).

(Des L. Vangelli. Photo)

1986 (14 Apr). *International Peace Year.* T **222** *and similar vert designs. Multicoloured.* P 14.
846	50l. Type **222**		10	10
847	350l. Messenger's feet ("How beautiful...are the feet...")		40	35
848	450l. Profiles and olive branch ("Blessed are the peacemakers...")		60	50
849	650l. Dove and sun ("Glory to God in the highest...")		75	65
850	2000l. Pope's hand releasing dove over rainbow ("Peace is a value with no frontiers...")		2·20	1·60
846/850	*Set of 5*		3·75	2·75

223/228 Vatican City (⅔-*size illustration*)

1986 (14 Apr). *World Heritage. Vatican City. Multicoloured.* P 13½ × 14.
851	**223**	550l. multicoloured	80	70
		a. Block of 6. Nos. 851/6	4·25	
852	224	550l. multicoloured	80	70
853	225	550l. multicoloured	80	70
854	226	550l. multicoloured	80	70
855	227	550l. multicoloured	80	70
856	228	550l. multicoloured	80	70
851/856	*Set of 6*		4·25	3·75

Nos. 851/6 were issued together in *se-tenant* blocks of six within the sheet, each block forming the composite design illustrated.

(Eng A. Ciaburro, Recess and litho)

1986 (12 June). *Centenary of Proclamation of St. Camillus de Lellis and St. John of God as Patron Saints of Hospitals and the Sick.* T **229** *and similar vert designs.* P 13½ × 14.
857	700l. deep green, dp violet & dp rose-red		85	70
858	700l. dp grey-blue, dp olive & dp rose-red		85	70
859	2000l. multicoloured		2·40	2·10

Designs:—No. 858, St. John supporting the sick (after Gomez Moreno); 859, Emblems of Ministers of the Sick and Brothers Hospitallers, and Pope John Paul II talking to patient.

(Eng P. Arghittu. Recess and litho)

1986 (2 Oct). *50th Anniv of Pontifical Academy of Sciences.* T **230** *and similar horiz design showing details from fresco "School of Athens" by Raphael. Multicoloured.* P 14 × 13½.
860	1500l. Type **230**		1·80	1·50
861	2500l. "The Scientists"		2·75	2·30

231 Pope and Young People (Central America)

232 "St. Augustine reading St. Paul's Epistles" (fresco, Benozzo Gozzoli)

(Des B. Cristiano. Photo)

1986 (20 Nov). AIR. *Pope John Paul II's Journeys (4th series).* T **231** *and similar horiz designs. Multicoloured.* P 14 × 13½.
862	350l. Type **231**		40	35
863	450l. Pope in prayer, Warsaw Cathedral and Our Lady of Czestochowa (Poland)		55	50
864	700l. Pope kneeling and crowd at Lourdes (France)		85	65
865	1000l. Sanctuary of Mariazell and St. Stephen's Cathedral, Vienna (Austria)		1·20	90
866	1500l. Pope and representatives of nations visited (Alaska, Asia and Pacific Islands)		1·60	1·30
867	2000l. Image of St. Nicholas of Flüe, Basilica of Einsiedeln and Pope (Switzerland)		2·20	1·50
868	2500l. "Crosses, Notre Dame Cathedral, Quebec" and Pope (Canada)		2·75	1·90
869	5000l. Pope, bishop and young people with cross (Spain, Dominican Republic and Puerto Rico)		5·50	3·75
862/869	*Set of 8*		13·50	9·75

467

VATICAN CITY   1987

1987 (7 Apr). *1600th Anniv of Conversion and Baptism of St. Augustine.* T **232** *and similar vert designs. Multicoloured. Photo.* P 13½ × 14.

870	300l. Type **232**	35	35
871	400l. "Baptism of St. Augustine" (Bartolomeo di Gentile)	45	45
872	500l. "Ecstasy of St. Augustine" (fresco, Benozzo Gozzoli)	55	50
873	2200l. "Dispute of the Sacrament" (detail of fresco, Raphael)	2·30	1·90
870/873	Set of 4	3·25	2·75

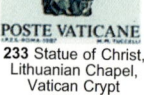

233 Statue of Christ, Lithuanian Chapel, Vatican Crypt

234 Chapter of Riga Church Seal

(Des Maria Tuccelli. Photo)

1987 (2 June). *600th Anniv of Conversion to Christianity of Lithuania.* T **233** *and similar vert designs. Multicoloured.* P 13½ × 14.

874	200l. Type **233**	30	20
875	700l. Statue of Virgin Mary with body of Christ and two angels	85	75
876	3000l. Lithuanian shrine	3·25	2·75

(Des M. Codoni. Photo)

1987 (2 June). *800th Anniv of Conversion to Christianity of Latvia.* T **234** *and similar vert design. Multicoloured.* P 13½ × 14.

877	700l. Type **234**	90	70
878	2400l. Basilica of the Assumption, Aglona	3·50	2·75

235 Judge

236 Stamp Room and 1929 5c. Stamp

(Des Rita Morena (**MS**883). Recess and litho)

1987 (29 Aug). *"Olymphilex '87" Olympic Stamps Exhibition, Rome.* T **235** *and similar vert designs showing figures from Caracalla Baths floor mosaic. Multicoloured.* P 14.

879	400l. Type **235**	45	40
880	500l. Runner	65	50
881	600l. Discus-thrower	75	50
882	2000l. Athlete	2·20	1·60
879/882	Set of 4	3·50	2·75
MS883	151 × 100 mm. As Nos. 879/82 but with Greek key borders	4·75	4·75

(Des Patrizia Gabriele. Photo)

1987 (29 Sept). *Inauguration of Philatelic and Numismatic Museum.* T **236** *and similar horiz design. Multicoloured.* P 14 × 13.

884	400l. Type **236**	45	40
885	3500l. Coin room and reverse of 1000l. 1986 coin	3·50	3·00

(Des R. Cristiano. Photo)

1987 (27 Oct). *Pope John Paul II's Journeys (5th series). Horiz designs as* T **231**. *Multicoloured.* P 14 × 13½.

886	50l. Youths, Pope and Machu Picchu (Venezuela, Ecuador, Peru, Trinidad and Tobago)	20	15
887	250l. Antwerp Cathedral, smoke stacks and Pope (Netherlands, Luxembourg and Belgium)	55	45
888	400l. People, buildings and Pope (Togo, Ivory Coast, Cameroun, Central African Republic, Zaire, Kenya and Morocco)	90	70
889	500l. Pope holding Cross and youths (Liechtenstein)	1·10	85
890	600l. Pope, Indians and Delhi Mosque (India)	1·30	1·00
891	700l. Pope, people, ceramic and Bogota Cathedral (Colombia and St. Lucia)	1·50	1·10
892	2500l. Pope, Curé d'Ars and Lyon Cathedral (France)	5·50	4·25
893	4000l. Hands releasing dove and symbols of countries visited (Bangladesh, Singapore, Fiji, New Zealand, Australia and Seychelles)	9·00	7·00
886/893	Set of 8	18·00	14·00

237 Arrival of Relics

238 Children and Sister of Institute of the Daughters of Mary Help of Christians

(Des L. Vangelli. Photo)

1987 (3 Dec). *900th Anniv of Transfer of St. Nicholas's Relics from Myra to Bari.* T **237** *and similar vert designs. Multicoloured.* P 13½ × 14.

894	500l. Type **237**	75	80
895	700l. St. Nicholas giving purses of gold to save from dishonour the three daughters of a poor man	1·10	1·10
896	3000l. St. Nicholas saving a ship	7·75	6·00

Nos. 894/6 were each issued in sheets of eight stamps and 16 labels depicting various popular images of St. Nicholas.

(Des Maria Perrini. Photo)

1988 (19 Apr). *Death Centenary of St. John Bosco (founder of Salesian Brothers).* T **238** *and similar vert designs. Multicoloured.* P 13½ × 14.

897	500l. Type **238**	55	50
	a. Horiz strip of 3. Nos. 897/9	3·50	
898	1000l. Bosco and children	90	90
899	2000l. Children and Salesian lay brother	1·80	1·90

Nos. 897/9 were issued together in horizontal *se-tenant* strips of three within the sheet, each strip forming a composite design.

468

VATICAN CITY   1988

239 The Annunciation
240 Prince Vladimir the Great (15th-century icon) 

(Des E. Woelfel (50l.), Maria Perrini (300l.), Anna Maresca (500l.), Maria Tuccelli (750l.), N. Suezawa (1000l.), Rita Fantini (2400l.). Photo)

1988 (16 June). *Marian Year.* T **239** *and similar vert designs. Multicoloured.* P 13½ × 14.
900	50l. Type **239**	10	10
901	300l. Nativity	30	25
902	500l. Pentecost	45	40
903	750l. The Assumption	65	55
904	1000l. Mother of the Church	90	75
905	2400l. Refuge of Sinners	2·00	1·80
900/905	Set of 6	4·00	3·50

(Des M. Codoni. Photo)

1988 (16 June). *Millenary of Conversion to Christianity of Rus of Kiev.* T **240** *and similar vert designs. Multicoloured.* P 13½ × 14.
906	450l. Type **240**	45	40
907	650l. St. Sophia's Cathedral, Kiev	65	60
908	2500l. "Mother of God in Prayer" (mosaic, St. Sophia's Cathedral)	2·20	2·00

241 "Marriage at Cana" (detail)
242 Angel with Olive Branch 

(Photo (650l.). Eng A. Ciaburro; recess (others))

1988 (29 Sept). *400th Death Anniv of Paolo Veronese* (painter). T **241** *and similar designs.* P 14 × 13½ (650l.) or 13½ × 14 (others).
909	550l. steel blue and crimson	75	55
910	650l. multicoloured	90	75
911	3000l. bright scarlet and deep brown	2·40	2·00

Designs: *Horiz*—650l. "Self-portrait". *Vert*—3000l. "Marriage at Cana" (different detail).

(Des R. Cristiano. Photo)

1988 (27 Oct). AIR. *Pope John Paul II's Journeys (6th series). Horiz designs as* T **231**. *Multicoloured.* P 14 × 13½.
912	450l. Hands releasing dove, St. Peter's, Rome, Santiago Cathedral and Sanctuary of Our Lady, Luján (Uruguay, Chile and Argentina)	55	50
913	650l. Pope in act of blessing, Speyer Cathedral and youths (German Federal Republic)	85	70
914	1000l. Hands releasing dove, Gdansk altar and intertwined flowers and thorns (Poland)	1·00	90
915	2500l. Skyscrapers and Pope blessing youths (U.S.A.)	2·75	2·20
916	5000l. Hands releasing dove, tepee at Fort Simpson and American Indians (Canada)	5·00	4·50
912/916	Set of 5	9·00	8·00

(Des L. Vangelli. Photo)

1988 (12 Dec). *Christmas.* T **242** *and similar vert designs. Multicoloured.* P 13½ × 14.
917	50l. Type **242**	10	10
918	400l. Angel holding olive branch in both hands	35	30
919	500l. Angel with olive branch (flying from right)	55	45
920	550l. Shepherds	60	50
921	850l. Nativity	85	70
922	1500l. Wise Men	1·30	1·10
917/922	Set of 6	3·25	2·75

MS923 120 × 140 mm. As Nos. 917/22 but with gold backgrounds ... 4·75 4·75

243 Head of Apis
244 The Annunciation 

(Eng Patrizia Gabriele. Recess and litho)

1989 (5 May). *150th Anniv of Gregorian Egyptian Museum. Sheet* 140 × 140 *mm containing* T **243** *and similar vert designs. Multicoloured.* P 14 × 13½.
MS924 l. Type **243**; 650l. Double-headed statue of Isis and Apis. 750l. Headless statue of physician Ugiahorresne, 2400l. Pharaoh Mentuhotep ... 4·75 4·75

1989 (5 May). *600th Anniv of Feast of Visitation of Virgin Mary.* T **244** *and similar vert designs showing illuminated initials. Multicoloured. Photo.* P 13½ × 14.
925	550l. Type **244**	65	55
926	750l. Virgin Mary and St. Elizabeth	75	65
927	2500l. Virgin Mary and St. Elizabeth with Jesus and John the Baptist as babies	2·30	2·00

245 Yellow-bibbed Lory ("Parrot")
246 Broken Bread (Congress emblem) 

(Photo Courvoisier)

1989 (13 June). *Birds featured in* Histoire Naturelle des Oiseaux *by Eleazar Albin.* T **245** *and similar vert designs. Multicoloured. Granite paper.* P 12.
928	100l. Type **245**	20	15
929	150l. Green woodpecker	20	20

469

VATICAN CITY   1989

930	200l. Goldcrest ("Crested Wren") and winter ("Common") wren	20	20
931	350l. Common kingfisher (Kingfisher)	30	30
932	500l. Common cardinal ("Red Gross Beak of Virginia")	45	45
933	700l. Northern bullfinch ("Bullfinch")	65	60
934	1500l. Norhtern lapwing ("Lapwing Plover")	1·40	1·30
935	3000l. Green-winged teal ("French Teal")	3·00	2·75
928/935	Set of 8	5·75	5·25

(Des M. Shin (550l.), H. Shim (others). Photo)

1989 (29 Sept). *44th International Eucharistic Congress, Seoul.* T **246** *and similar vert designs.* P 13½ × 14.

936	550l. rosine and blackish green	55	45
937	850l. multicoloured	85	70
938	1000l. multicoloured	1·00	85
939	2500l. slate-green, bright rose & brt violet	2·40	2·00
936/939	Set of 4	4·25	3·50

Designs—850l. Cross; 1000l. Cross and fishes; 2500l. Small cross on wafer.

247 Papel's Arms, Map of South America and Pope

248 Basilica of the Assumption, Baltimore

(Des Patrizia Gabriele and Anna Maresca. Photo)

1989 (9 Nov). *Pope John Paul II's Journeys (7th series).* T **247** *and similar horiz designs. Multicoloured.* P 14 × 13½.

940	50l. Type **247**	20	15
941	550l. Austria	55	50
942	800l. Southern Africa	1·00	75
943	1000l. France	1·20	1·00
944	4000l. Italy	4·25	3·50
940/944	Set of 5	6·25	4·25

(Photo Courvoisier)

1989 (9 Nov). *Bicentenary of First Catholic Diocese in U.S.A.* T **248** *and similar horiz designs, each agate and yellow-brown. Granite paper.* P 12.

945	450l. Type **248**	55	50
946	1350l. John Carroll (first Archbishop of Baltimore)	1·60	1·30
947	2400l. Cathedral of Mary Our Queen, Baltimore (after Martin Barry)	2·50	2·10

249 Vision of Ursulines on Mystical Stair

250 Ordination and Arrival in Frisia

(Des Sister A. Porro. Photo)

1990 (5 Apr). *450th Death Anniv of St. Angela Merici (founder of Company of St. Ursula).* T **249** *and similar vert designs. Multicoloured.* P 13½ × 14.

948	700l. Type **249**	85	70
949	800l. St. Angela teaching Ursulines	1·00	85
950	2800l. Ursulines	3·75	2·75

(Des P. Arghittu. Photo)

1990 (5 June). *1300th Anniv of Beginning of St. Willibrord's Missions.* T **250** *and similar vent designs. Multicoloured.* P 13½ × 14.

951	300l. Type **250**	30	30
952	700l. St. Willibrord in Antwerp, creation as bishop by Pope Sergius I and gift of part of Echternach by Abbess of Euren	75	65
953	3000l. Gift of Echternach by King Pepin and St. Willibrord's death	3·00	2·50

251 Abraham

252 Fishermen on Lake Peking

(Photo Courvoisier)

1990 (5 June). *40th Anniv of Caritas Internationalis.* T **251** *and similar square designs showing details of mosaic from Basilica of Sta. Maria Maggiore, Rome. Multicoloured. Granite paper.* P 12.

954	450l. Type **251**	55	50
955	650l. Three visitors	90	70
956	800l. Sarah making bread	1·10	95
957	2000l. Visitors seated at Abraham's table	2·50	2·20
954/957	Set of 4	4·50	4·00
MS958	100 × 135 mm. As Nos. 954/7 but without gold frame	6·00	6·00

1990 (2 Oct). *300th Anniv of Peking-Nanking Diocese.* T **252** *and similar vert designs, showing details of two enamelled bronze vases given by Peking Apostolic Delegate to Pope Plus IX. Multicoloured. Photo.* P 13½ × 14.

959	500l. Type **252**	45	45
960	750l. Church of the Immaculate Conception (first Peking church, 1650)	65	60
961	1500l. Lake Peking	1·50	1·30
962	2000l. Church of the Redeemer, Peking, 1703	1·80	1·60
959/962	Set of 4	4·00	3·50

253 Pope and African Landscape

254 Choir of Angels

(Photo Courvoisier)

1990 (27 Nov). *AIR. Pope John Paul II's Journeys (8th series).* T **253** *and similar horiz designs. Multicoloured. Granite paper.* P 11½.

963	500l. Type **253**	45	45
964	1000l. Northern European landscape (Scandinavia)	65	65
965	3000l. Cathedral (Santiago de Compostela, Spain)	1·50	1·50
966	5000l. Oriental landscape (Korea, Indonesia and Mauritius)	1·80	1·80
963/966	Set of 4	4·00	4·00

VATICAN CITY — 1990

(Photo State Ptg Wks, Paris)

1990 (27 Nov). *Christmas.* T **254** and similar multicoloured designs showing details of painting by Sebastiano Mainardi. P 12½ × 13 (2500l.) or 13 × 12½ (others).

967	50l. Type **254**	20	20
968	200l. St. Joseph	20	20
969	650l. Holy Child	75	75
970	750l. Virgin Mary	90	90
971	2500l. "Nativity" (complete picture) (vert)	2·75	2·75
967/971	Set of 5	4·25	4·25

255 "Eleazar" (left half)

256 Title Page and Pope Leo XIII's Arms

(Photo Courvoisier)

1991 (9 Apr). *Restoration of Sistine Chapel.* T **255** and similar horiz designs, depicting details of Lunettes of the Ancestors of Christ by Michelangelo. Multicoloured. Granite paper. P 11½.

972	50l. Type **255**	20	20
973	100l. "Eleazar" (right half)	20	20
	a. Booklet pane. No. 973 × 6	1·20	
974	150l. "Jacob" (left half)	20	20
	a. Booklet pane. No. 974 × 6	1·20	
975	250l. "Jacob" (right half)	20	20
976	350l. "Josiah" (left half)	30	30
977	400l. "Josiah" (right half)	35	35
978	500l. "Asa" (left half)	45	45
979	650l. "Asa" (right half)	60	60
	a. Booklet pane. No. 979 × 6	3·75	
980	800l. "Zerubbabel" (left half)	75	75
981	1000l. "Zerubbabel" (right half)	90	90
982	2000l. "Azor" (left half)	1·80	1·80
983	3000l. "Azor" (right half)	2·75	2·75
972/983	Set of 12	7·75	7·75

The booklet panes have a white margin around the block of stamps.

(Eng Maria Perrini (600l.), A Ciaburro (others). Recess)

1991 (23 May). *Centenary of Rerum Novarum (encyclical on workers' rights).* T **256** and similar horiz designs. P 14 × 13½.

984	600l. deep blue and myrtle green	55	55
985	750l. deep green and lake-brown	75	75
986	3500l. reddish purple and blue-black	3·50	3·00

Designs:—750l. Allegory of Church, workers and employers (from Leo XIII's 15th Anniversary medal, 1892), 3500l. Profile of Pope Leo XIII (from same medal).

(Photo Courvoisier)

1991 (1 Oct). *Centenary of Vatican Observatory.* T **257** and similar multicoloured designs. Granite paper. P 11½.

987	750l. Type **257**	65	60
988	1000l. Castelgandolfo observatory (horiz)	1·00	95
989	3000l. Vatican Observatory telescope, Mount Graham, Tucson, U.S.A.	3·00	2·50

(Photo Slate Ptg Wks, Paris)

1991 (1 Oct). *600th Anniv of Canonization of St. Bridget (founder of Order of the Holy Saviour).* T **258** and similar vert design. Multicoloured. P 12½ × 13.

990	1500l. Type **258**	1·40	1·20
991	2000l. "Revelation of Christ" (Puccini)	1·90	1·60

259 Cathedral of the Immaculate Conception, Ouagadougou

260 Colonnade of St. Peter's Cathedral, Rome

(Eng E. Donnini. Recess and litho)

1991 (11 Nov). *Pope John Paul II's Journeys (9th series).* T **259** and similar vert designs. Multicoloured. P 13½ × 14.

992	200l. Type **259** (Cape Verde, Guinea Bissau, Mali, Burkina Faso and Chad)	20	20
993	550l. St. Vitus's Cathedral, Prague (Czechoslovakia)	55	55
994	750l. Basilica of Our Lady of Guadaloupe (Mexico and Curacao)	75	75
995	1500l. Ta' Pinu Sanctuary, Gozo (Malta)	1·60	1·60
996	3500l. Cathedral of Christ the King, Giteca (Tanzania, Burundi, Rwanda and Ivory Coast)	4·25	4·25
992/996	Set of 5	6·50	6·50

(Des and eng J. Larrivière (500l.), C. Jumelet (others). Recess State Ptg Wks. Paris)

1991 (11 Nov). *Synod of Bishops' Special Assembly for Europe.* T **260** and similar horiz designs, each black and olive-brown. P 12½ × 13.

997	300l. Type **260**	30	30
	a. Horiz strip of 3. Nos. 997/9	4·75	
998	500l. St. Peter's Cathedral and square	45	45
999	4000l. Apostolic Palace and colonnade	4·00	4·00

Nos. 997/9 were issued together in horizontal *se-tenant* strips of three within the sheet, each strip forming a composite design.

257 Astrograph (astronomical camera)

258 "Apparition of Virgin Mary" (Biagio Puccini)

261 Christopher Columbus

262 "Our Lady of Childbirth"

VATICAN CITY 1992

(Photo Courvoisier)

1992 (24 Mar). *500th Anniv of Discovery of America by Columbus.* T **261** *and similar vert designs. Multicoloured. Granite paper.* P 11½.
1000	500l. Type **261**		45	45
1001	600l. St. Pedro Claver		55	55
1002	850l. "Virgin of the Catholic Kings"		75	70
1003	1000l. Bortolomé de las Cases		1·00	90
1004	2000l. Junipero Serra		2·00	1·80
1000/1004	Set of 5		4·25	4·00
MS1005	138 × 95 mm. 1500l., 2500l. Details of nautical chart from atlas of Battista Agnese		6·00	6·00

1992 (15 May). *500th Death Anniv of Piero della Francesca (painter).* T **262** *and similar vert designs. Photo. Multicoloured.* P 13½ × 14.
1006	300l. Type **262**		30	30
1007	750l. "Our Lady of Childbirth" (detail)		75	75
1008	1000l. "The Resurrection"		1·00	1·00
1009	3000l. "The Resurrection" (detail)		3·00	3·00
1006/1009	Set of 4		4·50	4·50

263 St. Giuseppe comforting the Sick

264 Maize (*Frumentum indicum*)

(Des G. Hajnal. Photo Courvoisier)

1992 (15 May). *150th Death Anniv of St. Giuseppe Benedetto Cottolengo.* T **263** *and similar vert design. Multicoloured.* P 11½.
1010	650l. Type **263**		65	65
1011	850l. St. Giuseppe holding Piccola Casa della Divina Provvidenza (infirmary), Turin		1·00	1·00

(Photo Courvoisier)

1992 (15 Sept). *Plants of the New World.* T **264** *and similar vert designs showing illustrations from the 18th-century* Phytanthoza Iconographia. *Multicoloured. Granite Paper.* P 11½.
1012	850l. Type **264**		80	80
	a. Block of 6. Nos. 1012/17		4·75	
1013	850l. Tomatoes (*Solanum pomiferum*)		80	75
1014	850l. Cactus (*Opuntia*)		80	80
1015	850l. Cacao (*Cacaos, Cacavifera*)		80	80
1016	850l. Peppers (*Solanum tuberosum*)		80	75
1017	850l. Pineapple (*Ananas sagitae*)		80	75
1012/1017	Set of 6		4·25	4·25

265 Our Lady of Guadalupe, Crucifix and Mitres

266 Pope, Dove and Map of Europe

(Des A. Canevari. Photo State Ptg Wks, Paris)

1992 (12 Oct). *Fourth Latin American Espiscopal Conference, Santo Domingo.* P 12½ × 13.
1018	265	700l. gold, emerald & lt yellowish green	85	85

(Des G. Contri. Photo)

1992 (24 Nov). AIR. *Pope John Paul II's Journeys (10th Series).* T **266** *and similar horiz designs. Multicoloured.* P 14.
1019	500l. Type **266** (Portugal)		45	45
1020	1000l. Map of Europe highlighting Poland		1·00	90
1021	4000l. Our Lady of Czestochowa and map highlighting Poland and Hungary		3·75	3·25
1022	6000l. Map of South America highlighting Brazil		6·50	5·00
1019/1022	Set of 4		10·50	10·00

267 "The Annunciation"

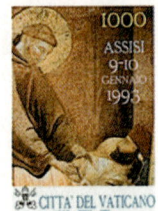

268 "St. Francis healing the Man from Ilerda" (fresco by Giotto in Upper Church, Assisi)

(Photo Courvoisier)

1992 (24 Nov). *Christmas.* T **267** *and similar square designs showing mosaics in Church of Sta. Maria Maggiore, Rome. Multicoloured. Granite paper.* P 11½.
1023	600l. Type **267**		75	75
1024	700l. "Nativity"		85	85
1025	1000l. "Adoration of the Kings"		1·20	1·20
1026	1500l. "Presentation in the Temple"		1·60	1·60
1023/1026	Set of 4		4·00	4·00

1993 (9 Jan). *"Peace in Europe' Prayer Meeting" Assisi. Litho.* P 13½ × 14.
1027	**268** 1000l. multicoloured		1·40	1·40

No. 1027 was issued with *se-tenant* label depicting St. Francis's Basilica, Assisi.

269 Dome of St. Peter's Cathedral

270 "The Sacrifice of Isaac"

(Photo Courvoisier)

1993 (23 Mar). *Architectural Treasures of Rome and the Vatican.* T **269** *and similar horiz designs. Multicoloured. Granite paper.* P 11½.
1028	200l. Type **269**		20	20
	a. Booklet pane. No. 1028 × 4		90	
1029	300l. St. John Lateran's Basilica		20	20
	a. Booklet pane. No. 1029 × 4		90	

472

VATICAN CITY   1993

1030	350l. Basilica of Sta. Maria Maggiore	30	30
	a. Booklet pane. No. 1030 × 4	1·30	
1031	500l. St. Paul's Basilica	45	45
	a. Booklet pane. No. 1031 × 4	1·90	
1032	600l. Apostolic Palace, Vatican	55	55
1033	700l. Apostolic Palace, Lateran	65	65
1034	850l. Papal Palace, Castelgandolfo	75	75
1035	1000l. Chancery Palace	90	90
1036	2000l. Palace of Propagation of the Faith	1·60	1·60
1037	3000l. San Calisto Palace	2·50	2·50
1028/1037	Set of 10	8·75	8·75

(Des and eng A. Ciaburro. Recess and photo)

1993 (22 May). *Ascension Day. T* **270** *and similar vert designs showing the bas-relief "Traditio Legis" from 4th-century sarcophagus. Multicoloured.* P 13½×14.

1038	200l. Type **270**	20	20
	a. Horiz strip of 3. Nos. 1038/40	4·50	
1039	750l. Jesus handing New Law to St. Peter	90	90
1040	3000l. Christ watching servant washing Pilate's hands	3·25	3·25

Nos. 1038/40 were issued together in horizontal *se-tenant* strips of three within the sheet, each strip forming a composite design.

273 St. John, Cross, Fish and Moldava River

274 Pope praying

(Des C. Bruscaglia and S. Isola. Litho)

1993 (29 Sept). *600th Death Anniv of St. John of Nepomuk (patron saint of Bohemia). T* **273** *and similar vert design. Multicoloured.* P 13½ × 14.

1047	1000l. Type **273**	90	90
1048	2000l. Charles Bridge, Prague	1·80	1·80

(Photo Courvoisier)

1993 (23 Nov). *Pope John Paul II's Journeys (11th series). T* **274** *and similar horiz designs. Multicoloured. Granite paper.* P 11½.

1049	600l. Type **274** (Senegal, Gambia and Guinea)	55	55
1050	1000l. Pope with Pastoral Staff (Angola and St. Thomas and Prince Islands)	1·10	1·10
1051	5000l. Pope with hands clasped in prayer (Dominican Republic)	5·00	5·00

271 Cross and Grape Vines

272 "Crucifixion" (Felice Casorati)

(Des G. Hajnal. Litho Enschedé)

1993 (22 May). *45th International Eucharistic Congress, Seville. T* **271** *and similar vert designs. Multicoloured.* P 14 × 13½.

1041	500l. Type **271**	45	45
1042	700l. Cross and hands offering broken bread	65	65
1043	1500l. Hands holding chalice	1·40	1·40
1044	2500l. Cross, banner and ears of wheat	2·30	2·30
1041/1044	Set of 4	4·25	4·25

275 "Madonna of Solothurn" (detail)

276 "Creation of the Planets" (left detail)

(Eng A. Ciaburro (700l.), P. Arghittu (1000l.), Rita Morena (1500l.). Recess and litho)

1993 (23 Nov). *450th Death Anniv of Hans Holbein the Younger (painter). T* **275** *and similar vert designs. Multicoloured.* P 13½ × 14.

1052	700l. Type **275**	75	75
1053	1000l. "Madonna of Solothurn"	1·10	1·10
1054	1500l. "Self-portrait"	1·60	1·60

(Photo French Govt Ptg Wks, Paris)

1993 (29 Sept). *Europa. Contemporary Art. T* **272** *and similar vert design. Multicoloured.* P 13.

1045	750l. Type **272**	65	75
1046	850l. "Rouen Cathedral" (Maurice Utrillo)	85	85

(Photo Courvoisier)

1994 (8 Apr). *Completion of Restoration of Sistine Chapel. T* **276** *and similar square designs. Multicoloured. Granite paper.* P 11½.

1055	350l. Type **276**	40	40
	a. Horiz pair. Nos. 1055/6	90	
1056	350l. God creating planets (right detail)	40	40
1057	500l. Adam (left detail, "The Creation of Man")	60	60
	a. Horiz pair. Nos. 1057/8	1·25	
1058	500l. God (right detail)	60	60
1059	1000l. Adam and Eve taking forbidden fruit (left detail, "The Original Sin")	1·20	1·20
	a. Horiz pair. Nos. 1059/60	2·50	
1060	1000l. Angel casting out Adam and Eve from the Garden (right detail)	1·20	1·20

VATICAN CITY 1994

1061	2000l. People climbing from swollen river (left detail, "The Flood")		2·40	2·40
	a. Horiz pair. Nos. 1061/2		5·00	
1062	2000l. Floodwaters surrounding temporary shelter (right detail)		2·40	2·40
1055/1062 Set of 8			8·25	8·25
MS1063	80 × 110 mm. 4000l. Christ and Virgin Mary (detail, "The Last Judgement"). P 12		5·00	5·00

Stamps of the same value were issued together in horizontal se-tenant pairs within their sheets, each pair forming a composite design.

277 Crosier and Dome

278 God creating Man and Woman

(Des Estella Francioso. Photo French Govt Ptg Wks, Paris)

1994 (8 Apr). *Special Assembly for Africa of Synod of Bishops*. T **277** and similar multicoloured design. P 12½ × 13 (850l.) or 13 × 12½ (1000l.).

1064	850l. Type **277**		75	75
1065	1000l. Crucifix, dome of St. Peter's and African scene (*horiz*)		90	90

(Des G. Hajnal. Litho)

1994 (31 May). *International Year of the Family*. T **278** and similar vert designs. Multicoloured. P 13½ × 14.

1066	400l. Type **278**		35	35
1067	750l. Family		65	65
1068	1000l. Parents teaching son		85	85
1069	2000l. Youth helping elderly couple		1·80	1·80
1066/1069 Set of 4			3·25	3·25

279 Timeline of Knowledge from Wheel to Atom

280 Bishop Euphrasius and Archdeacon Claudius

(Des G. Contri. Litho Enschedé)

1994 (31 May). *Europa. Discoveries*. T **279** and similar horiz design. Multicoloured. P 13½ × 14.

1070	750l. Type **279**		75	75
1071	850l. Galileo, solar system and scientific apparatus		90	90

(Des Maria Perrini. Litho)

1994 (27 Sept). *13th International Congress on Christian Archaeology, Split and Porec, Croatia*. T **280** and similar vert designs showing mosaics from Euphrasian Basilica, Porec. P 13½ × 14.

1072	700l. Type **280**		55	55
1073	1500l. Madonna and Child with two angels		1·30	1·30
1074	3000l. Jesus Christ between Apostles St. Peter and St. Paul		2·75	2·75

281 Route Map, Mongolian Village and Giovanni da Montecorvino

1994 (27 Sept). *700th Anniv of Evangelization of China*. Litho. P 14½ × 14.

1075	**281**	1000l. multicoloured	90	90

282 Houses, Mahdi's Mausoleum, Omdurman, and St. Mary's Basilica, Lodonga (Benin, Uganda and Sudan)

(Des and eng J. Larriviere. Recess French Govt Ptg Wks, Paris)

1994 (18 Nov). *Pope John Paul II's Journeys (12th series)*. T **282** and similar horiz designs. P 13.

1076	600l. lt brown, dp bluish grn & carm-red		55	55
1077	700l. violet, olive-sepia & yellow-green		65	65
1078	1000l. reddish brown, turquoise-blue and bright reddish violet		90	90
1079	2000l. black, bright new blue & Indian red		1·80	1·80
1080	3000l. dp blue, brt reddish vio & chestnut		2·75	2·75
1076/1080 Set of 5			6·00	6·00

Designs:—700l. St. Mary's Church, Apollonia, Mosque and statue of Skanderbeg, Tirana (Albania); 1000l. Church of the Saint, Huelva Region, and The Giralda, Real Maestranza and Golden Tower, Seville (Spain); 2000l. Skyscrapers and St. Thomas's Theological Seminary, Denver, "El Castillo" (pyramid), Kulkulkan, Jamaican girl and Mexican boy (Jamaica, Mexico and United States); 3000l. Tallin, "Hymn to Liberty" (monument), Riga, and Tower, Cathedral Square, Vilnius (Lithuania, Latvia and Estonia).

283 Holy Family

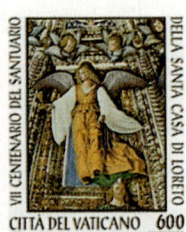

284 Angel with Chalice (Melozzo da Forli) (St. Mark's)

474

VATICAN CITY 1994

(Photo Courvoisier)

1994 (18 Nov). *Christmas.* T **283** *and similar horiz designs showing details of "Nativity" by Tintoretto. Multicoloured. Granite paper.* P 11 × 11½.
1081	700l. Type **283**	75	75
1082	1000l. Upper half of painting (45 × 28mm)	1·30	1·30
	a. Vert pair. Nos. 1082/3	2·75	
1083	1000l. Lower half of painting (45 × 28mm)	1·30	1·30

Nos. 1082/3 were issued together in vertical *se-tenant* pairs within the sheet, each pair forming a composite design of the complete painting.

(Photo Courvoisier)

1995 (25 Mar). *700th Anniv of Shrine of the Holy House, Loreto.* T **284** *and similar vert designs showing details from the vaults of sacristies. Multicoloured. Granite paper.* P 11½.
1084	600l. Type **284**	50	50
1085	700l. Angel with lamb (Melozzo) (Sacristy of St. Mark)	55	55
1086	1500l. Angel with lute (Luca Signorelli) (St. John's)	1·20	1·20
1087	2500l. Angel (Signorelli) (St. John's)	2·40	2·40
1084/1087 Set of 4		4·25	4·25
MS1088	75 × 110 mm. 3000l. Madonna and Child (detail of "Translation of the Holy House" (marble relief)) (35 × 35mm)	3·25	3·25

285 Hands and Broken Chains

286 Fountain of the Triton (Bernini), Vatican Gardens

(Des Gabriella Titotto. Photo)

1995 (25 Mar). *Europa. Peace and Freedom.* T **285** *and similar horiz designs. Multicoloured.* P 14 × 13½.
1089	750l. Type **285**	65	70
1090	850l. Globe, olive wreath, dove and handclasp	85	85

(Photo Courvoisier)

1995 (8 June). *European Nature Conservation Year.* T **286** *and similar vert designs. Multicoloured Granite paper.* P 12.
1091	200l. Type **286**	20	20
1092	300l. Avenue of roses, Castelgandolfo	30	30
	a. Booklet pane. No. 1092 × 3	1·00	
1093	400l. Statue of Apollo, Vatican Gardens	35	35
	a. Booklet pane. No. 1093 × 3	1·10	
1094	550l. Ruins of Domitian's Villa, Castelgandolfo	45	45
	a. Booklet pane. No. 1094 × 3	1·40	
1095	750l. Box elder, Vatican Gardens	65	65
	a. Booklet pane. No. 1095 × 3	2·00	
1096	1500l. Belvedere Gardens, Castelgandolfo	1·40	1·40
1097	2000l. Eagle fountain, Vatican Gardens	1·80	1·80
1098	3000l. Avenue of cypresses, Castelgandolfo	2·50	2·50
1091/1098 Set of 8		7·00	7·00

The booklet panes have a perforated margin around the stamps.

287 Guglielmo Marconi and Transmitter

288 St. Antony of Padua (statue by Donatello)

(Des E. Jünger (850l.), I. Fantini (1000l.). Litho German State Ptg Works, Berlin)

1995 (8 June). *One Hundred Years of Radio.* T **287** *and similar horiz design. Multicoloured. Phosphorescent paper.* P 14.
1099	850l. Type **287**	90	90
1100	1000l. Archangel Gabriel, Pope John Paul II with microphone and Vatican broadcasting station	1·10	1·10

(Eng F. Tulli (500l.), P. Arghittu (750l.), A. Ciaburro (3000l.). Recess)

1995 (3 Oct). *Saints' Anniversaries.* T **288** *and similar vert designs.* P 13½ × 14.
1101	500l. reddish brown and myrtle green	45	45
1102	750l. emerald and deep violet	65	65
1103	3000l. deep violet-blue and plum	2·75	2·75

Designs:—500l. Type **288** (800th birth anniv); 750l. St. John of God (founder of Order of Hospitallers, 500th birth anniv) (sculpture, Filippo Valle); 3000l. St. Philip Neri (founder of Friars of the Oratory, 400th death anniv) (sculpture, Giovanni Battista Maini).

289 Dove and Hearts

290 "The Annunciation" (Johannes of lenzenstein)

(Des P. Guiotto. Photo French Govt Ptg Wks, Paris)

1995 (3 Oct). *50th Anniv of United Nations Organization.* T **289** *and similar vert designs. Multicoloured.* P 13½ × 13.
1104	550l. Type **289**	45	45
1105	750l. Human faces	65	65
1106	850l. Doves	75	75
1107	1250l. Symbolic lymph system	1·10	1·10
1108	2000l. People gazing at "explosion" of flowers	1·80	1·80
1104/1108 Set of 5		4·25	4·25

(Photo Courvoisier)

1995 (20 Nov). *Holy Year 2000 (1st issue).* T **290** *and similar vert designs showing illustrations from illuminated manuscripts in Vatican Apostolic Library. Multicoloured. Granite paper.* P 12.
1109	400l. Type **290**	35	35
1110	850l. "Nativity" (from King Matthias I Corvinus's breviary)	75	75
1111	1250l. "Flight into Egypt" (from Book of Hours)	1·10	1·10

475

VATICAN CITY   1995

1112   2000l. "Jesus among the Teachers"
             (Pietro Lombardo) . . . . . .   2·20   2·20
1109/1112 *Set* of 4 . . . .   4·00   4·00
    See also Nos. 1132/5, 1167/70, 1197/1200, 1231/34, 1242/50 and 1265/8.

291 Pope, Statue of Virgin Mary and Zagreb Cathedral

292 Marco Polo receiving Golden Book from the Great Khan

(Litho Questa)

1995 (20 Nov). *Pope John Paul II's Journeys (13th series).* T **291** *and similar horiz design. Multicoloured.* P 14½ × 14.
1113   1000l. Type **291** (Croatia)   90   90
1114   2000l. Pope, Genoa Lantern, Orvieto
             Cathedral and Valley of the
             Temples, Agrigento (Italy) . . .   1·80   1·80

(Photo Courvoisier)

1996 (15 Mar). *700th Anniv of Marco Polo's Return from China.* T **292** *and similar designs. Multicoloured (except* 2000l.*). Granite paper.* P 11½.
1115   350l. Type **292**   30   30
1116   850l. The Great Khan giving alms to
             poor, Cambaluc   60   60
1117   1250l. Marco Polo delivering Pope
             Gregory X's letter to the Great
             Khan   90   90
1118   2500l. Marco Polo in Persia listening to
             Nativity story . . . .   2·20   2·20
1115/1118 *Set* of 4 . . . .   3·50   3·50
MS1119 138 × 100 mm. 2000l. black (Marco
Polo) (*vert*). P 12 . . . .   1·90   1·90
    The designs of Nos. 1115/18 are taken from miniatures held by the Bodleian Library, Oxford. The portrait on the 2000l. is from the first printed edition of Polo's work *Il Milione*.
    The miniature sheet also commemorates "China '96" International Stamp Exhibition, Peking.

293 Angel with Crosses

294 Gianna Molla (surgeon)

(Des G. Hajnal. Photo)

1996 (15 Mar). *Anniversaries.* T **293** *and similar vert design. Multicoloured.* P 13½ × 14.
1120   1250l. Type **293** (400th Anniv of Union
             of Brest-Litovsk)   90   90
1121   2000l. Latin and Byzantine mitres and
             Tree of Life (350th Anniv of Union
             of Uzhorod) . . . .   1·60   1·60

(Des and eng F. Tulli (750l.), A. Ciaburro (850l.). Recess)

1996 (7 May). *Europa. Famous Women.* T **294** *and similar vert design.* P 13½ × 14.
1122   750l. deep blue   65   75
1123   850l. lake-brown   75   80
Design:—850l. Edith Stein (Carmelite nun).

295 "Sun and Steel"

296 Wawel Cathedral

(Des P. Guiotto. Litho French Govt Ptg Wks, Paris)

1996 (7 May). *Centenary of Modern Olympic Games.* T **295** *and similar vert designs. Multicoloured.* P 13½.
1124   1250l. Type **295** . . . .   1·80   1·80
     a. Horiz strip of 5. Nos. 1124/8 . .   9·00
1125   1250l. "Solar Plexus" . . . .   1·80   1·80
1126   1250l. Hand and golden beams . .   1·80   1·80
1127   1250l. "Speculum Aevi" (athlete and
             shadow) . . . .   1·80   1·80
1128   1250l. Hercules . . . .   1·80   1·80
1124/1128 *Set* of 5 . . . .   8·00   8·00
Nos. 1124/8 were issued together in horizontal *se-tenant* strips of five stamps within the sheet.

(Des I. Fantini. Litho German State Ptg Wks, Berlin)

1996 (12 Oct). *50th Anniv of Ordination of Karol Wojtyla (Pope John Paul II) at Wawel Cathedral, Crakow, Poland.* T **296** *and similar horiz designs. Multicoloured.* P 14.
1129   500l. Type **296**   75   75
1130   750l. Pope John Paul II . . . . . .   1·10   1·10
1131   1250l. St. John Lateran's Basilica, Rome
             (seat of Bishop of Eternal City)   1·80   1·80

297 "Baptism of Jesus"

298 Philippines, Papua New Guinea, Australia and Sri Lanka

(Photo Courvoisier)

1996 (12 Oct). *Holy Year 2000 (2nd issue).* T **297** *and similar vert designs showing illustrations from 13th-century illuminated New Testament in Vatican Apostolic Library. Multicoloured. Granite paper.* P 12.
1132   550l. Type **297**   40   40
1133   850l. "Temptation in the Desert" .   60   60
1134   1500l. "Cure of a Leper" . . . . . .   1·10   1·10
1135   2500l. "Jesus the Teacher" . . . .   2·30   2·30
1132/1135 *Set* of 4 . . . .   4·00   4·00

(Des A. Ciaburro. Litho)

1996 (20 Nov). *Pope John Paul II's Journeys (14th series).* T **298** *and similar horiz designs.* P 14 × 13½.
1136   250l. blue and black   20   20
1137   500l. turquoise-green and black .   35   35
1138   750l. green and black   55   55
1139   1000l. brown and black   75   75
1140   2000l. brownish grey and black . .   1·80   1·80
1141   5000l. bright rose and black . . .   4·25   4·25
1136/1141 *Set* of 6 . . . .   7·25   7·25

476

VATICAN CITY   1996

Designs:—500l. Czech Republic and Poland; 750l. Belgium; 1000l. Slovakia, 2000l. Cameroun, South Africa and Kenya; 5000l. United States of America and United Nations Headquarters.

299 "Nativity" (Murillo)

300 Pope St. Celestine V

(Litho Ashton Potter Canada)

1996 (20 Nov). *Christmas.* P 13½.
| 1142 | 299 | 750l. multicoloured | 85 | 85 |

(Des I. Fantini. Litho Enschedé)

1996 (20 Nov). *Saints' Anniversaries.* T **300** and similar vert design. Multicoloured. P 14 × 13½.
| 1143 | 1250l. Type **300** (700th death) | 1·30 | 1·30 |
| 1144 | 1250l. St. Alfonso Maria de' Liguori (founder of Redemptorists Order) (300th birth) | 1·30 | 1·30 |

301 Travelling Carriage

302 Halberdier

(Photo Courvoisier)

1997 (20 Mar). *Papal Transport.* T **301** and similar horiz designs. Multicoloured. Granite paper. P 12.
1145	50l. Type **301**	10	10
1146	100l. Graham Paige motor car	10	10
	a. Booklet pane. No. 1146 × 4	40	
1147	300l. Ceremonial berlin (carriage)	20	20
	a. Booklet pane. No. 1147 × 4	80	
1148	500l. Citroën Lictoria VI motor car	35	35
	a. Booklet pane. No. 1148 × 4	1·40	
1149	750l. Grand ceremonial berlin	55	55
	a. Booklet pane. No. 1149 × 4	2·20	
1150	850l. Mercedes Benz motor car	60	60
1151	1000l. Semi-ceremonial berlin	85	85
1152	1250l. Mercedes Benz 300 SEL motor car	1·10	1·10
1153	2000l. Travelling carriage (different)	1·60	1·60
1154	4000l. Fiat Campagnola	3·75	3·75
1145/1154 *Set of* 10		5·50	5·50

The booklet panes have a perforated margin around the edges.

(Litho Ashton-Potter Canada)

1997 (20 Mar). *Europa. The Swiss Guard.* T **302** and similar vert design. Multicoloured. P 13½.
1155	750l. Type **302**	55	55
	a. Horiz strip. Nos. 1155/6 and 2 labels	1·20	
1156	850l. Swordsman	60	60

Nos. 1155/6 were issued together in horizontal strips of two stamps and two labels, showing either the Corps' flag or the ceremonial morion, within sheets of 8 stamps and 8 labels.

303 Aristotle describing the Species (De Historia Animalium by Aristotle)

304 St. Adalbert

1997 (23 Apr). *"Looking at The Classics" Exhibition.* T **303** and similar horiz designs showing illustrations from manuscripts of the Classics. Multicoloured. Photo. P 14.
1157	500l. Type **303**	35	35
1158	750l. Bacchus riding dragon (Metamorphoses by Ovid)	65	65
1159	1250l. General reviewing his soldiers (Iliad by Homer)	1·00	1·00
1160	2000l. Horsemen leaving Canne (Ab Urbe Condita by Livy)	1·60	1·60
1157/1160 *Set of* 4		3·25	3·25
MS1161 100 × 135 mm. 1000l. Male and female masks; 1000l. Two female masks; 1000l. Two male masks (Comedies by Terence). P 13½.		2·10	2·10

(Des V. Suchánek. Recess Germam State Ptg Wks, Berlin)

1997 (23 Apr). *Death Millenary of St. Adalbert (Bishop of Prague).* P 14.
| 1162 | **304** | 850l. deep lilac | 1·10 | 1·10 |

305 Eucharist and Arms of Wroclaw

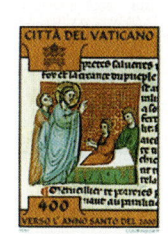

306 Jesus healing Paralysed Man

(Des Gabriella Titotto. Photo French State Ptg Wks, Paris)

1997 (27 May). *46th International Eucharistic Congress Wroclaw, Poland.* T **305** and similar vert designs. Multicoloured. P 13½ × 13.
1163	650l. Type **305**	45	45
1164	1000l. Last Supper and Congress emblem	80	80
1165	1250l. Wroclaw Cathedral and the Holy Dove	90	90
1166	2500l. Cross, doves and hands around globe	2·20	2·20
1163/1166 *Set of* 4		4·00	4·00

(Photo Courvoisier)

1997 (15 Sept). *Holy Year 2000 (3rd issue).* T **306** and similar vert designs showing illustrations from 14th century illuminated New Testament in Vatican Apostolic Library. Multicoloured. Granite paper. P 12.
| 1167 | 400l. Type **306** | 30 | 30 |
| 1168 | 800l. Calming the tempest | 65 | 65 |

477

VATICAN CITY 1997

1169	300l. Feeding the five thousand		1·60	1·60
1170	3600l. Peter acclaiming Christ as the Messiah		4·00	4·00
1167/1170 Set of 4			6·00	6·00

307 St. Ambrose and Ambrosiana Basilica

1997 (15 Sept). *1600th Death Anniv of St. Ambrose. Bishop of Milan. Photo.* P 13½ × 14.
1171	307	800l. multicoloured	1·10	1·10

308 Pope Paul VI

1997 (15 Sept). *Birth Centenary of Pope Paul VI. Litho.* P 13½ × 14.
1172	308	900l. multicoloured	65	65

No. 1172 was issued in sheetlets of four stamps and 16 labels showing four different coats of arms.

1997 (4 Oct). *Aid for Earthquake Victims. As No.* **MS**958 *but additionally inscr "PRO TERREMOTATI 1997" in the margin.*
MS1173 100 × 135 mm. As No. **MS**958 (sold at 8000l.) . . . . 15·00 16·00

No. **MS**1173 was issued in an illustrated folder.

309 Guatemala Pyramid and Amerindian Boy

(Des I. Fantini. Litho Enschedé)

1997 (11 Nov). *Pope John Paul II's Journeys (15th series).* T **309** *and similar vert designs. Multicoloured.* P 14 × 13½.
1174	400l. Type **301** (Guatemala, Nicaragua, El Salvador, Venezuela)		30	30
1175	900l. St. Francis de Paul and St. Olive's Cathedral and Mosque (Tunisia)		65	65
1176	1000l. St. Nicholas's Cathedral, Ljubljana, and Blessed Lady's monument, Maribor (Slovenia)		75	75
1177	1300l. Paderborn Cathedral and Brandenburg Gate, Berlin (Germany)		95	95
1178	2000l. St. Martin's Abbey, Pannonhalma and St. Stephen's crown (Hungary)		1·80	1·80
1179	4000l. Reims Cathedral, baptism of Clovis and St. Martin of Tours (France)		3·75	3·75
1174/1179 Set of 6			7·25	7·25

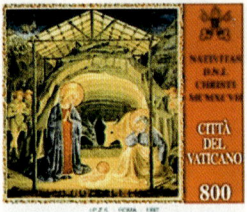

310 "Madonna of the Belt" (detail of altarpiece, Gozzoli)

1997 (11 Nov). *Christmas. 500th Death Anniv of Benozzo Gozzoli (artist). Photo.* P 14.
1180	310	800l. multicoloured	90	90

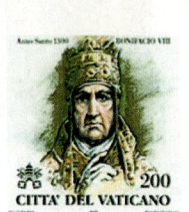

311 Pope Boniface VIII (1300)

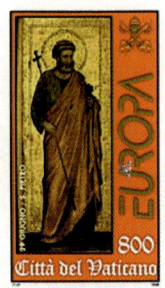

312 St. Peter

(Des I. Fantini. Litho German Sate Ptg Wks, Berlin)

1998 (24 Mar). *Popes and their Holy Years (1st series).* T **311** *and similar square designs. Multicoloured.* P 13½.
1181	200l. Type **311**	20	20
1182	400l. Clement VI (1350)	30	30
1183	500l. Boniface IX (1390 and 1400)	35	35
1184	700l. Martinus V (1423)	50	50
1185	800l. Nicholas V (1450)	75	75
1186	900l. Sistus IV (1475)	90	90
1187	1300l. Alexander VI (1500)	1·30	1·30
1188	3000l. Clement VII (1525)	4·00	4·00
1181/1188 Set of 8		7·50	7·50

Nos. 1181/8 were each issued with *se-tenant* labels showing the arms of the featured Pope within sheetlets of 5 stamps and 5 labels.

See also Nos. 1213/20 and 1255/64.

(Litho French State Ptg Wks, Paris)

1998 (24 Mar). *Europa. National Festival. The Feast of St. Peter and St. Paul.* T **312** *and similar vert design. Multicoloured.* P 13.
1189	800l. Type **312**	65	80
1190	900l. St. Paul	80	85

The designs are details from the Stefaneschi Triptych by Giotto.

VATICAN CITY   1998

313 Angel
314 Entry into Jerusalem 
317 "The Good Shepherd"
318 Pope and War Refugees

(Photo Courvoisier)

1998 (19 May). *Musical Angels from "The Ascension" by Melozzo da Forli in the Basilica of the Apostles, Rome*. T **313** and similar vert designs. Multicoloured. Granite paper. P 12.

1191	450l. Type **313**	35	35
1192	650l. Angel playing lute	45	45
1193	800l. Angel playing drum	60	60
1194	1000l. Angel playing viol	90	90
1195	1300l. Angel playing violin	1·20	1·20
1196	2000l. Angel with tamborine	2·00	2·00
1191/1196	*Set of* 6	5·00	5·00

(Photo Courvoisier)

1998 (19 May). *Holy Year 2000 (4th issue)*. T **314** and similar horiz designs showing illustrations from the illuminated New Testament in Vatican Apostolic Library. Multicoloured. Granite paper. P 12.

1197	500l. Type **314**	35	35
1198	800l. Washing of the Apostles' feet	60	60
1199	1500l. The Last Supper	1·00	1·00
1200	3000l. The Crucifixion	2·75	2·75
1197/1200	*Set of* 4	4·25	4·25

315 Turin Shroud

(Des Rita Morena. Recess and litho)

1998 (19 May). *Exhibition of the Holy Shroud, Turin Cathedral*. T **315** and similar vert design. P 13½ × 14.

1201	900l. chocolate and light turquoise-green	75	75
1202	2500l. black, flesh and turquoise-green	2·20	2·20

Design:—2500l. Turin Cathedral.

316 Pope John Paul II

(Des I. Fantini. Photo)

1998 (23 Oct). *"Italiá 98" International Stamp Exhibition, Milan (1st issue). Stamp Day*. P 14.
1203   **316**   800l. multicoloured . . . . 1·10   1·10

317 "The Good Shepherd"
318 Pope and War Refugees 

(Embossed and photo (**MS**1205), photo (1204) Courvoisier)

1998 (25 Oct). *"Italiá 98" International Stamp Exhibition, Milan (2nd issue). Art Day*. T **317** and similar designs showing sculptures from sarcophagi. Multicoloured. Granite paper. Imperf × 12.

1204	900l. Type **317**	75	75
	a. Booklet pane. No. 1204 × 5	3·75	

MS1205 106 × 130 mm. 600l. Peter's Denial; 900l. Praying woman; 1000l. Christ and the Cyrenean; 2000l. Christ with the Cross and two Apostles. P 12 . . . . 3·00   3·00
No. 1204 was only issued in stamp booklets.

(Des A. Mazzotta. Litho Ashton Potter Canada)

1998 (1 Dec). *Pope John Paul II's Journeys (16th series)*. T **318** and similar vert designs. Multicoloured. P 12½.

1206	300l. Type **318** (Bosnia and Herzegovina)	20	20
1207	600l. Kneeling in front of statue of Jesus (Czech Republic)	45	45
1208	800l. With girls (Lebanon)	60	60
1209	900l. Welcome by garlanded girls (Poland)	65	65
1210	1300l. With young people (France)	95	95
1211	5000l. With children (Brazil)	3·75	3·75
1206/1211	*Set of* 6	6·00	6·00

319 "Nativity" (Giulio Clovio)
320 Rose "John Paul II" 

(Litho Enschedé)

1998 (1 Dec). *Christmas*. P 14 × 13½.
1212   **319**   800l. multicoloured 65   65

(Des I. Fantini. Litho German State Ptg Wks, Berlin)

1999 (23 Mar). *Popes and their Holy Years (2nd series)*. Square designs as T **311**. Multicoloured. P 13½.

1213	300l. Julius III (1550)	35	35
1214	600l. Gregoy XIII (1575)	55	55
1215	800l. Clement VIII (1600)	75	75
1216	900l. Urban VIII (1625)	90	90
1217	1000l. Innocent X (1650)	1·10	1·10
1218	1300l. Clement X (1675)	1·30	1·30
1219	1500l. Innocent XII (1700)	1·60	1·60
1220	2000l. Benedict XIII (1725)	2·50	2·50
1213/1220	*Set of* 8	8·25	8·25

Nos. 1213/20 were each issued with *se-tenant* labels showing the arms of the featured Pope within sheetlets of five stamps and five labels.

VATICAN CITY 1999

(Litho Ashton Potter Canada)

1999 (23 Mar). *Europa. Parks and Gardens*. T **320** and similar vert design. Multicoloured. P 12½ × 13.
1221	800l. Type **320**	60	60
	a. Strip. Nos. 1221/2 plus label	1·40	1·40
1222	900l. Water lilies (Fountain of the Frogs, Vatican Gardens)	65	65

Nos. 1221/2 were issued together *se-tenant* with intervening label, showing a 16th-century mosaic of a heron, within sheets of ten stamps and five labels.

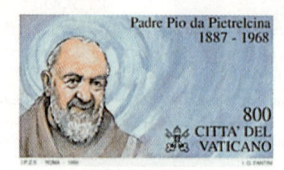

321 Father Pio

(Des I. Fantini. Litho)

1999 (27 Apr). *Beatification of Father Pio da Pietrelcina (Capuchin friar who bore the stigmata)*. T **321** and similar multicoloured designs. P 14 × 13½.
1223	800l. Type **321**	60	60
MS1224	86 × 115 mm. 300l. Monastery Church, San Giovanni Rotondo (29 × 39 mm); 600l. San Giovanni Rotondo new church (29 × 39 mm); 900l. Type **321** (59 × 39 mm). P 13½	1·30	1·30

322 Bethlehem

(Photo Courvoisier)

1999 (25 May). *Holy Places in Palestine*. T **322** and similar horiz designs. Multicoloured. Granite paper. P 11½.
1225	200l. Type **322**	20	20
1226	500l. Nazareth	35	35
1227	800l. Lake Tiberias	60	60
1228	900l. Jerusalem	65	65
1229	1300l. Mount Tabor	95	95
1225/1229	Set of 5	2·50	2·50
MS1230	110 × 86 mm. 1000l. × 4, composite design of map of the Holy Land (from 17th-century Geographia Blaviana) (each 50 × 38 mm). P 12 × 11½	2·75	2·75

Nos. 1225/9 are illustrations from The Holy Land by I. Messmer.

323 Deposition from the Cross

(Photo Courvoisier)

1999 (25 May). *Holy Year 2000 (5th issue)*. T **323** and similar horiz designs showing illustrations from an illuminated New Testament in Vatican Apostolic Library. Multicoloured. Granite paper. P 11½ × 12.
1231	400l. Type **323**	30	30
1232	700l. The Resurrection	50	50
1233	1300l. Pentecost	95	95
1234	3000l. The Last Judgement	2·20	2·20
1231/1234	Set of 4	3·50	3·50

(Photo Courvoisier)

1999 (25 May). *Kosovo Relief Fund*. Granite paper. P 12½.
1235	**324**	3600l. black	2·50	2·50

325 Visit to Cuba
326 Hot Air Balloons, Jigsaw Puzzle of Europe and Magnifying Glass 

(Des G. Hajnal. Litho Enschedé)

1999 (12 Oct). *Pope John Paul II's Journeys (17th series)*. T **325** and similar vert designs. Multicoloured. P 14 × 13½.
1236	600l. Type **325**	45	45
1237	800l. Stole over hands and staff (Nigeria)	55	55
1238	900l. Dove, cathedral and disabled people (Austria)	75	75
1239	1300l. With Crucifix and statue (Croatia)	1·10	1·10
1240	2000l. Quirinal Palace, Rome (Italy)	2·00	2·00
1236/1240	Set of 5	4·25	4·25

(Des Daniela Longo. Photo Courvoisier)

1999 (12 Oct). *50th Anniv of Council of Europe*. P 11½.
1241	**326**	1200l. multicoloured	60	60

327 "The Cherubim at the Doors of Paradise" and "The Banishment from the Garden of Eden"

(Photo Courvoisier)

1999 (24 Nov). *Holy Year 2000 (6th issue). Opening of Holy Door, St. Peter's Basilica*. T **327** and similar horiz designs showing panels from the door. Multicoloured. Granite paper. P 11½ × 12.
1242	200l. Type **327**	20	20
1243	300l. "The Annunciation" and "Angel"	20	20
1244	400l. "Baptism of Christ" and "Straying Sheep"	30	30
1245	500l. "The Merciful Father" and "Curing Paralysed Man"	35	35
1246	600l. "The Penitent Woman" and "The Obligation to Forgive"	45	45
1247	800l. "Peter's Denial" and "A Thief in Paradise"	65	65
1248	1000l. "Jesus appears to Thomas" and "Jesus appears to the Eleven"	90	90
1249	1200l. "Jesus appears to Saul" and "Opening of the Holy Door"	1·10	1·10
1242/1249	Set of 8	3·75	3·75
MS1250	106 × 142 mm. As Nos. 1242/9	4·50	4·50

Stamps from the miniature sheet have the design right up to the perforations whereas the sheet stamps have the design surrounded by a white margin.

VATICAN CITY   1999

328 St. Joseph (detail) 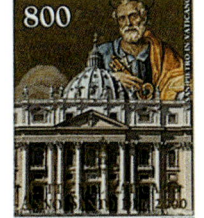   **329** St. Peter's Basilica

(Litho Ashton-Potter, Canada)

1999 (24 Nov). *Christmas. T* **328** *and similar vert designs depicting "St. Joseph, the Virgin Mary and the Holy Child" (Giovanni di Petro). Multicoloured.* P 13 × 12½.

1251	500l. Type **328**	35	35
1252	800l. Holy Child (detail)	55	55
1253	900l. Virgin Mary (detail)	90	90
1254	1200l. Complete painting	1·10	1·10
1251/1254	Set of 4	2·50	2·50

No. 1254 was issued in sheets with ten "priority" labels.

(Des I. Fantini. Litho German State Ptg Wks, Berlin)

2000 (4 Feb). *Popes and their Holy Years (3rd series). Square designs as T* **311**. *Multicoloured.* P 14.

1255	300l. Benedict XIV (1750)	30	30
1256	400l. Pius VI (1775)	35	35
1257	500l. Leo XII (1825)	45	45
1258	600l. Pius IX (1875)	55	55
1259	700l. Leo XIII (1900)	65	65
1260	800l. Pius XI (1925)	75	75
1261	1200l. Pius XII (1950)	1·10	1·10
1262	1500l. Paul VI (1975)	1·30	1·30
1263	2000l. John Paul II (2000)	2·00	2·00
1255/1263	Set of 9	6·50	6·50
MS1264	137 × 103 mm. 2000l. John Paul II resting face on hand	1·50	1·50

Nos. 1255/63 were each issued with *se-tenant* labels showing the arms of the featured Pope within sheetlets of five stamps and five labels.

(Des M. Padovan. Photo Courvoisier)

2000 (4 Feb). *Holy Year 2000 (7th issue). T* **329** *and similar vert designs. Multicoloured. Granite paper.* P 12 × 11½.

1265	800l. Type **329**	55	55
1266	1000l. St. John Lateran Basilica	75	75
1267	1200l. St. Mary Major Basilica	90	90
1268	2000l. St. Paul-outside-the-Walls Basilica	1·50	1·50
1265/1268	Set of 4	3·25	3·25

No. 1267 was issued in sheets with ten "priority" labels.

330 Embroidered Altar Frontal, Hólar Cathedral    **331** "Building Europe"

(Litho Enschedé)

2000 (4 Feb). *Millenary of Christianity in Iceland.* P 13½ × 14.
| 1269 | **330** | 1500l. multicoloured | 1·10 | 1·10 |

(Des J.-P. Cousin. Litho State Ptg Wks, Paris)

2000 (9 May). *Europa.* P 13½ × 13.
| 1270 | **331** | 1200l. multicoloured | 90 | 90 |

No. 1270 was issued in sheets with ten "priority" labels.

332 Pope John Paul II

(Des and eng C. Slania. Recess Stamp Printing Office, Sweden)

2000. *80th Birthday of Pope John Paul II. T* **332** *and similar vert designs.* P 13.

1271	800l. deep reddish lilac	55	55
1272	1200l. indigo	90	90
1273	2000l. deep blue-green	1·50	1·50

Designs:—1200l. Black Madonna of Czestochowa; 2000l. Pastoral Staff.

333 "The Calling of St. Peter and St. Andrew" (Domenico Ghirlandaio)

(Photo Courvoisier)

2000 (9 May). *Restoration of the Sistine Chapel (1st series). T* **333** *and similar horiz designs. Multicoloured. Granite paper.* P 11½ × 12.

1274	500l. Type **333**	35	35
1275	1000l. "The Trials of Moses" (Sandro Botticelli)	75	75
1276	1500l. "The Donation of the Keys" (Pietro Perugino)	1·10	1·10
1277	3000l. "The Worship of the Golden Calf" (Cosimo Rosselli)	2·20	2·20
1274/1277	Set of 4	4·00	4·00

See also Nos. 1294/7 and 1339/42.

334 Congress Emblem    **335** Pope John Paul II and Youths' Faces

(Litho Ashton-Potter, Canada)

2000 (19 June). *47th International Eucharistic Congress, Rome.* P 13 × 12½.
| 1278 | **334** | 1200l. multicoloured | 1·10 | 1·10 |

481

VATICAN CITY 2000

(Des P. Montozzi and G. Olcuire. Litho Enschedé)

2000 (19 June). *15th World Youth Day, Rome.* T **335** *and similar vert designs.*

(a) Sheet stamps. P 14 × 13½.
1279	800l. Type **335**		55	55
1280	1000l. Girl waving flag		65	65
1281	1200l. Youths' cheering		70	90
1282	1500l. Youth waving flag		1·20	1·20

(b) Self-adhesive booklet stamps. Die-cut perf 12
1283	1000l. As No. 1280		75	75
1279/1283 Set of 5			3·75	3·75

The stamps are peeled directly from the booklet cover and cannot therefore be collected as a separate pane.

336 Pope and Children

337 Pope John XXIII

(Des I. Fantini. Photo Couvoisier)

2000 (1 Sept). *Pope John Paul II's Journeys (18th series).* T **336** *and similar vert designs. Multicoloured. Granite paper.* P 12.
1284	1000l. Type **336** (Mexico and United States of America)		75	75
	a. Horiz strip of 5. Nos. 1284/8		4·00	
1285	1000l. Pope praying, building and children waving (Rumania)		75	75
1286	1000l. Holding Pastoral Staff (Poland)		75	75
1287	1000l. Pope and Bishop Anton Martin Slomsek (Slovenia)		75	75
1288	1000l. Pope, churches and crowd (India and Georgia)		75	75
1284/1288 Set of 5			3·50	3·50

Nos. 1284/8 were issued together in horizontal *se-tenant* strips of five stamps within the sheet.

(Des I. Fantini. Photo)

2000 (1 Sept). *Beatification of Pope John XXIII.* P 13½ × 14.
1289	337	1200l. multicoloured	90	90

338 Nativity (fresco)

(Photo Courvoisier)

2000 (7 Nov). *Christmas.* T **338** *and similar horiz designs showing Fresco by Giotto from St. Francis Basilica. Multicoloured. Granite paper.* P 12 × 11½.
1290	800l. Type **338**		55	55
1291	1200l. Baby Jesus (detail)		90	90
1292	1500l. Mary (detail)		1·10	1·10
1293	2000l. Joseph (detail)		1·50	1·50
1290/1293 Set of 4			3·75	3·75

(Photo Courvoisier)

2001 (15 Feb). *Restoration of the Sistine Chapel (2nd series). Horiz designs as* T **333**. *Multicoloured. Granite paper.* P 11½.
1294	800l. "The Baptism of Christ" (Pietro Perugino)		45	45
1295	1200l. "The Passage through the Red Sea" (Biagio d'Antonio)		65	65
1296	1500l. "The Punishment of Core, Datan and Abiron" (Botticelli)		85	85
1297	4000l. "The Sermon on the Mount" (Cosimo Rosselli)		2·20	2·20
1294/1297 Set of 4			3·75	3·75

339 Freedom of St. Gregory

340 Hands holding Water and Globe

(Photo Courvoisier)

2001 (15 Feb). *1700th Anniv of the Adoption of Christianity in Armenia.* T **339** *and similar vert designs. Multicoloured. Granite paper.* P 11½ × 12.
1298	1200l. Type **339**		65	65
1299	1500l. St. Gregory making Agatangel write		85	85
1300	2000l. St. Gregory and King Tirade meet Emperor Constantine and Pope Sylvester I		1·10	1·10

No. 1298 was issued in sheets with ten "Priority" labels.

(Des I. Fantini. Litho Cartor)

2001 (22 May). *Europa. Water Resources.* T **340** *and similar vert design. Multicoloured.* P 13½.
1301	800l. Type **340**		45	45
1302	1200l. Hand and catching rain water		65	65

341 Verdi and Score of Nabucco

342 Communication between People of Different Races

(Des G. Toffoletti. Litho Enschedé)

2001 (22 May). *Death Centenary of Giuseppe Verdi (composer).* T **341** *and similar horiz designs. Multicoloured.* P 13½ × 14½.
1303	800l. Type **341**		45	45
1304	1500l. Verdi and character from Aida		85	85
1305	2000l. Verdi and scene from Otello		1·10	1·10

(Des U. Golob. Litho Enschedé)

2001 (22 May). *"Dialogue between Civilizations".* P 14½ × 13½.
1306	342	1500l. multicoloured	85	85

VATICAN CITY 2001

343 Couple feeding Poor Man

344 Mount Sinai, Monastery of Holy Catherine and Pope

(Des Daniela Longo. Photo State Ptg Wks, Paris)

2001 (25 Sept). *Cancellation of Foreign Debt of Poor Countries. T* **343** *and similar square designs showing illustrations from "Works of Corporal Mercy" (15th-century panels by Carlo di Camerino). Multicoloured.* P 13.

1307	200l. Type **343**	20	20
1308	400l. Giving alms	20	20
1309	800l. Giving clothing	45	45
1310	1000l. Women caring for sick man	55	55
1311	1500l. Man visiting prisoner	85	85
1307/1311	*Set of 5*	2·00	2·00

(Des Daniela Longo. Litho Enschedé)

2001 (25 Sept). *Pope John Paul II's Journeys (19th series). The Holy Land. T* **344** *and similar square designs. Multicoloured.* P 13½.

1312	500l. Type **344**	30	30
1313	800l. Pope before Crucifix, Mount Nebo	45	45
1314	1200l. Pope celebrating Mass	65	65
1315	1500l. Pope at prayer Holy Sepulchre	85	85
1316	5000l. Pope praying at Shrine of Fatima	2·75	2·75
1312/1316	*Set of 5*	4·50	4·50
MS1317	85 × 115 mm. 3000l. Pope at Western Wall, Jerusalem (35 × 27mm)	2·10	2·10

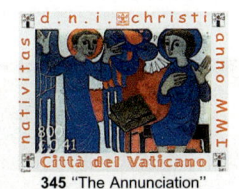

345 "The Annunciation"

(Litho Cartor)

2001 (22 Nov). *Christmas. T* **345** *and similar horiz designs showing scenes from "Life of Christ" (enamel, Egino G. Weinert). Multicoloured.* P 13 × 13½.

1318	800l. Type **345**	45	45
1319	1200l. "The Nativity"	65	65
	a. Perf 13 × 13½ (3 sides). Booklets	70	70
	b. Booklet pane. No. 1319a × 4, plus 4 "Priority" labels	2·00	
1320	1500l. "Adoration of the Magi"	85	85

The booklet pane consists of four stamps each with a "Priority" label attached either at left or right of stamp.

346 Fibula, 675–650 B.C.

(Photo Enschedé)

2001 (22 Nov). *Etruscan Museum Exhibits. T* **346** *and similar horiz designs. Multicoloured.* P 13½.

1321	800l. Type **346**	35	35
1322	1200l. 6th-century earrings	55	55
1323	1500l. Embossed Greek stud, 425–400 B.C.	70	70
1324	2000l. 3rd-century Greek head of Medusa	90	90
1321/1324	*Set of 4*	2·30	2·30

347 Emblem

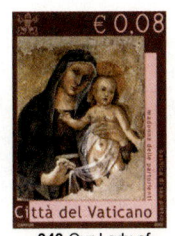

348 Our Lady of Women in Labour (14th-century fresco)

(Embossed and litho Cartor)

2001 (22 Nov). *80th Anniv of Guiseppe Toniolo Institute for Higher Studies and the Catholic University of the Sacred Heart.* P 12½.

1325	**347**	1200l. deep blue and vermilion	65	65

New Currency 100 cents = 1 euro

(Litho Cartor)

2002 (12 Mar). *Our Lady in the Vatican Basilica. T* **348** *and similar vert designs. Multicoloured.* P 13½ × 13.

1326	8c. Type **348**	15	15
1327	15c. Our Lady with people praying (mosaic)	25	25
1328	23c. Our Lady at the Tomb of Pius XII (15th-century fresco)	30	30
1329	31c. Our Lady of the Fever (13th-century)	45	45
1330	41c. Our Lady of the Slap	60	60
1331	52c. Mary Immaculate (mosaic)	75	75
1332	62c. Our Lady of Christians	90	90
1333	77c. The Virgin of the Deesis	1·10	1·10
1334	€1.03 L'Addolorata (painting, Lippo Memmi)	1·40	1·40
1335	€1.55 Presentation of Mary at the Temple (mosaic)	2·20	2·20
1326/1335	*Set of 10*	7·25	7·25

483

VATICAN CITY   2002

349 Pope Clement XI

(Des C. Slania. Recess Stamp Ptg Office, Sweden)

2002 (12 Mar). *300th Anniv of Pontifical Ecclesiastical Academy, Rome.* T **349** *and similar designs.* P 13.
1336	77c. blackish purple	1·10	1·10
	a. Horiz strip of 3. Nos. 1336/8	3·50	
1337	77c. deep dull green (46 × 33 mm)	1·10	1·10
1338	77c. blackish purple	1·10	1·10

Designs:—No. 1337 Façade of Piazza della Minerva Institute, Rome; 1338 Pope John Paul II.

351 "Christ and the Circus" (Aldo Carpi)

(Photo Enschedé)

2002 (13 June). *Europa. Circus.* T **350** *and similar horiz design. Multicoloured.* P 13½.
1347	41c. Type **350**	60	60
1348	62c. Christ with clown (detail of "Christ and the Circus")	90	90

(Photo Walsall Security Printers Ltd)

2002 (13 June). *Restoration of the Sistine Chapel (3rd series). Horiz designs as* T **333**. *Multicoloured. Granite paper.* P 11½ × 12.
1339	26c. "The Temptation of Christ" (Botticelli)	35	35
1340	41c. "The Last Supper" (Cosimo Rosselli)	60	60
1341	77c. "Moses' Journey into Egypt" (Pietro Perugino)	1·10	1·10
1342	€1.55, "The Last Days of Moses" (Luca Signorelli)	2·20	2·20
1339/1342	Set of 4	3·75	3·75

352 Crucifix, St. Dominic Church, Arezzo

(Photo Enschedé)

2002 (26 Sept). *700th Death Anniv of Cenni di Pepo (Cimabue) (artist).* T **351** *and similar vert designs showing the Crucifix and details thereof. Multicoloured.* P 13½ × 14.
1349	41c. Type **351**	60	60
1350	62c. Jesus	90	90
1351	77c. Mary	1·10	1·10
1352	€1.03 John the Baptist	1·40	1·40
1349/1352	Set of 4	3·50	3·50

(Des I. Fantini. Litho Cartor)

2002 (26 Sept). *Birth Millenary of Pope Leo IX.* T **352** *and similar horiz designs. Multicoloured.* P 13 × 13½.
1353	41c. Type **352**	60	60
1354	62c. Arrival in Rome as pilgrim and coronation as Pope	90	90
1355	€1.29 Leo IX in chains	1·90	1·90

No. 1354 was issued with a priority mail label attached.

350 Regina Viarum (Appian Way) and 1852 Papal States Stamp

(Photo State Ptg Wks, Paris)

2002 (13 June). *Centenary of Pontifical Stamps.* T **349** *and similar designs.* P 13 × 13½.
1343	41c. red-brown, deep dull purple and lake-brown	60	60
1344	52c. multicoloured	75	75
1345	€1.03 new blue, indigo and blue-green	1·40	1·40
MS1346	reddish brown, buff and deep purple, (circular)	2·30	2·30

Designs: As Type 349—No. 1344, Cassian Way and 1868 80c. Papal States stamp; 1345, Porta Angelica, Vatican and 1929 Vatican City 10c. stamp. **MS**1346, 104 × 83 mm Courtyard, Palazzo Madama, Rome.

354 "The Nativity" (15th-century painting in style of Di Baldeso)

(Photo State Ptg Wks, Paris)

2002 (21 Nov). *Christmas.* P 13.
1356	**354** 41c. multicoloured	60	60

A stamp of a similar design was issued by New Zealand.

VATICAN CITY 2002

355 Pope John Paul II (Malta)

(Litho Cartor)

2002 (21 Nov). *Journeys of Pope John Paul II in 2001.* T **355** and similar horiz designs. Multicoloured. P 13.

1357	41c. Type **355**	60	60
1358	62c. Praying (Ukraine)	90	90
1359	€1.55 Wearing mitre (Kazakhstan)	2·20	2·20

MACHINE LABELS

From 15 March 2000 gummed labels were available from automatic machines.

A set of five designs as Type A, multicoloured, featuring St. Paul's Basilica, Rome; St. Peter's Basilica, Vatican; St Mary's Basilica, Rome; St. John's Basilica, Rome and coat of arms.

On 22 May 2002 a set of five new designs featuring coins as Type B were issues.

Four new designs were issued on 12 March 2002, as Type C featuring Sts. Matthew, Mark, Luke and John.

STAMP BOOKLETS

The following checklist covers, in simplified form, booklets issued by the Vatican City. It is intended that it should be used in conjunction with the main listings and details of stamps and panes listed there are not repeated.

Prices are for complete booklets

Booklet No.	Date	Contents and Face Value	Price
SB1	8.4.82	Pope John Paul II's Journeys (2nd series) 1 pane. No. 768 × 8; 1 pane. No. 769 × 8:1 pane, No. 772x8, 1 pane, No. 773x8 (4800l.)	16·00
SB2	14.3.85	Pope John Paul II's Journeys (3rd series) 1 pane. No. 815a (5000l.)	7·50
SB3	9.4.91	Restoration of Sistine Chapel 1 pane, No. 973a; 1 pane, No. 974a; 1 pane, No. 979a (5400l.)	7·50
SB4	23.3.93	Architectural Treasures 1 pane, No. 1028a; 1 pane, No. 1029a; 1 pane, No. 1030a; 1 pane, No. 1031 a (5400l.)	5·75
SB5	8.6.95	European Nature Conservation Year 1 pane, No. 1092a; 1 pane, No. 1093a, 1 pane, No. 1094a; 1 pane, No. 1095a (6000l.)	5·75
SB6	20.3.97	Papal Transport 1 pane, No. 1146a, No. 1147a, 1 pane, 1 pane, No. 1148a, 1 pane, No. 1149a (6600l.)	5·50
SB7	25.10.98	"Italia 98" Art Day 1 pane, No. 1204a (4500l.)	4·00
SB8	19.6.00	World Youth Day No. 1283 × 4 (4000l.)	3·00
SB9	22.11.00	Christmas 1 pane 1319b	2·20